Hamilton, Said
Mastering Fractions

5-12A
5-32

A

Mastering Fractions

Book Title: Mastering Fractions

Author: Said Hamilton

Editor: Melvin DeGree

Cover design by: Kathleen Myers

First published in 1996

Hamilton Education Guides
P.O. Box 681
Vienna, Va. 22183

Library of Congress Catalog Card Number 95-95207
Library of Congress Cataloging-in-Publication Data

ISBN 0-9649954-0-9

This book is dedicated to my wife and children for their support and understanding.

General Contents

Appendix   ***Exercise Solutions***

Detailed Contents

Chapter 1 - Parentheses and Brackets

Appendix - Exercise Solutions

Acknowledgments

The primary motivating factor in writing this book was observing the difficulty my children have had in following the math concepts presented in the books used in their school programs. I therefore would like to acknowledge my children in giving me the inspiration to proceed with this project. My special thanks to Melvin DeGree for his editorial comments. His comments truly elevated the usefulness of this book. I would also like to acknowledge and give my sincere thanks to the following education professionals who reviewed and provided valuable comments to further enhance this book: Mrs. Linda Clark, Mrs. Sandra Levy, Mrs. Shirley Isler, Mrs. Sue Kunihiro, and various other contributors. My especial thanks to Mary Spaulding for her professional skill and support in typing and preparation of this book and to Kathleen Myers for her outstanding cover design. Finally, I would like to thank my family for their understanding and patience in allowing me to take on the task of writing this book. I hope users of this book will find it valuable.

Introduction and Overview

Solving and simplifying fractions was always a subject of "mystery" to me and many of my friends during my school years. Some decades later, among many of our school children the subject of fractions is still a "mystery". To alleviate this problem, the author has devoted this book in its entirety to fractions and how one can master fraction problems.

The author's purpose in writing this book is to enhance the younger generation's ability to solve fractional problems and to "demystify" mathematics. It is my belief that any subject, particularly mathematics, can be turned into an interesting subject if it is taught in simple terms and with clarity. To achieve that the author seeks to guide the student to gain greater proficiency by introduction of simple techniques on how to solve each class of problem. The techniques are presented using step by step easy to follow examples with solutions to exercises that show in detail how each problem can be solved.

The scope of this book is intended to be for educational levels ranging from the 6th grade to adult. The book can also be used by students in home study programs, parents, teachers, special education programs, preparatory schools, and adult educational programs up to the college level as a main text, a thorough reference, or a supplementary book. A fundamental understanding of how numbers are added, subtracted, multiplied, and divided is required.

This book is divided into nine chapters. Chapter 1 introduces the student to the concept and use of signed numbers and parentheses and brackets as math expressions in solving mathematical operations. What defines a fraction and the steps as to how fractions are simplified and converted from one form to another are discussed in chapter 2. Chapters 3, 4, and 5 discuss the three types of fractions, i.e., integer, decimal, and mixed fractions, respectively. The steps as to how these types of fractions are added, subtracted, multiplied, divided, and mixed are described in each respective chapter. In chapter 6 integer and decimal fractions are combined and the mathematical operations as to how they are solved are discussed. How to solve integer and mixed fractions is addressed in chapter 7. Chapter 8 combines decimal with mixed fractions and shows how mathematical operations are performed using these types of fractions. In chapter 9 integer, decimal, and mixed fractions are combined. The steps used to perform mathematical operations when the three types of fractions are combined are discussed. Finally, step by step solution to the exercises is provided in the Appendix.

It is the author's hope that this book stands apart from other fractions books as a more concise and understandable treatment of this important subject.

With best wishes,

Said Hamilton

Terminology

The following terminology is used throughout this book:

Absolute Value - The numerical value or magnitude of a quantity, as of a negative number, without regard to its sign. The symbol for absolute value is two parallel lines "$|\ |$". For example, $|-2| = |2| = 2$, $|-35| = |35| = 35$, $|-0.23| = |0.23| = 0.23$, $|-5.13| = |5.13| = 5.13$, etc.

Addend - Any of a set of numbers to be added.

Addition - The process of adding two or more numbers to get a number called the sum.

Algebraic Approach - An approach in which only numbers, letters, and arithmetic operations are used.

Associative - Pertaining to an operation in which the result is the same regardless of the way the elements are grouped, as, in addition, $2 + (4 + 5) = (2 + 4) + 5 = 11$ and, in multiplication, $2 \times (4 \times 5) = (2 \times 4) \times 5 = 40$.

Brackets - A pair of symbols, [ ], used to enclose a mathematical expression.

Case - Supporting facts offered in justification of a statement.

Change - To replace by another; alter; transform.

Common Denominator - A common multiple of the denominators of two or more fractions. For example, 10 is a common denominator of $\frac{1}{2}$ and $\frac{3}{5}$.

Common Fraction - A fraction whose numerator and denominator are both whole numbers. In this book a common fraction is the same as an integer fraction.

Commutative - Pertaining to an operation in which the order of the elements does not affect the result, as, in addition, $5 + 3 = 3 + 5$ and, in multiplication, $5 \times 3 = 3 \times 5$.

Complex Fraction - A fraction in which the numerator or denominator or both contain fractions. For example, $\dfrac{\frac{2}{15}}{\frac{5}{7}}$ is a complex fraction.

Conversion - A change in the form of a quantity or an expression without a change in the value.

Convert - To change from one form or use to another; transform.

Decimal Fraction - A fraction containing decimal number.

Decimal Number - Any number written using base 10 ; a number containing a decimal point.

Decimal Point - A period placed to the left of a decimal.

Denominator - The term below the line in a fraction; the divisor of the numerator.

Difference - The amount by which one quantity differs from another; remainder left after subtraction.

Distributive - Of the principle in multiplication that allows the multiplier to be used separately with each term of the multiplicand.

Dividend - A quantity to be divided.

Division - The process of finding how many times a number (the divisor) is contained in another number (the dividend). The number of times equals the quotient.

Divisor - The quantity by which another quantity, the dividend, is to be divided.

Equal - Of the same quantity, size, number, value, degree, intensity, quality, etc.

Equivalent Fractions - Fractions that are numerically the same.

Even Number - A number which is exactly divisible by two; not odd.

Exact Order - Not deviating in form or content; precise.

Exponential Notation - A way of expressing a number as the product of factor and 10 raised to some power. The factor is either a whole number or a decimal number. For example, the exponential notation form of 0.0353, 0.048, 489, 3987 are 3.53×10^{-2}, 48×10^{-3}, 4.89×10^{2}, and 3.987×10^{3}, respectively.

Factor - One of two or more quantities having a designated product. For example 3 and 5 are factors of 15.

Fraction - A number which indicates the ratio between two quantities in the form of $\dfrac{a}{b}$ such that a is any real number and b is any real number not equal to zero.

Greatest Common Factor - A greatest number that divides two or more numbers without a remainder. For example, 6 is the Greatest Common Factor (G.C.F.) among 6, 12, and 36.

Group - An assemblage of objects or numbers.

Imaginary Number - The positive square root of a negative number.

Improper Fraction - A fraction in which the numerator is larger than or equal to the denominator.

Integer Fraction - A fraction having positive or negative whole numbers in the numerator and the denominator.

Integer Number - Any member of the set of positive whole numbers $(1, 2, 3, 4, ...)$, negative whole numbers $(-1, -2, -3, -4, ...)$, and zero is an integer number.

Irrational Number - A number not capable of being expressed by an integer (a whole number) or an integer fraction (quotient of an integer). For example, $\sqrt{12}$, π, and $\sqrt[4]{7}$ are irrational numbers.

Lowest Term - Smallest value.

Mathematical Operations - The process of performing addition, subtraction, multiplication, and division in a specified sequence.

Minimize - To reduce to the least possible amount; reduce to a minimum.

Mixed Fraction - A fraction made up of a positive or negative whole number and an integer fraction.

Mixed Operation - Combining addition, subtraction, multiplication, and division in a math process is defined as a mixed operation.

Multiplicand - The number that is or is to be multiplied by another.

Multiplication - The process of finding the number obtained by repeated additions of a number a specified number of times: Multiplication is symbolized in various ways, i.e., $3 \times 4 = 12$ or $3 \cdot 4 = 12$, which means $3 + 3 + 3 + 3 = 12$, to add the number three together four times.

Multiplier - The number by which the multiplicand is multiplied. For example, if 3 is multiplied by 4, 3 is the multiplicand, 4 is the multiplier, and 12 is the product.

Not Applicable - In this book "Not Applicable" implies to a "Step" that can not be put to a specific use. A "Step" that is not relevant.

Numerator - The term above the line in a fraction.

Odd Number - A number having a remainder of one when divided by two; not even.

Operation - A process or action, such as addition, subtraction, multiplication, or division, performed in a specified sequence and in accordance with specific rules of procedure.

Parentheses - A pair of symbols, ( ), used to enclose a sum, product, or other mathematical expressions.

Prime Number - A number that has itself and unity as its only factors. For example, 2, 3, 5, 7, and 11 are prime numbers since they have no common divisor except unity.

Product - The quantity obtained by multiplying two or more quantities together.

Proper Fraction - A fraction in which the numerator is smaller than the denominator.

Quotient - The quantity resulting from division of one quantity by another.

Rational Number - A number that can be represented as an integer (a whole number) or an integer fraction (quotient of integers). For example, $\dfrac{1}{5}$, $-\dfrac{2}{15}$, $12 = \dfrac{12}{1}$, $-230 = -\dfrac{230}{1} = \dfrac{230}{-1}$, $-10 = -\dfrac{10}{1} = -\dfrac{100}{10} = -\dfrac{50}{5} = \dfrac{350}{-35}$, *etc.*, and $0.13 = \dfrac{13}{100} = \dfrac{130}{1000} = \dfrac{26}{200}$, *etc.* are rational numbers.

Real Number - A number that is either a rational number or an irrational number. For example, $\dfrac{3}{5}$, $-\dfrac{4}{13}$, -23, 0.13, $\sqrt{5}$, and π are real numbers.

Re-group - A repeated assemblage of objects or numbers.

Remainder - a) What is left when a smaller number is subtracted from a larger number. b) What is left undivided when one number is divided by another that is not one of its factors.

Sign - A mark or symbol having an accepted and specific meaning. For example, the sign " $+$ " implies addition.

Signed Number - A number which can have a positive or negative value as designated by " $+$ " or " $-$ " symbol. A signed number with no accompanying symbol is understood to be positive.

Simplify - Make easier; less complex.

Specific Example - An example that is precise and explicit.

Step - One of a series of actions or measures taken toward some end.

Sub-group - A distinct group within a group.

Subtraction - The mathematical process of finding the difference between two numbers.

Sum - The amount obtained as a result of adding two or more numbers together.

Symbol - A sign used to represent a mathematical operation.

Whole Number - A whole number is defined as an integer number.

The following references were used in developing this terminology:

1) *The Webster's New World Dictionary of American English, Victoria E. Neufeldt, editor in chief, third college edition, 1993.*
2) *The American Heritage Dictionary of the English Language, William Morris, editor, third edition, 1992.*

Chapter 1 - Parentheses and Brackets

The objective of this chapter is to teach the student the concept of grouping numbers. This is achieved by introduction of parentheses and brackets as tools for solving mathematical problems. In section 1.1 signed numbers are introduced and their use in addition, subtraction, multiplication, and division are discussed. Section 1.2 shows how numbers are grouped and solved in addition. Sections 1.3, 1.4, and 1.5 show how parentheses and brackets are used in subtraction, multiplication, and division, respectively. Section 1.6 show the use of parentheses and brackets in solving mixed operations. In addition, for completeness, the general algebraic approach as to how parentheses and brackets are used in grouping numbers is provided in each section. The student, depending on his or her grade level, can skip the algebraic approach and only learn how to solve the specific examples. To further enforce the objective of this chapter, additional examples as to how parentheses and brackets are used are provided at the end of each section.

1.1   Signed Numbers

In mathematics, "$+$" and "$-$" symbols are used to indicate the use of positive and negative numbers, respectively. If a signed number has no symbol it is understood to be a positive number. Although the intent of this book is not to teach algebra, the following algebraic concept is required prior to studying fractional operations. This concept is represented in basic terms using specific examples only, in keeping with the methodology used through out this book. Signed numbers are added, subtracted, multiplied, and divided as exemplified in the following cases:

Case I - Addition of Signed Numbers

When two numbers are added, the numbers are called **addends** and the result is called a **sum**. The sign of the sum dependents on the sign of the numbers. This is shown in the following cases with the sign change of two real numbers (see definition in the Terminology section) a and b:

Case I a.

$$\boxed{a+b} = \boxed{A}$$

For example,

1. $\boxed{5+6} = \boxed{11}$ 2. $\boxed{7+8} = \boxed{15}$ 3. $\boxed{1+0} = \boxed{1}$

4. $\boxed{3+15} = \boxed{18}$ 5. $\boxed{15+9} = \boxed{24}$

Case I b.

$$\boxed{-a+b} = \boxed{B}$$

For example,

1. $\boxed{-7+3} = \boxed{-4}$ 2. $\boxed{-9+0} = \boxed{-9}$ 3. $\boxed{-15+40} = \boxed{25}$

4. $\boxed{-35+18} = \boxed{-17}$ 5. $\boxed{-8+30} = \boxed{22}$

Case I c.

$$\boxed{a+(-b)} = \boxed{a-b} = \boxed{C}$$

For example,

1. $\boxed{2+(-5)} = \boxed{2-5} = \boxed{-3}$ 2. $\boxed{7+(-9)} = \boxed{7-9} = \boxed{-2}$

3. $\boxed{0+(-1)} = \boxed{0-1} = \boxed{-1}$ 4. $\boxed{8+(-45)} = \boxed{8-45} = \boxed{-37}$

5. $\boxed{40+(-9)} = \boxed{40-9} = \boxed{31}$

Case I d.

$$\boxed{(-a)+b} = \boxed{-a+b} = \boxed{D}$$ *Note:* $(-a) = -a$

For example,

1. $\boxed{(-3)+9} = \boxed{-3+9} = \boxed{6}$ 2. $\boxed{(-12)+8} = \boxed{-12+8} = \boxed{-4}$

3. $\boxed{(-7)+25} = \boxed{-7+25} = \boxed{18}$ 4. $\boxed{(-34)+10} = \boxed{-34+10} = \boxed{-24}$

5. $\boxed{(-1)+0} = \boxed{-1+0} = \boxed{-1}$

Case I e.

$$\boxed{(-a)+(-b)} = \boxed{-a-b} = \boxed{E}$$

For example,

1. $\boxed{(-6)+(-9)} = \boxed{-6-9} = \boxed{-15}$ 2. $\boxed{(-45)+(-6)} = \boxed{-45-6} = \boxed{-51}$

3. $\boxed{(-10)+(-55)} = \boxed{-10-55} = \boxed{-65}$ 4. $\boxed{(-35)+(-20)} = \boxed{-35-20} = \boxed{-55}$

5. $\boxed{(-5)+(-5)} = \boxed{-5-5} = \boxed{-10}$

Case II - Subtraction of Signed Numbers
When two numbers are subtracted the result is called the **difference**. The sign of the difference depends on the sign of the numbers. This is shown in the following cases with the sign change of two real numbers a and b:

Case II a.

$$\boxed{a - b} = \boxed{A}$$

For example,

1. $\boxed{15 - 6} = \boxed{\mathbf{9}}$ 2. $\boxed{17 - 47} = \boxed{\mathbf{-30}}$ 3. $\boxed{1 - 0} = \boxed{\mathbf{1}}$

4. $\boxed{3 - 15} = \boxed{\mathbf{-12}}$ 5. $\boxed{45 - 9} = \boxed{\mathbf{36}}$

Case II b.

$$\boxed{-a - b} = \boxed{B}$$

For example,

1. $\boxed{-7 - 3} = \boxed{\mathbf{-10}}$ 2. $\boxed{-1 + 0} = \boxed{\mathbf{-1}}$ 3. $\boxed{-15 - 45} = \boxed{\mathbf{-60}}$

4. $\boxed{-35 - 8} = \boxed{\mathbf{-43}}$ 5. $\boxed{-8 - 30} = \boxed{\mathbf{-38}}$

Case II c.

$$\boxed{a - (-b)} = \boxed{a + (b)} = \boxed{a + b} = \boxed{C}$$

For example,

1. $\boxed{12 - (-5)} = \boxed{12 + (5)} = \boxed{12 + 5} = \boxed{\mathbf{17}}$

2. $\boxed{7 - (-9)} = \boxed{7 + (9)} = \boxed{7 + 9} = \boxed{\mathbf{16}}$

3. $\boxed{0 - (-1)} = \boxed{0 + (1)} = \boxed{0 + 1} = \boxed{\mathbf{1}}$

4. $\boxed{30 - (-45)} = \boxed{30 + (45)} = \boxed{30 + 45} = \boxed{\mathbf{75}}$

5. $\boxed{10 - (-39)} = \boxed{10 + (39)} = \boxed{10 + 39} = \boxed{\mathbf{49}}$

Case II d.

$$\boxed{(-a) - (-b)} = \boxed{(-a) + (b)} = \boxed{-a + b} = \boxed{D}$$

For example,

1. $\boxed{(-3) - (-9)} = \boxed{(-3) + (9)} = \boxed{-3 + 9} = \boxed{\mathbf{6}}$

2. $\boxed{(-32)-(-8)} = \boxed{(-32)+(8)} = \boxed{-32+8} = \boxed{\mathbf{-24}}$

3. $\boxed{(-17)-(-25)} = \boxed{(-17)+(25)} = \boxed{-17+25} = \boxed{\mathbf{8}}$

4. $\boxed{(-35)-(-10)} = \boxed{(-35)+(10)} = \boxed{-35+10} = \boxed{\mathbf{-25}}$

5. $\boxed{(-1)-(-6)} = \boxed{(-1)+(6)} = \boxed{-1+6} = \boxed{\mathbf{5}}$.

Case III - Multiplication of Signed Numbers

When two numbers are multiplied, the numbers are called **factors** and the result is called a **product**. For example, when 12 is multiplied by 2 the result is 24.

$$\boxed{12\,(factor) \times 2\,(factor)} = \boxed{\mathbf{24}\,(product)}$$

Thus, 12 and 2 are the factors, and 24 is the product.

The sign of the product is positive if the factors had the same sign and is negative if the factors had different signs. This is shown in the following cases with the sign change of two real numbers a and b:

Case III a.

$$\boxed{a \times b} = \boxed{ab}$$

For example,

1. $\boxed{5 \times 6} = \boxed{\mathbf{30}}$ 2. $\boxed{7 \times 8} = \boxed{\mathbf{56}}$ 3. $\boxed{1 \times 0} = \boxed{\mathbf{0}}$

4. $\boxed{10 \times 7} = \boxed{\mathbf{70}}$ 5. $\boxed{15 \times 7} = \boxed{\mathbf{105}}$

Case III b.

$$\boxed{(-a) \times b} = \boxed{-a \times b} = \boxed{-ab}$$

For example,

1. $\boxed{(-7) \times 3} = \boxed{-7 \times 3} = \boxed{\mathbf{-21}}$ 2. $\boxed{(-1) \times 0} = \boxed{-1 \times 0} = \boxed{\mathbf{0}}$

3. $\boxed{(-15) \times 40} = \boxed{-15 \times 40} = \boxed{\mathbf{-600}}$ 4. $\boxed{(-25) \times 16} = \boxed{-25 \times 16} = \boxed{\mathbf{-400}}$

5. $\boxed{(-8) \times 20} = \boxed{-8 \times 20} = \boxed{\mathbf{-160}}$

Case III c.

$$\boxed{a \times (-b)} = \boxed{-a \times b} = \boxed{-ab}$$

For example,

1. $\boxed{2 \times (-5)} = \boxed{-2 \times 5} = \boxed{-10}$ 2. $\boxed{7 \times (-9)} = \boxed{-7 \times 9} = \boxed{-63}$

3. $\boxed{0 \times (-1)} = \boxed{0}$ 4. $\boxed{30 \times (-25)} = \boxed{-30 \times 25} = \boxed{-750}$

5. $\boxed{40 \times (-9)} = \boxed{-40 \times 9} = \boxed{-360}$

Case III d.

$$\boxed{(-a) \times (-b)} = \boxed{+ab} = \boxed{ab}$$

For example,

1. $\boxed{(-3) \times (-9)} = \boxed{+27} = \boxed{27}$ 2. $\boxed{(-12) \times (-4)} = \boxed{+48} = \boxed{48}$

3. $\boxed{(-8) \times (-150)} = \boxed{+1200} = \boxed{1200}$ 4. $\boxed{(-30) \times (-10)} = \boxed{+300} = \boxed{300}$

5. $\boxed{(-5) \times (-25)} = \boxed{+125} = \boxed{125}$

Case IV - Division of Signed Numbers

When one number is divided by another, the first numbers is called the **dividend**, the second number the **divisor**, and the result a **quotient**. For example, when 12 is divided by 2 the result is 6.

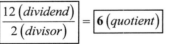

$$\boxed{\frac{12 \,(dividend)}{2 \,(divisor)}} = \boxed{6 \,(quotient)}$$

Thus, 12 is the dividend, 2 is the divisor, and 6 is the quotient.

The sign of the quotient is positive if the divisor and the dividend had the same sign and is negative if the divisor and the dividend had different signs. This is shown in the following cases with the sign change of two real numbers a and b:

Case IV a.

$$\boxed{\frac{a}{b}} = \boxed{A}$$

For example,

1. $\dfrac{9}{3} = \boxed{3}$ 2. $\dfrac{27}{3} = \boxed{9}$ 3. $\dfrac{75}{5} = \boxed{15}$

4. $\dfrac{18}{4} = \boxed{4.5}$ 5. $\dfrac{36}{6} = \boxed{6}$

Case IV b.

$$\dfrac{-a}{b} = -\dfrac{a}{b} = \boxed{B}$$

For example,

1. $\dfrac{-10}{2} = -\dfrac{10}{2} = \boxed{-5}$ 2. $\dfrac{-66}{3} = -\dfrac{66}{3} = \boxed{-22}$ 3. $\dfrac{-75}{5} = -\dfrac{75}{5} = \boxed{-15}$

4. $\dfrac{-8}{2} = -\dfrac{8}{2} = \boxed{-4}$ 5. $\dfrac{-5}{3} = -\dfrac{5}{3} = \boxed{-1.67}$

Case IV c.

$$\dfrac{a}{-b} = -\dfrac{a}{b} = \boxed{C}$$

For example,

1. $\dfrac{30}{-2} = -\dfrac{30}{2} = \boxed{-15}$ 2. $\dfrac{88}{-8} = -\dfrac{88}{8} = \boxed{-11}$ 3. $\dfrac{45}{-9} = -\dfrac{45}{9} = \boxed{-5}$

4. $\dfrac{18}{-5} = -\dfrac{18}{5} = \boxed{-3.6}$ 5. $\dfrac{35}{-7} = -\dfrac{35}{7} = \boxed{-5}$

Case IV d.

$$\dfrac{-a}{-b} = \dfrac{a}{b} = \boxed{D}$$

For example,

1. $\dfrac{-40}{-2} = \dfrac{40}{2} = \boxed{20}$ 2. $\dfrac{-66}{-3} = \dfrac{66}{3} = \boxed{22}$ 3. $\dfrac{-7}{-7} = \dfrac{7}{7} = \boxed{1}$

4. $\dfrac{-28}{-4} = \dfrac{28}{4} = \boxed{7}$ 5. $\dfrac{-8}{-3} = \dfrac{8}{3} = \boxed{2.67}$

General rules used in addition, subtraction, multiplication, and division of signed numbers.

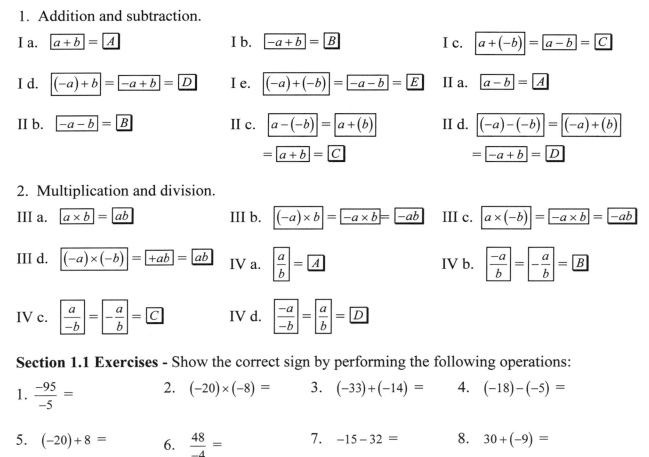

Summary of cases used in addition, subtraction, multiplication, and division of signed numbers:

1. Addition and subtraction.

I a. $\boxed{a+b}=\boxed{A}$ I b. $\boxed{-a+b}=\boxed{B}$ I c. $\boxed{a+(-b)}=\boxed{a-b}=\boxed{C}$

I d. $\boxed{(-a)+b}=\boxed{-a+b}=\boxed{D}$ I e. $\boxed{(-a)+(-b)}=\boxed{-a-b}=\boxed{E}$ II a. $\boxed{a-b}=\boxed{A}$

II b. $\boxed{-a-b}=\boxed{B}$ II c. $\boxed{a-(-b)}=\boxed{a+(b)}$ II d. $\boxed{(-a)-(-b)}=\boxed{(-a)+(b)}$

$=\boxed{a+b}=\boxed{C}$ $=\boxed{-a+b}=\boxed{D}$

2. Multiplication and division.

III a. $\boxed{a\times b}=\boxed{ab}$ III b. $\boxed{(-a)\times b}=\boxed{-a\times b}=\boxed{-ab}$ III c. $\boxed{a\times(-b)}=\boxed{-a\times b}=\boxed{-ab}$

III d. $\boxed{(-a)\times(-b)}=\boxed{+ab}=\boxed{ab}$ IV a. $\boxed{\dfrac{a}{b}}=\boxed{A}$ IV b. $\boxed{\dfrac{-a}{b}}=\boxed{-\dfrac{a}{b}}=\boxed{B}$

IV c. $\boxed{\dfrac{a}{-b}}=\boxed{-\dfrac{a}{b}}=\boxed{C}$ IV d. $\boxed{\dfrac{-a}{-b}}=\boxed{\dfrac{a}{b}}=\boxed{D}$

Section 1.1 Exercises - Show the correct sign by performing the following operations:

1. $\dfrac{-95}{-5}=$ 2. $(-20)\times(-8)=$ 3. $(-33)+(-14)=$ 4. $(-18)-(-5)=$

5. $(-20)+8=$ 6. $\dfrac{48}{-4}=$ 7. $-15-32=$ 8. $30+(-9)=$

9. $55-(-6)=$ 10. $8\times(-35)=$

1.2   Using Parentheses and Brackets in Addition

Parentheses and brackets are used to group numbers as a means to minimize mistakes in solving mathematical operations. In this section the use of parentheses and brackets are discussed in detail. However, two properties associated with addition are discussed first and are as follows:

1. Changing the order in which two numbers are added does not change the final answer. This property of real numbers is called the **Commutative Property of Addition**, e.g., for any two real numbers a and b

$$\boxed{a+b} = \boxed{b+a}$$

For example, $\boxed{9+7} = \boxed{16}$ and $\boxed{7+9} = \boxed{16}$

2. Re-grouping numbers does not change the final answer. This property of real numbers is called the **Associative Property of Addition**, e.g., for any real numbers a, b, and c

$$\boxed{(a+b)+c} = \boxed{a+(b+c)}$$

For example,

$$\boxed{(5+4)+7} = \boxed{(9)+7} = \boxed{9+7} = \boxed{16}$$

$$\boxed{5+(4+7)} = \boxed{5+(11)} = \boxed{5+11} = \boxed{16}$$

In this section, although changing the order in which numbers are added or grouped does not affect the final answer, it is important to learn how to solve math operations in the exact order in which parentheses or brackets are used. Learning how to use parentheses and brackets properly will minimize mistakes in solving mixed operations which are addressed in the proceeding chapters. Parentheses and brackets are used in different ways to group numbers. The use of parentheses and brackets in addition, using integer numbers, are discussed in the following cases:

Case I - Use of Parentheses in Addition
In addition, parentheses can be grouped in different ways as is shown in the following example cases:

Case I a - *Adding Integer Numbers Without Using Parentheses*
Integer numbers are added without the use of parentheses, as shown in the following general and specific example:

$$\boxed{a+b+c+d+e} =$$

Let $\boxed{a+b+c+d+e = A}$, then

$$\boxed{a+b+c+d+e} = \boxed{A}$$

Example 1.2-1

$$\boxed{2+3+5+6+10} =$$

Solution:

$$\boxed{2+3+5+6+10} = \boxed{26}$$

Case I b - *Adding Two Integer Numbers Grouped by Parentheses*
Two integer numbers that are grouped by parentheses are added in the following ways, as shown by general and specific example cases:

Case I b-1.

$$\boxed{(a+b)+(c+d)} =$$

Let $\boxed{k_1 = a+b}$, $\boxed{k_2 = c+d}$, and $\boxed{k_1 + k_2 = A}$, then

$$\boxed{(a+b)+(c+d)} = \boxed{(k_1)+(k_2)} = \boxed{k_1 + k_2} = \boxed{A}$$

Example 1.2-2

$$\boxed{(12+35)+(8+10)} =$$

Solution:

$$\boxed{(12+35)+(8+10)} = \boxed{(47)+(18)} = \boxed{47+18} = \boxed{65}$$

Case I b-2.

$$\boxed{a+(b+c)+(d+e)+f} =$$

Let $\boxed{k_1 = b+c}$, $\boxed{k_2 = d+e}$, and $\boxed{a+k_1+k_2+f = B}$, then

$$\boxed{a+(b+c)+(d+e)+f} = \boxed{a+(k_1)+(k_2)+f} = \boxed{a+k_1+k_2+f} = \boxed{B}$$

Example 1.2-3

$$\boxed{6+(5+12)+(8+7)+23} =$$

Solution:

$$\boxed{6+(5+12)+(8+7)+23} = \boxed{6+(17)+(15)+23} = \boxed{6+17+15+23} = \boxed{\mathbf{61}}$$

Case I b-3.

$$\boxed{(a+b)+(c+d)+(e+f)} =$$

Let $\boxed{k_1 = a+b}$, $\boxed{k_2 = c+d}$, $\boxed{k_3 = e+f}$, and $\boxed{k_1+k_2+k_3 = C}$, then

$$\boxed{(a+b)+(c+d)+(e+f)} = \boxed{(k_1)+(k_2)+(k_3)} = \boxed{k_1+k_2+k_3} = \boxed{C}$$

Example 1.2-4

$$\boxed{(2+5)+(7+10)+(9+12)} =$$

Solution:

$$\boxed{(2+5)+(7+10)+(9+12)} = \boxed{(7)+(17)+(21)} = \boxed{7+17+21} = \boxed{\mathbf{45}}$$

Case I c - *Adding Three Integer Numbers Grouped by Parentheses*
Three integer numbers that are grouped by parentheses are added in the following ways, as shown by general and specific example cases:

Case I c-1.

$$\boxed{a+(b+c+d)} =$$

Let $\boxed{k_1 = b+c+d}$, and $\boxed{a+k_1 = A}$, then

$$\boxed{a+(b+c+d)} = \boxed{a+(k_1)} = \boxed{a+k_1} = \boxed{A}$$

Example 1.2-5

$$\boxed{6+(22+16+5)} =$$

Solution:

$$\boxed{6+(22+16+5)} = \boxed{6+(43)} = \boxed{6+43} = \boxed{\mathbf{49}}$$

Case I c-2.

$$\left[(a + b + c) + (d + e + f)\right] =$$

Let $\boxed{k_1 = a + b + c}$, $\boxed{k_2 = d + e + f}$, and $\boxed{k_1 + k_2 = B}$, then

$$\left[(a + b + c) + (d + e + f)\right] = \left[(k_1) + (k_2)\right] = \boxed{k_1 + k_2} = \boxed{B}$$

Example 1.2-6

$$\left[(10 + 3 + 7) + (20 + 6 + 13)\right] =$$

Solution:

$$\left[(10 + 3 + 7) + (20 + 6 + 13)\right] = \left[(20) + (39)\right] = \boxed{20 + 39} = \boxed{59}$$

Case I d - *Adding Two and Three Integer Numbers Grouped by Parentheses*
Two and three integer numbers that are grouped by parentheses are added in the following ways, as shown by general and specific example cases:

Case I d-1.

$$\left[(a + b + c) + (d + e)\right] =$$

Let $\boxed{k_1 = a + b + c}$, $\boxed{k_2 = d + e}$, and $\boxed{k_1 + k_2 = A}$, then

$$\left[(a + b + c) + (d + e)\right] = \left[(k_1) + (k_2)\right] = \boxed{k_1 + k_2} = \boxed{A}$$

Example 1.2-7

$$\left[(22 + 13 + 8) + (6 + 24)\right] =$$

Solution:

$$\left[(22 + 13 + 8) + (6 + 24)\right] = \left[(43) + (30)\right] = \boxed{43 + 30} = \boxed{73}$$

Case I d-2.

$$\left[(a + b) + (c + d + e) + f\right] =$$

Let $\boxed{k_1 = a + b}$, $\boxed{k_2 = c + d + e}$, and $\boxed{k_1 + k_2 + f = B}$, then

$$\boxed{(a+b)+(c+d+e)+f} = \boxed{(k_1)+(k_2)+f} = \boxed{k_1+k_2+f} = \boxed{B}$$

Example 1.2-8

$$\boxed{(43+6)+(4+13+7)+9} =$$

Solution:

$$\boxed{(43+6)+(4+13+7)+9} = \boxed{(49)+(24)+9} = \boxed{49+24+9} = \boxed{82}$$

Case II - Use of Brackets in Addition

In addition, brackets are used in a similar way as parentheses. However, brackets are used to separate mathematical operations that contain integer numbers already grouped by parentheses. Brackets are also used to group numbers in different ways, as is shown in the following example cases:

Case II a - *Using Brackets to Add Two Integer Numbers Sub-grouped by Parentheses*
Two integer numbers, already grouped by parentheses, are regrouped by brackets and are added as in the following general and specific example cases:

Case II a-1.

$$\boxed{a+\big[(b+c)+(d+e)\big]} =$$

Let $\boxed{k_1 = b+c}$, $\boxed{k_2 = d+e}$, $\boxed{k_1+k_2 = k_3}$, and $\boxed{a+k_3 = A}$, then

$$\boxed{a+\big[(b+c)+(d+e)\big]} = \boxed{a+\big[(k_1)+(k_2)\big]} = \boxed{a+\big[k_1+k_2\big]} = \boxed{a+\big[k_3\big]} = \boxed{a+k_3} = \boxed{A}$$

Example 1.2-9

$$\boxed{6+\big[(10+3)+(4+5)\big]} =$$

Solution:

$$\boxed{6+\big[(10+3)+(4+5)\big]} = \boxed{6+\big[(13)+(9)\big]} = \boxed{6+[13+9]} = \boxed{6+[22]} = \boxed{6+22} = \boxed{28}$$

Case II a-2.

$$\boxed{\big[(a+b)+(c+d)\big]+(e+f)} =$$

Let $\boxed{k_1 = a+b}$, $\boxed{k_2 = c+d}$, $\boxed{k_3 = e+f}$, $\boxed{k_1+k_2 = k_4}$, and $\boxed{k_4+k_3 = B}$, then

$$\boxed{\big[(a+b)+(c+d)\big]+(e+f)} = \boxed{\big[(k_1)+(k_2)\big]+(k_3)} = \boxed{\big[k_1+k_2\big]+k_3} = \boxed{\big[k_4\big]+k_3} = \boxed{k_4+k_3} = \boxed{B}$$

Example 1.2-10

$$\left[\left[(4+7)+(5+9)\right]+(20+3)\right] =$$

Solution:

$$\left[\left[(4+7)+(5+9)\right]+(20+3)\right] = \left[\left[(11)+(14)\right]+(23)\right] = \left[\left[11+14\right]+23\right] = \left[\left[25\right]+23\right] = \left[25+23\right] = \boxed{\mathbf{48}}$$

Case II a-3.

$$\left[(a+b)+\left[(c+d)+(e+f)\right]\right] =$$

Let $\boxed{k_1 = a+b}$, $\boxed{k_2 = c+d}$, $\boxed{k_3 = e+f}$, $\boxed{k_2 + k_3 = k_4}$, and $\boxed{k_1 + k_4 = C}$, then

$$\left[(a+b)+\left[(c+d)+(e+f)\right]\right] = \left[(k_1)+\left[(k_2)+(k_3)\right]\right] = \left[k_1+\left[k_2+k_3\right]\right] = \left[k_1+\left[k_4\right]\right] = \left[k_1+k_4\right] = \boxed{C}$$

Example 1.2-11

$$\left[(7+12)+\left[(13+5)+(6+34)\right]\right] =$$

Solution:

$$\left[(7+12)+\left[(13+5)+(6+34)\right]\right] = \left[(19)+\left[(18)+(40)\right]\right] = \left[19+\left[18+40\right]\right] = \left[19+\left[58\right]\right] = \left[19+58\right] = \boxed{\mathbf{77}}$$

Case II b - *Using Brackets to Add Three Integer Numbers Sub-grouped by Parentheses*
Three integer numbers, already grouped by parentheses, are regrouped by brackets and are added as in the following general and specific example cases:

Case II b-1.

$$\left[\left[(a+b+c)+d\right]+e\right] =$$

Let $\boxed{k_1 = a+b+c}$, $\boxed{k_2 = k_1+d}$, and $\boxed{k_2 + e = A}$, then

$$\left[\left[(a+b+c)+d\right]+e\right] = \left[\left[(k_1)+d\right]+e\right] = \left[\left[k_1+d\right]+e\right] = \left[\left[k_2\right]+e\right] = \left[k_2+e\right] = \boxed{A}$$

Example 1.2-12

$$\left[\left[(7+3+25)+4\right]+6\right] =$$

Solution:

$$\boxed{\Big[\big[(7+3+25)+4\big]+6\Big]} = \boxed{\Big[\big[(35)+4\big]+6\Big]} = \boxed{\big[35+4\big]+6} = \boxed{\big[39\big]+6} = \boxed{39+6} = \boxed{\mathbf{45}}$$

Case II b-2.

$$\boxed{a+\Big[(b+c+d)+(e+f+g)\Big]} =$$

Let $\boxed{k_1 = b+c+d}$, $\boxed{k_2 = e+f+g}$, $\boxed{k_1+k_2 = k_3}$, and $\boxed{a+k_3 = B}$, then

$$\boxed{a+\Big[(b+c+d)+(e+f+g)\Big]} = \boxed{a+\Big[(k_1)+(k_2)\Big]} = \boxed{a+\big[k_1+k_2\big]} = \boxed{a+\big[k_3\big]} = \boxed{a+k_3} = \boxed{B}$$

Example 1.2-13

$$\boxed{20+\Big[(5+12+6)+(3+8+4)\Big]} =$$

Solution:

$$\boxed{20+\Big[(5+12+6)+(3+8+4)\Big]} = \boxed{20+\Big[(23)+(15)\Big]} = \boxed{20+\big[23+15\big]} = \boxed{20+\big[38\big]} = \boxed{20+38} = \boxed{\mathbf{58}}$$

Case II c - *Using Brackets to Add Two and Three Integer Numbers Sub-grouped by Parentheses*
Two and three integer numbers, already grouped by parentheses, are regrouped by brackets and are added as in the following general and specific example cases:

Case II c-1.

$$\boxed{a+\Big[(b+c)+(d+e+f)\Big]} =$$

Let $\boxed{k_1 = b+c}$, $\boxed{k_2 = d+e+f}$, $\boxed{k_1+k_2 = k_3}$, and $\boxed{a+k_3 = A}$, then

$$\boxed{a+\Big[(b+c)+(d+e+f)\Big]} = \boxed{a+\Big[(k_1)+(k_2)\Big]} = \boxed{a+\big[k_1+k_2\big]} = \boxed{a+\big[k_3\big]} = \boxed{a+k_3} = \boxed{A}$$

Example 1.2-14

$$\boxed{4+\Big[(3+12)+(9+15+23)\Big]} =$$

Solution:

$$\boxed{4+\Big[(3+12)+(9+15+23)\Big]} = \boxed{4+\Big[(15)+(47)\Big]} = \boxed{4+\big[15+47\big]} = \boxed{4+\big[62\big]} = \boxed{4+62} = \boxed{\mathbf{66}}$$

Case II c-2.

$$\left[\left[(a+b)+(c+d+e)+f\right]+g\right]=$$

Let $\boxed{k_1=a+b}$, $\boxed{k_2=c+d+e}$, $\boxed{k_1+k_2+f=k_3}$, and $\boxed{k_3+g=B}$, then

$$\left[\left[(a+b)+(c+d+e)+f\right]+g\right]=\left[\left[(k_1)+(k_2)+f\right]+g\right]=\left[\left[k_1+k_2+f\right]+g\right]=\left[\left[k_3\right]+g\right]=\boxed{k_3+g}=\boxed{B}$$

Example 1.2-15

$$\left[\left[(3+5)+(4+9+11)+6\right]+3\right]=$$

Solution:

$$\left[\left[(3+5)+(4+9+11)+6\right]+3\right]=\left[\left[(8)+(24)+6\right]+3\right]=\left[\left[8+24+6\right]+3\right]=\left[\left[38\right]+3\right]=\boxed{38+3}=\boxed{\mathbf{41}}$$

Case II c-3.

$$\left[(a+b)+\left[(c+d+e)+(f+g)+h\right]\right]=$$

Let $\boxed{k_1=a+b}$, $\boxed{k_2=c+d+e}$, $\boxed{k_3=f+g}$, $\boxed{k_2+k_3+h=k_4}$, and $\boxed{k_1+k_4=C}$, then

$$\left[(a+b)+\left[(c+d+e)+(f+g)+h\right]\right]=\left[(k_1)+\left[(k_2)+(k_3)+h\right]\right]=\left[k_1+\left[k_2+k_3+h\right]\right]=\left[k_1+\left[k_4\right]\right]=\boxed{k_1+k_4}=\boxed{C}$$

Example 1.2-16

$$\left[(4+3)+\left[(6+9+12)+(30+5)+1\right]\right]=$$

Solution:

$$\left[(4+3)+\left[(6+9+12)+(30+5)+1\right]\right]=\left[7+\left[(27)+(35)+1\right]\right]=\left[7+\left[27+35+1\right]\right]=\left[7+\left[63\right]\right]=\boxed{7+63}=\boxed{\mathbf{70}}$$

The following examples further illustrate how to use parentheses and brackets in addition:

Example 1.2-17

$$\left[5+(2+13+8)+(8+20)\right]=\boxed{5+(23)+(28)}=\boxed{5+23+28}=\boxed{\mathbf{56}}$$

Example 1.2-18

$$\left[(25+33)+(8+13)+7\right]=\left[(58)+(21)+7\right]=\boxed{58+21+7}=\boxed{\mathbf{86}}$$

Example 1.2-19

$$\boxed{18+(52+10+7)+15+(6+24)} = \boxed{18+(69)+15+(30)} = \boxed{18+69+15+30} = \boxed{\mathbf{132}}$$

Example 1.2-20

$$\boxed{12+\left[3+(16+4)+(2+13+5)\right]} = \boxed{12+\left[3+(20)+(20)\right]} = \boxed{12+\left[3+20+20\right]} = \boxed{12+\left[43\right]} = \boxed{12+43} = \boxed{\mathbf{55}}$$

Example 1.2-21

$$\boxed{(26+11+7)+\left[(2+13)+(23+8)+20\right]} = \boxed{(44)+\left[(15)+(31)+20\right]} = \boxed{44+\left[15+31+20\right]} = \boxed{44+\left[66\right]}$$

$$= \boxed{44+66} = \boxed{\mathbf{110}}$$

Example 1.2-22

$$\boxed{\left[2+(12+6)+(18+4+9)\right]+(16+5)} = \boxed{\left[2+(18)+(31)\right]+(21)} = \boxed{\left[2+18+31\right]+21} = \boxed{\left[51\right]+21} = \boxed{51+21}$$

$$= \boxed{\mathbf{72}}$$

Example 1.2-23

$$\boxed{23+(12+5)+\left[7+(12+9)\right]} = \boxed{23+(17)+\left[7+(21)\right]} = \boxed{23+17+\left[7+21\right]} = \boxed{23+17+\left[28\right]} = \boxed{23+17+28}$$

$$= \boxed{\mathbf{68}}$$

Example 1.2-24

$$\boxed{\left[(12+3+8)+(32+4)+3\right]+(5+20)} = \boxed{\left[(23)+(36)+3\right]+(25)} = \boxed{\left[23+36+3\right]+25} = \boxed{\left[62\right]+25} = \boxed{62+25}$$

$$= \boxed{\mathbf{87}}$$

Example 1.2-25

$$\boxed{(23+13)+7+\left[23+(12+9)\right]} = \boxed{(36)+7+\left[23+(21)\right]} = \boxed{36+7+\left[23+21\right]} = \boxed{43+\left[44\right]} = \boxed{43+44} = \boxed{\mathbf{87}}$$

Example 1.2-26

$$\boxed{\left[(25+13+2)+(16+84)\right]+(10+3)+5} = \boxed{\left[(40)+(100)\right]+(13)+5} = \boxed{\left[40+100\right]+13+5} = \boxed{\left[140\right]+18}$$

$$= \boxed{140+18} = \boxed{\mathbf{158}}$$

Section 1.2 Exercises - Add the following numbers in the order grouped:

1. $2+3+5+6 \ =$

2. $(2+5)+(6+3)+9 \ =$

3. $(6+3+8)+(2+3)+4 \ =$

4. $8+\left[(1+3+4)+(1+2)\right] \ =$

5. $\left[(18+4)+9\right]+\left[1+(2+3)\right] \ =$

6. $8+\left[(2+3)+(6+3)+15\right] \ =$

7. $(7+3+8)+\left[(7+2+3)+5\right] \ =$

8. $\left[(3+9+4)+1+(1+8)\right]+(8+2) \ =$

9. $\left[(2+3+6)+(1+8)\right]+\left[(1+3)+4\right] \ =$

10. $\left[\left[(3+5)+(4+3)+5\right]+(2+3+5)\right]+6 \ =$

1.3   Using Parentheses and Brackets in Subtraction

In this section the use of parentheses and brackets as applied to subtraction are discussed. Changing the order in which numbers are subtracted or grouped does affect the final answer. The following two properties associated with subtraction are discussed first and are as follows:

1. Changing the order in which two numbers are subtracted does change the final answer. For example, for any two real numbers a and b

    $$\boxed{a - b \neq b - a}$$ *Note:* The symbol "$\neq$" means not equal.

    For example, $\boxed{20-8} = \boxed{\mathbf{12}}$, but $\boxed{8-20} = \boxed{\mathbf{-12}}$

2. Re-grouping numbers does change the final answer. For example, for any real numbers a, b, and c

    $$\boxed{(a-b)-c \neq a-(b-c)}$$

    For example,

    $\boxed{(25-6)-8} = \boxed{(19)-8} = \boxed{19-8} = \boxed{\mathbf{11}}$, however

    $\boxed{25-(6-8)} = \boxed{25-(-2)} = \boxed{25+(2)} = \boxed{25+2} = \boxed{\mathbf{27}}$

In the following cases the use of parentheses and brackets in subtraction, using integer numbers, are discussed:

Case I - Use of Parentheses in Subtraction

In subtraction, parentheses can be grouped in different ways as is shown in the following example cases:

Case I a - *Subtracting Integer Numbers Without Using Parentheses*

Integer numbers are subtracted without the use of parentheses, as shown in the following general and specific example:

$$\boxed{a-b-c-d-e} =$$

Let $\boxed{a-b-c-d-e = A}$, then

$$\boxed{a-b-c-d-e} = \boxed{A}$$

Example 1.3-1

$$\boxed{24-5-13-7-8} =$$

Solution:

$$\boxed{24 - 5 - 13 - 7 - 8} = \boxed{-9}$$

Case I b - *Subtracting Two Integer Numbers Grouped by Parentheses*
Two integer numbers that are grouped by parentheses are subtracted in the following ways as shown by general and specific example cases:

Case I b-1.

$$\boxed{a - (b - c)} =$$

Let $\boxed{k_1 = b - c}$, and $\boxed{a - k_1 = A}$, then

$$\boxed{a - (b - c)} = \boxed{a - (k_1)} = \boxed{a - k_1} = \boxed{A}$$

Example 1.3-2

$$\boxed{20 - (15 - 45)} =$$

Solution:

$$\boxed{20 - (15 - 45)} = \boxed{20 - (-30)} = \boxed{20 + (30)} = \boxed{20 + 30} = \boxed{50}$$

Case I b-2.

$$\boxed{(a - b) - (c - d)} =$$

Let $\boxed{k_1 = a - b}$, $\boxed{k_2 = c - d}$, and $\boxed{k_1 - k_2 = B}$, then

$$\boxed{(a - b) - (c - d)} = \boxed{(k_1) - (k_2)} = \boxed{k_1 - k_2} = \boxed{B}$$

Example 1.3-3

$$\boxed{(20 - 25) - (7 - 5)} =$$

Solution:

$$\boxed{(20 - 25) - (7 - 5)} = \boxed{(-5) - (2)} = \boxed{-5 - 2} = \boxed{-7}$$

Case I b-3.

$$a-(b-c)-(d-e) =$$

Let $k_1 = b-c$, $k_2 = d-e$, and $a-k_1-k_2 = C$, then

$$a-(b-c)-(d-e) = a-(k_1)-(k_2) = a-k_1-k_2 = \boxed{C}$$

Example 1.3-4

$$25-(35-12)-(8-3) =$$

Solution:

$$25-(35-12)-(8-3) = 25-(23)-(5) = 25-23-5 = \boxed{-3}$$

Case I c - *Subtracting Three Integer Numbers Grouped by Parentheses*

Three integer numbers that are grouped by parentheses are subtracted in the following ways, as shown by general and specific example cases:

Case I c-1.

$$a-(b-c-d) =$$

Let $k_1 = b-c-d$, and $a-k_1 = A$, then

$$a-(b-c-d) = a-(k_1) = a-k_1 = \boxed{A}$$

Example 1.3-5

$$6-(22-16-8) =$$

Solution:

$$6-(22-16-8) = 6-(-2) = 6+(2) = 6+2 = \boxed{8}$$

Case I c-2.

$$(a-b-c)-(d-e-f) =$$

Let $k_1 = a-b-c$, $k_2 = d-e-f$, and $k_1-k_2 = B$, then

$$\left|(a-b-c)-(d-e-f)\right| = \left|(k_1)-(k_2)\right| = \left|k_1-k_2\right| = \boxed{B}$$

Example 1.3-6

$$\left|(15-3-8)-(40-9-34)\right| =$$

Solution:

$$\left|(15-3-8)-(40-9-34)\right| = \left|(4)-(-3)\right| = \boxed{4+(3)} = \boxed{4+3} = \boxed{7}$$

Case I d - *Subtracting Two and Three Integer Numbers Grouped by Parentheses*
Two and three integer numbers that are grouped by parentheses are subtracted in the following ways, as shown by general and specific example cases:

Case I d-1.

$$\left|(a-b)-(c-d-e)-f\right| =$$

Let $\boxed{k_1 = a-b}$, $\boxed{k_2 = c-d-e}$, and $\boxed{k_1 - k_2 - f = A}$, then

$$\left|(a-b)-(c-d-e)-f\right| = \left|(k_1)-(k_2)-f\right| = \boxed{k_1-k_2-f} = \boxed{A}$$

Example 1.3-7

$$\left|(43-6)-(54-13-7)-19\right| =$$

Solution:

$$\left|(43-6)-(54-13-7)-19\right| = \left|(37)-(34)-19\right| = \boxed{37-34-19} = \boxed{3-19} = \boxed{-16}$$

Case I d-2.

$$\left|(a-b-c)-(d-e)\right| =$$

Let $\boxed{k_1 = a-b-c}$, $\boxed{k_2 = d-e}$, and $\boxed{k_1 - k_2 = B}$, then

$$\left|(a-b-c)-(d-e)\right| = \left|(k_1)-(k_2)\right| = \boxed{k_1-k_2} = \boxed{B}$$

Example 1.3-8

$$\left|(8-13-10)-(6-36)\right| =$$

Solution:

$$\left|(8-13-10)-(6-36)\right| = \left|(-15)-(-30)\right| = \left|-15+(30)\right| = \left|-15+30\right| = \boxed{\mathbf{15}}$$

Case II - Use of Brackets in subtraction

In subtraction, brackets are used in a similar way as parentheses. However, brackets are used to separate mathematical operations that contain integer numbers already grouped by parentheses. Brackets are also used to group numbers in different ways, as is shown in the following example cases:

Case II a - *Using Brackets to Subtract Two Integer Numbers Sub-grouped by Parentheses*
Two integer numbers, already grouped by parentheses, are regrouped by brackets and subtracted as in the following general and specific example cases:

Case II a-1.

$$\left|\left[a-(b-c)\right]-d\right| =$$

Let $\boxed{k_1 = b - c}$, $\boxed{a - k_1 = k_2}$, and $\boxed{k_2 - d = A}$, then

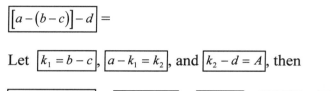

$$\left|\left[a-(b-c)\right]-d\right| = \left|\left[a-k_1\right]-d\right| = \left|\left[k_2\right]-d\right| = \left|k_2 - d\right| = \boxed{A}$$

Example 1.3-9

$$\left|\left[38-(12-9)\right]-30\right| =$$

Solution:

$$\left|\left[38-(12-9)\right]-30\right| = \left|\left[38-(3)\right]-30\right| = \left|\left[38-3\right]-30\right| = \left|\left[35\right]-30\right| = \left|35-30\right| = \boxed{\mathbf{5}}$$

Case II a-2.

$$\left|\left[(a-b)-c\right]-d\right| =$$

Let $\boxed{k_1 = a - b}$, $\boxed{k_2 = k_1 - c}$, and $\boxed{k_2 - d = B}$, then

$$\left|\left[(a-b)-c\right]-d\right| = \left|\left[(k_1)-c\right]-d\right| = \left|\left[k_1-c\right]-d\right| = \left|\left[k_2\right]-d\right| = \left|k_2 - d\right| = \boxed{B}$$

Example 1.3-10

$$\left|\left[(9-23)-12\right]-40\right| =$$

Solution:

$$\boxed{[(9-23)-12]-40} = \boxed{[(-14)-12]-40} = \boxed{[-14-12]-40} = \boxed{[-26]-40} = \boxed{-26-40} = \boxed{\mathbf{-66}}$$

Case II a-3.

$$\boxed{a-[(b-c)-d]} =$$

Let $\boxed{k_1 = b - c}$, $\boxed{k_2 = k_1 - d}$, and $\boxed{a - k_2 = C}$, then

$$\boxed{a-[(b-c)-d]} = \boxed{a-[(k_1)-d]} = \boxed{a-[k_1-d]} = \boxed{a-[k_2]} = \boxed{a-k_2} = \boxed{C}$$

Example 1.3-11

$$\boxed{5-[(18-7)-27]} =$$

Solution:

$$\boxed{5-[(18-7)-27]} = \boxed{5-[(11)-27]} = \boxed{5-[11-27]} = \boxed{5-[-16]} = \boxed{5+[16]} = \boxed{5+16} = \boxed{\mathbf{21}}$$

Case II a-4.

$$\boxed{a-[(b-c)-(d-e)]} =$$

Let $\boxed{k_1 = b - c}$, $\boxed{k_2 = d - e}$, $\boxed{k_1 - k_2 = k_3}$, and $\boxed{a - k_3 = D}$, then

$$\boxed{a-[(b-c)-(d-e)]} = \boxed{a-[(k_1)-(k_2)]} = \boxed{a-[k_1-k_2]} = \boxed{a-[k_3]} = \boxed{a-k_3} = \boxed{D}$$

Example 1.3-12

$$\boxed{26-[(10-6)-(4-9)]} =$$

Solution:

$$\boxed{26-[(10-6)-(4-9)]} = \boxed{26-[(4)-(-5)]} = \boxed{26-[4+(5)]} = \boxed{26-[4+5]} = \boxed{26-[9]} = \boxed{26-9} = \boxed{\mathbf{17}}$$

Case II a-5.

$$\boxed{(a-b)-[(c-d)-(e-f)]} =$$

Let; $\boxed{k_1 = a - b}$, $\boxed{k_2 = c - d}$, $\boxed{k_3 = e - f}$, $\boxed{k_2 - k_3 = k_4}$, and $\boxed{k_1 - k_4 = E}$, then

$$\boxed{(a-b)-\big[(c-d)-(e-f)\big]} = \boxed{(k_1)-\big[(k_2)-(k_3)\big]} = \boxed{k_1 -[k_2 - k_3]} = \boxed{k_1 -[k_4]} = \boxed{k_1 - k_4} = \boxed{E}$$

Example 1.3-13

$$\boxed{(27-14)-\big[(13-9)-(26-8)\big]} =$$

Solution:

$$\boxed{(27-14)-\big[(13-9)-(26-8)\big]} = \boxed{(13)-\big[(4)-(18)\big]} = \boxed{13-[4-18]} = \boxed{13-[-14]} = \boxed{13+[14]} = \boxed{13+14}$$

$$= \boxed{27}$$

Case II b - *Using Brackets to Subtract Three Integer Numbers Sub-grouped by Parentheses*
Three integer numbers, already grouped by parentheses, are regrouped by brackets and subtracted as in the following general and specific example cases:

Case II b-1.

$$\boxed{\big[(a-b-c)-d\big]-e} =$$

Let $\boxed{k_1 = a-b-c}$, $\boxed{k_2 = k_1 -d}$, and $\boxed{k_2 -e = A}$, then

$$\boxed{\big[(a-b-c)-d\big]-e} = \boxed{\big[(k_1)-d\big]-e} = \boxed{[k_1 -d]-e} = \boxed{[k_2]-e} = \boxed{k_2 -e} = \boxed{A}$$

Example 1.3-14

$$\boxed{\big[(45-13-7)-15\big]-20} =$$

Solution:

$$\boxed{\big[(45-13-7)-15\big]-20} = \boxed{\big[(25)-15\big]-20} = \boxed{[25-15]-20} = \boxed{[10]-20} = \boxed{10-20} = \boxed{-10}$$

Case II b-2.

$$\boxed{a-\big[(b-c-d)-(e-f-g)\big]} =$$

Let $\boxed{k_1 = b-c-d}$, $\boxed{k_2 = e-f-g}$, $\boxed{k_1 -k_2 = k_3}$, and $\boxed{a-k_3 = B}$, then

$$\boxed{a-\big[(b-c-d)-(e-f-g)\big]} = \boxed{a-\big[(k_1)-(k_2)\big]} = \boxed{a-[k_1 -k_2]} = \boxed{a-[k_3]} = \boxed{a-k_3} = \boxed{B}$$

Example 1.3-15

$$50 - \left[(5 - 25 - 7) - (36 - 12 - 5)\right] =$$

Solution:

$$50 - \left[(5 - 25 - 7) - (36 - 12 - 5)\right] = 50 - \left[(-27) - (19)\right] = 50 - \left[-27 - 19\right] = 50 - \left[-46\right] = 50 + \left[46\right]$$

$$= 50 + 46 = \boxed{96}$$

Case II c - *Using Brackets to Subtract Two and Three Integer Numbers Sub-grouped by Parentheses*

Two and three integer numbers, already grouped by parentheses, are regrouped by brackets and subtracted as in the following general and specific example cases:

Case II c-1.

$$\left[(a - b) - (c - d - e)\right] - f =$$

Let $k_1 = a - b$, $k_2 = c - d - e$, $k_1 - k_2 = k_3$, and $k_3 - f = A$, then

$$\left[(a - b) - (c - d - e)\right] - f = \left[(k_1) - (k_2)\right] - f = \left[k_1 - k_2\right] - f = \left[k_3\right] - f = k_3 - f = \boxed{A}$$

Example 1.3-16

$$\left[(300 - 450) - (100 - 35 - 55)\right] - 12 =$$

Solution:

$$\left[(300 - 450) - (100 - 35 - 55)\right] - 12 = \left[(-150) - (10)\right] - 12 = \left[-150 - 10\right] - 12 = \left[-160\right] - 12 = -160 - 12$$

$$= \boxed{-172}$$

Case II c-2.

$$a - \left[(b - c) - (d - e - f)\right] =$$

Let $k_1 = b - c$, $k_2 = d - e - f$, $k_1 - k_2 = k_3$, and $a - k_3 = B$, then

$$a - \left[(b - c) - (d - e - f)\right] = a - \left[(k_1) - (k_2)\right] = a - \left[k_1 - k_2\right] = a - \left[k_3\right] = a - k_3 = \boxed{B}$$

Example 1.3-17

$$34 - \big[(324 - 130) - (250 - 39 - 85)\big] =$$

Solution:

$$34 - \big[(324 - 130) - (250 - 39 - 85)\big] = 34 - \big[(194) - (126)\big] = 34 - [194 - 126] = 34 - [68] = 34 - 68$$

$$= \boxed{-34}$$

Case II c-3.

$$\big[(a - b) - (c - d - e) - f\big] - g =$$

Let $k_1 = a - b$, $k_2 = c - d - e$, $k_1 - k_2 - f = k_3$, and $k_3 - g = C$, then

$$\big[(a - b) - (c - d - e) - f\big] - g = \big[(k_1) - (k_2) - f\big] - g = \big[k_1 - k_2 - f\big] - g = \big[k_3\big] - g = k_3 - g = \boxed{C}$$

Example 1.3-18

$$\big[(13 - 8) - (24 - 9 - 15) - 6\big] - 30 =$$

Solution:

$$\big[(13 - 8) - (24 - 9 - 15) - 6\big] - 30 = \big[(5) - (0) - 6\big] - 30 = [5 - 0 - 6] - 30 = [-1] - 30 = -1 - 30 = \boxed{-31}$$

Case II c-4.

$$(a - b) - \big[(c - d - e) - (f - g)\big] =$$

Let $k_1 = a - b$, $k_2 = c - d - e$, $k_3 = f - g$, $k_2 - k_3 = k_4$, and $k_1 - k_4 = D$, then

$$(a - b) - \big[(c - d - e) - (f - g)\big] = (k_1) - \big[(k_2) - (k_3)\big] = k_1 - \big[k_2 - k_3\big] = k_1 - \big[k_4\big] = k_1 - k_4 = \boxed{D}$$

Example 1.3-19

$$(35 - 12) - \big[(8 - 6 - 4) - (20 - 18)\big] =$$

Solution:

$$\boxed{(35-12)-\left[(8-6-4)-(20-18)\right]} = \boxed{(23)-\left[(-2)-(2)\right]} = \boxed{(23)-[-2-2]} = \boxed{(23)-[-4]} = \boxed{23+[4]} = \boxed{23+4}$$

$$= \boxed{27}$$

Section 1.3 Exercises - Subtract the following numbers in the order grouped:

1. $(55-5)-3-8 =$

2. $59-38-12-(20-5) =$

3. $(20-5)-(11-2) =$

4. $\left[-25-(4-13)\right]-5 =$

5. $350-(25-38)-30 =$

6. $\left[(-30-3)-8\right]-(16-9) =$

7. $\left[(40-4)-(8-10)\right]-9 =$

8. $(35-56)-\left[(20-15)-8\right] =$

9. $\left[(-175-55)-245\right]-(5-6) =$

10. $(48-80)-\left[(12-2)-(15-37)\right] =$

1.4   Using Parentheses and Brackets in Multiplication

Parentheses and brackets are the tools used for grouping numbers. In this section the use of parentheses and brackets as applied to multiplication are discussed. The following properties associated with multiplication are discussed first and are as follows:

1. Changing the order in which two numbers are multiplied does not change the final answer. This property of real numbers is called the **Commutative Property of Multiplication**, e.g., for any two real numbers a and b

$$\boxed{a \times b} = \boxed{b \times a}$$

For example, $\boxed{3 \times 15} = \boxed{45}$ and $\boxed{15 \times 3} = \boxed{45}$

2. Re-grouping numbers does not change the final answer. This property of real numbers is called the **Associative Property of Multiplication**, e.g., for any real numbers a, b, and c

$$\boxed{(a \times b) \times c} = \boxed{a \times (b \times c)}$$

For example,

$$\boxed{(4 \times 8) \times 5} = \boxed{(32) \times 5} = \boxed{32 \times 5} = \boxed{160}$$

$$\boxed{4 \times (8 \times 5)} = \boxed{4 \times (40)} = \boxed{4 \times 40} = \boxed{160}$$

3. Multiplication can be distributed over addition. This property is called the **Distributive Property of multiplication**, e.g., for any real numbers a, b, and c

$$\boxed{a \times (b + c)} = \boxed{ab + ac}$$

For example,

$$\boxed{9 \times (4 + 5)} = \boxed{(9 \times 4) + (9 \times 5)} = \boxed{36 + 45} = \boxed{81}$$

Similar to addition (see Section 1.2), changing the order in which numbers are multiplied or grouped does not affect the final answer. However, again, it is important to learn how to solve math operations in the exact order in which parentheses or brackets are used in grouping numbers. The use of parentheses and brackets in multiplication, using integer numbers, are discussed in the following cases:

Case I - Use of Parentheses in Multiplication

In multiplication, parentheses can be grouped in different ways, as is shown in the following example cases:

Case I a - *Multiplying Integer Numbers Without Using Parentheses*

Integer numbers are multiplied without the use of parentheses, as shown in the following general and specific example:

$$\boxed{a \times b \times c \times d \times e} = \boxed{abcde}$$

Example 1.4-1

$$\boxed{3 \times 5 \times 7 \times 2 \times 4} =$$

Solution:

$$\boxed{3 \times 5 \times 7 \times 2 \times 4} = \boxed{\mathbf{840}}$$

Case I b - *Multiplying Two Integer Numbers Grouped by Parentheses*

Two integer numbers that are grouped by parentheses are multiplied in the following ways, as shown by general and specific example cases:

Case I b-1.

$$\boxed{(a \times b) \times (c \times d) \times (e \times f)} = \boxed{(ab) \times (cd) \times (ef)} = \boxed{ab \times cd \times ef} = \boxed{abcdef}$$

Example 1.4-2

$$\boxed{(2 \times 5) \times (7 \times 4) \times (1 \times 3)} =$$

Solution:

$$\boxed{(2 \times 5) \times (7 \times 4) \times (1 \times 3)} = \boxed{(10) \times (28) \times (3)} = \boxed{10 \times 28 \times 3} = \boxed{\mathbf{840}}$$

Case I b-2.

$$\boxed{a \times (b \times c) \times (d \times e) \times f} = \boxed{a \times (bc) \times (de) \times f} = \boxed{a \times bc \times de \times f} = \boxed{abcdef}$$

Example 1.4-3

$$\boxed{2 \times (5 \times 3) \times (6 \times 4) \times 7} =$$

Solution:

$$\boxed{2 \times (5 \times 3) \times (6 \times 4) \times 7} = \boxed{2 \times (15) \times (24) \times 7} = \boxed{2 \times 15 \times 24 \times 7} = \boxed{\mathbf{5040}}$$

Case I c - *Multiplying Three Integer Numbers Grouped by Parentheses*

Three integer numbers that are grouped by parentheses are multiplied in the following ways, as shown by general and specific example cases:

Case I c-1.

$$\boxed{a \times (b \times c \times d)} = \boxed{a \times (bcd)} = \boxed{a \times bcd} = \boxed{abcd}$$

Example 1.4-4

$$\boxed{2 \times (3 \times 8 \times 10)} =$$

Solution:

$$\boxed{2 \times (3 \times 8 \times 10)} = \boxed{2 \times (240)} = \boxed{2 \times 240} = \boxed{\mathbf{480}}$$

Case I c-2.

$$\boxed{(a \times b \times c) \times (d \times e \times f)} =$$

$$\boxed{(a \times b \times c) \times (d \times e \times f)} = \boxed{(abc) \times (def)} = \boxed{abc \times def} = \boxed{abcdef}$$

Example 1.4-5

$$\boxed{(5 \times 3 \times 2) \times (10 \times 4 \times 7)} =$$

Solution:

$$\boxed{(5 \times 3 \times 2) \times (10 \times 4 \times 7)} = \boxed{(30) \times (280)} = \boxed{30 \times 280} = \boxed{\mathbf{8400}}$$

Case I d - *Multiplying Two and Three Integer Numbers Grouped by Parentheses*

Two and three integer numbers that are grouped by parentheses are multiplied in the following ways, as shown by general and specific example cases:

Case I d-1.

$$\boxed{(a \times b) \times (c \times d \times e) \times f} = \boxed{(ab) \times (cde) \times f} = \boxed{abcdef}$$

Example 1.4-6

$$\boxed{(3 \times 1) \times (4 \times 5 \times 11) \times 2} =$$

Solution:

$$\boxed{(3 \times 1) \times (4 \times 5 \times 11) \times 2} = \boxed{(3) \times (220) \times 2} = \boxed{3 \times 220 \times 2} = \boxed{\mathbf{1320}}$$

Case I d-2.

$$\boxed{(a \times b \times c) \times (d \times e)} = \boxed{(abc) \times (de)} = \boxed{abc \times de} = \boxed{abcde}$$

Example 1.4-7

$$\boxed{(2 \times 9 \times 8) \times (6 \times 4)} =$$

Solution:

$$\boxed{(2 \times 9 \times 8) \times (6 \times 4)} = \boxed{(144) \times (24)} = \boxed{144 \times 24} = \boxed{\mathbf{3456}}$$

Case II - Use of Brackets in Multiplication

In multiplication, brackets are used in a similar way as parentheses. However, brackets are used to separate mathematical operations that contain integer numbers already grouped by parentheses. Brackets are also used to group numbers in different ways, as is shown in the following example cases:

Case II a - *Using Brackets to Multiply Two Integer Numbers Sub-grouped by Parentheses*

Two integer numbers already grouped by parentheses are regrouped by brackets and are multiplied as in the following general and specific example cases:

Case II a-1.

$$\boxed{a \times \left[(b \times c) \times (d \times e) \right]} = \boxed{a \times \left[(bc) \times (de) \right]} = \boxed{a \times \left[bc \times de \right]} = \boxed{a \times \left[bcde \right]} = \boxed{a \times bcde} = \boxed{abcde}$$

Example 1.4-8

$$\boxed{6 \times \left[(12 \times 3) \times (4 \times 1) \right]} =$$

Solution:

$$\boxed{6 \times \left[(12 \times 3) \times (4 \times 1) \right]} = \boxed{6 \times \left[(36) \times (4) \right]} = \boxed{6 \times \left[36 \times 4 \right]} = \boxed{6 \times \left[144 \right]} = \boxed{6 \times 144} = \boxed{\mathbf{864}}$$

Case II a-2.

$$\boxed{\left[(a \times b) \times (c \times d) \right] \times (e \times f)} = \boxed{\left[(ab) \times (cd) \right] \times (ef)} = \boxed{\left[ab \times cd \right] ef} = \boxed{\left[abcd \right] ef} = \boxed{abcdef}$$

Example 1.4-9

$$\left[\left[(4\times1)\times(5\times9)\right]\times(2\times3)\right]=$$

Solution:

$$\left[\left[(4\times1)\times(5\times9)\right]\times(2\times3)\right]=\left[\left[(4)\times(45)\right]\times(6)\right]=\left[\left[4\times45\right]\times6\right]=\left[\left[180\right]\times6\right]=\left[180\times6\right]=\boxed{\mathbf{1080}}$$

Case II a-3.

$$\left[(a\times b)\times\left[(c\times d)\times(e\times f)\right]\right]=\left[(ab)\times\left[(cd)\times(ef)\right]\right]=\left[ab\times\left[cd\times ef\right]\right]=\left[ab\times\left[cdef\right]\right]=\left[ab\times cdef\right]=\boxed{abcdef}$$

Example 1.4-10

$$\left[(7\times4)\times\left[(13\times2)\times(6\times1)\right]\right]=$$

Solution:

$$\left[(7\times4)\times\left[(13\times2)\times(6\times1)\right]\right]=\left[(28)\times\left[(26)\times(6)\right]\right]=\left[28\times\left[156\right]\right]=\left[28\times156\right]=\boxed{\mathbf{4368}}$$

Case II b - *Using Brackets to Multiply Three Integer Numbers Sub-grouped by Parentheses*
Three integer numbers, already grouped by parentheses, are regrouped by brackets and are multiplied as in the following general and specific example cases:

Case II b-1.

$$\left[\left[(a\times b\times c)\times d\right]\times e\right]=\left[\left[(abc)\times d\right]\times e\right]=\left[\left[abc\times d\right]\times e\right]=\left[\left[abcd\right]\times e\right]=\left[abcd\times e\right]=\boxed{abcde}$$

Example 1.4-11

$$\left[\left[(7\times3\times10)\times4\right]\times2\right]=$$

Solution:

$$\left[\left[(7\times3\times10)\times4\right]\times2\right]=\left[\left[(210)\times4\right]\times2\right]=\left[\left[210\times4\right]\times2\right]=\left[\left[840\right]\times2\right]=\left[840\times2\right]=\boxed{\mathbf{1680}}$$

Case II b-2.

$$a\times\left[\left[(b\times c\times d)\times(e\times f\times g)\right]\right]=a\times\left[\left[(bcd)\times(efg)\right]\right]=a\times\left[bcd\times efg\right]=a\times\left[bcdefg\right]=\boxed{a\times bcdefg}$$

$$=\boxed{abcdefg}$$

Example 1.4-12

$$2 \times \left[(5 \times 1 \times 6) \times (3 \times 8 \times 4)\right] =$$

Solution:

$$2 \times \left[(5 \times 1 \times 6) \times (3 \times 8 \times 4)\right] = 2 \times \left[(30) \times (96)\right] = 2 \times \left[30 \times 96\right] = 2 \times \left[2880\right] = 2 \times 2880 = \boxed{\mathbf{5760}}$$

Case II c - *Using Brackets to Multiply Two and Three Integer Numbers Sub-grouped by Parentheses*

Two and three integer numbers, already grouped by parentheses, are regrouped by brackets and are multiplied as in the following general and specific example cases:

Case II c-1.

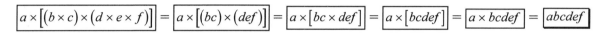

$$a \times \left[(b \times c) \times (d \times e \times f)\right] = a \times \left[(bc) \times (def)\right] = a \times \left[bc \times def\right] = a \times \left[bcdef\right] = a \times bcdef = \boxed{abcdef}$$

Example 1.4-13

$$2 \times \left[(3 \times 7) \times (1 \times 10 \times 5)\right] =$$

Solution:

$$2 \times \left[(3 \times 7) \times (1 \times 10 \times 5)\right] = 2 \times \left[(21) \times (50)\right] = 2 \times \left[21 \times 50\right] = 2 \times \left[1050\right] = 2 \times 1050 = \boxed{\mathbf{2100}}$$

Case II c-2.

$$\left[(a \times b) \times (c \times d \times e) \times f\right] \times g = \left[(ab) \times (cde) \times f\right] \times g = \left[ab \times cde \times f\right] \times g = \left[abcdef\right] \times g = abcdef \times g$$

$$= \boxed{abcdefg}$$

Example 1.4-14

$$\left[(3 \times 5) \times (4 \times 1 \times 7) \times 6\right] \times 2 =$$

Solution:

$$\left[(3 \times 5) \times (4 \times 1 \times 7) \times 6\right] \times 2 = \left[(15) \times (28) \times 6\right] \times 2 = \left[15 \times 28 \times 6\right] \times 2 = \left[2520\right] \times 2 = 2520 \times 2 = \boxed{\mathbf{5040}}$$

Case II c-3.

$$(a \times b) \times \left[(c \times d \times e) \times (f \times g) \times h\right] = (ab) \times \left[(cde) \times (fg) \times h\right] = ab \times \left[cde \times fg \times h\right] = ab \times \left[cdefgh\right]$$

$$= \boxed{ab \times cdefgh} = \boxed{abcdefgh}$$

Example 1.4-15

$$\boxed{(5 \times 3) \times \left[(6 \times 2 \times 8) \times (7 \times 4) \times 1\right]} =$$

Solution:

$$\boxed{(5 \times 3) \times \left[(6 \times 2 \times 8) \times (7 \times 4) \times 1\right]} = \boxed{(15) \times \left[(96) \times (28) \times 1\right]} = \boxed{15 \times [96 \times 28 \times 1]} = \boxed{15 \times [2688]} = \boxed{15 \times 2688}$$

$$= \boxed{40320}$$

The following examples further illustrate how to use parentheses and brackets in multiplication:

Example 1.4-16

$$\boxed{5 \times (2 \times 11 \times 8) \times (4 \times 6)} = \boxed{5 \times (176) \times (24)} = \boxed{5 \times 176 \times 24} = \boxed{\mathbf{21120}}$$

Example 1.4-17

$$\boxed{(6 \times 5) \times (8 \times 10) \times 3} = \boxed{(30) \times (80) \times 3} = \boxed{30 \times 80 \times 3} = \boxed{\mathbf{7200}}$$

Example 1.4-18

$$\boxed{(2 \times 10 \times 7) \times (6 \times 2) \times 4} = \boxed{(140) \times (12) \times 4} = \boxed{140 \times 12 \times 4} = \boxed{\mathbf{6720}}$$

Example 1.4-19

$$\boxed{9 \times \left[3 \times (10 \times 4) \times (2 \times 7 \times 5)\right]} = \boxed{9 \times \left[3 \times (40) \times (70)\right]} = \boxed{9 \times [3 \times 40 \times 70]} = \boxed{9 \times [8400]} = \boxed{9 \times 8400} = \boxed{\mathbf{75600}}$$

Example 1.4-20

$$\boxed{(20 \times 1 \times 5) \times \left[(2 \times 6) \times (4 \times 8) \times 3\right]} = \boxed{(100) \times \left[(12) \times (32) \times 3\right]} = \boxed{100 \times [12 \times 32 \times 3]} = \boxed{100 \times [1152]}$$

$$= \boxed{100 \times 1152} = \boxed{\mathbf{115200}}$$

Example 1.4-21

$$\boxed{\left[(5 \times 3) \times (11 \times 4 \times 2)\right] \times (6 \times 5)} = \boxed{\left[(15) \times (88)\right] \times (30)} = \boxed{[15 \times 88] \times 30} = \boxed{[1320] \times 30} = \boxed{1320 \times 30} = \boxed{\mathbf{39600}}$$

Example 1.4-22

$$5 \times (8 \times 5) \times [7 \times (4 \times 9)] = 5 \times (40) \times [7 \times (36)] = 5 \times 40 \times [7 \times 36] = 5 \times 40 \times [252] = 5 \times 40 \times 252$$

$$= \boxed{50400}$$

Example 1.4-23

$$[(12 \times 3 \times 1) \times (2 \times 4) \times 3] \times (5 \times 8) = [(36) \times (8) \times 3] \times (40) = [36 \times 8 \times 3] \times 40 = [864] \times 40 = 864 \times 40$$

$$= \boxed{34560}$$

Example 1.4-24

$$(5 \times 13 \times 3) \times [8 \times (10 \times 2)] \times 3 = (195) \times [8 \times (20)] \times 3 = 195 \times [8 \times 20] \times 3 = 195 \times [160] \times 3 = 195 \times 160 \times 3$$

$$= \boxed{93600}$$

Example 1.4-25

$$[(2 \times 7 \times 4) \times (6 \times 8)] \times (2 \times 3) \times 4 = [(56) \times (48)] \times (6) \times 4 = [56 \times 48] \times 6 \times 4 = [2688] \times 6 \times 4$$

$$= 2688 \times 6 \times 4 = \boxed{64512}$$

Section 1.4 Exercises - Multiply the following numbers in the order grouped:

1. $5 \times 2 \times 7 \times 4 =$

2. $(3 \times 5) \times (4 \times 2) \times 7 =$

3. $(20 \times 3 \times 4) \times (1 \times 2 \times 6) =$

4. $8 \times [(1 \times 5 \times 6) \times (7 \times 2)] =$

5. $[(2 \times 7) \times 4] \times [6 \times (5 \times 3)] =$

6. $(6 \times 8) \times [(2 \times 3) \times 5] \times 10 =$

7. $(2 \times 3 \times 9) \times [(4 \times 5) \times 0] \times 7 =$

8. $[(1 \times 6 \times 3) \times [(7 \times 3) \times 5]] \times 3 =$

9. $[(2 \times 3) \times (6 \times 5 \times 2)] \times [4 \times (2 \times 4)] =$

10. $[(2 \times 3) \times (6 \times 7) \times 2] \times [(4 \times 2) \times 5] =$

1.5   Using Parentheses and Brackets in Division

In this section the use of parentheses and brackets as applied to division are discussed. Similar to subtraction, discussed in Section 1.3, changing the order in which numbers are divided or grouped does affect the final answer. These two properties associated with division are discussed below:

1. Changing the order in which two numbers are divided does change the final answer. For example, for any two real numbers a and b

$$\boxed{a \div b \neq b \div a}$$ Note 1: $\dfrac{a}{b}$, $b \neq 0$ and $\dfrac{b}{a}$, $a \neq 0$ Note 2: $\dfrac{a}{0}$ is not defined.

For example, $\boxed{15 \div 5} = \boxed{3}$, but $\boxed{5 \div 15} = \boxed{0.33}$

2. Re-grouping numbers does change the final answer. For example, for any real numbers a, b, and c

$$\boxed{(a \div b) \div c \neq a \div (b \div c)}$$

For example,

$$\boxed{(28 \div 4) \div 2} = \boxed{(7) \div 2} = \boxed{7 \div 2} = \boxed{3.5}, \text{ however}$$

$$\boxed{28 \div (4 \div 2)} = \boxed{28 \div (2)} = \boxed{28 \div 2} = \boxed{14}$$

In the following cases the use of parentheses and brackets in division, using integer numbers, are discussed:

Case I - Use of Parentheses in Division

In division, parentheses can be grouped in different ways, as is shown in the following example cases:

Case I a - *Dividing Two Integer Numbers*

Two integer numbers are divided using the general division process. Following is the general and a specific example as to how two integer numbers are divided:

$$\boxed{a \div b} = \boxed{A}$$

Example 1.5-1

$$\boxed{135 \div 15} =$$

Solution:

$$\boxed{135 \div 15} = \boxed{9}$$

Case I b - *Dividing Two Integer Numbers Grouped by Parentheses*

Two integer numbers that are grouped by parentheses are divided in the following ways, as shown by general and specific example cases:

Case I b-1.

$$\boxed{a \div (b \div c)} =$$

Let $\boxed{b \div c = k_1}$ and $\boxed{a \div k_1 = B}$, then

$$\boxed{a \div (b \div c)} = \boxed{a \div (k_1)} = \boxed{a \div k_1} = \boxed{B}$$

Example 1.5-2

$$\boxed{38 \div (12 \div 3)} =$$

Solution:

$$\boxed{38 \div (12 \div 3)} = \boxed{38 \div (4)} = \boxed{38 \div 4} = \boxed{\mathbf{9.5}}$$

Case I b-2.

$$\boxed{(a \div b) \div c} =$$

Let $\boxed{a \div b = k_1}$ and $\boxed{k_1 \div c = C}$, then

$$\boxed{(a \div b) \div c} = \boxed{(k_1) \div c} = \boxed{k_1 \div c} = \boxed{C}$$

Example 1.5-3

$$\boxed{(125 \div 5) \div 4} =$$

Solution:

$$\boxed{(125 \div 5) \div 4} = \boxed{(25) \div 4} = \boxed{25 \div 4} = \boxed{\mathbf{6.25}}$$

Case I b-3.

$$\boxed{(a \div b) \div (c \div d)} =$$

Let $\boxed{a \div b = k_1}$, $\boxed{c \div d = k_2}$, and $\boxed{k_1 \div k_2 = D}$, then

$$\boxed{\boxed{(a \div b) \div (c \div d)} = \boxed{(k_1) \div (k_2)} = \boxed{k_1 \div k_2} = \boxed{D}}$$

Example 1.5-4

$$\boxed{(15 \div 4) \div (8 \div 3)} =$$

Solution:

$$\boxed{(15 \div 4) \div (8 \div 3)} = \boxed{(3.75) \div (2.67)} = \boxed{3.75 \div 2.67} = \boxed{\mathbf{1.41}}$$

Case II - Use of Brackets in Division

In division, brackets are used in a similar way as parentheses. However, brackets are used to separate mathematical operations that contain integer numbers already grouped by parentheses. Brackets are used to group numbers in different ways, as is shown in the following general and specific example cases:

Case II-1.

$$\boxed{[a \div (b \div c)] \div d} =$$

Let $\boxed{b \div c = k_1}$, $\boxed{a \div k_1 = k_2}$, and $\boxed{k_2 \div d = A}$, then

$$\boxed{[a \div (b \div c)] \div d} = \boxed{[a \div (k_1)] \div d} = \boxed{[a \div k_1] \div d} = \boxed{[k_2] \div d} = \boxed{k_2 \div d} = \boxed{A}$$

Example 1.5-5

$$\boxed{[15 \div (6 \div 4)] \div 2} =$$

Solution:

$$\boxed{[15 \div (6 \div 4)] \div 2} = \boxed{[15 \div (1.5)] \div 2} = \boxed{[15 \div 1.5] \div 2} = \boxed{[10] \div 2} = \boxed{10 \div 2} = \boxed{\mathbf{5}}$$

Case II-2.

$$\boxed{[(a \div b) \div c] \div d} =$$

Let $\boxed{a \div b = k_1}$, $\boxed{k_1 \div c = k_2}$, and $\boxed{k_2 \div d = B}$, then

$$\boxed{[(a \div b) \div c] \div d} = \boxed{[(k_1) \div c] \div d} = \boxed{[k_1 \div c] \div d} = \boxed{[k_2] \div d} = \boxed{k_2 \div d} = \boxed{B}$$

Example 1.5-6

$$\left[\left[\left(236 \div 12\right) \div 5\right] \div 3\right] =$$

Solution:

$$\left[\left[\left(236 \div 12\right) \div 5\right] \div 3\right] = \left[\left[\left(19.67\right) \div 5\right] \div 3\right] = \left[\left[19.67 \div 5\right] \div 3\right] = \left[\left[3.93\right] \div 3\right] = \boxed{3.93 \div 3} = \boxed{\mathbf{1.31}}$$

Case II-3.

$$\boxed{a \div \left[b \div \left(c \div d\right)\right]} =$$

Let $\boxed{c \div d = k_1}$, $\boxed{b \div k_1 = k_2}$, and $\boxed{a \div k_2 = C}$, then

$$\boxed{a \div \left[b \div \left(c \div d\right)\right]} = \boxed{a \div \left[b \div \left(k_1\right)\right]} = \boxed{a \div \left[b \div k_1\right]} = \boxed{a \div \left[k_2\right]} = \boxed{a \div k_2} = \boxed{C}$$

Example 1.5-7

$$\boxed{238 \div \left[24 \div \left(15 \div 5\right)\right]} =$$

Solution:

$$\boxed{238 \div \left[24 \div \left(15 \div 5\right)\right]} = \boxed{238 \div \left[24 \div \left(3\right)\right]} = \boxed{238 \div \left[24 \div 3\right]} = \boxed{238 \div \left[8\right]} = \boxed{238 \div 8} = \boxed{\mathbf{29.75}}$$

Case II-4.

$$\boxed{\left[\left(a \div b\right) \div \left(c \div d\right)\right] \div e} =$$

Let $\boxed{a \div b = k_1}$, $\boxed{c \div d = k_1}$, $\boxed{k_1 \div k_2 = k_3}$, and $\boxed{k_3 \div e = D}$, then

$$\boxed{\left[\left(a \div b\right) \div \left(c \div d\right)\right] \div e} = \boxed{\left[\left(k_1\right) \div \left(k_2\right)\right] \div e} = \boxed{\left[k_1 \div k_2\right] \div e} = \boxed{\left[k_3\right] \div e} = \boxed{k_3 \div e} = \boxed{D}$$

Example 1.5-8

$$\boxed{\left[\left(28 \div 13\right) \div \left(15 \div 4\right)\right] \div 2} =$$

Solution:

$$\boxed{\left[\left(28 \div 13\right) \div \left(15 \div 4\right)\right] \div 2} = \boxed{\left[\left(2.15\right) \div \left(3.75\right)\right] \div 2} = \boxed{\left[2.15 \div 3.75\right] \div 2} = \boxed{\left[0.57\right] \div 2} = \boxed{0.57 \div 2} = \boxed{\mathbf{0.285}}$$

Case II-5.

$$\left[\left[(a \div b) \div c\right] \div (d \div e)\right] =$$

Let $a \div b = k_1$, $k_1 \div c = k_2$, $d \div e = k_3$, and $k_2 \div k_3 = E$, then

$$\left[\left[(a \div b) \div c\right] \div (d \div e)\right] = \left[\left[(k_1) \div c\right] \div (k_3)\right] = \left[\left[k_1 \div c\right] \div k_3\right] = \left[\left[k_2\right] \div k_3\right] = \left[k_2 \div k_3\right] = \boxed{E}$$

Example 1.5-9

$$\left[\left[(29 \div 5) \div 2\right] \div (15 \div 6)\right] =$$

Solution:

$$\left[\left[(29 \div 5) \div 2\right] \div (15 \div 6)\right] = \left[\left[(5.8) \div 2\right] \div (2.5)\right] = \left[\left[5.8 \div 2\right] \div 2.5\right] = \left[\left[2.9\right] \div 2.5\right] = \left[2.9 \div 2.5\right] = \boxed{\mathbf{1.16}}$$

Case II-6.

$$\left[a \div \left[(b \div c) \div (d \div e)\right]\right] =$$

Let $b \div c = k_1$, $d \div e = k_2$, $k_1 \div k_2 = k_3$, and $a \div k_3 = F$, then

$$\left[a \div \left[(b \div c) \div (d \div e)\right]\right] = \left[a \div \left[(k_1) \div (k_2)\right]\right] = \left[a \div \left[k_1 \div k_2\right]\right] = \left[a \div \left[k_3\right]\right] = \left[a \div k_3\right] = \boxed{F}$$

Example 1.5-10

$$\left[238 \div \left[(35 \div 5) \div (14 \div 7)\right]\right] =$$

Solution:

$$\left[238 \div \left[(35 \div 5) \div (14 \div 7)\right]\right] = \left[238 \div \left[(7) \div (2)\right]\right] = \left[238 \div \left[7 \div 2\right]\right] = \left[238 \div \left[3.5\right]\right] = \left[238 \div 3.5\right] = \boxed{\mathbf{68}}$$

Case II-7.

$$\left[\left[(a \div b) \div (c \div d)\right] \div (e \div f)\right] =$$

Let $a \div b = k_1$, $c \div d = k_2$, $e \div f = k_3$, $k_1 \div k_2 = k_4$, and $k_4 \div k_3 = G$, then

$$\left[\left[(a \div b) \div (c \div d)\right] \div (e \div f)\right] = \left[\left[(k_1) \div (k_2)\right] \div (k_3)\right] = \left[\left[k_1 \div k_2\right] \div k_3\right] = \left[\left[k_4\right] \div k_3\right] = \left[k_4 \div k_3\right] = \boxed{G}$$

Example 1.5-11

$$\left[\left[(230 \div 5) \div (36 \div 4)\right] \div (25 \div 6)\right] =$$

Solution:

$$\left[\left[(230 \div 5) \div (36 \div 4)\right] \div (25 \div 6)\right] = \left[\left[(46) \div (9)\right] \div (4.17)\right] = \left[\left[46 \div 9\right] \div 4.17\right] = \left[\left[5.11\right] \div 4.17\right] = \boxed{5.11 \div 4.17} = \boxed{\mathbf{1.23}}$$

Case II-8.

$$\left[(a \div b) \div \left[(c \div d) \div (e \div f)\right]\right] =$$

Let $\boxed{a \div b = k_1}$, $\boxed{c \div d = k_2}$, $\boxed{e \div f = k_3}$, $\boxed{k_2 \div k_3 = k_4}$, and $\boxed{k_1 \div k_4 = H}$, then

$$\left[(a \div b) \div \left[(c \div d) \div (e \div f)\right]\right] = \left[(k_1) \div \left[(k_2) \div (k_3)\right]\right] = \boxed{k_1 \div \left[k_2 \div k_3\right]} = \boxed{k_1 \div \left[k_4\right]} = \boxed{k_1 \div k_4} = \boxed{H}$$

Example 1.5-12

$$\left[(358 \div 12) \div \left[(35 \div 7) \div (25 \div 2)\right]\right] =$$

Solution:

$$\left[(358 \div 12) \div \left[(35 \div 7) \div (25 \div 2)\right]\right] = \left[(29.83) \div \left[(5) \div (12.5)\right]\right] = \boxed{29.83 \div \left[5 \div 12.5\right]} = \boxed{29.83 \div \left[0.4\right]} = \boxed{29.83 \div 0.4}$$

$$= \boxed{\mathbf{74.58}}$$

The following examples further illustrate how to use parentheses and brackets in division:

Example 1.5-13

$$\left[(35 \div 5) \div 3\right] = \left[(7) \div 3\right] = \boxed{7 \div 3} = \boxed{\mathbf{2.33}}$$

Example 1.5-14

$$\boxed{240 \div (16 \div 2)} = \boxed{240 \div (8)} = \boxed{240 \div 8} = \boxed{\mathbf{30}}$$

Example 1.5-15

$$\left[(40 \div 2) \div (165 \div 15)\right] = \left[(20) \div (11)\right] = \boxed{20 \div 11} = \boxed{\mathbf{1.82}}$$

Example 1.5-16

$$28 \div \left[15 \div \left(36 \div 3\right)\right] = 28 \div \left[15 \div \left(12\right)\right] = 28 \div \left[15 \div 12\right] = 28 \div \left[1.25\right] = 28 \div 1.25 = \boxed{\mathbf{22.4}}$$

Example 1.5-17

$$\left[\left[\left(80 \div 2\right) \div 5\right] \div 4\right] = \left[\left[\left(40\right) \div 5\right] \div 4\right] = \left[\left[40 \div 5\right] \div 4\right] = \left[\left[8\right] \div 4\right] = \boxed{8 \div 4} = \boxed{\mathbf{2}}$$

Example 1.5-18

$$\left[\left(238 \div 4\right) \div \left[16 \div \left(8 \div 2\right)\right]\right] = \left[\left(59.5\right) \div \left[16 \div \left(4\right)\right]\right] = \boxed{59.5 \div \left[16 \div 4\right]} = \boxed{59.5 \div \left[4\right]} = \boxed{59.5 \div 4} = \boxed{\mathbf{14.88}}$$

Example 1.5-19

$$\left[\left[\left(30 \div 3\right) \div \left(28 \div 2\right)\right] \div 5\right] = \left[\left[\left(10\right) \div \left(14\right)\right] \div 5\right] = \left[\left[10 \div 14\right] \div 5\right] = \left[\left[0.71\right] \div 5\right] = \boxed{0.71 \div 5} = \boxed{\mathbf{0.14}}$$

Example 1.5-20

$$\left[\left[\left(81 \div 3\right) \div 3\right] \div \left(18 \div 2\right)\right] = \left[\left[\left(27\right) \div 3\right] \div \left(9\right)\right] = \left[\left[27 \div 3\right] \div 9\right] = \left[\left[9\right] \div 9\right] = \boxed{9 \div 9} = \boxed{\mathbf{1}}$$

Example 1.5-21

$$45 \div \left[25 \div \left(15 \div 5\right)\right] = 45 \div \left[25 \div \left(3\right)\right] = 45 \div \left[25 \div 3\right] = 45 \div \left[8.33\right] = \boxed{45 \div 8.33} = \boxed{\mathbf{5.4}}$$

Example 1.5-22

$$\left[\left(230 \div 10\right) \div \left[48 \div \left(24 \div 2\right)\right]\right] = \left[\left(23\right) \div \left[48 \div \left(12\right)\right]\right] = \left[23 \div \left[48 \div 12\right]\right] = \left[23 \div \left[4\right]\right] = \boxed{23 \div 4} = \boxed{\mathbf{5.75}}$$

Section 1.5 Exercises - Divide the following numbers in the order grouped:

1. $\left(16 \div 2\right) \div 4 =$

2. $\left(125 \div 5\right) \div \left(15 \div 5\right) =$

3. $\left[25 \div \left(8 \div 2\right)\right] \div 3 =$

4. $\left[\left(140 \div 10\right) \div 2\right] \div 6 =$

5. $\left[155 \div \left(15 \div 3\right)\right] \div 9 =$

6. $250 \div \left[\left(48 \div 2\right) \div 4\right] =$

7. $\left[\left(28 \div 4\right) \div \left(16 \div 3\right)\right] \div 8 =$

8. $66 \div \left[48 \div \left(14 \div 2\right)\right] =$

9. $\left(180 \div 2\right) \div \left[\left(88 \div 2\right) \div 4\right] =$

10. $\left[\left(48 \div 4\right) \div 2\right] \div \left(18 \div 3\right) =$

1.6   Using Parentheses and Brackets in Mixed Operations

In this section the use of parentheses and brackets as applied to addition, subtraction, multiplication, and division, using integer numbers, are discussed. Similar to subtraction and division, the order in which mixed operations are grouped does effect the final answer. This is discussed in the following cases:

Case I - Use of Parentheses in Addition, Subtraction, Multiplication, and Division

In mixed mathematical operations, parentheses can be grouped in different ways, as is shown in the following example cases:

Case I-1.

$$\boxed{a + (b \div c)} =$$

Let $\boxed{b \div c = k_1}$ and $\boxed{a + k_1 = A}$, then

$$\boxed{a + (b \div c)} = \boxed{a + (k_1)} = \boxed{a + k_1} = \boxed{A}$$

Example 1.6-1

$$\boxed{30 + (50 \div 5)} =$$

Solution:

$$\boxed{30 + (50 \div 5)} = \boxed{30 + (10)} = \boxed{30 + 10} = \boxed{40}$$

Case I-2.

$$\boxed{a \div (b \times c)} =$$

Let $\boxed{b \times c = k_1}$ and $\boxed{a \div k_1 = B}$, then

$$\boxed{a \div (b \times c)} = \boxed{a \div (k_1)} = \boxed{a \div k_1} = \boxed{B}$$

Example 1.6-2

$$\boxed{18 \div (4 \times 2)} =$$

Solution:

$$\boxed{18 \div (4 \times 2)} = \boxed{18 \div (8)} = \boxed{18 \div 8} = \boxed{2.25}$$

Case I-3.

$$\boxed{(a \times b) \div c} =$$

Let $\boxed{a \times b = k_1}$ and $\boxed{k_1 \div c = C}$, then

$$\boxed{(a \times b) \div c} = \boxed{(k_1) \div c} = \boxed{k_1 \div c} = \boxed{C}$$

Example 1.6-3

$$\boxed{(20 \times 5) \div 8} =$$

Solution:

$$\boxed{(20 \times 5) \div 8} = \boxed{(100) \div 8} = \boxed{100 \div 8} = \boxed{\mathbf{12.5}}$$

Case I-4.

$$\boxed{(a \div b) + c} =$$

Let $\boxed{a \div b = k_1}$ and $\boxed{k_1 + c = D}$, then

$$\boxed{(a \div b) + c} = \boxed{(k_1) + c} = \boxed{k_1 + c} = \boxed{D}$$

Example 1.6-4

$$\boxed{(45 \div 5) + 25} =$$

Solution:

$$\boxed{(45 \div 5) + 25} = \boxed{(9) + 25} = \boxed{9 + 25} = \boxed{\mathbf{34}}$$

Case I-5.

$$\boxed{(a + b) \div (c - d)} =$$

Let $\boxed{a + b = k_1}$, $\boxed{c - d = k_2}$, and $\boxed{k_1 \div k_2 = E}$, then

$$\boxed{(a + b) \div (c - d)} = \boxed{(k_1) \div (k_2)} = \boxed{k_1 \div k_2} = \boxed{E}$$

Example 1.6-5

$$\boxed{(23+5)\div(20-8)} =$$

Solution:

$$\boxed{(23+5)\div(20-8)} = \boxed{(28)\div(12)} = \boxed{28\div12} = \boxed{\textbf{2.33}}$$

Case I-6.

$$\boxed{(a\div b)-(c\times d)} =$$

Let $\boxed{a\div b = k_1}$, $\boxed{c\times d = k_2}$, and $\boxed{k_1 - k_2 = F}$, then

$$\boxed{(a\div b)-(c\times d)} = \boxed{(k_1)-(k_2)} = \boxed{k_1 - k_2} = \boxed{F}$$

Example 1.6-6

$$\boxed{(49\div5)-(12\times4)} =$$

Solution:

$$\boxed{(49\div5)-(12\times4)} = \boxed{(9.8)-(48)} = \boxed{9.8-48} = \boxed{\textbf{-38.2}}$$

Case II - Use of Brackets in Addition, Subtraction, Multiplication, and Division

In mixed operations, brackets are used in a similar way as parentheses. However, brackets are used to separate mathematical operations that contain integer numbers already grouped by parentheses. Brackets are used to group numbers in different ways, as is shown in the following general and specific example cases:

Case II-1.

$$\boxed{[a\div(b+c)]\div d} =$$

Let $\boxed{b+c = k_1}$, $\boxed{a\div k_1 = k_2}$, and $\boxed{k_2\div d = A}$, then

$$\boxed{[a\div(b+c)]\div d} = \boxed{[a\div(k_1)]\div d} = \boxed{[a\div k_1]\div d} = \boxed{[k_2]\div d} = \boxed{k_2\div d} = \boxed{A}$$

Example 1.6-7

$$\boxed{[350\div(12+8)]\div4} =$$

Solution:

$$\left[\left[350 \div (12+8)\right] \div 4\right] = \left[\left[350 \div (20)\right] \div 4\right] = \left[\left[350 \div 20\right] \div 4\right] = \left[\left[17.5\right] \div 4\right] = \left[17.5 \div 4\right] = \boxed{\textbf{4.38}}$$

Case II-2.

$$\left[\left[(a \times b) \div c\right] + d\right] =$$

Let $\boxed{a \times b = k_1}$, $\boxed{k_1 \div c = k_2}$, and $\boxed{k_2 + d = B}$, then

$$\left[\left[(a \times b) \div c\right] + d\right] = \left[\left[(k_1) \div c\right] + d\right] = \left[\left[k_1 \div c\right] + d\right] = \left[\left[k_2\right] + d\right] = \left[k_2 + d\right] = \boxed{B}$$

Example 1.6-8

$$\left[\left[(12 \times 4) \div 2\right] + 46\right] =$$

Solution:

$$\left[\left[(12 \times 4) \div 2\right] + 46\right] = \left[\left[(48) \div 2\right] + 46\right] = \left[\left[48 \div 2\right] + 46\right] = \left[\left[24\right] + 46\right] = \left[24 + 46\right] = \boxed{\textbf{70}}$$

Case II-3.

$$\left[a \times \left[b - (c+d)\right]\right] =$$

Let $\boxed{c + d = k_1}$, $\boxed{b - k_1 = k_2}$, and $\boxed{a k_2 = C}$, then

$$\left[a \times \left[b - (c+d)\right]\right] = \left[a \times \left[b - (k_1)\right]\right] = \left[a \times \left[b - k_1\right]\right] = \left[a \times \left[k_2\right]\right] = \left[a \times k_2\right] = \left[a k_2\right] = \boxed{C}$$

Example 1.6-9

$$\left[8 \times \left[10 - (5+9)\right]\right] =$$

Solution:

$$\left[8 \times \left[10 - (5+9)\right]\right] = \left[8 \times \left[10 - (14)\right]\right] = \left[8 \times \left[10 - 14\right]\right] = \left[8 \times \left[-4\right]\right] = \left[8 \times -4\right] = \boxed{\textbf{-32}}$$

Case II-4.

$$\left[\left[(a \times b) \div (c+d)\right] \div e\right] =$$

Let $\boxed{a \times b = k_1}$, $\boxed{c + d = k_2}$, $\boxed{k_1 \div k_2 = k_3}$, and $\boxed{k_3 \div e = D}$, then

$$\boxed{\left[(a \times b) \div (c + d) \right] \div e} = \boxed{\left[(k_1) \div (k_2) \right] \div e} = \boxed{\left[k_1 \div k_2 \right] \div e} = \boxed{\left[k_3 \right] \div e} = \boxed{k_3 \div e} = \boxed{D}$$

Example 1.6-10

$$\boxed{\left[(4 \times 5) \div (28 + 9) \right] \div 5} =$$

Solution:

$$\boxed{\left[(4 \times 5) \div (28 + 9) \right] \div 5} = \boxed{\left[(20) \div (37) \right] \div 5} = \boxed{\left[20 \div 37 \right] \div 5} = \boxed{\left[0.54 \right] \div 5} = \boxed{0.54 \div 5} = \boxed{\mathbf{0.108}}$$

Case II-5.

$$\boxed{\left[(a - b) - c \right] + (d + e)} =$$

Let $\boxed{a - b = k_1}$, $\boxed{k_1 - c = k_2}$, $\boxed{d + e = k_3}$, and $\boxed{k_2 + k_3 = E}$, then

$$\boxed{\left[(a - b) - c \right] + (d + e)} = \boxed{\left[(k_1) - c \right] + (k_3)} = \boxed{\left[k_1 - c \right] + k_3} = \boxed{\left[k_2 \right] + k_3} = \boxed{k_2 + k_3} = \boxed{E}$$

Example 1.6-11

$$\boxed{\left[(23 - 6) - 8 \right] + (12 + 7)} =$$

Solution:

$$\boxed{\left[(23 - 6) - 8 \right] + (12 + 7)} = \boxed{\left[(17) - 8 \right] + (19)} = \boxed{\left[17 - 8 \right] + 19} = \boxed{\left[9 \right] + 19} = \boxed{9 + 19} = \boxed{\mathbf{28}}$$

Case II-6.

$$\boxed{a + \left[(b + c) - (d \times e) \right]} =$$

Let $\boxed{b + c = k_1}$, $\boxed{d \times e = k_2}$, $\boxed{k_1 - k_2 = k_3}$, and $\boxed{a + k_3 = F}$, then

$$\boxed{a + \left[(b + c) - (d \times e) \right]} = \boxed{a + \left[(k_1) - (k_2) \right]} = \boxed{a + \left[k_1 - k_2 \right]} = \boxed{a + \left[k_3 \right]} = \boxed{a + k_3} = \boxed{F}$$

Example 1.6-12

$$\boxed{35 + \left[(12 + 5) - (4 \times 2) \right]} =$$

Solution:

$$35+\Big[(12+5)-(4\times2)\Big] = 35+\Big[(17)-(8)\Big] = 35+\Big[17-8\Big] = 35+\big[9\big] = 35+9 = \boxed{\mathbf{44}}$$

Case II-7.

$$\Big[\big[(a\div b)+(c\div d)\big]\times(e+f)\Big] =$$

Let $\boxed{a\div b=k_1}$, $\boxed{c\div d=k_2}$, $\boxed{e+f=k_3}$, $\boxed{k_1+k_2=k_4}$, and $\boxed{k_4k_3=G}$, then

$$\Big[\big[(a\div b)+(c\div d)\big]\times(e+f)\Big] = \Big[\big[(k_1)+(k_2)\big]\times(k_3)\Big] = \Big[\big[k_1+k_2\big]\times k_3\Big] = \Big[\big[k_4\big]\times k_3\Big] = \Big[k_4\times k_3\Big] = \boxed{k_4k_3} = \boxed{G}$$

Example 1.6-13

$$\Big[\big[(45\div9)+(12\div4)\big]\times(10+5)\Big] =$$

Solution:

$$\Big[\big[(45\div9)+(12\div4)\big]\times(10+5)\Big] = \Big[\big[(5)+(3)\big]\times(15)\Big] = \Big[\big[5+3\big]\times15\Big] = \Big[\big[8\big]\times15\Big] = \Big[8\times15\Big] = \boxed{\mathbf{120}}$$

Case II-8.

$$\Big[(a-b)+\big[(c\div d)\times(e\div f)\big]\Big] =$$

Let $\boxed{a-b=k_1}$, $\boxed{c\div d=k_2}$, $\boxed{e\div f=k_3}$, $\boxed{k_2k_3=k_4}$, and $\boxed{k_1+k_4=H}$, then

$$\Big[(a-b)+\big[(c\div d)\times(e\div f)\big]\Big] = \Big[(k_1)+\big[(k_2)\times(k_3)\big]\Big] = \Big[k_1+\big[k_2\times k_3\big]\Big] = \Big[k_1+\big[k_2k_3\big]\Big] = \Big[k_1+\big[k_4\big]\Big] = \Big[k_1+k_4\Big]$$

$$= \boxed{H}$$

Example 1.6-14

$$\Big[(45-6)+\big[(12\div4)\times(34\div4)\big]\Big] =$$

Solution:

$$\Big[(45-6)+\big[(12\div4)\times(34\div4)\big]\Big] = \Big[(39)+\big[(3)\times(8.5)\big]\Big] = \Big[39+\big[3\times8.5\big]\Big] = \Big[39+\big[25.5\big]\Big] = \Big[39+25.5\Big] = \boxed{\mathbf{64.5}}$$

Case II-9.

$$\left[(a+b+c)\div\left[d\times(e-f)\right]\right]=$$

Let $\boxed{a+b+c=k_1}$, $\boxed{e-f=k_2}$, $\boxed{dk_2=k_3}$, and $\boxed{k_1\div k_3=I}$, then

$$\left[(a+b+c)\div\left[d\times(e-f)\right]\right]=\left[(k_1)\div\left[d\times(k_2)\right]\right]=\left[k_1\div\left[d\times k_2\right]\right]=\left[k_1\div\left[dk_2\right]\right]=\left[k_1\div dk_2\right]=\left[k_1\div k_3\right]=\boxed{I}$$

Example 1.6-15

$$\left[(8+50+5)\div\left[3\times(25-12)\right]\right]=$$

Solution:

$$\left[(8+50+5)\div\left[3\times(25-12)\right]\right]=\left[(63)\div\left[3\times(13)\right]\right]=\left[63\div\left[3\times13\right]\right]=\left[63\div\left[39\right]\right]=\left[63\div39\right]=\boxed{1.62}$$

The following examples further illustrate how to use parentheses and brackets in mixed operations:

Example 1.6-16

$$\left[(39+5)\div4\right]=\left[(44)\div4\right]=\left[44\div4\right]=\boxed{11}$$

Example 1.6-17

$$\left[36\times(12+3)\right]=\left[36\times(15)\right]=\left[36\times15\right]=\boxed{540}$$

Example 1.6-18

$$\left[(23+5)\div(8\times2)\right]=\left[(28)\div(16)\right]=\left[28\div16\right]=\boxed{1.75}$$

Example 1.6-19

$$\left[38+\left[15\times(20\div2)\right]\right]=\left[38+\left[15\times(10)\right]\right]=\left[38+\left[15\times10\right]\right]=\left[38+\left[150\right]\right]=\left[38+150\right]=\boxed{188}$$

Example 1.6-20

$$\left[\left[(35\times2)+5\right]\div3\right]=\left[\left[(70)+5\right]\div3\right]=\left[\left[70+5\right]\div3\right]=\left[\left[75\right]\div3\right]=\left[75\div3\right]=\boxed{25}$$

Example 1.6-21

$$\left[(28-18)\times\left[16-(8-3)\right]\right]=\left[(10)\times\left[16-(5)\right]\right]=\left[10\times\left[16-5\right]\right]=\left[10\times\left[11\right]\right]=\left[10\times11\right]=\boxed{110}$$

Example 1.6-22

$$\left[\left[(20-4)+(15-5)\right]\div 2\right] = \left[\left[(16)+(10)\right]\div 2\right] = \left[\boxed{16+10}\div 2\right] = \left[\boxed{26}\div 2\right] = \boxed{26\div 2} = \boxed{\textbf{13}}$$

Example 1.6-23

$$\left[\left[(15+6)\div 3\right]\times(8\div 2)\right] = \left[\left[(21)\div 3\right]\times(4)\right] = \left[\boxed{21\div 3}\times 4\right] = \left[\boxed{7}\times 4\right] = \boxed{7\times 4} = \boxed{\textbf{28}}$$

Example 1.6-24

$$\boxed{30-\left[15\times(30+2)\right]} = \boxed{30-\left[15\times(32)\right]} = \boxed{30-\left[15\times 32\right]} = \boxed{30-[480]} = \boxed{30-480} = \boxed{\textbf{-450}}$$

Example 1.6-25

$$\left[(85\div 5)\times\left[20+(13-8)\right]\right] = \left[(17)\times\left[20+(5)\right]\right] = \boxed{17\times[20+5]} = \boxed{17\times[25]} = \boxed{17\times 25} = \boxed{\textbf{425}}$$

Section 1.6 Exercises - Perform the indicated operations in the order grouped:

1. $(28\div 4)\times 3 =$

2. $250+(15\div 3) =$

3. $28\div\left[(23+5)\times 8\right] =$

4. $\left[(255-15)\div 20\right]+8 =$

5. $\left[230\div(15\times 2)\right]+12 =$

6. $55\times\left[(28+2)\div 3\right] =$

7. $\left[(55\div 5)+(18-4)\right]\times 4 =$

8. $35-\left[400\div(16+4)\right] =$

9. $(230+5)\div\left[2\times(18+2)\right] =$

10. $\left[(38\div 4)+2\right]\times(15-3) =$

Chapter 2 - Simplifying and Converting Fractions

The objective of this chapter is to ensure the student learns how to simplify and convert fractions from one form to another. The description of what defines a fraction along with identifying the different types of fractions used in this book are discussed in Section 2.1. Section 2.2 shows the steps as to how improper fractions are changed to mixed fractions. Section 2.3 shows the steps on how to simplify fractions. The steps as to how decimal fractions and mixed fractions are changed to integer fractions are discussed in Sections 2.4 and 2.5, respectively. The additional examples along with the exercises provided at the end of each section further enforce the objective of this chapter.

Section 2.1   What is a Fraction?

A fraction is an indicated quotient of two quantities generally shown as $\left(\dfrac{a}{b}\right)$, where the top quantity (a) is referred to as the numerator and the bottom quantity (b) is referred to as the denominator. In this book, fractions are classified into three categories:

1. **Integer Fractions**
2. **Decimal Fractions**, and
3. **Mixed Fractions**

These fractions are defined as follows:

Integer Fractions: Integer fractions are a class of fractions where both the numerator and the denominator are integer numbers. For example, $-\dfrac{357}{110}$, $-\dfrac{12}{7}$, $-\dfrac{35}{80}$, $-\dfrac{2}{5}$, $-\dfrac{1}{3}$, $\dfrac{123}{325}$, $\dfrac{2}{5}$, $\dfrac{4}{6}$, $\dfrac{18}{7}$, $\dfrac{645}{12}$, etc. are integer fractions.

Integer fractions are divided to the following subclasses:

- **Proper Fractions**, and

- **Improper Fractions**

Proper fractions are integer fractions with absolute values (see definition in the Terminology section) of less than one. For example, $-\dfrac{3}{5}$, $-\dfrac{23}{27}$, $-\dfrac{12}{19}$, $-\dfrac{123}{327}$, $-\dfrac{347}{534}$, $\dfrac{1}{8}$, $\dfrac{7}{9}$, $\dfrac{12}{35}$, $\dfrac{125}{232}$, $\dfrac{238}{315}$, etc. are proper fractions.

Improper fractions are integer fractions with absolute values of greater than one. For example, $-\dfrac{8}{3}$, $-\dfrac{12}{5}$, $-\dfrac{38}{32}$, $-\dfrac{110}{23}$, $-\dfrac{437}{323}$, $\dfrac{10}{5}$, $\dfrac{12}{3}$, $\dfrac{75}{5}$, $\dfrac{136}{24}$, $\dfrac{354}{120}$, etc. are improper fractions.

In general, integer fractions are shown as $\left(\dfrac{a}{b}\right)$ where (a) and (b) are whole numbers. For example,

1. Let $a = 8$ and $b = 13$, then $\dfrac{a}{b} = \dfrac{8}{13}$.

2. Let $a = -3$ and $b = 7$, then $\dfrac{a}{b} = \dfrac{-3}{7} = -\dfrac{3}{7}$.

3. Let $a = 123$ and $b = -98$, then $\dfrac{a}{b} = \dfrac{123}{-98} = -\dfrac{123}{98}$.

Decimal Fractions: Decimal fractions are defined in this book as the type of fractions where either the numerator or the denominator or both are decimal numbers. For example, $-\dfrac{0.24}{0.3}$, $-\dfrac{3}{0.5}$, $-\dfrac{0.008}{0.14}$, $-\dfrac{12.8}{1.6}$, $-\dfrac{235.6}{5}$, $\dfrac{0.2}{0.5}$, $\dfrac{0.5}{1}$, $\dfrac{0.02}{0.3}$, $\dfrac{0.001}{0.5}$, $\dfrac{4}{0.12}$, etc. are decimal fractions.

- **Exponential Notation** - In general, decimal fractions are represented in exponential notation form as $\left(a \times 10^{-k}\right)$ where (a) is an integer number and (k) indicates the location of the decimal point k places to the left of where it is written. For example,

  1. Let $a = 382$ and $k = 1$, then $\left(a \times 10^{-k}\right) = 382 \times 10^{-1} = 38.2$.

  2. Let $a = 5$ and $k = 2$, then $\left(a \times 10^{-k}\right) = 5 \times 10^{-2} = 0.05$.

  3. Let $a = 75$ and $k = 3$, then $\left(a \times 10^{-k}\right) = 75 \times 10^{-3} = 0.075$.

  4. Let $a = 24$ and $k = 4$, then $\left(a \times 10^{-k}\right) = 24 \times 10^{-4} = 0.0024$.

  5. Let $a = 15$ and $k = 0$, then $\left(a \times 10^{-k}\right) = 15 \times 10^{-0} = 15 \times 1 = 15$.

  Note that any number (except zero) raised to the zero power is equal to one. For example, $250^0 = 1$, $-(233)^0 = -1$, $5^0 = 1$, $(-233)^0 = 1$, $12500000^0 = 1$, $17345^0 = 1$, etc.

Mixed Fractions: Mixed fractions are made up of a positive or negative whole number and an integer fraction, where the integer fraction value is less than one. For example, $-3\dfrac{2}{8}$, $-7\dfrac{2}{5}$, $-12\dfrac{5}{7}$, $-24\dfrac{12}{37}$, $-1\dfrac{2}{3}$, $1\dfrac{3}{5}$, $2\dfrac{1}{8}$, $6\dfrac{2}{3}$, $3\dfrac{5}{9}$, $1\dfrac{4}{13}$, etc. are mixed fractions.

In general, mixed fractions are shown as $\left(k\dfrac{a}{b}\right)$ where (k) is made up of a positive or negative whole number and $\dfrac{a}{b}$ is an integer fraction. For example,

1. Let $k = 3$ and $\dfrac{a}{b} = \dfrac{5}{7}$, then $k\dfrac{a}{b} = 3\dfrac{5}{7}$.

2. Let $k = -7$ and $\dfrac{a}{b} = \dfrac{3}{8}$, then $k\dfrac{a}{b} = -7\dfrac{3}{8}$.

3. Let $k = 23$ and $\dfrac{a}{b} = \dfrac{1}{5}$, then $k\dfrac{a}{b} = 23\dfrac{1}{5}$.

In addition, fractions that are numerically equal, i.e., the numerator and the denominator are multiplied or divided by the same non-zero number, are considered as **Equivalent Fractions**. For   example, $\left(\dfrac{0.2}{0.12}=\dfrac{0.4}{0.24}=\dfrac{0.6}{0.36}=\dfrac{0.8}{0.48},\cdots\right)$, $\left(-\dfrac{5}{3}=-\dfrac{10}{6}=-\dfrac{15}{9}=-\dfrac{20}{12},\cdots\right)$, $\left(\dfrac{2}{7}=\dfrac{4}{14}=\dfrac{6}{21}=\dfrac{8}{28},\cdots\right)$,

$\left(\dfrac{1}{5}=\dfrac{2}{10}=\dfrac{3}{15}=\dfrac{4}{20},\cdots\right)$, $\left(-\dfrac{5}{8}=-\dfrac{10}{16}=-\dfrac{15}{24}=-\dfrac{20}{32},\cdots\right)$, $\left(\dfrac{3.2}{0.3}=\dfrac{6.4}{0.6}=\dfrac{9.6}{0.9}=\dfrac{12.8}{1.2},\cdots\right)$, $\left(\dfrac{3}{4}=\dfrac{6}{8}=\dfrac{9}{12}=\dfrac{12}{16},\cdots\right)$,

etc. are equivalent fractions.

Section 2.1 Exercises - Name the following type of fractions:

1. $\dfrac{0.5}{0.2}$

2. $-\dfrac{3}{5}$

3. $1\dfrac{2}{3}$

4. $\dfrac{1}{0.1}$

5. $\left(\dfrac{5}{2}=\dfrac{10}{4}=\dfrac{15}{6}=\dfrac{20}{8}\right)$

6. $4\dfrac{3}{8}$

7. $\dfrac{1}{3}$

8. $-\dfrac{38}{13}$

9. $\dfrac{7}{2}$

10. $\left(\dfrac{0.3}{2.2}=\dfrac{0.6}{4.4}=\dfrac{0.9}{6.6}=\dfrac{1.2}{8.8}\right)$

2.2   Changing Improper Fractions to Mixed Fractions

Improper fractions of the form $\left(\dfrac{c}{b}\right)$ with absolute values of greater than one are changed to

mixed fractions of the form $\left(k\dfrac{a}{b}\right)$, where (k) is a positive or negative whole number and $\left(\dfrac{a}{b}\right)$ is

an integer fraction with value of less than one, using the following steps:

Step 1   Divide the dividend, i.e., the numerator of the improper fraction by the divisor, i.e., the denominator of the improper fraction using the general division process.

Step 2   a. Use the whole number portion of the quotient as the whole number portion of the mixed fraction.

b. Use the dividend of the remainder as the dividend (numerator) in the remainder portion of the quotient.

c. Use the divisor of the improper fraction as the divisor (denominator) in the remainder portion of the quotient.

The following examples show the steps as to how improper fractions are changed to mixed fractions:

Example 2.2-1

$$\boxed{\dfrac{86}{5}} =$$

Solution:

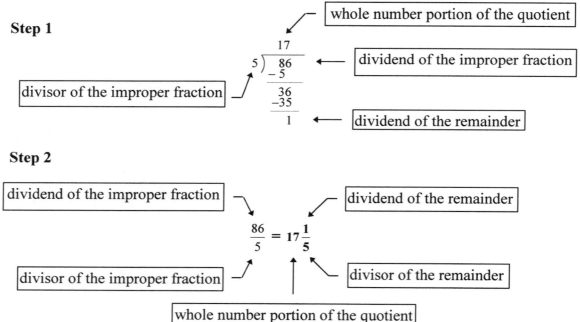

Example 2.2-2

$$\boxed{\dfrac{506}{3}} =$$

Solution:

Step 1

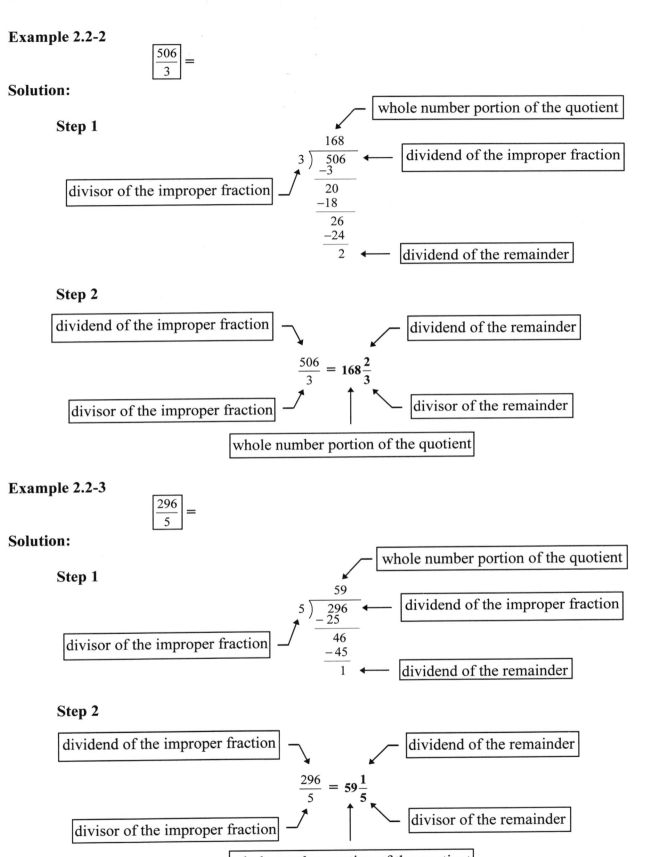

Step 2

Example 2.2-3

$$\boxed{\dfrac{296}{5}} =$$

Solution:

Step 1

Step 2

Example 2.2-4

$$\left| -\frac{597}{10} \right| =$$

Solution:

Step 1

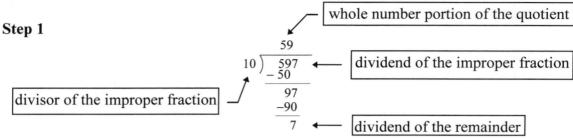

Step 2

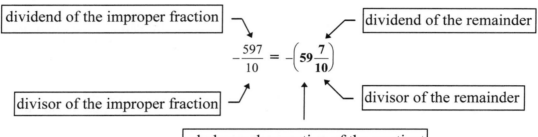

Example 2.2-5

$$\left| \frac{1428}{45} \right| =$$

Solution:

Step 1

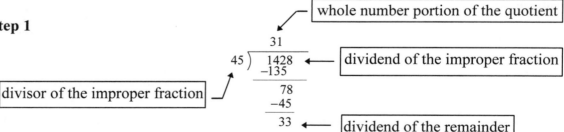

Step 2

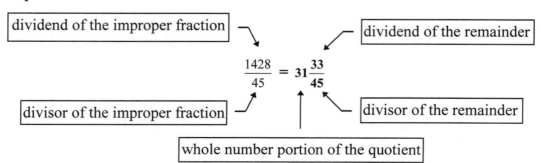

Example 2.2-6

$$\boxed{-\dfrac{38}{3}} =$$

Solution:

Step 1

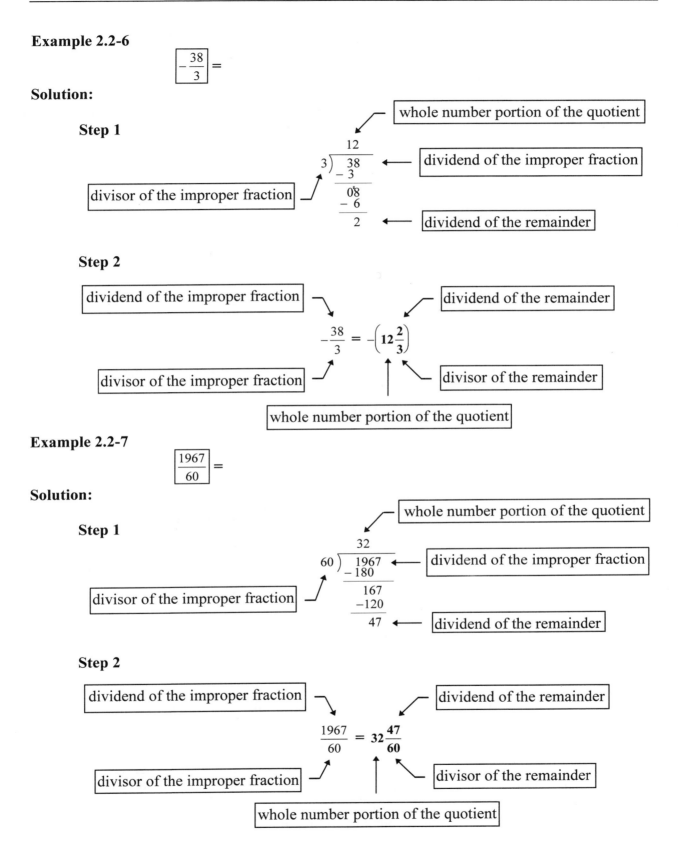

Step 2

Example 2.2-7

$$\boxed{\dfrac{1967}{60}} =$$

Solution:

Step 1

Step 2

Example 2.2-8

$$\boxed{-\frac{28}{13}} =$$

Solution:

Step 1

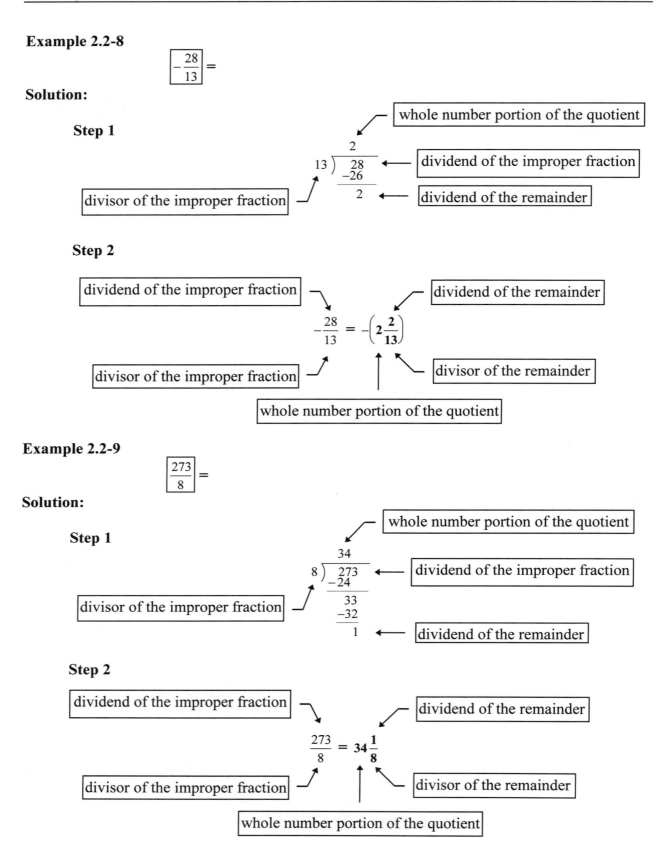

Step 2

Example 2.2-10

$$\boxed{-\dfrac{355}{102}} =$$

Solution:

Step 1

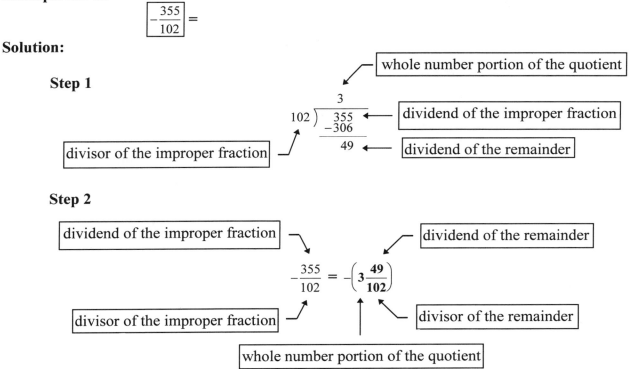

Step 2

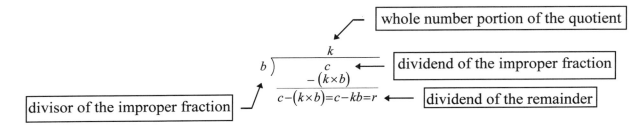

In general, an improper integer fraction $\left(\dfrac{c}{b}\right)$, where (c) is bigger than (b), is changed to a mixed fraction in the following way:

1. divide the numerator (c) by its denominator (b) using the general division process.

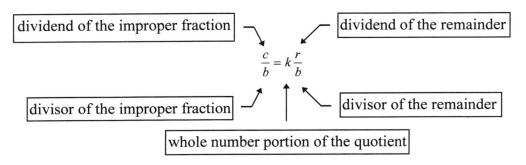

2. Use the whole number portion of the quotient (k), the dividend of the remainder (r), and the divisor of the improper fraction (b) to represent the mixed fraction as:

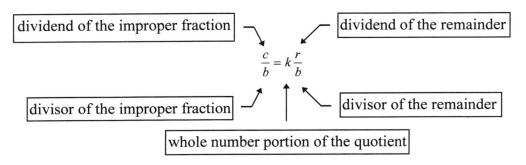

Note 1 - In the general equation $\left(\dfrac{c}{b} = k\dfrac{r}{b}\right)$; $\dfrac{c}{b}$ is the improper fraction, $k\dfrac{r}{b}$ is the quotient, k is the whole number portion of the quotient, and $\dfrac{r}{b}$ is the remainder portion of the quotient.

Note 2 - The divisor of the improper fraction is always used as the divisor of the remainder. This is shown in Step 2 of examples above.

Section 2.2 Exercises - Change the following improper fractions to mixed fractions:

1. $\dfrac{83}{4} =$

2. $\dfrac{13}{3} =$

3. $-\dfrac{26}{5} =$

4. $\dfrac{67}{10} =$

5. $\dfrac{9}{2} =$

6. $-\dfrac{332}{113} =$

7. $\dfrac{205}{9} =$

8. $-\dfrac{235}{14}$

9. $\dfrac{207}{11} =$

10. $-\dfrac{523}{101} =$

2.3   Simplifying Integer Fractions

Integer fractions $\left(\dfrac{a}{b}\right)$ where both the numerator (a) and the denominator (b) are integer numbers are simplified as in the following cases:

Case 1 - The Numerator and the Denominator are Even Numbers

Use the following steps to simplify the integer fractions if the numerator and the denominator are even numbers:

Step 1   Check the numerator and the denominator of the integer fraction to see if it is an $\dfrac{even}{even}$ type of fraction.

Step 2   Simplify the fraction to its lowest term by dividing the numerator and the denominator by their Greatest Common Factor (G.C.F.) which is an even number, i.e., $(2, 4, 6, 8, 10, 12, 14, ...)$. See page 70 on methods for finding G.C.F.

Step 3   Change the improper fraction to a mixed fraction if the fraction obtained from Step 2 is an improper fraction (see Section 2.2).

The following examples show the steps as to how integer fractions with even numerator and denominator are simplified

Example 2.3-1

$$\boxed{-\dfrac{366}{64}} =$$

Solution:

Step 1 $\boxed{-\dfrac{366}{64}} = \boxed{-\dfrac{366\,(is\ an\ even\ No.)}{64\,(is\ an\ even\ No.)}}$

Step 2 $\boxed{-\dfrac{366\,(is\ an\ even\ No.)}{64\,(is\ an\ even\ No.)}} = \boxed{-\dfrac{366 \div 2}{64 \div 2}} = \boxed{-\dfrac{183}{32}}$

Step 3 $\boxed{-\dfrac{183}{32}} = \boxed{-\left(5\dfrac{23}{32}\right)}$

Example 2.3-2

$$\boxed{\dfrac{400}{350}} =$$

Solution:

Step 1 $\boxed{\dfrac{400}{350}} = \boxed{\dfrac{400\,(is\ an\ even\ No.)}{350\,(is\ an\ even\ No.)}}$

Step 2 $\boxed{\dfrac{400\,(is\ an\ even\ No.)}{350\,(is\ an\ even\ No.)}} = \boxed{\dfrac{400 \div 50}{350 \div 50}} = \boxed{\dfrac{8}{7}}$

Step 3 $\boxed{\dfrac{8}{7}} = \boxed{1\dfrac{1}{7}}$

Example 2.3-3

$\boxed{\dfrac{2}{8}} =$

Solution:

Step 1 $\boxed{\dfrac{2}{8}} = \boxed{\dfrac{2\,(\text{is an even No.})}{8\,(\text{is an even No.})}}$

Step 2 $\boxed{\dfrac{2\,(\text{is an even No.})}{8\,(\text{is an even No.})}} = \boxed{\dfrac{2 \div 2}{8 \div 2}} = \boxed{\dfrac{1}{4}}$

Step 3 $\boxed{Not\ Applicable}$

Note: See definition of "Not Applicable" in the Terminology section.

Example 2.3-4

$\boxed{-\dfrac{18}{12}} =$

Solution:

Step 1 $\boxed{-\dfrac{18}{12}} = \boxed{-\dfrac{18\,(\text{is an even No.})}{12\,(\text{is an even No.})}}$

Step 2 $\boxed{-\dfrac{18\,(\text{is an even No.})}{12\,(\text{is an even No.})}} = \boxed{-\dfrac{18 \div 6}{12 \div 6}} = \boxed{-\dfrac{3}{2}}$

Step 3 $\boxed{-\dfrac{3}{2}} = \boxed{-\left(1\dfrac{1}{2}\right)}$

Example 2.3-5

$\boxed{\dfrac{16}{32}} =$

Solution:

Step 1 $\boxed{\dfrac{16}{32}} = \boxed{\dfrac{16\,(\text{is an even No.})}{32\,(\text{is an even No.})}}$

Step 2 $\boxed{\dfrac{16\,(\text{is an even No.})}{32\,(\text{is an even No.})}} = \boxed{\dfrac{16 \div 16}{32 \div 16}} = \boxed{\dfrac{1}{2}}$

Step 3 $\boxed{Not\ Applicable}$

Case 2 - The Numerator and the Denominator are Odd Numbers
Use the following steps to simplify the integer fractions if the numerator and the denominator are odd numbers:

Step 1   Check the numerator and the denominator of the integer fraction to see if it is an $\dfrac{odd}{odd}$ type of fraction.

Step 2   Simplify the fraction to its lowest term by dividing the numerator and the denominator by their Greatest Common Factor (G.C.F.) which is an odd number, i.e., $(3, 5, 7, 9, 11, 13, 15, ...)$. See page 70 on methods for finding G.C.F.

Step 3   Change the improper fraction to a mixed fraction if the fraction obtained from Step 2 is an improper fraction (see Section 2.2).

The following examples show the steps as to how integer fractions with odd numerator and denominator are simplified:

Example 2.3-6

$$\boxed{-\dfrac{3}{15}} =$$

Solution:

Step 1 $\boxed{-\dfrac{3}{15}} = \boxed{-\dfrac{3\,(is\ an\ odd\ No.)}{15\,(is\ an\ odd\ No.)}}$

Step 2 $\boxed{-\dfrac{3\,(is\ an\ odd\ No.)}{15\,(is\ an\ odd\ No.)}} = \boxed{-\dfrac{3 \div 3}{15 \div 3}} = \boxed{-\dfrac{1}{5}}$

Step 3 $\boxed{Not\ Applicable}$

Example 2.3-7

$$\boxed{\dfrac{7}{21}} =$$

Solution:

Step 1 $\boxed{\dfrac{7}{21}} = \boxed{\dfrac{7\,(is\ an\ odd\ No.)}{21\,(is\ an\ odd\ No.)}}$

Step 2 $\boxed{\dfrac{7\,(is\ an\ odd\ No.)}{21\,(is\ an\ odd\ No.)}} = \boxed{\dfrac{7 \div 7}{21 \div 7}} = \boxed{\dfrac{1}{3}}$

Step 3 $\boxed{Not\ Applicable}$

Example 2.3-8

$$\boxed{\dfrac{17}{21}} =$$

Solution:

Step 1 $\boxed{\dfrac{17}{21}} = \boxed{\dfrac{\mathbf{17}\,(\textit{is an odd No.})}{\mathbf{21}\,(\textit{is an odd No.})}}$

Step 2 $\boxed{\textit{Not Applicable}}$

Step 3 $\boxed{\textit{Not Applicable}}$

Note - In cases where the answer to Steps 2 and 3 are stated as "Not Applicable" this indicates that the fraction is in its lowest term and can not be simplified any further.

Example 2.3-9

$$\boxed{-\dfrac{305}{35}} =$$

Solution:

Step 1 $\boxed{-\dfrac{305}{35}} = \boxed{-\dfrac{305\,(\textit{is an odd No.})}{35\,(\textit{is an odd No.})}}$

Step 2 $\boxed{-\dfrac{305\,(\textit{is an odd No.})}{35\,(\textit{is an odd No.})}} = \boxed{-\dfrac{305 \div 5}{35 \div 5}} = \boxed{-\dfrac{61}{7}}$

Step 3 $\boxed{-\dfrac{61}{7}} = \boxed{-\left(8\dfrac{5}{7}\right)}$

Example 2.3-10

$$\boxed{\dfrac{105}{33}} =$$

Solution:

Step 1 $\boxed{\dfrac{105}{33}} = \boxed{\dfrac{105\,(\textit{is an odd No.})}{33\,(\textit{is an odd No.})}}$

Step 2 $\boxed{\dfrac{105\,(\textit{is an odd No.})}{33\,(\textit{is an odd No.})}} = \boxed{\dfrac{105 \div 3}{33 \div 3}} = \boxed{\dfrac{35}{11}}$

Step 3 $\boxed{\dfrac{35}{11}} = \boxed{3\dfrac{2}{11}}$

Case 3 - The Numerator is an Even Number and the Denominator is an Odd Number
Use the following steps to simplify the integer fractions if the numerator is an even number and the denominator is an odd number:

Step 1   Check the numerator and the denominator of the integer fraction to see if it is an $\dfrac{even}{odd}$ type of fraction.

Step 2   Simplify the fraction to its lowest term by dividing the numerator and the denominator by their Greatest Common Factor (G.C.F.) which is an odd number, i.e., $(\, 3, 5, 7, 9, 11, 13, 15, ...)$. See page 70 on methods for finding G.C.F.

Step 3   Change the improper fraction to a mixed fraction if the fraction obtained from Step 2 is an improper fraction (see Section 2.2).

The following examples show the steps as to how integer fractions with an even numerator and an odd denominator are simplified:

Example 2.3-11

$$\boxed{\dfrac{18}{27}} =$$

Solution:

Step 1 $\boxed{\dfrac{18}{27}} = \boxed{\dfrac{18\,(\textit{is an even No.})}{27\,(\textit{is an odd No.})}}$

Step 2 $\boxed{\dfrac{18\,(\textit{is an even No.})}{27\,(\textit{is an odd No.})}} = \boxed{\dfrac{18 \div 9}{27 \div 9}} = \boxed{\dfrac{2}{3}}$

Step 3 $\boxed{\textit{Not Applicable}}$

Example 2.3-12

$$\boxed{\dfrac{14}{25}} =$$

Solution:

Step 1 $\boxed{\dfrac{14}{25}} = \boxed{\dfrac{\mathbf{14}\,(\textit{is an even No.})}{\mathbf{25}\,(\textit{is an odd No.})}}$

Step 2 $\boxed{\textit{Not Applicable}}$

Step 3 $\boxed{\textit{Not Applicable}}$

Example 2.3-13

$$\boxed{\dfrac{334}{15}} =$$

Solution:

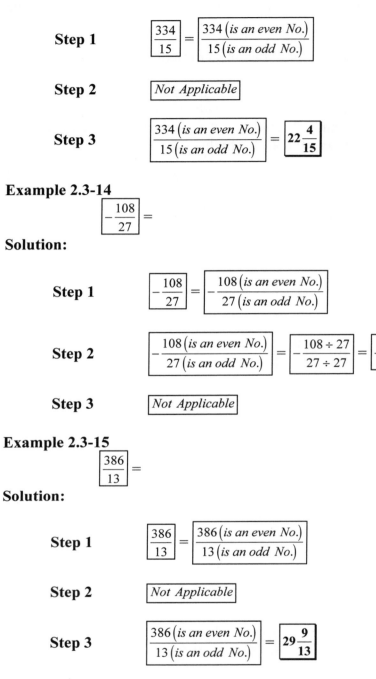

Step 1
$$\boxed{\dfrac{334}{15}} = \boxed{\dfrac{334\,(\textit{is an even No.})}{15\,(\textit{is an odd No.})}}$$

Step 2
$$\boxed{\textit{Not Applicable}}$$

Step 3
$$\boxed{\dfrac{334\,(\textit{is an even No.})}{15\,(\textit{is an odd No.})}} = \boxed{22\dfrac{4}{15}}$$

Example 2.3-14
$$\boxed{-\dfrac{108}{27}} =$$

Solution:

Step 1
$$\boxed{-\dfrac{108}{27}} = \boxed{-\dfrac{108\,(\textit{is an even No.})}{27\,(\textit{is an odd No.})}}$$

Step 2
$$\boxed{-\dfrac{108\,(\textit{is an even No.})}{27\,(\textit{is an odd No.})}} = \boxed{-\dfrac{108 \div 27}{27 \div 27}} = \boxed{-\dfrac{4}{1}} = \boxed{-4}$$

Step 3
$$\boxed{\textit{Not Applicable}}$$

Example 2.3-15
$$\boxed{\dfrac{386}{13}} =$$

Solution:

Step 1
$$\boxed{\dfrac{386}{13}} = \boxed{\dfrac{386\,(\textit{is an even No.})}{13\,(\textit{is an odd No.})}}$$

Step 2
$$\boxed{\textit{Not Applicable}}$$

Step 3
$$\boxed{\dfrac{386\,(\textit{is an even No.})}{13\,(\textit{is an odd No.})}} = \boxed{29\dfrac{9}{13}}$$

Case 4 - The Numerator is an Odd Number and the Denominator is an Even Number

Use the following steps to simplify the integer fractions if the numerator is an odd number and the denominator is an even number:

Step 1   Check the numerator and the denominator of the integer fraction to see if it is an $\frac{odd}{even}$ type of fraction.

Step 2   Simplify the fraction to its lowest term by dividing the numerator and the denominator by their Greatest Common Factor (G.C.F.) which is an odd number, i.e., $(3, 5, 7, 9, 11, 13, 15, ...)$. See page 70 on methods for finding G.C.F.

Step 3   Change the improper fraction to a mixed fraction if the fraction obtained from Step 2 is an improper fraction (see Section 2.2).

The following examples show the steps as to how integer fractions with an odd numerator and an even denominator are simplified:

Example 2.3-16

$$\boxed{\frac{15}{60}} =$$

Solution:

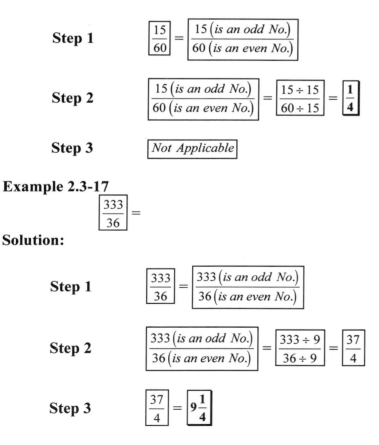

Step 1 $\boxed{\dfrac{15}{60}} = \boxed{\dfrac{15 \,(\textit{is an odd No.})}{60 \,(\textit{is an even No.})}}$

Step 2 $\boxed{\dfrac{15 \,(\textit{is an odd No.})}{60 \,(\textit{is an even No.})}} = \boxed{\dfrac{15 \div 15}{60 \div 15}} = \boxed{\dfrac{1}{4}}$

Step 3 $\boxed{\textit{Not Applicable}}$

Example 2.3-17

$$\boxed{\frac{333}{36}} =$$

Solution:

Step 1 $\boxed{\dfrac{333}{36}} = \boxed{\dfrac{333 \,(\textit{is an odd No.})}{36 \,(\textit{is an even No.})}}$

Step 2 $\boxed{\dfrac{333 \,(\textit{is an odd No.})}{36 \,(\textit{is an even No.})}} = \boxed{\dfrac{333 \div 9}{36 \div 9}} = \boxed{\dfrac{37}{4}}$

Step 3 $\boxed{\dfrac{37}{4}} = \boxed{9\dfrac{1}{4}}$

Example 2.3-18

$$\boxed{\dfrac{305}{200}} =$$

Solution:

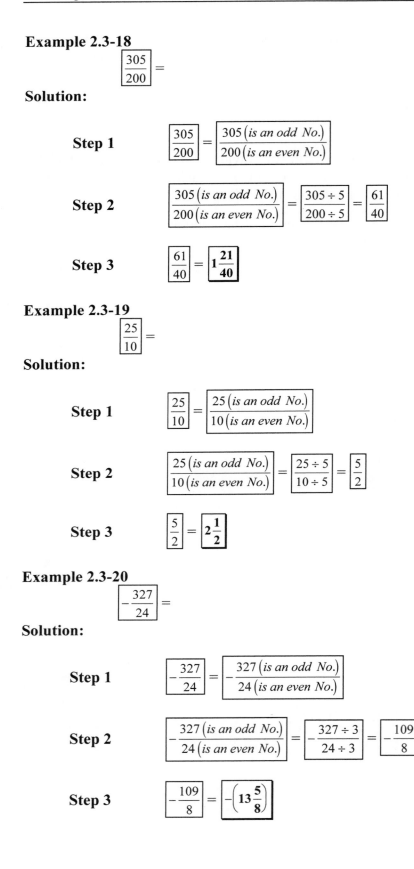

Step 1 $\boxed{\dfrac{305}{200}} = \boxed{\dfrac{305\,(is\ an\ odd\ No.)}{200\,(is\ an\ even\ No.)}}$

Step 2 $\boxed{\dfrac{305\,(is\ an\ odd\ No.)}{200\,(is\ an\ even\ No.)}} = \boxed{\dfrac{305 \div 5}{200 \div 5}} = \boxed{\dfrac{61}{40}}$

Step 3 $\boxed{\dfrac{61}{40}} = \boxed{\mathbf{1\dfrac{21}{40}}}$

Example 2.3-19

$$\boxed{\dfrac{25}{10}} =$$

Solution:

Step 1 $\boxed{\dfrac{25}{10}} = \boxed{\dfrac{25\,(is\ an\ odd\ No.)}{10\,(is\ an\ even\ No.)}}$

Step 2 $\boxed{\dfrac{25\,(is\ an\ odd\ No.)}{10\,(is\ an\ even\ No.)}} = \boxed{\dfrac{25 \div 5}{10 \div 5}} = \boxed{\dfrac{5}{2}}$

Step 3 $\boxed{\dfrac{5}{2}} = \boxed{\mathbf{2\dfrac{1}{2}}}$

Example 2.3-20

$$\boxed{-\dfrac{327}{24}} =$$

Solution:

Step 1 $\boxed{-\dfrac{327}{24}} = \boxed{-\dfrac{327\,(is\ an\ odd\ No.)}{24\,(is\ an\ even\ No.)}}$

Step 2 $\boxed{-\dfrac{327\,(is\ an\ odd\ No.)}{24\,(is\ an\ even\ No.)}} = \boxed{-\dfrac{327 \div 3}{24 \div 3}} = \boxed{-\dfrac{109}{8}}$

Step 3 $\boxed{-\dfrac{109}{8}} = \boxed{-\left(\mathbf{13\dfrac{5}{8}}\right)}$

Note that in Cases 2, 3, and 4 where the integer fractions are $\frac{odd}{odd}$, $\frac{even}{odd}$, and $\frac{odd}{even}$, respectively odd numbers are always used to simplify the fractions. The following examples further illustrate how to simplify integer fractions:

Example 2.3-21

$$\boxed{\frac{15}{3}} = \boxed{\frac{15\,(is\ an\ odd\ No.)}{3\,(is\ an\ odd\ No.)}} = \boxed{\frac{15 \div 3}{3 \div 3}} = \boxed{\frac{5}{1}} = \boxed{5}$$

Example 2.3-22

$$\boxed{-\frac{6}{8}} = \boxed{\frac{6\,(is\ an\ even\ No.)}{8\,(is\ an\ even\ No.)}} = \boxed{-\frac{6 \div 2}{8 \div 2}} = \boxed{-\frac{3}{4}}$$

Example 2.3-23

$$\boxed{\frac{12}{3}} = \boxed{\frac{12\,(is\ an\ even\ No.)}{3\,(is\ an\ odd\ No.)}} = \boxed{\frac{12 \div 3}{3 \div 3}} = \boxed{\frac{4}{1}} = \boxed{4}$$

Example 2.3-24

$$\boxed{\frac{35}{7}} = \boxed{\frac{35\,(is\ an\ odd\ No.)}{7\,(is\ an\ odd\ No.)}} = \boxed{\frac{35 \div 7}{7 \div 7}} = \boxed{\frac{5}{1}} = \boxed{5}$$

Example 2.3-25

$$\boxed{\frac{100}{3}} = \boxed{\frac{100\,(is\ an\ even\ No.)}{3\,(is\ an\ odd\ No.)}} = \boxed{33\frac{1}{3}}$$

Example 2.3-26

$$\boxed{\frac{112}{2}} = \boxed{\frac{112\,(is\ an\ even\ No.)}{2\,(is\ an\ even\ No.)}} = \boxed{\frac{112 \div 2}{2 \div 2}} = \boxed{\frac{56}{1}} = \boxed{56}$$

Example 2.3-27

$$\boxed{-\frac{325}{40}} = \boxed{-\frac{325\,(is\ an\ odd\ No.)}{40\,(is\ an\ even\ No.)}} = \boxed{-\frac{325 \div 5}{40 \div 5}} = \boxed{-\frac{65}{8}} = \boxed{-\left(8\frac{1}{8}\right)}$$

Example 2.3-28

$$\boxed{\frac{22}{6}} = \boxed{\frac{22\,(is\ an\ even\ No.)}{6\,(is\ an\ even\ No.)}} = \boxed{\frac{22 \div 2}{6 \div 2}} = \boxed{\frac{11}{3}} = \boxed{3\frac{2}{3}}$$

Example 2.3-29

$$\boxed{\frac{36}{3}} = \boxed{\frac{36\,(is\ an\ even\ No.)}{3\,(is\ an\ odd\ No.)}} = \boxed{\frac{36 \div 3}{3 \div 3}} = \boxed{\frac{12}{1}} = \boxed{\mathbf{12}}$$

Example 2.3-30

$$\boxed{\frac{6}{39}} = -\boxed{\frac{6\,(is\ an\ even\ No.)}{39\,(is\ an\ odd\ No.)}} = -\boxed{\frac{6 \div 3}{39 \div 3}} = -\boxed{\frac{2}{13}}$$

Greatest Common Factor (G.C.F.) can be found in two ways: 1. trial and error method, and 2. prime factoring method.

1. **Trial and Error Method**: In trial and error method the numerator and the denominator are divided by odd or even numbers until the largest divisor for both the numerator and the denominator is found.

2. **Prime Factoring Method**: The steps in using prime factoring method are:

   a. Rewrite both the numerator and the denominator by their equivalent prime number products.

   b. Identify the prime numbers that are common in both the numerator and the denominator.

   c. Multiply the common prime numbers in either the numerator or the denominator to obtain the G.C.F.

   The following are examples of how G.C.F. can be found using the prime factoring method:

   1. $\dfrac{24}{45} = \dfrac{2 \times 2 \times 2 \times 3}{3 \times 3 \times 5}$ 3 is common, therefore $G.C.F.= 3$

   2. $\dfrac{400}{350} = \dfrac{2 \times 2 \times 2 \times 2 \times 5 \times 5}{2 \times 5 \times 5 \times 7}$ 2, 5, and 5 are common, therefore $G.C.F.= 2 \times 5 \times 5 = 50$

   3. $\dfrac{15}{60} = \dfrac{3 \times 5}{2 \times 3 \times 2 \times 5}$ 3 and 5 are common, therefore $G.C.F.= 3 \times 5 = 15$

   4. $\dfrac{108}{27} = \dfrac{2 \times 2 \times 3 \times 3 \times 3}{3 \times 3 \times 3}$ 3, 3, and 3 are common, therefore $G.C.F.= 3 \times 3 \times 3 = 27$

Section 2.3 Exercises - Simplify the following integer fractions:

1. $\dfrac{60}{150} =$ 2. $\dfrac{8}{18} =$ 3. $\dfrac{355}{15} =$ 4. $\dfrac{3}{8} =$ 5. $\dfrac{27}{6} =$

6. $\dfrac{33}{6} =$ 7. $\dfrac{250}{1000} =$ 8. $\dfrac{4}{32} =$ 9. $\dfrac{284}{568} =$ 10. $\dfrac{45}{75} =$

2.4   Changing Decimal Fractions to Integer Fractions

Decimal fractions of the form $\left(\dfrac{a \times 10^{-k_1}}{b \times 10^{-k_2}}\right)$ where (a) and (b) are integer numbers and (k_1) and

(k_2) are equal to the number of decimal places are changed to integer fractions using the following steps:

Step 1   Change the decimal number of the form $\left(a \times 10^{-k_1}\right)$ to integer fraction of the form

$\left(\dfrac{a\ (outer\ numerator)}{10^{k_1}\ (inner\ deno\min ator)}\right)$ in the numerator, e.g., change 0.5 to $\dfrac{5}{10}$ in the numerator.

Step 2   Change the decimal number of the form $\left(b \times 10^{-k_2}\right)$ to integer fraction of the form

$\left(\dfrac{b\ (inner\ numerator)}{10^{k_2}\ (outer\ deno\min ator)}\right)$ in the denominator, e.g., change 2.38 to $\dfrac{238}{100}$ in the

denominator.

Step 3   Multiply the outer numerator (a) with the outer denominator $\left(10^{k_2}\right)$ and the inner

denominator $\left(10^{k_1}\right)$ with the inner numerator (b), e.g., change $\dfrac{\frac{5}{10}}{\frac{238}{100}}$ to

$\dfrac{5 \times 100}{10 \times 238} = \dfrac{500}{2380}$.

Step 4   Simplify the integer fraction to its lowest term (see Section 2.3).

Step 5   Change the improper fraction to a mixed fraction if the fraction obtained from Step 4 is an improper fraction (see Section 2.2).

The following examples show the steps as to how decimal fractions are changed to integer fractions:

Example 2.4-1

$\boxed{\dfrac{3.75}{0.005}} =$

Solution:

Step 1 $\boxed{\dfrac{3.75}{0.005}} = \boxed{\dfrac{\frac{375}{100}}{0.005}}$

Step 2 $\boxed{\dfrac{\frac{375}{100}}{0.005}} = \boxed{\dfrac{\frac{375}{100}}{\frac{5}{1000}}}$

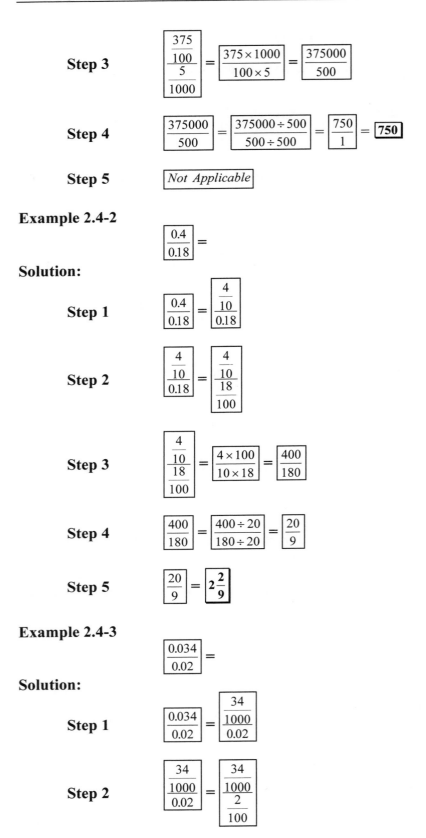

Step 3 $\dfrac{\dfrac{375}{100}}{\dfrac{5}{1000}} = \dfrac{375 \times 1000}{100 \times 5} = \dfrac{375000}{500}$

Step 4 $\dfrac{375000}{500} = \dfrac{375000 \div 500}{500 \div 500} = \dfrac{750}{1} = \boxed{750}$

Step 5 $\boxed{Not\ Applicable}$

Example 2.4-2

$\dfrac{0.4}{0.18} =$

Solution:

Step 1 $\dfrac{0.4}{0.18} = \dfrac{\dfrac{4}{10}}{0.18}$

Step 2 $\dfrac{\dfrac{4}{10}}{0.18} = \dfrac{\dfrac{4}{10}}{\dfrac{18}{100}}$

Step 3 $\dfrac{\dfrac{4}{10}}{\dfrac{18}{100}} = \dfrac{4 \times 100}{10 \times 18} = \dfrac{400}{180}$

Step 4 $\dfrac{400}{180} = \dfrac{400 \div 20}{180 \div 20} = \dfrac{20}{9}$

Step 5 $\dfrac{20}{9} = \boxed{2\dfrac{2}{9}}$

Example 2.4-3

$\dfrac{0.034}{0.02} =$

Solution:

Step 1 $\dfrac{0.034}{0.02} = \dfrac{\dfrac{34}{1000}}{0.02}$

Step 2 $\dfrac{\dfrac{34}{1000}}{0.02} = \dfrac{\dfrac{34}{1000}}{\dfrac{2}{100}}$

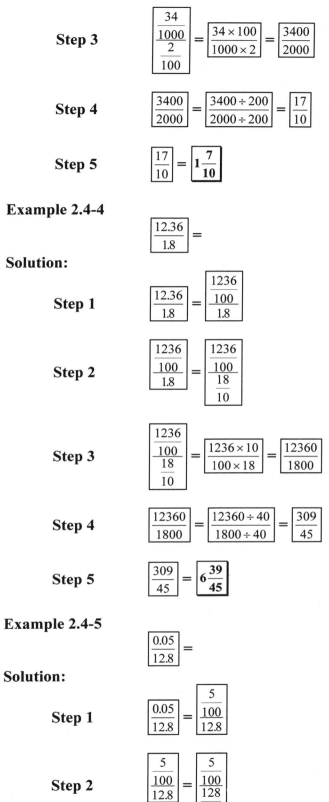

Step 3 $\dfrac{\dfrac{34}{1000}}{\dfrac{2}{100}} = \dfrac{34 \times 100}{1000 \times 2} = \dfrac{3400}{2000}$

Step 4 $\dfrac{3400}{2000} = \dfrac{3400 \div 200}{2000 \div 200} = \dfrac{17}{10}$

Step 5 $\dfrac{17}{10} = \mathbf{1\dfrac{7}{10}}$

Example 2.4-4

$\dfrac{12.36}{1.8} =$

Solution:

Step 1 $\dfrac{12.36}{1.8} = \dfrac{\dfrac{1236}{100}}{1.8}$

Step 2 $\dfrac{\dfrac{1236}{100}}{1.8} = \dfrac{\dfrac{1236}{100}}{\dfrac{18}{10}}$

Step 3 $\dfrac{\dfrac{1236}{100}}{\dfrac{18}{10}} = \dfrac{1236 \times 10}{100 \times 18} = \dfrac{12360}{1800}$

Step 4 $\dfrac{12360}{1800} = \dfrac{12360 \div 40}{1800 \div 40} = \dfrac{309}{45}$

Step 5 $\dfrac{309}{45} = \mathbf{6\dfrac{39}{45}}$

Example 2.4-5

$\dfrac{0.05}{12.8} =$

Solution:

Step 1 $\dfrac{0.05}{12.8} = \dfrac{\dfrac{5}{100}}{12.8}$

Step 2 $\dfrac{\dfrac{5}{100}}{12.8} = \dfrac{\dfrac{5}{100}}{\dfrac{128}{10}}$

Step 3   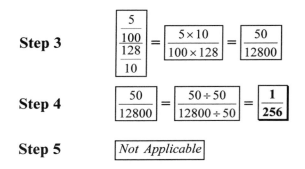

$$\boxed{\dfrac{\frac{5}{100}}{\frac{128}{10}}} = \boxed{\dfrac{5 \times 10}{100 \times 128}} = \boxed{\dfrac{50}{12800}}$$

Step 4 $\boxed{\dfrac{50}{12800}} = \boxed{\dfrac{50 \div 50}{12800 \div 50}} = \boxed{\dfrac{1}{256}}$

Step 5 $\boxed{\textit{Not Applicable}}$

In general, fractions with decimal numbers are categorized as in the following cases and are changed to integer fractions as shown below:

Case I. - *The numerator and the denominator are decimal numbers*

$$\boxed{\dfrac{a \times 10^{-k_1}}{b \times 10^{-k_2}}} = \boxed{\dfrac{\frac{a}{10^{k_1}}}{\frac{b}{10^{k_2}}}} = \boxed{\dfrac{a \times 10^{k_2}}{10^{k_1} \times b}}$$

Example 2.4-6

$$\boxed{\dfrac{38 \times 10^{-2}}{14 \times 10^{-1}}} = \boxed{\dfrac{0.38}{1.4}} = \boxed{\dfrac{\frac{38}{100}}{\frac{14}{10}}} = \boxed{\dfrac{38 \times 10}{100 \times 14}} = \boxed{\dfrac{\cancel{380}^{19}}{\cancel{1400}_{70}}} = \boxed{\dfrac{19}{70}}$$

Case II. - *The numerator is a decimal number and the denominator is an integer number*

$$\boxed{\dfrac{a \times 10^{-k_1}}{b}} = \boxed{\dfrac{\frac{a}{10^{k_1}}}{\frac{b}{1}}} = \boxed{\dfrac{a \times 1}{10^{k_1} \times b}} = \boxed{\dfrac{a}{10^{k_1} \times b}}$$

Example 2.4-7

$$\boxed{\dfrac{15 \times 10^{-3}}{26}} = \boxed{\dfrac{0.015}{26}} = \boxed{\dfrac{\frac{15}{1000}}{\frac{26}{1}}} = \boxed{\dfrac{15 \times 1}{1000 \times 26}} = \boxed{\dfrac{\cancel{15}^{3}}{\cancel{26000}_{5200}}} = \boxed{\dfrac{3}{5200}}$$

Case III. - *The numerator is an integer number and the denominator is a decimal number*

$$\boxed{\dfrac{a}{b \times 10^{-k_2}}} = \boxed{\dfrac{\frac{a}{1}}{\frac{b}{10^{k_2}}}} = \boxed{\dfrac{a \times 10^{k_2}}{1 \times b}} = \boxed{\dfrac{a \times 10^{k_2}}{b}}$$

Example 2.4-8

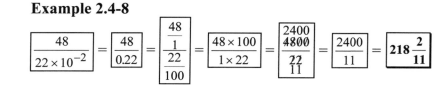

The following examples further illustrate how to change decimal fractions to integer fractions:

Example 2.4-9

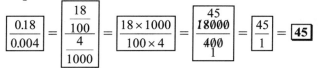

Example 2.4-10

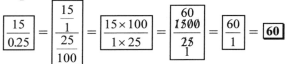

Example 2.4-11

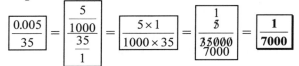

Example 2.4-12

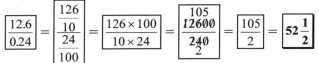

Example 2.4-13

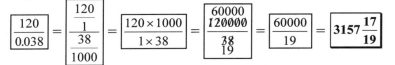

Example 2.4-14

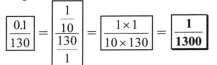

Example 2.4-15

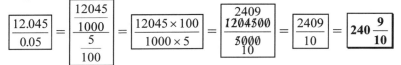

Example 2.4-16

$$\boxed{\frac{38}{112.4}} = \boxed{\frac{\frac{38}{1}}{\frac{1124}{10}}} = \boxed{\frac{38 \times 10}{1 \times 1124}} = \boxed{\frac{\overset{95}{\cancel{380}}}{\underset{281}{\cancel{1124}}}} = \boxed{\frac{95}{281}}$$

Example 2.4-17

$$\boxed{\frac{0.009}{1.23}} = \boxed{\frac{\frac{9}{1000}}{\frac{123}{100}}} = \boxed{\frac{9 \times 100}{1000 \times 123}} = \boxed{\frac{\overset{3}{\cancel{900}}}{\underset{410}{\cancel{123000}}}} = \boxed{\frac{3}{410}}$$

Example 2.4-18

$$\boxed{\frac{28}{12.24}} = \boxed{\frac{\frac{28}{1}}{\frac{1224}{100}}} = \boxed{\frac{28 \times 100}{1 \times 1224}} = \boxed{\frac{\overset{350}{\cancel{2800}}}{\underset{153}{\cancel{1224}}}} = \boxed{\frac{350}{153}} = \boxed{2\frac{44}{153}}$$

Note - An expression that contains fractions in the numerator and/or denominator is referred to as a **Complex Fraction**. For example, $\dfrac{\frac{2}{3}}{\frac{8}{15}}$, $\dfrac{\frac{5}{3}}{116}$, $\dfrac{\frac{2}{7}}{38}$, $\dfrac{0.5}{\frac{3}{5}}$, $\dfrac{\frac{2}{5}}{30.6}$, etc. are complex fractions.

Section 2.4 Exercises - Change the following decimal fractions to integer fractions:

1. $\dfrac{0.3}{0.05} =$ 2. $\dfrac{0.02}{4} =$ 3. $\dfrac{0.5}{0.01} =$ 4. $\dfrac{35}{0.005} =$

5. $\dfrac{12.3}{0.03} =$ 6. $\dfrac{6}{12.2} =$ 7. $\dfrac{0.008}{1.2} =$ 8. $\dfrac{0.9}{0.05} =$

9. $\dfrac{1}{0.2} =$ 10. $\dfrac{4.02}{12.8} =$

2.5   Changing Mixed Fractions to Integer Fractions

Mixed fractions of the form $\left(k\dfrac{a}{b}\right)$ where (k) is a whole number and $\left(\dfrac{a}{b}\right)$ is an integer fraction

for a number less than one are changed to integer fractions using the following steps:

Step 1   Multiply the whole number (k) by the denominator (b) and add the result to the numerator (a). The product $(k \times b) + a$ is the numerator of the integer fraction with

its denominator remaining as (b), e.g., change $2\dfrac{3}{5}$ to $\dfrac{(2 \times 5) + 3}{5} = \dfrac{10 + 3}{5} = \dfrac{13}{5}$.

Step 2   Simplify the integer fraction to its lowest term (see Section 2.3).

The following examples show the steps as to how mixed fractions are changed to integer fractions:

Example 2.5-1

$$\boxed{6\dfrac{2}{3}} =$$

Solution:

Step 1 $\boxed{6\dfrac{2}{3}} = \boxed{\dfrac{(6 \times 3) + 2}{3}} = \boxed{\dfrac{18 + 2}{3}} = \boxed{\dfrac{\mathbf{20}}{\mathbf{3}}}$

Step 2 $\boxed{Not\ Applicable}$

Example 2.5-2

$$\boxed{13\dfrac{2}{4}} =$$

Solution:

Step 1 $\boxed{13\dfrac{2}{4}} = \boxed{\dfrac{(13 \times 4) + 2}{4}} = \boxed{\dfrac{52 + 2}{4}} = \boxed{\dfrac{54}{4}}$

Step 2 $\boxed{\dfrac{54}{4}} = \boxed{\dfrac{54 \div 2}{4 \div 2}} = \boxed{\dfrac{\mathbf{17}}{\mathbf{2}}}$

Example 2.5-3

$$\boxed{3\dfrac{2}{8}} =$$

Solution:

Step 1 $\boxed{3\dfrac{2}{8}} = \boxed{\dfrac{(3 \times 8) + 2}{8}} = \boxed{\dfrac{24 + 2}{8}} = \boxed{\dfrac{26}{8}}$

Step 2 $\boxed{\dfrac{26}{8}} = \boxed{\dfrac{26 \div 2}{8 \div 2}} = \boxed{\dfrac{\mathbf{13}}{\mathbf{4}}}$

Example 2.5-4

$$2\frac{3}{5} =$$

Solution:

Step 1 $2\frac{3}{5} = \frac{(2 \times 5) + 3}{5} = \frac{10 + 3}{5} = \boxed{\frac{13}{5}}$

Step 2 $\boxed{Not\ Applicable}$

Example 2.5-5

$$5\frac{6}{8} =$$

Solution:

Step 1 $5\frac{6}{8} = \frac{5 \times 8 + 6}{8} = \frac{40 + 6}{8} = \frac{46}{8}$

Step 2 $\frac{46}{8} = \frac{46 \div 2}{8 \div 2} = \boxed{\frac{23}{4}}$

Note that conversion of mixed fractions to integer fractions result to having improper integer fractions which is a subclass of integer fractions (see Section 2.1). The following examples further illustrate how to change mixed fractions to improper integer fractions:

Example 2.5-6

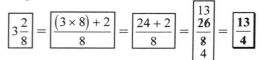

$$3\frac{2}{8} = \frac{(3 \times 8) + 2}{8} = \frac{24 + 2}{8} = \frac{\overset{13}{\cancel{26}}}{\underset{4}{\cancel{8}}} = \boxed{\frac{13}{4}}$$

Example 2.5-7

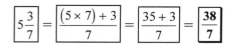

$$5\frac{3}{7} = \frac{(5 \times 7) + 3}{7} = \frac{35 + 3}{7} = \boxed{\frac{38}{7}}$$

Example 2.5-8

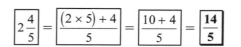

$$2\frac{4}{5} = \frac{(2 \times 5) + 4}{5} = \frac{10 + 4}{5} = \boxed{\frac{14}{5}}$$

Example 2.5-9

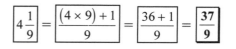

$$4\frac{1}{9} = \frac{(4 \times 9) + 1}{9} = \frac{36 + 1}{9} = \boxed{\frac{37}{9}}$$

Example 2.5-10

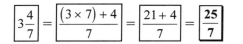

$$\boxed{3\frac{4}{7}} = \boxed{\frac{(3 \times 7) + 4}{7}} = \boxed{\frac{21 + 4}{7}} = \boxed{\frac{\mathbf{25}}{\mathbf{7}}}$$

Example 2.5-11

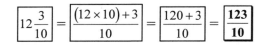

$$\boxed{12\frac{3}{10}} = \boxed{\frac{(12 \times 10) + 3}{10}} = \boxed{\frac{120 + 3}{10}} = \boxed{\frac{\mathbf{123}}{\mathbf{10}}}$$

Example 2.5-12

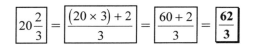

$$\boxed{20\frac{2}{3}} = \boxed{\frac{(20 \times 3) + 2}{3}} = \boxed{\frac{60 + 2}{3}} = \boxed{\frac{\mathbf{62}}{\mathbf{3}}}$$

Example 2.5-13

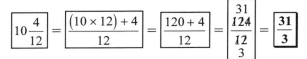

$$\boxed{10\frac{4}{12}} = \boxed{\frac{(10 \times 12) + 4}{12}} = \boxed{\frac{120 + 4}{12}} = \boxed{\frac{\overset{31}{\cancel{124}}}{\underset{3}{\cancel{12}}}} = \boxed{\frac{\mathbf{31}}{\mathbf{3}}}$$

Example 2.5-14

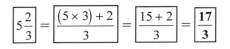

$$\boxed{5\frac{2}{3}} = \boxed{\frac{(5 \times 3) + 2}{3}} = \boxed{\frac{15 + 2}{3}} = \boxed{\frac{\mathbf{17}}{\mathbf{3}}}$$

Example 2.5-15

$$\boxed{6\frac{8}{11}} = \boxed{\frac{(6 \times 11) + 8}{11}} = \boxed{\frac{66 + 8}{11}} = \boxed{\frac{\mathbf{74}}{\mathbf{11}}}$$

Section 2.5 Exercises - Change the following mixed fractions to improper integer fractions:

1. $3\frac{2}{6} =$ 2. $4\frac{3}{8} =$ 3. $5\frac{1}{8} =$ 4. $8\frac{3}{5} =$

5. $7\frac{2}{3} =$ 6. $9\frac{3}{16} =$ 7. $12\frac{2}{4} =$ 8. $10\frac{4}{5} =$

9. $2\frac{5}{8} =$ 10. $3\frac{2}{15} =$

Chapter 3 - Integer Fractions

The objective of this chapter is to improve the student's ability in solving integer fractions. The steps in solving integer fractions along with examples illustrating the steps as to how to add (Section 3.1), subtract (Section 3.2), multiply (Section 3.3), and divide (Section 3.4) two or more integer fractions are given. Section 3.5 combines the mathematical operations using integer fractions. In addition, for completeness, the general algebraic approach in solving integer fractional operations is provided in each section. The student, depending on his or her grade level and ability, can skip the algebraic approach to integer fractions and only learn the techniques that are followed by examples. Focusing on the examples, and the steps shown to solve each problem, should be adequate to teach the student the mechanics of how integer fractions are mathematically operated on.

3.1   Adding Integer Fractions

Integer fractions, i.e., fractions where both the numerator and the denominator are integers, are added as in the following cases:

Case I   Adding Two or More Integer Fractions With Common Denominators

Integer fractions with two or more common denominators are added using the steps given as in each case below:

Case I-A   *Add two integer fractions with common denominators using the following steps:*

Step 1   a. Use the common denominator between the first and second fractions as the new denominator.

b. Add the numerators of the first and second fractions to obtain the new numerator.

Step 2   Simplify the fraction to its lowest term (see Section 2.3).

Step 3   Change the improper fraction to a mixed fraction if the fraction obtained from Step 2 is an improper fraction (see Section 2.2).

The following examples show the steps as to how two integer fractions with common denominators are added:

Example 3.1-1

$$\boxed{\frac{2}{3} + \frac{8}{3}} =$$

Solution:

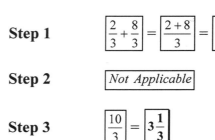

Step 1 $\boxed{\dfrac{2}{3} + \dfrac{8}{3}} = \boxed{\dfrac{2+8}{3}} = \boxed{\dfrac{10}{3}}$

Step 2 $\boxed{Not\ Applicable}$

Step 3 $\boxed{\dfrac{10}{3}} = \boxed{3\dfrac{1}{3}}$

Example 3.1-2

$$\boxed{\dfrac{15}{4} + \dfrac{9}{4}} =$$

Solution:

Step 1 $\boxed{\dfrac{15}{4} + \dfrac{9}{4}} = \boxed{\dfrac{15+9}{4}} = \boxed{\dfrac{24}{4}}$

Step 2 $\boxed{\dfrac{24}{4}} = \boxed{\dfrac{24 \div 4}{4 \div 4}} = \dfrac{6}{1} = \boxed{6}$

Step 3 $\boxed{Not\ Applicable}$

Example 3.1-3

$$\boxed{\dfrac{5}{9} + \dfrac{2}{9}} =$$

Solution:

Step 1 $\boxed{\dfrac{5}{9} + \dfrac{2}{9}} = \boxed{\dfrac{5+2}{9}} = \boxed{\dfrac{7}{9}}$

Step 2 $\boxed{Not\ Applicable}$

Step 3 $\boxed{Not\ Applicable}$

Example 3.1-4

$$\boxed{\dfrac{4}{7} + \dfrac{15}{7}} =$$

Solution:

Step 1 $\boxed{\dfrac{4}{7} + \dfrac{15}{7}} = \boxed{\dfrac{4+15}{7}} = \boxed{\dfrac{19}{7}}$

Step 2 $\boxed{Not\ Applicable}$

Step 3 $\boxed{\dfrac{19}{7}} = \boxed{2\dfrac{5}{7}}$

Example 3.1-5

$$\boxed{\dfrac{12}{5} + \dfrac{33}{5}} =$$

Solution:

Step 1 $\boxed{\dfrac{12}{5} + \dfrac{33}{5}} = \boxed{\dfrac{12+33}{5}} = \boxed{\dfrac{45}{5}}$

Step 2 $\boxed{\dfrac{45}{5}} = \boxed{\dfrac{45 \div 5}{5 \div 5}} = \boxed{\dfrac{9}{1}} = \boxed{9}$

Step 3 $\boxed{\textit{Not Applicable}}$

In general, two integer fractions with a common denominator are added in the following way:

$$\boxed{\dfrac{a}{d} + \dfrac{b}{d}} = \boxed{\dfrac{a+b}{d}}$$

Example 3.1-6

$$\boxed{\dfrac{5}{3} + \dfrac{13}{3}} = \boxed{\dfrac{5+13}{3}} = \boxed{\dfrac{\overset{6}{\cancel{18}}}{\underset{1}{\cancel{3}}}} = \boxed{\dfrac{6}{1}} = \boxed{6}$$

Case I-B   *Add three integer fractions with common denominators using the following steps:*

Step 1   a. Use the common denominator between the first, second, and third fractions as the new denominator.

  b. Add the numerators of the first, second, and third fractions to obtain the new denominator.

Step 2   Simplify the fraction to its lowest term (see Section 2.3).

Step 3   Change the improper fraction to a mixed fraction if the fraction obtained from Step 2 is an improper fraction (see Section 2.2).

The following examples show the steps as to how three integer fractions with common denominators are added:

Example 3.1-7

$$\boxed{\dfrac{3}{5} + \dfrac{4}{5} + \dfrac{1}{5}} =$$

Solution:

Step 1 $\boxed{\dfrac{3}{5} + \dfrac{4}{5} + \dfrac{1}{5}} = \boxed{\dfrac{3+4+1}{5}} = \boxed{\dfrac{8}{5}}$

Step 2 $\boxed{\textit{Not Applicable}}$

Step 3 $\boxed{\dfrac{8}{5}} = \boxed{1\dfrac{3}{5}}$

Example 3.1-8

$$\boxed{\dfrac{5}{8} + \dfrac{2}{8} + \dfrac{14}{8}} =$$

Solution:

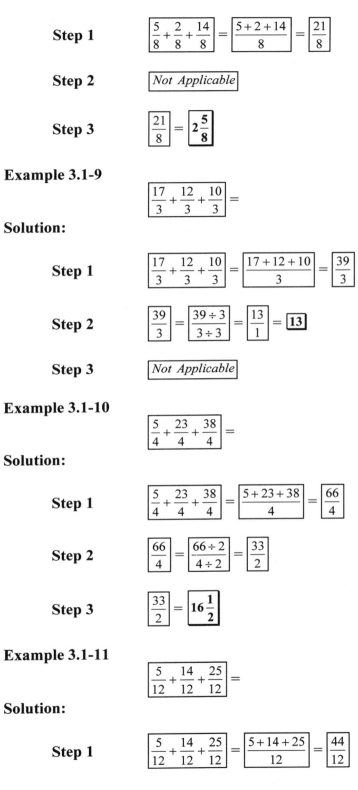

Step 1 $\boxed{\dfrac{5}{8} + \dfrac{2}{8} + \dfrac{14}{8}} = \boxed{\dfrac{5+2+14}{8}} = \boxed{\dfrac{21}{8}}$

Step 2 $\boxed{\textit{Not Applicable}}$

Step 3 $\boxed{\dfrac{21}{8}} = \boxed{\mathbf{2\dfrac{5}{8}}}$

Example 3.1-9

$\boxed{\dfrac{17}{3} + \dfrac{12}{3} + \dfrac{10}{3}} =$

Solution:

Step 1 $\boxed{\dfrac{17}{3} + \dfrac{12}{3} + \dfrac{10}{3}} = \boxed{\dfrac{17+12+10}{3}} = \boxed{\dfrac{39}{3}}$

Step 2 $\boxed{\dfrac{39}{3}} = \boxed{\dfrac{39 \div 3}{3 \div 3}} = \boxed{\dfrac{13}{1}} = \boxed{\mathbf{13}}$

Step 3 $\boxed{\textit{Not Applicable}}$

Example 3.1-10

$\boxed{\dfrac{5}{4} + \dfrac{23}{4} + \dfrac{38}{4}} =$

Solution:

Step 1 $\boxed{\dfrac{5}{4} + \dfrac{23}{4} + \dfrac{38}{4}} = \boxed{\dfrac{5+23+38}{4}} = \boxed{\dfrac{66}{4}}$

Step 2 $\boxed{\dfrac{66}{4}} = \boxed{\dfrac{66 \div 2}{4 \div 2}} = \boxed{\dfrac{33}{2}}$

Step 3 $\boxed{\dfrac{33}{2}} = \boxed{\mathbf{16\dfrac{1}{2}}}$

Example 3.1-11

$\boxed{\dfrac{5}{12} + \dfrac{14}{12} + \dfrac{25}{12}} =$

Solution:

Step 1 $\boxed{\dfrac{5}{12} + \dfrac{14}{12} + \dfrac{25}{12}} = \boxed{\dfrac{5+14+25}{12}} = \boxed{\dfrac{44}{12}}$

Step 2 $\boxed{\dfrac{44}{12}} = \boxed{\dfrac{44 \div 4}{12 \div 4}} = \boxed{\dfrac{11}{3}}$

Step 3 $\boxed{\dfrac{11}{3}} = \boxed{3\dfrac{2}{3}}$

In general, three integer fractions with a common denominator are added in the following way:

$$\boxed{\dfrac{a}{d} + \dfrac{b}{d} + \dfrac{c}{d}} = \boxed{\dfrac{a+b+c}{d}}$$

Example 3.1-12

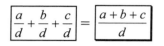

$$\boxed{\dfrac{3}{5} + \dfrac{2}{5} + \dfrac{5}{5}} = \boxed{\dfrac{3+2+5}{5}} = \boxed{\dfrac{\overset{2}{\cancel{10}}}{\underset{1}{\cancel{5}}}} = \boxed{\dfrac{2}{1}} = \boxed{2}$$

Case II   Adding Two or More Integer Fractions Without a Common Denominator

Two or more integer fractions without a common denominator are added using the steps given as in each case below:

Case II-A   *Add two integer fractions without a common denominator using the following steps:*

Step 1   Change the integer number (a) to an integer fraction of the form $\left(\dfrac{a}{1}\right)$, e.g., change 5 to $\dfrac{5}{1}$.

Step 2   a. Multiply the denominators of the first and second fractions to obtain the new denominator.

   b. Cross multiply the numerator of the first fraction with the denominator of the second fraction.

   c. Cross multiply the numerator of the second fraction with the denominator of the first fraction.

   d. Add the results from the steps 2b and 2c above to obtain the new numerator.

Step 3   Simplify the fraction to its lowest term (see Section 2.3).

Step 4   Change the improper fraction to a mixed fraction if the fraction obtained from Step 3 is an improper fraction (see Section 2.2).

The following examples show the steps as to how two integer fractions without a common denominator are added:

Example 3.1-13

$$\boxed{\dfrac{2}{5} + \dfrac{3}{4}} =$$

Solution:

Step 1 $\boxed{Not\ Applicable}$

Step 2 $\boxed{\dfrac{2}{5}+\dfrac{3}{4}}=\boxed{\dfrac{(2\times4)+(3\times5)}{5\times4}}=\boxed{\dfrac{8+15}{20}}=\boxed{\dfrac{23}{20}}$

Step 3 $\boxed{Not\ Applicable}$

Step 4 $\boxed{\dfrac{23}{20}}=\boxed{\mathbf{1\dfrac{3}{20}}}$

Example 3.1-14

$\boxed{40+\dfrac{4}{3}}=$

Solution:

Step 1 $\boxed{40+\dfrac{4}{3}}=\boxed{\dfrac{40}{1}+\dfrac{4}{3}}$

Step 2 $\boxed{\dfrac{40}{1}+\dfrac{4}{3}}=\boxed{\dfrac{(40\times3)+(4\times1)}{1\times3}}=\boxed{\dfrac{120+4}{3}}=\boxed{\dfrac{124}{3}}$

Step 3 $\boxed{Not\ Applicable}$

Step 4 $\boxed{\dfrac{124}{3}}=\boxed{\mathbf{41\dfrac{1}{3}}}$

Example 3.1-15

$\boxed{\dfrac{3}{5}+\dfrac{2}{7}}=$

Solution:

Step 1 $\boxed{Not\ Applicable}$

Step 2 $\boxed{\dfrac{3}{5}+\dfrac{2}{7}}=\boxed{\dfrac{(3\times7)+(2\times5)}{5\times7}}=\boxed{\dfrac{21+10}{35}}=\boxed{\mathbf{\dfrac{31}{35}}}$

Step 3 $\boxed{Not\ Applicable}$

Step 4 $\boxed{Not\ Applicable}$

Example 3.1-16

$$\boxed{\frac{8}{15}+\frac{3}{5}}=$$

Solution:

Step 1 $\boxed{\textit{Not Applicable}}$

Step 2 $\boxed{\frac{8}{15}+\frac{3}{5}}=\boxed{\frac{(8\times5)+(3\times15)}{15\times5}}=\boxed{\frac{40+45}{75}}=\boxed{\frac{85}{75}}$

Step 3 $\boxed{\frac{85}{75}}=\boxed{\frac{85\div5}{75\div5}}=\boxed{\frac{17}{15}}$

Step 4 $\boxed{\frac{17}{15}}=\boxed{1\frac{2}{15}}$

Example 3.1-17

$$\boxed{\frac{5}{6}+3}=$$

Solution:

Step 1 $\boxed{\frac{5}{6}+3}=\boxed{\frac{5}{6}+\frac{3}{1}}$

Step 2 $\boxed{\frac{5}{6}+\frac{3}{1}}=\boxed{\frac{(5\times1)+(3\times6)}{6\times1}}=\boxed{\frac{5+18}{6}}=\boxed{\frac{23}{6}}$

Step 3 $\boxed{\textit{Not Applicable}}$

Step 4 $\boxed{\frac{23}{6}}=\boxed{3\frac{5}{6}}$

In general, two integer fractions without a common denominator are added in the following way:

$$\boxed{\frac{a}{b}+\frac{c}{d}}=\boxed{\frac{(a\times d)+(c\times b)}{(b\times d)}}=\boxed{\frac{ad+cb}{bd}}$$

Example 3.1-18

$$\boxed{\frac{6}{3}+\frac{9}{4}}=\boxed{\frac{(6\times4)+(3\times9)}{3\times4}}=\boxed{\frac{24+27}{12}}=\boxed{\frac{\overset{17}{\cancel{51}}}{\underset{4}{\cancel{12}}}}=\boxed{\frac{17}{4}}=\boxed{4\frac{1}{4}}$$

Case II-B   *Add three integer fractions without a common denominator using the following steps:*

Step 1   Use parentheses to group the first and second fractions.

Step 2   Change the integer number (a) to an integer fraction of the form $\left(\dfrac{a}{1}\right)$, e.g., change 28 to $\dfrac{28}{1}$.

Step 3   a. Add the grouped fractions following Steps 2a through 2d, outlined in Section 3.1, Case II-A above, to obtain a new integer fraction.

b. Add the new integer fraction to the third fraction by repeating Steps 2a through 2d outlined in Section 3.1, Case II-A above.

Step 4   Simplify the fraction to its lowest term (see Section 2.3).

Step 5   Change the improper fraction to a mixed fraction if the fraction obtained from Step 4 is an improper fraction (see Section 2.2).

The following examples show the steps as to how three integer fractions without a common denominator are added:

Example 3.1-19

$$\boxed{\dfrac{3}{5}+\dfrac{4}{3}+\dfrac{1}{6}}=$$

Solution:

Step 1 $\boxed{\dfrac{3}{5}+\dfrac{4}{3}+\dfrac{1}{6}}=\boxed{\left(\dfrac{3}{5}+\dfrac{4}{3}\right)+\dfrac{1}{6}}$

Step 2 $\boxed{\textit{Not Applicable}}$

Step 3 $\boxed{\left(\dfrac{3}{5}+\dfrac{4}{3}\right)+\dfrac{1}{6}}=\boxed{\left(\dfrac{(3\times3)+(4\times5)}{5\times3}\right)+\dfrac{1}{6}}=\boxed{\left(\dfrac{9+20}{15}\right)+\dfrac{1}{6}}=\boxed{\left(\dfrac{29}{15}\right)+\dfrac{1}{6}}=\boxed{\dfrac{29}{15}+\dfrac{1}{6}}$

$=\boxed{\dfrac{(29\times6)+(1\times15)}{15\times6}}=\boxed{\dfrac{174+15}{90}}=\boxed{\dfrac{189}{90}}$

Step 4 $\boxed{\dfrac{189}{90}}=\boxed{\dfrac{189\div9}{90\div9}}=\boxed{\dfrac{21}{10}}$

Step 5 $\boxed{\dfrac{21}{10}}=\boxed{2\dfrac{1}{10}}$

Example 3.1-20

$$\boxed{\dfrac{4}{6}+\dfrac{2}{5}+\dfrac{1}{8}}=$$

Solution:

Step 1 $\dfrac{4}{6}+\dfrac{2}{5}+\dfrac{1}{8}=\boxed{\left(\dfrac{4}{6}+\dfrac{2}{5}\right)+\dfrac{1}{8}}$

Step 2 $\boxed{Not\ Applicable}$

Step 3 $\boxed{\left(\dfrac{4}{6}+\dfrac{2}{5}\right)+\dfrac{1}{8}}=\boxed{\left(\dfrac{(4\times5)+(2\times6)}{6\times5}\right)+\dfrac{1}{8}}=\boxed{\left(\dfrac{20+12}{30}\right)+\dfrac{1}{8}}=\boxed{\left(\dfrac{32}{30}\right)+\dfrac{1}{8}}=\boxed{\dfrac{32}{30}+\dfrac{1}{8}}$

$=\boxed{\dfrac{(32\times8)+(1\times30)}{30\times8}}=\boxed{\dfrac{256+30}{240}}=\boxed{\dfrac{286}{240}}$

Step 4 $\boxed{\dfrac{286}{240}}=\boxed{\dfrac{286\div2}{240\div2}}=\boxed{\dfrac{143}{120}}$

Step 5 $\boxed{\dfrac{143}{120}}=\boxed{\mathbf{1\dfrac{23}{120}}}$

Example 3.1-21

$\boxed{\dfrac{3}{5}+12+\dfrac{5}{8}}=$

Solution:

Step 1 $\boxed{\dfrac{3}{5}+12+\dfrac{5}{8}}=\boxed{\left(\dfrac{3}{5}+12\right)+\dfrac{5}{8}}$

Step 2 $\boxed{\left(\dfrac{3}{5}+12\right)+\dfrac{5}{8}}=\boxed{\left(\dfrac{3}{5}+\dfrac{12}{1}\right)+\dfrac{5}{8}}$

Step 3 $\boxed{\left(\dfrac{3}{5}+\dfrac{12}{1}\right)+\dfrac{5}{8}}=\boxed{\left(\dfrac{(3\times1)+(12\times5)}{5\times1}\right)+\dfrac{5}{8}}=\boxed{\left(\dfrac{3+60}{5}\right)+\dfrac{5}{8}}=\boxed{\left(\dfrac{63}{5}\right)+\dfrac{5}{8}}=\boxed{\dfrac{63}{5}+\dfrac{5}{8}}$

$=\boxed{\dfrac{(63\times8)+(5\times5)}{5\times8}}=\boxed{\dfrac{504+25}{40}}=\boxed{\dfrac{529}{40}}$

Step 4 $\boxed{Not\ Applicable}$

Step 5 $\boxed{\dfrac{529}{40}}=\boxed{\mathbf{13\dfrac{9}{40}}}$

Example 3.1-22

$\boxed{15+\dfrac{3}{4}+\dfrac{5}{6}}=$

Solution:

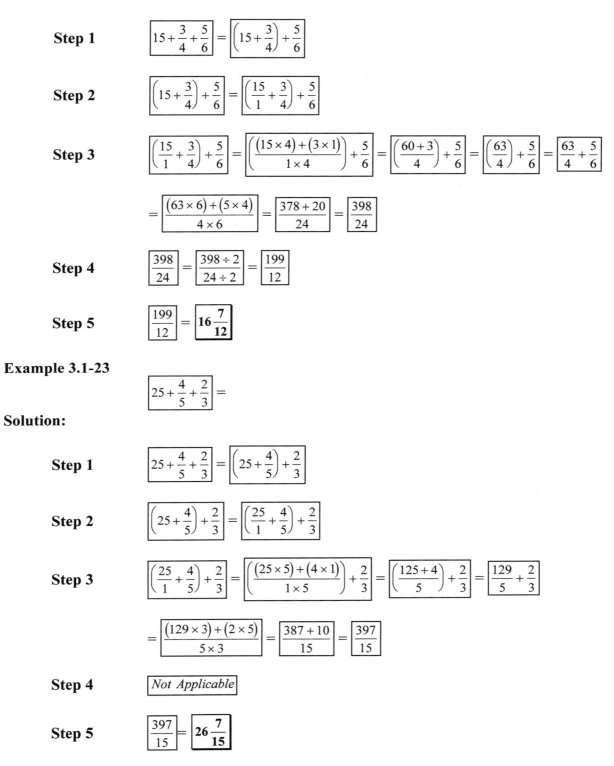

Step 1 $\boxed{15 + \dfrac{3}{4} + \dfrac{5}{6}} = \boxed{\left(15 + \dfrac{3}{4}\right) + \dfrac{5}{6}}$

Step 2 $\boxed{\left(15 + \dfrac{3}{4}\right) + \dfrac{5}{6}} = \boxed{\left(\dfrac{15}{1} + \dfrac{3}{4}\right) + \dfrac{5}{6}}$

Step 3 $\boxed{\left(\dfrac{15}{1} + \dfrac{3}{4}\right) + \dfrac{5}{6}} = \boxed{\left(\dfrac{(15 \times 4) + (3 \times 1)}{1 \times 4}\right) + \dfrac{5}{6}} = \boxed{\left(\dfrac{60 + 3}{4}\right) + \dfrac{5}{6}} = \boxed{\left(\dfrac{63}{4}\right) + \dfrac{5}{6}} = \boxed{\dfrac{63}{4} + \dfrac{5}{6}}$

$= \boxed{\dfrac{(63 \times 6) + (5 \times 4)}{4 \times 6}} = \boxed{\dfrac{378 + 20}{24}} = \boxed{\dfrac{398}{24}}$

Step 4 $\boxed{\dfrac{398}{24}} = \boxed{\dfrac{398 \div 2}{24 \div 2}} = \boxed{\dfrac{199}{12}}$

Step 5 $\boxed{\dfrac{199}{12}} = \boxed{\mathbf{16\dfrac{7}{12}}}$

Example 3.1-23

$\boxed{25 + \dfrac{4}{5} + \dfrac{2}{3}} =$

Solution:

Step 1 $\boxed{25 + \dfrac{4}{5} + \dfrac{2}{3}} = \boxed{\left(25 + \dfrac{4}{5}\right) + \dfrac{2}{3}}$

Step 2 $\boxed{\left(25 + \dfrac{4}{5}\right) + \dfrac{2}{3}} = \boxed{\left(\dfrac{25}{1} + \dfrac{4}{5}\right) + \dfrac{2}{3}}$

Step 3 $\boxed{\left(\dfrac{25}{1} + \dfrac{4}{5}\right) + \dfrac{2}{3}} = \boxed{\left(\dfrac{(25 \times 5) + (4 \times 1)}{1 \times 5}\right) + \dfrac{2}{3}} = \boxed{\left(\dfrac{125 + 4}{5}\right) + \dfrac{2}{3}} = \boxed{\dfrac{129}{5} + \dfrac{2}{3}}$

$= \boxed{\dfrac{(129 \times 3) + (2 \times 5)}{5 \times 3}} = \boxed{\dfrac{387 + 10}{15}} = \boxed{\dfrac{397}{15}}$

Step 4 $\boxed{\textit{Not Applicable}}$

Step 5 $\boxed{\dfrac{397}{15}} = \boxed{\mathbf{26\dfrac{7}{15}}}$

In general, three integer fractions without a common denominator are added as in the following cases:

Case I.

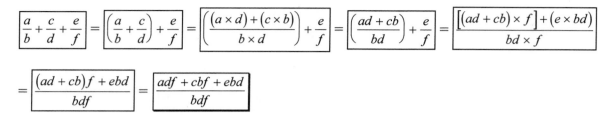

Example 3.1-24

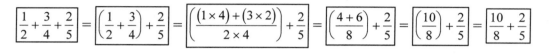

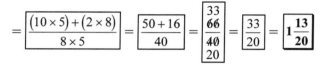

Case II.

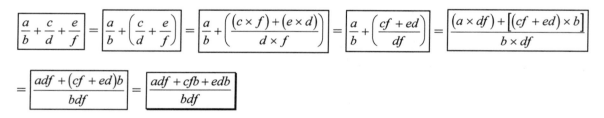

Example 3.1-25

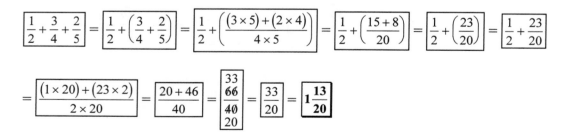

Note - In addition the use of parentheses does not change the final answer; the two examples above have the same answer (see Section 1.2).

The following examples further illustrate how to add integer fractions:

Note that throughout the remaining chapters of this book, the intent of these additional examples (which are given at the end of each section) is to show that:

1. *Fractional operations can be solved in different ways, and*

2. *Fractional operations do not necessarily have to be solved in the exact "Steps" order as is given in this and other chapters. For example, in many instances, the process of adding, subtracting, multiplying, and dividing fractions is greatly simplified if fractions are reduced to their lowest terms first. In some instances, fractions are simplified several times at various steps of an operation.*

Example 3.1-26

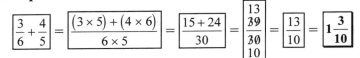

$$\boxed{\frac{3}{6}+\frac{4}{5}}=\boxed{\frac{(3\times5)+(4\times6)}{6\times5}}=\boxed{\frac{15+24}{30}}=\boxed{\frac{\frac{13}{39}}{\frac{30}{10}}}=\boxed{\frac{13}{10}}=\boxed{1\frac{3}{10}}$$

Example 3.1-27

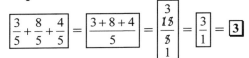

$$\boxed{\frac{3}{5}+\frac{8}{5}+\frac{4}{5}}=\boxed{\frac{3+8+4}{5}}=\boxed{\frac{\frac{3}{15}}{\frac{5}{1}}}=\boxed{\frac{3}{1}}=\boxed{3}$$

Example 3.1-28

$$\boxed{\frac{2}{5}+\frac{1}{4}+\frac{4}{3}}=\boxed{\left(\frac{2}{5}+\frac{1}{4}\right)+\frac{4}{3}}=\boxed{\left(\frac{(2\times4)+(1\times5)}{5\times4}\right)+\frac{4}{3}}=\boxed{\left(\frac{8+5}{20}\right)+\frac{4}{3}}=\boxed{\left(\frac{13}{20}\right)+\frac{4}{3}}=\boxed{\frac{13}{20}+\frac{4}{3}}$$

$$=\boxed{\frac{(13\times3)+(4\times20)}{20\times3}}=\boxed{\frac{39+80}{60}}=\boxed{\frac{119}{60}}=\boxed{1\frac{59}{60}}$$

Example 3.1-29

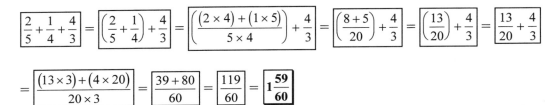

$$\boxed{\frac{1}{2}+\left(\frac{2}{3}+\frac{1}{5}\right)}=\boxed{\frac{1}{2}+\left(\frac{(2\times5)+(1\times3)}{3\times5}\right)}=\boxed{\frac{1}{2}+\left(\frac{10+3}{15}\right)}=\boxed{\frac{1}{2}+\left(\frac{13}{15}\right)}=\boxed{\frac{1}{2}+\frac{13}{15}}=\boxed{\frac{(1\times15)+(13\times2)}{2\times15}}$$

$$=\boxed{\frac{15+26}{30}}=\boxed{\frac{41}{30}}=\boxed{1\frac{11}{30}}$$

Example 3.1-30

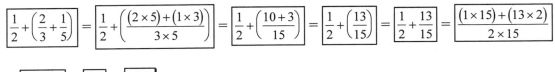

$$\boxed{6+\frac{4}{3}+\frac{8}{1}+\frac{9}{6}}=\boxed{\left(\frac{6}{1}+\frac{4}{3}\right)+\left(\frac{8}{1}+\frac{\frac{3}{9}}{\frac{6}{2}}\right)}=\boxed{\left(\frac{(6\times3)+(4\times1)}{1\times3}\right)+\left(\frac{8}{1}+\frac{3}{2}\right)}=\boxed{\left(\frac{18+4}{3}\right)+\left(\frac{(8\times2)+(3\times1)}{1\times2}\right)}$$

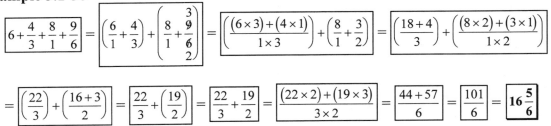

$$=\boxed{\left(\frac{22}{3}\right)+\left(\frac{16+3}{2}\right)}=\boxed{\frac{22}{3}+\left(\frac{19}{2}\right)}=\boxed{\frac{22}{3}+\frac{19}{2}}=\boxed{\frac{(22\times2)+(19\times3)}{3\times2}}=\boxed{\frac{44+57}{6}}=\boxed{\frac{101}{6}}=\boxed{16\frac{5}{6}}$$

Example 3.1-31

$$\left[\left(\frac{2}{3}+\frac{6}{3}\right)+\left(\frac{8}{6}+\frac{2}{6}+\frac{1}{6}\right)\right]=\left[\left(\frac{2+6}{3}\right)+\left(\frac{8+2+1}{6}\right)\right]=\left[\left(\frac{8}{3}\right)+\left(\frac{11}{6}\right)\right]=\frac{8}{3}+\frac{11}{6}=\frac{(8\times6)+(11\times3)}{3\times6}=\frac{48+33}{18}$$

$$=\frac{\overset{9}{\cancel{81}}}{\underset{2}{\cancel{18}}}=\frac{9}{2}=\boxed{4\frac{1}{2}}$$

Example 3.1-32

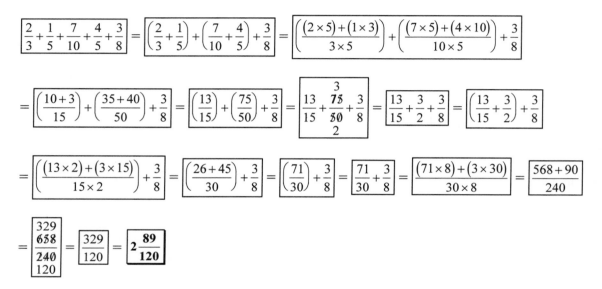

$$\frac{2}{3}+\frac{1}{5}+\frac{7}{10}+\frac{4}{5}+\frac{3}{8}=\left[\left(\frac{2}{3}+\frac{1}{5}\right)+\left(\frac{7}{10}+\frac{4}{5}\right)+\frac{3}{8}\right]=\left[\left(\frac{(2\times5)+(1\times3)}{3\times5}\right)+\left(\frac{(7\times5)+(4\times10)}{10\times5}\right)+\frac{3}{8}\right]$$

$$=\left[\left(\frac{10+3}{15}\right)+\left(\frac{35+40}{50}\right)+\frac{3}{8}\right]=\left[\left(\frac{13}{15}\right)+\left(\frac{75}{50}\right)+\frac{3}{8}\right]=\frac{13}{15}+\frac{\overset{3}{\cancel{75}}}{\underset{2}{\cancel{50}}}+\frac{3}{8}=\frac{13}{15}+\frac{3}{2}+\frac{3}{8}=\left[\left(\frac{13}{15}+\frac{3}{2}\right)+\frac{3}{8}\right]$$

$$=\left[\left(\frac{(13\times2)+(3\times15)}{15\times2}\right)+\frac{3}{8}\right]=\left[\left(\frac{26+45}{30}\right)+\frac{3}{8}\right]=\left[\left(\frac{71}{30}\right)+\frac{3}{8}\right]=\frac{71}{30}+\frac{3}{8}=\frac{(71\times8)+(3\times30)}{30\times8}=\frac{568+90}{240}$$

$$=\frac{\overset{329}{\cancel{658}}}{\underset{120}{\cancel{240}}}=\frac{329}{120}=\boxed{2\frac{89}{120}}$$

Example 3.1-33

$$2+\frac{0}{200}+\frac{5}{10}+\frac{4}{5}+6=\frac{2}{1}+0+\frac{5}{10}+\frac{4}{5}+\frac{6}{1}=\frac{2}{1}+\frac{5}{10}+\frac{4}{5}+\frac{6}{1}=\left[\left(\frac{2}{1}+\frac{5}{10}\right)+\left(\frac{4}{5}+\frac{6}{1}\right)\right]$$

$$=\left[\left(\frac{(2\times10)+(5\times1)}{1\times10}\right)+\left(\frac{(4\times1)+(6\times5)}{5\times1}\right)\right]=\left[\left(\frac{20+5}{10}\right)+\left(\frac{4+30}{5}\right)\right]=\left[\left(\frac{25}{10}\right)+\left(\frac{34}{5}\right)\right]=\frac{25}{10}+\frac{34}{5}$$

$$=\frac{(25\times5)+(34\times10)}{10\times5}=\frac{125+340}{50}=\frac{\overset{93}{\cancel{465}}}{\underset{10}{\cancel{50}}}=\frac{93}{10}=\boxed{9\frac{3}{10}}$$

Example 3.1-34

$$\frac{4}{5}+\left[\left(\frac{3}{4}+\frac{1}{5}\right)+\left(5+\frac{2}{3}\right)\right]=\frac{4}{5}+\left[\left(\frac{(3\times5)+(1\times4)}{4\times5}\right)+\left(\frac{5}{1}+\frac{2}{3}\right)\right]=\frac{4}{5}+\left[\left(\frac{15+4}{20}\right)+\left(\frac{(5\times3)+(2\times1)}{1\times3}\right)\right]$$

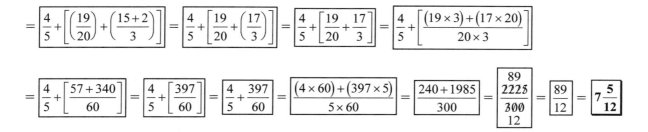

Example 3.1-35

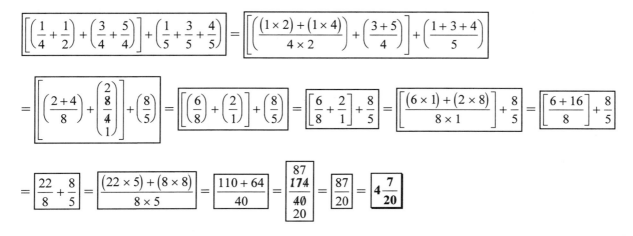

$$= \boxed{\dfrac{22}{8} + \dfrac{8}{5}} = \boxed{\dfrac{(22 \times 5) + (8 \times 8)}{8 \times 5}} = \boxed{\dfrac{110 + 64}{40}} = \boxed{\dfrac{\overset{87}{\cancel{174}}}{\underset{20}{\cancel{40}}}} = \boxed{\dfrac{87}{20}} = \boxed{4\dfrac{7}{20}}$$

Section 3.1 Exercises - Add the following integer fractions:

1. $\dfrac{4}{9} + \dfrac{2}{9} =$

2. $\dfrac{3}{8} + \dfrac{2}{5} =$

3. $\dfrac{3}{8} + \dfrac{2}{4} + \dfrac{5}{6} =$

4. $\dfrac{4}{5} + \dfrac{2}{5} + \dfrac{3}{5} =$

5. $5 + \dfrac{0}{10} + \dfrac{6}{1} + \dfrac{4}{8} =$

6. $\left(\dfrac{3}{16} + \dfrac{1}{8}\right) + \dfrac{1}{6} =$

7. $\left(\dfrac{4}{5} + \dfrac{2}{8}\right) + \left(\dfrac{2}{4} + \dfrac{1}{4} + \dfrac{3}{4}\right) =$

8. $\dfrac{2}{5} + \left(\dfrac{4}{9} + \dfrac{2}{9} + \dfrac{1}{9}\right) =$

9. $\dfrac{2}{5} + \dfrac{1}{2} + \dfrac{4}{5} + \dfrac{2}{3} + 12 =$

10. $\left[\dfrac{5}{8} + \left(\dfrac{3}{5} + \dfrac{1}{8}\right)\right] + \left(\dfrac{1}{8} + \dfrac{3}{8}\right) =$

3.2   Subtracting Integer Fractions

Integer fractions, i.e., fractions where both the numerator and the denominator are integer numbers are subtracted as in the following cases:

Case I   Subtracting Two or More Integer Fractions With Common Denominators

Integer fractions with two or more common denominators are subtracted using the steps given as in each case below:

Case I-A   *Subtract two integer fractions with common denominators using the following steps:*

Step 1   a. Use the common denominator between the first and second fractions as the new denominator.

             b. Subtract the numerators of the first and second fractions to obtain the new numerator.

Step 2   Simplify the fraction to its lowest term (see Section 2.3).

Step 3   Change the improper fraction to a mixed fraction if the fraction obtained from Step 2 is an improper fraction (see Section 2.2).

The following examples show the steps as to how two integer fractions with common denominators are subtracted:

Example 3.2-1

$$\frac{25}{3} - \frac{2}{3} =$$

Solution:

> **Step 1** $\frac{25}{3} - \frac{2}{3} = \frac{25-2}{3} = \frac{23}{3}$

> **Step 2** $\boxed{Not\ Applicable}$

> **Step 3** $\frac{23}{3} = 7\frac{2}{3}$

Example 3.2-2

$$\frac{40}{4} - \frac{10}{4} =$$

Solution:

> **Step 1** $\frac{40}{4} - \frac{10}{4} = \frac{40-10}{4} = \frac{30}{4}$

> **Step 2** $\frac{30}{4} = \frac{30 \div 2}{4 \div 2} = \frac{15}{2}$

Step 3 $\boxed{\dfrac{15}{2}} = \boxed{7\dfrac{1}{2}}$

Example 3.2-3

$$\boxed{\dfrac{9}{12} - \dfrac{22}{12}} =$$

Solution:

Step 1 $\boxed{\dfrac{9}{12} - \dfrac{22}{12}} = \boxed{\dfrac{9 - 22}{12}} = \boxed{\dfrac{-13}{12}}$

Step 2 $\boxed{\textit{Not Applicable}}$

Step 3 $\boxed{\dfrac{-13}{12}} = \boxed{-\left(1\dfrac{1}{12}\right)}$

Example 3.2-4

$$\boxed{\dfrac{5}{10} - \dfrac{14}{10}} =$$

Solution:

Step 1 $\boxed{\dfrac{5}{10} - \dfrac{14}{10}} = \boxed{\dfrac{5 - 14}{10}} = \boxed{\dfrac{-9}{10}}$

Step 2 $\boxed{\textit{Not Applicable}}$

Step 3 $\boxed{\textit{Not Applicable}}$

Example 3.2-5

$$\boxed{\dfrac{15}{6} - \dfrac{53}{6}} =$$

Solution:

Step 1 $\boxed{\dfrac{15}{6} - \dfrac{53}{6}} = \boxed{\dfrac{15 - 53}{6}} = \boxed{\dfrac{-38}{6}}$

Step 2 $\boxed{\dfrac{-38}{6}} = \boxed{\dfrac{-38 \div 2}{6 \div 2}} = \boxed{\dfrac{-19}{3}}$

Step 3 $\boxed{\dfrac{-19}{3}} = \boxed{-\left(6\dfrac{1}{3}\right)}$

In general, two integer fractions with a common denominator are subtracted in the following way:

$$\boxed{\dfrac{a}{d} - \dfrac{b}{d}} = \boxed{\dfrac{a-b}{d}}$$

Example 3.2-6

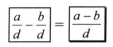

$$\boxed{\dfrac{6}{8} - \dfrac{4}{8}} = \boxed{\dfrac{6-4}{8}} = \boxed{\dfrac{\overset{1}{2}}{\underset{4}{8}}} = \boxed{\dfrac{1}{4}}$$

Case I-B   *Subtract three integer fractions with common denominators using the following steps:*

Step 1   a. Use the common denominator between the first, second, and third fractions as the new denominator.

   b. Subtract the numerators of the first, second, and third fractions to obtain the new numerator.

Step 2   Simplify the fraction to its lowest term (see Section 2.3).

Step 3   Change the improper fraction to a mixed fraction if the fraction obtained from Step 2 is an improper fraction (see Section 2.2).

The following examples show the steps as to how three integer fractions with common denominators are subtracted:

Example 3.2-7

$$\boxed{\dfrac{7}{4} - \dfrac{3}{4} - \dfrac{1}{4}} =$$

Solution:

Step 1 $\boxed{\dfrac{7}{4} - \dfrac{3}{4} - \dfrac{1}{4}} = \boxed{\dfrac{7-3-1}{4}} = \boxed{\dfrac{7-4}{4}} = \boxed{\dfrac{3}{4}}$

Step 2 $\boxed{Not\ Applicable}$

Step 3 $\boxed{Not\ Applicable}$

Example 3.2-8

$$\boxed{\dfrac{25}{8} - \dfrac{3}{8} - \dfrac{4}{8}} =$$

Solution:

Step 1 $\boxed{\dfrac{25}{8} - \dfrac{3}{8} - \dfrac{4}{8}} = \boxed{\dfrac{25-3-4}{8}} = \boxed{\dfrac{25-7}{8}} = \boxed{\dfrac{18}{8}}$

Step 2 $\boxed{\dfrac{18}{8}} = \boxed{\dfrac{18 \div 2}{8 \div 2}} = \boxed{\dfrac{9}{4}}$

Step 3 $\boxed{\dfrac{9}{4}} = \boxed{2\dfrac{1}{4}}$

Example 3.2-9

$\boxed{\dfrac{25}{6} - \dfrac{4}{6} - \dfrac{1}{6}} =$

Solution:

Step 1 $\boxed{\dfrac{25}{6} - \dfrac{4}{6} - \dfrac{1}{6}} = \boxed{\dfrac{25 - 4 - 1}{6}} = \boxed{\dfrac{25 - 5}{6}} = \boxed{\dfrac{20}{6}}$

Step 2 $\boxed{\dfrac{20}{6}} = \boxed{\dfrac{20 \div 2}{6 \div 2}} = \boxed{\dfrac{10}{3}}$

Step 3 $\boxed{\dfrac{10}{3}} = \boxed{3\dfrac{1}{3}}$

Example 3.2-10

$\boxed{\dfrac{12}{7} - \dfrac{28}{7} - \dfrac{13}{7}} =$

Solution:

Step 1 $\boxed{\dfrac{12}{7} - \dfrac{28}{7} - \dfrac{13}{7}} = \boxed{\dfrac{12 - 28 - 13}{7}} = \boxed{\dfrac{12 - 41}{7}} = \boxed{\dfrac{-29}{7}}$

Step 2 $\boxed{\textit{Not Applicable}}$

Step 3 $\boxed{\dfrac{-29}{7}} = \boxed{-\left(4\dfrac{1}{7}\right)}$

Example 3.2-11

$\boxed{\dfrac{125}{12} - \dfrac{25}{12} - \dfrac{360}{12}} =$

Solution:

Step 1 $\boxed{\dfrac{125}{12} - \dfrac{25}{12} - \dfrac{360}{12}} = \boxed{\dfrac{125 - 25 - 360}{12}} = \boxed{\dfrac{125 - 385}{12}} = \boxed{\dfrac{-260}{12}}$

Step 2 $\boxed{\dfrac{-260}{12}} = \boxed{\dfrac{-260 \div 4}{12 \div 4}} = \boxed{\dfrac{-65}{3}}$

Step 3
$$\left|\frac{-65}{3}\right| = \left|-\left(21\frac{2}{3}\right)\right|$$

In general, three integer fractions with a common denominator are subtracted in the following way:

$$\left|\frac{a}{d} - \frac{b}{d} - \frac{c}{d}\right| = \left|\frac{a-b-c}{d}\right|$$

Example 3.2-12

$$\left|\frac{5}{6} - \frac{2}{6} - \frac{1}{6}\right| = \left|\frac{5-2-1}{6}\right| = \left|\frac{5-3}{6}\right| = \left|\frac{\overset{1}{\underset{3}{\cancel{\frac{2}{6}}}}}{}\right| = \left|\frac{1}{3}\right|$$

Case II   Subtracting Two or More Integer Fractions Without a Common Denominator
Two or more integer fractions without a common denominator are subtracted using the steps given as in each case below:

Case II-A   *Subtract two integer fractions without a common denominator using the following steps:*

Step 1   Change the integer number (a) to an integer fraction of the form $\left(\frac{a}{1}\right)$, e.g., change 358 to $\frac{358}{1}$.

Step 2   a. Multiply the denominators of the first and second fractions to obtain the new denominator.

b. Cross multiply the numerator of the first fraction with the denominator of the second fraction.

c. Cross multiply the numerator of the second fraction with the denominator of the first fraction.

d. Subtract the results from steps 2b and 2c above to obtain the new numerator.

Step 3   Simplify the fraction to its lowest term (see Section 2.3).

Step 4   Change the improper fraction to a mixed fraction if the fraction obtained from Step 3 is an improper fraction (see Section 2.2).

The following examples show the steps as to how two integer fractions without a common denominator are subtracted:

Example 3.2-13

$$\left|5 - \frac{12}{8}\right| =$$

Solution:

Step 1
$$\left|5 - \frac{12}{8}\right| = \left|\frac{5}{1} - \frac{12}{8}\right|$$

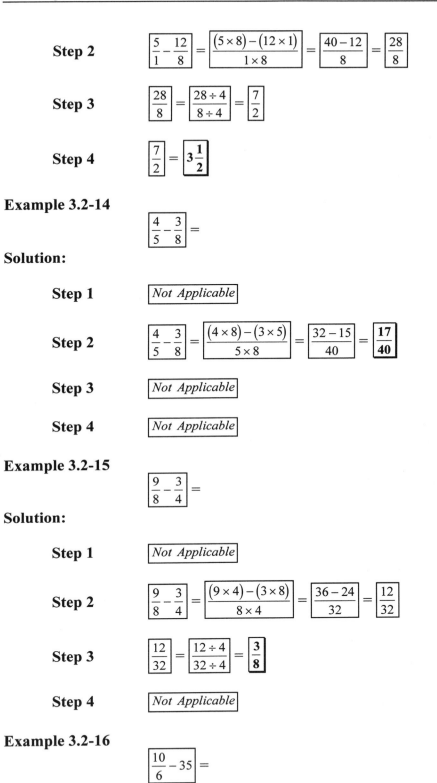

Step 2
$$\boxed{\frac{5}{1} - \frac{12}{8}} = \boxed{\frac{(5 \times 8) - (12 \times 1)}{1 \times 8}} = \boxed{\frac{40 - 12}{8}} = \boxed{\frac{28}{8}}$$

Step 3
$$\boxed{\frac{28}{8}} = \boxed{\frac{28 \div 4}{8 \div 4}} = \boxed{\frac{7}{2}}$$

Step 4
$$\boxed{\frac{7}{2}} = \boxed{3\frac{1}{2}}$$

Example 3.2-14
$$\boxed{\frac{4}{5} - \frac{3}{8}} =$$

Solution:

Step 1 $\boxed{Not\ Applicable}$

Step 2
$$\boxed{\frac{4}{5} - \frac{3}{8}} = \boxed{\frac{(4 \times 8) - (3 \times 5)}{5 \times 8}} = \boxed{\frac{32 - 15}{40}} = \boxed{\frac{17}{40}}$$

Step 3 $\boxed{Not\ Applicable}$

Step 4 $\boxed{Not\ Applicable}$

Example 3.2-15
$$\boxed{\frac{9}{8} - \frac{3}{4}} =$$

Solution:

Step 1 $\boxed{Not\ Applicable}$

Step 2
$$\boxed{\frac{9}{8} - \frac{3}{4}} = \boxed{\frac{(9 \times 4) - (3 \times 8)}{8 \times 4}} = \boxed{\frac{36 - 24}{32}} = \boxed{\frac{12}{32}}$$

Step 3
$$\boxed{\frac{12}{32}} = \boxed{\frac{12 \div 4}{32 \div 4}} = \boxed{\frac{3}{8}}$$

Step 4 $\boxed{Not\ Applicable}$

Example 3.2-16
$$\boxed{\frac{10}{6} - 35} =$$

Solution:

Step 1 $\boxed{\dfrac{10}{6} - 35} = \boxed{\dfrac{10}{6} - \dfrac{35}{1}}$

Step 2 $\boxed{\dfrac{10}{6} - \dfrac{35}{1}} = \boxed{\dfrac{(10 \times 1) - (35 \times 6)}{6 \times 1}} = \boxed{\dfrac{10 - 210}{6}} = \boxed{\dfrac{-200}{6}}$

Step 3 $\boxed{\dfrac{-200}{6}} = \boxed{\dfrac{-200 \div 2}{6 \div 2}} = \boxed{\dfrac{-100}{3}}$

Step 4 $\boxed{\dfrac{-100}{3}} = \boxed{-\left(33\dfrac{1}{3}\right)}$

Example 3.2-17

$\boxed{\dfrac{3}{9} - \dfrac{4}{15}} =$

Solution:

Step 1 $\boxed{Not\ Applicable}$

Step 2 $\boxed{\dfrac{3}{9} - \dfrac{4}{15}} = \boxed{\dfrac{(3 \times 15) - (4 \times 9)}{9 \times 15}} = \boxed{\dfrac{45 - 36}{135}} = \boxed{\dfrac{9}{135}}$

Step 3 $\boxed{\dfrac{9}{135}} = \boxed{\dfrac{9 \div 9}{135 \div 9}} = \boxed{\dfrac{1}{15}}$

Step 4 $\boxed{Not\ Applicable}$

In general, two integer fractions without a common denominator are subtracted in the following way:

$\boxed{\dfrac{a}{b} - \dfrac{c}{d}} = \boxed{\dfrac{(a \times d) - (c \times b)}{b \times d}} = \boxed{\dfrac{ad - cb}{bd}}$

Example 3.2-18

$\boxed{\dfrac{3}{4} - \dfrac{1}{8}} = \boxed{\dfrac{(3 \times 8) - (1 \times 4)}{4 \times 8}} = \boxed{\dfrac{24 - 4}{32}} = \boxed{\dfrac{\overset{5}{\cancel{20}}}{\underset{8}{\cancel{32}}}} = \boxed{\dfrac{5}{8}}$

Case II-B   *Subtract three integer fractions without a common denominator using the following steps:*

Step 1   Use parentheses to group the first and second fractions.

Step 2   Change the integer number (a) to an integer fraction of the form $\left(\dfrac{a}{1}\right)$, e.g., change 12

to $\dfrac{12}{1}$.

Step 3   a. Subtract the grouped fraction following Steps 2a through 2d, outlined in Section 3.2, Case II-A above, to obtain a new integer fraction.

b. Subtract the new integer fraction from the third fraction by repeating Steps 2a through 2d, outlined in Section 3.2, Case II-A above.

Step 4   Simplify the fraction to its lowest term (see Section 2.3).

Step 5   Change the improper fraction to a mixed fraction if the fraction obtained from Step 4 is an improper fraction (see Section 2.2).

The following examples show the steps as to how three integer fractions without a common denominator are subtracted:

Example 3.2-19

$$\boxed{\dfrac{4}{5} - \dfrac{1}{3} - \dfrac{2}{6}} =$$

Solution:

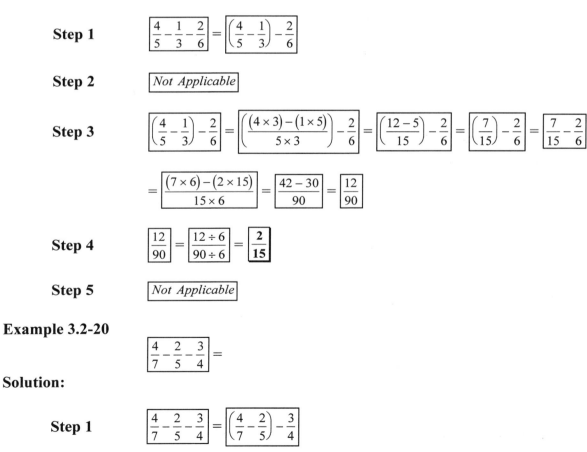

Step 1 $\boxed{\dfrac{4}{5} - \dfrac{1}{3} - \dfrac{2}{6}} = \boxed{\left(\dfrac{4}{5} - \dfrac{1}{3}\right) - \dfrac{2}{6}}$

Step 2 $\boxed{\textit{Not Applicable}}$

Step 3 $\boxed{\left(\dfrac{4}{5} - \dfrac{1}{3}\right) - \dfrac{2}{6}} = \boxed{\left(\dfrac{(4 \times 3) - (1 \times 5)}{5 \times 3}\right) - \dfrac{2}{6}} = \boxed{\left(\dfrac{12 - 5}{15}\right) - \dfrac{2}{6}} = \boxed{\left(\dfrac{7}{15}\right) - \dfrac{2}{6}} = \boxed{\dfrac{7}{15} - \dfrac{2}{6}}$

$= \boxed{\dfrac{(7 \times 6) - (2 \times 15)}{15 \times 6}} = \boxed{\dfrac{42 - 30}{90}} = \boxed{\dfrac{12}{90}}$

Step 4 $\boxed{\dfrac{12}{90}} = \boxed{\dfrac{12 \div 6}{90 \div 6}} = \boxed{\dfrac{2}{15}}$

Step 5 $\boxed{\textit{Not Applicable}}$

Example 3.2-20

$$\boxed{\dfrac{4}{7} - \dfrac{2}{5} - \dfrac{3}{4}} =$$

Solution:

Step 1 $\boxed{\dfrac{4}{7} - \dfrac{2}{5} - \dfrac{3}{4}} = \boxed{\left(\dfrac{4}{7} - \dfrac{2}{5}\right) - \dfrac{3}{4}}$

Step 2 $\boxed{Not\ Applicable}$

Step 3 $\boxed{\left(\dfrac{4}{7}-\dfrac{2}{5}\right)-\dfrac{3}{4}}=\boxed{\left(\dfrac{(4\times5)-(2\times7)}{7\times5}\right)-\dfrac{3}{4}}=\boxed{\left(\dfrac{20-14}{35}\right)-\dfrac{3}{4}}=\boxed{\left(\dfrac{6}{35}\right)-\dfrac{3}{4}}=\boxed{\dfrac{6}{35}-\dfrac{3}{4}}$

$=\boxed{\dfrac{(6\times4)-(3\times35)}{35\times4}}=\boxed{\dfrac{24-105}{140}}=\boxed{\dfrac{-81}{140}}$

Step 4 $\boxed{Not\ Applicable}$

Step 5 $\boxed{Not\ Applicable}$

Example 3.2-21

$\boxed{15-\dfrac{5}{8}-\dfrac{2}{3}}=$

Solution:

Step 1 $\boxed{15-\dfrac{5}{8}-\dfrac{2}{3}}=\boxed{\left(15-\dfrac{5}{8}\right)-\dfrac{2}{3}}$

Step 2 $\boxed{\left(15-\dfrac{5}{8}\right)-\dfrac{2}{3}}=\boxed{\left(\dfrac{15}{1}-\dfrac{5}{8}\right)-\dfrac{2}{3}}$

Step 3 $\boxed{\left(\dfrac{15}{1}-\dfrac{5}{8}\right)-\dfrac{2}{3}}=\boxed{\left(\dfrac{(15\times8)-(5\times1)}{1\times8}\right)-\dfrac{2}{3}}=\boxed{\left(\dfrac{120-5}{8}\right)-\dfrac{2}{3}}=\boxed{\left(\dfrac{115}{8}\right)-\dfrac{2}{3}}=\boxed{\dfrac{115}{8}-\dfrac{2}{3}}$

$=\boxed{\dfrac{(115\times3)-(2\times8)}{8\times3}}=\boxed{\dfrac{345-16}{24}}=\boxed{\dfrac{329}{24}}$

Step 4 $\boxed{Not\ Applicable}$

Step 5 $\boxed{\dfrac{329}{24}}=\boxed{13\dfrac{17}{24}}$

Example 3.2-22

$\boxed{25-\dfrac{3}{4}-\dfrac{32}{5}}=$

Solution:

Step 1 $\boxed{25-\dfrac{3}{4}-\dfrac{32}{5}}=\boxed{\left(25-\dfrac{3}{4}\right)-\dfrac{32}{5}}$

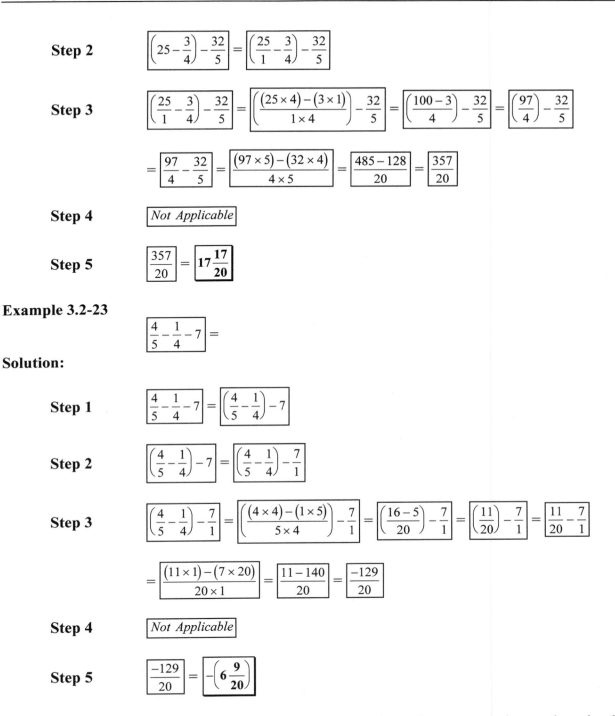

Step 2 $\left[\left(25-\dfrac{3}{4}\right)-\dfrac{32}{5}\right]=\left[\left(\dfrac{25}{1}-\dfrac{3}{4}\right)-\dfrac{32}{5}\right]$

Step 3 $\left[\left(\dfrac{25}{1}-\dfrac{3}{4}\right)-\dfrac{32}{5}\right]=\left[\left(\dfrac{(25\times4)-(3\times1)}{1\times4}\right)-\dfrac{32}{5}\right]=\left[\left(\dfrac{100-3}{4}\right)-\dfrac{32}{5}\right]=\left[\left(\dfrac{97}{4}\right)-\dfrac{32}{5}\right]$

$=\left[\dfrac{97}{4}-\dfrac{32}{5}\right]=\left[\dfrac{(97\times5)-(32\times4)}{4\times5}\right]=\left[\dfrac{485-128}{20}\right]=\left[\dfrac{357}{20}\right]$

Step 4 $\boxed{Not\ Applicable}$

Step 5 $\dfrac{357}{20}=\boxed{17\dfrac{17}{20}}$

Example 3.2-23

$\left[\dfrac{4}{5}-\dfrac{1}{4}-7\right]=$

Solution:

Step 1 $\left[\dfrac{4}{5}-\dfrac{1}{4}-7\right]=\left[\left(\dfrac{4}{5}-\dfrac{1}{4}\right)-7\right]$

Step 2 $\left[\left(\dfrac{4}{5}-\dfrac{1}{4}\right)-7\right]=\left[\left(\dfrac{4}{5}-\dfrac{1}{4}\right)-\dfrac{7}{1}\right]$

Step 3 $\left[\left(\dfrac{4}{5}-\dfrac{1}{4}\right)-\dfrac{7}{1}\right]=\left[\left(\dfrac{(4\times4)-(1\times5)}{5\times4}\right)-\dfrac{7}{1}\right]=\left[\left(\dfrac{16-5}{20}\right)-\dfrac{7}{1}\right]=\left[\left(\dfrac{11}{20}\right)-\dfrac{7}{1}\right]=\left[\dfrac{11}{20}-\dfrac{7}{1}\right]$

$=\left[\dfrac{(11\times1)-(7\times20)}{20\times1}\right]=\left[\dfrac{11-140}{20}\right]=\left[\dfrac{-129}{20}\right]$

Step 4 $\boxed{Not\ Applicable}$

Step 5 $\dfrac{-129}{20}=\boxed{-\left(6\dfrac{9}{20}\right)}$

In general, three integer fractions without a common denominator are subtracted as in the following cases:

Case I.

$$\left[\dfrac{a}{b}-\dfrac{c}{d}-\dfrac{e}{f}\right]=\left[\left(\dfrac{a}{b}-\dfrac{c}{d}\right)-\dfrac{e}{f}\right]=\left[\left(\dfrac{(a\times d)-(c\times b)}{b\times d}\right)-\dfrac{e}{f}\right]=\left[\left(\dfrac{ad-cb}{bd}\right)-\dfrac{e}{f}\right]=\left[\dfrac{[(ad-cb)\times f]-(e\times bd)}{bd\times f}\right]$$

$$= \boxed{\frac{[adf - cbf] - ebd}{bdf}} = \boxed{\frac{adf - cbf - ebd}{bdf}}$$

Example 3.2-24

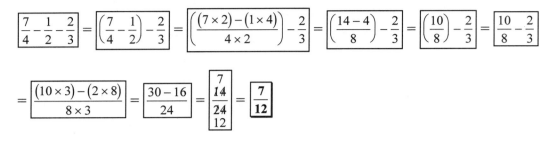

$$\boxed{\frac{7}{4} - \frac{1}{2} - \frac{2}{3}} = \boxed{\left(\frac{7}{4} - \frac{1}{2}\right) - \frac{2}{3}} = \boxed{\left(\frac{(7 \times 2) - (1 \times 4)}{4 \times 2}\right) - \frac{2}{3}} = \boxed{\left(\frac{14 - 4}{8}\right) - \frac{2}{3}} = \boxed{\left(\frac{10}{8}\right) - \frac{2}{3}} = \boxed{\frac{10}{8} - \frac{2}{3}}$$

$$= \boxed{\frac{(10 \times 3) - (2 \times 8)}{8 \times 3}} = \boxed{\frac{30 - 16}{24}} = \boxed{\frac{\overset{7}{14}}{\underset{12}{24}}} = \boxed{\frac{7}{12}}$$

Case II.

$$\boxed{\frac{a}{b} - \frac{c}{d} - \frac{e}{f}} = \boxed{\frac{a}{b} + \left(-\frac{c}{d} - \frac{e}{f}\right)} = \boxed{\frac{a}{b} + \left(\frac{-(c \times f) - (e \times d)}{d \times f}\right) - \frac{e}{f}} = \boxed{\frac{a}{b} + \left(\frac{-cf - ed}{df}\right)}$$

$$= \boxed{\frac{(a \times df) + [b \times (-cf - ed)]}{b \times df}} = \boxed{\frac{adf + [-bcf - bed]}{bdf}} = \boxed{\frac{adf - bcf - bed}{bdf}}$$

Example 3.2-25

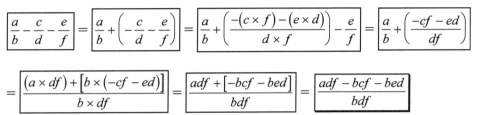

$$\boxed{\frac{7}{4} - \frac{1}{2} - \frac{2}{3}} = \boxed{\frac{7}{4} + \left(-\frac{1}{2} - \frac{2}{3}\right)} = \boxed{\frac{7}{4} + \left(\frac{-(1 \times 3) - (2 \times 2)}{2 \times 3}\right)} = \boxed{\frac{7}{4} + \left(\frac{-3 - 4}{6}\right)} = \boxed{\frac{7}{4} + \left(\frac{-7}{6}\right)} = \boxed{\frac{7}{4} - \frac{7}{6}}$$

$$= \boxed{\frac{(7 \times 6) - (7 \times 4)}{4 \times 6}} = \boxed{\frac{42 - 28}{24}} = \boxed{\frac{\overset{7}{14}}{\underset{12}{24}}} = \boxed{\frac{7}{12}}$$

The following examples further illustrate how to subtract integer fractions:

Example 3.2-26

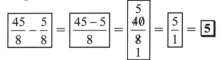

$$\boxed{\frac{45}{8} - \frac{5}{8}} = \boxed{\frac{45 - 5}{8}} = \boxed{\frac{\overset{5}{40}}{\underset{1}{8}}} = \boxed{\frac{5}{1}} = \boxed{5}$$

Example 3.2-27

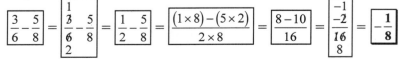

$$\boxed{\frac{3}{6} - \frac{5}{8}} = \boxed{\frac{\overset{1}{3}}{\underset{2}{6}} - \frac{5}{8}} = \boxed{\frac{1}{2} - \frac{5}{8}} = \boxed{\frac{(1 \times 8) - (5 \times 2)}{2 \times 8}} = \boxed{\frac{8 - 10}{16}} = \boxed{\frac{\overset{-1}{-2}}{\underset{8}{16}}} = \boxed{-\frac{1}{8}}$$

Example 3.2-28

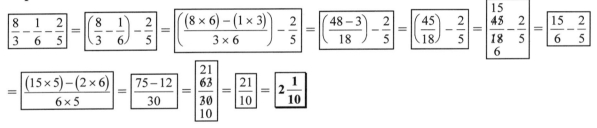

$$\boxed{\frac{8}{3} - \frac{1}{6} - \frac{2}{5}} = \boxed{\left(\frac{8}{3} - \frac{1}{6}\right) - \frac{2}{5}} = \boxed{\left(\frac{(8 \times 6) - (1 \times 3)}{3 \times 6}\right) - \frac{2}{5}} = \boxed{\left(\frac{48 - 3}{18}\right) - \frac{2}{5}} = \boxed{\left(\frac{\overset{15}{\cancel{45}}}{\underset{6}{\cancel{18}}}\right) - \frac{2}{5}} = \boxed{\frac{15}{6} - \frac{2}{5}}$$

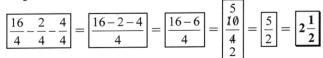

$$= \boxed{\frac{(15 \times 5) - (2 \times 6)}{6 \times 5}} = \boxed{\frac{75 - 12}{30}} = \boxed{\frac{\overset{21}{\cancel{63}}}{\underset{10}{\cancel{30}}}} = \boxed{\frac{21}{10}} = \boxed{2\frac{1}{10}}$$

Example 3.2-29

$$\boxed{\frac{16}{4} - \frac{2}{4} - \frac{4}{4}} = \boxed{\frac{16 - 2 - 4}{4}} = \boxed{\frac{16 - 6}{4}} = \boxed{\frac{\overset{5}{\cancel{10}}}{\underset{2}{\cancel{4}}}} = \boxed{\frac{5}{2}} = \boxed{2\frac{1}{2}}$$

Example 3.2-30

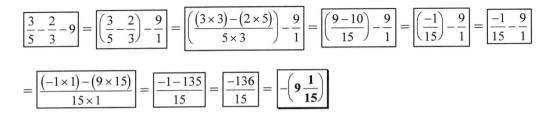

$$\boxed{\frac{3}{5} - \frac{2}{3} - 9} = \boxed{\left(\frac{3}{5} - \frac{2}{3}\right) - \frac{9}{1}} = \boxed{\left(\frac{(3 \times 3) - (2 \times 5)}{5 \times 3}\right) - \frac{9}{1}} = \boxed{\left(\frac{9 - 10}{15}\right) - \frac{9}{1}} = \boxed{\left(\frac{-1}{15}\right) - \frac{9}{1}} = \boxed{\frac{-1}{15} - \frac{9}{1}}$$

$$= \boxed{\frac{(-1 \times 1) - (9 \times 15)}{15 \times 1}} = \boxed{\frac{-1 - 135}{15}} = \boxed{\frac{-136}{15}} = \boxed{-\left(9\frac{1}{15}\right)}$$

Example 3.2-31

$$\boxed{\left(\frac{13}{8} - \frac{4}{3}\right) - \frac{1}{5}} = \boxed{\left(\frac{(13 \times 3) - (4 \times 8)}{8 \times 3}\right) - \frac{1}{5}} = \boxed{\left(\frac{39 - 32}{24}\right) - \frac{1}{5}} = \boxed{\left(\frac{7}{24}\right) - \frac{1}{5}} = \boxed{\frac{7}{24} - \frac{1}{5}} = \boxed{\frac{(7 \times 5) - (1 \times 24)}{24 \times 5}}$$

$$= \boxed{\frac{35 - 24}{120}} = \boxed{\frac{11}{120}}$$

Example 3.2-32

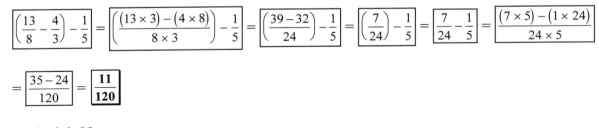

$$\boxed{\frac{2}{4} - \left(\frac{1}{3} - \frac{1}{5}\right)} = \boxed{\frac{\overset{1}{\cancel{2}}}{\underset{2}{\cancel{4}}} - \left(\frac{(5 \times 1) - (1 \times 3)}{3 \times 5}\right)} = \boxed{\frac{1}{2} - \left(\frac{5 - 3}{15}\right)} = \boxed{\frac{1}{2} - \left(\frac{2}{15}\right)} = \boxed{\frac{1}{2} - \frac{2}{15}} = \boxed{\frac{(1 \times 15) - (2 \times 2)}{2 \times 15}} = \boxed{\frac{15 - 4}{30}}$$

$$= \boxed{\frac{11}{30}}$$

Example 3.2-33

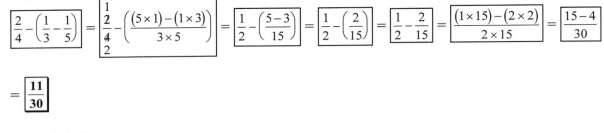

$$\boxed{\left(\frac{20}{3} - \frac{1}{5}\right) - \left(\frac{4}{7} - \frac{6}{7}\right)} = \boxed{\left(\frac{(20 \times 5) - (1 \times 3)}{3 \times 5}\right) - \left(\frac{4 - 6}{7}\right)} = \boxed{\left(\frac{100 - 3}{15}\right) - \left(\frac{-2}{7}\right)} = \boxed{\left(\frac{97}{15}\right) + \left(\frac{2}{7}\right)} = \boxed{\frac{97}{15} + \frac{2}{7}}$$

$$= \boxed{\frac{(97 \times 7)+(2 \times 15)}{15 \times 7}} = \boxed{\frac{679+30}{105}} = \boxed{\frac{709}{105}} = \boxed{6\frac{79}{105}}$$

Example 3.2-34

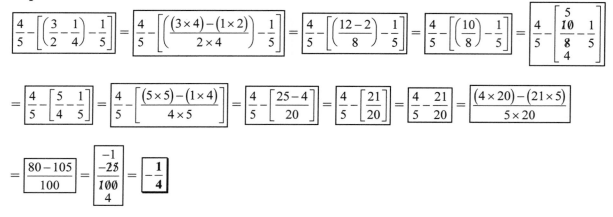

Example 3.2-35

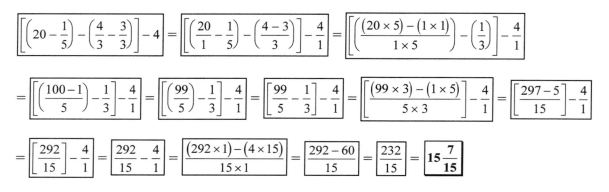

Section 3.2 Exercises - Subtract the following integer fractions:

1. $\dfrac{3}{5} - \dfrac{2}{5} =$

2. $\dfrac{2}{5} - \dfrac{3}{4} =$

3. $\dfrac{12}{15} - \dfrac{3}{15} - \dfrac{6}{15} =$

4. $\dfrac{5}{8} - \dfrac{3}{4} - \dfrac{1}{3} =$

5. $\left(\dfrac{2}{8} - \dfrac{1}{6}\right) - \dfrac{2}{5} =$

6. $28 - \left(\dfrac{1}{8} - \dfrac{2}{3}\right) =$

7. $\left(\dfrac{4}{6} - \dfrac{1}{8}\right) - \left(\dfrac{4}{5} - \dfrac{1}{2}\right) =$

8. $\left(20 - \dfrac{1}{6}\right) - \left(\dfrac{3}{4} - \dfrac{1}{2}\right) =$

9. $\left[\dfrac{18}{5} - \left(\dfrac{4}{3} - \dfrac{2}{3}\right)\right] - 2 =$

10. $\left[\left(18 - \dfrac{1}{2}\right) - \left(\dfrac{16}{2} - 2\right)\right] - \dfrac{1}{5} =$

3.3   Multiplying Integer Fractions

Two or more integer fractions with or without a common denominator are multiplied using the steps given as in each case below:

Case I   *Multiply two integer fractions with or without a common denominator using the following steps:*

Step 1   Change the integer number (a) to an integer fraction of the form $\left(\dfrac{a}{1}\right)$, e.g., change 300 to $\dfrac{300}{1}$.

Step 2   a. Multiply the numerator of the first fraction with the numerator of the second fraction to obtain the new numerator.

         b. Multiply the denominator of the first fraction with the denominator of the second fraction to obtain the new denominator.

Step 3   Simplify the fraction to its lowest term (see Section 2.3).

Step 4   Change the improper fraction to a mixed fraction if the fraction obtained from Step 3 is an improper fraction (see Section 2.2).

The following examples show the steps as to how two integer fractions with or without a common denominator are multiplied:

Example 3.3-1

$$\boxed{\dfrac{4}{5} \times \dfrac{3}{8}} =$$

Solution:

    Step 1 $\boxed{Not\ Applicable}$

    Step 2 $\boxed{\dfrac{4}{5} \times \dfrac{3}{8}} = \boxed{\dfrac{4 \times 3}{5 \times 8}} = \boxed{\dfrac{12}{40}}$

    Step 3 $\boxed{\dfrac{12}{40}} = \boxed{\dfrac{12 \div 4}{40 \div 4}} = \boxed{\dfrac{3}{10}}$

    Step 4 $\boxed{Not\ Applicable}$

Example 3.3-2

$$\boxed{25 \times \dfrac{5}{8}} =$$

Solution:

    Step 1 $\boxed{25 \times \dfrac{5}{8}} = \boxed{\dfrac{25}{1} \times \dfrac{5}{8}}$

    Step 2 $\boxed{\dfrac{25}{1} \times \dfrac{5}{8}} = \boxed{\dfrac{25 \times 5}{1 \times 8}} = \boxed{\dfrac{125}{8}}$

Step 3   Not Applicable

Step 4 $\boxed{\dfrac{125}{8}} = \boxed{15\dfrac{5}{8}}$

Example 3.3-3

$$\boxed{\dfrac{140}{3} \times \dfrac{1}{5}} =$$

Solution:

Step 1   Not Applicable

Step 2 $\boxed{\dfrac{140}{3} \times \dfrac{1}{5}} = \boxed{\dfrac{140 \times 1}{3 \times 5}} = \boxed{\dfrac{140}{15}}$

Step 3 $\boxed{\dfrac{140}{15}} = \boxed{\dfrac{140 \div 5}{15 \div 5}} = \boxed{\dfrac{28}{3}}$

Step 4 $\boxed{\dfrac{28}{3}} = \boxed{9\dfrac{1}{3}}$

Example 3.3-4

$$\boxed{36 \times \dfrac{4}{28}} =$$

Solution:

Step 1 $\boxed{36 \times \dfrac{4}{28}} = \boxed{\dfrac{36}{1} \times \dfrac{4}{28}}$

Step 2 $\boxed{\dfrac{36}{1} \times \dfrac{4}{28}} = \boxed{\dfrac{36 \times 4}{1 \times 28}} = \boxed{\dfrac{144}{28}}$

Step 3 $\boxed{\dfrac{144}{28}} = \boxed{\dfrac{144 \div 4}{28 \div 4}} = \boxed{\dfrac{36}{7}}$

Step 4 $\boxed{\dfrac{36}{7}} = \boxed{5\dfrac{1}{7}}$

Example 3.3-5

$$\boxed{\dfrac{9}{38} \times 12} =$$

Solution:

Step 1 $\boxed{\dfrac{9}{38} \times 12} = \boxed{\dfrac{9}{38} \times \dfrac{12}{1}}$

Step 2 $\boxed{\dfrac{9}{38} \times \dfrac{12}{1}} = \boxed{\dfrac{9 \times 12}{38 \times 1}} = \boxed{\dfrac{108}{38}}$

Step 3 $\boxed{\dfrac{108}{38}} = \boxed{\dfrac{108 \div 2}{38 \div 2}} = \boxed{\dfrac{54}{19}}$

Step 4 $\boxed{\dfrac{54}{19}} = \boxed{2\dfrac{16}{19}}$

In general, two integer fractions with or without a common denominator are multiplied in the following way:

$\boxed{\dfrac{a}{b} \times \dfrac{c}{d}} = \boxed{\dfrac{a \times c}{b \times d}} = \boxed{\dfrac{ac}{bd}}$

Example 3.3-6

$\boxed{\dfrac{2}{5} \times \dfrac{3}{4}} = \boxed{\dfrac{2 \times 3}{5 \times 4}} = \boxed{\dfrac{\overset{3}{\cancel{6}}}{\underset{10}{\cancel{20}}}} = \boxed{\dfrac{3}{10}}$

Case II   *Multiply three integer fractions with or without a common denominator using the following steps:*

Step 1   Change the integer number (a) to an integer fraction of the form $\left(\dfrac{a}{1}\right)$, e.g., change

25 to $\dfrac{25}{1}$.

Step 2   a. Multiply the numerators of the first, second, and third fractions to obtain the new numerator (see Section 1.4).

b. Multiply the denominator of the first, second, and third fractions to obtain the new denominator (see Section 1.4).

Step 3   Simplify the fraction to its lowest term (see Section 2.3).

Step 4   Change the improper fraction to a mixed fraction if the fraction obtained from Step 3 is an improper fraction(see Section 2.2).

The following examples show the steps as to how three integer fractions with or without a common denominator are multiplied:

Example 3.3-7

$\boxed{12 \times \dfrac{3}{5} \times \dfrac{1}{8}} =$

Solution:

Step 1 $\boxed{12 \times \dfrac{3}{5} \times \dfrac{1}{8}} = \boxed{\dfrac{12}{1} \times \dfrac{3}{5} \times \dfrac{1}{8}}$

Step 2 $\dfrac{12}{1} \times \dfrac{3}{5} \times \dfrac{1}{8} = \dfrac{12 \times 3 \times 1}{1 \times 5 \times 8} = \dfrac{36}{40}$

Step 3 $\dfrac{36}{40} = \dfrac{36 \div 4}{40 \div 4} = \boxed{\dfrac{9}{10}}$

Step 4 $\boxed{\textit{Not Applicable}}$

Example 3.3-8

$\boxed{\dfrac{25}{3} \times \dfrac{4}{7} \times \dfrac{6}{5}} =$

Solution:

Step 1 $\boxed{\textit{Not Applicable}}$

Step 2 $\dfrac{25}{3} \times \dfrac{4}{7} \times \dfrac{6}{5} = \dfrac{25 \times 4 \times 6}{3 \times 7 \times 5} = \dfrac{600}{105}$

Step 3 $\dfrac{600}{105} = \dfrac{600 \div 15}{105 \div 15} = \dfrac{40}{7}$

Step 4 $\dfrac{40}{7} = \boxed{5\dfrac{5}{7}}$

Example 3.3-9

$\boxed{\dfrac{25}{3} \times 14 \times \dfrac{9}{50}} =$

Solution:

Step 1 $\dfrac{25}{3} \times 14 \times \dfrac{9}{50} = \dfrac{25}{3} \times \dfrac{14}{1} \times \dfrac{9}{50}$

Step 2 $\dfrac{25}{3} \times \dfrac{14}{1} \times \dfrac{9}{50} = \dfrac{25 \times 14 \times 9}{3 \times 1 \times 50} = \dfrac{3150}{150}$

Step 3 $\dfrac{3150}{150} = \dfrac{3150 \div 150}{150 \div 150} = \dfrac{21}{1} = \boxed{21}$

Step 4 $\boxed{\textit{Not Applicable}}$

Example 3.3-10

$\boxed{\dfrac{9}{8} \times \dfrac{33}{5} \times \dfrac{5}{48}} =$

Solution:

Step 1 $\boxed{Not\ Applicable}$

Step 2 $\boxed{\dfrac{9}{8} \times \dfrac{33}{5} \times \dfrac{5}{48}} = \boxed{\dfrac{9 \times 33 \times 5}{8 \times 5 \times 48}} = \boxed{\dfrac{1485}{1920}}$

Step 3 $\boxed{\dfrac{1485}{1920}} = \boxed{\dfrac{1485 \div 15}{1920 \div 15}} = \boxed{\mathbf{\dfrac{99}{128}}}$

Step 4 $\boxed{Not\ Applicable}$

Example 3.3-11

$\boxed{\dfrac{125}{4} \times \dfrac{28}{13} \times 39} =$

Solution:

Step 1 $\boxed{\dfrac{125}{4} \times \dfrac{28}{13} \times 39} = \boxed{\dfrac{125}{4} \times \dfrac{28}{13} \times \dfrac{39}{1}}$

Step 2 $\boxed{\dfrac{125}{4} \times \dfrac{28}{13} \times \dfrac{39}{1}} = \boxed{\dfrac{125 \times 28 \times 39}{4 \times 13 \times 1}} = \boxed{\dfrac{136500}{52}}$

Step 3 $\boxed{\dfrac{136500}{52}} = \boxed{\dfrac{136500 \div 52}{52 \div 52}} = \boxed{\dfrac{2625}{1}} = \boxed{\mathbf{2625}}$

Step 4 $\boxed{Not\ Applicable}$

In general, three integer fractions with or without a common denominator are multiplied as in the following cases:

Case I.

$\boxed{\dfrac{a}{b} \times \dfrac{c}{d} \times \dfrac{e}{f}} = \boxed{\dfrac{a \times c \times e}{b \times d \times f}} = \boxed{\dfrac{ace}{bdf}}$

Example 3.3-12

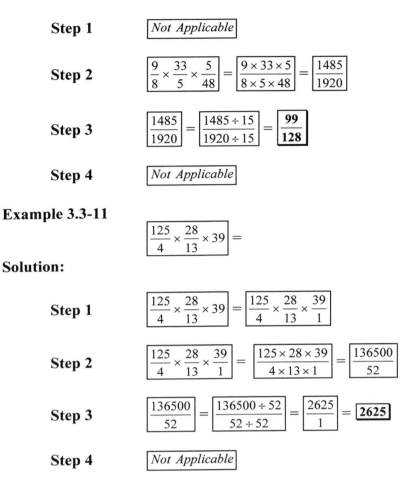

$\boxed{\dfrac{2}{3} \times \dfrac{3}{15} \times \dfrac{5}{2}} = \boxed{\dfrac{\overset{1}{2} \times \overset{1}{3} \times \overset{1}{\cancel{5}}}{\underset{1}{\cancel{3}} \times \underset{3}{\cancel{15}} \times \underset{1}{\cancel{2}}}} = \boxed{\dfrac{1 \times 1 \times 1}{1 \times 3 \times 1}} = \boxed{\mathbf{\dfrac{1}{3}}}$

Case II.

$\boxed{\dfrac{a}{b} \times \dfrac{c}{d} \times \dfrac{e}{f}} = \boxed{\left(\dfrac{a}{b} \times \dfrac{c}{d}\right) \times \dfrac{e}{f}} = \boxed{\left(\dfrac{a \times c}{b \times d}\right) \times \dfrac{e}{f}} = \boxed{\left(\dfrac{ac}{bd}\right) \times \dfrac{e}{f}} = \boxed{\dfrac{ac}{bd} \times \dfrac{e}{f}} = \boxed{\dfrac{ac \times e}{bd \times f}} = \boxed{\dfrac{ace}{bdf}}$

Example 3.3-13

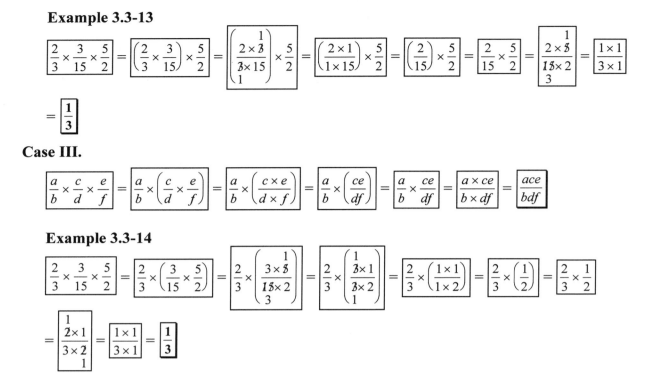

Case III.

$$\boxed{\frac{a}{b} \times \frac{c}{d} \times \frac{e}{f}} = \boxed{\frac{a}{b} \times \left(\frac{c}{d} \times \frac{e}{f}\right)} = \boxed{\frac{a}{b} \times \left(\frac{c \times e}{d \times f}\right)} = \boxed{\frac{a}{b} \times \left(\frac{ce}{df}\right)} = \boxed{\frac{a}{b} \times \frac{ce}{df}} = \boxed{\frac{a \times ce}{b \times df}} = \boxed{\frac{ace}{bdf}}$$

Example 3.3-14

Note - In multiplication the use of parentheses does not change the final answer; the three examples above have the same answer (see Section 1.4).

The following examples further illustrate how to multiply integer fractions:

Example 3.3-15

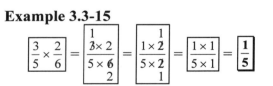

Example 3.3-16

$$\boxed{\frac{2}{3} \times 24} = \boxed{\frac{2}{3} \times \frac{24}{1}} = \boxed{\frac{2 \times \overset{8}{24}}{\underset{1}{3} \times 1}} = \boxed{\frac{2 \times 8}{1 \times 1}} = \boxed{\frac{16}{1}} = \boxed{16}$$

Example 3.3-17

$$\boxed{\frac{2}{5} \times \frac{4}{5} \times \frac{25}{8}} = \boxed{\frac{2 \times 4 \times \overset{5}{25}}{\underset{1}{5} \times 5 \times \underset{2}{8}}} = \boxed{\frac{\overset{1}{2} \times 1 \times \overset{1}{5}}{1 \times \underset{1}{5} \times \underset{1}{2}}} = \boxed{\frac{1 \times 1 \times 1}{1 \times 1 \times 1}} = \boxed{\frac{1}{1}} = \boxed{1}$$

Example 3.3-18

$$\boxed{\frac{6}{3} \times \frac{1}{3} \times \frac{0}{1}} = \boxed{\frac{6 \times 1 \times 0}{3 \times 3 \times 1}} = \boxed{\frac{0}{1}} = \boxed{0}$$

Example 3.3-19

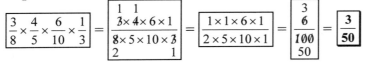

$$\boxed{1000 \times \frac{2}{100} \times \frac{1}{10} \times \frac{1}{2}} = \boxed{\frac{1000}{1} \times \frac{2}{100} \times \frac{1}{10} \times \frac{1}{2}} = \boxed{\frac{\overset{10}{\cancel{1000}} \times \overset{1}{\cancel{2}} \times 1 \times 1}{1 \times \underset{1}{\cancel{100}} \times 10 \times \underset{1}{\cancel{2}}}} = \boxed{\frac{\overset{1}{\cancel{10}} \times 1 \times 1 \times 1}{1 \times 1 \times \underset{1}{\cancel{10}} \times 1}} = \boxed{\frac{1 \times 1 \times 1 \times 1}{1 \times 1 \times 1 \times 1}} = \boxed{\frac{1}{1}} = \boxed{\boxed{1}}$$

Example 3.3-20

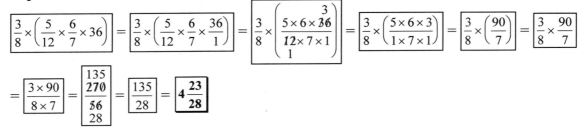

$$\boxed{\frac{3}{8} \times \frac{4}{5} \times \frac{6}{10} \times \frac{1}{3}} = \boxed{\frac{\overset{1}{\cancel{3}} \times \overset{1}{\cancel{4}} \times 6 \times 1}{\underset{2}{\cancel{8}} \times 5 \times 10 \times \underset{1}{\cancel{3}}}} = \boxed{\frac{1 \times 1 \times 6 \times 1}{2 \times 5 \times 10 \times 1}} = \boxed{\frac{\overset{3}{\cancel{6}}}{\underset{50}{\cancel{100}}}} = \boxed{\boxed{\frac{3}{50}}}$$

Example 3.3-21

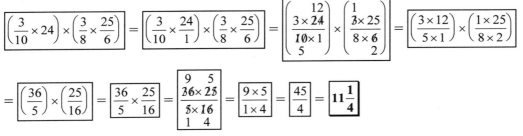

$$\boxed{\frac{3}{8} \times \left(\frac{5}{12} \times \frac{6}{7} \times 36 \right)} = \boxed{\frac{3}{8} \times \left(\frac{5}{12} \times \frac{6}{7} \times \frac{36}{1} \right)} = \boxed{\frac{3}{8} \times \left(\frac{5 \times 6 \times \overset{3}{\cancel{36}}}{\underset{1}{\cancel{12}} \times 7 \times 1} \right)} = \boxed{\frac{3}{8} \times \left(\frac{5 \times 6 \times 3}{1 \times 7 \times 1} \right)} = \boxed{\frac{3}{8} \times \left(\frac{90}{7} \right)} = \boxed{\frac{3}{8} \times \frac{90}{7}}$$

$$= \boxed{\frac{3 \times 90}{8 \times 7}} = \boxed{\frac{\overset{135}{\cancel{270}}}{\underset{28}{\cancel{56}}}} = \boxed{\frac{135}{28}} = \boxed{\boxed{4\frac{23}{28}}}$$

Example 3.3-22

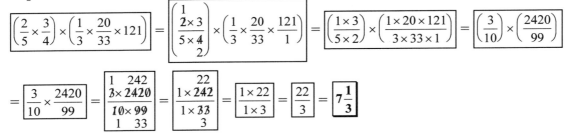

$$\boxed{\left(\frac{3}{10} \times 24 \right) \times \left(\frac{3}{8} \times \frac{25}{6} \right)} = \boxed{\left(\frac{3}{10} \times \frac{24}{1} \right) \times \left(\frac{3}{8} \times \frac{25}{6} \right)} = \boxed{\left(\frac{3 \times \overset{12}{\cancel{24}}}{\underset{5}{\cancel{10}} \times 1} \right) \times \left(\frac{\overset{1}{\cancel{3}} \times 25}{8 \times \underset{2}{\cancel{6}}} \right)} = \boxed{\left(\frac{3 \times 12}{5 \times 1} \right) \times \left(\frac{1 \times 25}{8 \times 2} \right)}$$

$$= \boxed{\left(\frac{36}{5} \right) \times \left(\frac{25}{16} \right)} = \boxed{\frac{36}{5} \times \frac{25}{16}} = \boxed{\frac{\overset{9}{\cancel{36}} \times \overset{5}{\cancel{25}}}{\underset{1}{\cancel{5}} \times \underset{4}{\cancel{16}}}} = \boxed{\frac{9 \times 5}{1 \times 4}} = \boxed{\frac{45}{4}} = \boxed{\boxed{11\frac{1}{4}}}$$

Example 3.3-23

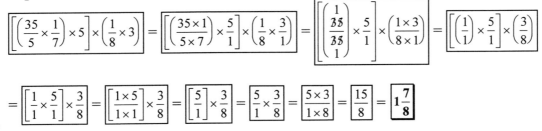

$$\boxed{\left(\frac{2}{5} \times \frac{3}{4} \right) \times \left(\frac{1}{3} \times \frac{20}{33} \times 121 \right)} = \boxed{\left(\frac{\overset{1}{\cancel{2}} \times 3}{5 \times \underset{2}{\cancel{4}}} \right) \times \left(\frac{1}{3} \times \frac{20}{33} \times \frac{121}{1} \right)} = \boxed{\left(\frac{1 \times 3}{5 \times 2} \right) \times \left(\frac{1 \times 20 \times 121}{3 \times 33 \times 1} \right)} = \boxed{\left(\frac{3}{10} \right) \times \left(\frac{2420}{99} \right)}$$

$$= \boxed{\frac{3}{10} \times \frac{2420}{99}} = \boxed{\frac{\overset{1}{\cancel{3}} \times \overset{242}{\cancel{2420}}}{10 \times \underset{33}{\cancel{99}}}} = \boxed{\frac{\overset{22}{\cancel{242}} \times 1}{1 \times \underset{3}{\cancel{33}}}} = \boxed{\frac{1 \times 22}{1 \times 3}} = \boxed{\frac{22}{3}} = \boxed{\boxed{7\frac{1}{3}}}$$

Example 3.3-24

$$\boxed{\left[\left(\frac{35}{5} \times \frac{1}{7} \right) \times 5 \right] \times \left(\frac{1}{8} \times 3 \right)} = \boxed{\left[\left(\frac{35 \times 1}{5 \times 7} \right) \times \frac{5}{1} \right] \times \left(\frac{1}{8} \times \frac{3}{1} \right)} = \boxed{\left[\left(\frac{\overset{1}{\cancel{35}}}{\underset{1}{\cancel{35}}} \right) \times \frac{5}{1} \right] \times \left(\frac{1 \times 3}{8 \times 1} \right)} = \boxed{\left[\left(\frac{1}{1} \right) \times \frac{5}{1} \right] \times \left(\frac{3}{8} \right)}$$

$$= \boxed{\left[\frac{1}{1} \times \frac{5}{1} \right] \times \frac{3}{8}} = \boxed{\left[\frac{1 \times 5}{1 \times 1} \right] \times \frac{3}{8}} = \boxed{\left[\frac{5}{1} \right] \times \frac{3}{8}} = \boxed{\frac{5}{1} \times \frac{3}{8}} = \boxed{\frac{5 \times 3}{1 \times 8}} = \boxed{\frac{15}{8}} = \boxed{\boxed{1\frac{7}{8}}}$$

Example 3.3-25

$$\left[\left(\frac{9}{80}\times 80\right)\times\left(\frac{1}{50}\times 5\right)\times\left(\frac{100}{2}\times\frac{50}{1}\right)\right] = \left[\left(\frac{9}{80}\times\frac{80}{1}\right)\times\left(\frac{1}{50}\times\frac{5}{1}\right)\times\left(\frac{\overset{50}{\cancel{100}}}{\underset{1}{2}}\times\frac{50}{1}\right)\right] = \left[\left(\frac{9\times\overset{1}{\cancel{80}}}{\underset{1}{80}\times 1}\right)\times\left(\frac{1\times\overset{1}{\cancel{5}}}{\underset{10}{\cancel{50}}\times 1}\right)\times\left(\frac{50\times 50}{1\times 1}\right)\right]$$

$$=\left[\left(\frac{9\times 1}{1\times 1}\right)\times\left(\frac{1\times 1}{10\times 1}\right)\times\left(\frac{2500}{1}\right)\right] = \left[\left(\frac{9}{1}\right)\times\left(\frac{1}{10}\right)\times\frac{2500}{1}\right] = \frac{9}{1}\times\frac{1}{10}\times\frac{2500}{1} = \frac{9\times 1\times\overset{250}{\cancel{2500}}}{1\times\underset{1}{\cancel{10}}\times 1} = \frac{9\times 1\times 250}{1\times 1\times 1}$$

$$=\frac{2250}{1} = \boxed{2250}$$

Section 3.3 Exercises - Multiply the following integer fractions:

1. $\dfrac{4}{8}\times\dfrac{3}{5} =$ 2. $\dfrac{4}{8}\times\dfrac{5}{6}\times 100 =$

3. $\dfrac{7}{3}\times\dfrac{9}{4}\times\dfrac{6}{3} =$ 4. $34\times\dfrac{1}{5}\times\dfrac{3}{17}\times\dfrac{1}{8}\times 20 =$

5. $\left(\dfrac{2}{55}\times 3\right)\times\left(\dfrac{4}{5}\times\dfrac{25}{8}\right) =$ 6. $\left(1000\times\dfrac{1}{5}\right)\times\left(\dfrac{25}{5}\times\dfrac{1}{8}\right)\times\dfrac{0}{100} =$

7. $\dfrac{2}{6}\times\dfrac{36}{1}\times\dfrac{1}{100}\times 10\times\dfrac{1}{6} =$ 8. $\left(\dfrac{7}{8}\times\dfrac{9}{4}\right)\times\left(\dfrac{4}{18}\times\dfrac{1}{14}\times\dfrac{1}{9}\right) =$

9. $\left[\left(18\times\dfrac{2}{8}\right)\times\left(\dfrac{1}{5}\times\dfrac{25}{3}\right)\right]\times\dfrac{2}{9} =$ 10. $\left(\dfrac{3}{8}\times\dfrac{4}{49}\times\dfrac{6}{5}\right)\times\left(\dfrac{7}{3}\times\dfrac{4}{8}\right)\times\dfrac{7}{2} =$

3.4   Dividing Integer Fractions

Two or more integer fractions with or without a common denominator are divided using the steps given as in each case below:

Case I *Divide two integer fractions with or without a common denominator using the following steps:*

Step 1 Change the integer number (a) to an integer fraction of the form $\left(\dfrac{a}{1}\right)$, e.g., change 39 to $\dfrac{39}{1}$.

Step 2 a. Change the division sign to a multiplication sign.

b. Replace the numerator of the second fraction with its denominator.

c. Replace the denominator of the second fraction with its numerator.

d. Multiply the numerator of the first fraction with the numerator of the second fraction to obtain the new numerator.

e. Multiply the denominator of the first fraction with the denominator of the second fraction to obtain the new denominator.

Step 3 Simplify the fraction to its lowest term (see Section 2.3).

Step 4 Change the improper fraction to a mixed fraction if the fraction obtained from Step 3 is an improper fraction (see Section 2.2).

The following examples show the steps as to how two integer fractions with or without a common denominator are divided:

Example 3.4-1

$$\boxed{\dfrac{3}{5} \div \dfrac{8}{15}} =$$

Solution:

Step 1 $\boxed{Not\ Applicable}$

Step 2 $\boxed{\dfrac{3}{5} \div \dfrac{8}{15}} = \boxed{\dfrac{3}{5} \times \dfrac{15}{8}} = \boxed{\dfrac{3 \times 15}{5 \times 8}} = \boxed{\dfrac{45}{40}}$

Step 3 $\boxed{\dfrac{45}{40}} = \boxed{\dfrac{45 \div 5}{40 \div 5}} = \boxed{\dfrac{9}{8}}$

Step 4 $\boxed{\dfrac{9}{8}} = \boxed{1\dfrac{1}{8}}$

Example 3.4-2

$$\boxed{9 \div \dfrac{6}{12}} =$$

Solution:

Step 1 $\boxed{9 \div \dfrac{6}{12}} = \boxed{\dfrac{9}{1} \div \dfrac{6}{12}}$

Step 2 $\boxed{\dfrac{9}{1} \div \dfrac{6}{12}} = \boxed{\dfrac{9}{1} \times \dfrac{12}{6}} = \boxed{\dfrac{9 \times 12}{1 \times 6}} = \boxed{\dfrac{108}{6}}$

Step 3 $\boxed{\dfrac{108}{6}} = \boxed{\dfrac{108 \div 6}{6 \div 6}} = \boxed{\dfrac{18}{1}} = \boxed{\mathbf{18}}$

Step 4 $\boxed{Not\ Applicable}$

Example 3.4-3

$$\boxed{\dfrac{320}{465} \div \dfrac{75}{100}} =$$

Solution:

Step 1 $\boxed{Not\ Applicable}$

Step 2 $\boxed{\dfrac{320}{465} \div \dfrac{75}{100}} = \boxed{\dfrac{320}{465} \times \dfrac{100}{75}} = \boxed{\dfrac{320 \times 100}{465 \times 75}} = \boxed{\dfrac{32000}{34875}}$

Step 3 $\boxed{\dfrac{32000}{34875}} = \boxed{\dfrac{32000 \div 25}{34875 \div 25}} = \boxed{\dfrac{1280}{1395}} = \boxed{\dfrac{1280 \div 5}{1395 \div 5}} = \boxed{\mathbf{\dfrac{256}{279}}}$

Step 4 $\boxed{Not\ Applicable}$

Example 3.4-4

$$\boxed{\dfrac{125}{65} \div 230} =$$

Solution:

Step 1 $\boxed{\dfrac{125}{65} \div 230} = \boxed{\dfrac{125}{65} \div \dfrac{230}{1}}$

Step 2 $\boxed{\dfrac{125}{65} \div \dfrac{230}{1}} = \boxed{\dfrac{125}{65} \times \dfrac{1}{230}} = \boxed{\dfrac{125 \times 1}{65 \times 230}} = \boxed{\dfrac{125}{14950}}$

Step 3 $\boxed{\dfrac{125}{14950}} = \boxed{\dfrac{125 \div 25}{14950 \div 25}} = \boxed{\mathbf{\dfrac{5}{598}}}$

Step 4 $\boxed{Not\ Applicable}$

Example 3.4-5

$$\boxed{\frac{32}{18} \div \frac{50}{12}} =$$

Solution:

Step 1 $\boxed{\textit{Not Applicable}}$

Step 2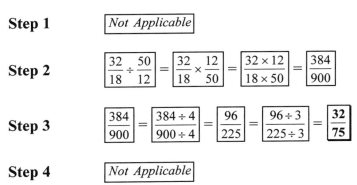

$$\boxed{\frac{32}{18} \div \frac{50}{12}} = \boxed{\frac{32}{18} \times \frac{12}{50}} = \boxed{\frac{32 \times 12}{18 \times 50}} = \boxed{\frac{384}{900}}$$

Step 3 $$\boxed{\frac{384}{900}} = \boxed{\frac{384 \div 4}{900 \div 4}} = \boxed{\frac{96}{225}} = \boxed{\frac{96 \div 3}{225 \div 3}} = \boxed{\frac{32}{75}}$$

Step 4 $\boxed{\textit{Not Applicable}}$

In general, two integer fractions with or without a common denominator are divided in the following way:

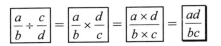

$$\boxed{\frac{a}{b} \div \frac{c}{d}} = \boxed{\frac{a}{b} \times \frac{d}{c}} = \boxed{\frac{a \times d}{b \times c}} = \boxed{\frac{ad}{bc}}$$

Example 3.4-6

$$\boxed{\frac{3}{5} \div \frac{2}{15}} = \boxed{\frac{3}{5} \times \frac{15}{2}} = \boxed{\frac{3 \times \overset{3}{\cancel{15}}}{\underset{1}{\cancel{5}} \times 2}} = \boxed{\frac{3 \times 3}{1 \times 2}} = \boxed{\frac{9}{2}} = \boxed{4\frac{1}{2}}$$

Case II   *Divide three integer fractions with or without a common denominator using the following steps:*

Step 1   Change the integer number (a) to an integer fraction of the form $\left(\frac{a}{1}\right)$, e.g., change

258 to $\frac{258}{1}$.

Step 2   a. Select the two fractions grouped by parentheses.

b. Divide the grouped fractions following Steps 2a through 2e, outlined in Section 3.4, Case I above, to obtain a new integer fraction.

c. Divide the new integer fraction by the third fraction by repeating Steps 2a through 2e, outlined in Section 3.4, Case I above.

Step 3   Simplify the fraction to its lowest term (see Section 2.3).

Step 4   Change the improper fraction to a mixed fraction if the fraction obtained from Step 3 is an improper fraction (see Section 2.2).

The following examples show the steps as to how three integer fractions are divided:

Example 3.4-7

$$\boxed{\left(\frac{3}{5} \div 4\right) \div \frac{9}{25}} =$$

Solution:

Step 1 $\boxed{\left(\frac{3}{5} \div 4\right) \div \frac{9}{25}} = \boxed{\left(\frac{3}{5} \div \frac{4}{1}\right) \div \frac{9}{25}}$

Step 2 $\boxed{\left(\frac{3}{5} \div \frac{4}{1}\right) \div \frac{9}{25}} = \boxed{\left(\frac{3}{5} \times \frac{1}{4}\right) \div \frac{9}{25}} = \boxed{\left(\frac{3 \times 1}{5 \times 4}\right) \div \frac{9}{25}} = \boxed{\left(\frac{3}{20}\right) \div \frac{9}{25}} = \boxed{\frac{3}{20} \div \frac{9}{25}}$

$= \boxed{\frac{3}{20} \times \frac{25}{9}} = \boxed{\frac{3 \times 25}{20 \times 9}} = \boxed{\frac{75}{180}}$

Step 3 $\boxed{\frac{75}{180}} = \boxed{\frac{75 \div 15}{180 \div 15}} = \boxed{\mathbf{\frac{5}{12}}}$

Step 4 $\boxed{\textit{Not Applicable}}$

Example 3.4-8

$$\boxed{235 \div \left(\frac{68}{15} \div \frac{33}{12}\right)} =$$

Solution:

Step 1 $\boxed{235 \div \left(\frac{68}{15} \div \frac{33}{12}\right)} = \boxed{\frac{235}{1} \div \left(\frac{68}{15} \div \frac{33}{12}\right)}$

Step 2 $\boxed{\frac{235}{1} \div \left(\frac{68}{15} \div \frac{33}{12}\right)} = \boxed{\frac{235}{1} \div \left(\frac{68}{15} \times \frac{12}{33}\right)} = \boxed{\frac{235}{1} \div \left(\frac{68 \times 12}{15 \times 33}\right)} = \boxed{\frac{235}{1} \div \left(\frac{816}{495}\right)}$

$= \boxed{\frac{235}{1} \div \frac{816}{495}} = \boxed{\frac{235}{1} \times \frac{495}{816}} = \boxed{\frac{235 \times 495}{1 \times 816}} = \boxed{\frac{116325}{816}}$

Step 3 $\boxed{\frac{116325}{816}} = \boxed{\frac{116325 \div 3}{816 \div 3}} = \boxed{\frac{38775}{272}}$

Step 4 $\boxed{\frac{38775}{272}} = \boxed{\mathbf{142\frac{151}{272}}}$

Example 3.4-9

$$\boxed{\left(\frac{4}{5} \div \frac{2}{3}\right) \div \frac{1}{5}} =$$

Solution:

> **Step 1** $\boxed{\textit{Not Applicable}}$

> **Step 2** $\boxed{\left(\dfrac{4}{5} \div \dfrac{2}{3}\right) \div \dfrac{1}{5}} = \boxed{\left(\dfrac{4}{5} \times \dfrac{3}{2}\right) \div \dfrac{1}{5}} = \boxed{\left(\dfrac{4 \times 3}{5 \times 2}\right) \div \dfrac{1}{5}} = \boxed{\left(\dfrac{12}{10}\right) \div \dfrac{1}{5}} = \boxed{\dfrac{12}{10} \div \dfrac{1}{5}} = \boxed{\dfrac{12}{10} \times \dfrac{5}{1}}$

> $= \boxed{\dfrac{12 \times 5}{10 \times 1}} = \boxed{\dfrac{60}{10}}$

> **Step 3** $\boxed{\dfrac{60}{10}} = \boxed{\dfrac{60 \div 10}{10 \div 10}} = \boxed{\dfrac{6}{1}} = \boxed{6}$

> **Step 4** $\boxed{\textit{Not Applicable}}$

Example 3.4-10

$$\boxed{\dfrac{12}{30} \div \left(\dfrac{15}{6} \div \dfrac{12}{5}\right)} =$$

Solution:

> **Step 1** $\boxed{\textit{Not Applicable}}$

> **Step 2** $\boxed{\dfrac{12}{30} \div \left(\dfrac{15}{6} \div \dfrac{12}{5}\right)} = \boxed{\dfrac{12}{30} \div \left(\dfrac{15}{6} \times \dfrac{5}{12}\right)} = \boxed{\dfrac{12}{30} \div \left(\dfrac{15 \times 5}{6 \times 12}\right)} = \boxed{\dfrac{12}{30} \div \left(\dfrac{75}{72}\right)} = \boxed{\dfrac{12}{30} \div \dfrac{75}{72}}$

> $= \boxed{\dfrac{12}{30} \times \dfrac{72}{75}} = \boxed{\dfrac{12 \times 72}{30 \times 75}} = \boxed{\dfrac{864}{2250}}$

> **Step 3** $\boxed{\dfrac{864}{2250}} = \boxed{\dfrac{864 \div 2}{2250 \div 2}} = \boxed{\dfrac{432}{1125}} = \boxed{\dfrac{432 \div 9}{1125 \div 9}} = \boxed{\dfrac{48}{125}}$

> **Step 4** $\boxed{\textit{Not Applicable}}$

Example 3.4-11

$$\boxed{\dfrac{9}{6} \div \left(\dfrac{7}{6} \div \dfrac{5}{6}\right)} =$$

Solution:

> **Step 1** $\boxed{\textit{Not Applicable}}$

> **Step 2** $\boxed{\dfrac{9}{6} \div \left(\dfrac{7}{6} \div \dfrac{5}{6}\right)} = \boxed{\dfrac{9}{6} \div \left(\dfrac{7}{6} \times \dfrac{6}{5}\right)} = \boxed{\dfrac{9}{6} \div \left(\dfrac{7 \times 6}{6 \times 5}\right)} = \boxed{\dfrac{9}{6} \div \left(\dfrac{42}{30}\right)} = \boxed{\dfrac{9}{6} \div \dfrac{42}{30}} = \boxed{\dfrac{9}{6} \times \dfrac{30}{42}}$

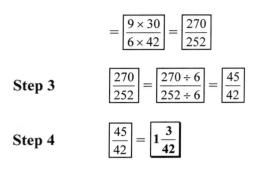

$$= \boxed{\frac{9 \times 30}{6 \times 42}} = \boxed{\frac{270}{252}}$$

Step 3
$$\boxed{\frac{270}{252}} = \boxed{\frac{270 \div 6}{252 \div 6}} = \boxed{\frac{45}{42}}$$

Step 4
$$\boxed{\frac{45}{42}} = \boxed{1\frac{3}{42}}$$

In general, three integer fractions with or without a common denominator are divided as in the following cases:

Case I.

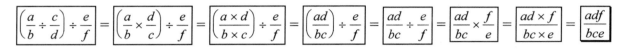

$$\boxed{\left(\frac{a}{b} \div \frac{c}{d}\right) \div \frac{e}{f}} = \boxed{\left(\frac{a}{b} \times \frac{d}{c}\right) \div \frac{e}{f}} = \boxed{\left(\frac{a \times d}{b \times c}\right) \div \frac{e}{f}} = \boxed{\left(\frac{ad}{bc}\right) \div \frac{e}{f}} = \boxed{\frac{ad}{bc} \div \frac{e}{f}} = \boxed{\frac{ad}{bc} \times \frac{f}{e}} = \boxed{\frac{ad \times f}{bc \times e}} = \boxed{\frac{adf}{bce}}$$

Example 3.4-12

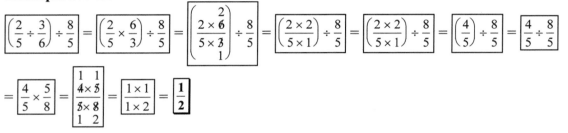

$$\boxed{\left(\frac{2}{5} \div \frac{3}{6}\right) \div \frac{8}{5}} = \boxed{\left(\frac{2}{5} \times \frac{6}{3}\right) \div \frac{8}{5}} = \boxed{\left(\frac{2 \times \overset{2}{\cancel{6}}}{5 \times \cancel{3}}\right) \div \frac{8}{5}} = \boxed{\left(\frac{2 \times 2}{5 \times 1}\right) \div \frac{8}{5}} = \boxed{\left(\frac{2 \times 2}{5 \times 1}\right) \div \frac{8}{5}} = \boxed{\left(\frac{4}{5}\right) \div \frac{8}{5}} = \boxed{\frac{4}{5} \div \frac{8}{5}}$$

$$= \boxed{\frac{4}{5} \times \frac{5}{8}} = \boxed{\frac{\overset{1}{\cancel{4}} \times \overset{1}{\cancel{5}}}{\underset{1}{\cancel{5}} \times \underset{2}{\cancel{8}}}} = \boxed{\frac{1 \times 1}{1 \times 2}} = \boxed{\frac{1}{2}}$$

Case II.

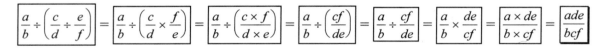

$$\boxed{\frac{a}{b} \div \left(\frac{c}{d} \div \frac{e}{f}\right)} = \boxed{\frac{a}{b} \div \left(\frac{c}{d} \times \frac{f}{e}\right)} = \boxed{\frac{a}{b} \div \left(\frac{c \times f}{d \times e}\right)} = \boxed{\frac{a}{b} \div \left(\frac{cf}{de}\right)} = \boxed{\frac{a}{b} \div \frac{cf}{de}} = \boxed{\frac{a}{b} \times \frac{de}{cf}} = \boxed{\frac{a \times de}{b \times cf}} = \boxed{\frac{ade}{bcf}}$$

Example 3.4-13

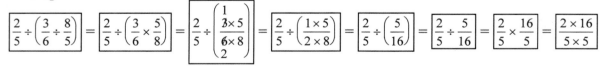

$$\boxed{\frac{2}{5} \div \left(\frac{3}{6} \div \frac{8}{5}\right)} = \boxed{\frac{2}{5} \div \left(\frac{3}{6} \times \frac{5}{8}\right)} = \boxed{\frac{2}{5} \div \left(\frac{\overset{1}{\cancel{3}} \times 5}{6 \times 8 \atop 2}\right)} = \boxed{\frac{2}{5} \div \left(\frac{1 \times 5}{2 \times 8}\right)} = \boxed{\frac{2}{5} \div \left(\frac{5}{16}\right)} = \boxed{\frac{2}{5} \div \frac{5}{16}} = \boxed{\frac{2}{5} \times \frac{16}{5}} = \boxed{\frac{2 \times 16}{5 \times 5}}$$

$$= \boxed{\frac{32}{25}} = \boxed{1\frac{7}{25}}$$

The following examples further illustrate how to divide integer fractions:

Example 3.4-14

$$\boxed{\frac{4}{5} \div \frac{2}{15}} = \boxed{\frac{4}{5} \times \frac{15}{2}} = \boxed{\frac{\overset{2}{\cancel{4}} \times \overset{3}{\cancel{15}}}{\underset{1}{\cancel{5}} \times \underset{1}{\cancel{2}}}} = \boxed{\frac{2 \times 3}{1 \times 1}} = \boxed{\frac{6}{1}} = \boxed{6}$$

Example 3.4-15

$$\boxed{\frac{3}{5} \div 24} = \boxed{\frac{3}{5} \div \frac{24}{1}} = \boxed{\frac{3}{5} \times \frac{1}{24}} = \boxed{\frac{\overset{1}{\cancel{3}} \times 1}{5 \times \underset{8}{\cancel{24}}}} = \boxed{\frac{1 \times 1}{5 \times 8}} = \boxed{\mathbf{\frac{1}{40}}}$$

Example 3.4-16

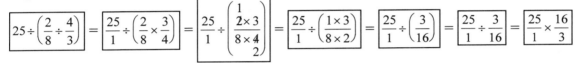

$$= \boxed{\frac{45}{4}} = \boxed{\mathbf{11\frac{1}{4}}}$$

Example 3.4-17

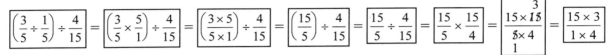

$$= \boxed{\frac{25 \times 16}{1 \times 3}} = \boxed{\frac{400}{3}} = \boxed{\mathbf{133\frac{1}{3}}}$$

Example 3.4-18

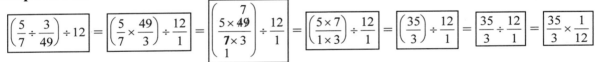

$$= \boxed{\frac{35 \times 1}{3 \times 12}} = \boxed{\mathbf{\frac{35}{36}}}$$

Example 3.4-19

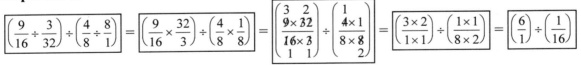

$$= \boxed{\frac{6}{1} \div \frac{1}{16}} = \boxed{\frac{6}{1} \times \frac{16}{1}} = \boxed{\frac{6 \times 16}{1 \times 1}} = \boxed{\frac{96}{1}} = \boxed{\mathbf{96}}$$

Example 3.4-20

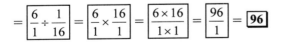

$$= \boxed{\frac{2}{3} \times \frac{2}{15}} = \boxed{\frac{2 \times 2}{3 \times 15}} = \boxed{\frac{4}{45}}$$

Example 3.4-21

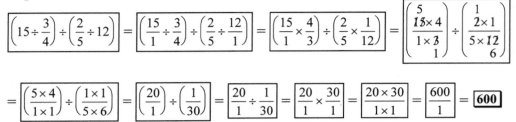

$$\boxed{\left(15 \div \frac{3}{4}\right) \div \left(\frac{2}{5} \div 12\right)} = \boxed{\left(\frac{15}{1} \div \frac{3}{4}\right) \div \left(\frac{2}{5} \div \frac{12}{1}\right)} = \boxed{\left(\frac{15}{1} \times \frac{4}{3}\right) \div \left(\frac{2}{5} \times \frac{1}{12}\right)} = \boxed{\left(\frac{\overset{5}{15} \times 4}{1 \times \underset{1}{3}}\right) \div \left(\frac{2 \times 1}{5 \times \underset{6}{12}}\right)}$$

$$= \boxed{\left(\frac{5 \times 4}{1 \times 1}\right) \div \left(\frac{1 \times 1}{5 \times 6}\right)} = \boxed{\left(\frac{20}{1}\right) \div \left(\frac{1}{30}\right)} = \boxed{\frac{20}{1} \div \frac{1}{30}} = \boxed{\frac{20}{1} \times \frac{30}{1}} = \boxed{\frac{20 \times 30}{1 \times 1}} = \boxed{\frac{600}{1}} = \boxed{\mathbf{600}}$$

Example 3.4-22

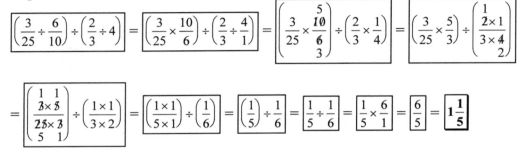

$$\boxed{\left(\frac{3}{25} \div \frac{6}{10}\right) \div \left(\frac{2}{3} \div 4\right)} = \boxed{\left(\frac{3}{25} \times \frac{10}{6}\right) \div \left(\frac{2}{3} \div \frac{4}{1}\right)} = \boxed{\left(\frac{3}{25} \times \frac{\overset{5}{10}}{\underset{3}{6}}\right) \div \left(\frac{2}{3} \times \frac{1}{4}\right)} = \boxed{\left(\frac{3}{25} \times \frac{5}{3}\right) \div \left(\frac{2 \times 1}{3 \times 4}\right)}$$

$$= \boxed{\left(\frac{\overset{1}{3} \times \overset{1}{5}}{\underset{5}{25} \times \underset{1}{3}}\right) \div \left(\frac{1 \times 1}{3 \times 2}\right)} = \boxed{\left(\frac{1 \times 1}{5 \times 1}\right) \div \left(\frac{1}{6}\right)} = \boxed{\left(\frac{1}{5}\right) \div \frac{1}{6}} = \boxed{\frac{1}{5} \div \frac{1}{6}} = \boxed{\frac{1}{5} \times \frac{6}{1}} = \boxed{\frac{6}{5}} = \boxed{\mathbf{1\frac{1}{5}}}$$

Example 3.4-23

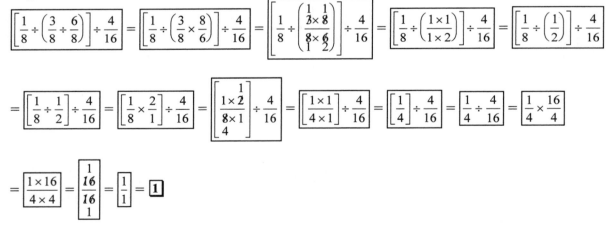

$$\boxed{\left[\frac{1}{8} \div \left(\frac{3}{8} \div \frac{6}{8}\right)\right] \div \frac{4}{16}} = \boxed{\left[\frac{1}{8} \div \left(\frac{3}{8} \times \frac{8}{6}\right)\right] \div \frac{4}{16}} = \boxed{\left[\frac{1}{8} \div \left(\frac{\overset{1}{3} \times \overset{1}{8}}{\underset{1}{8} \times \underset{2}{6}}\right)\right] \div \frac{4}{16}} = \boxed{\left[\frac{1}{8} \div \left(\frac{1 \times 1}{1 \times 2}\right)\right] \div \frac{4}{16}} = \boxed{\left[\frac{1}{8} \div \left(\frac{1}{2}\right)\right] \div \frac{4}{16}}$$

$$= \boxed{\left[\frac{1}{8} \div \frac{1}{2}\right] \div \frac{4}{16}} = \boxed{\left[\frac{1}{8} \times \frac{2}{1}\right] \div \frac{4}{16}} = \boxed{\left[\frac{1 \times \overset{1}{2}}{\underset{4}{8} \times 1}\right] \div \frac{4}{16}} = \boxed{\left[\frac{1 \times 1}{4 \times 1}\right] \div \frac{4}{16}} = \boxed{\left[\frac{1}{4}\right] \div \frac{4}{16}} = \boxed{\frac{1}{4} \div \frac{4}{16}} = \boxed{\frac{1}{4} \times \frac{16}{4}}$$

$$= \boxed{\frac{1 \times 16}{4 \times 4}} = \boxed{\frac{\overset{1}{16}}{\underset{1}{16}}} = \boxed{\frac{1}{1}} = \boxed{\mathbf{1}}$$

Example 3.4-24

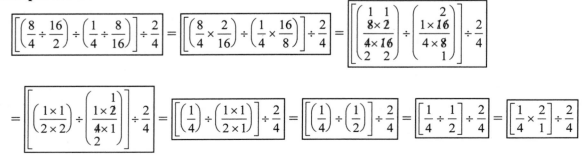

$$\boxed{\left[\left(\frac{8}{4} \div \frac{16}{2}\right) \div \left(\frac{1}{4} \div \frac{8}{16}\right)\right] \div \frac{2}{4}} = \boxed{\left[\left(\frac{8}{4} \times \frac{2}{16}\right) \div \left(\frac{1}{4} \times \frac{16}{8}\right)\right] \div \frac{2}{4}} = \boxed{\left[\left(\frac{\overset{1}{8} \times \overset{1}{2}}{\underset{2}{4} \times \underset{2}{16}}\right) \div \left(\frac{1 \times \overset{2}{16}}{4 \times \underset{1}{8}}\right)\right] \div \frac{2}{4}}$$

$$= \boxed{\left[\left(\frac{1 \times 1}{2 \times 2}\right) \div \left(\frac{1 \times \overset{1}{2}}{4 \times 1}\right)\right] \div \frac{2}{4}} = \boxed{\left[\left(\frac{1}{4}\right) \div \left(\frac{1 \times 1}{2 \times 1}\right)\right] \div \frac{2}{4}} = \boxed{\left[\left(\frac{1}{4}\right) \div \left(\frac{1}{2}\right)\right] \div \frac{2}{4}} = \boxed{\left[\frac{1}{4} \div \frac{1}{2}\right] \div \frac{2}{4}} = \boxed{\left[\frac{1}{4} \times \frac{2}{1}\right] \div \frac{2}{4}}$$

$$= \left[\frac{1}{\frac{1\times 2}{4\times 1}=2}\div\frac{2}{4}\right]=\left[\frac{1\times 1}{2\times 1}\div\frac{2}{4}\right]=\left[\frac{1}{2}\div\frac{2}{4}\right]=\frac{1}{2}\div\frac{2}{4}=\frac{1}{2}\times\frac{4}{2}=\frac{1\times 4}{2\times 2}=\frac{\frac{1}{4}}{\frac{4}{1}}=\frac{1}{1}=\boxed{1}$$

Section 3.4 Exercises - Divide the following integer fractions:

1. $\dfrac{8}{10}\div\dfrac{4}{30}=$

2. $\left(\dfrac{3}{8}\div\dfrac{12}{16}\right)\div\dfrac{4}{8}=$

3. $\left(\dfrac{4}{16}\div\dfrac{1}{32}\right)\div 8=$

4. $12\div\left(\dfrac{9}{8}\div\dfrac{27}{16}\right)=$

5. $\left(\dfrac{2}{20}\div\dfrac{4}{5}\right)\div 2=$

6. $\left(\dfrac{4}{15}\div\dfrac{8}{30}\right)\div\left(\dfrac{1}{5}\div\dfrac{4}{35}\right)=$

7. $\left(\dfrac{2}{5}\div\dfrac{4}{10}\right)\div\left(\dfrac{9}{1}\div\dfrac{18}{4}\right)=$

8. $\left(\dfrac{4}{5}\div\dfrac{2}{5}\right)\div\left(\dfrac{8}{5}\div 4\right)=$

9. $\left(\dfrac{6}{10}\div 1\right)\div\left(\dfrac{4}{6}\div\dfrac{1}{3}\right)=$

10. $\left[\left(\dfrac{9}{8}\div\dfrac{18}{16}\right)\div\dfrac{4}{2}\right]\div\dfrac{1}{8}=$

3.5   Solving Mixed Operations Using Integer Fractions

Mixed integer fractions, i.e., integer fractions that are being added, subtracted, multiplied, and divided are solved by using the following steps:

Step 1   Change the integer number (a) to an integer fraction of the form $\left(\dfrac{a}{1}\right)$, e.g., change

155 to $\dfrac{155}{1}$.

Step 2   Add, subtract, multiply, and divide the integer fractions by following the steps outlined in sections 3.1 through 3.4.

Step 3   Simplify the fraction to its lowest term (see Section 2.3).

Step 4   Change the improper fraction to a mixed fraction if the fraction obtained from Step 3 is an improper fraction (see Section 2.2).

The following examples show mathematical operations on integer fractions using the above steps:

Example 3.5-1

$$\left[\left(\frac{3}{5}\times\frac{4}{6}\right)+\left(\frac{4}{3}\div\frac{1}{5}\right)\right]=$$

Solution:

Step 1 $\boxed{Not\ Applicable}$

Step 2 $\left[\left(\frac{3}{5}\times\frac{4}{6}\right)+\left(\frac{4}{3}\div\frac{1}{5}\right)\right]=\left[\left(\frac{3\times4}{5\times6}\right)+\left(\frac{4}{3}\times\frac{5}{1}\right)\right]=\left[\left(\frac{12}{30}\right)+\left(\frac{4\times5}{3\times1}\right)\right]=\left[\frac{12}{30}+\left(\frac{20}{3}\right)\right]$

$=\left[\frac{12}{30}+\frac{20}{3}\right]=\left[\frac{(12\times3)+(20\times30)}{30\times3}\right]=\left[\frac{36+600}{90}\right]=\left[\frac{636}{90}\right]$

Step 3 $\left[\frac{636}{90}\right]=\left[\frac{636\div6}{90\div6}\right]=\left[\frac{106}{15}\right]$

Step 4 $\left[\frac{106}{15}\right]=\boxed{7\frac{1}{15}}$

Example 3.5-2

$$\left[\left(2+\frac{4}{3}\right)-\left(\frac{4}{5}-\frac{3}{2}\right)\right]=$$

Solution:

Step 1 $\left[\left(2+\frac{4}{3}\right)-\left(\frac{4}{5}-\frac{3}{2}\right)\right]=\left[\left(\frac{2}{1}+\frac{4}{3}\right)-\left(\frac{4}{5}-\frac{3}{2}\right)\right]$

Step 2 $\left[\left(\frac{2}{1}+\frac{4}{3}\right)-\left(\frac{4}{5}-\frac{3}{2}\right)\right]=\left[\left(\frac{(2\times3)+(4\times1)}{1\times3}\right)-\left(\frac{(4\times2)-(3\times5)}{5\times2}\right)\right]=\left[\left(\frac{6+4}{3}\right)-\left(\frac{8-15}{10}\right)\right]$

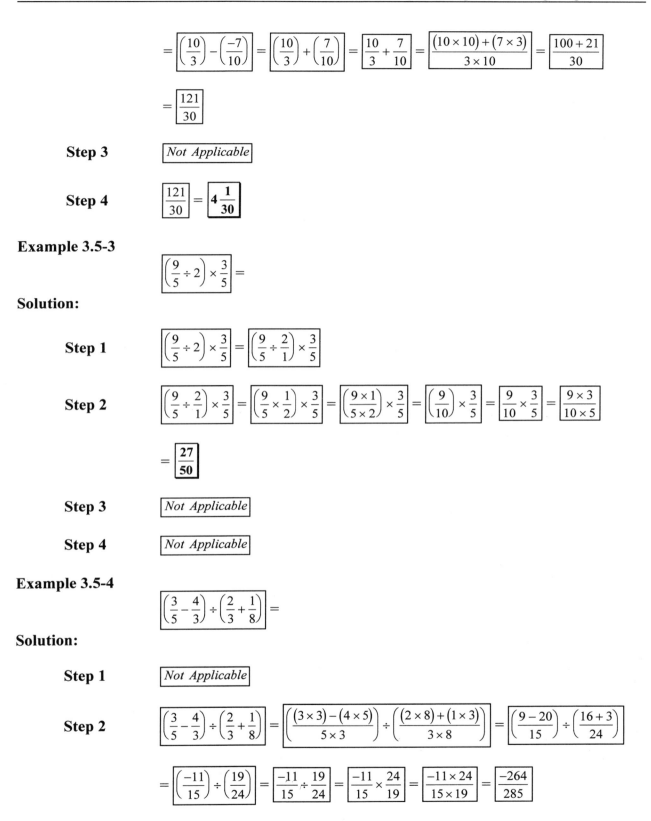

$$= \left[\left(\frac{10}{3}\right) - \left(\frac{-7}{10}\right)\right] = \left[\left(\frac{10}{3}\right) + \left(\frac{7}{10}\right)\right] = \left[\frac{10}{3} + \frac{7}{10}\right] = \left[\frac{(10 \times 10) + (7 \times 3)}{3 \times 10}\right] = \left[\frac{100 + 21}{30}\right]$$

$$= \left[\frac{121}{30}\right]$$

Step 3 $\boxed{Not\ Applicable}$

Step 4 $\left[\frac{121}{30}\right] = \boxed{4\frac{1}{30}}$

Example 3.5-3

$$\left[\left(\frac{9}{5} \div 2\right) \times \frac{3}{5}\right] =$$

Solution:

Step 1 $\left[\left(\frac{9}{5} \div 2\right) \times \frac{3}{5}\right] = \left[\left(\frac{9}{5} \div \frac{2}{1}\right) \times \frac{3}{5}\right]$

Step 2 $\left[\left(\frac{9}{5} \div \frac{2}{1}\right) \times \frac{3}{5}\right] = \left[\left(\frac{9}{5} \times \frac{1}{2}\right) \times \frac{3}{5}\right] = \left[\left(\frac{9 \times 1}{5 \times 2}\right) \times \frac{3}{5}\right] = \left[\left(\frac{9}{10}\right) \times \frac{3}{5}\right] = \left[\frac{9}{10} \times \frac{3}{5}\right] = \left[\frac{9 \times 3}{10 \times 5}\right]$

$$= \boxed{\frac{27}{50}}$$

Step 3 $\boxed{Not\ Applicable}$

Step 4 $\boxed{Not\ Applicable}$

Example 3.5-4

$$\left[\left(\frac{3}{5} - \frac{4}{3}\right) \div \left(\frac{2}{3} + \frac{1}{8}\right)\right] =$$

Solution:

Step 1 $\boxed{Not\ Applicable}$

Step 2 $\left[\left(\frac{3}{5} - \frac{4}{3}\right) \div \left(\frac{2}{3} + \frac{1}{8}\right)\right] = \left[\left(\frac{(3 \times 3) - (4 \times 5)}{5 \times 3}\right) \div \left(\frac{(2 \times 8) + (1 \times 3)}{3 \times 8}\right)\right] = \left[\left(\frac{9 - 20}{15}\right) \div \left(\frac{16 + 3}{24}\right)\right]$

$$= \left[\left(\frac{-11}{15}\right) \div \left(\frac{19}{24}\right)\right] = \left[\frac{-11}{15} \div \frac{19}{24}\right] = \left[\frac{-11}{15} \times \frac{24}{19}\right] = \left[\frac{-11 \times 24}{15 \times 19}\right] = \left[\frac{-264}{285}\right]$$

Step 3 $\dfrac{-264}{285} = \dfrac{-264 \div 3}{285 \div 3} = \boxed{-\dfrac{88}{95}}$

Step 4 $\boxed{\textit{Not Applicable}}$

Example 3.5-5

$$\left[5 \div \left(\frac{30}{4} \times \frac{1}{3}\right)\right] + \left(\frac{2}{3} + \frac{1}{5}\right) =$$

Solution:

Step 1 $\left[5 \div \left(\dfrac{30}{4} \times \dfrac{1}{3}\right)\right] + \left(\dfrac{2}{3} + \dfrac{1}{5}\right) = \left[\dfrac{5}{1} \div \left(\dfrac{30}{4} \times \dfrac{1}{3}\right)\right] + \left(\dfrac{2}{3} + \dfrac{1}{5}\right)$

Step 2 $\left[\dfrac{5}{1} \div \left(\dfrac{30}{4} \times \dfrac{1}{3}\right)\right] + \left(\dfrac{2}{3} + \dfrac{1}{5}\right) = \left[\dfrac{5}{1} \div \left(\dfrac{30 \times 1}{4 \times 3}\right)\right] + \left(\dfrac{(2 \times 5) + (1 \times 3)}{3 \times 5}\right)$

$= \left[\dfrac{5}{1} \div \left(\dfrac{30}{12}\right)\right] + \left(\dfrac{10 + 3}{15}\right) = \left[\dfrac{5}{1} \div \dfrac{30}{12}\right] + \left(\dfrac{13}{15}\right) = \left[\dfrac{5}{1} \times \dfrac{12}{30}\right] + \dfrac{13}{15} = \left[\dfrac{5 \times 12}{1 \times 30}\right] + \dfrac{13}{15}$

$= \left[\dfrac{60}{30}\right] + \dfrac{13}{15} = \dfrac{60}{30} + \dfrac{13}{15} = \dfrac{(60 \times 15) + (13 \times 30)}{30 \times 15} = \dfrac{900 + 390}{450} = \dfrac{1290}{450}$

Step 3 $\dfrac{1290}{450} = \dfrac{1290 \div 10}{450 \div 10} = \dfrac{129}{45} = \dfrac{129 \div 3}{45 \div 3} = \dfrac{43}{15}$

Step 4 $\dfrac{43}{15} = \boxed{2\dfrac{13}{15}}$

In general, integer fractions are added, subtracted, multiplied, and divided as in the following example cases which are followed by a specific example for each case:

Case I.

$$\left(\frac{a}{b} \times \frac{c}{d}\right) + \left(\frac{e}{f} \div \frac{g}{h}\right) = \left(\frac{a \times c}{b \times d}\right) + \left(\frac{e}{f} \times \frac{h}{g}\right) = \left(\frac{a \times c}{b \times d}\right) + \left(\frac{e \times h}{f \times g}\right) = \left(\frac{ac}{bd}\right) + \left(\frac{eh}{fg}\right) = \frac{ac}{bd} + \frac{eh}{fg}$$

$$= \frac{(ac \times fg) + (eh \times bd)}{bd \times fg} = \boxed{\frac{acfg + ehbd}{bdfg}}$$

Example 3.5-6

$$\left(\frac{3}{5} \times \frac{15}{6}\right) + \left(\frac{2}{8} \div \frac{1}{4}\right) = \left(\frac{\overset{1}{\cancel{3}} \times \overset{3}{\cancel{15}}}{\underset{1}{\cancel{5}} \times \underset{2}{\cancel{6}}}\right) + \left(\frac{2}{8} \times \frac{4}{1}\right) = \left(\frac{1 \times 3}{1 \times 2}\right) + \left(\frac{2 \times \overset{1}{\cancel{4}}}{\underset{2}{\cancel{8}} \times 1}\right) = \left(\frac{3}{2}\right) + \left(\frac{\overset{1}{\cancel{2}} \times 1}{\underset{1}{\cancel{2}} \times 1}\right) = \frac{3}{2} + \left(\frac{1 \times 1}{1 \times 1}\right)$$

$$= \boxed{\frac{3}{2} + \left(\frac{1}{1}\right)} = \boxed{\frac{3}{2} + \frac{1}{1}} = \boxed{\frac{(3 \times 1) + (1 \times 2)}{2 \times 1}} = \boxed{\frac{3+2}{2}} = \boxed{\frac{5}{2}} = \boxed{2\frac{1}{2}}$$

Case II.

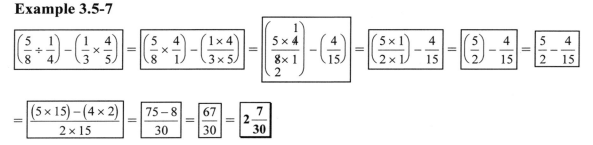

$$\boxed{\left(\frac{a}{b} \div \frac{c}{d}\right) - \left(\frac{e}{f} \times \frac{g}{h}\right)} = \boxed{\left(\frac{a}{b} \times \frac{d}{c}\right) - \left(\frac{e \times g}{f \times h}\right)} = \boxed{\left(\frac{a \times d}{b \times c}\right) - \left(\frac{e \times g}{f \times h}\right)} = \boxed{\left(\frac{ad}{bc}\right) - \left(\frac{eg}{fh}\right)} = \boxed{\frac{ad}{bc} - \frac{eg}{fh}}$$

$$= \boxed{\frac{(ad \times fh) - (eg \times bc)}{bc \times fh}} = \boxed{\frac{adfh - egbc}{bcfh}}$$

Example 3.5-7

$$\boxed{\left(\frac{5}{8} \div \frac{1}{4}\right) - \left(\frac{1}{3} \times \frac{4}{5}\right)} = \boxed{\left(\frac{5}{8} \times \frac{4}{1}\right) - \left(\frac{1 \times 4}{3 \times 5}\right)} = \boxed{\left(\frac{5 \times \overset{1}{4}}{\underset{2}{8} \times 1}\right) - \left(\frac{4}{15}\right)} = \boxed{\left(\frac{5 \times 1}{2 \times 1}\right) - \frac{4}{15}} = \boxed{\left(\frac{5}{2}\right) - \frac{4}{15}} = \boxed{\frac{5}{2} - \frac{4}{15}}$$

$$= \boxed{\frac{(5 \times 15) - (4 \times 2)}{2 \times 15}} = \boxed{\frac{75 - 8}{30}} = \boxed{\frac{67}{30}} = \boxed{2\frac{7}{30}}$$

Case III.

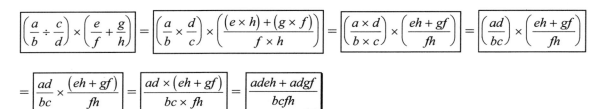

$$\boxed{\left(\frac{a}{b} \div \frac{c}{d}\right) \times \left(\frac{e}{f} + \frac{g}{h}\right)} = \boxed{\left(\frac{a}{b} \times \frac{d}{c}\right) \times \left(\frac{(e \times h) + (g \times f)}{f \times h}\right)} = \boxed{\left(\frac{a \times d}{b \times c}\right) \times \left(\frac{eh + gf}{fh}\right)} = \boxed{\left(\frac{ad}{bc}\right) \times \left(\frac{eh + gf}{fh}\right)}$$

$$= \boxed{\frac{ad}{bc} \times \frac{(eh + gf)}{fh}} = \boxed{\frac{ad \times (eh + gf)}{bc \times fh}} = \boxed{\frac{adeh + adgf}{bcfh}}$$

Example 3.5-8

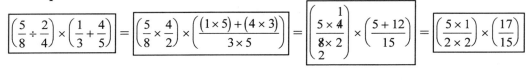

$$\boxed{\left(\frac{5}{8} \div \frac{2}{4}\right) \times \left(\frac{1}{3} + \frac{4}{5}\right)} = \boxed{\left(\frac{5}{8} \times \frac{4}{2}\right) \times \left(\frac{(1 \times 5) + (4 \times 3)}{3 \times 5}\right)} = \boxed{\left(\frac{5 \times \overset{1}{4}}{\underset{2}{8} \times 2}\right) \times \left(\frac{5 + 12}{15}\right)} = \boxed{\left(\frac{5 \times 1}{2 \times 2}\right) \times \left(\frac{17}{15}\right)}$$

$$= \boxed{\left(\frac{5}{4}\right) \times \left(\frac{17}{15}\right)} = \boxed{\frac{5}{4} \times \frac{17}{15}} = \boxed{\frac{\overset{1}{5} \times 17}{4 \times \underset{3}{15}}} = \boxed{\frac{1 \times 17}{4 \times 3}} = \boxed{\frac{17}{12}} = \boxed{1\frac{5}{12}}$$

Case IV.

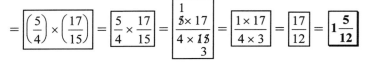

$$\boxed{\left(\frac{a}{b} - \frac{c}{d}\right) \div \left(\frac{e}{f} \times \frac{g}{h}\right)} = \boxed{\left(\frac{(a \times d) - (c \times b)}{b \times d}\right) \div \left(\frac{e \times g}{f \times h}\right)} = \boxed{\left(\frac{ad - cb}{bd}\right) \div \left(\frac{eg}{fh}\right)} = \boxed{\left(\frac{ad - cb}{bd}\right) \times \left(\frac{fh}{eg}\right)}$$

$$= \left|\frac{(ad - cb)}{bd} \times \frac{fh}{eg}\right| = \left|\frac{(ad - cb) \times fh}{bd \times eg}\right| = \boxed{\frac{adfh - cbfh}{bdeg}}$$

Example 3.5-9

$$\boxed{\left(\frac{5}{2} - \frac{1}{3}\right) \div \left(\frac{2}{5} \times \frac{10}{16}\right)} = \boxed{\left(\frac{(5 \times 3) - (1 \times 2)}{2 \times 3}\right) \div \left(\frac{\overset{1}{2} \times \overset{2}{10}}{\underset{1}{5} \times \underset{8}{16}}\right)} = \boxed{\left(\frac{15 - 2}{6}\right) \div \left(\frac{1 \times 2}{1 \times 8}\right)} = \boxed{\left(\frac{13}{6}\right) \div \left(\frac{1 \times 1}{1 \times 4}\right)}$$

$$= \boxed{\left(\frac{13}{6}\right) \div \left(\frac{1}{4}\right)} = \boxed{\frac{13}{6} \div \frac{1}{4}} = \boxed{\frac{13}{6} \times \frac{4}{1}} = \boxed{\frac{13 \times \overset{2}{4}}{\underset{3}{6} \times 1}} = \boxed{\frac{13 \times 2}{3 \times 1}} = \boxed{\frac{26}{3}} = \boxed{\mathbf{8\frac{2}{3}}}$$

Case V.

$$\boxed{\left(\frac{a}{b} - \frac{c}{d}\right) + \left(\frac{e}{f} \times \frac{g}{h}\right)} = \boxed{\left(\frac{(a \times d) - (c \times b)}{b \times d}\right) + \left(\frac{e \times g}{f \times h}\right)} = \boxed{\left(\frac{ad - cb}{bd}\right) + \left(\frac{eg}{fh}\right)} = \boxed{\frac{(ad - cb)}{bd} + \frac{eg}{fh}}$$

$$= \boxed{\frac{[(ad - cb) \times fh] + (eg \times bd)}{bd \times fh}} = \boxed{\frac{[adfh - cbfh] + egbd}{bdfh}} = \boxed{\frac{adfh - cbfh + egbd}{bdfh}}$$

Example 3.5-10

$$\boxed{\left(\frac{5}{4} - \frac{1}{3}\right) + \left(\frac{3}{5} \times \frac{4}{7}\right)} = \boxed{\left(\frac{(5 \times 3) - (1 \times 4)}{4 \times 3}\right) + \left(\frac{3 \times 4}{5 \times 7}\right)} = \boxed{\left(\frac{15 - 4}{12}\right) + \left(\frac{12}{35}\right)} = \boxed{\left(\frac{11}{12}\right) + \frac{12}{35}} = \boxed{\frac{11}{12} + \frac{12}{35}}$$

$$= \boxed{\frac{(11 \times 35) + (12 \times 12)}{12 \times 35}} = \boxed{\frac{385 + 144}{420}} = \boxed{\frac{529}{420}} = \boxed{\mathbf{1\frac{109}{420}}}$$

The following examples further illustrate how to add, subtract, multiply, and divide integer fractions:

Example 3.5-11

$$\boxed{\left(\frac{2}{3} \div \frac{5}{6}\right) \times \frac{3}{5}} = \boxed{\left(\frac{2}{3} \times \frac{6}{5}\right) \times \frac{3}{5}} = \boxed{\left(\frac{2 \times \overset{2}{6}}{\underset{1}{3} \times 5}\right) \times \frac{3}{5}} = \boxed{\left(\frac{2 \times 2}{1 \times 5}\right) \times \frac{3}{5}} = \boxed{\left(\frac{4}{5}\right) \times \frac{3}{5}} = \boxed{\frac{4}{5} \times \frac{3}{5}} = \boxed{\frac{4 \times 3}{5 \times 5}} = \boxed{\mathbf{\frac{12}{25}}}$$

Example 3.5-12

$$\boxed{25 \times \left(\frac{4}{7} + \frac{8}{10}\right)} = \boxed{\frac{25}{1} \times \left(\frac{4}{7} + \frac{\overset{4}{8}}{\underset{5}{10}}\right)} = \boxed{\frac{25}{1} \times \left(\frac{4}{7} + \frac{4}{5}\right)} = \boxed{\frac{25}{1} \times \left(\frac{(4 \times 5) + (4 \times 7)}{7 \times 5}\right)} = \boxed{\frac{25}{1} \times \left(\frac{20 + 28}{35}\right)}$$

$$= \boxed{\frac{25}{1} \times \left(\frac{48}{35}\right)} = \boxed{\frac{25}{1} \times \frac{48}{35}} = \boxed{\frac{\overset{5}{\cancel{25}} \times 48}{1 \times \underset{7}{\cancel{35}}}} = \boxed{\frac{5 \times 48}{1 \times 7}} = \boxed{\frac{240}{7}} = \boxed{34\frac{2}{7}}$$

Example 3.5-13

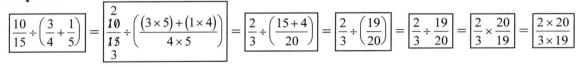

$$= \boxed{\frac{40}{57}}$$

Example 3.5-14

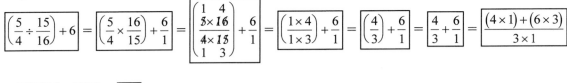

$$= \boxed{\frac{4+18}{3}} = \boxed{\frac{22}{3}} = \boxed{7\frac{1}{3}}$$

Example 3.5-15

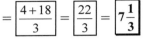

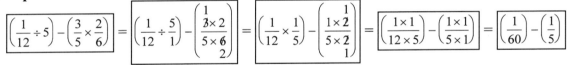

$$= \boxed{\frac{1}{60} - \frac{1}{5}} = \boxed{\frac{(1 \times 5) - (1 \times 60)}{60 \times 5}} = \boxed{\frac{5 - 60}{300}} = \boxed{\frac{\overset{-11}{\cancel{-55}}}{\underset{60}{\cancel{300}}}} = \boxed{-\frac{11}{60}}$$

Example 3.5-16

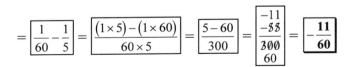

$$= \boxed{\left(\frac{4}{3}\right) \times \left(\frac{37}{20}\right)} = \boxed{\frac{4}{3} \times \frac{37}{20}} = \boxed{\frac{1}{3 \times \underset{5}{\cancel{20}}}} = \boxed{\frac{1 \times 37}{3 \times 5}} = \boxed{\frac{37}{15}} = \boxed{2\frac{7}{15}}$$

Example 3.5-17

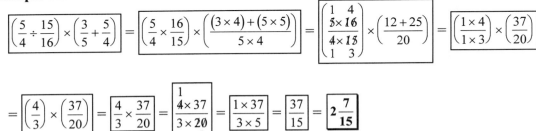

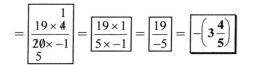

$$= \boxed{\dfrac{\overset{1}{19 \times 4}}{\underset{5}{2\!\!\!\!/0 \times -1}}} = \boxed{\dfrac{19 \times 1}{5 \times -1}} = \boxed{\dfrac{19}{-5}} = \boxed{-\left(3\dfrac{4}{5}\right)}$$

Example 3.5-18

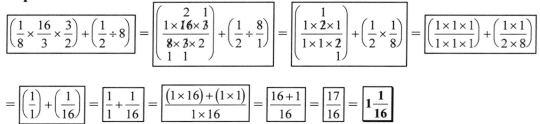

$$= \boxed{\left(\dfrac{1}{1}\right) + \left(\dfrac{1}{16}\right)} = \boxed{\dfrac{1}{1} + \dfrac{1}{16}} = \boxed{\dfrac{(1 \times 16) + (1 \times 1)}{1 \times 16}} = \boxed{\dfrac{16+1}{16}} = \boxed{\dfrac{17}{16}} = \boxed{\mathbf{1\dfrac{1}{16}}}$$

Example 3.5-19

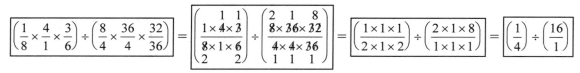

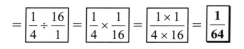

$$= \boxed{\dfrac{1}{4} \div \dfrac{16}{1}} = \boxed{\dfrac{1}{4} \times \dfrac{1}{16}} = \boxed{\dfrac{1 \times 1}{4 \times 16}} = \boxed{\dfrac{\mathbf{1}}{\mathbf{64}}}$$

Example 3.5-20

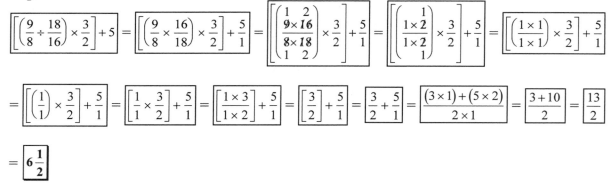

$$= \boxed{\left[\left(\dfrac{1}{1}\right) \times \dfrac{3}{2}\right] + \dfrac{5}{1}} = \boxed{\left[\dfrac{1}{1} \times \dfrac{3}{2}\right] + \dfrac{5}{1}} = \boxed{\left[\dfrac{1 \times 3}{1 \times 2}\right] + \dfrac{5}{1}} = \boxed{\dfrac{3}{2} + \dfrac{5}{1}} = \boxed{\dfrac{3}{2} + \dfrac{5}{1}} = \boxed{\dfrac{(3 \times 1) + (5 \times 2)}{2 \times 1}} = \boxed{\dfrac{3+10}{2}} = \boxed{\dfrac{13}{2}}$$

$$= \boxed{6\dfrac{1}{2}}$$

Example 3.5-21

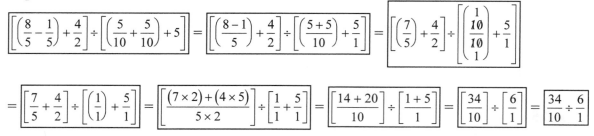

$$= \boxed{\left[\dfrac{7}{5} + \dfrac{4}{2}\right] \div \left[\left(\dfrac{1}{1}\right) + \dfrac{5}{1}\right]} = \boxed{\left[\dfrac{(7 \times 2) + (4 \times 5)}{5 \times 2}\right] \div \left[\dfrac{1}{1} + \dfrac{5}{1}\right]} = \boxed{\left[\dfrac{14+20}{10}\right] \div \left[\dfrac{1+5}{1}\right]} = \boxed{\left[\dfrac{34}{10}\right] \div \left[\dfrac{6}{1}\right]} = \boxed{\dfrac{34}{10} \div \dfrac{6}{1}}$$

$$= \boxed{\frac{34}{10} \times \frac{1}{6}} = \boxed{\frac{\overset{17}{\cancel{34}} \times 1}{10 \times \underset{3}{\cancel{6}}}} = \boxed{\frac{17 \times 1}{10 \times 3}} = \boxed{\frac{17}{30}}$$

Section 3.5 Exercises - Use the following integer fractions to perform the indicated operations:

1. $\left(\dfrac{5}{4} \times \dfrac{8}{1}\right) \div \dfrac{2}{3} =$

2. $\left(\dfrac{3}{4} \div 12\right) \times \dfrac{4}{15} =$

3. $\dfrac{3}{5} \times \left(\dfrac{2}{4} - \dfrac{1}{3}\right) =$

4. $\left(\dfrac{1}{5} \div \dfrac{4}{15}\right) \times \dfrac{2}{5} =$

5. $\left(\dfrac{4}{8} + 4\right) \div \left(\dfrac{2}{8} - \dfrac{1}{3}\right) =$

6. $\left(\dfrac{6}{5} - \dfrac{3}{4}\right) \times \left(\dfrac{4}{5} - \dfrac{1}{5}\right) =$

7. $\left(\dfrac{5}{4} \times \dfrac{8}{1}\right) \div \left(\dfrac{4}{5} \div \dfrac{8}{15}\right) =$

8. $\left(\dfrac{1}{6} \times \dfrac{12}{5} \times \dfrac{15}{20}\right) + \left(\dfrac{2}{3} - \dfrac{1}{5}\right) =$

9. $\left[\dfrac{2}{5} + \left(\dfrac{2}{4} + \dfrac{1}{2}\right)\right] \div \dfrac{1}{10} =$

10. $\left[\left(\dfrac{2}{5} - \dfrac{3}{5}\right) \times \left(12 - \dfrac{1}{3}\right)\right] - \dfrac{3}{2} =$

Chapter 4 - Decimal Fractions

The objective of this chapter is to improve the student's ability in solving decimal fractions. Decimal fractions are another class of fractions where the numerator and the denominator are decimal numbers. The steps used to solve decimal fractions with examples illustrating the steps as to how to add (Section 4.1), subtract (Section 4.2), multiply (Section 4.3), and divide (Section 4.4) two or more decimal fractions are given. Section 4.5 combines the mathematical operations using decimal fractions. In addition, for completeness, the general algebraic approach in solving decimal fractions is given in each section. The student, depending on his or her grade level and ability, can skip the algebraic approach to decimal fractions and only learn the techniques that are followed by examples. Focusing on the examples, and the steps shown to solve each problem, should be adequate to teach the student the mechanics of how decimal fractions are mathematically operated on.

4.1 Adding Decimal Fractions

Decimal fractions $\left(\dfrac{a \times 10^{-k_1}}{b \times 10^{-k_2}} \right)$, i.e., fractions where (a) and (b) are integer numbers and (k_1) and (k_2) are equal to the number of decimal places are added as in the following cases:

Case I Adding Two or More Decimal Fractions With Common Denominators
Decimal fractions with two or more common denominators are added using the steps given as in each case below:

Case I-A *Add two decimal fractions with common denominators using the following steps:*

Step 1 Add the decimal fractions in a similar way as integer fractions with common denominators are added (see Section 3.1, Case I-A).

Step 2 Change the decimal fractions to integer fractions (see Section 2.4).

Step 3 Simplify the fraction to its lowest term (see Section 2.3).

Step 4 Change the improper fraction to a mixed fraction if the fraction obtained from Step 3 is an improper fraction (see Section 2.2).

The following examples show the steps as to how two decimal fractions with common denominators are added:

Example 4.1-1

$$\boxed{\dfrac{0.29}{0.5} + \dfrac{0.8}{0.5}} =$$

Solution:

Step 1 $\boxed{\dfrac{0.29}{0.5} + \dfrac{0.8}{0.5}} = \boxed{\dfrac{0.29 + 0.8}{0.5}} = \boxed{\dfrac{1.09}{0.5}}$

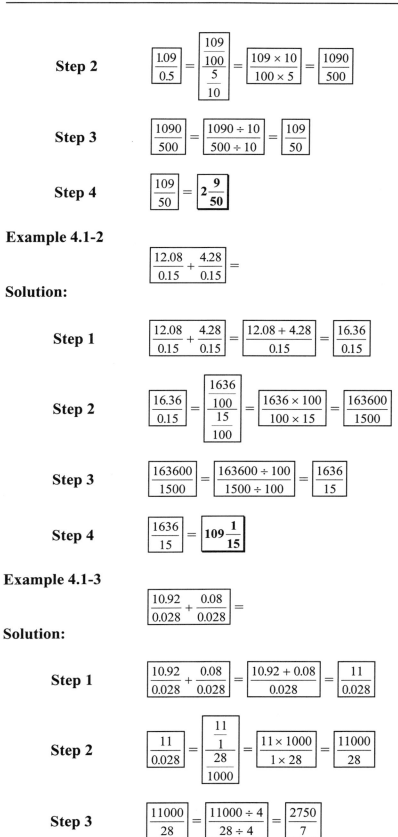

Step 2
$$\frac{1.09}{0.5} = \frac{\frac{109}{100}}{\frac{5}{10}} = \frac{109 \times 10}{100 \times 5} = \frac{1090}{500}$$

Step 3
$$\frac{1090}{500} = \frac{1090 \div 10}{500 \div 10} = \frac{109}{50}$$

Step 4
$$\frac{109}{50} = 2\frac{9}{50}$$

Example 4.1-2
$$\frac{12.08}{0.15} + \frac{4.28}{0.15} =$$

Solution:

Step 1
$$\frac{12.08}{0.15} + \frac{4.28}{0.15} = \frac{12.08 + 4.28}{0.15} = \frac{16.36}{0.15}$$

Step 2
$$\frac{16.36}{0.15} = \frac{\frac{1636}{100}}{\frac{15}{100}} = \frac{1636 \times 100}{100 \times 15} = \frac{163600}{1500}$$

Step 3
$$\frac{163600}{1500} = \frac{163600 \div 100}{1500 \div 100} = \frac{1636}{15}$$

Step 4
$$\frac{1636}{15} = 109\frac{1}{15}$$

Example 4.1-3
$$\frac{10.92}{0.028} + \frac{0.08}{0.028} =$$

Solution:

Step 1
$$\frac{10.92}{0.028} + \frac{0.08}{0.028} = \frac{10.92 + 0.08}{0.028} = \frac{11}{0.028}$$

Step 2
$$\frac{11}{0.028} = \frac{\frac{11}{1}}{\frac{28}{1000}} = \frac{11 \times 1000}{1 \times 28} = \frac{11000}{28}$$

Step 3
$$\frac{11000}{28} = \frac{11000 \div 4}{28 \div 4} = \frac{2750}{7}$$

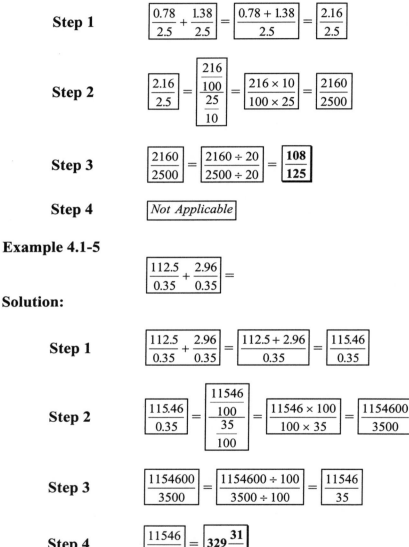

Step 4 $\dfrac{2750}{7} = \boxed{392\dfrac{6}{7}}$

Example 4.1-4

$\dfrac{0.78}{2.5} + \dfrac{1.38}{2.5} =$

Solution:

Step 1 $\dfrac{0.78}{2.5} + \dfrac{1.38}{2.5} = \dfrac{0.78 + 1.38}{2.5} = \dfrac{2.16}{2.5}$

Step 2 $\dfrac{2.16}{2.5} = \dfrac{\dfrac{216}{100}}{\dfrac{25}{10}} = \dfrac{216 \times 10}{100 \times 25} = \dfrac{2160}{2500}$

Step 3 $\dfrac{2160}{2500} = \dfrac{2160 \div 20}{2500 \div 20} = \boxed{\dfrac{108}{125}}$

Step 4 $\boxed{Not\ Applicable}$

Example 4.1-5

$\dfrac{112.5}{0.35} + \dfrac{2.96}{0.35} =$

Solution:

Step 1 $\dfrac{112.5}{0.35} + \dfrac{2.96}{0.35} = \dfrac{112.5 + 2.96}{0.35} = \dfrac{115.46}{0.35}$

Step 2 $\dfrac{115.46}{0.35} = \dfrac{\dfrac{11546}{100}}{\dfrac{35}{100}} = \dfrac{11546 \times 100}{100 \times 35} = \dfrac{1154600}{3500}$

Step 3 $\dfrac{1154600}{3500} = \dfrac{1154600 \div 100}{3500 \div 100} = \dfrac{11546}{35}$

Step 4 $\dfrac{11546}{35} = \boxed{329\dfrac{31}{35}}$

In general two decimal fractions with a common denominator are added in the following way:

$$\dfrac{a \times 10^{-k_1}}{d \times 10^{-k_3}} + \dfrac{b \times 10^{-k_2}}{d \times 10^{-k_3}} = \dfrac{a \times 10^{-k_1} + b \times 10^{-k_2}}{d \times 10^{-k_3}}$$

Let $\boxed{A_1 = a \times 10^{-k_1}}$, $\boxed{A_2 = b \times 10^{-k_2}}$, and $\boxed{A_3 = d \times 10^{-k_3}}$, then

$$\boxed{\dfrac{a \times 10^{-k_1} + b \times 10^{-k_2}}{d \times 10^{-k_3}}} = \boxed{\dfrac{A_1}{A_3} + \dfrac{A_2}{A_3}} = \boxed{\dfrac{A_1 + A_2}{A_3}}$$

Example 4.1-6

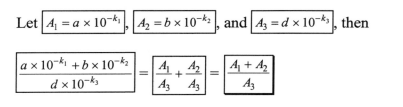

$$\boxed{\dfrac{5 \times 10^{-2}}{8 \times 10^{-1}} + \dfrac{2 \times 10^{-1}}{8 \times 10^{-1}}} = \boxed{\dfrac{0.05}{0.8} + \dfrac{0.2}{0.8}} = \boxed{\dfrac{0.05 + 0.2}{0.8}} = \boxed{\dfrac{0.25}{0.8}} = \boxed{\dfrac{\frac{25}{100}}{\frac{8}{10}}} = \boxed{\dfrac{25 \times 10}{100 \times 8}} = \boxed{\dfrac{250}{800}} = \boxed{\dfrac{5}{16}}$$

Case I-B   *Add three decimal fractions with common denominators using the following steps:*

Step 1   Add the decimal fractions in a similar way as integer fractions with common denominators are added (see Section 3.1, Case I-B).

Step 2   Change the decimal fractions to integer fractions (see Section 2.4).

Step 3   Simplify the fraction to its lowest term (see Section 2.3).

Step 4   Change the improper fraction to a mixed fraction if the fraction obtained from Step 3 is an improper fraction (see Section 2.2).

The following examples show the steps as to how three decimal fractions with common denominators are added:

Example 4.1-7

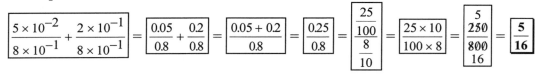

$$\boxed{\dfrac{0.32}{0.5} + \dfrac{0.8}{0.5} + \dfrac{0.04}{0.5}} =$$

Solution:

Step 1 $\boxed{\dfrac{0.32}{0.5} + \dfrac{0.8}{0.5} + \dfrac{0.04}{0.5}} = \boxed{\dfrac{0.32 + 0.8 + 0.04}{0.5}} = \boxed{\dfrac{1.16}{0.5}}$

Step 2 $\boxed{\dfrac{1.16}{0.5}} = \boxed{\dfrac{\frac{116}{100}}{\frac{5}{10}}} = \boxed{\dfrac{116 \times 10}{100 \times 5}} = \boxed{\dfrac{1160}{500}}$

Step 3 $\boxed{\dfrac{1160}{500}} = \boxed{\dfrac{1160 \div 20}{500 \div 20}} = \boxed{\dfrac{58}{25}}$

Step 4 $\boxed{\dfrac{58}{25}} = \boxed{2\dfrac{8}{25}}$

Example 4.1-8

$$\boxed{\dfrac{12.6}{0.4} + \dfrac{0.6}{0.4} + \dfrac{5.1}{0.4}} =$$

Solution:

Step 1
$$\boxed{\dfrac{12.6}{0.4} + \dfrac{0.6}{0.4} + \dfrac{5.1}{0.4}} = \boxed{\dfrac{12.6 + 0.6 + 5.1}{0.4}} = \boxed{\dfrac{18.3}{0.4}}$$

Step 2
$$\boxed{\dfrac{18.3}{0.4}} = \boxed{\dfrac{\dfrac{183}{10}}{\dfrac{4}{10}}} = \boxed{\dfrac{183 \times 10}{10 \times 4}} = \boxed{\dfrac{1830}{40}}$$

Step 3
$$\boxed{\dfrac{1830}{40}} = \boxed{\dfrac{1830 \div 10}{40 \div 10}} = \boxed{\dfrac{183}{4}}$$

Step 4
$$\boxed{\dfrac{183}{4}} = \boxed{45\dfrac{3}{4}}$$

Example 4.1-9
$$\boxed{\dfrac{2.32}{0.45} + \dfrac{0.8}{0.45} + \dfrac{0.2}{0.45}} =$$

Solution:

Step 1
$$\boxed{\dfrac{2.32}{0.45} + \dfrac{0.8}{0.45} + \dfrac{0.2}{0.45}} = \boxed{\dfrac{2.32 + 0.8 + 0.2}{0.45}} = \boxed{\dfrac{3.32}{0.45}}$$

Step 2
$$\boxed{\dfrac{3.32}{0.45}} = \boxed{\dfrac{\dfrac{332}{100}}{\dfrac{45}{100}}} = \boxed{\dfrac{332 \times 100}{100 \times 45}} = \boxed{\dfrac{33200}{4500}}$$

Step 3
$$\boxed{\dfrac{33200}{4500}} = \boxed{\dfrac{33200 \div 100}{4500 \div 100}} = \boxed{\dfrac{332}{45}}$$

Step 4
$$\boxed{\dfrac{332}{45}} = \boxed{7\dfrac{17}{45}}$$

Example 4.1-10
$$\boxed{\dfrac{25.56}{16.4} + \dfrac{1.35}{16.4} + \dfrac{20.2}{16.4}} =$$

Solution:

Step 1
$$\boxed{\dfrac{25.56}{16.4} + \dfrac{1.35}{16.4} + \dfrac{20.2}{16.4}} = \boxed{\dfrac{25.56 + 1.35 + 20.2}{16.4}} = \boxed{\dfrac{47.11}{16.4}}$$

Step 2 $\dfrac{47.11}{16.4} = \dfrac{\dfrac{4711}{100}}{\dfrac{164}{10}} = \dfrac{4711 \times 10}{100 \times 164} = \dfrac{47110}{16400}$

Step 3 $\dfrac{47110}{16400} = \dfrac{47110 \div 10}{16400 \div 10} = \dfrac{4711}{1640}$

Step 4 $\dfrac{4711}{1640} = \boxed{2\dfrac{1431}{1640}}$

Example 4.1-11

$$\dfrac{1.45}{1.35} + \dfrac{0.19}{1.35} + \dfrac{0.234}{1.35} =$$

Solution:

Step 1 $\dfrac{1.45}{1.35} + \dfrac{0.19}{1.35} + \dfrac{0.234}{1.35} = \dfrac{1.45 + 0.19 + 0.234}{1.35} = \dfrac{1.874}{1.35}$

Step 2 $\dfrac{1.874}{1.35} = \dfrac{\dfrac{1874}{1000}}{\dfrac{135}{100}} = \dfrac{1874 \times 100}{1000 \times 135} = \dfrac{187400}{135000}$

Step 3 $\dfrac{187400}{135000} = \dfrac{187400 \div 100}{135000 \div 100} = \dfrac{1874}{1350} = \dfrac{1874 \div 2}{1350 \div 2} = \dfrac{937}{675}$

Step 4 $\dfrac{937}{675} = \boxed{1\dfrac{262}{675}}$

In general, three decimal fractions with a common denominator are added in the following way:

$$\dfrac{a \times 10^{-k_1}}{d \times 10^{-k_4}} + \dfrac{b \times 10^{-k_2}}{d \times 10^{-k_4}} + \dfrac{c \times 10^{-k_3}}{d \times 10^{-k_4}} = \dfrac{a \times 10^{-k_1} + b \times 10^{-k_2} + c \times 10^{-k_3}}{d \times 10^{-k_4}}$$

Let $\boxed{A_1 = a \times 10^{-k_1}}$, $\boxed{A_2 = b \times 10^{-k_2}}$, $\boxed{A_3 = c \times 10^{-k_3}}$, and $\boxed{A_4 = d \times 10^{-k_4}}$, then

$$\dfrac{a \times 10^{-k_1} + b \times 10^{-k_2} + c \times 10^{-k_3}}{d \times 10^{-k_4}} = \dfrac{A_1}{A_4} + \dfrac{A_2}{A_4} + \dfrac{A_3}{A_4} = \boxed{\dfrac{A_1 + A_2 + A_3}{A_4}}$$

Example 4.1-12

$$\dfrac{15 \times 10^{-2}}{124 \times 10^{-3}} + \dfrac{3 \times 10^{-1}}{124 \times 10^{-3}} + \dfrac{4 \times 10^{-2}}{124 \times 10^{-3}} = \dfrac{0.15}{0.124} + \dfrac{0.3}{0.124} + \dfrac{0.04}{0.124} = \dfrac{0.15 + 0.3 + 0.04}{0.124} = \dfrac{0.49}{0.124} = \dfrac{\dfrac{49}{100}}{\dfrac{124}{1000}}$$

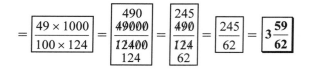

Case II   Adding Two or More Decimal Fractions Without a Common Denominator

Two or more decimal fractions without a common denominator are added using the steps given as in each case below:

Case II A   *Add two decimal fractions without a common denominator using the following steps:*

Step 1   a. Change the decimal fractions to integer fractions (see Section 2.4).

b. Change the decimal number $\left(a \times 10^{-k}\right)$ to an integer fraction of the form $\left(\dfrac{a}{10^k}\right)$,

e.g., change 0.05 to $\dfrac{5}{100}$.

Step 2   Add the integer fractions (see Section 3.1, Case II-A).

Step 3   Simplify the fraction to its lowest term (see Section 2.3).

Step 4   Change the improper fraction to a mixed fraction if the fraction obtained from Step 3 is an improper fraction (see Section 2.2).

The following examples show the steps as to how two decimal fractions without a common denominators are added:

Example 4.1-13

$$\boxed{\dfrac{0.5}{0.01} + \dfrac{0.3}{0.8}} =$$

Solution:

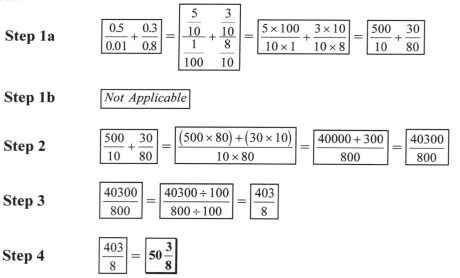

Example 4.1-14

$$\boxed{\dfrac{10.8}{0.2} + 12.5} =$$

Solution:

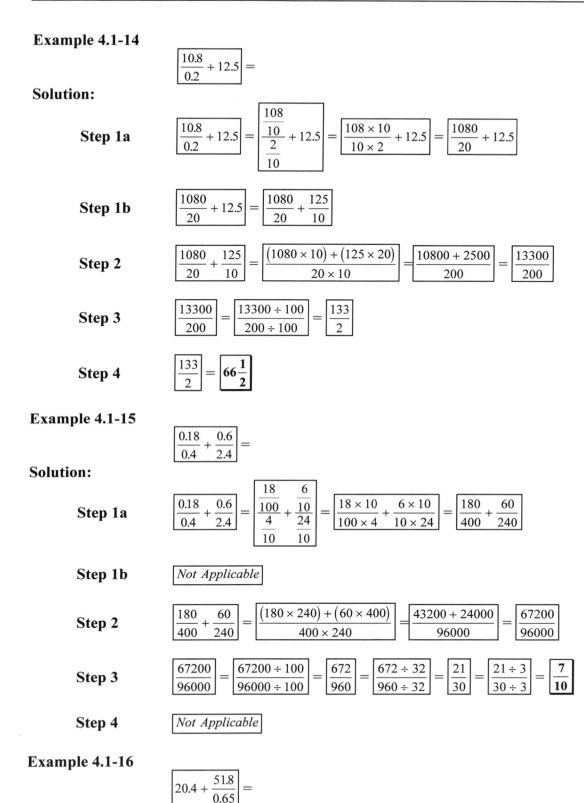

Step 1a $\boxed{\dfrac{10.8}{0.2} + 12.5} = \boxed{\dfrac{\dfrac{108}{10}}{\dfrac{2}{10}} + 12.5} = \boxed{\dfrac{108 \times 10}{10 \times 2} + 12.5} = \boxed{\dfrac{1080}{20} + 12.5}$

Step 1b $\boxed{\dfrac{1080}{20} + 12.5} = \boxed{\dfrac{1080}{20} + \dfrac{125}{10}}$

Step 2 $\boxed{\dfrac{1080}{20} + \dfrac{125}{10}} = \boxed{\dfrac{(1080 \times 10) + (125 \times 20)}{20 \times 10}} = \boxed{\dfrac{10800 + 2500}{200}} = \boxed{\dfrac{13300}{200}}$

Step 3 $\boxed{\dfrac{13300}{200}} = \boxed{\dfrac{13300 \div 100}{200 \div 100}} = \boxed{\dfrac{133}{2}}$

Step 4 $\boxed{\dfrac{133}{2}} = \boxed{\mathbf{66\dfrac{1}{2}}}$

Example 4.1-15

$$\boxed{\dfrac{0.18}{0.4} + \dfrac{0.6}{2.4}} =$$

Solution:

Step 1a $\boxed{\dfrac{0.18}{0.4} + \dfrac{0.6}{2.4}} = \boxed{\dfrac{\dfrac{18}{100}}{\dfrac{4}{10}} + \dfrac{\dfrac{6}{10}}{\dfrac{24}{10}}} = \boxed{\dfrac{18 \times 10}{100 \times 4} + \dfrac{6 \times 10}{10 \times 24}} = \boxed{\dfrac{180}{400} + \dfrac{60}{240}}$

Step 1b $\boxed{Not\ Applicable}$

Step 2 $\boxed{\dfrac{180}{400} + \dfrac{60}{240}} = \boxed{\dfrac{(180 \times 240) + (60 \times 400)}{400 \times 240}} = \boxed{\dfrac{43200 + 24000}{96000}} = \boxed{\dfrac{67200}{96000}}$

Step 3 $\boxed{\dfrac{67200}{96000}} = \boxed{\dfrac{67200 \div 100}{96000 \div 100}} = \boxed{\dfrac{672}{960}} = \boxed{\dfrac{672 \div 32}{960 \div 32}} = \boxed{\dfrac{21}{30}} = \boxed{\dfrac{21 \div 3}{30 \div 3}} = \boxed{\mathbf{\dfrac{7}{10}}}$

Step 4 $\boxed{Not\ Applicable}$

Example 4.1-16

$$\boxed{20.4 + \dfrac{51.8}{0.65}} =$$

Solution:

Step 1a
$$\boxed{20.4 + \frac{51.8}{0.65}} = \boxed{20.4 + \frac{\frac{518}{10}}{\frac{65}{100}}} = \boxed{20.4 + \frac{518 \times 100}{10 \times 65}} = \boxed{20.4 + \frac{51800}{650}}$$

Step 1b
$$\boxed{20.4 + \frac{51800}{650}} = \boxed{\frac{204}{10} + \frac{51800}{650}}$$

Step 2
$$\boxed{\frac{204}{10} + \frac{51800}{650}} = \boxed{\frac{(204 \times 650) + (51800 \times 10)}{10 \times 650}} = \boxed{\frac{132600 + 518000}{6500}}$$

$$= \boxed{\frac{650600}{6500}}$$

Step 3
$$\boxed{\frac{650600}{6500}} = \boxed{\frac{650600 \div 100}{6500 \div 100}} = \boxed{\frac{6506}{65}}$$

Step 4
$$\boxed{\frac{6506}{65}} = \boxed{\mathbf{100\frac{6}{65}}}$$

Example 4.1-17
$$\boxed{\frac{24.5}{0.2} + \frac{10.8}{0.08}} =$$

Solution:

Step 1a
$$\boxed{\frac{24.5}{0.2} + \frac{10.8}{0.08}} = \boxed{\frac{\frac{245}{10}}{\frac{2}{10}} + \frac{\frac{108}{10}}{\frac{8}{100}}} = \boxed{\frac{245 \times 10}{10 \times 2} + \frac{108 \times 100}{10 \times 8}} = \boxed{\frac{2450}{20} + \frac{10800}{80}}$$

Step 1b
$$\boxed{\textit{Not Applicable}}$$

Step 2
$$\boxed{\frac{2450}{20} + \frac{10800}{80}} = \boxed{\frac{(2450 \times 80) + (10800 \times 20)}{20 \times 80}} = \boxed{\frac{196000 + 216000}{1600}}$$

$$= \boxed{\frac{412000}{1600}}$$

Step 3
$$\boxed{\frac{412000}{1600}} = \boxed{\frac{412000 \div 400}{1600 \div 400}} = \boxed{\frac{1030}{4}} = \boxed{\frac{1030 \div 2}{4 \div 2}} = \boxed{\frac{515}{2}}$$

Step 4
$$\boxed{\frac{515}{2}} = \boxed{\mathbf{257\frac{1}{2}}}$$

In general, two decimal fractions without a common denominator are added in the following way:

$$\frac{a \times 10^{-k_1}}{b \times 10^{-k_2}} + \frac{c \times 10^{-k_3}}{d \times 10^{-k_4}} = \frac{\left[\left(a \times 10^{-k_1}\right) \times \left(d \times 10^{-k_4}\right)\right] + \left[\left(c \times 10^{-k_3}\right) \times \left(b \times 10^{-k_2}\right)\right]}{\left(b \times 10^{-k_2}\right) \times \left(d \times 10^{-k_4}\right)}$$

Let $\boxed{A_1 = a \times 10^{-k_1}}$, $\boxed{A_2 = b \times 10^{-k_2}}$, $\boxed{A_3 = c \times 10^{-k_3}}$, and $\boxed{A_4 = d \times 10^{-k_4}}$, then

$$\frac{\left[\left(a \times 10^{-k_1}\right) \times \left(d \times 10^{-k_4}\right)\right] + \left[\left(c \times 10^{-k_3}\right) \times \left(b \times 10^{-k_2}\right)\right]}{\left(b \times 10^{-k_2}\right) \times \left(d \times 10^{-k_4}\right)} = \frac{\left[A_1 \times A_4\right] + \left[A_3 \times A_2\right]}{A_2 \times A_4} = \frac{\left[A_1 A_4\right] + \left[A_3 A_2\right]}{A_2 A_4}$$

$$= \boxed{\frac{A_1 A_4 + A_3 A_2}{A_2 A_4}}$$

Example 4.1-18

$$\frac{2 \times 10^{-2}}{3 \times 10^{-1}} + \frac{4 \times 10^{-1}}{55 \times 10^{-2}} = \frac{0.02}{0.3} + \frac{0.4}{0.55} = \frac{\frac{2}{100}}{\frac{3}{10}} + \frac{\frac{4}{10}}{\frac{55}{100}} = \frac{2 \times 10}{100 \times 3} + \frac{4 \times 100}{10 \times 55} = \frac{20}{300} + \frac{400}{550}$$

$$= \frac{(20 \times 550) + (400 \times 300)}{300 \times 550} = \frac{11000 + 120000}{165000} = \frac{131000}{165000} = \boxed{\frac{131}{165}}$$

Case II-B *Add three decimal fractions without a common denominator using the following steps:*

Step 1   Use parentheses to group the first and second fractions.

Step 2   a. Change the decimal fractions to integer fractions (see Section 2.4).

b. Change the decimal number $\left(a \times 10^{-k}\right)$ to an integer fraction of the form $\left(\frac{a}{10^k}\right)$,

e.g., change 1.5 to $\frac{15}{10}$.

Step 3   Add the integer fractions (see Section 3.1, Case II-B).

Step 4   Simplify the fraction to its lowest term (see Section 2.3).

Step 5   Change the improper fraction to a mixed fraction if the fraction obtained from Step 4 is an improper fraction (see Section 2.2).

The following examples show the steps as to how three decimal fractions without a common denominators are added:

Example 4.1-19

$$\boxed{0.6 + \frac{0.8}{0.03} + \frac{1.5}{0.5}} =$$

Solution:

Step 1
$$0.6 + \frac{0.8}{0.03} + \frac{1.5}{0.5} = \left(0.6 + \frac{0.8}{0.03}\right) + \frac{1.5}{0.5}$$

Step 2a
$$\left(0.6 + \frac{0.8}{0.03}\right) + \frac{1.5}{0.5} = \left(0.6 + \frac{\frac{8}{10}}{\frac{3}{100}}\right) + \frac{\frac{15}{10}}{\frac{5}{10}} = \left(0.6 + \frac{8 \times 100}{10 \times 3}\right) + \frac{15 \times 10}{10 \times 5}$$

$$= \left(0.6 + \frac{800}{30}\right) + \frac{150}{50}$$

Step 2b
$$\left(0.6 + \frac{800}{30}\right) + \frac{150}{50} = \left(\frac{6}{10} + \frac{800}{30}\right) + \frac{150}{50}$$

Step 3
$$\left(\frac{6}{10} + \frac{800}{30}\right) + \frac{150}{50} = \left(\frac{(6 \times 30) + (800 \times 10)}{10 \times 30}\right) + \frac{150}{50} = \left(\frac{180 + 8000}{300}\right) + \frac{150}{50}$$

$$= \left(\frac{8180}{300}\right) + \frac{150}{50} = \frac{8180}{300} + \frac{150}{50} = \frac{(8180 \times 50) + (150 \times 300)}{300 \times 50} = \frac{409000 + 45000}{15000}$$

$$= \frac{454000}{15000}$$

Step 4
$$\frac{454000}{15000} = \frac{454000 \div 1000}{15000 \div 1000} = \frac{454}{15}$$

Step 5
$$\frac{454}{15} = 30\frac{4}{15}$$

Example 4.1-20
$$\frac{0.8}{0.03} + \frac{1.2}{0.5} + \frac{0.4}{0.02} =$$

Solution:

Step 1
$$\frac{0.8}{0.03} + \frac{1.2}{0.5} + \frac{0.4}{0.02} = \left(\frac{0.8}{0.03} + \frac{1.2}{0.5}\right) + \frac{0.4}{0.02}$$

Step 2a
$$\left(\frac{0.8}{0.03} + \frac{1.2}{0.5}\right) + \frac{0.4}{0.02} = \left(\frac{\frac{8}{10}}{\frac{3}{100}} + \frac{\frac{12}{10}}{\frac{5}{10}}\right) + \frac{\frac{4}{10}}{\frac{2}{100}} = \left(\frac{8 \times 100}{10 \times 3} + \frac{12 \times 10}{10 \times 5}\right) + \frac{4 \times 100}{10 \times 2}$$

$$= \left[\left(\frac{800}{30} + \frac{120}{50} \right) + \frac{400}{20} \right]$$

Step 2b $\boxed{Not\ Applicable}$

Step 3 $\left[\left(\frac{800}{30} + \frac{120}{50} \right) + \frac{400}{20} \right] = \left[\left(\frac{(800 \times 50) + (120 \times 30)}{30 \times 50} \right) + \frac{400}{20} \right] = \left[\left(\frac{40000 + 3600}{1500} \right) + \frac{400}{20} \right]$

$$= \left[\left(\frac{43600}{1500} \right) + \frac{400}{20} \right] = \left[\frac{43600}{1500} + \frac{400}{20} \right] = \left[\frac{(43600 \times 20) + (400 \times 1500)}{1500 \times 20} \right]$$

$$= \left[\frac{872000 + 600000}{30000} \right] = \left[\frac{1472000}{30000} \right]$$

Step 4 $\left[\frac{1472000}{30000} \right] = \left[\frac{1472000 \div 2000}{30000 \div 2000} \right] = \left[\frac{736}{15} \right]$

Step 5 $\left[\frac{736}{15} \right] = \boxed{\mathbf{49\frac{1}{15}}}$

Example 4.1-21

$$\left[\frac{0.4}{0.2} + \frac{0.3}{0.01} + 0.12 \right] =$$

Solution:

Step 1 $\left[\frac{0.4}{0.2} + \frac{0.3}{0.01} + 0.12 \right] = \left[\left(\frac{0.4}{0.2} + \frac{0.3}{0.01} \right) + 0.12 \right]$

Step 2a $\left[\left(\frac{0.4}{0.2} + \frac{0.3}{0.01} \right) + 0.12 \right] = \left[\left(\frac{\frac{4}{10}}{\frac{2}{10}} + \frac{\frac{3}{10}}{\frac{1}{100}} \right) + 0.12 \right] = \left[\left(\frac{4 \times 10}{10 \times 2} + \frac{3 \times 100}{10 \times 1} \right) + 0.12 \right]$

$$= \left[\left(\frac{40}{20} + \frac{300}{10} \right) + 0.12 \right]$$

Step 2b $\left[\left(\frac{40}{20} + \frac{300}{10} \right) + 0.12 \right] = \left[\left(\frac{40}{20} + \frac{300}{10} \right) + \frac{12}{100} \right]$

Step 3 $\left[\left(\frac{40}{20} + \frac{300}{10} \right) + \frac{12}{100} \right] = \left[\left(\frac{(40 \times 10) + (300 \times 20)}{20 \times 10} \right) + \frac{12}{100} \right] = \left[\left(\frac{400 + 6000}{200} \right) + \frac{12}{100} \right]$

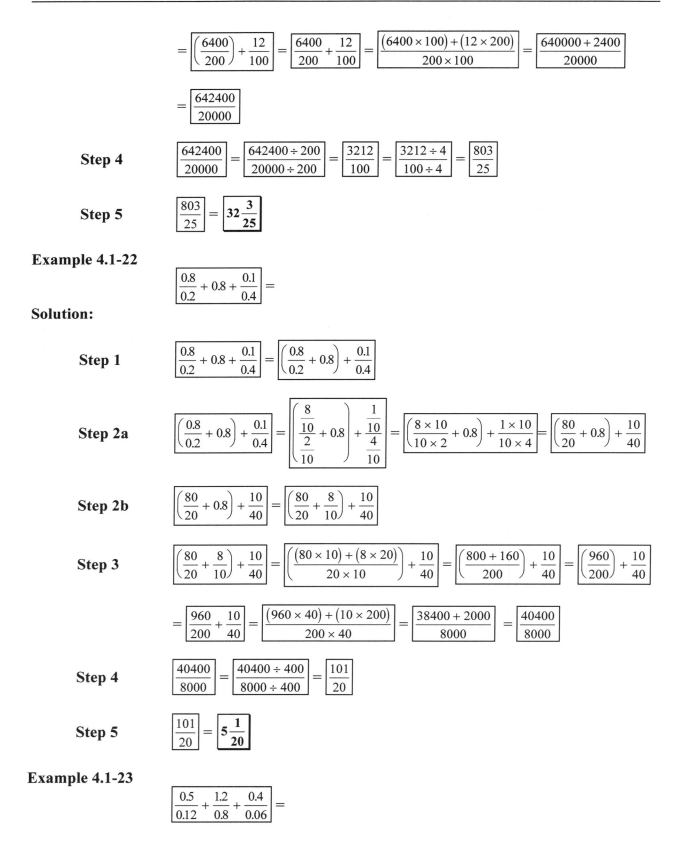

$$= \left| \left(\frac{6400}{200} \right) + \frac{12}{100} \right| = \left| \frac{6400}{200} + \frac{12}{100} \right| = \left| \frac{(6400 \times 100) + (12 \times 200)}{200 \times 100} \right| = \left| \frac{640000 + 2400}{20000} \right|$$

$$= \left| \frac{642400}{20000} \right|$$

Step 4 $\left| \frac{642400}{20000} \right| = \left| \frac{642400 \div 200}{20000 \div 200} \right| = \left| \frac{3212}{100} \right| = \left| \frac{3212 \div 4}{100 \div 4} \right| = \left| \frac{803}{25} \right|$

Step 5 $\left| \frac{803}{25} \right| = \boxed{32 \frac{3}{25}}$

Example 4.1-22

$$\left| \frac{0.8}{0.2} + 0.8 + \frac{0.1}{0.4} \right| =$$

Solution:

Step 1 $\left| \frac{0.8}{0.2} + 0.8 + \frac{0.1}{0.4} \right| = \left| \left(\frac{0.8}{0.2} + 0.8 \right) + \frac{0.1}{0.4} \right|$

Step 2a $\left| \left(\frac{0.8}{0.2} + 0.8 \right) + \frac{0.1}{0.4} \right| = \left| \left(\frac{\frac{8}{10}}{\frac{2}{10}} + 0.8 \right) + \frac{\frac{1}{10}}{\frac{4}{10}} \right| = \left| \left(\frac{8 \times 10}{10 \times 2} + 0.8 \right) + \frac{1 \times 10}{10 \times 4} \right| = \left| \left(\frac{80}{20} + 0.8 \right) + \frac{10}{40} \right|$

Step 2b $\left| \left(\frac{80}{20} + 0.8 \right) + \frac{10}{40} \right| = \left| \left(\frac{80}{20} + \frac{8}{10} \right) + \frac{10}{40} \right|$

Step 3 $\left| \left(\frac{80}{20} + \frac{8}{10} \right) + \frac{10}{40} \right| = \left| \left(\frac{(80 \times 10) + (8 \times 20)}{20 \times 10} \right) + \frac{10}{40} \right| = \left| \left(\frac{800 + 160}{200} \right) + \frac{10}{40} \right| = \left| \left(\frac{960}{200} \right) + \frac{10}{40} \right|$

$$= \left| \frac{960}{200} + \frac{10}{40} \right| = \left| \frac{(960 \times 40) + (10 \times 200)}{200 \times 40} \right| = \left| \frac{38400 + 2000}{8000} \right| = \left| \frac{40400}{8000} \right|$$

Step 4 $\left| \frac{40400}{8000} \right| = \left| \frac{40400 \div 400}{8000 \div 400} \right| = \left| \frac{101}{20} \right|$

Step 5 $\left| \frac{101}{20} \right| = \boxed{5 \frac{1}{20}}$

Example 4.1-23

$$\left| \frac{0.5}{0.12} + \frac{1.2}{0.8} + \frac{0.4}{0.06} \right| =$$

Solution:

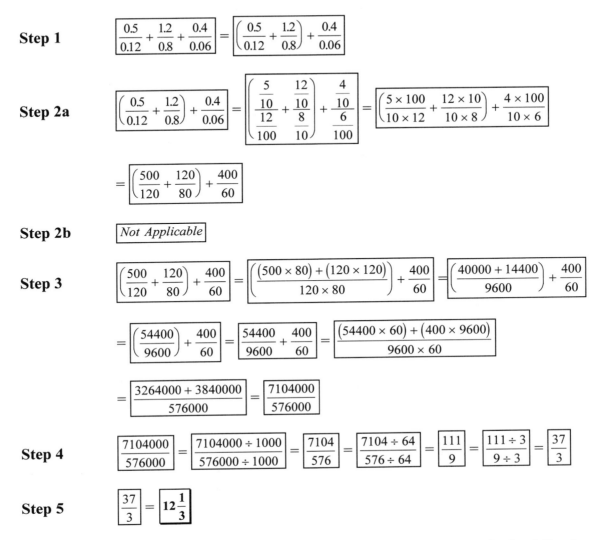

Step 1

$$\boxed{\frac{0.5}{0.12} + \frac{1.2}{0.8} + \frac{0.4}{0.06}} = \boxed{\left(\frac{0.5}{0.12} + \frac{1.2}{0.8}\right) + \frac{0.4}{0.06}}$$

Step 2a

$$\boxed{\left(\frac{0.5}{0.12} + \frac{1.2}{0.8}\right) + \frac{0.4}{0.06}} = \boxed{\left(\frac{\frac{5}{10}}{\frac{12}{100}} + \frac{\frac{12}{10}}{\frac{8}{10}}\right) + \frac{\frac{4}{10}}{\frac{6}{100}}} = \boxed{\left(\frac{5 \times 100}{10 \times 12} + \frac{12 \times 10}{10 \times 8}\right) + \frac{4 \times 100}{10 \times 6}}$$

$$= \boxed{\left(\frac{500}{120} + \frac{120}{80}\right) + \frac{400}{60}}$$

Step 2b

$$\boxed{\textit{Not Applicable}}$$

Step 3

$$\boxed{\left(\frac{500}{120} + \frac{120}{80}\right) + \frac{400}{60}} = \boxed{\left(\frac{(500 \times 80) + (120 \times 120)}{120 \times 80}\right) + \frac{400}{60}} = \boxed{\left(\frac{40000 + 14400}{9600}\right) + \frac{400}{60}}$$

$$= \boxed{\left(\frac{54400}{9600}\right) + \frac{400}{60}} = \boxed{\frac{54400}{9600} + \frac{400}{60}} = \boxed{\frac{(54400 \times 60) + (400 \times 9600)}{9600 \times 60}}$$

$$= \boxed{\frac{3264000 + 3840000}{576000}} = \boxed{\frac{7104000}{576000}}$$

Step 4

$$\boxed{\frac{7104000}{576000}} = \boxed{\frac{7104000 \div 1000}{576000 \div 1000}} = \boxed{\frac{7104}{576}} = \boxed{\frac{7104 \div 64}{576 \div 64}} = \boxed{\frac{111}{9}} = \boxed{\frac{111 \div 3}{9 \div 3}} = \boxed{\frac{37}{3}}$$

Step 5

$$\boxed{\frac{37}{3}} = \boxed{12\frac{1}{3}}$$

In general, three decimal fractions without a common denominator are added as in the following cases:

Case I.

$$\boxed{\frac{a \times 10^{-k_1}}{b \times 10^{-k_2}} + \frac{c \times 10^{-k_3}}{d \times 10^{-k_4}} + \frac{e \times 10^{-k_5}}{f \times 10^{-k_6}}} = \boxed{\left(\frac{a \times 10^{-k_1}}{b \times 10^{-k_2}} + \frac{c \times 10^{-k_3}}{d \times 10^{-k_4}}\right) + \frac{e \times 10^{-k_5}}{f \times 10^{-k_6}}}$$

$$= \boxed{\left(\frac{\left[\left(a \times 10^{-k_1}\right) \times \left(d \times 10^{-k_4}\right)\right] + \left[\left(c \times 10^{-k_3}\right) \times \left(b \times 10^{-k_2}\right)\right]}{\left(b \times 10^{-k_2}\right) \times \left(d \times 10^{-k_4}\right)}\right) + \frac{e \times 10^{-k_5}}{f \times 10^{-k_6}}}$$

Let $\boxed{A_1 = a \times 10^{-k_1}}$, $\boxed{A_2 = b \times 10^{-k_2}}$, $\boxed{A_3 = c \times 10^{-k_3}}$, $\boxed{A_4 = d \times 10^{-k_4}}$, $\boxed{A_5 = e \times 10^{-k_5}}$, and

$$\boxed{A_6 = f \times 10^{-k_6}}, \text{ then}$$

$$\boxed{\left(\frac{\left[\left(a \times 10^{-k_1}\right) \times \left(d \times 10^{-k_4}\right)\right] + \left[\left(c \times 10^{-k_3}\right) \times \left(b \times 10^{-k_2}\right)\right]}{\left(b \times 10^{-k_2}\right) \times \left(d \times 10^{-k_4}\right)}\right) + \frac{e \times 10^{-k_5}}{f \times 10^{-k_6}}} = \boxed{\left(\frac{\left[A_1 \times A_4\right] + \left[A_3 \times A_2\right]}{A_2 \times A_4}\right) + \frac{A_5}{A_6}}$$

$$= \boxed{\left(\frac{\left[A_1 A_4\right] + \left[A_3 A_2\right]}{A_2 A_4}\right) + \frac{A_5}{A_6}} = \boxed{\left(\frac{A_1 A_4 + A_3 A_2}{A_2 A_4}\right) + \frac{A_5}{A_6}} = \boxed{\frac{A_1 A_4 + A_3 A_2}{A_2 A_4} + \frac{A_5}{A_6}}$$

Let $\boxed{B_1 = A_1 A_4 + A_3 A_2}$ and $\boxed{B_2 = A_2 A_4}$, then

$$\boxed{\frac{A_1 A_4 + A_3 A_2}{A_2 A_4} + \frac{A_5}{A_6}} = \boxed{\frac{B_1}{B_2} + \frac{A_5}{A_6}} = \boxed{\frac{\left(B_1 \times A_6\right) + \left(A_5 \times B_2\right)}{B_2 \times A_6}} = \boxed{\frac{\left(B_1 A_6\right) + \left(A_5 B_2\right)}{B_2 A_6}} = \boxed{\frac{B_1 A_6 + A_5 B_2}{B_2 A_6}}$$

Example 4.1-24

$$\boxed{\frac{2 \times 10^{-1}}{45 \times 10^{-2}} + \frac{4 \times 10^{-2}}{3 \times 10^{-1}} + \frac{33 \times 10^{-2}}{15 \times 10^{-2}}} = \boxed{\frac{0.2}{0.45} + \frac{0.04}{0.3} + \frac{0.33}{0.15}} = \boxed{\left(\frac{0.2}{0.45} + \frac{0.04}{0.3}\right) + \frac{0.33}{0.15}} = \boxed{\left(\frac{\frac{2}{10}}{\frac{45}{100}} + \frac{\frac{4}{100}}{\frac{3}{10}}\right) + \frac{\frac{33}{100}}{\frac{15}{100}}}$$

$$= \boxed{\left(\frac{2 \times 100}{10 \times 45} + \frac{4 \times 10}{100 \times 3}\right) + \frac{33 \times 100}{100 \times 15}} = \boxed{\left(\frac{200}{450} + \frac{40}{300}\right) + \frac{3300}{1500}} = \boxed{\left(\frac{(200 \times 300) + (40 \times 450)}{450 \times 300}\right) + \frac{3300}{1500}}$$

$$= \boxed{\left(\frac{60000 + 18000}{135000}\right) + \frac{3300}{1500}} = \boxed{\left(\frac{78000}{135000}\right) + \frac{3300}{1500}} = \boxed{\frac{\overset{78}{\cancel{78000}}}{\underset{135}{\cancel{135000}}} + \frac{\overset{33}{\cancel{3300}}}{\underset{15}{\cancel{1500}}}} = \boxed{\frac{78}{135} + \frac{\overset{11}{\cancel{33}}}{\underset{5}{\cancel{15}}}} = \boxed{\frac{78}{135} + \frac{11}{5}}$$

$$= \boxed{\frac{(78 \times 5) + (11 \times 135)}{135 \times 5}} = \boxed{\frac{390 + 1485}{675}} = \boxed{\frac{\overset{75}{\cancel{1875}}}{\underset{27}{\cancel{675}}}} = \boxed{\frac{\overset{25}{\cancel{75}}}{\underset{9}{\cancel{27}}}} = \boxed{\frac{25}{9}} = \boxed{\mathbf{2\frac{7}{9}}}$$

Case II.

$$\boxed{\frac{a \times 10^{-k_1}}{b \times 10^{-k_2}} + \frac{c \times 10^{-k_3}}{d \times 10^{-k_4}} + \frac{e \times 10^{-k_5}}{f \times 10^{-k_6}}} = \boxed{\frac{a \times 10^{-k_1}}{b \times 10^{-k_2}} + \left(\frac{c \times 10^{-k_3}}{d \times 10^{-k_4}} + \frac{e \times 10^{-k_5}}{f \times 10^{-k_6}}\right)}$$

$$= \boxed{\frac{a \times 10^{-k_1}}{b \times 10^{-k_2}} + \left(\frac{\left[\left(c \times 10^{-k_3}\right) \times \left(f \times 10^{-k_6}\right)\right] + \left[\left(e \times 10^{-k_5}\right) \times \left(d \times 10^{-k_4}\right)\right]}{\left(d \times 10^{-k_4}\right) \times \left(f \times 10^{-k_6}\right)}\right)}$$

Let $\boxed{A_1 = a \times 10^{-k_1}}$, $\boxed{A_2 = b \times 10^{-k_2}}$, $\boxed{A_3 = c \times 10^{-k_3}}$, $\boxed{A_4 = d \times 10^{-k_4}}$, $\boxed{A_5 = e \times 10^{-k_5}}$, and

$\boxed{A_6 = f \times 10^{-k_6}}$, then

$$\boxed{\dfrac{a \times 10^{-k_1}}{b \times 10^{-k_2}} + \left(\dfrac{\left[\left(c \times 10^{-k_3}\right) \times \left(f \times 10^{-k_6}\right)\right] + \left[\left(e \times 10^{-k_5}\right) \times \left(d \times 10^{-k_4}\right)\right]}{\left(d \times 10^{-k_4}\right) \times \left(f \times 10^{-k_6}\right)} \right)} = \boxed{\dfrac{A_1}{A_2} + \left(\dfrac{[A_3 \times A_6] + [A_5 \times A_4]}{A_4 \times A_6} \right)}$$

$$\boxed{\dfrac{A_1}{A_2} + \left(\dfrac{[A_3 A_6] + [A_5 A_4]}{A_4 A_6} \right)} = \boxed{\dfrac{A_1}{A_2} + \left(\dfrac{A_3 A_6 + A_5 A_4}{A_4 A_6} \right)} = \boxed{\dfrac{A_1}{A_2} + \dfrac{A_3 A_6 + A_5 A_4}{A_4 A_6}}$$

Let $\boxed{B_1 = A_3 A_6 + A_5 A_4}$ and $\boxed{B_2 = A_4 A_6}$, then

$$\boxed{\dfrac{A_1}{A_2} + \dfrac{A_3 A_6 + A_5 A_4}{A_4 A_6}} = \boxed{\dfrac{A_1}{A_2} + \dfrac{B_1}{B_2}} = \boxed{\dfrac{\left(A_1 \times B_2\right) + \left(B_1 \times A_2\right)}{A_2 \times B_2}} = \boxed{\dfrac{\left(A_1 B_2\right) + \left(B_1 A_2\right)}{A_2 B_2}} = \boxed{\dfrac{A_1 B_2 + B_1 A_2}{A_2 B_2}}$$

Example 4.1-25

$$\boxed{\dfrac{2 \times 10^{-1}}{45 \times 10^{-2}} + \dfrac{4 \times 10^{-2}}{3 \times 10^{-1}} + \dfrac{33 \times 10^{-2}}{15 \times 10^{-2}}} = \boxed{\dfrac{0.2}{0.45} + \dfrac{0.04}{0.3} + \dfrac{0.33}{0.15}} = \boxed{\dfrac{0.2}{0.45} + \left(\dfrac{0.04}{0.3} + \dfrac{0.33}{0.15} \right)} = \boxed{\dfrac{\frac{2}{10}}{\frac{45}{100}} + \left(\dfrac{\frac{4}{100}}{\frac{3}{10}} + \dfrac{\frac{33}{100}}{\frac{15}{100}} \right)}$$

$$= \boxed{\dfrac{2 \times 100}{10 \times 45} + \left(\dfrac{4 \times 10}{100 \times 3} + \dfrac{33 \times 100}{100 \times 15} \right)} = \boxed{\dfrac{200}{450} + \left(\dfrac{40}{300} + \dfrac{3300}{1500} \right)} = \boxed{\dfrac{200}{450} + \left(\dfrac{(40 \times 1500) + (3300 \times 300)}{300 \times 1500} \right)}$$

$$= \boxed{\dfrac{200}{450} + \left(\dfrac{60000 + 990000}{450000} \right)} = \boxed{\dfrac{200}{450} + \left(\dfrac{1050000}{450000} \right)} = \boxed{\dfrac{\overset{4}{\cancel{200}}}{\underset{9}{\cancel{450}}} + \dfrac{\overset{105}{\cancel{1050000}}}{\underset{45}{\cancel{450000}}}} = \boxed{\dfrac{4}{9} + \dfrac{105}{45}} = \boxed{\dfrac{(4 \times 45) + (105 \times 9)}{9 \times 45}}$$

$$= \boxed{\dfrac{180 + 945}{405}} = \boxed{\dfrac{\overset{225}{\cancel{1125}}}{\underset{81}{\cancel{405}}}} = \boxed{\dfrac{\overset{25}{\cancel{225}}}{\underset{9}{\cancel{81}}}} = \boxed{\dfrac{25}{9}} = \boxed{2\dfrac{7}{9}}$$

Note - In addition the use of parentheses does not change the final answer; the two examples above have the same answer (see Section 1.2).

The following examples further illustrate how to add decimal fractions:

Example 4.1-26

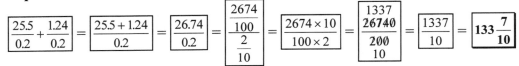

$$\boxed{\dfrac{25.5}{0.2} + \dfrac{1.24}{0.2}} = \boxed{\dfrac{25.5 + 1.24}{0.2}} = \boxed{\dfrac{26.74}{0.2}} = \boxed{\dfrac{\frac{2674}{100}}{\frac{2}{10}}} = \boxed{\dfrac{2674 \times 10}{100 \times 2}} = \boxed{\dfrac{\frac{1337}{26740}}{\frac{200}{10}}} = \boxed{\dfrac{1337}{10}} = \boxed{133\dfrac{7}{10}}$$

Example 4.1-27

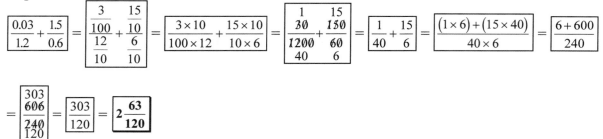

$$= \boxed{\dfrac{\dfrac{303}{606}}{\dfrac{240}{120}}} = \boxed{\dfrac{303}{120}} = \boxed{2\dfrac{63}{120}}$$

Example 4.1-28

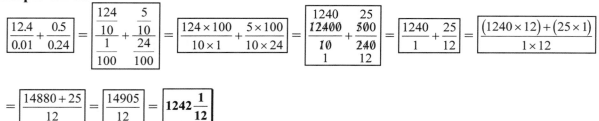

$$= \boxed{\dfrac{14880+25}{12}} = \boxed{\dfrac{14905}{12}} = \boxed{1242\dfrac{1}{12}}$$

Example 4.1-29

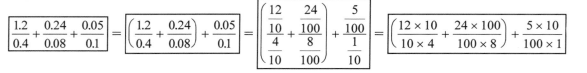

$$= \boxed{\left(\dfrac{\dfrac{3}{120}}{\dfrac{40}{1}} + \dfrac{\dfrac{3}{2400}}{\dfrac{800}{1}}\right) + \dfrac{\dfrac{1}{500}}{\dfrac{1000}{2}}} = \boxed{\left(\dfrac{3}{1}+\dfrac{3}{1}\right)+\dfrac{1}{2}} = \boxed{\left(\dfrac{3+3}{1}\right)+\dfrac{1}{2}} = \boxed{\left(\dfrac{6}{1}\right)+\dfrac{1}{2}} = \boxed{\dfrac{6}{1}+\dfrac{1}{2}} = \boxed{\dfrac{(6\times2)+(1\times1)}{1\times2}} = \boxed{\dfrac{12+1}{2}}$$

$$= \boxed{\dfrac{13}{2}} = \boxed{6\dfrac{1}{2}}$$

Example 4.1-30

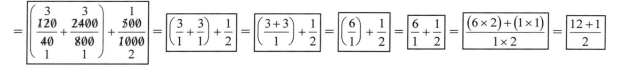

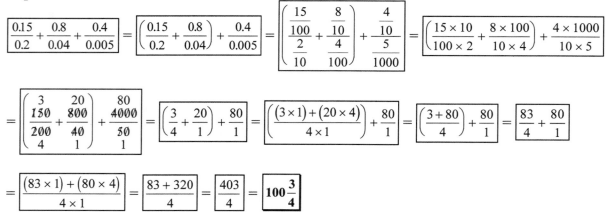

$$= \boxed{\dfrac{(83\times1)+(80\times4)}{4\times1}} = \boxed{\dfrac{83+320}{4}} = \boxed{\dfrac{403}{4}} = \boxed{100\dfrac{3}{4}}$$

Example 4.1-31

$$\left(\frac{0.6}{1.5}+\frac{0.8}{1.5}\right)+\frac{0.07}{0.15}=\left(\frac{0.6+0.8}{1.5}\right)+\frac{0.07}{0.15}=\left(\frac{1.4}{1.5}\right)+\frac{0.07}{0.15}=\frac{1.4}{1.5}+\frac{0.07}{0.15}=\frac{\frac{14}{10}}{\frac{15}{10}}+\frac{\frac{7}{100}}{\frac{15}{100}}$$

$$=\frac{14\times 10}{10\times 15}+\frac{7\times 100}{100\times 15}=\frac{\overset{14}{\cancel{140}}}{\underset{15}{\cancel{150}}}+\frac{\overset{7}{\cancel{700}}}{\underset{15}{\cancel{1500}}}=\frac{14}{15}+\frac{7}{15}=\frac{14+7}{15}=\frac{\overset{7}{\cancel{21}}}{\underset{5}{\cancel{15}}}=\frac{7}{5}=\boxed{1\frac{2}{5}}$$

Example 4.1-32

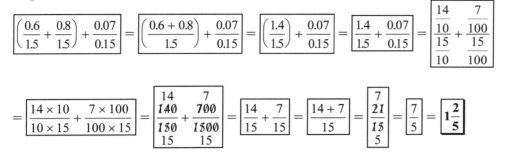

$$\left(\frac{0.06}{12.5}+\frac{0.8}{1.5}\right)+0.05=\left(\frac{\frac{6}{100}}{\frac{125}{10}}+\frac{\frac{8}{10}}{\frac{15}{10}}\right)+\frac{5}{100}=\left(\frac{6\times 10}{100\times 125}+\frac{8\times 10}{10\times 15}\right)+\frac{5}{100}=\left(\frac{\overset{3}{\cancel{60}}}{\underset{625}{\cancel{12500}}}+\frac{\overset{8}{\cancel{80}}}{\underset{15}{\cancel{150}}}\right)+\frac{\overset{1}{\cancel{5}}}{\underset{20}{\cancel{100}}}$$

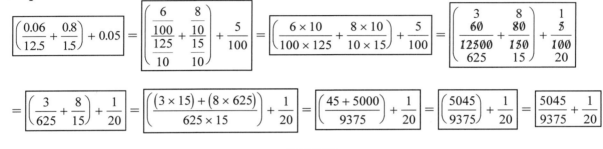

$$=\left(\frac{3}{625}+\frac{8}{15}\right)+\frac{1}{20}=\left(\frac{(3\times 15)+(8\times 625)}{625\times 15}\right)+\frac{1}{20}=\left(\frac{45+5000}{9375}\right)+\frac{1}{20}=\left(\frac{5045}{9375}\right)+\frac{1}{20}=\frac{5045}{9375}+\frac{1}{20}$$

$$=\frac{(5045\times 20)+(1\times 9375)}{9375\times 20}=\frac{100900+9375}{187500}=\frac{\overset{4411}{\cancel{110275}}}{\underset{7500}{\cancel{187500}}}=\boxed{\frac{4411}{7500}}$$

Example 4.1-33

$$12.45+\left(\frac{10.2}{0.5}+\frac{0.4}{0.06}\right)=\frac{1245}{100}+\left(\frac{\frac{102}{10}}{\frac{5}{10}}+\frac{\frac{4}{10}}{\frac{6}{100}}\right)=\frac{1245}{100}+\left(\frac{102\times 10}{10\times 5}+\frac{4\times 100}{10\times 6}\right)=\frac{1245}{100}+\left(\frac{1020}{50}+\frac{400}{60}\right)$$

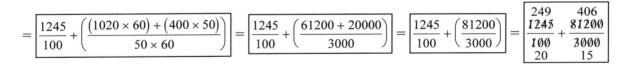

$$=\frac{1245}{100}+\left(\frac{(1020\times 60)+(400\times 50)}{50\times 60}\right)=\frac{1245}{100}+\left(\frac{61200+20000}{3000}\right)=\frac{1245}{100}+\left(\frac{81200}{3000}\right)=\frac{\overset{249}{\cancel{1245}}}{\underset{20}{\cancel{100}}}+\frac{\overset{406}{\cancel{81200}}}{\underset{15}{\cancel{3000}}}$$

$$=\frac{249}{20}+\frac{406}{15}=\frac{(249\times 15)+(406\times 20)}{20\times 15}=\frac{3735+8120}{300}=\frac{\overset{2371}{\cancel{11855}}}{\underset{60}{\cancel{300}}}=\frac{2371}{60}=\boxed{39\frac{31}{60}}$$

Example 4.1-34

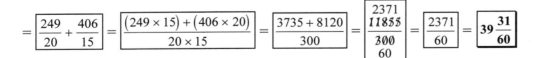

$$\left(\frac{0.7}{0.05}+\frac{0.08}{0.4}\right)+\left(\frac{0.4}{0.03}+0.05\right)=\left(\frac{\frac{7}{10}}{\frac{5}{100}}+\frac{\frac{8}{100}}{\frac{4}{10}}\right)+\left(\frac{\frac{4}{10}}{\frac{3}{100}}+\frac{1}{\frac{5}{100}}{20}\right)=\left(\frac{7\times 100}{10\times 5}+\frac{8\times 10}{100\times 4}\right)+\left(\frac{4\times 100}{10\times 3}+\frac{1}{20}\right)$$

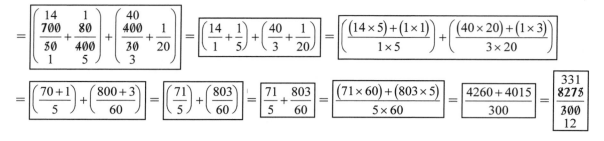

$$= \boxed{\frac{331}{12}} = \boxed{27\frac{7}{12}}$$

Example 4.1-35

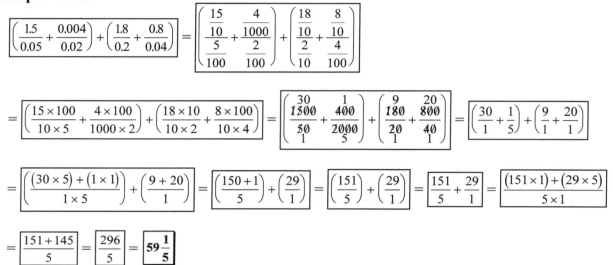

$$= \boxed{\left(\frac{(30\times5)+(1\times1)}{1\times5}\right)+\left(\frac{9+20}{1}\right)} = \boxed{\left(\frac{150+1}{5}\right)+\left(\frac{29}{1}\right)} = \boxed{\left(\frac{151}{5}\right)+\left(\frac{29}{1}\right)} = \boxed{\frac{151}{5}+\frac{29}{1}} = \boxed{\frac{(151\times1)+(29\times5)}{5\times1}}$$

$$= \boxed{\frac{151+145}{5}} = \boxed{\frac{296}{5}} = \boxed{59\frac{1}{5}}$$

Section 4.1 Exercises - Add the following decimal fractions:

1. $\dfrac{0.5}{1.5}+\dfrac{0.3}{1.5} =$

2. $\dfrac{0.02}{1.8}+\dfrac{0.4}{0.28} =$

3. $\dfrac{0.6}{0.5}+\dfrac{0.08}{0.3} =$

4. $\dfrac{3.3}{0.5}+\dfrac{0.15}{0.5}+\dfrac{0.1}{0.5} =$

5. $\dfrac{2.2}{0.2}+\dfrac{0.15}{0.5}+\dfrac{1.4}{0.4} =$

6. $\dfrac{1.2}{0.2}+\dfrac{0.5}{0.01}+\dfrac{1.5}{0.3} =$

7. $0.18+\left(\dfrac{0.4}{0.002}+\dfrac{1.4}{0.2}\right) =$

8. $\left(\dfrac{0.2}{0.4}+\dfrac{0.1}{0.8}\right)+0.15 =$

9. $\left(\dfrac{0.08}{0.2}+\dfrac{0}{0.1}\right)+\left(\dfrac{0.05}{0.15}+\dfrac{0.5}{1.5}\right) =$

10. $\left(\dfrac{4.9}{0.07}+3.6\right)+\left(\dfrac{0.5}{0.05}+\dfrac{0.15}{0.5}\right) =$

4.2   Subtracting Decimal Fractions

Decimal fractions $\left(\dfrac{a \times 10^{-k_1}}{b \times 10^{-k_2}}\right)$, i.e., fractions where (a) and (b) are integer numbers and (k_1) and (k_2) are equal to the number of decimal places are subtracted as in the following cases:

Case I   Subtracting Two or More Decimal Fractions With Common Denominators

Decimal fractions with two or more common denominators are subtracted using the steps given as in each case below:

Case I-A   *Subtract two decimal fractions with common denominators using the following steps:*

Step 1   Subtract the decimal fractions in a similar way as integer fractions with common denominators are subtracted (see Section 3.2, Case I-A).

Step 2   Change the decimal fractions to integer fractions (see Section 2.4).

Step 3   Simplify the fraction to its lowest term (see Section 2.3).

Step 4   Change the improper fraction to a mixed fraction if the fraction obtained from Step 3 is an improper fraction (see Section 2.2).

The following examples show the steps as to how two decimal fractions with common denominators are subtracted:

Example 4.2-1

$$\dfrac{\dfrac{0.9}{0.2} - \dfrac{0.8}{0.2}}{} =$$

Solution:

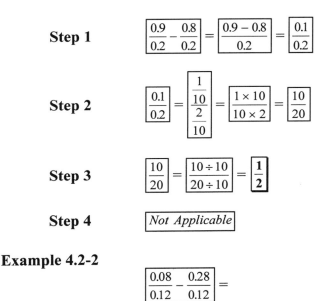

Step 1 $\dfrac{0.9}{0.2} - \dfrac{0.8}{0.2} = \dfrac{0.9 - 0.8}{0.2} = \dfrac{0.1}{0.2}$

Step 2 $\dfrac{0.1}{0.2} = \dfrac{\frac{1}{10}}{\frac{2}{10}} = \dfrac{1 \times 10}{10 \times 2} = \dfrac{10}{20}$

Step 3 $\dfrac{10}{20} = \dfrac{10 \div 10}{20 \div 10} = \dfrac{1}{2}$

Step 4 $\boxed{\text{Not Applicable}}$

Example 4.2-2

$$\dfrac{0.08}{0.12} - \dfrac{0.28}{0.12} =$$

Solution:

Step 1
$$\frac{0.08}{0.12} - \frac{0.28}{0.12} = \frac{0.08 - 0.28}{0.12} = \frac{-0.2}{0.12}$$

Step 2
$$\frac{-0.2}{0.12} = \frac{-\dfrac{2}{10}}{\dfrac{12}{100}} = \frac{-2 \times 100}{10 \times 12} = \frac{-200}{120}$$

Step 3
$$\frac{-200}{120} = \frac{-200 \div 40}{120 \div 40} = \frac{-5}{3}$$

Step 4
$$\frac{-5}{3} = -\left(1\frac{2}{3}\right)$$

Example 4.2-3
$$\frac{0.92}{0.025} - \frac{0.8}{0.025} =$$

Solution:

Step 1
$$\frac{0.92}{0.025} - \frac{0.8}{0.025} = \frac{0.92 - 0.8}{0.025} = \frac{0.12}{0.025}$$

Step 2
$$\frac{0.12}{0.025} = \frac{\dfrac{12}{100}}{\dfrac{25}{1000}} = \frac{12 \times 1000}{100 \times 25} = \frac{12000}{2500}$$

Step 3
$$\frac{12000}{2500} = \frac{12000 \div 500}{2500 \div 500} = \frac{24}{5}$$

Step 4
$$\frac{24}{5} = 4\frac{4}{5}$$

Example 4.2-4
$$\frac{0.78}{0.5} - \frac{0.18}{0.5} =$$

Solution:

Step 1
$$\frac{0.78}{0.5} - \frac{0.18}{0.5} = \frac{0.78 - 0.18}{0.5} = \frac{0.6}{0.5}$$

Step 2
$$\boxed{\frac{0.6}{0.5}} = \boxed{\frac{\frac{6}{10}}{\frac{5}{10}}} = \boxed{\frac{6 \times 10}{10 \times 5}} = \boxed{\frac{60}{50}}$$

Step 3
$$\boxed{\frac{60}{50}} = \boxed{\frac{60 \div 10}{50 \div 10}} = \boxed{\frac{6}{5}}$$

Step 4
$$\boxed{\frac{6}{5}} = \boxed{1\frac{1}{5}}$$

Example 4.2-5
$$\boxed{\frac{0.5}{0.032} - \frac{0.96}{0.032}} =$$

Solution:

Step 1
$$\boxed{\frac{0.5}{0.032} - \frac{0.96}{0.032}} = \boxed{\frac{0.5 - 0.96}{0.032}} = \boxed{\frac{-0.46}{0.032}}$$

Step 2
$$\boxed{\frac{-0.46}{0.032}} = \boxed{\frac{\frac{-46}{100}}{\frac{32}{1000}}} = \boxed{\frac{-46 \times 1000}{100 \times 32}} = \boxed{\frac{-46000}{3200}}$$

Step 3
$$\boxed{\frac{-46000}{3200}} = \boxed{\frac{-46000 \div 400}{3200 \div 400}} = \boxed{\frac{-115}{8}}$$

Step 4
$$\boxed{\frac{-115}{8}} = \boxed{-\left(14\frac{3}{8}\right)}$$

In general two decimal fractions with a common denominator are subtracted in the following way:

$$\boxed{\frac{a \times 10^{-k_1}}{d \times 10^{-k_3}} - \frac{b \times 10^{-k_2}}{d \times 10^{-k_3}}} = \boxed{\frac{a \times 10^{-k_1} - b \times 10^{-k_2}}{d \times 10^{-k_3}}}$$

Let $\boxed{A_1 = a \times 10^{-k_1}}$, $\boxed{A_2 = b \times 10^{-k_2}}$, and $\boxed{A_3 = d \times 10^{-k_3}}$, then

$$\boxed{\frac{a \times 10^{-k_1} - b \times 10^{-k_2}}{d \times 10^{-k_3}}} = \boxed{\frac{A_1}{A_3} - \frac{A_2}{A_3}} = \boxed{\frac{A_1 - A_2}{A_3}}$$

Example 4.2-6
$$\boxed{\frac{5 \times 10^{-1}}{6 \times 10^{-1}} - \frac{2 \times 10^{-2}}{6 \times 10^{-1}}} = \boxed{\frac{0.5}{0.6} - \frac{0.02}{0.6}} = \boxed{\frac{0.5 - 0.02}{0.6}} = \boxed{\frac{0.48}{0.6}} = \boxed{\frac{\frac{48}{100}}{\frac{6}{10}}} = \boxed{\frac{48 \times 10}{100 \times 6}} = \boxed{\frac{\cancel{480}^{24}}{\cancel{600}_{30}}} = \boxed{\frac{\cancel{24}^{4}}{\cancel{30}_{5}}} = \boxed{\frac{4}{5}}$$

Case I-B   *Subtract three decimal fractions with common denominators using the following steps:*

Step 1   Subtract the decimal fractions in a similar way as integer fractions with common denominators are subtracted (see Section 3.2, Case I-B).

Step 2   Change the decimal fractions to integer fractions (see Section 2.4).

Step 3   Simplify the fraction to its lowest term (see Section 2.3).

Step 4   Change the improper fraction to a mixed fraction if the fraction obtained from Step 3 is an improper fraction (see Section 2.2).

The following examples show the steps as to how three decimal fractions with common denominators are subtracted:

Example 4.2-7

$$\boxed{\dfrac{0.12}{0.6} - \dfrac{0.7}{0.6} - \dfrac{0.05}{0.6}} =$$

Solution:

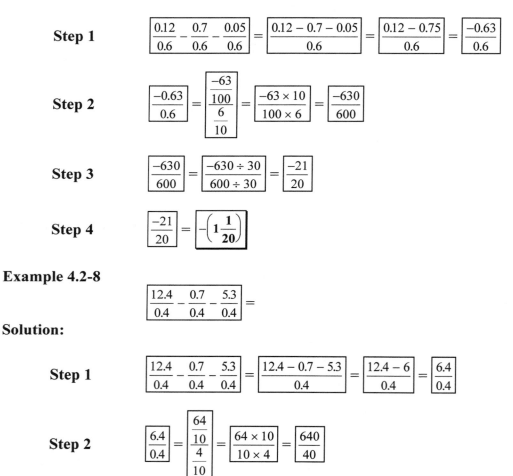

Step 1 $\boxed{\dfrac{0.12}{0.6} - \dfrac{0.7}{0.6} - \dfrac{0.05}{0.6}} = \boxed{\dfrac{0.12 - 0.7 - 0.05}{0.6}} = \boxed{\dfrac{0.12 - 0.75}{0.6}} = \boxed{\dfrac{-0.63}{0.6}}$

Step 2 $\boxed{\dfrac{-0.63}{0.6}} = \boxed{\dfrac{\frac{-63}{100}}{\frac{6}{10}}} = \boxed{\dfrac{-63 \times 10}{100 \times 6}} = \boxed{\dfrac{-630}{600}}$

Step 3 $\boxed{\dfrac{-630}{600}} = \boxed{\dfrac{-630 \div 30}{600 \div 30}} = \boxed{\dfrac{-21}{20}}$

Step 4 $\boxed{\dfrac{-21}{20}} = \boxed{-\left(1\dfrac{1}{20}\right)}$

Example 4.2-8

$$\boxed{\dfrac{12.4}{0.4} - \dfrac{0.7}{0.4} - \dfrac{5.3}{0.4}} =$$

Solution:

Step 1 $\boxed{\dfrac{12.4}{0.4} - \dfrac{0.7}{0.4} - \dfrac{5.3}{0.4}} = \boxed{\dfrac{12.4 - 0.7 - 5.3}{0.4}} = \boxed{\dfrac{12.4 - 6}{0.4}} = \boxed{\dfrac{6.4}{0.4}}$

Step 2 $\boxed{\dfrac{6.4}{0.4}} = \boxed{\dfrac{\frac{64}{10}}{\frac{4}{10}}} = \boxed{\dfrac{64 \times 10}{10 \times 4}} = \boxed{\dfrac{640}{40}}$

Step 3 $\boxed{\dfrac{640}{40}} = \boxed{\dfrac{640 \div 40}{40 \div 40}} = \boxed{\dfrac{16}{1}} = \boxed{\mathbf{16}}$

Step 4 $\boxed{Not\ Applicable}$

Example 4.2-9

$\boxed{\dfrac{4.12}{0.63} - \dfrac{0.7}{0.63} - \dfrac{0.25}{0.63}} =$

Solution:

Step 1 $\boxed{\dfrac{4.12}{0.63} - \dfrac{0.7}{0.63} - \dfrac{0.25}{0.63}} = \boxed{\dfrac{4.12 - 0.7 - 0.25}{0.63}} = \boxed{\dfrac{4.12 - 0.95}{0.63}} = \boxed{\dfrac{3.17}{0.63}}$

Step 2 $\boxed{\dfrac{3.17}{0.63}} = \boxed{\dfrac{\dfrac{317}{100}}{\dfrac{63}{100}}} = \boxed{\dfrac{317 \times 100}{100 \times 63}} = \boxed{\dfrac{31700}{6300}}$

Step 3 $\boxed{\dfrac{31700}{6300}} = \boxed{\dfrac{31700 \div 100}{6300 \div 100}} = \boxed{\dfrac{317}{63}}$

Step 4 $\boxed{\dfrac{317}{63}} = \boxed{\mathbf{5\dfrac{2}{63}}}$

Example 4.2-10

$\boxed{\dfrac{0.56}{15.8} - \dfrac{1.38}{15.8} - \dfrac{25.85}{15.8}} =$

Solution:

Step 1 $\boxed{\dfrac{0.56}{15.8} - \dfrac{1.38}{15.8} - \dfrac{25.85}{15.8}} = \boxed{\dfrac{0.56 - 1.38 - 25.85}{15.8}} = \boxed{\dfrac{0.56 - 27.23}{15.8}} = \boxed{\dfrac{-26.67}{15.8}}$

Step 2 $\boxed{\dfrac{-26.67}{15.8}} = \boxed{\dfrac{\dfrac{-2667}{100}}{\dfrac{158}{10}}} = \boxed{\dfrac{-2667 \times 10}{100 \times 158}} = \boxed{\dfrac{-26670}{15800}}$

Step 3 $\boxed{\dfrac{-26670}{15800}} = \boxed{\dfrac{-26670 \div 10}{15800 \div 10}} = \boxed{\dfrac{-2667}{1580}}$

Step 4 $\boxed{\dfrac{-2667}{1580}} = \boxed{-\left(\mathbf{1\dfrac{1087}{1580}}\right)}$

Example 4.2-11

$$\boxed{\dfrac{1.45}{12.45} - \dfrac{0.09}{12.45} - \dfrac{0.34}{12.45}} =$$

Solution:

Step 1

$$\boxed{\dfrac{1.45}{12.45} - \dfrac{0.09}{12.45} - \dfrac{0.34}{12.45}} = \boxed{\dfrac{1.45 - 0.09 - 0.34}{12.45}} = \boxed{\dfrac{1.45 - 0.43}{12.45}} = \boxed{\dfrac{1.02}{12.45}}$$

Step 2

$$\boxed{\dfrac{1.02}{12.45}} = \boxed{\dfrac{\frac{102}{100}}{\frac{1245}{100}}} = \boxed{\dfrac{102 \times 100}{100 \times 1245}} = \boxed{\dfrac{10200}{124500}}$$

Step 3

$$\boxed{\dfrac{10200}{124500}} = \boxed{\dfrac{10200 \div 100}{124500 \div 100}} = \boxed{\dfrac{102}{1245}} = \boxed{\dfrac{102 \div 3}{1245 \div 3}} = \boxed{\mathbf{\dfrac{34}{415}}}$$

Step 4 $\boxed{\textit{Not Applicable}}$

In general, three decimal fractions with a common denominator are subtracted in the following way:

$$\boxed{\dfrac{a \times 10^{-k_1}}{d \times 10^{-k_4}} - \dfrac{b \times 10^{-k_2}}{d \times 10^{-k_4}} - \dfrac{c \times 10^{-k_3}}{d \times 10^{-k_4}}} = \boxed{\dfrac{a \times 10^{-k_1} - b \times 10^{-k_2} - c \times 10^{-k_3}}{d \times 10^{-k_4}}}$$

Let $\boxed{A_1 = a \times 10^{-k_1}}$, $\boxed{A_2 = b \times 10^{-k_2}}$, $\boxed{A_3 = c \times 10^{-k_3}}$, and $\boxed{A_4 = d \times 10^{-k_4}}$, then

$$\boxed{\dfrac{a \times 10^{-k_1} - b \times 10^{-k_2} - c \times 10^{-k_3}}{d \times 10^{-k_4}}} = \boxed{\dfrac{A_1}{A_4} - \dfrac{A_2}{A_4} - \dfrac{A_3}{A_4}} = \boxed{\dfrac{A_1 - A_2 - A_3}{A_4}}$$

Example 4.2-12

$$\boxed{\dfrac{16 \times 10^{-2}}{12 \times 10^{-2}} - \dfrac{9 \times 10^{-3}}{12 \times 10^{-2}} - \dfrac{4 \times 10^{-1}}{12 \times 10^{-2}}} = \boxed{\dfrac{0.16}{0.12} - \dfrac{0.009}{0.12} - \dfrac{0.4}{0.12}} = \boxed{\dfrac{0.16 - 0.009 - 0.4}{0.12}} = \boxed{\dfrac{0.16 - 0.409}{0.12}}$$

$$= \boxed{\dfrac{-0.249}{0.12}} = \boxed{\dfrac{\frac{-249}{1000}}{\frac{12}{100}}} = \boxed{\dfrac{-249 \times 100}{1000 \times 12}} = \boxed{\dfrac{-249}{\cancel{24900}\,12000}\;^{-249}\;^{120}} = \boxed{\dfrac{-249}{120}} = \boxed{-\left(2\dfrac{9}{120}\right)}$$

Case II   Subtracting Two or More Decimal Fractions Without a Common Denominator
Two or more decimal fractions without a common denominator are subtracted using the steps given as in each case below:

Case II-A   *Subtract two decimal fractions without a common denominator using the following steps:*

Step 1   a. Change the decimal fractions to integer fractions (see Section 2.4).

b. Change the decimal number $\left(a \times 10^{-k}\right)$ to an integer fraction of the form $\left(\dfrac{a}{10^k}\right)$,

e.g., change 12.8 to $\dfrac{128}{10}$.

Step 2   Subtract the integer fractions (see Section 3.2, Case II-A).

Step 3   Simplify the fraction to its lowest term (see Section 2.3).

Step 4   Change the improper fraction to a mixed fraction if the fraction obtained from Step 3 is an improper fraction (see Section 2.2).

The following examples show the steps as to how two decimal fractions without a common denominators are subtracted:

Example 4.2-13

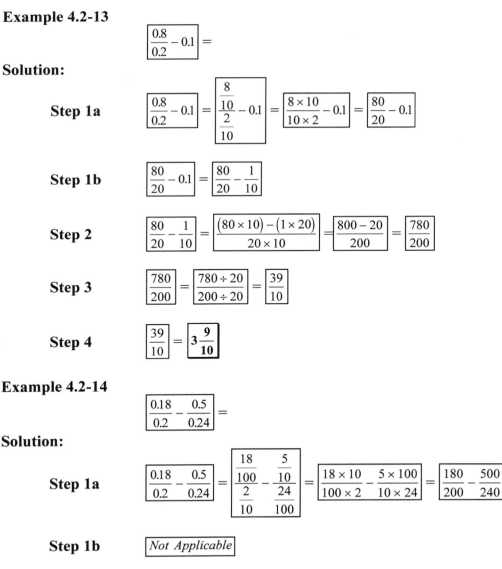

$$\boxed{\dfrac{0.8}{0.2} - 0.1} =$$

Solution:

Step 1a $\boxed{\dfrac{0.8}{0.2} - 0.1} = \boxed{\dfrac{\frac{8}{10}}{\frac{2}{10}} - 0.1} = \boxed{\dfrac{8 \times 10}{10 \times 2} - 0.1} = \boxed{\dfrac{80}{20} - 0.1}$

Step 1b $\boxed{\dfrac{80}{20} - 0.1} = \boxed{\dfrac{80}{20} - \dfrac{1}{10}}$

Step 2 $\boxed{\dfrac{80}{20} - \dfrac{1}{10}} = \boxed{\dfrac{(80 \times 10) - (1 \times 20)}{20 \times 10}} = \boxed{\dfrac{800 - 20}{200}} = \boxed{\dfrac{780}{200}}$

Step 3 $\boxed{\dfrac{780}{200}} = \boxed{\dfrac{780 \div 20}{200 \div 20}} = \boxed{\dfrac{39}{10}}$

Step 4 $\boxed{\dfrac{39}{10}} = \boxed{3\dfrac{9}{10}}$

Example 4.2-14

$$\boxed{\dfrac{0.18}{0.2} - \dfrac{0.5}{0.24}} =$$

Solution:

Step 1a $\boxed{\dfrac{0.18}{0.2} - \dfrac{0.5}{0.24}} = \boxed{\dfrac{\frac{18}{100}}{\frac{2}{10}} - \dfrac{\frac{5}{10}}{\frac{24}{100}}} = \boxed{\dfrac{18 \times 10}{100 \times 2} - \dfrac{5 \times 100}{10 \times 24}} = \boxed{\dfrac{180}{200} - \dfrac{500}{240}}$

Step 1b $\boxed{Not\ Applicable}$

Step 2 $\dfrac{180}{200} - \dfrac{500}{240} = \dfrac{(180 \times 240) - (500 \times 200)}{200 \times 240} = \dfrac{43200 - 100000}{48000} = \dfrac{-56800}{48000}$

Step 3 $\dfrac{-56800}{48000} = \dfrac{-56800 \div 100}{48000 \div 100} = \dfrac{-568}{480} = \dfrac{-568 \div 8}{480 \div 8} = \dfrac{-71}{60}$

Step 4 $\dfrac{-71}{60} = -\left(1\dfrac{11}{60}\right)$

Example 4.2-15

$\dfrac{1.2}{0.5} - \dfrac{0.38}{5.4} =$

Solution:

Step 1a $\dfrac{1.2}{0.5} - \dfrac{0.38}{5.4} = \dfrac{\frac{12}{10}}{\frac{5}{10}} - \dfrac{\frac{38}{100}}{\frac{54}{10}} = \dfrac{12 \times 10}{10 \times 5} - \dfrac{38 \times 10}{100 \times 54} = \dfrac{120}{50} - \dfrac{380}{5400}$

Step 1b *Not Applicable*

Step 2 $\dfrac{120}{50} - \dfrac{380}{5400} = \dfrac{(120 \times 5400) - (380 \times 50)}{50 \times 5400} = \dfrac{648000 - 19000}{270000} = \dfrac{629000}{270000}$

Step 3 $\dfrac{629000}{270000} = \dfrac{629000 \div 1000}{270000 \div 1000} = \dfrac{629}{270}$

Step 4 $\dfrac{629}{270} = 2\dfrac{89}{270}$

Example 4.2-16

$0.48 - \dfrac{1.8}{0.6} =$

Solution:

Step 1a $0.48 - \dfrac{1.8}{0.6} = 0.48 - \dfrac{\frac{18}{10}}{\frac{6}{10}} = 0.48 - \dfrac{18 \times 10}{10 \times 6} = 0.48 - \dfrac{180}{60}$

Step 1b $0.48 - \dfrac{180}{60} = \dfrac{48}{100} - \dfrac{180}{60}$

Step 2 $\dfrac{48}{100} - \dfrac{180}{60} = \dfrac{(48 \times 60) - (180 \times 100)}{100 \times 60} = \dfrac{2880 - 18000}{6000} = \dfrac{-15120}{6000}$

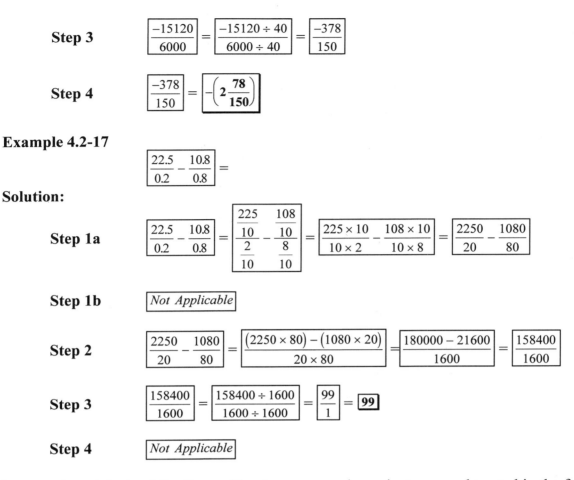

Step 3
$$\frac{-15120}{6000} = \frac{-15120 \div 40}{6000 \div 40} = \frac{-378}{150}$$

Step 4
$$\frac{-378}{150} = -\left(2\frac{78}{150}\right)$$

Example 4.2-17

$$\frac{22.5}{0.2} - \frac{10.8}{0.8} =$$

Solution:

Step 1a
$$\frac{22.5}{0.2} - \frac{10.8}{0.8} = \frac{\frac{225}{10}}{\frac{2}{10}} - \frac{\frac{108}{10}}{\frac{8}{10}} = \frac{225 \times 10}{10 \times 2} - \frac{108 \times 10}{10 \times 8} = \frac{2250}{20} - \frac{1080}{80}$$

Step 1b $\boxed{Not\ Applicable}$

Step 2
$$\frac{2250}{20} - \frac{1080}{80} = \frac{(2250 \times 80) - (1080 \times 20)}{20 \times 80} = \frac{180000 - 21600}{1600} = \frac{158400}{1600}$$

Step 3
$$\frac{158400}{1600} = \frac{158400 \div 1600}{1600 \div 1600} = \frac{99}{1} = \boxed{99}$$

Step 4 $\boxed{Not\ Applicable}$

In general, two decimal fractions without a common denominator are subtracted in the following way:

$$\frac{a \times 10^{-k_1}}{b \times 10^{-k_2}} - \frac{c \times 10^{-k_3}}{d \times 10^{-k_4}} = \frac{\left[\left(a \times 10^{-k_1}\right) \times \left(d \times 10^{-k_4}\right)\right] - \left[\left(c \times 10^{-k_3}\right) \times \left(b \times 10^{-k_2}\right)\right]}{\left(b \times 10^{-k_2}\right) \times \left(d \times 10^{-k_4}\right)}$$

Let $\boxed{A_1 = a \times 10^{-k_1}}$, $\boxed{A_2 = b \times 10^{-k_2}}$, $\boxed{A_3 = c \times 10^{-k_3}}$, and $\boxed{A_4 = d \times 10^{-k_4}}$, then

$$\frac{\left[\left(a \times 10^{-k_1}\right) \times \left(d \times 10^{-k_4}\right)\right] - \left[\left(c \times 10^{-k_3}\right) \times \left(b \times 10^{-k_2}\right)\right]}{\left(b \times 10^{-k_2}\right) \times \left(d \times 10^{-k_4}\right)} = \frac{[A_1 \times A_4] - [A_3 \times A_2]}{A_2 \times A_4} = \frac{[A_1 A_4] - [A_3 A_2]}{A_2 A_4}$$

$$= \frac{A_1 A_4 - A_3 A_2}{A_2 A_4}$$

Example 4.2-18

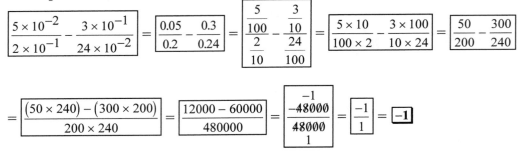

$$= \boxed{\frac{(50 \times 240) - (300 \times 200)}{200 \times 240}} = \boxed{\frac{12000 - 60000}{480000}} = \boxed{\frac{-1\atop{-48000}}{48000\atop 1}} = \boxed{\frac{-1}{1}} = \boxed{-1}$$

Case II-B   *Subtract three decimal fractions without a common denominator using the following steps:*

Step 1   Use parentheses to group the first and second fractions.

Step 2   a. Change the decimal fractions to integer fractions (see Section 2.4).

b. Change the decimal number $\left(a \times 10^{-k}\right)$ to an integer fraction of the form $\left(\frac{a}{10^k}\right)$,

e.g., change 0.08 to $\frac{8}{100}$.

Step 3   Subtract the integer fractions (see Section 3.2, Case II-B).

Step 4   Simplify the fraction to its lowest term (see Section 2.3).

Step 5   Change the improper fraction to a mixed fraction if the fraction obtained from Step 4 is an improper fraction (see Section 2.2).

The following examples show the steps as to how three decimal fractions without a common denominators are subtracted:

Example 4.2-19

$$\boxed{\frac{0.7}{0.6} - \frac{0.25}{0.2} - \frac{0.4}{0.01}} =$$

Solution:

Step 1 $\boxed{\dfrac{0.7}{0.6} - \dfrac{0.25}{0.2} - \dfrac{0.4}{0.01}} = \boxed{\left(\dfrac{0.7}{0.6} - \dfrac{0.25}{0.2}\right) - \dfrac{0.4}{0.01}}$

Step 2a $\boxed{\left(\dfrac{0.7}{0.6} - \dfrac{0.25}{0.2}\right) - \dfrac{0.4}{0.01}} = \boxed{\left(\dfrac{\frac{7}{10}}{\frac{6}{10}} - \dfrac{\frac{25}{100}}{\frac{2}{10}}\right) - \dfrac{\frac{4}{10}}{\frac{1}{100}}} = \boxed{\left(\dfrac{7 \times 10}{10 \times 6} - \dfrac{25 \times 10}{100 \times 2}\right) - \dfrac{4 \times 100}{10 \times 1}}$

$$= \boxed{\left(\dfrac{70}{60} - \dfrac{250}{200}\right) - \dfrac{400}{10}}$$

Step 2b $\boxed{\textit{Not Applicable}}$

Step 3

$$\left(\frac{70}{60} - \frac{250}{200}\right) - \frac{400}{10} = \left(\frac{(70 \times 200) - (250 \times 60)}{60 \times 200}\right) - \frac{400}{10} = \left(\frac{14000 - 15000}{12000}\right) - \frac{400}{10}$$

$$= \left(\frac{-1000}{12000}\right) - \frac{400}{10} = \frac{-1000}{12000} - \frac{400}{10} = \frac{(-1000 \times 10) - (400 \times 12000)}{12000 \times 10}$$

$$= \frac{-10000 - 4800000}{120000} = \frac{-4810000}{120000}$$

Step 4

$$\frac{-4810000}{120000} = \frac{-4810000 \div 10000}{120000 \div 10000} = \frac{-481}{12}$$

Step 5

$$\frac{-481}{12} = -\left(40\frac{1}{12}\right)$$

Example 4.2-20

$$0.8 - \frac{0.09}{0.1} - \frac{0.2}{0.5} =$$

Solution:

Step 1

$$0.8 - \frac{0.09}{0.1} - \frac{0.2}{0.5} = \left(0.8 - \frac{0.09}{0.1}\right) - \frac{0.2}{0.5}$$

Step 2a

$$\left(0.8 - \frac{0.09}{0.1}\right) - \frac{0.2}{0.5} = \left(0.8 - \frac{\frac{9}{100}}{\frac{1}{10}}\right) - \frac{\frac{2}{10}}{\frac{5}{10}} = \left(0.8 - \frac{9 \times 10}{100 \times 1}\right) - \frac{2 \times 10}{10 \times 5}$$

$$= \left(0.8 - \frac{90}{100}\right) - \frac{20}{50}$$

Step 2b

$$\left(0.8 - \frac{90}{100}\right) - \frac{20}{50} = \left(\frac{8}{10} - \frac{90}{100}\right) - \frac{20}{50}$$

Step 3

$$\left(\frac{8}{10} - \frac{90}{100}\right) - \frac{20}{50} = \left(\frac{(8 \times 100) - (90 \times 10)}{10 \times 100}\right) - \frac{20}{50} = \left(\frac{800 - 900}{1000}\right) - \frac{20}{50}$$

$$= \left(\frac{-100}{1000}\right) - \frac{20}{50} = \frac{-100}{1000} - \frac{20}{50} = \frac{(-100 \times 50) - (20 \times 1000)}{1000 \times 50} = \frac{-5000 - 20000}{50000}$$

$$= \frac{-25000}{50000}$$

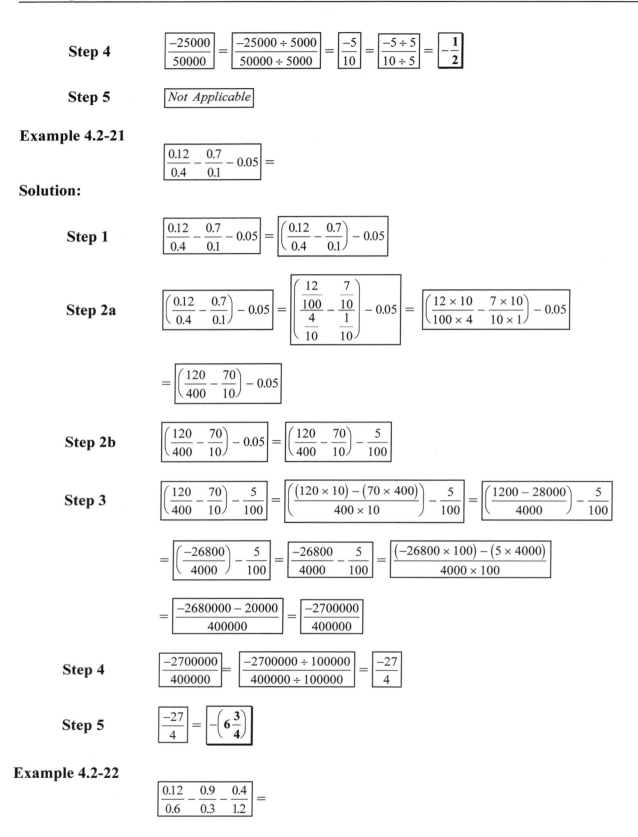

Step 4 $\dfrac{-25000}{50000} = \dfrac{-25000 \div 5000}{50000 \div 5000} = \dfrac{-5}{10} = \dfrac{-5 \div 5}{10 \div 5} = \boxed{-\dfrac{1}{2}}$

Step 5   *Not Applicable*

Example 4.2-21

$\dfrac{0.12}{0.4} - \dfrac{0.7}{0.1} - 0.05 =$

Solution:

Step 1 $\dfrac{0.12}{0.4} - \dfrac{0.7}{0.1} - 0.05 = \left(\dfrac{0.12}{0.4} - \dfrac{0.7}{0.1} \right) - 0.05$

Step 2a $\left(\dfrac{0.12}{0.4} - \dfrac{0.7}{0.1} \right) - 0.05 = \left(\dfrac{\frac{12}{100}}{\frac{4}{10}} - \dfrac{\frac{7}{10}}{\frac{1}{10}} \right) - 0.05 = \left(\dfrac{12 \times 10}{100 \times 4} - \dfrac{7 \times 10}{10 \times 1} \right) - 0.05$

$= \left(\dfrac{120}{400} - \dfrac{70}{10} \right) - 0.05$

Step 2b $\left(\dfrac{120}{400} - \dfrac{70}{10} \right) - 0.05 = \left(\dfrac{120}{400} - \dfrac{70}{10} \right) - \dfrac{5}{100}$

Step 3 $\left(\dfrac{120}{400} - \dfrac{70}{10} \right) - \dfrac{5}{100} = \left(\dfrac{(120 \times 10) - (70 \times 400)}{400 \times 10} \right) - \dfrac{5}{100} = \left(\dfrac{1200 - 28000}{4000} \right) - \dfrac{5}{100}$

$= \left(\dfrac{-26800}{4000} \right) - \dfrac{5}{100} = \dfrac{-26800}{4000} - \dfrac{5}{100} = \dfrac{(-26800 \times 100) - (5 \times 4000)}{4000 \times 100}$

$= \dfrac{-2680000 - 20000}{400000} = \dfrac{-2700000}{400000}$

Step 4 $\dfrac{-2700000}{400000} = \dfrac{-2700000 \div 100000}{400000 \div 100000} = \dfrac{-27}{4}$

Step 5 $\dfrac{-27}{4} = \boxed{-\left(6\dfrac{3}{4} \right)}$

Example 4.2-22

$\dfrac{0.12}{0.6} - \dfrac{0.9}{0.3} - \dfrac{0.4}{1.2} =$

Solution:

Step 1
$$\frac{0.12}{0.6} - \frac{0.9}{0.3} - \frac{0.4}{1.2} = \left(\frac{0.12}{0.6} - \frac{0.9}{0.3}\right) - \frac{0.4}{1.2}$$

Step 2a
$$\left(\frac{0.12}{0.6} - \frac{0.9}{0.3}\right) - \frac{0.4}{1.2} = \left(\frac{\frac{12}{100}}{\frac{6}{10}} - \frac{\frac{9}{10}}{\frac{3}{10}}\right) - \frac{\frac{4}{10}}{\frac{12}{10}} = \left(\frac{12 \times 10}{100 \times 6} - \frac{9 \times 10}{10 \times 3}\right) - \frac{4 \times 10}{10 \times 12}$$

$$= \left(\frac{120}{600} - \frac{90}{30}\right) - \frac{40}{120}$$

Step 2b
$$\boxed{Not\ Applicable}$$

Step 3
$$\left(\frac{120}{600} - \frac{90}{30}\right) - \frac{40}{120} = \left(\frac{(120 \times 30) - (90 \times 600)}{600 \times 30}\right) - \frac{40}{120} = \left(\frac{3600 - 54000}{18000}\right) - \frac{40}{120}$$

$$= \left(\frac{-50400}{18000}\right) - \frac{40}{120} = \frac{-50400}{18000} - \frac{40}{120} = \frac{(-50400 \times 120) - (40 \times 18000)}{18000 \times 120}$$

$$= \frac{-6048000 - 720000}{2160000} = \frac{-6768000}{2160000}$$

Step 4
$$\frac{-6768000}{2160000} = \frac{-6768000 \div 8000}{2160000 \div 8000} = \frac{-846}{270} = \frac{-846 \div 2}{270 \div 2} = \frac{-423}{135}$$

Step 5
$$\frac{-423}{135} = -\left(3\frac{18}{135}\right)$$

Example 4.2-23
$$4.5 - \frac{0.06}{0.3} - \frac{0.4}{0.5} =$$

Solution:

Step 1
$$4.5 - \frac{0.06}{0.3} - \frac{0.4}{0.5} = \left(4.5 - \frac{0.06}{0.3}\right) - \frac{0.4}{0.5}$$

Step 2a
$$\left(4.5 - \frac{0.06}{0.3}\right) - \frac{0.4}{0.5} = \left(4.5 - \frac{\frac{6}{100}}{\frac{3}{10}}\right) - \frac{\frac{4}{10}}{\frac{5}{10}} = \left(4.5 - \frac{6 \times 10}{100 \times 3}\right) - \frac{4 \times 10}{10 \times 5}$$

$$= \left[\left(4.5 - \frac{60}{300}\right) - \frac{40}{50}\right]$$

Step 2b $\left[\left(4.5 - \frac{60}{300}\right) - \frac{40}{50}\right] = \left[\left(\frac{45}{10} - \frac{60}{300}\right) - \frac{40}{50}\right]$

Step 3 $\left[\left(\frac{45}{10} - \frac{60}{300}\right) - \frac{40}{50}\right] = \left[\left(\frac{(45 \times 300) - (60 \times 10)}{10 \times 300}\right) - \frac{40}{50}\right] = \left[\left(\frac{13500 - 600}{3000}\right) - \frac{40}{50}\right]$

$$= \left[\left(\frac{12900}{3000}\right) - \frac{40}{50}\right] = \left[\frac{12900}{3000} - \frac{40}{50}\right] = \left[\frac{(12900 \times 50) - (40 \times 3000)}{3000 \times 50}\right] = \left[\frac{645000 - 120000}{150000}\right]$$

$$= \left[\frac{525000}{150000}\right]$$

Step 4 $\left[\frac{525000}{150000}\right] = \left[\frac{525000 \div 5000}{150000 \div 5000}\right] = \left[\frac{105}{30}\right] = \left[\frac{105 \div 15}{30 \div 15}\right] = \left[\frac{7}{2}\right]$

Step 5 $\left[\frac{7}{2}\right] = \left[3\frac{1}{2}\right]$

In general, three decimal fractions without a common denominator are subtracted as in the following cases:

Case I.

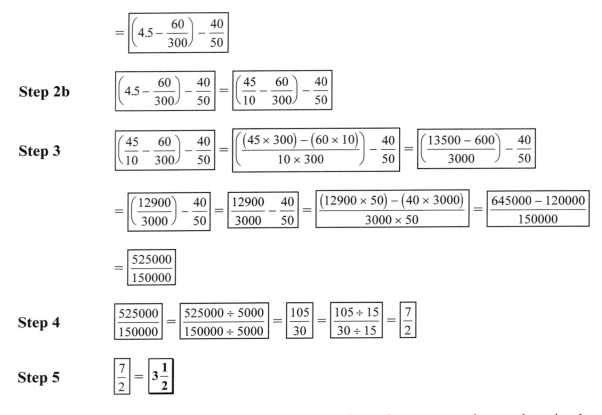

$$\left[\frac{a \times 10^{-k_1}}{b \times 10^{-k_2}} - \frac{c \times 10^{-k_3}}{d \times 10^{-k_4}} - \frac{e \times 10^{-k_5}}{f \times 10^{-k_6}}\right] = \left[\left(\frac{a \times 10^{-k_1}}{b \times 10^{-k_2}} - \frac{c \times 10^{-k_3}}{d \times 10^{-k_4}}\right) - \frac{e \times 10^{-k_5}}{f \times 10^{-k_6}}\right]$$

$$= \left[\left(\frac{\left[\left(a \times 10^{-k_1}\right) \times \left(d \times 10^{-k_4}\right)\right] - \left[\left(c \times 10^{-k_3}\right) \times \left(b \times 10^{-k_2}\right)\right]}{\left(b \times 10^{-k_2}\right) \times \left(d \times 10^{-k_4}\right)}\right) - \frac{e \times 10^{-k_5}}{f \times 10^{-k_6}}\right]$$

Let $\boxed{A_1 = a \times 10^{-k_1}}$, $\boxed{A_2 = b \times 10^{-k_2}}$, $\boxed{A_3 = c \times 10^{-k_3}}$, $\boxed{A_4 = d \times 10^{-k_4}}$, $\boxed{A_5 = e \times 10^{-k_5}}$, and

$\boxed{A_6 = f \times 10^{-k_6}}$, then

$$\left[\left(\frac{\left[\left(a \times 10^{-k_1}\right) \times \left(d \times 10^{-k_4}\right)\right] - \left[\left(c \times 10^{-k_3}\right) \times \left(b \times 10^{-k_2}\right)\right]}{\left(b \times 10^{-k_2}\right) \times \left(d \times 10^{-k_4}\right)}\right) - \frac{e \times 10^{-k_5}}{f \times 10^{-k_6}}\right] = \left[\left(\frac{[A_1 \times A_4] - [A_3 \times A_2]}{A_2 \times A_4}\right) - \frac{A_5}{A_6}\right]$$

$$= \left[\left(\frac{[A_1 A_4] - [A_3 A_2]}{A_2 A_4}\right) - \frac{A_5}{A_6}\right] = \left[\left(\frac{A_1 A_4 - A_3 A_2}{A_2 A_4}\right) - \frac{A_5}{A_6}\right] = \left[\frac{A_1 A_4 - A_3 A_2}{A_2 A_4} - \frac{A_5}{A_6}\right]$$

Let $\boxed{B_1 = A_1 A_4 - A_3 A_2}$ and $\boxed{B_2 = A_2 A_4}$, then

$$\boxed{\dfrac{A_1 A_4 - A_3 A_2}{A_2 A_4} - \dfrac{A_5}{A_6}} = \boxed{\dfrac{B_1}{B_2} - \dfrac{A_5}{A_6}} = \boxed{\dfrac{(B_1 \times A_6) - (A_5 \times B_2)}{B_2 \times A_6}} = \boxed{\dfrac{(B_1 A_6) - (A_5 B_2)}{B_2 A_6}} = \boxed{\dfrac{B_1 A_6 - A_5 B_2}{B_2 A_6}}$$

Example 4.2-24

$$\boxed{\dfrac{12 \times 10^{-1}}{4 \times 10^{-2}} - \dfrac{4 \times 10^{-2}}{6 \times 10^{-1}} - \dfrac{2 \times 10^{-1}}{5 \times 10^{-2}}} = \boxed{\dfrac{1.2}{0.04} - \dfrac{0.04}{0.6} - \dfrac{0.2}{0.05}} = \boxed{\left(\dfrac{1.2}{0.04} - \dfrac{0.04}{0.6}\right) - \dfrac{0.2}{0.05}} = \boxed{\left(\dfrac{\frac{12}{10}}{\frac{4}{100}} - \dfrac{\frac{4}{100}}{\frac{6}{10}}\right) - \dfrac{\frac{2}{10}}{\frac{5}{100}}}$$

$$= \boxed{\left(\dfrac{12 \times 100}{10 \times 4} - \dfrac{4 \times 10}{100 \times 6}\right) - \dfrac{2 \times 100}{10 \times 5}} = \boxed{\left(\dfrac{\frac{1200}{40}}{\frac{40}{1}} - \dfrac{\frac{40}{600}}{\frac{600}{15}}\right) - \dfrac{\frac{200}{50}}{\frac{50}{1}}} = \boxed{\left(\dfrac{30}{1} - \dfrac{1}{15}\right) - \dfrac{4}{1}} = \boxed{\left(\dfrac{(30 \times 15) - (1 \times 1)}{1 \times 15}\right) - \dfrac{4}{1}}$$

$$= \boxed{\left(\dfrac{450 - 1}{15}\right) - \dfrac{4}{1}} = \boxed{\left(\dfrac{449}{15}\right) - \dfrac{4}{1}} = \boxed{\dfrac{449}{15} - \dfrac{4}{1}} = \boxed{\dfrac{(449 \times 1) - (4 \times 15)}{15 \times 1}} = \boxed{\dfrac{449 - 60}{15}} = \boxed{\dfrac{389}{15}} = \boxed{25\dfrac{14}{15}}$$

Case II.

$$\boxed{\dfrac{a \times 10^{-k_1}}{b \times 10^{-k_2}} - \dfrac{c \times 10^{-k_3}}{d \times 10^{-k_4}} - \dfrac{e \times 10^{-k_5}}{f \times 10^{-k_6}}} = \boxed{\dfrac{a \times 10^{-k_1}}{b \times 10^{-k_2}} + \left(-\dfrac{c \times 10^{-k_3}}{d \times 10^{-k_4}} - \dfrac{e \times 10^{-k_5}}{f \times 10^{-k_6}}\right)}$$

$$= \boxed{\dfrac{a \times 10^{-k_1}}{b \times 10^{-k_2}} + \left(\dfrac{-\left[\left(c \times 10^{-k_3}\right) \times \left(f \times 10^{-k_6}\right)\right] - \left[\left(e \times 10^{-k_5}\right) \times \left(d \times 10^{-k_4}\right)\right]}{\left(d \times 10^{-k_4}\right) \times \left(f \times 10^{-k_6}\right)}\right)}$$

Let $\boxed{A_1 = a \times 10^{-k_1}}$, $\boxed{A_2 = b \times 10^{-k_2}}$, $\boxed{A_3 = c \times 10^{-k_3}}$, $\boxed{A_4 = d \times 10^{-k_4}}$, $\boxed{A_5 = e \times 10^{-k_5}}$, and

$\boxed{A_6 = f \times 10^{-k_6}}$, then

$$\boxed{\dfrac{a \times 10^{-k_1}}{b \times 10^{-k_2}} + \left(\dfrac{-\left[\left(c \times 10^{-k_3}\right) \times \left(f \times 10^{-k_6}\right)\right] - \left[\left(e \times 10^{-k_5}\right) \times \left(d \times 10^{-k_4}\right)\right]}{\left(d \times 10^{-k_4}\right) \times \left(f \times 10^{-k_6}\right)}\right)} = \boxed{\dfrac{A_1}{A_2} + \left(\dfrac{-[A_3 \times A_6] - [A_5 \times A_4]}{A_4 \times A_6}\right)}$$

$$\boxed{\dfrac{A_1}{A_2} + \left(\dfrac{-[A_3 A_6] - [A_5 A_4]}{A_4 A_6}\right)} = \boxed{\dfrac{A_1}{A_2} + \left(\dfrac{-A_3 A_6 - A_5 A_4}{A_4 A_6}\right)} = \boxed{\dfrac{A_1}{A_2} + \dfrac{-A_3 A_6 - A_5 A_4}{A_4 A_6}} = \boxed{\dfrac{A_1}{A_2} - \dfrac{A_3 A_6 + A_5 A_4}{A_4 A_6}}$$

Let $\boxed{B_1 = A_3 A_6 + A_5 A_4}$ and $\boxed{B_2 = A_4 A_6}$, then

$$\frac{A_1}{A_2} - \frac{A_3 A_6 + A_5 A_4}{A_4 A_6} = \frac{A_1}{A_2} - \frac{B_1}{B_2} = \frac{(A_1 \times B_2) - (B_1 \times A_2)}{A_2 \times B_2} = \frac{(A_1 B_2) - (B_1 A_2)}{A_2 B_2} = \boxed{\frac{A_1 B_2 - B_1 A_2}{A_2 B_2}}$$

Example 4.2-25

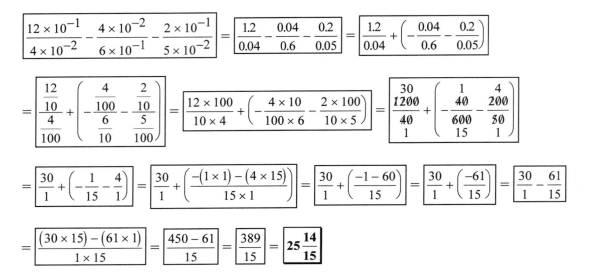

$$\frac{12 \times 10^{-1}}{4 \times 10^{-2}} - \frac{4 \times 10^{-2}}{6 \times 10^{-1}} - \frac{2 \times 10^{-1}}{5 \times 10^{-2}} = \frac{1.2}{0.04} - \frac{0.04}{0.6} - \frac{0.2}{0.05} = \frac{1.2}{0.04} + \left(-\frac{0.04}{0.6} - \frac{0.2}{0.05} \right)$$

$$= \frac{\frac{12}{10}}{\frac{4}{100}} + \left(-\frac{\frac{4}{100}}{\frac{6}{10}} - \frac{\frac{2}{10}}{\frac{5}{100}} \right) = \frac{12 \times 100}{10 \times 4} + \left(-\frac{4 \times 10}{100 \times 6} - \frac{2 \times 100}{10 \times 5} \right) = \frac{\overset{30}{\cancel{1200}}}{\cancel{40}} + \left(-\frac{\overset{1}{\cancel{40}}}{\cancel{600}} - \frac{\overset{4}{\cancel{200}}}{\cancel{50}} \right)$$

$$= \frac{30}{1} + \left(-\frac{1}{15} - \frac{4}{1} \right) = \frac{30}{1} + \left(\frac{-(1 \times 1) - (4 \times 15)}{15 \times 1} \right) = \frac{30}{1} + \left(\frac{-1 - 60}{15} \right) = \frac{30}{1} + \left(\frac{-61}{15} \right) = \frac{30}{1} - \frac{61}{15}$$

$$= \frac{(30 \times 15) - (61 \times 1)}{1 \times 15} = \frac{450 - 61}{15} = \frac{389}{15} = \boxed{25\frac{14}{15}}$$

The following examples further illustrate how to Subtract decimal fractions:

Example 4.2-26

$$\frac{1.5}{0.24} - \frac{2.3}{0.24} = \frac{1.5 - 2.3}{0.24} = \frac{-0.8}{0.24} = \frac{\frac{-8}{10}}{\frac{24}{100}} = \frac{-8 \times 100}{10 \times 24} = \frac{\overset{-10}{\cancel{-800}}}{\cancel{240}} = \frac{-10}{3} = \boxed{-\left(3\frac{1}{3} \right)}$$

Example 4.2-27

$$\frac{1.8}{0.02} - \frac{0.6}{0.2} = \frac{\frac{18}{10}}{\frac{2}{100}} - \frac{\frac{6}{10}}{\frac{2}{10}} = \frac{18 \times 100}{10 \times 2} - \frac{6 \times 10}{10 \times 2} = \frac{\overset{90}{\cancel{1800}}}{\underset{1}{\cancel{20}}} - \frac{\overset{3}{\cancel{60}}}{\underset{1}{\cancel{20}}} = \frac{90}{1} - \frac{3}{1} = \frac{90 - 3}{1} = \frac{87}{1} = \boxed{87}$$

Example 4.2-28

$$\frac{2.7}{0.09} - \frac{1.5}{0.05} = \frac{\frac{27}{10}}{\frac{9}{100}} - \frac{\frac{15}{10}}{\frac{5}{100}} = \frac{27 \times 100}{10 \times 9} - \frac{15 \times 100}{10 \times 5} = \frac{\overset{30}{\cancel{2700}}}{\underset{1}{\cancel{90}}} - \frac{\overset{30}{\cancel{1500}}}{\underset{1}{\cancel{50}}} = \frac{30}{1} - \frac{30}{1} = \frac{30 - 30}{1} = \frac{0}{1} = \boxed{0}$$

Example 4.2-29

$$\frac{2.8}{0.05} - \frac{0.1}{0.05} - \frac{3.8}{0.05} = \frac{2.8 - 0.1 - 3.8}{0.05} = \frac{-1.1}{0.05} = \frac{\frac{-11}{10}}{\frac{5}{100}} = \frac{-11 \times 100}{10 \times 5} = \frac{\overset{-22}{\cancel{-1100}}}{\underset{1}{\cancel{50}}} = \frac{-22}{1} = \boxed{-22}$$

Example 4.2-30

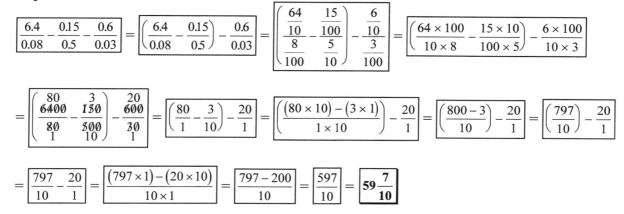

Example 4.2-31

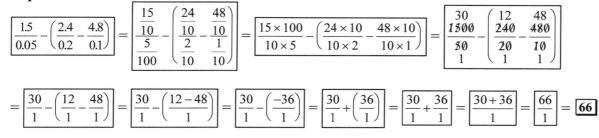

Example 4.2-32

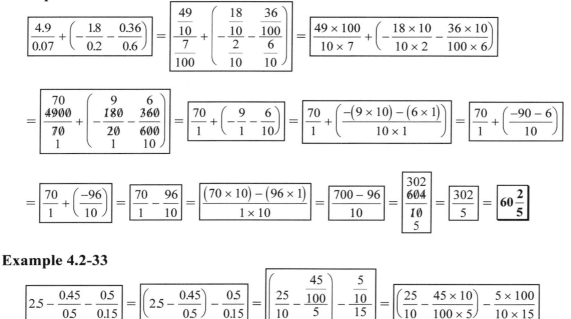

Example 4.2-33

$$\boxed{2.5 - \dfrac{0.45}{0.5} - \dfrac{0.5}{0.15}} = \boxed{\left(2.5 - \dfrac{0.45}{0.5}\right) - \dfrac{0.5}{0.15}} = \boxed{\left(25 \cdot \dfrac{10}{100} \cdot \dfrac{45}{100} \cdot \dfrac{45}{100} \cdot \dfrac{10}{10}\right) ...}$$

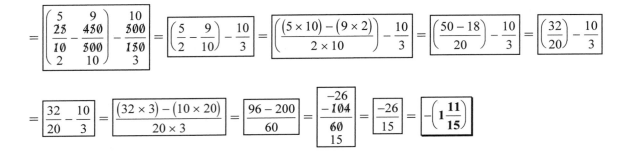

Example 4.2-34

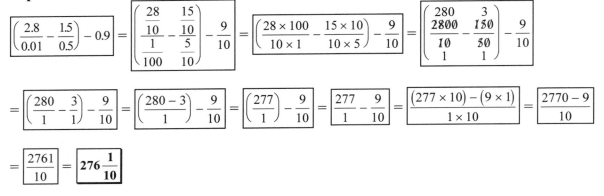

Example 4.2-35

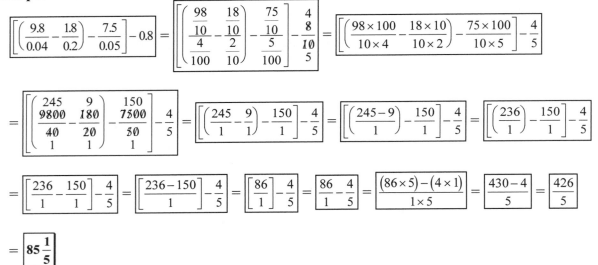

Section 4.2 Exercises - Subtract the following decimal fractions:

1. $\dfrac{3.6}{0.04} - \dfrac{0.8}{0.04} =$

2. $\dfrac{6.4}{0.04} - \dfrac{1.8}{0.01} =$

3. $\dfrac{3.6}{0.02} - \dfrac{1.8}{0.2} =$

4. $\dfrac{2.4}{0.12} - \dfrac{0.3}{0.12} - \dfrac{1.5}{0.12} =$

5. $\left(\dfrac{12.2}{0.04} - \dfrac{1.8}{0.2}\right) - \dfrac{4.9}{0.7} =$

6. $8.8 + \left(-\dfrac{0.9}{0.03} - \dfrac{0.4}{0.02}\right) =$

7. $\dfrac{2.2}{0.4} - \left(\dfrac{0.9}{0.03} - \dfrac{1.5}{0.5}\right) =$

8. $\left(9.8 - \dfrac{1.4}{0.2}\right) - \dfrac{0.1}{0.2} =$

9. $\dfrac{3.3}{0.03} - \dfrac{1.1}{0.1} - \dfrac{0}{0.5} =$

10. $\left[\left(\dfrac{3.6}{0.04} - \dfrac{0.3}{1.2}\right) - \dfrac{1.2}{0.2}\right] - 0.5 =$

4.3   Multiplying Decimal Fractions

Two or more decimal fractions with or without a common denominator are multiplied using the steps given as in each case below:

Case I   *Multiply two decimal fractions with or without a common denominator using the following steps:*

Step 1   a. Change the decimal fractions to integer fractions (see Section 2.4).

b. Change the decimal number $\left(a \times 10^{-k}\right)$ to an integer fraction of the form $\left(\dfrac{a}{10^k}\right)$,

e.g., change 0.003 to $\dfrac{3}{1000}$.

Step 2   Multiply the integer fractions (see Section 3.3, Case I).

Step 3   Simplify the fraction to its lowest term (see Section 2.3).

Step 4   Change the improper fraction to a mixed fraction if the fraction obtained from Step 3 is an improper fraction (see Section 2.2).

The following examples show the steps as to how two decimal fractions with or without a common denominator are multiplied:

Example 4.3-1

$$\boxed{\frac{12.2}{1.08} \times \frac{1.5}{0.4}} =$$

Solution:

Step 1a $\boxed{\dfrac{12.2}{1.08} \times \dfrac{1.5}{0.4}} = \boxed{\dfrac{\frac{122}{10}}{\frac{108}{100}} \times \dfrac{\frac{15}{10}}{\frac{4}{10}}} = \boxed{\dfrac{122 \times 100}{10 \times 108} \times \dfrac{15 \times 10}{10 \times 4}} = \boxed{\dfrac{12200}{1080} \times \dfrac{150}{40}}$

Step 1b $\boxed{\textit{Not Applicable}}$

Step 2 $\boxed{\dfrac{12200}{1080} \times \dfrac{150}{40}} = \boxed{\dfrac{12200 \times 150}{1080 \times 40}} = \boxed{\dfrac{1830000}{43200}}$

Step 3 $\boxed{\dfrac{1830000}{43200}} = \boxed{\dfrac{1830000 \div 400}{43200 \div 400}} = \boxed{\dfrac{4575}{108}} = \boxed{\dfrac{4575 \div 3}{108 \div 3}} = \boxed{\dfrac{1525}{36}}$

Step 4 $\boxed{\dfrac{1525}{36}} = \boxed{42\dfrac{13}{36}}$

Example 4.3-2

$$\boxed{\frac{0.2}{0.08} \times 0.5} =$$

Solution:

Step 1a $\boxed{\dfrac{0.2}{0.08} \times 0.5} = \boxed{\dfrac{\dfrac{2}{10}}{\dfrac{8}{100}} \times 0.5} = \boxed{\dfrac{2 \times 100}{10 \times 8} \times 0.5} = \boxed{\dfrac{200}{80} \times 0.5}$

Step 1b $\boxed{\dfrac{200}{80} \times 0.5} = \boxed{\dfrac{200}{80} \times \dfrac{5}{10}}$

Step 2 $\boxed{\dfrac{200}{80} \times \dfrac{5}{10}} = \boxed{\dfrac{200 \times 5}{80 \times 10}} = \boxed{\dfrac{1000}{800}}$

Step 3 $\boxed{\dfrac{1000}{800}} = \boxed{\dfrac{1000 \div 200}{800 \div 200}} = \boxed{\dfrac{5}{4}}$

Step 4 $\boxed{\dfrac{5}{4}} = \boxed{1\dfrac{1}{4}}$

Example 4.3-3

$\boxed{\dfrac{2.2}{0.04} \times \dfrac{1.8}{0.3}} =$

Solution:

Step 1a $\boxed{\dfrac{2.2}{0.04} \times \dfrac{1.8}{0.3}} = \boxed{\dfrac{\dfrac{22}{10}}{\dfrac{4}{100}} \times \dfrac{\dfrac{18}{10}}{\dfrac{3}{10}}} = \boxed{\dfrac{22 \times 100}{10 \times 4} \times \dfrac{18 \times 10}{10 \times 3}} = \boxed{\dfrac{2200}{40} \times \dfrac{180}{30}}$

Step 1b $\boxed{Not\ Applicable}$

Step 2 $\boxed{\dfrac{2200}{40} \times \dfrac{180}{30}} = \boxed{\dfrac{2200 \times 180}{40 \times 30}} = \boxed{\dfrac{396000}{1200}}$

Step 3 $\boxed{\dfrac{396000}{1200}} = \boxed{\dfrac{396000 \div 1200}{1200 \div 1200}} = \boxed{\dfrac{330}{1}} = \boxed{\mathbf{330}}$

Step 4 $\boxed{Not\ Applicable}$

Example 4.3-4

$\boxed{\dfrac{12.2}{4.8} \times \dfrac{0.05}{4.8}} =$

Solution:

Step 1a $\boxed{\dfrac{12.2}{4.8} \times \dfrac{0.05}{4.8}} = \boxed{\dfrac{\dfrac{122}{10}}{\dfrac{48}{10}} \times \dfrac{\dfrac{5}{100}}{\dfrac{48}{10}}} = \boxed{\dfrac{122 \times 10}{10 \times 48} \times \dfrac{5 \times 10}{100 \times 48}} = \boxed{\dfrac{1220}{480} \times \dfrac{50}{4800}}$

Step 1b   Not Applicable

Step 2 $\dfrac{1220}{480} \times \dfrac{50}{4800} = \dfrac{1220 \times 50}{480 \times 4800} = \dfrac{61000}{2304000}$

Step 3 $\dfrac{61000}{2304000} = \dfrac{61000 \div 1000}{2304000 \div 1000} = \dfrac{\mathbf{61}}{\mathbf{2304}}$

Step 4   Not Applicable

Example 4.3-5

$12.4 \times \dfrac{0.05}{0.8} =$

Solution:

Step 1a $12.4 \times \dfrac{0.05}{0.8} = 12.4 \times \dfrac{\frac{5}{100}}{\frac{8}{10}} = 12.4 \times \dfrac{5 \times 10}{100 \times 8} = 12.4 \times \dfrac{50}{800}$

Step 1b $12.4 \times \dfrac{50}{800} = \dfrac{124}{10} \times \dfrac{50}{800}$

Step 2 $\dfrac{124}{10} \times \dfrac{50}{800} = \dfrac{124 \times 50}{10 \times 800} = \dfrac{6200}{8000}$

Step 3 $\dfrac{6200}{8000} = \dfrac{6200 \div 200}{8000 \div 200} = \dfrac{\mathbf{31}}{\mathbf{40}}$

Step 4   Not Applicable

In general, two decimal fractions are multiplied in the following way:

$$\dfrac{a \times 10^{-k_1}}{b \times 10^{-k_2}} \times \dfrac{c \times 10^{-k_3}}{d \times 10^{-k_4}} = \dfrac{\left(a \times 10^{-k_1}\right) \times \left(c \times 10^{-k_3}\right)}{\left(b \times 10^{-k_2}\right) \times \left(d \times 10^{-k_4}\right)}$$

Let $A_1 = a \times 10^{-k_1}$, $A_2 = b \times 10^{-k_2}$, $A_3 = c \times 10^{-k_3}$, and $A_4 = d \times 10^{-k_4}$, then

$$\dfrac{\left(a \times 10^{-k_1}\right) \times \left(c \times 10^{-k_3}\right)}{\left(b \times 10^{-k_2}\right) \times \left(d \times 10^{-k_4}\right)} = \dfrac{A_1 \times A_3}{A_2 \times A_4} = \dfrac{A_1 A_3}{A_2 A_4}$$

Example 4.3-6

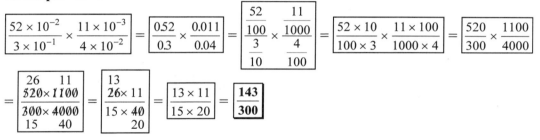

Case II   *Multiply three decimal fractions with or without a common denominator using the following steps:*

Step 1   a. Change the decimal fractions to integer fractions (see Section 2.4).

b. Change the decimal number $\left(a \times 10^{-k}\right)$ to an integer fraction of the form $\left(\dfrac{a}{10^k}\right)$,

e.g., change 13.9 to $\dfrac{139}{10}$.

Step 2   Multiply the integer fractions (see Section 3.3, Case II).

Step 3   Simplify the fraction to its lowest term (see Section 2.3).

Step 4   Change the improper fraction to a mixed fraction if the fraction obtained from Step 3 is an improper fraction (see Section 2.2).

The following examples show the steps as to how three decimal fractions with or without a common denominator are multiplied:

Example 4.3-7

$$\boxed{\dfrac{0.08}{0.5} \times \dfrac{0.1}{0.06} \times 0.3} =$$

Solution:

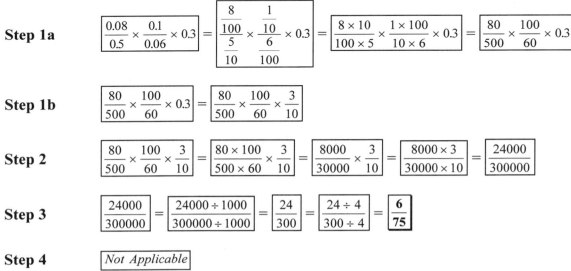

Example 4.3-8

$$\boxed{0.8 \times \frac{0.01}{0.8} \times \frac{0.75}{0.2} =}$$

Solution:

Step 1a

$$\boxed{0.8 \times \frac{0.01}{0.8} \times \frac{0.75}{0.2}} = \boxed{0.8 \times \frac{\frac{1}{100}}{\frac{8}{10}} \times \frac{\frac{75}{100}}{\frac{2}{10}}} = \boxed{0.8 \times \frac{1 \times 10}{100 \times 8} \times \frac{75 \times 10}{100 \times 2}} = \boxed{0.8 \times \frac{10}{800} \times \frac{750}{200}}$$

Step 1b

$$\boxed{0.8 \times \frac{10}{800} \times \frac{750}{200}} = \boxed{\frac{8}{10} \times \frac{10}{800} \times \frac{750}{200}}$$

Step 2

$$\boxed{\frac{8}{10} \times \frac{10}{800} \times \frac{750}{200}} = \boxed{\frac{8 \times 10 \times 750}{10 \times 800 \times 200}} = \boxed{\frac{60000}{1600000}}$$

Step 3

$$\boxed{\frac{60000}{1600000}} = \boxed{\frac{60000 \div 10000}{1600000 \div 10000}} = \boxed{\frac{6}{160}} = \boxed{\frac{6 \div 2}{160 \div 2}} = \boxed{\mathbf{\frac{3}{80}}}$$

Step 4 $\boxed{\textit{Not Applicable}}$

Example 4.3-9

$$\boxed{\frac{2.5}{0.4} \times \frac{0.02}{1.8} \times \frac{2.45}{0.4} =}$$

Solution:

Step 1a

$$\boxed{\frac{2.5}{0.4} \times \frac{0.02}{1.8} \times \frac{2.45}{0.4}} = \boxed{\frac{\frac{25}{10}}{\frac{4}{10}} \times \frac{\frac{2}{100}}{\frac{18}{10}} \times \frac{\frac{245}{100}}{\frac{4}{10}}} = \boxed{\frac{25 \times 10}{10 \times 4} \times \frac{2 \times 10}{100 \times 18} \times \frac{245 \times 10}{100 \times 4}}$$

$$= \boxed{\frac{250}{40} \times \frac{20}{1800} \times \frac{2450}{400}}$$

Step 1b $\boxed{\textit{Not Applicable}}$

Step 2

$$\boxed{\frac{250}{40} \times \frac{20}{1800} \times \frac{2450}{400}} = \boxed{\frac{250 \times 20 \times 2450}{40 \times 1800 \times 400}} = \boxed{\frac{12250000}{28800000}}$$

Step 3

$$\boxed{\frac{12250000}{28800000}} = \boxed{\frac{12250000 \div 50000}{28800000 \div 50000}} = \boxed{\mathbf{\frac{245}{576}}}$$

Step 4 $\boxed{\textit{Not Applicable}}$

Example 4.3-10

$$\boxed{0.09 \times \frac{0.1}{0.7} \times \frac{0.25}{0.6} =}$$

Solution:

Step 1a

$$0.09 \times \frac{0.1}{0.7} \times \frac{0.25}{0.6} = 0.09 \times \frac{\frac{1}{10}}{\frac{7}{10}} \times \frac{\frac{25}{100}}{\frac{6}{10}} = 0.09 \times \frac{1 \times 10}{10 \times 7} \times \frac{25 \times 10}{100 \times 6} = 0.09 \times \frac{10}{70} \times \frac{250}{600}$$

Step 1b

$$0.09 \times \frac{10}{70} \times \frac{250}{600} = \frac{9}{100} \times \frac{10}{70} \times \frac{250}{600}$$

Step 2

$$\frac{9}{100} \times \frac{10}{70} \times \frac{250}{600} = \frac{9 \times 10 \times 250}{100 \times 70 \times 600} = \frac{22500}{4200000}$$

Step 3

$$\frac{22500}{4200000} = \frac{22500 \div 500}{4200000 \div 500} = \frac{45}{8400} = \frac{45 \div 15}{8400 \div 15} = \boxed{\frac{3}{560}}$$

Step 4

$$\boxed{Not\ Applicable}$$

Example 4.3-11

$$\frac{0.9}{0.2} \times \frac{0.8}{0.1} \times \frac{0.5}{1.5} =$$

Solution:

Step 1a

$$\frac{0.9}{0.2} \times \frac{0.8}{0.1} \times \frac{0.5}{1.5} = \frac{\frac{9}{10}}{\frac{2}{10}} \times \frac{\frac{8}{10}}{\frac{1}{10}} \times \frac{\frac{5}{10}}{\frac{15}{10}} = \frac{9 \times 10}{10 \times 2} \times \frac{8 \times 10}{10 \times 1} \times \frac{5 \times 10}{10 \times 15} = \frac{90}{20} \times \frac{80}{10} \times \frac{50}{150}$$

Step 1b

$$\boxed{Not\ Applicable}$$

Step 2

$$\frac{90}{20} \times \frac{80}{10} \times \frac{50}{150} = \frac{90 \times 80 \times 50}{20 \times 10 \times 150} = \frac{360000}{30000}$$

Step 3

$$\frac{360000}{30000} = \frac{360000 \div 30000}{300000 \div 30000} = \frac{12}{1} = \boxed{12}$$

Step 4

$$\boxed{Not\ Applicable}$$

In general, three decimal fractions are multiplied as in the following cases:

Case I.

$$\frac{a \times 10^{-k_1}}{b \times 10^{-k_2}} \times \frac{c \times 10^{-k_3}}{d \times 10^{-k_4}} \times \frac{e \times 10^{-k_5}}{f \times 10^{-k_6}} = \frac{\left(a \times 10^{-k_1}\right) \times \left(c \times 10^{-k_3}\right) \times \left(e \times 10^{-k_5}\right)}{\left(b \times 10^{-k_2}\right) \times \left(d \times 10^{-k_4}\right) \times \left(f \times 10^{-k_6}\right)}$$

Let $\boxed{A_1 = a \times 10^{-k_1}}$, $\boxed{A_2 = b \times 10^{-k_2}}$, $\boxed{A_3 = c \times 10^{-k_3}}$, $\boxed{A_4 = d \times 10^{-k_4}}$, $\boxed{A_5 = e \times 10^{-k_5}}$, and

$\boxed{A_6 = f \times 10^{-k_6}}$, then

$$\boxed{\frac{\left(a \times 10^{-k_1}\right) \times \left(c \times 10^{-k_3}\right) \times \left(e \times 10^{-k_5}\right)}{\left(b \times 10^{-k_2}\right) \times \left(d \times 10^{-k_4}\right) \times \left(f \times 10^{-k_6}\right)}} = \boxed{\frac{A_1 \times A_3 \times A_5}{A_2 \times A_4 \times A_6}} = \boxed{\frac{A_1 A_3 A_5}{A_2 A_4 A_6}}$$

Example 4.3-12

$$\boxed{\frac{2 \times 10^{-1}}{5 \times 10^{-2}} \times \frac{24 \times 10^{-2}}{3 \times 10^{-1}} \times \frac{12 \times 10^{-3}}{14 \times 10^{-2}}} = \boxed{\frac{0.2}{0.05} \times \frac{0.24}{0.3} \times \frac{0.012}{0.14}} = \boxed{\frac{\frac{2}{10}}{\frac{5}{100}} \times \frac{\frac{24}{100}}{\frac{3}{10}} \times \frac{\frac{12}{1000}}{\frac{14}{100}}}$$

$$= \boxed{\frac{2 \times 100}{10 \times 5} \times \frac{24 \times 10}{100 \times 3} \times \frac{12 \times 100}{1000 \times 14}} = \boxed{\frac{200}{50} \times \frac{240}{300} \times \frac{1200}{14000}} = \boxed{\frac{\overset{4}{\cancel{200}} \times \overset{12}{\cancel{240}} \times \overset{3}{\cancel{1200}}}{\underset{1}{\cancel{50}} \times \underset{15}{\cancel{300}} \times \underset{35}{\cancel{14000}}}} = \boxed{\frac{4 \times 12 \times \cancel{3}}{1 \times \cancel{15} \times 35}} = \boxed{\frac{4 \times 12 \times 1}{1 \times 5 \times 35}}$$

$$= \boxed{\frac{48}{175}}$$

Case II.

$$\boxed{\frac{a \times 10^{-k_1}}{b \times 10^{-k_2}} \times \frac{c \times 10^{-k_3}}{d \times 10^{-k_4}} \times \frac{e \times 10^{-k_5}}{f \times 10^{-k_6}}} = \boxed{\left(\frac{a \times 10^{-k_1}}{b \times 10^{-k_2}} \times \frac{c \times 10^{-k_3}}{d \times 10^{-k_4}}\right) \times \frac{e \times 10^{-k_5}}{f \times 10^{-k_6}}}$$

$$= \boxed{\left(\frac{\left(a \times 10^{-k_1}\right) \times \left(c \times 10^{-k_3}\right)}{\left(b \times 10^{-k_2}\right) \times \left(d \times 10^{-k_4}\right)}\right) \times \frac{e \times 10^{-k_5}}{f \times 10^{-k_6}}}$$

Let $\boxed{A_1 = a \times 10^{-k_1}}$, $\boxed{A_2 = b \times 10^{-k_2}}$, $\boxed{A_3 = c \times 10^{-k_3}}$, $\boxed{A_4 = d \times 10^{-k_4}}$, $\boxed{A_5 = e \times 10^{-k_5}}$, and

$\boxed{A_6 = f \times 10^{-k_6}}$, then

$$\boxed{\left(\frac{\left(a \times 10^{-k_1}\right) \times \left(c \times 10^{-k_3}\right)}{\left(b \times 10^{-k_2}\right) \times \left(d \times 10^{-k_4}\right)}\right) \times \frac{e \times 10^{-k_5}}{f \times 10^{-k_6}}} = \boxed{\left(\frac{A_1 \times A_3}{A_2 \times A_4}\right) \times \frac{A_5}{A_6}} = \boxed{\left(\frac{A_1 A_3}{A_2 A_4}\right) \times \frac{A_5}{A_6}} = \boxed{\frac{A_1 A_3}{A_2 A_4} \times \frac{A_5}{A_6}}$$

$$= \boxed{\frac{A_1 A_3 \times A_5}{A_2 A_4 \times A_6}} = \boxed{\frac{A_1 A_3 A_5}{A_2 A_4 A_6}}$$

Example 4.3-13

$$\boxed{\frac{2 \times 10^{-1}}{5 \times 10^{-2}} \times \frac{24 \times 10^{-2}}{3 \times 10^{-1}} \times \frac{12 \times 10^{-3}}{14 \times 10^{-2}}} = \boxed{\frac{0.2}{0.05} \times \frac{0.24}{0.3} \times \frac{0.012}{0.14}} = \boxed{\left(\frac{\frac{2}{10}}{\frac{5}{100}} \times \frac{\frac{24}{100}}{\frac{3}{10}}\right) \times \frac{\frac{12}{1000}}{\frac{14}{100}}}$$

$$= \boxed{\left(\frac{2 \times 100}{10 \times 5} \times \frac{24 \times 10}{100 \times 3} \right) \times \frac{12 \times 100}{1000 \times 14}} = \boxed{\left(\frac{200}{50} \times \frac{240}{300} \right) \times \frac{1200}{14000}} = \boxed{\left(\frac{\overset{4}{200} \times \overset{12}{240}}{\underset{1}{50} \times \underset{15}{300}} \right) \frac{\overset{3}{1200}}{\underset{35}{14000}}} = \boxed{\left(\frac{4 \times 12}{1 \times 15} \right) \times \frac{3}{35}}$$

$$= \boxed{\left(\frac{4 \times 4}{1 \times 5} \right) \times \frac{3}{35}} = \boxed{\left(\frac{16}{5} \right) \times \frac{3}{35}} = \boxed{\frac{16}{5} \times \frac{3}{35}} = \boxed{\frac{16 \times 3}{5 \times 35}} = \boxed{\boxed{\frac{48}{175}}}$$

Case III.

$$\boxed{\frac{a \times 10^{-k_1}}{b \times 10^{-k_2}} \times \frac{c \times 10^{-k_3}}{d \times 10^{-k_4}} \times \frac{e \times 10^{-k_5}}{f \times 10^{-k_6}} = \frac{a \times 10^{-k_1}}{b \times 10^{-k_2}} \times \left(\frac{c \times 10^{-k_3}}{d \times 10^{-k_4}} \times \frac{e \times 10^{-k_5}}{f \times 10^{-k_6}} \right)}$$

$$= \boxed{\frac{a \times 10^{-k_1}}{b \times 10^{-k_2}} \times \left(\frac{\left(c \times 10^{-k_3} \right) \times \left(e \times 10^{-k_5} \right)}{\left(d \times 10^{-k_4} \right) \times \left(f \times 10^{-k_6} \right)} \right)}$$

Let $\boxed{A_1 = a \times 10^{-k_1}}$, $\boxed{A_2 = b \times 10^{-k_2}}$, $\boxed{A_3 = c \times 10^{-k_3}}$, $\boxed{A_4 = d \times 10^{-k_4}}$, $\boxed{A_5 = e \times 10^{-k_5}}$, and

$\boxed{A_6 = f \times 10^{-k_6}}$, then

$$\boxed{\frac{a \times 10^{-k_1}}{b \times 10^{-k_2}} \times \left(\frac{\left(c \times 10^{-k_3} \right) \times \left(e \times 10^{-k_5} \right)}{\left(d \times 10^{-k_4} \right) \times \left(f \times 10^{-k_6} \right)} \right)} = \boxed{\frac{A_1}{A_2} \times \left(\frac{A_3 \times A_5}{A_4 \times A_6} \right)} = \boxed{\frac{A_1}{A_2} \times \left(\frac{A_3 A_5}{A_4 A_6} \right)} = \boxed{\frac{A_1}{A_2} \times \frac{A_3 A_5}{A_4 A_6}}$$

$$= \boxed{\frac{A_1 \times A_3 A_5}{A_2 \times A_4 A_6}} = \boxed{\frac{A_1 A_3 A_5}{A_2 A_4 A_6}}$$

Example 4.3-14

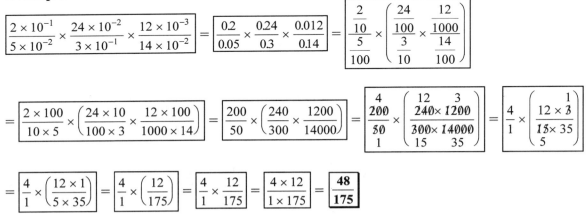

$$\boxed{\frac{2 \times 10^{-1}}{5 \times 10^{-2}} \times \frac{24 \times 10^{-2}}{3 \times 10^{-1}} \times \frac{12 \times 10^{-3}}{14 \times 10^{-2}}} = \boxed{\frac{0.2}{0.05} \times \frac{0.24}{0.3} \times \frac{0.012}{0.14}} = \boxed{\frac{\frac{2}{10}}{\frac{5}{100}} \times \left(\frac{\frac{24}{100}}{\frac{3}{10}} \times \frac{\frac{12}{1000}}{\frac{14}{100}} \right)}$$

$$= \boxed{\frac{2 \times 100}{10 \times 5} \times \left(\frac{24 \times 10}{100 \times 3} \times \frac{12 \times 100}{1000 \times 14} \right)} = \boxed{\frac{200}{50} \times \left(\frac{240}{300} \times \frac{1200}{14000} \right)} = \boxed{\frac{\overset{4}{200}}{\underset{1}{50}} \times \left(\frac{\overset{12}{240} \times \overset{3}{1200}}{\underset{15}{300} \times \underset{35}{14000}} \right)} = \boxed{\frac{4}{1} \times \left(\frac{12 \times 3}{15 \times 35} \right)}$$

$$= \boxed{\frac{4}{1} \times \left(\frac{12 \times 1}{5 \times 35} \right)} = \boxed{\frac{4}{1} \times \left(\frac{12}{175} \right)} = \boxed{\frac{4}{1} \times \frac{12}{175}} = \boxed{\frac{4 \times 12}{1 \times 175}} = \boxed{\boxed{\frac{48}{175}}}$$

Note - In multiplication the use of parentheses does not change the final answer; the three examples above have the same answer (see Section 1.4).

The following examples further illustrate how to multiply decimal fractions:

Example 4.3-15

$$\boxed{\frac{0.8}{0.01} \times \frac{0.05}{0.1}} = \boxed{\frac{\frac{8}{10}}{\frac{1}{100}} \times \frac{\frac{5}{100}}{\frac{1}{10}}} = \boxed{\frac{8 \times 100}{10 \times 1} \times \frac{5 \times 10}{100 \times 1}} = \boxed{\frac{\overset{80}{\cancel{800}}}{\underset{1}{\cancel{10}}} \times \frac{\overset{1}{\cancel{50}}}{\underset{2}{\cancel{100}}}} = \boxed{\frac{80}{1} \times \frac{1}{2}} = \boxed{\frac{\overset{40}{\cancel{80} \times 1}}{1 \times 2}} = \boxed{\frac{40 \times 1}{1 \times 1}} = \boxed{\frac{40}{1}}$$

$$= \boxed{40}$$

Example 4.3-16

$$\boxed{24.6 \times \frac{0.08}{1.6}} = \boxed{\frac{246}{10} \times \frac{\frac{8}{100}}{\frac{16}{10}}} = \boxed{\frac{246}{10} \times \frac{8 \times 10}{100 \times 16}} = \boxed{\frac{\overset{123}{\cancel{246}}}{\underset{5}{\cancel{10}}} \times \frac{\overset{1}{\cancel{80}}}{\underset{20}{\cancel{1600}}}} = \boxed{\frac{123}{5} \times \frac{1}{20}} = \boxed{\frac{123 \times 1}{5 \times 20}} = \boxed{\frac{123}{100}} = \boxed{1\frac{23}{100}}$$

Example 4.3-17

$$\boxed{\frac{0.18}{0.2} \times \frac{1.7}{0.04} \times \frac{0.8}{0.2}} = \boxed{\frac{\frac{18}{100}}{\frac{2}{10}} \times \frac{\frac{17}{10}}{\frac{4}{100}} \times \frac{\frac{8}{10}}{\frac{2}{10}}} = \boxed{\frac{18 \times 10}{100 \times 2} \times \frac{17 \times 100}{10 \times 4} \times \frac{8 \times 10}{10 \times 2}} = \boxed{\frac{\overset{9}{\cancel{180}}}{\underset{10}{\cancel{200}}} \times \frac{\overset{170}{\cancel{1700}}}{\underset{4}{\cancel{40}}} \times \frac{\overset{4}{\cancel{80}}}{\underset{1}{\cancel{20}}}} = \boxed{\frac{9}{10} \times \frac{170}{4} \times \frac{4}{1}}$$

$$= \boxed{\frac{9 \times \overset{17}{\cancel{170}} \times \overset{1}{\cancel{4}}}{\underset{1}{\cancel{10}} \times \underset{1}{\cancel{4}} \times 1}} = \boxed{\frac{9 \times 17 \times 1}{1 \times 1 \times 1}} = \boxed{\frac{153}{1}} = \boxed{153}$$

Example 4.3-18

$$\boxed{0.35 \times \frac{2.4}{0.04} \times \frac{1.8}{0.12}} = \boxed{\frac{35}{100} \times \frac{\frac{24}{10}}{\frac{4}{100}} \times \frac{\frac{18}{10}}{\frac{12}{100}}} = \boxed{\frac{35}{100} \times \frac{24 \times 100}{10 \times 4} \times \frac{18 \times 100}{10 \times 12}} = \boxed{\frac{\overset{7}{\cancel{35}} \times \overset{60}{\cancel{2400}} \times \overset{15}{\cancel{1800}}}{\underset{20}{\cancel{100}} \times \underset{1}{\cancel{40}} \times \underset{1}{\cancel{120}}}} = \boxed{\frac{7 \times 60 \times 15}{20 \times 1 \times 1}}$$

$$= \boxed{\frac{\overset{315}{\cancel{6300}}}{\underset{1}{\cancel{20}}}} = \boxed{\frac{315}{1}} = \boxed{315}$$

Example 4.3-19

$$\boxed{\left(\frac{0.5}{1.05} \times 10.5\right) \times \frac{2.8}{0.04}} = \boxed{\left(\frac{\frac{5}{10}}{\frac{105}{100}} \times \frac{105}{10}\right) \times \frac{\frac{28}{10}}{\frac{4}{100}}} = \boxed{\left(\frac{5 \times 100}{10 \times 105} \times \frac{105}{10}\right) \times \frac{28 \times 100}{10 \times 4}} = \boxed{\left(\frac{500}{1050} \times \frac{105}{10}\right) \times \frac{2800}{40}}$$

$$= \boxed{\left(\frac{\overset{10}{\cancel{500}}}{\underset{21}{\cancel{1050}}} \times \frac{\overset{21}{\cancel{105}}}{\underset{2}{\cancel{10}}}\right) \times \frac{\overset{70}{\cancel{2800}}}{\underset{1}{\cancel{40}}}} = \boxed{\left(\frac{10}{21} \times \frac{21}{2}\right) \times \frac{70}{1}} = \boxed{\left(\frac{\overset{5}{\cancel{10}} \times \overset{1}{\cancel{21}}}{\underset{1}{\cancel{21}} \times \underset{1}{\cancel{2}}}\right) \times \frac{70}{1}} = \boxed{\left(\frac{5 \times 1}{1 \times 1}\right) \times \frac{70}{1}} = \boxed{\left(\frac{5}{1}\right) \times \frac{70}{1}} = \boxed{\frac{5}{1} \times \frac{70}{1}}$$

$$= \boxed{\frac{5 \times 70}{1 \times 1}} = \boxed{\frac{350}{1}} = \boxed{350}$$

Example 4.3-20

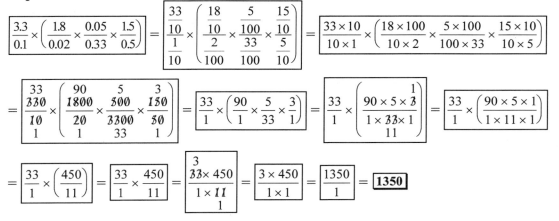

Example 4.3-21

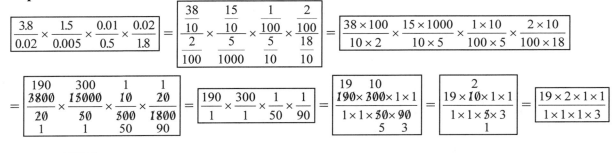

Example 4.3-22

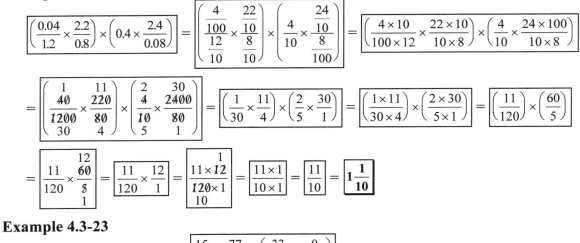

Example 4.3-23

$$\frac{1.5}{0.5} \times \frac{0.77}{0.02} \times \left(\frac{0.33}{0.7} \times \frac{0}{0.15} \right) = \frac{\frac{15}{10}}{\frac{5}{10}} \times \frac{\frac{77}{100}}{\frac{2}{100}} \times \left(\frac{\frac{33}{100}}{\frac{7}{10}} \times \frac{\frac{0}{1}}{\frac{15}{100}} \right) = \frac{15 \times 10}{10 \times 5} \times \frac{77 \times 100}{100 \times 2} \times \left(\frac{33 \times 10}{100 \times 7} \times \frac{100 \times 0}{1 \times 15} \right)$$

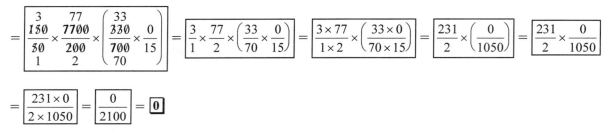

$$= \boxed{\frac{3}{130} \times \frac{77}{7700} \times \left(\frac{33}{330} \times \frac{0}{15}\right)} = \boxed{\frac{3}{1} \times \frac{77}{2} \times \left(\frac{33}{70} \times \frac{0}{15}\right)} = \boxed{\frac{3 \times 77}{1 \times 2} \times \left(\frac{33 \times 0}{70 \times 15}\right)} = \boxed{\frac{231}{2} \times \left(\frac{0}{1050}\right)} = \boxed{\frac{231}{2} \times \frac{0}{1050}}$$

$$= \boxed{\frac{231 \times 0}{2 \times 1050}} = \boxed{\frac{0}{2100}} = \boxed{0}$$

Note: Any number multiplied by zero is always equal to zero.

Example 4.3-24

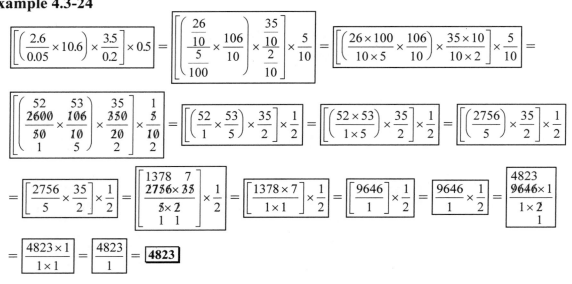

$$\boxed{\left[\left(\frac{2.6}{0.05} \times 10.6\right) \times \frac{3.5}{0.2}\right] \times 0.5} = \boxed{\left[\left(\frac{\frac{26}{10}}{\frac{5}{100}} \times \frac{106}{10}\right) \times \frac{\frac{35}{10}}{\frac{2}{10}}\right] \times \frac{5}{10}} = \boxed{\left[\left(\frac{26 \times 100}{10 \times 5} \times \frac{106}{10}\right) \times \frac{35 \times 10}{10 \times 2}\right] \times \frac{5}{10}} =$$

$$\boxed{\left[\left(\frac{52}{2600} \times \frac{53}{106} \times \frac{35}{350} \times \frac{1}{5}\right)\right]} = \boxed{\left[\left(\frac{52}{1} \times \frac{53}{5}\right) \times \frac{35}{2}\right] \times \frac{1}{2}} = \boxed{\left[\left(\frac{52 \times 53}{1 \times 5}\right) \times \frac{35}{2}\right] \times \frac{1}{2}} = \boxed{\left[\left(\frac{2756}{5}\right) \times \frac{35}{2}\right] \times \frac{1}{2}}$$

$$= \boxed{\left[\frac{2756}{5} \times \frac{35}{2}\right] \times \frac{1}{2}} = \boxed{\frac{2756 \times 35}{5 \times 2} \times \frac{1}{2}} = \boxed{\frac{1378 \times 7}{1 \times 1} \times \frac{1}{2}} = \boxed{\frac{9646}{1} \times \frac{1}{2}} = \boxed{\frac{9646}{1} \times \frac{1}{2}} = \boxed{\frac{9646 \times 1}{1 \times 2}}$$

$$= \boxed{\frac{4823 \times 1}{1 \times 1}} = \boxed{\frac{4823}{1}} = \boxed{4823}$$

Section 4.3 Exercises - Multiply the following decimal fractions:

1. $\dfrac{3.5}{0.07} \times \dfrac{0.7}{0.05} =$

2. $\dfrac{1.5}{0.05} \times \dfrac{0.1}{0.03} =$

3. $\left(\dfrac{1.8}{0.02} \times \dfrac{0.4}{0.04}\right) \times 0.07 =$

4. $\dfrac{1.5}{0.05} \times \dfrac{1.8}{0.2} \times \dfrac{0}{1.8} =$

5. $\dfrac{1.1}{0.2} \times \dfrac{0.44}{0.4} \times 3.8 =$

6. $\dfrac{7.5}{1.2} \times \dfrac{0.02}{0.8} \times \dfrac{0.12}{0.75} =$

7. $\left(\dfrac{3.9}{0.03} \times \dfrac{1.5}{0.05}\right) \times \dfrac{0.08}{0.39} =$

8. $1.45 \times \dfrac{7.5}{0.001} \times \dfrac{0.5}{0.45} =$

9. $\left(\dfrac{1.8}{0.04} \times 0.2\right) \times \left(\dfrac{0.4}{0.9} \times 0.12\right) =$

10. $\left[8.4 \times \left(\dfrac{5.5}{0.5} \times \dfrac{0.01}{0.1}\right)\right] \times 0.2 =$

4.4   Dividing Decimal Fractions

Two or more decimal fractions with or without a common denominator are divided using the steps given as in each case below:

Case I   *Divide two decimal fractions with or without a common denominator using the following steps:*

Step 1   a. Change the decimal fractions to integer fractions (see Section 2.4).

b. Change the decimal number $\left(a \times 10^{-k} \right)$ to an integer fraction of the form $\left(\dfrac{a}{10^k} \right)$,

e.g., change 238.6 to $\dfrac{2386}{10}$.

Step 2   Divide the integer fractions (see Section 3.4, Case I).

Step 3   Simplify the fraction to its lowest term (see Section 2.3).

Step 4   Change the improper fraction to a mixed fraction if the fraction obtained from Step 3 is an improper fraction (see Section 2.2).

The following examples show the steps as to how two decimal fractions with or without a common denominator are divided:

Example 4.4-1

$$\boxed{\dfrac{10.5}{0.06} \div \dfrac{12.4}{2.8}} =$$

Solution:

Step 1a $\boxed{\dfrac{10.5}{0.06} \div \dfrac{12.4}{2.8}} = \boxed{\dfrac{\frac{105}{10}}{\frac{6}{100}} \div \dfrac{\frac{124}{10}}{\frac{28}{10}}} = \boxed{\dfrac{105 \times 100}{10 \times 6} \div \dfrac{124 \times 10}{10 \times 28}} = \boxed{\dfrac{10500}{60} \div \dfrac{1240}{280}}$

Step 1b $\boxed{Not\ Applicable}$

Step 2 $\boxed{\dfrac{10500}{60} \div \dfrac{1240}{280}} = \boxed{\dfrac{10500}{60} \times \dfrac{280}{1240}} = \boxed{\dfrac{10500 \times 280}{60 \times 1240}} = \boxed{\dfrac{2940000}{74400}}$

Step 3 $\boxed{\dfrac{2940000}{74400}} = \boxed{\dfrac{2940000 \div 100}{74400 \div 100}} = \boxed{\dfrac{29400}{744}} = \boxed{\dfrac{29400 \div 24}{744 \div 24}} = \boxed{\dfrac{1225}{31}}$

Step 4 $\boxed{\dfrac{1225}{31}} = \boxed{39\dfrac{16}{31}}$

Example 4.4-2

$$\boxed{\dfrac{0.5}{0.08} \div 0.2} =$$

Solution:

Step 1a $\boxed{\dfrac{0.5}{0.08} \div 0.2} = \boxed{\dfrac{\frac{5}{10}}{\frac{8}{100}} \div 0.2} = \boxed{\dfrac{5 \times 100}{10 \times 8} \div 0.2} = \boxed{\dfrac{500}{80} \div 0.2}$

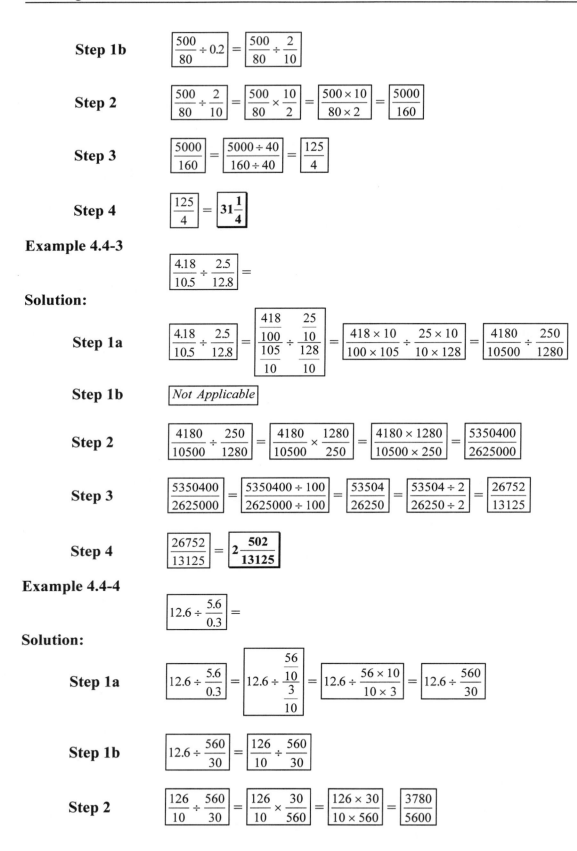

Step 1b $\boxed{\dfrac{500}{80} \div 0.2} = \boxed{\dfrac{500}{80} \div \dfrac{2}{10}}$

Step 2 $\boxed{\dfrac{500}{80} \div \dfrac{2}{10}} = \boxed{\dfrac{500}{80} \times \dfrac{10}{2}} = \boxed{\dfrac{500 \times 10}{80 \times 2}} = \boxed{\dfrac{5000}{160}}$

Step 3 $\boxed{\dfrac{5000}{160}} = \boxed{\dfrac{5000 \div 40}{160 \div 40}} = \boxed{\dfrac{125}{4}}$

Step 4 $\boxed{\dfrac{125}{4}} = \boxed{31\dfrac{1}{4}}$

Example 4.4-3

$\boxed{\dfrac{4.18}{10.5} \div \dfrac{2.5}{12.8}} =$

Solution:

Step 1a $\boxed{\dfrac{4.18}{10.5} \div \dfrac{2.5}{12.8}} = \boxed{\dfrac{\frac{418}{100}}{\frac{105}{10}} \div \dfrac{\frac{25}{10}}{\frac{128}{10}}} = \boxed{\dfrac{418 \times 10}{100 \times 105} \div \dfrac{25 \times 10}{10 \times 128}} = \boxed{\dfrac{4180}{10500} \div \dfrac{250}{1280}}$

Step 1b $\boxed{Not\ Applicable}$

Step 2 $\boxed{\dfrac{4180}{10500} \div \dfrac{250}{1280}} = \boxed{\dfrac{4180}{10500} \times \dfrac{1280}{250}} = \boxed{\dfrac{4180 \times 1280}{10500 \times 250}} = \boxed{\dfrac{5350400}{2625000}}$

Step 3 $\boxed{\dfrac{5350400}{2625000}} = \boxed{\dfrac{5350400 \div 100}{2625000 \div 100}} = \boxed{\dfrac{53504}{26250}} = \boxed{\dfrac{53504 \div 2}{26250 \div 2}} = \boxed{\dfrac{26752}{13125}}$

Step 4 $\boxed{\dfrac{26752}{13125}} = \boxed{2\dfrac{502}{13125}}$

Example 4.4-4

$\boxed{12.6 \div \dfrac{5.6}{0.3}} =$

Solution:

Step 1a $\boxed{12.6 \div \dfrac{5.6}{0.3}} = \boxed{12.6 \div \dfrac{\frac{56}{10}}{\frac{3}{10}}} = \boxed{12.6 \div \dfrac{56 \times 10}{10 \times 3}} = \boxed{12.6 \div \dfrac{560}{30}}$

Step 1b $\boxed{12.6 \div \dfrac{560}{30}} = \boxed{\dfrac{126}{10} \div \dfrac{560}{30}}$

Step 2 $\boxed{\dfrac{126}{10} \div \dfrac{560}{30}} = \boxed{\dfrac{126}{10} \times \dfrac{30}{560}} = \boxed{\dfrac{126 \times 30}{10 \times 560}} = \boxed{\dfrac{3780}{5600}}$

Step 3 $\dfrac{3780}{5600} = \dfrac{3780 \div 20}{5600 \div 20} = \boxed{\dfrac{\mathbf{189}}{\mathbf{280}}}$

Step 4 $\boxed{Not\ Applicable}$

Example 4.4-5

$\boxed{\dfrac{0.05}{1.5} \div \dfrac{3.6}{0.8}} =$

Solution:

Step 1a $\boxed{\dfrac{0.05}{1.5} \div \dfrac{3.6}{0.8}} = \boxed{\dfrac{\frac{5}{100}}{\frac{15}{10}} \div \dfrac{\frac{36}{10}}{\frac{8}{10}}} = \boxed{\dfrac{5 \times 10}{100 \times 15} \div \dfrac{36 \times 10}{10 \times 8}} = \boxed{\dfrac{50}{1500} \div \dfrac{360}{80}}$

Step 1b $\boxed{Not\ Applicable}$

Step 2 $\boxed{\dfrac{50}{1500} \div \dfrac{360}{80}} = \boxed{\dfrac{50}{1500} \times \dfrac{80}{360}} = \boxed{\dfrac{50 \times 80}{1500 \times 360}} = \boxed{\dfrac{4000}{540000}}$

Step 3 $\boxed{\dfrac{4000}{540000}} = \boxed{\dfrac{4000 \div 4000}{540000 \div 4000}} = \boxed{\dfrac{\mathbf{1}}{\mathbf{135}}}$

Step 4 $\boxed{Not\ Applicable}$

In general, two decimal fractions are divided in the following way:

$$\boxed{\dfrac{a \times 10^{-k_1}}{b \times 10^{-k_2}} \div \dfrac{c \times 10^{-k_3}}{d \times 10^{-k_4}}} = \boxed{\dfrac{a \times 10^{-k_1}}{b \times 10^{-k_2}} \times \dfrac{d \times 10^{-k_4}}{c \times 10^{-k_3}}} = \boxed{\dfrac{\left(a \times 10^{-k_1}\right) \times \left(d \times 10^{-k_4}\right)}{\left(b \times 10^{-k_2}\right) \times \left(c \times 10^{-k_3}\right)}}$$

Let $\boxed{A_1 = a \times 10^{-k_1}}$, $\boxed{A_2 = b \times 10^{-k_2}}$, $\boxed{A_3 = c \times 10^{-k_3}}$, and $\boxed{A_4 = d \times 10^{-k_4}}$, then

$$\boxed{\dfrac{\left(a \times 10^{-k_1}\right) \times \left(d \times 10^{-k_4}\right)}{\left(b \times 10^{-k_2}\right) \times \left(c \times 10^{-k_3}\right)}} = \boxed{\dfrac{A_1 \times A_4}{A_2 \times A_3}} = \boxed{\dfrac{A_1 A_4}{A_2 A_3}}$$

Example 4.4-6

$\boxed{\dfrac{5 \times 10^{-1}}{12 \times 10^{-2}} \times \dfrac{45 \times 10^{-3}}{6 \times 10^{-2}}} = \boxed{\dfrac{0.5}{0.12} \div \dfrac{0.045}{0.06}} = \boxed{\dfrac{\frac{5}{10}}{\frac{12}{100}} \div \dfrac{\frac{45}{1000}}{\frac{6}{100}}} = \boxed{\dfrac{5 \times 100}{10 \times 12} \div \dfrac{45 \times 100}{1000 \times 6}} = \boxed{\dfrac{500}{120} \div \dfrac{4500}{6000}}$

$= \boxed{\dfrac{500}{120} \times \dfrac{6000}{4500}} = \boxed{\dfrac{\overset{1}{\cancel{500}} \times \overset{50}{\cancel{6000}}}{\underset{1}{\cancel{120}} \times \underset{9}{\cancel{4500}}}} = \boxed{\dfrac{1 \times 50}{1 \times 9}} = \boxed{\dfrac{50}{9}} = \boxed{\mathbf{5\dfrac{5}{9}}}$

Case II   *Divide three decimal fractions with or without a common denominator using the following steps:*

Step 1   a. Change the decimal fractions to integer fractions (see Section 2.4).

b. Change the decimal number $\left(a \times 10^{-k}\right)$ to an integer fraction of the form $\left(\dfrac{a}{10^k}\right)$,

e.g., change 0.9 to $\dfrac{9}{10}$.

Step 2   Divide the integer fractions (see Section 3.4, Case II).

Step 3   Simplify the fraction to its lowest term (see Section 2.3).

Step 4   Change the improper fraction to a mixed fraction if the fraction obtained from Step 3 is an improper fraction (see Section 2.2).

The following examples show the steps as to how three decimal fractions with or without a common denominator are divided:

Example 4.4-7

$$\left[\left(\frac{0.12}{0.03} \div \frac{1.2}{0.5}\right) \div \frac{0.4}{0.9}\right] =$$

Solution:

Step 1a
$$\left[\left(\frac{0.12}{0.03} \div \frac{1.2}{0.5}\right) \div \frac{0.4}{0.9}\right] = \left[\left(\frac{\frac{12}{100}}{\frac{3}{100}} \div \frac{\frac{12}{10}}{\frac{5}{10}}\right) \div \frac{\frac{4}{10}}{\frac{9}{10}}\right] = \left[\left(\frac{12 \times 100}{100 \times 3} \div \frac{12 \times 10}{10 \times 5}\right) \div \frac{4 \times 10}{10 \times 9}\right]$$

$$= \left[\left(\frac{1200}{300} \div \frac{120}{50}\right) \div \frac{40}{90}\right]$$

Step 1b $\boxed{Not\ Applicable}$

Step 2
$$\left[\left(\frac{1200}{300} \div \frac{120}{50}\right) \div \frac{40}{90}\right] = \left[\left(\frac{1200}{300} \times \frac{50}{120}\right) \div \frac{40}{90}\right] = \left[\left(\frac{1200 \times 50}{300 \times 120}\right) \div \frac{40}{90}\right] = \left[\left(\frac{60000}{36000}\right) \div \frac{40}{90}\right]$$

$$= \left[\frac{60000}{36000} \div \frac{40}{90}\right] = \left[\frac{60000}{36000} \times \frac{90}{40}\right] = \left[\frac{60000 \times 90}{36000 \times 40}\right] = \left[\frac{5400000}{1440000}\right]$$

Step 3
$$\boxed{\frac{5400000}{1440000}} = \boxed{\frac{5400000 \div 10000}{1440000 \div 10000}} = \boxed{\frac{540}{144}} = \boxed{\frac{540 \div 36}{144 \div 36}} = \boxed{\frac{15}{4}}$$

Step 4
$$\boxed{\frac{15}{4}} = \boxed{3\frac{3}{4}}$$

Example 4.4-8

$$\left[0.03 \div \left(\frac{0.8}{0.5} \div 0.42\right)\right] =$$

Solution:

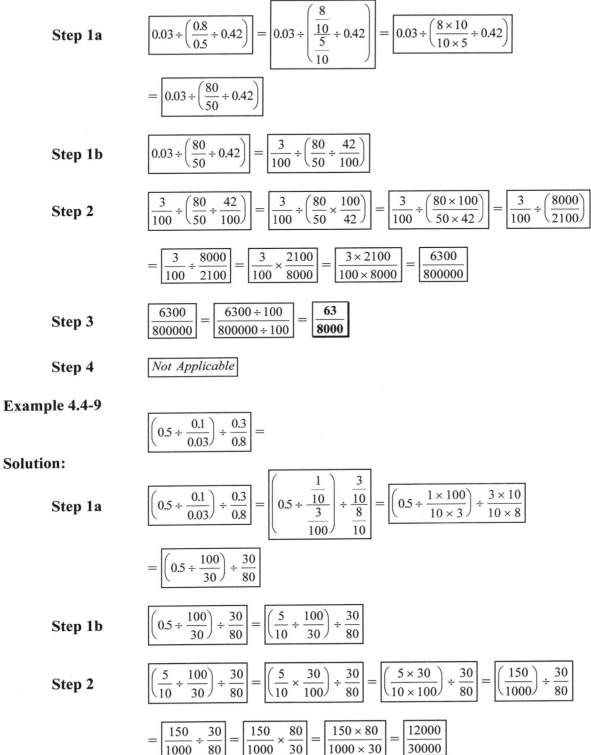

Step 1a $\boxed{0.03 \div \left(\dfrac{0.8}{0.5} \div 0.42 \right)} = \boxed{0.03 \div \left(\dfrac{\frac{8}{10}}{\frac{5}{10}} \div 0.42 \right)} = \boxed{0.03 \div \left(\dfrac{8 \times 10}{10 \times 5} \div 0.42 \right)}$

$= \boxed{0.03 \div \left(\dfrac{80}{50} \div 0.42 \right)}$

Step 1b $\boxed{0.03 \div \left(\dfrac{80}{50} \div 0.42 \right)} = \boxed{\dfrac{3}{100} \div \left(\dfrac{80}{50} \div \dfrac{42}{100} \right)}$

Step 2 $\boxed{\dfrac{3}{100} \div \left(\dfrac{80}{50} \div \dfrac{42}{100} \right)} = \boxed{\dfrac{3}{100} \div \left(\dfrac{80}{50} \times \dfrac{100}{42} \right)} = \boxed{\dfrac{3}{100} \div \left(\dfrac{80 \times 100}{50 \times 42} \right)} = \boxed{\dfrac{3}{100} \div \left(\dfrac{8000}{2100} \right)}$

$= \boxed{\dfrac{3}{100} \div \dfrac{8000}{2100}} = \boxed{\dfrac{3}{100} \times \dfrac{2100}{8000}} = \boxed{\dfrac{3 \times 2100}{100 \times 8000}} = \boxed{\dfrac{6300}{800000}}$

Step 3 $\boxed{\dfrac{6300}{800000}} = \boxed{\dfrac{6300 \div 100}{800000 \div 100}} = \boxed{\mathbf{\dfrac{63}{8000}}}$

Step 4 $\boxed{\textit{Not Applicable}}$

Example 4.4-9

$\boxed{\left(0.5 \div \dfrac{0.1}{0.03} \right) \div \dfrac{0.3}{0.8}} =$

Solution:

Step 1a $\boxed{\left(0.5 \div \dfrac{0.1}{0.03} \right) \div \dfrac{0.3}{0.8}} = \boxed{\left(0.5 \div \dfrac{\frac{1}{10}}{\frac{3}{100}} \right) \div \dfrac{\frac{3}{10}}{\frac{8}{10}}} = \boxed{\left(0.5 \div \dfrac{1 \times 100}{10 \times 3} \right) \div \dfrac{3 \times 10}{10 \times 8}}$

$= \boxed{\left(0.5 \div \dfrac{100}{30} \right) \div \dfrac{30}{80}}$

Step 1b $\boxed{\left(0.5 \div \dfrac{100}{30} \right) \div \dfrac{30}{80}} = \boxed{\left(\dfrac{5}{10} \div \dfrac{100}{30} \right) \div \dfrac{30}{80}}$

Step 2 $\boxed{\left(\dfrac{5}{10} \div \dfrac{100}{30} \right) \div \dfrac{30}{80}} = \boxed{\left(\dfrac{5}{10} \times \dfrac{30}{100} \right) \div \dfrac{30}{80}} = \boxed{\left(\dfrac{5 \times 30}{10 \times 100} \right) \div \dfrac{30}{80}} = \boxed{\left(\dfrac{150}{1000} \right) \div \dfrac{30}{80}}$

$= \boxed{\dfrac{150}{1000} \div \dfrac{30}{80}} = \boxed{\dfrac{150}{1000} \times \dfrac{80}{30}} = \boxed{\dfrac{150 \times 80}{1000 \times 30}} = \boxed{\dfrac{12000}{30000}}$

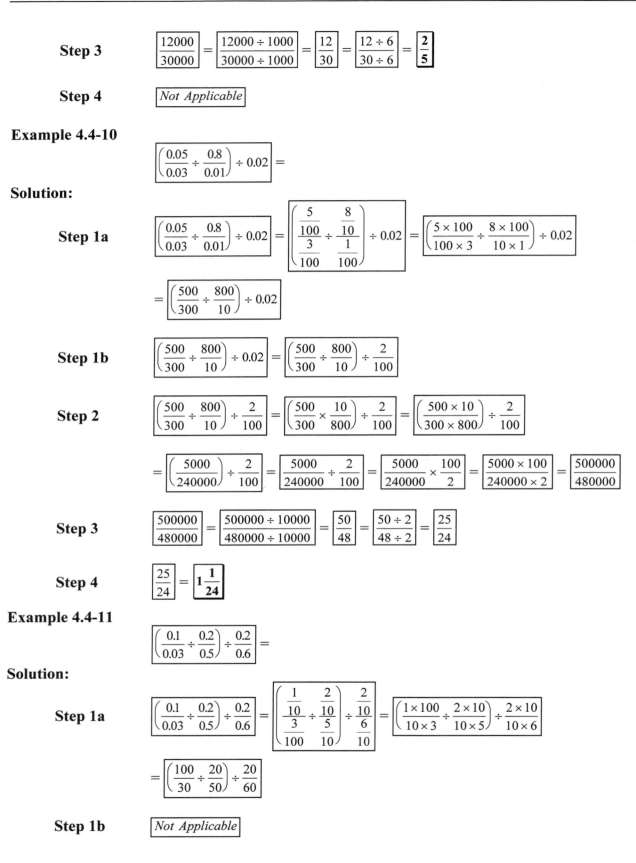

Step 3 $\dfrac{12000}{30000} = \dfrac{12000 \div 1000}{30000 \div 1000} = \dfrac{12}{30} = \dfrac{12 \div 6}{30 \div 6} = \boxed{\dfrac{2}{5}}$

Step 4 $\boxed{Not\ Applicable}$

Example 4.4-10

$\left(\dfrac{0.05}{0.03} \div \dfrac{0.8}{0.01} \right) \div 0.02 =$

Solution:

Step 1a $\left(\dfrac{0.05}{0.03} \div \dfrac{0.8}{0.01} \right) \div 0.02 = \left(\dfrac{\frac{5}{100}}{\frac{3}{100}} \div \dfrac{\frac{8}{10}}{\frac{1}{100}} \right) \div 0.02 = \left(\dfrac{5 \times 100}{100 \times 3} \div \dfrac{8 \times 100}{10 \times 1} \right) \div 0.02$

$= \left(\dfrac{500}{300} \div \dfrac{800}{10} \right) \div 0.02$

Step 1b $\left(\dfrac{500}{300} \div \dfrac{800}{10} \right) \div 0.02 = \left(\dfrac{500}{300} \div \dfrac{800}{10} \right) \div \dfrac{2}{100}$

Step 2 $\left(\dfrac{500}{300} \div \dfrac{800}{10} \right) \div \dfrac{2}{100} = \left(\dfrac{500}{300} \times \dfrac{10}{800} \right) \div \dfrac{2}{100} = \left(\dfrac{500 \times 10}{300 \times 800} \right) \div \dfrac{2}{100}$

$= \left(\dfrac{5000}{240000} \right) \div \dfrac{2}{100} = \dfrac{5000}{240000} \div \dfrac{2}{100} = \dfrac{5000}{240000} \times \dfrac{100}{2} = \dfrac{5000 \times 100}{240000 \times 2} = \dfrac{500000}{480000}$

Step 3 $\dfrac{500000}{480000} = \dfrac{500000 \div 10000}{480000 \div 10000} = \dfrac{50}{48} = \dfrac{50 \div 2}{48 \div 2} = \dfrac{25}{24}$

Step 4 $\dfrac{25}{24} = \boxed{1\dfrac{1}{24}}$

Example 4.4-11

$\left(\dfrac{0.1}{0.03} \div \dfrac{0.2}{0.5} \right) \div \dfrac{0.2}{0.6} =$

Solution:

Step 1a $\left(\dfrac{0.1}{0.03} \div \dfrac{0.2}{0.5} \right) \div \dfrac{0.2}{0.6} = \left(\dfrac{\frac{1}{10}}{\frac{3}{100}} \div \dfrac{\frac{2}{10}}{\frac{5}{10}} \right) \div \dfrac{\frac{2}{10}}{\frac{6}{10}} = \left(\dfrac{1 \times 100}{10 \times 3} \div \dfrac{2 \times 10}{10 \times 5} \right) \div \dfrac{2 \times 10}{10 \times 6}$

$= \left(\dfrac{100}{30} \div \dfrac{20}{50} \right) \div \dfrac{20}{60}$

Step 1b $\boxed{Not\ Applicable}$

Step 2

$$\left(\frac{100}{30} \div \frac{20}{50}\right) \div \frac{20}{60} = \left(\left(\frac{100}{30} \times \frac{50}{20}\right) \div \frac{20}{60}\right) = \left(\left(\frac{100 \times 50}{30 \times 20}\right) \div \frac{20}{60}\right) = \left(\left(\frac{5000}{600}\right) \div \frac{20}{60}\right)$$

$$= \left|\frac{5000}{600} \div \frac{20}{60}\right| = \left|\frac{5000}{600} \times \frac{60}{20}\right| = \left|\frac{5000 \times 60}{600 \times 20}\right| = \left|\frac{300000}{12000}\right|$$

Step 3

$$\left|\frac{300000}{12000}\right| = \left|\frac{30000 \div 3000}{12000 \div 3000}\right| = \left|\frac{100}{4}\right| = \left|\frac{100 \div 4}{4 \div 4}\right| = \left|\frac{25}{1}\right| = \boxed{25}$$

Step 4 $\boxed{\textit{Not Applicable}}$

In general, three decimal fractions are divided as in the following cases:

Case I.

$$\left(\frac{a \times 10^{-k_1}}{b \times 10^{-k_2}} \div \frac{c \times 10^{-k_3}}{d \times 10^{-k_4}}\right) \div \frac{e \times 10^{-k_5}}{f \times 10^{-k_6}} = \left(\left(\frac{a \times 10^{-k_1}}{b \times 10^{-k_2}} \times \frac{d \times 10^{-k_4}}{c \times 10^{-k_3}}\right) \div \frac{e \times 10^{-k_5}}{f \times 10^{-k_6}}\right)$$

$$= \left|\frac{\left(a \times 10^{-k_1}\right) \times \left(d \times 10^{-k_4}\right)}{\left(b \times 10^{-k_2}\right) \times \left(c \times 10^{-k_3}\right)} \div \frac{e \times 10^{-k_5}}{f \times 10^{-k_6}}\right|$$

Let $\boxed{A_1 = a \times 10^{-k_1}}$, $\boxed{A_2 = b \times 10^{-k_2}}$, $\boxed{A_3 = c \times 10^{-k_3}}$, $\boxed{A_4 = d \times 10^{-k_4}}$, $\boxed{A_5 = e \times 10^{-k_5}}$, and

$\boxed{A_6 = f \times 10^{-k_6}}$, then

$$\left|\frac{\left(a \times 10^{-k_1}\right) \times \left(d \times 10^{-k_4}\right)}{\left(b \times 10^{-k_2}\right) \times \left(c \times 10^{-k_3}\right)} \div \frac{e \times 10^{-k_5}}{f \times 10^{-k_6}}\right| = \left(\frac{A_1 \times A_4}{A_2 \times A_3}\right) \div \frac{A_5}{A_6} = \left(\frac{A_1 A_4}{A_2 A_3}\right) \div \frac{A_5}{A_6} = \frac{A_1 A_4}{A_2 A_3} \div \frac{A_5}{A_6}$$

$$= \frac{A_1 A_4}{A_2 A_3} \times \frac{A_6}{A_5} = \frac{A_1 A_4 \times A_6}{A_2 A_3 \times A_5} = \frac{A_1 A_4 A_6}{A_2 A_3 A_5}$$

Example 4.4-12

$$\left(\frac{4 \times 10^{-1}}{25 \times 10^{-2}} \div \frac{12 \times 10^{-2}}{3 \times 10^{-1}}\right) \div \frac{45 \times 10^{-3}}{6 \times 10^{-2}} = \left(\frac{0.4}{0.25} \div \frac{0.12}{0.3}\right) \div \frac{0.045}{0.06} = \left(\frac{\frac{4}{10}}{\frac{25}{100}} \div \frac{\frac{12}{100}}{\frac{3}{10}}\right) \div \frac{\frac{45}{1000}}{\frac{6}{100}}$$

$$= \left(\frac{4 \times 100}{10 \times 25} \div \frac{12 \times 10}{100 \times 3}\right) \div \frac{45 \times 100}{1000 \times 6} = \left(\frac{400}{250} \div \frac{120}{300}\right) \div \frac{4500}{6000} = \left(\frac{\cancel{400}}{\cancel{250}}^{8}_{5} \div \frac{\cancel{120}}{\cancel{300}}^{4}_{10}\right) \div \frac{\cancel{4500}}{\cancel{6000}}^{9}_{12} = \left(\frac{8}{5} \div \frac{4}{10}\right) \div \frac{9}{12}$$

$$= \left[\left(\frac{8}{5} \times \frac{10}{4} \right) \div \frac{9}{12} \right] = \left[\left(\frac{8 \times 10}{5 \times 4} \right) \div \frac{9}{12} \right] = \left[\left(\frac{80}{20} \right) \div \frac{9}{12} \right] = \left[\frac{\overset{4}{\cancel{80}}}{\underset{1}{\cancel{20}}} \div \frac{\overset{3}{\cancel{9}}}{\underset{4}{\cancel{12}}} \right] = \left[\frac{4}{1} \div \frac{3}{4} \right] = \left[\frac{4}{1} \times \frac{4}{3} \right] = \left[\frac{4 \times 4}{1 \times 3} \right] = \left[\frac{16}{3} \right]$$

$$= \boxed{5\frac{1}{3}}$$

Case II.

$$\left[\frac{a \times 10^{-k_1}}{b \times 10^{-k_2}} \div \left(\frac{c \times 10^{-k_3}}{d \times 10^{-k_4}} \div \frac{e \times 10^{-k_5}}{f \times 10^{-k_6}} \right) \right] = \left[\frac{a \times 10^{-k_1}}{b \times 10^{-k_2}} \div \left(\frac{c \times 10^{-k_3}}{d \times 10^{-k_4}} \times \frac{f \times 10^{-k_6}}{e \times 10^{-k_5}} \right) \right]$$

$$= \left[\frac{a \times 10^{-k_1}}{b \times 10^{-k_2}} \div \left(\frac{\left(c \times 10^{-k_3} \right) \times \left(f \times 10^{-k_6} \right)}{\left(d \times 10^{-k_4} \right) \times \left(e \times 10^{-k_5} \right)} \right) \right]$$

Let $\boxed{A_1 = a \times 10^{-k_1}}$, $\boxed{A_2 = b \times 10^{-k_2}}$, $\boxed{A_3 = c \times 10^{-k_3}}$, $\boxed{A_4 = d \times 10^{-k_4}}$, $\boxed{A_5 = e \times 10^{-k_5}}$, and

$\boxed{A_6 = f \times 10^{-k_6}}$, then

$$\left[\frac{a \times 10^{-k_1}}{b \times 10^{-k_2}} \div \left(\frac{\left(c \times 10^{-k_3} \right) \times \left(f \times 10^{-k_6} \right)}{\left(d \times 10^{-k_4} \right) \times \left(e \times 10^{-k_5} \right)} \right) \right] = \left[\frac{A_1}{A_2} \div \left(\frac{A_3 \times A_6}{A_4 \times A_5} \right) \right] = \left[\frac{A_1}{A_2} \div \left(\frac{A_3 A_6}{A_4 A_5} \right) \right] = \left[\frac{A_1}{A_2} \div \frac{A_3 A_6}{A_4 A_5} \right]$$

$$= \left[\frac{A_1}{A_2} \times \frac{A_4 A_5}{A_3 A_6} \right] = \left[\frac{A_1 \times A_4 A_5}{A_2 \times A_3 A_6} \right] = \boxed{\frac{A_1 A_4 A_5}{A_2 A_3 A_6}}$$

Example 4.4-13

$$\left[\frac{4 \times 10^{-1}}{25 \times 10^{-2}} \div \left(\frac{12 \times 10^{-2}}{3 \times 10^{-1}} \div \frac{45 \times 10^{-3}}{6 \times 10^{-2}} \right) \right] = \left[\frac{0.4}{0.25} \div \left(\frac{0.12}{0.3} \div \frac{0.045}{0.06} \right) \right] = \left[\frac{\frac{4}{10}}{\frac{25}{100}} \div \left(\frac{\frac{12}{100}}{\frac{3}{10}} \div \frac{\frac{45}{1000}}{\frac{6}{100}} \right) \right]$$

$$= \left[\frac{4 \times 100}{10 \times 25} \div \left(\frac{12 \times 10}{100 \times 3} \div \frac{45 \times 100}{1000 \times 6} \right) \right] = \left[\frac{400}{250} \div \left(\frac{120}{300} \div \frac{4500}{6000} \right) \right] = \left[\frac{\overset{8}{\cancel{400}}}{\underset{5}{\cancel{250}}} \div \left(\frac{\overset{4}{\cancel{120}}}{\underset{10}{\cancel{300}}} \div \frac{\overset{9}{\cancel{4500}}}{\underset{12}{\cancel{6000}}} \right) \right] = \left[\frac{8}{5} \div \left(\frac{4}{10} \div \frac{9}{12} \right) \right]$$

$$= \left[\frac{8}{5} \div \left(\frac{4}{10} \times \frac{12}{9} \right) \right] = \left[\frac{8}{5} \div \left(\frac{4 \times 12}{10 \times 9} \right) \right] = \left[\frac{8}{5} \div \left(\frac{48}{90} \right) \right] = \left[\frac{8}{5} \div \frac{\overset{24}{\cancel{48}}}{\underset{45}{\cancel{90}}} \right] = \left[\frac{8}{5} \div \frac{24}{45} \right] = \left[\frac{8}{5} \times \frac{45}{24} \right] = \left[\frac{\overset{1}{\cancel{8}} \times \overset{9}{\cancel{45}}}{\underset{1}{\cancel{5}} \times \underset{3}{\cancel{24}}} \right] = \left[\frac{1 \times 9}{1 \times 6} \right]$$

$$= \left[\frac{1 \times 9}{1 \times 3} \right] = \left[\frac{\overset{3}{\cancel{9}}}{\underset{1}{\cancel{3}}} \right] = \left[\frac{3}{1} \right] = \boxed{3}$$

The following examples further illustrate how to divide decimal fractions:

Example 4.4-14

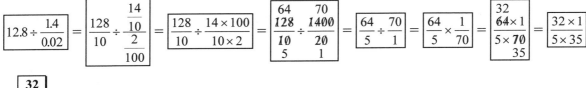

$$= \boxed{\frac{60}{1}} = \boxed{\mathbf{60}}$$

Example 4.4-15

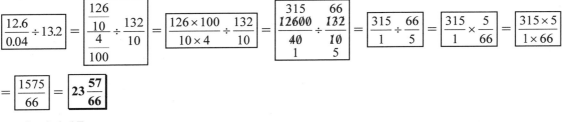

$$= \boxed{\frac{32}{175}}$$

Example 4.4-16

$$\boxed{\frac{12.6}{0.04} \div 13.2} = \boxed{\frac{\frac{126}{10}}{\frac{4}{100}} \div \frac{132}{10}} = \boxed{\frac{126 \times 100}{10 \times 4} \div \frac{132}{10}} = \boxed{\frac{\overset{315}{\underset{1}{\cancel{12600}}}}{\underset{1}{\cancel{40}}} \div \frac{132}{\underset{5}{\cancel{10}}}} = \boxed{\frac{315}{1} \div \frac{66}{5}} = \boxed{\frac{315}{1} \times \frac{5}{66}} = \boxed{\frac{315 \times 5}{1 \times 66}}$$

$$= \boxed{\frac{1575}{66}} = \boxed{\mathbf{23 \frac{57}{66}}}$$

Example 4.4-17

$$\boxed{\left(\frac{0.3}{0.05} \div \frac{0.1}{0.5}\right) \div \frac{0.4}{0.12}} = \boxed{\left(\frac{\frac{3}{10}}{\frac{5}{100}} \div \frac{\frac{1}{10}}{\frac{5}{10}}\right) \div \frac{\frac{4}{10}}{\frac{12}{100}}} = \boxed{\left(\frac{3 \times 100}{10 \times 5} \div \frac{1 \times 10}{10 \times 5}\right) \div \frac{4 \times 100}{10 \times 12}} = \boxed{\left(\frac{300}{50} \div \frac{10}{50}\right) \div \frac{400}{120}}$$

$$= \boxed{\left(\frac{300}{50} \times \frac{50}{10}\right) \div \frac{400}{120}} = \boxed{\left(\frac{\overset{30}{\cancel{300}} \times \overset{1}{\cancel{50}}}{\underset{1}{\cancel{50}} \times \underset{1}{\cancel{10}}}\right) \div \frac{\overset{10}{\cancel{400}}}{\underset{3}{\cancel{120}}}} = \boxed{\left(\frac{30 \times 1}{1 \times 1}\right) \div \frac{10}{3}} = \boxed{\left(\frac{30}{1}\right) \div \frac{10}{3}} = \boxed{\frac{30}{1} \div \frac{10}{3}} = \boxed{\frac{30}{1} \times \frac{3}{10}}$$

$$= \boxed{\frac{\overset{3}{\cancel{30}} \times 3}{1 \times \underset{1}{\cancel{10}}}} = \boxed{\frac{3 \times 3}{1 \times 1}} = \boxed{\frac{9}{1}} = \boxed{\mathbf{9}}$$

Example 4.4-18

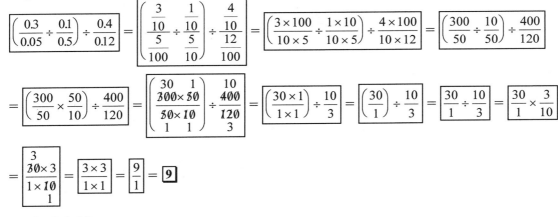

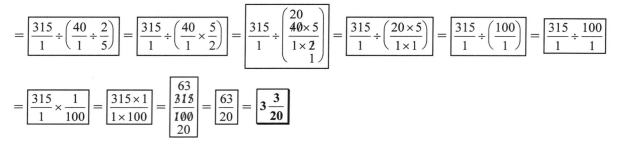

Example 4.4-19

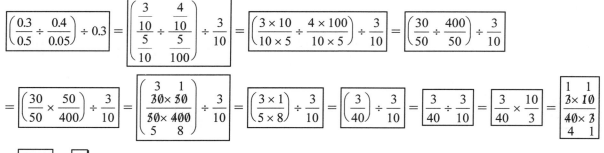

Example 4.4-20

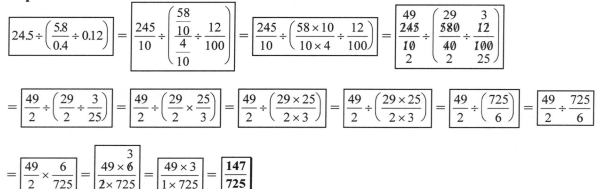

Example 4.4-21

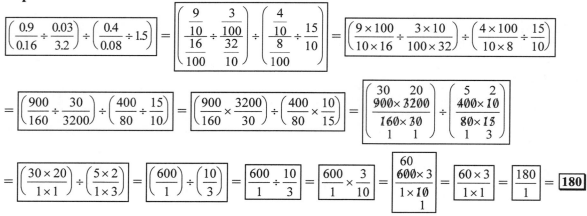

Example 4.4-22

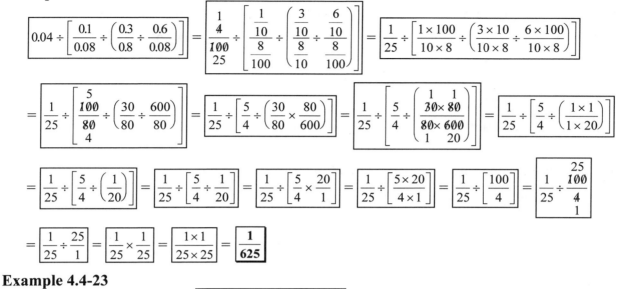

Example 4.4-23

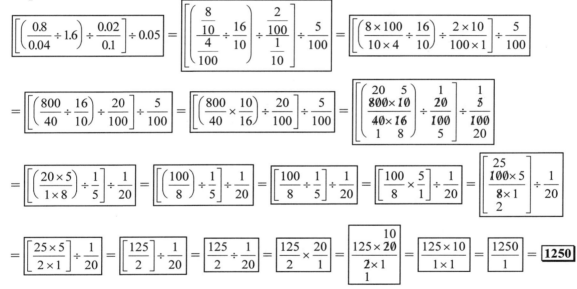

Section 4.4 Exercises - Divide the following decimal fractions:

1. $\dfrac{0.8}{0.01} \div \dfrac{0.04}{0.2} =$

2. $\dfrac{0.3}{0.08} \div \dfrac{1.2}{0.16} =$

3. $\dfrac{0.04}{0.05} \div 0.2 =$

4. $\left(\dfrac{0.9}{0.08} \div \dfrac{1.8}{0.16}\right) \div \dfrac{0.4}{0.02} =$

5. $0.6 \div \left(\dfrac{1.2}{0.64} \div \dfrac{0.04}{0.1}\right) =$

6. $\left(\dfrac{0.2}{0.05} \div \dfrac{0.4}{3.5}\right) \div \dfrac{0.8}{0.01} =$

7. $\dfrac{0.6}{0.01} \div \left(0.3 \div \dfrac{0.06}{0.4}\right) =$

8. $\dfrac{0.5}{0.04} \div \left(\dfrac{0.08}{0.1} \div 0.04\right) =$

9. $\left(\dfrac{0.9}{0.8} \div \dfrac{0.27}{1.6}\right) \div \dfrac{0.1}{0.09} =$

10. $\left[\left(\dfrac{0.1}{0.05} \div \dfrac{0.4}{0.02}\right) \div \dfrac{0.04}{0.1}\right] \div 0.2 =$

4.5   Solving Mixed Operations Using Decimal Fractions

Decimal fractions are added, subtracted, multiplied, and divided by using the following steps:

Step 1   a. Change the decimal fractions to integer fractions (see Section 2.4).

b. Change the decimal number $\left(a \times 10^{-k}\right)$ to an integer fraction of the form $\left(\frac{a}{10^k}\right)$,

e.g., change 0.038 to $\frac{38}{1000}$.

Step 2   Add, subtract, multiply, and divide the integer fractions by following the steps outlined in sections 3.1 through 3.4.

Step 3   Simplify the fraction to its lowest term (see Sections 2.3).

Step 4   Change the improper fraction to a mixed fraction if the fraction obtained from Step 3 is an improper fraction (see Section 2.2).

The following examples show mathematical operations on decimal fractions using the above steps:

Example 4.5-1

$$\left[\left(\frac{0.2}{0.06} \div 0.5\right) \times \frac{0.1}{0.3}\right] =$$

Solution:

Step 1a

$$\left[\left(\frac{0.2}{0.06} \div 0.5\right) \times \frac{0.1}{0.3}\right] = \left[\left(\frac{\frac{2}{10}}{\frac{6}{100}} \div 0.5\right) \times \frac{\frac{1}{10}}{\frac{3}{10}}\right] = \left[\left(\frac{2 \times 100}{10 \times 6} \div 0.5\right) \times \frac{1 \times 10}{10 \times 3}\right]$$

$$= \left[\left(\frac{200}{60} \div 0.5\right) \times \frac{10}{30}\right]$$

Step 1b

$$\left[\left(\frac{200}{60} \div 0.5\right) \times \frac{10}{30}\right] = \left[\left(\frac{200}{60} \div \frac{5}{10}\right) \times \frac{10}{30}\right]$$

Step 2

$$\left[\left(\frac{200}{60} \div \frac{5}{10}\right) \times \frac{10}{30}\right] = \left[\left(\frac{200}{60} \times \frac{10}{5}\right) \times \frac{10}{30}\right] = \left[\left(\frac{200 \times 10}{60 \times 5}\right) \times \frac{10}{30}\right] = \left[\left(\frac{2000}{300}\right) \times \frac{10}{30}\right]$$

$$= \left[\frac{2000}{300} \times \frac{10}{30}\right] = \left[\frac{2000 \times 10}{300 \times 30}\right] = \left[\frac{20000}{9000}\right]$$

Step 3

$$\left[\frac{20000}{9000}\right] = \left[\frac{20000 \div 1000}{9000 \div 1000}\right] = \left[\frac{20}{9}\right]$$

Step 4

$$\left[\frac{20}{9}\right] = \left[2\frac{2}{9}\right]$$

Example 4.5-2

$$\left(\frac{0.04}{0.5} + \frac{0.08}{0.5} \right) \times \frac{1.2}{0.1} =$$

Solution:

Step 1a

$$\left(\frac{0.04}{0.5} + \frac{0.08}{0.5} \right) \times \frac{1.2}{0.1} = \left(\frac{0.04 + 0.08}{0.5} \right) \times \frac{1.2}{0.1} = \left(\frac{0.12}{0.5} \right) \times \frac{1.2}{0.1} = \frac{0.12}{0.5} \times \frac{1.2}{0.1}$$

$$= \frac{\dfrac{12}{100}}{\dfrac{5}{10}} \times \frac{\dfrac{12}{10}}{\dfrac{1}{10}} = \frac{12 \times 10}{100 \times 5} \times \frac{12 \times 10}{10 \times 1} = \frac{120}{500} \times \frac{120}{10}$$

Step 1b   Not Applicable

Step 2

$$\frac{120}{500} \times \frac{120}{10} = \frac{120 \times 120}{500 \times 10} = \frac{14400}{5000}$$

Step 3

$$\frac{14400}{5000} = \frac{14400 \div 100}{5000 \div 100} = \frac{144}{50} = \frac{144 \div 2}{50 \div 2} = \frac{72}{25}$$

Step 4

$$\frac{72}{25} = \mathbf{2\frac{22}{25}}$$

Example 4.5-3

$$\left(\frac{0.15}{0.3} - \frac{0.1}{0.5} \right) \div \frac{1.2}{0.02} =$$

Solution:

Step 1a

$$\left(\frac{0.15}{0.3} - \frac{0.1}{0.5} \right) \div \frac{1.2}{0.02} = \left(\frac{\dfrac{15}{100}}{\dfrac{3}{10}} - \frac{\dfrac{1}{10}}{\dfrac{5}{10}} \right) \div \frac{\dfrac{12}{10}}{\dfrac{2}{100}} = \left(\frac{15 \times 10}{100 \times 3} - \frac{1 \times 10}{10 \times 5} \right) \div \frac{12 \times 100}{10 \times 2}$$

$$= \left(\frac{150}{300} - \frac{10}{50} \right) \div \frac{1200}{20}$$

Step 1b   Not Applicable

Step 2

$$\left(\frac{150}{300} - \frac{10}{50} \right) \div \frac{1200}{20} = \left(\frac{(150 \times 50) - (10 \times 300)}{300 \times 50} \right) \div \frac{1200}{20} = \left(\frac{7500 - 3000}{15000} \right) \div \frac{1200}{20}$$

$$= \left(\frac{4500}{15000} \right) \div \frac{1200}{20} = \frac{4500}{15000} \div \frac{1200}{20} = \frac{4500}{15000} \times \frac{20}{1200} = \frac{4500 \times 20}{15000 \times 1200}$$

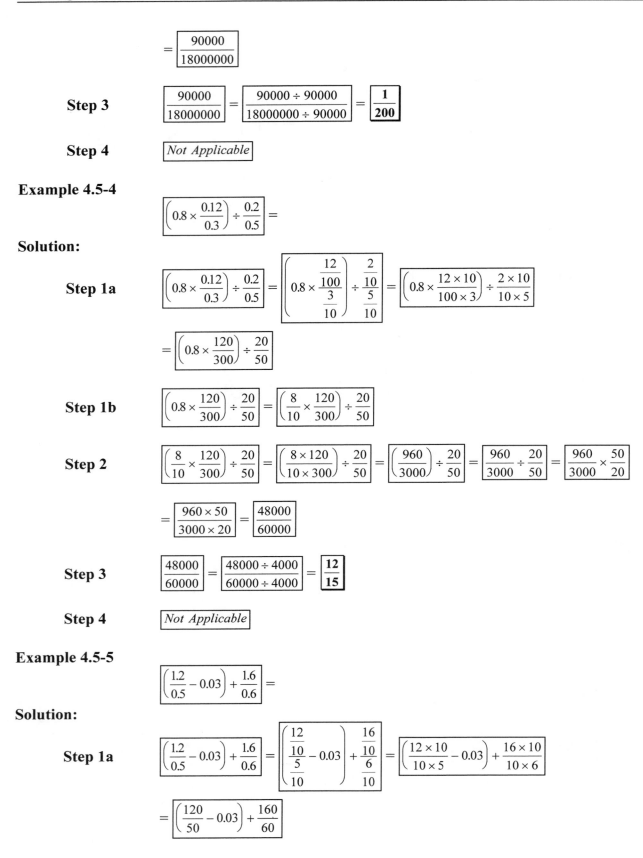

$$= \boxed{\dfrac{90000}{18000000}}$$

Step 3 $\boxed{\dfrac{90000}{18000000}} = \boxed{\dfrac{90000 \div 90000}{18000000 \div 90000}} = \boxed{\dfrac{1}{200}}$

Step 4 $\boxed{Not\ Applicable}$

Example 4.5-4

$$\boxed{\left(0.8 \times \dfrac{0.12}{0.3}\right) \div \dfrac{0.2}{0.5}} =$$

Solution:

Step 1a $\boxed{\left(0.8 \times \dfrac{0.12}{0.3}\right) \div \dfrac{0.2}{0.5}} = \boxed{\left(0.8 \times \dfrac{\frac{12}{100}}{\frac{3}{10}}\right) \div \dfrac{\frac{2}{10}}{\frac{5}{10}}} = \boxed{\left(0.8 \times \dfrac{12 \times 10}{100 \times 3}\right) \div \dfrac{2 \times 10}{10 \times 5}}$

$$= \boxed{\left(0.8 \times \dfrac{120}{300}\right) \div \dfrac{20}{50}}$$

Step 1b $\boxed{\left(0.8 \times \dfrac{120}{300}\right) \div \dfrac{20}{50}} = \boxed{\left(\dfrac{8}{10} \times \dfrac{120}{300}\right) \div \dfrac{20}{50}}$

Step 2 $\boxed{\left(\dfrac{8}{10} \times \dfrac{120}{300}\right) \div \dfrac{20}{50}} = \boxed{\left(\dfrac{8 \times 120}{10 \times 300}\right) \div \dfrac{20}{50}} = \boxed{\left(\dfrac{960}{3000}\right) \div \dfrac{20}{50}} = \boxed{\dfrac{960}{3000} \div \dfrac{20}{50}} = \boxed{\dfrac{960}{3000} \times \dfrac{50}{20}}$

$$= \boxed{\dfrac{960 \times 50}{3000 \times 20}} = \boxed{\dfrac{48000}{60000}}$$

Step 3 $\boxed{\dfrac{48000}{60000}} = \boxed{\dfrac{48000 \div 4000}{60000 \div 4000}} = \boxed{\dfrac{12}{15}}$

Step 4 $\boxed{Not\ Applicable}$

Example 4.5-5

$$\boxed{\left(\dfrac{1.2}{0.5} - 0.03\right) + \dfrac{1.6}{0.6}} =$$

Solution:

Step 1a $\boxed{\left(\dfrac{1.2}{0.5} - 0.03\right) + \dfrac{1.6}{0.6}} = \boxed{\left(\dfrac{\frac{12}{10}}{\frac{5}{10}} - 0.03\right) + \dfrac{\frac{16}{10}}{\frac{6}{10}}} = \boxed{\left(\dfrac{12 \times 10}{10 \times 5} - 0.03\right) + \dfrac{16 \times 10}{10 \times 6}}$

$$= \boxed{\left(\dfrac{120}{50} - 0.03\right) + \dfrac{160}{60}}$$

Step 1b
$$\left(\frac{120}{50} - 0.03\right) + \frac{160}{60} = \left(\frac{120}{50} - \frac{3}{100}\right) + \frac{160}{60}$$

Step 2
$$\left(\frac{120}{50} - \frac{3}{100}\right) + \frac{160}{60} = \left(\frac{(120 \times 100) - (3 \times 50)}{50 \times 100}\right) + \frac{160}{60} = \left(\frac{12000 - 150}{5000}\right) + \frac{160}{60}$$

$$= \left(\frac{11850}{5000}\right) + \frac{160}{60} = \frac{11850}{5000} + \frac{160}{60} = \frac{(11850 \times 60) + (160 \times 5000)}{5000 \times 60}$$

$$= \frac{711000 + 800000}{300000} = \frac{1511000}{300000}$$

Step 3
$$\frac{1511000}{300000} = \frac{1511000 \div 1000}{300000 \div 1000} = \frac{1511}{300}$$

Step 4
$$\frac{1511}{300} = 5\frac{11}{300}$$

In general, decimal fractions are added, subtracted, multiplied, and divided as in the following example cases which are followed by a specific example for each case:

Case I.

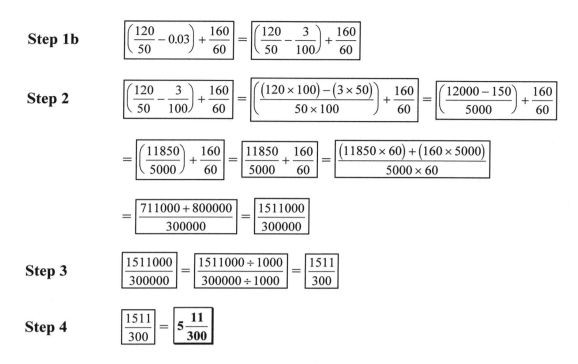

$$\left(\frac{a \times 10^{-k_1}}{b \times 10^{-k_2}} \div \frac{c \times 10^{-k_3}}{d \times 10^{-k_4}}\right) \times \frac{e \times 10^{-k_5}}{f \times 10^{-k_6}} = \left(\frac{a \times 10^{-k_1}}{b \times 10^{-k_2}} \times \frac{d \times 10^{-k_4}}{c \times 10^{-k_3}}\right) \times \frac{e \times 10^{-k_5}}{f \times 10^{-k_6}}$$

$$= \frac{\left(\left(a \times 10^{-k_1}\right) \times \left(d \times 10^{-k_4}\right)\right)}{\left(\left(b \times 10^{-k_2}\right) \times \left(c \times 10^{-k_3}\right)\right)} \times \frac{e \times 10^{-k_5}}{f \times 10^{-k_6}}$$

Let $A_1 = a \times 10^{-k_1}$, $A_2 = b \times 10^{-k_2}$, $A_3 = c \times 10^{-k_3}$, $A_4 = d \times 10^{-k_4}$, $A_5 = e \times 10^{-k_5}$, and

$A_6 = f \times 10^{-k_6}$, then

$$\frac{\left(\left(a \times 10^{-k_1}\right) \times \left(d \times 10^{-k_4}\right)\right)}{\left(\left(b \times 10^{-k_2}\right) \times \left(c \times 10^{-k_3}\right)\right)} \times \frac{e \times 10^{-k_5}}{f \times 10^{-k_6}} = \left(\frac{A_1 \times A_4}{A_2 \times A_3}\right) \times \frac{A_5}{A_6} = \left(\frac{A_1 A_4}{A_2 A_3}\right) \times \frac{A_5}{A_6} = \frac{A_1 A_4}{A_2 A_3} \times \frac{A_5}{A_6} = \frac{A_1 A_4 A_5}{A_2 A_3 A_6}$$

Example 4.5-6

$$\left(\frac{6 \times 10^{-2}}{13 \times 10^{-1}} \div \frac{24 \times 10^{-1}}{5 \times 10^{-2}}\right) \times \frac{26 \times 10^{-2}}{1 \times 10^{-1}} = \left(\frac{0.06}{1.3} \div \frac{2.4}{0.05}\right) \times \frac{0.26}{0.1} = \left(\frac{\frac{6}{100}}{\frac{13}{10}} \div \frac{\frac{24}{10}}{\frac{5}{100}}\right) \times \frac{\frac{26}{100}}{\frac{1}{10}}$$

$$= \left[\left(\frac{6 \times 10}{100 \times 13} \div \frac{24 \times 100}{10 \times 5} \right) \times \frac{26 \times 10}{100 \times 1} \right] = \left[\left(\frac{60}{1300} \div \frac{2400}{50} \right) \times \frac{260}{100} \right] = \left[\left(\frac{\overset{3}{\cancel{60}}}{\underset{65}{\cancel{1300}}} \div \frac{\overset{48}{\cancel{2400}}}{\underset{1}{\cancel{50}}} \right) \times \frac{\overset{13}{\cancel{260}}}{\underset{5}{\cancel{100}}} \right] = \left[\left(\frac{3}{65} \div \frac{48}{1} \right) \times \frac{13}{5} \right]$$

$$= \left[\left(\frac{3}{65} \times \frac{1}{48} \right) \times \frac{13}{5} \right] = \left[\left(\frac{3 \times 1}{65 \times 48} \right) \times \frac{13}{5} \right] = \left[\left(\frac{3}{3120} \right) \times \frac{13}{5} \right] = \left[\frac{3}{3120} \times \frac{13}{5} \right] = \left[\frac{3 \times \overset{1}{\cancel{13}}}{\underset{240}{\cancel{3120}} \times 5} \right] = \left[\frac{3 \times 1}{240 \times 5} \right] = \left[\frac{\overset{1}{\cancel{3}}}{\underset{80}{\cancel{240}} \times 5} \right]$$

$$= \left[\frac{1}{80 \times 5} \right] = \boxed{\frac{1}{400}}$$

Case II.

$$\left[\left(\frac{a \times 10^{-k_1}}{b \times 10^{-k_2}} + \frac{c \times 10^{-k_3}}{d \times 10^{-k_4}} \right) \div \frac{e \times 10^{-k_5}}{f \times 10^{-k_6}} \right]$$

$$= \left[\left(\frac{\left[\left(a \times 10^{-k_1} \right) \times \left(d \times 10^{-k_4} \right) \right] + \left[\left(c \times 10^{-k_3} \right) \times \left(b \times 10^{-k_2} \right) \right]}{\left(b \times 10^{-k_2} \right) \times \left(d \times 10^{-k_4} \right)} \right) \div \frac{e \times 10^{-k_5}}{f \times 10^{-k_6}} \right]$$

Let $\boxed{A_1 = a \times 10^{-k_1}}$, $\boxed{A_2 = b \times 10^{-k_2}}$, $\boxed{A_3 = c \times 10^{-k_3}}$, $\boxed{A_4 = d \times 10^{-k_4}}$, $\boxed{A_5 = e \times 10^{-k_5}}$, and

$\boxed{A_6 = f \times 10^{-k_6}}$, then

$$\left[\left(\frac{\left[\left(a \times 10^{-k_1} \right) \times \left(d \times 10^{-k_4} \right) \right] + \left[\left(c \times 10^{-k_3} \right) \times \left(b \times 10^{-k_2} \right) \right]}{\left(b \times 10^{-k_2} \right) \times \left(d \times 10^{-k_4} \right)} \right) \div \frac{e \times 10^{-k_5}}{f \times 10^{-k_6}} \right] = \left[\left(\frac{\left[A_1 \times A_4 \right] + \left[A_3 \times A_2 \right]}{A_2 \times A_4} \right) \div \frac{A_5}{A_6} \right]$$

$$= \left[\left(\frac{\left[A_1 A_4 \right] + \left[A_3 A_2 \right]}{A_2 A_4} \right) \div \frac{A_5}{A_6} \right] = \left[\left(\frac{A_1 A_4 + A_3 A_2}{A_2 A_4} \right) \div \frac{A_5}{A_6} \right]$$

Let $\boxed{B_1 = A_1 A_4 + A_3 A_2}$ and $\boxed{B_2 = A_2 A_4}$, then

$$\left[\left(\frac{A_1 A_4 + A_3 A_2}{A_2 A_4} \right) \div \frac{A_5}{A_6} \right] = \left[\left(\frac{B_1}{B_2} \right) \div \frac{A_5}{A_6} \right] = \left[\frac{B_1}{B_2} \div \frac{A_5}{A_6} \right] = \left[\frac{B_1}{B_2} \times \frac{A_6}{A_5} \right] = \left[\frac{B_1 \times A_6}{B_2 \times A_5} \right] = \boxed{\frac{B_1 A_6}{B_2 A_5}}$$

Example 4.5-7

$$\left[\left(\frac{5 \times 10^{-1}}{15 \times 10^{-2}} + \frac{1 \times 10^{-2}}{3 \times 10^{-1}} \right) \div \frac{2 \times 10^{-3}}{6 \times 10^{-2}} \right] = \left[\left(\frac{0.5}{0.15} + \frac{0.01}{0.3} \right) \div \frac{0.002}{0.06} \right] = \left[\left(\frac{\frac{5}{10}}{\frac{15}{100}} + \frac{\frac{1}{100}}{\frac{3}{10}} \right) \div \frac{\frac{2}{1000}}{\frac{6}{100}} \right]$$

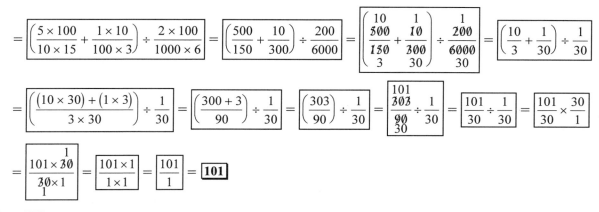

$$= \left[\left(\frac{5 \times 100}{10 \times 15} + \frac{1 \times 10}{100 \times 3} \right) \div \frac{2 \times 100}{1000 \times 6} \right] = \left[\left(\frac{500}{150} + \frac{10}{300} \right) \div \frac{200}{6000} \right] = \left[\left(\frac{\overset{10}{\cancel{500}}}{\underset{3}{\cancel{150}}} + \frac{\overset{1}{\cancel{10}}}{\underset{30}{\cancel{300}}} \right) \div \frac{\overset{1}{\cancel{200}}}{\underset{30}{\cancel{6000}}} \right] = \left[\left(\frac{10}{3} + \frac{1}{30} \right) \div \frac{1}{30} \right]$$

$$= \left[\left(\frac{(10 \times 30) + (1 \times 3)}{3 \times 30} \right) \div \frac{1}{30} \right] = \left[\left(\frac{300 + 3}{90} \right) \div \frac{1}{30} \right] = \left[\left(\frac{303}{90} \right) \div \frac{1}{30} \right] = \left[\frac{\overset{101}{\cancel{303}}}{\underset{30}{\cancel{90}}} \div \frac{1}{30} \right] = \left[\frac{101}{30} \div \frac{1}{30} \right] = \left[\frac{101}{30} \times \frac{30}{1} \right]$$

$$= \left[\frac{101 \times \overset{1}{\cancel{30}}}{\underset{1}{\cancel{30}} \times 1} \right] = \left[\frac{101 \times 1}{1 \times 1} \right] = \left[\frac{101}{1} \right] = \boxed{101}$$

Case III.

$$\left[\frac{a \times 10^{-k_1}}{b \times 10^{-k_2}} \div \left(\frac{c \times 10^{-k_3}}{d \times 10^{-k_4}} \times \frac{e \times 10^{-k_5}}{f \times 10^{-k_6}} \right) \right] = \left[\frac{a \times 10^{-k_1}}{b \times 10^{-k_2}} \div \left(\frac{\left(c \times 10^{-k_3} \right) \times \left(e \times 10^{-k_5} \right)}{\left(d \times 10^{-k_4} \right) \times \left(f \times 10^{-k_6} \right)} \right) \right]$$

Let $\boxed{A_1 = a \times 10^{-k_1}}$, $\boxed{A_2 = b \times 10^{-k_2}}$, $\boxed{A_3 = c \times 10^{-k_3}}$, $\boxed{A_4 = d \times 10^{-k_4}}$, $\boxed{A_5 = e \times 10^{-k_5}}$, and

$\boxed{A_6 = f \times 10^{-k_6}}$, then

$$\left[\frac{a \times 10^{-k_1}}{b \times 10^{-k_2}} \div \left(\frac{\left(c \times 10^{-k_3} \right) \times \left(e \times 10^{-k_5} \right)}{\left(d \times 10^{-k_4} \right) \times \left(f \times 10^{-k_6} \right)} \right) \right] = \left[\frac{A_1}{A_2} \div \left(\frac{A_3 \times A_5}{A_4 \times A_6} \right) \right] = \left[\frac{A_1}{A_2} \div \left(\frac{A_3 A_5}{A_4 A_6} \right) \right] = \left[\frac{A_1}{A_2} \div \frac{A_3 A_5}{A_4 A_6} \right]$$

$$= \left[\frac{A_1}{A_2} \times \frac{A_4 A_6}{A_3 A_5} \right] = \left[\frac{A_1 \times A_4 A_6}{A_2 \times A_3 A_5} \right] = \boxed{\frac{A_1 A_4 A_6}{A_2 A_3 A_5}}$$

Example 4.5-8

$$\left[\frac{4 \times 10^{-1}}{15 \times 10^{-3}} \div \left(\frac{12 \times 10^{-1}}{6 \times 10^{-2}} \times \frac{5 \times 10^{-1}}{8 \times 10^{-2}} \right) \right] = \left[\frac{0.4}{0.015} \div \left(\frac{1.2}{0.06} \times \frac{0.5}{0.08} \right) \right] = \left[\frac{\frac{4}{10}}{\frac{15}{1000}} \div \left(\frac{\frac{12}{10}}{\frac{6}{100}} \times \frac{\frac{5}{10}}{\frac{8}{100}} \right) \right]$$

$$= \left[\frac{4 \times 1000}{10 \times 15} \div \left(\frac{12 \times 100}{10 \times 6} \times \frac{5 \times 100}{10 \times 8} \right) \right] = \left[\frac{4000}{150} \div \left(\frac{1200}{60} \times \frac{500}{80} \right) \right] = \left[\frac{\overset{80}{\cancel{4000}}}{\underset{3}{\cancel{150}}} \div \left(\frac{\overset{20}{\cancel{1200}}}{\underset{1}{\cancel{60}}} \times \frac{\overset{25}{\cancel{500}}}{\underset{4}{\cancel{80}}} \right) \right] = \left[\frac{80}{3} \div \left(\frac{20}{1} \times \frac{25}{4} \right) \right]$$

$$= \left[\frac{80}{3} \div \left(\frac{20 \times 25}{1 \times 4} \right) \right] = \left[\frac{80}{3} \div \left(\frac{500}{4} \right) \right] = \left[\frac{80}{3} \div \frac{\overset{125}{\cancel{500}}}{\underset{1}{\cancel{4}}} \right] = \left[\frac{80}{3} \div \frac{125}{1} \right] = \left[\frac{80}{3} \times \frac{1}{125} \right] = \left[\frac{80 \times 1}{3 \times 125} \right] = \left[\frac{\overset{16}{\cancel{80}}}{\underset{75}{\cancel{375}}} \right] = \boxed{\frac{16}{75}}$$

Case IV.

$$\left(\frac{a \times 10^{-k_1}}{b \times 10^{-k_2}} - \frac{c \times 10^{-k_3}}{d \times 10^{-k_4}}\right) \times \frac{e \times 10^{-k_5}}{f \times 10^{-k_6}}$$

$$= \left(\frac{\left[\left(a \times 10^{-k_1}\right) \times \left(d \times 10^{-k_4}\right)\right] - \left[\left(c \times 10^{-k_3}\right) \times \left(b \times 10^{-k_2}\right)\right]}{\left(b \times 10^{-k_2}\right) \times \left(d \times 10^{-k_4}\right)}\right) \times \frac{e \times 10^{-k_5}}{f \times 10^{-k_6}}$$

Let $A_1 = a \times 10^{-k_1}$, $A_2 = b \times 10^{-k_2}$, $A_3 = c \times 10^{-k_3}$, $A_4 = d \times 10^{-k_4}$, $A_5 = e \times 10^{-k_5}$, and

$A_6 = f \times 10^{-k_6}$, then

$$\left(\frac{\left[\left(a \times 10^{-k_1}\right) \times \left(d \times 10^{-k_4}\right)\right] - \left[\left(c \times 10^{-k_3}\right) \times \left(b \times 10^{-k_2}\right)\right]}{\left(b \times 10^{-k_2}\right) \times \left(d \times 10^{-k_4}\right)}\right) \times \frac{e \times 10^{-k_5}}{f \times 10^{-k_6}} = \left(\frac{\left[A_1 \times A_4\right] - \left[A_3 \times A_2\right]}{A_2 \times A_4}\right) \times \frac{A_5}{A_6}$$

$$= \left(\frac{\left[A_1 A_4\right] - \left[A_3 A_2\right]}{A_2 A_4}\right) \times \frac{A_5}{A_6} = \left(\frac{A_1 A_4 - A_3 A_2}{A_2 A_4}\right) \times \frac{A_5}{A_6}$$

Let $B_1 = A_1 A_4 - A_3 A_2$ and $B_2 = A_2 A_4$, then

$$\left(\frac{A_1 A_4 - A_3 A_2}{A_2 A_4}\right) \times \frac{A_5}{A_6} = \left(\frac{B_1}{B_2}\right) \times \frac{A_5}{A_6} = \frac{B_1}{B_2} \times \frac{A_5}{A_6} = \frac{B_1 \times A_5}{B_2 \times A_6} = \frac{B_1 A_5}{B_2 A_6}$$

Example 4.5-9

$$\left(\frac{4 \times 10^{-2}}{3 \times 10^{-1}} - \frac{12 \times 10^{-2}}{6 \times 10^{-1}}\right) \times \frac{22 \times 10^{-2}}{5 \times 10^{-1}} = \left(\frac{0.04}{0.3} - \frac{0.12}{0.6}\right) \times \frac{0.22}{0.5} = \left(\frac{\frac{4}{100}}{\frac{3}{10}} - \frac{\frac{12}{100}}{\frac{6}{10}}\right) \times \frac{\frac{22}{100}}{\frac{5}{10}}$$

$$= \left(\frac{4 \times 10}{100 \times 3} - \frac{12 \times 10}{100 \times 6}\right) \times \frac{22 \times 10}{100 \times 5} = \left(\frac{40}{300} - \frac{120}{600}\right) \times \frac{220}{500} = \left(\frac{\overset{2}{\cancel{40}}}{\underset{15}{\cancel{300}}} - \frac{\overset{1}{\cancel{120}}}{\underset{5}{\cancel{600}}}\right) \times \frac{\overset{11}{\cancel{220}}}{\underset{25}{\cancel{500}}} = \left(\frac{2}{15} - \frac{1}{5}\right) \times \frac{11}{25}$$

$$= \left(\frac{(2 \times 5) - (1 \times 15)}{15 \times 5}\right) \times \frac{11}{25} = \left(\frac{10 - 15}{75}\right) \times \frac{11}{25} = \left(\frac{-5}{75}\right) \times \frac{11}{25} = \frac{\overset{-1}{\cancel{-5}}}{\underset{15}{\cancel{75}}} \times \frac{11}{25} = \frac{-1}{15} \times \frac{11}{25} = \frac{-1 \times 11}{15 \times 25} = \boxed{\frac{-11}{375}}$$

Case V.

$$\frac{a \times 10^{-k_1}}{b \times 10^{-k_2}} - \left(\frac{c \times 10^{-k_3}}{d \times 10^{-k_4}} \div \frac{e \times 10^{-k_5}}{f \times 10^{-k_6}}\right) = \frac{a \times 10^{-k_1}}{b \times 10^{-k_2}} - \left(\frac{c \times 10^{-k_3}}{d \times 10^{-k_4}} \times \frac{f \times 10^{-k_6}}{e \times 10^{-k_5}}\right)$$

$$= \left| \frac{a \times 10^{-k_1}}{b \times 10^{-k_2}} - \left(\frac{\left(c \times 10^{-k_3}\right) \times \left(f \times 10^{-k_6}\right)}{\left(d \times 10^{-k_4}\right) \times \left(e \times 10^{-k_5}\right)} \right) \right|$$

Let $\boxed{A_1 = a \times 10^{-k_1}}$, $\boxed{A_2 = b \times 10^{-k_2}}$, $\boxed{A_3 = c \times 10^{-k_3}}$, $\boxed{A_4 = d \times 10^{-k_4}}$, $\boxed{A_5 = e \times 10^{-k_5}}$, and

$\boxed{A_6 = f \times 10^{-k_6}}$, then

$$\left| \frac{a \times 10^{-k_1}}{b \times 10^{-k_2}} - \left(\frac{\left(c \times 10^{-k_3}\right) \times \left(f \times 10^{-k_6}\right)}{\left(d \times 10^{-k_4}\right) \times \left(e \times 10^{-k_5}\right)} \right) \right| = \left| \frac{A_1}{A_2} - \left(\frac{A_3 \times A_6}{A_4 \times A_5} \right) \right| = \left| \frac{A_1}{A_2} - \left(\frac{A_3 A_6}{A_4 A_5} \right) \right| = \left| \frac{A_1}{A_2} - \frac{A_3 A_6}{A_4 A_5} \right|$$

$$= \left| \frac{\left(A_1 \times A_4 A_5\right) - \left(A_3 A_6 \times A_2\right)}{A_2 \times A_4 A_5} \right| = \left| \frac{\left(A_1 A_4 A_5\right) - \left(A_3 A_6 A_2\right)}{A_2 A_4 A_5} \right| = \boxed{\frac{A_1 A_4 A_5 - A_3 A_6 A_2}{A_2 A_4 A_5}}$$

Example 4.5-10

$$\left| \frac{2 \times 10^{-1}}{1 \times 10^{-2}} - \left(\frac{5 \times 10^{-2}}{3 \times 10^{-1}} \div \frac{8 \times 10^{-3}}{3 \times 10^{-2}} \right) \right| = \left| \frac{0.2}{0.01} - \left(\frac{0.05}{0.3} \div \frac{0.008}{0.03} \right) \right| = \left| \frac{\frac{2}{10}}{\frac{1}{100}} - \left(\frac{\frac{5}{100}}{\frac{3}{10}} \div \frac{\frac{8}{1000}}{\frac{3}{100}} \right) \right|$$

$$= \left| \frac{2 \times 100}{10 \times 1} - \left(\frac{5 \times 10}{100 \times 3} \div \frac{8 \times 100}{1000 \times 3} \right) \right| = \left| \frac{200}{10} - \left(\frac{50}{300} \div \frac{800}{3000} \right) \right| = \left| \frac{\overset{20}{\cancel{200}}}{\underset{1}{\cancel{10}}} - \left(\frac{\overset{1}{\cancel{50}}}{\underset{6}{\cancel{300}}} \div \frac{\overset{4}{\cancel{800}}}{\underset{15}{\cancel{3000}}} \right) \right| = \left| \frac{20}{1} - \left(\frac{1}{6} \div \frac{4}{15} \right) \right|$$

$$= \left| \frac{20}{1} - \left(\frac{1}{6} \times \frac{15}{4} \right) \right| = \left| \frac{20}{1} - \left(\frac{1 \times 15}{6 \times 4} \right) \right| = \left| \frac{20}{1} - \left(\frac{15}{24} \right) \right| = \left| \frac{20}{1} - \frac{15}{24} \right| = \left| \frac{\left(20 \times 24\right) - \left(15 \times 1\right)}{1 \times 24} \right| = \left| \frac{480 - 15}{24} \right| = \left| \frac{465}{24} \right|$$

$$= \boxed{19 \frac{9}{24}}$$

The following examples further illustrate how to add, subtract, multiply, and divide decimal fractions:

Example 4.5-11

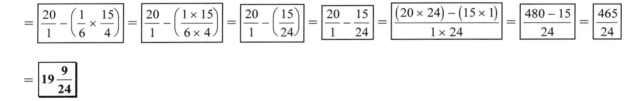

$$\left| \left(\frac{0.12}{0.3} \times \frac{0.8}{1.2} \right) + \frac{1.2}{0.05} \right| = \left| \left(\frac{\frac{12}{100}}{\frac{3}{10}} \times \frac{\frac{8}{10}}{\frac{12}{10}} \right) + \frac{\frac{12}{10}}{\frac{5}{100}} \right| = \left| \left(\frac{12 \times 10}{100 \times 3} \times \frac{8 \times 10}{10 \times 12} \right) + \frac{12 \times 100}{10 \times 5} \right| = \left| \left(\frac{120}{300} \times \frac{80}{120} \right) + \frac{1200}{50} \right|$$

$$= \left| \left(\frac{\overset{1}{\cancel{120}} \times \overset{4}{\cancel{80}}}{\underset{15}{\cancel{300}} \times \underset{1}{\cancel{120}}} \right) + \frac{\overset{24}{\cancel{1200}}}{\underset{1}{\cancel{50}}} \right| = \left| \left(\frac{1 \times 4}{15 \times 1} \right) + \frac{24}{1} \right| = \left| \left(\frac{4}{15} \right) + \frac{24}{1} \right| = \left| \frac{4}{15} + \frac{24}{1} \right| = \left| \frac{\left(4 \times 1\right) + \left(24 \times 15\right)}{15 \times 1} \right| = \left| \frac{4 + 360}{15} \right| = \left| \frac{364}{15} \right|$$

$$= \boxed{24\frac{4}{15}}$$

Example 4.5-12

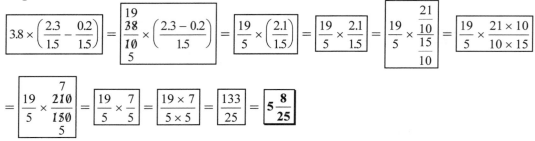

$$\boxed{3.8 \times \left(\frac{2.3}{1.5} - \frac{0.2}{1.5}\right)} = \boxed{\frac{19}{\frac{38}{10}} \times \left(\frac{2.3 - 0.2}{1.5}\right)} = \boxed{\frac{19}{5} \times \left(\frac{2.1}{1.5}\right)} = \boxed{\frac{19}{5} \times \frac{2.1}{1.5}} = \boxed{\frac{19}{5} \times \frac{\frac{21}{10}}{\frac{15}{10}}} = \boxed{\frac{19}{5} \times \frac{21 \times 10}{10 \times 15}}$$

$$= \boxed{\frac{19}{5} \times \frac{\overset{7}{\cancel{210}}}{\underset{5}{\cancel{150}}}} = \boxed{\frac{19}{5} \times \frac{7}{5}} = \boxed{\frac{19 \times 7}{5 \times 5}} = \boxed{\frac{133}{25}} = \boxed{5\frac{8}{25}}$$

Example 4.5-13

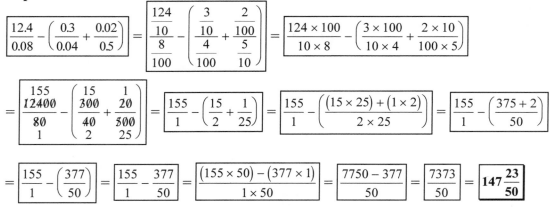

$$\boxed{\frac{12.4}{0.08} - \left(\frac{0.3}{0.04} + \frac{0.02}{0.5}\right)} = \boxed{\frac{\frac{124}{10}}{\frac{8}{100}} - \left(\frac{\frac{3}{10}}{\frac{4}{100}} + \frac{\frac{2}{100}}{\frac{5}{10}}\right)} = \boxed{\frac{124 \times 100}{10 \times 8} - \left(\frac{3 \times 100}{10 \times 4} + \frac{2 \times 10}{100 \times 5}\right)}$$

$$= \boxed{\frac{\overset{155}{\cancel{12400}}}{\underset{1}{\cancel{80}}} - \left(\frac{\overset{15}{\cancel{300}}}{\underset{2}{\cancel{40}}} + \frac{\overset{1}{\cancel{20}}}{\underset{25}{\cancel{500}}}\right)} = \boxed{\frac{155}{1} - \left(\frac{15}{2} + \frac{1}{25}\right)} = \boxed{\frac{155}{1} - \left(\frac{(15 \times 25) + (1 \times 2)}{2 \times 25}\right)} = \boxed{\frac{155}{1} - \left(\frac{375 + 2}{50}\right)}$$

$$= \boxed{\frac{155}{1} - \left(\frac{377}{50}\right)} = \boxed{\frac{155}{1} - \frac{377}{50}} = \boxed{\frac{(155 \times 50) - (377 \times 1)}{1 \times 50}} = \boxed{\frac{7750 - 377}{50}} = \boxed{\frac{7373}{50}} = \boxed{147\frac{23}{50}}$$

Example 4.5-14

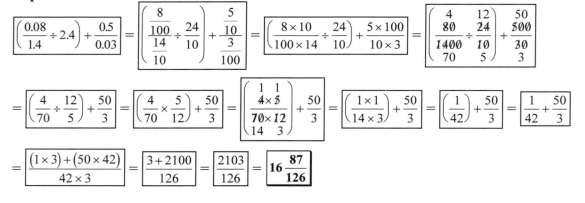

$$\boxed{\left(\frac{0.08}{1.4} \div 2.4\right) + \frac{0.5}{0.03}} = \boxed{\left(\frac{\frac{8}{100}}{\frac{14}{10}} \div \frac{24}{10}\right) + \frac{\frac{5}{10}}{\frac{3}{100}}} = \boxed{\left(\frac{8 \times 10}{100 \times 14} \div \frac{24}{10}\right) + \frac{5 \times 100}{10 \times 3}} = \boxed{\left(\frac{\overset{4}{\cancel{80}}}{\underset{70}{\cancel{1400}}} \div \frac{\overset{12}{\cancel{24}}}{\underset{5}{\cancel{10}}}\right) + \frac{\overset{50}{\cancel{500}}}{\underset{3}{\cancel{30}}}}$$

$$= \boxed{\left(\frac{4}{70} \div \frac{12}{5}\right) + \frac{50}{3}} = \boxed{\left(\frac{4}{70} \times \frac{5}{12}\right) + \frac{50}{3}} = \boxed{\left(\frac{\overset{1}{\cancel{4}} \times \overset{1}{\cancel{5}}}{\underset{14}{\cancel{70}} \times \underset{3}{\cancel{12}}}\right) + \frac{50}{3}} = \boxed{\left(\frac{1 \times 1}{14 \times 3}\right) + \frac{50}{3}} = \boxed{\left(\frac{1}{42}\right) + \frac{50}{3}} = \boxed{\frac{1}{42} + \frac{50}{3}}$$

$$= \boxed{\frac{(1 \times 3) + (50 \times 42)}{42 \times 3}} = \boxed{\frac{3 + 2100}{126}} = \boxed{\frac{2103}{126}} = \boxed{16\frac{87}{126}}$$

Example 4.5-15

$$\boxed{\left(\frac{0.5}{0.04} \div \frac{1.5}{1.6}\right) \times \left(\frac{0.3}{0.08} + \frac{0.02}{0.4}\right)} = \boxed{\left(\frac{\frac{5}{10}}{\frac{4}{100}} \div \frac{\frac{15}{10}}{\frac{16}{10}}\right) \times \left(\frac{\frac{3}{10}}{\frac{8}{100}} + \frac{\frac{2}{100}}{\frac{4}{10}}\right)} = \boxed{\left(\frac{5 \times 100}{10 \times 4} \div \frac{15 \times 10}{10 \times 16}\right) \times \left(\frac{3 \times 100}{10 \times 8} + \frac{2 \times 10}{100 \times 4}\right)}$$

$$= \left(\frac{\overset{25}{\cancel{\underset{\underset{2}{\cancel{40}}}{\cancel{500}}}}}{\cancel{40}} \div \frac{\overset{15}{\cancel{\underset{\underset{16}{\cancel{160}}}{\cancel{150}}}}}{\cancel{160}} \right) \times \left(\frac{\overset{15}{\cancel{\underset{4}{\cancel{300}}}}}{\cancel{80}} + \frac{\overset{1}{\cancel{\underset{20}{\cancel{20}}}}}{\cancel{400}} \right) = \left(\frac{25}{2} \div \frac{15}{16} \right) \times \left(\frac{15}{4} + \frac{1}{20} \right) = \left(\frac{25}{2} \times \frac{16}{15} \right) \times \left(\frac{(15 \times 20) + (1 \times 4)}{4 \times 20} \right)$$

$$= \left(\frac{\overset{5}{\cancel{25}} \times \overset{8}{\cancel{16}}}{\underset{1}{\cancel{2}} \times \underset{3}{\cancel{15}}} \right) \times \left(\frac{300 + 4}{80} \right) = \left(\frac{5 \times 8}{1 \times 3} \right) \times \left(\frac{304}{80} \right) = \left(\frac{40}{3} \right) \times \left(\frac{304}{80} \right) = \frac{40}{3} \times \frac{304}{80} = \frac{\overset{1}{\cancel{40}} \times 304}{3 \times \underset{2}{\cancel{80}}} = \frac{1 \times \overset{152}{\cancel{304}}}{3 \times \underset{1}{\cancel{2}}}$$

$$= \frac{1 \times 152}{3 \times 1} = \frac{152}{3} = \boxed{50 \frac{2}{3}}$$

Example 4.5-16

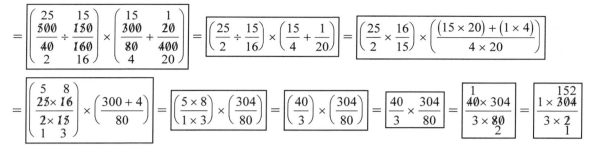

$$= \frac{105}{1} \times \left(\frac{104 \times 100}{10 \times 12} \right) = \frac{105}{1} \times \left(\frac{\overset{260}{\cancel{\underset{\underset{3}{\cancel{120}}}{\cancel{10400}}}}}{\cancel{120}} \right) = \frac{105}{1} \times \left(\frac{260}{3} \right) = \frac{105}{1} \times \frac{260}{3} = \frac{105 \times 260}{1 \times 3} = \frac{\overset{9100}{\cancel{\underset{\underset{1}{\cancel{3}}}{\cancel{27300}}}}}{\cancel{3}} = \frac{9100}{1}$$

$$= \boxed{9100}$$

Example 4.5-17

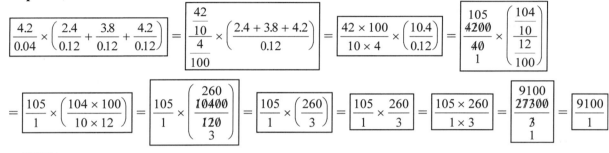

$$= \left(\frac{100}{80} \times \frac{40}{200} \times \frac{10}{500} \right) \div \frac{100}{350} = \left(\frac{1 \times \overset{1}{\cancel{40}} \times \overset{1}{\cancel{10}}}{\underset{2}{\cancel{80}} \times \underset{2}{\cancel{200}} \times \underset{50}{\cancel{500}}} \right) \div \frac{2}{7} = \left(\frac{1 \times 1 \times 1}{2 \times 2 \times 50} \right) \div \frac{2}{7} = \left(\frac{1}{200} \right) \div \frac{2}{7} = \frac{1}{200} \div \frac{2}{7}$$

$$= \frac{1}{200} \times \frac{7}{2} = \frac{1 \times 7}{200 \times 2} = \boxed{\frac{7}{400}}$$

Example 4.5-18

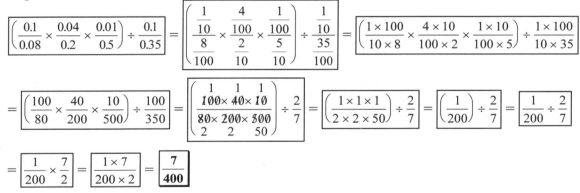

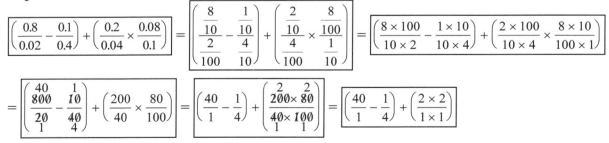

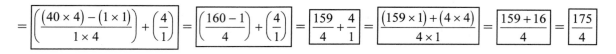

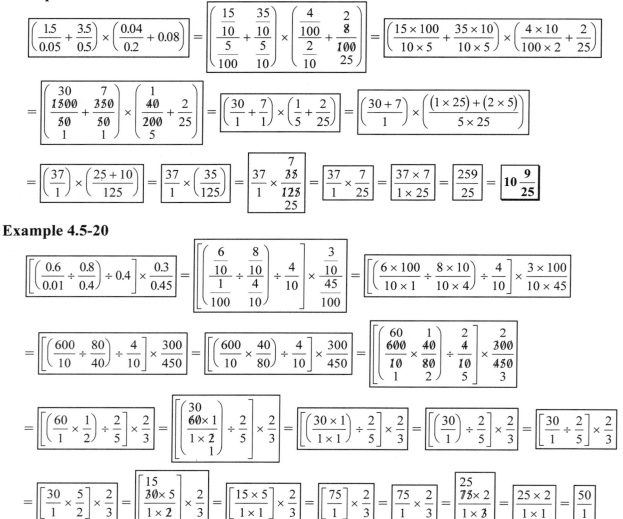

Example 4.5-19

Example 4.5-20

Section 4.5 Exercises - Use the following decimal fractions to perform the indicated operations:

1. $\dfrac{2.4}{0.3} \times \left(\dfrac{0.2}{1.2} + \dfrac{0.01}{0.5} \right) =$

2. $\left(\dfrac{0.04}{0.8} \div \dfrac{1.6}{0.02} \right) \times 0.08 =$

3. $\left(\dfrac{1.5}{0.5} + \dfrac{1.2}{0.03} + \dfrac{0}{0.4} \right) - \dfrac{2.4}{0.1} =$

4. $\dfrac{0.6}{0.2} + \left(\dfrac{4.9}{0.07} - 0.36 \right) =$

5. $\left(\dfrac{3.6}{0.06} \times \dfrac{0.3}{1.2} \right) \div 0.001 =$

6. $\left(\dfrac{0.9}{0.08} \div \dfrac{0.18}{1.6} \right) \times \dfrac{1.4}{0.2} =$

7. $\left(\dfrac{0.8}{0.05} - \dfrac{0.1}{0.05} \right) + \dfrac{0.4}{0.2} =$

8. $\dfrac{0.16}{0.2} \times \left(\dfrac{0.5}{0.06} \div \dfrac{0.3}{0.05} \right) =$

9. $\left(\dfrac{4.8}{0.04} \times \dfrac{0.1}{0.4} \right) \div \dfrac{7.5}{0.05} =$

10. $\left[\left(\dfrac{2.7}{0.09} + \dfrac{1.5}{0.05} \right) + 3.2 \right] - \dfrac{6.4}{0.02} =$

Chapter 5 - Mixed Fractions

The objective of this chapter is to improve the student's ability in solving mixed fractions. The steps used to solve mixed fractions with examples illustrating the steps as to how to add (Section 5.1), subtract (Section 5.2), multiply (Section 5.3), and divide (Section 5.4) two or more mixed fractions are given. Section 5.5 combines the mathematical operations using mixed fractions. In addition, for completeness, the general algebraic approach in solving mixed fractions is given in each section. The student, depending on his or her grade level and ability, can skip the algebraic approach to mixed fractions and only learn the techniques that are followed by examples. Focusing on the examples, and the steps shown to solve each problem, should be adequate to teach the student the mechanics of how mixed fractions are mathematically operated on.

5.1   Adding Mixed Fractions

Mixed fractions $\left(k\dfrac{a}{b} \right)$, i.e., fractions made up of a whole number (k) and an integer fraction $\left(\dfrac{a}{b} \right)$ are added as in the following cases:

Case I   Adding Two or More Mixed Fractions With Common Denominators

Mixed fractions with two or more common denominators are added using the steps given as in each case below:

Case I-A   *Add two mixed fractions with common denominators using the following steps:*

Step 1   Change the mixed fractions to integer fractions (see Section 2.5).

Step 2   Add the integer fractions (see Section 3.1, Case I-A).

Step 3   Simplify the fraction to its lowest term (see Section 2.3).

Step 4   Change the improper fraction to a mixed fraction if the fraction obtained from Step 3 is an improper fraction (see Section 2.2).

The following examples show the steps as to how two mixed fractions with common denominators are added:

Example 5.1-1

$$3\frac{1}{5} + 2\frac{1}{5} =$$

Solution:

Step 1 $3\dfrac{1}{5} + 2\dfrac{1}{5} = \dfrac{(3 \times 5)+1}{5} + \dfrac{(2 \times 5)+1}{5} = \dfrac{15+1}{5} + \dfrac{10+1}{5} = \dfrac{16}{5} + \dfrac{11}{5}$

Step 2 $\dfrac{16}{5} + \dfrac{11}{5} = \dfrac{16+11}{5} = \dfrac{27}{5}$

Step 3   Not Applicable

Step 4 $\dfrac{27}{5} = \boxed{5\dfrac{2}{5}}$

Example 5.1-2

$$\boxed{2\dfrac{3}{8} + 1\dfrac{1}{8}} =$$

Solution:

Step 1 $\boxed{2\dfrac{3}{8} + 1\dfrac{1}{8}} = \boxed{\dfrac{(2\times 8)+3}{8} + \dfrac{(1\times 8)+1}{8}} = \boxed{\dfrac{16+3}{8} + \dfrac{8+1}{8}} = \boxed{\dfrac{19}{8} + \dfrac{9}{8}}$

Step 2 $\boxed{\dfrac{19}{8} + \dfrac{9}{8}} = \boxed{\dfrac{19+9}{8}} = \boxed{\dfrac{28}{8}}$

Step 3 $\boxed{\dfrac{28}{8}} = \boxed{\dfrac{28\div 4}{8\div 4}} = \boxed{\dfrac{7}{2}}$

Step 4 $\boxed{\dfrac{7}{2}} = \boxed{3\dfrac{1}{2}}$

Example 5.1-3

$$\boxed{15\dfrac{2}{7} + 5\dfrac{1}{7}} =$$

Solution:

Step 1 $\boxed{15\dfrac{2}{7} + 5\dfrac{1}{7}} = \boxed{\dfrac{(15\times 7)+2}{7} + \dfrac{(5\times 7)+1}{7}} = \boxed{\dfrac{105+2}{7} + \dfrac{35+1}{7}} = \boxed{\dfrac{107}{7} + \dfrac{36}{7}}$

Step 2 $\boxed{\dfrac{107}{7} + \dfrac{36}{7}} = \boxed{\dfrac{107+36}{7}} = \boxed{\dfrac{143}{7}}$

Step 3 $\boxed{\textit{Not Applicable}}$

Step 4 $\boxed{\dfrac{143}{7}} = \boxed{20\dfrac{3}{7}}$

Example 5.1-4

$$\boxed{5\dfrac{1}{6} + 2\dfrac{5}{6}} =$$

Solution:

Step 1 $\boxed{5\dfrac{1}{6} + 2\dfrac{5}{6}} = \boxed{\dfrac{(5\times 6)+1}{6} + \dfrac{(2\times 6)+5}{6}} = \boxed{\dfrac{30+1}{6} + \dfrac{12+5}{6}} = \boxed{\dfrac{31}{6} + \dfrac{17}{6}}$

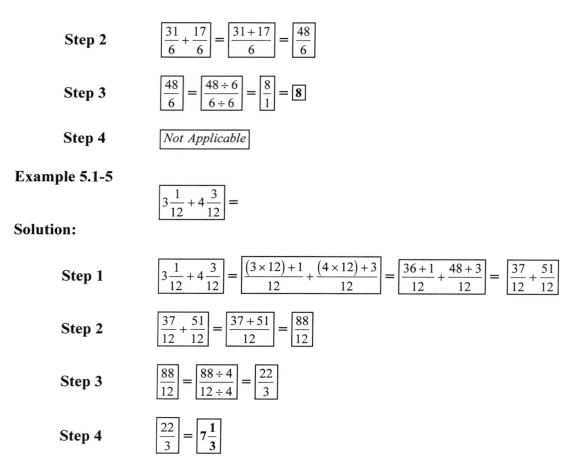

Step 2 $\dfrac{31}{6}+\dfrac{17}{6}=\dfrac{31+17}{6}=\dfrac{48}{6}$

Step 3 $\dfrac{48}{6}=\dfrac{48\div6}{6\div6}=\dfrac{8}{1}=\boxed{8}$

Step 4 $\boxed{\textit{Not Applicable}}$

Example 5.1-5

$$\boxed{3\dfrac{1}{12}+4\dfrac{3}{12}=}$$

Solution:

Step 1 $3\dfrac{1}{12}+4\dfrac{3}{12}=\dfrac{(3\times12)+1}{12}+\dfrac{(4\times12)+3}{12}=\dfrac{36+1}{12}+\dfrac{48+3}{12}=\dfrac{37}{12}+\dfrac{51}{12}$

Step 2 $\dfrac{37}{12}+\dfrac{51}{12}=\dfrac{37+51}{12}=\dfrac{88}{12}$

Step 3 $\dfrac{88}{12}=\dfrac{88\div4}{12\div4}=\dfrac{22}{3}$

Step 4 $\dfrac{22}{3}=7\dfrac{1}{3}$

In general two mixed fractions with a common denominator are added in the following way:

$$\boxed{k_1\dfrac{a}{d}+k_2\dfrac{b}{d}}=\dfrac{(k_1\times d)+a}{d}+\dfrac{(k_2\times d)+b}{d}=\dfrac{k_1d+a}{d}+\dfrac{k_2d+b}{d}$$

Let $\boxed{A_1=k_1d+a}$, and $\boxed{A_2=k_2d+b}$, then

$$\dfrac{k_1d+a}{d}+\dfrac{k_2d+b}{d}=\dfrac{A_1}{d}+\dfrac{A_2}{d}=\boxed{\dfrac{A_1+A_2}{d}}$$

Example 5.1-6

$$2\dfrac{1}{3}+4\dfrac{2}{3}=\dfrac{(2\times3)+1}{3}+\dfrac{(4\times3)+2}{3}=\dfrac{6+1}{3}+\dfrac{12+2}{3}=\dfrac{7}{3}+\dfrac{14}{3}=\dfrac{7+14}{3}=\dfrac{21}{\dfrac{3}{1}}=\dfrac{7}{1}=\boxed{7}$$

Case I-B   *Add three mixed fractions with common denominators using the following steps:*

Step 1   Change the mixed fractions to integer fractions (see Section 2.5).

Step 2   Add the integer fractions (see Section 3.1, Case I-B).

Step 3   Simplify the fraction to its lowest term (see Section 2.3).

Step 4   Change the improper fraction to a mixed fraction if the fraction obtained from Step 3 is an improper fraction (see Section 2.2).

The following examples show the steps as to how three mixed fractions with common denominators are added:

Example 5.1-7

$$3\frac{1}{5} + 2\frac{1}{5} + 1\frac{1}{5} =$$

Solution:

Step 1 $3\frac{1}{5} + 2\frac{1}{5} + 1\frac{1}{5} = \dfrac{(3 \times 5) + 1}{5} + \dfrac{(2 \times 5) + 1}{5} + \dfrac{(1 \times 5) + 1}{5} = \dfrac{15 + 1}{5} + \dfrac{10 + 1}{5} + \dfrac{5 + 1}{5}$

$$= \frac{16}{5} + \frac{11}{5} + \frac{6}{5}$$

Step 2 $\dfrac{16}{5} + \dfrac{11}{5} + \dfrac{6}{5} = \dfrac{16 + 11 + 6}{5} = \dfrac{33}{5}$

Step 3 $\boxed{\textit{Not Applicable}}$

Step 4 $\dfrac{33}{5} = 6\dfrac{3}{5}$

Example 5.1-8

$$18\frac{20}{10} + 1\frac{1}{10} + 2\frac{14}{10} =$$

Solution:

Step 1 $18\dfrac{20}{10} + 1\dfrac{1}{10} + 2\dfrac{14}{10} = \dfrac{(18 \times 10) + 20}{10} + \dfrac{(1 \times 10) + 1}{10} + \dfrac{(2 \times 10) + 14}{10}$

$$= \frac{180 + 20}{10} + \frac{10 + 1}{10} + \frac{20 + 14}{10} = \frac{200}{10} + \frac{11}{10} + \frac{34}{10}$$

Step 2 $\dfrac{200}{10} + \dfrac{11}{10} + \dfrac{34}{10} = \dfrac{200 + 11 + 34}{10} = \dfrac{245}{10}$

Step 3 $\dfrac{245}{10} = \dfrac{245 \div 5}{10 \div 5} = \dfrac{49}{2}$

Step 4 $\dfrac{49}{2} = 24\dfrac{1}{2}$

Example 5.1-9

$$5\frac{4}{7} + 2\frac{3}{7} + 3\frac{1}{7} =$$

Solution:

Step 1 $\quad 5\frac{4}{7} + 2\frac{3}{7} + 3\frac{1}{7} = \frac{(5\times 7)+4}{7} + \frac{(2\times 7)+3}{7} + \frac{(3\times 7)+1}{7} = \frac{35+4}{7} + \frac{14+3}{7} + \frac{21+1}{7}$

$$= \frac{39}{7} + \frac{17}{7} + \frac{22}{7}$$

Step 2 $\quad \frac{39}{7} + \frac{17}{7} + \frac{22}{7} = \frac{39+17+22}{7} = \frac{78}{7}$

Step 3 $\quad \boxed{Not\ Applicable}$

Step 4 $\quad \frac{78}{7} = \boxed{11\frac{1}{7}}$

Example 5.1-10

$$12\frac{4}{3} + 11\frac{1}{3} + 2\frac{2}{3} =$$

Solution:

Step 1 $\quad 12\frac{4}{3} + 11\frac{1}{3} + 2\frac{2}{3} = \frac{(12\times 3)+4}{3} + \frac{(11\times 3)+1}{3} + \frac{(2\times 3)+2}{3} = \frac{36+4}{3} + \frac{33+1}{3} + \frac{6+2}{3}$

$$= \frac{40}{3} + \frac{34}{3} + \frac{8}{3}$$

Step 2 $\quad \frac{40}{3} + \frac{34}{3} + \frac{8}{3} = \frac{40+34+8}{3} = \frac{82}{3}$

Step 3 $\quad \boxed{Not\ Applicable}$

Step 4 $\quad \frac{82}{3} = \boxed{27\frac{1}{3}}$

Example 5.1-11

$$2\frac{1}{8} + 3\frac{2}{8} + 5\frac{3}{8} =$$

Solution:

Step 1 $\quad 2\frac{1}{8} + 3\frac{2}{8} + 5\frac{3}{8} = \frac{(2\times 8)+1}{8} + \frac{(3\times 8)+2}{8} + \frac{(5\times 8)+3}{8} = \frac{16+1}{8} + \frac{24+2}{8} + \frac{40+3}{8}$

$$= \boxed{\frac{17}{8} + \frac{26}{8} + \frac{43}{8}}$$

Step 2 $\boxed{\frac{17}{8} + \frac{26}{8} + \frac{43}{8}} = \boxed{\frac{17 + 26 + 43}{8}} = \boxed{\frac{86}{8}}$

Step 3 $\boxed{\frac{86}{8}} = \boxed{\frac{86 \div 2}{8 \div 2}} = \boxed{\frac{43}{4}}$

Step 4 $\boxed{\frac{43}{4}} = \boxed{\mathbf{10\frac{3}{4}}}$

In general, three mixed fractions with a common denominator are added in the following way:

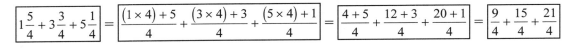

$$\boxed{k_1 \frac{a}{d} + k_2 \frac{b}{d} + k_3 \frac{c}{d}} = \boxed{\frac{(k_1 \times d) + a}{d} + \frac{(k_2 \times d) + b}{d} + \frac{(k_3 \times d) + c}{d}} = \boxed{\frac{k_1 d + a}{d} + \frac{k_2 d + b}{d} + \frac{k_3 d + c}{d}}$$

Let $\boxed{A_1 = k_1 d + a}$, $\boxed{A_2 = k_2 d + b}$, and $\boxed{A_3 = k_3 d + c}$, then

$$\boxed{\frac{k_1 d + a}{d} + \frac{k_2 d + b}{d} + \frac{k_3 d + c}{d}} = \boxed{\frac{A_1}{d} + \frac{A_2}{d} + \frac{A_3}{d}} = \boxed{\frac{A_1 + A_2 + A_3}{d}}$$

Example 5.1-12

$$\boxed{1\frac{5}{4} + 3\frac{3}{4} + 5\frac{1}{4}} = \boxed{\frac{(1 \times 4) + 5}{4} + \frac{(3 \times 4) + 3}{4} + \frac{(5 \times 4) + 1}{4}} = \boxed{\frac{4 + 5}{4} + \frac{12 + 3}{4} + \frac{20 + 1}{4}} = \boxed{\frac{9}{4} + \frac{15}{4} + \frac{21}{4}}$$

$$= \boxed{\frac{9 + 15 + 21}{4}} = \boxed{\frac{45}{4}} = \boxed{\mathbf{11\frac{1}{4}}}$$

Case II   Adding Two or More Mixed Fractions Without a Common Denominator
Two or more mixed fractions without a common denominator are added using the steps given as in each case below:

Case II-A   *Add two mixed fractions without a common denominator using the following steps:*

Step 1   Change the mixed fractions to integer fractions (see Section 2.5).

Step 2   Add the integer fractions (see Section 3.1, Case II-A).

Step 3   Simplify the fraction to its lowest term (see Section 2.3).

Step 4   Change the improper fraction to a mixed fraction if the fraction obtained from Step 3 is an improper fraction (see Section 2.2).

The following examples show the steps as to how two mixed fractions without a common denominators are added:

Example 5.1-13

$$\boxed{2\frac{1}{5}+3\frac{1}{3}=}$$

Solution:

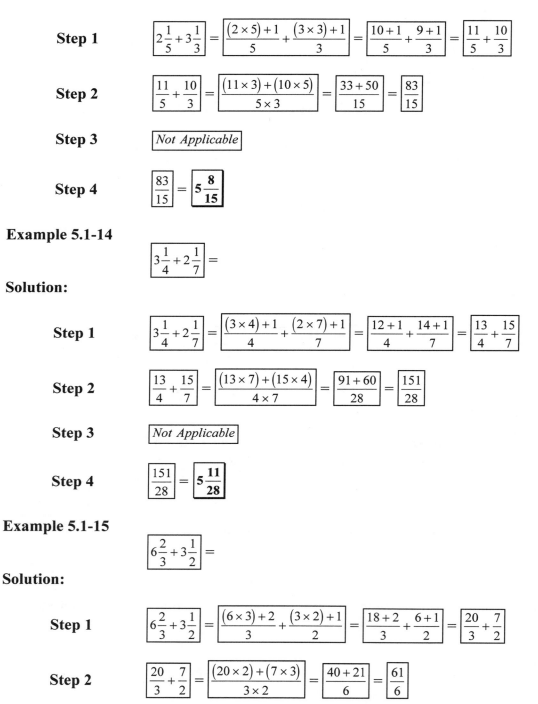

Step 1
$$\boxed{2\frac{1}{5}+3\frac{1}{3}}=\boxed{\frac{(2\times5)+1}{5}+\frac{(3\times3)+1}{3}}=\boxed{\frac{10+1}{5}+\frac{9+1}{3}}=\boxed{\frac{11}{5}+\frac{10}{3}}$$

Step 2
$$\boxed{\frac{11}{5}+\frac{10}{3}}=\boxed{\frac{(11\times3)+(10\times5)}{5\times3}}=\boxed{\frac{33+50}{15}}=\boxed{\frac{83}{15}}$$

Step 3 $\boxed{\textit{Not Applicable}}$

Step 4 $\boxed{\frac{83}{15}}=\boxed{\mathbf{5\frac{8}{15}}}$

Example 5.1-14

$$\boxed{3\frac{1}{4}+2\frac{1}{7}=}$$

Solution:

Step 1
$$\boxed{3\frac{1}{4}+2\frac{1}{7}}=\boxed{\frac{(3\times4)+1}{4}+\frac{(2\times7)+1}{7}}=\boxed{\frac{12+1}{4}+\frac{14+1}{7}}=\boxed{\frac{13}{4}+\frac{15}{7}}$$

Step 2
$$\boxed{\frac{13}{4}+\frac{15}{7}}=\boxed{\frac{(13\times7)+(15\times4)}{4\times7}}=\boxed{\frac{91+60}{28}}=\boxed{\frac{151}{28}}$$

Step 3 $\boxed{\textit{Not Applicable}}$

Step 4 $\boxed{\frac{151}{28}}=\boxed{\mathbf{5\frac{11}{28}}}$

Example 5.1-15

$$\boxed{6\frac{2}{3}+3\frac{1}{2}=}$$

Solution:

Step 1
$$\boxed{6\frac{2}{3}+3\frac{1}{2}}=\boxed{\frac{(6\times3)+2}{3}+\frac{(3\times2)+1}{2}}=\boxed{\frac{18+2}{3}+\frac{6+1}{2}}=\boxed{\frac{20}{3}+\frac{7}{2}}$$

Step 2
$$\boxed{\frac{20}{3}+\frac{7}{2}}=\boxed{\frac{(20\times2)+(7\times3)}{3\times2}}=\boxed{\frac{40+21}{6}}=\boxed{\frac{61}{6}}$$

Step 3   Not Applicable

Step 4 $\dfrac{61}{6} = \boxed{10\dfrac{1}{6}}$

Example 5.1-16

$7\dfrac{2}{5} + 3\dfrac{1}{8} =$

Solution:

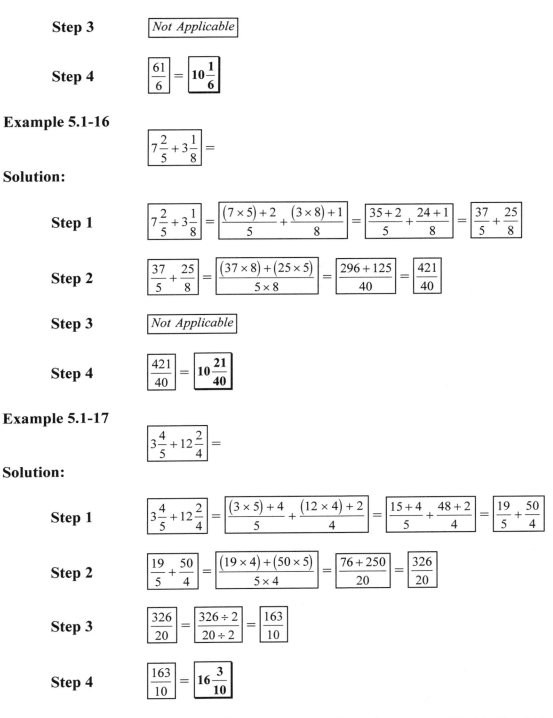

Step 1 $7\dfrac{2}{5} + 3\dfrac{1}{8} = \dfrac{(7 \times 5) + 2}{5} + \dfrac{(3 \times 8) + 1}{8} = \dfrac{35 + 2}{5} + \dfrac{24 + 1}{8} = \dfrac{37}{5} + \dfrac{25}{8}$

Step 2 $\dfrac{37}{5} + \dfrac{25}{8} = \dfrac{(37 \times 8) + (25 \times 5)}{5 \times 8} = \dfrac{296 + 125}{40} = \dfrac{421}{40}$

Step 3   Not Applicable

Step 4 $\dfrac{421}{40} = \boxed{10\dfrac{21}{40}}$

Example 5.1-17

$3\dfrac{4}{5} + 12\dfrac{2}{4} =$

Solution:

Step 1 $3\dfrac{4}{5} + 12\dfrac{2}{4} = \dfrac{(3 \times 5) + 4}{5} + \dfrac{(12 \times 4) + 2}{4} = \dfrac{15 + 4}{5} + \dfrac{48 + 2}{4} = \dfrac{19}{5} + \dfrac{50}{4}$

Step 2 $\dfrac{19}{5} + \dfrac{50}{4} = \dfrac{(19 \times 4) + (50 \times 5)}{5 \times 4} = \dfrac{76 + 250}{20} = \dfrac{326}{20}$

Step 3 $\dfrac{326}{20} = \dfrac{326 \div 2}{20 \div 2} = \dfrac{163}{10}$

Step 4 $\dfrac{163}{10} = \boxed{16\dfrac{3}{10}}$

In general, two mixed fractions without a common denominator are added in the following way:

$$k_1\dfrac{a}{b} + k_2\dfrac{c}{d} = \dfrac{(k_1 \times b) + a}{b} + \dfrac{(k_2 \times d) + c}{d} = \dfrac{k_1 b + a}{b} + \dfrac{k_2 d + c}{d}$$

Let $\boxed{A_1 = k_1 b + a}$, and $\boxed{A_2 = k_2 d + c}$, then

$$\boxed{\frac{k_1 b + a}{b} + \frac{k_2 d + c}{d}} = \boxed{\frac{A_1}{b} + \frac{A_2}{d}} = \boxed{\frac{(A_1 \times d) + (A_2 \times b)}{b \times d}} = \boxed{\boxed{\frac{A_1 d + A_2 b}{bd}}}$$

Example 5.1-18

$$\boxed{1\frac{2}{3} + 2\frac{1}{5}} = \boxed{\frac{(1 \times 3) + 2}{3} + \frac{(2 \times 5) + 1}{5}} = \boxed{\frac{3+2}{3} + \frac{10+1}{5}} = \boxed{\frac{5}{3} + \frac{11}{5}} = \boxed{\frac{(5 \times 5) + (11 \times 3)}{3 \times 5}} = \boxed{\frac{25+33}{15}} = \boxed{\frac{58}{15}}$$

$$= \boxed{3\frac{13}{15}}$$

Case II-B   *Add three mixed fractions without a common denominator using the following steps:*

Step 1   Use parentheses to group the first and second fractions.

Step 2   Change the mixed fractions to integer fractions (see Section 2.5).

Step 3   Add the integer fractions (see Section 3.1, Case II-B).

Step 4   Simplify the fraction to its lowest term (see Section 2.3).

Step 5   Change the improper fraction to a mixed fraction if the fraction obtained from Step 4 is an improper fraction (see Section 2.2).

The following examples show the steps as to how three mixed fractions without a common denominators are added:

Example 5.1-19

$$\boxed{2\frac{1}{5} + 3\frac{1}{2} + 2\frac{1}{3}} =$$

Solution:

Step 1 $$\boxed{2\frac{1}{5} + 3\frac{1}{2} + 2\frac{1}{3}} = \boxed{\left(2\frac{1}{5} + 3\frac{1}{2}\right) + 2\frac{1}{3}}$$

Step 2 $$\boxed{\left(2\frac{1}{5} + 3\frac{1}{2}\right) + 2\frac{1}{3}} = \boxed{\left(\frac{(2 \times 5) + 1}{5} + \frac{(3 \times 2) + 1}{2}\right) + \frac{(2 \times 3) + 1}{3}} = \boxed{\left(\frac{10+1}{5} + \frac{6+1}{2}\right) + \frac{6+1}{3}}$$

$$= \boxed{\left(\frac{11}{5} + \frac{7}{2}\right) + \frac{7}{3}}$$

Step 3 $$\boxed{\left(\frac{11}{5} + \frac{7}{2}\right) + \frac{7}{3}} = \boxed{\left(\frac{(11 \times 2) + (7 \times 5)}{5 \times 2}\right) + \frac{7}{3}} = \boxed{\left(\frac{22+35}{10}\right) + \frac{7}{3}} = \boxed{\left(\frac{57}{10}\right) + \frac{7}{3}} = \boxed{\frac{57}{10} + \frac{7}{3}}$$

$$= \boxed{\frac{(57 \times 3) + (7 \times 10)}{10 \times 3}} = \boxed{\frac{171+70}{30}} = \boxed{\frac{241}{30}}$$

Step 4 $\boxed{Not\ Applicable}$

Step 5 $\boxed{\dfrac{241}{30}} = \boxed{8\dfrac{1}{30}}$

Example 5.1-20

$$\boxed{3\dfrac{1}{8} + 2\dfrac{1}{2} + 4\dfrac{3}{5}} =$$

Solution:

Step 1 $\boxed{3\dfrac{1}{8} + 2\dfrac{1}{2} + 4\dfrac{3}{5}} = \boxed{\left(3\dfrac{1}{8} + 2\dfrac{1}{2}\right) + 4\dfrac{3}{5}}$

Step 2 $\boxed{\left(3\dfrac{1}{8} + 2\dfrac{1}{2}\right) + 4\dfrac{3}{5}} = \boxed{\left(\dfrac{(3\times 8)+1}{8} + \dfrac{(2\times 2)+1}{2}\right) + \dfrac{(4\times 5)+3}{5}}$

$= \boxed{\left(\dfrac{24+1}{8} + \dfrac{4+1}{2}\right) + \dfrac{20+3}{5}} = \boxed{\left(\dfrac{25}{8} + \dfrac{5}{2}\right) + \dfrac{23}{5}}$

Step 3 $\boxed{\left(\dfrac{25}{8} + \dfrac{5}{2}\right) + \dfrac{23}{5}} = \boxed{\left(\dfrac{(25\times 2)+(5\times 8)}{8\times 2}\right) + \dfrac{23}{5}} = \boxed{\left(\dfrac{50+40}{16}\right) + \dfrac{23}{5}} = \boxed{\left(\dfrac{90}{16}\right) + \dfrac{23}{5}}$

$= \boxed{\dfrac{90}{16} + \dfrac{23}{5}} = \boxed{\dfrac{(90\times 5)+(23\times 16)}{16\times 5}} = \boxed{\dfrac{450+368}{80}} = \boxed{\dfrac{818}{80}}$

Step 4 $\boxed{\dfrac{818}{80}} = \boxed{\dfrac{818\div 2}{80\div 2}} = \boxed{\dfrac{409}{40}}$

Step 5 $\boxed{\dfrac{409}{40}} = \boxed{10\dfrac{9}{40}}$

Example 5.1-21

$$\boxed{3\dfrac{2}{4} + 1\dfrac{2}{3} + 2\dfrac{1}{6}} =$$

Solution:

Step 1 $\boxed{3\dfrac{2}{4} + 1\dfrac{2}{3} + 2\dfrac{1}{6}} = \boxed{\left(3\dfrac{2}{4} + 1\dfrac{2}{3}\right) + 2\dfrac{1}{6}}$

Step 2 $\boxed{\left(3\dfrac{2}{4} + 1\dfrac{2}{3}\right) + 2\dfrac{1}{6}} = \boxed{\left(\dfrac{(3\times 4)+2}{4} + \dfrac{(1\times 3)+2}{3}\right) + \dfrac{(2\times 6)+1}{6}}$

$$= \left[\left(\frac{12+2}{4}+\frac{3+2}{3}\right)+\frac{12+1}{6}\right] = \left[\left(\frac{14}{4}+\frac{5}{3}\right)+\frac{13}{6}\right]$$

Step 3
$$\left[\left(\frac{14}{4}+\frac{5}{3}\right)+\frac{13}{6}\right] = \left[\left(\frac{(14\times3)+(5\times4)}{4\times3}\right)+\frac{13}{6}\right] = \left[\left(\frac{42+20}{12}\right)+\frac{13}{6}\right] = \left[\left(\frac{62}{12}\right)+\frac{13}{6}\right]$$

$$= \left[\frac{62}{12}+\frac{13}{6}\right] = \left[\frac{(62\times6)+(13\times12)}{12\times6}\right] = \left[\frac{372+156}{72}\right] = \left[\frac{528}{72}\right]$$

Step 4
$$\left[\frac{528}{72}\right] = \left[\frac{528\div8}{72\div8}\right] = \left[\frac{66}{9}\right] = \left[\frac{66\div3}{9\div3}\right] = \left[\frac{22}{3}\right]$$

Step 5
$$\left[\frac{22}{3}\right] = \boxed{7\frac{1}{3}}$$

Example 5.1-22

$$\left[5\frac{1}{2}+2\frac{1}{3}+4\frac{1}{8}\right] =$$

Solution:

Step 1
$$\left[5\frac{1}{2}+2\frac{1}{3}+4\frac{1}{8}\right] = \left[\left(5\frac{1}{2}+2\frac{1}{3}\right)+4\frac{1}{8}\right]$$

Step 2
$$\left[\left(5\frac{1}{2}+2\frac{1}{3}\right)+4\frac{1}{8}\right] = \left[\left(\frac{(5\times2)+1}{2}+\frac{(2\times3)+1}{3}\right)+\frac{(4\times8)+1}{8}\right]$$

$$= \left[\left(\frac{10+1}{2}+\frac{6+1}{3}\right)+\frac{32+1}{8}\right] = \left[\left(\frac{11}{2}+\frac{7}{3}\right)+\frac{33}{8}\right]$$

Step 3
$$\left[\left(\frac{11}{2}+\frac{7}{3}\right)+\frac{33}{8}\right] = \left[\left(\frac{(11\times3)+(7\times2)}{2\times3}\right)+\frac{33}{8}\right] = \left[\left(\frac{33+14}{6}\right)+\frac{33}{8}\right] = \left[\left(\frac{47}{6}\right)+\frac{33}{8}\right]$$

$$= \left[\frac{47}{6}+\frac{33}{8}\right] = \left[\frac{(47\times8)+(33\times6)}{6\times8}\right] = \left[\frac{376+198}{48}\right] = \left[\frac{574}{48}\right]$$

Step 4
$$\left[\frac{574}{48}\right] = \left[\frac{574\div2}{48\div2}\right] = \left[\frac{287}{24}\right]$$

Step 5
$$\left[\frac{287}{24}\right] = \boxed{11\frac{23}{24}}$$

Example 5.1-23

$$3\frac{1}{8} + 2\frac{1}{5} + 1\frac{2}{3} =$$

Solution:

Step 1
$$3\frac{1}{8} + 2\frac{1}{5} + 1\frac{2}{3} = \left(3\frac{1}{8} + 2\frac{1}{5}\right) + 1\frac{2}{3}$$

Step 2
$$\left(3\frac{1}{8} + 2\frac{1}{5}\right) + 1\frac{2}{3} = \left(\frac{(3\times 8)+1}{8} + \frac{(2\times 5)+1}{5}\right) + \frac{(1\times 3)+2}{3}$$

$$= \left(\frac{24+1}{8} + \frac{10+1}{5}\right) + \frac{3+2}{3} = \left(\frac{25}{8} + \frac{11}{5}\right) + \frac{5}{3}$$

Step 3
$$\left(\frac{25}{8} + \frac{11}{5}\right) + \frac{5}{3} = \left(\frac{(25\times 5)+(11\times 8)}{8\times 5}\right) + \frac{5}{3} = \left(\frac{125+88}{40}\right) + \frac{5}{3} = \left(\frac{213}{40}\right) + \frac{5}{3}$$

$$= \frac{213}{40} + \frac{5}{3} = \frac{(213\times 3)+(5\times 40)}{40\times 3} = \frac{639+200}{120} = \frac{839}{120}$$

Step 4
$$\boxed{\textit{Not Applicable}}$$

Step 5
$$\frac{839}{120} = 6\frac{119}{120}$$

In general, three mixed fractions without a common denominator are added as in the following cases:

Case I.

$$k_1\frac{a}{b} + k_2\frac{c}{d} + k_3\frac{e}{f} = \left(k_1\frac{a}{b} + k_2\frac{c}{d}\right) + k_3\frac{e}{f} = \left(\frac{(k_1\times b)+a}{b} + \frac{(k_2\times d)+c}{d}\right) + \frac{(k_3\times f)+e}{f}$$

$$= \left(\frac{k_1 b + a}{b} + \frac{k_2 d + c}{d}\right) + \frac{k_3 f + e}{f}$$

Let $\boxed{A_1 = k_1 b + a}$, $\boxed{A_2 = k_2 d + c}$, and $\boxed{A_3 = k_3 f + e}$, then

$$\left(\frac{k_1 b + a}{b} + \frac{k_2 d + c}{d}\right) + \frac{k_3 f + e}{f} = \left(\frac{A_1}{b} + \frac{A_2}{d}\right) + \frac{A_3}{f} = \left(\frac{(A_1\times d)+(A_2\times b)}{b\times d}\right) + \frac{A_3}{f} = \left(\frac{A_1 d + A_2 b}{bd}\right) + \frac{A_3}{f}$$

$$= \frac{(A_1 d + A_2 b)}{bd} + \frac{A_3}{f} = \frac{[(A_1 d + A_2 b)\times f]+(A_3\times bd)}{bd\times f} = \frac{[A_1 df + A_2 bf]+A_3 bd}{bdf} = \frac{A_1 df + A_2 bf + A_3 bd}{bdf}$$

Example 5.1-24

$$2\frac{2}{3} + 3\frac{5}{4} + 1\frac{3}{5} = \left(2\frac{2}{3} + 3\frac{5}{4}\right) + 1\frac{3}{5} = \left(\frac{(2\times3)+2}{3} + \frac{(3\times4)+5}{4}\right) + \frac{(1\times5)+3}{5} = \left(\frac{6+2}{3} + \frac{12+5}{4}\right) + \frac{5+3}{5}$$

$$= \left(\frac{8}{3} + \frac{17}{4}\right) + \frac{8}{5} = \left(\frac{(8\times4)+(17\times3)}{3\times4}\right) + \frac{8}{5} = \left(\frac{32+51}{12}\right) + \frac{8}{5} = \left(\frac{83}{12}\right) + \frac{8}{5} = \frac{83}{12} + \frac{8}{5}$$

$$= \frac{(83\times5)+(8\times12)}{12\times5} = \frac{415+96}{60} = \frac{511}{60} = 8\frac{31}{60}$$

Case II.

$$k_1\frac{a}{b} + k_2\frac{c}{d} + k_3\frac{e}{f} = k_1\frac{a}{b} + \left(k_2\frac{c}{d} + k_3\frac{e}{f}\right) = \frac{(k_1\times b)+a}{b} + \left(\frac{(k_2\times d)+c}{d} + \frac{(k_3\times f)+e}{f}\right)$$

$$= \frac{k_1 b + a}{b} + \left(\frac{k_2 d + c}{d} + \frac{k_3 f + e}{f}\right)$$

Let $\boxed{A_1 = k_1 b + a}$, $\boxed{A_2 = k_2 d + c}$, and $\boxed{A_3 = k_3 f + e}$, then

$$\frac{k_1 b + a}{b} + \left(\frac{k_2 d + c}{d} + \frac{k_3 f + e}{f}\right) = \frac{A_1}{b} + \left(\frac{A_2}{d} + \frac{A_3}{f}\right) = \frac{A_1}{b} + \left(\frac{(A_2\times f)+(A_3\times d)}{d\times f}\right) + = \frac{A_1}{b} + \left(\frac{A_2 f + A_3 d}{df}\right)$$

$$= \frac{A_1}{b} + \frac{(A_2 f + A_3 d)}{df} = \frac{(A_1\times df)+[(A_2 f + A_3 d)\times b]}{b\times df} = \frac{A_1 df + [A_2 fb + A_3 db]}{bdf} = \frac{A_1 df + A_2 fb + A_3 db}{bdf}$$

Example 5.1-25

$$2\frac{2}{3} + 3\frac{5}{4} + 1\frac{3}{5} = 2\frac{2}{3} + \left(3\frac{5}{4} + 1\frac{3}{5}\right) = \frac{(2\times3)+2}{3} + \left(\frac{(3\times4)+5}{4} + \frac{(1\times5)+3}{5}\right) = \frac{6+2}{3} + \left(\frac{12+5}{4} + \frac{5+3}{5}\right)$$

$$= \frac{8}{3} + \left(\frac{17}{4} + \frac{8}{5}\right) = \frac{8}{3} + \left(\frac{(17\times5)+(8\times4)}{4\times5}\right) = \frac{8}{3} + \left(\frac{85+32}{20}\right) = \frac{8}{3} + \left(\frac{117}{20}\right) = \frac{8}{3} + \frac{117}{20}$$

$$= \frac{(8\times20)+(117\times3)}{3\times20} = \frac{160+351}{60} = \frac{511}{60} = 8\frac{31}{60}$$

Note - In addition the use of parentheses does not change the final answer; the two examples above have the same answer (see Section 1.2).

The following examples further illustrate how to add mixed fractions:

Example 5.1-26

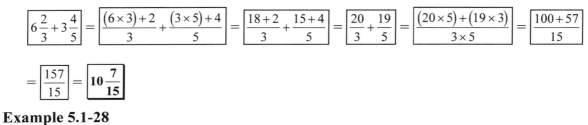

Example 5.1-27

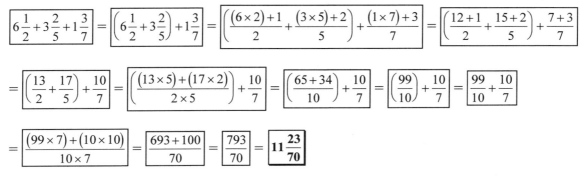

Example 5.1-28

$$6\frac{1}{2}+3\frac{2}{5}+1\frac{3}{7}=\left(6\frac{1}{2}+3\frac{2}{5}\right)+1\frac{3}{7}=\left(\frac{(6\times2)+1}{2}+\frac{(3\times5)+2}{5}\right)+\frac{(1\times7)+3}{7}=\left(\frac{12+1}{2}+\frac{15+2}{5}\right)+\frac{7+3}{7}$$

$$=\left(\frac{13}{2}+\frac{17}{5}\right)+\frac{10}{7}=\left(\frac{(13\times5)+(17\times2)}{2\times5}\right)+\frac{10}{7}=\left(\frac{65+34}{10}\right)+\frac{10}{7}=\left(\frac{99}{10}\right)+\frac{10}{7}=\frac{99}{10}+\frac{10}{7}$$

$$=\frac{(99\times7)+(10\times10)}{10\times7}=\frac{693+100}{70}=\frac{793}{70}=\boxed{11\frac{23}{70}}$$

Example 5.1-29

$$5\frac{4}{7}+2\frac{3}{7}+1\frac{2}{7}=\frac{(5\times7)+4}{7}+\frac{(2\times7)+3}{7}+\frac{(1\times7)+2}{7}=\frac{35+4}{7}+\frac{14+3}{7}+\frac{7+2}{7}=\frac{39}{7}+\frac{17}{7}+\frac{9}{7}$$

$$=\frac{39+17+9}{7}=\frac{65}{7}=\boxed{9\frac{2}{7}}$$

Example 5.1-30

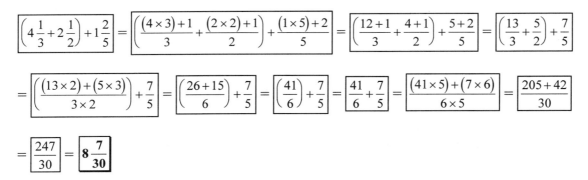

Example 5.1-31

$$8\frac{3}{4} + \left(2\frac{1}{3} + 1\frac{1}{2}\right) = \frac{(8\times 4)+3}{4} + \left(\frac{(2\times 3)+1}{3} + \frac{(1\times 2)+1}{2}\right) = \frac{32+3}{4} + \left(\frac{6+1}{3} + \frac{2+1}{2}\right) = \frac{35}{4} + \left(\frac{7}{3} + \frac{3}{2}\right)$$

$$= \frac{35}{4} + \left(\frac{(7\times 2)+(3\times 3)}{3\times 2}\right) = \frac{35}{4} + \left(\frac{14+9}{6}\right) = \frac{35}{4} + \left(\frac{23}{6}\right) = \frac{35}{4} + \frac{23}{6} = \frac{(35\times 6)+(23\times 4)}{4\times 6} = \frac{210+92}{24}$$

$$= \frac{\overset{151}{\cancel{302}}}{\underset{12}{24}} = \frac{151}{12} = \mathbf{12\frac{7}{12}}$$

Example 5.1-32

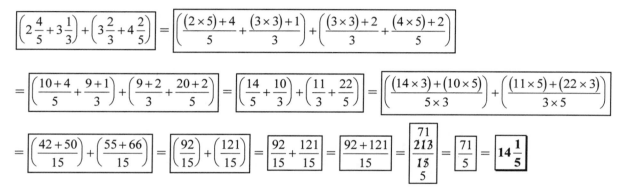

$$\left(2\frac{4}{5} + 3\frac{1}{3}\right) + \left(3\frac{2}{3} + 4\frac{2}{5}\right) = \left(\frac{(2\times 5)+4}{5} + \frac{(3\times 3)+1}{3}\right) + \left(\frac{(3\times 3)+2}{3} + \frac{(4\times 5)+2}{5}\right)$$

$$= \left(\frac{10+4}{5} + \frac{9+1}{3}\right) + \left(\frac{9+2}{3} + \frac{20+2}{5}\right) = \left(\frac{14}{5} + \frac{10}{3}\right) + \left(\frac{11}{3} + \frac{22}{5}\right) = \left(\frac{(14\times 3)+(10\times 5)}{5\times 3}\right) + \left(\frac{(11\times 5)+(22\times 3)}{3\times 5}\right)$$

$$= \left(\frac{42+50}{15}\right) + \left(\frac{55+66}{15}\right) = \left(\frac{92}{15}\right) + \left(\frac{121}{15}\right) = \frac{92}{15} + \frac{121}{15} = \frac{92+121}{15} = \frac{\overset{71}{\cancel{213}}}{\underset{5}{\cancel{15}}} = \frac{71}{5} = \mathbf{14\frac{1}{5}}$$

Example 5.1-33

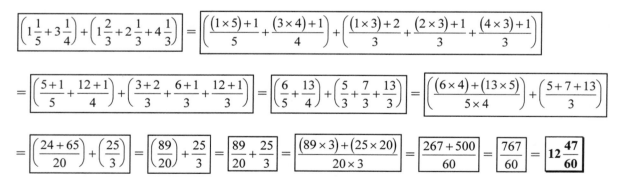

$$\left(1\frac{1}{5} + 3\frac{1}{4}\right) + \left(1\frac{2}{3} + 2\frac{1}{3} + 4\frac{1}{3}\right) = \left(\frac{(1\times 5)+1}{5} + \frac{(3\times 4)+1}{4}\right) + \left(\frac{(1\times 3)+2}{3} + \frac{(2\times 3)+1}{3} + \frac{(4\times 3)+1}{3}\right)$$

$$= \left(\frac{5+1}{5} + \frac{12+1}{4}\right) + \left(\frac{3+2}{3} + \frac{6+1}{3} + \frac{12+1}{3}\right) = \left(\frac{6}{5} + \frac{13}{4}\right) + \left(\frac{5}{3} + \frac{7}{3} + \frac{13}{3}\right) = \left(\frac{(6\times 4)+(13\times 5)}{5\times 4}\right) + \left(\frac{5+7+13}{3}\right)$$

$$= \left(\frac{24+65}{20}\right) + \left(\frac{25}{3}\right) = \left(\frac{89}{20}\right) + \frac{25}{3} = \frac{89}{20} + \frac{25}{3} = \frac{(89\times 3)+(25\times 20)}{20\times 3} = \frac{267+500}{60} = \frac{767}{60} = \mathbf{12\frac{47}{60}}$$

Example 5.1-34

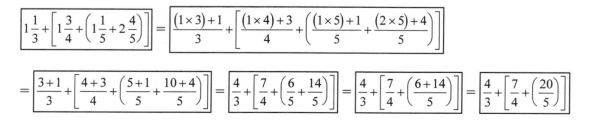

$$1\frac{1}{3} + \left[1\frac{3}{4} + \left(1\frac{1}{5} + 2\frac{4}{5}\right)\right] = \frac{(1\times 3)+1}{3} + \left[\frac{(1\times 4)+3}{4} + \left(\frac{(1\times 5)+1}{5} + \frac{(2\times 5)+4}{5}\right)\right]$$

$$= \frac{3+1}{3} + \left[\frac{4+3}{4} + \left(\frac{5+1}{5} + \frac{10+4}{5}\right)\right] = \frac{4}{3} + \left[\frac{7}{4} + \left(\frac{6}{5} + \frac{14}{5}\right)\right] = \frac{4}{3} + \left[\frac{7}{4} + \left(\frac{6+14}{5}\right)\right] = \frac{4}{3} + \left[\frac{7}{4} + \left(\frac{20}{5}\right)\right]$$

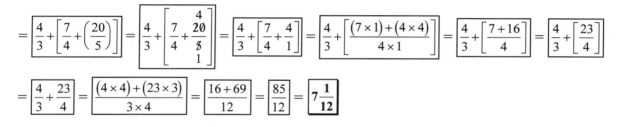

Example 5.1-35

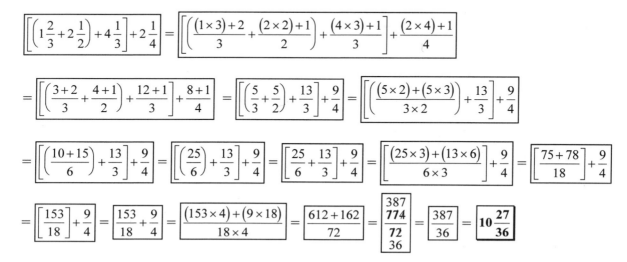

Section 5.1 Exercises - Add the following mixed fractions:

1. $1\dfrac{3}{4}+2\dfrac{5}{3}=$

2. $2\dfrac{3}{8}+3\dfrac{1}{8}=$

3. $1\dfrac{1}{2}+\left(1\dfrac{3}{4}+2\dfrac{1}{4}\right)=$

4. $\left(2\dfrac{3}{4}+3\dfrac{4}{5}\right)+1\dfrac{2}{3}=$

5. $2\dfrac{2}{3}+\left(1\dfrac{3}{8}+2\dfrac{1}{3}\right)=$

6. $3\dfrac{5}{8}+2\dfrac{7}{8}+4\dfrac{3}{8}+1\dfrac{4}{8}=$

7. $\left(1\dfrac{3}{2}+2\dfrac{5}{2}\right)+\left(1\dfrac{4}{3}+1\dfrac{2}{3}\right)=$

8. $\left(1\dfrac{2}{3}+2\dfrac{5}{4}\right)+\left(3\dfrac{3}{2}+2\dfrac{7}{2}\right)=$

9. $\left(6\dfrac{1}{2}+3\dfrac{2}{3}\right)+\left(1\dfrac{1}{5}+3\dfrac{1}{4}\right)=$

10. $1\dfrac{4}{3}+\left[2\dfrac{3}{5}+\left(1\dfrac{2}{5}+3\dfrac{4}{2}\right)\right]=$

5.2   Subtracting Mixed Fractions

Mixed fractions $\left(k\dfrac{a}{b}\right)$, i.e., fractions made up of a whole number (k) and an integer fraction $\left(\dfrac{a}{b}\right)$ are subtracted as in the following cases:

Case I   Subtracting Two or More Mixed Fractions With Common Denominators

Mixed fractions with two or more common denominators are subtracted using the steps given as in each case below:

Case I-A   *Subtract two mixed fractions with common denominators using the following steps:*

Step 1   Change the mixed fractions to integer fractions (see Section 2.5).

Step 2   Subtract the integer fractions (see Section 3.2, Case I-A).

Step 3   Simplify the fraction to its lowest term (see Section 2.3).

Step 4   Change the improper fraction to a mixed fraction if the fraction obtained from Step 3 is an improper fraction (see Section 2.2).

The following examples show the steps as to how two mixed fractions with common denominators are subtracted:

Example 5.2-1

$$\boxed{3\dfrac{1}{4} - 2\dfrac{1}{4}} =$$

Solution:

Step 1 $\boxed{3\dfrac{1}{4} - 2\dfrac{1}{4}} = \boxed{\dfrac{(3\times4)+1}{4} - \dfrac{(2\times4)+1}{4}} = \boxed{\dfrac{12+1}{4} - \dfrac{8+1}{4}} = \boxed{\dfrac{13}{4} - \dfrac{9}{4}}$

Step 2 $\boxed{\dfrac{13}{4} - \dfrac{9}{4}} = \boxed{\dfrac{13-9}{4}} = \boxed{\dfrac{4}{4}}$

Step 3 $\boxed{\dfrac{4}{4}} = \boxed{\dfrac{4\div4}{4\div4}} = \boxed{\dfrac{1}{1}} = \boxed{1}$

Step 4 $\boxed{Not\ Applicable}$

Example 5.2-2

$$\boxed{2\dfrac{1}{3} - 7\dfrac{2}{3}} =$$

Solution:

Step 1 $\boxed{2\dfrac{1}{3} - 7\dfrac{2}{3}} = \boxed{\dfrac{(2\times3)+1}{3} - \dfrac{(7\times3)+2}{3}} = \boxed{\dfrac{6+1}{3} - \dfrac{21+2}{3}} = \boxed{\dfrac{7}{3} - \dfrac{23}{3}}$

Step 2 $\boxed{\dfrac{7}{3}-\dfrac{23}{3}} = \boxed{\dfrac{7-23}{3}} = \boxed{\dfrac{-16}{3}}$

Step 3 $\boxed{\textit{Not Applicable}}$

Step 4 $\boxed{\dfrac{-16}{3}} = \boxed{-\left(5\dfrac{1}{3}\right)}$

Example 5.2-3

$\boxed{5\dfrac{1}{8}-3\dfrac{3}{8}} =$

Solution:

Step 1 $\boxed{5\dfrac{1}{8}-3\dfrac{3}{8}} = \boxed{\dfrac{(5\times8)+1}{8}-\dfrac{(3\times8)+3}{8}} = \boxed{\dfrac{40+1}{8}-\dfrac{24+3}{8}} = \boxed{\dfrac{41}{8}-\dfrac{27}{8}}$

Step 2 $\boxed{\dfrac{41}{8}-\dfrac{27}{8}} = \boxed{\dfrac{41-27}{8}} = \boxed{\dfrac{14}{8}}$

Step 3 $\boxed{\dfrac{14}{8}} = \boxed{\dfrac{14\div2}{8\div2}} = \boxed{\dfrac{7}{4}}$

Step 4 $\boxed{\dfrac{7}{4}} = \boxed{1\dfrac{3}{4}}$

Example 5.2-4

$\boxed{2\dfrac{1}{5}-5\dfrac{2}{5}} =$

Solution:

Step 1 $\boxed{2\dfrac{1}{5}-5\dfrac{2}{5}} = \boxed{\dfrac{(2\times5)+1}{5}-\dfrac{(5\times5)+2}{5}} = \boxed{\dfrac{10+1}{5}-\dfrac{25+2}{5}} = \boxed{\dfrac{11}{5}-\dfrac{27}{5}}$

Step 2 $\boxed{\dfrac{11}{5}-\dfrac{27}{5}} = \boxed{\dfrac{11-27}{5}} = \boxed{\dfrac{-16}{5}}$

Step 3 $\boxed{\textit{Not Applicable}}$

Step 4 $\boxed{\dfrac{-16}{5}} = \boxed{-\left(3\dfrac{1}{5}\right)}$

Example 5.2-5

$\boxed{25\dfrac{1}{2}-13\dfrac{3}{2}} =$

Solution:

Step 1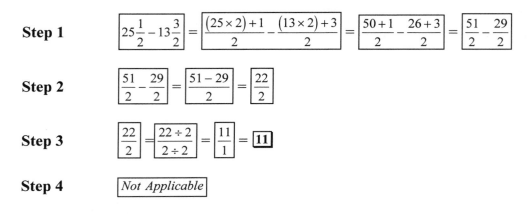

$$25\frac{1}{2} - 13\frac{3}{2} = \left| \frac{(25 \times 2) + 1}{2} - \frac{(13 \times 2) + 3}{2} \right| = \left| \frac{50 + 1}{2} - \frac{26 + 3}{2} \right| = \left| \frac{51}{2} - \frac{29}{2} \right|$$

Step 2 $$\left| \frac{51}{2} - \frac{29}{2} \right| = \left| \frac{51 - 29}{2} \right| = \left| \frac{22}{2} \right|$$

Step 3 $$\left| \frac{22}{2} \right| = \left| \frac{22 \div 2}{2 \div 2} \right| = \left| \frac{11}{1} \right| = \boxed{11}$$

Step 4 $\boxed{\textit{Not Applicable}}$

In general two mixed fractions with a common denominator are subtracted in the following way:

$$\left| k_1 \frac{a}{d} - k_2 \frac{b}{d} \right| = \left| \frac{(k_1 \times d) + a}{d} - \frac{(k_2 \times d) + b}{d} \right| = \left| \frac{k_1 d + a}{d} - \frac{k_2 d + b}{d} \right|$$

Let $\boxed{A_1 = k_1 d + a}$, and $\boxed{A_2 = k_2 d + b}$, then

$$\left| \frac{k_1 d + a}{d} - \frac{k_2 d + b}{d} \right| = \left| \frac{A_1}{d} - \frac{A_2}{d} \right| = \boxed{\frac{A_1 - A_2}{d}}$$

Example 5.2-6

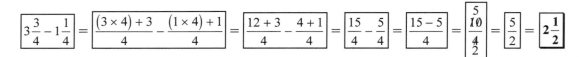

$$\left| 3\frac{3}{4} - 1\frac{1}{4} \right| = \left| \frac{(3 \times 4) + 3}{4} - \frac{(1 \times 4) + 1}{4} \right| = \left| \frac{12 + 3}{4} - \frac{4 + 1}{4} \right| = \left| \frac{15}{4} - \frac{5}{4} \right| = \left| \frac{15 - 5}{4} \right| = \left| \frac{\overset{5}{\cancel{10}}}{\underset{2}{\cancel{4}}} \right| = \left| \frac{5}{2} \right| = \boxed{2\frac{1}{2}}$$

Case I-B   *Subtract three mixed fractions with common denominators using the following steps:*

Step 1   Change the mixed fractions to integer fractions (see Section 2.5).

Step 2   Subtract the integer fractions (see Section 3.2, Case I-B).

Step 3   Simplify the fraction to its lowest term (see Section 2.3).

Step 4   Change the improper fraction to a mixed fraction if the fraction obtained from Step 3 is an improper fraction (see Section 2.2).

The following examples show the steps as to how three mixed fractions with common denominators are subtracted:

Example 5.2-7

$$\boxed{5\frac{1}{5} - 2\frac{1}{5} - 4\frac{2}{5}} =$$

Solution:

Step 1

$$5\frac{1}{5} - 2\frac{1}{5} - 4\frac{2}{5} = \frac{(5 \times 5) + 1}{5} - \frac{(2 \times 5) + 1}{5} - \frac{(4 \times 5) + 2}{5} = \frac{25 + 1}{5} - \frac{10 + 1}{5} - \frac{20 + 2}{5}$$

$$= \frac{26}{5} - \frac{11}{5} - \frac{22}{5}$$

Step 2

$$\frac{26}{5} - \frac{11}{5} - \frac{22}{5} = \frac{26 - 11 - 22}{5} = \frac{26 - 33}{5} = \frac{-7}{5}$$

Step 3 $\boxed{Not\ Applicable}$

Step 4 $\frac{-7}{5} = -\left(1\frac{2}{5}\right)$

Example 5.2-8

$$8\frac{1}{3} - 4\frac{1}{3} - 3\frac{2}{3} =$$

Solution:

Step 1

$$8\frac{1}{3} - 4\frac{1}{3} - 3\frac{2}{3} = \frac{(8 \times 3) + 1}{3} - \frac{(4 \times 3) + 1}{3} - \frac{(3 \times 3) + 2}{3} = \frac{24 + 1}{3} - \frac{12 + 1}{3} - \frac{9 + 2}{3}$$

$$= \frac{25}{3} - \frac{13}{3} - \frac{11}{3}$$

Step 2

$$\frac{25}{3} - \frac{13}{3} - \frac{11}{3} = \frac{25 - 13 - 11}{3} = \frac{25 - 24}{3} = \frac{1}{3}$$

Step 3 $\boxed{Not\ Applicable}$

Step 4 $\boxed{Not\ Applicable}$

Example 5.2-9

$$3\frac{1}{8} - 2\frac{3}{8} - 3\frac{2}{8} =$$

Solution:

Step 1

$$3\frac{1}{8} - 2\frac{3}{8} - 3\frac{2}{8} = \frac{(3 \times 8) + 1}{8} - \frac{(2 \times 8) + 3}{8} - \frac{(3 \times 8) + 2}{8} = \frac{24 + 1}{8} - \frac{16 + 3}{8} - \frac{24 + 2}{8}$$

$$= \frac{25}{8} - \frac{19}{8} - \frac{26}{8}$$

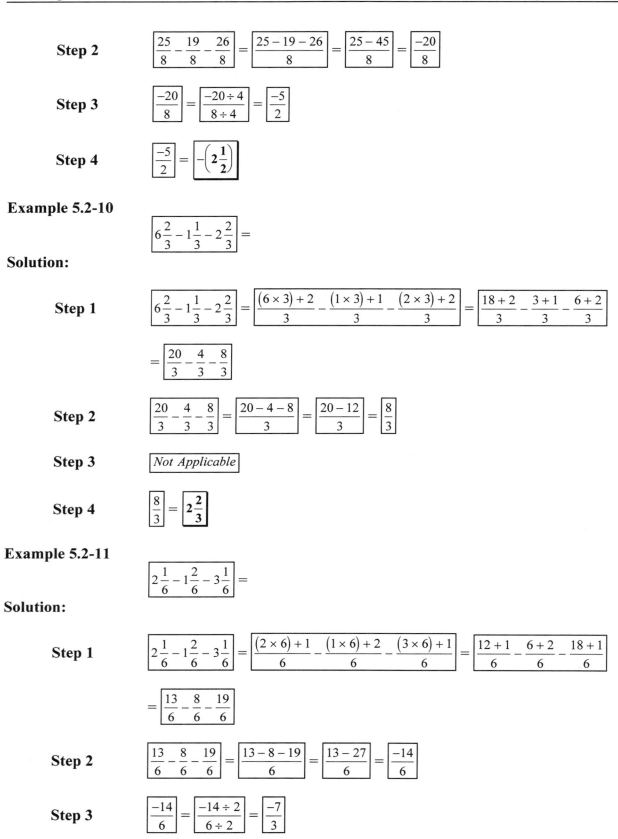

Step 2 $\boxed{\dfrac{25}{8} - \dfrac{19}{8} - \dfrac{26}{8}} = \boxed{\dfrac{25 - 19 - 26}{8}} = \boxed{\dfrac{25 - 45}{8}} = \boxed{\dfrac{-20}{8}}$

Step 3 $\boxed{\dfrac{-20}{8}} = \boxed{\dfrac{-20 \div 4}{8 \div 4}} = \boxed{\dfrac{-5}{2}}$

Step 4 $\boxed{\dfrac{-5}{2}} = \boxed{-\left(2\dfrac{1}{2}\right)}$

Example 5.2-10

$\boxed{6\dfrac{2}{3} - 1\dfrac{1}{3} - 2\dfrac{2}{3}} =$

Solution:

Step 1 $\boxed{6\dfrac{2}{3} - 1\dfrac{1}{3} - 2\dfrac{2}{3}} = \boxed{\dfrac{(6 \times 3) + 2}{3} - \dfrac{(1 \times 3) + 1}{3} - \dfrac{(2 \times 3) + 2}{3}} = \boxed{\dfrac{18 + 2}{3} - \dfrac{3 + 1}{3} - \dfrac{6 + 2}{3}}$

$= \boxed{\dfrac{20}{3} - \dfrac{4}{3} - \dfrac{8}{3}}$

Step 2 $\boxed{\dfrac{20}{3} - \dfrac{4}{3} - \dfrac{8}{3}} = \boxed{\dfrac{20 - 4 - 8}{3}} = \boxed{\dfrac{20 - 12}{3}} = \boxed{\dfrac{8}{3}}$

Step 3 $\boxed{\textit{Not Applicable}}$

Step 4 $\boxed{\dfrac{8}{3}} = \boxed{2\dfrac{2}{3}}$

Example 5.2-11

$\boxed{2\dfrac{1}{6} - 1\dfrac{2}{6} - 3\dfrac{1}{6}} =$

Solution:

Step 1 $\boxed{2\dfrac{1}{6} - 1\dfrac{2}{6} - 3\dfrac{1}{6}} = \boxed{\dfrac{(2 \times 6) + 1}{6} - \dfrac{(1 \times 6) + 2}{6} - \dfrac{(3 \times 6) + 1}{6}} = \boxed{\dfrac{12 + 1}{6} - \dfrac{6 + 2}{6} - \dfrac{18 + 1}{6}}$

$= \boxed{\dfrac{13}{6} - \dfrac{8}{6} - \dfrac{19}{6}}$

Step 2 $\boxed{\dfrac{13}{6} - \dfrac{8}{6} - \dfrac{19}{6}} = \boxed{\dfrac{13 - 8 - 19}{6}} = \boxed{\dfrac{13 - 27}{6}} = \boxed{\dfrac{-14}{6}}$

Step 3 $\boxed{\dfrac{-14}{6}} = \boxed{\dfrac{-14 \div 2}{6 \div 2}} = \boxed{\dfrac{-7}{3}}$

Step 4 $\boxed{\dfrac{-7}{3}} = \boxed{-\left(2\dfrac{1}{3}\right)}$

In general, three mixed fractions with a common denominator are subtracted in the following way:

$$\boxed{k_1\dfrac{a}{d} - k_2\dfrac{b}{d} - k_3\dfrac{c}{d}} = \boxed{\dfrac{(k_1 \times d) + a}{d} - \dfrac{(k_2 \times d) + b}{d} - \dfrac{(k_3 \times d) + c}{d}} = \boxed{\dfrac{k_1 d + a}{d} - \dfrac{k_2 d + b}{d} - \dfrac{k_3 d + c}{d}}$$

Let $\boxed{A_1 = k_1 d + a}$, $\boxed{A_2 = k_2 d + b}$, and $\boxed{A_3 = k_3 d + c}$, then

$$\boxed{\dfrac{k_1 d + a}{d} - \dfrac{k_2 d + b}{d} - \dfrac{k_3 d + c}{d}} = \boxed{\dfrac{A_1}{d} - \dfrac{A_2}{d} - \dfrac{A_3}{d}} = \boxed{\dfrac{A_1 - A_2 - A_3}{d}}$$

Example 5.2-12

$$\boxed{6\dfrac{5}{4} - 2\dfrac{2}{4} - 1\dfrac{3}{4}} = \boxed{\dfrac{(6 \times 4) + 5}{4} - \dfrac{(2 \times 4) + 2}{4} - \dfrac{(1 \times 4) + 3}{4}} = \boxed{\dfrac{24 + 5}{4} - \dfrac{8 + 2}{4} - \dfrac{4 + 3}{4}} = \boxed{\dfrac{29}{4} - \dfrac{10}{4} - \dfrac{7}{4}}$$

$$= \boxed{\dfrac{29 - 10 - 7}{4}} = \boxed{\dfrac{29 - 17}{4}} = \boxed{\dfrac{\overset{3}{\cancel{12}}}{\underset{1}{\cancel{4}}}} = \boxed{\dfrac{3}{1}} = \boxed{3}$$

Case II   Subtracting Two or More Mixed Fractions Without a Common Denominator

Two or more mixed fractions without a common denominator are subtracted using the steps given as in each case below:

Case II-A   *Subtract two mixed fractions without common denominators using the following steps:*

Step 1   Change the mixed fractions to integer fractions (see Section 2.5).

Step 2   Subtract the integer fractions (see Section 3.2, Case II-A).

Step 3   Simplify the fraction to its lowest term (see Section 2.3).

Step 4   Change the improper fraction to a mixed fraction if the fraction obtained from Step 3 is an improper fraction (see Section 2.2).

The following examples show the steps as to how two mixed fractions without common denominators are subtracted:

Example 5.2-13

$$\boxed{4\dfrac{3}{4} - 3\dfrac{1}{8}} =$$

Solution:

Step 1 $\boxed{4\dfrac{3}{4} - 3\dfrac{1}{8}} = \boxed{\dfrac{(4 \times 4) + 3}{4} - \dfrac{(3 \times 8) + 1}{8}} = \boxed{\dfrac{16 + 3}{4} - \dfrac{24 + 1}{8}} = \boxed{\dfrac{19}{4} - \dfrac{25}{8}}$

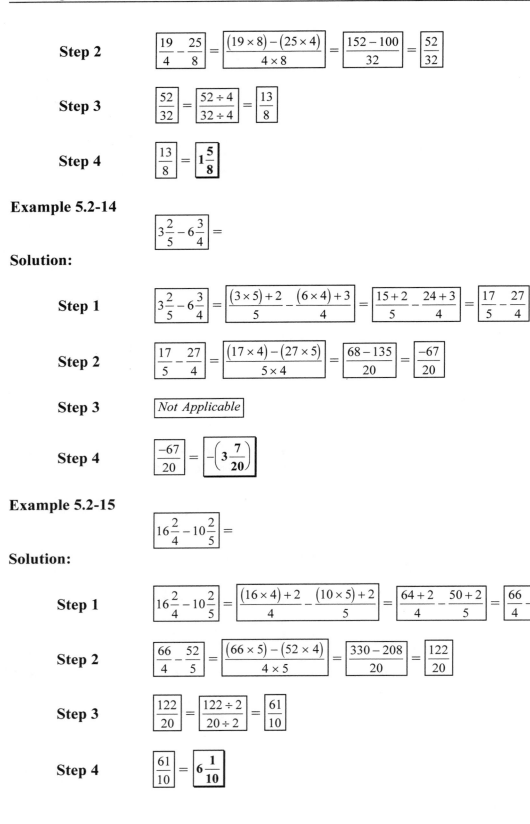

Step 2 $\boxed{\dfrac{19}{4}-\dfrac{25}{8}}=\boxed{\dfrac{(19\times 8)-(25\times 4)}{4\times 8}}=\boxed{\dfrac{152-100}{32}}=\boxed{\dfrac{52}{32}}$

Step 3 $\boxed{\dfrac{52}{32}}=\boxed{\dfrac{52\div 4}{32\div 4}}=\boxed{\dfrac{13}{8}}$

Step 4 $\boxed{\dfrac{13}{8}}=\boxed{1\dfrac{5}{8}}$

Example 5.2-14

$\boxed{3\dfrac{2}{5}-6\dfrac{3}{4}}=$

Solution:

Step 1 $\boxed{3\dfrac{2}{5}-6\dfrac{3}{4}}=\boxed{\dfrac{(3\times 5)+2}{5}-\dfrac{(6\times 4)+3}{4}}=\boxed{\dfrac{15+2}{5}-\dfrac{24+3}{4}}=\boxed{\dfrac{17}{5}-\dfrac{27}{4}}$

Step 2 $\boxed{\dfrac{17}{5}-\dfrac{27}{4}}=\boxed{\dfrac{(17\times 4)-(27\times 5)}{5\times 4}}=\boxed{\dfrac{68-135}{20}}=\boxed{\dfrac{-67}{20}}$

Step 3 $\boxed{Not\ Applicable}$

Step 4 $\boxed{\dfrac{-67}{20}}=\boxed{-\left(3\dfrac{7}{20}\right)}$

Example 5.2-15

$\boxed{16\dfrac{2}{4}-10\dfrac{2}{5}}=$

Solution:

Step 1 $\boxed{16\dfrac{2}{4}-10\dfrac{2}{5}}=\boxed{\dfrac{(16\times 4)+2}{4}-\dfrac{(10\times 5)+2}{5}}=\boxed{\dfrac{64+2}{4}-\dfrac{50+2}{5}}=\boxed{\dfrac{66}{4}-\dfrac{52}{5}}$

Step 2 $\boxed{\dfrac{66}{4}-\dfrac{52}{5}}=\boxed{\dfrac{(66\times 5)-(52\times 4)}{4\times 5}}=\boxed{\dfrac{330-208}{20}}=\boxed{\dfrac{122}{20}}$

Step 3 $\boxed{\dfrac{122}{20}}=\boxed{\dfrac{122\div 2}{20\div 2}}=\boxed{\dfrac{61}{10}}$

Step 4 $\boxed{\dfrac{61}{10}}=\boxed{6\dfrac{1}{10}}$

Example 5.2-16

$$3\frac{1}{5} - 4\frac{4}{3} =$$

Solution:

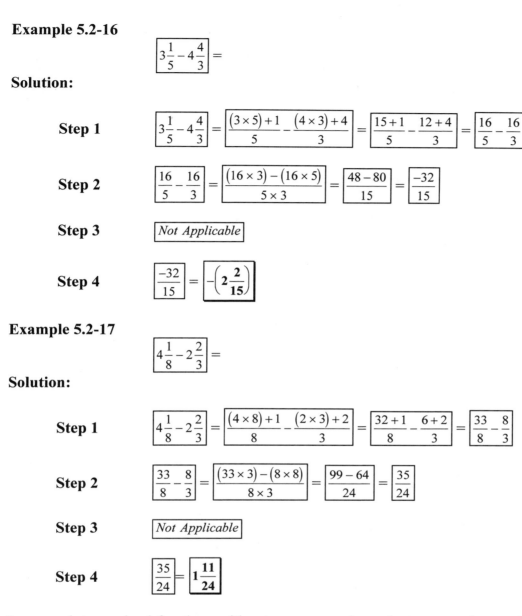

Step 1 $3\frac{1}{5} - 4\frac{4}{3} = \frac{(3 \times 5) + 1}{5} - \frac{(4 \times 3) + 4}{3} = \frac{15 + 1}{5} - \frac{12 + 4}{3} = \frac{16}{5} - \frac{16}{3}$

Step 2 $\frac{16}{5} - \frac{16}{3} = \frac{(16 \times 3) - (16 \times 5)}{5 \times 3} = \frac{48 - 80}{15} = \frac{-32}{15}$

Step 3 *Not Applicable*

Step 4 $\frac{-32}{15} = -\left(2\frac{2}{15}\right)$

Example 5.2-17

$$4\frac{1}{8} - 2\frac{2}{3} =$$

Solution:

Step 1 $4\frac{1}{8} - 2\frac{2}{3} = \frac{(4 \times 8) + 1}{8} - \frac{(2 \times 3) + 2}{3} = \frac{32 + 1}{8} - \frac{6 + 2}{3} = \frac{33}{8} - \frac{8}{3}$

Step 2 $\frac{33}{8} - \frac{8}{3} = \frac{(33 \times 3) - (8 \times 8)}{8 \times 3} = \frac{99 - 64}{24} = \frac{35}{24}$

Step 3 *Not Applicable*

Step 4 $\frac{35}{24} = 1\frac{11}{24}$

In general, two mixed fractions without a common denominator are subtracted in the following way:

$$k_1\frac{a}{b} - k_2\frac{c}{d} = \frac{(k_1 \times b) + a}{b} - \frac{(k_2 \times d) + c}{d} = \frac{k_1 b + a}{b} - \frac{k_2 d + c}{d}$$

Let $A_1 = k_1 b + a$, and $A_2 = k_2 d + c$, then

$$\frac{k_1 b + a}{b} - \frac{k_2 d + c}{d} = \frac{A_1}{b} - \frac{A_2}{d} = \frac{(A_1 \times d) - (A_2 \times b)}{b \times d} = \frac{A_1 d - A_2 b}{bd}$$

Example 5.2-18

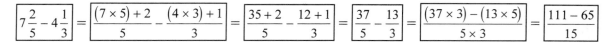

$$7\frac{2}{5} - 4\frac{1}{3} = \frac{(7 \times 5) + 2}{5} - \frac{(4 \times 3) + 1}{3} = \frac{35 + 2}{5} - \frac{12 + 1}{3} = \frac{37}{5} - \frac{13}{3} = \frac{(37 \times 3) - (13 \times 5)}{5 \times 3} = \frac{111 - 65}{15}$$

$$= \frac{46}{15} = 3\frac{1}{15}$$

Case II-B   *Subtract three mixed fractions without a common denominator using the following steps:*

Step 1   Use parentheses to group the first an second fractions.

Step 2   Change the mixed fractions to integer fractions (see Section 2.5).

Step 3   Subtract the integer fractions (see Section 3.2, Case II-B).

Step 4   Simplify the fraction to its lowest term (see Section 2.3).

Step 5   Change the improper fraction to a mixed fraction if the fraction obtained from Step 4 is an improper fraction (see Section 2.2).

The following examples show the steps as to how three mixed fractions without a common denominator are subtracted:

Example 5.2-19

$$3\frac{1}{4} - 2\frac{1}{3} - 1\frac{1}{2} =$$

Solution:

Step 1 $$3\frac{1}{4} - 2\frac{1}{3} - 1\frac{1}{2} = \left(3\frac{1}{4} - 2\frac{1}{3}\right) - 1\frac{1}{2}$$

Step 2 $$\left(3\frac{1}{4} - 2\frac{1}{3}\right) - 1\frac{1}{2} = \left(\frac{(3 \times 4) + 1}{4} - \frac{(2 \times 3) + 1}{3}\right) - \frac{(1 \times 2) + 1}{2} = \left(\frac{12 + 1}{4} - \frac{6 + 1}{3}\right) - \frac{2 + 1}{2}$$

$$= \left(\frac{13}{4} - \frac{7}{3}\right) - \frac{3}{2}$$

Step 3 $$\left(\frac{13}{4} - \frac{7}{3}\right) - \frac{3}{2} = \left(\frac{(13 \times 3) - (7 \times 4)}{4 \times 3}\right) - \frac{3}{2} = \left(\frac{39 - 28}{12}\right) - \frac{3}{2} = \left(\frac{11}{12}\right) - \frac{3}{2} = \frac{11}{12} - \frac{3}{2}$$

$$= \frac{(11 \times 2) - (3 \times 12)}{12 \times 2} = \frac{22 - 36}{24} = \frac{-14}{24}$$

Step 4 $$\frac{-14}{24} = \frac{-14 \div 2}{24 \div 2} = -\frac{7}{12}$$

Step 5 $\boxed{\textit{Not Applicable}}$

Example 5.2-20

$$\boxed{4\frac{1}{5} - 3\frac{1}{8} - 2\frac{1}{4}} =$$

Solution:

Step 1 $\boxed{4\frac{1}{5} - 3\frac{1}{8} - 2\frac{1}{4}} = \boxed{\left(4\frac{1}{5} - 3\frac{1}{8}\right) - 2\frac{1}{4}}$

Step 2 $\boxed{\left(4\frac{1}{5} - 3\frac{1}{8}\right) - 2\frac{1}{4}} = \boxed{\left(\frac{(4\times5)+1}{5} - \frac{(3\times8)+1}{8}\right) - \frac{(2\times4)+1}{4}}$

$$= \boxed{\left(\frac{20+1}{5} - \frac{24+1}{8}\right) - \frac{8+1}{4}} = \boxed{\left(\frac{21}{5} - \frac{25}{8}\right) - \frac{9}{4}}$$

Step 3 $\boxed{\left(\frac{21}{5} - \frac{25}{8}\right) - \frac{9}{4}} = \boxed{\left(\frac{(21\times8)-(25\times5)}{5\times8}\right) - \frac{9}{4}} = \boxed{\left(\frac{168-125}{40}\right) - \frac{9}{4}} = \boxed{\left(\frac{43}{40}\right) - \frac{9}{4}}$

$$= \boxed{\frac{43}{40} - \frac{9}{4}} = \boxed{\frac{(43\times4)-(9\times40)}{40\times4}} = \boxed{\frac{172-360}{160}} = \boxed{\frac{-188}{160}}$$

Step 4 $\boxed{\frac{-188}{160}} = \boxed{\frac{-188\div4}{160\div4}} = \boxed{\frac{-47}{40}}$

Step 5 $\boxed{\frac{-47}{40}} = \boxed{-\left(1\frac{7}{40}\right)}$

Example 5.2-21

$$\boxed{12\frac{1}{4} - 15\frac{2}{3} - 8\frac{1}{5}} =$$

Solution:

Step 1 $\boxed{12\frac{1}{4} - 15\frac{2}{3} - 8\frac{1}{5}} = \boxed{\left(12\frac{1}{4} - 15\frac{2}{3}\right) - 8\frac{1}{5}}$

Step 2 $\boxed{\left(12\frac{1}{4} - 15\frac{2}{3}\right) - 8\frac{1}{5}} = \boxed{\left(\frac{(12\times4)+1}{4} - \frac{(15\times3)+2}{3}\right) - \frac{(8\times5)+1}{5}}$

$$= \boxed{\left(\frac{48+1}{4} - \frac{45+2}{3}\right) - \frac{40+1}{5}} = \boxed{\left(\frac{49}{4} - \frac{47}{3}\right) - \frac{41}{5}}$$

Step 3

$$\left(\frac{49}{4} - \frac{47}{3}\right) - \frac{41}{5} = \left(\frac{(49 \times 3) - (47 \times 4)}{4 \times 3}\right) - \frac{41}{5} = \left(\frac{147 - 188}{12}\right) - \frac{41}{5} = \left(\frac{-41}{12}\right) - \frac{41}{5}$$

$$= \frac{-41}{12} - \frac{41}{5} = \frac{(-41 \times 5) - (41 \times 12)}{12 \times 2} = \frac{-205 - 492}{24} = \frac{-697}{24}$$

Step 4 $\boxed{\textit{Not Applicable}}$

Step 5 $\frac{-697}{24} = \boxed{-\left(11\frac{37}{60}\right)}$

Example 5.2-22

$$\boxed{6\frac{1}{5} - 2\frac{1}{3} - 1\frac{1}{2}} =$$

Solution:

Step 1 $6\frac{1}{5} - 2\frac{1}{3} - 1\frac{1}{2} = \left(6\frac{1}{5} - 2\frac{1}{3}\right) - 1\frac{1}{2}$

Step 2 $\left(6\frac{1}{5} - 2\frac{1}{3}\right) - 1\frac{1}{2} = \left(\frac{(6 \times 5) + 1}{5} - \frac{(2 \times 3) + 1}{3}\right) - \frac{(1 \times 2) + 1}{2} = \left(\frac{30 + 1}{5} - \frac{6 + 1}{3}\right) - \frac{2 + 1}{2}$

$$= \left(\frac{31}{5} - \frac{7}{3}\right) - \frac{3}{2}$$

Step 3 $\left(\frac{31}{5} - \frac{7}{3}\right) - \frac{3}{2} = \left(\frac{(31 \times 3) - (7 \times 5)}{5 \times 3}\right) - \frac{3}{2} = \left(\frac{93 - 35}{15}\right) - \frac{3}{2} = \left(\frac{58}{15}\right) - \frac{3}{2} = \frac{58}{15} - \frac{3}{2}$

$$= \frac{(58 \times 2) - (3 \times 15)}{15 \times 2} = \frac{116 - 45}{30} = \frac{71}{30}$$

Step 4 $\boxed{\textit{Not Applicable}}$

Step 5 $\frac{71}{30} = \boxed{2\frac{11}{30}}$

Example 5.2-23

$$\boxed{5\frac{3}{5} - 6\frac{1}{4} - 10\frac{2}{3}} =$$

Solution:

Step 1 $5\frac{3}{5} - 6\frac{1}{4} - 10\frac{2}{3} = \left(5\frac{3}{5} - 6\frac{1}{4}\right) - 10\frac{2}{3}$

Step 2 $$\left(5\dfrac{3}{5}-6\dfrac{1}{4}\right)-10\dfrac{2}{3}=\left(\dfrac{(5\times5)+3}{5}-\dfrac{(6\times4)+1}{4}\right)-\dfrac{(10\times3)+2}{3}$$

$$=\left(\dfrac{25+3}{5}-\dfrac{24+1}{4}\right)-\dfrac{30+2}{3}=\left(\dfrac{28}{5}-\dfrac{25}{4}\right)-\dfrac{32}{3}$$

Step 3 $$\left(\dfrac{28}{5}-\dfrac{25}{4}\right)-\dfrac{32}{3}=\left(\dfrac{(28\times4)-(25\times5)}{5\times4}\right)-\dfrac{32}{3}=\left(\dfrac{112-125}{20}\right)-\dfrac{32}{3}$$

$$=\left(\dfrac{-13}{20}\right)-\dfrac{32}{3}=\dfrac{-13}{20}-\dfrac{32}{3}=\dfrac{(-13\times3)-(32\times20)}{20\times3}=\dfrac{-39-640}{60}=\dfrac{-679}{60}$$

Step 4   Not Applicable

Step 5 $$\dfrac{-679}{60}=-\left(11\dfrac{19}{60}\right)$$

In general, three mixed fractions without a common denominator are subtracted as in the following cases:

Case I.

$$k_1\dfrac{a}{b}-k_2\dfrac{c}{d}-k_3\dfrac{e}{f}=\left(k_1\dfrac{a}{b}-k_2\dfrac{c}{d}\right)-k_3\dfrac{e}{f}=\left(\dfrac{(k_1\times b)+a}{b}-\dfrac{(k_2\times d)+c}{d}\right)-\dfrac{(k_3\times f)+e}{f}$$

$$=\left(\dfrac{k_1b+a}{b}-\dfrac{k_2d+c}{d}\right)-\dfrac{k_3f+e}{f}$$

Let $A_1=k_1b+a$, $A_2=k_2d+c$, and $A_3=k_3f+e$, then

$$\left(\dfrac{k_1b+a}{b}-\dfrac{k_2d+c}{d}\right)-\dfrac{k_3f+e}{f}=\left(\dfrac{A_1}{b}-\dfrac{A_2}{d}\right)-\dfrac{A_3}{f}=\left(\dfrac{(A_1\times d)-(A_2\times b)}{b\times d}\right)-\dfrac{A_3}{f}=\left(\dfrac{A_1d-A_2b}{bd}\right)-\dfrac{A_3}{f}$$

$$=\dfrac{(A_1d-A_2b)}{bd}-\dfrac{A_3}{f}=\dfrac{[(A_1d-A_2b)\times f]-(A_3\times bd)}{bd\times f}=\dfrac{[A_1df-A_2bf]-A_3bd}{bdf}=\dfrac{A_1df-A_2bf-A_3bd}{bdf}$$

Example 5.2-24

$$5\dfrac{2}{3}-2\dfrac{1}{2}-1\dfrac{4}{5}=\left(5\dfrac{2}{3}-2\dfrac{1}{2}\right)-1\dfrac{4}{5}=\left(\dfrac{(5\times3)+2}{3}-\dfrac{(2\times2)+1}{2}\right)-\dfrac{(1\times5)+4}{5}=\left(\dfrac{15+2}{3}-\dfrac{4+1}{2}\right)-\dfrac{5+4}{5}$$

$$= \left[\left(\frac{17}{3} - \frac{5}{2}\right) - \frac{9}{5}\right] = \left[\left(\frac{(17 \times 2) - (5 \times 3)}{3 \times 2}\right) - \frac{9}{5}\right] = \left[\left(\frac{34 - 15}{6}\right) - \frac{9}{5}\right] = \left[\left(\frac{19}{6}\right) - \frac{9}{5}\right] = \left[\frac{19}{6} - \frac{9}{5}\right]$$

$$= \left[\frac{(19 \times 5) - (9 \times 6)}{6 \times 5}\right] = \left[\frac{95 - 54}{30}\right] = \left[\frac{41}{30}\right] = \boxed{1\frac{11}{30}}$$

Case II.

$$\left[k_1 \frac{a}{b} - k_2 \frac{c}{d} - k_3 \frac{e}{f}\right] = \left[k_1 \frac{a}{b} + \left(-k_2 \frac{c}{d} - k_3 \frac{e}{f}\right)\right] = \left[\frac{(k_1 \times b) + a}{b} + \left(-\frac{(k_2 \times d) + c}{d} - \frac{(k_3 \times f) + e}{f}\right)\right]$$

$$= \left[\frac{k_1 b + a}{b} + \left(-\frac{k_2 d + c}{d} - \frac{k_3 f + e}{f}\right)\right]$$

Let $\boxed{A_1 = k_1 b + a}$, $\boxed{A_2 = k_2 d + c}$, and $\boxed{A_3 = k_3 f + e}$, then

$$\left[\frac{k_1 b + a}{b} + \left(-\frac{k_2 d + c}{d} - \frac{k_3 f + e}{f}\right)\right] = \left[\frac{A_1}{b} + \left(-\frac{A_2}{d} - \frac{A_3}{f}\right)\right] = \left[\frac{A_1}{b} + \left(\frac{-(A_2 \times f) - (A_3 \times d)}{d \times f}\right)\right]$$

$$= \left[\frac{A_1}{b} + \left(\frac{-A_2 f - A_3 d}{df}\right)\right] = \left[\frac{A_1}{b} + \frac{(-A_2 f - A_3 d)}{df}\right] = \left[\frac{(A_1 \times df) + \left[(-A_2 f - A_3 d) \times b\right]}{b \times df}\right]$$

$$= \left[\frac{A_1 df + \left[-A_2 fb - A_3 db\right]}{bdf}\right] = \boxed{\frac{A_1 df - A_2 fb - A_3 db}{bdf}}$$

Example 5.2-25

$$\left[5\frac{2}{3} - 2\frac{1}{2} - 1\frac{4}{5}\right] = \left[5\frac{2}{3} + \left(-2\frac{1}{2} - 1\frac{4}{5}\right)\right] = \left[\frac{(5 \times 3) + 2}{3} + \left(-\frac{(2 \times 2) + 1}{2} - \frac{(1 \times 5) + 4}{5}\right)\right]$$

$$= \left[\frac{15 + 2}{3} + \left(-\frac{4 + 1}{2} - \frac{5 + 4}{5}\right)\right] = \left[\frac{17}{3} + \left(-\frac{5}{2} - \frac{9}{5}\right)\right] = \left[\frac{17}{3} + \left(\frac{-(5 \times 5) - (9 \times 2)}{2 \times 5}\right)\right] = \left[\frac{17}{3} + \left(\frac{-25 - 18}{10}\right)\right]$$

$$= \left[\frac{17}{3} + \left(\frac{-43}{10}\right)\right] = \left[\frac{17}{3} + \frac{-43}{10}\right] = \left[\frac{17}{3} - \frac{43}{10}\right] = \left[\frac{(17 \times 10) - (43 \times 3)}{3 \times 10}\right] = \left[\frac{170 - 129}{30}\right] = \left[\frac{41}{30}\right] = \boxed{1\frac{11}{30}}$$

The following examples further illustrate how to subtract mixed fractions:

Example 5.2-26

$$\left[5\frac{3}{8} - 1\frac{1}{3}\right] = \left[\frac{(5 \times 8) + 3}{8} - \frac{(1 \times 3) + 1}{3}\right] = \left[\frac{40 + 3}{8} - \frac{3 + 1}{3}\right] = \left[\frac{43}{8} - \frac{4}{3}\right] = \left[\frac{(43 \times 3) - (4 \times 8)}{8 \times 3}\right] = \left[\frac{129 - 32}{24}\right] = \left[\frac{97}{24}\right]$$

$$= \boxed{4\frac{1}{24}}$$

Example 5.2-27

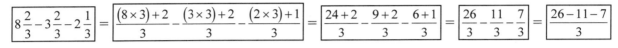

$$3\frac{4}{5} - 1\frac{2}{3} = \boxed{\frac{(3\times5)+4}{5} - \frac{(1\times3)+2}{3}} = \boxed{\frac{15+4}{5} - \frac{3+2}{3}} = \boxed{\frac{19}{5} - \frac{5}{3}} = \boxed{\frac{(19\times3)-(5\times5)}{5\times3}} = \boxed{\frac{57-25}{15}} = \boxed{\frac{32}{15}}$$

$$= \boxed{2\frac{2}{15}}$$

Example 5.2-28

$$8\frac{2}{3} - 3\frac{2}{3} - 2\frac{1}{3} = \boxed{\frac{(8\times3)+2}{3} - \frac{(3\times3)+2}{3} - \frac{(2\times3)+1}{3}} = \boxed{\frac{24+2}{3} - \frac{9+2}{3} - \frac{6+1}{3}} = \boxed{\frac{26}{3} - \frac{11}{3} - \frac{7}{3}} = \boxed{\frac{26-11-7}{3}}$$

$$= \boxed{\frac{8}{3}} = \boxed{2\frac{2}{3}}$$

Example 5.2-29

$$4\frac{1}{2} - 2\frac{1}{3} - 1\frac{1}{5} = \boxed{\left(4\frac{1}{2} - 2\frac{1}{3}\right) - 1\frac{1}{5}} = \boxed{\left(\frac{(4\times2)+1}{2} - \frac{(2\times3)+1}{3}\right) - \frac{(1\times5)+1}{5}} = \boxed{\left(\frac{8+1}{2} - \frac{6+1}{3}\right) - \frac{5+1}{5}}$$

$$= \boxed{\left(\frac{9}{2} - \frac{7}{3}\right) - \frac{6}{5}} = \boxed{\left(\frac{(9\times3)-(7\times2)}{2\times3}\right) - \frac{6}{5}} = \boxed{\left(\frac{27-14}{6}\right) - \frac{6}{5}} = \boxed{\left(\frac{13}{6}\right) - \frac{6}{5}} = \boxed{\frac{13}{6} - \frac{6}{5}} = \boxed{\frac{(13\times5)-(6\times6)}{6\times5}}$$

$$= \boxed{\frac{65-36}{30}} = \boxed{\frac{29}{30}}$$

Example 5.2-30

$$4\frac{3}{4} - \left(3\frac{4}{5} - 2\frac{1}{2}\right) = \boxed{\frac{(4\times4)+3}{4} - \left(\frac{(3\times5)+4}{5} - \frac{(2\times2)+1}{2}\right)} = \boxed{\frac{16+3}{4} - \left(\frac{15+4}{5} - \frac{4+1}{2}\right)}$$

$$= \boxed{\frac{19}{4} - \left(\frac{19}{5} - \frac{5}{2}\right)} = \boxed{\frac{19}{4} - \left(\frac{(19\times2)-(5\times5)}{5\times2}\right)} = \boxed{\frac{19}{4} - \left(\frac{38-25}{10}\right)} = \boxed{\frac{19}{4} - \left(\frac{13}{10}\right)} = \boxed{\frac{19}{4} - \frac{13}{10}}$$

$$= \boxed{\frac{(19\times10)-(13\times4)}{4\times10}} = \boxed{\frac{190-52}{40}} = \boxed{\frac{\overset{69}{\cancel{138}}}{\underset{20}{\cancel{40}}}} = \boxed{\frac{69}{20}} = \boxed{3\frac{9}{20}}$$

Example 5.2-31

$$\left(6\frac{2}{3} - 1\frac{1}{4}\right) - \left(4\frac{1}{8} - 2\frac{1}{4}\right) = \boxed{\left(\frac{(6\times3)+2}{3} - \frac{(1\times4)+1}{4}\right) - \left(\frac{(4\times8)+1}{8} - \frac{(2\times4)+1}{4}\right)}$$

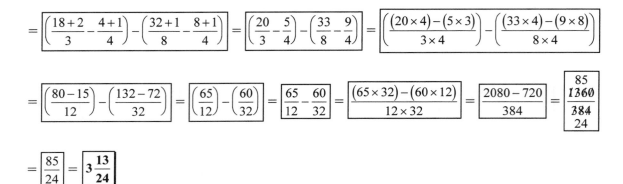

$$= \left[\left(\frac{18+2}{3} - \frac{4+1}{4}\right) - \left(\frac{32+1}{8} - \frac{8+1}{4}\right)\right] = \left[\left(\frac{20}{3} - \frac{5}{4}\right) - \left(\frac{33}{8} - \frac{9}{4}\right)\right] = \left[\left(\frac{(20\times4)-(5\times3)}{3\times4}\right) - \left(\frac{(33\times4)-(9\times8)}{8\times4}\right)\right]$$

$$= \left[\left(\frac{80-15}{12}\right) - \left(\frac{132-72}{32}\right)\right] = \left[\left(\frac{65}{12}\right) - \left(\frac{60}{32}\right)\right] = \left[\frac{65}{12} - \frac{60}{32}\right] = \left[\frac{(65\times32)-(60\times12)}{12\times32}\right] = \left[\frac{2080-720}{384}\right] = \frac{\overset{85}{\cancel{1360}}}{\underset{24}{\cancel{384}}}$$

$$= \left[\frac{85}{24}\right] = \boxed{3\frac{13}{24}}$$

Example 5.2-32

$$\left[\left(5\frac{2}{5} - 1\frac{3}{5}\right) - \left(1\frac{1}{5} - 2\frac{1}{3}\right)\right] = \left[\left(\frac{(5\times5)+2}{5} - \frac{(1\times5)+3}{5}\right) - \left(\frac{(1\times5)+1}{5} - \frac{(2\times3)+1}{3}\right)\right]$$

$$= \left[\left(\frac{25+2}{5} - \frac{5+3}{5}\right) - \left(\frac{5+1}{5} - \frac{6+1}{3}\right)\right] = \left[\left(\frac{27}{5} - \frac{8}{5}\right) - \left(\frac{6}{5} - \frac{7}{3}\right)\right] = \left[\left(\frac{27-8}{5}\right) - \left(\frac{(6\times3)-(7\times5)}{5\times3}\right)\right]$$

$$= \left[\left(\frac{19}{5}\right) - \left(\frac{18-35}{15}\right)\right] = \left[\frac{19}{5} - \left(\frac{-17}{15}\right)\right] = \left[\frac{19}{5} - \frac{-17}{15}\right] = \left[\frac{19}{5} + \frac{17}{15}\right] = \left[\frac{(19\times15)+(17\times5)}{5\times15}\right] = \left[\frac{285+85}{75}\right] = \frac{\overset{74}{\cancel{370}}}{\underset{15}{\cancel{75}}}$$

$$= \left[\frac{74}{15}\right] = \boxed{4\frac{14}{15}}$$

Example 5.2-33

$$\left[\left(8\frac{1}{4} - 1\frac{1}{2}\right) - \left(4\frac{1}{2} - 1\frac{1}{3}\right)\right] = \left[\left(\frac{(8\times4)+1}{4} - \frac{(1\times2)+1}{2}\right) - \left(\frac{(4\times2)+1}{2} - \frac{(1\times3)+1}{3}\right)\right]$$

$$= \left[\left(\frac{32+1}{4} - \frac{2+1}{2}\right) - \left(\frac{8+1}{2} - \frac{3+1}{3}\right)\right] = \left[\left(\frac{33}{4} - \frac{3}{2}\right) - \left(\frac{9}{2} - \frac{4}{3}\right)\right] = \left[\left(\frac{(33\times2)-(3\times4)}{4\times2}\right) - \left(\frac{(9\times3)-(4\times2)}{2\times3}\right)\right]$$

$$= \left[\left(\frac{66-12}{8}\right) - \left(\frac{27-8}{6}\right)\right] = \left[\left(\frac{54}{8}\right) - \left(\frac{19}{6}\right)\right] = \left[\frac{\overset{27}{\cancel{54}}}{\underset{4}{\cancel{8}}} - \frac{19}{6}\right] = \left[\frac{27}{4} - \frac{19}{6}\right] = \left[\frac{(27\times6)-(19\times4)}{4\times6}\right] = \left[\frac{162-76}{24}\right] = \frac{\overset{43}{\cancel{86}}}{\underset{12}{\cancel{24}}}$$

$$= \left[\frac{43}{12}\right] = \boxed{3\frac{7}{12}}$$

Example 5.2-34

$$\left[2\frac{3}{5} - \left[\left(3\frac{1}{3} - 1\frac{2}{3}\right) - 4\frac{2}{5}\right]\right] = \left[\frac{(2\times5)+3}{5} - \left[\left(\frac{(3\times3)+1}{3} - \frac{(1\times3)+2}{3}\right) - \frac{(4\times5)+2}{5}\right]\right]$$

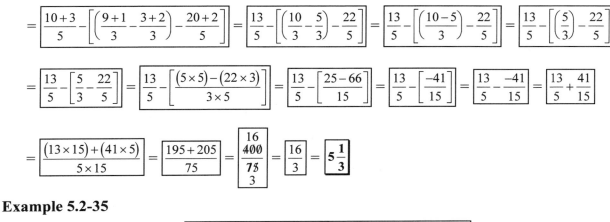

$$= \boxed{\frac{10+3}{5}-\left[\left(\frac{9+1}{3}-\frac{3+2}{3}\right)-\frac{20+2}{5}\right]} = \boxed{\frac{13}{5}-\left[\left(\frac{10}{3}-\frac{5}{3}\right)-\frac{22}{5}\right]} = \boxed{\frac{13}{5}-\left[\left(\frac{10-5}{3}\right)-\frac{22}{5}\right]} = \boxed{\frac{13}{5}-\left[\left(\frac{5}{3}\right)-\frac{22}{5}\right]}$$

$$= \boxed{\frac{13}{5}-\left[\frac{5}{3}-\frac{22}{5}\right]} = \boxed{\frac{13}{5}-\left[\frac{(5\times5)-(22\times3)}{3\times5}\right]} = \boxed{\frac{13}{5}-\left[\frac{25-66}{15}\right]} = \boxed{\frac{13}{5}-\left[\frac{-41}{15}\right]} = \boxed{\frac{13}{5}-\frac{-41}{15}} = \boxed{\frac{13}{5}+\frac{41}{15}}$$

$$= \boxed{\frac{(13\times15)+(41\times5)}{5\times15}} = \boxed{\frac{195+205}{75}} = \boxed{\frac{\frac{16}{400}}{\frac{75}{3}}} = \boxed{\frac{16}{3}} = \boxed{5\frac{1}{3}}$$

Example 5.2-35

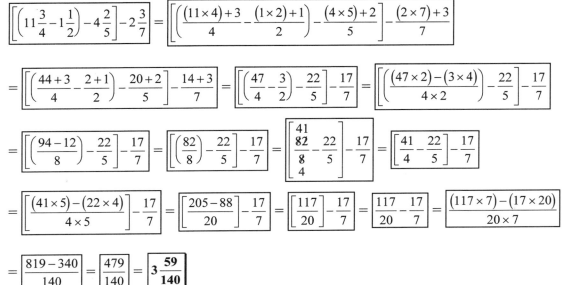

$$\boxed{\left[\left(11\frac{3}{4}-1\frac{1}{2}\right)-4\frac{2}{5}\right]-2\frac{3}{7}} = \boxed{\left[\left(\frac{(11\times4)+3}{4}-\frac{(1\times2)+1}{2}\right)-\frac{(4\times5)+2}{5}\right]-\frac{(2\times7)+3}{7}}$$

$$= \boxed{\left[\left(\frac{44+3}{4}-\frac{2+1}{2}\right)-\frac{20+2}{5}\right]-\frac{14+3}{7}} = \boxed{\left[\left(\frac{47}{4}-\frac{3}{2}\right)-\frac{22}{5}\right]-\frac{17}{7}} = \boxed{\left[\left(\frac{(47\times2)-(3\times4)}{4\times2}\right)-\frac{22}{5}\right]-\frac{17}{7}}$$

$$= \boxed{\left[\left(\frac{94-12}{8}\right)-\frac{22}{5}\right]-\frac{17}{7}} = \boxed{\left[\left(\frac{82}{8}\right)-\frac{22}{5}\right]-\frac{17}{7}} = \boxed{\left[\frac{\frac{41}{82}}{\frac{8}{4}}-\frac{22}{5}\right]-\frac{17}{7}} = \boxed{\left[\frac{41}{4}-\frac{22}{5}\right]-\frac{17}{7}}$$

$$= \boxed{\left[\frac{(41\times5)-(22\times4)}{4\times5}\right]-\frac{17}{7}} = \boxed{\left[\frac{205-88}{20}\right]-\frac{17}{7}} = \boxed{\left[\frac{117}{20}\right]-\frac{17}{7}} = \boxed{\frac{117}{20}-\frac{17}{7}} = \boxed{\frac{(117\times7)-(17\times20)}{20\times7}}$$

$$= \boxed{\frac{819-340}{140}} = \boxed{\frac{479}{140}} = \boxed{3\frac{59}{140}}$$

Section 5.2 Exercises - Subtract the following mixed fractions:

1. $4\frac{3}{7}-3\frac{1}{7} =$ 2. $3\frac{2}{5}-4\frac{2}{3} =$ 3. $\left(8\frac{1}{4}-2\frac{3}{4}\right)-1\frac{1}{3} =$

4. $6\frac{4}{5}-\left(2\frac{3}{4}-1\frac{2}{3}\right) =$ 5. $2\frac{3}{6}-4\frac{5}{6}-5\frac{1}{6} =$ 6. $4\frac{2}{3}-5\frac{5}{6}-2\frac{3}{5} =$

7. $3\frac{2}{5}-\left(4\frac{3}{8}-1\frac{2}{3}\right) =$ 8. $\left(6\frac{2}{3}-1\frac{1}{5}\right)-\left(2\frac{4}{3}-5\frac{2}{3}\right) =$ 9. $\left(3\frac{3}{4}-4\frac{2}{5}\right)-\left(3\frac{1}{8}-2\frac{3}{4}\right) =$

10. $\left[\left(5\frac{3}{4}-3\frac{5}{8}\right)-1\frac{2}{3}\right]-2\frac{3}{5} =$

5.3   Multiplying Mixed Fractions

Two or more mixed fractions with or without a common denominator are multiplied using the steps given as in each case below:

Case I   *Multiply two mixed fractions with or without a common denominator using the following steps:*

Step 1   Change the mixed fractions to integer fractions (see Section 2.5).

Step 2   Multiply the integer fractions (see Section 3.3, Case I).

Step 3   Simplify the fraction to its lowest term (see Section 2.3).

Step 4   Change the improper fraction to a mixed fraction if the fraction obtained from Step 3 is an improper fraction (see Section 2.2).

The following examples show the steps as to how two mixed fractions with or without a common denominator are multiplied:

Example 5.3-1

$$2\frac{3}{5} \times 1\frac{2}{3} =$$

Solution:

Step 1 $2\frac{3}{5} \times 1\frac{2}{3} = \frac{(2 \times 5) + 3}{5} \times \frac{(1 \times 3) + 2}{3} = \frac{10 + 3}{5} \times \frac{3 + 2}{3} = \frac{13}{5} \times \frac{5}{3}$

Step 2 $\frac{13}{5} \times \frac{5}{3} = \frac{13 \times 5}{5 \times 3} = \frac{65}{15}$

Step 3 $\frac{65}{15} = \frac{65 \div 5}{15 \div 5} = \frac{13}{3}$

Step 4 $\frac{13}{3} = 4\frac{1}{3}$

Example 5.3-2

$$3\frac{1}{3} \times 4\frac{1}{3} =$$

Solution:

Step 1 $3\frac{1}{3} \times 4\frac{1}{3} = \frac{(3 \times 3) + 1}{3} \times \frac{(4 \times 3) + 1}{3} = \frac{9 + 1}{3} \times \frac{12 + 1}{3} = \frac{10}{3} \times \frac{13}{3}$

Step 2 $\frac{10}{3} \times \frac{13}{3} = \frac{10 \times 13}{3 \times 3} = \frac{130}{9}$

Step 3 $\boxed{Not\ Applicable}$

Step 4 $\dfrac{130}{9} = \boxed{14\dfrac{4}{9}}$

Example 5.3-3

$$\boxed{15\dfrac{2}{3} \times 8\dfrac{1}{7}} =$$

Solution:

Step 1 $\boxed{15\dfrac{2}{3} \times 8\dfrac{1}{7}} = \boxed{\dfrac{(15 \times 3) + 2}{3} \times \dfrac{(8 \times 7) + 1}{7}} = \boxed{\dfrac{45 + 2}{3} \times \dfrac{56 + 1}{7}} = \boxed{\dfrac{47}{3} \times \dfrac{57}{7}}$

Step 2 $\boxed{\dfrac{47}{3} \times \dfrac{57}{7}} = \boxed{\dfrac{47 \times 57}{3 \times 7}} = \boxed{\dfrac{2679}{21}}$

Step 3 $\boxed{\dfrac{2679}{21}} = \boxed{\dfrac{2679 \div 3}{21 \div 3}} = \boxed{\dfrac{893}{7}}$

Step 4 $\boxed{\dfrac{893}{7}} = \boxed{127\dfrac{4}{7}}$

Example 5.3-4

$$\boxed{3\dfrac{1}{5} \times 5\dfrac{2}{5}} =$$

Solution:

Step 1 $\boxed{3\dfrac{1}{5} \times 5\dfrac{2}{5}} = \boxed{\dfrac{(3 \times 5) + 1}{5} \times \dfrac{(5 \times 5) + 2}{5}} = \boxed{\dfrac{15 + 1}{5} \times \dfrac{25 + 2}{5}} = \boxed{\dfrac{16}{5} \times \dfrac{27}{5}}$

Step 2 $\boxed{\dfrac{16}{5} \times \dfrac{27}{5}} = \boxed{\dfrac{16 \times 27}{5 \times 5}} = \boxed{\dfrac{432}{25}}$

Step 3 $\boxed{Not\ Applicable}$

Step 4 $\boxed{\dfrac{432}{25}} = \boxed{17\dfrac{7}{25}}$

Example 5.3-5

$$\boxed{5\dfrac{3}{8} \times 2\dfrac{5}{3}} =$$

Solution:

Step 1 $\boxed{5\dfrac{3}{8} \times 2\dfrac{5}{3}} = \boxed{\dfrac{(5 \times 8) + 3}{8} \times \dfrac{(2 \times 3) + 5}{3}} = \boxed{\dfrac{40 + 3}{8} \times \dfrac{6 + 5}{3}} = \boxed{\dfrac{43}{8} \times \dfrac{11}{3}}$

Step 2 $\boxed{\dfrac{43}{8} \times \dfrac{11}{3}} = \boxed{\dfrac{43 \times 11}{8 \times 3}} = \boxed{\dfrac{473}{24}}$

Step 3 $\boxed{\textit{Not Applicable}}$

Step 4 $\boxed{\dfrac{473}{24}} = \boxed{\mathbf{19\dfrac{17}{24}}}$

In general, two mixed fractions are multiplied in the following way:

$$\boxed{k_1\dfrac{a}{b} \times k_2\dfrac{c}{d}} = \boxed{\dfrac{(k_1 \times b) + a}{b} \times \dfrac{(k_2 \times d) + c}{d}} = \boxed{\dfrac{k_1 b + a}{b} \times \dfrac{k_2 d + c}{d}} = \boxed{\dfrac{(k_1 b + a) \times (k_2 d + c)}{b \times d}}$$

Let $\boxed{A_1 = k_1 b + a}$, and $\boxed{A_2 = k_2 d + c}$, then

$$\boxed{\dfrac{(k_1 b + a) \times (k_2 d + c)}{b \times d}} = \boxed{\dfrac{A_1 \times A_2}{b \times d}} = \boxed{\dfrac{A_1 A_2}{bd}}$$

Example 5.3-6

$$\boxed{5\dfrac{2}{3} \times 2\dfrac{1}{4}} = \boxed{\dfrac{(5 \times 3) + 2}{3} \times \dfrac{(2 \times 4) + 1}{4}} = \boxed{\dfrac{15 + 2}{3} \times \dfrac{8 + 1}{4}} = \boxed{\dfrac{17}{3} \times \dfrac{9}{4}} = \boxed{\dfrac{17 \times \overset{3}{\cancel{9}}}{\underset{1}{\cancel{3}} \times 4}} = \boxed{\dfrac{17 \times 3}{1 \times 4}} = \boxed{\dfrac{51}{4}} = \boxed{\mathbf{12\dfrac{3}{4}}}$$

Case II   *Multiply three mixed fractions with or without a common denominator using the following steps:*

Step 1   Change the mixed fractions to integer fractions (see Section 2.5).

Step 2   Multiply the integer fractions (see Section 3.3, Case II).

Step 3   Simplify the fraction to its lowest term (see Section 2.3).

Step 4   Change the improper fraction to a mixed fraction if the fraction obtained from Step 3 is an improper fraction (see Section 2.2).

The following examples show the steps as to how three mixed fractions with or without a common denominator are multiplied:

Example 5.3-7

$$\boxed{3\dfrac{2}{5} \times 1\dfrac{2}{3} \times 4\dfrac{1}{4}} =$$

Solution:

Step 1 $\boxed{3\dfrac{2}{5} \times 1\dfrac{2}{3} \times 4\dfrac{1}{4}} = \boxed{\dfrac{(3 \times 5) + 2}{5} \times \dfrac{(1 \times 3) + 2}{3} \times \dfrac{(4 \times 4) + 1}{4}} = \boxed{\dfrac{15 + 2}{5} \times \dfrac{3 + 2}{3} \times \dfrac{16 + 1}{4}}$

$= \boxed{\dfrac{17}{5} \times \dfrac{5}{3} \times \dfrac{17}{4}}$

Step 2 $\dfrac{17}{5} \times \dfrac{5}{3} \times \dfrac{17}{4} = \dfrac{17 \times 5 \times 17}{5 \times 3 \times 4} = \dfrac{1445}{60}$

Step 3 $\dfrac{1445}{60} = \dfrac{1445 \div 5}{60 \div 5} = \dfrac{289}{12}$

Step 4 $\dfrac{289}{12} = \boxed{24\dfrac{1}{12}}$

Example 5.3-8

$$2\dfrac{3}{2} \times 1\dfrac{1}{2} \times 3\dfrac{5}{2} =$$

Solution:

Step 1 $2\dfrac{3}{2} \times 1\dfrac{1}{2} \times 3\dfrac{5}{2} = \dfrac{(2 \times 2)+3}{2} \times \dfrac{(1 \times 2)+1}{2} \times \dfrac{(3 \times 2)+5}{2} = \dfrac{4+3}{2} \times \dfrac{2+1}{2} \times \dfrac{6+5}{2}$

$= \dfrac{7}{2} \times \dfrac{3}{2} \times \dfrac{11}{2}$

Step 2 $\dfrac{7}{2} \times \dfrac{3}{2} \times \dfrac{11}{2} = \dfrac{7 \times 3 \times 11}{2 \times 2 \times 2} = \dfrac{231}{8}$

Step 3 $\boxed{Not\ Applicable}$

Step 4 $\dfrac{231}{8} = \boxed{28\dfrac{7}{8}}$

Example 5.3-9

$$4\dfrac{1}{5} \times 2\dfrac{2}{3} \times 1\dfrac{1}{4} =$$

Solution:

Step 1 $4\dfrac{1}{5} \times 2\dfrac{2}{3} \times 1\dfrac{1}{4} = \dfrac{(4 \times 5)+1}{5} \times \dfrac{(2 \times 3)+2}{3} \times \dfrac{(1 \times 4)+1}{4} = \dfrac{20+1}{5} \times \dfrac{6+2}{3} \times \dfrac{4+1}{4}$

$= \dfrac{21}{5} \times \dfrac{8}{3} \times \dfrac{5}{4}$

Step 2 $\dfrac{21}{5} \times \dfrac{8}{3} \times \dfrac{5}{4} = \dfrac{21 \times 8 \times 5}{5 \times 3 \times 4} = \dfrac{840}{60}$

Step 3 $\dfrac{840}{60} = \dfrac{840 \div 60}{60 \div 60} = \dfrac{14}{1} = \boxed{14}$

Step 4 $\boxed{Not\ Applicable}$

Example 5.3-10

$$\boxed{4\frac{1}{3} \times 2\frac{2}{3} \times 6\frac{5}{3}} =$$

Solution:

Step 1 $\boxed{4\frac{1}{3} \times 2\frac{2}{3} \times 6\frac{5}{3}} = \boxed{\frac{(4\times 3)+1}{3} \times \frac{(2\times 3)+2}{3} \times \frac{(6\times 3)+5}{3}} = \boxed{\frac{12+1}{3} \times \frac{6+2}{3} \times \frac{18+5}{3}}$

$= \boxed{\frac{13}{3} \times \frac{8}{3} \times \frac{23}{3}}$

Step 2 $\boxed{\frac{13}{3} \times \frac{8}{3} \times \frac{23}{3}} = \boxed{\frac{13\times 8\times 23}{3\times 3\times 3}} = \boxed{\frac{2392}{27}}$

Step 3 $\boxed{Not\ Applicable}$

Step 4 $\boxed{\frac{2392}{27}} = \boxed{\mathbf{88\frac{16}{27}}}$

Example 5.3-11

$$\boxed{2\frac{1}{4} \times 4\frac{2}{8} \times 6\frac{4}{6}} =$$

Solution:

Step 1 $\boxed{2\frac{1}{4} \times 4\frac{2}{8} \times 6\frac{4}{6}} = \boxed{\frac{(2\times 4)+1}{4} \times \frac{(4\times 8)+2}{8} \times \frac{(6\times 6)+4}{6}} = \boxed{\frac{8+1}{4} \times \frac{32+2}{8} \times \frac{36+4}{6}}$

$= \boxed{\frac{9}{4} \times \frac{34}{8} \times \frac{40}{6}}$

Step 2 $\boxed{\frac{9}{4} \times \frac{34}{8} \times \frac{40}{6}} = \boxed{\frac{9\times 34\times 40}{4\times 8\times 6}} = \boxed{\frac{12240}{192}}$

Step 3 $\boxed{\frac{12240}{192}} = \boxed{\frac{12240\div 16}{192\div 16}} = \boxed{\frac{765}{12}} = \boxed{\frac{765\div 3}{12\div 3}} = \boxed{\frac{255}{4}}$

Step 4 $\boxed{\frac{255}{4}} = \boxed{\mathbf{63\frac{3}{4}}}$

In general, three mixed fractions are multiplied as in the following cases:

Case I.

$$\boxed{k_1\frac{a}{b} \times k_2\frac{c}{d} \times k_3\frac{e}{f}} = \boxed{\frac{(k_1 \times b)+a}{b} \times \frac{(k_2 \times d)+c}{d} \times \frac{(k_3 \times f)+e}{f}} = \boxed{\frac{k_1b+a}{b} \times \frac{k_2d+c}{d} \times \frac{k_3f+e}{f}}$$

Let $\boxed{A_1 = k_1b+a}$, $\boxed{A_2 = k_2d+c}$, and $\boxed{A_3 = k_3f+e}$, then

$$\boxed{\frac{k_1b+a}{b} \times \frac{k_2d+c}{d} \times \frac{k_3f+e}{f}} = \boxed{\frac{A_1}{b} \times \frac{A_2}{d} \times \frac{A_3}{f}} = \boxed{\frac{A_1 \times A_2 \times A_3}{b \times d \times f}} = \boxed{\frac{A_1A_2A_3}{bdf}}$$

Example 5.3-12

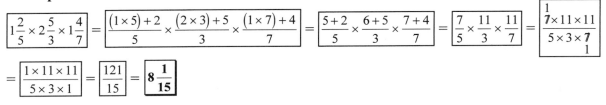

$$\boxed{1\frac{2}{5} \times 2\frac{5}{3} \times 1\frac{4}{7}} = \boxed{\frac{(1\times5)+2}{5} \times \frac{(2\times3)+5}{3} \times \frac{(1\times7)+4}{7}} = \boxed{\frac{5+2}{5} \times \frac{6+5}{3} \times \frac{7+4}{7}} = \boxed{\frac{7}{5} \times \frac{11}{3} \times \frac{11}{7}} = \boxed{\frac{\overset{1}{7}\times11\times11}{5\times3\times\underset{1}{7}}}$$

$$= \boxed{\frac{1\times11\times11}{5\times3\times1}} = \boxed{\frac{121}{15}} = \boxed{8\frac{1}{15}}$$

Case II.

$$\boxed{k_1\frac{a}{b} \times k_2\frac{c}{d} \times k_3\frac{e}{f}} = \boxed{\left(k_1\frac{a}{b} \times k_2\frac{c}{d}\right) \times k_3\frac{e}{f}} = \boxed{\left(\frac{(k_1 \times b)+a}{b} \times \frac{(k_2 \times d)+c}{d}\right) \times \frac{(k_3 \times f)+e}{f}}$$

$$= \boxed{\left(\frac{k_1b+a}{b} \times \frac{k_2d+c}{d}\right) \times \frac{k_3f+e}{f}}$$

Let $\boxed{A_1 = k_1b+a}$, $\boxed{A_2 = k_2d+c}$, and $\boxed{A_3 = k_3f+e}$, then

$$\boxed{\left(\frac{k_1b+a}{b} \times \frac{k_2d+c}{d}\right) \times \frac{k_3f+e}{f}} = \boxed{\left(\frac{A_1}{b} \times \frac{A_2}{d}\right) \times \frac{A_3}{f}} = \boxed{\left(\frac{A_1 \times A_2}{b \times d}\right) \times \frac{A_3}{f}} = \boxed{\left(\frac{A_1A_2}{bd}\right) \times \frac{A_3}{f}} = \boxed{\frac{A_1A_2}{bd} \times \frac{A_3}{f}}$$

$$= \boxed{\frac{A_1A_2A_3}{bdf}}$$

Example 5.3-13

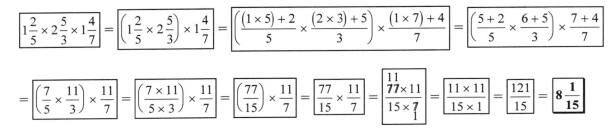

$$\boxed{1\frac{2}{5} \times 2\frac{5}{3} \times 1\frac{4}{7}} = \boxed{\left(1\frac{2}{5} \times 2\frac{5}{3}\right) \times 1\frac{4}{7}} = \boxed{\left(\frac{(1\times5)+2}{5} \times \frac{(2\times3)+5}{3}\right) \times \frac{(1\times7)+4}{7}} = \boxed{\left(\frac{5+2}{5} \times \frac{6+5}{3}\right) \times \frac{7+4}{7}}$$

$$= \boxed{\left(\frac{7}{5} \times \frac{11}{3}\right) \times \frac{11}{7}} = \boxed{\left(\frac{7\times11}{5\times3}\right) \times \frac{11}{7}} = \boxed{\left(\frac{77}{15}\right) \times \frac{11}{7}} = \boxed{\frac{77}{15} \times \frac{11}{7}} = \boxed{\frac{\overset{11}{77}\times11}{15\times\underset{1}{7}}} = \boxed{\frac{11\times11}{15\times1}} = \boxed{\frac{121}{15}} = \boxed{8\frac{1}{15}}$$

Case III.

$$k_1\frac{a}{b} \times k_2\frac{c}{d} \times k_3\frac{e}{f} = k_1\frac{a}{b} \times \left(k_2\frac{c}{d} \times k_3\frac{e}{f}\right) = \frac{(k_1 \times b) + a}{b} \times \left(\frac{(k_2 \times d) + c}{d} \times \frac{(k_3 \times f) + e}{f}\right)$$

$$= \frac{k_1b + a}{b} \times \left(\frac{k_2d + c}{d} \times \frac{k_3f + e}{f}\right)$$

Let $\boxed{A_1 = k_1b + a}$, $\boxed{A_2 = k_2d + c}$, and $\boxed{A_3 = k_3f + e}$, then

$$\frac{k_1b + a}{b} \times \left(\frac{k_2d + c}{d} \times \frac{k_3f + e}{f}\right) = \frac{A_1}{b} \times \left(\frac{A_2}{d} \times \frac{A_3}{f}\right) = \frac{A_1}{b} \times \left(\frac{A_2 \times A_3}{d \times f}\right) = \frac{A_1}{b} \times \left(\frac{A_2 A_3}{df}\right) = \frac{A_1}{b} \times \frac{A_2 A_3}{df}$$

$$= \frac{A_1 \times A_2 A_3}{b \times df} = \boxed{\frac{A_1 A_2 A_3}{bdf}}$$

Example 5.3-14

$$1\frac{2}{5} \times 2\frac{5}{3} \times 1\frac{4}{7} = 1\frac{2}{5} \times \left(2\frac{5}{3} \times 1\frac{4}{7}\right) = \frac{(1 \times 5) + 2}{5} \times \left(\frac{(2 \times 3) + 5}{3} \times \frac{(1 \times 7) + 4}{7}\right) = \frac{5 + 2}{5} \times \left(\frac{6 + 5}{3} \times \frac{7 + 4}{7}\right)$$

$$= \frac{7}{5} \times \left(\frac{11}{3} \times \frac{11}{7}\right) = \frac{7}{5} \times \left(\frac{11 \times 11}{3 \times 7}\right) = \frac{7}{5} \times \left(\frac{121}{21}\right) = \frac{7}{5} \times \frac{121}{21} = \frac{\overset{1}{7} \times 121}{5 \times \underset{3}{21}} = \frac{1 \times 121}{5 \times 3} = \frac{121}{15} = \boxed{8\frac{1}{15}}$$

Note - In multiplication the use of parentheses does not change the final answer; the three examples above have the same answer (see Section 1.4).

The following examples further illustrate how to multiply mixed fractions:

Example 5.3-15

$$3\frac{1}{4} \times 2\frac{3}{8} = \frac{(3 \times 4) + 1}{4} \times \frac{(2 \times 8) + 3}{8} = \frac{12 + 1}{4} \times \frac{16 + 3}{8} = \frac{13}{4} \times \frac{19}{8} = \frac{13 \times 19}{4 \times 8} = \frac{247}{32} = \boxed{7\frac{23}{32}}$$

Example 5.3-16

$$4\frac{2}{3} \times 2\frac{3}{7} = \frac{(4 \times 3) + 2}{3} \times \frac{(2 \times 7) + 3}{7} = \frac{12 + 2}{3} \times \frac{14 + 3}{7} = \frac{14}{3} \times \frac{17}{7} = \frac{\overset{2}{14} \times 17}{3 \times \underset{1}{7}} = \frac{2 \times 17}{3 \times 1} = \frac{34}{3} = \boxed{11\frac{1}{3}}$$

Example 5.3-17

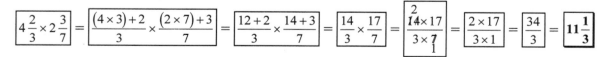

$$1\frac{5}{8} \times 4\frac{2}{8} \times 3\frac{1}{2} = \frac{(1 \times 8) + 5}{8} \times \frac{(4 \times 8) + 2}{8} \times \frac{(3 \times 2) + 1}{2} = \frac{8 + 5}{8} \times \frac{32 + 2}{8} \times \frac{6 + 1}{2} = \frac{13}{8} \times \frac{34}{8} \times \frac{7}{2}$$

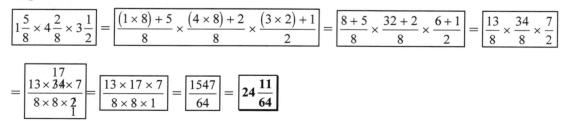

$$= \frac{13 \times \overset{17}{34} \times 7}{8 \times 8 \times \underset{1}{2}} = \frac{13 \times 17 \times 7}{8 \times 8 \times 1} = \frac{1547}{64} = \boxed{24\frac{11}{64}}$$

Example 5.3-18

$$\left(2\frac{2}{3} \times 1\frac{3}{5}\right) \times 3\frac{1}{2} = \left(\frac{(2 \times 3)+2}{3} \times \frac{(1 \times 5)+3}{5}\right) \times \frac{(3 \times 2)+1}{2} = \left(\frac{6+2}{3} \times \frac{5+3}{5}\right) \times \frac{6+1}{2} = \left(\frac{8}{3} \times \frac{8}{5}\right) \times \frac{7}{2}$$

$$= \left(\frac{8 \times 8}{3 \times 5}\right) \times \frac{7}{2} = \left(\frac{64}{15}\right) \times \frac{7}{2} = \frac{64}{15} \times \frac{7}{2} = \frac{\overset{32}{64} \times 7}{15 \times \underset{1}{2}} = \frac{32 \times 7}{15 \times 1} = \frac{224}{15} = \boxed{14\frac{14}{15}}$$

Example 5.3-19

$$2\frac{3}{4} \times \left(1\frac{3}{5} \times 3\frac{2}{10}\right) = \frac{(2 \times 4)+3}{4} \times \left(\frac{(1 \times 5)+3}{5} \times \frac{(3 \times 10)+2}{10}\right) = \frac{8+3}{4} \times \left(\frac{5+3}{5} \times \frac{30+2}{10}\right) = \frac{11}{4} \times \left(\frac{8}{5} \times \frac{32}{10}\right)$$

$$= \frac{11}{4} \times \left(\frac{\overset{4}{8} \times 32}{5 \times \underset{5}{10}}\right) = \frac{11}{4} \times \left(\frac{4 \times 32}{5 \times 5}\right) = \frac{11}{4} \times \left(\frac{128}{25}\right) = \frac{11}{4} \times \frac{128}{25} = \frac{11 \times \overset{32}{128}}{\underset{1}{4} \times 25} = \frac{11 \times 32}{1 \times 25} = \frac{352}{25} = \boxed{14\frac{2}{25}}$$

Example 5.3-20

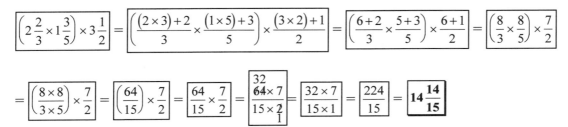

$$= \left(\frac{3+1}{3} \times \frac{10+4}{5} \times \frac{10+3}{5}\right) \times \frac{14+1}{14} = \left(\frac{4}{3} \times \frac{14}{5} \times \frac{13}{5}\right) \times \frac{15}{14} = \left(\frac{4 \times 14 \times 13}{3 \times 5 \times 5}\right) \times \frac{15}{14} = \left(\frac{728}{75}\right) \times \frac{15}{14} = \frac{728}{75} \times \frac{15}{14}$$

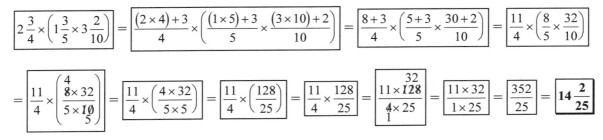

Example 5.3-21

$$1\frac{2}{3} \times \left(3\frac{1}{6} \times 2\frac{1}{2}\right) \times 1\frac{3}{5} = \frac{(1 \times 3)+2}{3} \times \left(\frac{(3 \times 6)+1}{6} \times \frac{(2 \times 2)+1}{2}\right) \times \frac{(5 \times 1)+3}{4}$$

$$= \frac{3+2}{3} \times \left(\frac{18+1}{6} \times \frac{4+1}{2}\right) \times \frac{5+3}{4} = \frac{5}{3} \times \left(\frac{19}{6} \times \frac{5}{2}\right) \times \frac{8}{5} = \frac{5}{3} \times \left(\frac{19 \times 5}{6 \times 2}\right) \times \frac{8}{5} = \frac{5}{3} \times \left(\frac{95}{12}\right) \times \frac{8}{5} = \frac{5}{3} \times \frac{95}{12} \times \frac{8}{5}$$

$$= \frac{\overset{1}{5} \times 95 \times \overset{2}{8}}{3 \times \underset{3}{12} \times \underset{1}{5}} = \frac{1 \times 95 \times 2}{3 \times 3 \times 1} = \frac{190}{9} = \boxed{21\frac{1}{9}}$$

Example 5.3-22

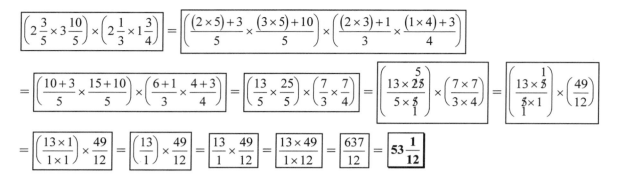

$$\left(2\frac{3}{5} \times 3\frac{10}{5}\right) \times \left(2\frac{1}{3} \times 1\frac{3}{4}\right) = \left[\left(\frac{(2\times5)+3}{5} \times \frac{(3\times5)+10}{5}\right) \times \left(\frac{(2\times3)+1}{3} \times \frac{(1\times4)+3}{4}\right)\right]$$

$$= \left[\left(\frac{10+3}{5} \times \frac{15+10}{5}\right) \times \left(\frac{6+1}{3} \times \frac{4+3}{4}\right)\right] = \left[\left(\frac{13}{5} \times \frac{25}{5}\right) \times \left(\frac{7}{3} \times \frac{7}{4}\right)\right] = \left[\left(\frac{13 \times \overset{5}{\cancel{25}}}{5 \times \underset{1}{\cancel{5}}}\right) \times \left(\frac{7\times7}{3\times4}\right)\right] = \left[\left(\frac{13 \times \overset{1}{\cancel{5}}}{\underset{1}{\cancel{5}} \times 1}\right) \times \left(\frac{49}{12}\right)\right]$$

$$= \left[\left(\frac{13\times1}{1\times1}\right) \times \frac{49}{12}\right] = \left[\left(\frac{13}{1}\right) \times \frac{49}{12}\right] = \frac{13}{1} \times \frac{49}{12} = \frac{13\times49}{1\times12} = \frac{637}{12} = \boxed{53\frac{1}{12}}$$

Example 5.3-23

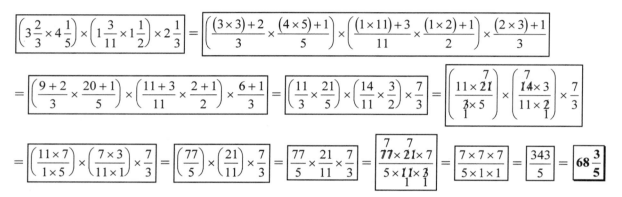

$$\left(3\frac{2}{3} \times 4\frac{1}{5}\right) \times \left(1\frac{3}{11} \times 1\frac{1}{2}\right) \times 2\frac{1}{3} = \left[\left(\frac{(3\times3)+2}{3} \times \frac{(4\times5)+1}{5}\right) \times \left(\frac{(1\times11)+3}{11} \times \frac{(1\times2)+1}{2}\right) \times \frac{(2\times3)+1}{3}\right]$$

$$= \left[\left(\frac{9+2}{3} \times \frac{20+1}{5}\right) \times \left(\frac{11+3}{11} \times \frac{2+1}{2}\right) \times \frac{6+1}{3}\right] = \left[\left(\frac{11}{3} \times \frac{21}{5}\right) \times \left(\frac{14}{11} \times \frac{3}{2}\right) \times \frac{7}{3}\right] = \left[\left(\frac{11 \times \overset{7}{\cancel{21}}}{\underset{1}{\cancel{3}} \times 5}\right) \times \left(\frac{\overset{7}{\cancel{14}} \times 3}{11 \times \underset{1}{\cancel{2}}}\right) \times \frac{7}{3}\right]$$

$$= \left[\left(\frac{11\times7}{1\times5}\right) \times \left(\frac{7\times3}{11\times1}\right) \times \frac{7}{3}\right] = \left[\left(\frac{77}{5}\right) \times \left(\frac{21}{11}\right) \times \frac{7}{3}\right] = \frac{77}{5} \times \frac{21}{11} \times \frac{7}{3} = \frac{\overset{7}{\cancel{77}} \times \overset{7}{\cancel{21}} \times 7}{5 \times \underset{1}{\cancel{11}} \times \underset{1}{\cancel{3}}} = \frac{7\times7\times7}{5\times1\times1} = \frac{343}{5} = \boxed{68\frac{3}{5}}$$

Example 5.3-24

$$4\frac{1}{8} \times \left[\left(6\frac{1}{2} \times 1\frac{2}{33}\right) \times 2\frac{1}{13}\right] = \frac{(4\times8)+1}{8} \times \left[\left(\frac{(6\times2)+1}{2} \times \frac{(1\times33)+2}{33}\right) \times \frac{(2\times13)+1}{13}\right]$$

$$= \frac{32+1}{8} \times \left[\left(\frac{12+1}{2} \times \frac{33+2}{33}\right) \times \frac{26+1}{13}\right] = \frac{33}{8} \times \left[\left(\frac{13}{2} \times \frac{35}{33}\right) \times \frac{27}{13}\right] = \frac{33}{8} \times \left[\left(\frac{13\times35}{2\times33}\right) \times \frac{27}{13}\right]$$

$$= \frac{33}{8} \times \left[\left(\frac{455}{66}\right) \times \frac{27}{13}\right] = \frac{33}{8} \times \left[\frac{455}{66} \times \frac{27}{13}\right] = \frac{33}{8} \times \left[\frac{455 \times \overset{9}{\cancel{27}}}{\underset{22}{\cancel{66}} \times 13}\right] = \frac{33}{8} \times \left[\frac{455\times9}{22\times13}\right] = \frac{33}{8} \times \left[\frac{4095}{286}\right]$$

$$= \frac{33}{8} \times \frac{4095}{286} = \frac{\overset{3}{\cancel{33}} \times 4095}{8 \times \underset{26}{\cancel{286}}} = \frac{3 \times \overset{315}{\cancel{4095}}}{8 \times \underset{2}{\cancel{26}}} = \frac{3\times315}{8\times2} = \frac{945}{16} = \boxed{59\frac{1}{16}}$$

Example 5.3-25

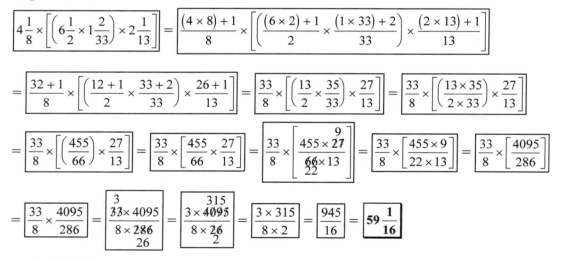

$$4\frac{3}{8} \times \left[2\frac{4}{5} \times \left(3\frac{5}{6} \times 1\frac{3}{5}\right)\right] = \frac{(4\times8)+3}{8} \times \left[\frac{(2\times5)+4}{5} \times \left(\frac{(3\times6)+5}{6} \times \frac{(1\times5)+3}{5}\right)\right]$$

$$= \boxed{\frac{32+3}{8} \times \left[\frac{10+4}{5} \times \left(\frac{18+5}{6} \times \frac{5+3}{5}\right)\right]} = \boxed{\frac{35}{8} \times \left[\frac{14}{5} \times \left(\frac{23}{6} \times \frac{8}{5}\right)\right]} = \boxed{\frac{35}{8} \times \left[\frac{14}{5} \times \left(\frac{23 \times \overset{4}{8}}{\underset{3}{6} \times 5}\right)\right]}$$

$$= \boxed{\frac{35}{8} \times \left[\frac{14}{5} \times \left(\frac{23 \times 4}{3 \times 5}\right)\right]} = \boxed{\frac{35}{8} \times \left[\frac{14}{5} \times \left(\frac{92}{15}\right)\right]} = \boxed{\frac{35}{8} \times \left[\frac{14}{5} \times \frac{92}{15}\right]} = \boxed{\frac{35}{8} \times \left[\frac{14 \times 92}{5 \times 15}\right]} = \boxed{\frac{35}{8} \times \left[\frac{1288}{75}\right]}$$

$$= \boxed{\frac{35}{8} \times \frac{1288}{75}} = \boxed{\frac{\overset{7}{\cancel{35}} \times \overset{161}{\cancel{1288}}}{\underset{1}{\cancel{8}} \times \underset{15}{\cancel{75}}}} = \boxed{\frac{7 \times 161}{1 \times 15}} = \boxed{\frac{1127}{15}} = \boxed{75\frac{2}{15}}$$

Section 5.3 Exercises - Multiply the following mixed fractions:

1. $1\frac{3}{4} \times 2\frac{1}{3} =$

2. $2\frac{1}{3} \times 1\frac{1}{4} \times 4\frac{5}{6} =$

3. $3\frac{1}{3} \times \left(1\frac{2}{5} \times 1\frac{2}{3}\right) =$

4. $\left(2\frac{3}{4} \times 5\frac{1}{2}\right) \times 3\frac{1}{5} =$

5. $2\frac{5}{6} \times 3\frac{2}{5} \times 1\frac{1}{3} \times 1\frac{1}{2} =$

6. $1\frac{1}{5} \times 2\frac{1}{3} \times \left(3\frac{2}{3} \times \frac{0}{1}\right) =$

7. $\left(1\frac{5}{6} \times 2\frac{1}{3}\right) \times \left(2\frac{3}{7} \times 1\frac{1}{7}\right) =$

8. $\left(2\frac{1}{2} \times 1\frac{3}{4}\right) \times \left(4\frac{1}{2} \times 2\frac{2}{3}\right) =$

9. $\left(3\frac{1}{2} \times 1\frac{2}{3} \times 3\frac{3}{5}\right) \times 1\frac{2}{3} =$

10. $2\frac{1}{3} \times \left[\left(3\frac{3}{5} \times 1\frac{1}{2}\right) \times 2\frac{2}{3}\right] =$

5.4   Dividing Mixed Fractions

Two or more mixed fractions with or without a common denominator are divided using the steps given as in each case below:

Case I   *Divide two mixed fractions with or without a common denominator using the following steps:*

Step 1   Change the mixed fractions to integer fractions (see Section 2.5).

Step 2   Divide the integer fractions (see Section 3.4, Case I).

Step 3   Simplify the fraction to its lowest term (see Section 2.3).

Step 4   Change the improper fraction to a mixed fraction if the fraction obtained from Step 3 is an improper fraction (see Section 2.2).

The following examples show the steps as to how two mixed fractions with or without a common denominator are divided:

Example 5.4-1

$$2\frac{3}{5} \div 1\frac{1}{3} =$$

Solution:

Step 1 $2\frac{3}{5} \div 1\frac{1}{3} = \frac{(2 \times 5) + 3}{5} \div \frac{(1 \times 3) + 1}{3} = \frac{10 + 3}{5} \div \frac{3 + 1}{3} = \frac{13}{5} \div \frac{4}{3}$

Step 2 $\frac{13}{5} \div \frac{4}{3} = \frac{13}{5} \times \frac{3}{4} = \frac{13 \times 3}{5 \times 4} = \frac{39}{20}$

Step 3 $\boxed{Not\ Applicable}$

Step 4 $\frac{39}{20} = \mathbf{1\frac{19}{20}}$

Example 5.4-2

$$3\frac{1}{5} \div 4\frac{1}{5} =$$

Solution:

Step 1 $3\frac{1}{5} \div 4\frac{1}{5} = \frac{(3 \times 5) + 1}{5} \div \frac{(4 \times 5) + 1}{5} = \frac{15 + 1}{5} \div \frac{20 + 1}{5} = \frac{16}{5} \div \frac{21}{5}$

Step 2 $\frac{16}{5} \div \frac{21}{5} = \frac{16}{5} \times \frac{5}{21} = \frac{16 \times 5}{5 \times 21} = \frac{80}{105}$

Step 3 $\frac{80}{105} = \frac{80 \div 5}{105 \div 5} = \mathbf{\frac{16}{21}}$

Step 4 $\boxed{Not\ Applicable}$

Example 5.4-3

$$15\frac{2}{3} \div 10\frac{1}{5} =$$

Solution:

Step 1 $15\frac{2}{3} \div 10\frac{1}{5} = \frac{(15 \times 3) + 2}{3} \div \frac{(10 \times 5) + 1}{5} = \frac{45 + 2}{3} \div \frac{50 + 1}{5} = \frac{47}{3} \div \frac{51}{5}$

Step 2 $\frac{47}{3} \div \frac{51}{5} = \frac{47}{3} \times \frac{5}{51} = \frac{47 \times 5}{3 \times 51} = \frac{235}{153}$

Step 3 $\boxed{Not\ Applicable}$

Step 4 $\frac{235}{153} = \boxed{1\frac{82}{153}}$

Example 5.4-4

$$2\frac{4}{6} \div 3\frac{1}{4} =$$

Solution:

Step 1 $2\frac{4}{6} \div 3\frac{1}{4} = \frac{(2 \times 6) + 4}{6} \div \frac{(3 \times 4) + 1}{4} = \frac{12 + 4}{6} \div \frac{12 + 1}{4} = \frac{16}{6} \div \frac{13}{4}$

Step 2 $\frac{16}{6} \div \frac{13}{4} = \frac{16}{6} \times \frac{4}{13} = \frac{16 \times 4}{6 \times 13} = \frac{64}{78}$

Step 3 $\frac{64}{78} = \frac{64 \div 2}{78 \div 2} = \boxed{\frac{32}{39}}$

Step 4 $\boxed{Not\ Applicable}$

Example 5.4-5

$$12\frac{2}{8} \div 6\frac{2}{4} =$$

Solution:

Step 1 $12\frac{2}{8} \div 6\frac{2}{4} = \frac{(12 \times 8) + 2}{8} \div \frac{(6 \times 4) + 2}{4} = \frac{96 + 2}{8} \div \frac{24 + 2}{4} = \frac{98}{8} \div \frac{26}{4}$

Step 2 $\frac{98}{8} \div \frac{26}{4} = \frac{98}{8} \times \frac{4}{26} = \frac{98 \times 4}{8 \times 26} = \frac{392}{208}$

Step 3 $\frac{392}{208} = \frac{392 \div 8}{208 \div 8} = \frac{49}{26}$

Step 4 $\boxed{\dfrac{49}{26}} = \boxed{1\dfrac{23}{26}}$

In general, two mixed fractions are divided in the following way:

$$\boxed{k_1\dfrac{a}{b} \div k_2\dfrac{c}{d}} = \boxed{\dfrac{(k_1 \times b) + a}{b} \div \dfrac{(k_2 \times d) + c}{d}} = \boxed{\dfrac{k_1b + a}{b} \div \dfrac{k_2d + c}{d}}$$

Let $\boxed{A_1 = k_1b + a}$, and $\boxed{A_2 = k_2d + c}$, then

$$\boxed{\dfrac{k_1b + a}{b} \div \dfrac{k_2d + c}{d}} = \boxed{\dfrac{A_1}{b} \div \dfrac{A_2}{d}} = \boxed{\dfrac{A_1}{b} \times \dfrac{d}{A_2}} = \boxed{\dfrac{A_1 \times d}{b \times A_2}} = \boxed{\dfrac{A_1 d}{bA_2}}$$

Example 5.4-6

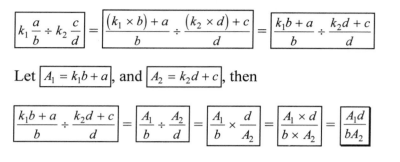

$$\boxed{1\dfrac{3}{5} \div 1\dfrac{2}{10}} = \boxed{\dfrac{(1 \times 5) + 3}{5} \div \dfrac{(1 \times 10) + 2}{10}} = \boxed{\dfrac{8}{5} \div \dfrac{12}{10}} = \boxed{\dfrac{8}{5} \times \dfrac{10}{12}} = \boxed{\dfrac{\overset{4}{8} \times \overset{2}{10}}{\underset{1}{5} \times \underset{6}{12}}} = \boxed{\dfrac{4 \times 2}{1 \times \overset{1}{6}_{3}}} = \boxed{\dfrac{4 \times 1}{1 \times 3}} = \boxed{\dfrac{4}{3}} = \boxed{1\dfrac{1}{3}}$$

Case II   *Divide three mixed fractions with or without a common denominator using the following steps:*

Step 1   Change the mixed fractions to integer fractions (see Section 2.5).

Step 2   Divide the integer fractions (see Section 3.4, Case II).

Step 3   Simplify the fraction to its lowest term (see Section 2.3).

Step 4   Change the improper fraction to a mixed fraction if the fraction obtained from Step 3 is an improper fraction (see Section 2.2).

The following examples show the steps as to how three mixed fractions with or without a common denominator are divided:

Example 5.4-7

$$\boxed{\left(3\dfrac{2}{5} \div 2\dfrac{1}{3}\right) \div 1\dfrac{2}{7}} =$$

Solution:

Step 1 $\boxed{\left(3\dfrac{2}{5} \div 2\dfrac{1}{3}\right) \div 1\dfrac{2}{7}} = \boxed{\left(\dfrac{(3 \times 5) + 2}{5} \div \dfrac{(2 \times 3) + 1}{3}\right) \div \dfrac{(1 \times 7) + 2}{7}} = \boxed{\left(\dfrac{15 + 2}{5} \div \dfrac{6 + 1}{3}\right) \div \dfrac{7 + 2}{7}}$

$$= \boxed{\left(\dfrac{17}{5} \div \dfrac{7}{3}\right) \div \dfrac{9}{7}}$$

Step 2 $\boxed{\left(\dfrac{17}{5} \div \dfrac{7}{3}\right) \div \dfrac{9}{7}} = \boxed{\left(\dfrac{17}{5} \times \dfrac{3}{7}\right) \div \dfrac{9}{7}} = \boxed{\left(\dfrac{17 \times 3}{5 \times 7}\right) \div \dfrac{9}{7}} = \boxed{\left(\dfrac{51}{35}\right) \div \dfrac{9}{7}} = \boxed{\dfrac{51}{35} \div \dfrac{9}{7}} = \boxed{\dfrac{51}{35} \times \dfrac{7}{9}}$

$$= \boxed{\frac{51 \times 7}{35 \times 9}} = \boxed{\frac{357}{315}}$$

Step 3 $\quad \boxed{\frac{357}{315}} = \boxed{\frac{357 \div 3}{315 \div 3}} = \boxed{\frac{119}{105}} = \boxed{\frac{119 \div 7}{105 \div 7}} = \boxed{\frac{17}{15}}$

Step 4 $\quad \boxed{\frac{17}{15}} = \boxed{\mathbf{1\frac{2}{15}}}$

Example 5.4-8

$$\boxed{2\frac{4}{5} \div \left(1\frac{2}{5} \div 3\frac{1}{3}\right)} =$$

Solution:

Step 1 $\quad \boxed{2\frac{4}{5} \div \left(1\frac{2}{5} \div 3\frac{1}{3}\right)} = \boxed{\frac{(2 \times 5) + 4}{5} \div \left(\frac{(1 \times 5) + 2}{5} \div \frac{(3 \times 3) + 1}{3}\right)} = \boxed{\frac{10 + 4}{5} \div \left(\frac{5 + 2}{5} \div \frac{9 + 1}{3}\right)}$

$$= \boxed{\frac{14}{5} \div \left(\frac{7}{5} \div \frac{10}{3}\right)}$$

Step 2 $\quad \boxed{\frac{14}{5} \div \left(\frac{7}{5} \div \frac{10}{3}\right)} = \boxed{\frac{14}{5} \div \left(\frac{7}{5} \times \frac{3}{10}\right)} = \boxed{\frac{14}{5} \div \left(\frac{7 \times 3}{5 \times 10}\right)} = \boxed{\frac{14}{5} \div \left(\frac{21}{50}\right)} = \boxed{\frac{14}{5} \div \frac{21}{50}}$

$$= \boxed{\frac{14}{5} \times \frac{50}{21}} = \boxed{\frac{14 \times 50}{5 \times 21}} = \boxed{\frac{700}{105}}$$

Step 3 $\quad \boxed{\frac{700}{105}} = \boxed{\frac{700 \div 5}{105 \div 5}} = \boxed{\frac{140}{21}} = \boxed{\frac{140 \div 7}{21 \div 7}} = \boxed{\frac{20}{3}}$

Step 4 $\quad \boxed{\frac{20}{3}} = \boxed{6\frac{2}{3}}$

Example 5.4-9

$$\boxed{\left(3\frac{2}{5} \div 2\frac{1}{5}\right) \div 1\frac{1}{5}} =$$

Solution:

Step 1 $\quad \boxed{\left(3\frac{2}{5} \div 2\frac{1}{5}\right) \div 1\frac{1}{5}} = \boxed{\left(\frac{(3 \times 5) + 2}{5} \div \frac{(2 \times 5) + 1}{5}\right) \div \frac{(1 \times 5) + 1}{5}} = \boxed{\left(\frac{15 + 2}{5} \div \frac{10 + 1}{5}\right) \div \frac{5 + 1}{5}}$

$$= \boxed{\left(\frac{17}{5} \div \frac{11}{5}\right) \div \frac{6}{5}}$$

Step 2 $\quad \boxed{\left(\frac{17}{5} \div \frac{11}{5}\right) \div \frac{6}{5}} = \boxed{\left(\frac{17}{5} \times \frac{5}{11}\right) \div \frac{6}{5}} = \boxed{\left(\frac{17 \times 5}{5 \times 11}\right) \div \frac{6}{5}} = \boxed{\left(\frac{85}{55}\right) \div \frac{6}{5}} = \boxed{\frac{85}{55} \div \frac{6}{5}} = \boxed{\frac{85}{55} \times \frac{5}{6}}$

$$= \boxed{\frac{85 \times 5}{55 \times 6}} = \boxed{\frac{425}{330}}$$

Step 3 $\boxed{\frac{425}{330}} = \boxed{\frac{425 \div 5}{330 \div 5}} = \boxed{\frac{85}{66}}$

Step 4 $\boxed{\frac{85}{66}} = \boxed{1\frac{19}{66}}$

Example 5.4-10

$$\boxed{2\frac{2}{5} \div \left(3\frac{1}{8} \div 4\frac{3}{5}\right) =}$$

Solution:

Step 1 $\boxed{2\frac{2}{5} \div \left(3\frac{1}{8} \div 4\frac{3}{5}\right)} = \boxed{\frac{(2 \times 5) + 2}{5} \div \left(\frac{(3 \times 8) + 1}{8} \div \frac{(4 \times 5) + 3}{5}\right)}$

$$= \boxed{\frac{10 + 2}{5} \div \left(\frac{24 + 1}{8} \div \frac{20 + 3}{5}\right)} = \boxed{\frac{12}{5} \div \left(\frac{25}{8} \div \frac{23}{5}\right)}$$

Step 2 $\boxed{\frac{12}{5} \div \left(\frac{25}{8} \div \frac{23}{5}\right)} = \boxed{\frac{12}{5} \div \left(\frac{25}{8} \times \frac{5}{23}\right)} = \boxed{\frac{12}{5} \div \left(\frac{25 \times 5}{8 \times 23}\right)} = \boxed{\frac{12}{5} \div \left(\frac{125}{184}\right)} = \boxed{\frac{12}{5} \div \frac{125}{184}}$

$$= \boxed{\frac{12}{5} \times \frac{184}{125}} = \boxed{\frac{12 \times 184}{5 \times 125}} = \boxed{\frac{2208}{625}}$$

Step 3 $\boxed{\textit{Not Applicable}}$

Step 4 $\boxed{\frac{2208}{625}} = \boxed{3\frac{333}{625}}$

Example 5.4-11

$$\boxed{\left(3\frac{4}{8} \div 1\frac{2}{5}\right) \div 4\frac{2}{3} =}$$

Solution:

Step 1 $\boxed{\left(3\frac{4}{8} \div 1\frac{2}{5}\right) \div 4\frac{2}{3}} = \boxed{\left(\frac{(3 \times 8) + 4}{8} \div \frac{(1 \times 5) + 2}{5}\right) \div \frac{(4 \times 3) + 2}{3}}$

$$= \boxed{\left(\frac{24 + 4}{8} \div \frac{5 + 2}{5}\right) \div \frac{12 + 2}{3}} = \boxed{\left(\frac{28}{8} \div \frac{7}{5}\right) \div \frac{14}{3}}$$

Step 2 $\boxed{\left(\frac{28}{8} \div \frac{7}{5}\right) \div \frac{14}{3}} = \boxed{\left(\frac{28}{8} \times \frac{5}{7}\right) \div \frac{14}{3}} = \boxed{\left(\frac{28 \times 5}{8 \times 7}\right) \div \frac{14}{3}} = \boxed{\left(\frac{140}{56}\right) \div \frac{14}{3}} = \boxed{\frac{140}{56} \div \frac{14}{3}}$

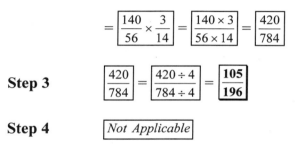

$$= \boxed{\frac{140}{56} \times \frac{3}{14}} = \boxed{\frac{140 \times 3}{56 \times 14}} = \boxed{\frac{420}{784}}$$

Step 3 $\qquad \boxed{\frac{420}{784}} = \boxed{\frac{420 \div 4}{784 \div 4}} = \boxed{\mathbf{\frac{105}{196}}}$

Step 4 $\qquad \boxed{\textit{Not Applicable}}$

In general, three mixed fractions are divided as in the following cases:

Case I.

$$\boxed{\left(k_1\frac{a}{b} \div k_2\frac{c}{d}\right) \div k_3\frac{e}{f}} = \boxed{\left(\frac{(k_1 \times b)+a}{b} \div \frac{(k_2 \times d)+c}{d}\right) \div \frac{(k_3 \times f)+e}{f}} = \boxed{\left(\frac{k_1b+a}{b} \div \frac{k_2d+c}{d}\right) \div \frac{k_3f+e}{f}}$$

Let $\boxed{A_1 = k_1b+a}$, $\boxed{A_2 = k_2d+c}$, and $\boxed{A_3 = k_3f+e}$

$$\boxed{\left(\frac{k_1b+a}{b} \div \frac{k_2d+c}{d}\right) \div \frac{k_3f+e}{f}} = \boxed{\left(\frac{A_1}{b} \div \frac{A_2}{d}\right) \div \frac{A_3}{f}} = \boxed{\left(\frac{A_1}{b} \times \frac{d}{A_2}\right) \div \frac{A_3}{f}} = \boxed{\left(\frac{A_1 \times d}{b \times A_2}\right) \div \frac{A_3}{f}} = \boxed{\left(\frac{A_1d}{bA_2}\right) \div \frac{A_3}{f}}$$

$$= \boxed{\frac{A_1d}{bA_2} \div \frac{A_3}{f}} = \boxed{\frac{A_1d}{bA_2} \times \frac{f}{A_3}} = \boxed{\frac{A_1d \times f}{bA_2 \times A_3}} = \boxed{\frac{A_1df}{bA_2A_3}}$$

Example 5.4-12

$$\boxed{\left(3\frac{1}{8} \div 1\frac{2}{3}\right) \div 1\frac{1}{4}} = \boxed{\left(\frac{(3 \times 8)+1}{8} \div \frac{(1 \times 3)+2}{3}\right) \div \frac{(1 \times 4)+1}{4}} = \boxed{\left(\frac{24+1}{8} \div \frac{3+2}{3}\right) \div \frac{4+1}{4}} = \boxed{\left(\frac{25}{8} \div \frac{5}{3}\right) \div \frac{5}{4}}$$

$$= \boxed{\left(\frac{25}{8} \times \frac{3}{5}\right) \div \frac{5}{4}} = \boxed{\left(\frac{25 \times 3}{8 \times 5}\right) \div \frac{5}{4}} = \boxed{\left(\frac{75}{40}\right) \div \frac{5}{4}} = \boxed{\frac{75}{40} \div \frac{5}{4}} = \boxed{\frac{15}{8} \div \frac{5}{4}} = \boxed{\frac{15}{8} \times \frac{4}{5}} = \boxed{\frac{\overset{3}{\cancel{15}} \times \overset{1}{\cancel{4}}}{\underset{2}{\cancel{8}} \times \underset{1}{\cancel{5}}}} = \boxed{\frac{3 \times 1}{2 \times 1}} = \boxed{\frac{3}{2}}$$

$$= \boxed{1\frac{1}{2}}$$

Case II.

$$\boxed{k_1\frac{a}{b} \div \left(k_2\frac{c}{d} \div k_3\frac{e}{f}\right)} = \boxed{\frac{(k_1 \times b)+a}{b} \div \left(\frac{(k_2 \times d)+c}{d} \div \frac{(k_3 \times f)+e}{f}\right)} = \boxed{\frac{k_1b+a}{b} \div \left(\frac{k_2d+c}{d} \div \frac{k_3f+e}{f}\right)}$$

Let $\boxed{A_1 = k_1b+a}$, $\boxed{A_2 = k_2d+c}$, and $\boxed{A_3 = k_3f+e}$, then

$$\boxed{\frac{k_1b+a}{b} \div \left(\frac{k_2d+c}{d} \div \frac{k_3f+e}{f}\right)} = \boxed{\frac{A_1}{b} \div \left(\frac{A_2}{d} \div \frac{A_3}{f}\right)} = \boxed{\frac{A_1}{b} \div \left(\frac{A_2}{d} \times \frac{f}{A_3}\right)} = \boxed{\frac{A_1}{b} \div \left(\frac{A_2 \times f}{d \times A_3}\right)}$$

$$= \boxed{\frac{A_1}{b} \div \left(\frac{A_2 f}{dA_3}\right)} = \boxed{\frac{A_1}{b} \div \frac{A_2 f}{dA_3}} = \boxed{\frac{A_1}{b} \times \frac{dA_3}{A_2 f}} = \boxed{\frac{A_1 \times dA_3}{b \times A_2 f}} = \boxed{\frac{A_1 dA_3}{bA_2 f}}$$

Example 5.4-13

$$\boxed{3\frac{1}{8} \div \left(1\frac{2}{3} \div 1\frac{1}{4}\right)} = \boxed{\frac{(3\times 8)+1}{8} \div \left(\frac{(1\times 3)+2}{3} \div \frac{(1\times 4)+1}{4}\right)} = \boxed{\frac{24+1}{8} \div \left(\frac{3+2}{3} \div \frac{4+1}{4}\right)} = \boxed{\frac{25}{8} \div \left(\frac{5}{3} \div \frac{5}{4}\right)}$$

$$= \boxed{\frac{25}{8} \div \left(\frac{5}{3} \times \frac{4}{5}\right)} = \boxed{\frac{25}{8} \div \left(\frac{5\times 4}{3\times 5}\right)} = \boxed{\frac{25}{8} \div \left(\frac{20}{15}\right)} = \boxed{\frac{25}{8} \div \frac{20}{15}} = \boxed{\frac{25}{8} \times \frac{15}{20}} = \boxed{\frac{\overset{5}{\cancel{25}}\times 15}{8\times \underset{4}{\cancel{20}}}} = \boxed{\frac{5\times 15}{8\times 4}} = \boxed{\frac{75}{32}}$$

$$= \boxed{2\frac{11}{32}}$$

The following examples further illustrate how to divide mixed fractions:

Example 5.4-14

$$\boxed{2\frac{3}{5} \div 1\frac{2}{3}} = \boxed{\frac{(2\times 5)+3}{5} \div \frac{(1\times 3)+2}{3}} = \boxed{\frac{10+3}{5} \div \frac{3+2}{3}} = \boxed{\frac{13}{5} \div \frac{5}{3}} = \boxed{\frac{13}{5} \times \frac{3}{5}} = \boxed{\frac{13\times 3}{5\times 5}} = \boxed{\frac{39}{25}} = \boxed{1\frac{14}{25}}$$

Example 5.4-15

$$\boxed{1\frac{1}{3} \div 4\frac{2}{3}} = \boxed{\frac{(1\times 3)+1}{3} \div \frac{(4\times 3)+2}{3}} = \boxed{\frac{3+1}{3} \div \frac{12+2}{3}} = \boxed{\frac{4}{3} \div \frac{14}{3}} = \boxed{\frac{4}{3} \times \frac{3}{14}} = \boxed{\frac{\overset{2}{\cancel{4}}\times \overset{1}{\cancel{3}}}{\underset{1}{\cancel{3}}\times \underset{7}{\cancel{14}}}} = \boxed{\frac{2\times 1}{1\times 7}} = \boxed{\frac{2}{7}}$$

Example 5.4-16

$$\boxed{3\frac{2}{3} \div \left(1\frac{2}{3} \div 2\frac{4}{5}\right)} = \boxed{\frac{(3\times 3)+2}{3} \div \left(\frac{(1\times 3)+2}{3} \div \frac{(2\times 5)+4}{5}\right)} = \boxed{\frac{9+2}{3} \div \left(\frac{3+2}{3} \div \frac{10+4}{5}\right)}$$

$$= \boxed{\frac{11}{3} \div \left(\frac{5}{3} \div \frac{14}{5}\right)} = \boxed{\frac{11}{3} \div \left(\frac{5}{3} \times \frac{5}{14}\right)} = \boxed{\frac{11}{3} \div \left(\frac{5\times 5}{3\times 14}\right)} = \boxed{\frac{11}{3} \div \left(\frac{25}{42}\right)} = \boxed{\frac{11}{3} \div \frac{25}{42}} = \boxed{\frac{11}{3} \times \frac{42}{25}} = \boxed{\frac{11\times \overset{14}{\cancel{42}}}{\underset{1}{\cancel{3}}\times 25}}$$

$$= \boxed{\frac{11\times 14}{1\times 25}} = \boxed{\frac{154}{25}} = \boxed{6\frac{4}{25}}$$

Example 5.4-17

$$\boxed{\left(1\frac{1}{3} \div 4\frac{2}{3}\right) \div 2\frac{3}{5}} = \boxed{\left(\frac{(1\times 3)+1}{3} \div \frac{(4\times 3)+2}{3}\right) \div \frac{(2\times 5)+3}{5}} = \boxed{\left(\frac{3+1}{3} \div \frac{12+2}{3}\right) \div \frac{10+3}{5}}$$

$$= \boxed{\left(\frac{4}{3} \div \frac{14}{3}\right) \div \frac{13}{5}} = \boxed{\left(\frac{4}{3} \times \frac{3}{14}\right) \div \frac{13}{5}} = \boxed{\left(\frac{\overset{2}{\cancel{4}}\times \overset{1}{\cancel{3}}}{\underset{1}{\cancel{3}}\times \underset{7}{\cancel{14}}}\right) \div \frac{13}{5}} = \boxed{\left(\frac{2\times 1}{1\times 7}\right) \div \frac{13}{5}} = \boxed{\left(\frac{2}{7}\right) \div \frac{13}{5}} = \boxed{\frac{2}{7} \div \frac{13}{5}} = \boxed{\frac{2}{7} \times \frac{5}{13}}$$

$$= \boxed{\dfrac{2 \times 5}{7 \times 13}} = \boxed{\dfrac{10}{91}}$$

Example 5.4-18

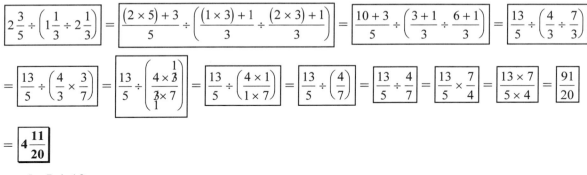

$$= \boxed{4\dfrac{11}{20}}$$

Example 5.4-19

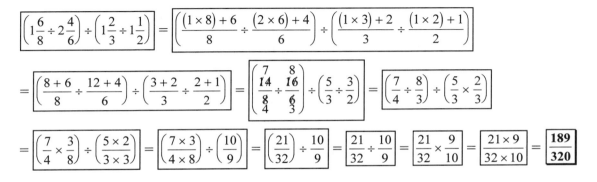

Example 5.4-20

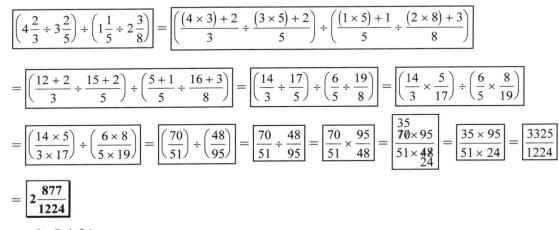

$$= \boxed{2\dfrac{877}{1224}}$$

Example 5.4-21

$$\boxed{\left(5\dfrac{2}{3} \div 2\dfrac{1}{4}\right) \div \left(1\dfrac{1}{6} \div 3\dfrac{2}{6}\right)} = \boxed{\left(\dfrac{(5 \times 3) + 2}{3} \div \dfrac{(2 \times 4) + 1}{4}\right) \div \left(\dfrac{(1 \times 6) + 1}{6} \div \dfrac{(3 \times 6) + 2}{6}\right)}$$

$$= \left[\left(\frac{15+2}{3} \div \frac{8+1}{4}\right) \div \left(\frac{6+1}{6} \div \frac{18+2}{6}\right)\right] = \left[\left(\frac{17}{3} \div \frac{9}{4}\right) \div \left(\frac{7}{6} \div \frac{\overset{10}{\cancel{20}}}{\underset{3}{\cancel{6}}}\right)\right] = \left[\left(\frac{17}{3} \times \frac{4}{9}\right) \div \left(\frac{7}{6} \div \frac{10}{3}\right)\right]$$

$$= \left[\left(\frac{17 \times 4}{3 \times 9}\right) \div \left(\frac{7}{6} \times \frac{3}{10}\right)\right] = \left[\left(\frac{68}{27}\right) \div \left(\frac{7 \times 3}{6 \times 10}\right)\right] = \left[\frac{68}{27} \div \left(\frac{21}{60}\right)\right] = \left[\frac{68}{27} \div \frac{21}{60}\right] = \left[\frac{68}{27} \times \frac{60}{21}\right] = \left[\frac{68 \times 60}{27 \times 21}\right] = \boxed{\frac{4080}{567}}$$

$$= \boxed{7\frac{111}{567}}$$

Example 5.4-22

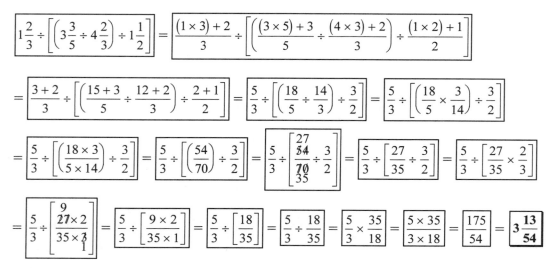

Example 5.4-23

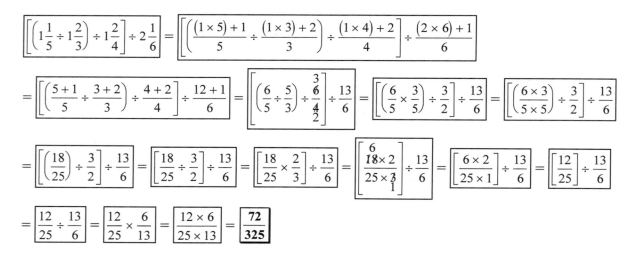

$$= \boxed{\frac{12}{25} \div \frac{13}{6}} = \boxed{\frac{12}{25} \times \frac{6}{13}} = \boxed{\frac{12 \times 6}{25 \times 13}} = \boxed{\frac{72}{325}}$$

Example 5.4-24

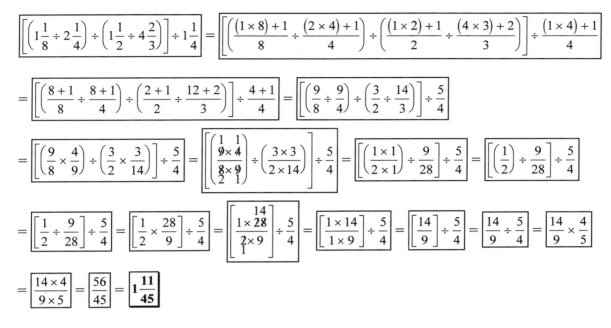

Section 5.4 Exercises - Divide the following mixed fractions:

1. $2\frac{1}{3} \div 1\frac{3}{5} =$

2. $3\frac{2}{5} \div 1\frac{3}{8} =$

3. $\left(3\frac{1}{2} \div 2\frac{3}{5}\right) \div 1\frac{2}{5} =$

4. $4\frac{1}{3} \div \left(2\frac{3}{4} \div 1\frac{3}{5}\right) =$

5. $\left(3\frac{2}{3} \div 2\frac{1}{5}\right) \div 2\frac{1}{2} =$

6. $\left(1\frac{3}{4} \div 2\frac{1}{3}\right) \div 1\frac{3}{5} =$

7. $\left(4\frac{2}{3} \div 2\frac{1}{4}\right) \div \left(2\frac{1}{5} \div 1\frac{3}{4}\right) =$

8. $\left(4\frac{2}{3} \div 2\frac{3}{4}\right) \div \left(2\frac{1}{5} \div 1\frac{1}{4}\right) =$

9. $\left[3\frac{2}{3} \div \left(2\frac{1}{3} \div 1\frac{1}{4}\right)\right] \div 2\frac{3}{5} =$

10. $\left[\left(4\frac{2}{5} \div 1\frac{2}{3}\right) \div \left(3\frac{1}{5} \div 1\frac{2}{3}\right)\right] \div 2\frac{1}{3} =$

5.5   Solving Mixed Operations Using Mixed Fractions

Mixed fractions are added, subtracted, multiplied, and divided by using the following steps:

Step 1   Change the mixed fractions to integer fractions (see Section 2.5).

Step 2   Add, subtract, multiply, and divide the integer fractions by following the steps outlined in sections 3.1 through 3.4.

Step 3   Simplify the fraction to its lowest term (see Sections 2.3).

Step 4   Change the improper fraction to a mixed fraction if the fraction obtained from Step 3 is an improper fraction (see Section 2.2).

The following examples show mathematical operations on mixed fractions using the above steps:

Example 5.5-1

$$\left[\left(3\frac{1}{5} \times 2\frac{5}{3}\right) + 1\frac{2}{3}\right] =$$

Solution:

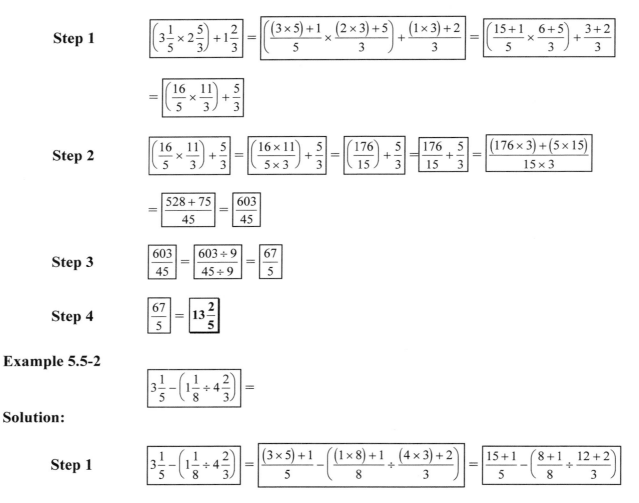

Step 1 $\left[\left(3\frac{1}{5} \times 2\frac{5}{3}\right) + 1\frac{2}{3}\right] = \left[\left(\frac{(3\times5)+1}{5} \times \frac{(2\times3)+5}{3}\right) + \frac{(1\times3)+2}{3}\right] = \left[\left(\frac{15+1}{5} \times \frac{6+5}{3}\right) + \frac{3+2}{3}\right]$

$= \left[\left(\frac{16}{5} \times \frac{11}{3}\right) + \frac{5}{3}\right]$

Step 2 $\left[\left(\frac{16}{5} \times \frac{11}{3}\right) + \frac{5}{3}\right] = \left[\left(\frac{16\times11}{5\times3}\right) + \frac{5}{3}\right] = \left[\left(\frac{176}{15}\right) + \frac{5}{3}\right] = \left[\frac{176}{15} + \frac{5}{3}\right] = \left[\frac{(176\times3)+(5\times15)}{15\times3}\right]$

$= \left[\frac{528+75}{45}\right] = \left[\frac{603}{45}\right]$

Step 3 $\left[\frac{603}{45}\right] = \left[\frac{603\div9}{45\div9}\right] = \left[\frac{67}{5}\right]$

Step 4 $\left[\frac{67}{5}\right] = \left[13\frac{2}{5}\right]$

Example 5.5-2

$$\left[3\frac{1}{5} - \left(1\frac{1}{8} \div 4\frac{2}{3}\right)\right] =$$

Solution:

Step 1 $\left[3\frac{1}{5} - \left(1\frac{1}{8} \div 4\frac{2}{3}\right)\right] = \left[\frac{(3\times5)+1}{5} - \left(\frac{(1\times8)+1}{8} \div \frac{(4\times3)+2}{3}\right)\right] = \left[\frac{15+1}{5} - \left(\frac{8+1}{8} \div \frac{12+2}{3}\right)\right]$

$$= \boxed{\frac{16}{5} - \left(\frac{9}{8} \div \frac{14}{3}\right)}$$

Step 2 $\boxed{\frac{16}{5} - \left(\frac{9}{8} \div \frac{14}{3}\right)} = \boxed{\frac{16}{5} - \left(\frac{9}{8} \times \frac{3}{14}\right)} = \boxed{\frac{16}{5} - \left(\frac{9 \times 3}{8 \times 14}\right)} = \boxed{\frac{16}{5} - \left(\frac{27}{112}\right)} = \boxed{\frac{16}{5} - \frac{27}{112}}$

$$= \boxed{\frac{(16 \times 112) - (27 \times 5)}{5 \times 112}} = \boxed{\frac{1792 - 135}{560}} = \boxed{\frac{1657}{560}}$$

Step 3 $\boxed{\textit{Not Applicable}}$

Step 4 $\boxed{\frac{1657}{560}} = \boxed{\mathbf{2\frac{537}{560}}}$

Example 5.5-3

$$\boxed{\left(2\frac{4}{5} + 1\frac{3}{5} + 1\frac{1}{5}\right) \div \left(2\frac{3}{4} \times 1\frac{1}{2}\right)} =$$

Solution:

Step 1 $\boxed{\left(2\frac{4}{5} + 1\frac{3}{5} + 1\frac{1}{5}\right) \div \left(2\frac{3}{4} \times 1\frac{1}{2}\right)}$

$$= \boxed{\left(\frac{(2 \times 5) + 4}{5} + \frac{(1 \times 5) + 3}{5} + \frac{(1 \times 5) + 1}{5}\right) \div \left(\frac{(2 \times 4) + 3}{4} \times \frac{(1 \times 2) + 1}{2}\right)}$$

$$= \boxed{\left(\frac{10 + 4}{5} + \frac{5 + 3}{5} + \frac{5 + 1}{5}\right) \div \left(\frac{8 + 3}{4} \times \frac{2 + 1}{2}\right)} = \boxed{\left(\frac{14}{5} + \frac{8}{5} + \frac{6}{5}\right) \div \left(\frac{11}{4} \times \frac{3}{2}\right)}$$

Step 2 $\boxed{\left(\frac{14}{5} + \frac{8}{5} + \frac{6}{5}\right) \div \left(\frac{11}{4} \times \frac{3}{2}\right)} = \boxed{\left(\frac{14 + 8 + 6}{5}\right) \div \left(\frac{11 \times 3}{4 \times 2}\right)} = \boxed{\left(\frac{28}{5}\right) \div \left(\frac{33}{8}\right)} = \boxed{\frac{28}{5} \div \frac{33}{8}}$

$$= \boxed{\frac{28}{5} \times \frac{8}{33}} = \boxed{\frac{28 \times 8}{5 \times 33}} = \boxed{\frac{224}{165}}$$

Step 3 $\boxed{\textit{Not Applicable}}$

Step 4 $\boxed{\frac{224}{165}} = \boxed{\mathbf{1\frac{59}{165}}}$

Example 5.5-4

$$\boxed{\left(3\frac{1}{2} \div 1\frac{1}{2}\right) \times \left(1\frac{2}{3} - 4\frac{1}{4}\right)} =$$

Solution:

Step 1
$$\left(3\frac{1}{2} \div 1\frac{1}{2}\right) \times \left(1\frac{2}{3} - 4\frac{1}{4}\right) = \left(\frac{(3\times 2)+1}{2} \div \frac{(1\times 2)+1}{2}\right) \times \left(\frac{(1\times 3)+2}{3} - \frac{(4\times 4)+1}{4}\right)$$

$$= \left(\frac{6+1}{2} \div \frac{2+1}{2}\right) \times \left(\frac{3+2}{3} - \frac{16+1}{4}\right) = \left(\frac{7}{2} \div \frac{3}{2}\right) \times \left(\frac{5}{3} - \frac{17}{4}\right)$$

Step 2
$$\left(\frac{7}{2} \div \frac{3}{2}\right) \times \left(\frac{5}{3} - \frac{17}{4}\right) = \left(\frac{7}{2} \times \frac{2}{3}\right) \times \left(\frac{(5\times 4)-(17\times 3)}{3\times 4}\right) = \left(\frac{7\times 2}{2\times 3}\right) \times \left(\frac{20-51}{12}\right)$$

$$= \left(\frac{14}{6}\right) \times \left(\frac{-31}{12}\right) = \frac{14}{6} \times \frac{-31}{12} = \frac{14\times -31}{6\times 12} = \frac{-434}{72}$$

Step 3
$$\frac{-434}{72} = \frac{-434 \div 2}{72 \div 2} = \frac{-217}{36}$$

Step 4
$$\frac{-217}{36} = -\left(6\frac{1}{36}\right)$$

Example 5.5-5

$$\left(3\frac{1}{2} + 2\frac{1}{5}\right) - \left(1\frac{2}{5} + 4\frac{1}{3}\right) =$$

Solution:

Step 1
$$\left(3\frac{1}{2} + 2\frac{1}{5}\right) - \left(1\frac{2}{5} + 4\frac{1}{3}\right) = \left(\frac{(3\times 2)+1}{2} + \frac{(2\times 5)+1}{5}\right) - \left(\frac{(1\times 5)+2}{5} + \frac{(4\times 3)+1}{3}\right)$$

$$= \left(\frac{6+1}{2} + \frac{10+1}{5}\right) - \left(\frac{5+2}{5} + \frac{12+1}{3}\right) = \left(\frac{7}{2} + \frac{11}{5}\right) - \left(\frac{7}{5} + \frac{13}{3}\right)$$

Step 2
$$\left(\frac{7}{2} + \frac{11}{5}\right) - \left(\frac{7}{5} + \frac{13}{3}\right) = \left(\frac{(7\times 5)+(11\times 2)}{2\times 5}\right) - \left(\frac{(7\times 3)+(13\times 5)}{5\times 3}\right)$$

$$= \left(\frac{35+22}{10}\right) - \left(\frac{21+65}{15}\right) = \left(\frac{57}{10}\right) - \left(\frac{86}{15}\right) = \frac{57}{10} - \frac{86}{15} = \frac{(57\times 15)-(86\times 10)}{10\times 15}$$

$$= \frac{855-860}{150} = \frac{-5}{150}$$

Step 3
$$\frac{-5}{150} = \frac{-5 \div 5}{150 \div 5} = -\frac{1}{30}$$

Step 4   Not Applicable

In general, mixed fractions are added, subtracted, multiplied, and divided as in the following example cases which are followed by a specific example for each case:

Case I.

$$\left[\left(k_1\frac{a}{b} \times k_2\frac{c}{d}\right)+\left(k_3\frac{e}{f} \div k_4\frac{g}{h}\right)\right] = \left[\left(\frac{(k_1 \times b)+a}{b} \times \frac{(k_2 \times d)+c}{d}\right)+\left(\frac{(k_3 \times f)+e}{f} \div \frac{(k_4 \times h)+g}{h}\right)\right]$$

$$= \left[\left(\frac{k_1 b+a}{b} \times \frac{k_2 d+c}{d}\right)+\left(\frac{k_3 f+e}{f} \div \frac{k_4 h+g}{h}\right)\right]$$

Let $A_1 = k_1 b+a$, $A_2 = k_2 d+c$, $A_3 = k_3 f+e$, and $A_4 = k_4 h+g$, then

$$\left[\left(\frac{k_1 b+a}{b} \times \frac{k_2 d+c}{d}\right)+\left(\frac{k_3 f+e}{f} \div \frac{k_4 h+g}{h}\right)\right] = \left[\left(\frac{A_1}{b} \times \frac{A_2}{d}\right)+\left(\frac{A_3}{f} \div \frac{A_4}{h}\right)\right] = \left[\left(\frac{A_1 \times A_2}{b \times d}\right)+\left(\frac{A_3}{f} \times \frac{h}{A_4}\right)\right]$$

$$= \left[\left(\frac{A_1 A_2}{bd}\right)+\left(\frac{A_3 \times h}{f \times A_4}\right)\right] = \frac{A_1 A_2}{bd}+\frac{A_3 h}{fA_4} = \frac{(A_1 A_2 \times fA_4)+(A_3 h \times bd)}{bd \times fA_4} = \frac{A_1 A_2 fA_4 + A_3 hbd}{bdfA_4}$$

Example 5.5-6

$$\left(2\frac{1}{4} \times 3\frac{2}{3}\right)+\left(3\frac{5}{2} \div 1\frac{4}{8}\right) = \left[\left(\frac{(2 \times 4)+1}{4} \times \frac{(3 \times 3)+2}{3}\right)+\left(\frac{(3 \times 2)+5}{2} \div \frac{(1 \times 8)+4}{8}\right)\right]$$

$$= \left[\left(\frac{8+1}{4} \times \frac{9+2}{3}\right)+\left(\frac{6+5}{2} \div \frac{8+4}{8}\right)\right] = \left[\left(\frac{9}{4} \times \frac{11}{3}\right)+\left(\frac{11}{2} \div \frac{12}{8}\right)\right] = \left[\left(\frac{\overset{3}{\cancel{9}} \times 11}{4 \times \underset{1}{\cancel{3}}}\right)+\left(\frac{11}{2} \times \frac{8}{12}\right)\right]$$

$$= \left[\left(\frac{3 \times 11}{4 \times 1}\right)+\left(\frac{11 \times \overset{4}{\cancel{8}}}{\underset{1}{\cancel{2}} \times 12}\right)\right] = \left[\left(\frac{33}{4}\right)+\left(\frac{11 \times \overset{1}{\cancel{4}}}{1 \times \underset{3}{\cancel{12}}}\right)\right] = \left[\left(\frac{33}{4}\right)+\left(\frac{11 \times 1}{1 \times 3}\right)\right] = \left[\left(\frac{33}{4}\right)+\left(\frac{11}{3}\right)\right] = \frac{33}{4}+\frac{11}{3}$$

$$= \frac{(33 \times 3)+(11 \times 4)}{4 \times 3} = \frac{99+44}{12} = \frac{143}{12} = 11\frac{11}{12}$$

Case II.

$$\left[\left(k_1\frac{a}{b} \div k_2\frac{c}{d}\right)-\left(k_3\frac{e}{f} \times k_4\frac{g}{h}\right)\right] = \left[\left(\frac{(k_1 \times b)+a}{b} \div \frac{(k_2 \times d)+c}{d}\right)-\left(\frac{(k_3 \times f)+e}{f} \times \frac{(k_4 \times h)+g}{h}\right)\right]$$

$$= \boxed{\left(\frac{k_1 b + a}{b} \div \frac{k_2 d + c}{d}\right) - \left(\frac{k_3 f + e}{f} \times \frac{k_4 h + g}{h}\right)}$$

Let $\boxed{A_1 = k_1 b + a}$, $\boxed{A_2 = k_2 d + c}$, $\boxed{A_3 = k_3 f + e}$, and $\boxed{A_4 = k_4 h + g}$, then

$$\boxed{\left(\frac{k_1 b + a}{b} \div \frac{k_2 d + c}{d}\right) - \left(\frac{k_3 f + e}{f} \times \frac{k_4 h + g}{h}\right)} = \boxed{\left(\frac{A_1}{b} \div \frac{A_2}{d}\right) - \left(\frac{A_3}{f} \times \frac{A_4}{h}\right)} = \boxed{\left(\frac{A_1}{b} \times \frac{d}{A_2}\right) - \left(\frac{A_3 \times A_4}{f \times h}\right)}$$

$$= \boxed{\left(\frac{A_1 \times d}{b \times A_2}\right) - \left(\frac{A_3 A_4}{fh}\right)} = \boxed{\left(\frac{A_1 d}{A_2 b}\right) - \left(\frac{A_3 A_4}{fh}\right)} = \boxed{\frac{(A_1 d \times fh) - (A_2 b \times A_3 A_4)}{A_2 bfh}} = \boxed{\frac{A_1 dfh - A_2 A_3 A_4 b}{A_2 bfh}}$$

Example 5.5-7

$$\boxed{\left(4\frac{3}{2} \div 1\frac{5}{4}\right) - \left(2\frac{1}{3} \times 1\frac{2}{6}\right)} = \boxed{\left(\frac{(4 \times 2) + 3}{2} \div \frac{(1 \times 4) + 5}{4}\right) - \left(\frac{(2 \times 3) + 1}{3} \times \frac{(1 \times 6) + 2}{6}\right)}$$

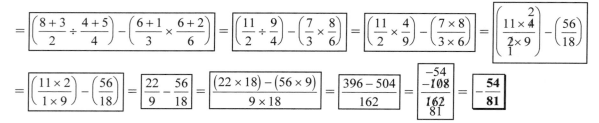

$$= \boxed{\left(\frac{8+3}{2} \div \frac{4+5}{4}\right) - \left(\frac{6+1}{3} \times \frac{6+2}{6}\right)} = \boxed{\left(\frac{11}{2} \div \frac{9}{4}\right) - \left(\frac{7}{3} \times \frac{8}{6}\right)} = \boxed{\left(\frac{11}{2} \times \frac{4}{9}\right) - \left(\frac{7 \times 8}{3 \times 6}\right)} = \boxed{\left(\frac{11 \times \overset{2}{4}}{\underset{1}{2} \times 9}\right) - \left(\frac{56}{18}\right)}$$

$$= \boxed{\left(\frac{11 \times 2}{1 \times 9}\right) - \left(\frac{56}{18}\right)} = \boxed{\frac{22}{9} - \frac{56}{18}} = \boxed{\frac{(22 \times 18) - (56 \times 9)}{9 \times 18}} = \boxed{\frac{396 - 504}{162}} = \boxed{\frac{\overset{-54}{\overset{-108}{\cancel{162}}}}{\underset{81}{}}} = \boxed{-\frac{54}{81}}$$

Case III.

$$\boxed{\left(k_1\frac{a}{b} - k_2\frac{c}{d}\right) \div \left(k_3\frac{e}{f} \times k_4\frac{g}{h}\right)} = \boxed{\left(\frac{(k_1 \times b) + a}{b} - \frac{(k_2 \times d) + c}{d}\right) \div \left(\frac{(k_3 \times f) + e}{f} \times \frac{(k_4 \times h) + g}{h}\right)}$$

$$= \boxed{\left(\frac{k_1 b + a}{b} - \frac{k_2 d + c}{d}\right) \div \left(\frac{k_3 f + e}{f} \times \frac{k_4 h + g}{h}\right)}$$

Let $\boxed{A_1 = k_1 b + a}$, $\boxed{A_2 = k_2 d + c}$, $\boxed{A_3 = k_3 f + e}$, and $\boxed{A_4 = k_4 h + g}$, then

$$\boxed{\left(\frac{k_1 b + a}{b} - \frac{k_2 d + c}{d}\right) \div \left(\frac{k_3 f + e}{f} \times \frac{k_4 h + g}{h}\right)} = \boxed{\left(\frac{A_1}{b} - \frac{A_2}{d}\right) \div \left(\frac{A_3}{f} \times \frac{A_4}{h}\right)}$$

$$= \boxed{\left(\frac{(A_1 \times d) - (A_2 \times b)}{b \times d}\right) \div \left(\frac{A_3 \times A_4}{f \times h}\right)} = \boxed{\left(\frac{A_1 d - A_2 b}{bd}\right) \div \left(\frac{A_3 A_4}{fh}\right)} = \boxed{\left(\frac{A_1 d - A_2 b}{bd}\right) \times \left(\frac{fh}{A_3 A_4}\right)}$$

$$= \boxed{\frac{(A_1 d - A_2 b) \times fh}{bd \times A_3 A_4}} = \boxed{\frac{A_1 dfh - A_2 bfh}{bd A_3 A_4}}$$

Example 5.5-8

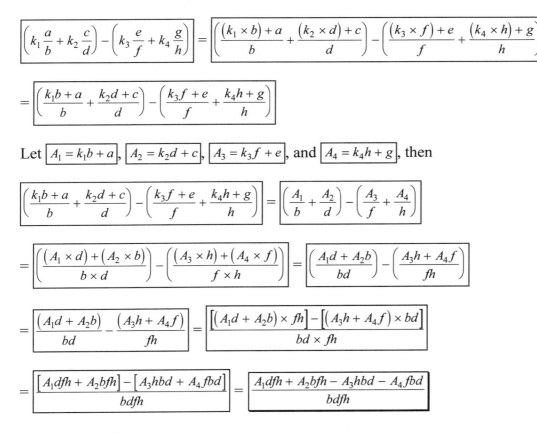

$$\left(8\frac{3}{2}-1\frac{5}{4}\right)\div\left(2\frac{1}{3}\times1\frac{2}{5}\right)=\left(\left(\frac{(8\times2)+3}{2}-\frac{(1\times4)+5}{4}\right)\div\left(\frac{(2\times3)+1}{3}\times\frac{(1\times5)+2}{5}\right)\right)$$

$$=\left(\left(\frac{16+3}{2}-\frac{4+5}{4}\right)\div\left(\frac{6+1}{3}\times\frac{5+2}{5}\right)\right)=\left(\left(\frac{19}{2}-\frac{9}{4}\right)\div\left(\frac{7}{3}\times\frac{7}{5}\right)\right)=\left(\left(\frac{(19\times4)-(9\times2)}{2\times4}\right)\div\left(\frac{7\times7}{3\times5}\right)\right)$$

$$=\left(\left(\frac{76-18}{8}\right)\div\left(\frac{49}{15}\right)\right)=\left(\left(\frac{58}{8}\right)\div\left(\frac{49}{15}\right)\right)=\frac{58}{8}\div\frac{49}{15}=\frac{58}{8}\times\frac{15}{49}=\frac{\overset{29}{\cancel{58}}\times15}{\underset{4}{\cancel{8}}\times49}=\frac{29\times15}{4\times49}=\frac{435}{196}=\mathbf{2\frac{43}{196}}$$

Case IV.

$$\left(k_1\frac{a}{b}+k_2\frac{c}{d}\right)-\left(k_3\frac{e}{f}+k_4\frac{g}{h}\right)=\left(\left(\frac{(k_1\times b)+a}{b}+\frac{(k_2\times d)+c}{d}\right)-\left(\frac{(k_3\times f)+e}{f}+\frac{(k_4\times h)+g}{h}\right)\right)$$

$$=\left(\left(\frac{k_1b+a}{b}+\frac{k_2d+c}{d}\right)-\left(\frac{k_3f+e}{f}+\frac{k_4h+g}{h}\right)\right)$$

Let $\boxed{A_1=k_1b+a}$, $\boxed{A_2=k_2d+c}$, $\boxed{A_3=k_3f+e}$, and $\boxed{A_4=k_4h+g}$, then

$$\left(\left(\frac{k_1b+a}{b}+\frac{k_2d+c}{d}\right)-\left(\frac{k_3f+e}{f}+\frac{k_4h+g}{h}\right)\right)=\left(\left(\frac{A_1}{b}+\frac{A_2}{d}\right)-\left(\frac{A_3}{f}+\frac{A_4}{h}\right)\right)$$

$$=\left(\left(\frac{(A_1\times d)+(A_2\times b)}{b\times d}\right)-\left(\frac{(A_3\times h)+(A_4\times f)}{f\times h}\right)\right)=\left(\left(\frac{A_1d+A_2b}{bd}\right)-\left(\frac{A_3h+A_4f}{fh}\right)\right)$$

$$=\frac{(A_1d+A_2b)}{bd}-\frac{(A_3h+A_4f)}{fh}=\frac{[(A_1d+A_2b)\times fh]-[(A_3h+A_4f)\times bd]}{bd\times fh}$$

$$=\frac{[A_1dfh+A_2bfh]-[A_3hbd+A_4fbd]}{bdfh}=\frac{A_1dfh+A_2bfh-A_3hbd-A_4fbd}{bdfh}$$

Example 5.5-9

$$\left(5\frac{3}{2}+1\frac{4}{3}\right)-\left(2\frac{2}{3}+1\frac{1}{5}\right)=\left(\left(\frac{(5\times2)+3}{2}+\frac{(1\times3)+4}{3}\right)-\left(\frac{(2\times3)+2}{3}+\frac{(1\times5)+1}{5}\right)\right)$$

$$=\left(\left(\frac{10+3}{2}+\frac{3+4}{3}\right)-\left(\frac{6+2}{3}+\frac{5+1}{5}\right)\right)=\left(\left(\frac{13}{2}+\frac{7}{3}\right)-\left(\frac{8}{3}+\frac{6}{5}\right)\right)=\left(\left(\frac{(13\times3)+(7\times2)}{2\times3}\right)-\left(\frac{(8\times5)+(6\times3)}{3\times5}\right)\right)$$

$$= \left[\left(\frac{39 + 14}{6} \right) - \left(\frac{40 + 18}{15} \right) \right] = \left[\left(\frac{53}{6} \right) - \left(\frac{58}{15} \right) \right] = \left[\frac{53}{6} - \frac{58}{15} \right] = \left[\frac{(53 \times 15) - (58 \times 6)}{6 \times 15} \right] = \left[\frac{795 - 348}{90} \right] = \boxed{\frac{\overset{149}{\cancel{447}}}{\underset{30}{\cancel{90}}}}$$

$$= \left[\frac{149}{30} \right] = \boxed{4\frac{29}{30}}$$

Case V.

$$\left[\left(k_1 \frac{a}{b} \div k_2 \frac{c}{d} \right) \times \left(k_3 \frac{e}{f} \div k_4 \frac{g}{h} \right) \right] = \left[\left(\frac{(k_1 \times b) + a}{b} \div \frac{(k_2 \times d) + c}{d} \right) \times \left(\frac{(k_3 \times f) + e}{f} \div \frac{(k_4 \times h) + g}{h} \right) \right]$$

$$= \left[\left(\frac{k_1 b + a}{b} \div \frac{k_2 d + c}{d} \right) \times \left(\frac{k_3 f + e}{f} \div \frac{k_4 h + g}{h} \right) \right]$$

Let $\boxed{A_1 = k_1 b + a}$, $\boxed{A_2 = k_2 d + c}$, $\boxed{A_3 = k_3 f + e}$, and $\boxed{A_4 = k_4 h + g}$, then

$$\left[\left(\frac{k_1 b + a}{b} \div \frac{k_2 d + c}{d} \right) \times \left(\frac{k_3 f + e}{f} \div \frac{k_4 h + g}{h} \right) \right] = \left[\left(\frac{A_1}{b} \div \frac{A_2}{d} \right) \times \left(\frac{A_3}{f} \div \frac{A_4}{h} \right) \right] = \left[\left(\frac{A_1}{b} \times \frac{d}{A_2} \right) \times \left(\frac{A_3}{f} \times \frac{h}{A_4} \right) \right]$$

$$= \left[\left(\frac{A_1 \times d}{b \times A_2} \right) \times \left(\frac{A_3 \times h}{f \times A_4} \right) \right] = \left[\left(\frac{A_1 d}{b A_2} \right) \times \left(\frac{A_3 h}{f A_4} \right) \right] = \left[\frac{A_1 d}{b A_2} \times \frac{A_3 h}{f A_4} \right] = \left[\frac{A_1 d \times A_3 h}{b A_2 \times f A_4} \right] = \boxed{\frac{A_1 d A_3 h}{b A_2 f A_4}}$$

Example 5.5-10

$$\left[\left(3\frac{3}{2} \div 2\frac{5}{4} \right) \times \left(4\frac{6}{7} \div 1\frac{2}{5} \right) \right] = \left[\left(\frac{(3 \times 2) + 3}{2} \div \frac{(2 \times 4) + 5}{4} \right) \times \left(\frac{(4 \times 7) + 6}{7} \div \frac{(1 \times 5) + 2}{5} \right) \right]$$

$$= \left[\left(\frac{6 + 3}{2} \div \frac{8 + 5}{4} \right) \times \left(\frac{28 + 6}{7} \div \frac{5 + 2}{5} \right) \right] = \left[\left(\frac{9}{2} \div \frac{13}{4} \right) \times \left(\frac{34}{7} \div \frac{7}{5} \right) \right] = \left[\left(\frac{9}{2} \times \frac{4}{13} \right) \times \left(\frac{34}{7} \times \frac{5}{7} \right) \right]$$

$$= \left[\left(\frac{9 \times \overset{2}{\cancel{4}}}{\underset{1}{\cancel{2}} \times 13} \right) \times \left(\frac{34 \times 5}{7 \times 7} \right) \right] = \left[\left(\frac{9 \times 2}{1 \times 13} \right) \times \left(\frac{34 \times 5}{7 \times 7} \right) \right] = \left[\left(\frac{18}{13} \right) \times \left(\frac{170}{49} \right) \right] = \left[\frac{18}{13} \times \frac{170}{49} \right] = \left[\frac{18 \times 170}{13 \times 49} \right] = \left[\frac{3060}{637} \right]$$

$$= \boxed{4\frac{512}{637}}$$

The following examples further illustrate how to add, subtract, multiply, and divide mixed fractions:

Example 5.5-11

$$\left[\left(5\frac{1}{4} \times 1\frac{4}{5} \right) \div 2\frac{3}{4} \right] = \left[\left(\frac{(5 \times 4) + 1}{4} \times \frac{(1 \times 5) + 4}{5} \right) \div \frac{(2 \times 4) + 3}{4} \right] = \left[\left(\frac{20 + 1}{4} \times \frac{5 + 4}{5} \right) \div \frac{8 + 3}{4} \right] = \left[\left(\frac{21}{4} \times \frac{9}{5} \right) \div \frac{11}{4} \right]$$

$$= \left[\left(\frac{21 \times 9}{4 \times 5}\right) \div \frac{11}{4}\right] = \left[\left(\frac{189}{20}\right) \div \frac{11}{4}\right] = \left[\frac{189}{20} \div \frac{11}{4}\right] = \left[\frac{189}{20} \times \frac{4}{11}\right] = \left[\frac{189 \times \overset{1}{4}}{\underset{5}{20} \times 11}\right] = \left[\frac{189 \times 1}{5 \times 11}\right] = \left[\frac{189}{55}\right] = \boxed{3\frac{24}{55}}$$

Example 5.5-12

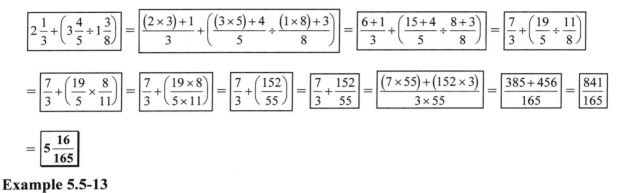

$$2\frac{1}{3} + \left(3\frac{4}{5} \div 1\frac{3}{8}\right) = \left[\frac{(2 \times 3) + 1}{3} + \left(\frac{(3 \times 5) + 4}{5} \div \frac{(1 \times 8) + 3}{8}\right)\right] = \left[\frac{6 + 1}{3} + \left(\frac{15 + 4}{5} \div \frac{8 + 3}{8}\right)\right] = \left[\frac{7}{3} + \left(\frac{19}{5} \div \frac{11}{8}\right)\right]$$

$$= \left[\frac{7}{3} + \left(\frac{19}{5} \times \frac{8}{11}\right)\right] = \left[\frac{7}{3} + \left(\frac{19 \times 8}{5 \times 11}\right)\right] = \left[\frac{7}{3} + \left(\frac{152}{55}\right)\right] = \left[\frac{7}{3} + \frac{152}{55}\right] = \left[\frac{(7 \times 55) + (152 \times 3)}{3 \times 55}\right] = \left[\frac{385 + 456}{165}\right] = \left[\frac{841}{165}\right]$$

$$= \boxed{5\frac{16}{165}}$$

Example 5.5-13

$$\left[\left(2\frac{5}{7} - 1\frac{1}{5}\right) + 2\frac{3}{4}\right] = \left[\left(\frac{(2 \times 7) + 5}{7} - \frac{(1 \times 5) + 1}{5}\right) + \frac{(2 \times 4) + 3}{4}\right] = \left[\left(\frac{14 + 5}{7} - \frac{5 + 1}{5}\right) + \frac{8 + 3}{4}\right] = \left[\left(\frac{19}{7} - \frac{6}{5}\right) + \frac{11}{4}\right]$$

$$= \left[\left(\frac{(19 \times 5) - (6 \times 7)}{7 \times 5}\right) + \frac{11}{4}\right] = \left[\left(\frac{95 - 42}{35}\right) + \frac{11}{4}\right] = \left[\left(\frac{53}{35}\right) + \frac{11}{4}\right] = \left[\frac{53}{35} + \frac{11}{4}\right] = \left[\frac{(53 \times 4) + (11 \times 35)}{35 \times 4}\right] = \left[\frac{212 + 385}{140}\right]$$

$$= \left[\frac{597}{140}\right] = \boxed{4\frac{37}{140}}$$

Example 5.5-14

$$3\frac{1}{3} \times \left(1\frac{2}{5} \div 2\frac{1}{10}\right) = \left[\frac{(3 \times 3) + 1}{3} \times \left(\frac{(1 \times 5) + 2}{5} \div \frac{(2 \times 10) + 1}{10}\right)\right] = \left[\frac{9 + 1}{3} \times \left(\frac{5 + 2}{5} \div \frac{20 + 1}{10}\right)\right] = \left[\frac{10}{3} \times \left(\frac{7}{5} \div \frac{21}{10}\right)\right]$$

$$= \left[\frac{10}{3} \times \left(\frac{7}{5} \times \frac{10}{21}\right)\right] = \left[\frac{10}{3} \times \left(\frac{7 \times 10}{5 \times 21}\right)\right] = \left[\frac{10}{3} \times \left(\frac{70}{105}\right)\right] = \left[\frac{10}{3} \times \frac{70}{105}\right] = \left[\frac{\overset{2}{10} \times 70}{3 \times \underset{21}{105}}\right] = \left[\frac{2 \times 70}{3 \times 21}\right] = \left[\frac{140}{63}\right] = \boxed{2\frac{14}{63}}$$

Example 5.5-15

$$\left[\left(5\frac{1}{4} \times 1\frac{4}{21}\right) \div \left(4\frac{1}{3} + 1\frac{1}{5}\right)\right] = \left[\left(\frac{(5 \times 4) + 1}{4} \times \frac{(1 \times 21) + 4}{21}\right) \div \left(\frac{(4 \times 3) + 1}{3} + \frac{(1 \times 5) + 1}{5}\right)\right]$$

$$= \left[\left(\frac{20 + 1}{4} \times \frac{21 + 4}{21}\right) \div \left(\frac{12 + 1}{3} + \frac{5 + 1}{5}\right)\right] = \left[\left(\frac{21}{4} \times \frac{25}{21}\right) \div \left(\frac{13}{3} + \frac{6}{5}\right)\right] = \left[\left(\frac{\overset{1}{21} \times 25}{4 \times \underset{1}{21}}\right) \div \left(\frac{(13 \times 5) + (6 \times 3)}{3 \times 5}\right)\right]$$

$$= \left[\left(\frac{1 \times 25}{4 \times 1}\right) \div \left(\frac{65 + 18}{15}\right)\right] = \left[\left(\frac{25}{4}\right) \div \left(\frac{83}{15}\right)\right] = \left[\frac{25}{4} \div \frac{83}{15}\right] = \left[\frac{25}{4} \times \frac{15}{83}\right] = \left[\frac{25 \times 15}{4 \times 83}\right] = \left[\frac{375}{332}\right] = \boxed{1\frac{43}{332}}$$

Example 5.5-16

$$\left(3\frac{2}{5} \div 1\frac{1}{10}\right) + \left(2\frac{2}{3} - 1\frac{1}{3}\right) = \left(\frac{(3\times5)+2}{5} \div \frac{(1\times10)+1}{10}\right) + \left(\frac{(2\times3)+2}{3} - \frac{(1\times3)+1}{3}\right)$$

$$= \left(\frac{15+2}{5} \div \frac{10+1}{10}\right) + \left(\frac{6+2}{3} - \frac{3+1}{3}\right) = \left(\frac{17}{5} \div \frac{11}{10}\right) + \left(\frac{8}{3} - \frac{4}{3}\right) = \left(\frac{17}{5} \times \frac{10}{11}\right) + \left(\frac{8-4}{3}\right) = \left(\frac{17 \times \overset{2}{\cancel{10}}}{\underset{1}{\cancel{5}} \times 11}\right) + \left(\frac{4}{3}\right)$$

$$= \left(\frac{17\times2}{1\times11}\right) + \frac{4}{3} = \left(\frac{34}{11}\right) + \frac{4}{3} = \frac{34}{11} + \frac{4}{3} = \frac{(34\times3)+(4\times11)}{11\times3} = \frac{102+44}{33} = \frac{146}{33} = \boxed{4\frac{14}{33}}$$

Example 5.5-17

$$\left(4\frac{2}{3} - 1\frac{4}{5}\right) \times \left(2\frac{1}{3} \div 1\frac{1}{9}\right) = \left(\frac{(4\times3)+2}{3} - \frac{(1\times5)+4}{5}\right) \times \left(\frac{(2\times3)+1}{3} \div \frac{(1\times9)+1}{9}\right)$$

$$= \left(\frac{12+2}{3} - \frac{5+4}{5}\right) \times \left(\frac{6+1}{3} \div \frac{9+1}{9}\right) = \left(\frac{14}{3} - \frac{9}{5}\right) \times \left(\frac{7}{3} \div \frac{10}{9}\right) = \left(\frac{(14\times5)-(9\times3)}{3\times5}\right) \times \left(\frac{7}{3} \times \frac{9}{10}\right)$$

$$= \left(\frac{70-27}{15}\right) \times \left(\frac{7 \times \overset{3}{\cancel{9}}}{\underset{1}{\cancel{3}} \times 10}\right) = \left(\frac{43}{15}\right) \times \left(\frac{7\times3}{1\times10}\right) = \frac{43}{15} \times \left(\frac{21}{10}\right) = \frac{43}{15} \times \frac{21}{10} = \frac{43 \times \overset{7}{\cancel{21}}}{\underset{5}{\cancel{15}} \times 10} = \frac{43\times7}{5\times10} = \frac{301}{50}$$

$$= \boxed{6\frac{1}{50}}$$

Example 5.5-18

$$3\frac{1}{4} \div \left(5\frac{4}{3} + 2\frac{5}{3} + 1\frac{2}{3}\right) = \frac{(3\times4)+1}{4} \div \left(\frac{(5\times3)+4}{3} + \frac{(2\times3)+5}{3} + \frac{(1\times3)+2}{3}\right)$$

$$= \frac{12+1}{4} \div \left(\frac{15+4}{3} + \frac{6+5}{3} + \frac{3+2}{3}\right) = \frac{13}{4} \div \left(\frac{19}{3} + \frac{11}{3} + \frac{5}{3}\right) = \frac{13}{4} \div \left(\frac{19+11+5}{3}\right) = \frac{13}{4} \div \left(\frac{35}{3}\right) = \frac{13}{4} \div \frac{35}{3}$$

$$= \frac{13}{4} \times \frac{3}{35} = \frac{13\times3}{4\times35} = \boxed{\frac{39}{140}}$$

Example 5.5-19

$$\left[\left(4\frac{2}{3} - 2\frac{1}{2}\right) \times 1\frac{3}{5}\right] - 1\frac{2}{3} = \left[\left(\frac{(4\times3)+2}{3} - \frac{(2\times2)+1}{2}\right) \times \frac{(1\times5)+3}{5}\right] - \frac{(1\times3)+2}{3}$$

$$= \left[\left(\frac{12+2}{3} - \frac{4+1}{2}\right) \times \frac{5+3}{5}\right] - \frac{3+2}{3} = \left[\left(\frac{14}{3} - \frac{5}{2}\right) \times \frac{8}{5}\right] - \frac{5}{3} = \left[\left(\frac{(14\times2)-(5\times3)}{3\times2}\right) \times \frac{8}{5}\right] - \frac{5}{3}$$

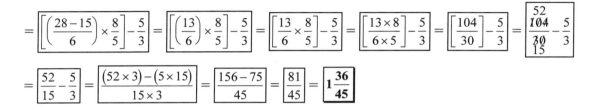

$$= \left[\frac{52}{15} - \frac{5}{3}\right] = \left[\frac{(52 \times 3) - (5 \times 15)}{15 \times 3}\right] = \left[\frac{156 - 75}{45}\right] = \left[\frac{81}{45}\right] = \boxed{1\frac{36}{45}}$$

Example 5.5-20

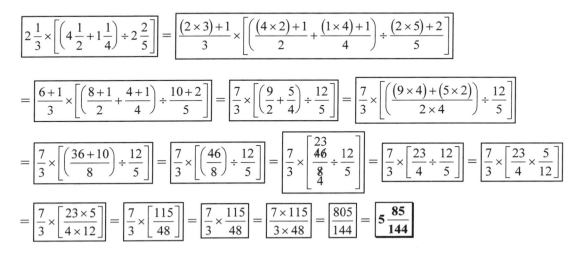

Section 5.5 Exercises - Use the following mixed fractions to perform the indicated operations:

1. $\left(4\frac{1}{2} \div 2\frac{3}{5}\right) \times 2\frac{3}{4} =$

2. $1\frac{3}{8} + \left(2\frac{1}{5} \div 1\frac{4}{5}\right) =$

3. $\left(1\frac{3}{4} \times 2\frac{1}{3}\right) \div 1\frac{2}{5} =$

4. $\left(2\frac{3}{4} - 2\frac{1}{4}\right) + 1\frac{3}{4} =$

5. $3\frac{1}{5} \div \left(4\frac{2}{3} + 1\frac{1}{3}\right) =$

6. $\left(2\frac{2}{3} \times 1\frac{1}{2}\right) + \left(2\frac{4}{5} \times 3\frac{1}{2}\right) =$

7. $\left(3\frac{3}{4} \div 2\frac{3}{5}\right) \div \left(1\frac{4}{5} \times 1\frac{2}{3}\right) =$

8. $\left(2\frac{1}{8} \times 1\frac{2}{5}\right) \div \left(2\frac{3}{5} + 2\frac{1}{5}\right) =$

9. $\left(1\frac{2}{3} + 3\frac{1}{4}\right) \div \left(2\frac{3}{5} - 1\frac{1}{3}\right) =$

10. $\left[\left(3\frac{1}{2} - 1\frac{2}{3}\right) + 1\frac{2}{5}\right] \times 2\frac{1}{3} =$

Chapter 6 - Integer and Decimal Fractions

The objective of this chapter is to improve the student's ability in solving integer and decimal fractions by grouping the two types of fractions together. The steps used to perform the combined fractional operations with examples illustrating how to add (Section 6.1), subtract (Section 6.2), multiply (Section 6.3), and divide (Section 6.4) two or more integer and decimal fractions are given. Section 6.5 mixes the mathematical operations using the two types of fractions. To further enhance the student's ability, each section is concluded by solving additional examples which do not follow the exact order as is given by the steps for each case.

6.1   Adding Integer and Decimal Fractions

Integer fractions of the form $\left(\dfrac{a}{b}\right)$ where both the numerator (a) and the denominator (b) are

integers, and decimal fractions of the form $\left(\dfrac{a \times 10^{-k_1}}{b \times 10^{-k_2}}\right)$ where (a) and (b) are integer numbers

and (k_1) and (k_2) are equal to the number of decimal places are added as in the following cases:

Case I   Adding Two Integer and Decimal Fractions

Add two integer and decimal fractions using the following steps:

Step 1   Change the integer number (a) to an integer fraction of the form $\left(\dfrac{a}{1}\right)$, e.g., change 5

to $\dfrac{5}{1}$.

Step 2   a. Change the decimal fraction to an integer fraction (see Section 2.4).

b. Change the decimal number $\left(a \times 10^{-k}\right)$ to an integer fraction of the form $\left(\dfrac{a}{10^k}\right)$,

e.g., change 12.5 to $\dfrac{125}{10}$.

Step 3   Add the integer fractions (see Section 3.1).

Step 4   Simplify the fraction to its lowest term (see Section 2.3).

Step 5   Change the improper fraction to a mixed fraction if the fraction obtained from Step 4 is an improper fraction (see Section 2.2).

The following examples show the steps as to how two integer and decimal fractions are added:

Example 6.1-1

$$\boxed{\dfrac{2}{8} + \dfrac{0.2}{0.01}} =$$

Solution:

Step 1 $\boxed{Not\ Applicable}$

Step 2a $\dfrac{2}{8} + \dfrac{0.2}{0.01} = \dfrac{2}{8} + \dfrac{\frac{2}{10}}{\frac{1}{100}} = \dfrac{2}{8} + \dfrac{2 \times 100}{10 \times 1} = \dfrac{2}{8} + \dfrac{200}{10}$

Step 2b $\boxed{Not\ Applicable}$

Step 3 $\dfrac{2}{8} + \dfrac{200}{10} = \dfrac{(2 \times 10) + (200 \times 8)}{8 \times 10} = \dfrac{20 + 1600}{80} = \dfrac{1620}{80}$

Step 4 $\dfrac{1620}{80} = \dfrac{1620 \div 20}{80 \div 20} = \dfrac{81}{4}$

Step 5 $\dfrac{81}{4} = \boxed{20\dfrac{1}{4}}$

Example 6.1-2

$$\dfrac{5}{6} + 0.3 =$$

Solution:

Step 1 $\boxed{Not\ Applicable}$

Step 2a $\boxed{Not\ Applicable}$

Step 2b $\dfrac{5}{6} + 0.3 = \dfrac{5}{6} + \dfrac{3}{10}$

Step 3 $\dfrac{5}{6} + \dfrac{3}{10} = \dfrac{(5 \times 10) + (3 \times 6)}{6 \times 10} = \dfrac{50 + 18}{60} = \dfrac{68}{60}$

Step 4 $\dfrac{68}{60} = \dfrac{68 \div 4}{60 \div 4} = \dfrac{17}{15}$

Step 5 $\dfrac{17}{15} = \boxed{1\dfrac{2}{15}}$

Example 6.1-3

$$24 + \dfrac{0.2}{0.05} =$$

Solution:

Step 1 $24 + \dfrac{0.2}{0.05} = \dfrac{24}{1} + \dfrac{0.2}{0.05}$

Step 2a

$$\boxed{\dfrac{24}{1} + \dfrac{0.2}{0.05}} = \boxed{\dfrac{24}{1} + \dfrac{\dfrac{2}{10}}{\dfrac{5}{100}}} = \boxed{\dfrac{24}{1} + \dfrac{2 \times 100}{10 \times 5}} = \boxed{\dfrac{24}{1} + \dfrac{200}{50}}$$

Step 2b $\boxed{Not\ Applicable}$

Step 3

$$\boxed{\dfrac{24}{1} + \dfrac{200}{50}} = \boxed{\dfrac{(24 \times 50) + (200 \times 1)}{1 \times 50}} = \boxed{\dfrac{1200 + 200}{50}} = \boxed{\dfrac{1400}{50}}$$

Step 4

$$\boxed{\dfrac{1400}{50}} = \boxed{\dfrac{1400 \div 50}{50 \div 50}} = \boxed{\dfrac{28}{1}} = \boxed{\mathbf{28}}$$

Step 5 $\boxed{Not\ Applicable}$

Example 6.1-4

$$\boxed{\dfrac{0.04}{1.2} + \dfrac{12}{30}} =$$

Solution:

Step 1 $\boxed{Not\ Applicable}$

Step 2a

$$\boxed{\dfrac{0.04}{1.2} + \dfrac{12}{30}} = \boxed{\dfrac{\dfrac{4}{100}}{\dfrac{12}{10}} + \dfrac{12}{30}} = \boxed{\dfrac{4 \times 10}{100 \times 12} + \dfrac{12}{30}} = \boxed{\dfrac{40}{1200} + \dfrac{12}{30}}$$

Step 2b $\boxed{Not\ Applicable}$

Step 3

$$\boxed{\dfrac{40}{1200} + \dfrac{12}{30}} = \boxed{\dfrac{(40 \times 30) + (12 \times 1200)}{1200 \times 30}} = \boxed{\dfrac{1200 + 14400}{36000}} = \boxed{\dfrac{15600}{36000}}$$

Step 4

$$\boxed{\dfrac{15600}{36000}} = \boxed{\dfrac{15600 \div 100}{36000 \div 100}} = \boxed{\dfrac{156}{360}} = \boxed{\dfrac{156 \div 12}{360 \div 12}} = \boxed{\mathbf{\dfrac{13}{30}}}$$

Step 5 $\boxed{Not\ Applicable}$

Example 6.1-5

$$\boxed{1.9 + \dfrac{3}{4}} =$$

Solution:

Step 1 $\boxed{Not\ Applicable}$

Step 2a $\boxed{Not\ Applicable}$

Step 2b $\boxed{1.9 + \dfrac{3}{4}} = \boxed{\dfrac{19}{10} + \dfrac{3}{4}} =$

Step 3 $\boxed{\dfrac{19}{10} + \dfrac{3}{4}} = \boxed{\dfrac{(19 \times 4) + (3 \times 10)}{10 \times 4}} = \boxed{\dfrac{76 + 30}{40}} = \boxed{\dfrac{106}{40}}$

Step 4 $\boxed{\dfrac{106}{40}} = \boxed{\dfrac{106 \div 2}{40 \div 2}} = \boxed{\dfrac{53}{20}}$

Step 5 $\boxed{\dfrac{53}{20}} = \boxed{2\dfrac{13}{20}}$

Case II   Adding Three Integer and Decimal Fractions

Add three integer and decimal fractions using the following steps:

Step 1   Use parentheses to group the first and second fractions.

Step 2   Change the integer number (a) to an integer fraction of the form $\left(\dfrac{a}{1}\right)$, e.g., change 23 to $\dfrac{23}{1}$.

Step 3   a. Change the decimal fraction(s) to integer fraction(s) (see Section 2.4).

   b. Change the decimal number $\left(a \times 10^{-k}\right)$ to an integer fraction of the form $\left(\dfrac{a}{10^{k}}\right)$, e.g., change 0.5 to $\dfrac{5}{10}$.

Step 4   Add the integer fractions (see Section 3.1).

Step 5   Simplify the fraction to its lowest term (see Section 2.3).

Step 6   Change the improper fraction to a mixed fraction if the fraction obtained from Step 5 is an improper fraction (see Section 2.2).

The following examples show the steps as to how three integer and decimal fractions are added:

Example 6.1-6

$$\boxed{\dfrac{2}{3} + \dfrac{0.3}{0.8} + 8} =$$

Solution:

Step 1 $\boxed{\dfrac{2}{3} + \dfrac{0.3}{0.8} + 8} = \boxed{\left(\dfrac{2}{3} + \dfrac{0.3}{0.8}\right) + 8}$

Step 2 $\boxed{\left(\dfrac{2}{3} + \dfrac{0.3}{0.8}\right) + 8} = \boxed{\left(\dfrac{2}{3} + \dfrac{0.3}{0.8}\right) + \dfrac{8}{1}}$

Step 3a
$$\left(\frac{2}{3} + \frac{0.3}{0.8}\right) + \frac{8}{1} = \left(\frac{2}{3} + \frac{\frac{3}{10}}{\frac{8}{10}}\right) + \frac{8}{1} = \left(\frac{2}{3} + \frac{3 \times 10}{10 \times 8}\right) + \frac{8}{1} = \left(\frac{2}{3} + \frac{30}{80}\right) + \frac{8}{1}$$

Step 3b $\boxed{Not\ Applicable}$

Step 4
$$\left(\frac{2}{3} + \frac{30}{80}\right) + \frac{8}{1} = \left(\frac{(2 \times 80) + (30 \times 3)}{3 \times 80}\right) + \frac{8}{1} = \left(\frac{160 + 90}{240}\right) + \frac{8}{1} = \frac{250}{240} + \frac{8}{1}$$

$$= \frac{(250 \times 1) + (8 \times 240)}{240} = \frac{250 + 1920}{240} = \frac{2170}{240}$$

Step 5
$$\frac{2170}{240} = \frac{2170 \div 10}{240 \div 10} = \frac{217}{24}$$

Step 6
$$\frac{217}{24} = \boxed{9\frac{1}{24}}$$

Example 6.1-7
$$\boxed{0.5 + \frac{3}{8} + \frac{0.5}{0.2}} =$$

Solution:

Step 1
$$0.5 + \frac{3}{8} + \frac{0.5}{0.2} = \left(0.5 + \frac{3}{8}\right) + \frac{0.5}{0.2}$$

Step 2 $\boxed{Not\ Applicable}$

Step 3a
$$\left(0.5 + \frac{3}{8}\right) + \frac{0.5}{0.2} = \left(0.5 + \frac{3}{8}\right) + \frac{\frac{5}{10}}{\frac{2}{10}} = \left(0.5 + \frac{3}{8}\right) + \frac{5 \times 10}{10 \times 2} = \left(0.5 + \frac{3}{8}\right) + \frac{50}{20}$$

Step 3b
$$\left(0.5 + \frac{3}{8}\right) + \frac{50}{20} = \left(\frac{5}{10} + \frac{3}{8}\right) + \frac{50}{20}$$

Step 4
$$\left(\frac{5}{10} + \frac{3}{8}\right) + \frac{50}{20} = \left(\frac{(5 \times 8) + (3 \times 10)}{10 \times 8}\right) + \frac{50}{20} = \left(\frac{40 + 30}{80}\right) + \frac{50}{20} = \frac{70}{80} + \frac{50}{20}$$

$$= \frac{(70 \times 20) + (50 \times 80)}{80 \times 20} = \frac{1400 + 4000}{1600} = \frac{54000}{1600}$$

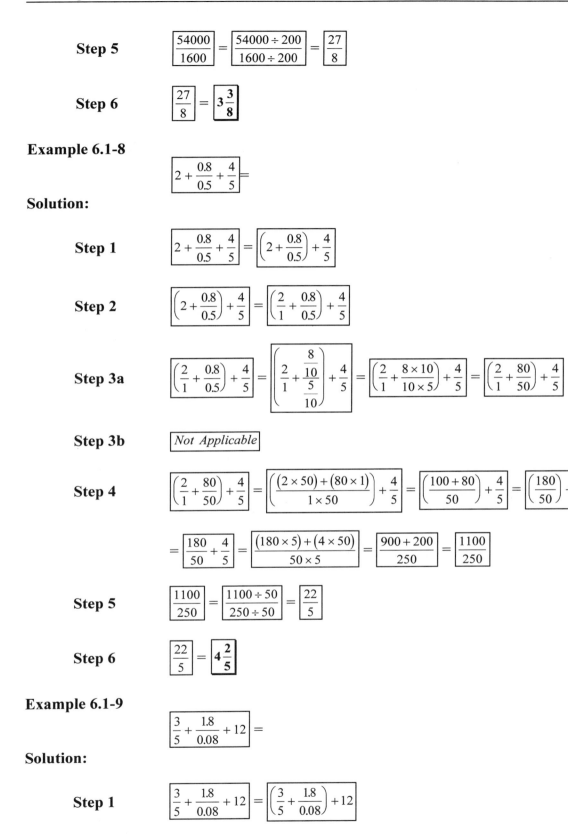

Step 5
$$\frac{54000}{1600} = \frac{54000 \div 200}{1600 \div 200} = \frac{27}{8}$$

Step 6
$$\frac{27}{8} = 3\frac{3}{8}$$

Example 6.1-8
$$2 + \frac{0.8}{0.5} + \frac{4}{5} =$$

Solution:

Step 1
$$2 + \frac{0.8}{0.5} + \frac{4}{5} = \left(2 + \frac{0.8}{0.5}\right) + \frac{4}{5}$$

Step 2
$$\left(2 + \frac{0.8}{0.5}\right) + \frac{4}{5} = \left(\frac{2}{1} + \frac{0.8}{0.5}\right) + \frac{4}{5}$$

Step 3a
$$\left(\frac{2}{1} + \frac{0.8}{0.5}\right) + \frac{4}{5} = \left(\frac{2}{1} + \frac{\frac{8}{10}}{\frac{5}{10}}\right) + \frac{4}{5} = \left(\frac{2}{1} + \frac{8 \times 10}{10 \times 5}\right) + \frac{4}{5} = \left(\frac{2}{1} + \frac{80}{50}\right) + \frac{4}{5}$$

Step 3b
Not Applicable

Step 4
$$\left(\frac{2}{1} + \frac{80}{50}\right) + \frac{4}{5} = \left(\frac{(2 \times 50) + (80 \times 1)}{1 \times 50}\right) + \frac{4}{5} = \left(\frac{100 + 80}{50}\right) + \frac{4}{5} = \left(\frac{180}{50}\right) + \frac{4}{5}$$

$$= \frac{180}{50} + \frac{4}{5} = \frac{(180 \times 5) + (4 \times 50)}{50 \times 5} = \frac{900 + 200}{250} = \frac{1100}{250}$$

Step 5
$$\frac{1100}{250} = \frac{1100 \div 50}{250 \div 50} = \frac{22}{5}$$

Step 6
$$\frac{22}{5} = 4\frac{2}{5}$$

Example 6.1-9
$$\frac{3}{5} + \frac{1.8}{0.08} + 12 =$$

Solution:

Step 1
$$\frac{3}{5} + \frac{1.8}{0.08} + 12 = \left(\frac{3}{5} + \frac{1.8}{0.08}\right) + 12$$

Step 2
$$\left(\frac{3}{5}+\frac{1.8}{0.08}\right)+12=\left(\frac{3}{5}+\frac{1.8}{0.08}\right)+\frac{12}{1}$$

Step 3a
$$\left(\frac{3}{5}+\frac{1.8}{0.08}\right)+\frac{12}{1}=\left(\frac{3}{5}+\frac{\frac{18}{10}}{\frac{8}{100}}\right)+\frac{12}{1}=\left(\frac{3}{5}+\frac{18\times100}{10\times8}\right)+\frac{12}{1}=\left(\frac{3}{5}+\frac{1800}{80}\right)+\frac{12}{1}$$

Step 3b
$$\boxed{Not\ Applicable}$$

Step 4
$$\left(\frac{3}{5}+\frac{1800}{80}\right)+\frac{12}{1}=\left(\frac{(3\times80)+(1800\times5)}{5\times80}\right)+\frac{12}{1}=\left(\frac{240+9000}{400}\right)+\frac{12}{1}$$

$$=\left(\frac{9240}{400}\right)+\frac{12}{1}=\frac{9240}{400}+\frac{12}{1}=\frac{(9240\times1)+(12\times400)}{400\times1}=\frac{9240+4800}{400}=\frac{14040}{400}$$

Step 5
$$\frac{14040}{400}=\frac{14040\div40}{400\div40}=\frac{351}{10}$$

Step 6
$$\frac{351}{10}=\boxed{35\frac{1}{10}}$$

Example 6.1-10
$$\frac{3}{8}+\frac{1.8}{0.02}+0.4=$$

Solution:

Step 1
$$\frac{3}{8}+\frac{1.8}{0.02}+0.4=\left(\frac{3}{8}+\frac{1.8}{0.02}\right)+0.4$$

Step 2
$$\boxed{Not\ Applicable}$$

Step 3a
$$\left(\frac{3}{8}+\frac{1.8}{0.02}\right)+0.4=\left(\frac{3}{8}+\frac{\frac{18}{10}}{\frac{2}{100}}\right)+0.4=\left(\frac{3}{8}+\frac{18\times100}{10\times2}\right)+0.4=\left(\frac{3}{8}+\frac{1800}{20}\right)+0.4$$

Step 3b
$$\left(\frac{3}{8}+\frac{1800}{20}\right)+0.4=\left(\frac{3}{8}+\frac{1800}{20}\right)+\frac{4}{10}$$

Step 4
$$\left(\frac{3}{8}+\frac{1800}{20}\right)+\frac{4}{10}=\left(\frac{(3\times20)+(1800\times8)}{8\times20}\right)+\frac{4}{10}=\left(\frac{60+14400}{160}\right)+\frac{4}{10}$$

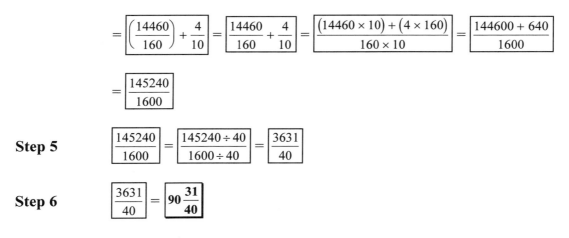

$$= \left[\left(\frac{14460}{160}\right) + \frac{4}{10}\right] = \left[\frac{14460}{160} + \frac{4}{10}\right] = \left[\frac{(14460 \times 10) + (4 \times 160)}{160 \times 10}\right] = \left[\frac{144600 + 640}{1600}\right]$$

$$= \left[\frac{145240}{1600}\right]$$

Step 5 $\qquad \left[\frac{145240}{1600}\right] = \left[\frac{145240 \div 40}{1600 \div 40}\right] = \left[\frac{3631}{40}\right]$

Step 6 $\qquad \left[\frac{3631}{40}\right] = \boxed{90\frac{31}{40}}$

The following examples further illustrate how to add integer and decimal fractions:

Example 6.1-11

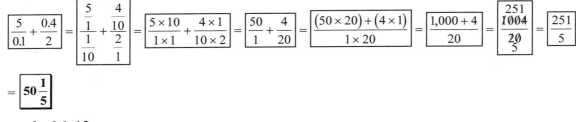

$$\left[\frac{3}{5} + \frac{0.12}{0.3}\right] = \left[\frac{3}{5} + \frac{\frac{12}{100}}{\frac{3}{10}}\right] = \left[\frac{3}{5} + \frac{12 \times 10}{100 \times 3}\right] = \left[\frac{3}{5} + \frac{\overset{2}{\cancel{120}}}{\underset{5}{\cancel{300}}}\right] = \left[\frac{3}{5} + \frac{2}{5}\right] = \left[\frac{3+2}{5}\right] = \left[\frac{\overset{1}{\cancel{5}}}{\underset{1}{\cancel{5}}}\right] = \left[\frac{1}{1}\right] = \boxed{1}$$

Example 6.1-12

$$\left[\frac{5}{0.1} + \frac{0.4}{2}\right] = \left[\frac{\frac{5}{1}}{\frac{1}{10}} + \frac{\frac{4}{10}}{\frac{2}{1}}\right] = \left[\frac{5 \times 10}{1 \times 1} + \frac{4 \times 1}{10 \times 2}\right] = \left[\frac{50}{1} + \frac{4}{20}\right] = \left[\frac{(50 \times 20) + (4 \times 1)}{1 \times 20}\right] = \left[\frac{1,000 + 4}{20}\right] = \left[\frac{\overset{251}{\cancel{1004}}}{\underset{5}{\cancel{20}}}\right] = \left[\frac{251}{5}\right]$$

$$= \boxed{50\frac{1}{5}}$$

Example 6.1-13

$$\left[\frac{8}{0.02} + 28\right] = \left[\frac{\frac{8}{1}}{\frac{2}{100}} + \frac{28}{1}\right] = \left[\frac{8 \times 100}{1 \times 2} + \frac{28}{1}\right] = \left[\frac{\overset{400}{\cancel{800}}}{\underset{1}{\cancel{2}}} + \frac{28}{1}\right] = \left[\frac{400}{1} + \frac{28}{1}\right] = \left[\frac{400 + 28}{1}\right] = \left[\frac{428}{1}\right] = \boxed{428}$$

Example 6.1-14

$$\left[\frac{3}{10} + 0.13\right] = \left[\frac{3}{10} + \frac{13}{100}\right] = \left[\frac{(3 \times 100) + (13 \times 10)}{10 \times 100}\right] = \left[\frac{300 + 130}{1000}\right] = \left[\frac{\overset{43}{\cancel{430}}}{\underset{100}{\cancel{1000}}}\right] = \boxed{\frac{43}{100}}$$

Example 6.1-15

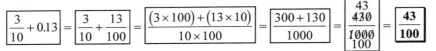
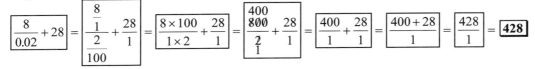

$$\left[\frac{5}{3} + \frac{0.04}{0.6} + \frac{3}{0.1}\right] = \left[\left(\frac{5}{3} + \frac{0.04}{0.6}\right) + \frac{3}{0.1}\right] = \left[\left(\frac{5}{3} + \frac{\frac{4}{100}}{\frac{6}{10}}\right) + \frac{\frac{3}{1}}{\frac{1}{10}}\right] = \left[\left(\frac{5}{3} + \frac{4 \times 10}{100 \times 6}\right) + \frac{3 \times 10}{1 \times 1}\right] = \left[\left(\frac{5}{3} + \frac{\overset{1}{\cancel{40}}}{\underset{15}{\cancel{600}}}\right) + \frac{30}{1}\right]$$

$$= \boxed{\left(\frac{5}{3}+\frac{1}{15}\right)+\frac{30}{1}} = \boxed{\left(\frac{(5\times15)+(1\times3)}{3\times15}\right)+\frac{30}{1}} = \boxed{\left(\frac{75+3}{45}\right)+\frac{30}{1}} = \boxed{\left(\frac{78}{45}\right)+\frac{30}{1}} = \boxed{\frac{78}{45}+\frac{30}{1}} = \boxed{\frac{(78\times1)+(30\times45)}{45\times1}}$$

$$= \boxed{\frac{78+1350}{45}} = \boxed{\frac{\overset{476}{\cancel{1428}}}{\underset{15}{\cancel{45}}}} = \boxed{\frac{476}{15}} = \boxed{\mathbf{31\frac{11}{15}}}$$

Example 6.1-16

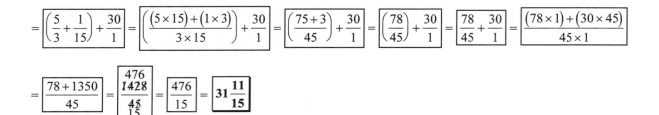

$$\boxed{\frac{4}{7}+\frac{0.1}{0.06}+5} = \boxed{\left(\frac{4}{7}+\frac{0.1}{0.06}\right)+5} = \boxed{\left(\frac{4}{7}+\frac{\frac{1}{10}}{\frac{6}{100}}\right)+\frac{5}{1}} = \boxed{\left(\frac{4}{7}+\frac{1\times100}{10\times6}\right)+\frac{5}{1}} = \boxed{\left(\frac{4}{7}+\frac{100}{60}\right)+\frac{5}{1}}$$

$$= \boxed{\left(\frac{(4\times60)+(100\times7)}{7\times60}\right)+\frac{5}{1}} = \boxed{\left(\frac{240+700}{420}\right)+\frac{5}{1}} = \boxed{\left(\frac{940}{420}\right)+\frac{5}{1}} = \boxed{\frac{\overset{47}{\cancel{940}}}{\underset{21}{\cancel{420}}}+\frac{5}{1}} = \boxed{\frac{47}{21}+\frac{5}{1}} = \boxed{\frac{(47\times1)+(5\times21)}{21\times1}}$$

$$= \boxed{\frac{47+105}{21}} = \boxed{\frac{152}{21}} = \boxed{\mathbf{7\frac{5}{21}}}$$

Example 6.1-17

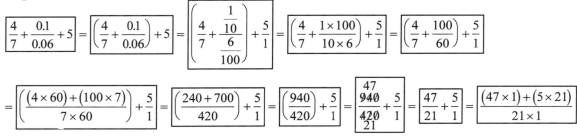

$$\boxed{\frac{5}{0.2}+\frac{3}{0.4}+3} = \boxed{\left(\frac{5}{0.2}+\frac{3}{0.4}\right)+3} = \boxed{\left(\frac{\frac{5}{1}}{\frac{2}{10}}+\frac{\frac{3}{1}}{\frac{4}{10}}\right)+\frac{3}{1}} = \boxed{\left(\frac{5\times10}{1\times2}+\frac{3\times10}{1\times4}\right)+\frac{3}{1}} = \boxed{\left(\frac{50}{2}+\frac{30}{4}\right)+\frac{3}{1}}$$

$$= \boxed{\left(\frac{(50\times4)+(30\times2)}{2\times4}\right)+\frac{3}{1}} = \boxed{\left(\frac{200+60}{8}\right)+\frac{3}{1}} = \boxed{\frac{\overset{65}{\cancel{260}}}{\underset{2}{\cancel{8}}}+\frac{3}{1}} = \boxed{\frac{65}{2}+\frac{3}{1}} = \boxed{\left(\frac{(65\times1)+(3\times2)}{2\times1}\right)} = \boxed{\frac{65+6}{2}} = \boxed{\frac{71}{2}}$$

$$= \boxed{\mathbf{35\frac{1}{2}}}$$

Example 6.1-18

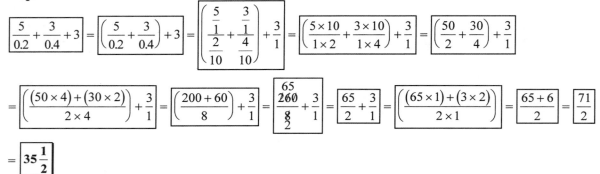

$$\boxed{\frac{0.12}{0.2}+\left(\frac{1}{5}+\frac{3}{8}\right)} = \boxed{\frac{\frac{12}{100}}{\frac{2}{10}}+\left(\frac{(1\times8)+(3\times5)}{5\times8}\right)} = \boxed{\frac{12\times10}{100\times2}+\left(\frac{8+15}{40}\right)} = \boxed{\frac{\overset{3}{\cancel{120}}}{\underset{5}{\cancel{200}}}+\left(\frac{23}{40}\right)} = \boxed{\frac{3}{5}+\frac{23}{40}}$$

$$= \boxed{\frac{(3\times40)+(23\times5)}{5\times40}} = \boxed{\frac{120+115}{200}} = \boxed{\frac{\overset{47}{\cancel{235}}}{\underset{40}{\cancel{200}}}} = \boxed{\frac{47}{40}} = \boxed{\mathbf{1\frac{7}{40}}}$$

Example 6.1-19

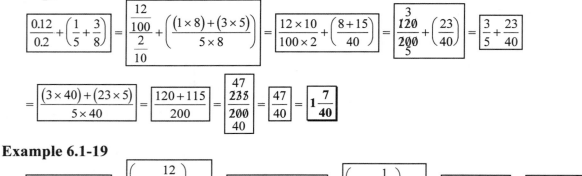

$$\boxed{\left(\frac{2}{5}+\frac{0.12}{0.6}\right)+\frac{1}{3}} = \boxed{\left(\frac{2}{5}+\frac{\frac{12}{100}}{\frac{6}{10}}\right)+\frac{1}{3}} = \boxed{\left(\frac{2}{5}+\frac{12\times10}{100\times6}\right)+\frac{1}{3}} = \boxed{\left(\frac{2}{5}+\frac{\overset{1}{\cancel{120}}}{\underset{5}{\cancel{600}}}\right)+\frac{1}{3}} = \boxed{\left(\frac{2}{5}+\frac{1}{5}\right)+\frac{1}{3}} = \boxed{\left(\frac{2+1}{5}\right)+\frac{1}{3}}$$

$$= \boxed{\left(\frac{3}{5}\right) + \frac{1}{3}} = \boxed{\frac{3}{5} + \frac{1}{3}} = \boxed{\frac{(3 \times 3) + (1 \times 5)}{5 \times 3}} = \boxed{\frac{9+5}{15}} = \boxed{\mathbf{\frac{14}{15}}}$$

Example 6.1-20

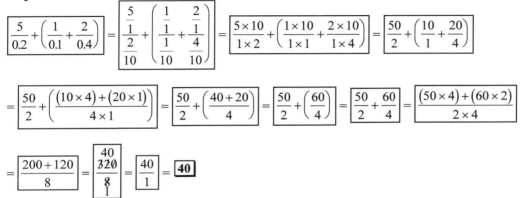

$$= \boxed{\frac{10}{1} + \frac{51}{10}} = \boxed{\frac{(10 \times 10) + (51 \times 1)}{1 \times 10}} = \boxed{\frac{100+51}{10}} = \boxed{\frac{151}{10}} = \boxed{\mathbf{15\frac{1}{10}}}$$

Example 6.1-21

$$\boxed{\frac{5}{0.2} + \left(\frac{1}{0.1} + \frac{2}{0.4}\right)} = \boxed{\frac{5}{\frac{1}{2}} + \left(\frac{1}{\frac{1}{10}} + \frac{2}{\frac{4}{10}}\right)} = \boxed{\frac{5 \times 10}{1 \times 2} + \left(\frac{1 \times 10}{1 \times 1} + \frac{2 \times 10}{1 \times 4}\right)} = \boxed{\frac{50}{2} + \left(\frac{10}{1} + \frac{20}{4}\right)}$$

$$= \boxed{\frac{50}{2} + \left(\frac{(10 \times 4) + (20 \times 1)}{4 \times 1}\right)} = \boxed{\frac{50}{2} + \left(\frac{40+20}{4}\right)} = \boxed{\frac{50}{2} + \left(\frac{60}{4}\right)} = \boxed{\frac{50}{2} + \frac{60}{4}} = \boxed{\frac{(50 \times 4) + (60 \times 2)}{2 \times 4}}$$

$$= \boxed{\frac{200+120}{8}} = \boxed{\frac{\overset{40}{\cancel{320}}}{\underset{1}{\cancel{8}}}} = \boxed{\frac{40}{1}} = \boxed{\mathbf{40}}$$

Section 6.1 Exercises - Add the following integer and decimal fractions:

1. $\dfrac{2}{5} + 0.01 =$

2. $\dfrac{3}{8} + \dfrac{0.2}{0.06} + 1 =$

3. $\dfrac{3}{5} + \dfrac{1.5}{0.2} + \dfrac{3}{0.4} =$

4. $\left(\dfrac{1}{2} + \dfrac{3}{4}\right) + \dfrac{0.8}{1.2} =$

5. $5.5 + \dfrac{3}{5} + \dfrac{0.2}{0.5} =$

6. $\left(\dfrac{6}{8} + \dfrac{1}{8} + \dfrac{3}{8}\right) + \dfrac{0.4}{0.08} =$

7. $\left(\dfrac{3}{4} + \dfrac{0.2}{0.1}\right) + \left(\dfrac{1}{0.1} + \dfrac{1}{5}\right) =$

8. $\dfrac{0.04}{1.2} + \left(2.2 + \dfrac{4}{5}\right) =$

9. $\left(\dfrac{1}{4} + \dfrac{5}{3}\right) + \left(\dfrac{1}{0.4} + \dfrac{5}{0.2}\right) =$

10. $\left(\dfrac{1}{4} + \dfrac{3}{2}\right) + \left(\dfrac{0.2}{0.04} + 2\right) =$

6.2   Subtracting Integer and Decimal Fractions

Integer fractions of the form $\left(\dfrac{a}{b}\right)$ where both the numerator (a) and the denominator (b) are

integers, and decimal fractions of the form $\left(\dfrac{a \times 10^{-k_1}}{b \times 10^{-k_2}}\right)$ where (a) and (b) are integer numbers

and (k_1) and (k_2) are equal to the number of decimal places are subtracted as in the following cases:

Case I   Subtracting Two Integer and Decimal Fractions

Subtract two integer and decimal fractions using the following steps:

Step 1   Change the integer number (a) to an integer fraction of the form $\left(\dfrac{a}{1}\right)$, e.g., change 13

to $\dfrac{13}{1}$.

Step 2   a. Change the decimal fraction to an integer fraction (see Section 2.4).

b. Change the decimal number $\left(a \times 10^{-k}\right)$ to an integer fraction of the form $\left(\dfrac{a}{10^k}\right)$,

e.g., change 0.123 to $\dfrac{123}{1000}$.

Step 3   Subtract the integer fractions (see Section 3.2).

Step 4   Simplify the fraction to its lowest term (see Section 2.3).

Step 5   Change the improper fraction to a mixed fraction if the fraction obtained from Step 4 is an improper fraction (see Section 2.2).

The following examples show the steps as to how two integer and decimal fractions are subtracted:

Example 6.2-1

$$\boxed{\dfrac{1.2}{0.03} - \dfrac{3}{5}} =$$

Solution:

Step 1 $\boxed{\textit{Not Applicable}}$

Step 2a $\boxed{\dfrac{1.2}{0.03} - \dfrac{3}{5}} = \boxed{\dfrac{\frac{12}{10}}{\frac{3}{100}} - \dfrac{3}{5}} = \boxed{\dfrac{12 \times 100}{10 \times 3} - \dfrac{3}{5}} = \boxed{\dfrac{1200}{30} - \dfrac{3}{5}}$

Step 2b $\boxed{\textit{Not Applicable}}$

Step 3 $\boxed{\dfrac{1200}{30} - \dfrac{3}{5}} = \boxed{\dfrac{(1200 \times 5) - (3 \times 30)}{30 \times 5}} = \boxed{\dfrac{6000 - 90}{150}} = \boxed{\dfrac{5910}{150}}$

Step 4 $\boxed{\dfrac{5910}{150}} = \boxed{\dfrac{5910 \div 10}{150 \div 10}} = \boxed{\dfrac{591}{15}}$

Step 5	$\dfrac{591}{15} = \boxed{39\dfrac{6}{15}}$

Example 6.2-2

$\boxed{0.8 - \dfrac{2}{3}} =$

Solution:

Step 1	$\boxed{\textit{Not Applicable}}$

Step 2a	$\boxed{\textit{Not Applicable}}$

Step 2b	$\boxed{0.8 - \dfrac{2}{3}} = \boxed{\dfrac{8}{10} - \dfrac{2}{3}}$

Step 3	$\boxed{\dfrac{8}{10} - \dfrac{2}{3}} = \boxed{\dfrac{(8 \times 3) - (2 \times 10)}{10 \times 3}} = \boxed{\dfrac{24 - 20}{30}} = \boxed{\dfrac{4}{30}}$

Step 4	$\boxed{\dfrac{4}{30}} = \boxed{\dfrac{4 \div 2}{30 \div 2}} = \boxed{\dfrac{2}{15}}$

Step 5	$\boxed{\textit{Not Applicable}}$

Example 6.2-3

$\boxed{24 - \dfrac{1.8}{0.04}} =$

Solution:

Step 1	$\boxed{24 - \dfrac{1.8}{0.04}} = \boxed{\dfrac{24}{1} - \dfrac{1.8}{0.04}}$

Step 2a	$\boxed{\dfrac{24}{1} - \dfrac{1.8}{0.04}} = \boxed{\dfrac{24}{1} - \dfrac{\dfrac{18}{10}}{\dfrac{4}{100}}} = \boxed{\dfrac{24}{1} - \dfrac{18 \times 100}{10 \times 4}} = \boxed{\dfrac{24}{1} - \dfrac{1800}{40}}$

Step 2b	$\boxed{\textit{Not Applicable}}$

Step 3	$\boxed{\dfrac{24}{1} - \dfrac{1800}{40}} = \boxed{\dfrac{(24 \times 40) - (1800 \times 1)}{1 \times 40}} = \boxed{\dfrac{960 - 1800}{40}} = \boxed{\dfrac{-840}{40}}$

Step 4	$\boxed{\dfrac{-840}{40}} = \boxed{\dfrac{-840 \div 40}{40 \div 40}} = \boxed{\dfrac{-21}{1}} = \boxed{-21}$

Step 5	$\boxed{\textit{Not Applicable}}$

Example 6.2-4

$$\boxed{\dfrac{0.3}{0.2} - \dfrac{3}{5}} =$$

Solution:

Step 1 $\boxed{\textit{Not Applicable}}$

Step 2a $\boxed{\dfrac{0.3}{0.2} - \dfrac{3}{5}} = \boxed{\dfrac{\frac{3}{10}}{\frac{2}{10}} - \dfrac{3}{5}} = \boxed{\dfrac{3 \times 10}{10 \times 2} - \dfrac{3}{5}} = \boxed{\dfrac{30}{20} - \dfrac{3}{5}}$

Step 2b $\boxed{\textit{Not Applicable}}$

Step 3 $\boxed{\dfrac{30}{20} - \dfrac{3}{5}} = \boxed{\dfrac{(30 \times 5) - (3 \times 20)}{20 \times 5}} = \boxed{\dfrac{150 - 60}{100}} = \boxed{\dfrac{90}{100}}$

Step 4 $\boxed{\dfrac{90}{100}} = \boxed{\dfrac{90 \div 10}{100 \div 10}} = \boxed{\mathbf{\dfrac{9}{10}}}$

Step 5 $\boxed{\textit{Not Applicable}}$

Example 6.2-5

$$\boxed{\dfrac{12}{5} - 0.015} =$$

Solution:

Step 1 $\boxed{\textit{Not Applicable}}$

Step 2a $\boxed{\textit{Not Applicable}}$

Step 2b $\boxed{\dfrac{12}{5} - 0.015} = \boxed{\dfrac{12}{5} - \dfrac{15}{1000}}$

Step 3 $\boxed{\dfrac{12}{5} - \dfrac{15}{1000}} = \boxed{\dfrac{(12 \times 1000) - (15 \times 5)}{5 \times 1000}} = \boxed{\dfrac{12000 - 75}{5000}} = \boxed{\dfrac{11925}{5000}}$

Step 4 $\boxed{\dfrac{11925}{5000}} = \boxed{\dfrac{11925 \div 25}{5000 \div 25}} = \boxed{\dfrac{477}{200}}$

Step 5 $\boxed{\dfrac{477}{200}} = \boxed{\mathbf{2\dfrac{77}{200}}}$

Case II   Subtracting Three Integer and Decimal Fractions

Subtract three integer and decimal fractions using the following steps:

Step 1   Use parentheses to group the first and second fractions.

Step 2   Change the integer number (a) to an integer fraction of the form $\left(\dfrac{a}{1}\right)$, e.g., change

129 to $\dfrac{129}{1}$.

Step 3   a. Change the decimal fraction(s) to integer fraction(s) (see Section 2.4).

b. Change the decimal number $\left(a \times 10^{-k}\right)$ to an integer fraction of the form $\left(\dfrac{a}{10^{k}}\right)$,

e.g., change 1.27 to $\dfrac{127}{100}$.

Step 4   Subtract the integer fractions (see Section 3.2).

Step 5   Simplify the fraction to its lowest term (see Section 2.3).

Step 6   Change the improper fraction to a mixed fraction if the fraction obtained from Step 5 is an improper fraction (see Section 2.2).

The following examples show the steps as to how three integer and decimal fractions are subtracted:

Example 6.2-6

$$\boxed{5 - \dfrac{0.2}{0.3} - \dfrac{3}{5}} =$$

Solution:

Step 1 $\boxed{5 - \dfrac{0.2}{0.3} - \dfrac{3}{5}} = \boxed{\left(5 - \dfrac{0.2}{0.3}\right) - \dfrac{3}{5}}$

Step 2 $\boxed{\left(5 - \dfrac{0.2}{0.3}\right) - \dfrac{3}{5}} = \boxed{\left(\dfrac{5}{1} - \dfrac{0.2}{0.3}\right) - \dfrac{3}{5}}$

Step 3a $\boxed{\left(\dfrac{5}{1} - \dfrac{0.2}{0.3}\right) - \dfrac{3}{5}} = \boxed{\left(\dfrac{5}{1} - \dfrac{\frac{2}{10}}{\frac{3}{10}}\right) - \dfrac{3}{5}} = \boxed{\left(\dfrac{5}{1} - \dfrac{2 \times 10}{10 \times 3}\right) - \dfrac{3}{5}} = \boxed{\left(\dfrac{5}{1} - \dfrac{20}{30}\right) - \dfrac{3}{5}}$

Step 3b $\boxed{Not\ Applicable}$

Step 4 $\boxed{\left(\dfrac{5}{1} - \dfrac{20}{30}\right) - \dfrac{3}{5}} = \boxed{\left(\dfrac{(5 \times 30) - (20 \times 1)}{1 \times 30}\right) - \dfrac{3}{5}} = \boxed{\left(\dfrac{150 - 20}{30}\right) - \dfrac{3}{5}} = \boxed{\left(\dfrac{130}{30}\right) - \dfrac{3}{5}}$

$= \boxed{\dfrac{130}{30} - \dfrac{3}{5}} = \boxed{\dfrac{(130 \times 5) - (3 \times 30)}{30 \times 5}} = \boxed{\dfrac{650 - 90}{150}} = \boxed{\dfrac{560}{150}}$

Step 5 $\boxed{\dfrac{560}{150}} = \boxed{\dfrac{560 \div 10}{150 \div 10}} = \boxed{\dfrac{56}{15}}$

Step 6 $\boxed{\dfrac{56}{15}} = \boxed{\mathbf{3\dfrac{11}{15}}}$

Example 6.2-7

$\boxed{0.2 - \dfrac{1}{3} - \dfrac{0.5}{0.4}} =$

Solution:

Step 1 $\boxed{0.2 - \dfrac{1}{3} - \dfrac{0.5}{0.4}} = \boxed{\left(0.2 - \dfrac{1}{3}\right) - \dfrac{0.5}{0.4}}$

Step 2 $\boxed{Not\ Applicable}$

Step 3a $\boxed{\left(0.2 - \dfrac{1}{3}\right) - \dfrac{0.5}{0.4}} = \boxed{\left(0.2 - \dfrac{1}{3}\right) - \dfrac{\frac{5}{10}}{\frac{4}{10}}} = \boxed{\left(0.2 - \dfrac{1}{3}\right) - \dfrac{5 \times 10}{10 \times 4}} = \boxed{\left(0.2 - \dfrac{1}{3}\right) - \dfrac{50}{40}}$

Step 3b $\boxed{\left(0.2 - \dfrac{1}{3}\right) - \dfrac{50}{40}} = \boxed{\left(\dfrac{2}{10} - \dfrac{1}{3}\right) - \dfrac{50}{40}}$

Step 4 $\boxed{\left(\dfrac{2}{10} - \dfrac{1}{3}\right) - \dfrac{50}{40}} = \boxed{\left(\dfrac{(2 \times 3) - (1 \times 10)}{10 \times 3}\right) - \dfrac{50}{40}} = \boxed{\left(\dfrac{6 - 10}{10}\right) - \dfrac{50}{40}} = \boxed{\left(\dfrac{-4}{30}\right) - \dfrac{50}{40}}$

$= \boxed{\dfrac{-4}{30} - \dfrac{50}{40}} = \boxed{\dfrac{(-4 \times 40) - (50 \times 30)}{30 \times 40}} = \boxed{\dfrac{-160 - 1500}{1200}} = \boxed{\dfrac{-1660}{1200}}$

Step 5 $\boxed{\dfrac{-1660}{1200}} = \boxed{\dfrac{-1660 \div 20}{1200 \div 20}} = \boxed{\dfrac{-83}{60}}$

Step 6 $\boxed{\dfrac{-83}{60}} = \boxed{-\left(1\dfrac{23}{60}\right)}$

Example 6.2-8

$\boxed{\dfrac{0.05}{1.2} - \dfrac{3}{8} - \dfrac{0.3}{0.8}} =$

Solution:

Step 1 $\boxed{\dfrac{0.05}{1.2} - \dfrac{3}{8} - \dfrac{0.3}{0.8}} = \boxed{\left(\dfrac{0.05}{1.2} - \dfrac{3}{8}\right) - \dfrac{0.3}{0.8}}$

Step 2 | Not Applicable |

Step 3a

$$\left(\frac{0.05}{1.2} - \frac{3}{8}\right) - \frac{0.3}{0.8} = \left(\frac{\frac{5}{100}}{\frac{12}{10}} - \frac{3}{8}\right) - \frac{\frac{3}{10}}{\frac{8}{10}} = \left(\frac{5 \times 10}{100 \times 12} - \frac{3}{8}\right) - \frac{3 \times 10}{10 \times 8}$$

$$= \left(\frac{50}{1200} - \frac{3}{8}\right) - \frac{30}{80}$$

Step 3b | Not Applicable |

Step 4

$$\left(\frac{50}{1200} - \frac{3}{8}\right) - \frac{30}{80} = \left(\frac{(50 \times 8) - (3 \times 1200)}{1200 \times 8}\right) - \frac{30}{80} = \left(\frac{400 - 3600}{9600}\right) - \frac{30}{80}$$

$$= \left(\frac{400 - 3600}{9600}\right) - \frac{30}{80} = \left(\frac{-3200}{9600}\right) - \frac{30}{80} = \frac{-3200}{9600} - \frac{30}{80}$$

$$= \frac{(-3200 \times 80) - (30 \times 9600)}{9600 \times 80} = \frac{-256000 - 288000}{768000} = \frac{-544000}{768000}$$

Step 5

$$\frac{-544000}{768000} = \frac{-544000 \div 1000}{768000 \div 1000} = \frac{-544}{768} = \frac{-544 \div 32}{768 \div 32} = -\frac{17}{24}$$

Step 6 | Not Applicable |

Example 6.2-9

$$\frac{2}{5} - 0.6 - \frac{0.4}{1.2} =$$

Solution:

Step 1

$$\frac{2}{5} - 0.6 - \frac{0.4}{1.2} = \left(\frac{2}{5} - 0.6\right) - \frac{0.4}{1.2}$$

Step 2 | Not Applicable |

Step 3a

$$\left(\frac{2}{5} - 0.6\right) - \frac{0.4}{1.2} = \left(\frac{2}{5} - 0.6\right) - \frac{\frac{4}{10}}{\frac{12}{10}} = \left(\frac{2}{5} - 0.6\right) - \frac{4 \times 10}{10 \times 12} = \left(\frac{2}{5} - 0.6\right) - \frac{40}{120}$$

Step 3b

$$\left(\frac{2}{5} - 0.6\right) - \frac{40}{120} = \left(\frac{2}{5} - \frac{6}{10}\right) - \frac{40}{120}$$

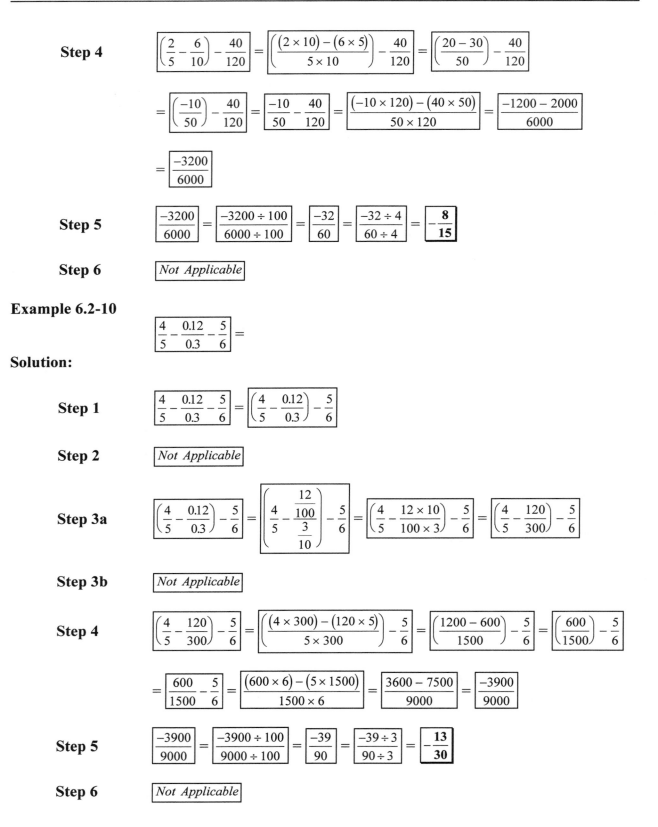

Step 4

$$\left[\left(\frac{2}{5}-\frac{6}{10}\right)-\frac{40}{120}\right]=\left[\left(\frac{(2\times10)-(6\times5)}{5\times10}\right)-\frac{40}{120}\right]=\left[\left(\frac{20-30}{50}\right)-\frac{40}{120}\right]$$

$$=\left[\left(\frac{-10}{50}\right)-\frac{40}{120}\right]=\left[\frac{-10}{50}-\frac{40}{120}\right]=\left[\frac{(-10\times120)-(40\times50)}{50\times120}\right]=\left[\frac{-1200-2000}{6000}\right]$$

$$=\left[\frac{-3200}{6000}\right]$$

Step 5

$$\left[\frac{-3200}{6000}\right]=\left[\frac{-3200\div100}{6000\div100}\right]=\left[\frac{-32}{60}\right]=\left[\frac{-32\div4}{60\div4}\right]=\boxed{-\frac{8}{15}}$$

Step 6 $\boxed{Not\ Applicable}$

Example 6.2-10

$$\boxed{\frac{4}{5}-\frac{0.12}{0.3}-\frac{5}{6}}=$$

Solution:

Step 1

$$\boxed{\frac{4}{5}-\frac{0.12}{0.3}-\frac{5}{6}}=\left[\left(\frac{4}{5}-\frac{0.12}{0.3}\right)-\frac{5}{6}\right]$$

Step 2 $\boxed{Not\ Applicable}$

Step 3a

$$\left[\left(\frac{4}{5}-\frac{0.12}{0.3}\right)-\frac{5}{6}\right]=\left[\left(\frac{4}{5}-\frac{\frac{12}{100}}{\frac{3}{10}}\right)-\frac{5}{6}\right]=\left[\left(\frac{4}{5}-\frac{12\times10}{100\times3}\right)-\frac{5}{6}\right]=\left[\left(\frac{4}{5}-\frac{120}{300}\right)-\frac{5}{6}\right]$$

Step 3b $\boxed{Not\ Applicable}$

Step 4

$$\left[\left(\frac{4}{5}-\frac{120}{300}\right)-\frac{5}{6}\right]=\left[\left(\frac{(4\times300)-(120\times5)}{5\times300}\right)-\frac{5}{6}\right]=\left[\left(\frac{1200-600}{1500}\right)-\frac{5}{6}\right]=\left[\left(\frac{600}{1500}\right)-\frac{5}{6}\right]$$

$$=\left[\frac{600}{1500}-\frac{5}{6}\right]=\left[\frac{(600\times6)-(5\times1500)}{1500\times6}\right]=\left[\frac{3600-7500}{9000}\right]=\left[\frac{-3900}{9000}\right]$$

Step 5

$$\left[\frac{-3900}{9000}\right]=\left[\frac{-3900\div100}{9000\div100}\right]=\left[\frac{-39}{90}\right]=\left[\frac{-39\div3}{90\div3}\right]=\boxed{-\frac{13}{30}}$$

Step 6 $\boxed{Not\ Applicable}$

The following examples further illustrate how to subtract integer and decimal fractions:

Example 6.2-11

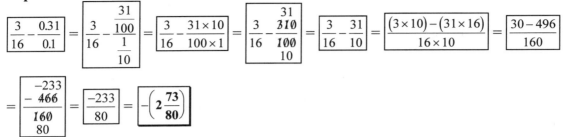

Example 6.2-12

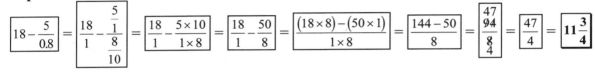

Example 6.2-13

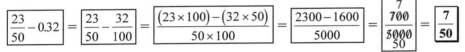

Example 6.2-14

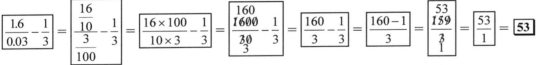

Example 6.2-15

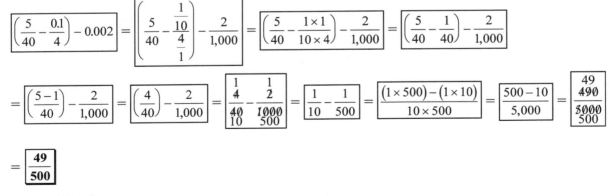

Example 6.2-16

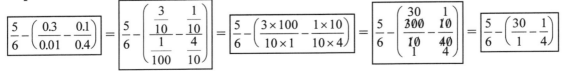

$$= \boxed{\frac{5}{6} - \left(\frac{(30\times4)-(1\times1)}{1\times4}\right)} = \boxed{\frac{5}{6} - \left(\frac{120-1}{4}\right)} = \boxed{\frac{5}{6} - \left(\frac{119}{4}\right)} = \boxed{\frac{5}{6} - \frac{119}{4}} = \boxed{\frac{(5\times4)-(119\times6)}{6\times4}} = \boxed{\frac{20-714}{24}}$$

$$= \boxed{\frac{\overset{-347}{-694}}{\underset{12}{24}}} = \boxed{\frac{-347}{12}} = \boxed{-\left(28\frac{11}{12}\right)}$$

Example 6.2-17

$$\boxed{\frac{8}{9} - \frac{12}{9} - \frac{0.3}{0.14}} = \boxed{\left(\frac{8}{9} - \frac{12}{9}\right) - \frac{0.3}{0.14}} = \boxed{\left(\frac{8-12}{9}\right) - \frac{\frac{3}{10}}{\frac{14}{100}}} = \boxed{\left(\frac{-4}{9}\right) - \frac{3\times100}{10\times14}} = \boxed{\frac{-4}{9} - \frac{\overset{15}{\cancel{300}}}{\underset{7}{\cancel{140}}}} = \boxed{\frac{4}{9} - \frac{15}{7}}$$

$$= \boxed{\frac{(-4\times7)-(15\times9)}{9\times7}} = \boxed{\frac{-28-135}{63}} = \boxed{\frac{-163}{63}} = \boxed{-\left(2\frac{37}{63}\right)}$$

Example 6.2-18

$$\boxed{\left(\frac{14}{2} - \frac{0.2}{4}\right) - \left(3 - \frac{0.1}{1}\right)} = \boxed{\left(\frac{14}{2} - \frac{\frac{2}{10}}{\frac{4}{1}}\right) - \left(\frac{3}{1} - \frac{\frac{1}{10}}{\frac{1}{1}}\right)} = \boxed{\left(\frac{\overset{7}{\cancel{14}}}{\underset{1}{\cancel{2}}} - \frac{2\times1}{10\times4}\right) - \left(\frac{3}{1} - \frac{1\times1}{10\times1}\right)} = \boxed{\left(\frac{7}{1} - \frac{2}{40}\right) - \left(\frac{3}{1} - \frac{1}{10}\right)}$$

$$= \boxed{\left(\frac{(7\times40)-(2\times1)}{1\times40}\right) - \left(\frac{(3\times10)-(1\times1)}{1\times10}\right)} = \boxed{\left(\frac{280-2}{40}\right) - \left(\frac{30-1}{10}\right)} = \boxed{\left(\frac{278}{40}\right) - \left(\frac{29}{10}\right)} = \boxed{\frac{\overset{139}{\cancel{278}}}{\underset{20}{\cancel{40}}} - \frac{29}{10}}$$

$$= \boxed{\frac{139}{20} - \frac{29}{10}} = \boxed{\frac{(139\times10)-(29\times20)}{20\times10}} = \boxed{\frac{1,390-580}{200}} = \boxed{\frac{\overset{81}{\cancel{810}}}{\underset{20}{\cancel{200}}}} = \boxed{\frac{81}{20}} = \boxed{4\frac{1}{20}}$$

Example 6.2-19

$$\boxed{\frac{6}{0.1} - \left(\frac{2}{5} - \frac{0.3}{2}\right)} = \boxed{\frac{6}{\frac{1}{10}} - \left(\frac{2}{5} - \frac{\frac{3}{10}}{\frac{2}{1}}\right)} = \boxed{\frac{6\times10}{1\times1} - \left(\frac{2}{5} - \frac{3\times1}{10\times2}\right)} = \boxed{\frac{60}{1} - \left(\frac{2}{5} - \frac{3}{20}\right)} = \boxed{\frac{60}{1} - \left(\frac{(2\times20)-(3\times5)}{5\times20}\right)}$$

$$= \boxed{\frac{60}{1} - \left(\frac{40-15}{100}\right)} = \boxed{\frac{60}{1} - \left(\frac{\overset{1}{\cancel{25}}}{\underset{4}{\cancel{100}}}\right)} = \boxed{\frac{60}{1} - \left(\frac{1}{4}\right)} = \boxed{\frac{60}{1} - \frac{1}{4}} = \boxed{\frac{(60\times4)-(1\times1)}{1\times4}} = \boxed{\frac{240-1}{4}} = \boxed{\frac{239}{4}} = \boxed{59\frac{3}{4}}$$

Example 6.2-20

$$\boxed{\left(\frac{5}{3} - \frac{1}{3}\right) - \left(\frac{0.2}{3} - \frac{0.1}{0.05}\right)} = \boxed{\left(\frac{5-1}{3}\right) - \left(\frac{\frac{2}{10}}{\frac{3}{1}} - \frac{\frac{1}{10}}{\frac{5}{100}}\right)} = \boxed{\left(\frac{4}{3}\right) - \left(\frac{2\times1}{10\times3} - \frac{1\times100}{10\times5}\right)} = \boxed{\frac{4}{3} - \left(\frac{2}{30} - \frac{100}{50}\right)}$$

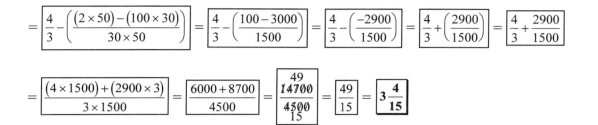

Example 6.2-21

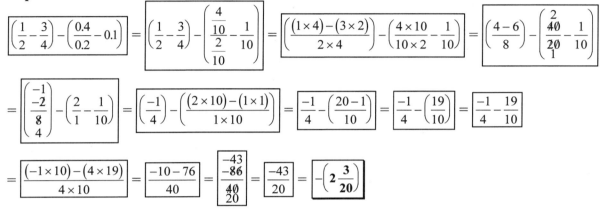

Section 6.2 Exercises - Subtract the following integer and decimal fractions:

1. $\dfrac{3}{8} - \dfrac{0.12}{0.3} =$

2. $\dfrac{0.3}{0.5} - \dfrac{4}{6} - 3 =$

3. $\left(\dfrac{5}{6} - \dfrac{1}{6}\right) - 1.25 =$

4. $\left(\dfrac{5}{2} - \dfrac{0.01}{0.4}\right) - \dfrac{3}{5} =$

5. $\dfrac{3}{4} - \dfrac{1}{3} - 0.2$

6. $\dfrac{5}{6} - \left(\dfrac{1}{10} - 0.01\right) =$

7. $8.5 - \dfrac{2}{10} - \dfrac{0.4}{0.5} =$

8. $12.5 - \left(\dfrac{3}{7} - \dfrac{2}{3}\right) =$

9. $\dfrac{0.2}{0.04} - \left(\dfrac{0.1}{2} - \dfrac{0.1}{4}\right) =$

10. $\left(\dfrac{8}{3} - \dfrac{4}{3}\right) - \left(\dfrac{0.4}{0.12} - \dfrac{2}{3}\right) =$

6.3   Multiplying Integer and Decimal Fractions

Two or more integer and decimal fractions of the forms:

1. $\left(\dfrac{a}{b}\right)$ where the numerator (a) and the denominator (b) are integers, and

2. $\left(\dfrac{a \times 10^{-k_1}}{b \times 10^{-k_2}}\right)$ where (a) and (b) are integer numbers and (k_1) and (k_2) are equal to the number

   of decimal places

are multiplied as in the following cases:

Case I   Multiplying Two Integer and Decimal Fractions

Multiply two integer and decimal fractions using the following steps:

Step 1   Change the integer number (a) to an integer fraction of the form $\left(\dfrac{a}{1}\right)$, e.g., change

119 to $\dfrac{119}{1}$.

Step 2   a. Change the decimal fraction to an integer fraction (see Section 2.4).

b. Change the decimal number $\left(a \times 10^{-k}\right)$ to an integer fraction of the form $\left(\dfrac{a}{10^k}\right)$,

e.g., change 23.8 to $\dfrac{238}{10}$.

Step 3   Multiply the integer fractions (see Section 3.3, Case I).

Step 4   Simplify the fraction to its lowest term (see Section 2.3).

Step 5   Change the improper fraction to a mixed fraction if the fraction obtained from Step 4 is an improper fraction (see Section 2.2).

The following examples show the steps as to how two integer and decimal fractions are multiplied:

Example 6.3-1

$$\boxed{\dfrac{12}{5} \times \dfrac{0.15}{0.6}} =$$

Solution:

Step 1 $\boxed{Not\ Applicable}$

Step 2a $\boxed{\dfrac{12}{5} \times \dfrac{0.15}{0.6}} = \boxed{\dfrac{12}{5} \times \dfrac{\frac{15}{100}}{\frac{6}{10}}} = \boxed{\dfrac{12}{5} \times \dfrac{15 \times 10}{100 \times 6}} = \boxed{\dfrac{12}{5} \times \dfrac{150}{600}}$

Step 2b $\boxed{Not\ Applicable}$

Step 3 $\boxed{\dfrac{12}{5} \times \dfrac{150}{600}} = \boxed{\dfrac{12 \times 150}{5 \times 600}} = \boxed{\dfrac{1800}{3000}}$

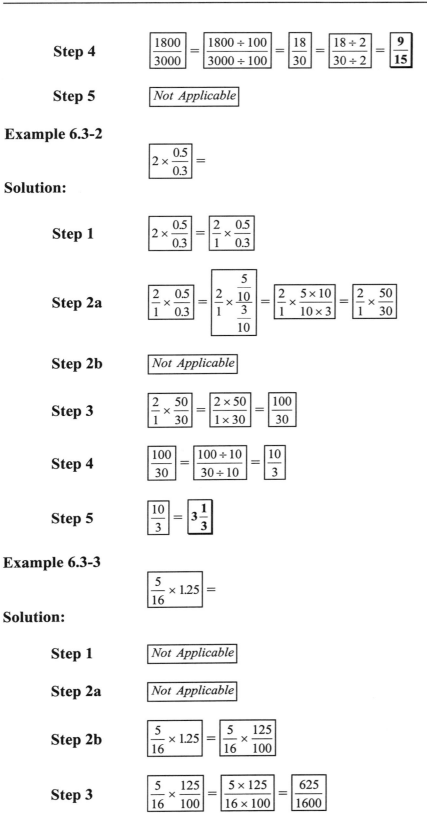

Step 4
$$\boxed{\frac{1800}{3000}} = \boxed{\frac{1800 \div 100}{3000 \div 100}} = \boxed{\frac{18}{30}} = \boxed{\frac{18 \div 2}{30 \div 2}} = \boxed{\frac{9}{15}}$$

Step 5 $\boxed{Not\ Applicable}$

Example 6.3-2
$$\boxed{2 \times \frac{0.5}{0.3}} =$$

Solution:

Step 1 $\boxed{2 \times \frac{0.5}{0.3}} = \boxed{\frac{2}{1} \times \frac{0.5}{0.3}}$

Step 2a $\boxed{\frac{2}{1} \times \frac{0.5}{0.3}} = \boxed{\frac{2}{1} \times \frac{\frac{5}{10}}{\frac{3}{10}}} = \boxed{\frac{2}{1} \times \frac{5 \times 10}{10 \times 3}} = \boxed{\frac{2}{1} \times \frac{50}{30}}$

Step 2b $\boxed{Not\ Applicable}$

Step 3 $\boxed{\frac{2}{1} \times \frac{50}{30}} = \boxed{\frac{2 \times 50}{1 \times 30}} = \boxed{\frac{100}{30}}$

Step 4 $\boxed{\frac{100}{30}} = \boxed{\frac{100 \div 10}{30 \div 10}} = \boxed{\frac{10}{3}}$

Step 5 $\boxed{\frac{10}{3}} = \boxed{3\frac{1}{3}}$

Example 6.3-3
$$\boxed{\frac{5}{16} \times 1.25} =$$

Solution:

Step 1 $\boxed{Not\ Applicable}$

Step 2a $\boxed{Not\ Applicable}$

Step 2b $\boxed{\frac{5}{16} \times 1.25} = \boxed{\frac{5}{16} \times \frac{125}{100}}$

Step 3 $\boxed{\frac{5}{16} \times \frac{125}{100}} = \boxed{\frac{5 \times 125}{16 \times 100}} = \boxed{\frac{625}{1600}}$

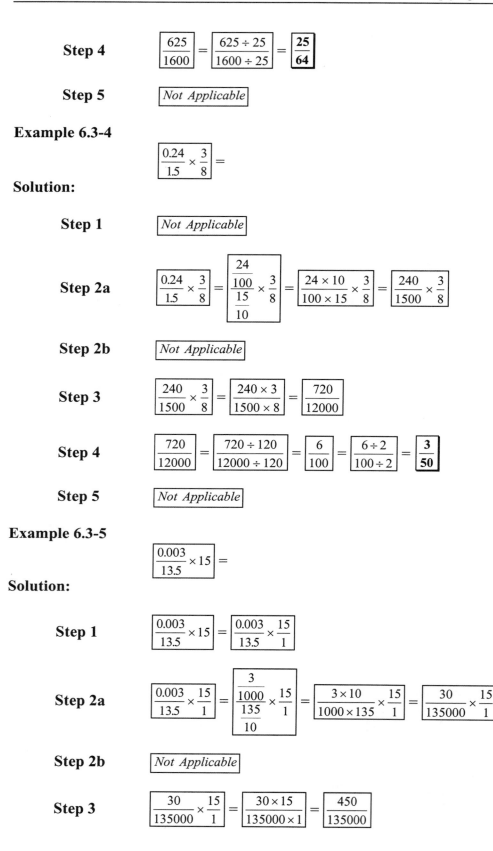

Step 4 $\dfrac{625}{1600} = \dfrac{625 \div 25}{1600 \div 25} = \boxed{\dfrac{25}{64}}$

Step 5   Not Applicable

Example 6.3-4

$\dfrac{0.24}{1.5} \times \dfrac{3}{8} =$

Solution:

Step 1   Not Applicable

Step 2a $\dfrac{0.24}{1.5} \times \dfrac{3}{8} = \dfrac{\dfrac{24}{100}}{\dfrac{15}{10}} \times \dfrac{3}{8} = \dfrac{24 \times 10}{100 \times 15} \times \dfrac{3}{8} = \dfrac{240}{1500} \times \dfrac{3}{8}$

Step 2b   Not Applicable

Step 3 $\dfrac{240}{1500} \times \dfrac{3}{8} = \dfrac{240 \times 3}{1500 \times 8} = \dfrac{720}{12000}$

Step 4 $\dfrac{720}{12000} = \dfrac{720 \div 120}{12000 \div 120} = \dfrac{6}{100} = \dfrac{6 \div 2}{100 \div 2} = \boxed{\dfrac{3}{50}}$

Step 5   Not Applicable

Example 6.3-5

$\dfrac{0.003}{13.5} \times 15 =$

Solution:

Step 1 $\dfrac{0.003}{13.5} \times 15 = \dfrac{0.003}{13.5} \times \dfrac{15}{1}$

Step 2a $\dfrac{0.003}{13.5} \times \dfrac{15}{1} = \dfrac{\dfrac{3}{1000}}{\dfrac{135}{10}} \times \dfrac{15}{1} = \dfrac{3 \times 10}{1000 \times 135} \times \dfrac{15}{1} = \dfrac{30}{135000} \times \dfrac{15}{1}$

Step 2b   Not Applicable

Step 3 $\dfrac{30}{135000} \times \dfrac{15}{1} = \dfrac{30 \times 15}{135000 \times 1} = \dfrac{450}{135000}$

Step 4 $\dfrac{450}{135000} = \dfrac{450 \div 450}{135000 \div 450} = \boxed{\dfrac{1}{300}}$

Step 5 $\boxed{Not\ Applicable}$

Case II   Multiplying Three Integer and Decimal Fractions

Multiply three integer and decimal fractions using the following steps:

Step 1   Change the integer number (a) an to integer fraction of the form $\left(\dfrac{a}{1}\right)$, e.g., change 26 to $\dfrac{26}{1}$.

Step 2   a. Change the decimal fraction(s) to integer fraction(s) (see Section 2.4).

b. Change the decimal number $\left(a \times 10^{-k}\right)$ to an integer fraction of the form $\left(\dfrac{a}{10^k}\right)$, e.g., change 0.25 to $\dfrac{25}{100}$.

Step 3   Multiply the integer fractions (see Section 3.3, Case II).

Step 4   Simplify the fraction to its lowest term (see Section 2.3).

Step 5   Change the improper fraction to a mixed fraction if the fraction obtained from Step 4 is an improper fraction (see Section 2.2).

The following examples show the steps as to how three integer and decimal fractions are multiplied:

Example 6.3-6

$\boxed{\dfrac{2}{5} \times 0.5 \times \dfrac{0.5}{0.8}} =$

Solution:

Step 1 $\boxed{Not\ Applicable}$

Step 2a $\boxed{\dfrac{2}{5} \times 0.5 \times \dfrac{0.5}{0.8}} = \boxed{\dfrac{2}{5} \times 0.5 \times \dfrac{\frac{5}{10}}{\frac{8}{10}}} = \boxed{\dfrac{2}{5} \times 0.5 \times \dfrac{5 \times 10}{10 \times 8}} = \boxed{\dfrac{2}{5} \times 0.5 \times \dfrac{50}{80}}$

Step 2b $\boxed{\dfrac{2}{5} \times 0.5 \times \dfrac{50}{80}} = \boxed{\dfrac{2}{5} \times \dfrac{5}{10} \times \dfrac{50}{80}}$

Step 3 $\boxed{\dfrac{2}{5} \times \dfrac{5}{10} \times \dfrac{50}{80}} = \boxed{\dfrac{2 \times 5 \times 50}{5 \times 10 \times 80}} = \boxed{\dfrac{500}{4000}}$

Step 4 $\boxed{\dfrac{500}{4000}} = \boxed{\dfrac{500 \div 500}{4000 \div 500}} = \boxed{\dfrac{1}{8}}$

Step 5 $\boxed{\textit{Not Applicable}}$

Example 6.3-7

$$\boxed{5 \times \dfrac{0.2}{0.08} \times \dfrac{4}{6}} =$$

Solution:

Step 1 $\boxed{5 \times \dfrac{0.2}{0.08} \times \dfrac{4}{6}} = \boxed{\dfrac{5}{1} \times \dfrac{0.2}{0.08} \times \dfrac{4}{6}}$

Step 2a $\boxed{\dfrac{5}{1} \times \dfrac{0.2}{0.08} \times \dfrac{4}{6}} = \boxed{\dfrac{5}{1} \times \dfrac{\dfrac{2}{10}}{\dfrac{8}{100}} \times \dfrac{4}{6}} = \boxed{\dfrac{5}{1} \times \dfrac{2 \times 100}{10 \times 8} \times \dfrac{4}{6}} = \boxed{\dfrac{5}{1} \times \dfrac{200}{80} \times \dfrac{4}{6}}$

Step 2b $\boxed{\textit{Not Applicable}}$

Step 3 $\boxed{\dfrac{5}{1} \times \dfrac{200}{80} \times \dfrac{4}{6}} = \boxed{\dfrac{5 \times 200 \times 4}{1 \times 80 \times 6}} = \boxed{\dfrac{4000}{480}}$

Step 4 $\boxed{\dfrac{4000}{480}} = \boxed{\dfrac{4000 \div 80}{480 \div 80}} = \boxed{\dfrac{50}{6}} = \boxed{\dfrac{50 \div 2}{6 \div 2}} = \boxed{\dfrac{25}{3}}$

Step 5 $\boxed{\dfrac{25}{3}} = \boxed{8\dfrac{1}{3}}$

Example 6.3-8

$$\boxed{\dfrac{5}{121} \times \dfrac{4.8}{0.06} \times \dfrac{3}{7}} =$$

Solution:

Step 1 $\boxed{\textit{Not Applicable}}$

Step 2a $\boxed{\dfrac{5}{121} \times \dfrac{4.8}{0.06} \times \dfrac{3}{7}} = \boxed{\dfrac{5}{121} \times \dfrac{\dfrac{48}{10}}{\dfrac{6}{100}} \times \dfrac{3}{7}} = \boxed{\dfrac{5}{121} \times \dfrac{48 \times 100}{10 \times 6} \times \dfrac{3}{7}} = \boxed{\dfrac{5}{121} \times \dfrac{4800}{60} \times \dfrac{3}{7}}$

Step 2b $\boxed{\textit{Not Applicable}}$

Step 3 $\boxed{\dfrac{5}{121} \times \dfrac{4800}{60} \times \dfrac{3}{7}} = \boxed{\dfrac{5 \times 4800 \times 3}{121 \times 60 \times 7}} = \boxed{\dfrac{72000}{50820}}$

Step 4 $\boxed{\dfrac{72000}{50820}} = \boxed{\dfrac{72000 \div 20}{50820 \div 20}} = \boxed{\dfrac{3600}{2541}} = \boxed{\dfrac{3600 \div 3}{2541 \div 3}} = \boxed{\dfrac{1200}{847}}$

Step 5 $\dfrac{1200}{847} = \boxed{1\dfrac{353}{847}}$

Example 6.3-9

$$12.45 \times \frac{0.2}{0.3} \times \frac{4}{5} =$$

Solution:

Step 1 $\boxed{Not\ Applicable}$

Step 2a $12.45 \times \dfrac{0.2}{0.3} \times \dfrac{4}{5} = 12.45 \times \dfrac{\frac{2}{10}}{\frac{3}{10}} \times \dfrac{4}{5} = 12.45 \times \dfrac{2 \times 10}{10 \times 3} \times \dfrac{4}{5} = 12.45 \times \dfrac{20}{30} \times \dfrac{4}{5}$

Step 2b $12.45 \times \dfrac{20}{30} \times \dfrac{4}{5} = \dfrac{1245}{100} \times \dfrac{20}{30} \times \dfrac{4}{5}$

Step 3 $\dfrac{1245}{100} \times \dfrac{20}{30} \times \dfrac{4}{5} = \dfrac{1245 \times 20 \times 4}{100 \times 30 \times 5} = \dfrac{99600}{15000}$

Step 4 $\dfrac{99600}{15000} = \dfrac{99600 \div 100}{15000 \div 100} = \dfrac{996}{150} = \dfrac{996 \div 2}{150 \div 2} = \dfrac{498}{75}$

Step 5 $\dfrac{498}{75} = \boxed{6\dfrac{48}{75}}$

Example 6.3-10

$$3 \times \frac{0.2}{0.6} \times 0.09 =$$

Solution:

Step 1 $3 \times \dfrac{0.2}{0.6} \times 0.09 = \dfrac{3}{1} \times \dfrac{0.2}{0.6} \times 0.09$

Step 2a $\dfrac{3}{1} \times \dfrac{0.2}{0.6} \times 0.09 = \dfrac{3}{1} \times \dfrac{\frac{2}{10}}{\frac{6}{10}} \times 0.09 = \dfrac{3}{1} \times \dfrac{2 \times 10}{10 \times 6} \times 0.09 = \dfrac{3}{1} \times \dfrac{20}{60} \times 0.09$

Step 2b $\dfrac{3}{1} \times \dfrac{20}{60} \times 0.09 = \dfrac{3}{1} \times \dfrac{20}{60} \times \dfrac{9}{100}$

Step 3 $\dfrac{3}{1} \times \dfrac{20}{60} \times \dfrac{9}{100} = \dfrac{3 \times 20 \times 9}{1 \times 60 \times 100} = \dfrac{540}{6000}$

Step 4 $\dfrac{540}{6000} = \dfrac{540 \div 20}{6000 \div 20} = \dfrac{27}{300} = \dfrac{27 \div 3}{300 \div 3} = \boxed{\dfrac{9}{100}}$

Step 5 $\boxed{Not \ Applicable}$

The following examples further illustrate how to multiply integer and decimal fractions:

Example 6.3-11

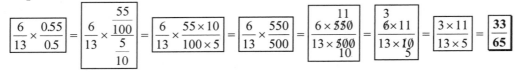

Example 6.3-12

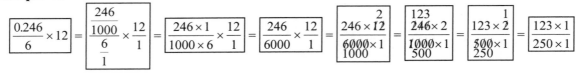

 $= \boxed{\dfrac{123}{250}}$

Example 6.3-13

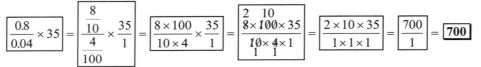

Example 6.3-14

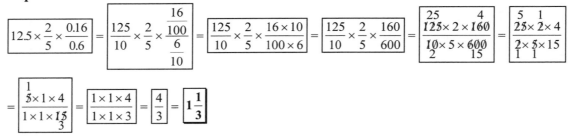

Example 6.3-15

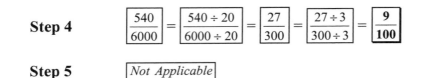

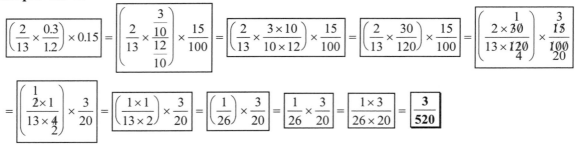

Example 6.3-16

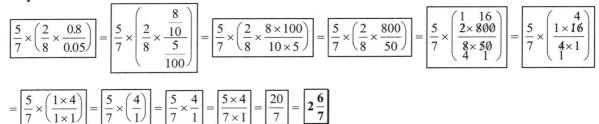

$$\frac{3}{5} \times \frac{5}{6} \times \frac{0.1}{0.02} = \frac{3}{5} \times \frac{5}{6} \times \frac{\frac{1}{10}}{\frac{2}{100}} = \frac{3}{5} \times \frac{5}{6} \times \frac{1 \times 100}{10 \times 2} = \frac{3}{5} \times \frac{5}{6} \times \frac{100}{20} = \frac{\overset{1}{3} \times \overset{1}{5} \times \overset{5}{100}}{\underset{1}{5} \times \underset{2}{6} \times \underset{1}{20}} = \frac{1 \times 1 \times 5}{1 \times 2 \times 1} = \frac{5}{2} = \boxed{2\frac{1}{2}}$$

Example 6.3-17

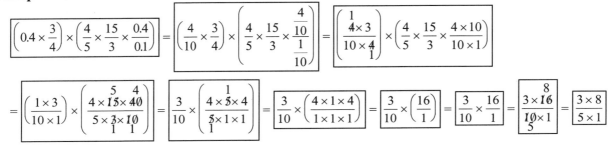

$$\frac{5}{7} \times \left(\frac{2}{8} \times \frac{0.8}{0.05} \right) = \frac{5}{7} \times \left(\frac{2}{8} \times \frac{\frac{8}{10}}{\frac{5}{100}} \right) = \frac{5}{7} \times \left(\frac{2}{8} \times \frac{8 \times 100}{10 \times 5} \right) = \frac{5}{7} \times \left(\frac{2}{8} \times \frac{800}{50} \right) = \frac{5}{7} \times \left(\frac{\overset{1}{2} \times \overset{16}{800}}{\underset{4}{8} \times \underset{1}{50}} \right) = \frac{5}{7} \times \left(\frac{\overset{4}{1 \times 16}}{\underset{1}{4 \times 1}} \right)$$

$$= \frac{5}{7} \times \left(\frac{1 \times 4}{1 \times 1} \right) = \frac{5}{7} \times \left(\frac{4}{1} \right) = \frac{5}{7} \times \frac{4}{1} = \frac{5 \times 4}{7 \times 1} = \frac{20}{7} = \boxed{2\frac{6}{7}}$$

Example 6.3-18

$$\left(0.4 \times \frac{3}{4} \right) \times \left(\frac{4}{5} \times \frac{15}{3} \times \frac{0.4}{0.1} \right) = \left(\frac{4}{10} \times \frac{3}{4} \right) \times \left(\frac{4}{5} \times \frac{15}{3} \times \frac{\frac{4}{10}}{\frac{1}{10}} \right) = \left(\frac{\overset{1}{4} \times 3}{10 \times \underset{1}{4}} \right) \times \left(\frac{4}{5} \times \frac{15}{3} \times \frac{4 \times 10}{10 \times 1} \right)$$

$$= \left(\frac{1 \times 3}{10 \times 1} \right) \times \left(\frac{4 \times \overset{5}{15} \times \overset{4}{40}}{5 \times \underset{1}{3} \times \underset{1}{10}} \right) = \frac{3}{10} \times \left(\frac{4 \times \overset{1}{5} \times 4}{\underset{1}{5} \times 1 \times 1} \right) = \frac{3}{10} \times \left(\frac{4 \times 1 \times 4}{1 \times 1 \times 1} \right) = \frac{3}{10} \times \left(\frac{16}{1} \right) = \frac{3}{10} \times \frac{16}{1} = \frac{3 \times \overset{8}{16}}{\underset{5}{10} \times 1} = \frac{3 \times 8}{5 \times 1}$$

$$= \frac{24}{5} = \boxed{4\frac{4}{5}}$$

Example 6.3-19

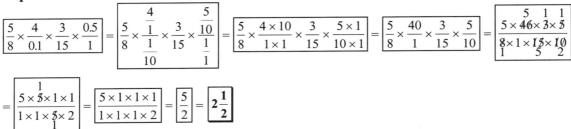

$$\frac{5}{8} \times \frac{4}{0.1} \times \frac{3}{15} \times \frac{0.5}{1} = \frac{5}{8} \times \frac{4}{\frac{1}{10}} \times \frac{3}{15} \times \frac{\frac{5}{10}}{\frac{1}{1}} = \frac{5}{8} \times \frac{4 \times 10}{1 \times 1} \times \frac{3}{15} \times \frac{5 \times 1}{10 \times 1} = \frac{5}{8} \times \frac{40}{1} \times \frac{3}{15} \times \frac{5}{10} = \frac{5 \times \overset{5}{40} \times \overset{1}{3} \times \overset{1}{5}}{8 \times 1 \times \underset{5}{15} \times \underset{2}{10}}$$

$$= \frac{5 \times \overset{1}{5} \times 1 \times 1}{1 \times 1 \times \underset{1}{5} \times 2} = \frac{5 \times 1 \times 1 \times 1}{1 \times 1 \times 1 \times 2} = \frac{5}{2} = \boxed{2\frac{1}{2}}$$

Example 6.3-20

$$\left(\frac{3}{8} \times 0.2 \times \frac{1}{0.3} \right) \times 0.004 = \left(\frac{3}{8} \times \frac{2}{10} \times \frac{1}{\frac{3}{10}} \right) \times \frac{4}{1000} = \left(\frac{3}{8} \times \frac{2}{10} \times \frac{1 \times 10}{1 \times 3} \right) \times \frac{4}{1000} = \left(\frac{3}{8} \times \frac{2}{10} \times \frac{10}{3} \right) \times \frac{4}{1000}$$

$$= \left(\frac{\overset{1}{3} \times \overset{1}{2} \times \overset{1}{10}}{\underset{4}{8} \times \underset{1}{10} \times \underset{1}{3}} \right) \times \frac{4}{1000} = \left(\frac{1 \times 1 \times 1}{4 \times 1 \times 1} \right) \times \frac{4}{1000} = \left(\frac{1}{4} \right) \times \frac{4}{1000} = \frac{1}{4} \times \frac{4}{1000} = \frac{1 \times \overset{1}{4}}{4 \times 1000} = \frac{1 \times 1}{1 \times 1000} = \boxed{\frac{1}{1000}}$$

Example 6.3-21

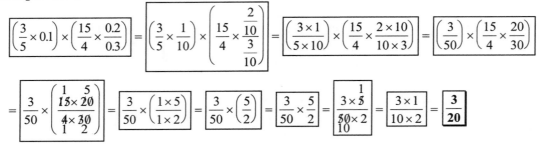

$$\left[\left(\frac{3}{5}\times0.1\right)\times\left(\frac{15}{4}\times\frac{0.2}{0.3}\right)\right]=\left[\left(\frac{3}{5}\times\frac{1}{10}\right)\times\left(\frac{15}{4}\times\frac{\frac{2}{10}}{\frac{3}{10}}\right)\right]=\left[\left(\frac{3\times1}{5\times10}\right)\times\left(\frac{15}{4}\times\frac{2\times10}{10\times3}\right)\right]=\left[\left(\frac{3}{50}\right)\times\left(\frac{15}{4}\times\frac{20}{30}\right)\right]$$

$$=\left[\frac{3}{50}\times\left(\frac{\overset{1}{\cancel{15}}\times\overset{5}{\cancel{20}}}{\underset{1}{\cancel{4}}\times\underset{2}{\cancel{30}}}\right)\right]=\left[\frac{3}{50}\times\left(\frac{1\times5}{1\times2}\right)\right]=\left[\frac{3}{50}\times\left(\frac{5}{2}\right)\right]=\left[\frac{3}{50}\times\frac{5}{2}\right]=\left[\frac{3\times\overset{1}{\cancel{5}}}{\underset{10}{\cancel{50}}\times2}\right]=\left[\frac{3\times1}{10\times2}\right]=\boxed{\frac{3}{20}}$$

Section 6.3 Exercises - Multiply the following integer and decimal fractions:

1. $\dfrac{3}{5}\times\dfrac{0.05}{0.1}=$

2. $5\times\dfrac{0.22}{0.001}\times\dfrac{1}{100}=$

3. $\left(\dfrac{2}{8}\times0.4\right)\times\dfrac{10}{2}=$

4. $\dfrac{2}{0.04}\times\left(\dfrac{0.5}{0.01}\times\dfrac{1}{4}\right)=$

5. $\dfrac{5}{8}\times0.8\times\dfrac{3}{0.05}=$

6. $\left(\dfrac{5}{3}\times0\right)\times\left(0.3\times\dfrac{1}{0.03}\right)=$

7. $\dfrac{7}{3}\times\left(\dfrac{1}{0.7}\times\dfrac{0.3}{5}\right)=$

8. $\left(\dfrac{5}{1}\times\dfrac{1}{3}\right)\times\left(0.03\times\dfrac{10}{0.2}\right)=$

9. $\dfrac{4}{3}\times\dfrac{0.3}{2}\times\dfrac{10}{0.1}\times0.4=$

10. $\left(\dfrac{3}{8}\times0.2\right)\times\left(2\times\dfrac{8}{6}\times\dfrac{1}{0.04}\right)=$

6.4   Dividing Integer and Decimal Fractions

Two or more integer and decimal fractions of the forms:

1. $\left(\dfrac{a}{b}\right)$ where the numerator (a) and the denominator (b) are integers, and

2. $\left(\dfrac{a \times 10^{-k_1}}{b \times 10^{-k_2}}\right)$ where (a) and (b) are integer numbers and (k_1) and (k_2) are equal to the number

of decimal places

are divided as in the following cases:

Case I   Dividing Two Integer and Decimal Fractions

Divide two integer and decimal fractions using the following steps:

Step 1   Change the integer number (a) to an integer fraction of the form $\left(\dfrac{a}{1}\right)$, e.g., change

238 to $\dfrac{238}{1}$.

Step 2   a. Change the decimal fraction to an integer fraction (see Section 2.4).

b. Change the decimal number $\left(a \times 10^{-k}\right)$ to an integer fraction of the form $\left(\dfrac{a}{10^k}\right)$,

e.g., change 22.13 to $\dfrac{2213}{100}$.

Step 3   Divide the integer fractions (see Section 3.4, Case I).

Step 4   Simplify the fraction to its lowest term (see Section 2.3).

Step 5   Change the improper fraction to a mixed fraction if the fraction obtained from Step 4 is an improper fraction (see Section 2.2).

The following examples show the steps as to how two integer and decimal fractions are divided:

Example 6.4-1

$$\boxed{0.5 \div \dfrac{2}{3} =}$$

Solution:

Step 1 $\boxed{\textit{Not Applicable}}$

Step 2a $\boxed{\textit{Not Applicable}}$

Step 2b $\boxed{0.5 \div \dfrac{2}{3}} = \boxed{\dfrac{5}{10} \div \dfrac{2}{3}}$

Step 3 $\boxed{\dfrac{5}{10} \div \dfrac{2}{3}} = \boxed{\dfrac{5}{10} \times \dfrac{3}{2}} = \boxed{\dfrac{5 \times 3}{10 \times 2}} = \boxed{\dfrac{15}{20}}$

Step 4 $\boxed{\dfrac{15}{20}} = \boxed{\dfrac{15 \div 5}{10 \div 5}} = \boxed{\dfrac{3}{4}}$

Step 5 $\boxed{Not\ Applicable}$

Example 6.4-2

$$\boxed{\dfrac{0.3}{0.5} \div \dfrac{5}{6}} =$$

Solution:

Step 1 $\boxed{Not\ Applicable}$

Step 2a $\boxed{\dfrac{0.3}{0.5} \div \dfrac{5}{6}} = \boxed{\dfrac{\dfrac{3}{10}}{\dfrac{5}{10}} \div \dfrac{5}{6}} = \boxed{\dfrac{3 \times 10}{10 \times 5} \div \dfrac{5}{6}} = \boxed{\dfrac{30}{50} \div \dfrac{5}{6}}$

Step 2b $\boxed{Not\ Applicable}$

Step 3 $\boxed{\dfrac{30}{50} \div \dfrac{5}{6}} = \boxed{\dfrac{30}{50} \times \dfrac{6}{5}} = \boxed{\dfrac{30 \times 6}{50 \times 5}} = \boxed{\dfrac{180}{250}}$

Step 4 $\boxed{\dfrac{180}{250}} = \boxed{\dfrac{180 \div 10}{250 \div 10}} = \boxed{\mathbf{\dfrac{18}{25}}}$

Step 5 $\boxed{Not\ Applicable}$

Example 6.4-3

$$\boxed{\dfrac{5}{24} \div \dfrac{0.06}{1.4}} =$$

Solution:

Step 1 $\boxed{Not\ Applicable}$

Step 2a $\boxed{\dfrac{5}{24} \div \dfrac{0.06}{1.4}} = \boxed{\dfrac{5}{24} \div \dfrac{\dfrac{6}{100}}{\dfrac{14}{10}}} = \boxed{\dfrac{5}{24} \div \dfrac{6 \times 10}{100 \times 14}} = \boxed{\dfrac{5}{24} \div \dfrac{60}{1400}}$

Step 2b $\boxed{Not\ Applicable}$

Step 3 $\boxed{\dfrac{5}{24} \div \dfrac{60}{1400}} = \boxed{\dfrac{5}{24} \times \dfrac{1400}{60}} = \boxed{\dfrac{5 \times 1400}{24 \times 60}} = \boxed{\dfrac{7000}{1440}}$

Step 4 $\boxed{\dfrac{7000}{1440}} = \boxed{\dfrac{7000 \div 40}{1440 \div 40}} = \boxed{\dfrac{175}{36}}$

Step 5 $\boxed{\dfrac{175}{36}} = \boxed{4\dfrac{31}{36}}$

Example 6.4-4

$\boxed{132 \div \dfrac{1.2}{0.006}} =$

Solution:

Step 1 $\boxed{132 \div \dfrac{1.2}{0.006}} = \boxed{\dfrac{132}{1} \div \dfrac{1.2}{0.006}}$

Step 2a $\boxed{\dfrac{132}{1} \div \dfrac{1.2}{0.006}} = \boxed{\dfrac{132}{1} \div \dfrac{\dfrac{12}{10}}{\dfrac{6}{1000}}} = \boxed{\dfrac{132}{1} \div \dfrac{12 \times 1000}{10 \times 6}} = \boxed{\dfrac{132}{1} \div \dfrac{12000}{60}}$

Step 2b $\boxed{\textit{Not Applicable}}$

Step 3 $\boxed{\dfrac{132}{1} \div \dfrac{12000}{60}} = \boxed{\dfrac{132}{1} \times \dfrac{60}{12000}} = \boxed{\dfrac{132 \times 60}{1 \times 12000}} = \boxed{\dfrac{7920}{12000}}$

Step 4 $\boxed{\dfrac{7920}{12000}} = \boxed{\dfrac{7920 \div 80}{12000 \div 80}} = \boxed{\dfrac{99}{150}} = \boxed{\dfrac{99 \div 3}{150 \div 3}} = \boxed{\dfrac{33}{50}}$

Step 5 $\boxed{\textit{Not Applicable}}$

Example 6.4-5

$\boxed{\dfrac{2.4}{0.05} \div 16} =$

Solution:

Step 1 $\boxed{\dfrac{2.4}{0.05} \div 16} = \boxed{\dfrac{2.4}{0.05} \div \dfrac{16}{1}}$

Step 2a $\boxed{\dfrac{2.4}{0.05} \div \dfrac{16}{1}} = \boxed{\dfrac{\dfrac{24}{10}}{\dfrac{5}{100}} \div \dfrac{16}{1}} = \boxed{\dfrac{24 \times 100}{10 \times 5} \div \dfrac{16}{1}} = \boxed{\dfrac{2400}{50} \div \dfrac{16}{1}}$

Step 2b $\boxed{\textit{Not Applicable}}$

Step 3 $\boxed{\dfrac{2400}{50} \div \dfrac{16}{1}} = \boxed{\dfrac{2400}{50} \times \dfrac{1}{16}} = \boxed{\dfrac{2400 \times 1}{50 \times 16}} = \boxed{\dfrac{2400}{800}}$

Step 4 $\boxed{\dfrac{2400}{800}} = \boxed{\dfrac{2400 \div 800}{800 \div 800}} = \boxed{\dfrac{3}{1}} = \boxed{3}$

Step 5 $\boxed{\textit{Not Applicable}}$

Case II   Dividing Three Integer and Decimal Fractions

Divide three integer and decimal fractions using the following steps:

Step 1   Change the integer number (a) to an integer fraction of the form $\left(\dfrac{a}{1}\right)$, e.g., change

22 to $\dfrac{22}{1}$.

Step 2   a. Change the decimal fraction(s) to integer fraction(s) (see Section 2.4).

b. Change the decimal number $\left(a \times 10^{-k}\right)$ to an integer fraction of the form $\left(\dfrac{a}{10^k}\right)$,

e.g., change 26.5 to $\dfrac{265}{10}$.

Step 3   Divide the integer fractions (see Section 3.4, Case II).

Step 4   Simplify the fraction to its lowest term (see Section 2.3).

Step 5   Change the improper fraction to a mixed fraction if the fraction obtained from Step 4 is an improper fraction (see Section 2.2).

The following examples show the steps as to how three integer and decimal fractions are divided:

Example 6.4-6

$$\boxed{\left(0.5 \div \frac{3}{8}\right) \div \frac{0.6}{0.5}} =$$

Solution:

Step 1 $\boxed{\textit{Not Applicable}}$

Step 2a $\boxed{\left(0.5 \div \frac{3}{8}\right) \div \frac{0.6}{0.5}} = \boxed{\left(0.5 \div \frac{3}{8}\right) \div \frac{\frac{6}{10}}{\frac{5}{10}}} = \boxed{\left(0.5 \div \frac{3}{8}\right) \div \frac{6 \times 10}{10 \times 5}} = \boxed{\left(0.5 \div \frac{3}{8}\right) \div \frac{60}{50}}$

Step 2b $\boxed{\left(0.5 \div \frac{3}{8}\right) \div \frac{60}{50}} = \boxed{\left(\frac{5}{10} \div \frac{3}{8}\right) \div \frac{60}{50}}$

Step 3 $\boxed{\left(\frac{5}{10} \div \frac{3}{8}\right) \div \frac{60}{50}} = \boxed{\left(\frac{5}{10} \times \frac{8}{3}\right) \div \frac{60}{50}} = \boxed{\left(\frac{5 \times 8}{10 \times 3}\right) \div \frac{60}{50}} = \boxed{\left(\frac{40}{30}\right) \div \frac{60}{50}} = \boxed{\frac{40}{30} \div \frac{60}{50}}$

$= \boxed{\frac{40}{30} \times \frac{50}{60}} = \boxed{\frac{40 \times 50}{30 \times 60}} = \boxed{\frac{2000}{1800}}$

Step 4 $\boxed{\frac{2000}{1800}} = \boxed{\frac{2000 \div 200}{1800 \div 200}} = \boxed{\frac{10}{9}}$

Step 5
$$\boxed{\frac{10}{9}} = \boxed{1\frac{1}{9}}$$

Example 6.4-7
$$\boxed{\frac{4}{5} \div \left(\frac{12.4}{0.5} \div \frac{0.6}{0.04} \right)} =$$

Solution:

Step 1 $\boxed{\textit{Not Applicable}}$

Step 2a
$$\boxed{\frac{4}{5} \div \left(\frac{12.4}{0.5} \div \frac{0.6}{0.04} \right)} = \boxed{\frac{4}{5} \div \left(\frac{\frac{124}{10}}{\frac{5}{10}} \div \frac{\frac{6}{10}}{\frac{4}{100}} \right)} = \boxed{\frac{4}{5} \div \left(\frac{124 \times 10}{10 \times 5} \div \frac{6 \times 100}{10 \times 4} \right)}$$

$$= \boxed{\frac{4}{5} \div \left(\frac{1240}{50} \div \frac{600}{40} \right)}$$

Step 2b $\boxed{\textit{Not Applicable}}$

Step 3
$$\boxed{\frac{4}{5} \div \left(\frac{1240}{50} \div \frac{600}{40} \right)} = \boxed{\frac{4}{5} \div \left(\frac{1240}{50} \times \frac{40}{600} \right)} = \boxed{\frac{4}{5} \div \left(\frac{1240 \times 40}{50 \times 600} \right)} = \boxed{\frac{4}{5} \div \left(\frac{49600}{30000} \right)}$$

$$= \boxed{\frac{4}{5} \div \frac{49600}{30000}} = \boxed{\frac{4}{5} \times \frac{30000}{49600}} = \boxed{\frac{4 \times 30000}{5 \times 49600}} = \boxed{\frac{120000}{248000}}$$

Step 4
$$\boxed{\frac{120000}{248000}} = \boxed{\frac{120000 \div 1000}{248000 \div 1000}} = \boxed{\frac{120}{248}} = \boxed{\frac{120 \div 8}{248 \div 8}} = \boxed{\mathbf{\frac{15}{31}}}$$

Step 5 $\boxed{\textit{Not Applicable}}$

Example 6.4-8
$$\boxed{\left(\frac{0.6}{0.07} \div 0.3 \right) \div \frac{3}{8}} =$$

Solution:

Step 1 $\boxed{\textit{Not Applicable}}$

Step 2a
$$\boxed{\left(\frac{0.6}{0.07} \div 0.3 \right) \div \frac{3}{8}} = \boxed{\left(\frac{\frac{6}{10}}{\frac{7}{100}} \div 0.3 \right) \div \frac{3}{8}} = \boxed{\left(\frac{6 \times 100}{10 \times 7} \div 0.3 \right) \div \frac{3}{8}} = \boxed{\left(\frac{600}{70} \div 0.3 \right) \div \frac{3}{8}}$$

Step 2b $\left(\dfrac{600}{70} \div 0.3\right) \div \dfrac{3}{8} = \left[\left(\dfrac{600}{70} \div \dfrac{3}{10}\right) \div \dfrac{3}{8}\right]$

Step 3 $\left(\dfrac{600}{70} \div \dfrac{3}{10}\right) \div \dfrac{3}{8} = \left[\left(\dfrac{600}{70} \times \dfrac{10}{3}\right) \div \dfrac{3}{8}\right] = \left[\left(\dfrac{600 \times 10}{70 \times 3}\right) \div \dfrac{3}{8}\right] = \left[\left(\dfrac{6000}{210}\right) \div \dfrac{3}{8}\right] = \left[\dfrac{6000}{210} \div \dfrac{3}{8}\right]$

$= \left[\dfrac{6000}{210} \times \dfrac{8}{3}\right] = \left[\dfrac{6000 \times 8}{210 \times 3}\right] = \left[\dfrac{48000}{630}\right]$

Step 4 $\dfrac{48000}{630} = \dfrac{48000 \div 10}{630 \div 10} = \dfrac{4800}{63} = \dfrac{4800 \div 3}{63 \div 3} = \dfrac{1600}{21}$

Step 5 $\dfrac{1600}{21} = \boxed{76\dfrac{4}{21}}$

Example 6.4-9

$\left[\left(\dfrac{0.9}{0.5} \div \dfrac{5}{3}\right) \div 6\right] =$

Solution:

Step 1 $\left(\dfrac{0.9}{0.5} \div \dfrac{5}{3}\right) \div 6 = \left[\left(\dfrac{0.9}{0.5} \div \dfrac{5}{3}\right) \div \dfrac{6}{1}\right]$

Step 2a $\left(\dfrac{0.9}{0.5} \div \dfrac{5}{3}\right) \div \dfrac{6}{1} = \left[\left(\dfrac{\dfrac{9}{10}}{\dfrac{5}{10}} \div \dfrac{5}{3}\right) \div \dfrac{6}{1}\right] = \left[\left(\dfrac{9 \times 10}{10 \times 5} \div \dfrac{5}{3}\right) \div \dfrac{6}{1}\right] = \left[\left(\dfrac{90}{50} \div \dfrac{5}{3}\right) \div \dfrac{6}{1}\right]$

Step 2b   *Not Applicable*

Step 3 $\left(\dfrac{90}{50} \div \dfrac{5}{3}\right) \div \dfrac{6}{1} = \left[\left(\dfrac{90}{50} \times \dfrac{3}{5}\right) \div \dfrac{6}{1}\right] = \left[\left(\dfrac{90 \times 3}{50 \times 5}\right) \div \dfrac{6}{1}\right] = \left[\left(\dfrac{270}{250}\right) \div \dfrac{6}{1}\right] = \left[\dfrac{270}{250} \div \dfrac{6}{1}\right]$

$= \left[\dfrac{270}{250} \times \dfrac{1}{6}\right] = \left[\dfrac{270 \times 1}{250 \times 6}\right] = \left[\dfrac{270}{1500}\right]$

Step 4 $\dfrac{270}{1500} = \dfrac{270 \div 30}{1500 \div 30} = \boxed{\dfrac{9}{50}}$

Step 5   *Not Applicable*

Example 6.4-10

$\dfrac{0.8}{0.12} \div \left(\dfrac{6}{8} \div 36\right) =$

Solution:

Step 1
$$\boxed{\dfrac{0.8}{0.12} \div \left(\dfrac{6}{8} \div 36\right)} = \boxed{\dfrac{0.8}{0.12} \div \left(\dfrac{6}{8} \div \dfrac{36}{1}\right)}$$

Step 2a
$$\boxed{\dfrac{0.8}{0.12} \div \left(\dfrac{6}{8} \div \dfrac{36}{1}\right)} = \boxed{\dfrac{\frac{8}{10}}{\frac{12}{100}} \div \left(\dfrac{6}{8} \div \dfrac{36}{1}\right)} = \boxed{\dfrac{8 \times 100}{10 \times 12} \div \left(\dfrac{6}{8} \div \dfrac{36}{1}\right)} = \boxed{\dfrac{800}{120} \div \left(\dfrac{6}{8} \div \dfrac{36}{1}\right)}$$

Step 2b
$\boxed{\textit{Not Applicable}}$

Step 3
$$\boxed{\dfrac{800}{120} \div \left(\dfrac{6}{8} \div \dfrac{36}{1}\right)} = \boxed{\dfrac{800}{120} \div \left(\dfrac{6}{8} \times \dfrac{1}{36}\right)} = \boxed{\dfrac{800}{120} \div \left(\dfrac{6 \times 1}{8 \times 36}\right)} = \boxed{\dfrac{800}{120} \div \left(\dfrac{6}{288}\right)} = \boxed{\dfrac{800}{120} \div \dfrac{6}{288}}$$

$$= \boxed{\dfrac{800}{120} \times \dfrac{288}{6}} = \boxed{\dfrac{800 \times 288}{120 \times 6}} = \boxed{\dfrac{230400}{720}}$$

Step 4
$$\boxed{\dfrac{230400}{720}} = \boxed{\dfrac{230400 \div 720}{720 \div 720}} = \boxed{\dfrac{320}{1}} = \boxed{\mathbf{320}}$$

Step 5
$\boxed{\textit{Not Applicable}}$

The following examples further illustrate how to divide integer and decimal fractions:

Example 6.4-11

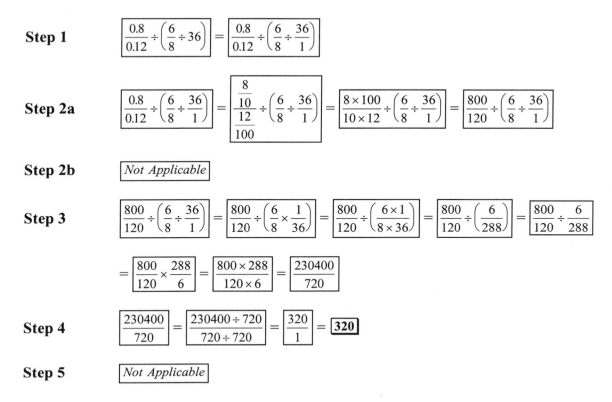

$$\boxed{\dfrac{3}{8} \div \dfrac{0.12}{0.5}} = \boxed{\dfrac{3}{8} \div \dfrac{\frac{12}{100}}{\frac{5}{10}}} = \boxed{\dfrac{3}{8} \div \dfrac{12 \times 10}{100 \times 5}} = \boxed{\dfrac{3}{8} \div \dfrac{120}{500}} = \boxed{\dfrac{3}{8} \times \dfrac{500}{120}} = \boxed{\dfrac{\overset{1}{3} \times \overset{125}{\cancel{500}}}{\underset{2}{\cancel{8}} \times \underset{40}{\cancel{120}}}} = \boxed{\dfrac{1 \times 125}{2 \times 40}} = \boxed{\dfrac{\overset{25}{\cancel{125}}}{\underset{16}{\cancel{80}}}} = \boxed{\dfrac{25}{16}} = \boxed{\mathbf{1\dfrac{9}{16}}}$$

Example 6.4-12

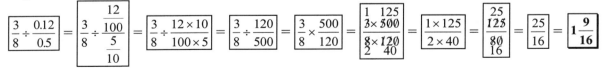

$$\boxed{\dfrac{2}{5} \div 12.5} = \boxed{\dfrac{2}{5} \div \dfrac{125}{10}} = \boxed{\dfrac{2}{5} \div \dfrac{\overset{25}{\cancel{125}}}{\underset{2}{\cancel{10}}}} = \boxed{\dfrac{2}{5} \div \dfrac{25}{2}} = \boxed{\dfrac{2}{5} \times \dfrac{2}{25}} = \boxed{\dfrac{2 \times 2}{5 \times 25}} = \boxed{\dfrac{\mathbf{4}}{\mathbf{125}}}$$

Example 6.4-13

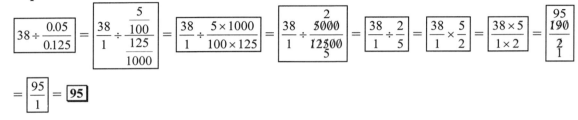

$$\boxed{38 \div \dfrac{0.05}{0.125}} = \boxed{\dfrac{38}{1} \div \dfrac{\frac{5}{100}}{\frac{125}{1000}}} = \boxed{\dfrac{38}{1} \div \dfrac{5 \times 1000}{100 \times 125}} = \boxed{\dfrac{38}{1} \div \dfrac{\overset{2}{\cancel{5000}}}{\underset{5}{\cancel{12500}}}} = \boxed{\dfrac{38}{1} \div \dfrac{2}{5}} = \boxed{\dfrac{38}{1} \times \dfrac{5}{2}} = \boxed{\dfrac{38 \times 5}{1 \times 2}} = \boxed{\dfrac{\overset{95}{\cancel{190}}}{\underset{1}{\cancel{2}}}}$$

$$= \boxed{\dfrac{95}{1}} = \boxed{\mathbf{95}}$$

Example 6.4-14

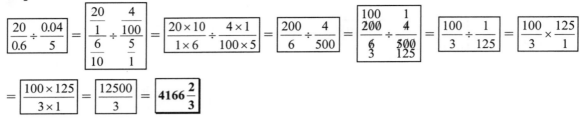

$$\boxed{\frac{\dfrac{20}{0.6} \div \dfrac{0.04}{5}}} = \boxed{\dfrac{\dfrac{20}{1}}{\dfrac{6}{10}} \div \dfrac{\dfrac{4}{100}}{\dfrac{5}{1}}} = \boxed{\dfrac{20 \times 10}{1 \times 6} \div \dfrac{4 \times 1}{100 \times 5}} = \boxed{\dfrac{200}{6} \div \dfrac{4}{500}} = \boxed{\dfrac{\overset{100}{\cancel{200}}}{\underset{3}{\cancel{6}}} \div \dfrac{\overset{1}{\cancel{4}}}{\underset{125}{\cancel{500}}}} = \boxed{\dfrac{100}{3} \div \dfrac{1}{125}} = \boxed{\dfrac{100}{3} \times \dfrac{125}{1}}$$

$$= \boxed{\dfrac{100 \times 125}{3 \times 1}} = \boxed{\dfrac{12500}{3}} = \boxed{\mathbf{4166\dfrac{2}{3}}}$$

Example 6.4-15

$$\boxed{\dfrac{0.3}{2} \div 8.024} = \boxed{\dfrac{\dfrac{3}{10}}{\dfrac{2}{1}} \div \dfrac{8024}{1000}} = \boxed{\dfrac{3 \times 1}{10 \times 2} \div \dfrac{\overset{1003}{\cancel{8024}}}{\underset{125}{\cancel{1000}}}} = \boxed{\dfrac{3}{20} \div \dfrac{1003}{125}} = \boxed{\dfrac{3}{20} \times \dfrac{125}{1003}} = \boxed{\dfrac{3 \times 125}{20 \times 1003}} = \boxed{\dfrac{\overset{75}{\cancel{375}}}{\underset{4012}{\cancel{20060}}}} = \boxed{\mathbf{\dfrac{75}{4012}}}$$

Example 6.4-16

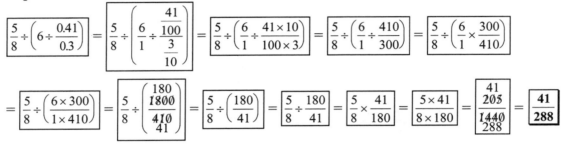

$$\boxed{\dfrac{5}{8} \div \left(6 \div \dfrac{0.41}{0.3}\right)} = \boxed{\dfrac{5}{8} \div \left(\dfrac{6}{1} \div \dfrac{\dfrac{41}{100}}{\dfrac{3}{10}}\right)} = \boxed{\dfrac{5}{8} \div \left(\dfrac{6}{1} \div \dfrac{41 \times 10}{100 \times 3}\right)} = \boxed{\dfrac{5}{8} \div \left(\dfrac{6}{1} \div \dfrac{410}{300}\right)} = \boxed{\dfrac{5}{8} \div \left(\dfrac{6}{1} \times \dfrac{300}{410}\right)}$$

$$= \boxed{\dfrac{5}{8} \div \left(\dfrac{6 \times 300}{1 \times 410}\right)} = \boxed{\dfrac{5}{8} \div \left(\dfrac{\overset{180}{\cancel{1800}}}{\underset{41}{\cancel{410}}}\right)} = \boxed{\dfrac{5}{8} \div \left(\dfrac{180}{41}\right)} = \boxed{\dfrac{5}{8} \div \dfrac{180}{41}} = \boxed{\dfrac{5}{8} \times \dfrac{41}{180}} = \boxed{\dfrac{5 \times 41}{8 \times 180}} = \boxed{\dfrac{\overset{41}{\cancel{205}}}{\underset{288}{\cancel{1440}}}} = \boxed{\mathbf{\dfrac{41}{288}}}$$

Example 6.4-17

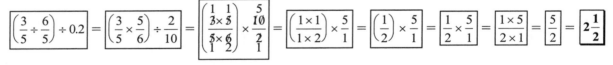

$$\boxed{\left(\dfrac{3}{5} \div \dfrac{6}{5}\right) \div 0.2} = \boxed{\left(\dfrac{3}{5} \times \dfrac{5}{6}\right) \div \dfrac{2}{10}} = \boxed{\left(\dfrac{\overset{1}{\cancel{3}} \times \overset{1}{\cancel{5}}}{\underset{1}{\cancel{5}} \times \underset{2}{\cancel{6}}}\right) \times \dfrac{\overset{5}{\cancel{10}}}{\underset{1}{\cancel{2}}}} = \boxed{\left(\dfrac{1 \times 1}{1 \times 2}\right) \times \dfrac{5}{1}} = \boxed{\left(\dfrac{1}{2}\right) \times \dfrac{5}{1}} = \boxed{\dfrac{1}{2} \times \dfrac{5}{1}} = \boxed{\dfrac{1 \times 5}{2 \times 1}} = \boxed{\dfrac{5}{2}} = \boxed{\mathbf{2\dfrac{1}{2}}}$$

Example 6.4-18

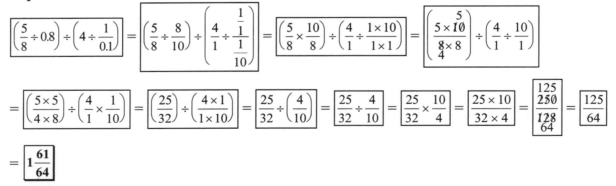

$$\boxed{\left(\dfrac{5}{8} \div 0.8\right) \div \left(4 \div \dfrac{1}{0.1}\right)} = \boxed{\left(\dfrac{5}{8} \div \dfrac{8}{10}\right) \div \left(\dfrac{4}{1} \div \dfrac{\dfrac{1}{1}}{\dfrac{1}{10}}\right)} = \boxed{\left(\dfrac{5}{8} \times \dfrac{10}{8}\right) \div \left(\dfrac{4}{1} \div \dfrac{1 \times 10}{1 \times 1}\right)} = \boxed{\left(\dfrac{5 \times \overset{5}{\cancel{10}}}{\underset{4}{\cancel{8}} \times 8}\right) \div \left(\dfrac{4}{1} \div \dfrac{10}{1}\right)}$$

$$= \boxed{\left(\dfrac{5 \times 5}{4 \times 8}\right) \div \left(\dfrac{4}{1} \times \dfrac{1}{10}\right)} = \boxed{\left(\dfrac{25}{32}\right) \div \left(\dfrac{4 \times 1}{1 \times 10}\right)} = \boxed{\dfrac{25}{32} \div \left(\dfrac{4}{10}\right)} = \boxed{\dfrac{25}{32} \div \dfrac{4}{10}} = \boxed{\dfrac{25}{32} \times \dfrac{10}{4}} = \boxed{\dfrac{25 \times 10}{32 \times 4}} = \boxed{\dfrac{\overset{125}{\cancel{250}}}{\underset{64}{\cancel{128}}}} = \boxed{\dfrac{125}{64}}$$

$$= \boxed{\mathbf{1\dfrac{61}{64}}}$$

Example 6.4-19

$$\boxed{\left(\dfrac{2}{5} \div \dfrac{1}{5}\right) \div \left(\dfrac{0.1}{0.02} \div 0.1\right)} = \boxed{\left(\dfrac{2}{5} \div \dfrac{1}{5}\right) \div \left(\dfrac{\dfrac{1}{10}}{\dfrac{2}{100}} \div \dfrac{1}{10}\right)} = \boxed{\left(\dfrac{2}{5} \times \dfrac{5}{1}\right) \div \left(\dfrac{1 \times 100}{10 \times 2} \div \dfrac{1}{10}\right)} = \boxed{\left(\dfrac{2 \times \overset{1}{\cancel{5}}}{\underset{1}{\cancel{5}} \times 1}\right) \div \left(\dfrac{100}{20} \div \dfrac{1}{10}\right)}$$

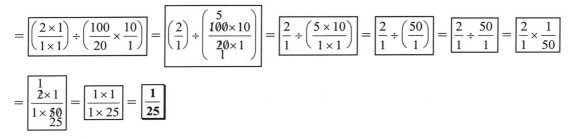

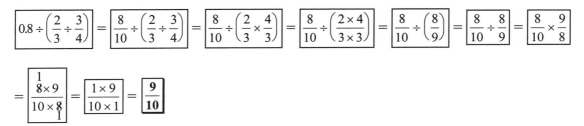

Example 6.4-20

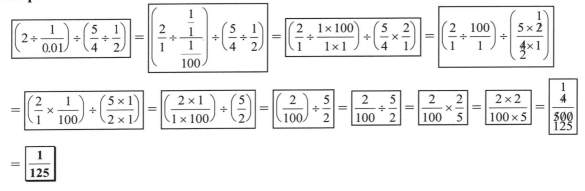

Example 6.4-21

$$\left[\left(2 \div \frac{1}{0.01}\right) \div \left(\frac{5}{4} \div \frac{1}{2}\right)\right] = \left[\left(\frac{2}{1} \div \frac{\frac{1}{1}}{\frac{1}{100}}\right) \div \left(\frac{5}{4} \div \frac{1}{2}\right)\right] = \left[\left(\frac{2}{1} \div \frac{1 \times 100}{1 \times 1}\right) \div \left(\frac{5}{4} \times \frac{2}{1}\right)\right] = \left[\left(\frac{2}{1} \div \frac{100}{1}\right) \div \left(\frac{5 \times 2}{\underset{2}{\overset{1}{4} \times 1}}\right)\right]$$

$$= \left[\left(\frac{2}{1} \times \frac{1}{100}\right) \div \left(\frac{5 \times 1}{2 \times 1}\right)\right] = \left[\left(\frac{2 \times 1}{1 \times 100}\right) \div \left(\frac{5}{2}\right)\right] = \left[\left(\frac{2}{100}\right) \div \frac{5}{2}\right] = \left[\frac{2}{100} \div \frac{5}{2}\right] = \left[\frac{2}{100} \times \frac{2}{5}\right] = \left[\frac{2 \times 2}{100 \times 5}\right] = \left[\frac{\overset{1}{4}}{\underset{125}{\cancel{500}}}\right]$$

$$= \boxed{\frac{1}{125}}$$

Section 6.4 Exercises - Divide the following integer and decimal fractions:

1. $\dfrac{5}{4} \div \dfrac{0.4}{1.2} =$

2. $0.2 \div \dfrac{5}{8} =$

3. $\left(\dfrac{1}{0.1} \div 1\right) \div 0.6 =$

4. $\left(\dfrac{9}{8} \div \dfrac{3}{8}\right) \div \dfrac{0.2}{0.3} =$

5. $\left(\dfrac{1}{0.04} \div \dfrac{1}{2}\right) \div 5 =$

6. $\left(\dfrac{4}{6} \div 0.3\right) \div \dfrac{2}{9} =$

7. $\left(\dfrac{0.8}{2.4} \div 0.02\right) \div \dfrac{5}{10} =$

8. $\left(0.04 \div \dfrac{2}{10}\right) \div \dfrac{1}{5} =$

9. $0.2 \div \left(\dfrac{1}{8} \div \dfrac{1}{4}\right) =$

10. $\left(\dfrac{1}{5} \div \dfrac{4}{5}\right) \div \left(0.2 \div \dfrac{0.1}{0.04}\right) =$

6.5   Solving Mixed Operations Using Integer and Decimal Fractions

Integer and decimal fractions of the forms:

1. $\left(\dfrac{a}{b}\right)$ where the numerator (a) and the denominator (b) are integers, and

2. $\left(\dfrac{a \times 10^{-k_1}}{b \times 10^{-k_2}}\right)$ where (a) and (b) are integer numbers and (k_1) and (k_2) are equal to the number

   of decimal places

are added, subtracted, multiplied, and divided by using the following steps:

Step 1   Change the integer number (a) to an integer fraction of the form $\left(\dfrac{a}{1}\right)$, e.g., change

200 to $\dfrac{200}{1}$.

Step 2   a. Change the decimal fraction(s) to integer fraction(s) (see Section 2.4).

   b. Change the decimal number(s) $\left(a \times 10^{-k}\right)$ to integer fraction(s) of the form $\left(\dfrac{a}{10^k}\right)$,

   e.g., change 26.1 to $\dfrac{261}{10}$.

Step 3   Add, subtract, multiply, and divide the integer fractions by following the steps outlined in sections 3.1 through 3.4.

Step 4   Simplify the fraction to its lowest term (see Sections 2.3).

Step 5   Change the improper fraction to a mixed fraction if the fraction obtained from Step 4 is an improper fraction (see Section 2.2).

The following examples show mathematical operations on integer and decimal fractions using the above steps:

Example 6.5-1

$$\left[\left(0.5 \times \frac{2}{3}\right) + \frac{0.3}{0.8}\right] =$$

Solution:

   Step 1 $\boxed{Not\ Applicable}$

   Step 2a $\left[\left(0.5 \times \dfrac{2}{3}\right) + \dfrac{0.3}{0.8}\right] = \left[\left(0.5 \times \dfrac{2}{3}\right) + \dfrac{\frac{3}{10}}{\frac{8}{10}}\right] = \left[\left(0.5 \times \dfrac{2}{3}\right) + \dfrac{3 \times 10}{10 \times 8}\right] = \left[\left(0.5 \times \dfrac{2}{3}\right) + \dfrac{30}{80}\right]$

   Step 2b $\left[\left(0.5 \times \dfrac{2}{3}\right) + \dfrac{30}{80}\right] = \left[\left(\dfrac{5}{10} \times \dfrac{2}{3}\right) + \dfrac{30}{80}\right]$

   Step 3 $\left[\left(\dfrac{5}{10} \times \dfrac{2}{3}\right) + \dfrac{30}{80}\right] = \left[\left(\dfrac{5 \times 2}{10 \times 3}\right) + \dfrac{30}{80}\right] = \left[\left(\dfrac{10}{30}\right) + \dfrac{30}{80}\right] = \left[\dfrac{10}{30} + \dfrac{30}{80}\right] = \left[\dfrac{(10 \times 80) + (30 \times 30)}{30 \times 80}\right]$

$$= \boxed{\frac{800 + 900}{2400}} = \boxed{\frac{1700}{2400}}$$

Step 4
$$\boxed{\frac{1700}{2400}} = \boxed{\frac{1700 \div 100}{2400 \div 100}} = \boxed{\mathbf{\frac{17}{24}}}$$

Step 5
$$\boxed{Not\ Applicable}$$

Example 6.5-2
$$\boxed{\left(7 + \frac{2}{5}\right) \times 0.8} =$$

Solution:

Step 1
$$\boxed{\left(7 + \frac{2}{5}\right) \times 0.8} = \boxed{\left(\frac{7}{1} + \frac{2}{5}\right) \times 0.8}$$

Step 2a
$$\boxed{Not\ Applicable}$$

Step 2b
$$\boxed{\left(\frac{7}{1} + \frac{2}{5}\right) \times 0.8} = \boxed{\left(\frac{7}{1} + \frac{2}{5}\right) \times \frac{8}{10}}$$

Step 3
$$\boxed{\left(\frac{7}{1} + \frac{2}{5}\right) \times \frac{8}{10}} = \boxed{\left(\frac{(7 \times 5) + (2 \times 1)}{1 \times 5}\right) \times \frac{8}{10}} = \boxed{\left(\frac{35 + 2}{5}\right) \times \frac{8}{10}} = \boxed{\left(\frac{37}{5}\right) \times \frac{8}{10}} = \boxed{\frac{37}{5} \times \frac{8}{10}}$$

$$= \boxed{\frac{37 \times 8}{5 \times 10}} = \boxed{\frac{296}{50}}$$

Step 4
$$\boxed{\frac{296}{50}} = \boxed{\frac{296 \div 2}{50 \div 2}} = \boxed{\frac{148}{25}}$$

Step 5
$$\boxed{\frac{148}{25}} = \boxed{\mathbf{5\frac{23}{25}}}$$

Example 6.5-3
$$\boxed{\left(5 - \frac{0.2}{0.7}\right) + \frac{2}{3}} =$$

Solution:

Step 1
$$\boxed{\left(5 - \frac{0.2}{0.7}\right) + \frac{2}{3}} = \boxed{\left(\frac{5}{1} - \frac{0.2}{0.7}\right) + \frac{2}{3}}$$

Step 2a
$$\left[\left(\frac{5}{1} - \frac{0.2}{0.7}\right) + \frac{2}{3}\right] = \left[\left(\frac{5}{1} - \frac{\frac{2}{10}}{\frac{7}{10}}\right) + \frac{2}{3}\right] = \left[\left(\frac{5}{1} - \frac{2 \times 10}{10 \times 7}\right) + \frac{2}{3}\right] = \left[\left(\frac{5}{1} - \frac{20}{70}\right) + \frac{2}{3}\right]$$

Step 2b   Not Applicable

Step 3
$$\left[\left(\frac{5}{1} - \frac{20}{70}\right) + \frac{2}{3}\right] = \left[\left(\frac{(5 \times 70) - (20 \times 1)}{1 \times 70}\right) + \frac{2}{3}\right] = \left[\left(\frac{350 - 20}{70}\right) + \frac{2}{3}\right] = \left[\left(\frac{330}{70}\right) + \frac{2}{3}\right]$$

$$= \left[\frac{330}{70} + \frac{2}{3}\right] = \left[\frac{(330 \times 3) + (2 \times 70)}{70 \times 3}\right] = \left[\frac{990 + 140}{210}\right] = \left[\frac{1130}{210}\right]$$

Step 4
$$\left|\frac{1130}{210}\right| = \left|\frac{1130 \div 10}{210 \div 10}\right| = \left|\frac{113}{21}\right|$$

Step 5
$$\left|\frac{113}{21}\right| = \boxed{5\frac{8}{21}}$$

Example 6.5-4
$$\left[\left(\frac{2}{3} \times 0.8\right) + \left(\frac{0.2}{0.5} \div 6\right)\right] =$$

Solution:

Step 1
$$\left[\left(\frac{2}{3} \times 0.8\right) + \left(\frac{0.2}{0.5} \div 6\right)\right] = \left[\left(\frac{2}{3} \times 0.8\right) + \left(\frac{0.2}{0.5} \div \frac{6}{1}\right)\right]$$

Step 2a
$$\left[\left(\frac{2}{3} \times 0.8\right) + \left(\frac{0.2}{0.5} \div \frac{6}{1}\right)\right] = \left[\left(\frac{2}{3} \times 0.8\right) + \left(\frac{\frac{2}{10}}{\frac{5}{10}} \div \frac{6}{1}\right)\right] = \left[\left(\frac{2}{3} \times 0.8\right) + \left(\frac{2 \times 10}{10 \times 5} \div \frac{6}{1}\right)\right]$$

$$= \left[\left(\frac{2}{3} \times 0.8\right) + \left(\frac{20}{50} \div \frac{6}{1}\right)\right]$$

Step 2b
$$\left[\left(\frac{2}{3} \times 0.8\right) + \left(\frac{20}{50} \div \frac{6}{1}\right)\right] = \left[\left(\frac{2}{3} \times \frac{8}{10}\right) + \left(\frac{20}{50} \div \frac{6}{1}\right)\right]$$

Step 3
$$\left[\left(\frac{2}{3} \times \frac{8}{10}\right) + \left(\frac{20}{50} \div \frac{6}{1}\right)\right] = \left[\left(\frac{2 \times 8}{3 \times 10}\right) + \left(\frac{20}{50} \times \frac{1}{6}\right)\right] = \left[\left(\frac{16}{30}\right) + \left(\frac{20 \times 1}{50 \times 6}\right)\right] = \left[\left(\frac{16}{30}\right) + \left(\frac{20}{300}\right)\right]$$

$$= \left[\frac{16}{30} + \frac{20}{300}\right] = \left[\frac{(16 \times 300) + (20 \times 30)}{30 \times 300}\right] = \left[\frac{4800 + 600}{9000}\right] = \left[\frac{5400}{9000}\right]$$

Step 4 $\dfrac{5400}{9000} = \dfrac{5400 \div 900}{9000 \div 900} = \dfrac{6}{10} = \dfrac{6 \div 2}{10 \div 2} = \boxed{\dfrac{3}{5}}$

Step 5 $\boxed{\textit{Not Applicable}}$

Example 6.5-5

$$\boxed{\left(0.06 + \frac{5}{6} \right) \div \left(5 \times \frac{0.2}{0.3} \times \frac{2}{5} \right) =}$$

Solution:

Step 1 $\boxed{\left(0.06 + \dfrac{5}{6} \right) \div \left(5 \times \dfrac{0.2}{0.3} \times \dfrac{2}{5} \right)} = \boxed{\left(0.06 + \dfrac{5}{6} \right) \div \left(\dfrac{5}{1} \times \dfrac{0.2}{0.3} \times \dfrac{2}{5} \right)}$

Step 2a $\boxed{\left(0.06 + \dfrac{5}{6} \right) \div \left(\dfrac{5}{1} \times \dfrac{0.2}{0.3} \times \dfrac{2}{5} \right)} = \boxed{\left(0.06 + \dfrac{5}{6} \right) \div \left(\dfrac{5}{1} \times \dfrac{\frac{2}{10}}{\frac{3}{10}} \times \dfrac{2}{5} \right)}$

$= \boxed{\left(0.06 + \dfrac{5}{6} \right) \div \left(\dfrac{5}{1} \times \dfrac{2 \times 10}{10 \times 3} \times \dfrac{2}{5} \right)} = \boxed{\left(0.06 + \dfrac{5}{6} \right) \div \left(\dfrac{5}{1} \times \dfrac{20}{30} \times \dfrac{2}{5} \right)}$

Step 2b $\boxed{\left(0.06 + \dfrac{5}{6} \right) \div \left(\dfrac{5}{1} \times \dfrac{20}{30} \times \dfrac{2}{5} \right)} = \boxed{\left(\dfrac{6}{100} + \dfrac{5}{6} \right) \div \left(\dfrac{5}{1} \times \dfrac{20}{30} \times \dfrac{2}{5} \right)}$

Step 3 $\boxed{\left(\dfrac{6}{100} + \dfrac{5}{6} \right) \div \left(\dfrac{5}{1} \times \dfrac{20}{30} \times \dfrac{2}{5} \right)} = \boxed{\left(\dfrac{(6 \times 6) + (5 \times 100)}{100 \times 6} \right) \div \left(\dfrac{5 \times 20 \times 2}{1 \times 30 \times 5} \right)}$

$= \boxed{\left(\dfrac{36 + 500}{600} \right) \div \left(\dfrac{200}{150} \right)} = \boxed{\left(\dfrac{536}{600} \right) \div \left(\dfrac{200}{150} \right)} = \boxed{\dfrac{536}{600} \div \dfrac{200}{150}} = \boxed{\dfrac{536}{600} \times \dfrac{150}{200}} = \boxed{\dfrac{536 \times 150}{600 \times 200}}$

$= \boxed{\dfrac{80400}{120000}}$

Step 4 $\boxed{\dfrac{80400}{120000}} = \boxed{\dfrac{80400 \div 400}{120000 \div 400}} = \boxed{\dfrac{201}{300}} = \boxed{\dfrac{201 \div 3}{300 \div 3}} = \boxed{\dfrac{67}{100}}$

Step 5 $\boxed{\textit{Not Applicable}}$

Example 6.5-6

$$\boxed{\left(0.5 + \frac{2}{3} \right) - \left(\frac{0.3}{0.5} + 6 \right) =}$$

Solution:

Step 1
$$\left[\left(0.5 + \frac{2}{3}\right) - \left(\frac{0.3}{0.5} + 6\right)\right] = \left[\left(0.5 + \frac{2}{3}\right) - \left(\frac{0.3}{0.5} + \frac{6}{1}\right)\right]$$

Step 2a
$$\left[\left(0.5 + \frac{2}{3}\right) - \left(\frac{0.3}{0.5} + \frac{6}{1}\right)\right] = \left[\left(0.5 + \frac{2}{3}\right) - \left(\frac{\frac{3}{10}}{\frac{5}{10}} + \frac{6}{1}\right)\right] = \left[\left(0.5 + \frac{2}{3}\right) - \left(\frac{3 \times 10}{10 \times 5} + \frac{6}{1}\right)\right]$$

$$= \left[\left(0.5 + \frac{2}{3}\right) - \left(\frac{30}{50} + \frac{6}{1}\right)\right]$$

Step 2b
$$\left[\left(0.5 + \frac{2}{3}\right) - \left(\frac{30}{50} + \frac{6}{1}\right)\right] = \left[\left(\frac{5}{10} + \frac{2}{3}\right) - \left(\frac{30}{50} + \frac{6}{1}\right)\right]$$

Step 3
$$\left[\left(\frac{5}{10} + \frac{2}{3}\right) - \left(\frac{30}{50} + \frac{6}{1}\right)\right] = \left[\left(\frac{(5 \times 3) + (2 \times 10)}{10 \times 3}\right) - \left(\frac{(30 \times 1) + (6 \times 50)}{50 \times 1}\right)\right]$$

$$= \left[\left(\frac{15 + 20}{30}\right) - \left(\frac{30 + 300}{50}\right)\right] = \left[\left(\frac{35}{30}\right) - \left(\frac{330}{50}\right)\right] = \left[\frac{35}{30} - \frac{330}{50}\right] = \left[\frac{(35 \times 50) - (330 \times 30)}{30 \times 50}\right]$$

$$= \left[\frac{1750 - 9900}{1500}\right] = \left[\frac{-8150}{1500}\right]$$

Step 4
$$\left[\frac{-8150}{1500}\right] = \left[\frac{-8150 \div 50}{1500 \div 50}\right] = \left[\frac{-163}{30}\right]$$

Step 5
$$\left[\frac{-163}{30}\right] = \left[-\left(5\frac{13}{30}\right)\right]$$

Example 6.5-7
$$\left[\left(5 - \frac{3}{5}\right) \times \left(10.5 + \frac{0.5}{0.2}\right)\right] =$$

Solution:

Step 1
$$\left[\left(5 - \frac{3}{5}\right) \times \left(10.5 + \frac{0.5}{0.2}\right)\right] = \left[\left(\frac{5}{1} - \frac{3}{5}\right) \times \left(10.5 + \frac{0.5}{0.2}\right)\right]$$

Step 2a
$$\left[\left(\frac{5}{1} - \frac{3}{5}\right) \times \left(10.5 + \frac{0.5}{0.2}\right)\right] = \left[\left(\frac{5}{1} - \frac{3}{5}\right) \times \left(10.5 + \frac{\frac{5}{10}}{\frac{2}{10}}\right)\right] = \left[\left(\frac{5}{1} - \frac{3}{5}\right) \times \left(10.5 + \frac{5 \times 10}{10 \times 2}\right)\right]$$

$$= \left[\left(\frac{5}{1} - \frac{3}{5} \right) \times \left(10.5 + \frac{50}{20} \right) \right]$$

Step 2b $\left[\left(\frac{5}{1} - \frac{3}{5} \right) \times \left(10.5 + \frac{50}{20} \right) \right] = \left[\left(\frac{5}{1} - \frac{3}{5} \right) \times \left(\frac{105}{10} + \frac{50}{20} \right) \right]$

Step 3 $\left[\left(\frac{5}{1} - \frac{3}{5} \right) \times \left(\frac{105}{10} + \frac{50}{20} \right) \right] = \left[\left(\frac{(5 \times 5) - (3 \times 1)}{1 \times 5} \right) \times \left(\frac{(105 \times 20) + (50 \times 10)}{10 \times 20} \right) \right]$

$$= \left[\left(\frac{25 - 3}{5} \right) \times \left(\frac{2100 + 500}{200} \right) \right] = \left[\left(\frac{22}{5} \right) \times \left(\frac{2600}{200} \right) \right] = \left[\frac{22}{5} \times \frac{2600}{200} \right] = \left[\frac{22 \times 2600}{5 \times 200} \right]$$

$$= \left[\frac{57200}{1000} \right]$$

Step 4 $\left[\frac{57200}{1000} \right] = \left[\frac{57200 \div 100}{1000 \div 100} \right] = \left[\frac{572}{10} \right] = \left[\frac{572 \div 2}{10 \div 2} \right] = \left[\frac{286}{5} \right]$

Step 5 $\left[\frac{286}{5} \right] = \left[\boxed{57\frac{1}{5}} \right]$

Example 6.5-8

$$\left[\left(0.5 \times \frac{0.2}{0.3} \right) \div \left(3 \times \frac{4}{5} \right) \right] =$$

Solution:

Step 1 $\left[\left(0.5 \times \frac{0.2}{0.3} \right) \div \left(3 \times \frac{4}{5} \right) \right] = \left[\left(0.5 \times \frac{0.2}{0.3} \right) \div \left(\frac{3}{1} \times \frac{4}{5} \right) \right]$

Step 2a $\left[\left(0.5 \times \frac{0.2}{0.3} \right) \div \left(\frac{3}{1} \times \frac{4}{5} \right) \right] = \left[\left(0.5 \times \frac{\frac{2}{10}}{\frac{3}{10}} \right) \div \left(\frac{3}{1} \times \frac{4}{5} \right) \right] = \left[\left(0.5 \times \frac{2 \times 10}{10 \times 3} \right) \div \left(\frac{3}{1} \times \frac{4}{5} \right) \right]$

$$= \left[\left(0.5 \times \frac{20}{30} \right) \div \left(\frac{3}{1} \times \frac{4}{5} \right) \right]$$

Step 2b $\left[\left(0.5 \times \frac{20}{30} \right) \div \left(\frac{3}{1} \times \frac{4}{5} \right) \right] = \left[\left(\frac{5}{10} \times \frac{20}{30} \right) \div \left(\frac{3}{1} \times \frac{4}{5} \right) \right]$

Step 3 $\left[\left(\frac{5}{10} \times \frac{20}{30} \right) \div \left(\frac{3}{1} \times \frac{4}{5} \right) \right] = \left[\left(\frac{5 \times 20}{10 \times 30} \right) \div \left(\frac{3 \times 4}{1 \times 5} \right) \right] = \left[\left(\frac{100}{300} \right) \div \left(\frac{12}{5} \right) \right] = \left[\frac{100}{300} \div \frac{12}{5} \right]$

$$= \boxed{\frac{100}{300} \times \frac{5}{12}} = \boxed{\frac{100 \times 5}{300 \times 12}} = \boxed{\frac{500}{3600}}$$

Step 4 $\qquad \boxed{\frac{500}{3600}} = \boxed{\frac{500 \div 100}{3600 \div 100}} = \boxed{\mathbf{\frac{5}{36}}}$

Step 5 $\qquad \boxed{Not\ Applicable}$

Example 6.5-9

$$\boxed{\left(3 \times \frac{0.2}{0.6} \times 0.09\right) \div \left(\frac{2}{3} + \frac{0.1}{0.06}\right)} =$$

Solution:

Step 1 $\qquad \boxed{\left(3 \times \frac{0.2}{0.6} \times 0.09\right) \div \left(\frac{2}{3} + \frac{0.1}{0.06}\right)} = \boxed{\left(\frac{3}{1} \times \frac{0.2}{0.6} \times 0.09\right) \div \left(\frac{2}{3} + \frac{0.1}{0.06}\right)}$

Step 2a $\qquad \boxed{\left(\frac{3}{1} \times \frac{0.2}{0.6} \times 0.09\right) \div \left(\frac{2}{3} + \frac{0.1}{0.06}\right)} = \boxed{\left(\frac{3}{1} \times \frac{\frac{2}{10}}{\frac{6}{10}} \times 0.09\right) \div \left(\frac{2}{3} + \frac{\frac{1}{10}}{\frac{6}{100}}\right)}$

$$= \boxed{\left(\frac{3}{1} \times \frac{2 \times 10}{10 \times 6} \times 0.09\right) \div \left(\frac{2}{3} + \frac{1 \times 100}{10 \times 6}\right)} = \boxed{\left(\frac{3}{1} \times \frac{20}{60} \times 0.09\right) \div \left(\frac{2}{3} + \frac{100}{60}\right)}$$

Step 2b $\qquad \boxed{\left(\frac{3}{1} \times \frac{20}{60} \times 0.09\right) \div \left(\frac{2}{3} + \frac{100}{60}\right)} = \boxed{\left(\frac{3}{1} \times \frac{20}{60} \times \frac{9}{100}\right) \div \left(\frac{2}{3} + \frac{100}{60}\right)}$

Step 3 $\qquad \boxed{\left(\frac{3}{1} \times \frac{20}{60} \times \frac{9}{100}\right) \div \left(\frac{2}{3} + \frac{100}{60}\right)} = \boxed{\left(\frac{3 \times 20 \times 9}{1 \times 60 \times 100}\right) \div \left(\frac{(2 \times 60) + (100 \times 3)}{3 \times 60}\right)}$

$$= \boxed{\left(\frac{540}{6000}\right) \div \left(\frac{120 + 300}{180}\right)} = \boxed{\left(\frac{540}{6000}\right) \div \left(\frac{420}{180}\right)} = \boxed{\frac{540}{6000} \div \frac{420}{180}} = \boxed{\frac{540}{6000} \times \frac{180}{420}}$$

$$= \boxed{\frac{540 \times 180}{6000 \times 420}} = \boxed{\frac{97200}{2520000}}$$

Step 4 $\qquad \boxed{\frac{97200}{2520000}} = \boxed{\frac{97200 \div 100}{2520000 \div 100}} = \boxed{\frac{972}{25200}} = \boxed{\frac{972 \div 4}{25200 \div 4}} = \boxed{\mathbf{\frac{243}{6300}}}$

Step 5 $\qquad \boxed{Not\ Applicable}$

Example 6.5-10

$$\left[\left(\frac{0.6}{0.07} \div 0.3\right) + \left(8 \div \frac{3}{8}\right)\right] =$$

Solution:

Step 1 $\left[\left(\frac{0.6}{0.07} \div 0.3\right) + \left(8 \div \frac{3}{8}\right)\right] = \left[\left(\frac{0.6}{0.07} \div 0.3\right) + \left(\frac{8}{1} \div \frac{3}{8}\right)\right]$

Step 2a $\left[\left(\frac{0.6}{0.07} \div 0.3\right) + \left(\frac{8}{1} \div \frac{3}{8}\right)\right] = \left[\left(\frac{\frac{6}{10}}{\frac{7}{100}} \div 0.3\right) + \left(\frac{8}{1} \div \frac{3}{8}\right)\right] = \left[\left(\frac{6 \times 100}{10 \times 7} \div 0.3\right) + \left(\frac{8}{1} \div \frac{3}{8}\right)\right]$

$= \left[\left(\frac{600}{70} \div 0.3\right) + \left(\frac{8}{1} \div \frac{3}{8}\right)\right]$

Step 2b $\left[\left(\frac{600}{70} \div 0.3\right) + \left(\frac{8}{1} \div \frac{3}{8}\right)\right] = \left[\left(\frac{600}{70} \div \frac{3}{10}\right) + \left(\frac{8}{1} \div \frac{3}{8}\right)\right]$

Step 3 $\left[\left(\frac{600}{70} \div \frac{3}{10}\right) + \left(\frac{8}{1} \div \frac{3}{8}\right)\right] = \left[\left(\frac{600}{70} \times \frac{10}{3}\right) + \left(\frac{8}{1} \times \frac{8}{3}\right)\right] = \left[\left(\frac{600 \times 10}{70 \times 3}\right) + \left(\frac{8 \times 8}{1 \times 3}\right)\right]$

$= \left[\left(\frac{6000}{210}\right) + \left(\frac{64}{3}\right)\right] = \left[\frac{6000}{210} + \frac{64}{3}\right] = \left[\frac{(6000 \times 3) + (64 \times 210)}{210 \times 3}\right] = \left[\frac{18000 + 13440}{630}\right]$

$= \left[\frac{31440}{630}\right]$

Step 4 $\frac{31440}{630} = \frac{31440 \div 10}{630 \div 10} = \frac{3144}{63} = \frac{3144 \div 3}{63 \div 3} = \frac{1048}{21}$

Step 5 $\frac{1048}{21} = \boxed{49\frac{19}{21}}$

The following examples further illustrate how to add, subtract, multiply, and divide integer and decimal fractions:

Example 6.5-11

$$\left[\left(\frac{3}{8} \times \frac{0.3}{1.2}\right) \div 0.25\right] = \left[\left(\frac{3}{8} \times \frac{\frac{3}{10}}{\frac{12}{10}}\right) \div \frac{25}{100}\right] = \left[\left(\frac{3}{8} \times \frac{3 \times 10}{10 \times 12}\right) \div \frac{\overset{1}{\cancel{25}}}{\underset{4}{\cancel{100}}}\right] = \left[\left(\frac{3}{8} \times \frac{\overset{1}{\cancel{30}}}{\underset{4}{\cancel{120}}}\right) \div \frac{1}{4}\right] = \left[\left(\frac{3}{8} \times \frac{1}{4}\right) \div \frac{1}{4}\right]$$

$$= \boxed{\left(\frac{3\times1}{8\times4}\right)\div\frac{1}{4}} = \boxed{\left(\frac{3}{32}\right)\div\frac{1}{4}} = \boxed{\frac{3}{32}\div\frac{1}{4}} = \boxed{\frac{3}{\underset{8}{\cancel{32}}}\times\frac{4}{1}} = \boxed{\frac{3\times\overset{1}{\cancel{4}}}{\underset{8}{\cancel{32}}\times1}} = \boxed{\frac{3\times1}{8\times1}} = \boxed{\mathbf{\frac{3}{8}}}$$

Example 6.5-12

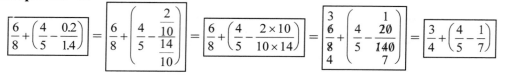

$$= \boxed{\frac{3}{4}+\left(\frac{(4\times7)-(1\times5)}{5\times7}\right)} = \boxed{\frac{3}{4}+\left(\frac{28-5}{35}\right)} = \boxed{\frac{3}{4}+\left(\frac{23}{35}\right)} = \boxed{\frac{3}{4}+\frac{23}{35}} = \boxed{\frac{(3\times35)+(23\times4)}{4\times35}} = \boxed{\frac{105+92}{140}}$$

$$= \boxed{\frac{197}{140}} = \boxed{\mathbf{1\frac{57}{140}}}$$

Example 6.5-13

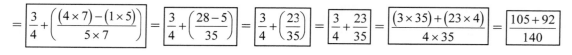

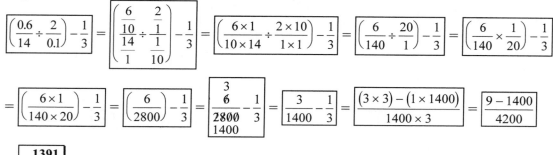

$$= \boxed{-\frac{1391}{4200}}$$

Example 6.5-14

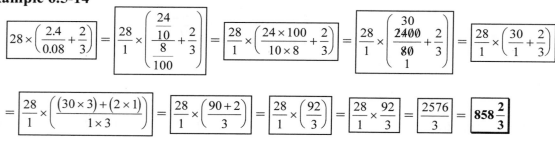

$$= \boxed{\frac{28}{1}\times\left(\frac{(30\times3)+(2\times1)}{1\times3}\right)} = \boxed{\frac{28}{1}\times\left(\frac{90+2}{3}\right)} = \boxed{\frac{28}{1}\times\left(\frac{92}{3}\right)} = \boxed{\frac{28}{1}\times\frac{92}{3}} = \boxed{\frac{2576}{3}} = \boxed{\mathbf{858\frac{2}{3}}}$$

Example 6.5-15

$$\boxed{\left(\frac{5}{0.1}+0.4\right)\times\frac{1}{504}} = \boxed{\left(\frac{\frac{5}{1}}{\frac{1}{10}}+\frac{4}{10}\right)\times\frac{1}{504}} = \boxed{\left(\frac{5\times10}{1\times1}+\frac{4}{10}\right)\times\frac{1}{504}} = \boxed{\left(\frac{50}{1}+\frac{4}{10}\right)\times\frac{1}{504}}$$

$= \left[\left(\dfrac{(50\times10)+(4\times1)}{1\times10} \right) \times \dfrac{1}{504} \right] = \left[\left(\dfrac{500+4}{10} \right) \times \dfrac{1}{504} \right] = \left[\left(\dfrac{504}{10} \right) \times \dfrac{1}{504} \right] = \left[\dfrac{504}{10} \times \dfrac{1}{504} \right] = \left[\dfrac{\overset{1}{\cancel{504}}\times 1}{10 \times \underset{1}{\cancel{504}}} \right] = \left[\dfrac{1\times1}{10\times1} \right]$

$= \boxed{\dfrac{1}{10}}$

Example 6.5-16

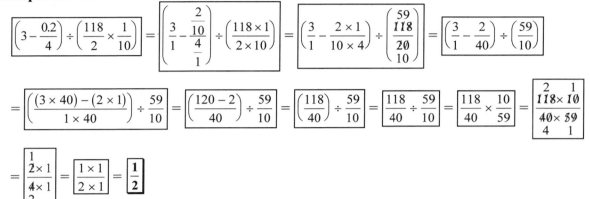

$\left[\left(3 - \dfrac{0.2}{4} \right) \div \left(\dfrac{118}{2} \times \dfrac{1}{10} \right) \right] = \left[\left(\dfrac{3}{1} - \dfrac{\frac{2}{10}}{\frac{4}{1}} \right) \div \left(\dfrac{118\times1}{2\times10} \right) \right] = \left[\left(\dfrac{3}{1} - \dfrac{2\times1}{10\times4} \right) \div \left(\dfrac{\frac{59}{118}}{\frac{20}{10}} \right) \right] = \left[\left(\dfrac{3}{1} - \dfrac{2}{40} \right) \div \left(\dfrac{59}{10} \right) \right]$

$= \left[\left(\dfrac{(3\times40)-(2\times1)}{1\times40} \right) \div \dfrac{59}{10} \right] = \left[\left(\dfrac{120-2}{40} \right) \div \dfrac{59}{10} \right] = \left[\left(\dfrac{118}{40} \right) \div \dfrac{59}{10} \right] = \left[\dfrac{118}{40} \div \dfrac{59}{10} \right] = \left[\dfrac{118}{40} \times \dfrac{10}{59} \right] = \left[\dfrac{\overset{2}{\cancel{118}}\times \overset{1}{\cancel{10}}}{\underset{4}{\cancel{40}}\times \underset{1}{\cancel{59}}} \right]$

$= \left[\dfrac{\frac{1}{2}\times1}{\frac{4}{2}\times1} \right] = \left[\dfrac{1\times1}{2\times1} \right] = \boxed{\dfrac{1}{2}}$

Example 6.5-17

$\left[\left(0.5 \times \dfrac{1}{5} \right) \div \left(0.05 \times \dfrac{3}{5} \right) \right] = \left[\left(\dfrac{5}{10} \times \dfrac{1}{5} \right) \div \left(\dfrac{5}{100} \times \dfrac{3}{5} \right) \right] = \left[\left(\dfrac{5\times1}{10\times5} \right) \div \left(\dfrac{5\times3}{100\times5} \right) \right] = \left[\left(\dfrac{5}{50} \right) \div \left(\dfrac{15}{500} \right) \right] = \left[\dfrac{5}{50} \div \dfrac{15}{500} \right]$

$= \left[\dfrac{5}{50} \times \dfrac{500}{15} \right] = \left[\dfrac{\overset{1}{\cancel{5}}\times \overset{10}{\cancel{500}}}{\underset{1}{\cancel{50}}\times \underset{3}{\cancel{15}}} \right] = \left[\dfrac{1\times10}{1\times3} \right] = \left[\dfrac{10}{3} \right] = \boxed{3\dfrac{1}{3}}$

Example 6.5-18

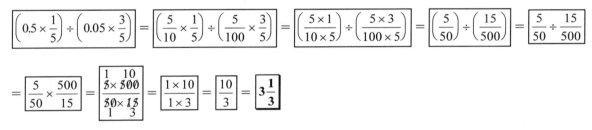

$\left[\left(\dfrac{0.3}{0.02} \times \dfrac{1}{6} \right) \div \left(\dfrac{4}{5} + \dfrac{31}{5} \right) \right] = \left[\left(\dfrac{\frac{3}{10}}{\frac{2}{100}} \times \dfrac{1}{6} \right) \div \left(\dfrac{4+31}{5} \right) \right] = \left[\left(\dfrac{3\times100}{10\times2} \times \dfrac{1}{6} \right) \div \left(\dfrac{35}{5} \right) \right] = \left[\left(\dfrac{\overset{15}{\cancel{300}}}{\underset{1}{\cancel{20}}} \times \dfrac{1}{6} \right) \div \dfrac{\overset{7}{\cancel{35}}}{\underset{1}{\cancel{5}}} \right]$

$= \left[\left(\dfrac{15}{1} \times \dfrac{1}{6} \right) \div \dfrac{7}{1} \right] = \left[\left(\dfrac{15\times1}{1\times6} \right) \div \dfrac{7}{1} \right] = \left[\left(\dfrac{15}{6} \right) \div \dfrac{7}{1} \right] = \left[\dfrac{15}{6} \div \dfrac{7}{1} \right] = \left[\dfrac{15}{6} \times \dfrac{1}{7} \right] = \left[\dfrac{15\times1}{6\times7} \right] = \left[\dfrac{\overset{5}{\cancel{15}}}{\underset{14}{\cancel{42}}} \right] = \boxed{\dfrac{5}{14}}$

Example 6.5-19

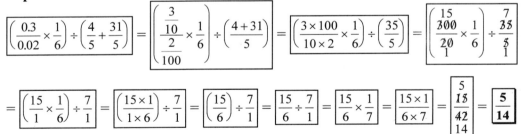

$\left[\left(\dfrac{3}{8} - \dfrac{0.02}{0.6} \right) + \left(2 + \dfrac{3}{4} \right) \right] = \left[\left(\dfrac{3}{8} - \dfrac{\frac{2}{100}}{\frac{6}{10}} \right) + \left(\dfrac{2}{1} + \dfrac{3}{4} \right) \right] = \left[\left(\dfrac{3}{8} - \dfrac{2\times10}{100\times6} \right) + \left(\dfrac{(2\times4)+(3\times1)}{1\times4} \right) \right]$

$= \left[\left(\dfrac{3}{8} - \dfrac{\overset{1}{\cancel{20}}}{\underset{30}{\cancel{600}}} \right) + \left(\dfrac{8+3}{4} \right) \right] = \left[\left(\dfrac{3}{8} - \dfrac{1}{30} \right) + \left(\dfrac{11}{4} \right) \right] = \left[\left(\dfrac{(3\times30)-(1\times8)}{8\times30} \right) + \dfrac{11}{4} \right] = \left[\left(\dfrac{90-8}{240} \right) + \dfrac{11}{4} \right] = \left[\left(\dfrac{82}{240} \right) + \dfrac{11}{4} \right]$

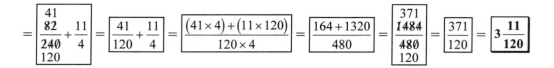

Example 6.5-20

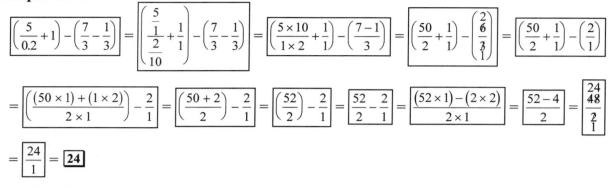

Example 6.5-21

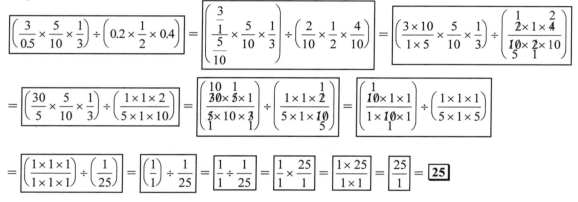

Section 6.5 Exercises - Use the following integer and decimal fractions to perform the indicated operations:

1. $\left(\dfrac{1}{4}+\dfrac{3}{2}\right)\div\dfrac{0.7}{2}=$

2. $\left(\dfrac{0.2}{1.4}+2\right)\times\dfrac{1}{4}=$

3. $\left(\dfrac{1}{5}\times0.5\right)+\dfrac{1}{10}=$

4. $\left(\dfrac{3}{5}+\dfrac{2}{3}\right)\times\dfrac{0.1}{1.5}=$

5. $\left(\dfrac{5}{3}-\dfrac{1}{3}\right)\div\dfrac{2.8}{0.12}=$

6. $\left(\dfrac{3}{8}\times4\right)\div\dfrac{0.05}{0.1}=$

7. $\left(\dfrac{0.3}{2.4}\times\dfrac{1}{3}\times2\right)\div\dfrac{1}{4}=$

8. $\left(\dfrac{3}{5}\times\dfrac{0.1}{4.4}\right)+400=$

9. $\left(\dfrac{1}{4}+\dfrac{2}{3}\right)\times\left(\dfrac{0.5}{0.02}\times\dfrac{1}{5}\right)=$

10. $\left[\left(\dfrac{5}{3}\times\dfrac{0.2}{1.2}\right)\div\dfrac{4}{9}\right]+\dfrac{3}{2}=$

Chapter 7 - Integer and Mixed Fractions

The objective of this chapter is to improve the student's ability in solving integer and mixed fractions by grouping the two types of fractions together. The steps used to perform the combined fractional operations with examples illustrating how to add (Section 7.1), subtract (Section 7.2), multiply (Section 7.3), and divide (Section 7.4) two or more integer and mixed fractions are given. Section 7.5 mixes the mathematical operations using the two types of fractions. To further enhance the student's ability, each section is concluded by solving additional examples which do not follow the exact order as is given by the steps for each case.

7.1 Adding Integer and Mixed Fractions

Integer fractions of the form $\left(\dfrac{a}{b}\right)$ where both the numerator (a) and the denominator (b) are integers, and mixed fractions of the form $\left(k\dfrac{a}{b}\right)$ where (k) is a whole number and $\left(\dfrac{a}{b}\right)$ is an integer fraction are added as in the following cases:

Case I Adding Two or More Integer and Mixed Fractions With Common Denominators

Integer and mixed fractions with two or more common denominators are added using the steps given as in each case below:

Case I-A *Add two integer and mixed fractions with common denominators using the following steps:*

Step 1 Change the mixed fraction to an integer fraction (see Section 2.5).

Step 2 Add the integer fractions (see Section 3.1, Case I-A).

Step 3 Simplify the fraction to its lowest term (see Section 2.3).

Step 4 Change the improper fraction to a mixed fraction if the fraction obtained from Step 3 is an improper fraction (see Section 2.2).

The following examples show the steps as to how two integer and mixed fractions with common denominators are added:

Example 7.1-1

$$25\dfrac{2}{5} + \dfrac{4}{5} =$$

Solution:

Step 1 $\quad 25\dfrac{2}{5} + \dfrac{4}{5} = \dfrac{(25 \times 5) + 2}{5} + \dfrac{4}{5} = \dfrac{125 + 2}{5} + \dfrac{4}{5} = \dfrac{127}{5} + \dfrac{4}{5}$

Step 2 $\quad \dfrac{127}{5} + \dfrac{4}{5} = \dfrac{127 + 4}{5} = \dfrac{131}{5}$

Step 3 $\boxed{Not\ Applicable}$

Step 4 $\boxed{\dfrac{131}{5}} = \boxed{\mathbf{26\dfrac{1}{5}}}$

Example 7.1-2

$$\boxed{9\dfrac{8}{30} + \dfrac{4}{30}} =$$

Solution:

Step 1 $\boxed{9\dfrac{8}{30} + \dfrac{4}{30}} = \boxed{\dfrac{(9 \times 30) + 8}{30} + \dfrac{4}{30}} = \boxed{\dfrac{270 + 8}{30} + \dfrac{4}{30}} = \boxed{\dfrac{278}{30} + \dfrac{4}{30}}$

Step 2 $\boxed{\dfrac{278}{30} + \dfrac{4}{30}} = \boxed{\dfrac{278 + 4}{30}} = \boxed{\dfrac{282}{30}}$

Step 3 $\boxed{\dfrac{282}{30}} = \boxed{\dfrac{282 \div 2}{30 \div 2}} = \boxed{\dfrac{141}{15}} = \boxed{\dfrac{141 \div 3}{15 \div 3}} = \boxed{\dfrac{47}{5}}$

Step 4 $\boxed{\dfrac{47}{5}} = \boxed{\mathbf{9\dfrac{2}{5}}}$

Example 7.1-3

$$\boxed{\dfrac{5}{26} + 3\dfrac{9}{26}} =$$

Solution:

Step 1 $\boxed{\dfrac{5}{26} + 3\dfrac{9}{26}} = \boxed{\dfrac{5}{26} + \dfrac{(3 \times 26) + 9}{26}} = \boxed{\dfrac{5}{26} + \dfrac{78 + 9}{26}} = \boxed{\dfrac{5}{26} + \dfrac{87}{26}}$

Step 2 $\boxed{\dfrac{5}{26} + \dfrac{87}{26}} = \boxed{\dfrac{5 + 87}{26}} = \boxed{\dfrac{92}{26}}$

Step 3 $\boxed{\dfrac{92}{26}} = \boxed{\dfrac{92 \div 2}{26 \div 2}} = \boxed{\dfrac{46}{13}}$

Step 4 $\boxed{\dfrac{46}{13}} = \boxed{\mathbf{3\dfrac{7}{13}}}$

Example 7.1-4

$$\boxed{2\dfrac{5}{13} + \dfrac{8}{13}} =$$

Solution:

Step 1 $2\dfrac{5}{13} + \dfrac{8}{13} = \dfrac{(2 \times 13) + 5}{13} + \dfrac{8}{13} = \dfrac{26 + 5}{13} + \dfrac{8}{13} = \dfrac{31}{13} + \dfrac{8}{13}$

Step 2 $\dfrac{31}{13} + \dfrac{8}{13} = \dfrac{31 + 8}{13} = \dfrac{39}{13}$

Step 3 $\dfrac{39}{13} = \dfrac{39 \div 13}{13 \div 13} = \dfrac{3}{1} = \boxed{3}$

Step 4 $\boxed{Not\ Applicable}$

Example 7.1-5

$$33\dfrac{5}{7} + \dfrac{6}{7} =$$

Solution:

Step 1 $33\dfrac{5}{7} + \dfrac{6}{7} = \dfrac{(33 \times 7) + 5}{7} + \dfrac{6}{7} = \dfrac{231 + 5}{7} + \dfrac{6}{7} = \dfrac{236}{7} + \dfrac{6}{7}$

Step 2 $\dfrac{236}{7} + \dfrac{6}{7} = \dfrac{236 + 6}{7} = \dfrac{242}{7}$

Step 3 $\boxed{Not\ Applicable}$

Step 4 $\dfrac{242}{7} = \boxed{34\dfrac{4}{7}}$

Case I-B   *Add three integer and mixed fractions with common denominators using the following steps:*

Step 1   Change the mixed fraction(s) to integer fraction(s) (see Section 2.5).

Step 2   Add the integer fractions (see Section 3.1, Case I-B).

Step 3   Simplify the fraction to its lowest term (see Section 2.3).

Step 4   Change the improper fraction to a mixed fraction if the fraction obtained from Step 3 is an improper fraction (see Section 2.2).

The following examples show the steps as to how three integer and mixed fractions with common denominators are added:

Example 7.1-6

$$24\dfrac{2}{5} + 6\dfrac{3}{5} + \dfrac{4}{5} =$$

Solution:

Step 1
$$\boxed{24\frac{2}{5} + 6\frac{3}{5} + \frac{4}{5}} = \boxed{\frac{(24 \times 5) + 2}{5} + \frac{(6 \times 5) + 3}{5} + \frac{4}{5}} = \boxed{\frac{120 + 2}{5} + \frac{30 + 3}{5} + \frac{4}{5}}$$

$$= \boxed{\frac{122}{5} + \frac{33}{5} + \frac{4}{5}}$$

Step 2
$$\boxed{\frac{122}{5} + \frac{33}{5} + \frac{4}{5}} = \boxed{\frac{122 + 33 + 4}{5}} = \boxed{\frac{159}{5}}$$

Step 3 $\boxed{Not\ Applicable}$

Step 4 $\boxed{\frac{159}{5}} = \boxed{\mathbf{31\frac{4}{5}}}$

Example 7.1-7
$$\boxed{2\frac{10}{23} + \frac{6}{23} + \frac{5}{23}} =$$

Solution:

Step 1
$$\boxed{2\frac{10}{23} + \frac{6}{23} + \frac{5}{23}} = \boxed{\frac{(2 \times 23) + 10}{23} + \frac{6}{23} + \frac{5}{23}} = \boxed{\frac{46 + 10}{23} + \frac{6}{23} + \frac{5}{23}} = \boxed{\frac{56}{23} + \frac{6}{23} + \frac{5}{23}}$$

Step 2
$$\boxed{\frac{56}{23} + \frac{6}{23} + \frac{5}{23}} = \boxed{\frac{56 + 6 + 5}{23}} = \boxed{\frac{67}{23}}$$

Step 3 $\boxed{Not\ Applicable}$

Step 4 $\boxed{\frac{67}{23}} = \boxed{\mathbf{2\frac{21}{23}}}$

Example 7.1-8
$$\boxed{4\frac{2}{4} + \frac{3}{4} + 6\frac{1}{4}} =$$

Solution:

Step 1
$$\boxed{4\frac{2}{4} + \frac{3}{4} + 6\frac{1}{4}} = \boxed{\frac{(4 \times 4) + 2}{4} + \frac{3}{4} + \frac{(6 \times 4) + 1}{4}} = \boxed{\frac{16 + 2}{4} + \frac{3}{4} + \frac{24 + 1}{4}}$$

$$= \boxed{\frac{18}{4} + \frac{3}{4} + \frac{25}{4}}$$

Step 2 $\dfrac{18}{4} + \dfrac{3}{4} + \dfrac{25}{4} = \dfrac{18 + 3 + 25}{4} = \dfrac{46}{4}$

Step 3 $\dfrac{46}{4} = \dfrac{46 \div 2}{4 \div 2} = \dfrac{23}{2}$

Step 4 $\dfrac{23}{2} = \mathbf{11\dfrac{1}{2}}$

Example 7.1-9

$$6\dfrac{2}{7} + 5\dfrac{3}{7} + \dfrac{5}{7} =$$

Solution:

Step 1 $6\dfrac{2}{7} + 5\dfrac{3}{7} + \dfrac{5}{7} = \dfrac{(6 \times 7) + 2}{7} + \dfrac{(5 \times 7) + 3}{7} + \dfrac{5}{7} = \dfrac{42 + 2}{7} + \dfrac{35 + 3}{7} + \dfrac{5}{7}$

$$= \dfrac{44}{7} + \dfrac{38}{7} + \dfrac{5}{7}$$

Step 2 $\dfrac{44}{7} + \dfrac{38}{7} + \dfrac{5}{7} = \dfrac{44 + 38 + 5}{7} = \dfrac{87}{7}$

Step 3 $\boxed{Not\ Applicable}$

Step 4 $\dfrac{87}{7} = \mathbf{12\dfrac{3}{7}}$

Example 7.1-10

$$\dfrac{5}{12} + \dfrac{8}{12} + 6\dfrac{5}{12} =$$

Solution:

Step 1 $\dfrac{5}{12} + \dfrac{8}{12} + 6\dfrac{5}{12} = \dfrac{5}{12} + \dfrac{8}{12} + \dfrac{(6 \times 12) + 5}{12} = \dfrac{5}{12} + \dfrac{8}{12} + \dfrac{72 + 5}{12} = \dfrac{5}{12} + \dfrac{8}{12} + \dfrac{77}{12}$

Step 2 $\dfrac{5}{12} + \dfrac{8}{12} + \dfrac{77}{12} = \dfrac{5 + 8 + 77}{12} = \dfrac{90}{12}$

Step 3 $\dfrac{90}{12} = \dfrac{90 \div 2}{12 \div 2} = \dfrac{45}{6} = \dfrac{45 \div 3}{6 \div 3} = \dfrac{15}{2}$

Step 4 $\dfrac{15}{2} = \mathbf{7\dfrac{1}{2}}$

Case II   Adding Two or More Integer and Mixed Fractions Without a Common Denominator

Two or more integer and mixed fractions without a common denominator are added using the steps given as in each case below:

Case II-A   *Add two integer and mixed fractions without a common denominator using the following steps:*

Step 1   Change the integer number (a) to an integer fraction of the form $\left(\dfrac{a}{1}\right)$, e.g., change 21

to $\dfrac{21}{1}$.

Step 2   Change the mixed fraction to an integer fraction (see Section 2.5).

Step 3   Add the integer fractions (see Section 3.1, Case II-A).

Step 4   Simplify the fraction to its lowest term (see Section 2.3).

Step 5   Change the improper fraction to a mixed fraction if the fraction obtained from Step 4 is an improper fraction (see Section 2.2).

The following examples show the steps as to how two integer and mixed fractions without a common denominator are added:

Example 7.1-11

$$\boxed{22\dfrac{3}{8} + \dfrac{4}{5}} =$$

Solution:

    Step 1 $\boxed{Not\ Applicable}$

    Step 2 $\boxed{22\dfrac{3}{8} + \dfrac{4}{5}} = \boxed{\dfrac{(22\times 8)+3}{8} + \dfrac{4}{5}} = \boxed{\dfrac{176+3}{8} + \dfrac{4}{5}} = \boxed{\dfrac{179}{8} + \dfrac{4}{5}}$

    Step 3 $\boxed{\dfrac{179}{8} + \dfrac{4}{5}} = \boxed{\dfrac{(179\times 5)+(4\times 8)}{8\times 5}} = \boxed{\dfrac{895+32}{40}} = \boxed{\dfrac{927}{40}}$

    Step 4 $\boxed{Not\ Applicable}$

    Step 5 $\boxed{\dfrac{927}{40}} = \boxed{\mathbf{23\dfrac{7}{40}}}$

Example 7.1-12

$$\boxed{12 + 4\dfrac{6}{9}} =$$

Solution:

    Step 1 $\boxed{12 + 4\dfrac{6}{9}} = \boxed{\dfrac{12}{1} + 4\dfrac{6}{9}}$

Step 2 $\boxed{\dfrac{12}{1} + 4\dfrac{6}{9}} = \boxed{\dfrac{12}{1} + \dfrac{(4 \times 9) + 6}{9}} = \boxed{\dfrac{12}{1} + \dfrac{36 + 6}{9}} = \boxed{\dfrac{12}{1} + \dfrac{42}{9}}$

Step 3 $\boxed{\dfrac{12}{1} + \dfrac{42}{9}} = \boxed{\dfrac{(12 \times 9) + (42 \times 1)}{1 \times 9}} = \boxed{\dfrac{108 + 42}{9}} = \boxed{\dfrac{150}{9}}$

Step 4 $\boxed{\dfrac{150}{9}} = \boxed{\dfrac{150 \div 3}{9 \div 3}} = \boxed{\dfrac{50}{3}}$

Step 5 $\boxed{\dfrac{50}{3}} = \boxed{\mathbf{16\dfrac{2}{3}}}$

Example 7.1-13

$\boxed{\dfrac{3}{5} + 4\dfrac{2}{3}} =$

Solution:

Step 1 $\boxed{Not\ Applicable}$

Step 2 $\boxed{\dfrac{3}{5} + 4\dfrac{2}{3}} = \boxed{\dfrac{3}{5} + \dfrac{(4 \times 3) + 2}{3}} = \boxed{\dfrac{3}{5} + \dfrac{12 + 2}{3}} = \boxed{\dfrac{3}{5} + \dfrac{14}{3}}$

Step 3 $\boxed{\dfrac{3}{5} + \dfrac{14}{3}} = \boxed{\dfrac{(3 \times 3) + (14 \times 5)}{5 \times 3}} = \boxed{\dfrac{9 + 70}{15}} = \boxed{\dfrac{79}{15}}$

Step 4 $\boxed{Not\ Applicable}$

Step 5 $\boxed{\dfrac{79}{15}} = \boxed{\mathbf{5\dfrac{4}{15}}}$

Example 7.1-14

$\boxed{10\dfrac{2}{4} + \dfrac{6}{8}} =$

Solution:

Step 1 $\boxed{Not\ Applicable}$

Step 2 $\boxed{10\dfrac{2}{4} + \dfrac{6}{8}} = \boxed{\dfrac{(10 \times 4) + 2}{4} + \dfrac{6}{8}} = \boxed{\dfrac{40 + 2}{4} + \dfrac{6}{8}} = \boxed{\dfrac{42}{4} + \dfrac{6}{8}}$

Step 3 $\boxed{\dfrac{42}{4} + \dfrac{6}{8}} = \boxed{\dfrac{(42 \times 8) + (6 \times 4)}{4 \times 8}} = \boxed{\dfrac{336 + 24}{32}} = \boxed{\dfrac{360}{32}}$

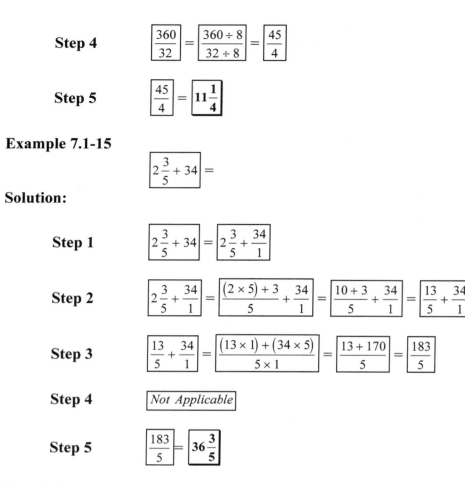

Step 4 $\boxed{\dfrac{360}{32}} = \boxed{\dfrac{360 \div 8}{32 \div 8}} = \boxed{\dfrac{45}{4}}$

Step 5 $\boxed{\dfrac{45}{4}} = \boxed{11\dfrac{1}{4}}$

Example 7.1-15

$$\boxed{2\dfrac{3}{5} + 34} =$$

Solution:

Step 1 $\boxed{2\dfrac{3}{5} + 34} = \boxed{2\dfrac{3}{5} + \dfrac{34}{1}}$

Step 2 $\boxed{2\dfrac{3}{5} + \dfrac{34}{1}} = \boxed{\dfrac{(2 \times 5) + 3}{5} + \dfrac{34}{1}} = \boxed{\dfrac{10 + 3}{5} + \dfrac{34}{1}} = \boxed{\dfrac{13}{5} + \dfrac{34}{1}}$

Step 3 $\boxed{\dfrac{13}{5} + \dfrac{34}{1}} = \boxed{\dfrac{(13 \times 1) + (34 \times 5)}{5 \times 1}} = \boxed{\dfrac{13 + 170}{5}} = \boxed{\dfrac{183}{5}}$

Step 4 $\boxed{\textit{Not Applicable}}$

Step 5 $\boxed{\dfrac{183}{5}} = \boxed{36\dfrac{3}{5}}$

Case II-B   *Add three integer and mixed fractions without a common denominator using the following steps:*

Step 1   Use parentheses to group the first and second fractions.

Step 2   Change the integer number (a) to an integer fraction of the form $\left(\dfrac{a}{1}\right)$, e.g., change 245 to $\dfrac{245}{1}$.

Step 3   Change the mixed fraction(s) to integer fraction(s) (see Section 2.5).

Step 4   Add the integer fractions (see Section 3.1, Case II-B).

Step 5   Simplify the fraction to its lowest term (see Section 2.3).

Step 6   Change the improper fraction to a mixed fraction if the fraction obtained from Step 5 is an improper fraction (see Section 2.2).

The following examples show the steps as to how three integer and mixed fractions without a common denominator are added:

Example 7.1-16

$$\boxed{3 + 2\dfrac{1}{3} + \dfrac{6}{8}} =$$

Solution:

Step 1 $\boxed{3+2\dfrac{1}{3}+\dfrac{6}{8}} = \boxed{\left(3+2\dfrac{1}{3}\right)+\dfrac{6}{8}}$

Step 2 $\boxed{\left(3+2\dfrac{1}{3}\right)+\dfrac{6}{8}} = \boxed{\left(\dfrac{3}{1}+2\dfrac{1}{3}\right)+\dfrac{6}{8}}$

Step 3 $\boxed{\left(\dfrac{3}{1}+2\dfrac{1}{3}\right)+\dfrac{6}{8}} = \boxed{\left(\dfrac{3}{1}+\dfrac{(2\times 3)+1}{3}\right)+\dfrac{6}{8}} = \boxed{\left(\dfrac{3}{1}+\dfrac{6+1}{3}\right)+\dfrac{6}{8}} = \boxed{\left(\dfrac{3}{1}+\dfrac{7}{3}\right)+\dfrac{6}{8}}$

Step 4 $\boxed{\left(\dfrac{3}{1}+\dfrac{7}{3}\right)+\dfrac{6}{8}} = \boxed{\left(\dfrac{(3\times 3)+(7\times 1)}{1\times 3}\right)+\dfrac{6}{8}} = \boxed{\left(\dfrac{9+7}{3}\right)+\dfrac{6}{8}} = \boxed{\left(\dfrac{16}{3}\right)+\dfrac{6}{8}} = \boxed{\dfrac{16}{3}+\dfrac{6}{8}}$

$= \boxed{\dfrac{(16\times 8)+(6\times 3)}{3\times 8}} = \boxed{\dfrac{128+18}{24}} = \boxed{\dfrac{146}{24}}$

Step 5 $\boxed{\dfrac{146}{24}} = \boxed{\dfrac{146\div 2}{24\div 2}} = \boxed{\dfrac{73}{12}}$

Step 6 $\boxed{\dfrac{73}{12}} = \boxed{\mathbf{6\dfrac{1}{12}}}$

Example 7.1-17

$\boxed{3\dfrac{2}{5}+\dfrac{6}{1}+1\dfrac{2}{3}} =$

Solution:

Step 1 $\boxed{3\dfrac{2}{5}+\dfrac{6}{1}+1\dfrac{2}{3}} = \boxed{\left(3\dfrac{2}{5}+\dfrac{6}{1}\right)+1\dfrac{2}{3}}$

Step 2 $\boxed{Not\ Applicable}$

Step 3 $\boxed{\left(3\dfrac{2}{5}+\dfrac{6}{1}\right)+1\dfrac{2}{3}} = \boxed{\left(\dfrac{(3\times 5)+2}{5}+\dfrac{6}{1}\right)+\dfrac{(1\times 3)+2}{3}} = \boxed{\left(\dfrac{15+2}{5}+\dfrac{6}{1}\right)+\dfrac{3+2}{3}}$

$= \boxed{\left(\dfrac{17}{5}+\dfrac{6}{1}\right)+\dfrac{5}{3}}$

Step 4 $\boxed{\left(\dfrac{17}{5}+\dfrac{6}{1}\right)+\dfrac{5}{3}} = \boxed{\left(\dfrac{(17\times 1)+(6\times 5)}{5\times 1}\right)+\dfrac{5}{3}} = \boxed{\left(\dfrac{17+30}{5}\right)+\dfrac{5}{3}} = \boxed{\left(\dfrac{47}{5}\right)+\dfrac{5}{3}} = \boxed{\dfrac{47}{5}+\dfrac{5}{3}}$

$$= \boxed{\frac{(47 \times 3) + (5 \times 5)}{5 \times 3}} = \boxed{\frac{141 + 25}{15}} = \boxed{\frac{166}{15}}$$

Step 5 $\boxed{Not\ Applicable}$

Step 6 $\boxed{\frac{166}{15}} = \boxed{11\frac{1}{15}}$

Example 7.1-18

$$\boxed{4\frac{3}{5} + 1\frac{4}{7} + 9} =$$

Solution:

Step 1 $\boxed{4\frac{3}{5} + 1\frac{4}{7} + 9} = \boxed{\left(4\frac{3}{5} + 1\frac{4}{7}\right) + 9}$

Step 2 $\boxed{\left(4\frac{3}{5} + 1\frac{4}{7}\right) + 9} = \boxed{\left(4\frac{3}{5} + 1\frac{4}{7}\right) + \frac{9}{1}}$

Step 3 $\boxed{\left(4\frac{3}{5} + 1\frac{4}{7}\right) + \frac{9}{1}} = \boxed{\left(\frac{(4 \times 5) + 3}{5} + \frac{(1 \times 7) + 4}{7}\right) + \frac{9}{1}} = \boxed{\left(\frac{20 + 3}{5} + \frac{7 + 4}{7}\right) + \frac{9}{1}}$

$$= \boxed{\left(\frac{23}{5} + \frac{11}{7}\right) + \frac{9}{1}}$$

Step 4 $\boxed{\left(\frac{23}{5} + \frac{11}{7}\right) + \frac{9}{1}} = \boxed{\left(\frac{(23 \times 7) + (11 \times 5)}{5 \times 7}\right) + \frac{9}{1}} = \boxed{\left(\frac{161 + 55}{35}\right) + \frac{9}{1}} = \boxed{\left(\frac{216}{35}\right) + \frac{9}{1}}$

$$= \boxed{\frac{216}{35} + \frac{9}{1}} = \boxed{\frac{(216 \times 1) + (9 \times 35)}{35 \times 1}} = \boxed{\frac{216 + 315}{35}} = \boxed{\frac{531}{35}}$$

Step 5 $\boxed{Not\ Applicable}$

Step 6 $\boxed{\frac{531}{35}} = \boxed{15\frac{6}{35}}$

Example 7.1-19

$$\boxed{6\frac{1}{5} + \frac{5}{8} + \frac{2}{3}} =$$

Solution:

Step 1 $\boxed{6\frac{1}{5} + \frac{5}{8} + \frac{2}{3}} = \boxed{\left(6\frac{1}{5} + \frac{5}{8}\right) + \frac{2}{3}}$

Step 2 $\boxed{Not\ Applicable}$

Step 3 $\boxed{\left(6\dfrac{1}{5}+\dfrac{5}{8}\right)+\dfrac{2}{3}} = \boxed{\left(\dfrac{(6\times 5)+1}{5}+\dfrac{5}{8}\right)+\dfrac{2}{3}} = \boxed{\left(\dfrac{30+1}{5}+\dfrac{5}{8}\right)+\dfrac{2}{3}} = \boxed{\left(\dfrac{31}{5}+\dfrac{5}{8}\right)+\dfrac{2}{3}}$

Step 4 $\boxed{\left(\dfrac{31}{5}+\dfrac{5}{8}\right)+\dfrac{2}{3}} = \boxed{\left(\dfrac{(31\times 8)+(5\times 5)}{5\times 8}\right)+\dfrac{2}{3}} = \boxed{\left(\dfrac{248+25}{40}\right)+\dfrac{2}{3}} = \boxed{\left(\dfrac{273}{40}\right)+\dfrac{2}{3}}$

$= \boxed{\dfrac{273}{40}+\dfrac{2}{3}} = \boxed{\dfrac{(273\times 3)+(2\times 40)}{40\times 3}} = \boxed{\dfrac{819+80}{120}} = \boxed{\dfrac{899}{120}}$

Step 5 $\boxed{Not\ Applicable}$

Step 6 $\boxed{\dfrac{899}{120}} = \boxed{\mathbf{7\dfrac{59}{120}}}$

Example 7.1-20

$\boxed{4\dfrac{2}{5}+24+\dfrac{6}{7}} =$

Solution:

Step 1 $\boxed{4\dfrac{2}{5}+24+\dfrac{6}{7}} = \boxed{\left(4\dfrac{2}{5}+24\right)+\dfrac{6}{7}}$

Step 2 $\boxed{\left(4\dfrac{2}{5}+24\right)+\dfrac{6}{7}} = \boxed{\left(4\dfrac{2}{5}+\dfrac{24}{1}\right)+\dfrac{6}{7}}$

Step 3 $\boxed{\left(4\dfrac{2}{5}+\dfrac{24}{1}\right)+\dfrac{6}{7}} = \boxed{\left(\dfrac{(4\times 5)+2}{5}+\dfrac{24}{1}\right)+\dfrac{6}{7}} = \boxed{\left(\dfrac{20+2}{5}+\dfrac{24}{1}\right)+\dfrac{6}{7}} = \boxed{\left(\dfrac{22}{5}+\dfrac{24}{1}\right)+\dfrac{6}{7}}$

Step 4 $\boxed{\left(\dfrac{22}{5}+\dfrac{24}{1}\right)+\dfrac{6}{7}} = \boxed{\left(\dfrac{(22\times 1)+(5\times 24)}{5\times 1}\right)+\dfrac{6}{7}} = \boxed{\left(\dfrac{22+120}{5}\right)+\dfrac{6}{7}} = \boxed{\left(\dfrac{142}{5}\right)+\dfrac{6}{7}}$

$= \boxed{\dfrac{142}{5}+\dfrac{6}{7}} = \boxed{\dfrac{(142\times 7)+(6\times 5)}{5\times 7}} = \boxed{\dfrac{994+30}{35}} = \boxed{\dfrac{1024}{35}}$

Step 5 $\boxed{Not\ Applicable}$

Step 6 $\boxed{\dfrac{1024}{35}} = \boxed{\mathbf{29\dfrac{9}{35}}}$

The following examples further illustrate how to add integer and mixed fractions:

Example 7.1-21

$$\boxed{\frac{3}{5}+5\frac{2}{5}} = \boxed{\frac{3}{5}+\frac{(5\times5)+2}{5}} = \boxed{\frac{3}{5}+\frac{25+2}{5}} = \boxed{\frac{3}{5}+\frac{27}{5}} = \boxed{\frac{3+27}{5}} = \boxed{\frac{\overset{6}{\cancel{30}}}{\underset{1}{\cancel{5}}}} = \boxed{\frac{6}{1}} = \boxed{6}$$

Example 7.1-22

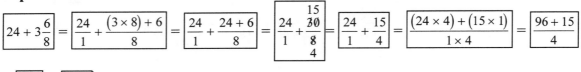

$$\boxed{24+3\frac{6}{8}} = \boxed{\frac{24}{1}+\frac{(3\times8)+6}{8}} = \boxed{\frac{24}{1}+\frac{24+6}{8}} = \boxed{\frac{24}{1}+\frac{\overset{15}{\cancel{30}}}{\underset{4}{\cancel{8}}}} = \boxed{\frac{24}{1}+\frac{15}{4}} = \boxed{\frac{(24\times4)+(15\times1)}{1\times4}} = \boxed{\frac{96+15}{4}}$$

$$= \boxed{\frac{111}{4}} = \boxed{27\frac{3}{4}}$$

Example 7.1-23

$$\boxed{10\frac{4}{5}+\frac{3}{8}} = \boxed{\frac{(10\times5)+4}{5}+\frac{3}{8}} = \boxed{\frac{50+4}{5}+\frac{3}{8}} = \boxed{\frac{54}{5}+\frac{3}{8}} = \boxed{\frac{(54\times8)+(3\times5)}{5\times8}} = \boxed{\frac{432+15}{40}} = \boxed{\frac{447}{40}}$$

$$= \boxed{11\frac{7}{40}}$$

Example 7.1-24

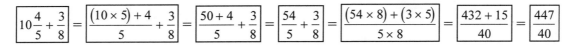

$$\boxed{\frac{2}{3}+5\frac{1}{3}+2\frac{1}{3}} = \boxed{\frac{2}{3}+\frac{(5\times3)+1}{3}+\frac{(2\times3)+1}{3}} = \boxed{\frac{2}{3}+\frac{15+1}{3}+\frac{6+1}{3}} = \boxed{\frac{2}{3}+\frac{16}{3}+\frac{7}{3}} = \boxed{\frac{2+16+7}{3}} = \boxed{\frac{25}{3}}$$

$$= \boxed{8\frac{1}{3}}$$

Example 7.1-25

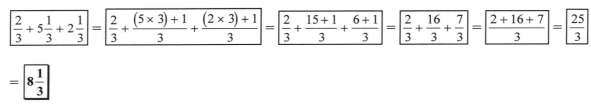

$$\boxed{\frac{3}{8}+5\frac{2}{3}+9} = \boxed{\left(\frac{3}{8}+5\frac{2}{3}\right)+9} = \boxed{\left(\frac{3}{8}+\frac{(5\times3)+2}{3}\right)+\frac{9}{1}} = \boxed{\left(\frac{3}{8}+\frac{15+2}{3}\right)+\frac{9}{1}} = \boxed{\left(\frac{3}{8}+\frac{17}{3}\right)+\frac{9}{1}}$$

$$= \boxed{\left(\frac{(3\times3)+(17\times8)}{8\times3}\right)+\frac{9}{1}} = \boxed{\left(\frac{9+136}{24}\right)+\frac{9}{1}} = \boxed{\left(\frac{145}{24}\right)+\frac{9}{1}} = \boxed{\frac{145}{24}+\frac{9}{1}} = \boxed{\frac{(145\times1)+(9\times24)}{24\times1}}$$

$$= \boxed{\frac{145+216}{24}} = \boxed{\frac{361}{24}} = \boxed{15\frac{1}{24}}$$

Example 7.1-26

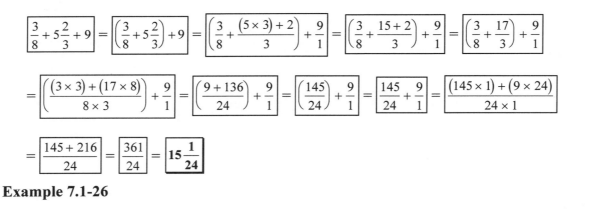

$$\boxed{\frac{2}{3}+\left(3\frac{4}{5}+\frac{5}{6}\right)} = \boxed{\frac{2}{3}+\left(\frac{(3\times5)+4}{5}+\frac{5}{6}\right)} = \boxed{\frac{2}{3}+\left(\frac{15+4}{5}+\frac{5}{6}\right)} = \boxed{\frac{2}{3}+\left(\frac{19}{5}+\frac{5}{6}\right)} = \boxed{\frac{2}{3}+\left(\frac{(19\times6)+(5\times5)}{5\times6}\right)}$$

$$= \boxed{\frac{2}{3} + \left(\frac{114+25}{30}\right)} = \boxed{\frac{2}{3} + \left(\frac{139}{30}\right)} = \boxed{\frac{2}{3} + \frac{139}{30}} = \boxed{\frac{(2\times30)+(139\times3)}{3\times30}} = \boxed{\frac{60+417}{90}} = \boxed{\frac{\overset{53}{\cancel{477}}}{\underset{10}{\cancel{90}}}} = \boxed{\frac{53}{10}} = \boxed{5\frac{3}{10}}$$

Example 7.1-27

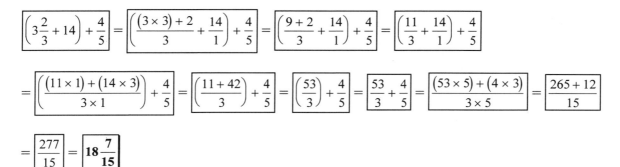

$$\boxed{\left(3\frac{2}{3}+14\right)+\frac{4}{5}} = \boxed{\left(\frac{(3\times3)+2}{3}+\frac{14}{1}\right)+\frac{4}{5}} = \boxed{\left(\frac{9+2}{3}+\frac{14}{1}\right)+\frac{4}{5}} = \boxed{\left(\frac{11}{3}+\frac{14}{1}\right)+\frac{4}{5}}$$

$$= \boxed{\left(\frac{(11\times1)+(14\times3)}{3\times1}\right)+\frac{4}{5}} = \boxed{\left(\frac{11+42}{3}\right)+\frac{4}{5}} = \boxed{\left(\frac{53}{3}\right)+\frac{4}{5}} = \boxed{\frac{53}{3}+\frac{4}{5}} = \boxed{\frac{(53\times5)+(4\times3)}{3\times5}} = \boxed{\frac{265+12}{15}}$$

$$= \boxed{\frac{277}{15}} = \boxed{18\frac{7}{15}}$$

Example 7.1-28

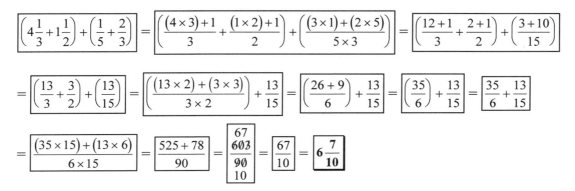

$$\boxed{\left(4\frac{1}{3}+1\frac{1}{2}\right)+\left(\frac{1}{5}+\frac{2}{3}\right)} = \boxed{\left(\frac{(4\times3)+1}{3}+\frac{(1\times2)+1}{2}\right)+\left(\frac{(3\times1)+(2\times5)}{5\times3}\right)} = \boxed{\left(\frac{12+1}{3}+\frac{2+1}{2}\right)+\left(\frac{3+10}{15}\right)}$$

$$= \boxed{\left(\frac{13}{3}+\frac{3}{2}\right)+\left(\frac{13}{15}\right)} = \boxed{\left(\frac{(13\times2)+(3\times3)}{3\times2}\right)+\frac{13}{15}} = \boxed{\left(\frac{26+9}{6}\right)+\frac{13}{15}} = \boxed{\left(\frac{35}{6}\right)+\frac{13}{15}} = \boxed{\frac{35}{6}+\frac{13}{15}}$$

$$= \boxed{\frac{(35\times15)+(13\times6)}{6\times15}} = \boxed{\frac{525+78}{90}} = \boxed{\frac{\overset{67}{\cancel{603}}}{\underset{10}{\cancel{90}}}} = \boxed{\frac{67}{10}} = \boxed{6\frac{7}{10}}$$

Example 7.1-29

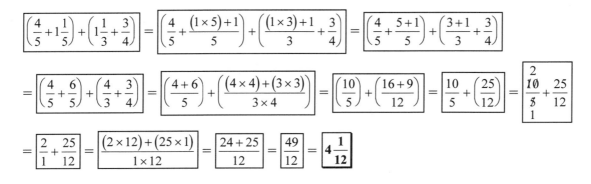

$$\boxed{\left(\frac{4}{5}+1\frac{1}{5}\right)+\left(1\frac{1}{3}+\frac{3}{4}\right)} = \boxed{\left(\frac{4}{5}+\frac{(1\times5)+1}{5}\right)+\left(\frac{(1\times3)+1}{3}+\frac{3}{4}\right)} = \boxed{\left(\frac{4}{5}+\frac{5+1}{5}\right)+\left(\frac{3+1}{3}+\frac{3}{4}\right)}$$

$$= \boxed{\left(\frac{4}{5}+\frac{6}{5}\right)+\left(\frac{4}{3}+\frac{3}{4}\right)} = \boxed{\left(\frac{4+6}{5}\right)+\left(\frac{(4\times4)+(3\times3)}{3\times4}\right)} = \boxed{\left(\frac{10}{5}\right)+\left(\frac{16+9}{12}\right)} = \boxed{\frac{10}{5}+\left(\frac{25}{12}\right)} = \boxed{\frac{\overset{2}{\cancel{10}}}{\underset{1}{\cancel{5}}}+\frac{25}{12}}$$

$$= \boxed{\frac{2}{1}+\frac{25}{12}} = \boxed{\frac{(2\times12)+(25\times1)}{1\times12}} = \boxed{\frac{24+25}{12}} = \boxed{\frac{49}{12}} = \boxed{4\frac{1}{12}}$$

Example 7.1-30

$$\boxed{\left[\left(1\frac{2}{3}+2\frac{1}{3}\right)+\frac{4}{5}\right]+\left(3\frac{1}{2}+\frac{1}{3}\right)} = \boxed{\left[\left(\frac{(1\times3)+2}{3}+\frac{(2\times3)+1}{3}\right)+\frac{4}{5}\right]+\left(\frac{(3\times2)+1}{2}+\frac{1}{3}\right)}$$

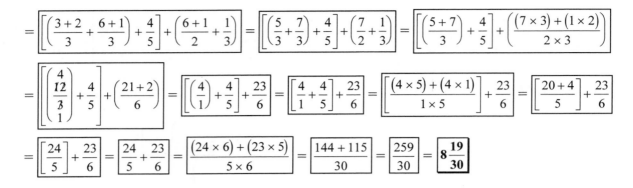

Example 7.1-31

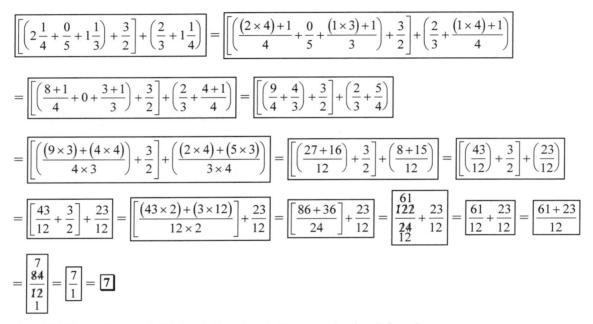

Section 7.1 Exercises - Add the following integer and mixed fractions:

1. $\dfrac{2}{3} + 2\dfrac{1}{3} =$

2. $1\dfrac{1}{3} + 2\dfrac{1}{5} + \dfrac{5}{6} =$

3. $1\dfrac{1}{5} + 2\dfrac{1}{3} + 4 =$

4. $\dfrac{3}{4} + \left(1\dfrac{1}{4} + 2\dfrac{1}{3}\right) =$

5. $\left(2\dfrac{1}{6} + \dfrac{3}{8}\right) + 12 =$

6. $\left(3\dfrac{1}{5} + 2\dfrac{1}{2}\right) + \dfrac{4}{5} =$

7. $1\dfrac{3}{5} + \left(\dfrac{2}{3} + \dfrac{4}{3} + \dfrac{1}{3}\right) =$

8. $3\dfrac{1}{4} + \left(2\dfrac{1}{2} + 5\right) =$

9. $\left(\dfrac{1}{3} + 2\dfrac{1}{3}\right) + \dfrac{4}{6} =$

10. $\left[\left(\dfrac{4}{5} + 2\dfrac{1}{3}\right) + 1\dfrac{1}{3}\right] + 22 =$

7.2 Subtracting Integer and Mixed Fractions

Integer fractions of the form $\left(\dfrac{a}{b}\right)$ where both the numerator (a) and the denominator (b) are integers, and mixed fractions of the form $\left(k\dfrac{a}{b}\right)$ where (k) is a whole number and $\left(\dfrac{a}{b}\right)$ is an integer fraction are subtracted as in the following cases:

Case I Subtracting Two or More Integer and Mixed Fractions With Common Denominators

Integer and mixed fractions with two or more common denominators are subtracted using the steps given as in each case below:

Case I-A *Subtract two integer and mixed fractions with common denominators using the following steps:*

Step 1 Change the mixed fraction to an integer fraction (see Section 2.5).

Step 2 Subtract the integer fractions (see Section 3.2, Case I-A).

Step 3 Simplify the fraction to its lowest term (see Section 2.3).

Step 4 Change the improper fraction to a mixed fraction if the fraction obtained from Step 3 is an improper fraction (see Section 2.2).

The following examples show the steps as to how two integer and mixed fractions with common denominators are subtracted:

Example 7.2-1

$$\boxed{15\dfrac{3}{5} - \dfrac{2}{5}} =$$

Solution:

Step 1 $\boxed{15\dfrac{3}{5} - \dfrac{2}{5}} = \boxed{\dfrac{(15 \times 5) + 3}{5} - \dfrac{2}{5}} = \boxed{\dfrac{75 + 3}{5} - \dfrac{2}{5}} = \boxed{\dfrac{78}{5} - \dfrac{2}{5}}$

Step 2 $\boxed{\dfrac{78}{5} - \dfrac{2}{5}} = \boxed{\dfrac{78 - 2}{5}} = \boxed{\dfrac{76}{5}}$

Step 3 $\boxed{Not\ Applicable}$

Step 4 $\boxed{\dfrac{76}{5}} = \boxed{\mathbf{15\dfrac{1}{5}}}$

Example 7.2-2

$$\boxed{\dfrac{9}{10} - 5\dfrac{4}{10}} =$$

Solution:

Step 1 $\boxed{\dfrac{9}{10} - 5\dfrac{4}{10}} = \boxed{\dfrac{9}{10} - \dfrac{(5 \times 10) + 4}{10}} = \boxed{\dfrac{9}{10} - \dfrac{50 + 4}{10}} = \boxed{\dfrac{9}{10} - \dfrac{54}{10}}$

Step 2 $\boxed{\dfrac{9}{10} - \dfrac{54}{10}} = \boxed{\dfrac{9 - 54}{10}} = \boxed{\dfrac{-45}{10}}$

Step 3 $\boxed{\dfrac{-45}{10}} = \boxed{\dfrac{-45 \div 5}{10 \div 5}} = \boxed{\dfrac{-9}{2}}$

Step 4 $\boxed{\dfrac{-9}{2}} = \boxed{-\left(4\dfrac{1}{2}\right)}$

Example 7.2-3

$\boxed{2\dfrac{5}{12} - \dfrac{7}{12}} =$

Solution:

Step 1 $\boxed{2\dfrac{5}{12} - \dfrac{7}{12}} = \boxed{\dfrac{(2 \times 12) + 5}{12} - \dfrac{7}{12}} = \boxed{\dfrac{24 + 5}{12} - \dfrac{7}{12}} = \boxed{\dfrac{29}{12} - \dfrac{7}{12}}$

Step 2 $\boxed{\dfrac{29}{12} - \dfrac{7}{12}} = \boxed{\dfrac{29 - 7}{12}} = \boxed{\dfrac{22}{12}}$

Step 3 $\boxed{\dfrac{22}{12}} = \boxed{\dfrac{22 \div 2}{12 \div 2}} = \boxed{\dfrac{11}{6}}$

Step 4 $\boxed{\dfrac{11}{6}} = \boxed{1\dfrac{5}{6}}$

Example 7.2-4

$\boxed{3\dfrac{1}{13} - \dfrac{9}{13}} =$

Solution:

Step 1 $\boxed{3\dfrac{1}{13} - \dfrac{9}{13}} = \boxed{\dfrac{(3 \times 13) + 1}{13} - \dfrac{9}{13}} = \boxed{\dfrac{39 + 1}{13} - \dfrac{9}{13}} = \boxed{\dfrac{40}{13} - \dfrac{9}{13}}$

Step 2 $\boxed{\dfrac{40}{13} - \dfrac{9}{13}} = \boxed{\dfrac{40 - 9}{13}} = \boxed{\dfrac{31}{13}}$

Step 3 $\boxed{\textit{Not Applicable}}$

Step 4 $\boxed{\dfrac{31}{13}} = \boxed{2\dfrac{5}{13}}$

Example 7.2-5

$$\boxed{\dfrac{2}{3} - 2\dfrac{1}{3}} =$$

Solution:

Step 1 $\boxed{\dfrac{2}{3} - 2\dfrac{1}{3}} = \boxed{\dfrac{2}{3} - \dfrac{(2 \times 3) + 1}{3}} = \boxed{\dfrac{2}{3} - \dfrac{6 + 1}{3}} = \boxed{\dfrac{2}{3} - \dfrac{7}{3}}$

Step 2 $\boxed{\dfrac{2}{3} - \dfrac{7}{3}} = \boxed{\dfrac{2 - 7}{3}} = \boxed{-\dfrac{5}{3}}$

Step 3 $\boxed{Not\ Applicable}$

Step 4 $\boxed{-\dfrac{5}{3}} = \boxed{-\left(1\dfrac{2}{3}\right)}$

Case I-B   *Subtract three integer and mixed fractions with common denominators using the following steps:*

Step 1   Change the mixed fraction(s) to integer fraction(s) (see Section 2.5).

Step 2   Subtract the integer fractions (see Section 3.2, Case I-B).

Step 3   Simplify the fraction to its lowest term (see Section 2.3).

Step 4   Change the improper fraction to a mixed fraction if the fraction obtained from Step 3 is an improper fraction (see Section 2.2).

The following examples show the steps as to how three integer and mixed fractions with common denominators are subtracted:

Example 7.2-6

$$\boxed{20\dfrac{3}{4} - 6\dfrac{1}{4} - \dfrac{2}{4}} =$$

Solution:

Step 1 $\boxed{20\dfrac{3}{4} - 6\dfrac{1}{4} - \dfrac{2}{4}} = \boxed{\dfrac{(20 \times 4) + 3}{4} - \dfrac{(6 \times 4) + 1}{4} - \dfrac{2}{4}} = \boxed{\dfrac{80 + 3}{4} - \dfrac{24 + 1}{4} - \dfrac{2}{4}}$

$$= \boxed{\dfrac{83}{4} - \dfrac{25}{4} - \dfrac{2}{4}}$$

Step 2 $\boxed{\dfrac{83}{4} - \dfrac{25}{4} - \dfrac{2}{4}} = \boxed{\dfrac{83 - 25 - 2}{4}} = \boxed{\dfrac{56}{4}}$

Step 3 $\left|\dfrac{56}{4}\right| = \left|\dfrac{56 \div 4}{4 \div 4}\right| = \left|\dfrac{14}{1}\right| = \boxed{14}$

Step 4 $\boxed{\textit{Not Applicable}}$

Example 7.2-7

$$\left|2\dfrac{10}{13} - \dfrac{5}{13} - \dfrac{9}{13}\right| =$$

Solution:

Step 1 $\left|2\dfrac{10}{13} - \dfrac{5}{13} - \dfrac{9}{13}\right| = \left|\dfrac{(2 \times 13) + 10}{13} - \dfrac{5}{13} - \dfrac{9}{13}\right| = \left|\dfrac{26 + 10}{13} - \dfrac{5}{13} - \dfrac{9}{13}\right|$

$= \left|\dfrac{36}{13} - \dfrac{5}{13} - \dfrac{9}{13}\right|$

Step 2 $\left|\dfrac{36}{13} - \dfrac{5}{13} - \dfrac{9}{13}\right| = \left|\dfrac{36 - 5 - 9}{13}\right| = \left|\dfrac{22}{13}\right|$

Step 3 $\boxed{\textit{Not Applicable}}$

Step 4 $\left|\dfrac{22}{13}\right| = \boxed{\mathbf{1\dfrac{9}{13}}}$

Example 7.2-8

$$\left|4\dfrac{1}{5} - \dfrac{2}{5} - 6\dfrac{3}{5}\right| =$$

Solution:

Step 1 $\left|4\dfrac{1}{5} - \dfrac{2}{5} - 6\dfrac{3}{5}\right| = \left|\dfrac{(4 \times 5) + 1}{5} - \dfrac{2}{5} - \dfrac{(6 \times 5) + 3}{5}\right| = \left|\dfrac{20 + 1}{5} - \dfrac{2}{5} - \dfrac{30 + 3}{5}\right|$

$= \left|\dfrac{21}{5} - \dfrac{2}{5} - \dfrac{33}{5}\right|$

Step 2 $\left|\dfrac{21}{5} - \dfrac{2}{5} - \dfrac{33}{5}\right| = \left|\dfrac{21 - 2 - 33}{5}\right| = \left|\dfrac{-14}{5}\right|$

Step 3 $\boxed{\textit{Not Applicable}}$

Step 4 $\left|\dfrac{-14}{5}\right| = \boxed{-\left(2\dfrac{4}{5}\right)}$

Example 7.2-9

$$6\frac{2}{7} - 5\frac{3}{7} - \frac{1}{7} =$$

Solution:

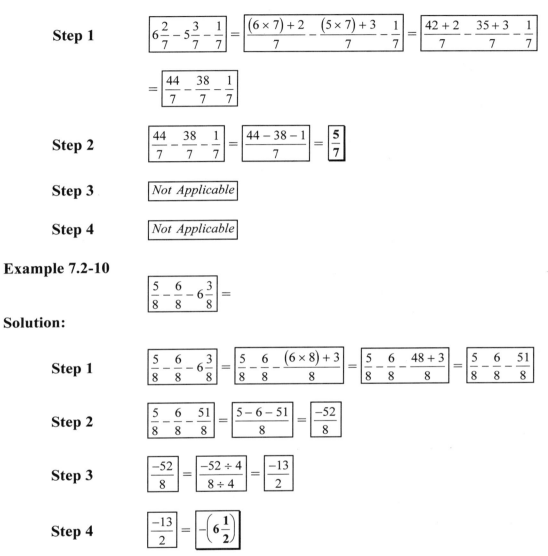

Step 1

$$6\frac{2}{7} - 5\frac{3}{7} - \frac{1}{7} = \frac{(6 \times 7) + 2}{7} - \frac{(5 \times 7) + 3}{7} - \frac{1}{7} = \frac{42 + 2}{7} - \frac{35 + 3}{7} - \frac{1}{7}$$

$$= \frac{44}{7} - \frac{38}{7} - \frac{1}{7}$$

Step 2

$$\frac{44}{7} - \frac{38}{7} - \frac{1}{7} = \frac{44 - 38 - 1}{7} = \boxed{\frac{5}{7}}$$

Step 3 $\boxed{Not\ Applicable}$

Step 4 $\boxed{Not\ Applicable}$

Example 7.2-10

$$\frac{5}{8} - \frac{6}{8} - 6\frac{3}{8} =$$

Solution:

Step 1

$$\frac{5}{8} - \frac{6}{8} - 6\frac{3}{8} = \frac{5}{8} - \frac{6}{8} - \frac{(6 \times 8) + 3}{8} = \frac{5}{8} - \frac{6}{8} - \frac{48 + 3}{8} = \frac{5}{8} - \frac{6}{8} - \frac{51}{8}$$

Step 2

$$\frac{5}{8} - \frac{6}{8} - \frac{51}{8} = \frac{5 - 6 - 51}{8} = \frac{-52}{8}$$

Step 3

$$\frac{-52}{8} = \frac{-52 \div 4}{8 \div 4} = \frac{-13}{2}$$

Step 4

$$\frac{-13}{2} = -\left(6\frac{1}{2}\right)$$

Case II   Subtracting Two or More Integer and Mixed Fractions Without a Common Denominator

Two or more integer and mixed fractions without a common denominator are subtracted using the steps given as in each case below:

Case II-A   *Subtract two integer and mixed fractions without a common denominator using the following steps:*

Step 1   Change the integer number (a) to an integer fraction of the form $\left(\dfrac{a}{1}\right)$, e.g., change

225 to $\dfrac{225}{1}$.

Step 2   Change the mixed fraction to an integer fraction (see Section 2.5).

Step 3   Subtract the integer fractions (see Section 3.2, Case II-A).

Step 4   Simplify the fraction to its lowest term (see Section 2.3).

Step 5   Change the improper fraction to a mixed fraction if the fraction obtained from Step 4 is an improper fraction (see Section 2.2).

The following examples show the steps as to how two integer and mixed fractions without a common denominator are subtracted:

Example 7.2-11

$$\boxed{10\dfrac{3}{8} - \dfrac{2}{5}} =$$

Solution:

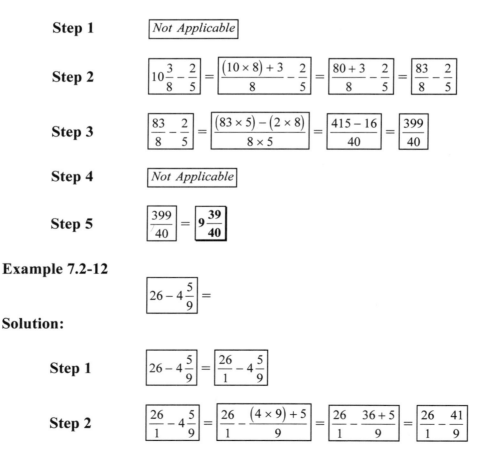

> **Step 1** $\boxed{Not\ Applicable}$
>
> **Step 2** $\boxed{10\dfrac{3}{8} - \dfrac{2}{5}} = \boxed{\dfrac{(10 \times 8) + 3}{8} - \dfrac{2}{5}} = \boxed{\dfrac{80 + 3}{8} - \dfrac{2}{5}} = \boxed{\dfrac{83}{8} - \dfrac{2}{5}}$
>
> **Step 3** $\boxed{\dfrac{83}{8} - \dfrac{2}{5}} = \boxed{\dfrac{(83 \times 5) - (2 \times 8)}{8 \times 5}} = \boxed{\dfrac{415 - 16}{40}} = \boxed{\dfrac{399}{40}}$
>
> **Step 4** $\boxed{Not\ Applicable}$
>
> **Step 5** $\boxed{\dfrac{399}{40}} = \boxed{9\dfrac{39}{40}}$

Example 7.2-12

$$\boxed{26 - 4\dfrac{5}{9}} =$$

Solution:

> **Step 1** $\boxed{26 - 4\dfrac{5}{9}} = \boxed{\dfrac{26}{1} - 4\dfrac{5}{9}}$
>
> **Step 2** $\boxed{\dfrac{26}{1} - 4\dfrac{5}{9}} = \boxed{\dfrac{26}{1} - \dfrac{(4 \times 9) + 5}{9}} = \boxed{\dfrac{26}{1} - \dfrac{36 + 5}{9}} = \boxed{\dfrac{26}{1} - \dfrac{41}{9}}$

Step 3 $\dfrac{26}{1}-\dfrac{41}{9}=\dfrac{(26\times 9)-(41\times 1)}{1\times 9}=\dfrac{234-41}{9}=\dfrac{193}{9}$

Step 4 $\boxed{\textit{Not Applicable}}$

Step 5 $\dfrac{193}{9}=\mathbf{21\dfrac{4}{9}}$

Example 7.2-13

$\dfrac{3}{5}-2\dfrac{1}{3}=$

Solution:

Step 1 $\boxed{\textit{Not Applicable}}$

Step 2 $\dfrac{3}{5}-2\dfrac{1}{3}=\dfrac{3}{5}-\dfrac{(2\times 3)+1}{3}=\dfrac{3}{5}-\dfrac{6+1}{3}=\dfrac{3}{5}-\dfrac{7}{3}$

Step 3 $\dfrac{3}{5}-\dfrac{7}{3}=\dfrac{(3\times 3)-(7\times 5)}{5\times 3}=\dfrac{9-35}{15}=\dfrac{-26}{15}$

Step 4 $\boxed{\textit{Not Applicable}}$

Step 5 $\dfrac{-26}{15}=\mathbf{-\left(1\dfrac{11}{15}\right)}$

Example 7.2-14

$6\dfrac{1}{4}-\dfrac{5}{8}=$

Solution:

Step 1 $\boxed{\textit{Not Applicable}}$

Step 2 $6\dfrac{1}{4}-\dfrac{5}{8}=\dfrac{(6\times 4)+1}{4}-\dfrac{5}{8}=\dfrac{24+1}{4}-\dfrac{5}{8}=\dfrac{25}{4}-\dfrac{5}{8}$

Step 3 $\dfrac{25}{4}-\dfrac{5}{8}=\dfrac{(25\times 8)-(5\times 4)}{4\times 8}=\dfrac{200-20}{32}=\dfrac{180}{32}$

Step 4 $\dfrac{180}{32}=\dfrac{180\div 4}{32\div 4}=\dfrac{45}{8}$

Step 5 $\dfrac{45}{8}=\mathbf{5\dfrac{5}{8}}$

Example 7.2-15

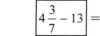

Solution:

Step 1 $\boxed{4\dfrac{3}{7} - 13} = \boxed{4\dfrac{3}{7} - \dfrac{13}{1}}$

Step 2 $\boxed{4\dfrac{3}{7} - \dfrac{13}{1}} = \boxed{\dfrac{(4 \times 7) + 3}{7} - \dfrac{13}{1}} = \boxed{\dfrac{28 + 3}{7} - \dfrac{13}{1}} = \boxed{\dfrac{31}{7} - \dfrac{13}{1}}$

Step 3 $\boxed{\dfrac{31}{7} - \dfrac{13}{1}} = \boxed{\dfrac{(31 \times 1) - (13 \times 7)}{7 \times 1}} = \boxed{\dfrac{31 - 91}{7}} = \boxed{-\dfrac{60}{7}}$

Step 4 $\boxed{\textit{Not Applicable}}$

Step 5 $\boxed{-\dfrac{60}{7}} = \boxed{-\left(8\dfrac{4}{7}\right)}$

Case II-B   *Subtract three integer and mixed fractions without a common denominator using the following steps:*

Step 1   Use parentheses to group the first and second fractions.

Step 2   Change the integer number (a) to an integer fraction of the form $\left(\dfrac{a}{1}\right)$, e.g., change

26 to $\dfrac{26}{1}$.

Step 3   Change the mixed fraction(s) to integer fraction(s) (see Section 2.5).

Step 4   Subtract the integer fractions (see Section 3.2, Case II-B).

Step 5   Simplify the fraction to its lowest term (see Section 2.3).

Step 6   Change the improper fraction to a mixed fraction if the fraction obtained from Step 5 is an improper fraction (see Section 2.2).

The following examples show the steps as to how three integer and mixed fractions without a common denominator are subtracted:

Example 7.2-16

$$\boxed{14 - 2\dfrac{1}{5} - \dfrac{6}{8}} =$$

Solution:

Step 1 $\boxed{14 - 2\dfrac{1}{5} - \dfrac{6}{8}} = \boxed{\left(14 - 2\dfrac{1}{5}\right) - \dfrac{6}{8}}$

Step 2
$$\left(14 - 2\frac{1}{5}\right) - \frac{6}{8} = \left[\left(\frac{14}{1} - 2\frac{1}{5}\right) - \frac{6}{8}\right]$$

Step 3
$$\left(\frac{14}{1} - 2\frac{1}{5}\right) - \frac{6}{8} = \left[\left(\frac{14}{1} - \frac{(2\times5)+1}{5}\right) - \frac{6}{8}\right] = \left[\left(\frac{14}{1} - \frac{10+1}{5}\right) - \frac{6}{8}\right] = \left[\left(\frac{14}{1} - \frac{11}{5}\right) - \frac{6}{8}\right]$$

Step 4
$$\left(\frac{14}{1} - \frac{11}{5}\right) - \frac{6}{8} = \left[\left(\frac{(14\times5)-(11\times1)}{1\times5}\right) - \frac{6}{8}\right] = \left[\left(\frac{70-11}{5}\right) - \frac{6}{8}\right] = \left[\left(\frac{59}{5}\right) - \frac{6}{8}\right]$$

$$= \left[\frac{59}{5} - \frac{6}{8}\right] = \left[\frac{(59\times8)-(6\times5)}{5\times8}\right] = \left[\frac{472-30}{40}\right] = \left[\frac{442}{40}\right]$$

Step 5
$$\frac{442}{40} = \frac{442\div2}{40\div2} = \frac{221}{20}$$

Step 6
$$\frac{221}{20} = \mathbf{11\frac{1}{20}}$$

Example 7.2-17
$$4\frac{2}{5} - \frac{1}{3} - 1\frac{2}{4} =$$

Solution:

Step 1
$$4\frac{2}{5} - \frac{1}{3} - 1\frac{2}{4} = \left(4\frac{2}{5} - \frac{1}{3}\right) - 1\frac{2}{4}$$

Step 2
Not Applicable

Step 3
$$\left(4\frac{2}{5} - \frac{1}{3}\right) - 1\frac{2}{4} = \left[\left(\frac{(4\times5)+2}{5} - \frac{1}{3}\right) - \frac{(1\times4)+2}{4}\right] = \left[\left(\frac{20+2}{5} - \frac{1}{3}\right) - \frac{4+2}{4}\right]$$

$$= \left[\left(\frac{22}{5} - \frac{1}{3}\right) - \frac{6}{4}\right]$$

Step 4
$$\left(\frac{22}{5} - \frac{1}{3}\right) - \frac{6}{4} = \left[\left(\frac{(22\times3)-(1\times5)}{5\times3}\right) - \frac{6}{4}\right] = \left[\left(\frac{66-5}{15}\right) - \frac{6}{4}\right] = \left[\left(\frac{61}{15}\right) - \frac{6}{4}\right] = \left[\frac{61}{15} - \frac{6}{4}\right]$$

$$= \left[\frac{(61\times4)-(6\times15)}{15\times4}\right] = \left[\frac{244-90}{60}\right] = \left[\frac{154}{60}\right]$$

Step 5
$$\frac{154}{60} = \frac{154\div2}{60\div2} = \frac{77}{30}$$

Step 6 $\boxed{\dfrac{77}{30}} = \boxed{2\dfrac{17}{30}}$

Example 7.2-18

$$\boxed{2\dfrac{3}{5} - 1\dfrac{2}{3} - 12} =$$

Solution:

Step 1 $\boxed{2\dfrac{3}{5} - 1\dfrac{2}{3} - 12} = \boxed{\left(2\dfrac{3}{5} - 1\dfrac{2}{3}\right) - 12}$

Step 2 $\boxed{\left(2\dfrac{3}{5} - 1\dfrac{2}{3}\right) - 12} = \boxed{\left(2\dfrac{3}{5} - 1\dfrac{2}{3}\right) - \dfrac{12}{1}}$

Step 3 $\boxed{\left(2\dfrac{3}{5} - 1\dfrac{2}{3}\right) - \dfrac{12}{1}} = \boxed{\left(\dfrac{(2\times 5)+3}{5} - \dfrac{(1\times 3)+2}{3}\right) - \dfrac{12}{1}} = \boxed{\left(\dfrac{10+3}{5} - \dfrac{3+2}{3}\right) - \dfrac{12}{1}}$

$$= \boxed{\left(\dfrac{13}{5} - \dfrac{5}{3}\right) - \dfrac{12}{1}}$$

Step 4 $\boxed{\left(\dfrac{13}{5} - \dfrac{5}{3}\right) - \dfrac{12}{1}} = \boxed{\left(\dfrac{(13\times 3)-(5\times 5)}{5\times 3}\right) - \dfrac{12}{1}} = \boxed{\left(\dfrac{39-25}{15}\right) - \dfrac{12}{1}} = \boxed{\left(\dfrac{14}{15}\right) - \dfrac{12}{1}}$

$$= \boxed{\dfrac{14}{15} - \dfrac{12}{1}} = \boxed{\dfrac{(14\times 1)-(12\times 15)}{15\times 1}} = \boxed{\dfrac{14-180}{15}} = \boxed{\dfrac{-166}{15}}$$

Step 5 $\boxed{\textit{Not Applicable}}$

Step 6 $\boxed{\dfrac{-166}{15}} = \boxed{-\left(11\dfrac{1}{15}\right)}$

Example 7.2-19

$$\boxed{4\dfrac{1}{2} - \dfrac{2}{8} - \dfrac{4}{10}} =$$

Solution:

Step 1 $\boxed{4\dfrac{1}{2} - \dfrac{2}{8} - \dfrac{4}{10}} = \boxed{\left(4\dfrac{1}{2} - \dfrac{2}{8}\right) - \dfrac{4}{10}}$

Step 2 $\boxed{\textit{Not Applicable}}$

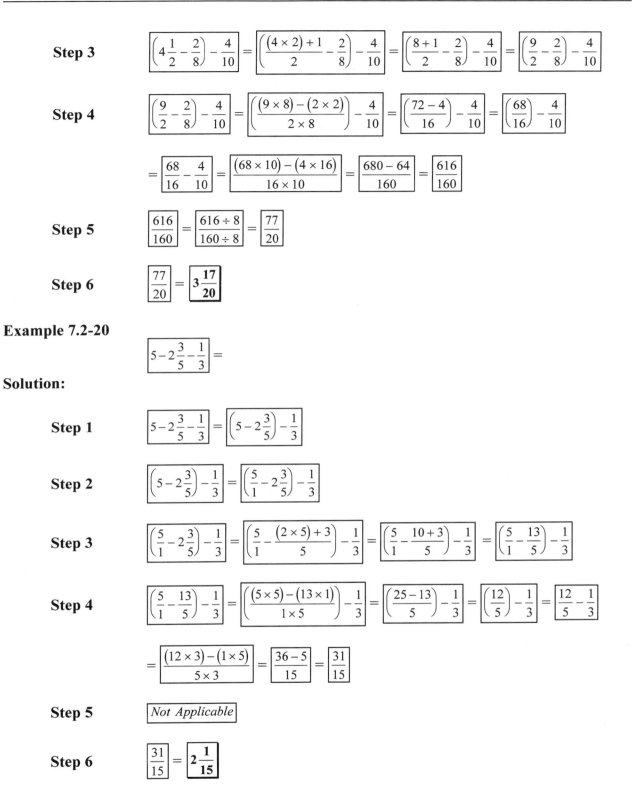

Step 3
$$\left(4\frac{1}{2}-\frac{2}{8}\right)-\frac{4}{10}=\left(\frac{(4\times2)+1}{2}-\frac{2}{8}\right)-\frac{4}{10}=\left(\frac{8+1}{2}-\frac{2}{8}\right)-\frac{4}{10}=\left(\frac{9}{2}-\frac{2}{8}\right)-\frac{4}{10}$$

Step 4
$$\left(\frac{9}{2}-\frac{2}{8}\right)-\frac{4}{10}=\left(\frac{(9\times8)-(2\times2)}{2\times8}\right)-\frac{4}{10}=\left(\frac{72-4}{16}\right)-\frac{4}{10}=\left(\frac{68}{16}\right)-\frac{4}{10}$$

$$=\frac{68}{16}-\frac{4}{10}=\frac{(68\times10)-(4\times16)}{16\times10}=\frac{680-64}{160}=\frac{616}{160}$$

Step 5
$$\frac{616}{160}=\frac{616\div8}{160\div8}=\frac{77}{20}$$

Step 6
$$\frac{77}{20}=3\frac{17}{20}$$

Example 7.2-20
$$5-2\frac{3}{5}-\frac{1}{3}=$$

Solution:

Step 1
$$5-2\frac{3}{5}-\frac{1}{3}=\left(5-2\frac{3}{5}\right)-\frac{1}{3}$$

Step 2
$$\left(5-2\frac{3}{5}\right)-\frac{1}{3}=\left(\frac{5}{1}-2\frac{3}{5}\right)-\frac{1}{3}$$

Step 3
$$\left(\frac{5}{1}-2\frac{3}{5}\right)-\frac{1}{3}=\left(\frac{5}{1}-\frac{(2\times5)+3}{5}\right)-\frac{1}{3}=\left(\frac{5}{1}-\frac{10+3}{5}\right)-\frac{1}{3}=\left(\frac{5}{1}-\frac{13}{5}\right)-\frac{1}{3}$$

Step 4
$$\left(\frac{5}{1}-\frac{13}{5}\right)-\frac{1}{3}=\left(\frac{(5\times5)-(13\times1)}{1\times5}\right)-\frac{1}{3}=\left(\frac{25-13}{5}\right)-\frac{1}{3}=\left(\frac{12}{5}\right)-\frac{1}{3}=\frac{12}{5}-\frac{1}{3}$$

$$=\frac{(12\times3)-(1\times5)}{5\times3}=\frac{36-5}{15}=\frac{31}{15}$$

Step 5
Not Applicable

Step 6
$$\frac{31}{15}=2\frac{1}{15}$$

The following examples further illustrate how to subtract integer and mixed fractions:

Example 7.2-21

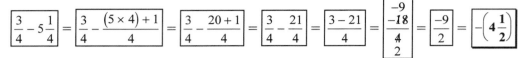

$$\boxed{\frac{3}{4}-5\frac{1}{4}}=\boxed{\frac{3}{4}-\frac{(5\times4)+1}{4}}=\boxed{\frac{3}{4}-\frac{20+1}{4}}=\boxed{\frac{3}{4}-\frac{21}{4}}=\boxed{\frac{3-21}{4}}=\boxed{\frac{\overset{-9}{\overset{-18}{\cancel{}}}}{\underset{2}{\cancel{4}}}}=\boxed{\frac{-9}{2}}=\boxed{-\left(4\frac{1}{2}\right)}$$

Example 7.2-22

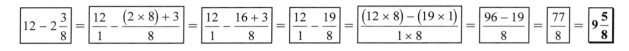

$$\boxed{12-2\frac{3}{8}}=\boxed{\frac{12}{1}-\frac{(2\times8)+3}{8}}=\boxed{\frac{12}{1}-\frac{16+3}{8}}=\boxed{\frac{12}{1}-\frac{19}{8}}=\boxed{\frac{(12\times8)-(19\times1)}{1\times8}}=\boxed{\frac{96-19}{8}}=\boxed{\frac{77}{8}}=\boxed{9\frac{5}{8}}$$

Example 7.2-23

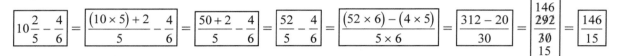

$$\boxed{10\frac{2}{5}-\frac{4}{6}}=\boxed{\frac{(10\times5)+2}{5}-\frac{4}{6}}=\boxed{\frac{50+2}{5}-\frac{4}{6}}=\boxed{\frac{52}{5}-\frac{4}{6}}=\boxed{\frac{(52\times6)-(4\times5)}{5\times6}}=\boxed{\frac{312-20}{30}}=\boxed{\frac{\overset{146}{\cancel{292}}}{\underset{15}{\cancel{30}}}}=\boxed{\frac{146}{15}}$$

$$=\boxed{9\frac{11}{15}}$$

Example 7.2-24

$$\boxed{\frac{2}{4}-5\frac{1}{4}-2\frac{3}{4}}=\boxed{\frac{2}{4}-\frac{(5\times4)+1}{4}-\frac{(2\times4)+3}{4}}=\boxed{\frac{2}{4}-\frac{20+1}{4}-\frac{8+3}{4}}=\boxed{\frac{2}{4}-\frac{21}{4}-\frac{11}{4}}=\boxed{\frac{2-21-11}{4}}$$

$$=\boxed{\frac{\overset{-15}{\overset{-30}{\cancel{}}}}{\underset{2}{\cancel{4}}}}=\boxed{\frac{-15}{2}}=\boxed{-\left(7\frac{1}{2}\right)}$$

Example 7.2-25

$$\boxed{\frac{3}{5}-4\frac{2}{3}-5}=\boxed{\left(\frac{3}{5}-4\frac{2}{3}\right)-5}=\boxed{\left(\frac{3}{5}-\frac{(4\times3)+2}{3}\right)-\frac{5}{1}}=\boxed{\left(\frac{3}{5}-\frac{12+2}{3}\right)-\frac{5}{1}}=\boxed{\left(\frac{3}{5}-\frac{14}{3}\right)-\frac{5}{1}}$$

$$=\boxed{\left(\frac{(3\times3)-(14\times5)}{5\times3}\right)-\frac{5}{1}}=\boxed{\left(\frac{9-70}{15}\right)-\frac{5}{1}}=\boxed{\left(\frac{-61}{15}\right)-\frac{5}{1}}=\boxed{\frac{-61}{15}-\frac{5}{1}}=\boxed{\frac{(-61\times1)-(5\times15)}{15\times1}}=\boxed{\frac{-61-75}{15}}$$

$$=\boxed{\frac{-136}{15}}=\boxed{-\left(9\frac{1}{15}\right)}$$

Example 7.2-26

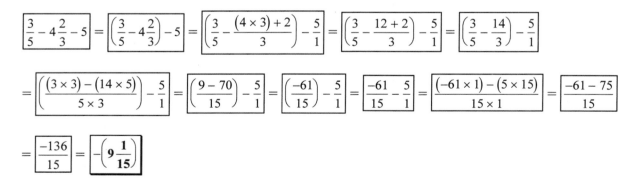

$$\boxed{\left(3\frac{2}{3}-14\right)-\frac{2}{3}}=\boxed{\left(\frac{(3\times3)+2}{3}-\frac{14}{1}\right)-\frac{2}{3}}=\boxed{\left(\frac{9+2}{3}-\frac{14}{1}\right)-\frac{2}{3}}=\boxed{\left(\frac{11}{3}-\frac{14}{1}\right)-\frac{2}{3}}$$

$$= \left[\left(\frac{(11 \times 1) - (14 \times 3)}{3 \times 1}\right) - \frac{2}{3}\right] = \left[\left(\frac{11 - 42}{3}\right) - \frac{2}{3}\right] = \left[\left(\frac{-31}{3}\right) - \frac{2}{3}\right] = \left[\frac{-31}{3} - \frac{2}{3}\right] = \left[\frac{-31 - 2}{3}\right] = \left[\frac{\frac{-11}{-33}}{\frac{3}{1}}\right] = \left[\frac{-11}{1}\right]$$

$$= \boxed{-11}$$

Example 7.2-27

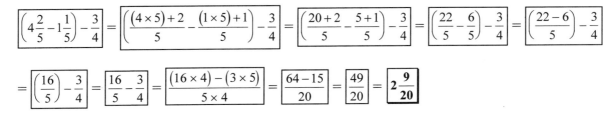

$$\left[\left(4\frac{2}{5} - 1\frac{1}{5}\right) - \frac{3}{4}\right] = \left[\left(\frac{(4 \times 5) + 2}{5} - \frac{(1 \times 5) + 1}{5}\right) - \frac{3}{4}\right] = \left[\left(\frac{20 + 2}{5} - \frac{5 + 1}{5}\right) - \frac{3}{4}\right] = \left[\left(\frac{22}{5} - \frac{6}{5}\right) - \frac{3}{4}\right] = \left[\left(\frac{22 - 6}{5}\right) - \frac{3}{4}\right]$$

$$= \left[\left(\frac{16}{5}\right) - \frac{3}{4}\right] = \left[\frac{16}{5} - \frac{3}{4}\right] = \left[\frac{(16 \times 4) - (3 \times 5)}{5 \times 4}\right] = \left[\frac{64 - 15}{20}\right] = \left[\frac{49}{20}\right] = \boxed{2\frac{9}{20}}$$

Example 7.2-28

$$\left[\left(\frac{14}{8} - \frac{1}{8}\right) - \left(1\frac{1}{2} - \frac{1}{4}\right)\right] = \left[\left(\frac{14 - 1}{8}\right) - \left(\frac{(1 \times 2) + 1}{2} - \frac{1}{4}\right)\right] = \left[\left(\frac{13}{8}\right) - \left(\frac{2 + 1}{2} - \frac{1}{4}\right)\right] = \left[\left(\frac{13}{8}\right) - \left(\frac{3}{2} - \frac{1}{4}\right)\right]$$

$$= \left[\frac{13}{8} - \left(\frac{(3 \times 4) - (1 \times 2)}{2 \times 4}\right)\right] = \left[\frac{13}{8} - \left(\frac{12 - 2}{8}\right)\right] = \left[\frac{13}{8} - \left(\frac{10}{8}\right)\right] = \left[\frac{13}{8} - \frac{10}{8}\right] = \left[\frac{13 - 10}{8}\right] = \boxed{\frac{3}{8}}$$

Example 7.2-29

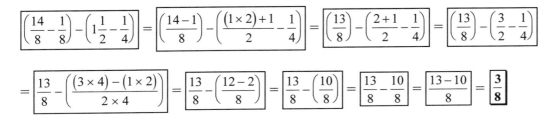

$$\left[\left(2\frac{1}{6} - 1\frac{1}{3}\right) - \left(\frac{2}{3} - \frac{1}{6}\right)\right] = \left[\left(\frac{(2 \times 6) + 1}{6} - \frac{(1 \times 3) + 1}{3}\right) - \left(\frac{(2 \times 6) - (1 \times 3)}{3 \times 6}\right)\right] = \left[\left(\frac{12 + 1}{6} - \frac{3 + 1}{3}\right) - \left(\frac{12 - 3}{18}\right)\right]$$

$$= \left[\left(\frac{13}{6} - \frac{4}{3}\right) - \left(\frac{\overset{1}{\cancel{9}}}{\underset{2}{\cancel{18}}}\right)\right] = \left[\left(\frac{(13 \times 3) - (4 \times 6)}{6 \times 3}\right) - \left(\frac{1}{2}\right)\right] = \left[\left(\frac{39 - 24}{18}\right) - \frac{1}{2}\right] = \left[\left(\frac{15}{18}\right) - \frac{1}{2}\right] = \left[\frac{15}{18} - \frac{1}{2}\right]$$

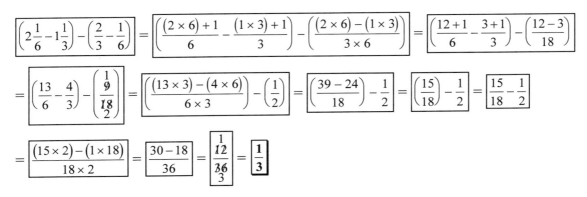

$$= \left[\frac{(15 \times 2) - (1 \times 18)}{18 \times 2}\right] = \left[\frac{30 - 18}{36}\right] = \left[\frac{\overset{1}{\cancel{12}}}{\underset{3}{\cancel{36}}}\right] = \boxed{\frac{1}{3}}$$

Example 7.2-30

$$\left[\left[\left(\frac{5}{2} - \frac{1}{4}\right) - \frac{1}{3}\right] - 1\frac{1}{4}\right] = \left[\left[\left(\frac{(5 \times 4) - (1 \times 2)}{2 \times 4}\right) - \frac{1}{3}\right] - \frac{(1 \times 4) + 1}{4}\right] = \left[\left[\left(\frac{20 - 2}{8}\right) - \frac{1}{3}\right] - \frac{4 + 1}{4}\right] = \left[\left[\left(\frac{18}{8}\right) - \frac{1}{3}\right] - \frac{5}{4}\right]$$

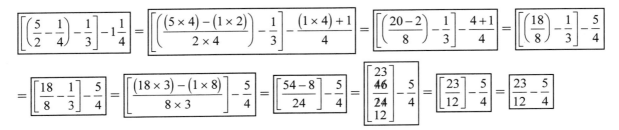

$$= \left[\left[\frac{18}{8} - \frac{1}{3}\right] - \frac{5}{4}\right] = \left[\left[\frac{(18 \times 3) - (1 \times 8)}{8 \times 3}\right] - \frac{5}{4}\right] = \left[\left[\frac{54 - 8}{24}\right] - \frac{5}{4}\right] = \left[\left[\frac{\overset{23}{\cancel{46}}}{\underset{12}{\cancel{24}}}\right] - \frac{5}{4}\right] = \left[\left[\frac{23}{12}\right] - \frac{5}{4}\right] = \left[\frac{23}{12} - \frac{5}{4}\right]$$

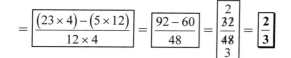

Example 7.2-31

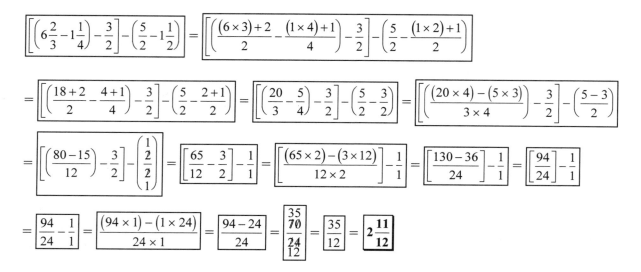

Section 7.2 Exercises - Subtract the following integer and mixed fractions:

1. $5\dfrac{2}{3} - \dfrac{1}{6} =$

2. $7\dfrac{1}{2} - \dfrac{2}{3} - 1\dfrac{5}{8} =$

3. $\dfrac{2}{6} - 3\dfrac{5}{6} - 1\dfrac{1}{6} =$

4. $6\dfrac{2}{3} - 1\dfrac{1}{2} - 5 =$

5. $\left(4\dfrac{1}{3} - \dfrac{3}{5}\right) - 12 =$

6. $1\dfrac{2}{3} - \dfrac{3}{5} - \dfrac{1}{4} =$

7. $7\dfrac{1}{3} - \left(\dfrac{3}{4} - \dfrac{1}{4}\right) =$

8. $\left(\dfrac{2}{5} - 1\dfrac{1}{2}\right) - \dfrac{3}{4} =$

9. $\left(3\dfrac{5}{6} - 8\right) - 1\dfrac{1}{6} =$

10. $\left(4\dfrac{2}{3} - \dfrac{1}{6}\right) - \left(\dfrac{3}{4} - \dfrac{1}{3}\right) =$

7.3   Multiplying Integer and Mixed Fractions

Integer fractions of the form $\left(\dfrac{a}{b}\right)$ where both the numerator (a) and the denominator (b) are

integers, and mixed fractions of the form $\left(k\dfrac{a}{b}\right)$ where (k) is a whole number and $\left(\dfrac{a}{b}\right)$ is an

integer fraction are multiplied as in the following cases:

Case I   *Multiply two integer and mixed fractions with or without a common denominator using the following steps:*

Step 1   Change the integer number (a) to an integer fraction of the form $\left(\dfrac{a}{1}\right)$, e.g., change

257 to $\dfrac{257}{1}$.

Step 2   Change the mixed fraction to an integer fraction (see Section 2.5).

Step 3   Multiply the integer fractions (see Section 3.3, Case I).

Step 4   Simplify the fraction to its lowest term (see Section 2.3).

Step 5   Change the improper fraction to a mixed fraction if the fraction obtained from Step 4 is an improper fraction (see Section 2.2).

The following examples show the steps as to how two integer and mixed fractions with or without a common denominator are multiplied:

Example 7.3-1

$$\boxed{2\dfrac{1}{5} \times \dfrac{7}{8}} =$$

Solution:

> **Step 1** $\boxed{\textit{Not Applicable}}$

> **Step 2** $\boxed{2\dfrac{1}{5} \times \dfrac{7}{8}} = \boxed{\dfrac{(2\times5)+1}{5} \times \dfrac{7}{8}} = \boxed{\dfrac{10+1}{5} \times \dfrac{7}{8}} = \boxed{\dfrac{11}{5} \times \dfrac{7}{8}}$

> **Step 3** $\boxed{\dfrac{11}{5} \times \dfrac{7}{8}} = \boxed{\dfrac{11\times7}{5\times8}} = \boxed{\dfrac{77}{40}}$

> **Step 4** $\boxed{\textit{Not Applicable}}$

> **Step 5** $\boxed{\dfrac{77}{40}} = \boxed{1\dfrac{37}{40}}$

Example 7.3-2

$$\boxed{\dfrac{1}{8} \times 2\dfrac{4}{6}} =$$

Solution:

Step 1 $\boxed{\textit{Not Applicable}}$

Step 2 $\boxed{\dfrac{1}{8} \times 2\dfrac{4}{6}} = \boxed{\dfrac{1}{8} \times \dfrac{(2 \times 6) + 4}{6}} = \boxed{\dfrac{1}{8} \times \dfrac{12 + 4}{6}} = \boxed{\dfrac{1}{8} \times \dfrac{16}{6}}$

Step 3 $\boxed{\dfrac{1}{8} \times \dfrac{16}{6}} = \boxed{\dfrac{1 \times 16}{8 \times 6}} = \boxed{\dfrac{16}{48}}$

Step 4 $\boxed{\dfrac{16}{48}} = \boxed{\dfrac{16 \div 16}{48 \div 16}} = \boxed{\dfrac{\mathbf{1}}{\mathbf{3}}}$

Step 5 $\boxed{\textit{Not Applicable}}$

Example 7.3-3

$\boxed{24 \times 3\dfrac{2}{3}} =$

Solution:

Step 1 $\boxed{24 \times 3\dfrac{2}{3}} = \boxed{\dfrac{24}{1} \times 3\dfrac{2}{3}}$

Step 2 $\boxed{\dfrac{24}{1} \times 3\dfrac{2}{3}} = \boxed{\dfrac{24}{1} \times \dfrac{(3 \times 3) + 2}{3}} = \boxed{\dfrac{24}{1} \times \dfrac{9 + 2}{3}} = \boxed{\dfrac{24}{1} \times \dfrac{11}{3}}$

Step 3 $\boxed{\dfrac{24}{1} \times \dfrac{11}{3}} = \boxed{\dfrac{24 \times 11}{1 \times 3}} = \boxed{\dfrac{264}{3}}$

Step 4 $\boxed{\dfrac{264}{3}} = \boxed{\dfrac{264 \div 3}{3 \div 3}} = \boxed{\dfrac{88}{1}} = \boxed{\mathbf{88}}$

Step 5 $\boxed{\textit{Not Applicable}}$

Example 7.3-4

$\boxed{24\dfrac{1}{8} \times \dfrac{6}{8}} =$

Solution:

Step 1 $\boxed{\textit{Not Applicable}}$

Step 2 $\boxed{24\dfrac{1}{8} \times \dfrac{6}{8}} = \boxed{\dfrac{(24 \times 8) + 1}{8} \times \dfrac{6}{8}} = \boxed{\dfrac{192 + 1}{8} \times \dfrac{6}{8}} = \boxed{\dfrac{193}{8} \times \dfrac{6}{8}}$

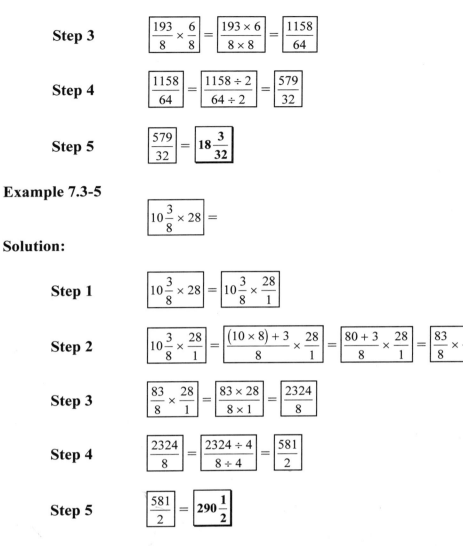

Step 3 $\boxed{\dfrac{193}{8} \times \dfrac{6}{8}} = \boxed{\dfrac{193 \times 6}{8 \times 8}} = \boxed{\dfrac{1158}{64}}$

Step 4 $\boxed{\dfrac{1158}{64}} = \boxed{\dfrac{1158 \div 2}{64 \div 2}} = \boxed{\dfrac{579}{32}}$

Step 5 $\boxed{\dfrac{579}{32}} = \boxed{18\dfrac{3}{32}}$

Example 7.3-5

$\boxed{10\dfrac{3}{8} \times 28} =$

Solution:

Step 1 $\boxed{10\dfrac{3}{8} \times 28} = \boxed{10\dfrac{3}{8} \times \dfrac{28}{1}}$

Step 2 $\boxed{10\dfrac{3}{8} \times \dfrac{28}{1}} = \boxed{\dfrac{(10 \times 8) + 3}{8} \times \dfrac{28}{1}} = \boxed{\dfrac{80 + 3}{8} \times \dfrac{28}{1}} = \boxed{\dfrac{83}{8} \times \dfrac{28}{1}}$

Step 3 $\boxed{\dfrac{83}{8} \times \dfrac{28}{1}} = \boxed{\dfrac{83 \times 28}{8 \times 1}} = \boxed{\dfrac{2324}{8}}$

Step 4 $\boxed{\dfrac{2324}{8}} = \boxed{\dfrac{2324 \div 4}{8 \div 4}} = \boxed{\dfrac{581}{2}}$

Step 5 $\boxed{\dfrac{581}{2}} = \boxed{290\dfrac{1}{2}}$

Case II *Multiply three integer and mixed fractions with or without a common denominator using the following steps:*

Step 1 Change the integer number (a) to an integer fraction of the form $\left(\dfrac{a}{1}\right)$, e.g., change 55

to $\dfrac{55}{1}$.

Step 2 Change the mixed fraction(s) to integer fraction(s) (see Section 2.5).

Step 3 Multiply the integer fractions (see Section 3.3, Case II).

Step 4 Simplify the fraction to its lowest term (see Section 2.3).

Step 5 Change the improper fraction to a mixed fraction if the fraction obtained from Step 4 is an improper fraction (see Section 2.2).

The following examples show the steps as to how three integer and mixed fractions with or without a common denominator are multiplied:

Example 7.3-6

$$\boxed{3 \times 2\dfrac{4}{5} \times \dfrac{5}{8}} =$$

Solution:

> **Step 1** $\quad \boxed{3 \times 2\dfrac{4}{5} \times \dfrac{5}{8}} = \boxed{\dfrac{3}{1} \times 2\dfrac{4}{5} \times \dfrac{5}{8}}$

> **Step 2** $\quad \boxed{\dfrac{3}{1} \times 2\dfrac{4}{5} \times \dfrac{5}{8}} = \boxed{\dfrac{3}{1} \times \dfrac{(2 \times 5) + 4}{5} \times \dfrac{5}{8}} = \boxed{\dfrac{3}{1} \times \dfrac{10 + 4}{5} \times \dfrac{5}{8}} = \boxed{\dfrac{3}{1} \times \dfrac{14}{5} \times \dfrac{5}{8}}$

> **Step 3** $\quad \boxed{\dfrac{3}{1} \times \dfrac{14}{5} \times \dfrac{5}{8}} = \boxed{\dfrac{3 \times 14 \times 5}{1 \times 5 \times 8}} = \boxed{\dfrac{210}{40}}$

> **Step 4** $\quad \boxed{\dfrac{210}{40}} = \boxed{\dfrac{210 \div 10}{40 \div 10}} = \boxed{\dfrac{21}{4}}$

> **Step 5** $\quad \boxed{\dfrac{21}{4}} = \boxed{5\dfrac{1}{4}}$

Example 7.3-7

$$\boxed{\dfrac{9}{8} \times 3\dfrac{1}{5} \times 4} =$$

Solution:

> **Step 1** $\quad \boxed{\dfrac{9}{8} \times 3\dfrac{1}{5} \times 4} = \boxed{\dfrac{9}{8} \times 3\dfrac{1}{5} \times \dfrac{4}{1}}$

> **Step 2** $\quad \boxed{\dfrac{9}{8} \times 3\dfrac{1}{5} \times \dfrac{4}{1}} = \boxed{\dfrac{9}{8} \times \dfrac{(3 \times 5) + 1}{5} \times \dfrac{4}{1}} = \boxed{\dfrac{9}{8} \times \dfrac{15 + 1}{5} \times \dfrac{4}{1}} = \boxed{\dfrac{9}{8} \times \dfrac{16}{5} \times \dfrac{4}{1}}$

> **Step 3** $\quad \boxed{\dfrac{9}{8} \times \dfrac{16}{5} \times \dfrac{4}{1}} = \boxed{\dfrac{9 \times 16 \times 4}{8 \times 5 \times 1}} = \boxed{\dfrac{576}{40}}$

> **Step 4** $\quad \boxed{\dfrac{576}{40}} = \boxed{\dfrac{576 \div 8}{40 \div 8}} = \boxed{\dfrac{72}{5}}$

> **Step 5** $\quad \boxed{\dfrac{72}{5}} = \boxed{14\dfrac{2}{5}}$

Example 7.3-8

$$\boxed{3\dfrac{1}{8} \times \dfrac{2}{5} \times 2\dfrac{3}{5}} =$$

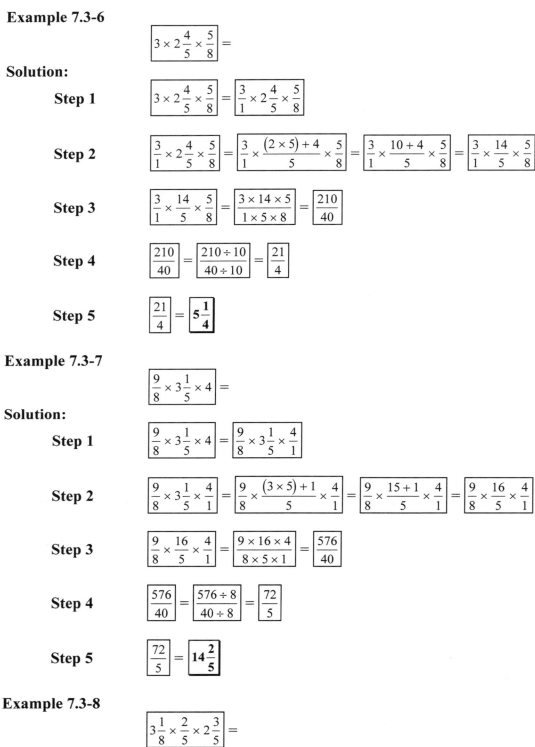

Solution:

Step 1 $\boxed{\textit{Not Applicable}}$

Step 2 $\boxed{3\dfrac{1}{8} \times \dfrac{2}{5} \times 2\dfrac{3}{5}} = \boxed{\dfrac{(3 \times 8)+1}{8} \times \dfrac{2}{5} \times \dfrac{(2 \times 5)+3}{5}} = \boxed{\dfrac{24+1}{8} \times \dfrac{2}{5} \times \dfrac{10+3}{5}} = \boxed{\dfrac{25}{8} \times \dfrac{2}{5} \times \dfrac{13}{5}}$

Step 3 $\boxed{\dfrac{25}{8} \times \dfrac{2}{5} \times \dfrac{13}{5}} = \boxed{\dfrac{25 \times 2 \times 13}{8 \times 5 \times 5}} = \boxed{\dfrac{650}{200}}$

Step 4 $\boxed{\dfrac{650}{200}} = \boxed{\dfrac{650 \div 50}{200 \div 50}} = \boxed{\dfrac{13}{4}}$

Step 5 $\boxed{\dfrac{13}{4}} = \boxed{\mathbf{3\dfrac{1}{4}}}$

Example 7.3-9

$\boxed{2\dfrac{3}{5} \times \dfrac{4}{5} \times \dfrac{3}{2}} =$

Solution:

Step 1 $\boxed{\textit{Not Applicable}}$

Step 2 $\boxed{2\dfrac{3}{5} \times \dfrac{4}{5} \times \dfrac{3}{2}} = \boxed{\dfrac{(2 \times 5)+3}{5} \times \dfrac{4}{5} \times \dfrac{3}{2}} = \boxed{\dfrac{10+3}{5} \times \dfrac{4}{5} \times \dfrac{3}{2}} = \boxed{\dfrac{13}{5} \times \dfrac{4}{5} \times \dfrac{3}{2}}$

Step 3 $\boxed{\dfrac{13}{5} \times \dfrac{4}{5} \times \dfrac{3}{2}} = \boxed{\dfrac{13 \times 4 \times 3}{5 \times 5 \times 2}} = \boxed{\dfrac{156}{50}}$

Step 4 $\boxed{\dfrac{156}{50}} = \boxed{\dfrac{156 \div 2}{50 \div 2}} = \boxed{\dfrac{78}{25}}$

Step 5 $\boxed{\dfrac{78}{25}} = \boxed{\mathbf{3\dfrac{3}{25}}}$

Example 7.3-10

$\boxed{10\dfrac{2}{3} \times 24 \times 2\dfrac{4}{5}} =$

Solution:

Step 1 $\boxed{10\dfrac{2}{3} \times 24 \times 2\dfrac{4}{5}} = \boxed{10\dfrac{2}{3} \times \dfrac{24}{1} \times 2\dfrac{4}{5}}$

Step 2 $$\boxed{10\frac{2}{3} \times \frac{24}{1} \times 2\frac{4}{5}} = \boxed{\frac{(10 \times 3) + 2}{3} \times \frac{24}{1} \times \frac{(2 \times 5) + 4}{5}} = \boxed{\frac{30 + 2}{3} \times \frac{24}{1} \times \frac{10 + 4}{5}}$$

$$= \boxed{\frac{32}{3} \times \frac{24}{1} \times \frac{14}{5}}$$

Step 3 $$\boxed{\frac{32}{3} \times \frac{24}{1} \times \frac{14}{5}} = \boxed{\frac{32 \times 24 \times 14}{3 \times 1 \times 5}} = \boxed{\frac{10752}{15}}$$

Step 4 $$\boxed{\frac{10752}{15}} = \boxed{\frac{10752 \div 3}{15 \div 3}} = \boxed{\frac{3584}{5}}$$

Step 5 $$\boxed{\frac{3584}{5}} = \boxed{\mathbf{716\frac{4}{5}}}$$

The following examples further illustrate how to multiply integer and mixed fractions:

Example 7.3-11

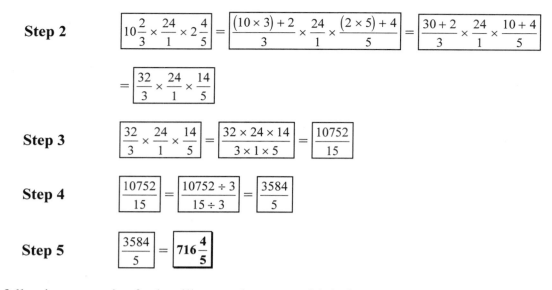

$$\boxed{1\frac{1}{4} \times \frac{2}{5}} = \boxed{\frac{(1 \times 4) + 1}{4} \times \frac{2}{5}} = \boxed{\frac{4 + 1}{4} \times \frac{2}{5}} = \boxed{\frac{5}{4} \times \frac{2}{5}} = \boxed{\frac{\overset{1}{\cancel{5}} \times \overset{1}{\cancel{2}}}{\underset{2}{\cancel{4}} \times \underset{1}{\cancel{5}}}} = \boxed{\frac{1 \times 1}{2 \times 1}} = \boxed{\mathbf{\frac{1}{2}}}$$

Example 7.3-12

$$\boxed{26 \times 3\frac{4}{5}} = \boxed{\frac{26}{1} \times \frac{(3 \times 5) + 4}{5}} = \boxed{\frac{26}{1} \times \frac{15 + 4}{5}} = \boxed{\frac{26}{1} \times \frac{19}{5}} = \boxed{\frac{26 \times 19}{1 \times 5}} = \boxed{\frac{494}{5}} = \boxed{\mathbf{98\frac{4}{5}}}$$

Example 7.3-13

$$\boxed{5\frac{3}{4} \times \frac{6}{7} \times 49} = \boxed{\frac{(5 \times 4) + 3}{4} \times \frac{6}{7} \times \frac{49}{1}} = \boxed{\frac{20 + 3}{4} \times \frac{6}{7} \times \frac{49}{1}} = \boxed{\frac{23}{4} \times \frac{6}{7} \times \frac{49}{1}} = \boxed{\frac{23 \times \overset{3}{\cancel{6}} \times \overset{7}{\cancel{49}}}{\underset{2}{\cancel{4}} \times \underset{1}{\cancel{7}} \times 1}} = \boxed{\frac{23 \times 3 \times 7}{2 \times 1 \times 1}}$$

$$= \boxed{\frac{483}{2}} = \boxed{\mathbf{241\frac{1}{2}}}$$

Example 7.3-14

$$\boxed{1\frac{1}{4} \times 2\frac{1}{3} \times \frac{2}{7}} = \boxed{\frac{(1 \times 4) + 1}{4} \times \frac{(2 \times 3) + 1}{3} \times \frac{2}{7}} = \boxed{\frac{4 + 1}{4} \times \frac{6 + 1}{3} \times \frac{2}{7}} = \boxed{\frac{5}{4} \times \frac{7}{3} \times \frac{2}{7}} = \boxed{\frac{5 \times \overset{1}{\cancel{7}} \times \overset{1}{\cancel{2}}}{\underset{2}{\cancel{4}} \times 3 \times \underset{1}{\cancel{7}}}} = \boxed{\frac{5 \times 1 \times 1}{2 \times 3 \times 1}} = \boxed{\mathbf{\frac{5}{6}}}$$

Example 7.3-15

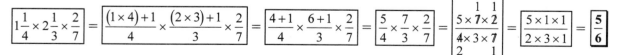

$$\boxed{3\frac{8}{9} \times 2\frac{4}{9} \times \frac{1}{9}} = \boxed{\frac{(3 \times 9) + 8}{9} \times \frac{(2 \times 9) + 4}{9} \times \frac{1}{9}} = \boxed{\frac{27 + 8}{9} \times \frac{18 + 4}{9} \times \frac{1}{9}} = \boxed{\frac{35}{9} \times \frac{22}{9} \times \frac{1}{9}} = \boxed{\frac{35 \times 22 \times 1}{9 \times 9 \times 9}}$$

$$= \boxed{\frac{770}{729}} = \boxed{1\frac{41}{729}}$$

Example 7.3-16

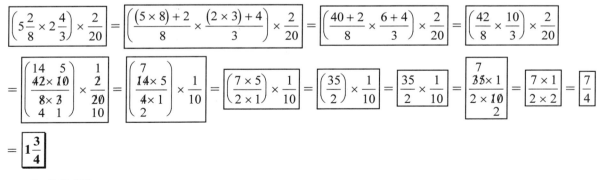

$$\left(5\frac{2}{8} \times 2\frac{4}{3}\right) \times \frac{2}{20} = \left(\frac{(5\times 8)+2}{8} \times \frac{(2\times 3)+4}{3}\right) \times \frac{2}{20} = \left(\frac{40+2}{8} \times \frac{6+4}{3}\right) \times \frac{2}{20} = \left(\frac{42}{8} \times \frac{10}{3}\right) \times \frac{2}{20}$$

$$= \left(\frac{\overset{14}{\cancel{42}}\times\overset{5}{\cancel{10}}}{\underset{4}{\cancel{8}}\times\underset{1}{\cancel{3}}}\right) \times \frac{\overset{1}{\cancel{2}}}{\underset{10}{\cancel{20}}} = \left(\frac{14\times 5}{4\times 1}\right) \times \frac{1}{10} = \left(\frac{7\times 5}{2\times 1}\right) \times \frac{1}{10} = \left(\frac{35}{2}\right) \times \frac{1}{10} = \frac{35}{2} \times \frac{1}{10} = \frac{\overset{7}{\cancel{35}}\times 1}{2 \times \underset{2}{\cancel{10}}} = \frac{7\times 1}{2\times 2} = \frac{7}{4}$$

$$= \boxed{1\frac{3}{4}}$$

Example 7.3-17

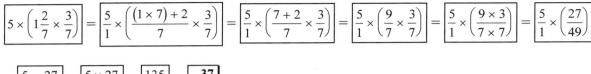

$$5 \times \left(1\frac{2}{7} \times \frac{3}{7}\right) = \frac{5}{1} \times \left(\frac{(1\times 7)+2}{7} \times \frac{3}{7}\right) = \frac{5}{1} \times \left(\frac{7+2}{7} \times \frac{3}{7}\right) = \frac{5}{1} \times \left(\frac{9}{7} \times \frac{3}{7}\right) = \frac{5}{1} \times \left(\frac{9\times 3}{7\times 7}\right) = \frac{5}{1} \times \left(\frac{27}{49}\right)$$

$$= \frac{5}{1} \times \frac{27}{49} = \frac{5\times 27}{1\times 49} = \frac{135}{49} = \boxed{2\frac{37}{49}}$$

Example 7.3-18

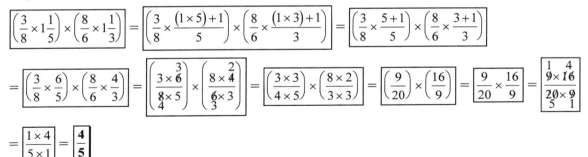

$$\left(\frac{3}{8} \times 1\frac{1}{5}\right) \times \left(\frac{8}{6} \times 1\frac{1}{3}\right) = \left(\frac{3}{8} \times \frac{(1\times 5)+1}{5}\right) \times \left(\frac{8}{6} \times \frac{(1\times 3)+1}{3}\right) = \left(\frac{3}{8} \times \frac{5+1}{5}\right) \times \left(\frac{8}{6} \times \frac{3+1}{3}\right)$$

$$= \left(\frac{3}{8} \times \frac{6}{5}\right) \times \left(\frac{8}{6} \times \frac{4}{3}\right) = \left(\frac{3\times\overset{3}{\cancel{6}}}{\underset{4}{\cancel{8}}\times 5}\right) \times \left(\frac{8\times 4}{\underset{3}{\cancel{6}}\times 3}\right) = \left(\frac{3\times 3}{4\times 5}\right) \times \left(\frac{8\times 2}{3\times 3}\right) = \left(\frac{9}{20}\right) \times \left(\frac{16}{9}\right) = \frac{9}{20} \times \frac{16}{9} = \frac{\overset{1}{\cancel{9}}\times\overset{4}{\cancel{16}}}{\underset{5}{\cancel{20}}\times\underset{1}{\cancel{9}}}$$

$$= \frac{1\times 4}{5\times 1} = \boxed{\frac{4}{5}}$$

Example 7.3-19

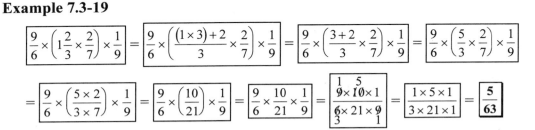

$$\frac{9}{6} \times \left(1\frac{2}{3} \times \frac{2}{7}\right) \times \frac{1}{9} = \frac{9}{6} \times \left(\frac{(1\times 3)+2}{3} \times \frac{2}{7}\right) \times \frac{1}{9} = \frac{9}{6} \times \left(\frac{3+2}{3} \times \frac{2}{7}\right) \times \frac{1}{9} = \frac{9}{6} \times \left(\frac{5}{3} \times \frac{2}{7}\right) \times \frac{1}{9}$$

$$= \frac{9}{6} \times \left(\frac{5\times 2}{3\times 7}\right) \times \frac{1}{9} = \frac{9}{6} \times \left(\frac{10}{21}\right) \times \frac{1}{9} = \frac{9}{6} \times \frac{10}{21} \times \frac{1}{9} = \frac{\overset{1}{\cancel{9}}\times\overset{5}{\cancel{10}}\times 1}{\underset{3}{\cancel{6}}\times 21 \times\underset{1}{\cancel{9}}} = \frac{1\times 5\times 1}{3\times 21\times 1} = \boxed{\frac{5}{63}}$$

Example 7.3-20

$$\left(\frac{7}{8} \times 2 \times 1\frac{1}{3}\right) \times \left(\frac{3}{7} \times 1\frac{1}{5}\right) = \left(\frac{7}{8} \times \frac{2}{1} \times \frac{(1\times 3)+1}{3}\right) \times \left(\frac{3}{7} \times \frac{(1\times 5)+1}{5}\right) = \left(\frac{7}{8} \times \frac{2}{1} \times \frac{3+1}{3}\right) \times \left(\frac{3}{7} \times \frac{5+1}{5}\right)$$

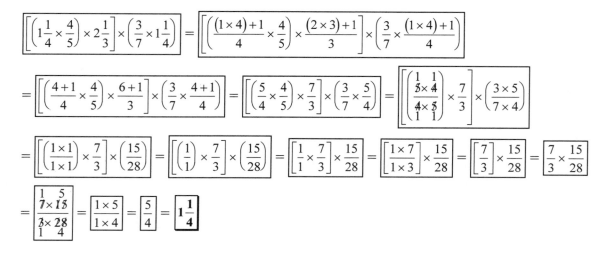

Example 7.3-21

$$\left[\left(1\frac{1}{4}\times\frac{4}{5}\right)\times2\frac{1}{3}\right]\times\left(\frac{3}{7}\times1\frac{1}{4}\right)=\left[\left(\frac{(1\times4)+1}{4}\times\frac{4}{5}\right)\times\frac{(2\times3)+1}{3}\right]\times\left(\frac{3}{7}\times\frac{(1\times4)+1}{4}\right)$$

$$=\left[\left(\frac{4+1}{4}\times\frac{4}{5}\right)\times\frac{6+1}{3}\right]\times\left(\frac{3}{7}\times\frac{4+1}{4}\right)=\left[\left(\frac{5}{4}\times\frac{4}{5}\right)\times\frac{7}{3}\right]\times\left(\frac{3}{7}\times\frac{5}{4}\right)=\left[\left(\frac{\overset{1}{\cancel{5}}\times\overset{1}{\cancel{4}}}{\underset{1}{\cancel{4}}\times\underset{1}{\cancel{5}}}\right)\times\frac{7}{3}\right]\times\left(\frac{3\times5}{7\times4}\right)$$

$$=\left[\left(\frac{1\times1}{1\times1}\right)\times\frac{7}{3}\right]\times\left(\frac{15}{28}\right)=\left[\left(\frac{1}{1}\right)\times\frac{7}{3}\right]\times\left(\frac{15}{28}\right)=\left[\frac{1}{1}\times\frac{7}{3}\right]\times\frac{15}{28}=\left[\frac{1\times7}{1\times3}\right]\times\frac{15}{28}=\left[\frac{7}{3}\right]\times\frac{15}{28}=\frac{7}{3}\times\frac{15}{28}$$

$$=\frac{\overset{1}{\cancel{7}}\times\overset{5}{\cancel{15}}}{\underset{1}{\cancel{3}}\times\underset{4}{\cancel{28}}}=\frac{1\times5}{1\times4}=\frac{5}{4}=1\frac{1}{4}$$

Section 7.3 Exercises - Multiply the following integer and mixed fractions:

1. $\dfrac{2}{8}\times1\dfrac{1}{4}=$

2. $2\dfrac{1}{5}\times5\dfrac{1}{3}\times\dfrac{3}{11}=$

3. $\left(1\dfrac{1}{3}\times2\dfrac{1}{3}\right)\times\dfrac{3}{8}=$

4. $\left(\dfrac{5}{8}\times1\dfrac{1}{3}\right)\times\left(\dfrac{3}{8}\times\dfrac{4}{5}\right)=$

5. $15\times\left(5\dfrac{1}{2}\times\dfrac{2}{11}\right)=$

6. $\left(1\dfrac{1}{4}\times2\dfrac{1}{3}\right)\times\left(1\dfrac{1}{5}\times\dfrac{2}{7}\right)=$

7. $\left(5\times\dfrac{3}{5}\times\dfrac{1}{4}\right)\times\left(\dfrac{2}{3}\times2\dfrac{1}{2}\right)=$

8. $2\dfrac{1}{3}\times\left(\dfrac{3}{8}\times1\dfrac{4}{7}\right)=$

9. $1\dfrac{1}{5}\times\dfrac{2}{3}\times\dfrac{1}{6}\times\dfrac{5}{4}=$

10. $3\dfrac{1}{3}\times\left[\dfrac{2}{3}\times\dfrac{5}{2}\times\left(1\dfrac{1}{5}\times0\right)\right]=$

7.4   Dividing Integer and Mixed Fractions

Integer fractions of the form $\left(\dfrac{a}{b}\right)$ where both the numerator (a) and the denominator (b) are integers, and mixed fractions of the form $\left(k\dfrac{a}{b}\right)$ where (k) is a whole number and $\left(\dfrac{a}{b}\right)$ is an integer fraction are divided as in the following cases:

Case I   *Divide two integer and mixed fractions with or without a common denominator using the following steps:*

Step 1   Change the integer number (a) to an integer fraction of the form $\left(\dfrac{a}{1}\right)$, e.g., change

300 to $\dfrac{300}{1}$.

Step 2   Change the mixed fraction to an integer fraction (see Section 2.5).

Step 3   Divide the integer fractions (see Section 3.4, Case I).

Step 4   Simplify the fraction to its lowest term (see Section 2.3).

Step 5   Change the improper fraction to a mixed fraction if the fraction obtained from Step 4 is an improper fraction (see Section 2.2).

The following examples show the steps as to how two integer and mixed fractions with or without a common denominator are divided:

Example 7.4-1

$$\boxed{\dfrac{3}{8} \div 1\dfrac{2}{5}} =$$

Solution:

Step 1 $\boxed{\textit{Not Applicable}}$

Step 2 $\boxed{\dfrac{3}{8} \div 1\dfrac{2}{5}} = \boxed{\dfrac{3}{8} \div \dfrac{(1 \times 5) + 2}{5}} = \boxed{\dfrac{3}{8} \div \dfrac{5 + 2}{5}} = \boxed{\dfrac{3}{8} \div \dfrac{7}{5}}$

Step 3 $\boxed{\dfrac{3}{8} \div \dfrac{7}{5}} = \boxed{\dfrac{3}{8} \times \dfrac{5}{7}} = \boxed{\dfrac{3 \times 5}{8 \times 7}} = \boxed{\dfrac{\mathbf{15}}{\mathbf{56}}}$

Step 4 $\boxed{\textit{Not Applicable}}$

Step 5 $\boxed{\textit{Not Applicable}}$

Example 7.4-2

$$\boxed{16 \div 2\dfrac{3}{4}} =$$

Solution:

Step 1 $\boxed{16 \div 2\dfrac{3}{4}} = \boxed{\dfrac{16}{1} \div 2\dfrac{3}{4}}$

Step 2 $\boxed{\dfrac{16}{1} \div 2\dfrac{3}{4}} = \boxed{\dfrac{16}{1} \div \dfrac{(2 \times 4) + 3}{4}} = \boxed{\dfrac{16}{1} \div \dfrac{8 + 3}{4}} = \boxed{\dfrac{16}{1} \div \dfrac{11}{4}}$

Step 3 $\boxed{\dfrac{16}{1} \div \dfrac{11}{4}} = \boxed{\dfrac{16}{1} \times \dfrac{4}{11}} = \boxed{\dfrac{16 \times 4}{1 \times 11}} = \boxed{\dfrac{64}{11}}$

Step 4 $\boxed{\textit{Not Applicable}}$

Step 5 $\boxed{\dfrac{64}{11}} = \boxed{\mathbf{5\dfrac{9}{11}}}$

Example 7.4-3

$\boxed{24\dfrac{2}{5} \div \dfrac{3}{5}} =$

Solution:

Step 1 $\boxed{\textit{Not Applicable}}$

Step 2 $\boxed{24\dfrac{2}{5} \div \dfrac{3}{5}} = \boxed{\dfrac{(24 \times 5) + 2}{5} \div \dfrac{3}{5}} = \boxed{\dfrac{120 + 2}{5} \div \dfrac{3}{5}} = \boxed{\dfrac{122}{5} \div \dfrac{3}{5}}$

Step 3 $\boxed{\dfrac{122}{5} \div \dfrac{3}{5}} = \boxed{\dfrac{122}{5} \times \dfrac{5}{3}} = \boxed{\dfrac{122 \times 5}{5 \times 3}} = \boxed{\dfrac{610}{15}}$

Step 4 $\boxed{\dfrac{610}{15}} = \boxed{\dfrac{610 \div 5}{15 \div 5}} = \boxed{\dfrac{122}{3}}$

Step 5 $\boxed{\dfrac{122}{3}} = \boxed{\mathbf{40\dfrac{2}{3}}}$

Example 7.4-4

$\boxed{12\dfrac{4}{5} \div 36} =$

Solution:

Step 1 $\boxed{12\dfrac{4}{5} \div 36} = \boxed{12\dfrac{4}{5} \div \dfrac{36}{1}}$

Step 2 $\boxed{12\dfrac{4}{5} \div \dfrac{36}{1}} = \boxed{\dfrac{(12 \times 5) + 4}{5} \div \dfrac{36}{1}} = \boxed{\dfrac{60 + 4}{5} \div \dfrac{36}{1}} = \boxed{\dfrac{64}{5} \div \dfrac{36}{1}}$

Step 3 $\boxed{\dfrac{64}{5} \div \dfrac{36}{1}} = \boxed{\dfrac{64}{5} \times \dfrac{1}{36}} = \boxed{\dfrac{64 \times 1}{5 \times 36}} = \boxed{\dfrac{64}{180}}$

Step 4 $\boxed{\dfrac{64}{180}} = \boxed{\dfrac{64 \div 4}{180 \div 4}} = \boxed{\dfrac{16}{45}}$

Step 5 $\boxed{Not\ Applicable}$

Example 7.4-5

$\boxed{6\dfrac{2}{3} \div \dfrac{12}{20}} =$

Solution:

Step 1 $\boxed{Not\ Applicable}$

Step 2 $\boxed{6\dfrac{2}{3} \div \dfrac{12}{20}} = \boxed{\dfrac{(6 \times 3) + 2}{3} \div \dfrac{12}{20}} = \boxed{\dfrac{18 + 2}{3} \div \dfrac{12}{20}} = \boxed{\dfrac{20}{3} \div \dfrac{12}{20}}$

Step 3 $\boxed{\dfrac{20}{3} \div \dfrac{12}{20}} = \boxed{\dfrac{20}{3} \times \dfrac{20}{12}} = \boxed{\dfrac{20 \times 20}{3 \times 12}} = \boxed{\dfrac{400}{36}}$

Step 4 $\boxed{\dfrac{400}{36}} = \boxed{\dfrac{400 \div 4}{36 \div 4}} = \boxed{\dfrac{100}{9}}$

Step 5 $\boxed{\dfrac{100}{9}} = \boxed{11\dfrac{1}{9}}$

Case II *Divide three integer and mixed fractions with or without a common denominator using the following steps:*

Step 1 Change the integer number (a) to an integer fraction of the form $\left(\dfrac{a}{1}\right)$, e.g., change

20 to $\dfrac{20}{1}$.

Step 2 Change the mixed fraction(s) to integer fraction(s) (see Section 2.5).

Step 3 Divide the integer fractions (see Section 3.4, Case II).

Step 4 Simplify the fraction to its lowest term (see Section 2.3).

Step 5 Change the improper fraction to a mixed fraction if the fraction obtained from Step 4 is an improper fraction (see Section 2.2).

The following examples show the steps as to how three integer and mixed fractions with or without a common denominator are divided:

Example 7.4-6

$$\left(2\frac{3}{8} \div 5\right) \div \frac{3}{5} =$$

Solution:

Step 1

$$\left(2\frac{3}{8} \div 5\right) \div \frac{3}{5} = \left(2\frac{3}{8} \div \frac{5}{1}\right) \div \frac{3}{5}$$

Step 2

$$\left(2\frac{3}{8} \div \frac{5}{1}\right) \div \frac{3}{5} = \left(\frac{(2 \times 8) + 3}{8} \div \frac{5}{1}\right) \div \frac{3}{5} = \left(\frac{16 + 3}{8} \div \frac{5}{1}\right) \div \frac{3}{5} = \left(\frac{19}{8} \div \frac{5}{1}\right) \div \frac{3}{5}$$

Step 3

$$\left(\frac{19}{8} \div \frac{5}{1}\right) \div \frac{3}{5} = \left(\frac{19}{8} \times \frac{1}{5}\right) \div \frac{3}{5} = \left(\frac{19 \times 1}{8 \times 5}\right) \div \frac{3}{5} = \left(\frac{19}{40}\right) \div \frac{3}{5} = \frac{19}{40} \div \frac{3}{5} = \frac{19}{40} \times \frac{5}{3}$$

$$= \frac{19 \times 5}{40 \times 3} = \frac{95}{120}$$

Step 4

$$\frac{95}{120} = \frac{95 \div 5}{120 \div 5} = \boxed{\frac{19}{24}}$$

Step 5

Not Applicable

Example 7.4-7

$$5 \div \left(3\frac{2}{3} \div 2\frac{3}{4}\right) =$$

Solution:

Step 1

$$5 \div \left(3\frac{2}{3} \div 2\frac{3}{4}\right) = \frac{5}{1} \div \left(3\frac{2}{3} \div 2\frac{3}{4}\right)$$

Step 2

$$\frac{5}{1} \div \left(3\frac{2}{3} \div 2\frac{3}{4}\right) = \frac{5}{1} \div \left(\frac{(3 \times 3) + 2}{3} \div \frac{(2 \times 4) + 3}{4}\right) = \frac{5}{1} \div \left(\frac{9 + 2}{3} \div \frac{8 + 3}{4}\right)$$

$$= \frac{5}{1} \div \left(\frac{11}{3} \div \frac{11}{4}\right)$$

Step 3

$$\frac{5}{1} \div \left(\frac{11}{3} \div \frac{11}{4}\right) = \frac{5}{1} \div \left(\frac{11}{3} \times \frac{4}{11}\right) = \frac{5}{1} \div \left(\frac{11 \times 4}{3 \times 11}\right) = \frac{5}{1} \div \left(\frac{44}{33}\right) = \frac{5}{1} \div \frac{44}{33} = \frac{5}{1} \times \frac{33}{44}$$

$$= \boxed{\frac{5 \times 33}{1 \times 44}} = \boxed{\frac{165}{44}}$$

Step 4 $\boxed{\frac{165}{44}} = \boxed{\frac{165 \div 11}{44 \div 11}} = \boxed{\frac{15}{4}}$

Step 5 $\boxed{\frac{15}{4}} = \boxed{\mathbf{3\frac{3}{4}}}$

Example 7.4-8

$$\boxed{\left(2\frac{3}{5} \div \frac{1}{6}\right) \div \frac{2}{3}} =$$

Solution:

Step 1 $\boxed{\textit{Not Applicable}}$

Step 2 $\boxed{\left(2\frac{3}{5} \div \frac{1}{6}\right) \div \frac{2}{3}} = \boxed{\left(\frac{(2 \times 5) + 3}{5} \div \frac{1}{6}\right) \div \frac{2}{3}} = \boxed{\left(\frac{10 + 3}{5} \div \frac{1}{6}\right) \div \frac{2}{3}} = \boxed{\left(\frac{13}{5} \div \frac{1}{6}\right) \div \frac{2}{3}}$

Step 3 $\boxed{\left(\frac{13}{5} \div \frac{1}{6}\right) \div \frac{2}{3}} = \boxed{\left(\frac{13}{5} \times \frac{6}{1}\right) \div \frac{2}{3}} = \boxed{\left(\frac{13 \times 6}{5 \times 1}\right) \div \frac{2}{3}} = \boxed{\left(\frac{78}{5}\right) \div \frac{2}{3}} = \boxed{\frac{78}{5} \div \frac{2}{3}} = \boxed{\frac{78}{5} \times \frac{3}{2}}$

$$= \boxed{\frac{78 \times 3}{5 \times 2}} = \boxed{\frac{234}{10}}$$

Step 4 $\boxed{\frac{234}{10}} = \boxed{\frac{234 \div 2}{10 \div 2}} = \boxed{\frac{117}{5}}$

Step 5 $\boxed{\frac{117}{5}} = \boxed{\mathbf{23\frac{2}{5}}}$

Example 7.4-9

$$\boxed{\frac{4}{5} \div \left(14 \div 2\frac{3}{4}\right)} =$$

Solution:

Step 1 $\boxed{\frac{4}{5} \div \left(14 \div 2\frac{3}{4}\right)} = \boxed{\frac{4}{5} \div \left(\frac{14}{1} \div 2\frac{3}{4}\right)}$

Step 2 $\boxed{\frac{4}{5} \div \left(\frac{14}{1} \div 2\frac{3}{4}\right)} = \boxed{\frac{4}{5} \div \left(\frac{14}{1} \div \frac{(2 \times 4) + 3}{4}\right)} = \boxed{\frac{4}{5} \div \left(\frac{14}{1} \div \frac{8 + 3}{4}\right)} = \boxed{\frac{4}{5} \div \left(\frac{14}{1} \div \frac{11}{4}\right)}$

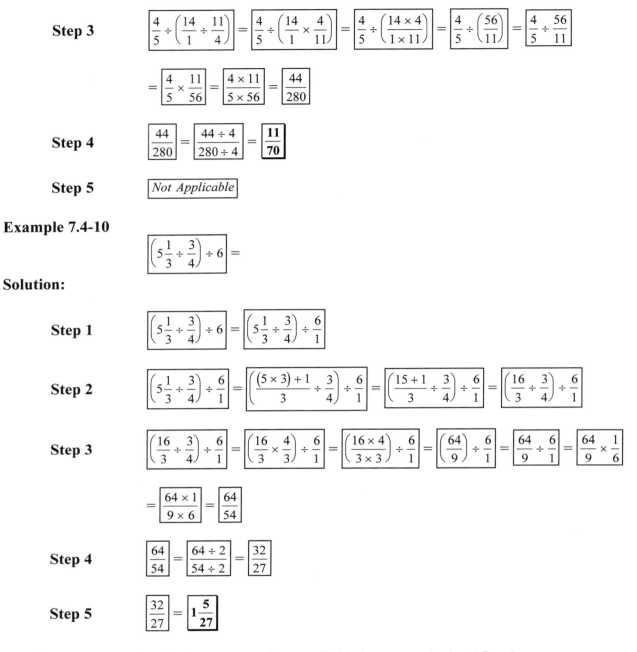

Step 3 $\dfrac{4}{5} \div \left(\dfrac{14}{1} \div \dfrac{11}{4}\right) = \dfrac{4}{5} \div \left(\dfrac{14}{1} \times \dfrac{4}{11}\right) = \dfrac{4}{5} \div \left(\dfrac{14 \times 4}{1 \times 11}\right) = \dfrac{4}{5} \div \left(\dfrac{56}{11}\right) = \dfrac{4}{5} \div \dfrac{56}{11}$

$= \dfrac{4}{5} \times \dfrac{11}{56} = \dfrac{4 \times 11}{5 \times 56} = \dfrac{44}{280}$

Step 4 $\dfrac{44}{280} = \dfrac{44 \div 4}{280 \div 4} = \boxed{\dfrac{11}{70}}$

Step 5   *Not Applicable*

Example 7.4-10

$\left(5\dfrac{1}{3} \div \dfrac{3}{4}\right) \div 6 =$

Solution:

Step 1 $\left(5\dfrac{1}{3} \div \dfrac{3}{4}\right) \div 6 = \left(5\dfrac{1}{3} \div \dfrac{3}{4}\right) \div \dfrac{6}{1}$

Step 2 $\left(5\dfrac{1}{3} \div \dfrac{3}{4}\right) \div \dfrac{6}{1} = \left(\dfrac{(5 \times 3) + 1}{3} \div \dfrac{3}{4}\right) \div \dfrac{6}{1} = \left(\dfrac{15 + 1}{3} \div \dfrac{3}{4}\right) \div \dfrac{6}{1} = \left(\dfrac{16}{3} \div \dfrac{3}{4}\right) \div \dfrac{6}{1}$

Step 3 $\left(\dfrac{16}{3} \div \dfrac{3}{4}\right) \div \dfrac{6}{1} = \left(\dfrac{16}{3} \times \dfrac{4}{3}\right) \div \dfrac{6}{1} = \left(\dfrac{16 \times 4}{3 \times 3}\right) \div \dfrac{6}{1} = \left(\dfrac{64}{9}\right) \div \dfrac{6}{1} = \dfrac{64}{9} \div \dfrac{6}{1} = \dfrac{64}{9} \times \dfrac{1}{6}$

$= \dfrac{64 \times 1}{9 \times 6} = \dfrac{64}{54}$

Step 4 $\dfrac{64}{54} = \dfrac{64 \div 2}{54 \div 2} = \dfrac{32}{27}$

Step 5 $\dfrac{32}{27} = \boxed{1\dfrac{5}{27}}$

The following examples further illustrate how to divide integer and mixed fractions:

Example 7.4-11

$1\dfrac{2}{5} \div \dfrac{3}{10} = \dfrac{(1 \times 5) + 2}{5} \div \dfrac{3}{10} = \dfrac{5 + 2}{5} \div \dfrac{3}{10} = \dfrac{7}{5} \div \dfrac{3}{10} = \dfrac{7}{5} \times \dfrac{10}{3} = \dfrac{7 \times \overset{2}{\cancel{10}}}{\underset{1}{\cancel{5}} \times 3} = \dfrac{7 \times 2}{1 \times 3} = \dfrac{14}{3} = \boxed{4\dfrac{2}{3}}$

Example 7.4-12

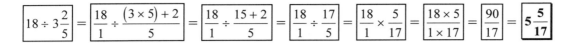

$$18 \div 3\frac{2}{5} = \frac{18}{1} \div \frac{(3 \times 5) + 2}{5} = \frac{18}{1} \div \frac{15 + 2}{5} = \frac{18}{1} \div \frac{17}{5} = \frac{18}{1} \times \frac{5}{17} = \frac{18 \times 5}{1 \times 17} = \frac{90}{17} = 5\frac{5}{17}$$

Example 7.4-13

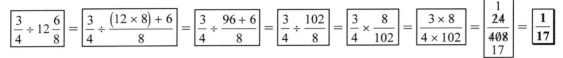

$$\frac{3}{4} \div 12\frac{6}{8} = \frac{3}{4} \div \frac{(12 \times 8) + 6}{8} = \frac{3}{4} \div \frac{96 + 6}{8} = \frac{3}{4} \div \frac{102}{8} = \frac{3}{4} \times \frac{8}{102} = \frac{3 \times 8}{4 \times 102} = \frac{\overset{1}{24}}{\underset{17}{408}} = \frac{1}{17}$$

Example 7.4-14

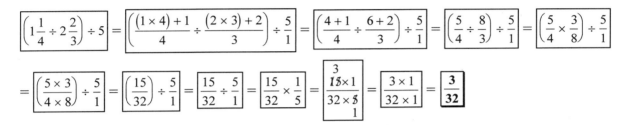

$$\left(1\frac{1}{4} \div 2\frac{2}{3}\right) \div 5 = \left(\frac{(1 \times 4) + 1}{4} \div \frac{(2 \times 3) + 2}{3}\right) \div \frac{5}{1} = \left(\frac{4 + 1}{4} \div \frac{6 + 2}{3}\right) \div \frac{5}{1} = \left(\frac{5}{4} \div \frac{8}{3}\right) \div \frac{5}{1} = \left(\frac{5}{4} \times \frac{3}{8}\right) \div \frac{5}{1}$$

$$= \left(\frac{5 \times 3}{4 \times 8}\right) \div \frac{5}{1} = \left(\frac{15}{32}\right) \div \frac{5}{1} = \frac{15}{32} \div \frac{5}{1} = \frac{15}{32} \times \frac{1}{5} = \frac{\overset{3}{15} \times 1}{32 \times \underset{1}{5}} = \frac{3 \times 1}{32 \times 1} = \frac{3}{32}$$

Example 7.4-15

$$2\frac{5}{6} \div \left(\frac{3}{4} \div 24\right) = \frac{(2 \times 6) + 5}{6} \div \left(\frac{3}{4} \div \frac{24}{1}\right) = \frac{12 + 5}{6} \div \left(\frac{3}{4} \times \frac{1}{24}\right) = \frac{17}{6} \div \left(\frac{\overset{1}{3} \times 1}{4 \times \underset{8}{24}}\right) = \frac{17}{6} \div \left(\frac{1 \times 1}{4 \times 8}\right)$$

$$= \frac{17}{6} \div \left(\frac{1}{32}\right) = \frac{17}{6} \div \frac{1}{32} = \frac{17}{6} \times \frac{32}{1} = \frac{17 \times \overset{16}{32}}{\underset{3}{6} \times 1} = \frac{17 \times 16}{3 \times 1} = \frac{272}{3} = 90\frac{2}{3}$$

Example 7.4-16

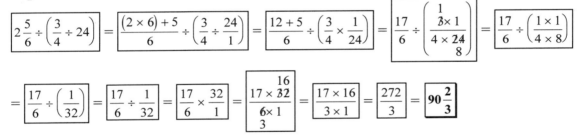

$$\left(6 \div 1\frac{2}{3}\right) \div 2\frac{3}{5} = \left(\frac{6}{1} \div \frac{(1 \times 3) + 2}{3}\right) \div \frac{(2 \times 5) + 3}{5} = \left(\frac{6}{1} \div \frac{3 + 2}{3}\right) \div \frac{10 + 3}{5} = \left(\frac{6}{1} \div \frac{5}{3}\right) \div \frac{13}{5}$$

$$= \left(\frac{6}{1} \times \frac{3}{5}\right) \div \frac{13}{5} = \left(\frac{6 \times 3}{1 \times 5}\right) \div \frac{13}{5} = \left(\frac{18}{5}\right) \div \frac{13}{5} = \frac{18}{5} \div \frac{13}{5} = \frac{18}{5} \times \frac{5}{13} = \frac{18 \times \overset{1}{5}}{\underset{1}{5} \times 13} = \frac{18 \times 1}{1 \times 13} = \frac{18}{13}$$

$$= 1\frac{5}{13}$$

Example 7.4-17

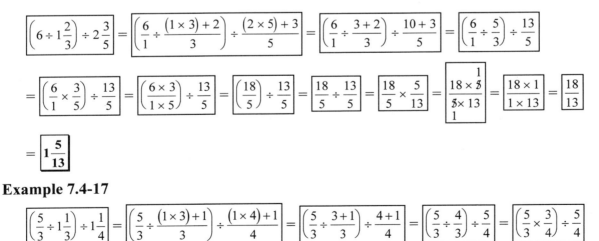

$$\left(\frac{5}{3} \div 1\frac{1}{3}\right) \div 1\frac{1}{4} = \left(\frac{5}{3} \div \frac{(1 \times 3) + 1}{3}\right) \div \frac{(1 \times 4) + 1}{4} = \left(\frac{5}{3} \div \frac{3 + 1}{3}\right) \div \frac{4 + 1}{4} = \left(\frac{5}{3} \div \frac{4}{3}\right) \div \frac{5}{4} = \left(\frac{5}{3} \times \frac{3}{4}\right) \div \frac{5}{4}$$

$$= \left(\frac{5 \times \overset{1}{\cancel{3}}}{\underset{1}{\cancel{3} \times 4}}\right) \div \frac{5}{4} = \left(\frac{5 \times 1}{1 \times 4}\right) \div \frac{5}{4} = \left(\frac{5}{4}\right) \div \frac{5}{4} = \frac{5}{4} \div \frac{5}{4} = \frac{5}{4} \times \frac{4}{5} = \frac{\overset{1}{\cancel{5}} \times \overset{1}{\cancel{4}}}{\underset{1}{\cancel{4} \times \cancel{5}}} = \frac{1 \times 1}{1 \times 1} = \frac{1}{1} = \boxed{1}$$

Example 7.4-18

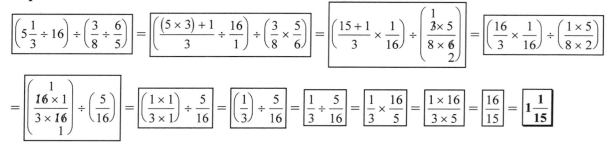

$$= \left(\frac{\overset{1}{\cancel{16}} \times 1}{3 \times \underset{1}{\cancel{16}}}\right) \div \left(\frac{5}{16}\right) = \left(\frac{1 \times 1}{3 \times 1}\right) \div \frac{5}{16} = \left(\frac{1}{3}\right) \div \frac{5}{16} = \frac{1}{3} \div \frac{5}{16} = \frac{1}{3} \times \frac{16}{5} = \frac{1 \times 16}{3 \times 5} = \frac{16}{15} = \boxed{1\frac{1}{15}}$$

Example 7.4-19

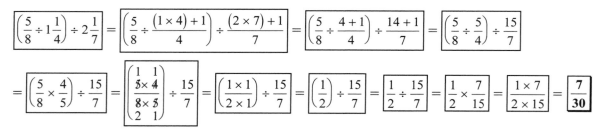

$$= \left(\frac{5}{8} \times \frac{4}{5}\right) \div \frac{15}{7} = \left(\frac{\overset{1}{\cancel{5}} \times \overset{1}{\cancel{4}}}{\underset{2}{\cancel{8}} \times \underset{1}{\cancel{5}}}\right) \div \frac{15}{7} = \left(\frac{1 \times 1}{2 \times 1}\right) \div \frac{15}{7} = \left(\frac{1}{2}\right) \div \frac{15}{7} = \frac{1}{2} \div \frac{15}{7} = \frac{1}{2} \times \frac{7}{15} = \frac{1 \times 7}{2 \times 15} = \boxed{\frac{7}{30}}$$

Example 7.4-20

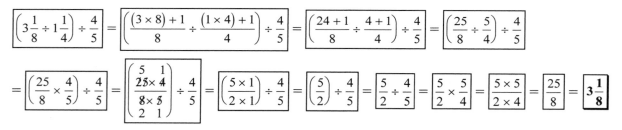

$$= \left(\frac{25}{8} \times \frac{4}{5}\right) \div \frac{4}{5} = \left(\frac{\overset{5}{\cancel{25}} \times \overset{1}{\cancel{4}}}{\underset{2}{\cancel{8}} \times \underset{1}{\cancel{5}}}\right) \div \frac{4}{5} = \left(\frac{5 \times 1}{2 \times 1}\right) \div \frac{4}{5} = \left(\frac{5}{2}\right) \div \frac{4}{5} = \frac{5}{2} \div \frac{4}{5} = \frac{5}{2} \times \frac{5}{4} = \frac{5 \times 5}{2 \times 4} = \frac{25}{8} = \boxed{3\frac{1}{8}}$$

Example 7.4-21

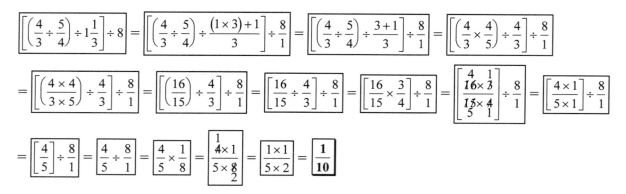

$$= \left[\frac{4}{5}\right] \div \frac{8}{1} = \frac{4}{5} \div \frac{8}{1} = \frac{4}{5} \times \frac{1}{8} = \frac{\overset{1}{\cancel{4}} \times 1}{5 \times \underset{2}{\cancel{8}}} = \frac{1 \times 1}{5 \times 2} = \boxed{\frac{1}{10}}$$

Section 7.4 Exercises - Divide the following integer and mixed fractions:

1. $2\dfrac{1}{3} \div \dfrac{5}{6} =$

2. $2\dfrac{3}{5} \div 6 =$

3. $\dfrac{6}{10} \div 2\dfrac{4}{5} =$

4. $5 \div \left(\dfrac{1}{3} \div \dfrac{3}{5}\right) =$

5. $\dfrac{1}{8} \div \left(1\dfrac{1}{4} \div \dfrac{3}{5}\right) =$

6. $\left(\dfrac{3}{7} \div \dfrac{4}{7}\right) \div 2\dfrac{3}{4} =$

7. $\dfrac{5}{6} \div \left(1\dfrac{1}{5} \div \dfrac{4}{5}\right) =$

8. $\left(3\dfrac{1}{8} \div \dfrac{5}{6}\right) \div 12 =$

9. $\left(1\dfrac{1}{4} \div \dfrac{3}{45}\right) \div \dfrac{2}{5} =$

10. $\left(1\dfrac{5}{8} \div 5\right) \div \left(2\dfrac{3}{4} \div \dfrac{1}{2}\right) =$

7.5 Solving Mixed Operations Using Integer and Mixed Fractions

Integer and mixed fractions of the forms:

1. $\left(\dfrac{a}{b}\right)$ where both the numerator (a) and the denominator (b) are integers, and

2. $\left(k\dfrac{a}{b}\right)$ where (k) is a whole number and $\left(\dfrac{a}{b}\right)$ is an integer fraction

are added, subtracted, multiplied, and divided by using the following steps:

Step 1 Change the integer number (a) to an integer fraction of the form $\left(\dfrac{a}{1}\right)$, e.g., change 7

to $\dfrac{7}{1}$.

Step 2 Change the mixed fraction(s) to integer fraction(s) (see Section 2.5).

Step 3 Add, subtract, multiply, and divide the integer fractions by following the steps outlined in sections 3.1 through 3.4.

Step 4 Simplify the fraction to its lowest term (see Sections 2.3).

Step 5 Change the improper fraction to a mixed fraction if the fraction obtained from Step 4 is an improper fraction (see Section 2.2).

The following examples show mathematical operations on integer and mixed fractions using the above steps:

Example 7.5-1

$$\boxed{\left(2\dfrac{3}{6}\times\dfrac{4}{5}\right)+\dfrac{2}{3}=}$$

Solution:

Step 1 $\boxed{\textit{Not Applicable}}$

Step 2 $\boxed{\left(2\dfrac{3}{6}\times\dfrac{4}{5}\right)+\dfrac{2}{3}}=\boxed{\left(\dfrac{(2\times6)+3}{6}\times\dfrac{4}{5}\right)+\dfrac{2}{3}}=\boxed{\left(\dfrac{12+3}{6}\times\dfrac{4}{5}\right)+\dfrac{2}{3}}=\boxed{\left(\dfrac{15}{6}\times\dfrac{4}{5}\right)+\dfrac{2}{3}}$

Step 3 $\boxed{\left(\dfrac{15}{6}\times\dfrac{4}{5}\right)+\dfrac{2}{3}}=\boxed{\left(\dfrac{15\times4}{6\times5}\right)+\dfrac{2}{3}}=\boxed{\left(\dfrac{60}{30}\right)+\dfrac{2}{3}}=\boxed{\dfrac{60}{30}+\dfrac{2}{3}}=\boxed{\dfrac{(60\times3)+(2\times30)}{30\times3}}$

$=\boxed{\dfrac{180+60}{90}}=\boxed{\dfrac{240}{90}}$

Step 4 $\boxed{\dfrac{240}{90}}=\boxed{\dfrac{240\div30}{90\div30}}=\boxed{\dfrac{8}{3}}$

Step 5 $\boxed{\dfrac{8}{3}}=\boxed{2\dfrac{2}{3}}$

Example 7.5-2

$$\left(5 - \frac{3}{4}\right) \div 2\frac{3}{5} =$$

Solution:

Step 1 $\left(5 - \frac{3}{4}\right) \div 2\frac{3}{5} = \left[\left(\frac{5}{1} - \frac{3}{4}\right) \div 2\frac{3}{5}\right]$

Step 2 $\left(\frac{5}{1} - \frac{3}{4}\right) \div 2\frac{3}{5} = \left[\left(\frac{5}{1} - \frac{3}{4}\right) \div \frac{(2 \times 5) + 3}{5}\right] = \left[\left(\frac{5}{1} - \frac{3}{4}\right) \div \frac{10 + 3}{5}\right] = \left[\left(\frac{5}{1} - \frac{3}{4}\right) \div \frac{13}{5}\right]$

Step 3 $\left(\frac{5}{1} - \frac{3}{4}\right) \div \frac{13}{5} = \left[\left(\frac{(5 \times 4) - (3 \times 1)}{1 \times 4}\right) \div \frac{13}{5}\right] = \left[\left(\frac{20 - 3}{4}\right) \div \frac{13}{5}\right] = \left[\left(\frac{17}{4}\right) \div \frac{13}{5}\right]$

$= \left[\frac{17}{4} \div \frac{13}{5}\right] = \left[\frac{17}{4} \times \frac{5}{13}\right] = \left[\frac{17 \times 5}{4 \times 13}\right] = \left[\frac{85}{52}\right]$

Step 4 $\boxed{Not\ Applicable}$

Step 5 $\frac{85}{52} = \boxed{1\frac{33}{52}}$

Example 7.5-3

$$\left(\frac{3}{8} \times \frac{2}{5}\right) \div \left(\frac{2}{3} + 1\frac{2}{3}\right) =$$

Solution:

Step 1 $\boxed{Not\ Applicable}$

Step 2 $\left(\frac{3}{8} \times \frac{2}{5}\right) \div \left(\frac{2}{3} + 1\frac{2}{3}\right) = \left[\left(\frac{3}{8} \times \frac{2}{5}\right) \div \left(\frac{2}{3} + \frac{(1 \times 3) + 2}{3}\right)\right] = \left[\left(\frac{3}{8} \times \frac{2}{5}\right) \div \left(\frac{2}{3} + \frac{3 + 2}{3}\right)\right]$

$= \left[\left(\frac{3}{8} \times \frac{2}{5}\right) \div \left(\frac{2}{3} + \frac{5}{3}\right)\right]$

Step 3 $\left[\left(\frac{3}{8} \times \frac{2}{5}\right) \div \left(\frac{2}{3} + \frac{5}{3}\right)\right] = \left[\left(\frac{3 \times 2}{8 \times 5}\right) \div \left(\frac{2 + 5}{3}\right)\right] = \left[\left(\frac{6}{40}\right) \div \left(\frac{7}{3}\right)\right] = \left[\frac{6}{40} \div \frac{7}{3}\right] = \left[\frac{6}{40} \times \frac{3}{7}\right]$

$= \left[\frac{6 \times 3}{40 \times 7}\right] = \left[\frac{18}{280}\right]$

Step 4 $\frac{18}{280} = \left[\frac{18 \div 2}{280 \div 2}\right] = \boxed{\frac{9}{140}}$

Step 5 $\boxed{Not\ Applicable}$

Example 7.5-4

$$\boxed{\left(3\frac{1}{5} - 2\frac{1}{3}\right) \times \left(\frac{2}{3} + 5\right)} =$$

Solution:

Step 1 $\boxed{\left(3\frac{1}{5} - 2\frac{1}{3}\right) \times \left(\frac{2}{3} + 5\right)} = \boxed{\left(3\frac{1}{5} - 2\frac{1}{3}\right) \times \left(\frac{2}{3} + \frac{5}{1}\right)}$

Step 2 $\boxed{\left(3\frac{1}{5} - 2\frac{1}{3}\right) \times \left(\frac{2}{3} + \frac{5}{1}\right)} = \boxed{\left(\frac{(3\times5)+1}{5} - \frac{(2\times3)+1}{3}\right) \times \left(\frac{2}{3} + \frac{5}{1}\right)}$

$= \boxed{\left(\frac{15+1}{5} - \frac{6+1}{3}\right) \times \left(\frac{2}{3} + \frac{5}{1}\right)} = \boxed{\left(\frac{16}{5} - \frac{7}{3}\right) \times \left(\frac{2}{3} + \frac{5}{1}\right)}$

Step 3 $\boxed{\left(\frac{16}{5} - \frac{7}{3}\right) \times \left(\frac{2}{3} + \frac{5}{1}\right)} = \boxed{\left(\frac{(16\times3)-(7\times5)}{5\times3}\right) \times \left(\frac{(2\times1)+(5\times3)}{3\times1}\right)}$

$= \boxed{\left(\frac{48-35}{15}\right) \times \left(\frac{2+15}{3}\right)} = \boxed{\left(\frac{13}{15}\right) \times \left(\frac{17}{3}\right)} = \boxed{\frac{13}{15} \times \frac{17}{3}} = \boxed{\frac{13\times17}{15\times3}} = \boxed{\frac{221}{45}}$

Step 4 $\boxed{Not\ Applicable}$

Step 5 $\boxed{\frac{221}{45}} = \boxed{\mathbf{4\frac{41}{45}}}$

Example 7.5-5

$$\boxed{\left(\frac{2}{3} \div 1\frac{1}{5}\right) \div \left(2\frac{1}{3} \times \frac{2}{5}\right)} =$$

Solution:

Step 1 $\boxed{Not\ Applicable}$

Step 2 $\boxed{\left(\frac{2}{3} \div 1\frac{1}{5}\right) \div \left(2\frac{1}{3} \times \frac{2}{5}\right)} = \boxed{\left(\frac{2}{3} \div \frac{(1\times5)+1}{5}\right) \div \left(\frac{(2\times3)+1}{3} \times \frac{2}{5}\right)}$

$= \boxed{\left(\frac{2}{3} \div \frac{5+1}{5}\right) \div \left(\frac{6+1}{3} \times \frac{2}{5}\right)} = \boxed{\left(\frac{2}{3} \div \frac{6}{5}\right) \div \left(\frac{7}{3} \times \frac{2}{5}\right)}$

Step 3 $\boxed{\left(\frac{2}{3} \div \frac{6}{5}\right) \div \left(\frac{7}{3} \times \frac{2}{5}\right)} = \boxed{\left(\frac{2}{3} \times \frac{5}{6}\right) \div \left(\frac{7\times2}{3\times5}\right)} = \boxed{\left(\frac{2\times5}{3\times6}\right) \div \left(\frac{14}{15}\right)} = \boxed{\left(\frac{10}{18}\right) \div \left(\frac{14}{15}\right)}$

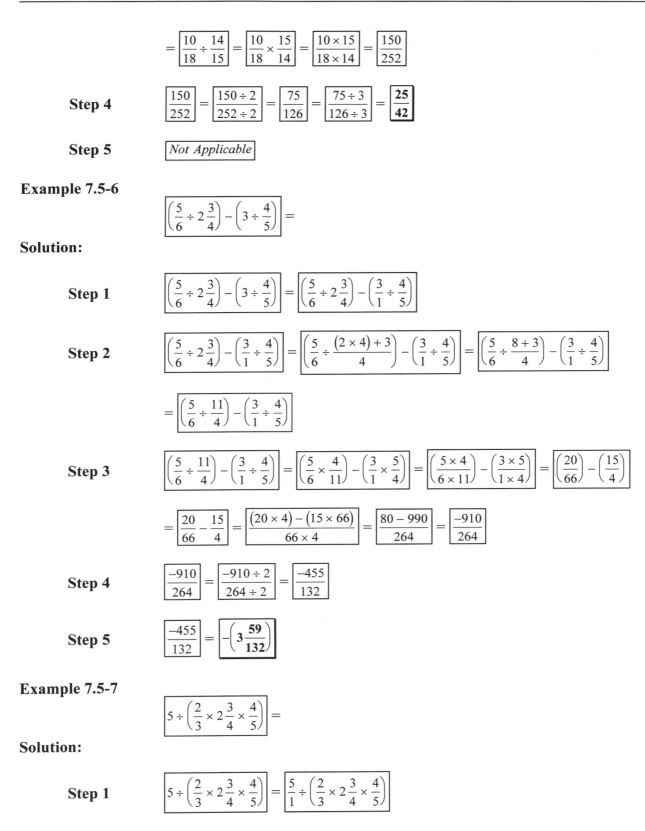

$$= \boxed{\frac{10}{18} \div \frac{14}{15}} = \boxed{\frac{10}{18} \times \frac{15}{14}} = \boxed{\frac{10 \times 15}{18 \times 14}} = \boxed{\frac{150}{252}}$$

Step 4 $\boxed{\frac{150}{252}} = \boxed{\frac{150 \div 2}{252 \div 2}} = \boxed{\frac{75}{126}} = \boxed{\frac{75 \div 3}{126 \div 3}} = \boxed{\mathbf{\frac{25}{42}}}$

Step 5 $\boxed{\textit{Not Applicable}}$

Example 7.5-6

$$\boxed{\left(\frac{5}{6} \div 2\frac{3}{4}\right) - \left(3 \div \frac{4}{5}\right)} =$$

Solution:

Step 1 $\boxed{\left(\frac{5}{6} \div 2\frac{3}{4}\right) - \left(3 \div \frac{4}{5}\right)} = \boxed{\left(\frac{5}{6} \div 2\frac{3}{4}\right) - \left(\frac{3}{1} \div \frac{4}{5}\right)}$

Step 2 $\boxed{\left(\frac{5}{6} \div 2\frac{3}{4}\right) - \left(\frac{3}{1} \div \frac{4}{5}\right)} = \boxed{\left(\frac{5}{6} \div \frac{(2 \times 4) + 3}{4}\right) - \left(\frac{3}{1} \div \frac{4}{5}\right)} = \boxed{\left(\frac{5}{6} \div \frac{8 + 3}{4}\right) - \left(\frac{3}{1} \div \frac{4}{5}\right)}$

$$= \boxed{\left(\frac{5}{6} \div \frac{11}{4}\right) - \left(\frac{3}{1} \div \frac{4}{5}\right)}$$

Step 3 $\boxed{\left(\frac{5}{6} \div \frac{11}{4}\right) - \left(\frac{3}{1} \div \frac{4}{5}\right)} = \boxed{\left(\frac{5}{6} \times \frac{4}{11}\right) - \left(\frac{3}{1} \times \frac{5}{4}\right)} = \boxed{\left(\frac{5 \times 4}{6 \times 11}\right) - \left(\frac{3 \times 5}{1 \times 4}\right)} = \boxed{\left(\frac{20}{66}\right) - \left(\frac{15}{4}\right)}$

$$= \boxed{\frac{20}{66} - \frac{15}{4}} = \boxed{\frac{(20 \times 4) - (15 \times 66)}{66 \times 4}} = \boxed{\frac{80 - 990}{264}} = \boxed{\frac{-910}{264}}$$

Step 4 $\boxed{\frac{-910}{264}} = \boxed{\frac{-910 \div 2}{264 \div 2}} = \boxed{\frac{-455}{132}}$

Step 5 $\boxed{\frac{-455}{132}} = \boxed{-\left(3\frac{59}{132}\right)}$

Example 7.5-7

$$\boxed{5 \div \left(\frac{2}{3} \times 2\frac{3}{4} \times \frac{4}{5}\right)} =$$

Solution:

Step 1 $\boxed{5 \div \left(\frac{2}{3} \times 2\frac{3}{4} \times \frac{4}{5}\right)} = \boxed{\frac{5}{1} \div \left(\frac{2}{3} \times 2\frac{3}{4} \times \frac{4}{5}\right)}$

Step 2
$$\frac{5}{1} \div \left(\frac{2}{3} \times 2\frac{3}{4} \times \frac{4}{5} \right) = \frac{5}{1} \div \left(\frac{2}{3} \times \frac{(2 \times 4) + 3}{4} \times \frac{4}{5} \right) = \frac{5}{1} \div \left(\frac{2}{3} \times \frac{8 + 3}{4} \times \frac{4}{5} \right)$$

$$= \frac{5}{1} \div \left(\frac{2}{3} \times \frac{11}{4} \times \frac{4}{5} \right)$$

Step 3
$$\frac{5}{1} \div \left(\frac{2}{3} \times \frac{11}{4} \times \frac{4}{5} \right) = \frac{5}{1} \div \left(\frac{2 \times 11 \times 4}{3 \times 4 \times 5} \right) = \frac{5}{1} \div \left(\frac{88}{60} \right) = \frac{5}{1} \div \frac{88}{60} = \frac{5}{1} \times \frac{60}{88} = \frac{5 \times 60}{1 \times 88}$$

$$= \frac{300}{88}$$

Step 4
$$\frac{300}{88} = \frac{300 \div 4}{88 \div 4} = \frac{75}{22}$$

Step 5
$$\frac{75}{22} = 3\frac{9}{22}$$

Example 7.5-8
$$\left(5 - \frac{2}{3} \right) \div \left(\frac{5}{6} + 1\frac{2}{6} + 3\frac{4}{6} \right) =$$

Solution:

Step 1
$$\left(5 - \frac{2}{3} \right) \div \left(\frac{5}{6} + 1\frac{2}{6} + 3\frac{4}{6} \right) = \left(\frac{5}{1} - \frac{2}{3} \right) \div \left(\frac{5}{6} + 1\frac{2}{6} + 3\frac{4}{6} \right)$$

Step 2
$$\left(\frac{5}{1} - \frac{2}{3} \right) \div \left(\frac{5}{6} + 1\frac{2}{6} + 3\frac{4}{6} \right) = \left(\frac{5}{1} - \frac{2}{3} \right) \div \left(\frac{5}{6} + \frac{(1 \times 6) + 2}{6} + \frac{(3 \times 6) + 4}{6} \right)$$

$$= \left(\frac{5}{1} - \frac{2}{3} \right) \div \left(\frac{5}{6} + \frac{6 + 2}{6} + \frac{18 + 4}{6} \right) = \left(\frac{5}{1} - \frac{2}{3} \right) \div \left(\frac{5}{6} + \frac{8}{6} + \frac{22}{6} \right)$$

Step 3
$$\left(\frac{5}{1} - \frac{2}{3} \right) \div \left(\frac{5}{6} + \frac{8}{6} + \frac{22}{6} \right) = \left(\frac{(5 \times 3) - (2 \times 1)}{1 \times 3} \right) \div \left(\frac{5 + 8 + 22}{6} \right) = \left(\frac{15 - 2}{3} \right) \div \left(\frac{35}{6} \right)$$

$$= \left(\frac{13}{3} \right) \div \frac{35}{6} = \frac{13}{3} \div \frac{35}{6} = \frac{13}{3} \times \frac{6}{35} = \frac{13 \times \overset{2}{6}}{\underset{1}{3} \times 35} = \frac{13 \times 2}{1 \times 35} = \frac{26}{35}$$

Step 4   *Not Applicable*

Step 5   *Not Applicable*

Example 7.5-9

$$\left[\left(3+2\frac{1}{5}\right)+\left(\frac{3}{8}+\frac{5}{8}\right)\right]\div\frac{2}{3}=$$

Solution:

Step 1

$$\left[\left(3+2\frac{1}{5}\right)+\left(\frac{3}{8}+\frac{5}{8}\right)\right]\div\frac{2}{3}=\left[\left(\frac{3}{1}+2\frac{1}{5}\right)+\left(\frac{3}{8}+\frac{5}{8}\right)\right]\div\frac{2}{3}$$

Step 2

$$\left[\left(\frac{3}{1}+2\frac{1}{5}\right)+\left(\frac{3}{8}+\frac{5}{8}\right)\right]\div\frac{2}{3}=\left[\left(\frac{3}{1}+\frac{(2\times5)+1}{5}\right)+\left(\frac{3}{8}+\frac{5}{8}\right)\right]\div\frac{2}{3}$$

$$=\left[\left(\frac{3}{1}+\frac{10+1}{5}\right)+\left(\frac{3}{8}+\frac{5}{8}\right)\right]\div\frac{2}{3}=\left[\left(\frac{3}{1}+\frac{11}{5}\right)+\left(\frac{3}{8}+\frac{5}{8}\right)\right]\div\frac{2}{3}$$

Step 3

$$\left[\left(\frac{3}{1}+\frac{11}{5}\right)+\left(\frac{3}{8}+\frac{5}{8}\right)\right]\div\frac{2}{3}=\left[\left(\frac{(3\times5)+(11\times1)}{1\times5}\right)+\left(\frac{3+5}{8}\right)\right]\div\frac{2}{3}$$

$$=\left[\left(\frac{15+11}{5}\right)+\left(\frac{8}{8}\right)\right]\div\frac{2}{3}=\left[\left(\frac{26}{5}\right)+\left(\frac{8}{8}\right)\right]\div\frac{2}{3}=\left[\frac{26}{5}+\frac{8}{8}\right]\div\frac{2}{3}$$

$$=\left[\frac{(26\times8)+(8\times5)}{5\times8}\right]\div\frac{2}{3}=\left[\frac{208+40}{40}\right]\div\frac{2}{3}=\left[\frac{248}{40}\right]\div\frac{2}{3}=\frac{248}{40}\div\frac{2}{3}=\frac{248}{40}\times\frac{3}{2}$$

$$=\frac{248\times3}{40\times2}=\frac{744}{80}$$

Step 4

$$\frac{744}{80}=\frac{744\div8}{80\div8}=\frac{93}{10}$$

Step 5

$$\frac{93}{10}=9\frac{3}{10}$$

Example 7.5-10

$$\left[8-\left(\frac{3}{5}-1\frac{2}{5}\right)\right]+\frac{3}{4}=$$

Solution:

Step 1

$$\left[8-\left(\frac{3}{5}-1\frac{2}{5}\right)\right]+\frac{3}{4}=\left[\frac{8}{1}-\left(\frac{3}{5}-1\frac{2}{5}\right)\right]+\frac{3}{4}$$

Step 2
$$\left[\frac{8}{1}-\left(\frac{3}{5}-1\frac{2}{5}\right)\right]+\frac{3}{4}=\left[\frac{8}{1}-\left(\frac{3}{5}-\frac{(1\times5)+2}{5}\right)\right]+\frac{3}{4}=\left[\frac{8}{1}-\left(\frac{3}{5}-\frac{5+2}{5}\right)\right]+\frac{3}{4}$$

$$=\left[\frac{8}{1}-\left(\frac{3}{5}-\frac{7}{5}\right)\right]+\frac{3}{4}$$

Step 3
$$\left[\frac{8}{1}-\left(\frac{3}{5}-\frac{7}{5}\right)\right]+\frac{3}{4}=\left[\frac{8}{1}-\left(\frac{3-7}{5}\right)\right]+\frac{3}{4}=\left[\frac{8}{1}-\left(\frac{-4}{5}\right)\right]+\frac{3}{4}=\left[\frac{8}{1}+\left(\frac{4}{5}\right)\right]+\frac{3}{4}$$

$$=\left[\frac{8}{1}+\frac{4}{5}\right]+\frac{3}{4}=\left[\frac{(8\times5)+(4\times1)}{1\times5}\right]+\frac{3}{4}=\left[\frac{40+4}{5}\right]+\frac{3}{4}=\left[\frac{44}{5}\right]+\frac{3}{4}=\frac{44}{5}+\frac{3}{4}$$

$$=\frac{(44\times4)+(3\times5)}{5\times4}=\frac{176+15}{20}=\frac{191}{20}$$

Step 4   Not Applicable

Step 5 $\frac{191}{20}=9\frac{11}{20}$

The following examples further illustrate how to add, subtract, multiply, and divide integer and mixed fractions:

Example 7.5-11

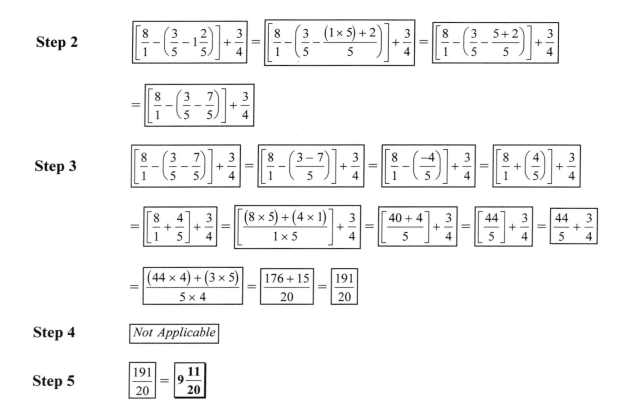

$$\frac{3}{4}\times\left(3\frac{2}{3}\div2\frac{1}{4}\right)=\frac{3}{4}\times\left(\frac{(3\times3)+2}{3}\div\frac{(2\times4)+1}{4}\right)=\frac{3}{4}\times\left(\frac{9+2}{3}\div\frac{8+1}{4}\right)=\frac{3}{4}\times\left(\frac{11}{3}\div\frac{9}{4}\right)$$

$$=\frac{3}{4}\times\left(\frac{11}{3}\times\frac{4}{9}\right)=\frac{3}{4}\times\left(\frac{11\times4}{3\times9}\right)=\frac{3}{4}\times\left(\frac{44}{27}\right)=\frac{3}{4}\times\frac{44}{27}=\frac{\overset{1}{\cancel{3}}\times\overset{11}{\cancel{44}}}{\underset{1}{\cancel{4}}\times\underset{9}{\cancel{27}}}=\frac{1\times11}{1\times9}=\frac{11}{9}=1\frac{2}{9}$$

Example 7.5-12

$$\left(2\frac{1}{3}+\frac{2}{3}\right)-5=\left(\frac{(2\times3)+1}{3}+\frac{2}{3}\right)-\frac{5}{1}=\left(\frac{6+1}{3}+\frac{2}{3}\right)-\frac{5}{1}=\left(\frac{7}{3}+\frac{2}{3}\right)-\frac{5}{1}=\left(\frac{7+2}{3}\right)-\frac{5}{1}=\left(\frac{9}{3}\right)-\frac{5}{1}$$

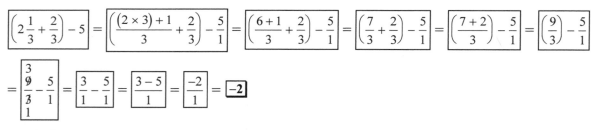

$$=\frac{\overset{3}{\cancel{9}}}{\underset{1}{\cancel{3}}}-\frac{5}{1}=\frac{3}{1}-\frac{5}{1}=\frac{3-5}{1}=\frac{-2}{1}=-2$$

Example 7.5-13

$$\left(2\frac{7}{8}\times6\right)+\left(2\frac{1}{4}-\frac{2}{4}\right)=\left(\frac{(2\times8)+7}{8}\times\frac{6}{1}\right)+\left(\frac{(2\times4)+1}{4}-\frac{2}{4}\right)=\left(\frac{16+7}{8}\times\frac{6}{1}\right)+\left(\frac{8+1}{4}-\frac{2}{4}\right)$$

$$= \left[\left(\frac{23}{8}\times\frac{6}{1}\right)+\left(\frac{9}{4}-\frac{2}{4}\right)\right] = \left[\left(\frac{23\times\overset{3}{\cancel{6}}}{\underset{4}{\cancel{8}\times 1}}\right)+\left(\frac{9-2}{4}\right)\right] = \left[\left(\frac{23\times 3}{4\times 1}\right)+\left(\frac{7}{4}\right)\right] = \left[\left(\frac{69}{4}\right)+\frac{7}{4}\right] = \left[\frac{69}{4}+\frac{7}{4}\right] = \left[\frac{69+7}{4}\right]$$

$$= \left[\frac{\overset{19}{\cancel{76}}}{\underset{1}{\cancel{4}}}\right] = \left[\frac{19}{1}\right] = \boxed{19}$$

Example 7.5-14

$$\left[\left(3\frac{1}{4}\div\frac{1}{4}\right)\times\left(\frac{4}{13}\times 1\frac{1}{2}\right)\right] = \left[\left(\frac{(3\times 4)+1}{4}\div\frac{1}{4}\right)\times\left(\frac{4}{13}\times\frac{(1\times 2)+1}{2}\right)\right] = \left[\left(\frac{12+1}{4}\div\frac{1}{4}\right)\times\left(\frac{4}{13}\times\frac{2+1}{2}\right)\right]$$

$$= \left[\left(\frac{13}{4}\div\frac{1}{4}\right)\times\left(\frac{4}{13}\times\frac{3}{2}\right)\right] = \left[\left(\frac{13}{4}\times\frac{4}{1}\right)\times\left(\frac{\overset{2}{4}\times 3}{13\times\underset{1}{\cancel{2}}}\right)\right] = \left[\left(\frac{13\times\overset{1}{\cancel{4}}}{\underset{1}{\cancel{4}}\times 1}\right)\times\left(\frac{2\times 3}{13\times 1}\right)\right] = \left[\left(\frac{13\times 1}{1\times 1}\right)\times\left(\frac{6}{13}\right)\right] = \left[\left(\frac{13}{1}\right)\times\left(\frac{6}{13}\right)\right]$$

$$= \left[\frac{13}{1}\times\frac{6}{13}\right] = \left[\frac{\overset{1}{\cancel{13}}\times 6}{1\times\underset{1}{\cancel{13}}}\right] = \left[\frac{1\times 6}{1\times 1}\right] = \left[\frac{6}{1}\right] = \boxed{6}$$

Example 7.5-15

$$\left[\left(\frac{2}{3}+2\frac{1}{3}+\frac{1}{3}\right)-\frac{2}{5}\right] = \left[\left(\frac{2}{3}+\frac{(2\times 3)+1}{3}+\frac{1}{3}\right)-\frac{2}{5}\right] = \left[\left(\frac{2}{3}+\frac{6+1}{3}+\frac{1}{3}\right)-\frac{2}{5}\right] = \left[\left(\frac{2}{3}+\frac{7}{3}+\frac{1}{3}\right)-\frac{2}{5}\right]$$

$$= \left[\left(\frac{2+7+1}{3}\right)-\frac{2}{5}\right] = \left[\left(\frac{10}{3}\right)-\frac{2}{5}\right] = \left[\frac{10}{3}-\frac{2}{5}\right] = \left[\frac{(10\times 5)-(2\times 3)}{3\times 5}\right] = \left[\frac{50-6}{15}\right] = \left[\frac{44}{15}\right] = \boxed{2\frac{14}{15}}$$

Example 7.5-16

$$\left[\left(2\frac{1}{3}\times\frac{3}{6}\times 1\frac{1}{7}\right)\div 12\right] = \left[\left(\frac{(2\times 3)+1}{3}\times\frac{3}{6}\times\frac{(1\times 7)+1}{7}\right)\div\frac{12}{1}\right] = \left[\left(\frac{6+1}{3}\times\frac{3}{6}\times\frac{7+1}{7}\right)\div\frac{12}{1}\right]$$

$$= \left[\left(\frac{7}{3}\times\frac{3}{6}\times\frac{8}{7}\right)\div\frac{12}{1}\right] = \left[\left(\frac{\overset{1}{\cancel{7}}\times\overset{1}{\cancel{3}}\times\overset{4}{\cancel{8}}}{\underset{1}{\cancel{3}}\times\underset{1}{\cancel{6}}\times\underset{1}{\cancel{7}}}\right)\div\frac{12}{1}\right] = \left[\left(\frac{1\times 1\times 4}{1\times 3\times 1}\right)\div\frac{12}{1}\right] = \left[\left(\frac{4}{3}\right)\div\frac{12}{1}\right] = \left[\frac{4}{3}\div\frac{12}{1}\right] = \left[\frac{4}{3}\times\frac{1}{12}\right]$$

$$= \left[\frac{\overset{1}{\cancel{4}}\times 1}{3\times\underset{3}{\cancel{12}}}\right] = \left[\frac{1\times 1}{3\times 3}\right] = \boxed{\frac{1}{9}}$$

Example 7.5-17

$$\left[\left(\frac{12}{3}-\frac{1}{2}\right)\times\left(5\times\frac{3}{5}\times\frac{1}{4}\right)\right] = \left[\left(\frac{(12\times 2)-(3\times 1)}{3\times 2}\right)\times\left(\frac{5}{1}\times\frac{3}{5}\times\frac{1}{4}\right)\right] = \left[\left(\frac{24-3}{6}\right)\times\left(\frac{\overset{1}{\cancel{5}}\times 3\times 1}{1\times\underset{1}{\cancel{5}}\times 4}\right)\right]$$

$$= \left[\left(\frac{21}{6}\right) \times \left(\frac{1 \times 3 \times 1}{1 \times 1 \times 4}\right)\right] = \left[\frac{21}{6} \times \left(\frac{3}{4}\right)\right] = \left[\frac{21}{6} \times \frac{3}{4}\right] = \left[\frac{21 \times \overset{1}{3}}{\underset{2}{6} \times 4}\right] = \left[\frac{21 \times 1}{2 \times 4}\right] = \left[\frac{21}{8}\right] = \boxed{2\frac{5}{8}}$$

Example 7.5-18

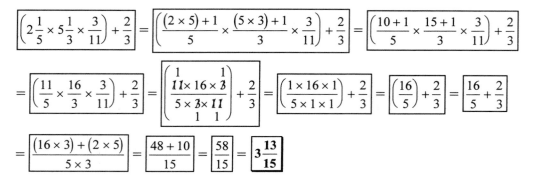

$$\left[\left(2\frac{1}{5} \times 5\frac{1}{3} \times \frac{3}{11}\right) + \frac{2}{3}\right] = \left[\left(\frac{(2 \times 5) + 1}{5} \times \frac{(5 \times 3) + 1}{3} \times \frac{3}{11}\right) + \frac{2}{3}\right] = \left[\left(\frac{10+1}{5} \times \frac{15+1}{3} \times \frac{3}{11}\right) + \frac{2}{3}\right]$$

$$= \left[\left(\frac{11}{5} \times \frac{16}{3} \times \frac{3}{11}\right) + \frac{2}{3}\right] = \left[\left(\frac{\overset{1}{11} \times 16 \times \overset{1}{3}}{5 \times \underset{1}{3} \times \underset{1}{11}}\right) + \frac{2}{3}\right] = \left[\left(\frac{1 \times 16 \times 1}{5 \times 1 \times 1}\right) + \frac{2}{3}\right] = \left[\left(\frac{16}{5}\right) + \frac{2}{3}\right] = \left[\frac{16}{5} + \frac{2}{3}\right]$$

$$= \left[\frac{(16 \times 3) + (2 \times 5)}{5 \times 3}\right] = \left[\frac{48 + 10}{15}\right] = \left[\frac{58}{15}\right] = \boxed{3\frac{13}{15}}$$

Example 7.5-19

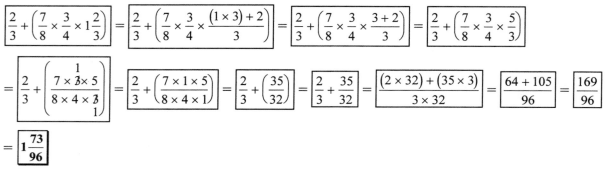

$$\left[\frac{2}{3} + \left(\frac{7}{8} \times \frac{3}{4} \times 1\frac{2}{3}\right)\right] = \left[\frac{2}{3} + \left(\frac{7}{8} \times \frac{3}{4} \times \frac{(1 \times 3) + 2}{3}\right)\right] = \left[\frac{2}{3} + \left(\frac{7}{8} \times \frac{3}{4} \times \frac{3+2}{3}\right)\right] = \left[\frac{2}{3} + \left(\frac{7}{8} \times \frac{3}{4} \times \frac{5}{3}\right)\right]$$

$$= \left[\frac{2}{3} + \left(\frac{7 \times \overset{1}{3} \times 5}{8 \times 4 \times \underset{1}{3}}\right)\right] = \left[\frac{2}{3} + \left(\frac{7 \times 1 \times 5}{8 \times 4 \times 1}\right)\right] = \left[\frac{2}{3} + \left(\frac{35}{32}\right)\right] = \left[\frac{2}{3} + \frac{35}{32}\right] = \left[\frac{(2 \times 32) + (35 \times 3)}{3 \times 32}\right] = \left[\frac{64 + 105}{96}\right] = \left[\frac{169}{96}\right]$$

$$= \boxed{1\frac{73}{96}}$$

Example 7.5-20

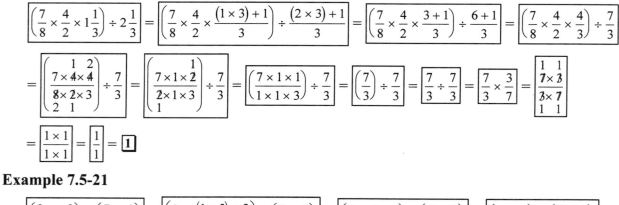

$$\left[\left(\frac{7}{8} \times \frac{4}{2} \times 1\frac{1}{3}\right) \div 2\frac{1}{3}\right] = \left[\left(\frac{7}{8} \times \frac{4}{2} \times \frac{(1 \times 3) + 1}{3}\right) \div \frac{(2 \times 3) + 1}{3}\right] = \left[\left(\frac{7}{8} \times \frac{4}{2} \times \frac{3+1}{3}\right) \div \frac{6+1}{3}\right] = \left[\left(\frac{7}{8} \times \frac{4}{2} \times \frac{4}{3}\right) \div \frac{7}{3}\right]$$

$$= \left[\left(\frac{7 \times \overset{1}{4} \times \overset{2}{4}}{\underset{2}{8} \times \underset{1}{2} \times 3}\right) \div \frac{7}{3}\right] = \left[\left(\frac{7 \times 1 \times \overset{1}{2}}{\underset{1}{2} \times 1 \times 3}\right) \div \frac{7}{3}\right] = \left[\left(\frac{7 \times 1 \times 1}{1 \times 1 \times 3}\right) \div \frac{7}{3}\right] = \left[\left(\frac{7}{3}\right) \div \frac{7}{3}\right] = \left[\frac{7}{3} \div \frac{7}{3}\right] = \left[\frac{7}{3} \times \frac{3}{7}\right] = \left[\frac{\overset{1}{7} \times \overset{1}{3}}{\underset{1}{3} \times \underset{1}{7}}\right]$$

$$= \left[\frac{1 \times 1}{1 \times 1}\right] = \left[\frac{1}{1}\right] = \boxed{1}$$

Example 7.5-21

$$\left[\left(\frac{2}{3} + 1\frac{2}{5}\right) \times \left(\frac{7}{8} \div \frac{1}{4}\right)\right] = \left[\left(\frac{2}{3} + \frac{(1 \times 5) + 2}{5}\right) \times \left(\frac{7}{8} \div \frac{1}{4}\right)\right] = \left[\left(\frac{2}{3} + \frac{5+2}{5}\right) \times \left(\frac{7}{8} \div \frac{1}{4}\right)\right] = \left[\left(\frac{2}{3} + \frac{7}{5}\right) \times \left(\frac{7}{8} \div \frac{1}{4}\right)\right]$$

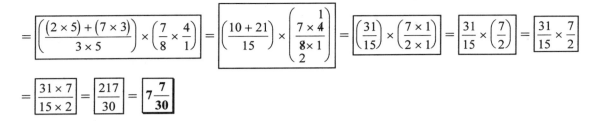

$$= \left[\left(\frac{(2 \times 5)+(7 \times 3)}{3 \times 5} \right) \times \left(\frac{7}{8} \times \frac{4}{1} \right) \right] = \left[\left(\frac{10+21}{15} \right) \times \left(\frac{7 \times \overset{1}{4}}{\underset{2}{8 \times 1}} \right) \right] = \left[\left(\frac{31}{15} \right) \times \left(\frac{7 \times 1}{2 \times 1} \right) \right] = \left[\frac{31}{15} \times \left(\frac{7}{2} \right) \right] = \left[\frac{31}{15} \times \frac{7}{2} \right]$$

$$= \left[\frac{31 \times 7}{15 \times 2} \right] = \left[\frac{217}{30} \right] = \boxed{7\frac{7}{30}}$$

Section 7.5 Exercises - Perform the indicated operations using integer and mixed fractions:

1. $\left(\frac{2}{3} \times 4\frac{1}{5} \right) + 2\frac{3}{4} =$

2. $\frac{8}{7} \times \left(2\frac{1}{3} \div 1\frac{4}{5} \right) =$

3. $12 + \left(3\frac{1}{2} - 1\frac{1}{4} \right) =$

4. $5 \div \left(\frac{4}{9} \times 3\frac{2}{5} \right) =$

5. $\left(\frac{4}{5} + 5\frac{1}{6} \right) - \left(2\frac{1}{3} - \frac{2}{3} \right) =$

6. $\left(\frac{2}{3} \times \frac{5}{4} \right) \div \left(\frac{3}{4} \times 2\frac{1}{3} \right) =$

7. $\left(\frac{4}{5} + 1\frac{1}{2} \right) \times \frac{3}{8} =$

8. $\left(2\frac{1}{3} \times 1\frac{1}{5} \times \frac{5}{4} \right) \div \frac{3}{8} =$

9. $\left(\frac{2}{3} + \frac{1}{3} \right) \times \left(2\frac{3}{8} \times 4 \right) =$

10. $\left(4\frac{2}{3} - \frac{1}{6} \right) \div \left(\frac{6}{25} \times \frac{5}{3} \right) =$

Chapter 8 - Decimal and Mixed Fractions

The objective of this chapter is to improve the student's ability in solving decimal and mixed fractions by grouping the two types of fractions together. The steps used to perform the combined fractional operations with examples illustrating how to add (Section 8.1), subtract (Section 8.2), multiply (Section 8.3), and divide (Section 8.4) two or more decimal and mixed fractions are given. Section 8.5 mixes the mathematical operations using the two types of fractions. To further enhance the student's ability, each section is concluded by solving additional examples which do not follow the exact order as is given by the steps for each case.

8.1   Adding Decimal and Mixed Fractions

Decimal fractions of the form $\left(\dfrac{a \times 10^{-k_1}}{b \times 10^{-k_2}} \right)$ where (a) and (b) are integer numbers and (k_1) and

(k_2) are equal to the number of decimal places, and mixed fractions of the form $\left(k \dfrac{a}{b} \right)$ where (k)

is made up of a whole number and $\left(\dfrac{a}{b} \right)$ is an integer fraction are added as in the following cases:

Case I   Adding Two Decimal and Mixed Fractions
Add two decimal and mixed fractions using the following steps:

Step 1   Change the mixed fraction to an integer fraction (see Section 2.5).

Step 2   a. Change the decimal fraction to an integer fraction (see Section 2.4).

   b. Change the decimal number $\left(a \times 10^{-k} \right)$ to an integer fraction of the form $\left(\dfrac{a}{10^k} \right)$,

   e.g., change 13.5 to $\dfrac{135}{10}$.

Step 3   Add the integer fractions (see Section 3.1).

Step 4   Simplify the fraction to its lowest term (see Section 2.3).

Step 5   Change the improper fraction to a mixed fraction if the fraction obtained from Step 4 is an improper fraction (see Section 2.2).

The following examples show the steps as to how two decimal and mixed fractions are added:

Example 8.1-1

$$\boxed{2\dfrac{3}{5} + \dfrac{0.5}{0.3}} =$$

Solution:

Step 1 $\boxed{2\dfrac{3}{5} + \dfrac{0.5}{0.3}} = \boxed{\dfrac{(2 \times 5) + 3}{5} + \dfrac{0.5}{0.3}} = \boxed{\dfrac{10 + 3}{5} + \dfrac{0.5}{0.3}} = \boxed{\dfrac{13}{5} + \dfrac{0.5}{0.3}}$

Step 2a
$$\frac{13}{5}+\frac{0.5}{0.3}=\frac{13}{5}+\frac{\dfrac{5}{10}}{\dfrac{3}{10}}=\frac{13}{5}+\frac{5\times10}{10\times3}=\frac{13}{5}+\frac{50}{30}$$

Step 2b $\boxed{Not\ Applicable}$

Step 3
$$\frac{13}{5}+\frac{50}{30}=\frac{(13\times30)+(50\times5)}{5\times30}=\frac{390+250}{150}=\frac{640}{150}$$

Step 4
$$\frac{640}{150}=\frac{640\div10}{150\div10}=\frac{64}{15}$$

Step 5
$$\frac{64}{15}=4\frac{4}{15}$$

Example 8.1-2
$$\frac{1.2}{0.04}+3\frac{2}{5}=$$

Solution:

Step 1
$$\frac{1.2}{0.04}+3\frac{2}{5}=\frac{1.2}{0.04}+\frac{(3\times5)+2}{5}=\frac{1.2}{0.04}+\frac{15+2}{5}=\frac{1.2}{0.04}+\frac{17}{5}$$

Step 2a
$$\frac{1.2}{0.04}+\frac{17}{5}=\frac{\dfrac{12}{10}}{\dfrac{4}{100}}+\frac{17}{5}=\frac{12\times100}{10\times4}+\frac{17}{5}=\frac{1200}{40}+\frac{17}{5}$$

Step 2b $\boxed{Not\ Applicable}$

Step 3
$$\frac{1200}{40}+\frac{17}{5}=\frac{(1200\times5)+(17\times40)}{40\times5}=\frac{6000+680}{200}=\frac{6680}{200}$$

Step 4
$$\frac{6680}{200}=\frac{6680\div40}{200\div40}=\frac{167}{5}$$

Step 5
$$\frac{167}{5}=33\frac{2}{5}$$

Example 8.1-3
$$6\frac{2}{3}+1.24=$$

Solution:

Step 1 $\boxed{6\dfrac{2}{3}+1.24}=\boxed{\dfrac{(6\times3)+2}{3}+1.24}=\boxed{\dfrac{18+2}{3}+1.24}=\boxed{\dfrac{20}{3}+1.24}$

Step 2a $\boxed{\textit{Not Applicable}}$

Step 2b $\boxed{\dfrac{20}{3}+1.24}=\boxed{\dfrac{20}{3}+\dfrac{124}{100}}$

Step 3 $\boxed{\dfrac{20}{3}+\dfrac{124}{100}}=\boxed{\dfrac{(20\times100)+(124\times3)}{3\times100}}=\boxed{\dfrac{2000+372}{300}}=\boxed{\dfrac{2372}{300}}$

Step 4 $\boxed{\dfrac{2372}{300}}=\boxed{\dfrac{2372\div4}{300\div4}}=\boxed{\dfrac{593}{75}}$

Step 5 $\boxed{\dfrac{593}{75}}=\boxed{\mathbf{7\dfrac{68}{75}}}$

Example 8.1-4

$\boxed{12\dfrac{1}{8}+\dfrac{1.4}{0.03}}=$

Solution:

Step 1 $\boxed{12\dfrac{1}{8}+\dfrac{1.4}{0.03}}=\boxed{\dfrac{(12\times8)+1}{8}+\dfrac{1.4}{0.03}}=\boxed{\dfrac{96+1}{8}+\dfrac{1.4}{0.03}}=\boxed{\dfrac{97}{8}+\dfrac{1.4}{0.03}}$

Step 2a $\boxed{\dfrac{97}{8}+\dfrac{1.4}{0.03}}=\boxed{\dfrac{97}{8}+\dfrac{\dfrac{14}{10}}{\dfrac{3}{100}}}=\boxed{\dfrac{97}{8}+\dfrac{14\times100}{10\times3}}=\boxed{\dfrac{97}{8}+\dfrac{1400}{30}}$

Step 2b $\boxed{\textit{Not Applicable}}$

Step 3 $\boxed{\dfrac{97}{8}+\dfrac{1400}{30}}=\boxed{\dfrac{(97\times30)+(1400\times8)}{8\times30}}=\boxed{\dfrac{2910+11200}{240}}=\boxed{\dfrac{14110}{240}}$

Step 4 $\boxed{\dfrac{14110}{240}}=\boxed{\dfrac{14110\div10}{240\div10}}=\boxed{\dfrac{1411}{24}}$

Step 5 $\boxed{\dfrac{1411}{24}}=\boxed{\mathbf{58\dfrac{19}{24}}}$

Example 8.1-5

$$\boxed{8.25 + 6\frac{5}{7}} =$$

Solution:

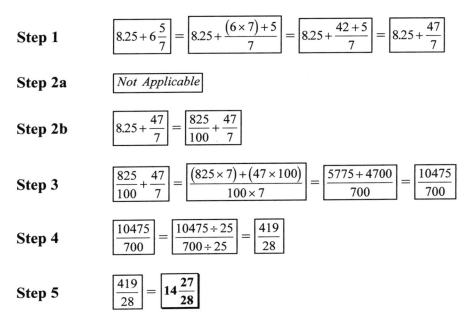

Step 1 $\boxed{8.25 + 6\frac{5}{7}} = \boxed{8.25 + \frac{(6\times 7)+5}{7}} = \boxed{8.25 + \frac{42+5}{7}} = \boxed{8.25 + \frac{47}{7}}$

Step 2a $\boxed{\textit{Not Applicable}}$

Step 2b $\boxed{8.25 + \frac{47}{7}} = \boxed{\frac{825}{100} + \frac{47}{7}}$

Step 3 $\boxed{\frac{825}{100} + \frac{47}{7}} = \boxed{\frac{(825\times 7)+(47\times 100)}{100\times 7}} = \boxed{\frac{5775+4700}{700}} = \boxed{\frac{10475}{700}}$

Step 4 $\boxed{\frac{10475}{700}} = \boxed{\frac{10475 \div 25}{700 \div 25}} = \boxed{\frac{419}{28}}$

Step 5 $\boxed{\frac{419}{28}} = \boxed{14\frac{27}{28}}$

Case II   Adding Three Decimal and Mixed Fractions

Add three decimal and mixed fractions using the following steps:

Step 1   Use parentheses to group the first and second fractions.

Step 2   Change the mixed fraction(s) to integer fraction(s) (see Section 2.5).

Step 3   a. Change the decimal fraction(s) to integer fraction(s) (see Section 2.4).

b. Change the decimal number $\left(a\times 10^{-k}\right)$ to an integer fraction of the form $\left(\frac{a}{10^{k}}\right)$,

e.g., change 0.005 to $\frac{5}{1000}$.

Step 4   Add the integer fractions (see Section 3.1).

Step 5   Simplify the fraction to its lowest term (see Section 2.3).

Step 6   Change the improper fraction to a mixed fraction if the fraction obtained from Step 5 is an improper fraction (see Section 2.2).

The following examples show the steps as to how three decimal and mixed fractions are added:

Example 8.1-6

$$\boxed{0.6 + 3\frac{1}{8} + 4\frac{1}{5} =}$$

Solution:

Step 1

$$\boxed{0.6 + 3\frac{1}{8} + 4\frac{1}{5}} = \boxed{\left(0.6 + 3\frac{1}{8}\right) + 4\frac{1}{5}}$$

Step 2

$$\boxed{\left(0.6 + 3\frac{1}{8}\right) + 4\frac{1}{5}} = \boxed{\left(0.6 + \frac{(3\times 8)+1}{8}\right) + \frac{(4\times 5)+1}{5}} = \boxed{\left(0.6 + \frac{24+1}{8}\right) + \frac{20+1}{5}}$$

$$= \boxed{\left(0.6 + \frac{25}{8}\right) + \frac{21}{5}}$$

Step 3a

$$\boxed{Not\ Applicable}$$

Step 3b

$$\boxed{\left(0.6 + \frac{25}{8}\right) + \frac{21}{5}} = \boxed{\left(\frac{6}{10} + \frac{25}{8}\right) + \frac{21}{5}}$$

Step 4

$$\boxed{\left(\frac{6}{10} + \frac{25}{8}\right) + \frac{21}{5}} = \boxed{\left(\frac{(6\times 8)+(25\times 10)}{10\times 8}\right) + \frac{21}{5}} = \boxed{\left(\frac{48+250}{80}\right) + \frac{21}{5}} = \boxed{\left(\frac{298}{80}\right) + \frac{21}{5}}$$

$$= \boxed{\frac{298}{80} + \frac{21}{5}} = \boxed{\frac{(298\times 5)+(21\times 80)}{80\times 5}} = \boxed{\frac{1490+1680}{400}} = \boxed{\frac{3170}{400}}$$

Step 5

$$\boxed{\frac{3170}{400}} = \boxed{\frac{3170\div 10}{400\div 10}} = \boxed{\frac{317}{40}}$$

Step 6

$$\boxed{\frac{317}{40}} = \boxed{\mathbf{7\frac{37}{40}}}$$

Example 8.1-7

$$\boxed{\frac{0.3}{0.8} + 2\frac{3}{5} + 0.2 =}$$

Solution:

Step 1

$$\boxed{\frac{0.3}{0.8} + 2\frac{3}{5} + 0.2} = \boxed{\left(\frac{0.3}{0.8} + 2\frac{3}{5}\right) + 0.2}$$

Step 2

$$\boxed{\left(\frac{0.3}{0.8} + 2\frac{3}{5}\right) + 0.2} = \boxed{\left(\frac{0.3}{0.8} + \frac{(2\times 5)+3}{5}\right) + 0.2} = \boxed{\left(\frac{0.3}{0.8} + \frac{10+3}{5}\right) + 0.2}$$

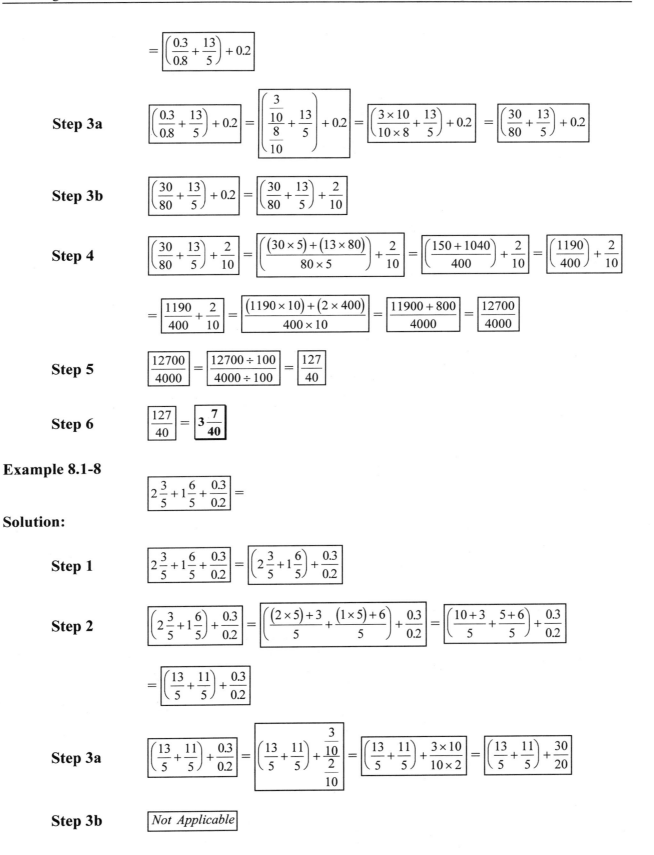

$$= \left[\left(\frac{0.3}{0.8} + \frac{13}{5}\right) + 0.2\right]$$

Step 3a $\left[\left(\frac{0.3}{0.8} + \frac{13}{5}\right) + 0.2\right] = \left[\left(\frac{\frac{3}{10}}{\frac{8}{10}} + \frac{13}{5}\right) + 0.2\right] = \left[\left(\frac{3 \times 10}{10 \times 8} + \frac{13}{5}\right) + 0.2\right] = \left[\left(\frac{30}{80} + \frac{13}{5}\right) + 0.2\right]$

Step 3b $\left[\left(\frac{30}{80} + \frac{13}{5}\right) + 0.2\right] = \left[\left(\frac{30}{80} + \frac{13}{5}\right) + \frac{2}{10}\right]$

Step 4 $\left[\left(\frac{30}{80} + \frac{13}{5}\right) + \frac{2}{10}\right] = \left[\left(\frac{(30 \times 5) + (13 \times 80)}{80 \times 5}\right) + \frac{2}{10}\right] = \left[\left(\frac{150 + 1040}{400}\right) + \frac{2}{10}\right] = \left[\left(\frac{1190}{400}\right) + \frac{2}{10}\right]$

$$= \left[\frac{1190}{400} + \frac{2}{10}\right] = \left[\frac{(1190 \times 10) + (2 \times 400)}{400 \times 10}\right] = \left[\frac{11900 + 800}{4000}\right] = \left[\frac{12700}{4000}\right]$$

Step 5 $\left[\frac{12700}{4000}\right] = \left[\frac{12700 \div 100}{4000 \div 100}\right] = \left[\frac{127}{40}\right]$

Step 6 $\left[\frac{127}{40}\right] = \boxed{3\frac{7}{40}}$

Example 8.1-8

$$\boxed{2\frac{3}{5} + 1\frac{6}{5} + \frac{0.3}{0.2}} =$$

Solution:

Step 1 $\boxed{2\frac{3}{5} + 1\frac{6}{5} + \frac{0.3}{0.2}} = \left[\left(2\frac{3}{5} + 1\frac{6}{5}\right) + \frac{0.3}{0.2}\right]$

Step 2 $\left[\left(2\frac{3}{5} + 1\frac{6}{5}\right) + \frac{0.3}{0.2}\right] = \left[\left(\frac{(2 \times 5) + 3}{5} + \frac{(1 \times 5) + 6}{5}\right) + \frac{0.3}{0.2}\right] = \left[\left(\frac{10 + 3}{5} + \frac{5 + 6}{5}\right) + \frac{0.3}{0.2}\right]$

$$= \left[\left(\frac{13}{5} + \frac{11}{5}\right) + \frac{0.3}{0.2}\right]$$

Step 3a $\left[\left(\frac{13}{5} + \frac{11}{5}\right) + \frac{0.3}{0.2}\right] = \left[\left(\frac{13}{5} + \frac{11}{5}\right) + \frac{\frac{3}{10}}{\frac{2}{10}}\right] = \left[\left(\frac{13}{5} + \frac{11}{5}\right) + \frac{3 \times 10}{10 \times 2}\right] = \left[\left(\frac{13}{5} + \frac{11}{5}\right) + \frac{30}{20}\right]$

Step 3b $\boxed{Not\ Applicable}$

Step 4
$$\left(\frac{13}{5}+\frac{11}{5}\right)+\frac{30}{20}=\left(\frac{13+11}{5}\right)+\frac{30}{20}=\left(\frac{24}{5}\right)+\frac{30}{20}=\frac{24}{5}+\frac{30}{20}=\frac{(24\times20)+(30\times5)}{5\times20}$$

$$=\frac{480+150}{100}=\frac{630}{100}$$

Step 5
$$\frac{630}{100}=\frac{630\div10}{100\div10}=\frac{63}{10}$$

Step 6
$$\frac{63}{10}=6\frac{3}{10}$$

Example 8.1-9
$$1\frac{4}{5}+\frac{0.06}{1.4}+\frac{0.1}{0.5}=$$

Solution:

Step 1
$$1\frac{4}{5}+\frac{0.06}{1.4}+\frac{0.1}{0.5}=\left(1\frac{4}{5}+\frac{0.06}{1.4}\right)+\frac{0.1}{0.5}$$

Step 2
$$\left(1\frac{4}{5}+\frac{0.06}{1.4}\right)+\frac{0.1}{0.5}=\left(\frac{(1\times5)+4}{5}+\frac{0.06}{1.4}\right)+\frac{0.1}{0.5}=\left(\frac{5+4}{5}+\frac{0.06}{1.4}\right)+\frac{0.1}{0.5}$$

$$=\left(\frac{9}{5}+\frac{0.06}{1.4}\right)+\frac{0.1}{0.5}$$

Step 3a
$$\left(\frac{9}{5}+\frac{0.06}{1.4}\right)+\frac{0.1}{0.5}=\left(\frac{9}{5}+\frac{\frac{6}{100}}{\frac{14}{10}}\right)+\frac{\frac{1}{10}}{\frac{5}{10}}=\left(\frac{9}{5}+\frac{6\times10}{100\times14}\right)+\frac{1\times10}{10\times5}=\left(\frac{9}{5}+\frac{60}{1400}\right)+\frac{10}{50}$$

Step 3b
$$\boxed{\textit{Not Applicable}}$$

Step 4
$$\left(\frac{9}{5}+\frac{60}{1400}\right)+\frac{10}{50}=\left(\frac{(9\times1400)+(60\times5)}{5\times1400}\right)+\frac{10}{50}=\left(\frac{12600+300}{7000}\right)+\frac{10}{50}$$

$$=\left(\frac{12900}{7000}\right)+\frac{10}{50}=\frac{12900}{7000}+\frac{10}{50}=\frac{(12900\times50)+(10\times7000)}{7000\times50}=\frac{645000+70000}{350000}$$

$$=\frac{715000}{350000}$$

Step 5
$$\frac{715000}{350000}=\frac{715000\div1000}{350000\div1000}=\frac{715}{350}=\frac{715\div5}{350\div5}=\frac{143}{70}$$

Step 6 $\boxed{\dfrac{143}{70}} = \boxed{2\dfrac{3}{70}}$

Example 8.1-10

$$\boxed{12.8 + \frac{1.4}{0.3} + 4\frac{6}{11}} =$$

Solution:

Step 1 $\boxed{12.8 + \dfrac{1.4}{0.3} + 4\dfrac{6}{11}} = \boxed{\left(12.8 + \dfrac{1.4}{0.3}\right) + 4\dfrac{6}{11}}$

Step 2 $\boxed{\left(12.8 + \dfrac{1.4}{0.3}\right) + 4\dfrac{6}{11}} = \boxed{\left(12.8 + \dfrac{1.4}{0.3}\right) + \dfrac{(4 \times 11) + 6}{11}} = \boxed{\left(12.8 + \dfrac{1.4}{0.3}\right) + \dfrac{44 + 6}{11}}$

$= \boxed{\left(12.8 + \dfrac{1.4}{0.3}\right) + \dfrac{50}{11}}$

Step 3a $\boxed{\left(12.8 + \dfrac{1.4}{0.3}\right) + \dfrac{50}{11}} = \boxed{\left(12.8 + \dfrac{\frac{14}{10}}{\frac{3}{10}}\right) + \dfrac{50}{11}} = \boxed{\left(12.8 + \dfrac{14 \times 10}{10 \times 3}\right) + \dfrac{50}{11}} = \boxed{\left(12.8 + \dfrac{140}{30}\right) + \dfrac{50}{11}}$

Step 3b $\boxed{\left(12.8 + \dfrac{140}{30}\right) + \dfrac{50}{11}} = \boxed{\left(\dfrac{128}{10} + \dfrac{140}{30}\right) + \dfrac{50}{11}}$

Step 4 $\boxed{\left(\dfrac{128}{10} + \dfrac{140}{30}\right) + \dfrac{50}{11}} = \boxed{\left(\dfrac{(128 \times 30) + (140 \times 10)}{10 \times 30}\right) + \dfrac{50}{11}} = \boxed{\left(\dfrac{3840 + 1400}{300}\right) + \dfrac{50}{11}}$

$= \boxed{\left(\dfrac{5240}{300}\right) + \dfrac{50}{11}} = \boxed{\dfrac{5240}{300} + \dfrac{50}{11}} = \boxed{\dfrac{(5240 \times 11) + (50 \times 300)}{300 \times 11}} = \boxed{\dfrac{57640 + 15000}{3300}}$

$= \boxed{\dfrac{72640}{3300}}$

Step 5 $\boxed{\dfrac{72640}{3300}} = \boxed{\dfrac{72640 \div 20}{3300 \div 20}} = \boxed{\dfrac{3632}{165}}$

Step 6 $\boxed{\dfrac{3632}{165}} = \boxed{22\dfrac{2}{165}}$

The following examples further illustrate how to add decimal and mixed fractions:

Example 8.1-11

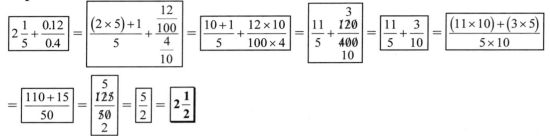

$$= \frac{110+15}{50} = \frac{\overset{5}{\cancel{125}}}{\underset{2}{\cancel{50}}} = \frac{5}{2} = 2\frac{1}{2}$$

Example 8.1-12

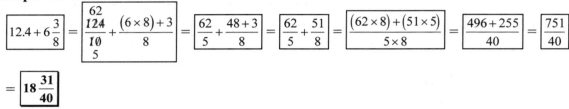

$$= 18\frac{31}{40}$$

Example 8.1-13

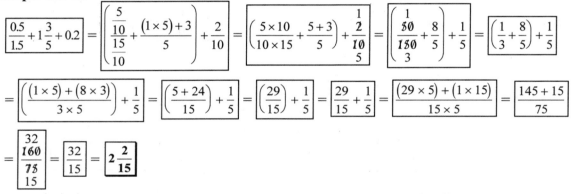

$$= \frac{\overset{32}{\cancel{160}}}{\underset{15}{\cancel{75}}} = \frac{32}{15} = 2\frac{2}{15}$$

Example 8.1-14

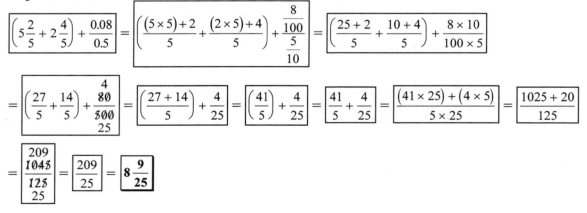

$$= \frac{\overset{209}{\cancel{1045}}}{\underset{25}{\cancel{125}}} = \frac{209}{25} = 8\frac{9}{25}$$

Example 8.1-15

$$6\frac{2}{5} + \left(0.8 + \frac{1.2}{0.06}\right) = \frac{(6 \times 5) + 2}{5} + \left(\frac{8}{10} + \frac{\frac{12}{10}}{\frac{6}{100}}\right) = \frac{30 + 2}{5} + \left(\frac{8}{10} + \frac{12 \times 100}{10 \times 6}\right) = \frac{32}{5} + \left(\frac{\cancel{8}^4}{\cancel{10}_5} + \frac{\cancel{1200}^{20}}{\cancel{60}_1}\right)$$

$$= \frac{32}{5} + \left(\frac{4}{5} + \frac{20}{1}\right) = \frac{32}{5} + \left(\frac{(4 \times 1) + (20 \times 5)}{5 \times 1}\right) = \frac{32}{5} + \left(\frac{4 + 100}{5}\right) = \frac{32}{5} + \left(\frac{104}{5}\right) = \frac{32}{5} + \frac{104}{5} = \frac{32 + 104}{5}$$

$$= \frac{136}{5} = 27\frac{1}{5}$$

Example 8.1-16

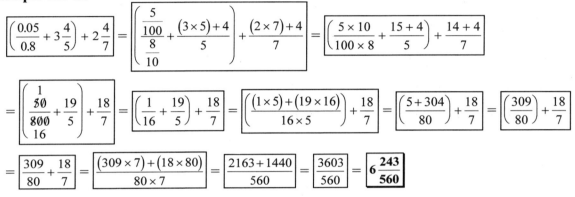

$$\left(\frac{0.05}{0.8} + 3\frac{4}{5}\right) + 2\frac{4}{7} = \left(\frac{\frac{5}{100}}{\frac{8}{10}} + \frac{(3 \times 5) + 4}{5}\right) + \frac{(2 \times 7) + 4}{7} = \left(\frac{5 \times 10}{100 \times 8} + \frac{15 + 4}{5}\right) + \frac{14 + 4}{7}$$

$$= \left(\frac{\cancel{50}^1}{\cancel{800}_{16}} + \frac{19}{5}\right) + \frac{18}{7} = \left(\frac{1}{16} + \frac{19}{5}\right) + \frac{18}{7} = \left(\frac{(1 \times 5) + (19 \times 16)}{16 \times 5}\right) + \frac{18}{7} = \left(\frac{5 + 304}{80}\right) + \frac{18}{7} = \left(\frac{309}{80}\right) + \frac{18}{7}$$

$$= \frac{309}{80} + \frac{18}{7} = \frac{(309 \times 7) + (18 \times 80)}{80 \times 7} = \frac{2163 + 1440}{560} = \frac{3603}{560} = 6\frac{243}{560}$$

Example 8.1-17

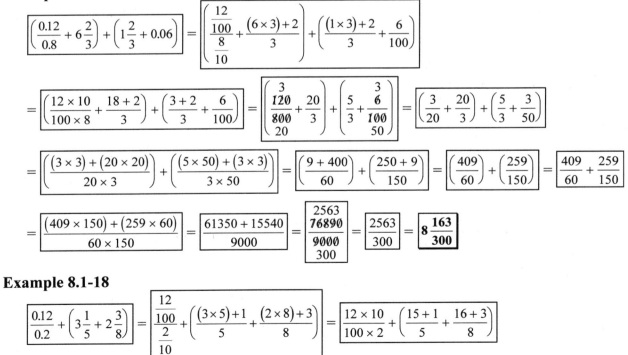

$$\left(\frac{0.12}{0.8} + 6\frac{2}{3}\right) + \left(1\frac{2}{3} + 0.06\right) = \left(\frac{\frac{12}{100}}{\frac{8}{10}} + \frac{(6 \times 3) + 2}{3}\right) + \left(\frac{(1 \times 3) + 2}{3} + \frac{6}{100}\right)$$

$$= \left(\frac{12 \times 10}{100 \times 8} + \frac{18 + 2}{3}\right) + \left(\frac{3 + 2}{3} + \frac{6}{100}\right) = \left(\frac{\cancel{3}}{\cancel{120}_{20}} + \frac{20}{3}\right) + \left(\frac{5}{3} + \frac{\cancel{6}^3}{\cancel{100}_{50}}\right) = \left(\frac{3}{20} + \frac{20}{3}\right) + \left(\frac{5}{3} + \frac{3}{50}\right)$$

$$= \left(\frac{(3 \times 3) + (20 \times 20)}{20 \times 3}\right) + \left(\frac{(5 \times 50) + (3 \times 3)}{3 \times 50}\right) = \left(\frac{9 + 400}{60}\right) + \left(\frac{250 + 9}{150}\right) = \left(\frac{409}{60}\right) + \left(\frac{259}{150}\right) = \frac{409}{60} + \frac{259}{150}$$

$$= \frac{(409 \times 150) + (259 \times 60)}{60 \times 150} = \frac{61350 + 15540}{9000} = \frac{\cancel{76890}^{2563}}{\cancel{9000}_{300}} = \frac{2563}{300} = 8\frac{163}{300}$$

Example 8.1-18

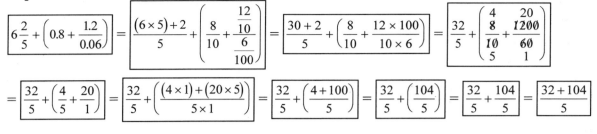

$$\frac{0.12}{0.2} + \left(3\frac{1}{5} + 2\frac{3}{8}\right) = \frac{\frac{12}{100}}{\frac{2}{10}} + \left(\frac{(3 \times 5) + 1}{5} + \frac{(2 \times 8) + 3}{8}\right) = \frac{12 \times 10}{100 \times 2} + \left(\frac{15 + 1}{5} + \frac{16 + 3}{8}\right)$$

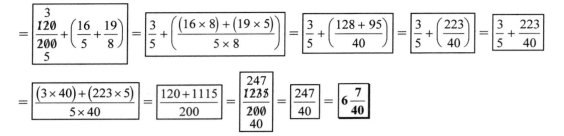

$$= \boxed{\begin{array}{c}3\\\dfrac{\cancel{120}}{200}\\5\end{array} + \left(\dfrac{16}{5} + \dfrac{19}{8}\right)} = \boxed{\dfrac{3}{5} + \left(\dfrac{(16 \times 8) + (19 \times 5)}{5 \times 8}\right)} = \boxed{\dfrac{3}{5} + \left(\dfrac{128 + 95}{40}\right)} = \boxed{\dfrac{3}{5} + \left(\dfrac{223}{40}\right)} = \boxed{\dfrac{3}{5} + \dfrac{223}{40}}$$

$$= \boxed{\dfrac{(3 \times 40) + (223 \times 5)}{5 \times 40}} = \boxed{\dfrac{120 + 1115}{200}} = \boxed{\begin{array}{c}247\\\dfrac{\cancel{1235}}{\cancel{200}}\\40\end{array}} = \boxed{\dfrac{247}{40}} = \boxed{6\dfrac{7}{40}}$$

Example 8.1-19

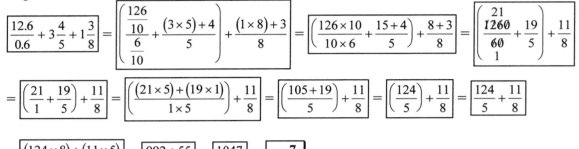

$$\boxed{\dfrac{12.6}{0.6} + 3\dfrac{4}{5} + 1\dfrac{3}{8}} = \boxed{\left(\dfrac{\frac{126}{10}}{\frac{6}{10}} + \dfrac{(3 \times 5) + 4}{5}\right) + \dfrac{(1 \times 8) + 3}{8}} = \boxed{\left(\dfrac{126 \times 10}{10 \times 6} + \dfrac{15 + 4}{5}\right) + \dfrac{8 + 3}{8}} = \boxed{\left(\begin{array}{c}21\\\dfrac{\cancel{1260}}{60}\\1\end{array} + \dfrac{19}{5}\right) + \dfrac{11}{8}}$$

$$= \boxed{\left(\dfrac{21}{1} + \dfrac{19}{5}\right) + \dfrac{11}{8}} = \boxed{\left(\dfrac{(21 \times 5) + (19 \times 1)}{1 \times 5}\right) + \dfrac{11}{8}} = \boxed{\left(\dfrac{105 + 19}{5}\right) + \dfrac{11}{8}} = \boxed{\left(\dfrac{124}{5}\right) + \dfrac{11}{8}} = \boxed{\dfrac{124}{5} + \dfrac{11}{8}}$$

$$= \boxed{\dfrac{(124 \times 8) + (11 \times 5)}{5 \times 8}} = \boxed{\dfrac{992 + 55}{40}} = \boxed{\dfrac{1047}{40}} = \boxed{26\dfrac{7}{40}}$$

Example 8.1-20

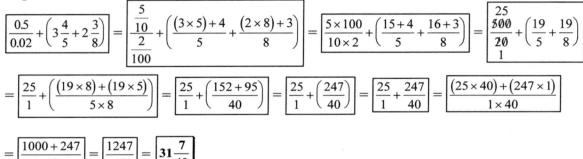

$$\boxed{\dfrac{0.5}{0.02} + \left(3\dfrac{4}{5} + 2\dfrac{3}{8}\right)} = \boxed{\dfrac{\frac{5}{10}}{\frac{2}{100}} + \left(\dfrac{(3 \times 5) + 4}{5} + \dfrac{(2 \times 8) + 3}{8}\right)} = \boxed{\dfrac{5 \times 100}{10 \times 2} + \left(\dfrac{15 + 4}{5} + \dfrac{16 + 3}{8}\right)} = \boxed{\begin{array}{c}25\\\dfrac{\cancel{500}}{20}\\1\end{array} + \left(\dfrac{19}{5} + \dfrac{19}{8}\right)}$$

$$= \boxed{\dfrac{25}{1} + \left(\dfrac{(19 \times 8) + (19 \times 5)}{5 \times 8}\right)} = \boxed{\dfrac{25}{1} + \left(\dfrac{152 + 95}{40}\right)} = \boxed{\dfrac{25}{1} + \left(\dfrac{247}{40}\right)} = \boxed{\dfrac{25}{1} + \dfrac{247}{40}} = \boxed{\dfrac{(25 \times 40) + (247 \times 1)}{1 \times 40}}$$

$$= \boxed{\dfrac{1000 + 247}{40}} = \boxed{\dfrac{1247}{40}} = \boxed{31\dfrac{7}{40}}$$

Example 8.1-21

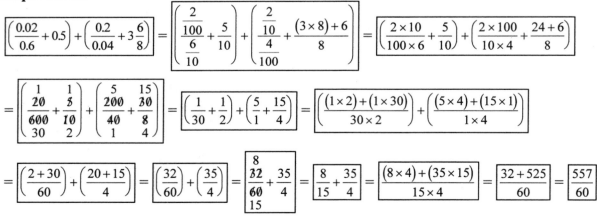

$$\boxed{\left(\dfrac{0.02}{0.6} + 0.5\right) + \left(\dfrac{0.2}{0.04} + 3\dfrac{6}{8}\right)} = \boxed{\left(\dfrac{\frac{2}{100}}{\frac{6}{10}} + \dfrac{5}{10}\right) + \left(\dfrac{\frac{2}{10}}{\frac{4}{100}} + \dfrac{(3 \times 8) + 6}{8}\right)} = \boxed{\left(\dfrac{2 \times 10}{100 \times 6} + \dfrac{5}{10}\right) + \left(\dfrac{2 \times 100}{10 \times 4} + \dfrac{24 + 6}{8}\right)}$$

$$= \boxed{\left(\begin{array}{c}1\\\dfrac{\cancel{20}}{\cancel{600}}\\30\end{array} + \begin{array}{c}1\\\dfrac{\cancel{5}}{\cancel{10}}\\2\end{array}\right) + \left(\begin{array}{c}5\\\dfrac{\cancel{200}}{40}\\1\end{array} + \begin{array}{c}15\\\dfrac{\cancel{30}}{\cancel{8}}\\4\end{array}\right)} = \boxed{\left(\dfrac{1}{30} + \dfrac{1}{2}\right) + \left(\dfrac{5}{1} + \dfrac{15}{4}\right)} = \boxed{\left(\dfrac{(1 \times 2) + (1 \times 30)}{30 \times 2}\right) + \left(\dfrac{(5 \times 4) + (15 \times 1)}{1 \times 4}\right)}$$

$$= \boxed{\left(\dfrac{2 + 30}{60}\right) + \left(\dfrac{20 + 15}{4}\right)} = \boxed{\left(\dfrac{32}{60}\right) + \left(\dfrac{35}{4}\right)} = \boxed{\begin{array}{c}8\\\dfrac{\cancel{32}}{60}\\15\end{array} + \dfrac{35}{4}} = \boxed{\dfrac{8}{15} + \dfrac{35}{4}} = \boxed{\dfrac{(8 \times 4) + (35 \times 15)}{15 \times 4}} = \boxed{\dfrac{32 + 525}{60}} = \boxed{\dfrac{557}{60}}$$

$$= \boxed{9\frac{17}{60}}$$

Section 8.1 Exercises - Add the following decimal and mixed fractions:

1. $3\frac{2}{5} + \frac{0.01}{0.5} =$

2. $0.12 + 6\frac{2}{10} =$

3. $\frac{0.03}{0.5} + 3\frac{4}{5} =$

4. $\left(3\frac{1}{2} + 2\frac{3}{4}\right) + \frac{0.8}{1.2} =$

5. $3\frac{5}{8} + \frac{0.02}{0.14} + \frac{0.2}{0.5} =$

6. $\left(3\frac{6}{8} + 5\frac{1}{8}\right) + \frac{0.4}{0.08} =$

7. $\left(5\frac{3}{4} + \frac{0.2}{0.1}\right) + 0.24 =$

8. $\frac{0.04}{1.2} + \left(4\frac{5}{6} + 2\frac{4}{5}\right) =$

9. $3\frac{2}{7} + \left(\frac{0.2}{0.04} + 0.4\right) =$

10. $\left(3\frac{1}{4} + 2\frac{4}{5}\right) + \left(\frac{0.12}{0.4} + \frac{0.5}{0.2}\right) =$

8.2   Subtracting Decimal and Mixed Fractions

Decimal fractions of the form $\left(\dfrac{a \times 10^{-k_1}}{b \times 10^{-k_2}} \right)$ where (a) and (b) are integer numbers and (k_1) and

(k_2) are equal to the number of decimal places, and mixed fractions of the form $\left(k\dfrac{a}{b} \right)$ where (k)

is made up of a whole number and $\left(\dfrac{a}{b} \right)$ is an integer fraction are subtracted as in the following

cases:

Case I   Subtracting Two Decimal and Mixed Fractions
Subtract two decimal and mixed fractions using the following steps:

Step 1   Change the mixed fraction to an integer fraction (see Section 2.5).

Step 2   a. Change the decimal fraction to an integer fraction (see Section 2.4).

   b. Change the decimal number $\left(a \times 10^{-k} \right)$ to an integer fraction of the form $\left(\dfrac{a}{10^k} \right)$,

   e.g., change 2.38 to $\dfrac{238}{100}$.

Step 3   Subtract the integer fractions (see Section 3.2).

Step 4   Simplify the fraction to its lowest term (see Section 2.3).

Step 5   Change the improper fraction to a mixed fraction if the fraction obtained from Step 4 is an improper fraction (see Section 2.2).

The following examples show the steps as to how two decimal and mixed fractions are subtracted:

Example 8.2-1

$$\boxed{2\frac{4}{7} - \frac{0.3}{0.2}} =$$

Solution:

Step 1 $\boxed{2\frac{4}{7} - \frac{0.3}{0.2}} = \boxed{\frac{(2 \times 7) + 4}{7} - \frac{0.3}{0.2}} = \boxed{\frac{14 + 4}{7} - \frac{0.3}{0.2}} = \boxed{\frac{18}{7} - \frac{0.3}{0.2}}$

Step 2a $\boxed{\frac{18}{7} - \frac{0.3}{0.2}} = \boxed{\frac{18}{7} - \frac{\frac{3}{10}}{\frac{2}{10}}} = \boxed{\frac{18}{7} - \frac{3 \times 10}{10 \times 2}} = \boxed{\frac{18}{7} - \frac{30}{20}}$

Step 2b $\boxed{Not\ Applicable}$

Step 3 $\boxed{\frac{18}{7} - \frac{30}{20}} = \boxed{\frac{(18 \times 20) - (30 \times 7)}{7 \times 20}} = \boxed{\frac{360 - 210}{140}} = \boxed{\frac{150}{140}}$

Step 4 $\boxed{\frac{150}{140}} = \boxed{\frac{150 \div 10}{140 \div 10}} = \boxed{\frac{15}{14}}$

Step 5 $\dfrac{15}{14} = \boxed{1\dfrac{1}{14}}$

Example 8.2-2

$$\boxed{0.35 - 2\dfrac{4}{5}} =$$

Solution:

Step 1 $\boxed{0.35 - 2\dfrac{4}{5}} = \boxed{0.35 - \dfrac{(2\times 5)+4}{5}} = \boxed{0.35 - \dfrac{10+4}{5}} = \boxed{0.35 - \dfrac{14}{5}}$

Step 2a $\boxed{\textit{Not Applicable}}$

Step 2b $\boxed{0.35 - \dfrac{14}{5}} = \boxed{\dfrac{35}{100} - \dfrac{14}{5}}$

Step 3 $\boxed{\dfrac{35}{100} - \dfrac{14}{5}} = \boxed{\dfrac{(35\times 5)-(14\times 100)}{100\times 5}} = \boxed{\dfrac{175-1400}{500}} = \boxed{\dfrac{-1225}{500}}$

Step 4 $\boxed{\dfrac{-1225}{500}} = \boxed{\dfrac{-1225\div 25}{500\div 25}} = \boxed{\dfrac{-49}{20}}$

Step 5 $\boxed{\dfrac{-49}{20}} = \boxed{-\left(2\dfrac{9}{20}\right)}$

Example 8.2-3

$$\boxed{\dfrac{0.12}{0.6} - 3\dfrac{5}{12}} =$$

Solution:

Step 1 $\boxed{\dfrac{0.12}{0.6} - 3\dfrac{5}{12}} = \boxed{\dfrac{0.12}{0.6} - \dfrac{(3\times 12)+5}{12}} = \boxed{\dfrac{0.12}{0.6} - \dfrac{36+5}{12}} = \boxed{\dfrac{0.12}{0.6} - \dfrac{41}{12}}$

Step 2a $\boxed{\dfrac{0.12}{0.6} - \dfrac{41}{12}} = \boxed{\dfrac{\frac{12}{100}}{\frac{6}{10}} - \dfrac{41}{12}} = \boxed{\dfrac{12\times 10}{100\times 6} - \dfrac{41}{12}} = \boxed{\dfrac{120}{600} - \dfrac{41}{12}}$

Step 2b $\boxed{\textit{Not Applicable}}$

Step 3 $\boxed{\dfrac{120}{600} - \dfrac{41}{12}} = \boxed{\dfrac{(120\times 12)-(41\times 600)}{600\times 12}} = \boxed{\dfrac{1440-24600}{7200}} = \boxed{\dfrac{-23160}{7200}}$

Step 4 $\boxed{\dfrac{-23160}{7200}} = \boxed{\dfrac{-23160\div 40}{7200\div 40}} = \boxed{\dfrac{-579}{180}} = \boxed{\dfrac{-579\div 3}{180\div 3}} = \boxed{\dfrac{-193}{60}}$

Step 5 $\dfrac{-193}{60} = -\left(3\dfrac{13}{60}\right)$

Example 8.2-4

$6\dfrac{7}{10} - 0.05 =$

Solution:

Step 1 $6\dfrac{7}{10} - 0.05 = \dfrac{(6\times 10)+7}{10} - 0.05 = \dfrac{60+7}{10} - 0.05 = \dfrac{67}{10} - 0.05$

Step 2a $\boxed{Not\ Applicable}$

Step 2b $\dfrac{67}{10} - 0.05 = \dfrac{67}{10} - \dfrac{5}{100}$

Step 3 $\dfrac{67}{10} - \dfrac{5}{100} = \dfrac{(67\times 100)-(5\times 10)}{10\times 100} = \dfrac{6700-50}{1000} = \dfrac{6650}{1000}$

Step 4 $\dfrac{6650}{1000} = \dfrac{6650\div 50}{1000\div 50} = \dfrac{133}{20}$

Step 5 $\dfrac{133}{20} = 6\dfrac{13}{20}$

Example 8.2-5

$3\dfrac{5}{8} - \dfrac{12.8}{0.02} =$

Solution:

Step 1 $3\dfrac{5}{8} - \dfrac{12.8}{0.02} = \dfrac{(3\times 8)+5}{8} - \dfrac{12.8}{0.02} = \dfrac{24+5}{8} - \dfrac{12.8}{0.02} = \dfrac{29}{8} - \dfrac{12.8}{0.02}$

Step 2a $\dfrac{29}{8} - \dfrac{12.8}{0.02} = \dfrac{29}{8} - \dfrac{\frac{128}{10}}{\frac{2}{100}} = \dfrac{29}{8} - \dfrac{128\times 100}{10\times 2} = \dfrac{29}{8} - \dfrac{12800}{20}$

Step 2b $\boxed{Not\ Applicable}$

Step 3 $\dfrac{29}{8} - \dfrac{12800}{20} = \dfrac{(29\times 20)-(12800\times 8)}{8\times 20} = \dfrac{580-102400}{160} = \dfrac{-101820}{160}$

Step 4 $\dfrac{-101820}{160} = \dfrac{-101820\div 20}{160\div 20} = \dfrac{-5091}{8}$

Step 5 $$\boxed{\dfrac{-5091}{8}} = \boxed{-\left(636\dfrac{3}{8}\right)}$$

Case II   Subtracting Three Decimal and Mixed Fractions

Subtract three decimal and mixed fractions using the following steps:

Step 1   Use parentheses to group the first and second fractions.

Step 2   Change the mixed fraction(s) to integer fraction(s) (see Section 2.5).

Step 3   a. Change the decimal fraction(s) to integer fraction(s) (see Section 2.4).

   b. Change the decimal number $\left(a \times 10^{-k}\right)$ to an integer fraction of the form $\left(\dfrac{a}{10^k}\right)$,

   e.g., change 0.028 to $\dfrac{28}{1000}$.

Step 4   Subtract the integer fractions (see Section 3.2).

Step 5   Simplify the fraction to its lowest term (see Section 2.3).

Step 6   Change the improper fraction to a mixed fraction if the fraction obtained from Step 5 is an improper fraction (see Section 2.2).

The following examples show the steps as to how three decimal and mixed fractions are subtracted:

Example 8.2-6

$$\boxed{\dfrac{0.01}{0.8} - 2\dfrac{3}{4} - \dfrac{0.4}{0.6}} =$$

Solution:

Step 1 $$\boxed{\dfrac{0.01}{0.8} - 2\dfrac{3}{4} - \dfrac{0.4}{0.6}} = \boxed{\left(\dfrac{0.01}{0.8} - 2\dfrac{3}{4}\right) - \dfrac{0.4}{0.6}}$$

Step 2 $$\boxed{\left(\dfrac{0.01}{0.8} - 2\dfrac{3}{4}\right) - \dfrac{0.4}{0.6}} = \boxed{\left(\dfrac{0.01}{0.8} - \dfrac{(2 \times 4) + 3}{4}\right) - \dfrac{0.4}{0.6}} = \boxed{\left(\dfrac{0.01}{0.8} - \dfrac{8 + 3}{4}\right) - \dfrac{0.4}{0.6}}$$

$$= \boxed{\left(\dfrac{0.01}{0.8} - \dfrac{11}{4}\right) - \dfrac{0.4}{0.6}}$$

Step 3a $$\boxed{\left(\dfrac{0.01}{0.8} - \dfrac{11}{4}\right) - \dfrac{0.4}{0.6}} = \boxed{\left(\dfrac{\frac{1}{100}}{\frac{8}{10}} - \dfrac{11}{4}\right) - \dfrac{\frac{4}{10}}{\frac{6}{10}}} = \boxed{\left(\dfrac{1 \times 10}{100 \times 8} - \dfrac{11}{4}\right) - \dfrac{4 \times 10}{10 \times 6}}$$

$$= \boxed{\left(\dfrac{10}{800} - \dfrac{11}{4}\right) - \dfrac{40}{60}}$$

Step 3b $\boxed{\textit{Not Applicable}}$

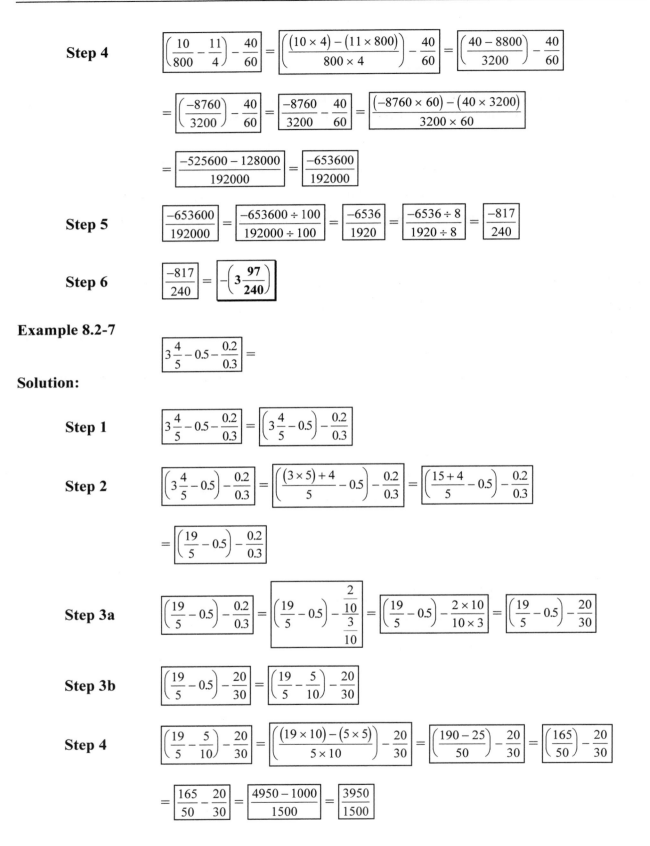

Step 4

$$\left(\frac{10}{800} - \frac{11}{4}\right) - \frac{40}{60} = \left(\frac{(10 \times 4) - (11 \times 800)}{800 \times 4}\right) - \frac{40}{60} = \left(\frac{40 - 8800}{3200}\right) - \frac{40}{60}$$

$$= \left(\frac{-8760}{3200}\right) - \frac{40}{60} = \frac{-8760}{3200} - \frac{40}{60} = \frac{(-8760 \times 60) - (40 \times 3200)}{3200 \times 60}$$

$$= \frac{-525600 - 128000}{192000} = \frac{-653600}{192000}$$

Step 5

$$\frac{-653600}{192000} = \frac{-653600 \div 100}{192000 \div 100} = \frac{-6536}{1920} = \frac{-6536 \div 8}{1920 \div 8} = \frac{-817}{240}$$

Step 6

$$\frac{-817}{240} = -\left(3\frac{97}{240}\right)$$

Example 8.2-7

$$3\frac{4}{5} - 0.5 - \frac{0.2}{0.3} =$$

Solution:

Step 1

$$3\frac{4}{5} - 0.5 - \frac{0.2}{0.3} = \left(3\frac{4}{5} - 0.5\right) - \frac{0.2}{0.3}$$

Step 2

$$\left(3\frac{4}{5} - 0.5\right) - \frac{0.2}{0.3} = \left(\frac{(3 \times 5) + 4}{5} - 0.5\right) - \frac{0.2}{0.3} = \left(\frac{15 + 4}{5} - 0.5\right) - \frac{0.2}{0.3}$$

$$= \left(\frac{19}{5} - 0.5\right) - \frac{0.2}{0.3}$$

Step 3a

$$\left(\frac{19}{5} - 0.5\right) - \frac{0.2}{0.3} = \left(\frac{19}{5} - 0.5\right) - \frac{\frac{2}{10}}{\frac{3}{10}} = \left(\frac{19}{5} - 0.5\right) - \frac{2 \times 10}{10 \times 3} = \left(\frac{19}{5} - 0.5\right) - \frac{20}{30}$$

Step 3b

$$\left(\frac{19}{5} - 0.5\right) - \frac{20}{30} = \left(\frac{19}{5} - \frac{5}{10}\right) - \frac{20}{30}$$

Step 4

$$\left(\frac{19}{5} - \frac{5}{10}\right) - \frac{20}{30} = \left(\frac{(19 \times 10) - (5 \times 5)}{5 \times 10}\right) - \frac{20}{30} = \left(\frac{190 - 25}{50}\right) - \frac{20}{30} = \left(\frac{165}{50}\right) - \frac{20}{30}$$

$$= \frac{165}{50} - \frac{20}{30} = \frac{4950 - 1000}{1500} = \frac{3950}{1500}$$

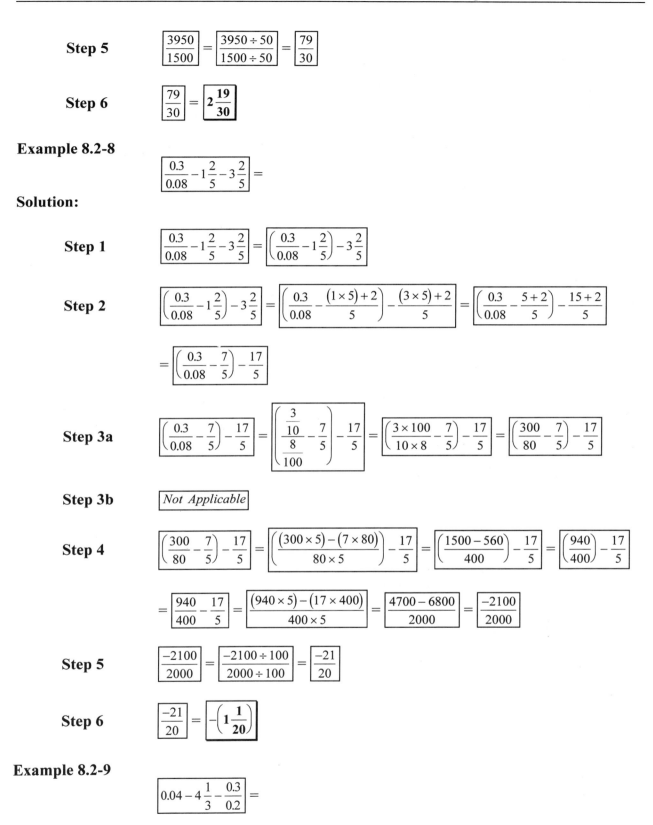

Step 5

$$\boxed{\frac{3950}{1500}} = \boxed{\frac{3950 \div 50}{1500 \div 50}} = \boxed{\frac{79}{30}}$$

Step 6

$$\boxed{\frac{79}{30}} = \boxed{2\frac{19}{30}}$$

Example 8.2-8

$$\boxed{\frac{0.3}{0.08} - 1\frac{2}{5} - 3\frac{2}{5}} =$$

Solution:

Step 1

$$\boxed{\frac{0.3}{0.08} - 1\frac{2}{5} - 3\frac{2}{5}} = \boxed{\left(\frac{0.3}{0.08} - 1\frac{2}{5}\right) - 3\frac{2}{5}}$$

Step 2

$$\boxed{\left(\frac{0.3}{0.08} - 1\frac{2}{5}\right) - 3\frac{2}{5}} = \boxed{\left(\frac{0.3}{0.08} - \frac{(1\times 5)+2}{5}\right) - \frac{(3\times 5)+2}{5}} = \boxed{\left(\frac{0.3}{0.08} - \frac{5+2}{5}\right) - \frac{15+2}{5}}$$

$$= \boxed{\left(\frac{0.3}{0.08} - \frac{7}{5}\right) - \frac{17}{5}}$$

Step 3a

$$\boxed{\left(\frac{0.3}{0.08} - \frac{7}{5}\right) - \frac{17}{5}} = \boxed{\left(\frac{\frac{3}{10}}{\frac{8}{100}} - \frac{7}{5}\right) - \frac{17}{5}} = \boxed{\left(\frac{3\times 100}{10\times 8} - \frac{7}{5}\right) - \frac{17}{5}} = \boxed{\left(\frac{300}{80} - \frac{7}{5}\right) - \frac{17}{5}}$$

Step 3b

$$\boxed{\textit{Not Applicable}}$$

Step 4

$$\boxed{\left(\frac{300}{80} - \frac{7}{5}\right) - \frac{17}{5}} = \boxed{\left(\frac{(300\times 5)-(7\times 80)}{80\times 5}\right) - \frac{17}{5}} = \boxed{\left(\frac{1500-560}{400}\right) - \frac{17}{5}} = \boxed{\left(\frac{940}{400}\right) - \frac{17}{5}}$$

$$= \boxed{\frac{940}{400} - \frac{17}{5}} = \boxed{\frac{(940\times 5)-(17\times 400)}{400\times 5}} = \boxed{\frac{4700-6800}{2000}} = \boxed{\frac{-2100}{2000}}$$

Step 5

$$\boxed{\frac{-2100}{2000}} = \boxed{\frac{-2100 \div 100}{2000 \div 100}} = \boxed{\frac{-21}{20}}$$

Step 6

$$\boxed{\frac{-21}{20}} = \boxed{-\left(1\frac{1}{20}\right)}$$

Example 8.2-9

$$\boxed{0.04 - 4\frac{1}{3} - \frac{0.3}{0.2}} =$$

Solution:

Step 1
$$\boxed{0.04 - 4\frac{1}{3} - \frac{0.3}{0.2}} = \boxed{\left(0.04 - 4\frac{1}{3}\right) - \frac{0.3}{0.2}}$$

Step 2
$$\boxed{\left(0.04 - 4\frac{1}{3}\right) - \frac{0.3}{0.2}} = \boxed{\left(0.04 - \frac{(4\times 3)+1}{3}\right) - \frac{0.3}{0.2}} = \boxed{\left(0.04 - \frac{12+1}{3}\right) - \frac{0.3}{0.2}}$$

$$= \boxed{\left(0.04 - \frac{13}{3}\right) - \frac{0.3}{0.2}}$$

Step 3a
$$\boxed{\left(0.04 - \frac{13}{3}\right) - \frac{0.3}{0.2}} = \boxed{\left(0.04 - \frac{13}{3}\right) - \frac{\frac{3}{10}}{\frac{2}{10}}} = \boxed{\left(0.04 - \frac{13}{3}\right) - \frac{3\times 10}{10\times 2}} = \boxed{\left(0.04 - \frac{13}{3}\right) - \frac{30}{20}}$$

Step 3b
$$\boxed{\left(0.04 - \frac{13}{3}\right) - \frac{30}{20}} = \boxed{\left(\frac{4}{100} - \frac{13}{3}\right) - \frac{30}{20}}$$

Step 4
$$\boxed{\left(\frac{4}{100} - \frac{13}{3}\right) - \frac{30}{20}} = \boxed{\left(\frac{(4\times 3)-(13\times 100)}{100\times 3}\right) - \frac{30}{20}} = \boxed{\left(\frac{12-1300}{300}\right) - \frac{30}{20}} = \boxed{\left(\frac{-1288}{300}\right) - \frac{30}{20}}$$

$$= \boxed{\frac{-1288}{300} - \frac{30}{20}} = \boxed{\frac{(-1288\times 20)-(30\times 300)}{300\times 20}} = \boxed{\frac{-25760-9000}{6000}} = \boxed{\frac{-34760}{6000}}$$

Step 5
$$\boxed{\frac{-34760}{6000}} = \boxed{\frac{-34760\div 40}{6000\div 40}} = \boxed{\frac{-869}{150}}$$

Step 6
$$\boxed{\frac{-869}{150}} = \boxed{-\left(5\frac{119}{150}\right)}$$

Example 8.2-10
$$\boxed{4\frac{1}{8} - \frac{0.3}{0.2} - \frac{0.5}{0.4}} =$$

Solution:

Step 1
$$\boxed{4\frac{1}{8} - \frac{0.3}{0.2} - \frac{0.5}{0.4}} = \boxed{\left(4\frac{1}{8} - \frac{0.3}{0.2}\right) - \frac{0.5}{0.4}}$$

Step 2
$$\boxed{\left(4\frac{1}{8} - \frac{0.3}{0.2}\right) - \frac{0.5}{0.4}} = \boxed{\left(\frac{(4\times 8)+1}{8} - \frac{0.3}{0.2}\right) - \frac{0.5}{0.4}} = \boxed{\left(\frac{32+1}{8} - \frac{0.3}{0.2}\right) - \frac{0.5}{0.4}}$$

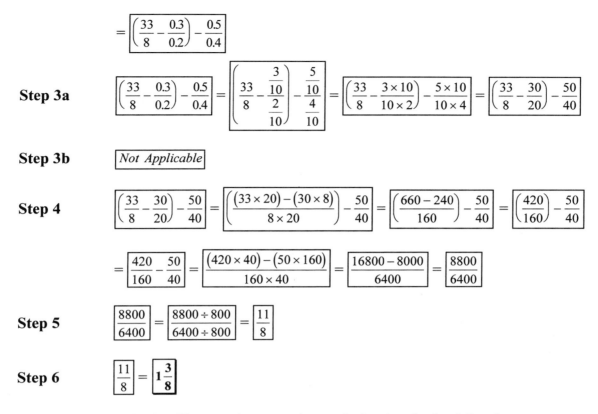

$$= \left[\left(\frac{33}{8} - \frac{0.3}{0.2}\right) - \frac{0.5}{0.4}\right]$$

Step 3a

$$\left[\left(\frac{33}{8} - \frac{0.3}{0.2}\right) - \frac{0.5}{0.4}\right] = \left[\left(\frac{33}{8} - \frac{\frac{3}{10}}{\frac{2}{10}}\right) - \frac{\frac{5}{10}}{\frac{4}{10}}\right] = \left[\left(\frac{33}{8} - \frac{3 \times 10}{10 \times 2}\right) - \frac{5 \times 10}{10 \times 4}\right] = \left[\left(\frac{33}{8} - \frac{30}{20}\right) - \frac{50}{40}\right]$$

Step 3b

Not Applicable

Step 4

$$\left[\left(\frac{33}{8} - \frac{30}{20}\right) - \frac{50}{40}\right] = \left[\left(\frac{(33 \times 20) - (30 \times 8)}{8 \times 20}\right) - \frac{50}{40}\right] = \left[\left(\frac{660 - 240}{160}\right) - \frac{50}{40}\right] = \left[\left(\frac{420}{160}\right) - \frac{50}{40}\right]$$

$$= \left[\frac{420}{160} - \frac{50}{40}\right] = \left[\frac{(420 \times 40) - (50 \times 160)}{160 \times 40}\right] = \left[\frac{16800 - 8000}{6400}\right] = \left[\frac{8800}{6400}\right]$$

Step 5

$$\left[\frac{8800}{6400}\right] = \left[\frac{8800 \div 800}{6400 \div 800}\right] = \left[\frac{11}{8}\right]$$

Step 6

$$\left[\frac{11}{8}\right] = \left[1\frac{3}{8}\right]$$

The following examples further illustrate how to subtract decimal and mixed fractions:

Example 8.2-11

$$\left[3\frac{1}{4} - \frac{0.24}{0.8}\right] = \left[\frac{(3 \times 4) + 1}{4} - \frac{\frac{24}{100}}{\frac{8}{10}}\right] = \left[\frac{12 + 1}{4} - \frac{24 \times 10}{100 \times 8}\right] = \left[\frac{13}{4} - \frac{\cancel{240}}{\cancel{800}}\right] = \left[\frac{13}{4} - \frac{3}{10}\right] = \left[\frac{(13 \times 10) - (3 \times 4)}{4 \times 10}\right]$$

$$= \left[\frac{130 - 12}{40}\right] = \left[\frac{\cancel{118}}{\cancel{40}}\right] = \left[\frac{59}{20}\right] = \left[2\frac{19}{20}\right]$$

Example 8.2-12

$$\left[2\frac{3}{8} - 12.4\right] = \left[\frac{(2 \times 8) + 3}{8} - \frac{\cancel{124}}{\cancel{10}}\right] = \left[\frac{16 + 3}{8} - \frac{62}{5}\right] = \left[\frac{19}{8} - \frac{62}{5}\right] = \left[\frac{(19 \times 5) - (62 \times 8)}{8 \times 5}\right] = \left[\frac{95 - 496}{40}\right] = \left[\frac{-401}{40}\right]$$

$$= \left[-\left(10\frac{1}{40}\right)\right]$$

Example 8.2-13

$$\left[\frac{14.2}{0.028} - 2\frac{3}{8}\right] = \left[\frac{\frac{142}{10}}{\frac{28}{1000}} - \frac{(2 \times 8) + 3}{8}\right] = \left[\frac{142 \times 1000}{10 \times 28} - \frac{16 + 3}{8}\right] = \left[\frac{\cancel{3550}}{\cancel{280}} - \frac{19}{8}\right] = \left[\frac{3550}{7} - \frac{19}{8}\right]$$

$$= \boxed{\dfrac{(3550 \times 8) - (19 \times 7)}{7 \times 8}} = \boxed{\dfrac{28400 - 133}{56}} = \boxed{\dfrac{28267}{56}} = \boxed{\mathbf{504\dfrac{43}{56}}}$$

Example 8.2-14

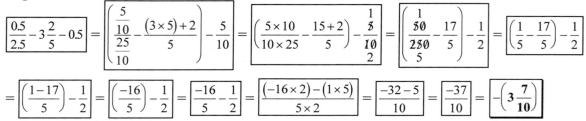

$$= \boxed{\left(\dfrac{1-17}{5}\right) - \dfrac{1}{2}} = \boxed{\left(\dfrac{-16}{5}\right) - \dfrac{1}{2}} = \boxed{\dfrac{-16}{5} - \dfrac{1}{2}} = \boxed{\dfrac{(-16 \times 2) - (1 \times 5)}{5 \times 2}} = \boxed{\dfrac{-32 - 5}{10}} = \boxed{\dfrac{-37}{10}} = \boxed{-\left(\mathbf{3\dfrac{7}{10}}\right)}$$

Example 8.2-15

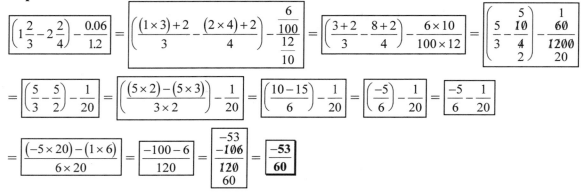

$$= \boxed{\left(\dfrac{5}{3} - \dfrac{5}{2}\right) - \dfrac{1}{20}} = \boxed{\left(\dfrac{(5 \times 2) - (5 \times 3)}{3 \times 2}\right) - \dfrac{1}{20}} = \boxed{\left(\dfrac{10 - 15}{6}\right) - \dfrac{1}{20}} = \boxed{\left(\dfrac{-5}{6}\right) - \dfrac{1}{20}} = \boxed{\dfrac{-5}{6} - \dfrac{1}{20}}$$

$$= \boxed{\dfrac{(-5 \times 20) - (1 \times 6)}{6 \times 20}} = \boxed{\dfrac{-100 - 6}{120}} = \boxed{\dfrac{\dfrac{-53}{-106}}{\dfrac{120}{60}}} = \boxed{\dfrac{\mathbf{-53}}{\mathbf{60}}}$$

Example 8.2-16

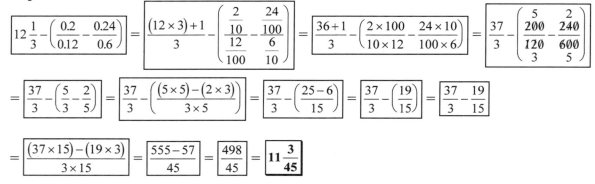

$$= \boxed{\dfrac{37}{3} - \left(\dfrac{5}{3} - \dfrac{2}{5}\right)} = \boxed{\dfrac{37}{3} - \left(\dfrac{(5 \times 5) - (2 \times 3)}{3 \times 5}\right)} = \boxed{\dfrac{37}{3} - \left(\dfrac{25 - 6}{15}\right)} = \boxed{\dfrac{37}{3} - \left(\dfrac{19}{15}\right)} = \boxed{\dfrac{37}{3} - \dfrac{19}{15}}$$

$$= \boxed{\dfrac{(37 \times 15) - (19 \times 3)}{3 \times 15}} = \boxed{\dfrac{555 - 57}{45}} = \boxed{\dfrac{498}{45}} = \boxed{\mathbf{11\dfrac{3}{45}}}$$

Example 8.2-17

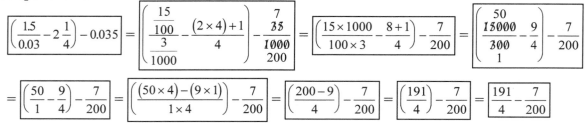

$$= \boxed{\left(\dfrac{50}{1} - \dfrac{9}{4}\right) - \dfrac{7}{200}} = \boxed{\left(\dfrac{(50 \times 4) - (9 \times 1)}{1 \times 4}\right) - \dfrac{7}{200}} = \boxed{\left(\dfrac{200 - 9}{4}\right) - \dfrac{7}{200}} = \boxed{\left(\dfrac{191}{4}\right) - \dfrac{7}{200}} = \boxed{\dfrac{191}{4} - \dfrac{7}{200}}$$

$$= \boxed{\frac{(191 \times 200) - (7 \times 4)}{4 \times 200}} = \boxed{\frac{38200 - 28}{800}} = \boxed{\frac{\overset{9543}{\cancel{38172}}}{\underset{200}{\cancel{800}}}} = \boxed{\frac{9543}{200}} = \boxed{47\frac{143}{200}}$$

Example 8.2-18

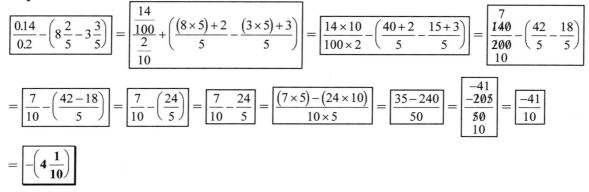

$$\boxed{\frac{0.14}{0.2} - \left(8\frac{2}{5} - 3\frac{3}{5}\right)} = \boxed{\frac{\frac{14}{100}}{\frac{2}{10}} + \left(\frac{(8\times5)+2}{5} - \frac{(3\times5)+3}{5}\right)} = \boxed{\frac{14\times10}{100\times2} - \left(\frac{40+2}{5} - \frac{15+3}{5}\right)} = \boxed{\frac{\overset{7}{\cancel{140}}}{\underset{10}{\cancel{200}}} - \left(\frac{42}{5} - \frac{18}{5}\right)}$$

$$= \boxed{\frac{7}{10} - \left(\frac{42-18}{5}\right)} = \boxed{\frac{7}{10} - \left(\frac{24}{5}\right)} = \boxed{\frac{7}{10} - \frac{24}{5}} = \boxed{\frac{(7\times5)-(24\times10)}{10\times5}} = \boxed{\frac{35-240}{50}} = \boxed{\frac{\overset{-41}{\cancel{-205}}}{\underset{10}{\cancel{50}}}} = \boxed{\frac{-41}{10}}$$

$$= \boxed{-\left(4\frac{1}{10}\right)}$$

Example 8.2-19

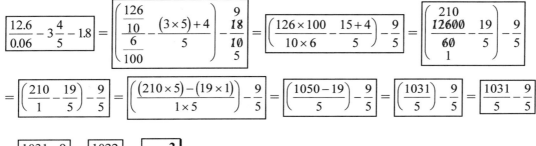

$$\boxed{\frac{12.6}{0.06} - 3\frac{4}{5} - 1.8} = \boxed{\left(\frac{\frac{126}{10}}{\frac{6}{100}} - \frac{(3\times5)+4}{5}\right) - \frac{\overset{9}{\cancel{18}}}{\underset{5}{\cancel{10}}}} = \boxed{\left(\frac{126\times100}{10\times6} - \frac{15+4}{5}\right) - \frac{9}{5}} = \boxed{\left(\frac{\overset{210}{\cancel{12600}}}{\underset{1}{\cancel{60}}} - \frac{19}{5}\right) - \frac{9}{5}}$$

$$= \boxed{\left(\frac{210}{1} - \frac{19}{5}\right) - \frac{9}{5}} = \boxed{\left(\frac{(210\times5)-(19\times1)}{1\times5}\right) - \frac{9}{5}} = \boxed{\left(\frac{1050-19}{5}\right) - \frac{9}{5}} = \boxed{\left(\frac{1031}{5}\right) - \frac{9}{5}} = \boxed{\frac{1031}{5} - \frac{9}{5}}$$

$$= \boxed{\frac{1031-9}{5}} = \boxed{\frac{1022}{5}} = \boxed{204\frac{2}{5}}$$

Example 8.2-20

$$\boxed{\frac{1.3}{0.013} - \left(6\frac{1}{8} - 2\frac{5}{6}\right)} = \boxed{\frac{\frac{13}{10}}{\frac{13}{1000}} - \left(\frac{(6\times8)+1}{8} - \frac{(2\times6)+5}{6}\right)} = \boxed{\frac{13\times1000}{10\times13} - \left(\frac{48+1}{8} - \frac{12+5}{6}\right)}$$

$$= \boxed{\frac{\overset{100}{\cancel{13000}}}{\underset{1}{\cancel{130}}} - \left(\frac{49}{8} - \frac{17}{6}\right)} = \boxed{\frac{100}{1} - \left(\frac{49}{8} - \frac{17}{6}\right)} = \boxed{\frac{100}{1} - \left(\frac{(49\times6)-(17\times8)}{8\times6}\right)} = \boxed{\frac{100}{1} - \left(\frac{294-136}{48}\right)}$$

$$= \boxed{\frac{100}{1} - \left(\frac{158}{48}\right)} = \boxed{\frac{100}{1} - \frac{\overset{79}{\cancel{158}}}{\underset{24}{\cancel{48}}}} = \boxed{\frac{100}{1} - \frac{79}{24}} = \boxed{\frac{(100\times24)-(79\times1)}{1\times24}} = \boxed{\frac{2400-79}{24}} = \boxed{\frac{2321}{24}} = \boxed{96\frac{17}{24}}$$

Example 8.2-21

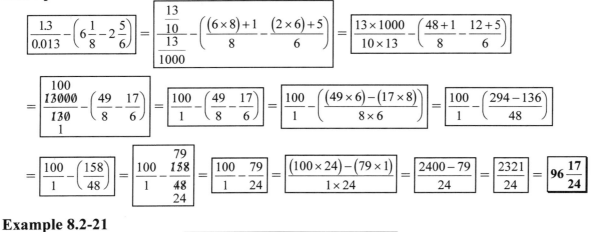

$$\boxed{\left(1\frac{2}{3} - \frac{0.4}{1.2}\right) - \left(1.28 - 2\frac{3}{5}\right)} = \boxed{\left(\frac{(1\times3)+2}{3} - \frac{\frac{4}{10}}{\frac{12}{10}}\right) - \left(\frac{128}{100} - \frac{(2\times5)+3}{5}\right)} = \boxed{\left(\frac{3+2}{3} - \frac{4\times10}{10\times12}\right) - \left(\frac{128}{100} - \frac{10+3}{5}\right)}$$

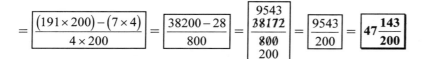

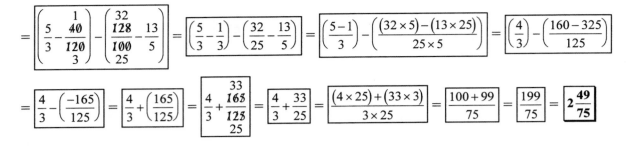

$$= \left[\left(\dfrac{5}{\dfrac{3}{120}}\dfrac{\dfrac{1}{40}}{\dfrac{120}{3}}\right)-\left(\dfrac{32}{\dfrac{128}{\dfrac{100}{25}}}-\dfrac{13}{5}\right)\right] = \left[\left(\dfrac{5}{3}-\dfrac{1}{3}\right)-\left(\dfrac{32}{25}-\dfrac{13}{5}\right)\right] = \left[\left(\dfrac{5-1}{3}\right)-\left(\dfrac{(32\times5)-(13\times25)}{25\times5}\right)\right] = \left[\left(\dfrac{4}{3}\right)-\left(\dfrac{160-325}{125}\right)\right]$$

$$= \left[\dfrac{4}{3}-\left(\dfrac{-165}{125}\right)\right] = \dfrac{4}{3}+\left(\dfrac{165}{125}\right) = \dfrac{4}{3}+\dfrac{\overset{33}{\cancel{165}}}{\underset{25}{\cancel{125}}} = \dfrac{4}{3}+\dfrac{33}{25} = \dfrac{(4\times25)+(33\times3)}{3\times25} = \dfrac{100+99}{75} = \dfrac{199}{75} = \boxed{2\dfrac{49}{75}}$$

Section 8.2 Exercises - Subtract the following decimal and mixed fractions:

1. $2\dfrac{1}{6}-\dfrac{0.02}{0.5}=$

2. $\dfrac{0.03}{1.5}-4\dfrac{2}{3}=$

3. $12.2-3\dfrac{4}{5}=$

4. $\left(3\dfrac{1}{2}-1\dfrac{3}{4}\right)-\dfrac{1.8}{0.9}=$

5. $2\dfrac{3}{8}-\dfrac{1.2}{0.06}-\dfrac{0.2}{0.5}=$

6. $\left(5\dfrac{2}{8}-1\dfrac{3}{8}\right)-\dfrac{0.4}{0.08}=$

7. $\left(15\dfrac{3}{4}-0.12\right)-\dfrac{0.8}{1.2}=$

8. $\dfrac{0.24}{1.2}-\left(2\dfrac{3}{5}-3\dfrac{4}{9}\right)=$

9. $3\dfrac{1}{8}-\left(\dfrac{0.8}{0.04}-1.2\right)=$

10. $\left(15.8-2\dfrac{3}{5}\right)-\left(\dfrac{0.12}{0.3}-\dfrac{0.5}{0.15}\right)=$

8.3   Multiplying Decimal and Mixed Fractions

Two or more decimal and mixed fractions of the forms:

1. $\left(\dfrac{a \times 10^{-k_1}}{b \times 10^{-k_2}}\right)$ where (a) and (b) are integer numbers and (k_1) and (k_2) are equal to the number

    of decimal places, and

2. $\left(k\dfrac{a}{b}\right)$ where (k) is made up of a whole number and $\left(\dfrac{a}{b}\right)$ is an integer fraction

are multiplied as in the following cases:

Case I   Multiplying Two Decimal and Mixed Fractions

Multiply two decimal and mixed fractions using the following steps:

Step 1   Change the mixed fraction to an integer fraction (see Section 2.5).

Step 2   a. Change the decimal fraction to an integer fraction (see Section 2.4).

            b. Change the decimal number $\left(a \times 10^{-k}\right)$ to an integer fraction of the form $\left(\dfrac{a}{10^k}\right)$,

            e.g., change 1.25 to $\dfrac{125}{100}$.

Step 3   Multiply the integer fractions (see Section 3.3, Case I).

Step 4   Simplify the fraction to its lowest term (see Section 2.3).

Step 5   Change the improper fraction to a mixed fraction if the fraction obtained from Step 4 is an improper fraction (see Section 2.2).

The following examples show the steps as to how two decimal and mixed fractions are multiplied:

Example 8.3-1

$$\boxed{\dfrac{0.12}{0.5} \times 2\dfrac{5}{13}} =$$

Solution:

Step 1 $\boxed{\dfrac{0.12}{0.5} \times 2\dfrac{5}{13}} = \boxed{\dfrac{0.12}{0.5} \times \dfrac{(2 \times 13) + 5}{13}} = \boxed{\dfrac{0.12}{0.5} \times \dfrac{26 + 5}{13}} = \boxed{\dfrac{0.12}{0.5} \times \dfrac{31}{13}}$

Step 2a $\boxed{\dfrac{0.12}{0.5} \times \dfrac{31}{13}} = \boxed{\dfrac{\frac{12}{100}}{\frac{5}{10}} \times \dfrac{31}{13}} = \boxed{\dfrac{12 \times 10}{100 \times 5} \times \dfrac{31}{13}} = \boxed{\dfrac{120}{500} \times \dfrac{31}{13}}$

Step 2b $\boxed{\textit{Not Applicable}}$

Step 3 $\boxed{\dfrac{120}{500} \times \dfrac{31}{13}} = \boxed{\dfrac{120 \times 31}{500 \times 13}} = \boxed{\dfrac{3720}{6500}}$

Step 4 $\boxed{\dfrac{3720}{6500}} = \boxed{\dfrac{3720 \div 40}{6500 \div 40}} = \boxed{\dfrac{\mathbf{186}}{\mathbf{325}}}$

Step 5 $\boxed{\textit{Not Applicable}}$

Example 8.3-2

$$\boxed{3\frac{4}{3} \times 0.8} =$$

Solution:

Step 1 $\boxed{3\frac{4}{3} \times 0.8} = \boxed{\frac{(3 \times 3) + 4}{3} \times 0.8} = \boxed{\frac{9 + 4}{3} \times 0.8} = \boxed{\frac{13}{3} \times 0.8}$

Step 2a $\boxed{\textit{Not Applicable}}$

Step 2b $\boxed{\frac{13}{3} \times 0.8} = \boxed{\frac{13}{3} \times \frac{8}{10}}$

Step 3 $\boxed{\frac{13}{3} \times \frac{8}{10}} = \boxed{\frac{13 \times 8}{3 \times 10}} = \boxed{\frac{104}{30}}$

Step 4 $\boxed{\frac{104}{30}} = \boxed{\frac{104 \div 2}{30 \div 2}} = \boxed{\frac{52}{15}}$

Step 5 $\boxed{\frac{52}{15}} = \boxed{\mathbf{3\frac{7}{15}}}$

Example 8.3-3

$$\boxed{\frac{12.8}{0.35} \times 4\frac{3}{7}} =$$

Solution:

Step 1 $\boxed{\frac{12.8}{0.35} \times 4\frac{3}{7}} = \boxed{\frac{12.8}{0.35} \times \frac{(4 \times 7) + 3}{7}} = \boxed{\frac{12.8}{0.35} \times \frac{28 + 3}{7}} = \boxed{\frac{12.8}{0.35} \times \frac{31}{7}}$

Step 2a $\boxed{\frac{12.8}{0.35} \times \frac{31}{7}} = \boxed{\dfrac{\frac{128}{10}}{\frac{35}{100}} \times \frac{31}{7}} = \boxed{\frac{128 \times 100}{10 \times 35} \times \frac{31}{7}} = \boxed{\frac{12800}{350} \times \frac{31}{7}}$

Step 2b $\boxed{\textit{Not Applicable}}$

Step 3 $\boxed{\frac{12800}{350} \times \frac{31}{7}} = \boxed{\frac{12800 \times 31}{350 \times 7}} = \boxed{\frac{396800}{2450}}$

Step 4 $\boxed{\frac{396800}{2450}} = \boxed{\frac{396800 \div 25}{2450 \div 25}} = \boxed{\frac{15872}{98}} = \boxed{\frac{15872 \div 2}{98 \div 2}} = \boxed{\frac{7936}{49}}$

Step 5 $\boxed{\dfrac{7936}{49}} = \boxed{\mathbf{161\dfrac{47}{49}}}$

Example 8.3-4

$$\boxed{0.236 \times 2\dfrac{5}{8} =}$$

Solution:

Step 1 $\boxed{0.236 \times 2\dfrac{5}{8}} = \boxed{0.236 \times \dfrac{(2\times 8)+5}{8}} = \boxed{0.236 \times \dfrac{16+5}{8}} = \boxed{0.236 \times \dfrac{21}{8}}$

Step 2a $\boxed{\textit{Not Applicable}}$

Step 2b $\boxed{0.236 \times \dfrac{21}{8}} = \boxed{\dfrac{236}{1000} \times \dfrac{21}{8}}$

Step 3 $\boxed{\dfrac{236}{1000} \times \dfrac{21}{8}} = \boxed{\dfrac{236 \times 21}{1000 \times 8}} = \boxed{\dfrac{4956}{8000}}$

Step 4 $\boxed{\dfrac{4956}{8000}} = \boxed{\dfrac{4956 \div 4}{8000 \div 4}} = \boxed{\mathbf{\dfrac{1239}{2000}}}$

Step 5 $\boxed{\textit{Not Applicable}}$

Example 8.3-5

$$\boxed{1\dfrac{7}{9} \times \dfrac{5.06}{2.8} =}$$

Solution:

Step 1 $\boxed{1\dfrac{7}{9} \times \dfrac{5.06}{2.8}} = \boxed{\dfrac{(1\times 9)+7}{9} \times \dfrac{5.06}{2.8}} = \boxed{\dfrac{9+7}{9} \times \dfrac{5.06}{2.8}} = \boxed{\dfrac{16}{9} \times \dfrac{5.06}{2.8}}$

Step 2a $\boxed{\dfrac{16}{9} \times \dfrac{5.06}{2.8}} = \boxed{\dfrac{16}{9} \times \dfrac{\frac{506}{100}}{\frac{28}{10}}} = \boxed{\dfrac{16}{9} \times \dfrac{506 \times 10}{100 \times 28}} = \boxed{\dfrac{16}{9} \times \dfrac{5060}{2800}}$

Step 2b $\boxed{\textit{Not Applicable}}$

Step 3 $\boxed{\dfrac{16}{9} \times \dfrac{5060}{2800}} = \boxed{\dfrac{16 \times 5060}{9 \times 2800}} = \boxed{\dfrac{80960}{25200}}$

Step 4 $\boxed{\dfrac{80960}{25200}} = \boxed{\dfrac{80960 \div 80}{25200 \div 80}} = \boxed{\dfrac{1012}{315}}$

Step 5 $$\boxed{\dfrac{1012}{315}} = \boxed{3\dfrac{67}{315}}$$

Case II   Multiplying Three Decimal and Mixed Fractions

Multiply three decimal and mixed fractions using the following steps:

Step 1   Change the mixed fraction(s) to integer fraction(s) (see Section 2.5).

Step 2   a. Change the decimal fraction(s) to integer fraction(s) (see Section 2.4).

        b. Change the decimal number $\left(a \times 10^{-k}\right)$ to an integer fraction of the form $\left(\dfrac{a}{10^k}\right)$,

        e.g., change 0.05 to $\dfrac{5}{100}$.

Step 3   Multiply the integer fractions (see Section 3.3, Case II).

Step 4   Simplify the fraction to its lowest term (see Section 2.3).

Step 5   Change the improper fraction to a mixed fraction if the fraction obtained from Step 4 is an improper fraction (see Section 2.2).

The following examples show the steps as to how three decimal and mixed fractions are multiplied:

Example 8.3-6

$$\boxed{4\dfrac{1}{5} \times \dfrac{0.7}{0.03} \times 0.9} =$$

Solution:

Step 1 $$\boxed{4\dfrac{1}{5} \times \dfrac{0.7}{0.03} \times 0.9} = \boxed{\dfrac{(4 \times 5)+1}{5} \times \dfrac{0.7}{0.03} \times 0.9} = \boxed{\dfrac{20+1}{5} \times \dfrac{0.7}{0.03} \times 0.9} = \boxed{\dfrac{21}{5} \times \dfrac{0.7}{0.03} \times 0.9}$$

Step 2a $$\boxed{\dfrac{21}{5} \times \dfrac{0.7}{0.03} \times 0.9} = \boxed{\dfrac{21}{5} \times \dfrac{\dfrac{7}{10}}{\dfrac{3}{100}} \times 0.9} = \boxed{\dfrac{21}{5} \times \dfrac{7 \times 100}{10 \times 3} \times 0.9} = \boxed{\dfrac{21}{5} \times \dfrac{700}{30} \times 0.9}$$

Step 2b $$\boxed{\dfrac{21}{5} \times \dfrac{700}{30} \times 0.9} = \boxed{\dfrac{21}{5} \times \dfrac{700}{30} \times \dfrac{9}{10}}$$

Step 3 $$\boxed{\dfrac{21}{5} \times \dfrac{700}{30} \times \dfrac{9}{10}} = \boxed{\dfrac{21 \times 700 \times 9}{5 \times 30 \times 10}} = \boxed{\dfrac{132300}{1500}}$$

Step 4 $$\boxed{\dfrac{132300}{1500}} = \boxed{\dfrac{132300 \div 300}{1500 \div 300}} = \boxed{\dfrac{441}{5}}$$

Step 5 $$\boxed{\dfrac{441}{5}} = \boxed{88\dfrac{1}{5}}$$

Example 8.3-7

$$\left| 2\frac{4}{5} \times 1\frac{3}{2} \times \frac{0.2}{0.3} \right| =$$

Solution:

Step 1

$$\left| 2\frac{4}{5} \times 1\frac{3}{2} \times \frac{0.2}{0.3} \right| = \left| \frac{(2 \times 5) + 4}{5} \times \frac{(1 \times 2) + 3}{2} \times \frac{0.2}{0.3} \right| = \left| \frac{10 + 4}{5} \times \frac{2 + 3}{2} \times \frac{0.2}{0.3} \right|$$

$$= \left| \frac{14}{5} \times \frac{5}{2} \times \frac{0.2}{0.3} \right|$$

Step 2a

$$\left| \frac{14}{5} \times \frac{5}{2} \times \frac{0.2}{0.3} \right| = \left| \frac{14}{5} \times \frac{5}{2} \times \frac{\frac{2}{10}}{\frac{3}{10}} \right| = \left| \frac{14}{5} \times \frac{5}{2} \times \frac{2 \times 10}{10 \times 3} \right| = \left| \frac{14}{5} \times \frac{5}{2} \times \frac{20}{30} \right|$$

Step 2b

$$\boxed{Not\ Applicable}$$

Step 3

$$\left| \frac{14}{5} \times \frac{5}{2} \times \frac{20}{30} \right| = \left| \frac{14 \times 5 \times 20}{5 \times 2 \times 30} \right| = \left| \frac{1400}{300} \right|$$

Step 4

$$\left| \frac{1400}{300} \right| = \left| \frac{1400 \div 100}{300 \div 100} \right| = \left| \frac{14}{3} \right|$$

Step 5

$$\left| \frac{14}{3} \right| = \boxed{4\frac{2}{3}}$$

Example 8.3-8

$$\left| 2\frac{4}{6} \times 1\frac{2}{3} \times 0.3 \right| =$$

Solution:

Step 1

$$\left| 2\frac{4}{6} \times 1\frac{2}{3} \times 0.3 \right| = \left| \frac{(2 \times 6) + 4}{6} \times \frac{(1 \times 3) + 2}{3} \times 0.3 \right| = \left| \frac{12 + 4}{6} \times \frac{3 + 2}{3} \times 0.3 \right|$$

$$= \left| \frac{16}{6} \times \frac{5}{3} \times 0.3 \right|$$

Step 2a

$$\boxed{Not\ Applicable}$$

Step 2b

$$\left| \frac{16}{6} \times \frac{5}{3} \times 0.3 \right| = \left| \frac{16}{6} \times \frac{5}{3} \times \frac{3}{10} \right|$$

Step 3

$$\left| \frac{16}{6} \times \frac{5}{3} \times \frac{3}{10} \right| = \left| \frac{16 \times 5 \times 3}{6 \times 3 \times 10} \right| = \left| \frac{240}{180} \right|$$

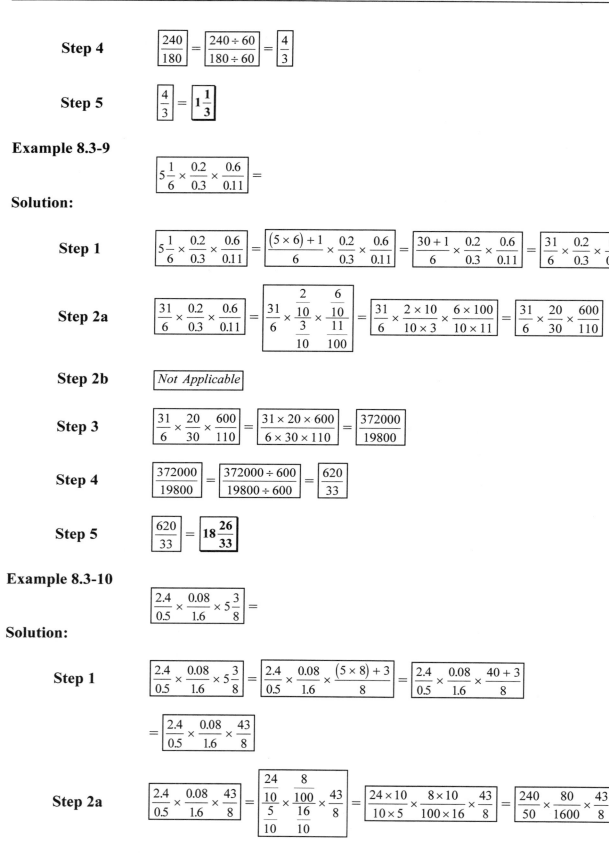

Step 4 $\boxed{\dfrac{240}{180}} = \boxed{\dfrac{240 \div 60}{180 \div 60}} = \boxed{\dfrac{4}{3}}$

Step 5 $\boxed{\dfrac{4}{3}} = \boxed{1\dfrac{1}{3}}$

Example 8.3-9

$\boxed{5\dfrac{1}{6} \times \dfrac{0.2}{0.3} \times \dfrac{0.6}{0.11}} =$

Solution:

Step 1 $\boxed{5\dfrac{1}{6} \times \dfrac{0.2}{0.3} \times \dfrac{0.6}{0.11}} = \boxed{\dfrac{(5 \times 6) + 1}{6} \times \dfrac{0.2}{0.3} \times \dfrac{0.6}{0.11}} = \boxed{\dfrac{30 + 1}{6} \times \dfrac{0.2}{0.3} \times \dfrac{0.6}{0.11}} = \boxed{\dfrac{31}{6} \times \dfrac{0.2}{0.3} \times \dfrac{0.6}{0.11}}$

Step 2a $\boxed{\dfrac{31}{6} \times \dfrac{0.2}{0.3} \times \dfrac{0.6}{0.11}} = \boxed{\dfrac{31}{6} \times \dfrac{\frac{2}{10}}{\frac{3}{10}} \times \dfrac{\frac{6}{10}}{\frac{11}{100}}} = \boxed{\dfrac{31}{6} \times \dfrac{2 \times 10}{10 \times 3} \times \dfrac{6 \times 100}{10 \times 11}} = \boxed{\dfrac{31}{6} \times \dfrac{20}{30} \times \dfrac{600}{110}}$

Step 2b $\boxed{\textit{Not Applicable}}$

Step 3 $\boxed{\dfrac{31}{6} \times \dfrac{20}{30} \times \dfrac{600}{110}} = \boxed{\dfrac{31 \times 20 \times 600}{6 \times 30 \times 110}} = \boxed{\dfrac{372000}{19800}}$

Step 4 $\boxed{\dfrac{372000}{19800}} = \boxed{\dfrac{372000 \div 600}{19800 \div 600}} = \boxed{\dfrac{620}{33}}$

Step 5 $\boxed{\dfrac{620}{33}} = \boxed{18\dfrac{26}{33}}$

Example 8.3-10

$\boxed{\dfrac{2.4}{0.5} \times \dfrac{0.08}{1.6} \times 5\dfrac{3}{8}} =$

Solution:

Step 1 $\boxed{\dfrac{2.4}{0.5} \times \dfrac{0.08}{1.6} \times 5\dfrac{3}{8}} = \boxed{\dfrac{2.4}{0.5} \times \dfrac{0.08}{1.6} \times \dfrac{(5 \times 8) + 3}{8}} = \boxed{\dfrac{2.4}{0.5} \times \dfrac{0.08}{1.6} \times \dfrac{40 + 3}{8}}$

$= \boxed{\dfrac{2.4}{0.5} \times \dfrac{0.08}{1.6} \times \dfrac{43}{8}}$

Step 2a $\boxed{\dfrac{2.4}{0.5} \times \dfrac{0.08}{1.6} \times \dfrac{43}{8}} = \boxed{\dfrac{\frac{24}{10}}{\frac{5}{10}} \times \dfrac{\frac{8}{100}}{\frac{16}{10}} \times \dfrac{43}{8}} = \boxed{\dfrac{24 \times 10}{10 \times 5} \times \dfrac{8 \times 10}{100 \times 16} \times \dfrac{43}{8}} = \boxed{\dfrac{240}{50} \times \dfrac{80}{1600} \times \dfrac{43}{8}}$

Step 2b $\boxed{Not\ Applicable}$

Step 3 $\boxed{\dfrac{240}{50} \times \dfrac{80}{1600} \times \dfrac{43}{8}} = \boxed{\dfrac{240 \times 80 \times 43}{50 \times 1600 \times 8}} = \boxed{\dfrac{825600}{640000}}$

Step 4 $\boxed{\dfrac{825600}{640000}} = \boxed{\dfrac{825600 \div 100}{640000 \div 100}} = \boxed{\dfrac{8256}{6400}} = \boxed{\dfrac{8256 \div 64}{6400 \div 64}} = \boxed{\dfrac{129}{100}}$

Step 5 $\boxed{\dfrac{129}{100}} = \boxed{1\dfrac{29}{100}}$

The following examples further illustrate how to multiply decimal and mixed fractions:

Example 8.3-11

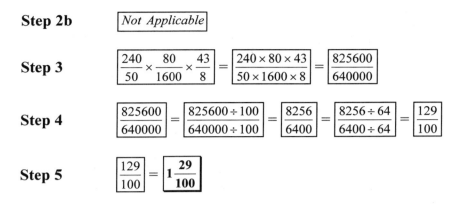

$$\boxed{2\frac{3}{12} \times \frac{1.25}{0.5}} = \boxed{\frac{(2\times12)+3}{12} \times \frac{\frac{125}{100}}{\frac{5}{10}}} = \boxed{\frac{24+3}{12} \times \frac{125\times10}{100\times5}} = \boxed{\frac{\overset{9}{27}}{\underset{4}{12}} \times \frac{\overset{5}{1250}}{\underset{2}{500}}} = \boxed{\frac{9}{4} \times \frac{5}{2}} = \boxed{\frac{9\times5}{4\times2}} = \boxed{\frac{45}{8}} = \boxed{5\frac{5}{8}}$$

Example 8.3-12

$$\boxed{\frac{0.125}{1.2} \times 3\frac{4}{5}} = \boxed{\frac{\frac{125}{1000}}{\frac{12}{10}} \times \frac{(3\times5)+4}{5}} = \boxed{\frac{125\times10}{1000\times12} \times \frac{15+4}{5}} = \boxed{\frac{\overset{5}{1250}}{\underset{48}{12000}} \times \frac{19}{5}} = \boxed{\frac{5}{48} \times \frac{19}{5}} = \boxed{\frac{\overset{1}{5}\times19}{48\times\underset{1}{5}}} = \boxed{\frac{1\times19}{48\times1}}$$

$$= \boxed{\frac{19}{48}}$$

Example 8.3-13

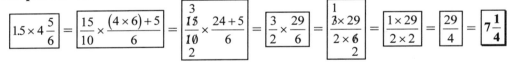

$$\boxed{1.5 \times 4\frac{5}{6}} = \boxed{\frac{15}{10} \times \frac{(4\times6)+5}{6}} = \boxed{\frac{\overset{3}{15}}{\underset{2}{10}} \times \frac{24+5}{6}} = \boxed{\frac{3}{2} \times \frac{29}{6}} = \boxed{\frac{\overset{1}{3}\times29}{2\times\underset{2}{6}}} = \boxed{\frac{1\times29}{2\times2}} = \boxed{\frac{29}{4}} = \boxed{7\frac{1}{4}}$$

Example 8.3-14

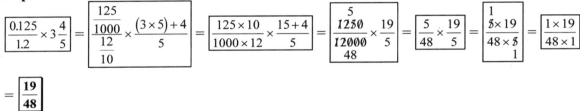

$$\boxed{12.5 \times 4\frac{5}{8} \times \frac{0.24}{0.6}} = \boxed{\frac{125}{10} \times \frac{(4\times8)+5}{8} \times \frac{\frac{24}{100}}{\frac{6}{10}}} = \boxed{\frac{\overset{25}{125}}{\underset{2}{10}} \times \frac{32+5}{8} \times \frac{24\times10}{100\times6}} = \boxed{\frac{25}{2} \times \frac{37}{8} \times \frac{\overset{2}{240}}{\underset{5}{600}}} = \boxed{\frac{25}{2} \times \frac{37}{8} \times \frac{2}{5}}$$

$$= \boxed{\frac{\overset{5}{25}\times37\times2}{2\times8\times\underset{1}{5}}} = \boxed{\frac{5\times37\times1}{1\times8\times1}} = \boxed{\frac{185}{8}} = \boxed{23\frac{1}{8}}$$

Example 8.3-15

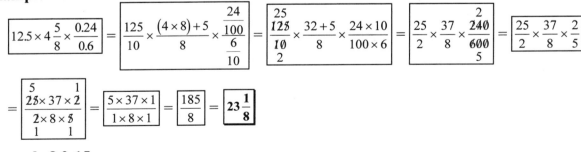

$$\boxed{\left(3\frac{1}{7} \times 4\frac{8}{12}\right) \times 0.15} = \boxed{\left(\frac{(3\times7)+1}{7} \times \frac{(4\times12)+8}{12}\right) \times \frac{15}{100}} = \boxed{\left(\frac{21+1}{7} \times \frac{48+8}{12}\right) \times \frac{\overset{3}{15}}{\underset{20}{100}}} = \boxed{\left(\frac{22}{7} \times \frac{\overset{14}{56}}{\underset{3}{12}}\right) \times \frac{3}{20}}$$

$$= \left[\left(\frac{22}{7} \times \frac{14}{3}\right) \times \frac{3}{20}\right] = \left[\left(\frac{22 \times \overset{2}{14}}{\underset{1}{7 \times 3}}\right) \times \frac{3}{20}\right] = \left[\left(\frac{22 \times 2}{1 \times 3}\right) \times \frac{3}{20}\right] = \left[\left(\frac{44}{3}\right) \times \frac{3}{20}\right] = \left[\frac{44}{3} \times \frac{3}{20}\right] = \left[\frac{\overset{11}{44} \times \overset{1}{3}}{\underset{1}{3} \times \underset{5}{20}}\right] = \left[\frac{11 \times 1}{1 \times 5}\right]$$

$$= \left[\frac{11}{5}\right] = \boxed{2\frac{1}{5}}$$

Example 8.3-16

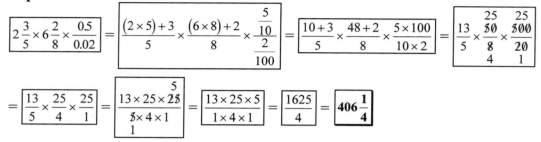

$$= \left[\frac{13}{5} \times \frac{25}{4} \times \frac{25}{1}\right] = \left[\frac{13 \times 25 \times \overset{5}{25}}{\underset{1}{5} \times 4 \times 1}\right] = \left[\frac{13 \times 25 \times 5}{1 \times 4 \times 1}\right] = \left[\frac{1625}{4}\right] = \boxed{406\frac{1}{4}}$$

Example 8.3-17

$$\left[4\frac{5}{6} \times \left(7\frac{1}{8} \times \frac{1.8}{0.04}\right)\right] = \left[\frac{(4 \times 6)+5}{6} \times \left(\frac{(7 \times 8)+1}{8} \times \frac{\frac{18}{10}}{\frac{4}{100}}\right)\right] = \left[\frac{24+5}{6} \times \left(\frac{56+1}{8} \times \frac{18 \times 100}{10 \times 4}\right)\right] = \left[\frac{29}{6} \times \left(\frac{57}{8} \times \frac{\overset{45}{1800}}{\underset{1}{40}}\right)\right]$$

$$= \left[\frac{29}{6} \times \left(\frac{57}{8} \times \frac{45}{1}\right)\right] = \left[\frac{29}{6} \times \left(\frac{57 \times 45}{8 \times 1}\right)\right] = \left[\frac{29}{6} \times \left(\frac{2565}{8}\right)\right] = \left[\frac{29}{6} \times \frac{2565}{8}\right] = \left[\frac{29 \times 2565}{6 \times 8}\right] = \left[\frac{74385}{48}\right] = \boxed{1549\frac{33}{48}}$$

Example 8.3-18

$$\left[\left(3\frac{4}{7} \times \frac{0.3}{1.4}\right) \times \left(\frac{0.2}{0.01} \times 2\frac{3}{5}\right)\right] = \left[\left(\frac{(3 \times 7)+4}{7} \times \frac{\frac{3}{10}}{\frac{14}{10}}\right) \times \left(\frac{\frac{2}{10}}{\frac{1}{100}} \times \frac{(2 \times 5)+3}{5}\right)\right]$$

$$= \left[\left(\frac{21+4}{7} \times \frac{3 \times 10}{10 \times 14}\right) \times \left(\frac{2 \times 100}{10 \times 1} \times \frac{10+3}{5}\right)\right] = \left[\left(\frac{25}{7} \times \frac{3}{\underset{14}{\overset{3}{140}}}\right) \times \left(\frac{\overset{20}{200}}{\underset{1}{10}} \times \frac{13}{5}\right)\right] = \left[\left(\frac{25}{7} \times \frac{3}{14}\right) \times \left(\frac{20}{1} \times \frac{13}{5}\right)\right]$$

$$= \left[\left(\frac{25 \times 3}{7 \times 14}\right) \times \left(\frac{\overset{4}{20} \times 13}{1 \times \underset{1}{5}}\right)\right] = \left[\left(\frac{25 \times 3}{7 \times 14}\right) \times \left(\frac{4 \times 13}{1 \times 1}\right)\right] = \left[\left(\frac{75}{98}\right) \times \left(\frac{52}{1}\right)\right] = \left[\frac{75}{98} \times \frac{52}{1}\right] = \left[\frac{75 \times 52}{98 \times 1}\right] = \left[\frac{\overset{1950}{3900}}{\underset{49}{98}}\right] = \left[\frac{1950}{49}\right]$$

$$= \boxed{39\frac{39}{49}}$$

Example 8.3-19

$$\left[3\frac{1}{8} \times \frac{1.26}{0.1} \times \frac{0.5}{0.15} \times 4\frac{2}{9}\right] = \left[\frac{(3 \times 8)+1}{8} \times \frac{\frac{126}{100}}{\frac{1}{10}} \times \frac{\frac{5}{10}}{\frac{15}{100}} \times \frac{(4 \times 9)+2}{9}\right] = \left[\frac{24+1}{8} \times \frac{126 \times 10}{100 \times 1} \times \frac{5 \times 100}{10 \times 15} \times \frac{36+2}{9}\right]$$

$$= \boxed{\dfrac{25}{8} \times \dfrac{\overset{63}{\cancel{1260}}}{100} \times \dfrac{\overset{10}{\cancel{300}}}{\underset{3}{\cancel{150}}} \times \dfrac{38}{9}} = \boxed{\dfrac{25}{8} \times \dfrac{63}{5} \times \dfrac{10}{3} \times \dfrac{38}{9}} = \boxed{\dfrac{25 \times \overset{21}{\cancel{63}} \times \overset{2}{\cancel{10}} \times \overset{19}{\cancel{38}}}{\underset{4}{\cancel{8}} \times \underset{1}{\cancel{5}} \times \underset{1}{\cancel{3}} \times 9}} = \boxed{\dfrac{25 \times 21 \times 2 \times 19}{\underset{2}{\cancel{4}} \times 1 \times 1 \times \underset{3}{\cancel{9}}}} = \boxed{\dfrac{25 \times 7 \times 1 \times 19}{2 \times 1 \times 1 \times 3}}$$

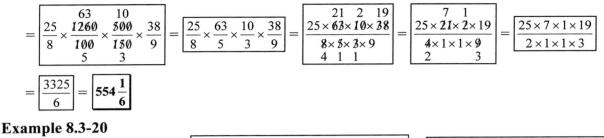

$$= \boxed{\dfrac{3325}{6}} = \boxed{\mathbf{554\dfrac{1}{6}}}$$

Example 8.3-20

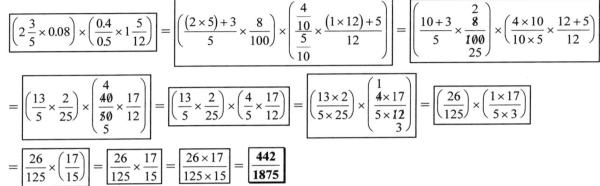

$$\boxed{\left(2\dfrac{3}{5} \times 0.08\right) \times \left(\dfrac{0.4}{0.5} \times 1\dfrac{5}{12}\right)} = \boxed{\left(\dfrac{(2\times5)+3}{5} \times \dfrac{8}{100}\right) \times \left(\dfrac{\frac{4}{\cancel{10}}}{\frac{5}{\cancel{10}}} \times \dfrac{(1\times12)+5}{12}\right)} = \boxed{\left(\dfrac{10+3}{5} \times \dfrac{\overset{2}{\cancel{8}}}{\underset{25}{\cancel{100}}}\right) \times \left(\dfrac{4\times10}{10\times5} \times \dfrac{12+5}{12}\right)}$$

$$= \boxed{\left(\dfrac{13}{5} \times \dfrac{2}{25}\right) \times \left(\dfrac{\overset{4}{\cancel{40}}}{\underset{5}{\cancel{50}}} \times \dfrac{17}{12}\right)} = \boxed{\left(\dfrac{13}{5} \times \dfrac{2}{25}\right) \times \left(\dfrac{4}{5} \times \dfrac{17}{12}\right)} = \boxed{\left(\dfrac{13\times2}{5\times25}\right) \times \left(\dfrac{\overset{1}{\cancel{4}}\times17}{5\times\underset{3}{\cancel{12}}}\right)} = \boxed{\left(\dfrac{26}{125}\right) \times \left(\dfrac{1\times17}{5\times3}\right)}$$

$$= \boxed{\dfrac{26}{125} \times \left(\dfrac{17}{15}\right)} = \boxed{\dfrac{26}{125} \times \dfrac{17}{15}} = \boxed{\dfrac{26\times17}{125\times15}} = \boxed{\mathbf{\dfrac{442}{1875}}}$$

Example 8.3-21

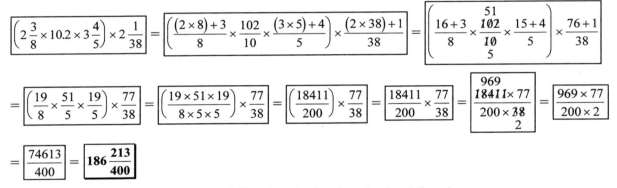

$$\boxed{\left(2\dfrac{3}{8} \times 10.2 \times 3\dfrac{4}{5}\right) \times 2\dfrac{1}{38}} = \boxed{\left(\dfrac{(2\times8)+3}{8} \times \dfrac{102}{10} \times \dfrac{(3\times5)+4}{5}\right) \times \dfrac{(2\times38)+1}{38}} = \boxed{\left(\dfrac{16+3}{8} \times \dfrac{\overset{51}{\cancel{102}}}{\underset{5}{\cancel{10}}} \times \dfrac{15+4}{5}\right) \times \dfrac{76+1}{38}}$$

$$= \boxed{\left(\dfrac{19}{8} \times \dfrac{51}{5} \times \dfrac{19}{5}\right) \times \dfrac{77}{38}} = \boxed{\left(\dfrac{19\times51\times19}{8\times5\times5}\right) \times \dfrac{77}{38}} = \boxed{\left(\dfrac{18411}{200}\right) \times \dfrac{77}{38}} = \boxed{\dfrac{18411}{200} \times \dfrac{77}{38}} = \boxed{\dfrac{\overset{969}{\cancel{18411}}\times77}{200\times\underset{2}{\cancel{38}}}} = \boxed{\dfrac{969\times77}{200\times2}}$$

$$= \boxed{\dfrac{74613}{400}} = \boxed{\mathbf{186\dfrac{213}{400}}}$$

Section 8.3 Exercises - Multiply the following decimal and mixed fractions:

1. $2\dfrac{1}{5} \times \dfrac{0.04}{0.8} =$

2. $\dfrac{0.22}{0.001} \times 2\dfrac{4}{5} =$

3. $3\dfrac{1}{8} \times 0.4 =$

4. $2\dfrac{3}{7} \times \left(\dfrac{0.6}{0.01} \times 3\dfrac{1}{5}\right) =$

5. $3\dfrac{5}{8} \times \dfrac{1.2}{0.05} \times 14.8 =$

6. $0.002 \times \left(2\dfrac{3}{5} \times \dfrac{0.8}{0.04}\right) =$

7. $2\dfrac{1}{3} \times \left(5\dfrac{6}{15} \times \dfrac{0.3}{0.15}\right) =$

8. $\left(3\dfrac{5}{7} \times \dfrac{1.8}{2.48}\right) \times \left(0.12 \times 3\dfrac{10}{12}\right) =$

9. $5\dfrac{2}{3} \times \dfrac{0.3}{12.8} \times 4\dfrac{9}{13} =$

10. $\left(2\dfrac{3}{8} \times \dfrac{0.1}{0.01}\right) \times \left(1\dfrac{2}{3} \times 1\dfrac{4}{5}\right) =$

8.4 Dividing Decimal and Mixed Fractions

Two or more decimal and mixed fractions of the forms:

1. $\left(\dfrac{a \times 10^{-k_1}}{b \times 10^{-k_2}}\right)$ where (a) and (b) are integer numbers and (k_1) and (k_2) are equal to the number of decimal places, and

2. $\left(k\dfrac{a}{b}\right)$ where (k) is made up of a whole number and $\left(\dfrac{a}{b}\right)$ is an integer fraction

are divided as in the following cases:

Case I Dividing Two Decimal and Mixed Fractions

Divide two decimal and mixed fractions using the following steps:

Step 1   Change the mixed fraction to an integer fraction (see Section 2.5).

Step 2   a. Change the decimal fraction to an integer fraction (see Section 2.4).

b. Change the decimal number $\left(a \times 10^{-k}\right)$ to an integer fraction of the form $\left(\dfrac{a}{10^k}\right)$,

e.g., change 28.5 to $\dfrac{285}{10}$.

Step 3   Divide the integer fractions (see Section 3.4, Case I).

Step 4   Simplify the fraction to its lowest term (see Section 2.3).

Step 5   Change the improper fraction to a mixed fraction if the fraction obtained from Step 4 is an improper fraction (see Section 2.2).

The following examples show the steps as to how two decimal and mixed fractions are divided:

Example 8.4-1

$$\boxed{4\dfrac{1}{3} \div \dfrac{0.6}{0.5}} =$$

Solution:

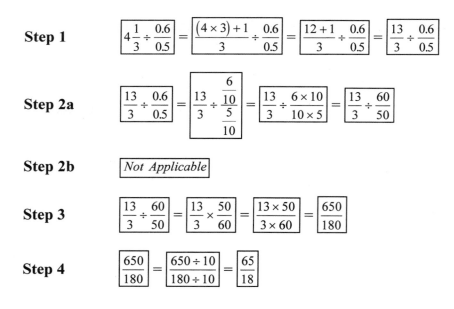

Step 5 $\dfrac{65}{18} = \boxed{3\dfrac{11}{18}}$

Example 8.4-2

$$\boxed{0.015 \div 3\dfrac{4}{5}} =$$

Solution:

Step 1 $\boxed{0.015 \div 3\dfrac{4}{5}} = \boxed{0.015 \div \dfrac{(3\times5)+4}{5}} = \boxed{0.015 \div \dfrac{15+4}{5}} = \boxed{0.015 \div \dfrac{19}{5}}$

Step 2a $\boxed{Not\ Applicable}$

Step 2b $\boxed{0.015 \div \dfrac{19}{5}} = \boxed{\dfrac{15}{1000} \div \dfrac{19}{5}}$

Step 3 $\boxed{\dfrac{15}{1000} \div \dfrac{19}{5}} = \boxed{\dfrac{15}{1000} \times \dfrac{5}{19}} = \boxed{\dfrac{15\times5}{1000\times19}} = \boxed{\dfrac{75}{19000}}$

Step 4 $\boxed{\dfrac{75}{19000}} = \boxed{\dfrac{75\div25}{19000\div25}} = \boxed{\dfrac{3}{760}}$

Step 5 $\boxed{Not\ Applicable}$

Example 8.4-3

$$\boxed{12\dfrac{2}{5} \div \dfrac{1.2}{0.08}} =$$

Solution:

Step 1 $\boxed{12\dfrac{2}{5} \div \dfrac{1.2}{0.08}} = \boxed{\dfrac{(12\times5)+2}{5} \div \dfrac{1.2}{0.08}} = \boxed{\dfrac{60+2}{5} \div \dfrac{1.2}{0.08}} = \boxed{\dfrac{62}{5} \div \dfrac{1.2}{0.08}}$

Step 2a $\boxed{\dfrac{62}{5} \div \dfrac{1.2}{0.08}} = \boxed{\dfrac{62}{5} \div \dfrac{\frac{12}{10}}{\frac{8}{100}}} = \boxed{\dfrac{62}{5} \div \dfrac{12\times100}{10\times8}} = \boxed{\dfrac{62}{5} \div \dfrac{1200}{80}}$

Step 2b $\boxed{Not\ Applicable}$

Step 3 $\boxed{\dfrac{62}{5} \div \dfrac{1200}{80}} = \boxed{\dfrac{62}{5} \times \dfrac{80}{1200}} = \boxed{\dfrac{62\times80}{5\times1200}} = \boxed{\dfrac{4960}{6000}}$

Step 4 $\boxed{\dfrac{4960}{6000}} = \boxed{\dfrac{4960\div80}{6000\div80}} = \boxed{\dfrac{62}{75}}$

Step 5 $\boxed{Not\ Applicable}$

Example 8.4-4

$$\boxed{18\frac{1}{3} \div 24.05} =$$

Solution:

Step 1 $\boxed{18\frac{1}{3} \div 24.05} = \boxed{\frac{(18 \times 3)+1}{3} \div 24.05} = \boxed{\frac{54+1}{3} \div 24.05} = \boxed{\frac{55}{3} \div 24.05}$

Step 2a $\boxed{Not\ Applicable}$

Step 2b $\boxed{\frac{55}{3} \div 24.05} = \boxed{\frac{55}{3} \div \frac{2405}{100}}$

Step 3 $\boxed{\frac{55}{3} \div \frac{2405}{100}} = \boxed{\frac{55}{3} \times \frac{100}{2405}} = \boxed{\frac{55 \times 100}{3 \times 2405}} = \boxed{\frac{5500}{7215}}$

Step 4 $\boxed{\frac{5500}{7215}} = \boxed{\frac{5500 \div 5}{7215 \div 5}} = \boxed{\mathbf{\frac{1100}{1443}}}$

Step 5 $\boxed{Not\ Applicable}$

Example 8.4-5

$$\boxed{5\frac{2}{3} \div \frac{1.08}{0.4}} =$$

Solution:

Step 1 $\boxed{5\frac{2}{3} \div \frac{1.08}{0.4}} = \boxed{\frac{(5 \times 3)+2}{3} \div \frac{1.08}{0.4}} = \boxed{\frac{15+2}{3} \div \frac{1.08}{0.4}} = \boxed{\frac{17}{3} \div \frac{1.08}{0.4}}$

Step 2a $\boxed{\frac{17}{3} \div \frac{1.08}{0.4}} = \boxed{\frac{17}{3} \div \frac{\frac{108}{100}}{\frac{4}{10}}} = \boxed{\frac{17}{3} \div \frac{108 \times 10}{100 \times 4}} = \boxed{\frac{17}{3} \div \frac{1080}{400}}$

Step 2b $\boxed{Not\ Applicable}$

Step 3 $\boxed{\frac{17}{3} \div \frac{1080}{400}} = \boxed{\frac{17}{3} \times \frac{400}{1080}} = \boxed{\frac{17 \times 400}{3 \times 1080}} = \boxed{\frac{6800}{3240}}$

Step 4 $\boxed{\frac{6800}{3240}} = \boxed{\frac{6800 \div 40}{3240 \div 40}} = \boxed{\frac{170}{81}}$

Step 5 $\boxed{\dfrac{170}{81}} = \boxed{2\dfrac{8}{81}}$

Case II   Dividing Three Decimal and Mixed Fractions

Divide three decimal and mixed fractions using the following steps:

Step 1   Change the mixed fraction(s) to integer fraction(s) (see Section 2.5).

Step 2   a. Change the decimal fraction(s) to integer fraction(s) (see Section 2.4).

b. Change the decimal number $\left(a \times 10^{-k}\right)$ to an integer fraction of the form $\left(\dfrac{a}{10^k}\right)$,

e.g., change 12.38 to $\dfrac{1238}{100}$.

Step 3   Divide the integer fractions (see Section 3.4, Case II).

Step 4   Simplify the fraction to its lowest term (see Section 2.3).

Step 5   Change the improper fraction to a mixed fraction if the fraction obtained from Step 4 is an improper fraction (see Section 2.2).

The following examples show the steps as to how three decimal and mixed fractions are divided:

Example 8.4-6

$$\boxed{\left(3\dfrac{1}{5} \div 0.6\right) \div 4\dfrac{1}{8}} =$$

Solution:

Step 1 $\boxed{\left(3\dfrac{1}{5} \div 0.6\right) \div 4\dfrac{1}{8}} = \boxed{\left(\dfrac{(3\times 5)+1}{5} \div 0.6\right) \div \dfrac{(4\times 8)+1}{8}} = \boxed{\left(\dfrac{15+1}{5} \div 0.6\right) \div \dfrac{32+1}{8}}$

$= \boxed{\left(\dfrac{16}{5} \div 0.6\right) \div \dfrac{33}{8}}$

Step 2a $\boxed{\textit{Not Applicable}}$

Step 2b $\boxed{\left(\dfrac{16}{5} \div 0.6\right) \div \dfrac{33}{8}} = \boxed{\left(\dfrac{16}{5} \div \dfrac{6}{10}\right) \div \dfrac{33}{8}}$

Step 3 $\boxed{\left(\dfrac{16}{5} \div \dfrac{6}{10}\right) \div \dfrac{33}{8}} = \boxed{\left(\dfrac{16}{5} \times \dfrac{10}{6}\right) \div \dfrac{33}{8}} = \boxed{\left(\dfrac{16 \times 10}{5 \times 6}\right) \div \dfrac{33}{8}} = \boxed{\left(\dfrac{16 \times 10}{5 \times 6}\right) \div \dfrac{33}{8}}$

$= \boxed{\dfrac{160}{30} \div \dfrac{33}{8}} = \boxed{\dfrac{160}{30} \times \dfrac{8}{33}} = \boxed{\dfrac{160 \times 8}{30 \times 33}} = \boxed{\dfrac{1280}{990}}$

Step 4 $\boxed{\dfrac{1280}{990}} = \boxed{\dfrac{1280 \div 10}{990 \div 10}} = \boxed{\dfrac{128}{99}}$

Step 5
$$\frac{128}{99} = \boxed{1\frac{29}{99}}$$

Example 8.4-7

$$\boxed{\left(\frac{0.6}{0.4} \div 0.5\right) \div 1\frac{3}{4}} =$$

Solution:

Step 1
$$\boxed{\left(\frac{0.6}{0.4} \div 0.5\right) \div 1\frac{3}{4}} = \boxed{\left(\frac{0.6}{0.4} \div 0.5\right) \div \frac{(1\times 4)+3}{4}} = \boxed{\left(\frac{0.6}{0.4} \div 0.5\right) \div \frac{4+3}{4}} = \boxed{\left(\frac{0.6}{0.4} \div 0.5\right) \div \frac{7}{4}}$$

Step 2a
$$\boxed{\left(\frac{0.6}{0.4} \div 0.5\right) \div \frac{7}{4}} = \boxed{\left(\frac{\frac{6}{10}}{\frac{4}{10}} \div 0.5\right) \div \frac{7}{4}} = \boxed{\left(\frac{6\times 10}{10\times 4} \div 0.5\right) \div \frac{7}{4}} = \boxed{\left(\frac{60}{40} \div 0.5\right) \div \frac{7}{4}}$$

Step 2b
$$\boxed{\left(\frac{60}{40} \div 0.5\right) \div \frac{7}{4}} = \boxed{\left(\frac{60}{40} \div \frac{5}{10}\right) \div \frac{7}{4}}$$

Step 3
$$\boxed{\left(\frac{60}{40} \div \frac{5}{10}\right) \div \frac{7}{4}} = \boxed{\left(\frac{60}{40} \times \frac{10}{5}\right) \div \frac{7}{4}} = \boxed{\left(\frac{60\times 10}{40\times 5}\right) \div \frac{7}{4}} = \boxed{\left(\frac{600}{200}\right) \div \frac{7}{4}} = \boxed{\frac{600}{200} \div \frac{7}{4}}$$

$$= \boxed{\frac{600}{200} \times \frac{4}{7}} = \boxed{\frac{600\times 4}{200\times 7}} = \boxed{\frac{2400}{1400}}$$

Step 4
$$\boxed{\frac{2400}{1400}} = \boxed{\frac{2400\div 200}{1400\div 200}} = \boxed{\frac{12}{7}}$$

Step 5
$$\boxed{\frac{12}{7}} = \boxed{1\frac{5}{7}}$$

Example 8.4-8

$$\boxed{\frac{0.2}{0.05} \div \left(3\frac{1}{5} \div 0.2\right)} =$$

Solution:

Step 1
$$\boxed{\frac{0.2}{0.05} \div \left(3\frac{1}{5} \div 0.2\right)} = \boxed{\frac{0.2}{0.05} \div \left(\frac{(3\times 5)+1}{5} \div 0.2\right)} = \boxed{\frac{0.2}{0.05} \div \left(\frac{15+1}{5} \div 0.2\right)}$$

$$= \boxed{\frac{0.2}{0.05} \div \left(\frac{16}{5} \div 0.2\right)}$$

Step 2a

$$\frac{0.2}{0.05} \div \left(\frac{16}{5} \div 0.2\right) = \frac{\frac{2}{10}}{\frac{5}{100}} \div \left(\frac{16}{5} \div 0.2\right) = \frac{2 \times 100}{10 \times 5} \div \left(\frac{16}{5} \div 0.2\right) = \frac{200}{50} \div \left(\frac{16}{5} \div 0.2\right)$$

Step 2b

$$\frac{200}{50} \div \left(\frac{16}{5} \div 0.2\right) = \frac{200}{50} \div \left(\frac{16}{5} \div \frac{2}{10}\right)$$

Step 3

$$\frac{200}{50} \div \left(\frac{16}{5} \div \frac{2}{10}\right) = \frac{200}{50} \div \left(\frac{16}{5} \times \frac{10}{2}\right) = \frac{200}{50} \div \left(\frac{16 \times 10}{5 \times 2}\right) = \frac{200}{50} \div \left(\frac{160}{10}\right)$$

$$= \frac{200}{50} \div \frac{160}{10} = \frac{200}{50} \times \frac{10}{160} = \frac{200 \times 10}{50 \times 160} = \frac{2000}{8000}$$

Step 4

$$\frac{2000}{8000} = \frac{2000 \div 2000}{8000 \div 2000} = \boxed{\frac{1}{4}}$$

Step 5

$\boxed{Not\ Applicable}$

Example 8.4-9

$$\left(0.6 \div 1\frac{2}{3}\right) \div \frac{0.3}{0.01} =$$

Solution:

Step 1

$$\left(0.6 \div 1\frac{2}{3}\right) \div \frac{0.3}{0.01} = \left(0.6 \div \frac{(1 \times 3) + 2}{3}\right) \div \frac{0.3}{0.01} = \left(0.6 \div \frac{3 + 2}{3}\right) \div \frac{0.3}{0.01}$$

$$= \left(0.6 \div \frac{5}{3}\right) \div \frac{0.3}{0.01}$$

Step 2a

$$\left(0.6 \div \frac{5}{3}\right) \div \frac{0.3}{0.01} = \left(0.6 \div \frac{5}{3}\right) \div \frac{\frac{3}{10}}{\frac{1}{100}} = \left(0.6 \div \frac{5}{3}\right) \div \frac{3 \times 100}{10 \times 1} = \left(0.6 \div \frac{5}{3}\right) \div \frac{300}{10}$$

Step 2b

$$\left(0.6 \div \frac{5}{3}\right) \div \frac{300}{10} = \left(\frac{6}{10} \div \frac{5}{3}\right) \div \frac{300}{10}$$

Step 3

$$\left(\frac{6}{10} \div \frac{5}{3}\right) \div \frac{300}{10} = \left(\frac{6}{10} \times \frac{3}{5}\right) \div \frac{300}{10} = \left(\frac{6 \times 3}{10 \times 5}\right) \div \frac{300}{10} = \left(\frac{18}{50}\right) \div \frac{300}{10} = \frac{18}{50} \div \frac{300}{10}$$

$$= \frac{18}{50} \times \frac{10}{300} = \frac{18 \times 10}{50 \times 300} = \frac{180}{15000}$$

Step 4 $\dfrac{180}{15000} = \dfrac{180 \div 20}{15000 \div 20} = \dfrac{9}{750} = \dfrac{9 \div 3}{750 \div 3} = \boxed{\dfrac{3}{250}}$

Step 5 $\boxed{Not\ Applicable}$

Example 8.4-10

$$\boxed{4\frac{2}{5} \div \left(\frac{0.01}{12.4} \div 0.3\right) =}$$

Solution:

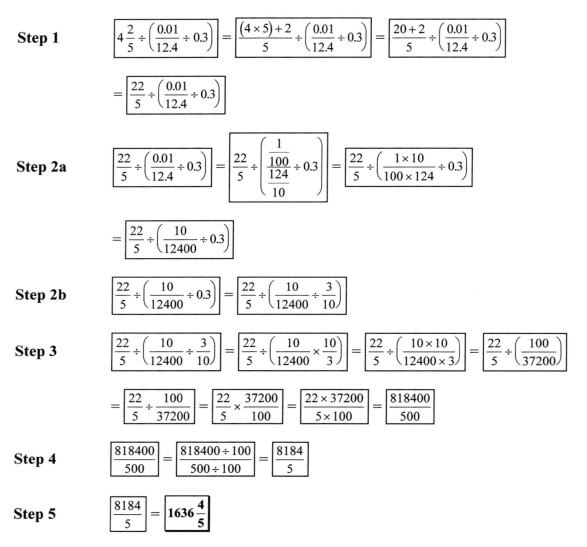

Step 1 $\boxed{4\dfrac{2}{5} \div \left(\dfrac{0.01}{12.4} \div 0.3\right)} = \boxed{\dfrac{(4\times 5)+2}{5} \div \left(\dfrac{0.01}{12.4} \div 0.3\right)} = \boxed{\dfrac{20+2}{5} \div \left(\dfrac{0.01}{12.4} \div 0.3\right)}$

$= \boxed{\dfrac{22}{5} \div \left(\dfrac{0.01}{12.4} \div 0.3\right)}$

Step 2a $\boxed{\dfrac{22}{5} \div \left(\dfrac{0.01}{12.4} \div 0.3\right)} = \boxed{\dfrac{22}{5} \div \left(\dfrac{\frac{1}{100}}{\frac{124}{10}} \div 0.3\right)} = \boxed{\dfrac{22}{5} \div \left(\dfrac{1\times 10}{100\times 124} \div 0.3\right)}$

$= \boxed{\dfrac{22}{5} \div \left(\dfrac{10}{12400} \div 0.3\right)}$

Step 2b $\boxed{\dfrac{22}{5} \div \left(\dfrac{10}{12400} \div 0.3\right)} = \boxed{\dfrac{22}{5} \div \left(\dfrac{10}{12400} \div \dfrac{3}{10}\right)}$

Step 3 $\boxed{\dfrac{22}{5} \div \left(\dfrac{10}{12400} \div \dfrac{3}{10}\right)} = \boxed{\dfrac{22}{5} \div \left(\dfrac{10}{12400} \times \dfrac{10}{3}\right)} = \boxed{\dfrac{22}{5} \div \left(\dfrac{10\times 10}{12400\times 3}\right)} = \boxed{\dfrac{22}{5} \div \left(\dfrac{100}{37200}\right)}$

$= \boxed{\dfrac{22}{5} \div \dfrac{100}{37200}} = \boxed{\dfrac{22}{5} \times \dfrac{37200}{100}} = \boxed{\dfrac{22\times 37200}{5\times 100}} = \boxed{\dfrac{818400}{500}}$

Step 4 $\boxed{\dfrac{818400}{500}} = \boxed{\dfrac{818400 \div 100}{500 \div 100}} = \boxed{\dfrac{8184}{5}}$

Step 5 $\boxed{\dfrac{8184}{5}} = \boxed{1636\dfrac{4}{5}}$

The following examples further illustrate how to divide decimal and mixed fractions:

Example 8.4-11

$$2\frac{3}{8} \div \frac{0.05}{0.3} = \frac{(2 \times 8) + 3}{8} \div \frac{\frac{5}{100}}{\frac{3}{10}} = \frac{16 + 3}{8} \div \frac{5 \times 10}{100 \times 3} = \frac{19}{8} \div \frac{\overset{1}{\cancel{50}}}{\underset{6}{\cancel{300}}} = \frac{19}{8} \div \frac{1}{6} = \frac{19}{8} \times \frac{6}{1} = \frac{19 \times \overset{3}{\cancel{6}}}{\underset{4}{\cancel{8}} \times 1} = \frac{19 \times 3}{4 \times 1}$$

$$= \frac{57}{4} = \boxed{14\frac{1}{4}}$$

Example 8.4-12

$$1\frac{2}{3} \div 24.6 = \frac{(1 \times 3) + 2}{3} \div \frac{246}{10} = \frac{3 + 2}{3} \div \frac{\overset{123}{\cancel{246}}}{\underset{5}{\cancel{10}}} = \frac{5}{3} \div \frac{123}{5} = \frac{5}{3} \times \frac{5}{123} = \frac{5 \times 5}{3 \times 123} = \boxed{\frac{25}{369}}$$

Example 8.4-13

$$0.25 \div 5\frac{1}{6} = \frac{25}{100} \div \frac{(5 \times 6) + 1}{6} = \frac{\overset{1}{\cancel{25}}}{\underset{4}{\cancel{100}}} \div \frac{30 + 1}{6} = \frac{1}{4} \div \frac{31}{6} = \frac{1}{4} \times \frac{6}{31} = \frac{1 \times \overset{3}{\cancel{6}}}{4 \times 31} = \frac{1 \times 3}{2 \times 31} = \boxed{\frac{3}{62}}$$

Example 8.4-14

$$\frac{0.01}{0.6} \div 12\frac{2}{5} = \frac{\frac{1}{100}}{\frac{6}{10}} \div \frac{(12 \times 5) + 2}{5} = \frac{1 \times 10}{100 \times 6} \div \frac{60 + 2}{5} = \frac{\overset{1}{\cancel{10}}}{\underset{60}{\cancel{600}}} \div \frac{62}{5} = \frac{1}{60} \div \frac{62}{5} = \frac{1}{60} \times \frac{5}{62} = \frac{1 \times \overset{1}{\cancel{5}}}{\underset{12}{\cancel{60}} \times 62}$$

$$= \frac{1 \times 1}{12 \times 62} = \boxed{\frac{1}{744}}$$

Example 8.4-15

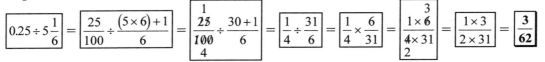

$$\frac{0.3}{0.12} \div \left(\frac{0.2}{1.2} \div 3\frac{2}{7} \right) = \frac{\frac{3}{10}}{\frac{12}{100}} \div \left(\frac{\frac{2}{10}}{\frac{12}{10}} \div \frac{(3 \times 7) + 2}{7} \right) = \frac{3 \times 100}{10 \times 12} \div \left(\frac{2 \times 10}{10 \times 12} \div \frac{21 + 2}{7} \right) = \frac{\overset{5}{\cancel{300}}}{\underset{2}{\cancel{120}}} \div \left(\frac{\overset{1}{\cancel{20}}}{\underset{6}{\cancel{120}}} \div \frac{23}{7} \right)$$

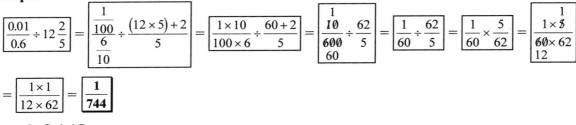

$$= \frac{5}{2} \div \left(\frac{1}{6} \div \frac{23}{7} \right) = \frac{5}{2} \div \left(\frac{1}{6} \times \frac{7}{23} \right) = \frac{5}{2} \div \left(\frac{1 \times 7}{6 \times 23} \right) = \frac{5}{2} \div \left(\frac{7}{138} \right) = \frac{5}{2} \div \frac{7}{138} = \frac{5}{2} \times \frac{138}{7} = \frac{5 \times \overset{69}{\cancel{138}}}{\underset{1}{\cancel{2}} \times 7}$$

$$= \frac{5 \times 69}{1 \times 7} = \frac{345}{7} = \boxed{49\frac{2}{7}}$$

Example 8.4-16

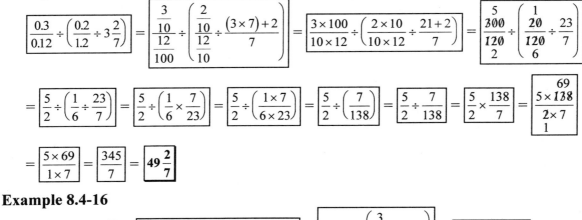

$$3\frac{5}{8} \div \left(0.6 \div 2\frac{1}{3} \right) = \frac{(3 \times 8) + 5}{8} \div \left(\frac{6}{10} \div \frac{(2 \times 3) + 1}{3} \right) = \frac{24 + 5}{8} \div \left(\frac{\overset{3}{\cancel{6}}}{\underset{5}{\cancel{10}}} \div \frac{6 + 1}{3} \right) = \frac{29}{8} \div \left(\frac{3}{5} \div \frac{7}{3} \right)$$

$$= \boxed{\frac{29}{8} \div \left(\frac{3}{5} \times \frac{3}{7}\right)} = \boxed{\frac{29}{8} \div \left(\frac{3 \times 3}{5 \times 7}\right)} = \boxed{\frac{29}{8} \div \left(\frac{9}{35}\right)} = \boxed{\frac{29}{8} \div \frac{9}{35}} = \boxed{\frac{29}{8} \times \frac{35}{9}} = \boxed{\frac{29 \times 35}{8 \times 9}} = \boxed{\frac{1015}{72}} = \boxed{\mathbf{14\frac{7}{72}}}$$

Example 8.4-17

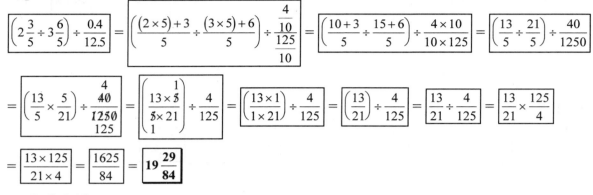

$$= \boxed{\frac{13 \times 125}{21 \times 4}} = \boxed{\frac{1625}{84}} = \boxed{\mathbf{19\frac{29}{84}}}$$

Example 8.4-18

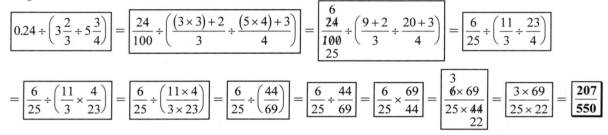

Example 8.4-19

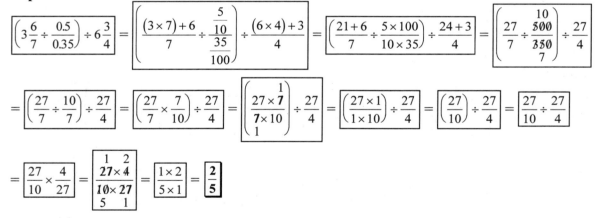

Example 8.4-20

$$\boxed{\left(3\frac{4}{5} \div 0.8\right) \div \left(2\frac{1}{3} \div \frac{0.02}{0.1}\right)} = \boxed{\left(\frac{(3 \times 5) + 4}{5} \div \frac{8}{10}\right) \div \left(\frac{(2 \times 3) + 1}{3} \div \frac{\frac{2}{100}}{\frac{1}{10}}\right)} = \boxed{\left(\frac{15 + 4}{5} \div \frac{\overset{4}{\cancel{8}}}{\underset{5}{\cancel{10}}}\right) \div \left(\frac{6 + 1}{3} \div \frac{2 \times 10}{100 \times 1}\right)}$$

$$= \boxed{\left(\frac{19}{5} \div \frac{4}{5}\right) \div \left(\frac{7}{3} \div \frac{\overset{1}{\cancel{20}}}{\underset{5}{\cancel{100}}}\right)} = \boxed{\left(\frac{19}{5} \div \frac{4}{5}\right) \div \left(\frac{7}{3} \div \frac{1}{5}\right)} = \boxed{\left(\frac{19}{5} \times \frac{5}{4}\right) \div \left(\frac{7}{3} \times \frac{5}{1}\right)} = \boxed{\left(\frac{19 \times \overset{1}{\cancel{5}}}{\underset{1}{\cancel{5}} \times 4}\right) \div \left(\frac{7 \times 5}{3 \times 1}\right)}$$

$$= \left[\left(\frac{19 \times 1}{1 \times 4}\right) \div \left(\frac{35}{3}\right)\right] = \left[\left(\frac{19}{4}\right) \div \frac{35}{3}\right] = \left[\frac{19}{4} \div \frac{35}{3}\right] = \left[\frac{19}{4} \times \frac{3}{35}\right] = \left[\frac{19 \times 3}{4 \times 35}\right] = \boxed{\mathbf{\frac{57}{140}}}$$

Example 8.4-21

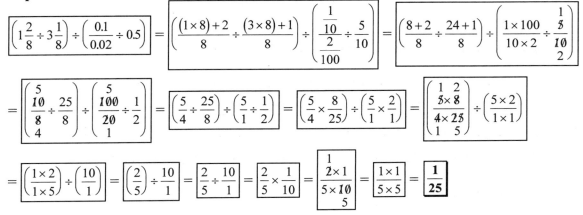

Section 8.4 Exercises - Divide the following decimal and mixed fractions:

1. $1\frac{3}{4} \div \frac{0.4}{1.2} =$

2. $0.4 \div 2\frac{3}{8} =$

3. $\left(\frac{0.05}{0.1} \div 2\frac{5}{8}\right) \div 0.6 =$

4. $\left(1\frac{3}{8} \div 2\frac{6}{8}\right) \div \frac{0.2}{0.3} =$

5. $\left(\frac{0.1}{0.04} \div 3\frac{1}{2}\right) \div 5\frac{2}{3} =$

6. $\left(2\frac{5}{6} \div 0.3\right) \div 1\frac{2}{9} =$

7. $\left(\frac{0.8}{2.4} \div 0.04\right) \div 2\frac{4}{5} =$

8. $\left(0.04 \div 3\frac{1}{10}\right) \div 3\frac{1}{5} =$

9. $0.2 \div \left(3\frac{1}{8} \div 2\frac{1}{4}\right) =$

10. $\left(3\frac{1}{5} \div 4\frac{4}{5}\right) \div \left(0.02 \div \frac{0.12}{0.4}\right) =$

8.5   Solving Mixed Operations Using Decimal and Mixed Fractions

Decimal and mixed fractions of the forms:

1. $\left(\dfrac{a \times 10^{-k_1}}{b \times 10^{-k_2}}\right)$ where (a) and (b) are integer numbers and (k_1) and (k_2) are equal to the number

   of decimal places, and

2. $\left(k\dfrac{a}{b}\right)$ where (k) is made up of a whole number and $\left(\dfrac{a}{b}\right)$ is an integer fraction

are added, subtracted, multiplied, and divided by using the following steps:

Step 1   Change the mixed fraction(s) to integer fraction(s) (see Section 2.5).

Step 2   a. Change the decimal fraction(s) to integer fraction(s) (see Section 2.4).

   b. Change the decimal number $\left(a \times 10^{-k}\right)$ to integer fraction of the form $\left(\dfrac{a}{10^k}\right)$,

   e.g., change 0.06 to $\dfrac{6}{100}$.

Step 3   Add, subtract, multiply, and divide the integer fractions by following the steps outlined in sections 3.1 through 3.4.

Step 4   Simplify the fraction to its lowest term (see Sections 2.3).

Step 5   Change the improper fraction to a mixed fraction if the fraction obtained from Step 4 is an improper fraction (see Section 2.2).

The following examples show mathematical operations on decimal and mixed fractions using the above steps:

Example 8.5-1

$$\left[\left(0.2 \div 2\frac{1}{5}\right) + 1\frac{2}{3}\right] =$$

Solution:

Step 1 $\left[\left(0.2 \div 2\frac{1}{5}\right) + 1\frac{2}{3}\right] = \left[\left(0.2 \div \frac{(2 \times 5) + 1}{5}\right) + \frac{(1 \times 3) + 2}{3}\right] = \left[\left(0.2 \div \frac{10 + 1}{5}\right) + \frac{3 + 2}{3}\right]$

$= \left[\left(0.2 \div \frac{11}{5}\right) + \frac{5}{3}\right]$

Step 2a $\boxed{Not\ Applicable}$

Step 2b $\left[\left(0.2 \div \frac{11}{5}\right) + \frac{5}{3}\right] = \left[\left(\frac{2}{10} \div \frac{11}{5}\right) + \frac{5}{3}\right]$

Step 3 $\left[\left(\frac{2}{10} \div \frac{11}{5}\right) + \frac{5}{3}\right] = \left[\left(\frac{2}{10} \times \frac{5}{11}\right) + \frac{5}{3}\right] = \left[\left(\frac{2 \times 5}{10 \times 11}\right) + \frac{5}{3}\right] = \left[\left(\frac{10}{110}\right) + \frac{5}{3}\right] = \left[\frac{10}{110} + \frac{5}{3}\right]$

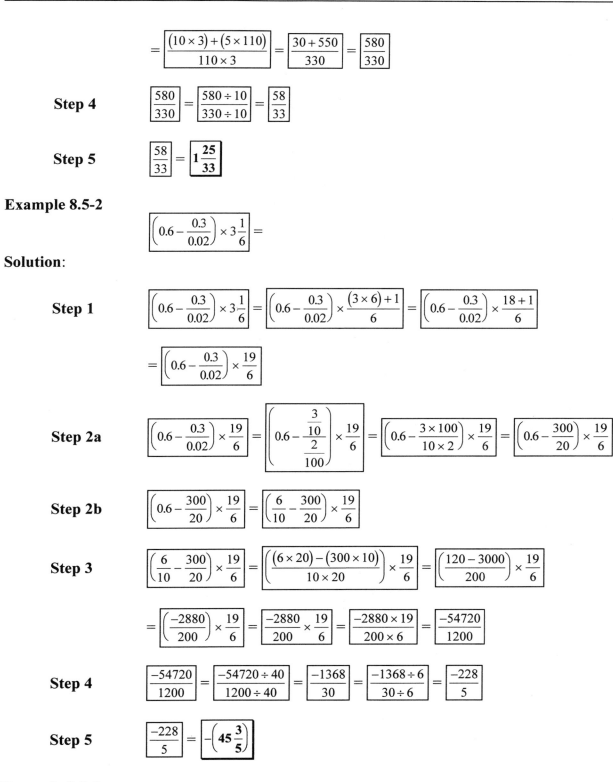

$$= \boxed{\frac{(10 \times 3) + (5 \times 110)}{110 \times 3}} = \boxed{\frac{30 + 550}{330}} = \boxed{\frac{580}{330}}$$

Step 4 $\quad \boxed{\frac{580}{330}} = \boxed{\frac{580 \div 10}{330 \div 10}} = \boxed{\frac{58}{33}}$

Step 5 $\quad \boxed{\frac{58}{33}} = \boxed{1\frac{25}{33}}$

Example 8.5-2

$$\boxed{\left(0.6 - \frac{0.3}{0.02}\right) \times 3\frac{1}{6}} =$$

Solution:

Step 1 $\quad \boxed{\left(0.6 - \frac{0.3}{0.02}\right) \times 3\frac{1}{6}} = \boxed{\left(0.6 - \frac{0.3}{0.02}\right) \times \frac{(3 \times 6) + 1}{6}} = \boxed{\left(0.6 - \frac{0.3}{0.02}\right) \times \frac{18 + 1}{6}}$

$$= \boxed{\left(0.6 - \frac{0.3}{0.02}\right) \times \frac{19}{6}}$$

Step 2a $\quad \boxed{\left(0.6 - \frac{0.3}{0.02}\right) \times \frac{19}{6}} = \boxed{\left(0.6 - \frac{\frac{3}{10}}{\frac{2}{100}}\right) \times \frac{19}{6}} = \boxed{\left(0.6 - \frac{3 \times 100}{10 \times 2}\right) \times \frac{19}{6}} = \boxed{\left(0.6 - \frac{300}{20}\right) \times \frac{19}{6}}$

Step 2b $\quad \boxed{\left(0.6 - \frac{300}{20}\right) \times \frac{19}{6}} = \boxed{\left(\frac{6}{10} - \frac{300}{20}\right) \times \frac{19}{6}}$

Step 3 $\quad \boxed{\left(\frac{6}{10} - \frac{300}{20}\right) \times \frac{19}{6}} = \boxed{\left(\frac{(6 \times 20) - (300 \times 10)}{10 \times 20}\right) \times \frac{19}{6}} = \boxed{\left(\frac{120 - 3000}{200}\right) \times \frac{19}{6}}$

$$= \boxed{\left(\frac{-2880}{200}\right) \times \frac{19}{6}} = \boxed{\frac{-2880}{200} \times \frac{19}{6}} = \boxed{\frac{-2880 \times 19}{200 \times 6}} = \boxed{\frac{-54720}{1200}}$$

Step 4 $\quad \boxed{\frac{-54720}{1200}} = \boxed{\frac{-54720 \div 40}{1200 \div 40}} = \boxed{\frac{-1368}{30}} = \boxed{\frac{-1368 \div 6}{30 \div 6}} = \boxed{\frac{-228}{5}}$

Step 5 $\quad \boxed{\frac{-228}{5}} = \boxed{-\left(45\frac{3}{5}\right)}$

Example 8.5-3

$$\boxed{\left(1.4 + \frac{0.2}{0.5}\right) - 2\frac{3}{5}} =$$

Solution:

Step 1
$$\boxed{\left(1.4+\frac{0.2}{0.5}\right)-2\frac{3}{5}}=\boxed{\left(1.4+\frac{0.2}{0.5}\right)-\frac{(2\times5)+3}{5}}=\boxed{\left(1.4+\frac{0.2}{0.5}\right)-\frac{10+3}{5}}=\boxed{\left(1.4+\frac{0.2}{0.5}\right)-\frac{13}{5}}$$

Step 2a
$$\boxed{\left(1.4+\frac{0.2}{0.5}\right)-\frac{13}{5}}=\boxed{\left(1.4+\frac{\frac{2}{10}}{\frac{5}{10}}\right)-\frac{13}{5}}=\boxed{\left(1.4+\frac{2\times10}{10\times5}\right)-\frac{13}{5}}=\boxed{\left(1.4+\frac{20}{50}\right)-\frac{13}{5}}$$

Step 2b
$$\boxed{\left(1.4+\frac{20}{50}\right)-\frac{13}{5}}=\boxed{\left(\frac{14}{10}+\frac{20}{50}\right)-\frac{13}{5}}$$

Step 3
$$\boxed{\left(\frac{14}{10}+\frac{20}{50}\right)-\frac{13}{5}}=\boxed{\left(\frac{(14\times50)+(20\times10)}{10\times50}\right)-\frac{13}{5}}=\boxed{\left(\frac{700+200}{500}\right)-\frac{13}{5}}=\boxed{\left(\frac{900}{500}\right)-\frac{13}{5}}$$

$$=\boxed{\frac{900}{500}-\frac{13}{5}}=\boxed{\frac{(900\times5)-(13\times500)}{500\times5}}=\boxed{\frac{4500-6500}{2500}}=\boxed{\frac{-2000}{2500}}$$

Step 4
$$\boxed{\frac{-2000}{2500}}=\boxed{\frac{-2000\div500}{2500\div500}}=\boxed{-\frac{4}{5}}$$

Step 5
$$\boxed{\textit{Not Applicable}}$$

Example 8.5-4
$$\boxed{\left(\frac{0.3}{0.12}\times2\frac{3}{6}\right)+1\frac{3}{5}}=$$

Solution:

Step 1
$$\boxed{\left(\frac{0.3}{0.12}\times2\frac{3}{6}\right)+1\frac{3}{5}}=\boxed{\left(\frac{0.3}{0.12}\times\frac{(2\times6)+3}{6}\right)+\frac{(1\times5)+3}{5}}=\boxed{\left(\frac{0.3}{0.12}\times\frac{12+3}{6}\right)+\frac{5+3}{5}}$$

$$=\boxed{\left(\frac{0.3}{0.12}\times\frac{15}{6}\right)+\frac{8}{5}}$$

Step 2a
$$\boxed{\left(\frac{0.3}{0.12}\times\frac{15}{6}\right)+\frac{8}{5}}=\boxed{\left(\frac{\frac{3}{10}}{\frac{12}{100}}\times\frac{15}{6}\right)+\frac{8}{5}}=\boxed{\left(\frac{3\times100}{10\times12}\times\frac{15}{6}\right)+\frac{8}{5}}=\boxed{\left(\frac{300}{120}\times\frac{15}{6}\right)+\frac{8}{5}}$$

Step 2b
$$\boxed{\textit{Not Applicable}}$$

Step 3

$$\left[\left(\frac{300}{120} \times \frac{15}{6}\right) + \frac{8}{5}\right] = \left[\left(\frac{300 \times 15}{120 \times 6}\right) + \frac{8}{5}\right] = \left[\left(\frac{4500}{720}\right) + \frac{8}{5}\right] = \left[\frac{4500}{720} + \frac{8}{5}\right]$$

$$= \left[\frac{(4500 \times 5) + (8 \times 720)}{720 \times 5}\right] = \left[\frac{22500 + 5760}{3600}\right] = \left[\frac{28260}{3600}\right]$$

Step 4

$$\left[\frac{28260}{3600}\right] = \left[\frac{28260 \div 60}{3600 \div 60}\right] = \left[\frac{471}{60}\right] = \left[\frac{471 \div 3}{60 \div 3}\right] = \left[\frac{157}{20}\right]$$

Step 5

$$\left[\frac{157}{20}\right] = \boxed{7\frac{17}{20}}$$

Example 8.5-5

$$\left[\left(0.5 \div \frac{0.2}{0.3}\right) - \left(2\frac{3}{5} \times 0.8\right)\right] =$$

Solution:

Step 1

$$\left[\left(0.5 \div \frac{0.2}{0.3}\right) - \left(2\frac{3}{5} \times 0.8\right)\right] = \left[\left(0.5 \div \frac{0.2}{0.3}\right) - \left(\frac{(2 \times 5) + 3}{5} \times 0.8\right)\right]$$

$$= \left[\left(0.5 \div \frac{0.2}{0.3}\right) - \left(\frac{10 + 3}{5} \times 0.8\right)\right] = \left[\left(0.5 \div \frac{0.2}{0.3}\right) - \left(\frac{13}{5} \times 0.8\right)\right]$$

Step 2a

$$\left[\left(0.5 \div \frac{0.2}{0.3}\right) - \left(\frac{13}{5} \times 0.8\right)\right] = \left[\left(0.5 \div \frac{\frac{2}{10}}{\frac{3}{10}}\right) - \left(\frac{13}{5} \times 0.8\right)\right] = \left[\left(0.5 \div \frac{2 \times 10}{10 \times 3}\right) - \left(\frac{13}{5} \times 0.8\right)\right]$$

$$= \left[\left(0.5 \div \frac{20}{30}\right) - \left(\frac{13}{5} \times 0.8\right)\right]$$

Step 2b

$$\left[\left(0.5 \div \frac{20}{30}\right) - \left(\frac{13}{5} \times 0.8\right)\right] = \left[\left(\frac{5}{10} \div \frac{20}{30}\right) - \left(\frac{13}{5} \times \frac{8}{10}\right)\right]$$

Step 3

$$\left[\left(\frac{5}{10} \div \frac{20}{30}\right) - \left(\frac{13}{5} \times \frac{8}{10}\right)\right] = \left[\left(\frac{5}{10} \times \frac{30}{20}\right) - \left(\frac{13 \times 8}{5 \times 10}\right)\right] = \left[\left(\frac{5 \times 30}{10 \times 20}\right) - \left(\frac{104}{50}\right)\right]$$

$$= \left[\left(\frac{150}{200}\right) - \left(\frac{104}{50}\right)\right] = \left[\frac{150}{200} - \frac{104}{50}\right] = \left[\frac{(150 \times 50) - (104 \times 200)}{200 \times 50}\right] = \left[\frac{7500 - 20800}{10000}\right]$$

$$= \left[\frac{-13300}{10000}\right]$$

Step 4 $\boxed{\dfrac{-13300}{10000}} = \boxed{\dfrac{-13300 \div 100}{10000 \div 100}} = \boxed{\dfrac{-133}{100}}$

Step 5 $\boxed{\dfrac{-133}{100}} = \boxed{-\left(1\dfrac{33}{100}\right)}$

Example 8.5-6

$$\boxed{3\dfrac{2}{5} \times \left(\dfrac{0.12}{0.4} + 2\dfrac{5}{8}\right)} =$$

Solution:

Step 1 $\boxed{3\dfrac{2}{5} \times \left(\dfrac{0.12}{0.4} + 2\dfrac{5}{8}\right)} = \boxed{\dfrac{(3\times5)+2}{5} \times \left(\dfrac{0.12}{0.4} + \dfrac{(2\times8)+5}{8}\right)} = \boxed{\dfrac{15+2}{5} \times \left(\dfrac{0.12}{0.4} + \dfrac{16+5}{8}\right)}$

$= \boxed{\dfrac{17}{5} \times \left(\dfrac{0.12}{0.4} + \dfrac{21}{8}\right)}$

Step 2a $\boxed{\dfrac{17}{5} \times \left(\dfrac{0.12}{0.4} + \dfrac{21}{8}\right)} = \boxed{\dfrac{17}{5} \times \left(\dfrac{\frac{12}{100}}{\frac{4}{10}} + \dfrac{21}{8}\right)} = \boxed{\dfrac{17}{5} \times \left(\dfrac{12\times10}{100\times4} + \dfrac{21}{8}\right)} = \boxed{\dfrac{17}{5} \times \left(\dfrac{120}{400} + \dfrac{21}{8}\right)}$

Step 2b $\boxed{Not\ Applicable}$

Step 3 $\boxed{\dfrac{17}{5} \times \left(\dfrac{120}{400} + \dfrac{21}{8}\right)} = \boxed{\dfrac{17}{5} \times \left(\dfrac{(120\times8)+(21\times400)}{400\times8}\right)} = \boxed{\dfrac{17}{5} \times \left(\dfrac{960+8400}{3200}\right)}$

$= \boxed{\dfrac{17}{5} \times \left(\dfrac{9360}{3200}\right)} = \boxed{\dfrac{17}{5} \times \dfrac{9360}{3200}} = \boxed{\dfrac{17\times9360}{5\times3200}} = \boxed{\dfrac{159120}{16000}}$

Step 4 $\boxed{\dfrac{159120}{16000}} = \boxed{\dfrac{159120 \div 80}{160000 \div 80}} = \boxed{\dfrac{1989}{200}}$

Step 5 $\boxed{\dfrac{1989}{200}} = \boxed{9\dfrac{189}{200}}$

Example 8.5-7

$$\boxed{\left(\dfrac{1.4}{0.02} - 3\dfrac{1}{20}\right) \div 0.45} =$$

Solution:

Step 1 $\boxed{\left(\dfrac{1.4}{0.02} - 3\dfrac{1}{20}\right) \div 0.45} = \boxed{\left(\dfrac{1.4}{0.02} - \dfrac{(3\times20)+1}{20}\right) \div 0.45} = \boxed{\left(\dfrac{1.4}{0.02} - \dfrac{60+1}{20}\right) \div 0.45}$

$$= \boxed{\left(\frac{1.4}{0.02} - \frac{61}{20}\right) \div 0.45}$$

Step 2a $\boxed{\left(\frac{1.4}{0.02} - \frac{61}{20}\right) \div 0.45} = \boxed{\left(\frac{\frac{14}{10}}{\frac{2}{100}} - \frac{61}{20}\right) \div 0.45} = \boxed{\left(\frac{14 \times 100}{10 \times 2} - \frac{61}{20}\right) \div 0.45}$

$$= \boxed{\left(\frac{1400}{20} - \frac{61}{20}\right) \div 0.45}$$

Step 2b $\boxed{\left(\frac{1400}{20} - \frac{61}{20}\right) \div 0.45} = \boxed{\left(\frac{1400}{20} - \frac{61}{20}\right) \div \frac{45}{100}}$

Step 3 $\boxed{\left(\frac{1400}{20} - \frac{61}{20}\right) \div \frac{45}{100}} = \boxed{\left(\frac{1400 - 61}{20}\right) \div \frac{45}{100}} = \boxed{\left(\frac{1339}{20}\right) \div \frac{45}{100}} = \boxed{\frac{1339}{20} \div \frac{45}{100}}$

$$= \boxed{\frac{1339}{20} \times \frac{100}{45}} = \boxed{\frac{1339 \times 100}{20 \times 45}} = \boxed{\frac{133900}{900}}$$

Step 4 $\boxed{\frac{133900}{900}} = \boxed{\frac{133900 \div 100}{900 \div 100}} = \boxed{\frac{1339}{9}}$

Step 5 $\boxed{\frac{1339}{9}} = \boxed{\mathbf{148\frac{7}{9}}}$

Example 8.5-8

$$\boxed{\left(0.3 + 2\frac{4}{5}\right) - \left(\frac{0.6}{0.4} + 0.8\right)} =$$

Solution:

Step 1 $\boxed{\left(0.3 + 2\frac{4}{5}\right) - \left(\frac{0.6}{0.4} + 0.8\right)} = \boxed{\left(0.3 + \frac{(2 \times 5) + 4}{5}\right) - \left(\frac{0.6}{0.4} + 0.8\right)}$

$$= \boxed{\left(0.3 + \frac{10 + 4}{5}\right) - \left(\frac{0.6}{0.4} + 0.8\right)} = \boxed{\left(0.3 + \frac{14}{5}\right) - \left(\frac{0.6}{0.4} + 0.8\right)}$$

Step 2a $\boxed{\left(0.3 + \frac{14}{5}\right) - \left(\frac{0.6}{0.4} + 0.8\right)} = \boxed{\left(0.3 + \frac{14}{5}\right) - \left(\frac{\frac{6}{10}}{\frac{4}{10}} + 0.8\right)} = \boxed{\left(0.3 + \frac{14}{5}\right) - \left(\frac{6 \times 10}{10 \times 4} + 0.8\right)}$

$$= \boxed{\left(0.3 + \frac{14}{5}\right) - \left(\frac{60}{40} + 0.8\right)}$$

Step 2b $$\left[\left(0.3+\frac{14}{5}\right)-\left(\frac{60}{40}+0.8\right)\right]=\left[\left(\frac{3}{10}+\frac{14}{5}\right)-\left(\frac{60}{40}+\frac{8}{10}\right)\right]$$

Step 3 $$\left[\left(\frac{3}{10}+\frac{14}{5}\right)-\left(\frac{60}{40}+\frac{8}{10}\right)\right]=\left[\left(\frac{(3\times5)+(14\times10)}{10\times5}\right)-\left(\frac{(60\times10)+(8\times40)}{40\times10}\right)\right]$$

$$=\left[\left(\frac{15+140}{50}\right)-\left(\frac{600+320}{400}\right)\right]=\left[\left(\frac{155}{50}\right)-\left(\frac{920}{400}\right)\right]=\left[\frac{155}{50}-\frac{920}{400}\right]$$

$$=\left[\frac{(155\times400)-(920\times50)}{50\times400}\right]=\left[\frac{62000-46000}{20000}\right]=\left[\frac{16000}{20000}\right]$$

Step 4 $$\left[\frac{16000}{20000}\right]=\left[\frac{16000\div4000}{20000\div4000}\right]=\boxed{\frac{4}{5}}$$

Step 5 $\boxed{Not\ Applicable}$

Example 8.5-9

$$\left[\left(2\frac{4}{5}\times1\frac{3}{2}\right)\div\left(0.5\times\frac{0.2}{0.3}\right)\right]=$$

Solution:

Step 1 $$\left[\left(2\frac{4}{5}\times1\frac{3}{2}\right)\div\left(0.5\times\frac{0.2}{0.3}\right)\right]=\left[\left(\frac{(2\times5)+4}{5}\times\frac{(1\times2)+3}{2}\right)\div\left(0.5\times\frac{0.2}{0.3}\right)\right]$$

$$=\left[\left(\frac{10+4}{5}\times\frac{2+3}{2}\right)\div\left(0.5\times\frac{0.2}{0.3}\right)\right]=\left[\left(\frac{14}{5}\times\frac{5}{2}\right)\div\left(0.5\times\frac{0.2}{0.3}\right)\right]$$

Step 2a $$\left[\left(\frac{14}{5}\times\frac{5}{2}\right)\div\left(0.5\times\frac{0.2}{0.3}\right)\right]=\left[\left(\frac{14}{5}\times\frac{5}{2}\right)\div\left(0.5\times\frac{\frac{2}{10}}{\frac{3}{10}}\right)\right]=\left[\left(\frac{14}{5}\times\frac{5}{2}\right)\div\left(0.5\times\frac{2\times10}{10\times3}\right)\right]$$

$$=\left[\left(\frac{14}{5}\times\frac{5}{2}\right)\div\left(0.5\times\frac{20}{30}\right)\right]$$

Step 2b $$\left[\left(\frac{14}{5}\times\frac{5}{2}\right)\div\left(0.5\times\frac{20}{30}\right)\right]=\left[\left(\frac{14}{5}\times\frac{5}{2}\right)\div\left(\frac{5}{10}\times\frac{20}{30}\right)\right]$$

Step 3 $$\left[\left(\frac{14}{5}\times\frac{5}{2}\right)\div\left(\frac{5}{10}\times\frac{20}{30}\right)\right]=\left[\left(\frac{14\times5}{5\times2}\right)\div\left(\frac{5\times20}{10\times30}\right)\right]=\left[\left(\frac{70}{10}\right)\div\left(\frac{100}{300}\right)\right]=\left[\frac{70}{10}\div\frac{100}{300}\right]$$

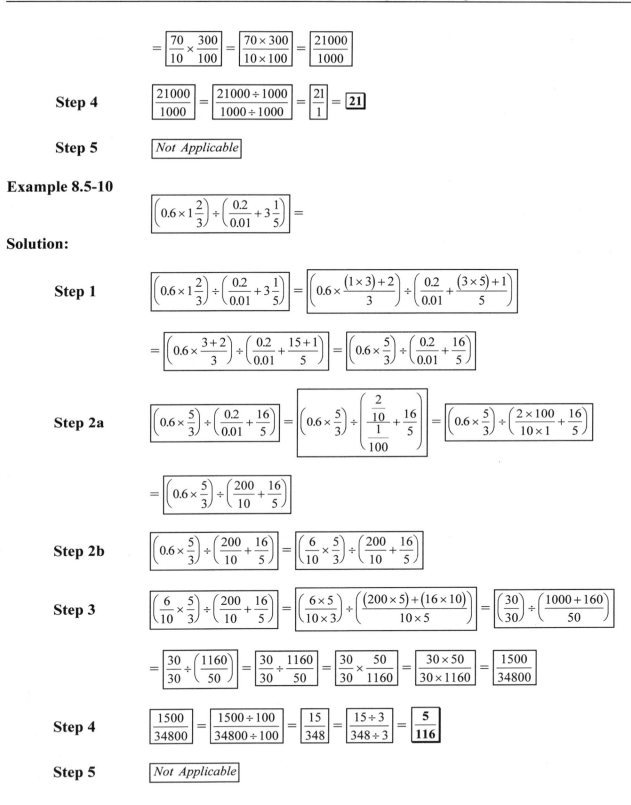

$$= \left|\frac{70}{10} \times \frac{300}{100}\right| = \left|\frac{70 \times 300}{10 \times 100}\right| = \left|\frac{21000}{1000}\right|$$

Step 4 $\quad \left|\frac{21000}{1000}\right| = \left|\frac{21000 \div 1000}{1000 \div 1000}\right| = \left|\frac{21}{1}\right| = \boxed{21}$

Step 5 $\quad \boxed{Not\ Applicable}$

Example 8.5-10

$$\left[\left(0.6 \times 1\frac{2}{3}\right) \div \left(\frac{0.2}{0.01} + 3\frac{1}{5}\right)\right] =$$

Solution:

Step 1 $\quad \left[\left(0.6 \times 1\frac{2}{3}\right) \div \left(\frac{0.2}{0.01} + 3\frac{1}{5}\right)\right] = \left[\left(0.6 \times \frac{(1 \times 3)+2}{3}\right) \div \left(\frac{0.2}{0.01} + \frac{(3 \times 5)+1}{5}\right)\right]$

$$= \left[\left(0.6 \times \frac{3+2}{3}\right) \div \left(\frac{0.2}{0.01} + \frac{15+1}{5}\right)\right] = \left[\left(0.6 \times \frac{5}{3}\right) \div \left(\frac{0.2}{0.01} + \frac{16}{5}\right)\right]$$

Step 2a $\quad \left[\left(0.6 \times \frac{5}{3}\right) \div \left(\frac{0.2}{0.01} + \frac{16}{5}\right)\right] = \left[\left(0.6 \times \frac{5}{3}\right) \div \left(\frac{\frac{2}{10}}{\frac{1}{100}} + \frac{16}{5}\right)\right] = \left[\left(0.6 \times \frac{5}{3}\right) \div \left(\frac{2 \times 100}{10 \times 1} + \frac{16}{5}\right)\right]$

$$= \left[\left(0.6 \times \frac{5}{3}\right) \div \left(\frac{200}{10} + \frac{16}{5}\right)\right]$$

Step 2b $\quad \left[\left(0.6 \times \frac{5}{3}\right) \div \left(\frac{200}{10} + \frac{16}{5}\right)\right] = \left[\left(\frac{6}{10} \times \frac{5}{3}\right) \div \left(\frac{200}{10} + \frac{16}{5}\right)\right]$

Step 3 $\quad \left[\left(\frac{6}{10} \times \frac{5}{3}\right) \div \left(\frac{200}{10} + \frac{16}{5}\right)\right] = \left[\left(\frac{6 \times 5}{10 \times 3}\right) \div \left(\frac{(200 \times 5)+(16 \times 10)}{10 \times 5}\right)\right] = \left[\left(\frac{30}{30}\right) \div \left(\frac{1000+160}{50}\right)\right]$

$$= \left[\frac{30}{30} \div \left(\frac{1160}{50}\right)\right] = \left[\frac{30}{30} \div \frac{1160}{50}\right] = \left[\frac{30}{30} \times \frac{50}{1160}\right] = \left[\frac{30 \times 50}{30 \times 1160}\right] = \left[\frac{1500}{34800}\right]$$

Step 4 $\quad \left|\frac{1500}{34800}\right| = \left|\frac{1500 \div 100}{34800 \div 100}\right| = \left|\frac{15}{348}\right| = \left|\frac{15 \div 3}{348 \div 3}\right| = \boxed{\frac{5}{116}}$

Step 5 $\quad \boxed{Not\ Applicable}$

The following examples further illustrate how to add, subtract, multiply, and divide decimal and mixed fractions:

Example 8.5-11

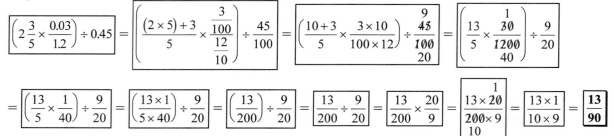

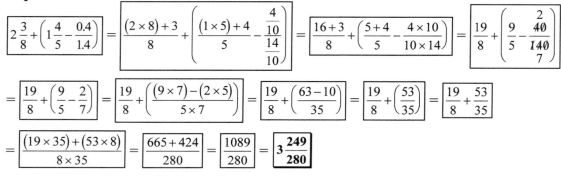

Example 8.5-12

Example 8.5-13

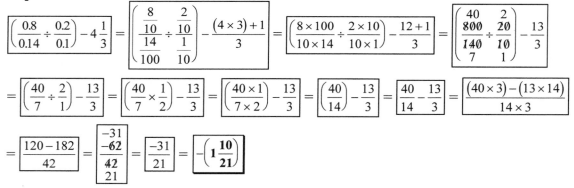

Example 8.5-14

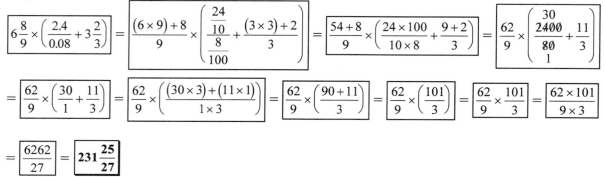

Example 8.5-15

$$\left(2\frac{5}{12}+0.4\right)\times\frac{0.01}{0.6} = \left(\frac{(2\times12)+5}{12}+\frac{4}{10}\right)\times\frac{\frac{1}{100}}{\frac{6}{10}} = \left(\frac{24+5}{12}+\frac{\overset{2}{\cancel{4}}}{\underset{5}{\cancel{10}}}\right)\times\frac{1\times10}{100\times6} = \left(\frac{29}{12}+\frac{2}{5}\right)\times\frac{\overset{1}{\cancel{10}}}{\underset{60}{\cancel{600}}}$$

$$= \left(\frac{29}{12}+\frac{2}{5}\right)\times\frac{1}{60} = \left(\frac{(29\times5)+(2\times12)}{12\times5}\right)\times\frac{1}{60} = \left(\frac{145+24}{60}\right)\times\frac{1}{60} = \left(\frac{169}{60}\right)\times\frac{1}{60} = \frac{169}{60}\times\frac{1}{60} = \frac{169\times1}{60\times60}$$

$$= \boxed{\frac{169}{3600}}$$

Example 8.5-16

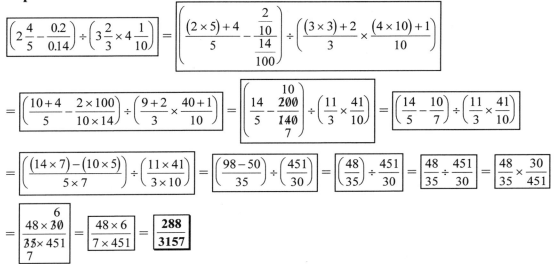

$$\left(2\frac{4}{5}-\frac{0.2}{0.14}\right)\div\left(3\frac{2}{3}\times4\frac{1}{10}\right) = \left(\frac{(2\times5)+4}{5}-\frac{\frac{2}{10}}{\frac{14}{100}}\right)\div\left(\frac{(3\times3)+2}{3}\times\frac{(4\times10)+1}{10}\right)$$

$$= \left(\frac{10+4}{5}-\frac{2\times100}{10\times14}\right)\div\left(\frac{9+2}{3}\times\frac{40+1}{10}\right) = \left(\frac{14}{5}-\frac{\overset{10}{\cancel{200}}}{\underset{7}{\cancel{140}}}\right)\div\left(\frac{11}{3}\times\frac{41}{10}\right) = \left(\frac{14}{5}-\frac{10}{7}\right)\div\left(\frac{11}{3}\times\frac{41}{10}\right)$$

$$= \left(\frac{(14\times7)-(10\times5)}{5\times7}\right)\div\left(\frac{11\times41}{3\times10}\right) = \left(\frac{98-50}{35}\right)\div\left(\frac{451}{30}\right) = \left(\frac{48}{35}\right)\div\frac{451}{30} = \frac{48}{35}\div\frac{451}{30} = \frac{48}{35}\times\frac{30}{451}$$

$$= \frac{48\times\overset{6}{\cancel{30}}}{\underset{7}{\cancel{35}}\times451} = \frac{48\times6}{7\times451} = \boxed{\frac{288}{3157}}$$

Example 8.5-17

$$\left(\frac{0.5}{0.25}\times3\frac{1}{5}\right)\div\left(0.5\times4\frac{3}{5}\right) = \left(\frac{\frac{5}{10}}{\frac{25}{100}}\times\frac{(3\times5)+1}{5}\right)\div\left(\frac{5}{10}\times\frac{(4\times5)+3}{5}\right) = \left(\frac{5\times100}{10\times25}\times\frac{15+1}{5}\right)\div\left(\frac{\overset{1}{\cancel{5}}}{\underset{2}{\cancel{10}}}\times\frac{20+3}{5}\right)$$

$$= \left(\frac{500}{250}\times\frac{16}{5}\right)\div\left(\frac{1}{2}\times\frac{23}{5}\right) = \left(\frac{\overset{2}{\cancel{500}}}{\underset{1}{\cancel{250}}}\times\frac{16}{5}\right)\div\left(\frac{1}{2}\times\frac{23}{5}\right) = \left(\frac{2}{1}\times\frac{16}{5}\right)\div\left(\frac{1\times23}{2\times5}\right) = \left(\frac{2\times16}{1\times5}\right)\div\left(\frac{23}{10}\right)$$

$$= \left(\frac{32}{5}\right)\div\frac{23}{10} = \frac{32}{5}\div\frac{23}{10} = \frac{32}{5}\times\frac{10}{23} = \frac{32\times\overset{2}{\cancel{10}}}{\underset{1}{\cancel{5}}\times23} = \frac{32\times2}{1\times23} = \frac{64}{23} = \boxed{2\frac{18}{23}}$$

Example 8.5-18

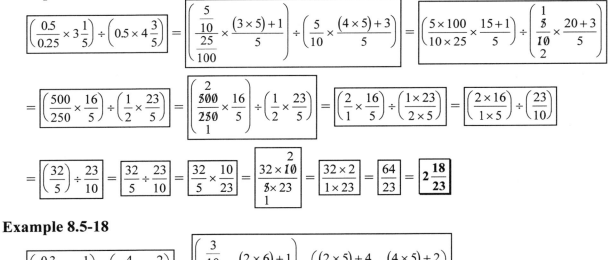

$$\left(\frac{0.3}{0.12}\times2\frac{1}{6}\right)\div\left(2\frac{4}{5}+4\frac{2}{5}\right) = \left(\frac{\frac{3}{10}}{\frac{12}{100}}\times\frac{(2\times6)+1}{6}\right)\div\left(\frac{(2\times5)+4}{5}+\frac{(4\times5)+2}{5}\right)$$

$$= \left[\left(\frac{3\times100}{10\times12}\times\frac{12+1}{6}\right)\div\left(\frac{10+4}{5}+\frac{20+2}{5}\right)\right] = \left[\left(\frac{\overset{5}{\cancel{300}}}{\underset{2}{\cancel{120}}}\times\frac{13}{6}\right)\div\left(\frac{14}{5}+\frac{22}{5}\right)\right] = \left[\left(\frac{5}{2}\times\frac{13}{6}\right)\div\left(\frac{14+22}{5}\right)\right]$$

$$= \left[\left(\frac{5\times13}{2\times6}\right)\div\left(\frac{36}{5}\right)\right] = \left[\left(\frac{65}{12}\right)\div\frac{36}{5}\right] = \frac{65}{12}\div\frac{36}{5} = \frac{65}{12}\times\frac{5}{36} = \frac{65\times5}{12\times36} = \boxed{\mathbf{\frac{325}{432}}}$$

Example 8.5-19

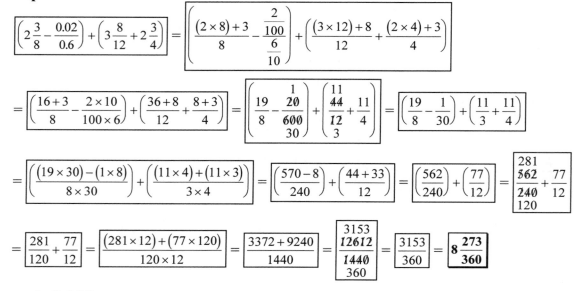

$$\left[\left(2\frac{3}{8}-\frac{0.02}{0.6}\right)+\left(3\frac{8}{12}+2\frac{3}{4}\right)\right] = \left[\left(\frac{(2\times8)+3}{8}-\frac{\frac{2}{100}}{\frac{6}{10}}\right)+\left(\frac{(3\times12)+8}{12}+\frac{(2\times4)+3}{4}\right)\right]$$

$$= \left[\left(\frac{16+3}{8}-\frac{2\times10}{100\times6}\right)+\left(\frac{36+8}{12}+\frac{8+3}{4}\right)\right] = \left[\left(\frac{19}{8}-\frac{\overset{1}{\cancel{20}}}{\underset{30}{\cancel{600}}}\right)+\left(\frac{\overset{11}{\cancel{44}}}{\underset{3}{\cancel{12}}}+\frac{11}{4}\right)\right] = \left[\left(\frac{19}{8}-\frac{1}{30}\right)+\left(\frac{11}{3}+\frac{11}{4}\right)\right]$$

$$= \left[\left(\frac{(19\times30)-(1\times8)}{8\times30}\right)+\left(\frac{(11\times4)+(11\times3)}{3\times4}\right)\right] = \left[\left(\frac{570-8}{240}\right)+\left(\frac{44+33}{12}\right)\right] = \left[\left(\frac{562}{240}\right)+\left(\frac{77}{12}\right)\right] = \frac{\overset{281}{\cancel{562}}}{\underset{120}{\cancel{240}}}+\frac{77}{12}$$

$$= \frac{281}{120}+\frac{77}{12} = \frac{(281\times12)+(77\times120)}{120\times12} = \frac{3372+9240}{1440} = \frac{\overset{3153}{\cancel{12612}}}{\underset{360}{\cancel{1440}}} = \frac{3153}{360} = \boxed{\mathbf{8\frac{273}{360}}}$$

Example 8.5-20

$$\left[\left(\frac{1.5}{0.2}+3\frac{6}{8}\right)-\left(2\frac{4}{5}\times2\frac{1}{3}\right)\right] = \left[\left(\frac{\frac{15}{10}}{\frac{2}{10}}+\frac{(3\times8)+6}{8}\right)-\left(\frac{(2\times5)+4}{5}\times\frac{(2\times3)+1}{3}\right)\right]$$

$$= \left[\left(\frac{15\times10}{10\times2}+\frac{24+6}{8}\right)-\left(\frac{10+4}{5}\times\frac{6+1}{3}\right)\right] = \left[\left(\frac{\overset{15}{\cancel{150}}}{\underset{2}{\cancel{20}}}+\frac{\overset{15}{\cancel{30}}}{\underset{4}{\cancel{8}}}\right)-\left(\frac{14}{5}\times\frac{7}{3}\right)\right] = \left[\left(\frac{15}{2}+\frac{15}{4}\right)-\left(\frac{14}{5}\times\frac{7}{3}\right)\right]$$

$$= \left[\left(\frac{(15\times4)+(15\times2)}{2\times4}\right)-\left(\frac{14\times7}{5\times3}\right)\right] = \left[\left(\frac{60+30}{2\times4}\right)-\left(\frac{98}{15}\right)\right] = \left[\left(\frac{90}{8}\right)-\left(\frac{98}{15}\right)\right] = \frac{\overset{45}{\cancel{90}}}{\underset{4}{\cancel{8}}}-\frac{98}{15} = \frac{45}{4}-\frac{98}{15}$$

$$= \frac{(45\times15)-(98\times4)}{4\times15} = \frac{675-392}{60} = \frac{283}{60} = \boxed{\mathbf{4\frac{43}{60}}}$$

Example 8.5-21

$$\left[\left(\frac{0.15}{0.5}\times2\frac{4}{10}\right)\div\left(0.2\times3\frac{1}{2}\times\frac{0.2}{0.04}\right)\right] = \left[\left(\frac{\frac{15}{100}}{\frac{5}{10}}\times\frac{(2\times10)+4}{10}\right)\div\left(\frac{2}{10}\times\frac{(3\times2)+1}{2}\times\frac{\frac{2}{10}}{\frac{4}{100}}\right)\right]$$

$$= \left[\left(\frac{15\times10}{100\times5}\times\frac{20+4}{10}\right)\div\left(\frac{2}{10}\times\frac{6+1}{2}\times\frac{2\times100}{10\times4}\right)\right] = \left[\left(\frac{\overset{3}{\cancel{150}}}{\underset{10}{\cancel{500}}}\times\frac{\overset{12}{\cancel{24}}}{\underset{5}{\cancel{10}}}\right)\div\left(\frac{\overset{1}{\cancel{2}}}{\underset{5}{\cancel{10}}}\times\frac{7}{2}\times\frac{\overset{5}{\cancel{200}}}{\underset{1}{\cancel{40}}}\right)\right] = \left[\left(\frac{3}{10}\times\frac{12}{5}\right)\div\left(\frac{1}{5}\times\frac{7}{2}\times\frac{5}{1}\right)\right]$$

$$= \left[\left(\frac{3\times\overset{6}{\cancel{12}}}{\underset{5}{\cancel{10}}\times5}\right)\div\left(\frac{1\times7\times\overset{1}{\cancel{5}}}{\underset{1}{\cancel{5}}\times2\times1}\right)\right] = \left[\left(\frac{3\times6}{5\times5}\right)\div\left(\frac{1\times7\times1}{1\times2\times1}\right)\right] = \left[\left(\frac{18}{25}\right)\div\left(\frac{7}{2}\right)\right] = \left[\frac{18}{25}\div\frac{7}{2}\right] = \left[\frac{18}{25}\times\frac{2}{7}\right] = \left[\frac{18\times2}{25\times7}\right] = \boxed{\frac{36}{175}}$$

Section 8.5 Exercises - Use the following decimal and mixed fractions to perform the indicated operations:

1. $\left(2\frac{1}{4}+3\frac{3}{5}\right)\div\frac{0.4}{0.24} =$

2. $\left(\frac{0.2}{1.4}+2\frac{3}{8}\right)\times3\frac{1}{4} =$

3. $\left(2\frac{1}{5}\times0.5\right)+4\frac{3}{10} =$

4. $\left(1\frac{3}{5}-3\frac{2}{3}\right)\times\frac{0.1}{1.5} =$

5. $\left(4\frac{5}{3}-3\frac{1}{3}\right)\div\frac{4.8}{0.12} =$

6. $\left(2\frac{3}{8}\times2\frac{6}{14}\right)\div\frac{0.01}{0.6} =$

7. $\left(\frac{0.3}{2.4}\times4\frac{1}{3}\right)\div3\frac{1}{4} =$

8. $\left(2\frac{3}{5}\times\frac{0.1}{1.4}\right)+4\frac{7}{3} =$

9. $\left(3\frac{1}{5}+2\frac{2}{5}\right)\times\left(\frac{0.5}{0.08}\times4\frac{1}{3}\right) =$

10. $\left[\left(2\frac{1}{3}\times\frac{0.2}{1.2}\right)\div3\frac{4}{5}\right]-1\frac{1}{2} =$

Chapter 9 - Integer, Decimal, and Mixed Fractions

The objective of this chapter is to improve the student's ability in solving integer, decimal, and mixed fractions. In this chapter the tools learned in the previous chapters are used together by performing math operations when integer, decimal, and mixed fractions are combined. The steps used to perform the fractional operations with examples illustrating how to add (Section 9.1), subtract (Section 9.2), multiply (Section 9.3), and divide (Section 9.4) three or more integer, decimal, and mixed fractions are given. Section 9.5 mixes the mathematical operations using the three types of fractions. To further enhance the student's ability, each section is concluded by solving additional examples which do not follow the exact order as is given by the steps for each case. It is the author's hope that by the time the student has finished this chapter he or she has "mastered" how to solve all types of fractional operations covered in this book.

9.1   Adding Integer, Decimal, and Mixed Fractions

Fractions of the following forms:

1. $\left(\dfrac{a}{b} \right)$ where (a) and (b) are integers,

2. $\left(\dfrac{a \times 10^{-k_1}}{b \times 10^{-k_2}} \right)$ where (a) and (b) are integer numbers and (k_1) and (k_2) are equal to the number of decimal places, and

3. $\left(k \dfrac{a}{b} \right)$ where (k) is made up of a whole number and $\left(\dfrac{a}{b} \right)$ is an integer fraction for a number less than one

are added as in the following cases:

Case I   Adding Integer, Decimal, and Mixed Fractions With Three Terms Only
Add three integer, decimal, and mixed fractions using the following steps:

Step 1   Use parentheses to group the first and second fractions.

Step 2   Change the integer number (a) to an integer fraction of the form $\left(\dfrac{a}{1} \right)$, e.g., change 6 to $\dfrac{6}{1}$.

Step 3   Change the mixed fraction to an integer fraction (see Section 2.5).

Step 4   a. Change the decimal fraction to an integer fraction (see Section 2.4).

b. Change the decimal number $\left(a \times 10^{-k} \right)$ to an integer fraction of the form $\left(\dfrac{a}{10^k} \right)$, e.g., change 0.25 to $\dfrac{25}{100}$.

Step 5   Add the integer fractions (see Section 3.1).

Step 6   Simplify the fraction to its lowest term (see Section 2.3).

Step 7   Change the improper fraction to a mixed fraction if the fraction obtained from Step 6 is an improper fraction (see Section 2.2).

The following examples show the steps as to how integer, decimal and mixed fractions with three terms only are added:

Example 9.1-1

$$\frac{4}{5} + 1\frac{3}{8} + \frac{0.5}{1.2} =$$

Solution:

Step 1 $\frac{4}{5} + 1\frac{3}{8} + \frac{0.5}{1.2} = \left[\left(\frac{4}{5} + 1\frac{3}{8}\right) + \frac{0.5}{1.2}\right]$

Step 2   Not Applicable

Step 3 $\left[\left(\frac{4}{5} + 1\frac{3}{8}\right) + \frac{0.5}{1.2}\right] = \left[\left(\frac{4}{5} + \frac{(1\times 8)+3}{8}\right) + \frac{0.5}{1.2}\right] = \left[\left(\frac{4}{5} + \frac{8+3}{8}\right) + \frac{0.5}{1.2}\right] = \left[\left(\frac{4}{5} + \frac{11}{8}\right) + \frac{0.5}{1.2}\right]$

Step 4a $\left[\left(\frac{4}{5} + \frac{11}{8}\right) + \frac{0.5}{1.2}\right] = \left[\left(\frac{4}{5} + \frac{11}{8}\right) + \frac{\frac{5}{10}}{\frac{12}{10}}\right] = \left[\left(\frac{4}{5} + \frac{11}{8}\right) + \frac{5\times 10}{10\times 12}\right] = \left[\left(\frac{4}{5} + \frac{11}{8}\right) + \frac{50}{120}\right]$

Step 4b   Not Applicable

Step 5 $\left[\left(\frac{4}{5} + \frac{11}{8}\right) + \frac{50}{120}\right] = \left[\left(\frac{(4\times 8)+(11\times 5)}{5\times 8}\right) + \frac{50}{120}\right] = \left[\left(\frac{32+55}{40}\right) + \frac{50}{120}\right] = \left[\left(\frac{87}{40}\right) + \frac{50}{120}\right]$

$= \left[\frac{87}{40} + \frac{50}{120}\right] = \left[\frac{(87\times 120)+(50\times 40)}{40\times 120}\right] = \left[\frac{10440+2000}{4800}\right] = \left[\frac{12440}{4800}\right]$

Step 6 $\left[\frac{12440}{4800}\right] = \left[\frac{12440\div 40}{4800\div 40}\right] = \left[\frac{311}{120}\right]$

Step 7 $\left[\frac{311}{120}\right] = \left[2\frac{71}{120}\right]$

Example 9.1-2

$$12 + 3\frac{4}{7} + \frac{0.05}{4.5} =$$

Solution:

Step 1 $12 + 3\frac{4}{7} + \frac{0.05}{4.5} = \left[\left(12 + 3\frac{4}{7}\right) + \frac{0.05}{4.5}\right]$

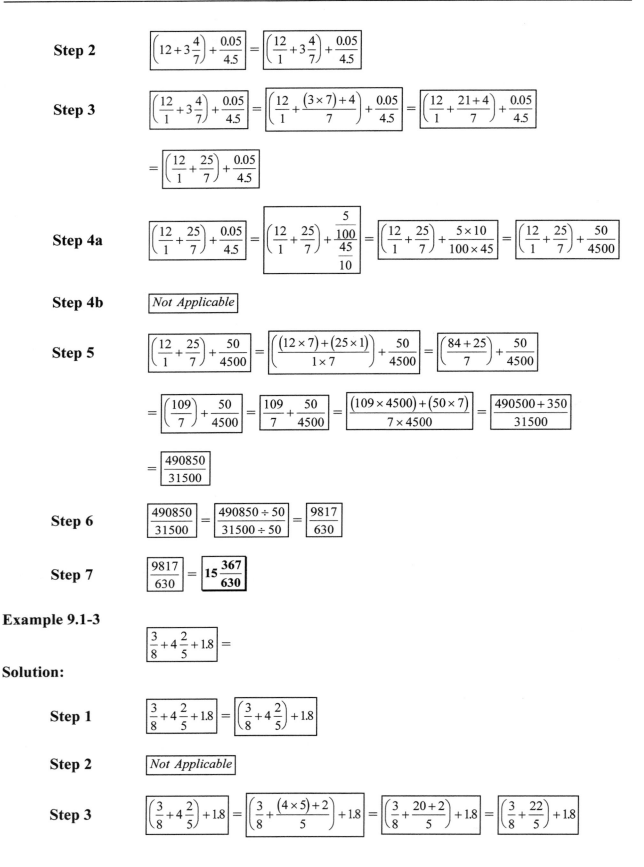

Step 2
$$\left[\left(12+3\frac{4}{7}\right)+\frac{0.05}{4.5}\right]=\left[\left(\frac{12}{1}+3\frac{4}{7}\right)+\frac{0.05}{4.5}\right]$$

Step 3
$$\left[\left(\frac{12}{1}+3\frac{4}{7}\right)+\frac{0.05}{4.5}\right]=\left[\left(\frac{12}{1}+\frac{(3\times 7)+4}{7}\right)+\frac{0.05}{4.5}\right]=\left[\left(\frac{12}{1}+\frac{21+4}{7}\right)+\frac{0.05}{4.5}\right]$$

$$=\left[\left(\frac{12}{1}+\frac{25}{7}\right)+\frac{0.05}{4.5}\right]$$

Step 4a
$$\left[\left(\frac{12}{1}+\frac{25}{7}\right)+\frac{0.05}{4.5}\right]=\left[\left(\frac{12}{1}+\frac{25}{7}\right)+\frac{\frac{5}{100}}{\frac{45}{10}}\right]=\left[\left(\frac{12}{1}+\frac{25}{7}\right)+\frac{5\times 10}{100\times 45}\right]=\left[\left(\frac{12}{1}+\frac{25}{7}\right)+\frac{50}{4500}\right]$$

Step 4b | *Not Applicable* |

Step 5
$$\left[\left(\frac{12}{1}+\frac{25}{7}\right)+\frac{50}{4500}\right]=\left[\left(\frac{(12\times 7)+(25\times 1)}{1\times 7}\right)+\frac{50}{4500}\right]=\left[\left(\frac{84+25}{7}\right)+\frac{50}{4500}\right]$$

$$=\left[\left(\frac{109}{7}\right)+\frac{50}{4500}\right]=\left[\frac{109}{7}+\frac{50}{4500}\right]=\left[\frac{(109\times 4500)+(50\times 7)}{7\times 4500}\right]=\left[\frac{490500+350}{31500}\right]$$

$$=\left[\frac{490850}{31500}\right]$$

Step 6
$$\frac{490850}{31500}=\frac{490850\div 50}{31500\div 50}=\frac{9817}{630}$$

Step 7
$$\frac{9817}{630}=\mathbf{15\frac{367}{630}}$$

Example 9.1-3
$$\frac{3}{8}+4\frac{2}{5}+1.8=$$

Solution:

Step 1
$$\frac{3}{8}+4\frac{2}{5}+1.8=\left[\left(\frac{3}{8}+4\frac{2}{5}\right)+1.8\right]$$

Step 2 | *Not Applicable* |

Step 3
$$\left[\left(\frac{3}{8}+4\frac{2}{5}\right)+1.8\right]=\left[\left(\frac{3}{8}+\frac{(4\times 5)+2}{5}\right)+1.8\right]=\left[\left(\frac{3}{8}+\frac{20+2}{5}\right)+1.8\right]=\left[\left(\frac{3}{8}+\frac{22}{5}\right)+1.8\right]$$

Step 4a $\boxed{\textit{Not Applicable}}$

Step 4b $\boxed{\left(\dfrac{3}{8}+\dfrac{22}{5}\right)+1.8} = \boxed{\left(\dfrac{3}{8}+\dfrac{22}{5}\right)+\dfrac{18}{10}}$

Step 5 $\boxed{\left(\dfrac{3}{8}+\dfrac{22}{5}\right)+\dfrac{18}{10}} = \boxed{\left(\dfrac{(3\times5)+(22\times8)}{8\times5}\right)+\dfrac{18}{10}} = \boxed{\left(\dfrac{15+176}{40}\right)+\dfrac{18}{10}} = \boxed{\left(\dfrac{191}{40}\right)+\dfrac{18}{10}}$

$= \boxed{\dfrac{191}{40}+\dfrac{18}{10}} = \boxed{\dfrac{(191\times10)+(18\times40)}{40\times10}} = \boxed{\dfrac{1910+720}{400}} = \boxed{\dfrac{2630}{400}}$

Step 6 $\boxed{\dfrac{2630}{400}} = \boxed{\dfrac{2630\div10}{400\div10}} = \boxed{\dfrac{263}{40}}$

Step 7 $\boxed{\dfrac{263}{40}} = \boxed{6\dfrac{23}{40}}$

Example 9.1-4

$\boxed{5\dfrac{2}{9}+\dfrac{4}{9}+\dfrac{0.15}{3.5}} =$

Solution:

Step 1 $\boxed{5\dfrac{2}{9}+\dfrac{4}{9}+\dfrac{0.15}{3.5}} = \boxed{\left(5\dfrac{2}{9}+\dfrac{4}{9}\right)+\dfrac{0.15}{3.5}}$

Step 2 $\boxed{\textit{Not Applicable}}$

Step 3 $\boxed{\left(5\dfrac{2}{9}+\dfrac{4}{9}\right)+\dfrac{0.15}{3.5}} = \boxed{\left(\dfrac{(5\times9)+2}{9}+\dfrac{4}{9}\right)+\dfrac{0.15}{3.5}} = \boxed{\left(\dfrac{45+2}{9}+\dfrac{4}{9}\right)+\dfrac{0.15}{3.5}} = \boxed{\left(\dfrac{47}{9}+\dfrac{4}{9}\right)+\dfrac{0.15}{3.5}}$

Step 4a $\boxed{\left(\dfrac{47}{9}+\dfrac{4}{9}\right)+\dfrac{0.15}{3.5}} = \boxed{\left(\dfrac{47}{9}+\dfrac{4}{9}\right)+\dfrac{\dfrac{15}{100}}{\dfrac{35}{10}}} = \boxed{\left(\dfrac{47}{9}+\dfrac{4}{9}\right)+\dfrac{15\times10}{100\times35}} = \boxed{\left(\dfrac{47}{9}+\dfrac{4}{9}\right)+\dfrac{150}{3500}}$

Step 4b $\boxed{\textit{Not Applicable}}$

Step 5 $\boxed{\left(\dfrac{47}{9}+\dfrac{4}{9}\right)+\dfrac{150}{3500}} = \boxed{\left(\dfrac{47+4}{9}\right)+\dfrac{150}{3500}} = \boxed{\left(\dfrac{51}{9}\right)+\dfrac{150}{3500}} = \boxed{\dfrac{51}{9}+\dfrac{150}{3500}}$

$$= \boxed{\frac{(51 \times 3500) + (150 \times 9)}{9 \times 3500}} = \boxed{\frac{178500 + 1350}{31500}} = \boxed{\frac{179850}{31500}}$$

Step 6 $\boxed{\frac{179850}{31500}} = \boxed{\frac{179850 \div 50}{31500 \div 50}} = \boxed{\frac{3597}{630}}$

Step 7 $\boxed{\frac{3597}{630}} = \boxed{\mathbf{5\frac{447}{630}}}$

Example 9.1-5

$$\boxed{0.28 + \frac{5}{6} + 3\frac{3}{5} =}$$

Solution:

Step 1 $\boxed{0.28 + \frac{5}{6} + 3\frac{3}{5}} = \boxed{\left(0.28 + \frac{5}{6}\right) + 3\frac{3}{5}}$

Step 2 $\boxed{\textit{Not Applicable}}$

Step 3 $\boxed{\left(0.28 + \frac{5}{6}\right) + 3\frac{3}{5}} = \boxed{\left(0.28 + \frac{5}{6}\right) + \frac{(3 \times 5) + 3}{5}} = \boxed{\left(0.28 + \frac{5}{6}\right) + \frac{15 + 3}{5}} = \boxed{\left(0.28 + \frac{5}{6}\right) + \frac{18}{5}}$

Step 4a $\boxed{\textit{Not Applicable}}$

Step 4b $\boxed{\left(0.28 + \frac{5}{6}\right) + \frac{18}{5}} = \boxed{\left(\frac{28}{100} + \frac{5}{6}\right) + \frac{18}{5}}$

Step 5 $\boxed{\left(\frac{28}{100} + \frac{5}{6}\right) + \frac{18}{5}} = \boxed{\left(\frac{(28 \times 6) + (5 \times 100)}{100 \times 6}\right) + \frac{18}{5}} = \boxed{\left(\frac{168 + 500}{600}\right) + \frac{18}{5}} = \boxed{\left(\frac{668}{600}\right) + \frac{18}{5}}$

$$= \boxed{\frac{668}{600} + \frac{18}{5}} = \boxed{\frac{(668 \times 5) + (18 \times 600)}{600 \times 5}} = \boxed{\frac{3340 + 10800}{3000}} = \boxed{\frac{14140}{3000}}$$

Step 6 $\boxed{\frac{14140}{3000}} = \boxed{\frac{14140 \div 20}{3000 \div 20}} = \boxed{\frac{707}{150}}$

Step 7 $\boxed{\frac{707}{150}} = \boxed{\mathbf{4\frac{107}{150}}}$

Case II Adding Integer, Decimal, and Mixed Fractions With More Than Three Terms

Add integer, decimal, and mixed fractions having more than three terms by using the following steps:

Step 1   Use parentheses to group the numbers in pairs, e.g., group the first and second numbers, third and fourth numbers, fifth and sixth numbers, etc. together.

Step 2   Change the integer number(s) (a) to integer fraction(s) of the form $\left(\dfrac{a}{1}\right)$, e.g., change

125 to $\dfrac{125}{1}$.

Step 3   Change the mixed fraction(s) to integer fraction(s) (see Section 2.5).

Step 4   a. Change the decimal fraction(s) to integer fraction(s) (see Section 2.4).

b. Change the decimal number(s) $\left(a \times 10^{-k}\right)$ to integer fraction(s) of the form $\left(\dfrac{a}{10^k}\right)$,

e.g., change 0.235 to $\dfrac{235}{1000}$.

Step 5   Add the integer fractions (see Section 3.1).

Step 6   Simplify the fraction to its lowest term (see Section 2.3).

Step 7   Change the improper fraction to a mixed fraction if the fraction obtained from Step 6 is an improper fraction (see Section 2.2).

The following examples show the steps as to how integer, decimal and mixed fractions with more than three terms are added:

Example 9.1-6

$$\boxed{\dfrac{6}{8} + 4 + 5\dfrac{2}{3} + 0.15} =$$

Solution:

Step 1 $\boxed{\dfrac{6}{8} + 4 + 5\dfrac{2}{3} + 0.15} = \boxed{\left(\dfrac{6}{8} + 4\right) + \left(5\dfrac{2}{3} + 0.15\right)}$

Step 2 $\boxed{\left(\dfrac{6}{8} + 4\right) + \left(5\dfrac{2}{3} + 0.15\right)} = \boxed{\left(\dfrac{6}{8} + \dfrac{4}{1}\right) + \left(5\dfrac{2}{3} + 0.15\right)}$

Step 3 $\boxed{\left(\dfrac{6}{8} + \dfrac{4}{1}\right) + \left(5\dfrac{2}{3} + 0.15\right)} = \boxed{\left(\dfrac{6}{8} + \dfrac{4}{1}\right) + \left(\dfrac{(5 \times 3) + 2}{3} + 0.15\right)}$

$= \boxed{\left(\dfrac{6}{8} + \dfrac{4}{1}\right) + \left(\dfrac{15 + 2}{3} + 0.15\right)} = \boxed{\left(\dfrac{6}{8} + \dfrac{4}{1}\right) + \left(\dfrac{17}{3} + 0.15\right)}$

Step 4a $\boxed{\textit{Not Applicable}}$

Step 4b
$$\left[\left(\frac{6}{8}+\frac{4}{1}\right)+\left(\frac{17}{3}+0.15\right)\right]=\left[\left(\frac{6}{8}+\frac{4}{1}\right)+\left(\frac{17}{3}+\frac{15}{100}\right)\right]$$

Step 5
$$\left[\left(\frac{6}{8}+\frac{4}{1}\right)+\left(\frac{17}{3}+\frac{15}{100}\right)\right]=\left[\left(\frac{(6\times1)+(4\times8)}{8\times1}\right)+\left(\frac{(17\times100)+(15\times3)}{3\times100}\right)\right]$$

$$=\left[\left(\frac{6+32}{8}\right)+\left(\frac{1700+45}{300}\right)\right]=\left[\left(\frac{38}{8}\right)+\left(\frac{1745}{300}\right)\right]=\left[\frac{38}{8}+\frac{1745}{300}\right]=\left[\frac{(38\times300)+(1745\times8)}{8\times300}\right]$$

$$=\left[\frac{11400+13960}{2400}\right]=\left[\frac{25360}{2400}\right]$$

Step 6
$$\frac{25360}{2400}=\frac{25360\div80}{2400\div80}=\frac{317}{30}$$

Step 7
$$\frac{317}{30}=\boxed{10\frac{17}{30}}$$

Example 9.1-7
$$\frac{3}{4}+0.2+1\frac{1}{5}+\frac{0.25}{0.3}=$$

Solution:

Step 1
$$\frac{3}{4}+0.2+1\frac{1}{5}+\frac{0.25}{0.3}=\left[\left(\frac{3}{4}+0.2\right)+\left(1\frac{1}{5}+\frac{0.25}{0.3}\right)\right]$$

Step 2
$$\boxed{\textit{Not Applicable}}$$

Step 3
$$\left[\left(\frac{3}{4}+0.2\right)+\left(1\frac{1}{5}+\frac{0.25}{0.3}\right)\right]=\left[\left(\frac{3}{4}+0.2\right)+\left(\frac{(1\times5)+1}{5}+\frac{0.25}{0.3}\right)\right]=\left[\left(\frac{3}{4}+0.2\right)+\left(\frac{5+1}{5}+\frac{0.25}{0.3}\right)\right]$$

$$=\left[\left(\frac{3}{4}+0.2\right)+\left(\frac{6}{5}+\frac{0.25}{0.3}\right)\right]$$

Step 4a
$$\left[\left(\frac{3}{4}+0.2\right)+\left(\frac{6}{5}+\frac{0.25}{0.3}\right)\right]=\left[\left(\frac{3}{4}+0.2\right)+\left(\frac{6}{5}+\frac{\frac{25}{100}}{\frac{3}{10}}\right)\right]=\left[\left(\frac{3}{4}+0.2\right)+\left(\frac{6}{5}+\frac{25\times10}{100\times3}\right)\right]$$

$$=\left[\left(\frac{3}{4}+0.2\right)+\left(\frac{6}{5}+\frac{250}{300}\right)\right]$$

Step 4b
$$\left[\left(\frac{3}{4}+0.2\right)+\left(\frac{6}{5}+\frac{250}{300}\right)\right]=\left[\left(\frac{3}{4}+\frac{2}{10}\right)+\left(\frac{6}{5}+\frac{250}{300}\right)\right]$$

Step 5
$$\left[\left(\frac{3}{4}+\frac{2}{10}\right)+\left(\frac{6}{5}+\frac{250}{300}\right)\right]=\left[\left(\frac{(3\times10)+(2\times4)}{4\times10}\right)+\left(\frac{(6\times300)+(250\times5)}{5\times300}\right)\right]$$

$$=\left[\left(\frac{30+8}{40}\right)+\left(\frac{1800+1250}{1500}\right)\right]=\left[\left(\frac{38}{40}\right)+\left(\frac{3050}{1500}\right)\right]=\left[\frac{38}{40}+\frac{3050}{1500}\right]$$

$$=\left[\frac{(38\times1500)+(3050\times40)}{40\times1500}\right]=\left[\frac{57000+122000}{60000}\right]=\left[\frac{179000}{60000}\right]$$

Step 6
$$\left[\frac{179000}{60000}\right]=\left[\frac{179000\div1000}{60000\div1000}\right]=\left[\frac{179}{60}\right]$$

Step 7
$$\left[\frac{179}{60}\right]=\left[\mathbf{2\frac{59}{60}}\right]$$

Example 9.1-8
$$\left[2\frac{1}{4}+\frac{0.1}{0.02}+4+\frac{3}{4}\right]=$$

Solution:

Step 1
$$\left[2\frac{1}{4}+\frac{0.1}{0.02}+4+\frac{3}{4}\right]=\left[\left(2\frac{1}{4}+\frac{0.1}{0.02}\right)+\left(4+\frac{3}{4}\right)\right]$$

Step 2
$$\left[\left(2\frac{1}{4}+\frac{0.1}{0.02}\right)+\left(4+\frac{3}{4}\right)\right]=\left[\left(2\frac{1}{4}+\frac{0.1}{0.02}\right)+\left(\frac{4}{1}+\frac{3}{4}\right)\right]$$

Step 3
$$\left[\left(2\frac{1}{4}+\frac{0.1}{0.02}\right)+\left(\frac{4}{1}+\frac{3}{4}\right)\right]=\left[\left(\frac{(2\times4)+1}{4}+\frac{0.1}{0.02}\right)+\left(\frac{4}{1}+\frac{3}{4}\right)\right]=\left[\left(\frac{8+1}{4}+\frac{0.1}{0.02}\right)+\left(\frac{4}{1}+\frac{3}{4}\right)\right]$$

$$=\left[\left(\frac{9}{4}+\frac{0.1}{0.02}\right)+\left(\frac{4}{1}+\frac{3}{4}\right)\right]$$

Step 4a
$$\left[\left(\frac{9}{4}+\frac{0.1}{0.02}\right)+\left(\frac{4}{1}+\frac{3}{4}\right)\right]=\left[\left(\frac{9}{4}+\frac{\frac{1}{10}}{\frac{2}{100}}\right)+\left(\frac{4}{1}+\frac{3}{4}\right)\right]=\left[\left(\frac{9}{4}+\frac{1\times100}{10\times2}\right)+\left(\frac{4}{1}+\frac{3}{4}\right)\right]$$

$$=\left[\left(\frac{9}{4}+\frac{100}{20}\right)+\left(\frac{4}{1}+\frac{3}{4}\right)\right]$$

Step 4b $\boxed{Not\ Applicable}$

Step 5 $\boxed{\left(\dfrac{9}{4}+\dfrac{100}{20}\right)+\left(\dfrac{4}{1}+\dfrac{3}{4}\right)}=\boxed{\left(\dfrac{(9\times20)+(100\times4)}{4\times20}\right)+\left(\dfrac{(4\times4)+(3\times1)}{1\times4}\right)}$

$=\boxed{\left(\dfrac{180+400}{80}\right)+\left(\dfrac{16+3}{4}\right)}=\boxed{\left(\dfrac{580}{80}\right)+\left(\dfrac{19}{4}\right)}=\boxed{\dfrac{580}{80}+\dfrac{19}{4}}=\boxed{\left(\dfrac{(580\times4)+(19\times80)}{80\times4}\right)}$

$=\boxed{\dfrac{2320+1520}{320}}=\boxed{\dfrac{3840}{320}}$

Step 6 $\boxed{\dfrac{3840}{320}}=\boxed{\dfrac{3840\div320}{320\div320}}=\boxed{\dfrac{12}{1}}=\boxed{\boxed{12}}$

Step 7 $\boxed{Not\ Applicable}$

Example 9.1-9

$\boxed{2\dfrac{4}{5}+3\dfrac{2}{5}+\dfrac{0.12}{0.1}+0.15+\dfrac{2}{3}=}$

Solution:

Step 1 $\boxed{2\dfrac{4}{5}+3\dfrac{2}{5}+\dfrac{0.12}{0.1}+0.15+\dfrac{2}{3}}=\boxed{\left(2\dfrac{4}{5}+3\dfrac{2}{5}\right)+\left(\dfrac{0.12}{0.1}+0.15\right)+\dfrac{2}{3}}$

Step 2 $\boxed{Not\ Applicable}$

Step 3 $\boxed{\left(2\dfrac{4}{5}+3\dfrac{2}{5}\right)+\left(\dfrac{0.12}{0.1}+0.15\right)+\dfrac{2}{3}}=\boxed{\left(\dfrac{(2\times5)+4}{5}+\dfrac{(3\times5)+2}{5}\right)+\left(\dfrac{0.12}{0.1}+0.15\right)+\dfrac{2}{3}}$

$=\boxed{\left(\dfrac{10+4}{5}+\dfrac{15+2}{5}\right)+\left(\dfrac{0.12}{0.1}+0.15\right)+\dfrac{2}{3}}=\boxed{\left(\dfrac{14}{5}+\dfrac{17}{5}\right)+\left(\dfrac{0.12}{0.1}+0.15\right)+\dfrac{2}{3}}$

Step 4a $\boxed{\left(\dfrac{14}{5}+\dfrac{17}{5}\right)+\left(\dfrac{0.12}{0.1}+0.15\right)+\dfrac{2}{3}}=\boxed{\left(\dfrac{14}{5}+\dfrac{17}{5}\right)+\left(\dfrac{\frac{12}{100}}{\frac{1}{10}}+0.15\right)+\dfrac{2}{3}}$

$=\boxed{\left(\dfrac{14}{5}+\dfrac{17}{5}\right)+\left(\dfrac{12\times10}{100\times1}+0.15\right)+\dfrac{2}{3}}=\boxed{\left(\dfrac{14}{5}+\dfrac{17}{5}\right)+\left(\dfrac{120}{100}+0.15\right)+\dfrac{2}{3}}$

Step 4b $\boxed{\left(\dfrac{14}{5}+\dfrac{17}{5}\right)+\left(\dfrac{120}{100}+0.15\right)+\dfrac{2}{3}}=\boxed{\left(\dfrac{14}{5}+\dfrac{17}{5}\right)+\left(\dfrac{120}{100}+\dfrac{15}{100}\right)+\dfrac{2}{3}}$

Step 5
$$\left[\left(\frac{14}{5}+\frac{17}{5}\right)+\left(\frac{120}{100}+\frac{15}{100}\right)+\frac{2}{3}\right]=\left[\left(\frac{14+17}{5}\right)+\left(\frac{120+15}{100}\right)+\frac{2}{3}\right]=\left[\left(\frac{31}{5}\right)+\left(\frac{135}{100}\right)+\frac{2}{3}\right]$$

$$=\left[\frac{31}{5}+\frac{135}{100}+\frac{2}{3}\right]=\left[\left(\frac{31}{5}+\frac{135}{100}\right)+\frac{2}{3}\right]=\left[\left(\frac{(31\times100)+(135\times5)}{5\times100}\right)+\frac{2}{3}\right]$$

$$=\left[\left(\frac{3100+675}{500}\right)+\frac{2}{3}\right]=\left[\left(\frac{3775}{500}\right)+\frac{2}{3}\right]=\left[\frac{3775}{500}+\frac{2}{3}\right]=\left[\frac{(3775\times3)+(2\times500)}{500\times3}\right]$$

$$=\left[\frac{11325+1000}{1500}\right]=\left[\frac{12325}{1500}\right]$$

Step 6
$$\left[\frac{12325}{1500}\right]=\left[\frac{12325\div25}{1500\div25}\right]=\left[\frac{493}{60}\right]$$

Step 7
$$\left[\frac{493}{60}\right]=\left[8\frac{13}{60}\right]$$

Example 9.1-10
$$\left[1\frac{2}{3}+0.8+\frac{2}{5}+\frac{1}{5}+2\frac{1}{4}+\frac{0.2}{1.8}\right]=$$

Solution:

Step 1
$$\left[1\frac{2}{3}+0.8+\frac{2}{5}+\frac{1}{5}+2\frac{1}{4}+\frac{0.2}{1.8}\right]=\left[\left(1\frac{2}{3}+0.8\right)+\left(\frac{2}{5}+\frac{1}{5}\right)+\left(2\frac{1}{4}+\frac{0.2}{1.8}\right)\right]$$

Step 2
$$\boxed{Not\ Applicable}$$

Step 3
$$\left[\left(1\frac{2}{3}+0.8\right)+\left(\frac{2}{5}+\frac{1}{5}\right)+\left(2\frac{1}{4}+\frac{0.2}{1.8}\right)\right]=\left[\left(\frac{(1\times3)+2}{3}+0.8\right)+\left(\frac{2}{5}+\frac{1}{5}\right)+\left(\frac{(2\times4)+1}{4}+\frac{0.2}{1.8}\right)\right]$$

$$=\left[\left(\frac{3+2}{3}+0.8\right)+\left(\frac{2}{5}+\frac{1}{5}\right)+\left(\frac{8+1}{4}+\frac{0.2}{1.8}\right)\right]=\left[\left(\frac{5}{3}+0.8\right)+\left(\frac{2}{5}+\frac{1}{5}\right)+\left(\frac{9}{4}+\frac{0.2}{1.8}\right)\right]$$

Step 4a
$$\left[\left(\frac{5}{3}+0.8\right)+\left(\frac{2}{5}+\frac{1}{5}\right)+\left(\frac{9}{4}+\frac{0.2}{1.8}\right)\right]=\left[\left(\frac{5}{3}+0.8\right)+\left(\frac{2}{5}+\frac{1}{5}\right)+\left(\frac{9}{4}+\frac{\frac{2}{10}}{\frac{18}{10}}\right)\right]$$

$$=\left[\left(\frac{5}{3}+0.8\right)+\left(\frac{2}{5}+\frac{1}{5}\right)+\left(\frac{9}{4}+\frac{2\times10}{10\times18}\right)\right]=\left[\left(\frac{5}{3}+0.8\right)+\left(\frac{2}{5}+\frac{1}{5}\right)+\left(\frac{9}{4}+\frac{20}{180}\right)\right]$$

Step 4b
$$\left(\frac{5}{3}+0.8\right)+\left(\frac{2}{5}+\frac{1}{5}\right)+\left(\frac{9}{4}+\frac{20}{180}\right)=\left(\frac{5}{3}+\frac{8}{10}\right)+\left(\frac{2}{5}+\frac{1}{5}\right)+\left(\frac{9}{4}+\frac{20}{180}\right)$$

Step 5
$$\left(\frac{5}{3}+\frac{8}{10}\right)+\left(\frac{2}{5}+\frac{1}{5}\right)+\left(\frac{9}{4}+\frac{20}{180}\right)=\left(\frac{(5\times10)+(8\times3)}{3\times10}\right)+\left(\frac{2+1}{5}\right)+\left(\frac{(9\times180)+(20\times4)}{4\times180}\right)$$

$$=\left(\frac{50+24}{30}\right)+\left(\frac{3}{5}\right)+\left(\frac{1620+80}{720}\right)=\left(\frac{74}{30}\right)+\frac{3}{5}+\left(\frac{1700}{720}\right)=\frac{74}{30}+\frac{3}{5}+\frac{1700}{720}$$

$$=\left(\frac{74}{30}+\frac{3}{5}\right)+\frac{1700}{720}=\left(\frac{(74\times5)+(3\times30)}{30\times5}\right)+\frac{1700}{720}=\left(\frac{370+90}{150}\right)+\frac{1700}{720}$$

$$=\left(\frac{460}{150}\right)+\frac{1700}{720}=\frac{460}{150}+\frac{1700}{720}=\frac{(460\times720)+(1700\times150)}{150\times720}=\frac{331200+255000}{108000}$$

$$=\frac{586200}{108000}$$

Step 6
$$\frac{586200}{108000}=\frac{586200\div100}{108000\div100}=\frac{5862}{1080}=\frac{5862\div2}{1080\div2}=\frac{2931}{540}$$

Step 7
$$\frac{2931}{540}=5\frac{231}{540}$$

The following examples further illustrate how to add integer, decimal, and mixed fractions:

Example 9.1-11

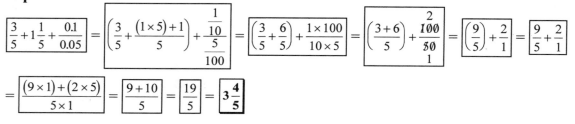

$$\frac{3}{5}+1\frac{1}{5}+\frac{0.1}{0.05}=\left(\frac{3}{5}+\frac{(1\times5)+1}{5}\right)+\frac{\frac{1}{10}}{\frac{5}{100}}=\left(\frac{3}{5}+\frac{6}{5}\right)+\frac{1\times100}{10\times5}=\left(\frac{3+6}{5}\right)+\frac{\overset{2}{\cancel{100}}}{\underset{1}{\cancel{50}}}=\left(\frac{9}{5}\right)+\frac{2}{1}=\frac{9}{5}+\frac{2}{1}$$

$$=\frac{(9\times1)+(2\times5)}{5\times1}=\frac{9+10}{5}=\frac{19}{5}=3\frac{4}{5}$$

Example 9.1-12

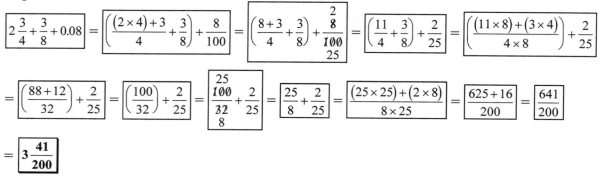

$$2\frac{3}{4}+\frac{3}{8}+0.08=\left(\frac{(2\times4)+3}{4}+\frac{3}{8}\right)+\frac{8}{100}=\left(\frac{8+3}{4}+\frac{3}{8}\right)+\frac{\overset{2}{\cancel{8}}}{\underset{25}{\cancel{100}}}=\left(\frac{11}{4}+\frac{3}{8}\right)+\frac{2}{25}=\left(\frac{(11\times8)+(3\times4)}{4\times8}\right)+\frac{2}{25}$$

$$=\left(\frac{88+12}{32}\right)+\frac{2}{25}=\left(\frac{100}{32}\right)+\frac{2}{25}=\frac{\overset{25}{\cancel{100}}}{\underset{8}{\cancel{32}}}+\frac{2}{25}=\frac{25}{8}+\frac{2}{25}=\frac{(25\times25)+(2\times8)}{8\times25}=\frac{625+16}{200}=\frac{641}{200}$$

$$=3\frac{41}{200}$$

Example 9.1-13

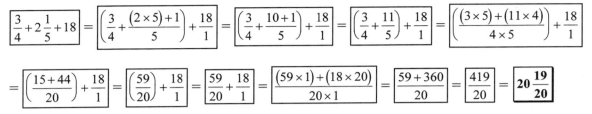

$$\frac{3}{4} + 2\frac{1}{5} + 18 = \left[\left(\frac{3}{4} + \frac{(2 \times 5)+1}{5}\right) + \frac{18}{1}\right] = \left[\left(\frac{3}{4} + \frac{10+1}{5}\right) + \frac{18}{1}\right] = \left[\left(\frac{3}{4} + \frac{11}{5}\right) + \frac{18}{1}\right] = \left[\left(\frac{(3 \times 5)+(11 \times 4)}{4 \times 5}\right) + \frac{18}{1}\right]$$

$$= \left[\left(\frac{15+44}{20}\right) + \frac{18}{1}\right] = \left[\left(\frac{59}{20}\right) + \frac{18}{1}\right] = \left[\frac{59}{20} + \frac{18}{1}\right] = \frac{(59 \times 1)+(18 \times 20)}{20 \times 1} = \frac{59+360}{20} = \frac{419}{20} = \boxed{20\frac{19}{20}}$$

Example 9.1-14

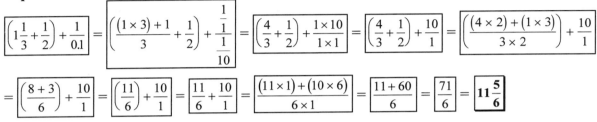

$$\left[\left(1\frac{1}{3} + \frac{1}{2}\right) + \frac{1}{0.1}\right] = \left[\left(\frac{(1 \times 3)+1}{3} + \frac{1}{2}\right) + \frac{1}{\frac{1}{10}}\right] = \left[\left(\frac{4}{3} + \frac{1}{2}\right) + \frac{1 \times 10}{1 \times 1}\right] = \left[\left(\frac{4}{3} + \frac{1}{2}\right) + \frac{10}{1}\right] = \left[\left(\frac{(4 \times 2)+(1 \times 3)}{3 \times 2}\right) + \frac{10}{1}\right]$$

$$= \left[\left(\frac{8+3}{6}\right) + \frac{10}{1}\right] = \left[\left(\frac{11}{6}\right) + \frac{10}{1}\right] = \left[\frac{11}{6} + \frac{10}{1}\right] = \frac{(11 \times 1)+(10 \times 6)}{6 \times 1} = \frac{11+60}{6} = \frac{71}{6} = \boxed{11\frac{5}{6}}$$

Example 9.1-15

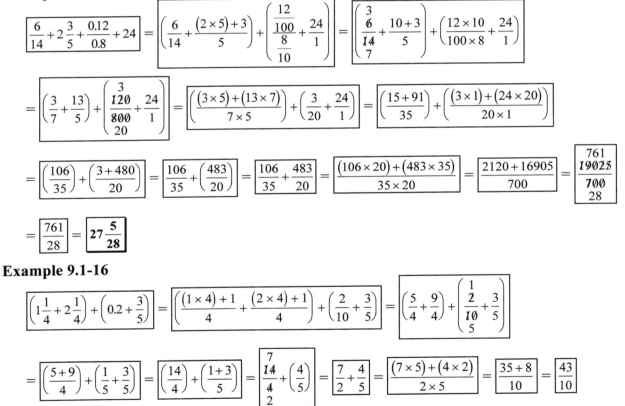

$$\frac{6}{14} + 2\frac{3}{5} + \frac{0.12}{0.8} + 24 = \left[\left(\frac{6}{14} + \frac{(2 \times 5)+3}{5}\right) + \left(\frac{\frac{12}{100}}{\frac{8}{10}} + \frac{24}{1}\right)\right] = \left[\left(\frac{\overset{3}{\cancel{6}}}{\underset{7}{\cancel{14}}} + \frac{10+3}{5}\right) + \left(\frac{12 \times 10}{100 \times 8} + \frac{24}{1}\right)\right]$$

$$= \left[\left(\frac{3}{7} + \frac{13}{5}\right) + \left(\frac{\overset{3}{\cancel{120}}}{\underset{20}{\cancel{800}}} + \frac{24}{1}\right)\right] = \left[\left(\frac{(3 \times 5)+(13 \times 7)}{7 \times 5}\right) + \left(\frac{3}{20} + \frac{24}{1}\right)\right] = \left[\left(\frac{15+91}{35}\right) + \left(\frac{(3 \times 1)+(24 \times 20)}{20 \times 1}\right)\right]$$

$$= \left[\left(\frac{106}{35}\right) + \left(\frac{3+480}{20}\right)\right] = \left[\frac{106}{35} + \left(\frac{483}{20}\right)\right] = \left[\frac{106}{35} + \frac{483}{20}\right] = \frac{(106 \times 20)+(483 \times 35)}{35 \times 20} = \frac{2120+16905}{700} = \frac{\overset{19025}{\cancel{19025}}}{\underset{28}{\cancel{700}}}$$

$$= \frac{761}{28} = \boxed{27\frac{5}{28}}$$

Example 9.1-16

$$\left[\left(1\frac{1}{4} + 2\frac{1}{4}\right) + \left(0.2 + \frac{3}{5}\right)\right] = \left[\left(\frac{(1 \times 4)+1}{4} + \frac{(2 \times 4)+1}{4}\right) + \left(\frac{2}{10} + \frac{3}{5}\right)\right] = \left[\left(\frac{5}{4} + \frac{9}{4}\right) + \left(\frac{\frac{1}{2}}{\underset{5}{\cancel{10}}} + \frac{3}{5}\right)\right]$$

$$= \left[\left(\frac{5+9}{4}\right) + \left(\frac{1}{5} + \frac{3}{5}\right)\right] = \left[\left(\frac{14}{4}\right) + \left(\frac{1+3}{5}\right)\right] = \frac{\overset{7}{\cancel{14}}}{\underset{2}{\cancel{4}}} + \left(\frac{4}{5}\right) = \frac{7}{2} + \frac{4}{5} = \frac{(7 \times 5)+(4 \times 2)}{2 \times 5} = \frac{35+8}{10} = \frac{43}{10}$$

$$= \boxed{4\frac{3}{10}}$$

Example 9.1-17

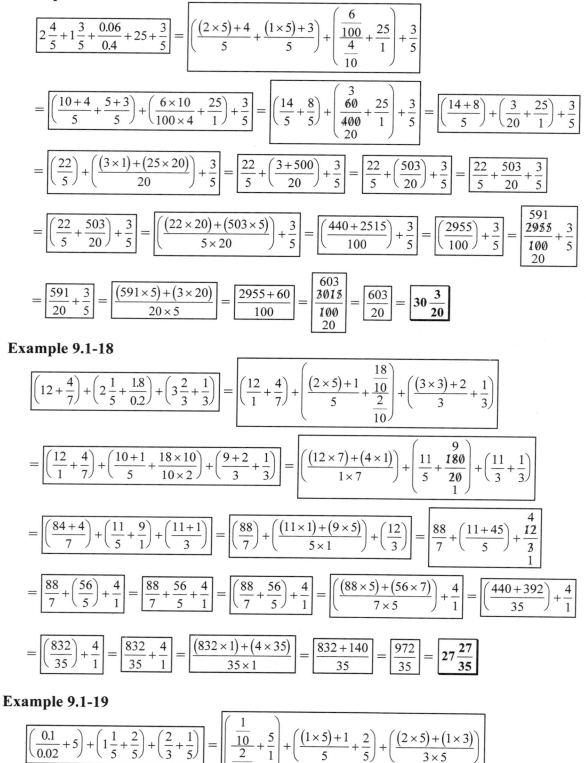

$$2\frac{4}{5}+1\frac{3}{5}+\frac{0.06}{0.4}+25+\frac{3}{5}=\left(\left(\frac{(2\times5)+4}{5}+\frac{(1\times5)+3}{5}\right)+\left(\frac{\frac{6}{100}}{\frac{4}{10}}+\frac{25}{1}\right)+\frac{3}{5}\right)$$

$$=\left(\left(\frac{10+4}{5}+\frac{5+3}{5}\right)+\left(\frac{6\times10}{100\times4}+\frac{25}{1}\right)+\frac{3}{5}\right)=\left(\left(\frac{14}{5}+\frac{8}{5}\right)+\left(\frac{\frac{3}{60}}{\frac{400}{20}}+\frac{25}{1}\right)+\frac{3}{5}\right)=\left(\left(\frac{14+8}{5}\right)+\left(\frac{3}{20}+\frac{25}{1}\right)+\frac{3}{5}\right)$$

$$=\left(\left(\frac{22}{5}\right)+\left(\frac{(3\times1)+(25\times20)}{20}\right)+\frac{3}{5}\right)=\frac{22}{5}+\left(\frac{3+500}{20}\right)+\frac{3}{5}=\frac{22}{5}+\left(\frac{503}{20}\right)+\frac{3}{5}=\frac{22}{5}+\frac{503}{20}+\frac{3}{5}$$

$$=\left(\left(\frac{22}{5}+\frac{503}{20}\right)+\frac{3}{5}\right)=\left(\left(\frac{(22\times20)+(503\times5)}{5\times20}\right)+\frac{3}{5}\right)=\left(\frac{440+2515}{100}\right)+\frac{3}{5}=\left(\frac{2955}{100}\right)+\frac{3}{5}=\frac{\overset{591}{\cancel{2955}}}{\underset{20}{\cancel{100}}}+\frac{3}{5}$$

$$=\frac{591}{20}+\frac{3}{5}=\frac{(591\times5)+(3\times20)}{20\times5}=\frac{2955+60}{100}=\frac{\overset{603}{\cancel{3015}}}{\underset{20}{\cancel{100}}}=\frac{603}{20}=\boxed{30\frac{3}{20}}$$

Example 9.1-18

$$\left(12+\frac{4}{7}\right)+\left(2\frac{1}{5}+\frac{1.8}{0.2}\right)+\left(3\frac{2}{3}+\frac{1}{3}\right)=\left(\left(\frac{12}{1}+\frac{4}{7}\right)+\left(\frac{(2\times5)+1}{5}+\frac{\frac{18}{10}}{\frac{2}{10}}\right)+\left(\frac{(3\times3)+2}{3}+\frac{1}{3}\right)\right)$$

$$=\left(\left(\frac{12}{1}+\frac{4}{7}\right)+\left(\frac{10+1}{5}+\frac{18\times10}{10\times2}\right)+\left(\frac{9+2}{3}+\frac{1}{3}\right)\right)=\left(\left(\frac{(12\times7)+(4\times1)}{1\times7}\right)+\left(\frac{11}{5}+\frac{\overset{9}{\cancel{180}}}{\underset{1}{\cancel{20}}}\right)+\left(\frac{11}{3}+\frac{1}{3}\right)\right)$$

$$=\left(\left(\frac{84+4}{7}\right)+\left(\frac{11}{5}+\frac{9}{1}\right)+\left(\frac{11+1}{3}\right)\right)=\left(\left(\frac{88}{7}\right)+\left(\frac{(11\times1)+(9\times5)}{5\times1}\right)+\left(\frac{12}{3}\right)\right)=\frac{88}{7}+\left(\frac{11+45}{5}\right)+\frac{\overset{4}{\cancel{12}}}{\underset{1}{\cancel{3}}}$$

$$=\frac{88}{7}+\left(\frac{56}{5}\right)+\frac{4}{1}=\frac{88}{7}+\frac{56}{5}+\frac{4}{1}=\left(\frac{88}{7}+\frac{56}{5}\right)+\frac{4}{1}=\left(\frac{(88\times5)+(56\times7)}{7\times5}\right)+\frac{4}{1}=\left(\frac{440+392}{35}\right)+\frac{4}{1}$$

$$=\left(\frac{832}{35}\right)+\frac{4}{1}=\frac{832}{35}+\frac{4}{1}=\frac{(832\times1)+(4\times35)}{35\times1}=\frac{832+140}{35}=\frac{972}{35}=\boxed{27\frac{27}{35}}$$

Example 9.1-19

$$\left(\frac{0.1}{0.02}+5\right)+\left(1\frac{1}{5}+\frac{2}{5}\right)+\left(\frac{2}{3}+\frac{1}{5}\right)=\left(\left(\frac{\frac{1}{10}}{\frac{2}{100}}+\frac{5}{1}\right)+\left(\frac{(1\times5)+1}{5}+\frac{2}{5}\right)+\left(\frac{(2\times5)+(1\times3)}{3\times5}\right)\right)$$

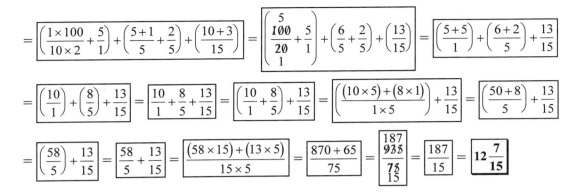

$$= \left[\left(\frac{1\times100}{10\times2}+\frac{5}{1}\right)+\left(\frac{5+1}{5}+\frac{2}{5}\right)+\left(\frac{10+3}{15}\right)\right] = \left[\left(\frac{\overset{5}{\cancel{100}}}{\underset{1}{\cancel{20}}}+\frac{5}{1}\right)+\left(\frac{6}{5}+\frac{2}{5}\right)+\left(\frac{13}{15}\right)\right] = \left[\left(\frac{5+5}{1}\right)+\left(\frac{6+2}{5}\right)+\frac{13}{15}\right]$$

$$= \left[\left(\frac{10}{1}\right)+\left(\frac{8}{5}\right)+\frac{13}{15}\right] = \left[\frac{10}{1}+\frac{8}{5}+\frac{13}{15}\right] = \left[\left(\frac{10}{1}+\frac{8}{5}\right)+\frac{13}{15}\right] = \left[\left(\frac{(10\times5)+(8\times1)}{1\times5}\right)+\frac{13}{15}\right] = \left[\left(\frac{50+8}{5}\right)+\frac{13}{15}\right]$$

$$= \left[\left(\frac{58}{5}\right)+\frac{13}{15}\right] = \left[\frac{58}{5}+\frac{13}{15}\right] = \frac{(58\times15)+(13\times5)}{15\times5} = \frac{870+65}{75} = \frac{\overset{187}{\cancel{935}}}{\underset{15}{\cancel{75}}} = \frac{187}{15} = \boxed{12\frac{7}{15}}$$

Example 9.1-20

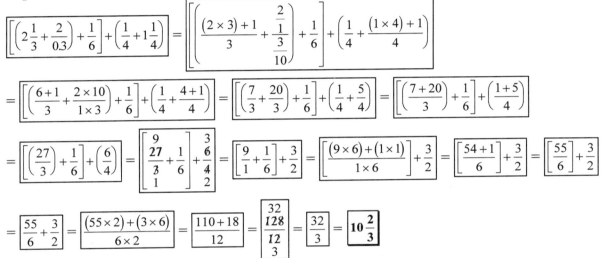

$$\left[\left(2\frac{1}{3}+\frac{2}{0.3}\right)+\frac{1}{6}\right]+\left(\frac{1}{4}+1\frac{1}{4}\right) = \left[\left(\frac{(2\times3)+1}{3}+\frac{\frac{2}{1}}{\frac{3}{10}}\right)+\frac{1}{6}\right]+\left(\frac{1}{4}+\frac{(1\times4)+1}{4}\right)$$

$$= \left[\left(\frac{6+1}{3}+\frac{2\times10}{1\times3}\right)+\frac{1}{6}\right]+\left(\frac{1}{4}+\frac{4+1}{4}\right) = \left[\left(\frac{7}{3}+\frac{20}{3}\right)+\frac{1}{6}\right]+\left(\frac{1}{4}+\frac{5}{4}\right) = \left[\left(\frac{7+20}{3}\right)+\frac{1}{6}\right]+\left(\frac{1+5}{4}\right)$$

$$= \left[\left(\frac{27}{3}\right)+\frac{1}{6}\right]+\left(\frac{6}{4}\right) = \left[\frac{\overset{9}{\cancel{27}}}{\underset{1}{\cancel{3}}}+\frac{1}{6}+\frac{\overset{3}{\cancel{6}}}{\underset{2}{\cancel{4}}}\right] = \left[\frac{9}{1}+\frac{1}{6}\right]+\frac{3}{2} = \left[\frac{(9\times6)+(1\times1)}{1\times6}\right]+\frac{3}{2} = \left[\frac{54+1}{6}\right]+\frac{3}{2} = \left[\frac{55}{6}\right]+\frac{3}{2}$$

$$= \frac{55}{6}+\frac{3}{2} = \frac{(55\times2)+(3\times6)}{6\times2} = \frac{110+18}{12} = \frac{\overset{32}{\cancel{128}}}{\underset{3}{\cancel{12}}} = \frac{32}{3} = \boxed{10\frac{2}{3}}$$

Example 9.1-21

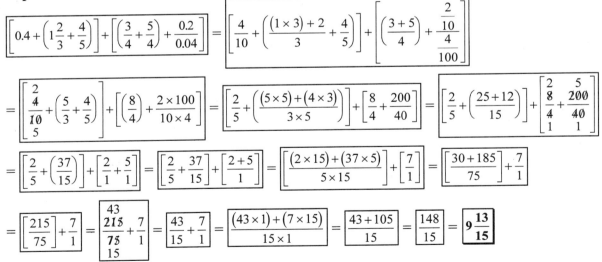

$$\left[0.4+\left(1\frac{2}{3}+\frac{4}{5}\right)\right]+\left[\left(\frac{3}{4}+\frac{5}{4}\right)+\frac{0.2}{0.04}\right] = \left[\frac{4}{10}+\left(\frac{(1\times3)+2}{3}+\frac{4}{5}\right)\right]+\left[\left(\frac{3+5}{4}\right)+\frac{\frac{2}{10}}{\frac{4}{100}}\right]$$

$$= \left[\frac{\overset{2}{\cancel{4}}}{\underset{5}{\cancel{10}}}+\left(\frac{5}{3}+\frac{4}{5}\right)\right]+\left[\left(\frac{8}{4}\right)+\frac{2\times100}{10\times4}\right] = \left[\frac{2}{5}+\left(\frac{(5\times5)+(4\times3)}{3\times5}\right)\right]+\left[\frac{8}{4}+\frac{200}{40}\right] = \left[\frac{2}{5}+\left(\frac{25+12}{15}\right)\right]+\left[\frac{\overset{2}{\cancel{8}}}{\underset{1}{\cancel{4}}}+\frac{\overset{5}{\cancel{200}}}{\underset{1}{\cancel{40}}}\right]$$

$$= \left[\frac{2}{5}+\left(\frac{37}{15}\right)\right]+\left[\frac{2}{1}+\frac{5}{1}\right] = \left[\frac{2}{5}+\frac{37}{15}\right]+\left[\frac{2+5}{1}\right] = \left[\frac{(2\times15)+(37\times5)}{5\times15}\right]+\left[\frac{7}{1}\right] = \left[\frac{30+185}{75}\right]+\frac{7}{1}$$

$$= \left[\frac{215}{75}\right]+\frac{7}{1} = \frac{\overset{43}{\cancel{215}}}{\underset{15}{\cancel{75}}}+\frac{7}{1} = \frac{43}{15}+\frac{7}{1} = \frac{(43\times1)+(7\times15)}{15\times1} = \frac{43+105}{15} = \frac{148}{15} = \boxed{9\frac{13}{15}}$$

Section 9.1 Exercises - Add the following integer, decimal, and mixed fractions:

1. $1\dfrac{2}{5} + \dfrac{3}{5} + 0.5 =$

2. $2\dfrac{1}{3} + \dfrac{3}{4} + \dfrac{0.12}{0.1} =$

3. $1\dfrac{3}{5} + \dfrac{0.3}{0.8} + 6 =$

4. $4\dfrac{3}{5} + \dfrac{3}{8} + \dfrac{0.1}{1.2} + 4 =$

5. $\dfrac{2}{8} + \dfrac{3}{8} + 1\dfrac{1}{5} + 2.8 =$

6. $\left(\dfrac{3}{4} + 2\right) + \left(1\dfrac{1}{5} + 0.5\right) =$

7. $\dfrac{3}{5} + 1\dfrac{1}{2} + 2.4 + \dfrac{6}{10} =$

8. $2\dfrac{3}{4} + \dfrac{1}{5} + \dfrac{3}{8} + 0.4 + 3\dfrac{2}{3} =$

9. $\left(\dfrac{3}{7} + 2\dfrac{1}{7}\right) + \left(3\dfrac{4}{5} + 1\dfrac{2}{5}\right) + \dfrac{0.1}{0.01} =$

10. $\dfrac{3}{5} + \left(\dfrac{3.2}{1.6} + 3\dfrac{2}{3}\right) + \left(\dfrac{0.3}{2.6} + 2\right) =$

9.2   Subtracting Integer, Decimal, and Mixed Fractions

Fractions of the following forms:

1. $\left(\dfrac{a}{b}\right)$ where (a) and (b) are integers,

2. $\left(\dfrac{a \times 10^{-k_1}}{b \times 10^{-k_2}}\right)$ where (a) and (b) are integer numbers and (k_1) and (k_2) are equal to the number

   of decimal places, and

3. $\left(k\dfrac{a}{b}\right)$ where (k) is made up of a whole number and $\left(\dfrac{a}{b}\right)$ is an integer fraction for a number

   less than one

are subtracted as in the following cases:

Case I   Subtracting Integer, Decimal, and Mixed Fractions With Three Terms Only

Subtract three integer, decimal, and mixed fractions using the following steps:

Step 1   Use parentheses to group the first and second fractions.

Step 2   Change the integer number (a) to an integer fraction of the form $\left(\dfrac{a}{1}\right)$, e.g., change 5

   to $\dfrac{5}{1}$.

Step 3   Change the mixed fraction to an integer fraction (see Section 2.5).

Step 4   a. Change the decimal fraction to an integer fraction (see Section 2.4).

   b. Change the decimal number $\left(a \times 10^{-k}\right)$ to an integer fraction of the form $\left(\dfrac{a}{10^k}\right)$,

   e.g., change 0.08 to $\dfrac{8}{100}$.

Step 5   Subtract the integer fractions (see Section 3.2).

Step 6   Simplify the fraction to its lowest term (see Section 2.3).

Step 7   Change the improper fraction to a mixed fraction if the fraction obtained from Step 6
   is an improper fraction (see Section 2.2).

The following examples show the steps as to how integer, decimal and mixed fractions with
three terms only are subtracted:

Example 9.2-1

$$\boxed{\dfrac{4}{5} - 2\dfrac{3}{8} - \dfrac{0.3}{2.4}} =$$

Solution:

Step 1 $\boxed{\dfrac{4}{5} - 2\dfrac{3}{8} - \dfrac{0.3}{2.4}} = \boxed{\left(\dfrac{4}{5} - 2\dfrac{3}{8}\right) - \dfrac{0.3}{2.4}}$

Step 2 $\boxed{Not\ Applicable}$

Step 3 $\boxed{\left(\dfrac{4}{5} - 2\dfrac{3}{8}\right) - \dfrac{0.3}{2.4}} = \boxed{\left(\dfrac{4}{5} - \dfrac{(2\times8)+3}{8}\right) - \dfrac{0.3}{2.4}} = \boxed{\left(\dfrac{4}{5} - \dfrac{16+3}{8}\right) - \dfrac{0.3}{2.4}} = \boxed{\left(\dfrac{4}{5} - \dfrac{19}{8}\right) - \dfrac{0.3}{2.4}}$

Step 4a $\boxed{\left(\dfrac{4}{5} - \dfrac{19}{8}\right) - \dfrac{0.3}{2.4}} = \boxed{\left(\dfrac{4}{5} - \dfrac{19}{8}\right) - \dfrac{\dfrac{3}{10}}{\dfrac{24}{10}}} = \boxed{\left(\dfrac{4}{5} - \dfrac{19}{8}\right) - \dfrac{3\times10}{10\times24}} = \boxed{\left(\dfrac{4}{5} - \dfrac{19}{8}\right) - \dfrac{30}{240}}$

Step 4b $\boxed{\textit{Not Applicable}}$

Step 5 $\boxed{\left(\dfrac{4}{5} - \dfrac{19}{8}\right) - \dfrac{30}{240}} = \boxed{\left(\dfrac{(4\times8)-(19\times5)}{5\times8}\right) - \dfrac{30}{240}} = \boxed{\left(\dfrac{32-95}{40}\right) - \dfrac{30}{240}} = \boxed{\left(\dfrac{-63}{40}\right) - \dfrac{30}{240}}$

$= \boxed{\dfrac{-63}{40} - \dfrac{30}{240}} = \boxed{\dfrac{(-63\times240)-(30\times40)}{40\times240}} = \boxed{\dfrac{-15120-1200}{9600}} = \boxed{\dfrac{-16320}{9600}}$

Step 6 $\boxed{\dfrac{-16320}{9600}} = \boxed{\dfrac{-16320\div320}{9600\div320}} = \boxed{\dfrac{-51}{30}}$

Step 7 $\boxed{\dfrac{-51}{30}} = \boxed{-\left(1\dfrac{21}{30}\right)}$

Example 9.2-2

$\boxed{12\dfrac{1}{5} - \dfrac{2}{3} - 0.5} =$

Solution:

Step 1 $\boxed{12\dfrac{1}{5} - \dfrac{2}{3} - 0.5} = \boxed{\left(12\dfrac{1}{5} - \dfrac{2}{3}\right) - 0.5}$

Step 2 $\boxed{\textit{Not Applicable}}$

Step 3 $\boxed{\left(12\dfrac{1}{5} - \dfrac{2}{3}\right) - 0.5} = \boxed{\left(\dfrac{(12\times5)+1}{5} - \dfrac{2}{3}\right) - 0.5} = \boxed{\left(\dfrac{(12\times5)+1}{5} - \dfrac{2}{3}\right) - 0.5}$

$= \boxed{\left(\dfrac{60+1}{5} - \dfrac{2}{3}\right) - 0.5} = \boxed{\left(\dfrac{61}{5} - \dfrac{2}{3}\right) - 0.5}$

Step 4a $\boxed{\textit{Not Applicable}}$

Step 4b $\boxed{\left(\dfrac{61}{5} - \dfrac{2}{3}\right) - 0.5} = \boxed{\left(\dfrac{61}{5} - \dfrac{2}{3}\right) - \dfrac{5}{10}}$

Step 5
$$\left(\frac{61}{5}-\frac{2}{3}\right)-\frac{5}{10}=\left(\frac{(61\times3)-(2\times5)}{5\times3}\right)-\frac{5}{10}=\left(\frac{183-10}{15}\right)-\frac{5}{10}=\left(\frac{173}{15}\right)-\frac{5}{10}$$

$$=\frac{173}{15}-\frac{5}{10}=\frac{(173\times10)-(5\times15)}{15\times10}=\frac{1730-75}{150}=\frac{1655}{150}$$

Step 6
$$\frac{1655}{150}=\frac{1655\div5}{150\div5}=\frac{331}{30}$$

Step 7
$$\frac{331}{30}=11\frac{1}{30}$$

Example 9.2-3

$$12-1\frac{2}{3}-\frac{0.6}{0.02}=$$

Solution:

Step 1
$$12-1\frac{2}{3}-\frac{0.6}{0.02}=\left(12-1\frac{2}{3}\right)-\frac{0.6}{0.02}$$

Step 2
$$\left(12-1\frac{2}{3}\right)-\frac{0.6}{0.02}=\left(\frac{12}{1}-1\frac{2}{3}\right)-\frac{0.6}{0.02}$$

Step 3
$$\left(\frac{12}{1}-1\frac{2}{3}\right)-\frac{0.6}{0.02}=\left(\frac{12}{1}-\frac{(1\times3)+2}{3}\right)-\frac{0.6}{0.02}=\left(\frac{12}{1}-\frac{3+2}{3}\right)-\frac{0.6}{0.02}$$

$$=\left(\frac{12}{1}-\frac{5}{3}\right)-\frac{0.6}{0.02}$$

Step 4a
$$\left(\frac{12}{1}-\frac{5}{3}\right)-\frac{0.6}{0.02}=\left(\frac{12}{1}-\frac{5}{3}\right)-\frac{\frac{6}{10}}{\frac{2}{100}}=\left(\frac{12}{1}-\frac{5}{3}\right)-\frac{6\times100}{10\times2}=\left(\frac{12}{1}-\frac{5}{3}\right)-\frac{600}{20}$$

Step 4b   Not Applicable

Step 5
$$\left(\frac{12}{1}-\frac{5}{3}\right)-\frac{600}{20}=\left(\frac{(12\times3)-(5\times1)}{1\times3}\right)-\frac{600}{20}=\left(\frac{36-5}{3}\right)-\frac{600}{20}=\left(\frac{31}{3}\right)-\frac{600}{20}$$

$$=\frac{31}{3}-\frac{600}{20}=\frac{(31\times20)-(600\times3)}{3\times20}=\frac{620-1800}{60}=\frac{-1180}{60}$$

Step 6
$$\frac{-1180}{60}=\frac{-1180\div20}{60\div20}=\frac{-59}{3}$$

Step 7 $\boxed{\dfrac{-59}{3}} = \boxed{-\left(19\dfrac{2}{3}\right)}$

Example 9.2-4

$\boxed{\dfrac{3}{5} - \dfrac{2.5}{0.03} - 3\dfrac{2}{5}} =$

Solution:

Step 1 $\boxed{\dfrac{3}{5} - \dfrac{2.5}{0.03} - 3\dfrac{2}{5}} = \boxed{\left(\dfrac{3}{5} - \dfrac{2.5}{0.03}\right) - 3\dfrac{2}{5}}$

Step 2 $\boxed{\textit{Not Applicable}}$

Step 3 $\boxed{\left(\dfrac{3}{5} - \dfrac{2.5}{0.03}\right) - 3\dfrac{2}{5}} = \boxed{\left(\dfrac{3}{5} - \dfrac{2.5}{0.03}\right) - \dfrac{(3\times 5)+2}{5}} = \boxed{\left(\dfrac{3}{5} - \dfrac{2.5}{0.03}\right) - \dfrac{15+2}{5}} = \boxed{\left(\dfrac{3}{5} - \dfrac{2.5}{0.03}\right) - \dfrac{17}{5}}$

Step 4a $\boxed{\left(\dfrac{3}{5} - \dfrac{2.5}{0.03}\right) - \dfrac{17}{5}} = \boxed{\left(\dfrac{3}{5} - \dfrac{\frac{25}{10}}{\frac{3}{100}}\right) - \dfrac{17}{5}} = \boxed{\left(\dfrac{3}{5} - \dfrac{25\times 100}{10\times 3}\right) - \dfrac{17}{5}} = \boxed{\left(\dfrac{3}{5} - \dfrac{2500}{30}\right) - \dfrac{17}{5}}$

Step 4b $\boxed{\textit{Not Applicable}}$

Step 5 $\boxed{\left(\dfrac{3}{5} - \dfrac{2500}{30}\right) - \dfrac{17}{5}} = \boxed{\left(\dfrac{(3\times 30)-(2500\times 5)}{5\times 30}\right) - \dfrac{17}{5}} = \boxed{\left(\dfrac{90-12500}{150}\right) - \dfrac{17}{5}}$

$= \boxed{\left(\dfrac{-12410}{150}\right) - \dfrac{17}{5}} = \boxed{\dfrac{-12410}{150} - \dfrac{17}{5}} = \boxed{\dfrac{(-12410\times 5)-(17\times 150)}{150\times 5}} = \boxed{\dfrac{-62050-2550}{750}}$

$= \boxed{\dfrac{-64600}{750}}$

Step 6 $\boxed{\dfrac{-64600}{750}} = \boxed{\dfrac{-64600\div 50}{750\div 50}} = \boxed{\dfrac{-1292}{15}}$

Step 7 $\boxed{\dfrac{-1292}{15}} = \boxed{-\left(86\dfrac{2}{15}\right)}$

Example 9.2-5

$$\boxed{\dfrac{0.22}{0.06} - 24 - 2\dfrac{5}{8}} =$$

Solution:

Step 1
$$\boxed{\dfrac{0.22}{0.06} - 24 - 2\dfrac{5}{8}} = \boxed{\left(\dfrac{0.22}{0.06} - 24\right) - 2\dfrac{5}{8}}$$

Step 2
$$\boxed{\left(\dfrac{0.22}{0.06} - 24\right) - 2\dfrac{5}{8}} = \boxed{\left(\dfrac{0.22}{0.06} - \dfrac{24}{1}\right) - 2\dfrac{5}{8}}$$

Step 3
$$\boxed{\left(\dfrac{0.22}{0.06} - \dfrac{24}{1}\right) - 2\dfrac{5}{8}} = \boxed{\left(\dfrac{0.22}{0.06} - \dfrac{24}{1}\right) - \dfrac{(2\times8)+5}{8}} = \boxed{\left(\dfrac{0.22}{0.06} - \dfrac{24}{1}\right) - \dfrac{16+5}{8}}$$

$$= \boxed{\left(\dfrac{0.22}{0.06} - \dfrac{24}{1}\right) - \dfrac{21}{8}}$$

Step 4a
$$\boxed{\left(\dfrac{0.22}{0.06} - \dfrac{24}{1}\right) - \dfrac{21}{8}} = \boxed{\left(\dfrac{\dfrac{22}{100}}{\dfrac{6}{100}} - \dfrac{24}{1}\right) - \dfrac{21}{8}} = \boxed{\left(\dfrac{22\times100}{100\times6} - \dfrac{24}{1}\right) - \dfrac{21}{8}} = \boxed{\left(\dfrac{2200}{600} - \dfrac{24}{1}\right) - \dfrac{21}{8}}$$

Step 4b
$$\boxed{\textit{Not Applicable}}$$

Step 5
$$\boxed{\left(\dfrac{2200}{600} - \dfrac{24}{1}\right) - \dfrac{21}{8}} = \boxed{\left(\dfrac{(2200\times1)-(24\times600)}{600\times1}\right) - \dfrac{21}{8}} = \boxed{\left(\dfrac{2200-14400}{600}\right) - \dfrac{21}{8}}$$

$$= \boxed{\left(\dfrac{-12200}{600}\right) - \dfrac{21}{8}} = \boxed{\dfrac{-12200}{600} - \dfrac{21}{8}} = \boxed{\dfrac{(-12200\times8)-(21\times600)}{600\times8}} = \boxed{\dfrac{-97600-12600}{4800}}$$

$$= \boxed{\dfrac{-110200}{4800}}$$

Step 6
$$\boxed{\dfrac{-110200}{4800}} = \boxed{\dfrac{-110200\div200}{4800\div200}} = \boxed{\dfrac{-551}{24}}$$

Step 7
$$\boxed{\dfrac{-551}{24}} = \boxed{-\left(\mathbf{22\dfrac{23}{24}}\right)}$$

Case II   Subtracting Integer, Decimal, and Mixed Fractions With More Than Three Terms

Subtract integer, decimal, and mixed fractions having more than three terms by using the following steps:

Step 1   Use parentheses to group the numbers in pairs, e.g., group the first and second numbers, third and fourth numbers, fifth and sixth numbers, etc. together.

Step 2   Change the integer number(s) (a) to an integer fraction(s) of the form $\left(\dfrac{a}{1}\right)$, e.g., change 38 to $\dfrac{38}{1}$.

Step 3   Change the mixed fraction(s) to integer fraction(s) (see Section 2.5).

Step 4   a. Change the decimal fraction(s) to integer fraction(s) (see Section 2.4).

b. Change the decimal number(s) $\left(a \times 10^{-k}\right)$ to integer fraction(s) of the form $\left(\dfrac{a}{10^k}\right)$, e.g., change 2.05 to $\dfrac{205}{100}$.

Step 5   Subtract the integer fractions (see Section 3.2).

Step 6   Simplify the fraction to its lowest term (see Section 2.3).

Step 7   Change the improper fraction to a mixed fraction if the fraction obtained from Step 6 is an improper fraction (see Section 2.2).

The following examples show the steps as to how integer, decimal and mixed fractions having more than three terms are subtracted:

Example 9.2-6

$$8 - \frac{2}{3} - 1\frac{2}{8} - \frac{0.2}{3.2} =$$

Solution:

Step 1

$$8 - \frac{2}{3} - 1\frac{2}{8} - \frac{0.2}{3.2} = \left[\left(8 - \frac{2}{3}\right) + \left(-1\frac{2}{8} - \frac{0.2}{3.2}\right)\right]$$

Step 2

$$\left[\left(8 - \frac{2}{3}\right) + \left(-1\frac{2}{8} - \frac{0.2}{3.2}\right)\right] = \left[\left(\frac{8}{1} - \frac{2}{3}\right) + \left(-1\frac{2}{8} - \frac{0.2}{3.2}\right)\right]$$

Step 3

$$\left[\left(\frac{8}{1} - \frac{2}{3}\right) + \left(-1\frac{2}{8} - \frac{0.2}{3.2}\right)\right] = \left[\left(\frac{8}{1} - \frac{2}{3}\right) + \left(-\frac{(1\times 8)+2}{8} - \frac{0.2}{3.2}\right)\right] = \left[\left(\frac{8}{1} - \frac{2}{3}\right) + \left(-\frac{8+2}{8} - \frac{0.2}{3.2}\right)\right]$$

$$= \left[\left(\frac{8}{1} - \frac{2}{3}\right) + \left(-\frac{10}{8} - \frac{0.2}{3.2}\right)\right]$$

Step 4a $$\left(\dfrac{8}{1}-\dfrac{2}{3}\right)+\left(-\dfrac{10}{8}-\dfrac{0.2}{3.2}\right)=\left(\dfrac{8}{1}-\dfrac{2}{3}\right)+\left(-\dfrac{10}{8}-\dfrac{\frac{2}{10}}{\frac{32}{10}}\right)=\left(\dfrac{8}{1}-\dfrac{2}{3}\right)+\left(-\dfrac{10}{8}-\dfrac{2\times10}{10\times32}\right)$$

$$=\left(\dfrac{8}{1}-\dfrac{2}{3}\right)+\left(-\dfrac{10}{8}-\dfrac{20}{320}\right)$$

Step 4b $\boxed{Not\ Applicable}$

Step 5 $$\left(\dfrac{8}{1}-\dfrac{2}{3}\right)+\left(-\dfrac{10}{8}-\dfrac{20}{320}\right)=\left(\dfrac{(8\times3)-(2\times1)}{1\times3}\right)+\left(\dfrac{(-10\times320)-(20\times8)}{8\times320}\right)$$

$$=\left(\dfrac{24-2}{3}\right)+\left(\dfrac{-3200-160}{2560}\right)=\left(\dfrac{22}{3}\right)+\left(\dfrac{-3360}{2560}\right)=\dfrac{22}{3}+\dfrac{-3360}{2560}=\dfrac{22}{3}-\dfrac{3360}{2560}$$

$$=\dfrac{(22\times2560)-(3360\times3)}{3\times2560}=\dfrac{56320-10080}{7680}=\dfrac{46240}{7680}$$

Step 6 $$\dfrac{46240}{7680}=\dfrac{46240\div160}{7680\div160}=\dfrac{289}{48}$$

Step 7 $$\dfrac{289}{48}=\boxed{6\dfrac{1}{48}}$$

Example 9.2-7

$$6\dfrac{2}{3}-\dfrac{1}{3}-\dfrac{0.15}{0.5}-0.12=$$

Solution:

Step 1 $$6\dfrac{2}{3}-\dfrac{1}{3}-\dfrac{0.15}{0.5}-0.12=\left(6\dfrac{2}{3}-\dfrac{1}{3}\right)+\left(-\dfrac{0.15}{0.5}-0.12\right)$$

Step 2 $\boxed{Not\ Applicable}$

Step 3 $$\left(6\dfrac{2}{3}-\dfrac{1}{3}\right)+\left(-\dfrac{0.15}{0.5}-0.12\right)=\left(\dfrac{(6\times3)+2}{3}-\dfrac{1}{3}\right)+\left(-\dfrac{0.15}{0.5}-0.12\right)$$

$$=\left(\dfrac{18+2}{3}-\dfrac{1}{3}\right)+\left(-\dfrac{0.15}{0.5}-0.12\right)=\left(\dfrac{20}{3}-\dfrac{1}{3}\right)+\left(-\dfrac{0.15}{0.5}-0.12\right)$$

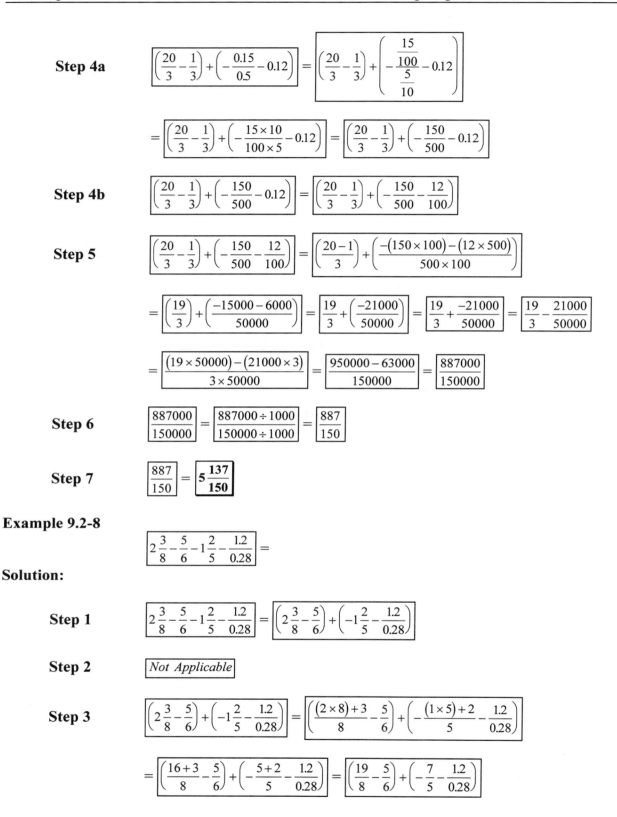

Step 4a $\left[\left(\dfrac{20}{3}-\dfrac{1}{3}\right)+\left(-\dfrac{0.15}{0.5}-0.12\right)\right]=\left[\left(\dfrac{20}{3}-\dfrac{1}{3}\right)+\left(-\dfrac{\dfrac{15}{100}}{\dfrac{5}{10}}-0.12\right)\right]$

$=\left[\left(\dfrac{20}{3}-\dfrac{1}{3}\right)+\left(-\dfrac{15\times10}{100\times5}-0.12\right)\right]=\left[\left(\dfrac{20}{3}-\dfrac{1}{3}\right)+\left(-\dfrac{150}{500}-0.12\right)\right]$

Step 4b $\left[\left(\dfrac{20}{3}-\dfrac{1}{3}\right)+\left(-\dfrac{150}{500}-0.12\right)\right]=\left[\left(\dfrac{20}{3}-\dfrac{1}{3}\right)+\left(-\dfrac{150}{500}-\dfrac{12}{100}\right)\right]$

Step 5 $\left[\left(\dfrac{20}{3}-\dfrac{1}{3}\right)+\left(-\dfrac{150}{500}-\dfrac{12}{100}\right)\right]=\left[\left(\dfrac{20-1}{3}\right)+\left(\dfrac{-(150\times100)-(12\times500)}{500\times100}\right)\right]$

$=\left[\left(\dfrac{19}{3}\right)+\left(\dfrac{-15000-6000}{50000}\right)\right]=\left[\dfrac{19}{3}+\left(\dfrac{-21000}{50000}\right)\right]=\left[\dfrac{19}{3}+\dfrac{-21000}{50000}\right]=\left[\dfrac{19}{3}-\dfrac{21000}{50000}\right]$

$=\left[\dfrac{(19\times50000)-(21000\times3)}{3\times50000}\right]=\left[\dfrac{950000-63000}{150000}\right]=\left[\dfrac{887000}{150000}\right]$

Step 6 $\left[\dfrac{887000}{150000}\right]=\left[\dfrac{887000\div1000}{150000\div1000}\right]=\left[\dfrac{887}{150}\right]$

Step 7 $\left[\dfrac{887}{150}\right]=\boxed{5\dfrac{137}{150}}$

Example 9.2-8

$\boxed{2\dfrac{3}{8}-\dfrac{5}{6}-1\dfrac{2}{5}-\dfrac{1.2}{0.28}}=$

Solution:

Step 1 $\boxed{2\dfrac{3}{8}-\dfrac{5}{6}-1\dfrac{2}{5}-\dfrac{1.2}{0.28}}=\left[\left(2\dfrac{3}{8}-\dfrac{5}{6}\right)+\left(-1\dfrac{2}{5}-\dfrac{1.2}{0.28}\right)\right]$

Step 2 $\boxed{Not\ Applicable}$

Step 3 $\left[\left(2\dfrac{3}{8}-\dfrac{5}{6}\right)+\left(-1\dfrac{2}{5}-\dfrac{1.2}{0.28}\right)\right]=\left[\left(\dfrac{(2\times8)+3}{8}-\dfrac{5}{6}\right)+\left(-\dfrac{(1\times5)+2}{5}-\dfrac{1.2}{0.28}\right)\right]$

$=\left[\left(\dfrac{16+3}{8}-\dfrac{5}{6}\right)+\left(-\dfrac{5+2}{5}-\dfrac{1.2}{0.28}\right)\right]=\left[\left(\dfrac{19}{8}-\dfrac{5}{6}\right)+\left(-\dfrac{7}{5}-\dfrac{1.2}{0.28}\right)\right]$

Step 4a
$$\left[\left(\frac{19}{8}-\frac{5}{6}\right)+\left(-\frac{7}{5}-\frac{1.2}{0.28}\right)\right]=\left[\left(\frac{19}{8}-\frac{5}{6}\right)+\left(-\frac{7}{5}-\frac{\frac{12}{10}}{\frac{28}{100}}\right)\right]=\left[\left(\frac{19}{8}-\frac{5}{6}\right)+\left(-\frac{7}{5}-\frac{12\times100}{10\times28}\right)\right]$$

$$=\left[\left(\frac{19}{8}-\frac{5}{6}\right)+\left(-\frac{7}{5}-\frac{1200}{280}\right)\right]$$

Step 4b   Not Applicable

Step 5
$$\left[\left(\frac{19}{8}-\frac{5}{6}\right)+\left(-\frac{7}{5}-\frac{1200}{280}\right)\right]=\left[\left(\frac{(19\times6)-(5\times8)}{8\times6}\right)+\left(\frac{(-7\times280)-(1200\times5)}{5\times280}\right)\right]$$

$$=\left[\left(\frac{114-40}{48}\right)+\left(\frac{-1960-6000}{1400}\right)\right]=\left[\left(\frac{74}{48}\right)+\left(\frac{-7960}{1400}\right)\right]=\left[\frac{74}{48}+\frac{-7960}{1400}\right]=\left[\frac{74}{48}-\frac{7960}{1400}\right]$$

$$=\left[\frac{(74\times1400)-(7960\times48)}{48\times1400}\right]=\left[\frac{103600-382080}{67200}\right]=\left[\frac{-278480}{67200}\right]$$

Step 6
$$\left[\frac{-278480}{67200}\right]=\left[\frac{-278480\div80}{67200\div80}\right]=\left[\frac{-3481}{840}\right]$$

Step 7
$$\left[\frac{-3481}{840}\right]=\left[-\left(4\frac{121}{840}\right)\right]$$

Example 9.2-9
$$\left[\frac{6}{7}-2\frac{1}{3}-3\frac{2}{5}-\frac{2}{5}-0.14\right]=$$

Solution:

Step 1
$$\left[\frac{6}{7}-2\frac{1}{3}-3\frac{2}{5}-\frac{2}{5}-0.14\right]=\left[\left(\frac{6}{7}-2\frac{1}{3}\right)+\left(-3\frac{2}{5}-\frac{2}{5}\right)-0.14\right]$$

Step 2   Not Applicable

Step 3
$$\left[\left(\frac{6}{7}-2\frac{1}{3}\right)+\left(-3\frac{2}{5}-\frac{2}{5}\right)-0.14\right]=\left[\left(\frac{6}{7}-\frac{(2\times3)+1}{3}\right)+\left(-\frac{(3\times5)+2}{5}-\frac{2}{5}\right)-0.14\right]$$

$$=\left[\left(\frac{6}{7}-\frac{6+1}{3}\right)+\left(-\frac{15+2}{5}-\frac{2}{5}\right)-0.14\right]=\left[\left(\frac{6}{7}-\frac{7}{3}\right)+\left(-\frac{17}{5}-\frac{2}{5}\right)-0.14\right]$$

Step 4a   Not Applicable

Step 4b
$$\left(\frac{6}{7}-\frac{7}{3}\right)+\left(-\frac{17}{5}-\frac{2}{5}\right)-0.14 = \left(\frac{6}{7}-\frac{7}{3}\right)+\left(-\frac{17}{5}-\frac{2}{5}\right)-\frac{14}{100}$$

Step 5
$$\left(\frac{6}{7}-\frac{7}{3}\right)+\left(-\frac{17}{5}-\frac{2}{5}\right)-\frac{14}{100} = \left(\frac{(6\times3)-(7\times7)}{7\times3}\right)+\left(\frac{-17-2}{5}\right)-\frac{14}{100}$$

$$= \left(\frac{18-49}{21}\right)+\left(\frac{-19}{5}\right)-\frac{14}{100} = \left(\frac{-31}{21}\right)+\frac{-19}{5}-\frac{14}{100} = \frac{-31}{21}+\frac{-19}{5}-\frac{14}{100}$$

$$= \frac{-31}{21}-\frac{19}{5}-\frac{14}{100} = \left(\frac{-31}{21}-\frac{19}{5}\right)-\frac{14}{100} = \left(\frac{(-31\times5)-(19\times21)}{21\times5}\right)-\frac{14}{100}$$

$$= \left(\frac{-155-399}{105}\right)-\frac{14}{100} = \left(\frac{-554}{105}\right)-\frac{14}{100} = \frac{-554}{105}-\frac{14}{100} = \frac{(-554\times100)-(14\times105)}{105\times100}$$

$$= \frac{-55400-1470}{10500} = \frac{-56870}{10500}$$

Step 6
$$\frac{-56870}{10500} = \frac{-56870\div10}{10500\div10} = \frac{-5687}{1050}$$

Step 7
$$\frac{-5687}{1050} = -\left(5\frac{437}{1050}\right)$$

Example 9.2-10
$$28-\frac{3}{10}-1\frac{3}{5}-\frac{2.2}{0.4}-0.8-\frac{4}{5} =$$

Solution:

Step 1
$$28-\frac{3}{10}-1\frac{3}{5}-\frac{2.2}{0.4}-0.8-\frac{4}{5} = \left(28-\frac{3}{10}\right)+\left(-1\frac{3}{5}-\frac{2.2}{0.4}\right)+\left(-0.8-\frac{4}{5}\right)$$

Step 2
$$\left(28-\frac{3}{10}\right)+\left(-1\frac{3}{5}-\frac{2.2}{0.4}\right)+\left(-0.8-\frac{4}{5}\right) = \left(\frac{28}{1}-\frac{3}{10}\right)+\left(-1\frac{3}{5}-\frac{2.2}{0.4}\right)+\left(-0.8-\frac{4}{5}\right)$$

Step 3
$$\left(\frac{28}{1}-\frac{3}{10}\right)+\left(-1\frac{3}{5}-\frac{2.2}{0.4}\right)+\left(-0.8-\frac{4}{5}\right) = \left(\frac{28}{1}-\frac{3}{10}\right)+\left(-\frac{(1\times5)+3}{5}-\frac{2.2}{0.4}\right)+\left(-0.8-\frac{4}{5}\right)$$

$$= \left(\frac{28}{1}-\frac{3}{10}\right)+\left(-\frac{5+3}{5}-\frac{2.2}{0.4}\right)+\left(-0.8-\frac{4}{5}\right) = \left(\frac{28}{1}-\frac{3}{10}\right)+\left(-\frac{8}{5}-\frac{2.2}{0.4}\right)+\left(-0.8-\frac{4}{5}\right)$$

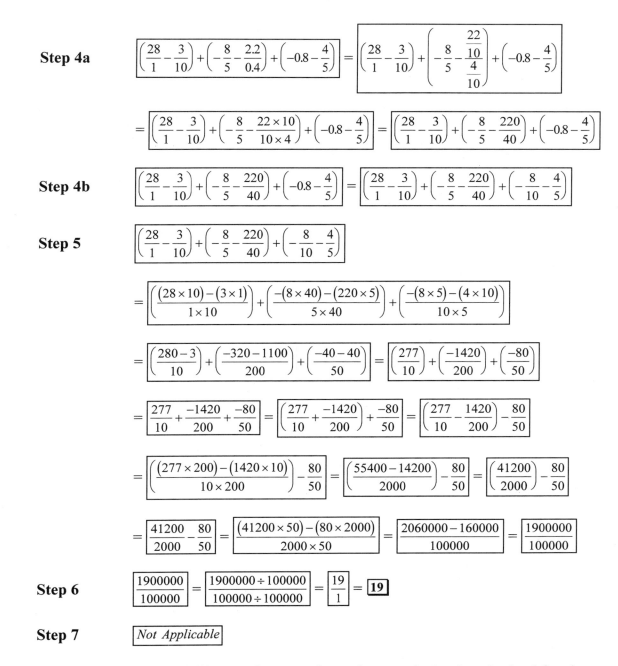

Step 4a

$$\left[\left(\frac{28}{1}-\frac{3}{10}\right)+\left(-\frac{8}{5}-\frac{2.2}{0.4}\right)+\left(-0.8-\frac{4}{5}\right)\right]=\left[\left(\frac{28}{1}-\frac{3}{10}\right)+\left(-\frac{8}{5}-\frac{\frac{22}{10}}{\frac{4}{10}}\right)+\left(-0.8-\frac{4}{5}\right)\right]$$

$$=\left[\left(\frac{28}{1}-\frac{3}{10}\right)+\left(-\frac{8}{5}-\frac{22\times10}{10\times4}\right)+\left(-0.8-\frac{4}{5}\right)\right]=\left[\left(\frac{28}{1}-\frac{3}{10}\right)+\left(-\frac{8}{5}-\frac{220}{40}\right)+\left(-0.8-\frac{4}{5}\right)\right]$$

Step 4b

$$\left[\left(\frac{28}{1}-\frac{3}{10}\right)+\left(-\frac{8}{5}-\frac{220}{40}\right)+\left(-0.8-\frac{4}{5}\right)\right]=\left[\left(\frac{28}{1}-\frac{3}{10}\right)+\left(-\frac{8}{5}-\frac{220}{40}\right)+\left(-\frac{8}{10}-\frac{4}{5}\right)\right]$$

Step 5

$$\left[\left(\frac{28}{1}-\frac{3}{10}\right)+\left(-\frac{8}{5}-\frac{220}{40}\right)+\left(-\frac{8}{10}-\frac{4}{5}\right)\right]$$

$$=\left[\left(\frac{(28\times10)-(3\times1)}{1\times10}\right)+\left(\frac{-(8\times40)-(220\times5)}{5\times40}\right)+\left(\frac{-(8\times5)-(4\times10)}{10\times5}\right)\right]$$

$$=\left[\left(\frac{280-3}{10}\right)+\left(\frac{-320-1100}{200}\right)+\left(\frac{-40-40}{50}\right)\right]=\left[\left(\frac{277}{10}\right)+\left(\frac{-1420}{200}\right)+\left(\frac{-80}{50}\right)\right]$$

$$=\left[\frac{277}{10}+\frac{-1420}{200}+\frac{-80}{50}\right]=\left[\left(\frac{277}{10}+\frac{-1420}{200}\right)+\frac{-80}{50}\right]=\left[\left(\frac{277}{10}-\frac{1420}{200}\right)-\frac{80}{50}\right]$$

$$=\left[\left(\frac{(277\times200)-(1420\times10)}{10\times200}\right)-\frac{80}{50}\right]=\left[\left(\frac{55400-14200}{2000}\right)-\frac{80}{50}\right]=\left[\left(\frac{41200}{2000}\right)-\frac{80}{50}\right]$$

$$=\left[\frac{41200}{2000}-\frac{80}{50}\right]=\left[\frac{(41200\times50)-(80\times2000)}{2000\times50}\right]=\frac{2060000-160000}{100000}=\frac{1900000}{100000}$$

Step 6

$$\boxed{\frac{1900000}{100000}}=\boxed{\frac{1900000\div100000}{100000\div100000}}=\boxed{\frac{19}{1}}=\boxed{\mathbf{19}}$$

Step 7

$$\boxed{Not\ Applicable}$$

The following examples further illustrate how to subtract integer, decimal, and mixed fractions:

Example 9.2-11

$$\boxed{\frac{0.18}{1.4}-\frac{3}{4}-3\frac{2}{5}}=\left[\left(\frac{\frac{18}{100}}{\frac{14}{10}}-\frac{3}{4}\right)-\frac{(3\times5)+2}{5}\right]=\left[\left(\frac{18\times10}{100\times14}-\frac{3}{4}\right)-\frac{15+2}{5}\right]=\left[\left(\frac{180}{1400}-\frac{3}{4}\right)-\frac{17}{5}\right]$$

$$= \left(\dfrac{\frac{9}{\cancel{180}}}{\frac{\cancel{1400}}{70}} - \dfrac{3}{4} \right) - \dfrac{17}{5} = \left(\dfrac{9}{70} - \dfrac{3}{4} \right) - \dfrac{17}{5} = \left(\dfrac{(9 \times 4) - (3 \times 70)}{70 \times 4} \right) - \dfrac{17}{5} = \left(\dfrac{36 - 210}{280} \right) - \dfrac{17}{5} = \left(\dfrac{-174}{280} \right) - \dfrac{17}{5}$$

$$= \dfrac{\frac{-87}{\cancel{-174}}}{\frac{\cancel{280}}{140}} - \dfrac{17}{5} = \dfrac{-87}{140} - \dfrac{17}{5} = \dfrac{(-87 \times 5) - (17 \times 140)}{140 \times 5} = \dfrac{-435 - 2380}{700} = \dfrac{\frac{-563}{\cancel{-2815}}}{\frac{\cancel{700}}{140}} = \dfrac{-563}{140} = -\left(4\dfrac{3}{140} \right)$$

Example 9.2-12

$$4\dfrac{1}{5} - \dfrac{3}{5} - 0.124 = \left(\dfrac{(4 \times 5) + 1}{5} - \dfrac{3}{5} \right) - \dfrac{124}{1000} = \left(\dfrac{21}{5} - \dfrac{3}{5} \right) - \dfrac{\frac{31}{\cancel{124}}}{\frac{\cancel{1000}}{250}} = \left(\dfrac{21 - 3}{5} \right) - \dfrac{31}{250} = \left(\dfrac{18}{5} \right) - \dfrac{31}{250}$$

$$= \dfrac{18}{5} - \dfrac{31}{250} = \dfrac{(18 \times 250) - (31 \times 5)}{5 \times 250} = \dfrac{4500 - 155}{1250} = \dfrac{\frac{869}{\cancel{4345}}}{\frac{\cancel{1250}}{250}} = \dfrac{869}{250} = 3\dfrac{119}{250}$$

Example 9.2-13

$$3\dfrac{2}{5} - \left(4\dfrac{2}{3} - \dfrac{0.01}{0.2} \right) = \dfrac{(3 \times 5) + 2}{5} - \left(\dfrac{(4 \times 3) + 2}{3} - \dfrac{\frac{1}{100}}{\frac{2}{10}} \right) = \dfrac{15 + 2}{5} - \left(\dfrac{12 + 2}{3} - \dfrac{1 \times 10}{100 \times 2} \right) = \dfrac{17}{5} - \left(\dfrac{14}{3} - \dfrac{\frac{1}{\cancel{10}}}{\frac{\cancel{200}}{20}} \right)$$

$$= \dfrac{17}{5} - \left(\dfrac{14}{3} - \dfrac{1}{20} \right) = \dfrac{17}{5} - \left(\dfrac{(14 \times 20) - (1 \times 3)}{3 \times 20} \right) = \dfrac{17}{5} - \left(\dfrac{280 - 3}{60} \right) = \dfrac{17}{5} - \left(\dfrac{277}{60} \right) = \dfrac{17}{5} - \dfrac{277}{60}$$

$$= \dfrac{(17 \times 60) - (277 \times 5)}{5 \times 60} = \dfrac{1020 - 1385}{300} = \dfrac{\frac{-73}{\cancel{-365}}}{\frac{\cancel{300}}{60}} = \dfrac{-73}{60} = -\left(1\dfrac{13}{60} \right)$$

Example 9.2-14

$$\dfrac{5}{14} - 1\dfrac{3}{5} - \dfrac{0.12}{0.5} - 30 = \left(\dfrac{5}{14} - \dfrac{(1 \times 5) + 3}{5} \right) + \left(-\dfrac{\frac{12}{100}}{\frac{5}{10}} - \dfrac{30}{1} \right) = \left(\dfrac{5}{14} - \dfrac{5 + 3}{5} \right) + \left(-\dfrac{12 \times 10}{100 \times 5} - \dfrac{30}{1} \right)$$

$$= \left(\dfrac{5}{14} - \dfrac{8}{5} \right) + \left(-\dfrac{\frac{6}{\cancel{120}}}{\frac{\cancel{500}}{25}} - \dfrac{30}{1} \right) = \left(\dfrac{(5 \times 5) - (8 \times 14)}{14 \times 5} \right) + \left(-\dfrac{6}{25} - \dfrac{30}{1} \right) = \left(\dfrac{25 - 112}{70} \right) + \left(\dfrac{-(6 \times 1) - (30 \times 25)}{25 \times 1} \right)$$

$$= \left(\dfrac{-87}{70} \right) + \left(\dfrac{-6 - 750}{25} \right) = \dfrac{-87}{70} + \left(\dfrac{-756}{25} \right) = \dfrac{-87}{70} + \dfrac{-756}{25} = \dfrac{-87}{70} - \dfrac{756}{25} = \dfrac{(-87 \times 25) - (756 \times 70)}{70 \times 25}$$

$$= \dfrac{-2175 - 52920}{1750} = \dfrac{\frac{-11019}{\cancel{-55095}}}{\frac{\cancel{1750}}{350}} = \dfrac{-11019}{350} = -\left(31\dfrac{169}{350} \right)$$

Example 9.2-15

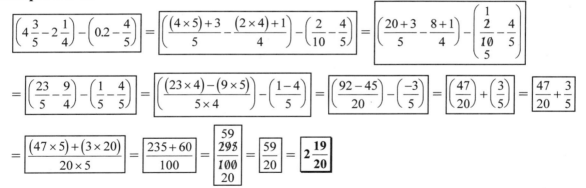

$$\boxed{\left(4\frac{3}{5} - 2\frac{1}{4}\right) - \left(0.2 - \frac{4}{5}\right)} = \boxed{\left(\frac{(4\times5)+3}{5} - \frac{(2\times4)+1}{4}\right) - \left(\frac{2}{10} - \frac{4}{5}\right)} = \boxed{\left(\frac{20+3}{5} - \frac{8+1}{4}\right) - \left(\frac{\frac{1}{2}}{\frac{10}{5}} - \frac{4}{5}\right)}$$

$$= \boxed{\left(\frac{23}{5} - \frac{9}{4}\right) - \left(\frac{1}{5} - \frac{4}{5}\right)} = \boxed{\left(\frac{(23\times4)-(9\times5)}{5\times4}\right) - \left(\frac{1-4}{5}\right)} = \boxed{\left(\frac{92-45}{20}\right) - \left(\frac{-3}{5}\right)} = \boxed{\left(\frac{47}{20}\right) + \left(\frac{3}{5}\right)} = \boxed{\frac{47}{20} + \frac{3}{5}}$$

$$= \boxed{\frac{(47\times5)+(3\times20)}{20\times5}} = \boxed{\frac{235+60}{100}} = \boxed{\frac{\overset{59}{\cancel{295}}}{\underset{20}{\cancel{100}}}} = \boxed{\frac{59}{20}} = \boxed{\mathbf{2\frac{19}{20}}}$$

Example 9.2-16

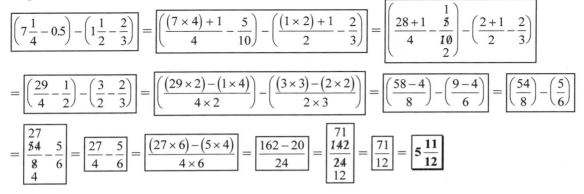

$$\boxed{\left(7\frac{1}{4} - 0.5\right) - \left(1\frac{1}{2} - \frac{2}{3}\right)} = \boxed{\left(\frac{(7\times4)+1}{4} - \frac{5}{10}\right) - \left(\frac{(1\times2)+1}{2} - \frac{2}{3}\right)} = \boxed{\left(\frac{28+1}{4} - \frac{\overset{1}{\cancel{5}}}{\underset{2}{\cancel{10}}}\right) - \left(\frac{2+1}{2} - \frac{2}{3}\right)}$$

$$= \boxed{\left(\frac{29}{4} - \frac{1}{2}\right) - \left(\frac{3}{2} - \frac{2}{3}\right)} = \boxed{\left(\frac{(29\times2)-(1\times4)}{4\times2}\right) - \left(\frac{(3\times3)-(2\times2)}{2\times3}\right)} = \boxed{\left(\frac{58-4}{8}\right) - \left(\frac{9-4}{6}\right)} = \boxed{\left(\frac{54}{8}\right) - \left(\frac{5}{6}\right)}$$

$$= \boxed{\frac{\overset{27}{\cancel{54}}}{\underset{4}{\cancel{8}}} - \frac{5}{6}} = \boxed{\frac{27}{4} - \frac{5}{6}} = \boxed{\frac{(27\times6)-(5\times4)}{4\times6}} = \boxed{\frac{162-20}{24}} = \boxed{\frac{\overset{71}{\cancel{142}}}{\underset{12}{\cancel{24}}}} = \boxed{\frac{71}{12}} = \boxed{\mathbf{5\frac{11}{12}}}$$

Example 9.2-17

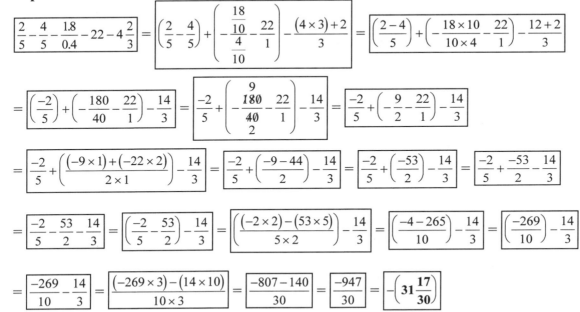

$$\boxed{\frac{2}{5} - \frac{4}{5} - \frac{1.8}{0.4} - 22 - 4\frac{2}{3}} = \boxed{\left(\frac{2}{5} - \frac{4}{5}\right) + \left(-\frac{\frac{18}{10}}{\frac{4}{10}} - \frac{22}{1}\right) - \frac{(4\times3)+2}{3}} = \boxed{\left(\frac{2-4}{5}\right) + \left(-\frac{18\times10}{10\times4} - \frac{22}{1}\right) - \frac{12+2}{3}}$$

$$= \boxed{\left(\frac{-2}{5}\right) + \left(-\frac{180}{40} - \frac{22}{1}\right) - \frac{14}{3}} = \boxed{\frac{-2}{5} + \left(-\frac{\overset{9}{\cancel{180}}}{\underset{2}{\cancel{40}}} - \frac{22}{1}\right) - \frac{14}{3}} = \boxed{\frac{-2}{5} + \left(-\frac{9}{2} - \frac{22}{1}\right) - \frac{14}{3}}$$

$$= \boxed{\frac{-2}{5} + \left(\frac{(-9\times1)+(-22\times2)}{2\times1}\right) - \frac{14}{3}} = \boxed{\frac{-2}{5} + \left(\frac{-9-44}{2}\right) - \frac{14}{3}} = \boxed{\frac{-2}{5} + \left(\frac{-53}{2}\right) - \frac{14}{3}} = \boxed{\frac{-2}{5} + \frac{-53}{2} - \frac{14}{3}}$$

$$= \boxed{\frac{-2}{5} - \frac{53}{2} - \frac{14}{3}} = \boxed{\left(\frac{-2}{5} - \frac{53}{2}\right) - \frac{14}{3}} = \boxed{\left(\frac{(-2\times2)-(53\times5)}{5\times2}\right) - \frac{14}{3}} = \boxed{\left(\frac{-4-265}{10}\right) - \frac{14}{3}} = \boxed{\left(\frac{-269}{10}\right) - \frac{14}{3}}$$

$$= \boxed{\frac{-269}{10} - \frac{14}{3}} = \boxed{\frac{(-269\times3)-(14\times10)}{10\times3}} = \boxed{\frac{-807-140}{30}} = \boxed{\frac{-947}{30}} = \boxed{-\left(\mathbf{31\frac{17}{30}}\right)}$$

Example 9.2-18

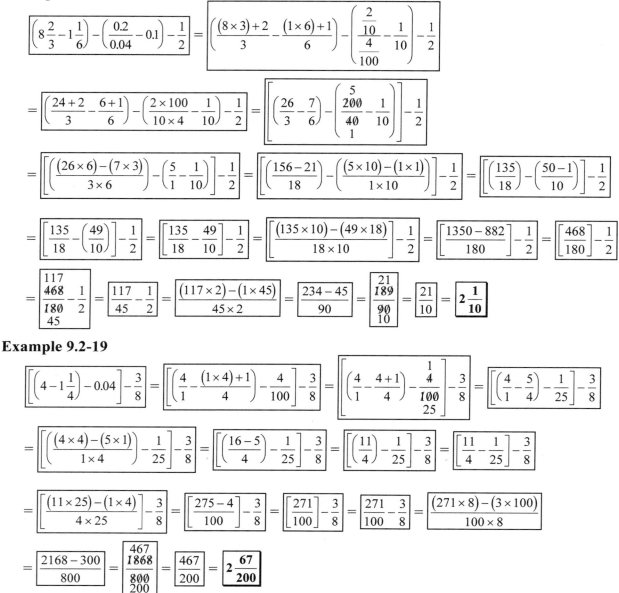

$$\left(8\frac{2}{3} - 1\frac{1}{6}\right) - \left(\frac{0.2}{0.04} - 0.1\right) - \frac{1}{2} = \left(\frac{(8\times3)+2}{3} - \frac{(1\times6)+1}{6}\right) - \left(\frac{\frac{2}{10}}{\frac{4}{100}} - \frac{1}{10}\right) - \frac{1}{2}$$

$$= \left(\frac{24+2}{3} - \frac{6+1}{6}\right) - \left(\frac{2\times100}{10\times4} - \frac{1}{10}\right) - \frac{1}{2} = \left(\frac{26}{3} - \frac{7}{6}\right) - \left(\frac{\frac{5}{200}}{\frac{40}{1}} - \frac{1}{10}\right) - \frac{1}{2}$$

$$= \left(\frac{(26\times6)-(7\times3)}{3\times6} - \left(\frac{5}{1} - \frac{1}{10}\right)\right) - \frac{1}{2} = \left(\frac{156-21}{18} - \left(\frac{(5\times10)-(1\times1)}{1\times10}\right)\right) - \frac{1}{2} = \left(\left(\frac{135}{18}\right) - \left(\frac{50-1}{10}\right)\right) - \frac{1}{2}$$

$$= \left(\frac{135}{18} - \left(\frac{49}{10}\right)\right) - \frac{1}{2} = \left(\frac{135}{18} - \frac{49}{10}\right) - \frac{1}{2} = \left(\frac{(135\times10)-(49\times18)}{18\times10}\right) - \frac{1}{2} = \left(\frac{1350-882}{180}\right) - \frac{1}{2} = \left(\frac{468}{180}\right) - \frac{1}{2}$$

$$= \frac{\frac{117}{468}}{\frac{180}{45}} - \frac{1}{2} = \frac{117}{45} - \frac{1}{2} = \frac{(117\times2)-(1\times45)}{45\times2} = \frac{234-45}{90} = \frac{\frac{21}{189}}{\frac{90}{10}} = \frac{21}{10} = 2\frac{1}{10}$$

Example 9.2-19

$$\left[\left(4-1\frac{1}{4}\right) - 0.04\right] - \frac{3}{8} = \left[\left(\frac{4}{1} - \frac{(1\times4)+1}{4}\right) - \frac{4}{100}\right] - \frac{3}{8} = \left[\left(\frac{4}{1} - \frac{4+1}{4}\right) - \frac{\frac{1}{4}}{\frac{100}{25}}\right] - \frac{3}{8} = \left[\left(\frac{4}{1} - \frac{5}{4}\right) - \frac{1}{25}\right] - \frac{3}{8}$$

$$= \left[\left(\frac{(4\times4)-(5\times1)}{1\times4}\right) - \frac{1}{25}\right] - \frac{3}{8} = \left[\left(\frac{16-5}{4}\right) - \frac{1}{25}\right] - \frac{3}{8} = \left[\left(\frac{11}{4}\right) - \frac{1}{25}\right] - \frac{3}{8} = \left[\frac{11}{4} - \frac{1}{25}\right] - \frac{3}{8}$$

$$= \left[\frac{(11\times25)-(1\times4)}{4\times25}\right] - \frac{3}{8} = \left[\frac{275-4}{100}\right] - \frac{3}{8} = \left[\frac{271}{100}\right] - \frac{3}{8} = \frac{271}{100} - \frac{3}{8} = \frac{(271\times8)-(3\times100)}{100\times8}$$

$$= \frac{2168-300}{800} = \frac{\frac{467}{1868}}{\frac{800}{200}} = \frac{467}{200} = 2\frac{67}{200}$$

Example 9.2-20

$$\left[\left(8\frac{1}{5} - 1\frac{1}{4}\right) - 2\right] - \left(\frac{3}{4} - 0.02\right) = \left[\left(\frac{(8\times5)+1}{5} - \frac{(1\times4)+1}{4}\right) - \frac{2}{1}\right] - \left(\frac{3}{4} - \frac{2}{100}\right)$$

$$= \left[\left(\frac{40+1}{5} - \frac{4+1}{4}\right) - \frac{2}{1}\right] - \left(\frac{3}{4} - \frac{\frac{1}{2}}{\frac{100}{50}}\right) = \left[\left(\frac{41}{5} - \frac{5}{4}\right) - \frac{2}{1}\right] - \left(\frac{3}{4} - \frac{1}{50}\right)$$

$$= \left[\left(\frac{(41\times4)-(5\times5)}{5\times4}\right) - \frac{2}{1}\right] - \left(\frac{(3\times50)-(1\times4)}{4\times50}\right) = \left[\left(\frac{164-25}{20}\right) - \frac{2}{1}\right] - \left(\frac{150-4}{200}\right) = \left[\left(\frac{139}{20}\right) - \frac{2}{1}\right] - \left(\frac{146}{200}\right)$$

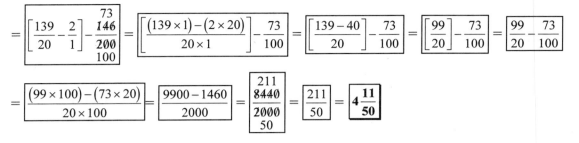

Example 9.2-21

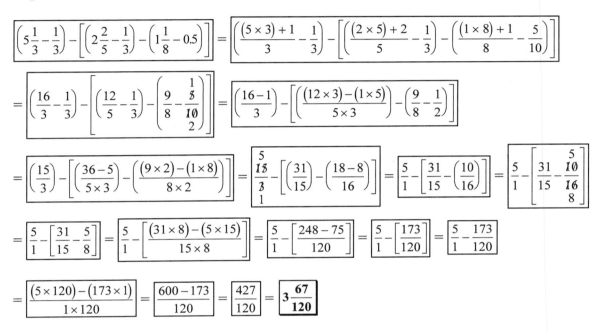

Section 9.2 Exercises - Subtract the following integer, decimal, and mixed fractions:

1. $2\dfrac{1}{6} - \dfrac{3}{5} - \dfrac{1.4}{0.4} =$

2. $\dfrac{5}{8} - 2\dfrac{4}{5} - 0.1 =$

3. $\left(1\dfrac{3}{4} - 0.2\right) - \dfrac{2}{3} =$

4. $\left(4\dfrac{2}{3} - 8\right) - \dfrac{0.01}{0.1} =$

5. $1\dfrac{3}{5} - \left(\dfrac{1}{8} - \dfrac{0.14}{0.2}\right) =$

6. $7 - \dfrac{2}{3} - 1\dfrac{1}{4} - 0.25 =$

7. $\left(3\dfrac{2}{3} - \dfrac{1}{3}\right) - \left(0.9 - \dfrac{2}{5}\right) =$

8. $\left(\dfrac{1}{3} - 1\dfrac{1}{4}\right) - \left(\dfrac{4}{5} - \dfrac{1}{5}\right) - 0.6 =$

9. $\left[4 - \left(\dfrac{2}{5} - 1\dfrac{2}{3}\right)\right] - 0.04 =$

10. $\left[\left(5\dfrac{2}{3} - 1\dfrac{1}{4}\right) - 0.2\right] - \dfrac{2}{5} =$

9.3   Multiplying Integer, Decimal, and Mixed Fractions

Fractions of the following forms:

1. $\left(\dfrac{a}{b}\right)$ where (a) and (b) are integers,

2. $\left(\dfrac{a \times 10^{-k_1}}{b \times 10^{-k_2}}\right)$ where (a) and (b) are integer numbers and (k_1) and (k_2) are equal to the number

    of decimal places, and

3. $\left(k\dfrac{a}{b}\right)$ where (k) is made up of a whole number and $\left(\dfrac{a}{b}\right)$ is an integer fraction for a number

    less than one

are multiplied as in the following cases:

Case I   Multiplying Integer, Decimal, and Mixed Fractions With Three Terms Only

Multiply three integer, decimal, and mixed fractions using the following steps:

Step 1   Change the integer number (a) to an integer fraction of the form $\left(\dfrac{a}{1}\right)$, e.g., change

  235 to $\dfrac{235}{1}$.

Step 2   Change the mixed fraction to an integer fraction (see Section 2.5).

Step 3   a. Change the decimal fraction to an integer fraction (see Section 2.4).

   b. Change the decimal number $\left(a \times 10^{-k}\right)$ to an integer fraction of the form $\left(\dfrac{a}{10^k}\right)$,

   e.g., change 239 to $\dfrac{239}{100}$.

Step 4   Multiply the integer fractions (see Section 3.3).

Step 5   Simplify the fraction to its lowest term (see Section 2.3).

Step 6   Change the improper fraction to a mixed fraction if the fraction obtained from Step 5 is an improper fraction (see Section 2.2).

The following examples show the steps as to how integer, decimal and mixed fractions with three terms only are multiplied:

Example 9.3-1

$$\boxed{\dfrac{4}{5} \times 1\dfrac{3}{8} \times \dfrac{0.8}{1.21}} =$$

Solution:

Step 1 $\boxed{\textit{Not Applicable}}$

Step 2 $\boxed{\dfrac{4}{5} \times 1\dfrac{3}{8} \times \dfrac{0.8}{1.21}} = \boxed{\dfrac{4}{5} \times \dfrac{(1\times 8)+3}{8} \times \dfrac{0.8}{1.21}} = \boxed{\dfrac{4}{5} \times \dfrac{8+3}{8} \times \dfrac{0.8}{1.21}} = \boxed{\dfrac{4}{5} \times \dfrac{11}{8} \times \dfrac{0.8}{1.21}}$

Step 3a $\dfrac{4}{5} \times \dfrac{11}{8} \times \dfrac{0.8}{1.21} = \dfrac{4}{5} \times \dfrac{11}{8} \times \dfrac{\frac{8}{10}}{\frac{121}{100}} = \dfrac{4}{5} \times \dfrac{11}{8} \times \dfrac{8 \times 100}{10 \times 121} = \dfrac{4}{5} \times \dfrac{11}{8} \times \dfrac{800}{1210}$

Step 3b $\boxed{Not\ Applicable}$

Step 4 $\dfrac{4}{5} \times \dfrac{11}{8} \times \dfrac{800}{1210} = \dfrac{4 \times 11 \times 800}{5 \times 8 \times 1210} = \dfrac{35200}{48400}$

Step 5 $\dfrac{35200}{48400} = \dfrac{35200 \div 100}{48400 \div 100} = \dfrac{352}{484} = \dfrac{352 \div 4}{484 \div 4} = \boxed{\dfrac{88}{121}}$

Step 6 $\boxed{Not\ Applicable}$

Example 9.3-2

$$\dfrac{3}{5} \times 2\dfrac{4}{7} \times 12.8 =$$

Solution:

Step 1 $\boxed{Not\ Applicable}$

Step 2 $\dfrac{3}{5} \times 2\dfrac{4}{7} \times 12.8 = \dfrac{3}{5} \times \dfrac{(2 \times 7) + 4}{7} \times 12.8 = \dfrac{3}{5} \times \dfrac{14 + 4}{7} \times 12.8 = \dfrac{3}{5} \times \dfrac{18}{7} \times 12.8$

Step 3a $\boxed{Not\ Applicable}$

Step 3b $\dfrac{3}{5} \times \dfrac{18}{7} \times 12.8 = \dfrac{3}{5} \times \dfrac{18}{7} \times \dfrac{128}{10}$

Step 4 $\dfrac{3}{5} \times \dfrac{18}{7} \times \dfrac{128}{10} = \dfrac{3 \times 18 \times 128}{5 \times 7 \times 10} = \dfrac{6912}{350}$

Step 5 $\dfrac{6912}{350} = \dfrac{6912 \div 2}{350 \div 2} = \dfrac{3456}{175}$

Step 6 $\dfrac{3456}{175} = \boxed{19\dfrac{131}{175}}$

Example 9.3-3

$$4\dfrac{5}{8} \times \dfrac{0.66}{0.1} \times 24 =$$

Solution:

Step 1
$$4\frac{5}{8} \times \frac{0.66}{0.1} \times 24 = 4\frac{5}{8} \times \frac{0.66}{0.1} \times \frac{24}{1}$$

Step 2
$$4\frac{5}{8} \times \frac{0.66}{0.1} \times \frac{24}{1} = \frac{(4 \times 8) + 5}{8} \times \frac{0.66}{0.1} \times \frac{24}{1} = \frac{32 + 5}{8} \times \frac{0.66}{0.1} \times \frac{24}{1}$$

$$= \frac{37}{8} \times \frac{0.66}{0.1} \times \frac{24}{1}$$

Step 3a
$$\frac{37}{8} \times \frac{0.66}{0.1} \times \frac{24}{1} = \frac{37}{8} \times \frac{\frac{66}{100}}{\frac{1}{10}} \times \frac{24}{1} = \frac{37}{8} \times \frac{66 \times 10}{100 \times 1} \times \frac{24}{1} = \frac{37}{8} \times \frac{660}{100} \times \frac{24}{1}$$

Step 3b
$$\boxed{Not\ Applicable}$$

Step 4
$$\frac{37}{8} \times \frac{660}{100} \times \frac{24}{1} = \frac{37 \times 660 \times 24}{8 \times 100 \times 1} = \frac{586080}{800}$$

Step 5
$$\frac{586080}{800} = \frac{586080 \div 80}{800 \div 80} = \frac{7326}{10} = \frac{7326 \div 2}{10 \div 2} = \frac{3663}{5}$$

Step 6
$$\frac{3663}{5} = \mathbf{732\frac{3}{5}}$$

Example 9.3-4
$$4 \times 1\frac{3}{8} \times 0.5 =$$

Solution:

Step 1
$$4 \times 1\frac{3}{8} \times 0.5 = \frac{4}{1} \times 1\frac{3}{8} \times 0.5$$

Step 2
$$\frac{4}{1} \times 1\frac{3}{8} \times 0.5 = \frac{4}{1} \times \frac{(1 \times 8) + 3}{8} \times 0.5 = \frac{4}{1} \times \frac{8 + 3}{8} \times 0.5 = \frac{4}{1} \times \frac{11}{8} \times 0.5$$

Step 3a
$$\boxed{Not\ Applicable}$$

Step 3b
$$\frac{4}{1} \times \frac{11}{8} \times 0.5 = \frac{4}{1} \times \frac{11}{8} \times \frac{5}{10}$$

Step 4
$$\frac{4}{1} \times \frac{11}{8} \times \frac{5}{10} = \frac{4 \times 11 \times 5}{1 \times 8 \times 10} = \frac{220}{80}$$

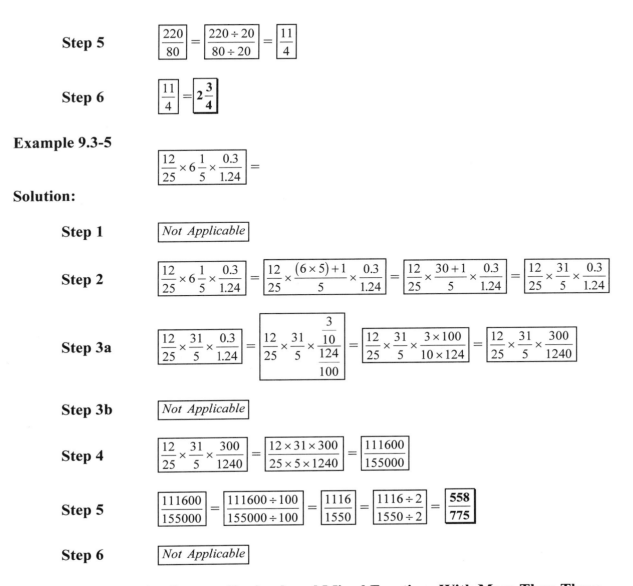

Step 5 $\boxed{\dfrac{220}{80}} = \boxed{\dfrac{220 \div 20}{80 \div 20}} = \boxed{\dfrac{11}{4}}$

Step 6 $\boxed{\dfrac{11}{4}} = \boxed{2\dfrac{3}{4}}$

Example 9.3-5

$\boxed{\dfrac{12}{25} \times 6\dfrac{1}{5} \times \dfrac{0.3}{1.24}} =$

Solution:

Step 1 $\boxed{\textit{Not Applicable}}$

Step 2 $\boxed{\dfrac{12}{25} \times 6\dfrac{1}{5} \times \dfrac{0.3}{1.24}} = \boxed{\dfrac{12}{25} \times \dfrac{(6 \times 5)+1}{5} \times \dfrac{0.3}{1.24}} = \boxed{\dfrac{12}{25} \times \dfrac{30+1}{5} \times \dfrac{0.3}{1.24}} = \boxed{\dfrac{12}{25} \times \dfrac{31}{5} \times \dfrac{0.3}{1.24}}$

Step 3a $\boxed{\dfrac{12}{25} \times \dfrac{31}{5} \times \dfrac{0.3}{1.24}} = \boxed{\dfrac{12}{25} \times \dfrac{31}{5} \times \dfrac{\frac{3}{10}}{\frac{124}{100}}} = \boxed{\dfrac{12}{25} \times \dfrac{31}{5} \times \dfrac{3 \times 100}{10 \times 124}} = \boxed{\dfrac{12}{25} \times \dfrac{31}{5} \times \dfrac{300}{1240}}$

Step 3b $\boxed{\textit{Not Applicable}}$

Step 4 $\boxed{\dfrac{12}{25} \times \dfrac{31}{5} \times \dfrac{300}{1240}} = \boxed{\dfrac{12 \times 31 \times 300}{25 \times 5 \times 1240}} = \boxed{\dfrac{111600}{155000}}$

Step 5 $\boxed{\dfrac{111600}{155000}} = \boxed{\dfrac{111600 \div 100}{155000 \div 100}} = \boxed{\dfrac{1116}{1550}} = \boxed{\dfrac{1116 \div 2}{1550 \div 2}} = \boxed{\dfrac{558}{775}}$

Step 6 $\boxed{\textit{Not Applicable}}$

Case II   Multiplying Integer, Decimal, and Mixed Fractions With More Than Three Terms

Multiply integer, decimal, and mixed fractions having more than three terms by using the following steps:

Step 1   Change the integer number(s) (a) to integer fraction(s) of the form $\left(\dfrac{a}{1}\right)$, e.g., change

29 to $\dfrac{29}{1}$.

Step 2   Change the mixed fraction(s) to integer fraction(s) (see Section 2.5).

Step 3   a. Change the decimal fraction(s) to integer fraction(s) (see Section 2.4).

b. Change the decimal number(s) $\left(a \times 10^{-k}\right)$ to integer fraction(s) of the form $\left(\dfrac{a}{10^k}\right)$, e.g., change 0.0018 to $\dfrac{18}{10000}$.

Step 4   Multiply the integer fractions (see Section 3.3).

Step 5   Simplify the fraction to its lowest term (see Section 2.3).

Step 6   Change the improper fraction to a mixed fraction if the fraction obtained from Step 5 is an improper fraction (see Section 2.2).

The following examples show the steps as to how integer, decimal and mixed fractions with more than three terms are multiplied:

Example 9.3-6

$$\left[\frac{0.5}{0.025}\times 1\frac{3}{8}\times\frac{0.08}{0.2}\times 6\right]=$$

Solution:

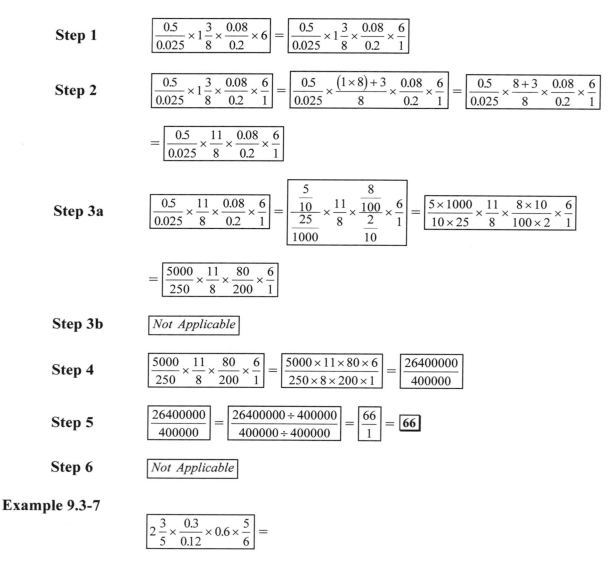

Example 9.3-7

$$\left[2\frac{3}{5}\times\frac{0.3}{0.12}\times 0.6\times\frac{5}{6}\right]=$$

Solution:

Step 1 $\boxed{Not\ Applicable}$

Step 2 $\boxed{2\dfrac{3}{5} \times \dfrac{0.3}{0.12} \times 0.6 \times \dfrac{5}{6}} = \boxed{\dfrac{(2 \times 5) + 3}{5} \times \dfrac{0.3}{0.12} \times 0.6 \times \dfrac{5}{6}} = \boxed{\dfrac{10 + 3}{5} \times \dfrac{0.3}{0.12} \times 0.6 \times \dfrac{5}{6}}$

$= \boxed{\dfrac{13}{5} \times \dfrac{0.3}{0.12} \times 0.6 \times \dfrac{5}{6}}$

Step 3a $\boxed{\dfrac{13}{5} \times \dfrac{0.3}{0.12} \times 0.6 \times \dfrac{5}{6}} = \boxed{\dfrac{13}{5} \times \dfrac{\dfrac{3}{10}}{\dfrac{12}{100}} \times 0.6 \times \dfrac{5}{6}} = \boxed{\dfrac{13}{5} \times \dfrac{3 \times 100}{10 \times 12} \times 0.6 \times \dfrac{5}{6}}$

$= \boxed{\dfrac{13}{5} \times \dfrac{300}{120} \times 0.6 \times \dfrac{5}{6}}$

Step 3b $\boxed{\dfrac{13}{5} \times \dfrac{300}{120} \times 0.6 \times \dfrac{5}{6}} = \boxed{\dfrac{13}{5} \times \dfrac{300}{120} \times \dfrac{6}{10} \times \dfrac{5}{6}}$

Step 4 $\boxed{\dfrac{13}{5} \times \dfrac{300}{120} \times \dfrac{6}{10} \times \dfrac{5}{6}} = \boxed{\dfrac{13 \times 300 \times 6 \times 5}{5 \times 120 \times 10 \times 6}} = \boxed{\dfrac{117000}{36000}}$

Step 5 $\boxed{\dfrac{117000}{36000}} = \boxed{\dfrac{117000 \div 1000}{36000 \div 1000}} = \boxed{\dfrac{117}{36}} = \boxed{\dfrac{117 \div 9}{36 \div 9}} = \boxed{\dfrac{13}{4}}$

Step 6 $\boxed{\dfrac{13}{4}} = \boxed{3\dfrac{1}{4}}$

Example 9.3-8

$\boxed{1\dfrac{2}{5} \times \dfrac{3}{8} \times \dfrac{0.3}{0.24} \times 2\dfrac{6}{8}} =$

Solution:

Step 1 $\boxed{Not\ Applicable}$

Step 2 $\boxed{1\dfrac{2}{5} \times \dfrac{3}{8} \times \dfrac{0.3}{0.24} \times 2\dfrac{6}{8}} = \boxed{\dfrac{(1 \times 5) + 2}{5} \times \dfrac{3}{8} \times \dfrac{0.3}{0.24} \times \dfrac{(2 \times 8) + 6}{8}} = \boxed{\dfrac{5 + 2}{5} \times \dfrac{3}{8} \times \dfrac{0.3}{0.24} \times \dfrac{16 + 6}{8}}$

$= \boxed{\dfrac{7}{5} \times \dfrac{3}{8} \times \dfrac{0.3}{0.24} \times \dfrac{22}{8}}$

Step 3a
$$\frac{7}{5} \times \frac{3}{8} \times \frac{0.3}{0.24} \times \frac{22}{8} = \frac{7}{5} \times \frac{3}{8} \times \frac{\frac{3}{10}}{\frac{24}{100}} \times \frac{22}{8} = \frac{7}{5} \times \frac{3}{8} \times \frac{3 \times 100}{10 \times 24} \times \frac{22}{8} = \frac{7}{5} \times \frac{3}{8} \times \frac{300}{240} \times \frac{22}{8}$$

Step 3b $\boxed{Not\ Applicable}$

Step 4
$$\frac{7}{5} \times \frac{3}{8} \times \frac{300}{240} \times \frac{22}{8} = \frac{7 \times 3 \times 300 \times 22}{5 \times 8 \times 240 \times 8} = \frac{138600}{76800}$$

Step 5
$$\frac{138600}{76800} = \frac{138600 \div 100}{76800 \div 100} = \frac{1386}{768} = \frac{1386}{768} = \frac{1386 \div 6}{768 \div 6} = \frac{231}{128}$$

Step 6
$$\frac{231}{128} = \boxed{1\frac{103}{128}}$$

Example 9.3-9
$$6 \times 2\frac{3}{4} \times 3\frac{1}{8} \times \frac{0.4}{0.12} \times \frac{3}{11} =$$

Solution:

Step 1
$$6 \times 2\frac{3}{4} \times 3\frac{1}{8} \times \frac{0.4}{0.12} \times \frac{3}{11} = \frac{6}{1} \times 2\frac{3}{4} \times 3\frac{1}{8} \times \frac{0.4}{0.12} \times \frac{3}{11}$$

Step 2
$$\frac{6}{1} \times 2\frac{3}{4} \times 3\frac{1}{8} \times \frac{0.4}{0.12} \times \frac{3}{11} = \frac{6}{1} \times \frac{(2 \times 4)+3}{4} \times \frac{(3 \times 8)+1}{8} \times \frac{0.4}{0.12} \times \frac{3}{11}$$

$$= \frac{6}{1} \times \frac{8+3}{4} \times \frac{24+1}{8} \times \frac{0.4}{0.12} \times \frac{3}{11} = \frac{6}{1} \times \frac{11}{4} \times \frac{25}{8} \times \frac{0.4}{0.12} \times \frac{3}{11}$$

Step 3a
$$\frac{6}{1} \times \frac{11}{4} \times \frac{25}{8} \times \frac{0.4}{0.12} \times \frac{3}{11} = \frac{6}{1} \times \frac{11}{4} \times \frac{25}{8} \times \frac{\frac{4}{10}}{\frac{12}{100}} \times \frac{3}{11} = \frac{6}{1} \times \frac{11}{4} \times \frac{25}{8} \times \frac{4 \times 100}{10 \times 12} \times \frac{3}{11}$$

$$= \frac{6}{1} \times \frac{11}{4} \times \frac{25}{8} \times \frac{400}{120} \times \frac{3}{11}$$

Step 3b $\boxed{Not\ Applicable}$

Step 4
$$\frac{6}{1} \times \frac{11}{4} \times \frac{25}{8} \times \frac{400}{120} \times \frac{3}{11} = \frac{6 \times 11 \times 25 \times 400 \times 3}{1 \times 4 \times 8 \times 120 \times 11} = \frac{1980000}{42240}$$

Step 5
$$\frac{1980000}{42240} = \frac{1980000 \div 440}{42240 \div 440} = \frac{4500}{96} = \frac{4500 \div 12}{96 \div 12} = \frac{375}{8}$$

Step 6 $\boxed{\dfrac{375}{8}} = \boxed{46\dfrac{7}{8}}$

Example 9.3-10

$$\boxed{8 \times 1\dfrac{3}{5} \times \dfrac{1}{16} \times \dfrac{10.4}{0.12} \times 2\dfrac{3}{4} \times 0.01} =$$

Solution:

Step 1 $\boxed{8 \times 1\dfrac{3}{5} \times \dfrac{1}{16} \times \dfrac{10.4}{0.12} \times 2\dfrac{3}{4} \times 0.01} = \boxed{\dfrac{8}{1} \times 1\dfrac{3}{5} \times \dfrac{1}{16} \times \dfrac{10.4}{0.12} \times 2\dfrac{3}{4} \times 0.01}$

Step 2 $\boxed{\dfrac{8}{1} \times 1\dfrac{3}{5} \times \dfrac{1}{16} \times \dfrac{10.4}{0.12} \times 2\dfrac{3}{4} \times 0.01} = \boxed{\dfrac{8}{1} \times \dfrac{(1 \times 5)+3}{5} \times \dfrac{1}{16} \times \dfrac{10.4}{0.12} \times \dfrac{(2 \times 4)+3}{4} \times 0.01}$

$= \boxed{\dfrac{8}{1} \times \dfrac{5+3}{5} \times \dfrac{1}{16} \times \dfrac{10.4}{0.12} \times \dfrac{8+3}{4} \times 0.01} = \boxed{\dfrac{8}{1} \times \dfrac{8}{5} \times \dfrac{1}{16} \times \dfrac{10.4}{0.12} \times \dfrac{11}{4} \times 0.01}$

Step 3a $\boxed{\dfrac{8}{1} \times \dfrac{8}{5} \times \dfrac{1}{16} \times \dfrac{10.4}{0.12} \times \dfrac{11}{4} \times 0.01} = \boxed{\dfrac{8}{1} \times \dfrac{8}{5} \times \dfrac{1}{16} \times \dfrac{\dfrac{104}{10}}{\dfrac{12}{100}} \times \dfrac{11}{4} \times 0.01}$

$= \boxed{\dfrac{8}{1} \times \dfrac{8}{5} \times \dfrac{1}{16} \times \dfrac{104 \times 100}{10 \times 12} \times \dfrac{11}{4} \times 0.01} = \boxed{\dfrac{8}{1} \times \dfrac{8}{5} \times \dfrac{1}{16} \times \dfrac{10400}{120} \times \dfrac{11}{4} \times 0.01}$

Step 3b $\boxed{\dfrac{8}{1} \times \dfrac{8}{5} \times \dfrac{1}{16} \times \dfrac{10400}{120} \times \dfrac{11}{4} \times 0.01} = \boxed{\dfrac{8}{1} \times \dfrac{8}{5} \times \dfrac{1}{16} \times \dfrac{10400}{120} \times \dfrac{11}{4} \times \dfrac{1}{100}}$

Step 4 $\boxed{\dfrac{8}{1} \times \dfrac{8}{5} \times \dfrac{1}{16} \times \dfrac{10400}{120} \times \dfrac{11}{4} \times \dfrac{1}{100}} = \boxed{\dfrac{8 \times 8 \times 1 \times 10400 \times 11 \times 1}{1 \times 5 \times 16 \times 120 \times 4 \times 100}} = \boxed{\dfrac{7321600}{3840000}}$

Step 5 $\boxed{\dfrac{7321600}{3840000}} = \boxed{\dfrac{7321600 \div 800}{3840000 \div 800}} = \boxed{\dfrac{9152}{4800}} = \boxed{\dfrac{9152 \div 64}{4800 \div 64}} = \boxed{\dfrac{143}{75}}$

Step 6 $\boxed{\dfrac{143}{75}} = \boxed{1\dfrac{68}{75}}$

The following examples further illustrate how to multiply integer, decimal, and mixed fractions:

Example 9.3-11

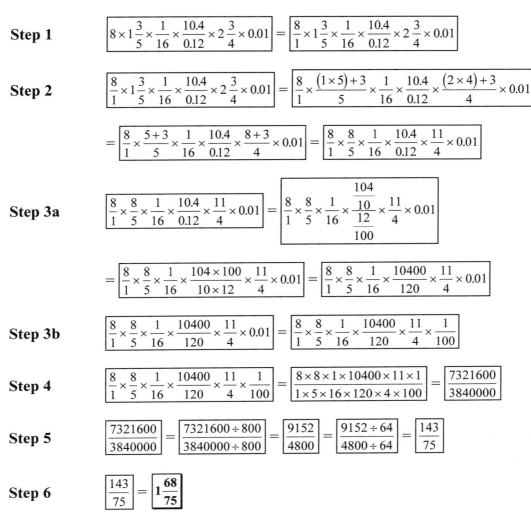

$= \boxed{\dfrac{2 \times 3 \times 1}{1 \times 1 \times 1}} = \boxed{\dfrac{6}{1}} = \boxed{6}$

Example 9.3-12

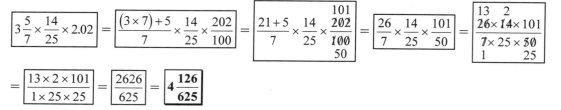

$$= \boxed{\frac{13 \times 2 \times 101}{1 \times 25 \times 25}} = \boxed{\frac{2626}{625}} = \boxed{4\frac{126}{625}}$$

Example 9.3-13

Example 9.3-14

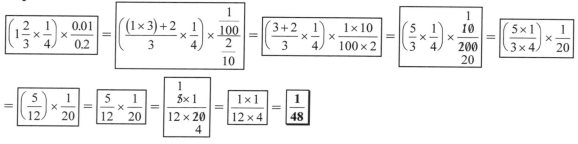

$$= \boxed{\left(\frac{5}{12}\right) \times \frac{1}{20}} = \boxed{\frac{5}{12} \times \frac{1}{20}} = \boxed{\frac{\overset{1}{\cancel{5}} \times 1}{12 \times \underset{4}{\cancel{20}}}} = \boxed{\frac{1 \times 1}{12 \times 4}} = \boxed{\mathbf{\frac{1}{48}}}$$

Example 9.3-15

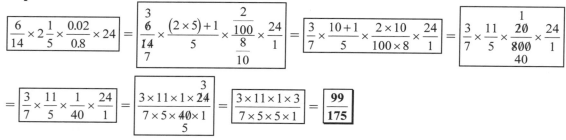

$$= \boxed{\frac{3}{7} \times \frac{11}{5} \times \frac{1}{40} \times \frac{24}{1}} = \boxed{\frac{3 \times 11 \times 1 \times \overset{3}{\cancel{24}}}{7 \times 5 \times \underset{5}{\cancel{40}} \times 1}} = \boxed{\frac{3 \times 11 \times 1 \times 3}{7 \times 5 \times 5 \times 1}} = \boxed{\mathbf{\frac{99}{175}}}$$

Example 9.3-16

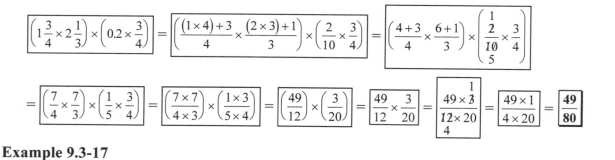

$$= \boxed{\left(\frac{7}{4} \times \frac{7}{3}\right) \times \left(\frac{1}{5} \times \frac{3}{4}\right)} = \boxed{\left(\frac{7 \times 7}{4 \times 3}\right) \times \left(\frac{1 \times 3}{5 \times 4}\right)} = \boxed{\left(\frac{49}{12}\right) \times \left(\frac{3}{20}\right)} = \boxed{\frac{49}{12} \times \frac{3}{20}} = \boxed{\frac{49 \times \overset{1}{\cancel{3}}}{\underset{4}{\cancel{12}} \times 20}} = \boxed{\frac{49 \times 1}{4 \times 20}} = \boxed{\mathbf{\frac{49}{80}}}$$

Example 9.3-17

$$\boxed{\left(4\frac{1}{3} \times \frac{1}{0.5}\right) \times \left(\frac{3}{2} \times 5\right)} = \boxed{\left(\frac{(4 \times 3) + 1}{1} \times \frac{\frac{1}{1}}{\frac{5}{10}}\right) \times \left(\frac{3}{2} \times \frac{5}{1}\right)} = \boxed{\left(\frac{13}{3} \times \frac{1 \times 10}{1 \times 5}\right) \times \left(\frac{3}{2} \times \frac{5}{1}\right)} = \boxed{\left(\frac{13}{3} \times \frac{10}{5}\right) \times \left(\frac{3 \times 5}{2 \times 1}\right)}$$

$$= \left(\left(\frac{13 \times \overset{2}{\cancel{10}}}{3 \times \underset{1}{\cancel{5}}}\right) \times \left(\frac{15}{2}\right)\right) = \left(\left(\frac{13 \times 2}{3 \times 1}\right) \times \left(\frac{15}{2}\right)\right) = \left(\frac{26}{3}\right) \times \frac{15}{2} = \frac{26}{3} \times \frac{15}{2} = \frac{\overset{13}{\cancel{26}} \times \overset{5}{\cancel{15}}}{\underset{1}{\cancel{3}} \times \underset{1}{\cancel{2}}} = \frac{13 \times 5}{1 \times 1} = \frac{65}{1} = \boxed{65}$$

Example 9.3-18

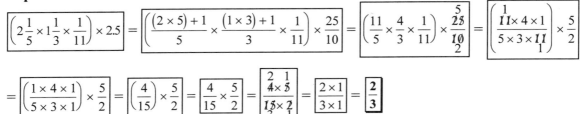

$$\left(2\frac{1}{5} \times 1\frac{1}{3} \times \frac{1}{11}\right) \times 2.5 = \left(\left(\frac{(2\times5)+1}{5} \times \frac{(1\times3)+1}{3} \times \frac{1}{11}\right) \times \frac{25}{10}\right) = \left(\frac{11}{5} \times \frac{4}{3} \times \frac{1}{11}\right) \times \frac{\overset{5}{\cancel{25}}}{\underset{2}{\cancel{10}}} = \left(\frac{\overset{1}{\cancel{11}} \times 4 \times 1}{5 \times 3 \times \underset{1}{\cancel{11}}}\right) \times \frac{5}{2}$$

$$= \left(\frac{1 \times 4 \times 1}{5 \times 3 \times 1}\right) \times \frac{5}{2} = \left(\frac{4}{15}\right) \times \frac{5}{2} = \frac{4}{15} \times \frac{5}{2} = \frac{\overset{2}{\cancel{4}} \times \overset{1}{\cancel{5}}}{\underset{3}{\cancel{15}} \times \underset{1}{\cancel{2}}} = \frac{2 \times 1}{3 \times 1} = \boxed{\frac{2}{3}}$$

Example 9.3-19

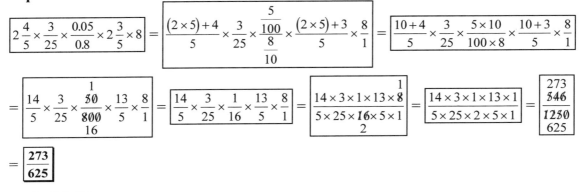

$$2\frac{4}{5} \times \frac{3}{25} \times \frac{0.05}{0.8} \times 2\frac{3}{5} \times 8 = \frac{(2\times5)+4}{5} \times \frac{3}{25} \times \frac{\frac{5}{100}}{\frac{8}{10}} \times \frac{(2\times5)+3}{5} \times \frac{8}{1} = \frac{10+4}{5} \times \frac{3}{25} \times \frac{5\times10}{100\times8} \times \frac{10+3}{5} \times \frac{8}{1}$$

$$= \frac{14}{5} \times \frac{3}{25} \times \frac{\overset{1}{\cancel{50}}}{\underset{16}{\cancel{800}}} \times \frac{13}{5} \times \frac{8}{1} = \frac{14}{5} \times \frac{3}{25} \times \frac{1}{16} \times \frac{13}{5} \times \frac{8}{1} = \frac{14\times3\times1\times13\times\overset{1}{\cancel{8}}}{5\times25\times\underset{2}{\cancel{16}}\times5\times1} = \frac{14\times3\times1\times13\times1}{5\times25\times2\times5\times1} = \frac{\overset{273}{\cancel{546}}}{\underset{625}{\cancel{1250}}}$$

$$= \boxed{\frac{273}{625}}$$

Example 9.3-20

$$\left(3\frac{1}{5} \times \frac{5}{8} \times 0.1\right) \times \left(\frac{2}{3} \times \frac{1}{16} \times \frac{0.3}{1.2}\right) = \left(\frac{(3\times5)+1}{5} \times \frac{5}{8} \times \frac{1}{10}\right) \times \left(\frac{2}{3} \times \frac{1}{16} \times \frac{\frac{3}{10}}{\frac{12}{10}}\right)$$

$$= \left(\frac{15+1}{5} \times \frac{5}{8} \times \frac{1}{10}\right) \times \left(\frac{2}{3} \times \frac{1}{16} \times \frac{3\times10}{10\times12}\right) = \left(\frac{16}{5} \times \frac{5}{8} \times \frac{1}{10}\right) \times \left(\frac{2}{3} \times \frac{1}{16} \times \frac{\overset{1}{\cancel{30}}}{\underset{4}{\cancel{120}}}\right) = \left(\frac{16}{5} \times \frac{5}{8} \times \frac{1}{10}\right) \times \left(\frac{2}{3} \times \frac{1}{16} \times \frac{1}{4}\right)$$

$$= \left(\frac{\overset{2}{\cancel{16}} \times \overset{1}{\cancel{5}} \times 1}{\underset{1}{\cancel{5}} \times 8 \times 10}\right) \times \left(\frac{\overset{1}{\cancel{2}} \times 1 \times 1}{3 \times 16 \times \underset{2}{\cancel{4}}}\right) = \left(\frac{2\times1\times1}{1\times1\times10}\right) \times \left(\frac{1\times1\times1}{3\times16\times2}\right) = \left(\frac{2}{10}\right) \times \left(\frac{1}{96}\right) = \frac{2}{10} \times \frac{1}{96} = \frac{\overset{1}{\cancel{2}} \times 1}{\underset{5}{\cancel{10}} \times 96} = \frac{1\times1}{5\times96}$$

$$= \boxed{\frac{1}{480}}$$

Example 9.3-21

$$\left(12 \times \frac{4}{7}\right) \times \left(2\frac{1}{10} \times \frac{0.014}{0.11}\right) \times 25 = \left(\frac{12}{1} \times \frac{4}{7}\right) \times \left(\frac{(2\times10)+1}{10} \times \frac{\frac{14}{1000}}{\frac{11}{100}}\right) \times \frac{25}{1}$$

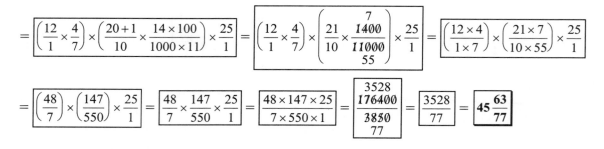

Section 9.3 Exercises - Multiply the following integer, decimal, and mixed fractions:

1. $\dfrac{3}{5} \times 1\dfrac{2}{3} \times 0.2 =$

2. $1\dfrac{3}{8} \times \dfrac{2}{3} \times 0.5 =$

3. $\dfrac{1}{3} \times \dfrac{3}{4} \times 0.04 \times 1\dfrac{2}{3} =$

4. $\left(2\dfrac{1}{5} \times \dfrac{3}{11} \times 1\dfrac{1}{3} \right) \times \dfrac{0.2}{0.01} =$

5. $0.08 \times \left(\dfrac{1}{4} \times 2\dfrac{1}{4} \right) =$

6. $\left(2\dfrac{4}{5} \times 1\dfrac{2}{3} \right) \times \left(\dfrac{5}{8} \times \dfrac{0.4}{0.05} \right) =$

7. $\dfrac{20}{27} \times 1\dfrac{3}{4} \times \dfrac{3}{6} \times \dfrac{0.008}{0.04} =$

8. $\left(2\dfrac{3}{5} \times 0.2 \right) \times \left(\dfrac{5}{13} \times \dfrac{0.2}{0.24} \right) =$

9. $\left(3\dfrac{2}{3} \times \dfrac{1}{11} \times 0.9 \right) \times \dfrac{1}{27} =$

10. $\left(\dfrac{0.5}{1.5} \times 2\dfrac{1}{10} \times 0.8 \right) \times \left(\dfrac{1}{21} \times \dfrac{1}{0.4} \right)$

9.4   Dividing Integer, Decimal, and Mixed Fractions

Fractions of the following forms:

1. $\left(\dfrac{a}{b}\right)$ where (a) and (b) are integers,

2. $\left(\dfrac{a \times 10^{-k_1}}{b \times 10^{-k_2}}\right)$ where (a) and (b) are integer numbers and (k_1) and (k_2) are equal to the number

of decimal places, and

3. $\left(k\dfrac{a}{b}\right)$ where (k) is made up of a whole number and $\left(\dfrac{a}{b}\right)$ is an integer fraction for a number

less than one

are divided as in the following cases:

Case I   Dividing Integer, Decimal, and Mixed Fractions With Three Terms Only

Divide three integer, decimal, and mixed fractions using the following steps:

Step 1   Change the integer number (a) to an integer fraction of the form $\left(\dfrac{a}{1}\right)$, e.g., change

29 to $\dfrac{29}{1}$.

Step 2   Change the mixed fraction to an integer fraction (see Section 2.5).

Step 3   a. Change the decimal fraction to an integer fraction (see Section 2.4).

b. Change the decimal number $\left(a \times 10^{-k}\right)$ to an integer fraction of the form $\left(\dfrac{a}{10^k}\right)$,

e.g., change 0.25 to $\dfrac{25}{100}$.

Step 4   Divide the integer fractions (see Section 3.4).

Step 5   Simplify the fraction to its lowest term (see Section 2.3).

Step 6   Change the improper fraction to a mixed fraction if the fraction obtained from Step 5
is an improper fraction (see Section 2.2).

The following examples show the steps as to how integer, decimal, and mixed fractions with
three terms only are divided:

Example 9.4-1

$$\left(2\frac{4}{5} \div \frac{3}{8}\right) \div \frac{0.9}{0.12} =$$

Solution:

Step 1 $\boxed{\textit{Not Applicable}}$

Step 2 $\left(2\dfrac{4}{5} \div \dfrac{3}{8}\right) \div \dfrac{0.9}{0.12} = \left(\dfrac{(2\times5)+4}{5} \div \dfrac{3}{8}\right) \div \dfrac{0.9}{0.12} = \left(\dfrac{10+4}{5} \div \dfrac{3}{8}\right) \div \dfrac{0.9}{0.12} = \left(\dfrac{14}{5} \div \dfrac{3}{8}\right) \div \dfrac{0.9}{0.12}$

Step 3a $\left(\left(\dfrac{14}{5}\div\dfrac{3}{8}\right)\div\dfrac{0.9}{0.12}\right)=\left(\left(\dfrac{14}{5}\div\dfrac{3}{8}\right)\div\dfrac{\frac{9}{10}}{\frac{12}{100}}\right)=\left(\left(\dfrac{14}{5}\div\dfrac{3}{8}\right)\div\dfrac{9\times100}{10\times12}\right)=\left(\left(\dfrac{14}{5}\div\dfrac{3}{8}\right)\div\dfrac{900}{120}\right)$

Step 3b $\boxed{Not\ Applicable}$

Step 4 $\left(\left(\dfrac{14}{5}\div\dfrac{3}{8}\right)\div\dfrac{900}{120}\right)=\left(\left(\dfrac{14}{5}\times\dfrac{8}{3}\right)\div\dfrac{900}{120}\right)=\left(\left(\dfrac{14\times8}{5\times3}\right)\div\dfrac{900}{120}\right)=\left(\left(\dfrac{112}{15}\right)\div\dfrac{900}{120}\right)=\left(\dfrac{112}{15}\div\dfrac{900}{120}\right)$

$=\left(\dfrac{112}{15}\times\dfrac{120}{900}\right)=\left(\dfrac{112\times120}{15\times900}\right)=\dfrac{13440}{13500}$

Step 5 $\dfrac{13440}{13500}=\dfrac{13440\div20}{13500\div20}=\boxed{\dfrac{672}{675}}$

Step 6 $\boxed{Not\ Applicable}$

Example 9.4-2

$4\dfrac{1}{5}\div\left(3\div\dfrac{0.8}{0.3}\right)=$

Solution:

Step 1 $4\dfrac{1}{5}\div\left(3\div\dfrac{0.8}{0.3}\right)=4\dfrac{1}{5}\div\left(\dfrac{3}{1}\div\dfrac{0.8}{0.3}\right)$

Step 2 $4\dfrac{1}{5}\div\left(\dfrac{3}{1}\div\dfrac{0.8}{0.3}\right)=\dfrac{(4\times5)+1}{5}\div\left(\dfrac{3}{1}\div\dfrac{0.8}{0.3}\right)=\dfrac{20+1}{5}\div\left(\dfrac{3}{1}\div\dfrac{0.8}{0.3}\right)=\dfrac{21}{5}\div\left(\dfrac{3}{1}\div\dfrac{0.8}{0.3}\right)$

Step 3a $\dfrac{21}{5}\div\left(\dfrac{3}{1}\div\dfrac{0.8}{0.3}\right)=\dfrac{21}{5}\div\left(\dfrac{3}{1}\div\dfrac{\frac{8}{10}}{\frac{3}{10}}\right)=\dfrac{21}{5}\div\left(\dfrac{3}{1}\div\dfrac{8\times10}{10\times3}\right)=\dfrac{21}{5}\div\left(\dfrac{3}{1}\div\dfrac{80}{30}\right)$

Step 3b $\boxed{Not\ Applicable}$

Step 4 $\dfrac{21}{5}\div\left(\dfrac{3}{1}\div\dfrac{80}{30}\right)=\dfrac{21}{5}\div\left(\dfrac{3}{1}\times\dfrac{30}{80}\right)=\dfrac{21}{5}\div\left(\dfrac{3\times30}{1\times80}\right)=\dfrac{21}{5}\div\left(\dfrac{90}{80}\right)=\dfrac{21}{5}\div\dfrac{90}{80}$

$=\dfrac{21}{5}\times\dfrac{80}{90}=\dfrac{21\times80}{5\times90}=\dfrac{1680}{450}$

Step 5 $\dfrac{1680}{450}=\dfrac{1680\div30}{450\div30}=\dfrac{56}{15}$

Step 6 $\boxed{\dfrac{56}{15}} = \boxed{3\dfrac{11}{15}}$

Example 9.4-3

$$\boxed{\left(\dfrac{3}{5} \div 12.8\right) \div 2\dfrac{5}{6}} =$$

Solution:

Step 1 $\boxed{Not\ Applicable}$

Step 2 $\boxed{\left(\dfrac{3}{5} \div 12.8\right) \div 2\dfrac{5}{6}} = \boxed{\left(\dfrac{3}{5} \div 12.8\right) \div \dfrac{(2 \times 6)+5}{6}} = \boxed{\left(\dfrac{3}{5} \div 12.8\right) \div \dfrac{12+5}{6}} = \boxed{\left(\dfrac{3}{5} \div 12.8\right) \div \dfrac{17}{6}}$

Step 3a $\boxed{Not\ Applicable}$

Step 3b $\boxed{\left(\dfrac{3}{5} \div 12.8\right) \div \dfrac{17}{6}} = \boxed{\left(\dfrac{3}{5} \div \dfrac{128}{10}\right) \div \dfrac{17}{6}}$

Step 4 $\boxed{\left(\dfrac{3}{5} \div \dfrac{128}{10}\right) \div \dfrac{17}{6}} = \boxed{\left(\dfrac{3}{5} \times \dfrac{10}{128}\right) \div \dfrac{17}{6}} = \boxed{\left(\dfrac{3 \times 10}{5 \times 128}\right) \div \dfrac{17}{6}} = \boxed{\left(\dfrac{30}{640}\right) \div \dfrac{17}{6}} = \boxed{\dfrac{30}{640} \div \dfrac{17}{6}}$

$= \boxed{\dfrac{30}{640} \times \dfrac{6}{17}} = \boxed{\dfrac{30 \times 6}{640 \times 17}} = \boxed{\dfrac{180}{10880}}$

Step 5 $\boxed{\dfrac{180}{10880}} = \boxed{\dfrac{180 \div 20}{10880 \div 20}} = \boxed{\dfrac{9}{544}}$

Step 6 $\boxed{Not\ Applicable}$

Example 9.4-4

$$\boxed{\dfrac{0.3}{0.15} \div \left(8\dfrac{1}{5} \div 6\right)} =$$

Solution:

Step 1 $\boxed{\dfrac{0.3}{0.15} \div \left(8\dfrac{1}{5} \div 6\right)} = \boxed{\dfrac{0.3}{0.15} \div \left(8\dfrac{1}{5} \div \dfrac{6}{1}\right)}$

Step 2 $\boxed{\dfrac{0.3}{0.15} \div \left(8\dfrac{1}{5} \div \dfrac{6}{1}\right)} = \boxed{\dfrac{0.3}{0.15} \div \left(\dfrac{(8 \times 5)+1}{5} \div \dfrac{6}{1}\right)} = \boxed{\dfrac{0.3}{0.15} \div \left(\dfrac{40+1}{5} \div \dfrac{6}{1}\right)} = \boxed{\dfrac{0.3}{0.15} \div \left(\dfrac{41}{5} \div \dfrac{6}{1}\right)}$

Step 3a $\boxed{\dfrac{0.3}{0.15} \div \left(\dfrac{41}{5} \div \dfrac{6}{1}\right)} = \boxed{\dfrac{\frac{3}{10}}{\frac{15}{100}} \div \left(\dfrac{41}{5} \div \dfrac{6}{1}\right)} = \boxed{\dfrac{3 \times 100}{10 \times 15} \div \left(\dfrac{41}{5} \div \dfrac{6}{1}\right)} = \boxed{\dfrac{300}{150} \div \left(\dfrac{41}{5} \div \dfrac{6}{1}\right)}$

Step 3b $\boxed{Not\ Applicable}$

Step 4 $\boxed{\dfrac{300}{150} \div \left(\dfrac{41}{5} \div \dfrac{6}{1} \right)} = \boxed{\dfrac{300}{150} \div \left(\dfrac{41}{5} \times \dfrac{1}{6} \right)} = \boxed{\dfrac{300}{150} \div \left(\dfrac{41 \times 1}{5 \times 6} \right)} = \boxed{\dfrac{300}{150} \div \left(\dfrac{41}{30} \right)} = \boxed{\dfrac{300}{150} \div \dfrac{41}{30}}$

$= \boxed{\dfrac{300}{150} \times \dfrac{30}{41}} = \boxed{\dfrac{300 \times 30}{150 \times 41}} = \boxed{\dfrac{9000}{6150}}$

Step 5 $\boxed{\dfrac{9000}{6150}} = \boxed{\dfrac{9000 \div 50}{6150 \div 50}} = \boxed{\dfrac{180}{123}} = \boxed{\dfrac{180 \div 3}{123 \div 3}} = \boxed{\dfrac{60}{41}}$

Step 6 $\boxed{\dfrac{60}{41}} = \boxed{\boxed{1\dfrac{19}{41}}}$

Example 9.4-5

$$\boxed{\left(\dfrac{2}{7} \div 2\dfrac{4}{7} \right) \div 10.5} =$$

Solution:

Step 1 $\boxed{Not\ Applicable}$

Step 2 $\boxed{\left(\dfrac{2}{7} \div 2\dfrac{4}{7} \right) \div 10.5} = \boxed{\left(\dfrac{2}{7} \div \dfrac{(2 \times 7) + 4}{7} \right) \div 10.5} = \boxed{\left(\dfrac{2}{7} \div \dfrac{14 + 4}{7} \right) \div 10.5} = \boxed{\left(\dfrac{2}{7} \div \dfrac{18}{7} \right) \div 10.5}$

Step 3a $\boxed{Not\ Applicable}$

Step 3b $\boxed{\left(\dfrac{2}{7} \div \dfrac{18}{7} \right) \div 10.5} = \boxed{\left(\dfrac{2}{7} \div \dfrac{18}{7} \right) \div \dfrac{105}{10}}$

Step 4 $\boxed{\left(\dfrac{2}{7} \div \dfrac{18}{7} \right) \div \dfrac{105}{10}} = \boxed{\left(\dfrac{2}{7} \times \dfrac{7}{18} \right) \div \dfrac{105}{10}} = \boxed{\left(\dfrac{2 \times 7}{7 \times 18} \right) \div \dfrac{105}{10}} = \boxed{\left(\dfrac{14}{126} \right) \div \dfrac{105}{10}} = \boxed{\dfrac{14}{126} \div \dfrac{105}{10}}$

$= \boxed{\dfrac{14}{126} \times \dfrac{10}{105}} = \boxed{\dfrac{14 \times 10}{126 \times 105}} = \boxed{\dfrac{140}{13230}}$

Step 5 $\boxed{\dfrac{140}{13230}} = \boxed{\dfrac{140 \div 10}{13230 \div 10}} = \boxed{\dfrac{14 \div 7}{1323 \div 7}} = \boxed{\boxed{\dfrac{2}{189}}}$

Step 6 $\boxed{Not\ Applicable}$

Case II   Dividing Integer, Decimal, and Mixed Fractions With More Than Three Terms

Divide integer, decimal, and mixed fractions having more than three terms by using the following steps:

Step 1   Change the integer number(s) (a) to integer fraction(s) of the form $\left(\dfrac{a}{1}\right)$, e.g., change

486 to $\dfrac{486}{1}$.

Step 2   Change the mixed fraction(s) to integer fraction(s) (see Section 2.5).

Step 3   a. Change the decimal fraction(s) to integer fraction(s) (see Section 2.4).

b. Change the decimal number(s) $\left(a \times 10^{-k}\right)$ to integer fraction(s) of the form $\left(\dfrac{a}{10^{k}}\right)$,

e.g., change 0.039 to $\dfrac{39}{1000}$.

Step 4   Divide the integer fractions (see Section 3.4).

Step 5   Simplify the fraction to its lowest term (see Section 2.3).

Step 6   Change the improper fraction to a mixed fraction if the fraction obtained from Step 5 is an improper fraction (see Section 2.2).

The following examples show the steps as to how integer, decimal, and mixed fractions with more than three terms are divided:

Example 9.4-6

$$\left[\left(4\frac{2}{5} \div \frac{4}{5}\right) \div \left(5 \div \frac{0.8}{0.05}\right)\right] =$$

Solution:

Step 1
$$\left[\left(4\frac{2}{5} \div \frac{4}{5}\right) \div \left(5 \div \frac{0.8}{0.05}\right)\right] = \left[\left(4\frac{2}{5} \div \frac{4}{5}\right) \div \left(\frac{5}{1} \div \frac{0.8}{0.05}\right)\right]$$

Step 2
$$\left[\left(4\frac{2}{5} \div \frac{4}{5}\right) \div \left(\frac{5}{1} \div \frac{0.8}{0.05}\right)\right] = \left[\left(\frac{(4\times5)+2}{5} \div \frac{4}{5}\right) \div \left(\frac{5}{1} \div \frac{0.8}{0.05}\right)\right] = \left[\left(\frac{20+2}{5} \div \frac{4}{5}\right) \div \left(\frac{5}{1} \div \frac{0.8}{0.05}\right)\right]$$

$$= \left[\left(\frac{22}{5} \div \frac{4}{5}\right) \div \left(\frac{5}{1} \div \frac{0.8}{0.05}\right)\right]$$

Step 3a
$$\left[\left(\frac{22}{5} \div \frac{4}{5}\right) \div \left(\frac{5}{1} \div \frac{0.8}{0.05}\right)\right] = \left[\left(\frac{22}{5} \div \frac{4}{5}\right) \div \left(\frac{5}{1} \div \frac{\frac{8}{10}}{\frac{5}{100}}\right)\right] = \left[\left(\frac{22}{5} \div \frac{4}{5}\right) \div \left(\frac{5}{1} \div \frac{8\times100}{10\times5}\right)\right]$$

$$= \left[\left(\frac{22}{5} \div \frac{4}{5}\right) \div \left(\frac{5}{1} \div \frac{800}{50}\right)\right]$$

Step 3b   Not Applicable

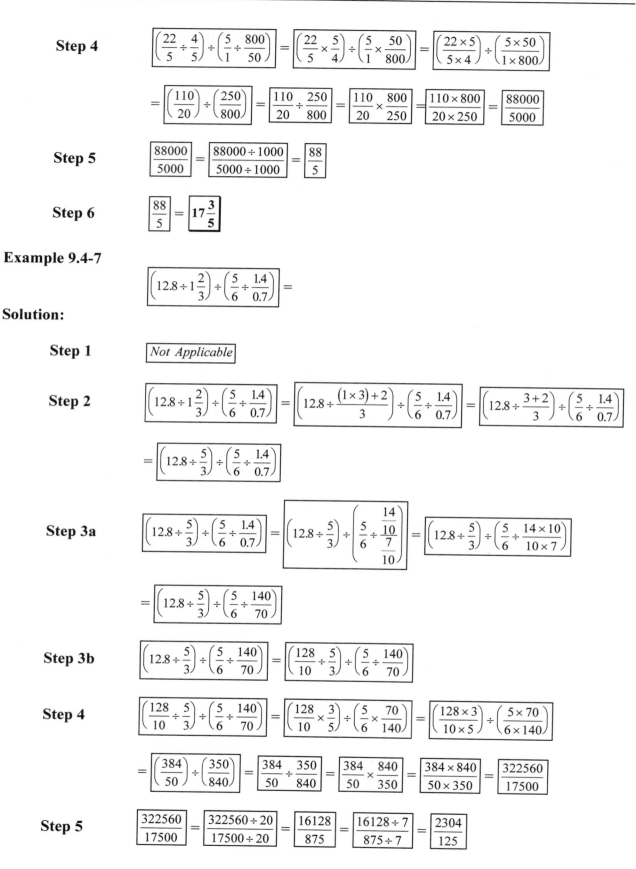

Step 4

$$\left(\frac{22}{5}\div\frac{4}{5}\right)\div\left(\frac{5}{1}\div\frac{800}{50}\right)=\left(\frac{22}{5}\times\frac{5}{4}\right)\div\left(\frac{5}{1}\times\frac{50}{800}\right)=\left(\frac{22\times5}{5\times4}\right)\div\left(\frac{5\times50}{1\times800}\right)$$

$$=\left(\frac{110}{20}\right)\div\left(\frac{250}{800}\right)=\frac{110}{20}\div\frac{250}{800}=\frac{110}{20}\times\frac{800}{250}=\frac{110\times800}{20\times250}=\frac{88000}{5000}$$

Step 5

$$\frac{88000}{5000}=\frac{88000\div1000}{5000\div1000}=\frac{88}{5}$$

Step 6

$$\frac{88}{5}=\boxed{17\frac{3}{5}}$$

Example 9.4-7

$$\left(12.8\div1\frac{2}{3}\right)\div\left(\frac{5}{6}\div\frac{1.4}{0.7}\right)=$$

Solution:

Step 1

Not Applicable

Step 2

$$\left(12.8\div1\frac{2}{3}\right)\div\left(\frac{5}{6}\div\frac{1.4}{0.7}\right)=\left(12.8\div\frac{(1\times3)+2}{3}\right)\div\left(\frac{5}{6}\div\frac{1.4}{0.7}\right)=\left(12.8\div\frac{3+2}{3}\right)\div\left(\frac{5}{6}\div\frac{1.4}{0.7}\right)$$

$$=\left(12.8\div\frac{5}{3}\right)\div\left(\frac{5}{6}\div\frac{1.4}{0.7}\right)$$

Step 3a

$$\left(12.8\div\frac{5}{3}\right)\div\left(\frac{5}{6}\div\frac{1.4}{0.7}\right)=\left(12.8\div\frac{5}{3}\right)\div\left(\frac{5}{6}\div\frac{\frac{14}{10}}{\frac{7}{10}}\right)=\left(12.8\div\frac{5}{3}\right)\div\left(\frac{5}{6}\div\frac{14\times10}{10\times7}\right)$$

$$=\left(12.8\div\frac{5}{3}\right)\div\left(\frac{5}{6}\div\frac{140}{70}\right)$$

Step 3b

$$\left(12.8\div\frac{5}{3}\right)\div\left(\frac{5}{6}\div\frac{140}{70}\right)=\left(\frac{128}{10}\div\frac{5}{3}\right)\div\left(\frac{5}{6}\div\frac{140}{70}\right)$$

Step 4

$$\left(\frac{128}{10}\div\frac{5}{3}\right)\div\left(\frac{5}{6}\div\frac{140}{70}\right)=\left(\frac{128}{10}\times\frac{3}{5}\right)\div\left(\frac{5}{6}\times\frac{70}{140}\right)=\left(\frac{128\times3}{10\times5}\right)\div\left(\frac{5\times70}{6\times140}\right)$$

$$=\left(\frac{384}{50}\right)\div\left(\frac{350}{840}\right)=\frac{384}{50}\div\frac{350}{840}=\frac{384}{50}\times\frac{840}{350}=\frac{384\times840}{50\times350}=\frac{322560}{17500}$$

Step 5

$$\frac{322560}{17500}=\frac{322560\div20}{17500\div20}=\frac{16128}{875}=\frac{16128\div7}{875\div7}=\frac{2304}{125}$$

Step 6 $\boxed{\dfrac{2304}{125}} = \boxed{18\dfrac{54}{125}}$

Example 9.4-8

$$\boxed{\left[8 \div \left(2\dfrac{1}{5} \div 0.5\right)\right] \div \dfrac{1}{4}} =$$

Solution:

Step 1 $\boxed{\left[8 \div \left(2\dfrac{1}{5} \div 0.5\right)\right] \div \dfrac{1}{4}} = \boxed{\left[\dfrac{8}{1} \div \left(2\dfrac{1}{5} \div 0.5\right)\right] \div \dfrac{1}{4}}$

Step 2 $\boxed{\left[\dfrac{8}{1} \div \left(2\dfrac{1}{5} \div 0.5\right)\right] \div \dfrac{1}{4}} = \boxed{\left[\dfrac{8}{1} \div \left(\dfrac{(2\times5)+1}{5} \div 0.5\right)\right] \div \dfrac{1}{4}} = \boxed{\left[\dfrac{8}{1} \div \left(\dfrac{10+1}{5} \div 0.5\right)\right] \div \dfrac{1}{4}}$

$$= \boxed{\left[\dfrac{8}{1} \div \left(\dfrac{11}{5} \div 0.5\right)\right] \div \dfrac{1}{4}}$$

Step 3a $\boxed{Not\ Applicable}$

Step 3b $\boxed{\left[\dfrac{8}{1} \div \left(\dfrac{11}{5} \div 0.5\right)\right] \div \dfrac{1}{4}} = \boxed{\left[\dfrac{8}{1} \div \left(\dfrac{11}{5} \div \dfrac{5}{10}\right)\right] \div \dfrac{1}{4}}$

Step 4 $\boxed{\left[\dfrac{8}{1} \div \left(\dfrac{11}{5} \div \dfrac{5}{10}\right)\right] \div \dfrac{1}{4}} = \boxed{\left[\dfrac{8}{1} \div \left(\dfrac{11}{5} \times \dfrac{10}{5}\right)\right] \div \dfrac{1}{4}} = \boxed{\left[\dfrac{8}{1} \div \left(\dfrac{11\times10}{5\times5}\right)\right] \div \dfrac{1}{4}}$

$$= \boxed{\left[\dfrac{8}{1} \div \left(\dfrac{110}{25}\right)\right] \div \dfrac{1}{4}} = \boxed{\left[\dfrac{8}{1} \div \dfrac{110}{25}\right] \div \dfrac{1}{4}} = \boxed{\left[\dfrac{8}{1} \times \dfrac{25}{110}\right] \div \dfrac{1}{4}} = \boxed{\left[\dfrac{8\times25}{1\times110}\right] \div \dfrac{1}{4}}$$

$$= \boxed{\left[\dfrac{200}{110}\right] \div \dfrac{1}{4}} = \boxed{\dfrac{200}{110} \div \dfrac{1}{4}} = \boxed{\dfrac{200}{110} \times \dfrac{4}{1}} = \boxed{\dfrac{200\times4}{110\times1}} = \boxed{\dfrac{800}{110}}$$

Step 5 $\boxed{\dfrac{800}{110}} = \boxed{\dfrac{800\div10}{110\div10}} = \boxed{\dfrac{80}{11}}$

Step 6 $\boxed{\dfrac{80}{11}} = \boxed{7\dfrac{3}{11}}$

Example 9.4-9

$$\boxed{\left(\dfrac{2}{15} \div \dfrac{0.2}{0.12}\right) \div \left(6 \div 1\dfrac{2}{5}\right)} =$$

Solution:

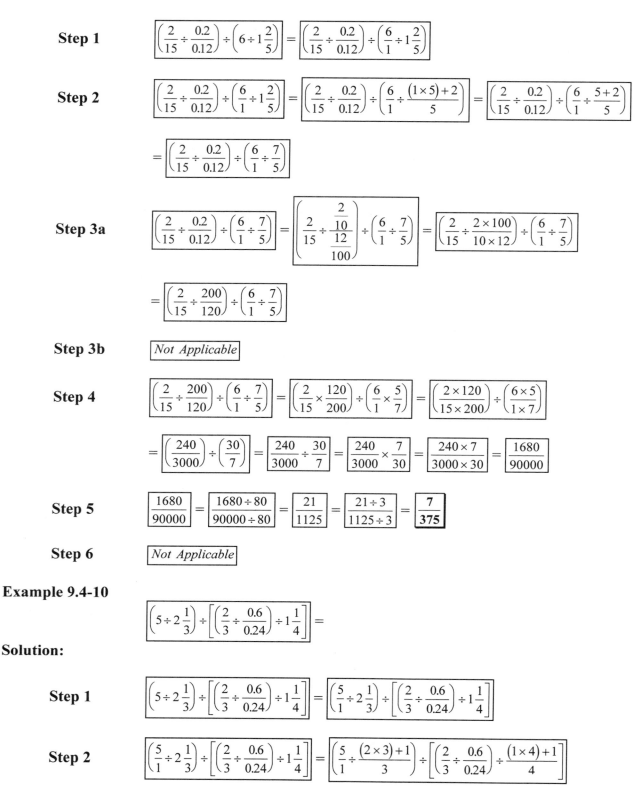

Step 1
$$\left(\frac{2}{15} \div \frac{0.2}{0.12}\right) \div \left(6 \div 1\frac{2}{5}\right) = \left[\left(\frac{2}{15} \div \frac{0.2}{0.12}\right) \div \left(\frac{6}{1} \div 1\frac{2}{5}\right)\right]$$

Step 2
$$\left[\left(\frac{2}{15} \div \frac{0.2}{0.12}\right) \div \left(\frac{6}{1} \div 1\frac{2}{5}\right)\right] = \left[\left(\frac{2}{15} \div \frac{0.2}{0.12}\right) \div \left(\frac{6}{1} \div \frac{(1\times 5)+2}{5}\right)\right] = \left[\left(\frac{2}{15} \div \frac{0.2}{0.12}\right) \div \left(\frac{6}{1} \div \frac{5+2}{5}\right)\right]$$

$$= \left[\left(\frac{2}{15} \div \frac{0.2}{0.12}\right) \div \left(\frac{6}{1} \div \frac{7}{5}\right)\right]$$

Step 3a
$$\left[\left(\frac{2}{15} \div \frac{0.2}{0.12}\right) \div \left(\frac{6}{1} \div \frac{7}{5}\right)\right] = \left[\left(\frac{2}{15} \div \frac{\frac{2}{10}}{\frac{12}{100}}\right) \div \left(\frac{6}{1} \div \frac{7}{5}\right)\right] = \left[\left(\frac{2}{15} \div \frac{2\times 100}{10\times 12}\right) \div \left(\frac{6}{1} \div \frac{7}{5}\right)\right]$$

$$= \left[\left(\frac{2}{15} \div \frac{200}{120}\right) \div \left(\frac{6}{1} \div \frac{7}{5}\right)\right]$$

Step 3b   Not Applicable

Step 4
$$\left[\left(\frac{2}{15} \div \frac{200}{120}\right) \div \left(\frac{6}{1} \div \frac{7}{5}\right)\right] = \left[\left(\frac{2}{15} \times \frac{120}{200}\right) \div \left(\frac{6}{1} \times \frac{5}{7}\right)\right] = \left[\left(\frac{2\times 120}{15\times 200}\right) \div \left(\frac{6\times 5}{1\times 7}\right)\right]$$

$$= \left[\left(\frac{240}{3000}\right) \div \left(\frac{30}{7}\right)\right] = \frac{240}{3000} \div \frac{30}{7} = \frac{240}{3000} \times \frac{7}{30} = \frac{240\times 7}{3000\times 30} = \frac{1680}{90000}$$

Step 5
$$\frac{1680}{90000} = \frac{1680\div 80}{90000\div 80} = \frac{21}{1125} = \frac{21\div 3}{1125\div 3} = \boxed{\frac{7}{375}}$$

Step 6   Not Applicable

Example 9.4-10
$$\left(5 \div 2\frac{1}{3}\right) \div \left[\left(\frac{2}{3} \div \frac{0.6}{0.24}\right) \div 1\frac{1}{4}\right] =$$

Solution:

Step 1
$$\left(5 \div 2\frac{1}{3}\right) \div \left[\left(\frac{2}{3} \div \frac{0.6}{0.24}\right) \div 1\frac{1}{4}\right] = \left[\left(\frac{5}{1} \div 2\frac{1}{3}\right) \div \left[\left(\frac{2}{3} \div \frac{0.6}{0.24}\right) \div 1\frac{1}{4}\right]\right]$$

Step 2
$$\left[\left(\frac{5}{1} \div 2\frac{1}{3}\right) \div \left[\left(\frac{2}{3} \div \frac{0.6}{0.24}\right) \div 1\frac{1}{4}\right]\right] = \left[\left(\frac{5}{1} \div \frac{(2\times 3)+1}{3}\right) \div \left[\left(\frac{2}{3} \div \frac{0.6}{0.24}\right) \div \frac{(1\times 4)+1}{4}\right]\right]$$

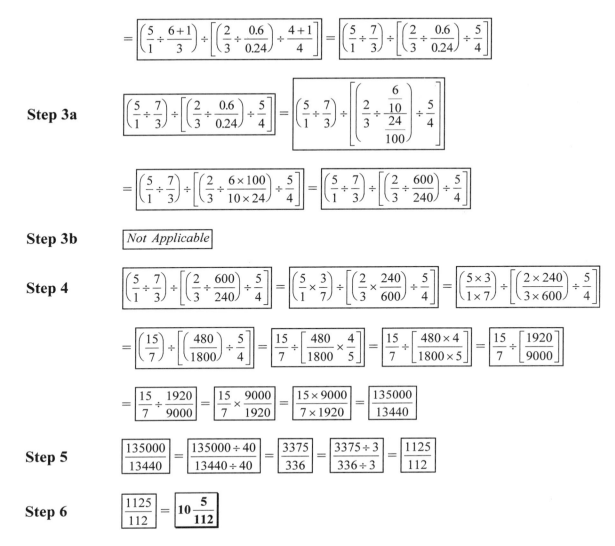

$$= \left[\left(\frac{5}{1} \div \frac{6+1}{3}\right) \div \left[\left(\frac{2}{3} \div \frac{0.6}{0.24}\right) \div \frac{4+1}{4}\right]\right] = \left[\left(\frac{5}{1} \div \frac{7}{3}\right) \div \left[\left(\frac{2}{3} \div \frac{0.6}{0.24}\right) \div \frac{5}{4}\right]\right]$$

Step 3a
$$\left[\left(\frac{5}{1} \div \frac{7}{3}\right) \div \left[\left(\frac{2}{3} \div \frac{0.6}{0.24}\right) \div \frac{5}{4}\right]\right] = \left[\left(\frac{5}{1} \div \frac{7}{3}\right) \div \left[\left(\frac{2}{3} \div \frac{\frac{6}{10}}{\frac{24}{100}}\right) \div \frac{5}{4}\right]\right]$$

$$= \left[\left(\frac{5}{1} \div \frac{7}{3}\right) \div \left[\left(\frac{2}{3} \div \frac{6 \times 100}{10 \times 24}\right) \div \frac{5}{4}\right]\right] = \left[\left(\frac{5}{1} \div \frac{7}{3}\right) \div \left[\left(\frac{2}{3} \div \frac{600}{240}\right) \div \frac{5}{4}\right]\right]$$

Step 3b   Not Applicable

Step 4
$$\left[\left(\frac{5}{1} \div \frac{7}{3}\right) \div \left[\left(\frac{2}{3} \div \frac{600}{240}\right) \div \frac{5}{4}\right]\right] = \left[\left(\frac{5}{1} \times \frac{3}{7}\right) \div \left[\left(\frac{2}{3} \times \frac{240}{600}\right) \div \frac{5}{4}\right]\right] = \left[\left(\frac{5 \times 3}{1 \times 7}\right) \div \left[\left(\frac{2 \times 240}{3 \times 600}\right) \div \frac{5}{4}\right]\right]$$

$$= \left[\left(\frac{15}{7}\right) \div \left[\left(\frac{480}{1800}\right) \div \frac{5}{4}\right]\right] = \left[\frac{15}{7} \div \left[\frac{480}{1800} \times \frac{4}{5}\right]\right] = \left[\frac{15}{7} \div \left[\frac{480 \times 4}{1800 \times 5}\right]\right] = \left[\frac{15}{7} \div \left[\frac{1920}{9000}\right]\right]$$

$$= \left[\frac{15}{7} \div \frac{1920}{9000}\right] = \left[\frac{15}{7} \times \frac{9000}{1920}\right] = \left[\frac{15 \times 9000}{7 \times 1920}\right] = \left[\frac{135000}{13440}\right]$$

Step 5
$$\frac{135000}{13440} = \frac{135000 \div 40}{13440 \div 40} = \frac{3375}{336} = \frac{3375 \div 3}{336 \div 3} = \frac{1125}{112}$$

Step 6
$$\frac{1125}{112} = \boxed{10 \frac{5}{112}}$$

The following examples further illustrate how to divide integer, decimal, and mixed fractions:

Example 9.4-11

$$\left[\frac{0.12}{0.4} \div \left(2\frac{1}{4} \div \frac{2}{8}\right)\right] = \left[\frac{\frac{12}{100}}{\frac{4}{10}} \div \left(\frac{(2 \times 4)+1}{4} \div \frac{\frac{1}{2}}{\frac{2}{8}}\right)\right] = \left[\frac{12 \times 10}{100 \times 4} \div \left(\frac{8+1}{4} \div \frac{1}{4}\right)\right] = \left[\frac{\overset{3}{\cancel{120}}}{\underset{10}{\cancel{400}}} \div \left(\frac{9}{4} \div \frac{1}{4}\right)\right] = \left[\frac{3}{10} \div \left(\frac{9}{4} \times \frac{4}{1}\right)\right]$$

$$= \left[\frac{3}{10} \div \left(\frac{9 \times 4}{4 \times 1}\right)\right] = \left[\frac{3}{10} \div \left(\frac{36}{4}\right)\right] = \left[\frac{3}{10} \div \frac{36}{4}\right] = \left[\frac{3}{10} \times \frac{4}{36}\right] = \left[\frac{\overset{1}{3} \times 4}{10 \times \underset{9}{\cancel{36}}}\right] = \left[\frac{\overset{1}{\cancel{3}} \times 1}{10 \times \underset{3}{\cancel{9}}}\right] = \left[\frac{1 \times 1}{10 \times 3}\right] = \boxed{\frac{1}{30}}$$

Example 9.4-12

$$\left[\left(1\frac{3}{5} \div \frac{2}{5}\right) \div 0.2\right] = \left[\left(\frac{(1 \times 5)+3}{5} \div \frac{2}{5}\right) \div \frac{\frac{1}{2}}{\frac{2}{10}}\right] = \left[\left(\frac{5+3}{5} \div \frac{2}{5}\right) \div \frac{1}{5}\right] = \left[\left(\frac{8}{5} \div \frac{2}{5}\right) \div \frac{1}{5}\right] = \left[\left(\frac{8}{5} \times \frac{5}{2}\right) \div \frac{1}{5}\right]$$

$$= \left(\frac{\overset{4}{\cancel{8}} \times \overset{1}{\cancel{5}}}{\underset{1}{\cancel{5}} \times \underset{1}{\cancel{2}}} \div \frac{1}{5} \right) = \left(\frac{4 \times 1}{1 \times 1} \div \frac{1}{5} \right) = \left(\frac{4}{1} \right) \div \frac{1}{5} = \frac{4}{1} \div \frac{1}{5} = \frac{4}{1} \times \frac{5}{1} = \frac{4 \times 5}{1 \times 1} = \frac{20}{1} = \boxed{20}$$

Example 9.4-13

$$\left(2\frac{4}{5} \div 0.2 \right) \div \frac{2}{5} = \left(\frac{(2 \times 5) + 4}{5} \div \frac{2}{10} \right) \div \frac{2}{5} = \left(\frac{10 + 4}{5} \div \frac{\overset{1}{\cancel{2}}}{\underset{5}{\cancel{10}}} \right) \div \frac{2}{5} = \left(\frac{14}{5} \div \frac{1}{5} \right) \div \frac{2}{5} = \left(\frac{14}{5} \times \frac{5}{1} \right) \div \frac{2}{5}$$

$$= \left(\frac{14 \times \overset{1}{\cancel{5}}}{\underset{1}{\cancel{5}} \times 1} \div \frac{2}{5} \right) = \left(\frac{14 \times 1}{1 \times 1} \div \frac{2}{5} \right) = \left(\frac{14}{1} \right) \div \frac{2}{5} = \frac{14}{1} \div \frac{2}{5} = \frac{14}{1} \times \frac{5}{2} = \frac{\overset{7}{\cancel{14}} \times 5}{1 \times \underset{1}{\cancel{2}}} = \frac{7 \times 5}{1 \times 1} = \frac{35}{1} = \boxed{35}$$

Example 9.4-14

$$\left(2\frac{3}{4} \div \frac{1}{16} \right) \div 0.04 = \left(\frac{(2 \times 4) + 3}{4} \div \frac{1}{16} \right) \div \frac{\overset{1}{\cancel{4}}}{\underset{25}{\cancel{100}}} = \left(\frac{8 + 3}{4} \div \frac{1}{16} \right) \div \frac{1}{25} = \left(\frac{11}{4} \div \frac{1}{16} \right) \div \frac{1}{25}$$

$$= \left(\frac{11}{4} \times \frac{16}{1} \right) \div \frac{1}{25} = \left(\frac{11 \times \overset{4}{\cancel{16}}}{\underset{1}{\cancel{4}} \times 1} \div \frac{1}{25} \right) = \left(\frac{11 \times 4}{1 \times 1} \div \frac{1}{25} \right) = \left(\frac{44}{1} \right) \div \frac{1}{25} = \frac{44}{1} \div \frac{1}{25} = \frac{44}{1} \times \frac{25}{1} = \frac{44 \times 25}{1 \times 1}$$

$$= \frac{44 \times 5}{1 \times 1} = \frac{1100}{1} = \boxed{1100}$$

Example 9.4-15

$$25 \div \left(4\frac{3}{5} \div \frac{1}{10} \right) = \frac{25}{1} \div \left(\frac{(4 \times 5) + 3}{5} \div \frac{1}{10} \right) = \frac{25}{1} \div \left(\frac{20 + 3}{5} \div \frac{1}{10} \right) = \frac{25}{1} \div \left(\frac{23}{5} \div \frac{1}{10} \right) = \frac{25}{1} \div \left(\frac{23}{5} \times \frac{10}{1} \right)$$

$$= \frac{25}{1} \div \left(\frac{23 \times \overset{2}{\cancel{10}}}{\underset{1}{\cancel{5}} \times 1} \right) = \frac{25}{1} \div \left(\frac{23 \times 2}{1 \times 1} \right) = \frac{25}{1} \div \left(\frac{46}{1} \right) = \frac{25}{1} \div \frac{46}{1} = \frac{25}{1} \times \frac{1}{46} = \frac{25 \times 1}{1 \times 46} = \boxed{\frac{25}{46}}$$

Example 9.4-16

$$\left(2\frac{2}{3} \div 4 \right) \div \frac{0.8}{0.12} = \left(\frac{(2 \times 3) + 2}{3} \div \frac{4}{1} \right) \div \frac{\frac{8}{10}}{\frac{12}{100}} = \left(\frac{6 + 2}{3} \div \frac{4}{1} \right) \div \frac{8 \times 100}{10 \times 12} = \left(\frac{8}{3} \div \frac{4}{1} \right) \div \frac{\overset{20}{\cancel{800}}}{\underset{3}{\cancel{120}}} = \left(\frac{8}{3} \times \frac{1}{4} \right) \div \frac{20}{3}$$

$$= \left(\frac{\overset{2}{\cancel{8}} \times 1}{3 \times \underset{1}{\cancel{4}}} \div \frac{20}{3} \right) = \left(\frac{2 \times 1}{3 \times 1} \div \frac{20}{3} \right) = \left(\frac{2}{3} \right) \div \frac{20}{3} = \frac{2}{3} \div \frac{20}{3} = \frac{2}{3} \times \frac{3}{20} = \frac{\overset{1}{\cancel{2}} \times \overset{1}{\cancel{3}}}{\underset{1}{\cancel{3}} \times \underset{10}{\cancel{20}}} = \frac{1 \times 1}{1 \times 10} = \boxed{\frac{1}{10}}$$

Example 9.4-17

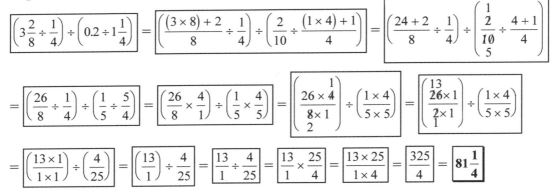

$$\left(3\frac{2}{8} \div \frac{1}{4}\right) \div \left(0.2 \div 1\frac{1}{4}\right) = \left(\left(\frac{(3\times8)+2}{8} \div \frac{1}{4}\right) \div \left(\frac{2}{10} \div \frac{(1\times4)+1}{4}\right)\right) = \left(\left(\frac{24+2}{8} \div \frac{1}{4}\right) \div \left(\frac{\overset{1}{\cancel{2}}}{\underset{5}{\cancel{10}}} \div \frac{4+1}{4}\right)\right)$$

$$= \left(\left(\frac{26}{8} \div \frac{1}{4}\right) \div \left(\frac{1}{5} \div \frac{5}{4}\right)\right) = \left(\left(\frac{26}{8} \times \frac{4}{1}\right) \div \left(\frac{1}{5} \times \frac{4}{5}\right)\right) = \left(\left(\frac{26\times\overset{1}{\cancel{4}}}{\underset{2}{\cancel{8}}\times1}\right) \div \left(\frac{1\times4}{5\times5}\right)\right) = \left(\left(\frac{\overset{13}{\cancel{26}}\times1}{\underset{1}{\cancel{2}}\times1}\right) \div \left(\frac{1\times4}{5\times5}\right)\right)$$

$$= \left(\left(\frac{13\times1}{1\times1}\right) \div \left(\frac{4}{25}\right)\right) = \left(\left(\frac{13}{1}\right) \div \frac{4}{25}\right) = \frac{13}{1} \div \frac{4}{25} = \frac{13}{1} \times \frac{25}{4} = \frac{13\times25}{1\times4} = \frac{325}{4} = \boxed{81\frac{1}{4}}$$

Example 9.4-18

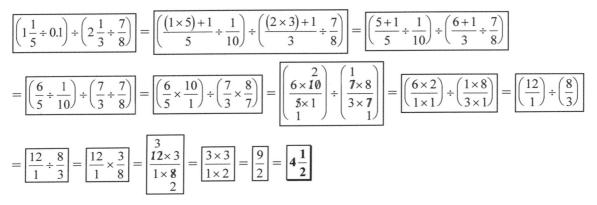

$$\left(1\frac{1}{5} \div 0.1\right) \div \left(2\frac{1}{3} \div \frac{7}{8}\right) = \left(\left(\frac{(1\times5)+1}{5} \div \frac{1}{10}\right) \div \left(\frac{(2\times3)+1}{3} \div \frac{7}{8}\right)\right) = \left(\left(\frac{5+1}{5} \div \frac{1}{10}\right) \div \left(\frac{6+1}{3} \div \frac{7}{8}\right)\right)$$

$$= \left(\left(\frac{6}{5} \div \frac{1}{10}\right) \div \left(\frac{7}{3} \div \frac{7}{8}\right)\right) = \left(\left(\frac{6}{5} \times \frac{10}{1}\right) \div \left(\frac{7}{3} \times \frac{8}{7}\right)\right) = \left(\frac{6\times\overset{2}{\cancel{10}}}{\underset{1}{\cancel{5}}\times1} \div \frac{\overset{1}{\cancel{7}}\times8}{3\times\underset{1}{\cancel{7}}}\right) = \left(\left(\frac{6\times2}{1\times1}\right) \div \left(\frac{1\times8}{3\times1}\right)\right) = \left(\left(\frac{12}{1}\right) \div \left(\frac{8}{3}\right)\right)$$

$$= \frac{12}{1} \div \frac{8}{3} = \frac{12}{1} \times \frac{3}{8} = \frac{\overset{3}{\cancel{12}}\times3}{1\times\underset{2}{\cancel{8}}} = \frac{3\times3}{1\times2} = \frac{9}{2} = \boxed{4\frac{1}{2}}$$

Example 9.4-19

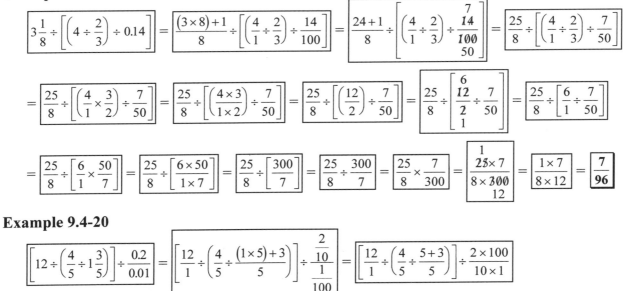

$$3\frac{1}{8} \div \left[\left(4 \div \frac{2}{3}\right) \div 0.14\right] = \frac{(3\times8)+1}{8} \div \left[\left(\frac{4}{1} \div \frac{2}{3}\right) \div \frac{14}{100}\right] = \frac{24+1}{8} \div \left[\left(\frac{4}{1} \div \frac{2}{3}\right) \div \frac{\overset{7}{\cancel{14}}}{\underset{50}{\cancel{100}}}\right] = \frac{25}{8} \div \left[\left(\frac{4}{1} \div \frac{2}{3}\right) \div \frac{7}{50}\right]$$

$$= \frac{25}{8} \div \left[\left(\frac{4}{1} \times \frac{3}{2}\right) \div \frac{7}{50}\right] = \frac{25}{8} \div \left[\left(\frac{4\times3}{1\times2}\right) \div \frac{7}{50}\right] = \frac{25}{8} \div \left[\left(\frac{12}{2}\right) \div \frac{7}{50}\right] = \frac{25}{8} \div \left[\frac{\overset{6}{\cancel{12}}}{\underset{1}{\cancel{2}}} \div \frac{7}{50}\right] = \frac{25}{8} \div \left[\frac{6}{1} \div \frac{7}{50}\right]$$

$$= \frac{25}{8} \div \left[\frac{6}{1} \times \frac{50}{7}\right] = \frac{25}{8} \div \left[\frac{6\times50}{1\times7}\right] = \frac{25}{8} \div \left[\frac{300}{7}\right] = \frac{25}{8} \div \frac{300}{7} = \frac{25}{8} \times \frac{7}{300} = \frac{\overset{1}{\cancel{25}}\times7}{8\times\underset{12}{\cancel{300}}} = \frac{1\times7}{8\times12} = \boxed{\frac{7}{96}}$$

Example 9.4-20

$$\left[12 \div \left(\frac{4}{5} \div 1\frac{3}{5}\right)\right] \div \frac{0.2}{0.01} = \left[\frac{12}{1} \div \left(\frac{4}{5} \div \frac{(1\times5)+3}{5}\right)\right] \div \frac{\frac{2}{10}}{\frac{1}{100}} = \left[\frac{12}{1} \div \left(\frac{4}{5} \div \frac{5+3}{5}\right)\right] \div \frac{2\times100}{10\times1}$$

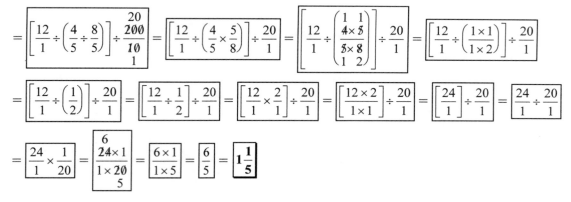

$$= \left[\frac{12}{1} \div \left(\frac{4}{5} \div \frac{8}{5}\right)\right] \div \frac{\frac{20}{200}}{\frac{10}{1}} = \left[\frac{12}{1} \div \left(\frac{4}{5} \times \frac{5}{8}\right)\right] \div \frac{20}{1} = \left[\frac{12}{1} \div \left(\frac{\overset{1}{4} \times \overset{1}{5}}{\underset{1}{5} \times \underset{2}{8}}\right)\right] \div \frac{20}{1} = \left[\frac{12}{1} \div \left(\frac{1 \times 1}{1 \times 2}\right)\right] \div \frac{20}{1}$$

$$= \left[\frac{12}{1} \div \left(\frac{1}{2}\right)\right] \div \frac{20}{1} = \left[\frac{12}{1} \div \frac{1}{2}\right] \div \frac{20}{1} = \left[\frac{12}{1} \times \frac{2}{1}\right] \div \frac{20}{1} = \left[\frac{12 \times 2}{1 \times 1}\right] \div \frac{20}{1} = \left[\frac{24}{1}\right] \div \frac{20}{1} = \frac{24}{1} \div \frac{20}{1}$$

$$= \frac{24}{1} \times \frac{1}{20} = \frac{\overset{6}{24} \times 1}{1 \times \underset{5}{20}} = \frac{6 \times 1}{1 \times 5} = \frac{6}{5} = \boxed{1\frac{1}{5}}$$

Example 9.4-21

$$\left(1\frac{3}{8} \div \frac{8}{1}\right) \div \left[0.5 \div \left(1\frac{1}{5} \div 11\right)\right] = \left(\frac{(1 \times 8) + 3}{8} \div \frac{8}{1}\right) \div \left[\frac{5}{10} \div \left(\frac{(1 \times 5) + 1}{5} \div \frac{11}{1}\right)\right]$$

$$= \left(\frac{8+3}{8} \div \frac{8}{1}\right) \div \left[\frac{\overset{1}{5}}{\underset{2}{10}} \div \left(\frac{5+1}{5} \div \frac{11}{1}\right)\right] = \left(\frac{11}{8} \div \frac{8}{1}\right) \div \left[\frac{1}{2} \div \left(\frac{6}{5} \div \frac{11}{1}\right)\right] = \left(\frac{11}{8} \times \frac{1}{8}\right) \div \left[\frac{1}{2} \div \left(\frac{6}{5} \times \frac{1}{11}\right)\right]$$

$$= \left(\frac{11 \times 1}{8 \times 8}\right) \div \left[\frac{1}{2} \div \left(\frac{6 \times 1}{5 \times 11}\right)\right] = \left(\frac{11}{64}\right) \div \left[\frac{1}{2} \div \left(\frac{6}{55}\right)\right] = \frac{11}{64} \div \left[\frac{1}{2} \div \frac{6}{55}\right] = \frac{11}{64} \div \left[\frac{1}{2} \times \frac{55}{6}\right] = \frac{11}{64} \div \left[\frac{1 \times 55}{2 \times 6}\right]$$

$$= \frac{11}{64} \div \left[\frac{1 \times 55}{2 \times 6}\right] = \frac{11}{64} \div \left[\frac{55}{12}\right] = \frac{11}{64} \div \frac{55}{12} = \frac{11}{64} \times \frac{12}{55} = \frac{\overset{1}{11} \times \overset{3}{12}}{\underset{16}{64} \times \underset{5}{55}} = \frac{1 \times 3}{16 \times 5} = \boxed{\frac{3}{80}}$$

Section 9.4 Exercises - Divide the following integer, decimal, and mixed fractions:

1. $\left(1\frac{1}{5} \div 25\right) \div \frac{0.1}{0.25} =$

2. $\left(2\frac{1}{3} \div 0.5\right) \div \frac{1}{3} =$

3. $\left(2\frac{3}{4} \div \frac{2}{6}\right) \div 1.1 =$

4. $\left(\frac{2}{3} \div 1\frac{1}{3}\right) \div \left(0.3 \div \frac{1}{6}\right) =$

5. $0.05 \div \left(2\frac{1}{3} \div 7\right) =$

6. $\left(\frac{2}{3} \div 0.2\right) \div \left(1\frac{1}{3} \div 4\right) =$

7. $\left(2\frac{4}{3} \div 1\frac{2}{3}\right) \div \left(\frac{3}{4} \div 0.1\right) =$

8. $\left(\frac{5}{8} \div 3\frac{1}{8}\right) \div 0.2 =$

9. $\left(3\frac{1}{4} \div \frac{2}{16}\right) \div \left(1\frac{2}{3} \div \frac{1}{0.3}\right) =$

10. $12 \div \left[1\frac{1}{3} \div \left(\frac{1}{5} \div 0.5\right)\right] =$

9.5   Solving Mixed Operations Using Integer, Decimal, and Mixed Fractions

Integer, decimal, and mixed fractions of the following forms:

1. $\left(\dfrac{a}{b}\right)$ where (a) and (b) are integers,

2. $\left(\dfrac{a \times 10^{-k_1}}{b \times 10^{-k_2}}\right)$ where (a) and (b) are integer numbers and (k_1) and (k_2) are equal to the number

    of decimal places, and

3. $\left(k\dfrac{a}{b}\right)$ where (k) is made up of a whole number and $\left(\dfrac{a}{b}\right)$ is an integer fraction for a number

    less than one

are added, subtracted, multiplied, and divided as in the following cases:

Case I   Adding, Subtracting, Multiplying, and Dividing Integer, Decimal, and Mixed Fractions With Three Terms Only

Add, subtract, multiply, and divide three integer, decimal, and mixed fractions using the following steps:

Step 1   Change the integer number (a) to an integer fraction of the form $\left(\dfrac{a}{1}\right)$, e.g., change 19

to $\dfrac{19}{1}$.

Step 2   Change the mixed fraction to an integer fraction (see Section 2.5).

Step 3   a. Change the decimal fraction to an integer fraction (see Section 2.4).

b. Change the decimal number $\left(a \times 10^{-k}\right)$ to an integer fraction of the form $\left(\dfrac{a}{10^k}\right)$,

e.g., change 0.9 to $\dfrac{9}{10}$.

Step 4   Add, subtract, multiply, and divide the integer fractions (see Sections 3.1 through 3.4).

Step 5   Simplify the fraction to its lowest term (see Section 2.3).

Step 6   Change the improper fraction to a mixed fraction if the fraction obtained from Step 5 is an improper fraction (see Section 2.2).

The following examples show mathematical operations on integer, decimal, and mixed fractions with three terms only:

Example 9.5-1

$$\left[\left(\frac{4}{9} \times 1\frac{3}{8}\right) + \frac{0.68}{0.2}\right] =$$

Solution:

Step 1 $\boxed{Not\ Applicable}$

Step 2 $\left[\left(\dfrac{4}{9} \times 1\dfrac{3}{8}\right) + \dfrac{0.68}{0.2}\right] = \left[\left(\dfrac{4}{9} \times \dfrac{(1 \times 8) + 3}{8}\right) + \dfrac{0.68}{0.2}\right] = \left[\left(\dfrac{4}{9} \times \dfrac{8 + 3}{8}\right) + \dfrac{0.68}{0.2}\right] = \left[\left(\dfrac{4}{9} \times \dfrac{11}{8}\right) + \dfrac{0.68}{0.2}\right]$

Step 3a $\left[\left(\dfrac{4}{9}\times\dfrac{11}{8}\right)+\dfrac{0.68}{0.2}\right]=\left[\left(\dfrac{4}{9}\times\dfrac{11}{8}\right)+\dfrac{\frac{68}{100}}{\frac{2}{10}}\right]=\left[\left(\dfrac{4}{9}\times\dfrac{11}{8}\right)+\dfrac{68\times10}{100\times2}\right]=\left[\left(\dfrac{4}{9}\times\dfrac{11}{8}\right)+\dfrac{680}{200}\right]$

Step 3b $\boxed{Not\ Applicable}$

Step 4 $\left[\left(\dfrac{4}{9}\times\dfrac{11}{8}\right)+\dfrac{680}{200}\right]=\left[\left(\dfrac{4\times11}{9\times8}\right)+\dfrac{680}{200}\right]=\left[\left(\dfrac{44}{72}\right)+\dfrac{680}{200}\right]=\left[\dfrac{44}{72}+\dfrac{680}{200}\right]$

$=\left[\dfrac{(44\times200)+(680\times72)}{72\times200}\right]=\left[\dfrac{8800+48960}{14400}\right]=\left[\dfrac{57760}{14400}\right]$

Step 5 $\left[\dfrac{57760}{14400}\right]=\left[\dfrac{57760\div80}{14400\div80}\right]=\left[\dfrac{722}{180}\right]=\left[\dfrac{722\div2}{180\div2}\right]=\left[\dfrac{361}{90}\right]$

Step 6 $\left[\dfrac{361}{90}\right]=\boxed{4\dfrac{1}{90}}$

Example 9.5-2

$\left[\dfrac{2}{3}\div\left(0.28\times3\dfrac{2}{5}\right)\right]=$

Solution:

Step 1 $\boxed{Not\ Applicable}$

Step 2 $\left[\dfrac{2}{3}\div\left(0.28\times3\dfrac{2}{5}\right)\right]=\left[\dfrac{2}{3}\div\left(0.28\times\dfrac{(3\times5)+2}{5}\right)\right]=\left[\dfrac{2}{3}\div\left(0.28\times\dfrac{15+2}{5}\right)\right]$

$=\left[\dfrac{2}{3}\div\left(0.28\times\dfrac{17}{5}\right)\right]$

Step 3a $\boxed{Not\ Applicable}$

Step 3b $\left[\dfrac{2}{3}\div\left(0.28\times\dfrac{17}{5}\right)\right]=\left[\dfrac{2}{3}\div\left(\dfrac{28}{100}\times\dfrac{17}{5}\right)\right]$

Step 4 $\left[\dfrac{2}{3}\div\left(\dfrac{28}{100}\times\dfrac{17}{5}\right)\right]=\left[\dfrac{2}{3}\div\left(\dfrac{28\times17}{100\times5}\right)\right]=\left[\dfrac{2}{3}\div\left(\dfrac{476}{500}\right)\right]=\left[\dfrac{2}{3}\div\dfrac{476}{500}\right]=\left[\dfrac{2}{3}\times\dfrac{500}{476}\right]$

$=\left[\dfrac{2\times500}{3\times476}\right]=\left[\dfrac{1000}{1428}\right]$

Step 5 $\boxed{\dfrac{1000}{1428}} = \boxed{\dfrac{1000 \div 4}{1428 \div 4}} = \boxed{\dfrac{250}{357}}$

Step 6 $\boxed{\text{Not Applicable}}$

Example 9.5-3

$\boxed{\left(6 \times 3\dfrac{4}{5}\right) - 0.7} =$

Solution:

Step 1 $\boxed{\left(6 \times 3\dfrac{4}{5}\right) - 0.7} = \boxed{\left(\dfrac{6}{1} \times 3\dfrac{4}{5}\right) - 0.7}$

Step 2 $\boxed{\left(\dfrac{6}{1} \times 3\dfrac{4}{5}\right) - 0.7} = \boxed{\left(\dfrac{6}{1} \times \dfrac{(3 \times 5) + 4}{5}\right) - 0.7} = \boxed{\left(\dfrac{6}{1} \times \dfrac{15 + 4}{5}\right) - 0.7} = \boxed{\left(\dfrac{6}{1} \times \dfrac{19}{5}\right) - 0.7}$

Step 3a $\boxed{\text{Not Applicable}}$

Step 3b $\boxed{\left(\dfrac{6}{1} \times \dfrac{19}{5}\right) - 0.7} = \boxed{\left(\dfrac{6}{1} \times \dfrac{19}{5}\right) - \dfrac{7}{10}}$

Step 4 $\boxed{\left(\dfrac{6}{1} \times \dfrac{19}{5}\right) - \dfrac{7}{10}} = \boxed{\left(\dfrac{6 \times 19}{1 \times 5}\right) - \dfrac{7}{10}} = \boxed{\left(\dfrac{114}{5}\right) - \dfrac{7}{10}} = \boxed{\dfrac{114}{5} - \dfrac{7}{10}} = \boxed{\dfrac{(114 \times 10) - (7 \times 5)}{5 \times 10}}$

$= \boxed{\dfrac{1140 - 35}{50}} = \boxed{\dfrac{1105}{50}}$

Step 5 $\boxed{\dfrac{1105}{50}} = \boxed{\dfrac{1105 \div 5}{50 \div 5}} = \boxed{\dfrac{221}{10}}$

Step 6 $\boxed{\dfrac{221}{10}} = \boxed{22\dfrac{1}{10}}$

Example 9.5-4

$\boxed{2\dfrac{5}{6} + \left(\dfrac{4}{7} - 12.8\right)} =$

Solution:

Step 1 $\boxed{\text{Not Applicable}}$

Step 2 $\boxed{2\dfrac{5}{6} + \left(\dfrac{4}{7} - 12.8\right)} = \boxed{\dfrac{(2 \times 6) + 5}{6} + \left(\dfrac{4}{7} - 12.8\right)} = \boxed{\dfrac{12 + 5}{6} + \left(\dfrac{4}{7} - 12.8\right)}$

$$= \boxed{\dfrac{17}{6} + \left(\dfrac{4}{7} - 12.8\right)}$$

Step 3a $\boxed{Not\ Applicable}$

Step 3b $\boxed{\dfrac{17}{6} + \left(\dfrac{4}{7} - 12.8\right)} = \boxed{\dfrac{17}{6} + \left(\dfrac{4}{7} - \dfrac{128}{10}\right)}$

Step 4 $\boxed{\dfrac{17}{6} + \left(\dfrac{4}{7} - \dfrac{128}{10}\right)} = \boxed{\dfrac{17}{6} + \left(\dfrac{(4 \times 10) - (128 \times 7)}{7 \times 10}\right)} = \boxed{\dfrac{17}{6} + \left(\dfrac{40 - 896}{70}\right)} = \boxed{\dfrac{17}{6} + \left(\dfrac{-856}{70}\right)}$

$$= \boxed{\dfrac{17}{6} + \dfrac{-856}{70}} = \boxed{\dfrac{17}{6} - \dfrac{856}{70}} = \boxed{\dfrac{(17 \times 70) - (856 \times 6)}{6 \times 70}} = \boxed{\dfrac{1190 - 5136}{420}} = \boxed{\dfrac{-3946}{420}}$$

Step 5 $\boxed{\dfrac{-3946}{420}} = \boxed{\dfrac{-3946 \div 2}{420 \div 2}} = \boxed{\dfrac{-1973}{210}}$

Step 6 $\boxed{\dfrac{-1973}{210}} = \boxed{-\left(\mathbf{9\dfrac{83}{210}}\right)}$

Example 9.5-5

$$\boxed{\left(2\dfrac{8}{10} \div \dfrac{0.3}{1.5}\right) - \dfrac{5}{6}} =$$

Solution:

Step 1 $\boxed{Not\ Applicable}$

Step 2 $\boxed{\left(2\dfrac{8}{10} \div \dfrac{0.3}{1.5}\right) - \dfrac{5}{6}} = \boxed{\left(\dfrac{(2 \times 10) + 8}{10} \div \dfrac{0.3}{1.5}\right) - \dfrac{5}{6}} = \boxed{\left(\dfrac{20 + 8}{10} \div \dfrac{0.3}{1.5}\right) - \dfrac{5}{6}}$

$$= \boxed{\left(\dfrac{28}{10} \div \dfrac{0.3}{1.5}\right) - \dfrac{5}{6}}$$

Step 3a $\boxed{\left(\dfrac{28}{10} \div \dfrac{0.3}{1.5}\right) - \dfrac{5}{6}} = \boxed{\left(\dfrac{28}{10} \div \dfrac{\frac{3}{10}}{\frac{15}{10}}\right) - \dfrac{5}{6}} = \boxed{\left(\dfrac{28}{10} \div \dfrac{3 \times 10}{10 \times 15}\right) - \dfrac{5}{6}} = \boxed{\left(\dfrac{28}{10} \div \dfrac{30}{150}\right) - \dfrac{5}{6}}$

Step 3b $\boxed{Not\ Applicable}$

Step 4 $\boxed{\left(\dfrac{28}{10} \div \dfrac{30}{150}\right) - \dfrac{5}{6}} = \boxed{\left(\dfrac{28}{10} \times \dfrac{150}{30}\right) - \dfrac{5}{6}} = \boxed{\left(\dfrac{28 \times 150}{10 \times 30}\right) - \dfrac{5}{6}} = \boxed{\left(\dfrac{4200}{300}\right) - \dfrac{5}{6}}$

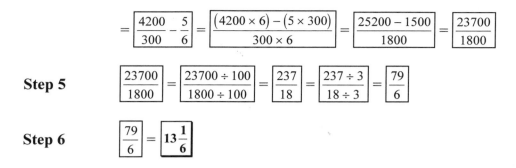

$$= \boxed{\frac{4200}{300} - \frac{5}{6}} = \boxed{\frac{(4200 \times 6) - (5 \times 300)}{300 \times 6}} = \boxed{\frac{25200 - 1500}{1800}} = \boxed{\frac{23700}{1800}}$$

Step 5 $\boxed{\dfrac{23700}{1800}} = \boxed{\dfrac{23700 \div 100}{1800 \div 100}} = \boxed{\dfrac{237}{18}} = \boxed{\dfrac{237 \div 3}{18 \div 3}} = \boxed{\dfrac{79}{6}}$

Step 6 $\boxed{\dfrac{79}{6}} = \boxed{13\dfrac{1}{6}}$

Case II   **Adding, Subtracting, Multiplying, and Dividing Integer, Decimal, and Mixed Fractions With More Than Three Terms**

Add, subtract, multiply, and divide more than three integer, decimal, and mixed fractions by using the following steps:

Step 1   Change the integer number(s) (a) to integer fraction(s) of the form $\left(\dfrac{a}{1}\right)$, e.g., change 258 to $\dfrac{258}{1}$.

Step 2   Change the mixed fraction(s) to integer fraction(s) (see Section 2.5).

Step 3   a. Change the decimal fraction(s) to integer fraction(s) (see Section 2.4).

   b. Change the decimal number(s) $\left(a \times 10^{-k}\right)$ to integer fraction(s) of the form $\left(\dfrac{a}{10^k}\right)$,

   e.g., change 0.003 to $\dfrac{3}{1000}$.

Step 4   Add, subtract, multiply, and divide the integer fractions (see Sections 3.1 through 3.4).

Step 5   Simplify the fraction to its lowest term (see Section 2.3).

Step 6   Change the improper fraction to a mixed fraction if the fraction obtained from Step 5 is an improper fraction (see Section 2.2).

The following examples show mathematical operations on integer, decimal, and mixed fractions with more than three terms:

Example 9.5-6

$$\boxed{\left(5 \div \frac{1}{3}\right) \times \left(2\frac{1}{80} + \frac{0.3}{1.8}\right)} =$$

Solution:

Step 1 $\boxed{\left(5 \div \dfrac{1}{3}\right) \times \left(2\dfrac{1}{80} + \dfrac{0.3}{1.8}\right)} = \boxed{\left(\dfrac{5}{1} \div \dfrac{1}{3}\right) \times \left(2\dfrac{1}{80} + \dfrac{0.3}{1.8}\right)}$

Step 2 $\boxed{\left(\dfrac{5}{1} \div \dfrac{1}{3}\right) \times \left(2\dfrac{1}{80} + \dfrac{0.3}{1.8}\right)} = \boxed{\left(\dfrac{5}{1} \div \dfrac{1}{3}\right) \times \left(\dfrac{(2 \times 80) + 1}{80} + \dfrac{0.3}{1.8}\right)} = \boxed{\left(\dfrac{5}{1} \div \dfrac{1}{3}\right) \times \left(\dfrac{160 + 1}{80} + \dfrac{0.3}{1.8}\right)}$

$$= \boxed{\left(\dfrac{5}{1} \div \dfrac{1}{3}\right) \times \left(\dfrac{161}{80} + \dfrac{0.3}{1.8}\right)}$$

Step 3a

$$\left(\left(\frac{5}{1}\div\frac{1}{3}\right)\times\left(\frac{161}{80}+\frac{0.3}{1.8}\right)\right)=\left(\left(\frac{5}{1}\div\frac{1}{3}\right)\times\left(\frac{161}{80}+\frac{\frac{3}{10}}{\frac{18}{10}}\right)\right)=\left(\left(\frac{5}{1}\div\frac{1}{3}\right)\times\left(\frac{161}{80}+\frac{3\times10}{10\times18}\right)\right)$$

$$=\left(\left(\frac{5}{1}\div\frac{1}{3}\right)\times\left(\frac{161}{80}+\frac{30}{180}\right)\right)$$

Step 3b $\boxed{Not\ Applicable}$

Step 4

$$\left(\left(\frac{5}{1}\div\frac{1}{3}\right)\times\left(\frac{161}{80}+\frac{30}{180}\right)\right)=\left(\left(\frac{5}{1}\times\frac{3}{1}\right)\times\left(\frac{(161\times180)+(30\times80)}{80\times180}\right)\right)$$

$$=\left(\left(\frac{5\times3}{1\times1}\right)\times\left(\frac{28980+2400}{14400}\right)\right)=\left(\left(\frac{15}{1}\right)\times\left(\frac{31380}{14400}\right)\right)=\left(\frac{15}{1}\times\frac{31380}{14400}\right)=\left(\frac{15\times31380}{1\times14400}\right)$$

$$=\boxed{\frac{470700}{14400}}$$

Step 5 $\dfrac{470700}{14400}=\dfrac{470700\div100}{14400\div100}=\dfrac{4707}{144}$

Step 6 $\dfrac{4707}{144}=\boxed{\mathbf{32\dfrac{99}{144}}}$

Example 9.5-7

$$\left(\left(3\frac{2}{5}\times2\frac{1}{3}\right)\div\left(\frac{3}{8}-0.24\right)\right)=$$

Solution:

Step 1 $\boxed{Not\ Applicable}$

Step 2

$$\left(\left(3\frac{2}{5}\times2\frac{1}{3}\right)\div\left(\frac{3}{8}-0.24\right)\right)=\left(\left(\frac{(3\times5)+2}{5}\times\frac{(2\times3)+1}{3}\right)\div\left(\frac{3}{8}-0.24\right)\right)$$

$$=\left(\left(\frac{15+2}{5}\times\frac{6+1}{3}\right)\div\left(\frac{3}{8}-0.24\right)\right)=\left(\left(\frac{17}{5}\times\frac{7}{3}\right)\div\left(\frac{3}{8}-0.24\right)\right)$$

Step 3a $\boxed{Not\ Applicable}$

Step 3b

$$\left(\left(\frac{17}{5}\times\frac{7}{3}\right)\div\left(\frac{3}{8}-0.24\right)\right)=\left(\left(\frac{17}{5}\times\frac{7}{3}\right)\div\left(\frac{3}{8}-\frac{24}{100}\right)\right)$$

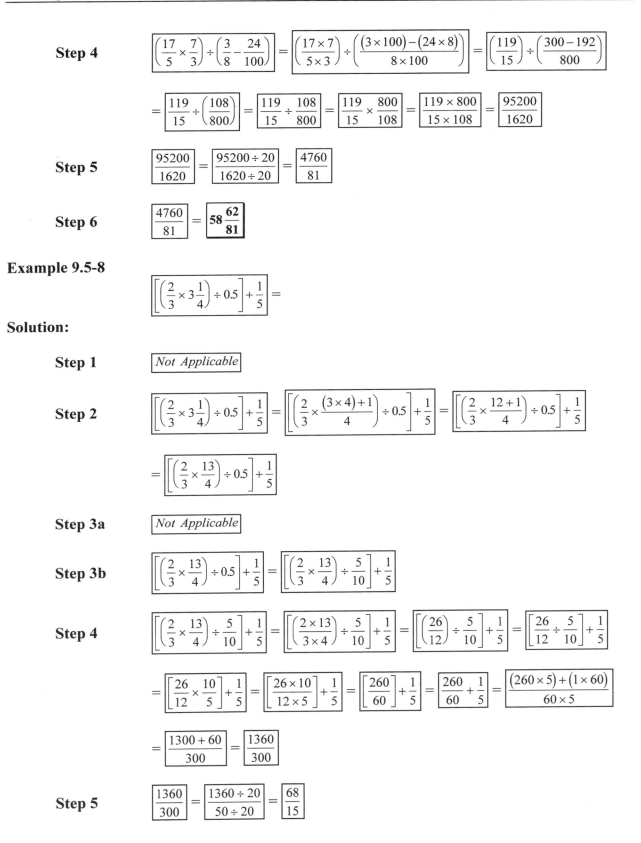

Step 4
$$\left(\frac{17}{5} \times \frac{7}{3}\right) \div \left(\frac{3}{8} - \frac{24}{100}\right) = \left(\frac{17 \times 7}{5 \times 3}\right) \div \left(\frac{(3 \times 100) - (24 \times 8)}{8 \times 100}\right) = \left(\frac{119}{15}\right) \div \left(\frac{300 - 192}{800}\right)$$

$$= \frac{119}{15} \div \left(\frac{108}{800}\right) = \frac{119}{15} \div \frac{108}{800} = \frac{119}{15} \times \frac{800}{108} = \frac{119 \times 800}{15 \times 108} = \frac{95200}{1620}$$

Step 5
$$\frac{95200}{1620} = \frac{95200 \div 20}{1620 \div 20} = \frac{4760}{81}$$

Step 6
$$\frac{4760}{81} = \mathbf{58\frac{62}{81}}$$

Example 9.5-8
$$\left[\left(\frac{2}{3} \times 3\frac{1}{4}\right) \div 0.5\right] + \frac{1}{5} =$$

Solution:

Step 1
$$\boxed{Not\ Applicable}$$

Step 2
$$\left[\left(\frac{2}{3} \times 3\frac{1}{4}\right) \div 0.5\right] + \frac{1}{5} = \left[\left(\frac{2}{3} \times \frac{(3 \times 4) + 1}{4}\right) \div 0.5\right] + \frac{1}{5} = \left[\left(\frac{2}{3} \times \frac{12 + 1}{4}\right) \div 0.5\right] + \frac{1}{5}$$

$$= \left[\left(\frac{2}{3} \times \frac{13}{4}\right) \div 0.5\right] + \frac{1}{5}$$

Step 3a
$$\boxed{Not\ Applicable}$$

Step 3b
$$\left[\left(\frac{2}{3} \times \frac{13}{4}\right) \div 0.5\right] + \frac{1}{5} = \left[\left(\frac{2}{3} \times \frac{13}{4}\right) \div \frac{5}{10}\right] + \frac{1}{5}$$

Step 4
$$\left[\left(\frac{2}{3} \times \frac{13}{4}\right) \div \frac{5}{10}\right] + \frac{1}{5} = \left[\left(\frac{2 \times 13}{3 \times 4}\right) \div \frac{5}{10}\right] + \frac{1}{5} = \left[\left(\frac{26}{12}\right) \div \frac{5}{10}\right] + \frac{1}{5} = \left[\frac{26}{12} \div \frac{5}{10}\right] + \frac{1}{5}$$

$$= \left[\frac{26}{12} \times \frac{10}{5}\right] + \frac{1}{5} = \left[\frac{26 \times 10}{12 \times 5}\right] + \frac{1}{5} = \left[\frac{260}{60}\right] + \frac{1}{5} = \frac{260}{60} + \frac{1}{5} = \frac{(260 \times 5) + (1 \times 60)}{60 \times 5}$$

$$= \frac{1300 + 60}{300} = \frac{1360}{300}$$

Step 5
$$\frac{1360}{300} = \frac{1360 \div 20}{50 \div 20} = \frac{68}{15}$$

Step 6 $\boxed{\dfrac{68}{15}} = \boxed{\mathbf{4\dfrac{8}{15}}}$

Example 9.5-9

$$\boxed{\left[25 \times \left(2\dfrac{1}{6} + \dfrac{5}{6}\right)\right] \div \left(2\dfrac{3}{8} - \dfrac{0.12}{0.4}\right)} =$$

Solution:

Step 1 $\boxed{\left[25 \times \left(2\dfrac{1}{6} + \dfrac{5}{6}\right)\right] \div \left(2\dfrac{3}{8} - \dfrac{0.12}{0.4}\right)} = \boxed{\left[\dfrac{25}{1} \times \left(2\dfrac{1}{6} + \dfrac{5}{6}\right)\right] \div \left(2\dfrac{3}{8} - \dfrac{0.12}{0.4}\right)}$

Step 2 $\boxed{\left[\dfrac{25}{1} \times \left(2\dfrac{1}{6} + \dfrac{5}{6}\right)\right] \div \left(2\dfrac{3}{8} - \dfrac{0.12}{0.4}\right)} = \boxed{\left[\dfrac{25}{1} \times \left(\dfrac{(2\times 6)+1}{6} + \dfrac{5}{6}\right)\right] \div \left(\dfrac{(2\times 8)+3}{8} - \dfrac{0.12}{0.4}\right)}$

$= \boxed{\left[\dfrac{25}{1} \times \left(\dfrac{12+1}{6} + \dfrac{5}{6}\right)\right] \div \left(\dfrac{16+3}{8} - \dfrac{0.12}{0.4}\right)} = \boxed{\left[\dfrac{25}{1} \times \left(\dfrac{13}{6} + \dfrac{5}{6}\right)\right] \div \left(\dfrac{19}{8} - \dfrac{0.12}{0.4}\right)} =$

Step 3a $\boxed{\left[\dfrac{25}{1} \times \left(\dfrac{13}{6} + \dfrac{5}{6}\right)\right] \div \left(\dfrac{19}{8} - \dfrac{0.12}{0.4}\right)} = \boxed{\left[\dfrac{25}{1} \times \left(\dfrac{13}{6} + \dfrac{5}{6}\right)\right] \div \left(\dfrac{19}{8} - \dfrac{\dfrac{12}{100}}{\dfrac{4}{10}}\right)}$

$= \boxed{\left[\dfrac{25}{1} \times \left(\dfrac{13}{6} + \dfrac{5}{6}\right)\right] \div \left(\dfrac{19}{8} - \dfrac{12\times 10}{100\times 4}\right)} = \boxed{\left[\dfrac{25}{1} \times \left(\dfrac{13}{6} + \dfrac{5}{6}\right)\right] \div \left(\dfrac{19}{8} - \dfrac{120}{400}\right)}$

Step 3b $\boxed{\textit{Not Applicable}}$

Step 4 $\boxed{\left[\dfrac{25}{1} \times \left(\dfrac{13}{6} + \dfrac{5}{6}\right)\right] \div \left(\dfrac{19}{8} - \dfrac{120}{400}\right)} = \boxed{\left[\dfrac{25}{1} \times \left(\dfrac{13+5}{6}\right)\right] \div \left(\dfrac{(19\times 400)-(120\times 8)}{8\times 400}\right)}$

$= \boxed{\left[\dfrac{25}{1} \times \left(\dfrac{18}{6}\right)\right] \div \left(\dfrac{7600-960}{3200}\right)} = \boxed{\left[\dfrac{25}{1} \times \dfrac{18}{6}\right] \div \left(\dfrac{6640}{3200}\right)} = \boxed{\left[\dfrac{25\times 18}{1\times 6}\right] \div \dfrac{6640}{3200}}$

$= \boxed{\left[\dfrac{450}{6}\right] \div \dfrac{6640}{3200}} = \boxed{\dfrac{450}{6} \div \dfrac{6640}{3200}} = \boxed{\dfrac{450}{6} \times \dfrac{3200}{6640}} = \boxed{\dfrac{450\times 3200}{6\times 6640}} = \boxed{\dfrac{1440000}{39840}}$

Step 5 $\boxed{\dfrac{1440000}{39840}} = \boxed{\dfrac{1440000 \div 160}{39840 \div 160}} = \boxed{\dfrac{9000}{249}} = \boxed{\dfrac{9000 \div 3}{249 \div 3}} = \boxed{\dfrac{3000}{83}}$

Step 6 $\boxed{\dfrac{3000}{83}} = \boxed{\mathbf{36\dfrac{12}{83}}}$

Example 9.5-10

$$\left[\left(2\frac{4}{5}\times\frac{3}{8}\right)\div0.8\right]+\left(\frac{3}{5}+\frac{1}{5}\right)=$$

Solution:

Step 1 $\boxed{Not\ Applicable}$

Step 2 $$\left[\left(2\frac{4}{5}\times\frac{3}{8}\right)\div0.8\right]+\left(\frac{3}{5}+\frac{1}{5}\right)=\left[\left(\frac{(2\times5)+4}{5}\times\frac{3}{8}\right)\div0.8\right]+\left(\frac{3}{5}+\frac{1}{5}\right)$$

$$=\left[\left(\frac{10+4}{5}\times\frac{3}{8}\right)\div0.8\right]+\left(\frac{3}{5}+\frac{1}{5}\right)=\left[\left(\frac{14}{5}\times\frac{3}{8}\right)\div0.8\right]+\left(\frac{3}{5}+\frac{1}{5}\right)$$

Step 3a $\boxed{Not\ Applicable}$

Step 3b $$\left[\left(\frac{14}{5}\times\frac{3}{8}\right)\div0.8\right]+\left(\frac{3}{5}+\frac{1}{5}\right)=\left[\left(\frac{14}{5}\times\frac{3}{8}\right)\div\frac{8}{10}\right]+\left(\frac{3}{5}+\frac{1}{5}\right)$$

Step 4 $$\left[\left(\frac{14}{5}\times\frac{3}{8}\right)\div\frac{8}{10}\right]+\left(\frac{3}{5}+\frac{1}{5}\right)=\left[\left(\frac{14\times3}{5\times8}\right)\div\frac{8}{10}\right]+\left(\frac{3+1}{5}\right)=\left[\left(\frac{42}{40}\right)\div\frac{8}{10}\right]+\left(\frac{4}{5}\right)$$

$$=\left[\frac{42}{40}\div\frac{8}{10}\right]+\frac{4}{5}=\left[\frac{42}{40}\times\frac{10}{8}\right]+\frac{4}{5}=\left[\frac{42\times10}{40\times8}\right]+\frac{4}{5}=\left[\frac{420}{320}\right]+\frac{4}{5}=\frac{420}{320}+\frac{4}{5}$$

$$=\frac{(420\times5)+(4\times320)}{320\times5}=\frac{2100+1280}{1600}=\frac{3380}{1600}$$

Step 5 $$\frac{3380}{1600}=\frac{3380\div20}{1600\div20}=\frac{169}{80}$$

Step 6 $$\frac{169}{80}=2\frac{9}{80}$$

The following examples further illustrate how to add, subtract, multiply, and divide integer, decimal, and mixed fractions:

Example 9.5-11

$$\left(3\frac{2}{5}\times\frac{1}{17}\right)\div\frac{0.12}{0.8}=\left(\frac{(3\times5)+2}{5}\times\frac{1}{17}\right)\div\frac{\frac{12}{100}}{\frac{8}{10}}=\left(\frac{15+2}{5}\times\frac{1}{17}\right)\div\frac{12\times10}{100\times8}=\left(\frac{17}{5}\times\frac{1}{17}\right)\div\frac{\overset{3}{\cancel{120}}}{\underset{20}{\cancel{800}}}$$

$$= \left[\left(\frac{\overset{1}{17}\times 1}{5\times \underset{1}{17}}\right)\div\frac{3}{20}\right] = \left[\left(\frac{1\times 1}{5\times 1}\right)\div\frac{3}{20}\right] = \left[\left(\frac{1}{5}\right)\div\frac{3}{20}\right] = \left[\frac{1}{5}\div\frac{3}{20}\right] = \left[\frac{1}{5}\times\frac{20}{3}\right] = \left[\frac{1\times\overset{4}{20}}{\underset{1}{5}\times 3}\right] = \left[\frac{1\times 4}{1\times 3}\right] = \left[\frac{4}{3}\right] = \boxed{1\frac{1}{3}}$$

Example 9.5-12

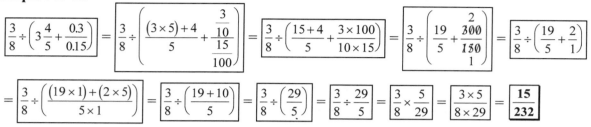

$$\frac{3}{8}\div\left(3\frac{4}{5}+\frac{0.3}{0.15}\right) = \frac{3}{8}\div\left(\frac{(3\times 5)+4}{5}+\frac{\frac{3}{10}}{\frac{15}{100}}\right) = \frac{3}{8}\div\left(\frac{15+4}{5}+\frac{3\times 100}{10\times 15}\right) = \frac{3}{8}\div\left(\frac{19}{5}+\frac{\overset{2}{300}}{\underset{1}{150}}\right) = \frac{3}{8}\div\left(\frac{19}{5}+\frac{2}{1}\right)$$

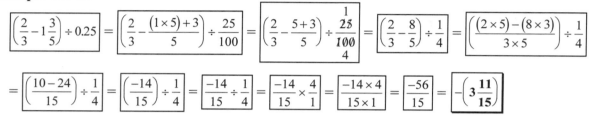

$$= \frac{3}{8}\div\left(\frac{(19\times 1)+(2\times 5)}{5\times 1}\right) = \frac{3}{8}\div\left(\frac{19+10}{5}\right) = \frac{3}{8}\div\left(\frac{29}{5}\right) = \frac{3}{8}\div\frac{29}{5} = \frac{3}{8}\times\frac{5}{29} = \frac{3\times 5}{8\times 29} = \boxed{\frac{15}{232}}$$

Example 9.5-13

$$\left[\left(\frac{2}{3}-1\frac{3}{5}\right)\div 0.25\right] = \left[\left(\frac{2}{3}-\frac{(1\times 5)+3}{5}\right)\div\frac{25}{100}\right] = \left[\left(\frac{2}{3}-\frac{5+3}{5}\right)\div\frac{\overset{1}{25}}{\underset{4}{100}}\right] = \left[\left(\frac{2}{3}-\frac{8}{5}\right)\div\frac{1}{4}\right] = \left[\left(\frac{(2\times 5)-(8\times 3)}{3\times 5}\right)\div\frac{1}{4}\right]$$

$$= \left[\left(\frac{10-24}{15}\right)\div\frac{1}{4}\right] = \left[\left(\frac{-14}{15}\right)\div\frac{1}{4}\right] = \left[\frac{-14}{15}\div\frac{1}{4}\right] = \left[\frac{-14}{15}\times\frac{4}{1}\right] = \left[\frac{-14\times 4}{15\times 1}\right] = \left[\frac{-56}{15}\right] = \boxed{-\left(3\frac{11}{15}\right)}$$

Example 9.5-14

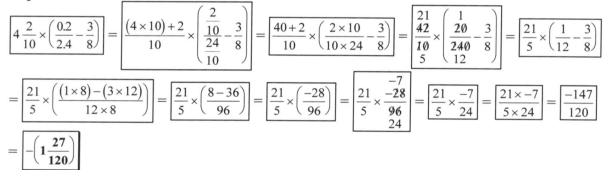

$$4\frac{2}{10}\times\left(\frac{0.2}{2.4}-\frac{3}{8}\right) = \frac{(4\times 10)+2}{10}\times\left(\frac{\frac{2}{10}}{\frac{24}{10}}-\frac{3}{8}\right) = \frac{40+2}{10}\times\left(\frac{2\times 10}{10\times 24}-\frac{3}{8}\right) = \frac{\overset{21}{42}}{\underset{5}{10}}\times\left(\frac{\overset{1}{20}}{\underset{12}{240}}-\frac{3}{8}\right) = \frac{21}{5}\times\left(\frac{1}{12}-\frac{3}{8}\right)$$

$$= \frac{21}{5}\times\left(\frac{(1\times 8)-(3\times 12)}{12\times 8}\right) = \frac{21}{5}\times\left(\frac{8-36}{96}\right) = \frac{21}{5}\times\left(\frac{-28}{96}\right) = \frac{21}{5}\times\frac{\overset{-7}{-28}}{\underset{24}{96}} = \frac{21}{5}\times\frac{-7}{24} = \frac{21\times -7}{5\times 24} = \frac{-147}{120}$$

$$= \boxed{-\left(1\frac{27}{120}\right)}$$

Example 9.5-15

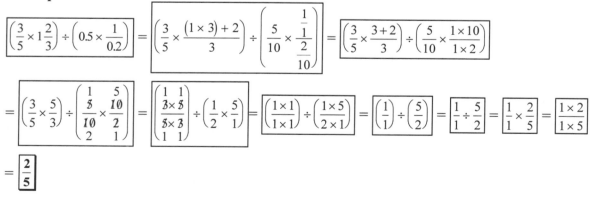

$$\left[\left(\frac{3}{5}\times 1\frac{2}{3}\right)\div\left(0.5\times\frac{1}{0.2}\right)\right] = \left[\left(\frac{3}{5}\times\frac{(1\times 3)+2}{3}\right)\div\left(\frac{5}{10}\times\frac{\frac{1}{1}}{\frac{2}{10}}\right)\right] = \left[\left(\frac{3}{5}\times\frac{3+2}{3}\right)\div\left(\frac{5}{10}\times\frac{1\times 10}{1\times 2}\right)\right]$$

$$= \left[\left(\frac{3}{5}\times\frac{5}{3}\right)\div\left(\frac{\overset{1}{5}}{\underset{2}{10}}\times\frac{\overset{5}{10}}{\underset{1}{2}}\right)\right] = \left[\left(\frac{1}{\underset{1}{3}}\times\frac{1}{\underset{1}{5}}\times\frac{\overset{1}{5}}{\underset{1}{3}}\right)\div\left(\frac{1}{2}\times\frac{5}{1}\right)\right] = \left[\left(\frac{1\times 1}{1\times 1}\right)\div\left(\frac{1\times 5}{2\times 1}\right)\right] = \left[\left(\frac{1}{1}\right)\div\left(\frac{5}{2}\right)\right] = \left[\frac{1}{1}\div\frac{5}{2}\right] = \left[\frac{1}{1}\times\frac{2}{5}\right] = \left[\frac{1\times 2}{1\times 5}\right]$$

$$= \boxed{\frac{2}{5}}$$

Example 9.5-16

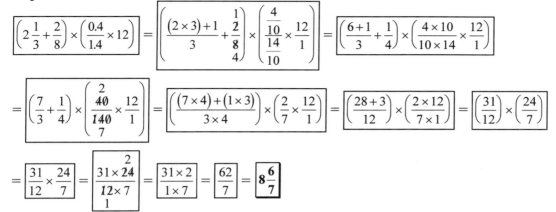

$$\boxed{\left(2\frac{1}{3}+\frac{2}{8}\right)\times\left(\frac{0.4}{1.4}\times12\right)}=\boxed{\left(\frac{(2\times3)+1}{3}+\frac{\overset{1}{2}}{\underset{4}{8}}\right)\times\left(\frac{\frac{4}{10}}{\frac{14}{10}}\times\frac{12}{1}\right)}=\boxed{\left(\frac{6+1}{3}+\frac{1}{4}\right)\times\left(\frac{4\times10}{10\times14}\times\frac{12}{1}\right)}$$

$$=\boxed{\left(\frac{7}{3}+\frac{1}{4}\right)\times\left(\frac{\overset{2}{40}}{\underset{7}{140}}\times\frac{12}{1}\right)}=\boxed{\left(\frac{(7\times4)+(1\times3)}{3\times4}\right)\times\left(\frac{2}{7}\times\frac{12}{1}\right)}=\boxed{\left(\frac{28+3}{12}\right)\times\left(\frac{2\times12}{7\times1}\right)}=\boxed{\left(\frac{31}{12}\right)\times\left(\frac{24}{7}\right)}$$

$$=\boxed{\frac{31}{12}\times\frac{24}{7}}=\boxed{\frac{31\times\overset{2}{24}}{\underset{1}{12}\times7}}=\boxed{\frac{31\times2}{1\times7}}=\boxed{\frac{62}{7}}=\boxed{\mathbf{8\frac{6}{7}}}$$

Example 9.5-17

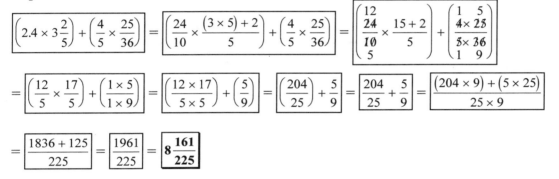

$$\boxed{\left(2.4\times3\frac{2}{5}\right)+\left(\frac{4}{5}\times\frac{25}{36}\right)}=\boxed{\left(\frac{24}{10}\times\frac{(3\times5)+2}{5}\right)+\left(\frac{4}{5}\times\frac{25}{36}\right)}=\boxed{\left(\frac{\overset{12}{24}}{\underset{5}{10}}\times\frac{15+2}{5}\right)+\left(\frac{\overset{1}{4}\times\overset{5}{25}}{\underset{1}{5}\times\underset{9}{36}}\right)}$$

$$=\boxed{\left(\frac{12}{5}\times\frac{17}{5}\right)+\left(\frac{1\times5}{1\times9}\right)}=\boxed{\left(\frac{12\times17}{5\times5}\right)+\left(\frac{5}{9}\right)}=\boxed{\left(\frac{204}{25}\right)+\frac{5}{9}}=\boxed{\frac{204}{25}+\frac{5}{9}}=\boxed{\frac{(204\times9)+(5\times25)}{25\times9}}$$

$$=\boxed{\frac{1836+125}{225}}=\boxed{\frac{1961}{225}}=\boxed{\mathbf{8\frac{161}{225}}}$$

Example 9.5-18

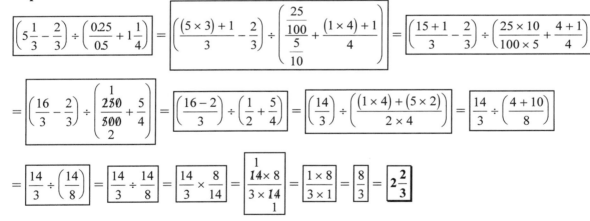

$$\boxed{\left(5\frac{1}{3}-\frac{2}{3}\right)\div\left(\frac{0.25}{0.5}+1\frac{1}{4}\right)}=\boxed{\left(\frac{(5\times3)+1}{3}-\frac{2}{3}\right)\div\left(\frac{\frac{25}{100}}{\frac{5}{10}}+\frac{(1\times4)+1}{4}\right)}=\boxed{\left(\frac{15+1}{3}-\frac{2}{3}\right)\div\left(\frac{25\times10}{100\times5}+\frac{4+1}{4}\right)}$$

$$=\boxed{\left(\frac{16}{3}-\frac{2}{3}\right)\div\left(\frac{\overset{1}{250}}{\underset{2}{500}}+\frac{5}{4}\right)}=\boxed{\left(\frac{16-2}{3}\right)\div\left(\frac{1}{2}+\frac{5}{4}\right)}=\boxed{\left(\frac{14}{3}\right)\div\left(\frac{(1\times4)+(5\times2)}{2\times4}\right)}=\boxed{\frac{14}{3}\div\left(\frac{4+10}{8}\right)}$$

$$=\boxed{\frac{14}{3}\div\left(\frac{14}{8}\right)}=\boxed{\frac{14}{3}\div\frac{14}{8}}=\boxed{\frac{14}{3}\times\frac{8}{14}}=\boxed{\frac{\overset{1}{14}\times8}{3\times\underset{1}{14}}}=\boxed{\frac{1\times8}{3\times1}}=\boxed{\frac{8}{3}}=\boxed{\mathbf{2\frac{2}{3}}}$$

Example 9.5-19

$$\boxed{\left[\left(3\frac{1}{5}+\frac{2}{3}\right)-0.5\right]\times\frac{1}{10}}=\boxed{\left[\left(\frac{(3\times5)+1}{5}+\frac{2}{3}\right)-\frac{5}{10}\right]\times\frac{1}{10}}=\boxed{\left[\left(\frac{15+1}{5}+\frac{2}{3}\right)-\frac{\overset{1}{5}}{\underset{2}{10}}\right]\times\frac{1}{10}}$$

$$=\boxed{\left[\left(\frac{16}{5}+\frac{2}{3}\right)-\frac{1}{2}\right]\times\frac{1}{10}}=\boxed{\left[\frac{(16\times3)+(2\times5)}{5\times3}-\frac{1}{2}\right]\times\frac{1}{10}}=\boxed{\left[\frac{48+10}{15}-\frac{1}{2}\right]\times\frac{1}{10}}=\boxed{\left[\frac{58}{15}-\frac{1}{2}\right]\times\frac{1}{10}}$$

$$= \left[\left[\frac{(58 \times 2) - (1 \times 15)}{15 \times 2}\right] \times \frac{1}{10}\right] = \left[\left[\frac{116 - 15}{30}\right] \times \frac{1}{10}\right] = \left[\frac{101}{30} \times \frac{1}{10}\right] = \left[\frac{101 \times 1}{30 \times 10}\right] = \boxed{\mathbf{\frac{101}{300}}}$$

Example 9.5-20

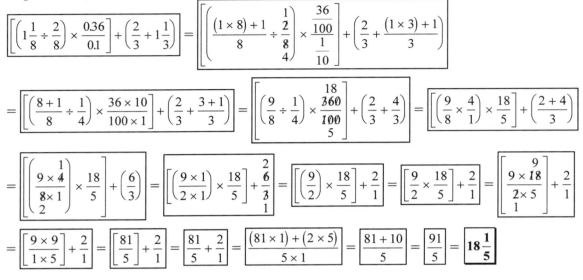

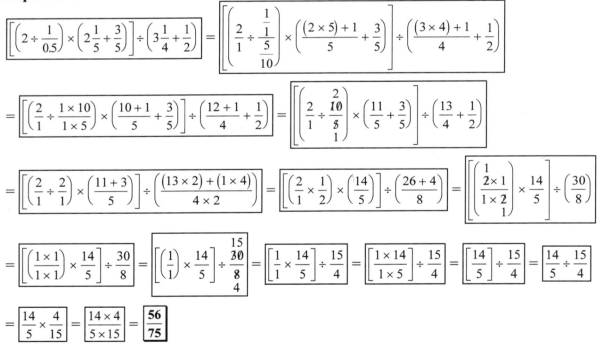

Example 9.5-21

Section 9.5 Exercises - Use the following integer, decimal, and mixed fractions to perform the indicated operations:

1. $\left(2\dfrac{4}{5}-\dfrac{1}{5}\right)\div 45 =$

2. $\left(1\dfrac{1}{4}+\dfrac{2}{3}\right)\times\dfrac{0.24}{0.2} =$

3. $\dfrac{3}{8}\times\left(3\dfrac{2}{5}-0.2\right) =$

4. $3\dfrac{1}{8}-\left(\dfrac{0.12}{0.6}+\dfrac{2}{3}\right) =$

5. $\left(1\dfrac{1}{4}+\dfrac{2}{3}\right)\times\left(\dfrac{1}{0.2}\times\dfrac{1}{5}\right) =$

6. $\left(\dfrac{2}{3}+2\dfrac{2}{3}\right)\div\left(15\times\dfrac{1}{5}\right) =$

7. $\left[\left(4\dfrac{1}{7}-\dfrac{1}{4}\right)\times 0.02\right]\div\dfrac{1}{14} =$

8. $\left[\left(2\dfrac{1}{5}+\dfrac{1.5}{0.01}\right)\div\dfrac{1}{5}\right]\times 4 =$

9. $\left(2\dfrac{1}{5}-\dfrac{1}{5}\right)\div\left(0.2\times\dfrac{3}{5}\right) =$

10. $2.8\div\left[\left(2\dfrac{1}{6}+\dfrac{2}{3}\right)+\dfrac{1}{18}\right] =$

Appendix - Exercise Solutions
Chapter 1 Solutions:
Section 1.1 Solutions:

1. $\dfrac{-95}{-5} = \dfrac{95}{5} = \mathbf{19}$

2. $(-20) \times (-8) = +160 = \mathbf{160}$

3. $(-33) + (-14) = -33 - 14 = \mathbf{-47}$

4. $(-18) - (-5) = (-18) + (5) = -18 + 5 = \mathbf{-13}$

5. $(-20) + 8 = -20 + 8 = \mathbf{-12}$

6. $\dfrac{48}{-4} = -\dfrac{48}{4} = \mathbf{-12}$

7. $-15 - 32 = \mathbf{-47}$

8. $30 + (-9) = 30 - 9 = \mathbf{21}$

9. $55 - (-6) = 55 + (6) = 55 + 6 = \mathbf{61}$

10. $8 \times (-35) = -8 \times 35 = \mathbf{-280}$

Section 1.2 Solutions:

1. $2 + 3 + 5 + 6 = \mathbf{16}$

2. $(2 + 5) + (6 + 3) + 9 = (7) + (9) + 9 = 7 + 9 + 9 = \mathbf{25}$

3. $(6 + 3 + 8) + (2 + 3) + 4 = (17) + (5) + 4 = 17 + 5 + 4 = \mathbf{26}$

4. $8 + \left[(1 + 3 + 4) + (1 + 2) \right] = 8 + \left[(8) + (3) \right] = 8 + [8 + 3] = 8 + [11] = 8 + 11 = \mathbf{19}$

5. $\left[(18 + 4) + 9 \right] + \left[1 + (2 + 3) \right] = \left[(22) + 9 \right] + \left[1 + (5) \right] = [22 + 9] + [1 + 5] = [31] + [6] = 31 + 6 = \mathbf{37}$

6. $8 + \left[(2 + 3) + (6 + 3) + 15 \right] = 8 + \left[(5) + (9) + 15 \right] = 8 + [5 + 9 + 15] = 8 + [29] = 8 + 29 = \mathbf{37}$

7. $(7 + 3 + 8) + \left[(7 + 2 + 3) + 5 \right] = (18) + \left[(12) + 5 \right] = 18 + [12 + 5] = 18 + [17] = 18 + 17 = \mathbf{35}$

8. $\left[(3 + 9 + 4) + 1 + (1 + 8) \right] + (8 + 2) = \left[(16) + 1 + (9) \right] + (10) = [16 + 1 + 9] + 10 = [26] + 10 = 26 + 10 = \mathbf{36}$

9. $\left[(2 + 3 + 6) + (1 + 8) \right] + \left[(1 + 3) + 4 \right] = \left[(11) + (9) \right] + \left[(4) + 4 \right] = [11 + 9] + [4 + 4] = [20] + [8] = 20 + 8 = \mathbf{28}$

10. $\left[\left[(3 + 5) + (4 + 3) + 5 \right] + (2 + 3 + 5) \right] + 6 = \left[\left[(8) + (7) + 5 \right] + (10) \right] + 6 = \left[[8 + 7 + 5] + 10 \right] + 6 = \left[[20] + 10 \right] + 6 = [20 + 10] + 6$

    $= [30] + 6 = 30 + 6 = \mathbf{36}$

Section 1.3 Solutions:

1. $(55 - 5) - 3 - 8 = (50) - 11 = 50 - 11 = \mathbf{39}$

2. $59 - 38 - 12 - (20 - 5) = 21 - 12 - (15) = 9 - 15 = \mathbf{-6}$

3. $(20 - 5) - (11 - 2) = (15) - (9) = 15 - 9 = \mathbf{6}$

4. $\left[-25-(4-13)\right]-5 = \left[-25-(-9)\right]-5 = \left[-25+(9)\right]-5 = \left[-25+9\right]-5 = \left[-16\right]-5 = -16-5 = -21$

5. $350-(25-38)-30 = 350-(-13)-30 = 350+(13)-30 = 350+13-30 = 363-30 = 333$

6. $\left[(-30-3)-8\right]-(16-9) = \left[(-33)-8\right]-(7) = \left[-33-8\right]-7 = \left[-41\right]-7 = -41-7 = -48$

7. $\left[(40-4)-(8-10)\right]-9 = \left[(36)-(-2)\right]-9 = \left[36+(2)\right]-9 = \left[36+2\right]-9 = \left[38\right]-9 = 38-9 = 29$

8. $(35-56)-\left[(20-15)-8\right] = (-21)-\left[(5)-8\right] = -21-\left[5-8\right] = -21-\left[-3\right] = -21+\left[3\right] = -21+3 = -18$

9. $\left[(-175-55)-245\right]-(5-6) = \left[(-230)-245\right]-(-1) = \left[-230-245\right]+(1) = \left[-475\right]+1 = -475+1 = -474$

10. $(48-80)-\left[(12-2)-(15-37)\right] = (-32)-\left[(10)-(-22)\right] = -32-\left[10+(22)\right] = -32-\left[10+22\right] = -32-\left[32\right] = -32-32$

    $= -64$

Section 1.4 Solutions:

1. $5\times2\times7\times4 = 280$

2. $(3\times5)\times(4\times2)\times7 = (15)\times(8)\times7 = 15\times8\times7 = 840$

3. $(20\times3\times4)\times(1\times2\times6) = (240)\times(12) = 240\times12 = 2880$

4. $8\times\left[(1\times5\times6)\times(7\times2)\right] = 8\times\left[(30)\times(14)\right] = 8\times\left[30\times14\right] = 8\times\left[420\right] = 8\times420 = 3360$

5. $\left[(2\times7)\times4\right]\times\left[6\times(5\times3)\right] = \left[(14)\times4\right]\times\left[6\times(15)\right] = \left[14\times4\right]\times\left[6\times15\right] = \left[56\right]\times\left[90\right] = 56\times90 = 5040$

6. $(6\times8)\times\left[(2\times3)\times5\right]\times10 = (48)\times\left[(6)\times5\right]\times10 = 48\times\left[6\times5\right]\times10 = 48\times\left[30\right]\times10 = 48\times30\times10 = 14400$

7. $(2\times3\times9)\times\left[(4\times5)\times0\right]\times7 = 0$

8. $\left[(1\times6\times3)\times\left[(7\times3)\times5\right]\right]\times3 = \left[(18)\times\left[(21)\times5\right]\right]\times3 = \left[18\times\left[21\times5\right]\right]\times3 = \left[18\times\left[105\right]\right]\times3 = \left[18\times105\right]\times3 = \left[1890\right]\times3$

   $= 1890\times3 = 5670$

9. $\left[(2\times3)\times(6\times5\times2)\right]\times\left[4\times(2\times4)\right] = \left[(6)\times(60)\right]\times\left[4\times(8)\right] = \left[6\times60\right]\times\left[4\times8\right] = \left[360\right]\times\left[32\right] = 360\times32 = 11520$

10. $\left[(2\times3)\times(6\times7)\times2\right]\times\left[(4\times2)\times5\right] = \left[(6)\times(42)\times2\right]\times\left[(8)\times5\right] = \left[6\times42\times2\right]\times\left[8\times5\right] = \left[504\right]\times\left[40\right] = 504\times40$

    $= 20160$

Section 1.5 Solutions:

1. $(16\div2)\div4 = (8)\div4 = 8\div4 = 2$

2. $(125\div5)\div(15\div5) = (25)\div(3) = 25\div3 = 8.33$

3. $\left[25 \div (8 \div 2)\right] \div 3 = \left[25 \div (4)\right] \div 3 = \left[25 \div 4\right] \div 3 = \left[6.25\right] \div 3 = 6.25 \div 3 = \mathbf{2.08}$

4. $\left[(140 \div 10) \div 2\right] \div 6 = \left[(14) \div 2\right] \div 6 = \left[14 \div 2\right] \div 6 = \left[7\right] \div 6 = 7 \div 6 = \mathbf{1.17}$

5. $\left[155 \div (15 \div 3)\right] \div 9 = \left[155 \div (5)\right] \div 9 = \left[155 \div 5\right] \div 9 = \left[31\right] \div 9 = 31 \div 9 = \mathbf{3.44}$

6. $250 \div \left[(48 \div 2) \div 4\right] = 250 \div \left[(24) \div 4\right] = 250 \div \left[24 \div 4\right] = 250 \div \left[6\right] = 250 \div 6 = \mathbf{41.67}$

7. $\left[(28 \div 4) \div (16 \div 3)\right] \div 8 = \left[(7) \div (5.33)\right] \div 8 = \left[7 \div 5.33\right] \div 8 = \left[1.31\right] \div 8 = 1.31 \div 8 = \mathbf{0.164}$

8. $66 \div \left[48 \div (14 \div 2)\right] = 66 \div \left[48 \div (7)\right] = 66 \div \left[48 \div 7\right] = 66 \div \left[6.86\right] = 66 \div 6.86 = \mathbf{9.62}$

9. $(180 \div 2) \div \left[(88 \div 2) \div 4\right] = (90) \div \left[(44) \div 4\right] = 90 \div \left[44 \div 4\right] = 90 \div \left[11\right] = 90 \div 11 = \mathbf{8.18}$

10. $\left[(48 \div 4) \div 2\right] \div (18 \div 3) = \left[(12) \div 2\right] \div (6) = \left[12 \div 2\right] \div 6 = \left[6\right] \div 6 = 6 \div 6 = \mathbf{1}$

Section 1.6 Solutions:

1. $(28 \div 4) \times 3 = (7) \times 3 = 7 \times 3 = \mathbf{21}$

2. $250 + (15 \div 3) = 250 + (5) = 250 + 5 = \mathbf{255}$

3. $28 \div \left[(23 + 5) \times 8\right] = 28 \div \left[(28) \times 8\right] = 28 \div \left[28 \times 8\right] = 28 \div \left[224\right] = 28 \div 224 = \mathbf{0.125}$

4. $\left[(255 - 15) \div 20\right] + 8 = \left[(240) \div 20\right] + 8 = \left[240 \div 20\right] + 8 = \left[12\right] + 8 = 12 + 8 = \mathbf{20}$

5. $\left[230 \div (15 \times 2)\right] + 12 = \left[230 \div (30)\right] + 12 = \left[230 \div 30\right] + 12 = \left[7.67\right] + 12 = 7.67 + 12 = \mathbf{19.67}$

6. $55 \times \left[(28 + 2) \div 3\right] = 55 \times \left[(30) \div 3\right] = 55 \times \left[30 \div 3\right] = 55 \times \left[10\right] = 55 \times 10 = \mathbf{550}$

7. $\left[(55 \div 5) + (18 - 4)\right] \times 4 = \left[(11) + (14)\right] \times 4 = \left[11 + 14\right] \times 4 = \left[25\right] \times 4 = 25 \times 4 = \mathbf{100}$

8. $35 - \left[400 \div (16 + 4)\right] = 35 - \left[400 \div (20)\right] = 35 - \left[400 \div 20\right] = 35 - \left[20\right] = 35 - 20 = \mathbf{15}$

9. $(230 + 5) \div \left[2 \times (18 + 2)\right] = (235) \div \left[2 \times (20)\right] = 235 \div \left[2 \times 20\right] = 235 \div \left[40\right] = 235 \div 40 = \mathbf{5.875}$

10. $\left[(38 \div 4) + 2\right] \times (15 - 3) = \left[(9.5) + 2\right] \times (12) = \left[9.5 + 2\right] \times 12 = \left[11.5\right] \times 12 = 11.5 \times 12 = \mathbf{138}$

Chapter 2 Solutions:

Section 2.1 Solutions:

1. $\dfrac{0.5}{0.2}$ is a decimal fraction.

2. $-\dfrac{3}{5}$ is a proper integer fraction.

3. $1\dfrac{2}{3}$ is a mixed fraction.

4. $\dfrac{1}{0.1}$ is a decimal fraction.

5. $\left(\dfrac{5}{2}=\dfrac{10}{4}=\dfrac{15}{6}=\dfrac{20}{8}\right)$ is an equivalent fraction.

6. $4\dfrac{3}{8}$ is a mixed fraction.

7. $\dfrac{1}{3}$ is a proper integer fraction.

8. $-\dfrac{38}{13}$ is an improper integer fraction.

9. $\dfrac{7}{2}$ is an improper integer fraction.

10. $\left(\dfrac{0.3}{2.2}=\dfrac{0.6}{4.4}=\dfrac{0.9}{6.6}=\dfrac{1.2}{8.8}\right)$ is an equivalent fraction.

Section 2.2 Solutions:

1. $\dfrac{83}{4}=20\dfrac{3}{4}$

2. $\dfrac{13}{3}=4\dfrac{1}{3}$

3. $-\dfrac{26}{5}=-\left(5\dfrac{1}{5}\right)$

4. $\dfrac{67}{10}=6\dfrac{7}{10}$

5. $\dfrac{9}{2}=4\dfrac{1}{2}$

6. $-\dfrac{332}{113}=-\left(2\dfrac{106}{113}\right)$

7. $\dfrac{205}{9}=22\dfrac{7}{9}$

8. $-\dfrac{235}{14}=-\left(16\dfrac{11}{14}\right)$

9. $\dfrac{207}{11}=18\dfrac{9}{11}$

10. $-\dfrac{523}{101}=-\left(5\dfrac{18}{101}\right)$

Section 2.3 Solutions:

1. $\dfrac{60}{150}=\dfrac{60\div30}{150\div30}=\dfrac{2}{5}$

2. $\dfrac{8}{18}=\dfrac{8\div2}{18\div2}=\dfrac{4}{9}$

3. $\dfrac{355}{15}=\dfrac{355\div5}{15\div5}=\dfrac{71}{3}=23\dfrac{2}{3}$

4. $\dfrac{3}{8}$ is in its lowest term.

5. $\dfrac{27}{6}=\dfrac{27\div3}{6\div3}=\dfrac{9}{2}=4\dfrac{1}{2}$

6. $\dfrac{33}{6}=\dfrac{33\div3}{6\div3}=\dfrac{11}{2}=5\dfrac{1}{2}$

7. $\dfrac{250}{1000}=\dfrac{250\div250}{1000\div250}=\dfrac{1}{4}$

8. $\dfrac{4}{32}=\dfrac{4\div4}{32\div4}=\dfrac{1}{8}$

9. $\dfrac{284}{568}=\dfrac{284\div4}{568\div4}=\dfrac{71}{142}=\dfrac{71\div71}{142\div71}=\dfrac{1}{2}$

10. $\dfrac{45}{75}=\dfrac{45\div15}{75\div15}=\dfrac{3}{5}$

Section 2.4 Solutions:

1. $\dfrac{0.3}{0.05} = \dfrac{\dfrac{3}{10}}{\dfrac{5}{100}} = \dfrac{3 \times 100}{10 \times 5} = \dfrac{\overset{6}{\cancel{300}}}{\underset{1}{\cancel{50}}} = \dfrac{6}{1} = \mathbf{6}$

2. $\dfrac{0.02}{4} = \dfrac{\dfrac{2}{100}}{\dfrac{4}{1}} = \dfrac{2 \times 1}{100 \times 4} = \dfrac{\overset{1}{\cancel{2}}}{\underset{200}{\cancel{400}}} = \mathbf{\dfrac{1}{200}}$

3. $\dfrac{0.5}{0.01} = \dfrac{\dfrac{5}{10}}{\dfrac{1}{100}} = \dfrac{5 \times 100}{10 \times 1} = \dfrac{\overset{50}{\cancel{500}}}{\underset{1}{\cancel{10}}} = \dfrac{50}{1} = \mathbf{50}$

4. $\dfrac{35}{0.005} = \dfrac{\dfrac{35}{1}}{\dfrac{5}{1000}} = \dfrac{35 \times 1000}{1 \times 5} = \dfrac{\overset{7000}{\cancel{35000}}}{\underset{1}{\cancel{5}}} = \dfrac{7000}{1}$

   $= \mathbf{7000}$

5. $\dfrac{12.3}{0.03} = \dfrac{\dfrac{123}{10}}{\dfrac{3}{100}} = \dfrac{123 \times 100}{10 \times 3} = \dfrac{\overset{410}{\cancel{12300}}}{\underset{1}{\cancel{30}}} = \dfrac{410}{1} = \mathbf{410}$

6. $\dfrac{6}{12.2} = \dfrac{\dfrac{6}{1}}{\dfrac{122}{10}} = \dfrac{6 \times 10}{1 \times 122} = \dfrac{\overset{30}{\cancel{60}}}{\underset{61}{\cancel{122}}} = \mathbf{\dfrac{30}{61}}$

7. $\dfrac{0.008}{1.2} = \dfrac{\dfrac{8}{1000}}{\dfrac{12}{10}} = \dfrac{8 \times 10}{1000 \times 12} = \dfrac{\overset{1}{\cancel{80}}}{\underset{150}{\cancel{12000}}} = \mathbf{\dfrac{1}{150}}$

8. $\dfrac{0.9}{0.05} = \dfrac{\dfrac{9}{10}}{\dfrac{5}{100}} = \dfrac{9 \times 100}{10 \times 5} = \dfrac{\overset{18}{\cancel{900}}}{\underset{1}{\cancel{50}}} = \dfrac{18}{1} = \mathbf{18}$

9. $\dfrac{1}{0.2} = \dfrac{\dfrac{1}{1}}{\dfrac{2}{10}} = \dfrac{1 \times 10}{1 \times 2} = \dfrac{\overset{5}{\cancel{10}}}{\underset{1}{\cancel{2}}} = \dfrac{5}{1} = \mathbf{5}$

10. $\dfrac{4.02}{12.8} = \dfrac{\dfrac{402}{100}}{\dfrac{128}{10}} = \dfrac{402 \times 10}{100 \times 128} = \dfrac{\overset{201}{\cancel{4020}}}{\underset{640}{\cancel{12800}}} = \mathbf{\dfrac{201}{640}}$

Section 2.5 Solutions:

1. $3\dfrac{2}{6} = \dfrac{(3 \times 6) + 2}{6} = \dfrac{18 + 2}{6} = \dfrac{\overset{10}{\cancel{20}}}{\underset{3}{\cancel{6}}} = \mathbf{\dfrac{10}{3}}$

2. $4\dfrac{3}{8} = \dfrac{(4 \times 8) + 3}{8} = \dfrac{32 + 3}{8} = \mathbf{\dfrac{35}{8}}$

3. $5\dfrac{1}{8} = \dfrac{(5 \times 8) + 1}{8} = \dfrac{40 + 1}{8} = \mathbf{\dfrac{41}{8}}$

4. $8\dfrac{3}{5} = \dfrac{(8 \times 5) + 3}{5} = \dfrac{40 + 3}{5} = \mathbf{\dfrac{43}{5}}$

5. $7\dfrac{2}{3} = \dfrac{(7 \times 3) + 2}{3} = \dfrac{21 + 2}{3} = \mathbf{\dfrac{23}{3}}$

6. $9\dfrac{3}{16} = \dfrac{(9 \times 16) + 3}{16} = \dfrac{144 + 3}{16} = \mathbf{\dfrac{147}{16}}$

7. $12\dfrac{2}{4} = \dfrac{(12 \times 4) + 2}{4} = \dfrac{48 + 2}{4} = \dfrac{\overset{25}{\cancel{50}}}{\underset{2}{\cancel{4}}} = \mathbf{\dfrac{25}{2}}$

8. $10\dfrac{4}{5} = \dfrac{(10 \times 5) + 4}{5} = \dfrac{50 + 4}{5} = \mathbf{\dfrac{54}{5}}$

9. $2\dfrac{5}{8} = \dfrac{(2 \times 8) + 5}{8} = \dfrac{16 + 5}{8} = \mathbf{\dfrac{21}{8}}$

10. $3\dfrac{2}{15} = \dfrac{(3 \times 15) + 2}{15} = \dfrac{45 + 2}{15} = \mathbf{\dfrac{47}{15}}$

Chapter 3 Solutions:

Section 3.1 Solutions:

1. $\dfrac{4}{9}+\dfrac{2}{9} = \dfrac{4+2}{9} = \dfrac{\overset{2}{\cancel{6}}}{\underset{3}{\cancel{9}}} = \dfrac{2}{3}$

2. $\dfrac{3}{8}+\dfrac{2}{5} = \dfrac{3}{8}+\dfrac{2}{5} = \dfrac{(3\times5)+(2\times8)}{8\times5} = \dfrac{15+16}{40} = \dfrac{31}{40}$

3. $\dfrac{3}{8}+\dfrac{2}{4}+\dfrac{5}{6} = \left(\dfrac{3}{8}+\dfrac{2}{4}\right)+\dfrac{5}{6} = \left(\dfrac{(3\times4)+(2\times8)}{8\times4}\right)+\dfrac{5}{6} = \left(\dfrac{12+16}{32}\right)+\dfrac{5}{6} = \left(\dfrac{28}{32}\right)+\dfrac{5}{6} = \dfrac{28}{32}+\dfrac{5}{6} = \dfrac{(28\times6)+(5\times32)}{32\times6}$

   $= \dfrac{168+160}{192} = \dfrac{\overset{41}{\cancel{328}}}{\underset{24}{\cancel{192}}} = \dfrac{41}{24} = 1\dfrac{17}{24}$

4. $\dfrac{4}{5}+\dfrac{2}{5}+\dfrac{3}{5} = \dfrac{4+2+3}{5} = \dfrac{9}{5} = 1\dfrac{4}{5}$

5. $5+\dfrac{0}{10}+\dfrac{6}{1}+\dfrac{4}{8} = \left(\dfrac{5}{1}+\dfrac{0}{10}\right)+\left(\dfrac{6}{1}+\dfrac{4}{8}\right) = \left(\dfrac{5}{1}+0\right)+\left(\dfrac{(6\times8)+(4\times1)}{1\times8}\right) = \left(\dfrac{5}{1}\right)+\left(\dfrac{48+4}{8}\right) = \dfrac{5}{1}+\left(\dfrac{52}{8}\right) = \dfrac{5}{1}+\dfrac{52}{8}$

   $= \dfrac{(5\times8)+(52\times1)}{1\times8} = \dfrac{40+52}{8} = \dfrac{\overset{23}{\cancel{92}}}{\underset{2}{\cancel{8}}} = \dfrac{23}{2} = 11\dfrac{1}{2}$

6. $\left(\dfrac{3}{16}+\dfrac{1}{8}\right)+\dfrac{1}{6} = \left(\dfrac{(3\times8)+(1\times16)}{16\times8}\right)+\dfrac{1}{6} = \left(\dfrac{24+16}{128}\right)+\dfrac{1}{6} = \left(\dfrac{40}{128}\right)+\dfrac{1}{6} = \dfrac{\overset{5}{\cancel{40}}}{\underset{16}{\cancel{128}}}+\dfrac{1}{6} = \dfrac{5}{16}+\dfrac{1}{6} = \dfrac{(5\times6)+(1\times16)}{16\times6}$

   $= \dfrac{30+16}{96} = \dfrac{\overset{23}{\cancel{46}}}{\underset{48}{\cancel{96}}} = \dfrac{23}{48}$

7. $\left(\dfrac{4}{5}+\dfrac{2}{8}\right)+\left(\dfrac{2}{4}+\dfrac{1}{4}+\dfrac{3}{4}\right) = \left(\dfrac{(4\times8)+(2\times5)}{5\times8}\right)+\left(\dfrac{2+1+3}{4}\right) = \left(\dfrac{32+10}{40}\right)+\left(\dfrac{6}{4}\right) = \left(\dfrac{42}{40}\right)+\dfrac{6}{4} = \dfrac{\overset{21}{\cancel{42}}}{\underset{20}{\cancel{40}}}+\dfrac{\overset{3}{\cancel{6}}}{\underset{2}{\cancel{4}}} = \dfrac{21}{20}+\dfrac{3}{2}$

   $= \dfrac{(21\times2)+(3\times20)}{20\times2} = \dfrac{42+60}{40} = \dfrac{\overset{51}{\cancel{102}}}{\underset{20}{\cancel{40}}} = \dfrac{51}{20} = 2\dfrac{11}{20}$

8. $\dfrac{2}{5}+\left(\dfrac{4}{9}+\dfrac{2}{9}+\dfrac{1}{9}\right) = \dfrac{2}{5}+\left(\dfrac{4+2+1}{9}\right) = \dfrac{2}{5}+\left(\dfrac{7}{9}\right) = \dfrac{2}{5}+\dfrac{7}{9} = \dfrac{(2\times9)+(7\times5)}{5\times9} = \dfrac{18+35}{45} = \dfrac{53}{45} = 1\dfrac{8}{45}$

9. $\dfrac{2}{5}+\dfrac{1}{2}+\dfrac{4}{5}+\dfrac{2}{3}+12 = \left(\dfrac{2}{5}+\dfrac{1}{2}\right)+\left(\dfrac{4}{5}+\dfrac{2}{3}\right)+\dfrac{12}{1} = \left(\dfrac{(2\times2)+(1\times5)}{5\times2}\right)+\left(\dfrac{(4\times3)+(2\times5)}{5\times3}\right)+\dfrac{12}{1}$

   $= \left(\dfrac{4+5}{10}\right)+\left(\dfrac{12+10}{15}\right)+\dfrac{12}{1} = \left(\dfrac{9}{10}\right)+\left(\dfrac{22}{15}\right)+\dfrac{12}{1} = \dfrac{9}{10}+\dfrac{22}{15}+\dfrac{12}{1} = \left(\dfrac{9}{10}+\dfrac{22}{15}\right)+\dfrac{12}{1} = \left(\dfrac{(9\times15)+(22\times10)}{10\times15}\right)+\dfrac{12}{1}$

$$= \left(\frac{135+220}{150}\right) + \frac{12}{1} = \left(\frac{355}{150}\right) + \frac{12}{1} = \frac{\overset{71}{\cancel{355}}}{\underset{30}{\cancel{150}}} + \frac{12}{1} = \frac{71}{30} + \frac{12}{1} = \frac{(71\times1)+(12\times30)}{30\times1} = \frac{71+360}{30} = \frac{431}{30} = \mathbf{14\frac{11}{30}}$$

10. $\left[\frac{5}{8}+\left(\frac{3}{5}+\frac{1}{8}\right)\right]+\left(\frac{1}{8}+\frac{3}{8}\right) = \left[\frac{5}{8}+\left(\frac{(3\times8)+(1\times5)}{5\times8}\right)\right]+\left(\frac{1+3}{8}\right) = \left[\frac{5}{8}+\left(\frac{24+5}{40}\right)\right]+\left(\frac{4}{8}\right) = \left[\frac{5}{8}+\left(\frac{29}{40}\right)\right]+\frac{4}{8}$

$$= \left[\frac{5}{8}+\frac{29}{40}\right]+\frac{\overset{1}{\cancel{4}}}{\underset{2}{\cancel{8}}} = \left[\frac{(5\times40)+(29\times8)}{8\times40}\right]+\frac{1}{2} = \left[\frac{200+232}{320}\right]+\frac{1}{2} = \left[\frac{432}{320}\right]+\frac{1}{2} = \frac{\overset{27}{\cancel{432}}}{\underset{20}{\cancel{320}}}+\frac{1}{2} = \frac{27}{20}+\frac{1}{2}$$

$$= \frac{(27\times2)+(1\times20)}{20\times2} = \frac{54+20}{40} = \frac{\overset{37}{\cancel{74}}}{\underset{20}{\cancel{40}}} = \frac{37}{20} = \mathbf{1\frac{17}{20}}$$

Section 3.2 Solutions:

1. $\frac{3}{5}-\frac{2}{5} = \frac{3-2}{5} = \mathbf{\frac{1}{5}}$

2. $\frac{2}{5}-\frac{3}{4} = \frac{(2\times4)-(3\times5)}{5\times4} = \frac{8-15}{20} = -\mathbf{\frac{7}{20}}$

3. $\frac{12}{15}-\frac{3}{15}-\frac{6}{15} = \frac{12-3-6}{15} = \frac{\overset{1}{\cancel{3}}}{\underset{5}{\cancel{15}}} = \mathbf{\frac{1}{5}}$

4. $\frac{5}{8}-\frac{3}{4}-\frac{1}{3} = \left(\frac{5}{8}-\frac{3}{4}\right)-\frac{1}{3} = \left(\frac{(5\times4)-(3\times8)}{8\times4}\right)-\frac{1}{3} = \left(\frac{20-24}{32}\right)-\frac{1}{3} = \left(\frac{-4}{32}\right)-\frac{1}{3} = \frac{\overset{-1}{\cancel{-4}}}{\underset{8}{\cancel{32}}}-\frac{1}{3} = \frac{-1}{8}-\frac{1}{3}$

$$= \frac{(-1\times3)-(1\times8)}{8\times3} = \frac{-3-8}{24} = -\mathbf{\frac{11}{24}}$$

5. $\left(\frac{2}{8}-\frac{1}{6}\right)-\frac{2}{5} = \left(\frac{(2\times6)-(1\times8)}{8\times6}\right)-\frac{2}{5} = \left(\frac{12-8}{48}\right)-\frac{2}{5} = \left(\frac{4}{48}\right)-\frac{2}{5} = \frac{\overset{1}{\cancel{4}}}{\underset{12}{\cancel{48}}}-\frac{2}{5} = \frac{1}{12}-\frac{2}{5} = \frac{(1\times5)-(2\times12)}{12\times5} = \frac{5-24}{60}$

$$= -\mathbf{\frac{19}{60}}$$

6. $28-\left(\frac{1}{8}-\frac{2}{3}\right) = \frac{28}{1}-\left(\frac{(1\times3)-(2\times8)}{8\times3}\right) = \frac{28}{1}-\left(\frac{3-16}{24}\right) = \frac{28}{1}-\left(\frac{-13}{24}\right) = \frac{28}{1}-\frac{-13}{24} = \frac{28}{1}+\frac{13}{24} = \frac{(28\times24)+(13\times1)}{1\times24}$

$$= \frac{672+13}{24} = \frac{685}{24} = \mathbf{28\frac{13}{24}}$$

7. $\left(\frac{4}{6}-\frac{1}{8}\right)-\left(\frac{4}{5}-\frac{1}{2}\right) = \left(\frac{(4\times8)-(1\times6)}{6\times8}\right)-\left(\frac{(4\times2)-(1\times5)}{5\times2}\right) = \left(\frac{32-6}{48}\right)-\left(\frac{8-5}{10}\right) = \left(\frac{26}{48}\right)-\left(\frac{3}{10}\right) = \frac{\overset{13}{\cancel{26}}}{\underset{24}{\cancel{48}}}-\frac{3}{10}$

$$= \frac{13}{24}-\frac{3}{10} = \frac{(13\times10)-(3\times24)}{24\times10} = \frac{130-72}{240} = \frac{\overset{29}{\cancel{58}}}{\underset{120}{\cancel{240}}} = \mathbf{\frac{29}{120}}$$

8. $\left(20-\frac{1}{6}\right)-\left(\frac{3}{4}-\frac{1}{2}\right) = \left(\frac{20}{1}-\frac{1}{6}\right)-\left(\frac{(3\times2)-(1\times4)}{4\times2}\right) = \left(\frac{(20\times6)-(1\times1)}{1\times6}\right)-\left(\frac{6-4}{8}\right) = \left(\frac{120-1}{6}\right)-\left(\frac{2}{8}\right) = \left(\frac{119}{6}\right)-\frac{2}{8}$

$= \dfrac{119}{6} - \dfrac{\overset{1}{\cancel{2}}}{\underset{4}{\cancel{8}}} = \dfrac{119}{6} - \dfrac{1}{4} = \dfrac{(119 \times 4) - (1 \times 6)}{6 \times 4} = \dfrac{476 - 6}{24} = \dfrac{\overset{235}{\cancel{470}}}{\underset{12}{\cancel{24}}} = \dfrac{235}{12} = \mathbf{19\dfrac{7}{12}}$

9. $\left[\dfrac{18}{5} - \left(\dfrac{4}{3} - \dfrac{2}{3}\right)\right] - 2 = \left[\dfrac{18}{5} - \left(\dfrac{4-2}{3}\right)\right] - \dfrac{2}{1} = \left[\dfrac{18}{5} - \left(\dfrac{2}{3}\right)\right] - \dfrac{2}{1} = \left[\dfrac{18}{5} - \dfrac{2}{3}\right] - \dfrac{2}{1} = \left[\dfrac{(18 \times 3) - (2 \times 5)}{5 \times 3}\right] - \dfrac{2}{1} = \left[\dfrac{54 - 10}{15}\right] - \dfrac{2}{1}$

$= \left[\dfrac{44}{15}\right] - \dfrac{2}{1} = \dfrac{44}{15} - \dfrac{2}{1} = \dfrac{(44 \times 1) - (2 \times 15)}{15 \times 1} = \dfrac{44 - 30}{15} = \mathbf{\dfrac{14}{15}}$

10. $\left[\left(18 - \dfrac{1}{2}\right) - \left(\dfrac{16}{2} - 2\right)\right] - \dfrac{1}{5} = \left[\left(\dfrac{18}{1} - \dfrac{1}{2}\right) - \left(\dfrac{16}{2} - \dfrac{2}{1}\right)\right] - \dfrac{1}{5} = \left[\left(\dfrac{(18 \times 2) - (1 \times 1)}{1 \times 2}\right) - \left(\dfrac{(16 \times 1) - (2 \times 2)}{2 \times 1}\right)\right] - \dfrac{1}{5}$

$= \left[\left(\dfrac{36-1}{2}\right) - \left(\dfrac{16-4}{2}\right)\right] - \dfrac{1}{5} = \left[\left(\dfrac{35}{2}\right) - \left(\dfrac{12}{2}\right)\right] - \dfrac{1}{5} = \left[\dfrac{35}{2} - \dfrac{12}{2}\right] - \dfrac{1}{5} = \left[\dfrac{35-12}{2}\right] - \dfrac{1}{5} = \left[\dfrac{23}{2}\right] - \dfrac{1}{5} = \dfrac{23}{2} - \dfrac{1}{5}$

$= \dfrac{(23 \times 5) - (1 \times 2)}{2 \times 5} = \dfrac{115 - 2}{10} = \dfrac{113}{10} = \mathbf{11\dfrac{3}{10}}$

Section 3.3 Solutions:

1. $\dfrac{4}{8} \times \dfrac{3}{5} = \dfrac{4 \times 3}{\underset{2}{\cancel{8}} \times 5} = \dfrac{1 \times 3}{2 \times 5} = \mathbf{\dfrac{3}{10}}$

2. $\dfrac{4}{8} \times \dfrac{5}{6} \times 100 = \dfrac{4}{8} \times \dfrac{5}{6} \times \dfrac{100}{1} = \dfrac{4 \times 5 \times 100}{8 \times 6 \times 1} = \dfrac{\overset{125}{\cancel{2000}}}{\underset{3}{\cancel{48}}} = \dfrac{125}{3} = \mathbf{41\dfrac{2}{3}}$

3. $\dfrac{7}{3} \times \dfrac{9}{4} \times \dfrac{6}{3} = \dfrac{7 \times \overset{3}{\cancel{9}} \times \overset{2}{\cancel{6}}}{\underset{1}{\cancel{3}} \times 4 \times \underset{1}{\cancel{3}}} = \dfrac{7 \times 3 \times 2}{1 \times 4 \times 1} = \dfrac{7 \times 3 \times \overset{1}{\cancel{2}}}{1 \times \underset{2}{\cancel{4}} \times 1} = \dfrac{7 \times 3 \times 1}{1 \times 2 \times 1} = \dfrac{21}{2} = \mathbf{10\dfrac{1}{2}}$

4. $34 \times \dfrac{1}{5} \times \dfrac{3}{17} \times \dfrac{1}{8} \times 20 = \dfrac{34}{1} \times \dfrac{1}{5} \times \dfrac{3}{17} \times \dfrac{1}{8} \times \dfrac{20}{1} = \dfrac{\overset{2}{\cancel{34}} \times 1 \times 3 \times 1 \times \overset{4}{\cancel{20}}}{1 \times \underset{1}{\cancel{5}} \times \underset{1}{\cancel{17}} \times 8 \times 1} = \dfrac{2 \times 1 \times 3 \times 1 \times 4}{1 \times 1 \times 1 \times 8 \times 1} = \dfrac{\overset{3}{\cancel{24}}}{\underset{1}{\cancel{8}}} = \dfrac{3}{1} = \mathbf{3}$

5. $\left(\dfrac{2}{55} \times 3\right) \times \left(\dfrac{4}{5} \times \dfrac{25}{8}\right) = \left(\dfrac{2}{55} \times \dfrac{3}{1}\right) \times \left(\dfrac{\overset{1}{\cancel{4}} \times \overset{5}{\cancel{25}}}{\underset{1}{\cancel{5}} \times \underset{2}{\cancel{8}}}\right) = \left(\dfrac{2 \times 3}{55 \times 1}\right) \times \left(\dfrac{1 \times 5}{1 \times 2}\right) = \left(\dfrac{6}{55}\right) \times \left(\dfrac{5}{2}\right) = \dfrac{6}{55} \times \dfrac{5}{2} = \dfrac{\overset{3}{\cancel{6}} \times \overset{1}{\cancel{5}}}{\underset{11}{\cancel{55}} \times \underset{1}{\cancel{2}}} = \dfrac{3 \times 1}{11 \times 1} = \mathbf{\dfrac{3}{11}}$

6. $\left(1000 \times \dfrac{1}{5}\right) \times \left(\dfrac{25}{5} \times \dfrac{1}{8}\right) \times \dfrac{0}{100} = \mathbf{0}$

7. $\dfrac{2}{6} \times \dfrac{36}{1} \times \dfrac{1}{100} \times 10 \times \dfrac{1}{6} = \dfrac{2}{6} \times \dfrac{36}{1} \times \dfrac{1}{100} \times \dfrac{10}{1} \times \dfrac{1}{6} = \dfrac{\overset{1}{\cancel{2}} \times \overset{6}{\cancel{36}} \times 1 \times \overset{1}{\cancel{10}} \times 1}{\underset{1}{\cancel{6}} \times 1 \times \underset{10}{\cancel{100}} \times 1 \times \underset{3}{\cancel{6}}} = \dfrac{1 \times 6 \times 1 \times 1 \times 1}{1 \times 1 \times 10 \times 1 \times 3} = \dfrac{\overset{1}{\cancel{6}}}{\underset{5}{\cancel{30}}} = \mathbf{\dfrac{1}{5}}$

8. $\left(\dfrac{7}{8} \times \dfrac{9}{4}\right) \times \left(\dfrac{4}{18} \times \dfrac{1}{14} \times \dfrac{1}{9}\right) = \left(\dfrac{7 \times 9}{8 \times 4}\right) \times \left(\dfrac{\overset{2}{\cancel{4}} \times 1 \times 1}{\underset{9}{\cancel{18}} \times 14 \times 9}\right) = \left(\dfrac{63}{32}\right) \times \left(\dfrac{2 \times 1 \times 1}{9 \times 14 \times 9}\right) = \dfrac{63}{32} \times \left(\dfrac{\overset{1}{\cancel{2}} \times 1 \times 1}{9 \times \underset{7}{\cancel{14}} \times 9}\right) = \dfrac{63}{32} \times \left(\dfrac{1 \times 1 \times 1}{9 \times 7 \times 9}\right)$

$= \dfrac{63}{32} \times \left(\dfrac{1}{567}\right) = \dfrac{63}{32} \times \dfrac{1}{567} = \dfrac{\overset{1}{\cancel{63}} \times 1}{32 \times \underset{9}{\cancel{567}}} = \dfrac{1 \times 1}{32 \times 9} = \mathbf{\dfrac{1}{288}}$

9. $$\left[\left(18\times\frac{2}{8}\right)\times\left(\frac{1}{5}\times\frac{25}{3}\right)\right]\times\frac{2}{9} = \left[\left(\frac{18}{1}\times\frac{2}{8}\right)\times\left(\frac{1\times\overset{5}{25}}{\underset{1}{5}\times 3}\right)\right]\times\frac{2}{9} = \left[\left(\frac{18\times\overset{1}{2}}{1\times\underset{4}{8}}\right)\times\left(\frac{1\times 5}{1\times 3}\right)\right]\times\frac{2}{9} = \left[\left(\frac{18\times 1}{1\times 4}\right)\times\left(\frac{5}{3}\right)\right]\times\frac{2}{9}$$

$$= \left[\left(\frac{18}{4}\right)\times\frac{5}{3}\right]\times\frac{2}{9} = \left[\frac{\overset{9}{18}}{\underset{2}{4}}\times\frac{5}{3}\right]\times\frac{2}{9} = \left[\frac{9}{2}\times\frac{5}{3}\right]\times\frac{2}{9} = \left[\frac{9\times 5}{2\times 3}\right]\times\frac{2}{9} = \left[\frac{45}{6}\right]\times\frac{2}{9} = \frac{45}{6}\times\frac{2}{9} = \frac{\overset{5}{45}\times\overset{1}{2}}{\underset{3}{6}\times\underset{1}{9}} = \frac{5\times 1}{3\times 1} = \frac{5}{3}$$

$$= 1\frac{2}{3}$$

10. $$\left(\frac{3}{8}\times\frac{4}{49}\times\frac{6}{5}\right)\times\left(\frac{7}{3}\times\frac{4}{8}\right)\times\frac{7}{2} = \left(\frac{3\times 4\times\overset{3}{6}}{8\times 49\times 5}\right)\times\left(\frac{7\times\overset{1}{4}}{3\times\underset{2}{8}}\right)\times\frac{7}{2} = \left(\frac{3\times 4\times 3}{4\times 49\times 5}\right)\times\left(\frac{7\times 1}{3\times 2}\right)\times\frac{7}{2} = \left(\frac{36}{980}\right)\times\left(\frac{7}{6}\right)\times\frac{7}{2}$$

$$= \frac{36}{980}\times\frac{7}{6}\times\frac{7}{2} = \frac{\overset{6}{36}\times 7\times 7}{980\times\underset{1}{6}\times 2} = \frac{6\times 7\times 7}{980\times 1\times 2} = \frac{\overset{147}{294}}{\underset{980}{1960}} = \frac{147}{980}$$

Section 3.4 Solutions:

1. $$\frac{8}{10}\div\frac{4}{30} = \frac{8}{10}\times\frac{30}{4} = \frac{\overset{2}{8}\times\overset{3}{30}}{\underset{1}{10}\times\underset{1}{4}} = \frac{2\times 3}{1\times 1} = \frac{6}{1} = 6$$

2. $$\left(\frac{3}{8}\div\frac{12}{16}\right)\div\frac{4}{8} = \left(\frac{3}{8}\times\frac{16}{12}\right)\div\frac{4}{8} = \left(\frac{\overset{1}{3}\times\overset{2}{16}}{\underset{1}{8}\times\underset{4}{12}}\right)\div\frac{\overset{1}{4}}{\underset{2}{8}} = \left(\frac{1\times 2}{1\times 4}\right)\div\frac{1}{2} = \left(\frac{2}{4}\right)\div\frac{1}{2} = \frac{2}{4}\div\frac{1}{2} = \frac{2}{4}\times\frac{2}{1} = \frac{2\times 2}{4\times 1} = \frac{\overset{1}{4}}{\underset{1}{4}} = \frac{1}{1} = 1$$

3. $$\left(\frac{4}{16}\div\frac{1}{32}\right)\div 8 = \left(\frac{4}{16}\times\frac{32}{1}\right)\div\frac{8}{1} = \left(\frac{4\times\overset{2}{32}}{\underset{1}{16}\times 1}\right)\div\frac{8}{1} = \left(\frac{4\times 2}{1\times 1}\right)\div\frac{8}{1} = \left(\frac{8}{1}\right)\div\frac{8}{1} = \frac{8}{1}\div\frac{8}{1} = \frac{8}{1}\times\frac{1}{8} = \frac{\overset{1}{8}\times 1}{1\times\underset{1}{8}} = \frac{1\times 1}{1\times 1}$$

$$= \frac{1}{1} = 1$$

4. $$12\div\left(\frac{9}{8}\div\frac{27}{16}\right) = \frac{12}{1}\div\left(\frac{9}{8}\times\frac{16}{27}\right) = \frac{12}{1}\div\left(\frac{\overset{1}{9}\times\overset{2}{16}}{\underset{1}{8}\times\underset{3}{27}}\right) = \frac{12}{1}\div\left(\frac{1\times 2}{1\times 3}\right) = \frac{12}{1}\div\left(\frac{2}{3}\right) = \frac{12}{1}\div\frac{2}{3} = \frac{12}{1}\times\frac{3}{2} = \frac{\overset{6}{12}\times 3}{1\times\underset{1}{2}} = \frac{6\times 3}{1\times 1}$$

$$= \frac{18}{1} = 18$$

5. $$\left(\frac{2}{20}\div\frac{4}{5}\right)\div 2 = \left(\frac{2}{20}\times\frac{5}{4}\right)\div\frac{2}{1} = \left(\frac{\overset{1}{2}\times\overset{1}{5}}{\underset{4}{20}\times\underset{2}{4}}\right)\div\frac{2}{1} = \left(\frac{1\times 1}{4\times 2}\right)\div\frac{2}{1} = \left(\frac{1}{8}\right)\div\frac{2}{1} = \frac{1}{8}\div\frac{2}{1} = \frac{1}{8}\times\frac{1}{2} = \frac{1\times 1}{8\times 2} = \frac{1}{16}$$

6. $$\left(\frac{4}{15}\div\frac{8}{30}\right)\div\left(\frac{1}{5}\div\frac{4}{35}\right) = \left(\frac{4}{15}\times\frac{30}{8}\right)\div\left(\frac{1}{5}\times\frac{35}{4}\right) = \left(\frac{\overset{1}{4}\times\overset{2}{30}}{\underset{1}{15}\times\underset{2}{8}}\right)\div\left(\frac{1\times\overset{7}{35}}{\underset{1}{5}\times 4}\right) = \left(\frac{1\times 2}{1\times 2}\right)\div\left(\frac{1\times 7}{1\times 4}\right) = \left(\frac{2}{2}\right)\div\left(\frac{7}{4}\right) = \frac{2}{2}\div\frac{7}{4}$$

$$= \frac{2}{2}\times\frac{4}{7} = \frac{2\times\overset{2}{4}}{\underset{1}{2}\times 7} = \frac{2\times 2}{1\times 7} = \frac{4}{7}$$

7. $$\left(\frac{2}{5}\div\frac{4}{10}\right)\div\left(\frac{9}{1}\div\frac{18}{4}\right) = \left(\frac{2}{5}\times\frac{10}{4}\right)\div\left(\frac{9}{1}\times\frac{4}{18}\right) = \left(\frac{\overset{1}{2}\times\overset{2}{10}}{\underset{1}{5}\times\underset{2}{4}}\right)\div\left(\frac{\overset{1}{9}\times 4}{1\times\underset{2}{18}}\right) = \left(\frac{1\times 2}{1\times 2}\right)\div\left(\frac{1\times 4}{1\times 2}\right) = \left(\frac{2}{2}\right)\div\left(\frac{4}{2}\right) = \frac{\overset{1}{2}}{\underset{1}{2}}\div\frac{\overset{2}{4}}{\underset{1}{2}}$$

$$= \frac{1}{1} \div \frac{2}{1} = \frac{1}{1} \times \frac{1}{2} = \frac{1 \times 1}{1 \times 2} = \mathbf{\frac{1}{2}}$$

8. $\left(\frac{4}{5} \div \frac{2}{5} \right) \div \left(\frac{8}{5} \div 4 \right) = \left(\frac{4}{5} \times \frac{5}{2} \right) \div \left(\frac{8}{5} \div \frac{4}{1} \right) = \left(\frac{\overset{2}{\cancel{4}} \times \overset{1}{\cancel{5}}}{\underset{1}{\cancel{5}} \times \underset{1}{\cancel{2}}} \right) \div \left(\frac{8}{5} \times \frac{1}{4} \right) = \left(\frac{2 \times 1}{1 \times 1} \right) \div \left(\frac{\overset{2}{\cancel{8}} \times 1}{5 \times \underset{1}{\cancel{4}}} \right) = \left(\frac{2}{1} \right) \div \left(\frac{2 \times 1}{5 \times 1} \right) = \frac{2}{1} \div \left(\frac{2}{5} \right)$

$$= \frac{2}{1} \div \frac{2}{5} = \frac{2}{1} \times \frac{5}{2} = \frac{\overset{1}{\cancel{2}} \times 5}{1 \times \underset{1}{\cancel{2}}} = \frac{1 \times 5}{1 \times 1} = \frac{5}{1} = \mathbf{5}$$

9. $\left(\frac{6}{10} \div 1 \right) \div \left(\frac{4}{6} \div \frac{1}{3} \right) = \left(\frac{6}{10} \div \frac{1}{1} \right) \div \left(\frac{4}{6} \times \frac{3}{1} \right) = \left(\frac{6}{10} \times \frac{1}{1} \right) \div \left(\frac{4 \times \overset{1}{\cancel{3}}}{\underset{2}{\cancel{6}} \times 1} \right) = \left(\frac{\overset{3}{\cancel{6}} \times 1}{\underset{5}{\cancel{10}} \times 1} \right) \div \left(\frac{\overset{2}{\cancel{4}} \times 1}{\underset{1}{\cancel{2}} \times 1} \right) = \left(\frac{3 \times 1}{5 \times 1} \right) \div \left(\frac{2 \times 1}{1 \times 1} \right) = \left(\frac{3}{5} \right) \div \left(\frac{2}{1} \right)$

$$= \frac{3}{5} \div \frac{2}{1} = \frac{3}{5} \times \frac{1}{2} = \frac{3 \times 1}{5 \times 2} = \mathbf{\frac{3}{10}}$$

10. $\left[\left(\frac{9}{8} \div \frac{18}{16} \right) \div \frac{4}{2} \right] \div \frac{1}{8} = \left[\left(\frac{9}{8} \times \frac{16}{18} \right) \div \frac{4}{2} \right] \div \frac{1}{8} = \left[\left(\frac{\overset{1}{\cancel{9}} \times \overset{2}{\cancel{16}}}{\underset{1}{\cancel{8}} \times \underset{2}{\cancel{18}}} \right) \div \frac{4}{2} \right] \div \frac{1}{8} = \left[\left(\frac{1 \times 2}{1 \times 2} \right) \div \frac{4}{2} \right] \div \frac{1}{8} = \left[\left(\frac{1 \times 1}{1 \times 1} \right) \div \frac{4}{2} \right] \div \frac{1}{8} =$

$$\left[\left(\frac{1}{1} \right) \div \frac{4}{2} \right] \div \frac{1}{8} = \left[\frac{1}{1} \div \frac{4}{2} \right] \div \frac{1}{8} = \left[\frac{1}{1} \times \frac{2}{4} \right] \div \frac{1}{8} = \left[\frac{1 \times \overset{1}{\cancel{2}}}{1 \times \underset{2}{\cancel{4}}} \right] \div \frac{1}{8} = \left[\frac{1 \times 1}{1 \times 2} \right] \div \frac{1}{8} = \left[\frac{1}{2} \right] \div \frac{1}{8} = \frac{1}{2} \div \frac{1}{8} = \frac{1}{2} \times \frac{8}{1} = \frac{1 \times \overset{4}{\cancel{8}}}{\underset{1}{\cancel{2}} \times 1}$$

$$= \frac{1 \times 4}{1 \times 1} = \frac{4}{1} = \mathbf{4}$$

Section 3.5 Solutions:

1. $\left(\frac{5}{4} \times \frac{8}{1} \right) \div \frac{2}{3} = \left(\frac{5 \times 8}{4 \times 1} \right) \div \frac{2}{3} = \left(\frac{40}{4} \right) \div \frac{2}{3} = \frac{\overset{10}{\cancel{40}}}{\underset{1}{\cancel{4}}} \div \frac{2}{3} = \frac{10}{1} \div \frac{2}{3} = \frac{10}{1} \times \frac{3}{2} = \frac{\overset{5}{\cancel{10}} \times 3}{1 \times \underset{1}{\cancel{2}}} = \frac{5 \times 3}{1 \times 1} = \frac{15}{1} = \mathbf{15}$

2. $\left(\frac{3}{4} \div 12 \right) \times \frac{4}{15} = \left(\frac{3}{4} \div \frac{12}{1} \right) \times \frac{4}{15} = \left(\frac{3}{4} \times \frac{1}{12} \right) \times \frac{4}{15} = \left(\frac{\overset{1}{\cancel{3}} \times 1}{4 \times \underset{4}{\cancel{12}}} \right) \times \frac{4}{15} = \left(\frac{1 \times 1}{4 \times 4} \right) \times \frac{4}{15} = \left(\frac{1}{16} \right) \times \frac{4}{15} = \frac{1}{16} \times \frac{4}{15} = \frac{1 \times \overset{1}{\cancel{4}}}{\underset{4}{\cancel{16}} \times 15}$

$$= \frac{1 \times 1}{4 \times 15} = \mathbf{\frac{1}{60}}$$

3. $\frac{3}{5} \times \left(\frac{2}{4} - \frac{1}{3} \right) = \frac{3}{5} \times \left(\frac{(2 \times 3) - (1 \times 4)}{4 \times 3} \right) = \frac{3}{5} \times \left(\frac{6-4}{12} \right) = \frac{3}{5} \times \left(\frac{2}{12} \right) = \frac{3}{5} \times \frac{2}{12} = \frac{\overset{1}{\cancel{3}} \times 2}{5 \times \underset{4}{\cancel{12}}} = \frac{1 \times 2}{5 \times 4} = \frac{\overset{1}{\cancel{2}}}{\underset{10}{\cancel{20}}} = \mathbf{\frac{1}{10}}$

4. $\left(\frac{1}{5} \div \frac{4}{15} \right) \times \frac{2}{5} = \left(\frac{1}{5} \times \frac{15}{4} \right) \times \frac{2}{5} = \left(\frac{1 \times \overset{3}{\cancel{15}}}{\underset{1}{\cancel{5}} \times 4} \right) \times \frac{2}{5} = \left(\frac{1 \times 3}{1 \times 4} \right) \times \frac{2}{5} = \left(\frac{3}{4} \right) \times \frac{2}{5} = \frac{3}{4} \times \frac{2}{5} = \frac{3 \times \overset{1}{\cancel{2}}}{\underset{2}{\cancel{4}} \times 5} = \frac{3 \times 1}{2 \times 5} = \mathbf{\frac{3}{10}}$

5. $\left(\frac{4}{8} + 4 \right) \div \left(\frac{2}{8} - \frac{1}{3} \right) = \left(\frac{4}{8} + \frac{4}{1} \right) \div \left(\frac{(2 \times 3) - (1 \times 8)}{8 \times 3} \right) = \left(\frac{(4 \times 1) + (4 \times 8)}{8 \times 1} \right) \div \left(\frac{6-8}{24} \right) = \left(\frac{4 + 32}{8} \right) \div \left(\frac{-2}{24} \right) = \left(\frac{36}{8} \right) \div \frac{-2}{24}$

$$= \frac{\overset{9}{\cancel{36}}}{\underset{2}{\cancel{8}}} \div \frac{\overset{-1}{\cancel{-2}}}{\underset{12}{\cancel{24}}} = \frac{9}{2} \div \frac{-1}{12} = \frac{9}{2} \times \frac{12}{-1} = \frac{9 \times \overset{54}{\cancel{12}}}{2 \times \underset{-1}{\cancel{-1}}} \dots = \frac{\overset{54}{\cancel{108}}}{\underset{-1}{\cancel{-2}}} = \frac{54}{-1} = \mathbf{-54}$$

6. $\left(\frac{6}{5} - \frac{3}{4} \right) \times \left(\frac{4}{5} - \frac{1}{5} \right) = \left(\frac{(6 \times 4) - (3 \times 5)}{5 \times 4} \right) \times \left(\frac{4-1}{5} \right) = \left(\frac{24-15}{20} \right) \times \left(\frac{3}{5} \right) = \left(\frac{9}{20} \right) \times \left(\frac{3}{5} \right) = \frac{9}{20} \times \frac{3}{5} = \frac{9 \times 3}{20 \times 5} = \mathbf{\frac{27}{100}}$

7. $\left(\dfrac{5}{4}\times\dfrac{8}{1}\right)\div\left(\dfrac{4}{5}\div\dfrac{8}{15}\right) = \left(\dfrac{5\times\overset{2}{\cancel{8}}}{\underset{1}{\cancel{4}}\times 1}\right)\div\left(\dfrac{4}{5}\times\dfrac{15}{8}\right) = \left(\dfrac{5\times2}{1\times1}\right)\div\left(\dfrac{4\times15}{5\times8}\right) = \left(\dfrac{10}{1}\right)\div\left(\dfrac{\overset{1}{\cancel{4}}\times\overset{3}{\cancel{15}}}{\underset{1}{\cancel{5}}\times\underset{2}{\cancel{8}}}\right) = \dfrac{10}{1}\div\left(\dfrac{1\times3}{1\times2}\right) = \dfrac{10}{1}\div\left(\dfrac{3}{2}\right)$

$= \dfrac{10}{1}\div\dfrac{3}{2} = \dfrac{10}{1}\times\dfrac{2}{3} = \dfrac{10\times2}{1\times3} = \dfrac{20}{3} = \mathbf{6\dfrac{2}{3}}$

8. $\left(\dfrac{1}{6}\times\dfrac{12}{5}\times\dfrac{15}{20}\right)+\left(\dfrac{2}{3}-\dfrac{1}{5}\right) = \left(\dfrac{1\times\overset{2}{\cancel{12}}\times\overset{3}{\cancel{15}}}{\underset{1}{\cancel{6}}\times\underset{1}{\cancel{5}}\times20}\right)+\left(\dfrac{(2\times5)-(1\times3)}{3\times5}\right) = \left(\dfrac{1\times2\times3}{1\times1\times20}\right)+\left(\dfrac{10-3}{15}\right) = \left(\dfrac{6}{20}\right)+\left(\dfrac{7}{15}\right) = \dfrac{\overset{3}{\cancel{6}}}{\underset{10}{\cancel{20}}}+\dfrac{7}{15}$

$= \dfrac{3}{10}+\dfrac{7}{15} = \dfrac{(3\times15)+(7\times10)}{10\times15} = \dfrac{45+70}{150} = \dfrac{\overset{23}{\cancel{115}}}{\underset{30}{\cancel{150}}} = \dfrac{\mathbf{23}}{\mathbf{30}}$

9. $\left[\dfrac{2}{5}+\left(\dfrac{2}{4}+\dfrac{1}{2}\right)\right]\div\dfrac{1}{10} = \left[\dfrac{2}{5}+\left(\dfrac{(2\times2)+(1\times4)}{4\times2}\right)\right]\div\dfrac{1}{10} = \left[\dfrac{2}{5}+\left(\dfrac{4+4}{8}\right)\right]\div\dfrac{1}{10} = \left[\dfrac{2}{5}+\left(\dfrac{8}{8}\right)\right]\div\dfrac{1}{10} = \left[\dfrac{2}{5}+\dfrac{\overset{1}{\cancel{8}}}{\underset{1}{\cancel{8}}}\right]\div\dfrac{1}{10}$

$= \left[\dfrac{2}{5}+\dfrac{1}{1}\right]\div\dfrac{1}{10} = \left[\dfrac{(2\times1)+(1\times5)}{5\times1}\right]\div\dfrac{1}{10} = \left[\dfrac{2+5}{5}\right]\div\dfrac{1}{10} = \left[\dfrac{7}{5}\right]\div\dfrac{1}{10} = \dfrac{7}{5}\div\dfrac{1}{10} = \dfrac{7}{5}\times\dfrac{10}{1} = \dfrac{7\times\overset{2}{\cancel{10}}}{\underset{1}{\cancel{5}}\times1} = \dfrac{7\times2}{1\times1} = \dfrac{14}{1}$

$= \mathbf{14}$

10. $\left[\left(\dfrac{2}{5}-\dfrac{3}{5}\right)\times\left(12-\dfrac{1}{3}\right)\right]-\dfrac{3}{2} = \left[\left(\dfrac{2-3}{5}\right)\times\left(\dfrac{12}{1}-\dfrac{1}{3}\right)\right]-\dfrac{3}{2} = \left[\left(\dfrac{-1}{5}\right)\times\left(\dfrac{(12\times3)-(1\times1)}{1\times3}\right)\right]-\dfrac{3}{2} = \left[\dfrac{-1}{5}\times\left(\dfrac{36-1}{3}\right)\right]-\dfrac{3}{2}$

$= \left[\dfrac{-1}{5}\times\left(\dfrac{35}{3}\right)\right]-\dfrac{3}{2} = \left[\dfrac{-1}{5}\times\dfrac{35}{3}\right]-\dfrac{3}{2} = \left[\dfrac{-1\times\overset{7}{\cancel{35}}}{\underset{1}{\cancel{5}}\times3}\right]-\dfrac{3}{2} = \left[\dfrac{-1\times7}{1\times3}\right]-\dfrac{3}{2} = \left[\dfrac{-7}{3}\right]-\dfrac{3}{2} = \dfrac{-7}{3}-\dfrac{3}{2} = \dfrac{(-7\times2)-(3\times3)}{3\times2}$

$= \dfrac{-14-9}{6} = \dfrac{-23}{6} = -\left(\mathbf{3\dfrac{5}{6}}\right)$

Chapter 4 Solutions:

Section 4.1 Solutions:

1. $\dfrac{0.5}{1.5}+\dfrac{0.3}{1.5}=\dfrac{0.5+0.3}{1.5}=\dfrac{0.8}{1.5}=\dfrac{\frac{8}{10}}{\frac{15}{10}}=\dfrac{8\times10}{10\times15}=\dfrac{\overset{8}{\cancel{80}}}{\underset{15}{\cancel{150}}}=\mathbf{\dfrac{8}{15}}$

2. $\dfrac{0.02}{1.8}+\dfrac{0.4}{0.28}=\dfrac{\frac{2}{100}}{\frac{18}{10}}+\dfrac{\frac{4}{10}}{\frac{28}{100}}=\dfrac{2\times10}{100\times18}+\dfrac{4\times100}{10\times28}=\dfrac{\overset{1}{\cancel{20}}}{\underset{90}{\cancel{1800}}}+\dfrac{\overset{10}{\cancel{400}}}{\underset{7}{\cancel{280}}}=\dfrac{1}{90}+\dfrac{10}{7}=\dfrac{(1\times7)+(10\times90)}{90\times7}=\dfrac{7+900}{630}=\dfrac{907}{630}$

$=\mathbf{1\dfrac{277}{630}}$

3. $\dfrac{0.6}{0.5}+\dfrac{0.08}{0.3}=\dfrac{\frac{6}{10}}{\frac{5}{10}}+\dfrac{\frac{8}{100}}{\frac{3}{10}}=\dfrac{6\times10}{10\times5}+\dfrac{8\times10}{100\times3}=\dfrac{\overset{6}{\cancel{60}}}{\underset{5}{\cancel{50}}}+\dfrac{\overset{4}{\cancel{80}}}{\underset{15}{\cancel{300}}}=\dfrac{6}{5}+\dfrac{4}{15}=\dfrac{(6\times15)+(4\times5)}{5\times15}=\dfrac{90+20}{75}=\dfrac{\overset{22}{\cancel{110}}}{\underset{15}{\cancel{75}}}=\dfrac{22}{15}$

$=\mathbf{1\dfrac{7}{15}}$

4. $\dfrac{3.3}{0.5}+\dfrac{0.15}{0.5}+\dfrac{0.1}{0.5}=\dfrac{3.3+0.15+0.1}{0.5}=\dfrac{3.55}{0.5}=\dfrac{\frac{355}{100}}{\frac{5}{10}}=\dfrac{355\times10}{100\times5}=\dfrac{\overset{71}{\cancel{3550}}}{\underset{10}{\cancel{500}}}=\dfrac{71}{10}=\mathbf{7\dfrac{1}{10}}$

5. $\dfrac{2.2}{0.2}+\dfrac{0.15}{0.5}+\dfrac{1.4}{0.4}=\left(\dfrac{2.2}{0.2}+\dfrac{0.15}{0.5}\right)+\dfrac{1.4}{0.4}=\left(\dfrac{\frac{22}{10}}{\frac{2}{10}}+\dfrac{\frac{15}{100}}{\frac{5}{10}}\right)+\dfrac{\frac{14}{10}}{\frac{4}{10}}=\left(\dfrac{22\times10}{10\times2}+\dfrac{15\times10}{100\times5}\right)+\dfrac{14\times10}{10\times4}=\left(\dfrac{\overset{11}{\cancel{220}}}{\underset{1}{\cancel{20}}}+\dfrac{\overset{3}{\cancel{150}}}{\underset{10}{\cancel{500}}}\right)+\dfrac{\overset{7}{\cancel{140}}}{\underset{2}{\cancel{40}}}$

$=\left(\dfrac{11}{1}+\dfrac{3}{10}\right)+\dfrac{7}{2}=\left(\dfrac{(11\times10)+(3\times1)}{1\times10}\right)+\dfrac{7}{2}=\left(\dfrac{110+3}{10}\right)+\dfrac{7}{2}=\left(\dfrac{113}{10}\right)+\dfrac{7}{2}=\dfrac{113}{10}+\dfrac{7}{2}=\dfrac{(113\times2)+(7\times10)}{10\times2}$

$=\dfrac{226+70}{20}=\dfrac{\overset{74}{\cancel{296}}}{\underset{5}{\cancel{20}}}=\dfrac{74}{5}=\mathbf{14\dfrac{4}{5}}$

6. $\dfrac{1.2}{0.2}+\dfrac{0.5}{0.01}+\dfrac{1.5}{0.3}=\left(\dfrac{1.2}{0.2}+\dfrac{0.5}{0.01}\right)+\dfrac{1.5}{0.3}=\left(\dfrac{\frac{12}{10}}{\frac{2}{10}}+\dfrac{\frac{5}{10}}{\frac{1}{100}}\right)+\dfrac{\frac{15}{10}}{\frac{3}{10}}=\left(\dfrac{12\times10}{10\times2}+\dfrac{5\times100}{10\times1}\right)+\dfrac{15\times10}{10\times3}=\left(\dfrac{\overset{6}{\cancel{120}}}{\underset{1}{\cancel{20}}}+\dfrac{\overset{50}{\cancel{500}}}{\underset{1}{\cancel{10}}}\right)+\dfrac{\overset{5}{\cancel{150}}}{\underset{1}{\cancel{30}}}$

$=\left(\dfrac{6}{1}+\dfrac{50}{1}\right)+\dfrac{5}{1}=\left(\dfrac{6+50}{1}\right)+\dfrac{5}{1}=\left(\dfrac{56}{1}\right)+\dfrac{5}{1}=\dfrac{56}{1}+\dfrac{5}{1}=\dfrac{56+5}{1}=\dfrac{61}{1}=\mathbf{61}$

7. $0.18+\left(\dfrac{0.4}{0.002}+\dfrac{1.4}{0.2}\right)=\dfrac{18}{100}+\left(\dfrac{\frac{4}{10}}{\frac{2}{1000}}+\dfrac{\frac{14}{10}}{\frac{2}{10}}\right)=\dfrac{18}{100}+\left(\dfrac{4\times1000}{10\times2}+\dfrac{14\times10}{10\times2}\right)=\dfrac{\overset{9}{\cancel{18}}}{\underset{50}{\cancel{100}}}+\left(\dfrac{\overset{200}{\cancel{4000}}}{\underset{1}{\cancel{20}}}+\dfrac{\overset{7}{\cancel{140}}}{\underset{1}{\cancel{20}}}\right)=\dfrac{9}{50}+\left(\dfrac{200}{1}+\dfrac{7}{1}\right)$

$=\dfrac{9}{50}+\left(\dfrac{200+7}{1}\right)=\dfrac{9}{50}+\left(\dfrac{207}{1}\right)=\dfrac{9}{50}+\dfrac{207}{1}=\dfrac{(9\times1)+(207\times50)}{50\times1}=\dfrac{9+10350}{50}=\dfrac{10359}{50}=\mathbf{207\dfrac{9}{50}}$

8. $\left(\dfrac{0.2}{0.4}+\dfrac{0.1}{0.8}\right)+0.15=\left(\dfrac{\frac{2}{10}}{\frac{4}{10}}+\dfrac{\frac{1}{10}}{\frac{8}{10}}\right)+\dfrac{15}{100}=\left(\dfrac{2\times10}{10\times4}+\dfrac{1\times10}{10\times8}\right)+\dfrac{15}{100}=\left(\dfrac{\overset{1}{\cancel{20}}}{\underset{2}{\cancel{40}}}+\dfrac{\overset{1}{\cancel{10}}}{\underset{8}{\cancel{80}}}\right)+\dfrac{\overset{3}{\cancel{15}}}{\underset{20}{\cancel{100}}}=\left(\dfrac{1}{2}+\dfrac{1}{8}\right)+\dfrac{3}{20}$

$$= \left(\frac{(1 \times 8) + (1 \times 2)}{2 \times 8} \right) + \frac{3}{20} = \left(\frac{8+2}{16} \right) + \frac{3}{20} = \left(\frac{10}{16} \right) + \frac{3}{20} = \frac{\overset{5}{\cancel{10}}}{\underset{8}{\cancel{16}}} + \frac{3}{20} = \frac{5}{8} + \frac{3}{20} = \frac{(5 \times 20) + (3 \times 8)}{8 \times 20} = \frac{100 + 24}{160} = \frac{\overset{31}{\cancel{124}}}{\underset{40}{\cancel{160}}}$$

$$= \frac{31}{40}$$

9. $$\left(\frac{0.08}{0.2} + \frac{0}{0.1} \right) + \left(\frac{0.05}{0.15} + \frac{0.5}{1.5} \right) = \left(\frac{\frac{8}{100}}{\frac{2}{10}} + \frac{\frac{0}{1}}{\frac{1}{10}} \right) + \left(\frac{\frac{5}{100}}{\frac{15}{100}} + \frac{\frac{5}{10}}{\frac{15}{10}} \right) = \left(\frac{8 \times 10}{100 \times 2} + \frac{0 \times 10}{1 \times 1} \right) + \left(\frac{5 \times 100}{100 \times 15} + \frac{5 \times 10}{10 \times 15} \right)$$

$$= \left(\frac{\overset{2}{\cancel{80}}}{\underset{5}{\cancel{200}}} + \frac{0}{1} \right) + \left(\frac{\overset{1}{\cancel{500}}}{\underset{3}{\cancel{1500}}} + \frac{\overset{1}{\cancel{50}}}{\underset{3}{\cancel{150}}} \right) = \left(\frac{2}{5} + \frac{0}{1} \right) + \left(\frac{1}{3} + \frac{1}{3} \right) = \left(\frac{2}{5} + 0 \right) + \left(\frac{1+1}{3} \right) = \left(\frac{2}{5} \right) + \left(\frac{2}{3} \right) = \frac{2}{5} + \frac{2}{3} = \frac{(2 \times 3) + (2 \times 5)}{5 \times 3}$$

$$= \frac{6+10}{15} = \frac{16}{15} = 1\frac{1}{15}$$

10. $$\left(\frac{4.9}{0.07} + 3.6 \right) + \left(\frac{0.5}{0.05} + \frac{0.15}{0.5} \right) = \left(\frac{\frac{49}{10}}{\frac{7}{100}} + \frac{36}{10} \right) + \left(\frac{\frac{5}{10}}{\frac{5}{100}} + \frac{\frac{15}{100}}{\frac{5}{10}} \right) = \left(\frac{49 \times 100}{10 \times 7} + \frac{36}{10} \right) + \left(\frac{5 \times 100}{10 \times 5} + \frac{15 \times 10}{100 \times 5} \right)$$

$$= \left(\frac{\overset{70}{\cancel{4900}}}{\underset{1}{\cancel{70}}} + \frac{\overset{18}{\cancel{36}}}{\underset{5}{\cancel{10}}} \right) + \left(\frac{\overset{10}{\cancel{500}}}{\underset{1}{\cancel{50}}} + \frac{\overset{3}{\cancel{150}}}{\underset{10}{\cancel{500}}} \right) = \left(\frac{70}{1} + \frac{18}{5} \right) + \left(\frac{10}{1} + \frac{3}{10} \right) = \left(\frac{(70 \times 5) + (18 \times 1)}{1 \times 5} \right) + \left(\frac{(10 \times 10) + (3 \times 1)}{1 \times 10} \right)$$

$$= \left(\frac{350 + 18}{5} \right) + \left(\frac{100 + 3}{10} \right) = \left(\frac{368}{5} \right) + \left(\frac{103}{10} \right) = \frac{368}{5} + \frac{103}{10} = \frac{(368 \times 10) + (103 \times 5)}{5 \times 10} = \frac{3680 + 515}{50} = \frac{\overset{839}{\cancel{4195}}}{\underset{10}{\cancel{50}}} = \frac{839}{10}$$

$$= 83\frac{9}{10}$$

Section 4.2 Solutions:

1. $$\frac{3.6}{0.04} - \frac{0.8}{0.04} = \frac{3.6 - 0.8}{0.04} = \frac{2.8}{0.04} = \frac{\frac{28}{10}}{\frac{4}{100}} = \frac{28 \times 100}{10 \times 4} = \frac{\overset{70}{\cancel{2800}}}{\underset{1}{\cancel{40}}} = \frac{70}{1} = 70$$

2. $$\frac{6.4}{0.04} - \frac{1.8}{0.01} = \frac{\frac{64}{10}}{\frac{4}{100}} - \frac{\frac{18}{10}}{\frac{1}{100}} = \frac{64 \times 100}{10 \times 4} - \frac{18 \times 100}{10 \times 1} = \frac{\overset{160}{\cancel{6400}}}{\underset{1}{\cancel{40}}} - \frac{\overset{180}{\cancel{1800}}}{\underset{1}{\cancel{10}}} = \frac{160}{1} - \frac{180}{1} = \frac{-20}{1} = -20$$

3. $$\frac{3.6}{0.02} - \frac{1.8}{0.2} = \frac{\frac{36}{10}}{\frac{2}{100}} - \frac{\frac{18}{10}}{\frac{2}{10}} = \frac{36 \times 100}{10 \times 2} - \frac{18 \times 10}{10 \times 2} = \frac{3600}{20} - \frac{180}{20} = \frac{3600 - 180}{20} = \frac{\overset{171}{\cancel{3420}}}{\underset{1}{\cancel{20}}} = \frac{171}{1} = 171$$

4. $$\frac{2.4}{0.12} - \frac{0.3}{0.12} - \frac{1.5}{0.12} = \frac{2.4 - 0.3 - 1.5}{0.12} = \frac{0.6}{0.12} = \frac{\frac{6}{10}}{\frac{12}{100}} = \frac{6 \times 100}{10 \times 12} = \frac{\overset{5}{\cancel{600}}}{\underset{1}{\cancel{120}}} = \frac{5}{1} = 5$$

5. $$\left(\frac{12.2}{0.04} - \frac{1.8}{0.2} \right) - \frac{4.9}{0.7} = \left(\frac{\frac{122}{10}}{\frac{4}{100}} - \frac{\frac{18}{10}}{\frac{2}{10}} \right) - \frac{\frac{49}{10}}{\frac{7}{10}} = \left(\frac{122 \times 100}{10 \times 4} - \frac{18 \times 10}{10 \times 2} \right) - \frac{49 \times 10}{10 \times 7} = \left(\frac{\overset{305}{\cancel{12200}}}{\underset{1}{\cancel{40}}} - \frac{\overset{9}{\cancel{180}}}{\underset{1}{\cancel{20}}} \right) - \frac{\overset{7}{\cancel{490}}}{\underset{1}{\cancel{70}}} = \left(\frac{305}{1} - \frac{9}{1} \right) - \frac{7}{1}$$

$$= \left(\frac{305-9}{1}\right) - \frac{7}{1} = \left(\frac{296}{1}\right) - \frac{7}{1} = \frac{296}{1} - \frac{7}{1} = \frac{296-7}{1} = \frac{289}{1} = \mathbf{289}$$

6. $\displaystyle 8.8 + \left(-\frac{0.9}{0.03} - \frac{0.4}{0.02}\right) = \frac{88}{10} + \left(-\frac{\frac{9}{10}}{\frac{3}{100}} - \frac{\frac{4}{10}}{\frac{2}{100}}\right) = \frac{88}{10} + \left(-\frac{9 \times 100}{10 \times 3} - \frac{4 \times 100}{10 \times 2}\right) = \frac{\overset{44}{\cancel{88}}}{\underset{5}{\cancel{10}}} + \left(-\frac{\overset{30}{\cancel{900}}}{\underset{1}{\cancel{30}}} - \frac{\overset{20}{\cancel{400}}}{\underset{1}{\cancel{20}}}\right)$

$$= \frac{44}{5} + \left(-\frac{30}{1} - \frac{20}{1}\right) = \frac{44}{5} + \left(\frac{-30-20}{1}\right) = \frac{44}{5} + \left(\frac{-50}{1}\right) = \frac{44}{5} + \frac{-50}{1} = \frac{44}{5} - \frac{50}{1} = \frac{(44 \times 1) - (50 \times 5)}{5 \times 1} = \frac{44-250}{5}$$

$$= \frac{-206}{5} = -\left(\mathbf{41\frac{1}{5}}\right)$$

7. $\displaystyle \frac{2.2}{0.4} - \left(\frac{0.9}{0.03} - \frac{1.5}{0.5}\right) = \frac{\frac{22}{10}}{\frac{4}{10}} - \left(\frac{\frac{9}{10}}{\frac{3}{100}} - \frac{\frac{15}{10}}{\frac{5}{10}}\right) = \frac{22 \times 10}{10 \times 4} - \left(\frac{9 \times 100}{10 \times 3} - \frac{15 \times 10}{10 \times 5}\right) = \frac{\overset{11}{\cancel{220}}}{\underset{2}{\cancel{40}}} - \left(\frac{\overset{30}{\cancel{900}}}{\underset{1}{\cancel{30}}} - \frac{\overset{3}{\cancel{150}}}{\underset{1}{\cancel{50}}}\right) = \frac{11}{2} - \left(\frac{30}{1} - \frac{3}{1}\right)$

$$= \frac{11}{2} - \left(\frac{30-3}{1}\right) = \frac{11}{2} - \left(\frac{27}{1}\right) = \frac{11}{2} - \frac{27}{1} = \frac{(11 \times 1) - (27 \times 2)}{2 \times 1} = \frac{11-54}{2} = \frac{-43}{2} = -\left(\mathbf{21\frac{1}{2}}\right)$$

8. $\displaystyle \left(9.8 - \frac{1.4}{0.2}\right) - \frac{0.1}{0.2} = \left(\frac{98}{10} - \frac{\frac{14}{10}}{\frac{2}{10}}\right) - \frac{\frac{1}{10}}{\frac{2}{10}} = \left(\frac{98}{10} - \frac{14 \times 10}{10 \times 2}\right) - \frac{1 \times 10}{10 \times 2} = \left(\frac{\overset{49}{\cancel{98}}}{\underset{5}{\cancel{10}}} - \frac{\overset{7}{\cancel{140}}}{\underset{1}{\cancel{20}}}\right) - \frac{\overset{1}{\cancel{10}}}{\underset{2}{\cancel{20}}} = \left(\frac{49}{5} - \frac{7}{1}\right) - \frac{1}{2}$

$$= \left(\frac{(49 \times 1) - (7 \times 5)}{5 \times 1}\right) - \frac{1}{2} = \left(\frac{49-35}{5}\right) - \frac{1}{2} = \left(\frac{14}{5}\right) - \frac{1}{2} = \frac{14}{5} - \frac{1}{2} = \frac{(14 \times 2) - (1 \times 5)}{5 \times 2} = \frac{28-5}{10} = \frac{23}{10} = \mathbf{2\frac{3}{10}}$$

9. $\displaystyle \frac{3.3}{0.03} - \frac{1.1}{0.1} - \frac{0}{0.5} = \left(\frac{3.3}{0.03} - \frac{1.1}{0.1}\right) - \frac{0}{0.5} = \left(\frac{\frac{33}{10}}{\frac{3}{100}} - \frac{\frac{11}{10}}{\frac{1}{10}}\right) - \frac{0}{\frac{5}{10}} = \left(\frac{33 \times 100}{10 \times 3} - \frac{11 \times 10}{10 \times 1}\right) - \frac{0 \times 10}{1 \times 5} = \left(\frac{\overset{110}{\cancel{3300}}}{\underset{1}{\cancel{30}}} - \frac{\overset{11}{\cancel{110}}}{\underset{1}{\cancel{10}}}\right) - \frac{0}{5}$

$$= \left(\frac{110}{1} - \frac{11}{1}\right) - 0 = \left(\frac{110-11}{1}\right) = \left(\frac{99}{1}\right) = \frac{99}{1} = \mathbf{99}$$

10. $\displaystyle \left[\left(\frac{3.6}{0.04} - \frac{0.3}{1.2}\right) - \frac{1.2}{0.2}\right] - 0.5 = \left[\left(\frac{\frac{36}{10}}{\frac{4}{100}} - \frac{\frac{3}{10}}{\frac{12}{10}}\right) - \frac{\frac{12}{10}}{\frac{2}{10}}\right] - \frac{5}{10} = \left[\left(\frac{36 \times 100}{10 \times 4} - \frac{3 \times 10}{10 \times 12}\right) - \frac{12 \times 10}{10 \times 2}\right] - \frac{5}{10}$

$$= \left[\left(\frac{\overset{90}{\cancel{3600}}}{\underset{1}{\cancel{40}}} - \frac{\overset{1}{\cancel{30}}}{\underset{4}{\cancel{120}}}\right) - \frac{\overset{6}{\cancel{120}}}{\underset{1}{\cancel{20}}}\right] - \frac{\overset{1}{\cancel{5}}}{\underset{2}{\cancel{10}}} = \left[\left(\frac{90}{1} - \frac{1}{4}\right) - \frac{6}{1}\right] - \frac{1}{2} = \left[\left(\frac{(90 \times 4) - (1 \times 1)}{1 \times 4}\right) - \frac{6}{1}\right] - \frac{1}{2} = \left[\left(\frac{360-1}{4}\right) - \frac{6}{1}\right] - \frac{1}{2}$$

$$= \left[\left(\frac{359}{4}\right) - \frac{6}{1}\right] - \frac{1}{2} = \left[\frac{359}{4} - \frac{6}{1}\right] - \frac{1}{2} = \left[\frac{(359 \times 1) - (6 \times 4)}{4 \times 1}\right] - \frac{1}{2} = \left[\frac{359-24}{4}\right] - \frac{1}{2} = \left[\frac{335}{4}\right] - \frac{1}{2} = \frac{335}{4} - \frac{1}{2}$$

$$= \frac{(335 \times 2) - (1 \times 4)}{4 \times 2} = \frac{670-4}{8} = \frac{\overset{333}{\cancel{666}}}{\underset{4}{\cancel{8}}} = \frac{333}{4} = \mathbf{83\frac{1}{4}}$$

Section 4.3 Solutions:

1. $\dfrac{3.5}{0.07} \times \dfrac{0.7}{0.05} = \dfrac{\frac{35}{10}}{\frac{7}{100}} \times \dfrac{\frac{7}{10}}{\frac{5}{100}} = \dfrac{35 \times 100}{10 \times 7} \times \dfrac{7 \times 100}{10 \times 5} = \dfrac{3500}{70} \times \dfrac{700}{50} = \dfrac{\overset{70}{\cancel{3500}} \times \overset{10}{\cancel{700}}}{\underset{1}{\cancel{70}} \times \underset{1}{\cancel{50}}} = \dfrac{70 \times 10}{1 \times 1} = \dfrac{700}{1} = \mathbf{700}$

2. $\dfrac{1.5}{0.05} \times \dfrac{0.1}{0.03} = \dfrac{\frac{15}{10}}{\frac{5}{100}} \times \dfrac{\frac{1}{10}}{\frac{3}{100}} = \dfrac{15 \times 100}{10 \times 5} \times \dfrac{1 \times 100}{10 \times 3} = \dfrac{1500}{50} \times \dfrac{100}{30} = \dfrac{\overset{30}{\cancel{1500}} \times \overset{10}{\cancel{100}}}{\underset{1}{\cancel{50}} \times \underset{3}{\cancel{30}}} = \dfrac{30 \times 10}{1 \times 3} = \dfrac{\overset{100}{\cancel{300}}}{\underset{1}{\cancel{3}}} = \dfrac{100}{1} = \mathbf{100}$

3. $\left(\dfrac{1.8}{0.02} \times \dfrac{0.4}{0.04} \right) \times 0.07 = \left(\dfrac{\frac{18}{10}}{\frac{2}{100}} \times \dfrac{\frac{4}{10}}{\frac{4}{100}} \right) \times \dfrac{7}{100} = \left(\dfrac{18 \times 100}{10 \times 2} \times \dfrac{4 \times 100}{10 \times 4} \right) \times \dfrac{7}{100} = \left(\dfrac{1800}{20} \times \dfrac{400}{40} \right) \times \dfrac{7}{100}$

$= \left(\dfrac{\overset{90}{\cancel{1800}} \times \overset{10}{\cancel{400}}}{\underset{1}{\cancel{20}} \times \underset{1}{\cancel{40}}} \right) \times \dfrac{7}{100} = \left(\dfrac{90 \times 10}{1 \times 1} \right) \times \dfrac{7}{100} = \left(\dfrac{900}{1} \right) \times \dfrac{7}{100} = \dfrac{900}{1} \times \dfrac{7}{100} = \dfrac{\overset{9}{\cancel{900}} \times 7}{1 \times \underset{1}{\cancel{100}}} = \dfrac{9 \times 7}{1 \times 1} = \dfrac{63}{1} = \mathbf{63}$

4. $\dfrac{1.5}{0.05} \times \dfrac{1.8}{0.2} \times \dfrac{0}{1.8} = \mathbf{0}$

5. $\dfrac{1.1}{0.2} \times \dfrac{0.44}{0.4} \times 3.8 = \dfrac{\frac{11}{10}}{\frac{2}{10}} \times \dfrac{\frac{44}{100}}{\frac{4}{10}} \times \dfrac{38}{10} = \dfrac{11 \times 10}{10 \times 2} \times \dfrac{44 \times 10}{100 \times 4} \times \dfrac{38}{10} = \dfrac{110}{20} \times \dfrac{440}{400} \times \dfrac{38}{10} = \dfrac{\overset{11}{\cancel{110}} \times \overset{11}{\cancel{440}} \times \overset{19}{\cancel{38}}}{\underset{2}{\cancel{20}} \times \underset{10}{\cancel{400}} \times \underset{5}{\cancel{10}}} = \dfrac{11 \times 11 \times 19}{2 \times 10 \times 5}$

$= \dfrac{2299}{100} = \mathbf{22\dfrac{99}{100}}$

6. $\dfrac{7.5}{1.2} \times \dfrac{0.02}{0.8} \times \dfrac{0.12}{0.75} = \dfrac{\frac{75}{10}}{\frac{12}{10}} \times \dfrac{\frac{2}{100}}{\frac{8}{10}} \times \dfrac{\frac{12}{100}}{\frac{75}{100}} = \dfrac{75 \times 10}{10 \times 12} \times \dfrac{2 \times 10}{100 \times 8} \times \dfrac{12 \times 100}{100 \times 75} = \dfrac{750}{120} \times \dfrac{20}{800} \times \dfrac{1200}{7500} = \dfrac{\overset{1}{\cancel{750}} \times \overset{1}{\cancel{20}} \times \overset{10}{\cancel{1200}}}{\underset{1}{\cancel{120}} \times \underset{40}{\cancel{800}} \times \underset{10}{\cancel{7500}}}$

$= \dfrac{1 \times 1 \times 10}{1 \times 40 \times 10} = \dfrac{\overset{1}{\cancel{10}}}{\underset{40}{\cancel{400}}} = \mathbf{\dfrac{1}{40}}$

7. $\left(\dfrac{3.9}{0.03} \times \dfrac{1.5}{0.05} \right) \times \dfrac{0.08}{0.39} = \left(\dfrac{\frac{39}{10}}{\frac{3}{100}} \times \dfrac{\frac{15}{10}}{\frac{5}{100}} \right) \times \dfrac{\frac{8}{100}}{\frac{39}{100}} = \left(\dfrac{39 \times 100}{10 \times 3} \times \dfrac{15 \times 100}{10 \times 5} \right) \times \dfrac{8 \times 100}{100 \times 39} = \left(\dfrac{3900}{30} \times \dfrac{1500}{50} \right) \times \dfrac{800}{3900}$

$= \left(\dfrac{\overset{130}{\cancel{3900}} \times \overset{30}{\cancel{1500}}}{\underset{1}{\cancel{30}} \times \underset{1}{\cancel{50}}} \right) \times \dfrac{\overset{8}{\cancel{800}}}{\underset{39}{\cancel{3900}}} = \left(\dfrac{130 \times 30}{1 \times 1} \right) \times \dfrac{8}{39} = \left(\dfrac{3900}{1} \right) \times \dfrac{8}{39} = \dfrac{3900}{1} \times \dfrac{8}{39} = \dfrac{\overset{100}{\cancel{3900}} \times 8}{1 \times \underset{1}{\cancel{39}}} = \dfrac{100 \times 8}{1 \times 1} = \dfrac{800}{1} = \mathbf{800}$

8. $1.45 \times \dfrac{7.5}{0.001} \times \dfrac{0.5}{0.45} = \dfrac{145}{100} \times \dfrac{\frac{75}{10}}{\frac{1}{1000}} \times \dfrac{\frac{5}{10}}{\frac{45}{100}} = \dfrac{145}{100} \times \dfrac{75 \times 1000}{10 \times 1} \times \dfrac{5 \times 100}{10 \times 45} = \dfrac{145}{100} \times \dfrac{75000}{10} \times \dfrac{500}{450} = \dfrac{\overset{29}{\cancel{145}} \times \overset{1500}{\cancel{75000}} \times \overset{5}{\cancel{500}}}{\underset{1}{\cancel{100}} \times \underset{2}{\cancel{10}} \times \underset{9}{\cancel{450}}}$

$= \dfrac{29 \times 1500 \times 5}{1 \times 2 \times 9} = \dfrac{\overset{36250}{\cancel{217500}}}{\underset{3}{\cancel{18}}} = \dfrac{36250}{3} = \mathbf{12083\dfrac{1}{3}}$

9. $\left(\dfrac{1.8}{0.04} \times 0.2\right) \times \left(\dfrac{0.4}{0.9} \times 0.12\right) = \left(\dfrac{\frac{18}{10}}{\frac{4}{100}} \times \dfrac{2}{10}\right) \times \left(\dfrac{\frac{4}{10}}{\frac{9}{10}} \times \dfrac{12}{100}\right) = \left(\dfrac{18\times100}{10\times4} \times \dfrac{2}{10}\right) \times \left(\dfrac{4\times10}{10\times9} \times \dfrac{12}{100}\right)$

$= \left(\dfrac{1800}{40} \times \dfrac{2}{10}\right) \times \left(\dfrac{40}{90} \times \dfrac{12}{100}\right) = \left(\dfrac{\overset{45}{\cancel{1800}}\times\overset{1}{\cancel{2}}}{\underset{1}{\cancel{40}}\times\underset{5}{\cancel{10}}}\right) \times \left(\dfrac{\overset{4}{\cancel{40}}\times\overset{3}{\cancel{12}}}{\underset{9}{\cancel{90}}\times\underset{25}{\cancel{100}}}\right) = \left(\dfrac{45\times1}{1\times5}\right) \times \left(\dfrac{4\times3}{9\times25}\right) = \left(\dfrac{45}{5}\right) \times \left(\dfrac{12}{225}\right) = \dfrac{\overset{9}{\cancel{45}}}{\underset{1}{\cancel{5}}} \times \dfrac{\overset{4}{\cancel{12}}}{\underset{75}{\cancel{225}}}$

$= \dfrac{9}{1} \times \dfrac{4}{75} = \dfrac{9\times4}{1\times75} = \dfrac{\overset{12}{\cancel{36}}}{\underset{25}{\cancel{75}}} = \dfrac{12}{25}$

10. $\left[8.4 \times \left(\dfrac{5.5}{0.5} \times \dfrac{0.01}{0.1}\right)\right] \times 0.2 = \left[\dfrac{84}{10} \times \left(\dfrac{\frac{55}{10}}{\frac{5}{10}} \times \dfrac{\frac{1}{100}}{\frac{1}{10}}\right)\right] \times \dfrac{2}{10} = \left[\dfrac{84}{10} \times \left(\dfrac{55\times10}{10\times5} \times \dfrac{1\times10}{100\times1}\right)\right] \times \dfrac{2}{10} = \left[\dfrac{84}{10} \times \left(\dfrac{550}{50} \times \dfrac{10}{100}\right)\right] \times \dfrac{2}{10}$

$= \left[\dfrac{\overset{42}{\cancel{84}}}{\underset{5}{\cancel{10}}} \times \left(\dfrac{\overset{11}{\cancel{550}}\times\overset{1}{\cancel{10}}}{\underset{1}{\cancel{50}}\times\underset{10}{\cancel{100}}}\right)\right] \times \dfrac{\overset{1}{\cancel{2}}}{\underset{5}{\cancel{10}}} = \left[\dfrac{42}{5} \times \left(\dfrac{11\times1}{1\times10}\right)\right] \times \dfrac{1}{5} = \left[\dfrac{42}{5} \times \left(\dfrac{11}{10}\right)\right] \times \dfrac{1}{5} = \left[\dfrac{42}{5} \times \dfrac{11}{10}\right] \times \dfrac{1}{5} = \left[\dfrac{\overset{21}{\cancel{42}}\times11}{5\times\underset{5}{\cancel{10}}}\right] \times \dfrac{1}{5} = \left[\dfrac{21\times11}{5\times5}\right] \times \dfrac{1}{5}$

$= \left[\dfrac{231}{25}\right] \times \dfrac{1}{5} = \dfrac{231}{25} \times \dfrac{1}{5} = \dfrac{231\times1}{25\times5} = \dfrac{231}{125} = 1\dfrac{106}{125}$

Section 4.4 Solutions:

1. $\dfrac{0.8}{0.01} \div \dfrac{0.04}{0.2} = \dfrac{\frac{8}{10}}{\frac{1}{100}} \div \dfrac{\frac{4}{100}}{\frac{2}{10}} = \dfrac{8\times100}{10\times1} \div \dfrac{4\times10}{100\times2} = \dfrac{\overset{80}{\cancel{800}}}{\underset{1}{\cancel{10}}} \div \dfrac{\overset{1}{\cancel{40}}}{\underset{5}{\cancel{200}}} = \dfrac{80}{1} \div \dfrac{1}{5} = \dfrac{80}{1} \times \dfrac{5}{1} = \dfrac{80\times5}{1\times1} = \dfrac{400}{1} = 400$

2. $\dfrac{0.3}{0.08} \div \dfrac{1.2}{0.16} = \dfrac{\frac{3}{10}}{\frac{8}{100}} \div \dfrac{\frac{12}{10}}{\frac{16}{100}} = \dfrac{3\times100}{10\times8} \div \dfrac{12\times100}{10\times16} = \dfrac{\overset{15}{\cancel{300}}}{\underset{4}{\cancel{80}}} \div \dfrac{\overset{15}{\cancel{1200}}}{\underset{2}{\cancel{160}}} = \dfrac{15}{4} \div \dfrac{15}{2} = \dfrac{15}{4} \times \dfrac{2}{15} = \dfrac{\overset{1}{\cancel{15}}\times\overset{1}{\cancel{2}}}{\underset{2}{\cancel{4}}\times\underset{1}{\cancel{15}}} = \dfrac{1\times1}{2\times1} = \dfrac{1}{2}$

3. $\dfrac{0.04}{0.05} \div 0.2 = \dfrac{\frac{4}{100}}{\frac{5}{100}} \div \dfrac{2}{10} = \dfrac{4\times100}{100\times5} \div \dfrac{2}{10} = \dfrac{\overset{4}{\cancel{400}}}{\underset{5}{\cancel{500}}} \div \dfrac{\overset{1}{\cancel{2}}}{\underset{5}{\cancel{10}}} = \dfrac{4}{5} \div \dfrac{1}{5} = \dfrac{4}{5} \times \dfrac{5}{1} = \dfrac{4\times\overset{1}{\cancel{5}}}{\underset{1}{\cancel{5}}\times1} = \dfrac{4\times1}{1\times1} = \dfrac{4}{1} = 4$

4. $\left(\dfrac{0.9}{0.08} \div \dfrac{1.8}{0.16}\right) \div \dfrac{0.4}{0.02} = \left(\dfrac{\frac{9}{10}}{\frac{8}{100}} \div \dfrac{\frac{18}{10}}{\frac{16}{100}}\right) \div \dfrac{\frac{4}{10}}{\frac{2}{100}} = \left(\dfrac{9\times100}{10\times8} \div \dfrac{18\times100}{10\times16}\right) \div \dfrac{4\times100}{10\times2} = \left(\dfrac{\overset{45}{\cancel{900}}}{\underset{4}{\cancel{80}}} \div \dfrac{\overset{45}{\cancel{1800}}}{\underset{4}{\cancel{160}}}\right) \div \dfrac{\overset{20}{\cancel{400}}}{\underset{1}{\cancel{20}}}$

$= \left(\dfrac{45}{4} \div \dfrac{45}{4}\right) \div \dfrac{20}{1} = \left(\dfrac{45}{4} \times \dfrac{4}{45}\right) \div \dfrac{20}{1} = \left(\dfrac{\overset{1}{\cancel{45}}\times\overset{1}{\cancel{4}}}{\underset{1}{\cancel{4}}\times\underset{1}{\cancel{45}}}\right) \div \dfrac{20}{1} = \left(\dfrac{1\times1}{1\times1}\right) \div \dfrac{20}{1} = \left(\dfrac{1}{1}\right) \div \dfrac{20}{1} = \dfrac{1}{1} \div \dfrac{20}{1} = \dfrac{1}{1} \times \dfrac{1}{20} = \dfrac{1\times1}{1\times20}$

$= \dfrac{1}{20}$

5. $0.6 \div \left(\dfrac{1.2}{0.64} \div \dfrac{0.04}{0.1}\right) = \dfrac{6}{10} \div \left(\dfrac{\frac{12}{10}}{\frac{64}{100}} \div \dfrac{\frac{4}{100}}{\frac{1}{10}}\right) = \dfrac{6}{10} \div \left(\dfrac{12\times100}{10\times64} \div \dfrac{4\times10}{100\times1}\right) = \dfrac{\overset{3}{\cancel{6}}}{\underset{5}{\cancel{10}}} \div \left(\dfrac{\overset{15}{\cancel{1200}}}{\underset{8}{\cancel{640}}} \div \dfrac{\overset{2}{\cancel{40}}}{\underset{5}{\cancel{100}}}\right) = \dfrac{3}{5} \div \left(\dfrac{15}{8} \div \dfrac{2}{5}\right)$

$$= \frac{3}{5} \div \left(\frac{15}{8} \times \frac{5}{2} \right) = \frac{3}{5} \div \left(\frac{75}{16} \right) = \frac{3}{5} \div \frac{75}{16} = \frac{3}{5} \times \frac{16}{75} = \frac{3 \times 16}{5 \times \overset{1}{\underset{25}{75}}} = \frac{1 \times 16}{5 \times 25} = \mathbf{\frac{16}{125}}$$

6. $$\left(\frac{0.2}{0.05} \div \frac{0.4}{3.5} \right) \div \frac{0.8}{0.01} = \left(\frac{\frac{2}{10}}{\frac{5}{100}} \div \frac{\frac{4}{10}}{\frac{35}{10}} \right) \div \frac{\frac{8}{10}}{\frac{1}{100}} = \left(\frac{2 \times 100}{10 \times 5} \div \frac{4 \times 10}{10 \times 35} \right) \div \frac{8 \times 100}{10 \times 1} = \left(\frac{\overset{4}{\underset{1}{200}}}{\underset{1}{\cancel{50}}} \div \frac{\overset{4}{\underset{35}{40}}}{\underset{35}{350}} \right) \div \frac{\overset{80}{800}}{\underset{1}{10}} = \left(\frac{4}{1} \div \frac{4}{35} \right) \div \frac{80}{1}$$

$$= \left(\frac{4}{1} \times \frac{35}{4} \right) \div \frac{80}{1} = \left(\frac{\overset{1}{4} \times 35}{1 \times \underset{1}{4}} \right) \div \frac{80}{1} = \left(\frac{1 \times 35}{1 \times 1} \right) \div \frac{80}{1} = \left(\frac{35}{1} \right) \div \frac{80}{1} = \frac{35}{1} \div \frac{80}{1} = \frac{35}{1} \times \frac{1}{80} = \frac{\overset{7}{35} \times 1}{1 \times \underset{16}{80}} = \frac{7 \times 1}{1 \times 16} = \mathbf{\frac{7}{16}}$$

7. $$\frac{0.6}{0.01} \div \left(0.3 \div \frac{0.06}{0.4} \right) = \frac{\frac{6}{10}}{\frac{1}{100}} \div \left(\frac{3}{10} \div \frac{\frac{6}{100}}{\frac{4}{10}} \right) = \frac{6 \times 100}{10 \times 1} \div \left(\frac{3}{10} \div \frac{6 \times 10}{100 \times 4} \right) = \frac{\overset{60}{600}}{\underset{1}{10}} \div \left(\frac{3}{10} \div \frac{\overset{3}{60}}{\underset{20}{400}} \right) = \frac{60}{1} \div \left(\frac{3}{10} \div \frac{3}{20} \right)$$

$$= \frac{60}{1} \div \left(\frac{3}{10} \times \frac{20}{3} \right) = \frac{60}{1} \div \left(\frac{\overset{1}{3} \times \overset{2}{20}}{\underset{1}{10} \times \underset{1}{3}} \right) = \frac{60}{1} \div \left(\frac{1 \times 2}{1 \times 1} \right) = \frac{60}{1} \div \left(\frac{2}{1} \right) = \frac{60}{1} \div \frac{2}{1} = \frac{60}{1} \times \frac{1}{2} = \frac{\overset{30}{60} \times 1}{1 \times 1} = \frac{30}{1} = \mathbf{30}$$

8. $$\frac{0.5}{0.04} \div \left(\frac{0.08}{0.1} \div 0.04 \right) = \frac{\frac{5}{10}}{\frac{4}{100}} \div \left(\frac{\frac{8}{100}}{\frac{1}{10}} \div \frac{4}{100} \right) = \frac{5 \times 100}{10 \times 4} \div \left(\frac{8 \times 10}{100 \times 1} \div \frac{4}{100} \right) = \frac{\overset{25}{500}}{\underset{2}{40}} \div \left(\frac{\overset{4}{80}}{\underset{5}{100}} \div \frac{\overset{1}{4}}{\underset{25}{100}} \right) = \frac{25}{2} \div \left(\frac{4}{5} \div \frac{1}{25} \right)$$

$$= \frac{25}{2} \div \left(\frac{4}{5} \times \frac{25}{1} \right) = \frac{25}{2} \div \left(\frac{4 \times \overset{5}{25}}{\underset{1}{5} \times 1} \right) = \frac{25}{2} \div \left(\frac{4 \times 5}{1 \times 1} \right) = \frac{25}{2} \div \left(\frac{20}{1} \right) = \frac{25}{2} \div \frac{20}{1} = \frac{25}{2} \times \frac{1}{20} = \frac{\overset{5}{25} \times 1}{2 \times \underset{4}{20}} = \frac{5 \times 1}{2 \times 4} = \mathbf{\frac{5}{8}}$$

9. $$\left(\frac{0.9}{0.8} \div \frac{0.27}{1.6} \right) \div \frac{0.1}{0.09} = \left(\frac{\frac{9}{10}}{\frac{8}{10}} \div \frac{\frac{27}{100}}{\frac{16}{10}} \right) \div \frac{\frac{1}{10}}{\frac{9}{100}} = \left(\frac{9 \times 10}{10 \times 8} \div \frac{27 \times 10}{100 \times 16} \right) \div \frac{1 \times 100}{10 \times 9} = \left(\frac{\overset{9}{90}}{\underset{8}{80}} \div \frac{\overset{27}{270}}{\underset{160}{1600}} \right) \div \frac{\overset{10}{100}}{\underset{9}{90}} = \left(\frac{9}{8} \div \frac{27}{160} \right) \div \frac{10}{9}$$

$$= \left(\frac{9}{8} \times \frac{160}{27} \right) \div \frac{10}{9} = \left(\frac{\overset{1}{9} \times \overset{20}{160}}{\underset{1}{8} \times \underset{3}{27}} \right) \div \frac{10}{9} = \left(\frac{1 \times 20}{1 \times 3} \right) \div \frac{10}{9} = \left(\frac{20}{3} \right) \div \frac{10}{9} = \frac{20}{3} \div \frac{10}{9} = \frac{20}{3} \times \frac{9}{10} = \frac{\overset{2}{20} \times \overset{3}{9}}{\underset{1}{3} \times \underset{1}{10}} = \frac{2 \times 3}{1 \times 1} = \frac{6}{1}$$

$$= \mathbf{6}$$

10. $$\left[\left(\frac{0.1}{0.05} \div \frac{0.4}{0.02} \right) \div \frac{0.04}{0.1} \right] \div 0.2 = \left[\left(\frac{\frac{1}{10}}{\frac{5}{100}} \div \frac{\frac{4}{10}}{\frac{2}{100}} \right) \div \frac{\frac{4}{100}}{\frac{1}{10}} \right] \div \frac{2}{10} = \left[\left(\frac{1 \times 100}{10 \times 5} \div \frac{4 \times 100}{10 \times 2} \right) \div \frac{4 \times 10}{100 \times 1} \right] \div \frac{2}{10}$$

$$= \left[\left(\frac{\overset{2}{100}}{\underset{1}{\cancel{50}}} \div \frac{\overset{20}{400}}{\underset{1}{20}} \right) \div \frac{\overset{2}{40}}{\underset{5}{100}} \right] \div \frac{\overset{1}{2}}{\underset{5}{10}} = \left[\left(\frac{2}{1} \div \frac{20}{1} \right) \div \frac{2}{5} \right] \div \frac{1}{5} = \left[\left(\frac{2}{1} \times \frac{1}{20} \right) \div \frac{2}{5} \right] \div \frac{1}{5} = \left[\left(\frac{\overset{1}{2} \times 1}{1 \times \underset{10}{20}} \right) \div \frac{2}{5} \right] \div \frac{1}{5} = \left[\left(\frac{1 \times 1}{1 \times 10} \right) \div \frac{2}{5} \right] \div \frac{1}{5}$$

$$= \left[\left(\frac{1}{10} \right) \div \frac{2}{5} \right] \div \frac{1}{5} = \left[\frac{1}{10} \div \frac{2}{5} \right] \div \frac{1}{5} = \left[\frac{1}{10} \times \frac{5}{2} \right] \div \frac{1}{5} = \left[\frac{1 \times \overset{1}{5}}{\underset{2}{10} \times 2} \right] \div \frac{1}{5} = \left[\frac{1 \times 1}{2 \times 2} \right] \div \frac{1}{5} = \left[\frac{1}{4} \right] \div \frac{1}{5} = \frac{1}{4} \div \frac{1}{5} = \frac{1}{4} \times \frac{5}{1}$$

$$= \frac{1 \times 5}{4 \times 1} = \frac{5}{4} = 1\frac{1}{4}$$

Section 4.5 Solutions:

1. $\dfrac{2.4}{0.3} \times \left(\dfrac{0.2}{1.2} + \dfrac{0.01}{0.5} \right) = \dfrac{\frac{24}{10}}{\frac{3}{10}} \times \left(\dfrac{\frac{2}{10}}{\frac{12}{10}} + \dfrac{\frac{1}{100}}{\frac{5}{10}} \right) = \dfrac{24 \times 10}{10 \times 3} \times \left(\dfrac{2 \times 10}{10 \times 12} + \dfrac{1 \times 10}{100 \times 5} \right) = \dfrac{\overset{8}{240}}{\underset{1}{30}} \times \left(\dfrac{\overset{1}{20}}{\underset{6}{120}} + \dfrac{\overset{1}{10}}{\underset{50}{500}} \right) = \dfrac{8}{1} \times \left(\dfrac{1}{6} + \dfrac{1}{50} \right)$

   $= \dfrac{8}{1} \times \left(\dfrac{(1 \times 50) + (1 \times 6)}{6 \times 50} \right) = \dfrac{8}{1} \times \left(\dfrac{50 + 6}{300} \right) = \dfrac{8}{1} \times \left(\dfrac{56}{300} \right) = \dfrac{8}{1} \times \dfrac{56}{300} = \dfrac{\overset{2}{8} \times 56}{1 \times \underset{75}{300}} = \dfrac{2 \times 56}{1 \times 75} = \dfrac{112}{75} = 1\dfrac{37}{75}$

2. $\left(\dfrac{0.04}{0.8} \div \dfrac{1.6}{0.02} \right) \times 0.08 = \left(\dfrac{\frac{4}{100}}{\frac{8}{10}} \div \dfrac{\frac{16}{10}}{\frac{2}{100}} \right) \times \dfrac{8}{100} = \left(\dfrac{4 \times 10}{100 \times 8} \div \dfrac{16 \times 100}{10 \times 2} \right) \times \dfrac{8}{100} = \left(\dfrac{\overset{1}{40}}{\underset{20}{800}} \div \dfrac{\overset{80}{1600}}{\underset{1}{20}} \right) \times \dfrac{\overset{2}{8}}{\underset{25}{100}} = \left(\dfrac{1}{20} \div \dfrac{80}{1} \right) \times \dfrac{2}{25}$

   $= \left(\dfrac{1}{20} \times \dfrac{1}{80} \right) \times \dfrac{2}{25} = \left(\dfrac{1 \times 1}{20 \times 80} \right) \times \dfrac{2}{25} = \left(\dfrac{1}{1600} \right) \times \dfrac{2}{25} = \dfrac{1}{1600} \times \dfrac{2}{25} = \dfrac{1 \times \overset{1}{2}}{\underset{800}{1600} \times 25} = \dfrac{1 \times 1}{800 \times 25} = \dfrac{1}{20000}$

3. $\left(\dfrac{1.5}{0.5} + \dfrac{1.2}{0.03} + \dfrac{0}{0.4} \right) - \dfrac{2.4}{0.1} = \left(\dfrac{\frac{15}{10}}{\frac{5}{10}} + \dfrac{\frac{12}{10}}{\frac{3}{100}} + \dfrac{\frac{0}{1}}{\frac{4}{10}} \right) - \dfrac{\frac{24}{10}}{\frac{1}{10}} = \left(\dfrac{15 \times 10}{10 \times 5} + \dfrac{12 \times 100}{10 \times 3} + \dfrac{0 \times 10}{1 \times 4} \right) - \dfrac{24 \times 10}{10 \times 1}$

   $= \left(\dfrac{\overset{3}{150}}{\underset{1}{50}} + \dfrac{\overset{40}{1200}}{\underset{1}{30}} + \dfrac{0}{4} \right) - \dfrac{\overset{24}{240}}{\underset{1}{10}} = \left(\dfrac{3}{1} + \dfrac{40}{1} + 0 \right) - \dfrac{24}{1} = \left(\dfrac{3 + 40}{1} \right) - \dfrac{24}{1} = \left(\dfrac{43}{1} \right) - \dfrac{24}{1} = \dfrac{43}{1} - \dfrac{24}{1} = \dfrac{43 - 24}{1} = \dfrac{19}{1} = 19$

4. $\dfrac{0.6}{0.2} + \left(\dfrac{4.9}{0.07} - 0.36 \right) = \dfrac{\frac{6}{10}}{\frac{2}{10}} + \left(\dfrac{\frac{49}{10}}{\frac{7}{100}} - \dfrac{36}{100} \right) = \dfrac{6 \times 10}{10 \times 2} + \left(\dfrac{49 \times 100}{10 \times 7} - \dfrac{36}{100} \right) = \dfrac{\overset{3}{60}}{\underset{1}{20}} + \left(\dfrac{\overset{70}{4900}}{\underset{1}{70}} - \dfrac{\overset{9}{36}}{\underset{25}{100}} \right) = \dfrac{3}{1} + \left(\dfrac{70}{1} - \dfrac{9}{25} \right)$

   $= \dfrac{3}{1} + \left(\dfrac{(70 \times 25) - (9 \times 1)}{1 \times 25} \right) = \dfrac{3}{1} + \left(\dfrac{1750 - 9}{25} \right) = \dfrac{3}{1} + \left(\dfrac{1741}{25} \right) = \dfrac{3}{1} + \dfrac{1741}{25} = \dfrac{(3 \times 25) + (1741 \times 1)}{1 \times 25} = \dfrac{75 + 1741}{25} = \dfrac{1816}{25}$

   $= 72\dfrac{16}{25}$

5. $\left(\dfrac{3.6}{0.06} \times \dfrac{0.3}{1.2} \right) \div 0.001 = \left(\dfrac{\frac{36}{10}}{\frac{6}{100}} \times \dfrac{\frac{3}{10}}{\frac{12}{10}} \right) \div \dfrac{1}{1000} = \left(\dfrac{36 \times 100}{10 \times 6} \times \dfrac{3 \times 10}{10 \times 12} \right) \div \dfrac{1}{1000} = \left(\dfrac{\overset{60}{3600}}{\underset{1}{60}} \times \dfrac{\overset{1}{30}}{\underset{4}{120}} \right) \div \dfrac{1}{1000}$

   $= \left(\dfrac{60}{1} \times \dfrac{1}{4} \right) \div \dfrac{1}{1000} = \left(\dfrac{\overset{15}{60} \times 1}{1 \times \underset{1}{4}} \right) \div \dfrac{1}{1000} = \left(\dfrac{15 \times 1}{1 \times 1} \right) \div \dfrac{1}{1000} = \left(\dfrac{15}{1} \right) \div \dfrac{1}{1000} = \dfrac{15}{1} \div \dfrac{1}{1000} = \dfrac{15}{1} \times \dfrac{1000}{1} = \dfrac{15 \times 1000}{1 \times 1}$

   $= \dfrac{15000}{1} = 15000$

6. $\left(\dfrac{0.9}{0.08} \div \dfrac{0.18}{1.6}\right) \times \dfrac{1.4}{0.2} = \left(\dfrac{\frac{9}{10}}{\frac{8}{100}} \div \dfrac{\frac{18}{100}}{\frac{16}{10}}\right) \times \dfrac{\frac{14}{10}}{\frac{2}{10}} = \left(\dfrac{9 \times 100}{10 \times 8} \div \dfrac{18 \times 10}{100 \times 16}\right) \times \dfrac{14 \times 10}{10 \times 2} = \left(\dfrac{\overset{45}{\cancel{900}}}{\underset{4}{\cancel{80}}} \div \dfrac{\overset{9}{\cancel{180}}}{\underset{80}{\cancel{1600}}}\right) \times \dfrac{\overset{7}{\cancel{140}}}{\underset{1}{\cancel{20}}} = \left(\dfrac{45}{4} \div \dfrac{9}{80}\right) \times \dfrac{7}{1}$

$= \left(\dfrac{45}{4} \times \dfrac{80}{9}\right) \times \dfrac{7}{1} = \left(\dfrac{\overset{5}{\cancel{45}} \times \overset{20}{\cancel{80}}}{\underset{1}{\cancel{4}} \times \underset{1}{\cancel{9}}}\right) \times \dfrac{7}{1} = \left(\dfrac{5 \times 20}{1 \times 1}\right) \times \dfrac{7}{1} = \left(\dfrac{100}{1}\right) \times \dfrac{7}{1} = \dfrac{100}{1} \times \dfrac{7}{1} = \dfrac{100 \times 7}{1 \times 1} = \dfrac{700}{1} = \textbf{700}$

7. $\left(\dfrac{0.8}{0.05} - \dfrac{0.1}{0.05}\right) + \dfrac{0.4}{0.2} = \left(\dfrac{\frac{8}{10}}{\frac{5}{100}} - \dfrac{\frac{1}{10}}{\frac{5}{100}}\right) + \dfrac{\frac{4}{10}}{\frac{2}{10}} = \left(\dfrac{8 \times 100}{10 \times 5} - \dfrac{1 \times 100}{10 \times 5}\right) + \dfrac{4 \times 10}{10 \times 2} = \left(\dfrac{800}{50} - \dfrac{100}{50}\right) + \dfrac{\overset{2}{\cancel{40}}}{\underset{1}{\cancel{20}}} = \left(\dfrac{800 - 100}{50}\right) + \dfrac{2}{1}$

$= \left(\dfrac{700}{50}\right) + \dfrac{2}{1} = \dfrac{\overset{14}{\cancel{700}}}{\underset{1}{\cancel{50}}} + \dfrac{2}{1} = \dfrac{14}{1} + \dfrac{2}{1} = \dfrac{14 + 2}{1} = \dfrac{16}{1} = \textbf{16}$

8. $\dfrac{0.16}{0.2} \times \left(\dfrac{0.5}{0.06} \div \dfrac{0.3}{0.05}\right) = \dfrac{\frac{16}{100}}{\frac{2}{10}} \times \left(\dfrac{\frac{5}{10}}{\frac{6}{100}} \div \dfrac{\frac{3}{10}}{\frac{5}{100}}\right) = \dfrac{16 \times 10}{100 \times 2} \times \left(\dfrac{5 \times 100}{10 \times 6} \div \dfrac{3 \times 100}{10 \times 5}\right) = \dfrac{\overset{4}{\cancel{160}}}{\underset{5}{\cancel{200}}} \times \left(\dfrac{\overset{25}{\cancel{500}}}{\underset{3}{\cancel{60}}} \div \dfrac{\overset{6}{\cancel{300}}}{\underset{1}{\cancel{50}}}\right) = \dfrac{4}{5} \times \left(\dfrac{25}{3} \div \dfrac{6}{1}\right)$

$= \dfrac{4}{5} \times \left(\dfrac{25}{3} \times \dfrac{1}{6}\right) = \dfrac{4}{5} \times \left(\dfrac{25 \times 1}{3 \times 6}\right) = \dfrac{4}{5} \times \left(\dfrac{25}{18}\right) = \dfrac{4}{5} \times \dfrac{25}{18} = \dfrac{\overset{2}{\cancel{4}} \times \overset{5}{\cancel{25}}}{\underset{1}{\cancel{5}} \times \underset{9}{\cancel{18}}} = \dfrac{2 \times 5}{1 \times 9} = \dfrac{10}{9} = \textbf{1}\dfrac{\textbf{1}}{\textbf{9}}$

9. $\left(\dfrac{4.8}{0.04} \times \dfrac{0.1}{0.4}\right) \div \dfrac{7.5}{0.05} = \left(\dfrac{\frac{48}{10}}{\frac{4}{100}} \times \dfrac{\frac{1}{10}}{\frac{4}{10}}\right) \div \dfrac{\frac{75}{10}}{\frac{5}{100}} = \left(\dfrac{48 \times 100}{10 \times 4} \times \dfrac{1 \times 10}{10 \times 4}\right) \div \dfrac{75 \times 100}{10 \times 5} = \left(\dfrac{\overset{120}{\cancel{4800}}}{\underset{1}{\cancel{40}}} \times \dfrac{\overset{1}{\cancel{10}}}{\underset{4}{\cancel{40}}}\right) \div \dfrac{\overset{150}{\cancel{7500}}}{\underset{1}{\cancel{50}}}$

$= \left(\dfrac{120}{1} \times \dfrac{1}{4}\right) \div \dfrac{150}{1} = \left(\dfrac{\overset{30}{\cancel{120}} \times 1}{1 \times \underset{1}{\cancel{4}}}\right) \div \dfrac{150}{1} = \left(\dfrac{30 \times 1}{1 \times 1}\right) \div \dfrac{150}{1} = \left(\dfrac{30}{1}\right) \div \dfrac{150}{1} = \dfrac{30}{1} \div \dfrac{150}{1} = \dfrac{30}{1} \times \dfrac{1}{150} = \dfrac{\overset{1}{\cancel{30}} \times 1}{1 \times \underset{5}{\cancel{150}}} = \dfrac{1 \times 1}{1 \times 5}$

$= \dfrac{\textbf{1}}{\textbf{5}}$

10. $\left[\left(\dfrac{2.7}{0.09} + \dfrac{1.5}{0.05}\right) + 3.2\right] - \dfrac{6.4}{0.02} = \left[\left(\dfrac{\frac{27}{10}}{\frac{9}{100}} + \dfrac{\frac{15}{10}}{\frac{5}{100}}\right) + \dfrac{32}{10}\right] - \dfrac{\frac{64}{10}}{\frac{2}{100}} = \left[\left(\dfrac{27 \times 100}{10 \times 9} + \dfrac{15 \times 100}{10 \times 5}\right) + \dfrac{32}{10}\right] - \dfrac{64 \times 100}{10 \times 2}$

$= \left[\left(\dfrac{\overset{30}{\cancel{2700}}}{\underset{1}{\cancel{90}}} + \dfrac{\overset{30}{\cancel{1500}}}{\underset{1}{\cancel{50}}}\right) + \dfrac{\overset{16}{\cancel{32}}}{\underset{5}{\cancel{10}}}\right] - \dfrac{\overset{320}{\cancel{6400}}}{\underset{1}{\cancel{20}}} = \left[\left(\dfrac{30}{1} + \dfrac{30}{1}\right) + \dfrac{16}{5}\right] - \dfrac{320}{1} = \left[\left(\dfrac{30 + 30}{1}\right) + \dfrac{16}{5}\right] - \dfrac{320}{1} = \left[\left(\dfrac{60}{1}\right) + \dfrac{16}{5}\right] - \dfrac{320}{1}$

$= \left[\dfrac{60}{1} + \dfrac{16}{5}\right] - \dfrac{320}{1} = \left[\dfrac{(60 \times 5) + (16 \times 1)}{1 \times 5}\right] - \dfrac{320}{1} = \left[\dfrac{300 + 16}{5}\right] - \dfrac{320}{1} = \left[\dfrac{316}{5}\right] - \dfrac{320}{1} = \dfrac{316}{5} - \dfrac{320}{1}$

$= \dfrac{(316 \times 1) - (320 \times 5)}{5 \times 1} = \dfrac{316 - 1600}{5} = \dfrac{-1284}{5} = -\left(\textbf{256}\dfrac{\textbf{4}}{\textbf{5}}\right)$

Chapter 5 Solutions:

Section 5.1 Solutions:

1. $1\frac{3}{4}+2\frac{5}{3} = \frac{(1\times 4)+3}{4}+\frac{(2\times 3)+5}{3} = \frac{4+3}{4}+\frac{6+5}{3} = \frac{7}{4}+\frac{11}{3} = \frac{(7\times 3)+(11\times 4)}{4\times 3} = \frac{21+44}{12} = \frac{65}{12} = \mathbf{5\frac{5}{12}}$

2. $2\frac{3}{8}+3\frac{1}{8} = \frac{(2\times 8)+3}{8}+\frac{(3\times 8)+1}{8} = \frac{16+3}{8}+\frac{24+1}{8} = \frac{19}{8}+\frac{25}{8} = \frac{19+25}{8} = \frac{\overset{11}{\cancel{44}}}{\underset{2}{\cancel{8}}} = \frac{11}{2} = \mathbf{5\frac{1}{2}}$

3. $1\frac{1}{2}+\left(1\frac{3}{4}+2\frac{1}{4}\right) = \frac{(1\times 2)+1}{2}+\left(\frac{(1\times 4)+3}{4}+\frac{(2\times 4)+1}{4}\right) = \frac{2+1}{2}+\left(\frac{4+3}{4}+\frac{8+1}{4}\right) = \frac{3}{2}+\left(\frac{7}{4}+\frac{9}{4}\right) = \frac{3}{2}+\left(\frac{7+9}{4}\right)$

    $= \frac{3}{2}+\left(\frac{16}{4}\right) = \frac{3}{2}+\frac{\overset{8}{\cancel{16}}}{\underset{2}{\cancel{4}}} = \frac{3}{2}+\frac{8}{2} = \frac{3+8}{2} = \frac{11}{2} = \mathbf{5\frac{1}{2}}$

4. $\left(2\frac{3}{4}+3\frac{4}{5}\right)+1\frac{2}{3} = \left(\frac{(2\times 4)+3}{4}+\frac{(3\times 5)+4}{5}\right)+\frac{(1\times 3)+2}{3} = \left(\frac{8+3}{4}+\frac{15+4}{5}\right)+\frac{3+2}{3} = \left(\frac{11}{4}+\frac{19}{5}\right)+\frac{5}{3}$

    $= \left(\frac{(11\times 5)+(19\times 4)}{4\times 5}\right)+\frac{5}{3} = \left(\frac{55+76}{20}\right)+\frac{5}{3} = \left(\frac{131}{20}\right)+\frac{5}{3} = \frac{131}{20}+\frac{5}{3} = \frac{(131\times 3)+(5\times 20)}{20\times 3} = \frac{393+100}{60}$

    $= \frac{493}{60} = \mathbf{8\frac{13}{60}}$

5. $2\frac{2}{3}+\left(1\frac{3}{8}+2\frac{1}{3}\right) = \frac{(2\times 3)+2}{3}+\left(\frac{(1\times 8)+3}{8}+\frac{(2\times 3)+1}{3}\right) = \frac{6+2}{3}+\left(\frac{8+3}{8}+\frac{6+1}{3}\right) = \frac{8}{3}+\left(\frac{11}{8}+\frac{7}{3}\right)$

    $= \frac{8}{3}+\left(\frac{(11\times 3)+(7\times 8)}{8\times 3}\right) = \frac{8}{3}+\left(\frac{33+56}{24}\right) = \frac{8}{3}+\left(\frac{89}{24}\right) = \frac{8}{3}+\frac{89}{24} = \frac{(8\times 24)+(89\times 3)}{3\times 24} = \frac{192+267}{72}$

    $= \frac{\overset{153}{\cancel{459}}}{\underset{24}{\cancel{72}}} = \frac{153}{24} = \mathbf{6\frac{9}{24}}$

6. $3\frac{5}{8}+2\frac{7}{8}+4\frac{3}{8}+1\frac{4}{8} = \frac{(3\times 8)+5}{8}+\frac{(2\times 8)+7}{8}+\frac{(4\times 8)+3}{8}+\frac{(1\times 8)+4}{8} = \frac{24+5}{8}+\frac{16+7}{8}+\frac{32+3}{8}+\frac{8+4}{8}$

    $= \frac{29}{8}+\frac{23}{8}+\frac{35}{8}+\frac{12}{8} = \frac{29+23+35+12}{8} = \frac{99}{8} = \mathbf{12\frac{3}{8}}$

7. $\left(1\frac{3}{2}+2\frac{5}{2}\right)+\left(1\frac{4}{3}+1\frac{2}{3}\right) = \left(\frac{(1\times 2)+3}{2}+\frac{(2\times 2)+5}{2}\right)+\left(\frac{(1\times 3)+4}{3}+\frac{(1\times 3)+2}{3}\right) = \left(\frac{2+3}{2}+\frac{4+5}{2}\right)+\left(\frac{3+4}{3}+\frac{3+2}{3}\right)$

    $= \left(\frac{5}{2}+\frac{9}{2}\right)+\left(\frac{7}{3}+\frac{5}{3}\right) = \left(\frac{5+9}{2}\right)+\left(\frac{7+5}{3}\right) = \left(\frac{14}{2}\right)+\left(\frac{12}{3}\right) = \frac{\overset{7}{\cancel{14}}}{\underset{1}{\cancel{2}}}+\frac{\overset{4}{\cancel{12}}}{\underset{1}{\cancel{3}}} = \frac{7}{1}+\frac{4}{1} = \frac{7+4}{1} = \frac{11}{1} = \mathbf{11}$

8. $\left(1\frac{2}{3}+2\frac{5}{4}\right)+\left(3\frac{3}{2}+2\frac{7}{2}\right) = \left(\frac{(1\times 3)+2}{3}+\frac{(2\times 4)+5}{4}\right)+\left(\frac{(3\times 2)+3}{2}+\frac{(2\times 2)+7}{2}\right) = \left(\frac{3+2}{3}+\frac{8+5}{4}\right)+\left(\frac{6+3}{2}+\frac{4+7}{2}\right)$

    $= \left(\frac{5}{3}+\frac{13}{4}\right)+\left(\frac{9}{2}+\frac{11}{2}\right) = \left(\frac{(5\times 4)+(13\times 3)}{3\times 4}\right)+\left(\frac{9+11}{2}\right) = \left(\frac{20+39}{12}\right)+\left(\frac{20}{2}\right) = \frac{59}{12}+\frac{\overset{10}{\cancel{20}}}{\underset{1}{\cancel{2}}} = \frac{59}{12}+\frac{10}{1}$

$$= \frac{(59 \times 1) + (10 \times 12)}{12 \times 1} = \frac{59 + 120}{12} = \frac{179}{12} = 14\frac{11}{12}$$

9. $\left(6\frac{1}{2} + 3\frac{2}{3}\right) + \left(1\frac{1}{5} + 3\frac{1}{4}\right) = \left(\frac{(6 \times 2) + 1}{2} + \frac{(3 \times 3) + 2}{3}\right) + \left(\frac{(1 \times 5) + 1}{5} + \frac{(3 \times 4) + 1}{4}\right) = \left(\frac{12 + 1}{2} + \frac{9 + 2}{3}\right) + \left(\frac{5 + 1}{5} + \frac{12 + 1}{4}\right)$

$\quad = \left(\frac{13}{2} + \frac{11}{3}\right) + \left(\frac{6}{5} + \frac{13}{4}\right) = \left(\frac{(13 \times 3) + (11 \times 2)}{2 \times 3}\right) + \left(\frac{(6 \times 4) + (13 \times 5)}{5 \times 4}\right) = \left(\frac{39 + 22}{6}\right) + \left(\frac{24 + 65}{20}\right) = \left(\frac{61}{6}\right) + \left(\frac{89}{20}\right)$

$\quad = \frac{61}{6} + \frac{89}{20} = \frac{(61 \times 20) + (89 \times 6)}{6 \times 20} = \frac{1220 + 534}{120} = \frac{\overset{877}{\cancel{1754}}}{\underset{60}{\cancel{120}}} = \frac{877}{60} = 14\frac{37}{60}$

10. $1\frac{4}{3} + \left[2\frac{3}{5} + \left(1\frac{2}{5} + 3\frac{4}{2}\right)\right] = \frac{(1 \times 3) + 4}{3} + \left[\frac{(2 \times 5) + 3}{5} + \left(\frac{(1 \times 5) + 2}{5} + \frac{(3 \times 2) + 4}{2}\right)\right] = \frac{3 + 4}{3} + \left[\frac{10 + 3}{5} + \left(\frac{5 + 2}{5} + \frac{6 + 4}{2}\right)\right]$

$\quad = \frac{7}{3} + \left[\frac{13}{5} + \left(\frac{7}{5} + \frac{10}{2}\right)\right] = \frac{7}{3} + \left[\frac{13}{5} + \left(\frac{(7 \times 2) + (10 \times 5)}{5 \times 2}\right)\right] = \frac{7}{3} + \left[\frac{13}{5} + \left(\frac{14 + 50}{10}\right)\right] = \frac{7}{3} + \left[\frac{13}{5} + \left(\frac{64}{10}\right)\right] = \frac{7}{3} + \left[\frac{13}{5} + \frac{\overset{32}{\cancel{64}}}{\underset{5}{\cancel{10}}}\right]$

$\quad = \frac{7}{3} + \left[\frac{13}{5} + \frac{32}{5}\right] = \frac{7}{3} + \left[\frac{13 + 32}{5}\right] = \frac{7}{3} + \left[\frac{45}{5}\right] = \frac{7}{3} + \frac{\overset{9}{\cancel{45}}}{\underset{1}{\cancel{5}}} = \frac{7}{3} + \frac{9}{1} = \frac{(7 \times 1) + (9 \times 3)}{3 \times 1} = \frac{7 + 27}{3} = \frac{34}{3} = 11\frac{1}{3}$

Section 5.2 Solutions:

1. $4\frac{3}{7} - 3\frac{1}{7} = \frac{(4 \times 7) + 3}{7} - \frac{(3 \times 7) + 1}{7} = \frac{28 + 3}{7} - \frac{21 + 1}{7} = \frac{31}{7} - \frac{22}{7} = \frac{31 - 22}{7} = \frac{9}{7} = 1\frac{2}{7}$

2. $3\frac{2}{5} - 4\frac{2}{3} = \frac{(3 \times 5) + 2}{5} - \frac{(4 \times 3) + 2}{3} = \frac{15 + 2}{5} - \frac{12 + 2}{3} = \frac{17}{5} - \frac{14}{3} = \frac{(17 \times 3) - (14 \times 5)}{5 \times 3} = \frac{51 - 70}{15} = \frac{-19}{15} = -\left(1\frac{4}{15}\right)$

3. $\left(8\frac{1}{4} - 2\frac{3}{4}\right) - 1\frac{1}{3} = \left(\frac{(8 \times 4) + 1}{4} - \frac{(2 \times 4) + 3}{4}\right) - \frac{(1 \times 3) + 1}{3} = \left(\frac{32 + 1}{4} - \frac{8 + 3}{4}\right) - \frac{3 + 1}{3} = \left(\frac{33}{4} - \frac{11}{4}\right) - \frac{4}{3} = \left(\frac{33 - 11}{4}\right) - \frac{4}{3}$

$\quad = \left(\frac{22}{4}\right) - \frac{4}{3} = \frac{\overset{11}{\cancel{22}}}{\underset{2}{\cancel{4}}} - \frac{4}{3} = \frac{11}{2} - \frac{4}{3} = \frac{(11 \times 3) - (4 \times 2)}{2 \times 3} = \frac{33 - 8}{6} = \frac{25}{6} = 4\frac{1}{6}$

4. $6\frac{4}{5} - \left(2\frac{3}{4} - 1\frac{2}{3}\right) = \frac{(6 \times 5) + 4}{5} - \left(\frac{(2 \times 4) + 3}{4} - \frac{(1 \times 3) + 2}{3}\right) = \frac{30 + 4}{5} - \left(\frac{8 + 3}{4} - \frac{3 + 2}{3}\right) = \frac{34}{5} - \left(\frac{11}{4} - \frac{5}{3}\right)$

$\quad = \frac{34}{5} - \left(\frac{(11 \times 3) - (5 \times 4)}{4 \times 3}\right) = \frac{34}{5} - \left(\frac{33 - 20}{12}\right) = \frac{34}{5} - \frac{13}{12} = \frac{(34 \times 12) - (13 \times 5)}{5 \times 12} = \frac{408 - 65}{60} = \frac{343}{60} = 5\frac{43}{60}$

5. $2\frac{3}{6} - 4\frac{5}{6} - 5\frac{1}{6} = \frac{(2 \times 6) + 3}{6} - \frac{(4 \times 6) + 5}{6} - \frac{(5 \times 6) + 1}{6} = \frac{12 + 3}{6} - \frac{24 + 5}{6} - \frac{30 + 1}{6} = \frac{15}{6} - \frac{29}{6} - \frac{31}{6} = \frac{15 - 29 - 31}{6}$

$\quad = \frac{\overset{-15}{\cancel{-45}}}{\underset{2}{\cancel{6}}} = \frac{-15}{2} = -\left(7\frac{1}{2}\right)$

6. $4\frac{2}{3} - 5\frac{5}{6} - 2\frac{3}{5} = \left(4\frac{2}{3} - 5\frac{5}{6}\right) - 2\frac{3}{5} = \left(\frac{(4 \times 3) + 2}{3} - \frac{(5 \times 6) + 5}{6}\right) - \frac{(2 \times 5) + 3}{5} = \left(\frac{12 + 2}{3} - \frac{30 + 5}{6}\right) - \frac{10 + 3}{5}$

$$= \left(\frac{14}{3} - \frac{35}{6}\right) - \frac{13}{5} = \left(\frac{(14 \times 6) - (35 \times 3)}{3 \times 6}\right) - \frac{13}{5} = \left(\frac{84 - 105}{18}\right) - \frac{13}{5} = \left(\frac{-21}{18}\right) - \frac{13}{5} = \frac{-21}{18} - \frac{13}{5} = \frac{(-21 \times 5) - (13 \times 18)}{18 \times 5}$$

$$= \frac{-105 - 234}{90} = \frac{\overset{-113}{\cancel{-339}}}{\underset{30}{\cancel{90}}} = \frac{-113}{30} = -\left(3\frac{23}{30}\right)$$

7. $3\frac{2}{5} - \left(4\frac{3}{8} - 1\frac{2}{3}\right) = \frac{(3 \times 5) + 2}{5} - \left(\frac{(4 \times 8) + 3}{8} - \frac{(1 \times 3) + 2}{3}\right) = \frac{15 + 2}{5} - \left(\frac{32 + 3}{8} - \frac{3 + 2}{3}\right) = \frac{17}{5} - \left(\frac{35}{8} - \frac{5}{3}\right)$

$$= \frac{17}{5} - \left(\frac{(35 \times 3) - (5 \times 8)}{8 \times 3}\right) = \frac{17}{5} - \left(\frac{105 - 40}{24}\right) = \frac{17}{5} - \left(\frac{65}{24}\right) = \frac{17}{5} - \frac{65}{24} = \frac{(17 \times 24) - (65 \times 5)}{5 \times 24} = \frac{408 - 325}{120} = \frac{83}{120}$$

8. $\left(6\frac{2}{3} - 1\frac{1}{5}\right) - \left(2\frac{4}{3} - 5\frac{2}{3}\right) = \left(\frac{(6 \times 3) + 2}{3} - \frac{(1 \times 5) + 1}{5}\right) - \left(\frac{(2 \times 3) + 4}{3} - \frac{(5 \times 3) + 2}{3}\right) = \left(\frac{18 + 2}{3} - \frac{5 + 1}{5}\right) - \left(\frac{6 + 4}{3} - \frac{15 + 2}{3}\right)$

$$= \left(\frac{20}{3} - \frac{6}{5}\right) - \left(\frac{10}{3} - \frac{17}{3}\right) = \left(\frac{(20 \times 5) - (6 \times 3)}{3 \times 5}\right) - \left(\frac{10 - 17}{3}\right) = \left(\frac{100 - 18}{15}\right) - \left(\frac{-7}{3}\right) = \left(\frac{82}{15}\right) + \left(\frac{7}{3}\right) = \frac{82}{15} + \frac{7}{3}$$

$$= \frac{(82 \times 3) + (7 \times 15)}{15 \times 3} = \frac{246 + 105}{45} = \frac{\overset{117}{\cancel{351}}}{\underset{15}{\cancel{45}}} = \frac{117}{15} = 7\frac{12}{15}$$

9. $\left(3\frac{3}{4} - 4\frac{2}{5}\right) - \left(3\frac{1}{8} - 2\frac{3}{4}\right) = \left(\frac{(3 \times 4) + 3}{4} - \frac{(4 \times 5) + 2}{5}\right) - \left(\frac{(3 \times 8) + 1}{8} - \frac{(2 \times 4) + 3}{4}\right) = \left(\frac{12 + 3}{4} - \frac{20 + 2}{5}\right) - \left(\frac{24 + 1}{8} - \frac{8 + 3}{4}\right)$

$$= \left(\frac{15}{4} - \frac{22}{5}\right) - \left(\frac{25}{8} - \frac{11}{4}\right) = \left(\frac{(15 \times 5) - (22 \times 4)}{4 \times 5}\right) - \left(\frac{(25 \times 4) - (11 \times 8)}{8 \times 4}\right) = \left(\frac{75 - 88}{20}\right) - \left(\frac{100 - 88}{32}\right) = \left(\frac{-13}{20}\right) - \left(\frac{12}{32}\right)$$

$$= \frac{-13}{20} - \frac{12}{32} = \frac{(-13 \times 32) - (12 \times 20)}{20 \times 32} = \frac{-416 - 240}{640} = \frac{\overset{-41}{\cancel{-656}}}{\underset{40}{\cancel{640}}} = \frac{-41}{40} = -\left(1\frac{1}{40}\right)$$

10. $\left[\left(5\frac{3}{4} - 3\frac{5}{8}\right) - 1\frac{2}{3}\right] - 2\frac{3}{5} = \left[\left(\frac{(5 \times 4) + 3}{4} - \frac{(3 \times 8) + 5}{8}\right) - \frac{(1 \times 3) + 2}{3}\right] - \frac{(2 \times 5) + 3}{5} = \left[\left(\frac{20 + 3}{4} - \frac{24 + 5}{8}\right) - \frac{3 + 2}{3}\right] - \frac{10 + 3}{5}$

$$= \left[\left(\frac{23}{4} - \frac{29}{8}\right) - \frac{5}{3}\right] - \frac{13}{5} = \left[\left(\frac{(23 \times 8) - (29 \times 4)}{4 \times 8}\right) - \frac{5}{3}\right] - \frac{13}{5} = \left[\left(\frac{184 - 116}{32}\right) - \frac{5}{3}\right] - \frac{13}{5} = \left[\left(\frac{68}{32}\right) - \frac{5}{3}\right] - \frac{13}{5}$$

$$= \left[\frac{\overset{17}{\cancel{68}}}{\underset{8}{\cancel{32}}} - \frac{5}{3}\right] - \frac{13}{5} = \left[\frac{17}{8} - \frac{5}{3}\right] - \frac{13}{5} = \left[\frac{(17 \times 3) - (5 \times 8)}{8 \times 3}\right] - \frac{13}{5} = \left[\frac{51 - 40}{24}\right] - \frac{13}{5} = \left[\frac{11}{24}\right] - \frac{13}{5} = \frac{11}{24} - \frac{13}{5}$$

$$= \frac{(11 \times 5) - (13 \times 24)}{24 \times 5} = \frac{55 - 312}{120} = \frac{-257}{120} = -\left(2\frac{17}{120}\right)$$

Section 5.3 Solutions:

1. $1\frac{3}{4} \times 2\frac{1}{3} = \frac{(1 \times 4) + 3}{4} \times \frac{(2 \times 3) + 1}{3} = \frac{4 + 3}{4} \times \frac{6 + 1}{3} = \frac{7}{4} \times \frac{7}{3} = \frac{7 \times 7}{4 \times 3} = \frac{49}{12} = 4\frac{1}{12}$

2. $2\frac{1}{3} \times 1\frac{1}{4} \times 4\frac{5}{6} = \frac{(2 \times 3) + 1}{3} \times \frac{(1 \times 4) + 1}{4} \times \frac{(4 \times 6) + 5}{6} = \frac{6 + 1}{3} \times \frac{4 + 1}{4} \times \frac{24 + 5}{6} = \frac{7}{3} \times \frac{5}{4} \times \frac{29}{6} = \frac{7 \times 5 \times 29}{3 \times 4 \times 6} = \frac{1015}{72}$

$$= 14\frac{7}{72}$$

3. $3\frac{1}{3} \times \left(1\frac{2}{5} \times 1\frac{2}{3}\right) = \frac{(3\times 3)+1}{3} \times \left(\frac{(1\times 5)+2}{5} \times \frac{(1\times 3)+2}{3}\right) = \frac{9+1}{3} \times \left(\frac{5+2}{5} \times \frac{3+2}{3}\right) = \frac{10}{3} \times \left(\frac{7}{5} \times \frac{5}{3}\right) = \frac{10}{3} \times \left(\frac{7\times \overset{1}{\cancel{5}}}{\underset{1}{\cancel{5}}\times 3}\right)$

$= \frac{10}{3} \times \left(\frac{7\times 1}{1\times 3}\right) = \frac{10}{3} \times \left(\frac{7}{3}\right) = \frac{10}{3} \times \frac{7}{3} = \frac{10\times 7}{3\times 3} = \frac{70}{9} = \mathbf{7\frac{7}{9}}$

4. $\left(2\frac{3}{4} \times 5\frac{1}{2}\right) \times 3\frac{1}{5} = \left(\frac{(2\times 4)+3}{4} \times \frac{(5\times 2)+1}{2}\right) \times \frac{(3\times 5)+1}{5} = \left(\frac{8+3}{4} \times \frac{10+1}{2}\right) \times \frac{15+1}{5} = \left(\frac{11}{4} \times \frac{11}{2}\right) \times \frac{16}{5} = \left(\frac{11\times 11}{4\times 2}\right) \times \frac{16}{5}$

$= \left(\frac{121}{8}\right) \times \frac{16}{5} = \frac{121}{8} \times \frac{16}{5} = \frac{121\times \overset{2}{\cancel{16}}}{\underset{1}{\cancel{8}}\times 5} = \frac{121\times 2}{1\times 5} = \frac{242}{5} = \mathbf{48\frac{2}{5}}$

5. $2\frac{5}{6} \times 3\frac{2}{5} \times 1\frac{1}{3} \times 1\frac{1}{2} = \frac{(2\times 6)+5}{6} \times \frac{(3\times 5)+2}{5} \times \frac{(1\times 3)+1}{3} \times \frac{(1\times 2)+1}{2} = \frac{12+5}{6} \times \frac{15+2}{5} \times \frac{3+1}{3} \times \frac{2+1}{2} = \frac{17}{6} \times \frac{17}{5} \times \frac{4}{3} \times \frac{3}{2}$

$= \frac{17\times 17\times \overset{2}{\cancel{4}}\times \overset{1}{\cancel{3}}}{\underset{1}{\cancel{6}}\times 5\times \underset{1}{\cancel{3}}\times 2} = \frac{17\times 17\times \overset{1}{\cancel{2}}\times 1}{\underset{3}{\cancel{6}}\times 5\times 1\times 1} = \frac{17\times 17\times 1\times 1}{3\times 5\times 1\times 1} = \frac{289}{15} = \mathbf{19\frac{4}{15}}$

6. $1\frac{1}{5} \times 2\frac{1}{3} \times \left(3\frac{2}{3} \times \frac{0}{1}\right) = \mathbf{0}$

7. $\left(1\frac{5}{6} \times 2\frac{1}{3}\right) \times \left(2\frac{3}{7} \times 1\frac{1}{7}\right) = \left(\frac{(1\times 6)+5}{6} \times \frac{(2\times 3)+1}{3}\right) \times \left(\frac{(2\times 7)+3}{7} \times \frac{(1\times 7)+1}{7}\right) = \left(\frac{6+5}{6} \times \frac{6+1}{3}\right) \times \left(\frac{14+3}{7} \times \frac{7+1}{7}\right)$

$= \left(\frac{11}{6} \times \frac{7}{3}\right) \times \left(\frac{17}{7} \times \frac{8}{7}\right) = \left(\frac{11\times 7}{6\times 3}\right) \times \left(\frac{17\times 8}{7\times 7}\right) = \left(\frac{77}{18}\right) \times \left(\frac{136}{49}\right) = \frac{77}{18} \times \frac{136}{49} = \frac{77\times \overset{68}{\cancel{136}}}{\underset{9}{\cancel{18}}\times 49} = \frac{77\times 68}{9\times 49} = \frac{5236}{441}$

$= \mathbf{11\frac{385}{441}}$

8. $\left(2\frac{1}{2} \times 1\frac{3}{4}\right) \times \left(4\frac{1}{2} \times 2\frac{2}{3}\right) = \left(\frac{(2\times 2)+1}{2} \times \frac{(1\times 4)+3}{4}\right) \times \left(\frac{(4\times 2)+1}{2} \times \frac{(2\times 3)+2}{3}\right) = \left(\frac{4+1}{2} \times \frac{4+3}{4}\right) \times \left(\frac{8+1}{2} \times \frac{6+2}{3}\right)$

$= \left(\frac{5}{2} \times \frac{7}{4}\right) \times \left(\frac{9}{2} \times \frac{8}{3}\right) = \left(\frac{5\times 7}{2\times 4}\right) \times \left(\frac{\overset{3}{\cancel{9}}\times \overset{4}{\cancel{8}}}{\underset{1}{\cancel{2}}\times \underset{1}{\cancel{3}}}\right) = \left(\frac{35}{8}\right) \times \left(\frac{3\times 4}{1\times 1}\right) = \frac{35}{8} \times \left(\frac{12}{1}\right) = \frac{35}{8} \times \frac{12}{1} = \frac{35\times \overset{3}{\cancel{12}}}{\underset{2}{\cancel{8}}\times 1} = \frac{35\times 3}{2\times 1} = \frac{105}{2}$

$= \mathbf{52\frac{1}{2}}$

9. $\left(3\frac{1}{2} \times 1\frac{2}{3} \times 3\frac{3}{5}\right) \times 1\frac{2}{3} = \left(\frac{(3\times 2)+1}{2} \times \frac{(1\times 3)+2}{3} \times \frac{(3\times 5)+3}{5}\right) \times \frac{(1\times 3)+2}{3} = \left(\frac{6+1}{2} \times \frac{3+2}{3} \times \frac{15+3}{5}\right) \times \frac{3+2}{3}$

$= \left(\frac{7}{2} \times \frac{5}{3} \times \frac{18}{5}\right) \times \frac{5}{3} = \left(\frac{7\times \overset{1}{\cancel{5}}\times \overset{6}{\cancel{18}}}{2\times \underset{1}{\cancel{3}}\times \underset{1}{\cancel{5}}}\right) \times \frac{5}{3} = \left(\frac{7\times 1\times 6}{2\times 1\times 1}\right) \times \frac{5}{3} = \left(\frac{42}{2}\right) \times \frac{5}{3} = \frac{42}{2} \times \frac{5}{3} = \frac{\overset{21}{\cancel{42}}\times 5}{\underset{1}{\cancel{2}}\times 3} = \frac{\overset{7}{\cancel{21}}\times 5}{1\times \underset{1}{\cancel{3}}} = \frac{7\times 5}{1\times 1} = \frac{35}{1}$

$= \mathbf{35}$

10. $2\frac{1}{3} \times \left[\left(3\frac{3}{5} \times 1\frac{1}{2}\right) \times 2\frac{2}{3}\right] = \frac{(2\times 3)+1}{3} \times \left[\left(\frac{(3\times 5)+3}{5} \times \frac{(1\times 2)+1}{2}\right) \times \frac{(2\times 3)+2}{3}\right] = \frac{6+1}{3} \times \left[\left(\frac{15+3}{5} \times \frac{2+1}{2}\right) \times \frac{6+2}{3}\right]$

$= \frac{7}{3} \times \left[\left(\frac{18}{5} \times \frac{3}{2}\right) \times \frac{8}{3}\right] = \frac{7}{3} \times \left[\left(\frac{\overset{9}{\cancel{18}}\times 3}{5\times \underset{1}{\cancel{2}}}\right) \times \frac{8}{3}\right] = \frac{7}{3} \times \left[\left(\frac{9\times 3}{5\times 1}\right) \times \frac{8}{3}\right] = \frac{7}{3} \times \left[\left(\frac{27}{5}\right) \times \frac{8}{3}\right] = \frac{7}{3} \times \left[\frac{27}{5} \times \frac{8}{3}\right] = \frac{7}{3} \times \left[\frac{\overset{9}{\cancel{27}}\times 8}{5\times \underset{1}{\cancel{3}}}\right]$

$$= \frac{7}{3} \times \left[\frac{9 \times 8}{5 \times 1} \right] = \frac{7}{3} \times \left[\frac{72}{5} \right] = \frac{7}{3} \times \frac{72}{5} = \frac{7 \times \overset{24}{\cancel{72}}}{\underset{1}{\cancel{3} \times 5}} = \frac{7 \times 24}{1 \times 5} = \frac{168}{5} = 33\frac{3}{5}$$

Section 5.4 Solutions:

1. $2\frac{1}{3} \div 1\frac{3}{5} = \frac{(2 \times 3)+1}{3} \div \frac{(1 \times 5)+3}{5} = \frac{6+1}{3} \div \frac{5+3}{5} = \frac{7}{3} \div \frac{8}{5} = \frac{7}{3} \times \frac{5}{8} = \frac{7 \times 5}{3 \times 8} = \frac{35}{24} = 1\frac{11}{24}$

2. $3\frac{2}{5} \div 1\frac{3}{8} = \frac{(3 \times 5)+2}{5} \div \frac{(1 \times 8)+3}{8} = \frac{15+2}{5} \div \frac{8+3}{8} = \frac{17}{5} \div \frac{11}{8} = \frac{17}{5} \times \frac{8}{11} = \frac{17 \times 8}{5 \times 11} = \frac{136}{55} = 2\frac{26}{55}$

3. $\left(3\frac{1}{2} \div 2\frac{3}{5} \right) \div 1\frac{2}{5} = \left(\frac{(3 \times 2)+1}{2} \div \frac{(2 \times 5)+3}{5} \right) \div \frac{(1 \times 5)+2}{5} = \left(\frac{6+1}{2} \div \frac{10+3}{5} \right) \div \frac{5+2}{5} = \left(\frac{7}{2} \div \frac{13}{5} \right) \div \frac{7}{5} = \left(\frac{7}{2} \times \frac{5}{13} \right) \div \frac{7}{5}$

    $= \left(\frac{7 \times 5}{2 \times 13} \right) \div \frac{7}{5} = \left(\frac{35}{26} \right) \div \frac{7}{5} = \frac{35}{26} \div \frac{7}{5} = \frac{35}{26} \times \frac{5}{7} = \frac{\overset{5}{\cancel{35}} \times 5}{26 \times \underset{1}{\cancel{7}}} = \frac{5 \times 5}{26 \times 1} = \frac{25}{26}$

4. $4\frac{1}{3} \div \left(2\frac{3}{4} \div 1\frac{3}{5} \right) = \frac{(4 \times 3)+1}{3} \div \left(\frac{(2 \times 4)+3}{4} \div \frac{(1 \times 5)+3}{5} \right) = \frac{12+1}{3} \div \left(\frac{8+3}{4} \div \frac{5+3}{5} \right) = \frac{13}{3} \div \left(\frac{11}{4} \div \frac{8}{5} \right) = \frac{13}{3} \div \left(\frac{11}{4} \times \frac{5}{8} \right)$

    $= \frac{13}{3} \div \left(\frac{11 \times 5}{4 \times 8} \right) = \frac{13}{3} \div \left(\frac{55}{32} \right) = \frac{13}{3} \div \frac{55}{32} = \frac{13}{3} \times \frac{32}{55} = \frac{13 \times 32}{3 \times 55} = \frac{416}{165} = 2\frac{86}{165}$

5. $\left(3\frac{2}{3} \div 2\frac{1}{5} \right) \div 2\frac{1}{2} = \left(\frac{(3 \times 3)+2}{3} \div \frac{(2 \times 5)+1}{5} \right) \div \frac{(2 \times 2)+1}{2} = \left(\frac{9+2}{3} \div \frac{10+1}{5} \right) \div \frac{4+1}{2} = \left(\frac{11}{3} \div \frac{11}{5} \right) \div \frac{5}{2} = \left(\frac{11}{3} \times \frac{5}{11} \right) \div \frac{5}{2}$

    $= \left(\frac{\overset{1}{\cancel{11}} \times 5}{3 \times \underset{1}{\cancel{11}}} \right) \div \frac{5}{2} = \left(\frac{1 \times 5}{3 \times 1} \right) \div \frac{5}{2} = \left(\frac{5}{3} \right) \div \frac{5}{2} = \frac{5}{3} \div \frac{5}{2} = \frac{5}{3} \times \frac{2}{5} = \frac{\overset{1}{\cancel{5}} \times 2}{3 \times \underset{1}{\cancel{5}}} = \frac{1 \times 2}{3 \times 1} = \frac{2}{3}$

6. $\left(1\frac{3}{4} \div 2\frac{1}{3} \right) \div 1\frac{3}{5} = \left(\frac{(1 \times 4)+3}{4} \div \frac{(2 \times 3)+1}{3} \right) \div \frac{(1 \times 5)+3}{5} = \left(\frac{4+3}{4} \div \frac{6+1}{3} \right) \div \frac{5+3}{5} = \left(\frac{7}{4} \div \frac{7}{3} \right) \div \frac{8}{5} = \left(\frac{7}{4} \times \frac{3}{7} \right) \div \frac{8}{5}$

    $= \left(\frac{\overset{1}{\cancel{7}} \times 3}{4 \times \underset{1}{\cancel{7}}} \right) \div \frac{8}{5} = \left(\frac{1 \times 3}{4 \times 1} \right) \div \frac{8}{5} = \left(\frac{3}{4} \right) \div \frac{8}{5} = \frac{3}{4} \div \frac{8}{5} = \frac{3}{4} \times \frac{5}{8} = \frac{3 \times 5}{4 \times 8} = \frac{15}{32}$

7. $\left(4\frac{2}{3} \div 2\frac{1}{4} \right) \div \left(2\frac{1}{5} \div 1\frac{3}{4} \right) = \left(\frac{(4 \times 3)+2}{3} \div \frac{(2 \times 4)+1}{4} \right) \div \left(\frac{(2 \times 5)+1}{5} \div \frac{(1 \times 4)+3}{4} \right) = \left(\frac{12+2}{3} \div \frac{8+1}{4} \right) \div \left(\frac{10+1}{5} \div \frac{4+3}{4} \right)$

    $= \left(\frac{14}{3} \div \frac{9}{4} \right) \div \left(\frac{11}{5} \div \frac{7}{4} \right) = \left(\frac{14}{3} \times \frac{4}{9} \right) \div \left(\frac{11}{5} \times \frac{4}{7} \right) = \left(\frac{14 \times 4}{3 \times 9} \right) \div \left(\frac{11 \times 4}{5 \times 7} \right) = \left(\frac{56}{27} \right) \div \left(\frac{44}{35} \right) = \frac{56}{27} \div \frac{44}{35} = \frac{56}{27} \times \frac{35}{44}$

    $= \frac{\overset{14}{\cancel{56}} \times 35}{27 \times \underset{11}{\cancel{44}}} = \frac{14 \times 35}{27 \times 11} = \frac{490}{297} = 1\frac{193}{297}$

8. $\left(4\frac{2}{3} \div 2\frac{3}{4} \right) \div \left(2\frac{1}{5} \div 1\frac{1}{4} \right) = \left(\frac{(4 \times 3)+2}{3} \div \frac{(2 \times 4)+3}{4} \right) \div \left(\frac{(2 \times 5)+1}{5} \div \frac{(1 \times 4)+1}{4} \right) = \left(\frac{12+2}{3} \div \frac{8+3}{4} \right) \div \left(\frac{10+1}{5} \div \frac{4+1}{4} \right)$

    $= \left(\frac{14}{3} \div \frac{11}{4} \right) \div \left(\frac{11}{5} \div \frac{5}{4} \right) = \left(\frac{14}{3} \times \frac{4}{11} \right) \div \left(\frac{11}{5} \times \frac{4}{5} \right) = \left(\frac{14 \times 4}{3 \times 11} \right) \div \left(\frac{11 \times 4}{5 \times 5} \right) = \left(\frac{56}{33} \right) \div \left(\frac{44}{25} \right) = \frac{56}{33} \div \frac{44}{25} = \frac{56}{33} \times \frac{25}{44}$

$$= \frac{\overset{14}{\cancel{56}} \times 25}{33 \times \underset{11}{\cancel{44}}} = \frac{14 \times 25}{33 \times 11} = \mathbf{\frac{350}{363}}$$

9. $\left[3\frac{2}{3} \div \left(2\frac{1}{3} \div 1\frac{1}{4} \right) \right] \div 2\frac{3}{5} = \left[\frac{(3 \times 3) + 2}{3} \div \left(\frac{(2 \times 3) + 1}{3} \div \frac{(1 \times 4) + 1}{4} \right) \right] \div \frac{(2 \times 5) + 3}{5} = \left[\frac{9 + 2}{3} \div \left(\frac{6 + 1}{3} \div \frac{4 + 1}{4} \right) \right] \div \frac{10 + 3}{5}$

$= \left[\frac{11}{3} \div \left(\frac{7}{3} \div \frac{5}{4} \right) \right] \div \frac{13}{5} = \left[\frac{11}{3} \div \left(\frac{7}{3} \times \frac{4}{5} \right) \right] \div \frac{13}{5} = \left[\frac{11}{3} \div \left(\frac{7 \times 4}{3 \times 5} \right) \right] \div \frac{13}{5} = \left[\frac{11}{3} \div \left(\frac{28}{15} \right) \right] \div \frac{13}{5} = \left[\frac{11}{3} \div \frac{28}{15} \right] \div \frac{13}{5}$

$= \left[\frac{11}{3} \times \frac{15}{28} \right] \div \frac{13}{5} = \left[\frac{11 \times \overset{5}{\cancel{15}}}{\underset{1}{\cancel{3}} \times 28} \right] \div \frac{13}{5} = \left[\frac{11 \times 5}{1 \times 28} \right] \div \frac{13}{5} = \left[\frac{55}{28} \right] \div \frac{13}{5} = \frac{55}{28} \div \frac{13}{5} = \frac{55}{28} \times \frac{5}{13} = \frac{55 \times 5}{28 \times 13} = \mathbf{\frac{275}{364}}$

10. $\left[\left(4\frac{2}{5} \div 1\frac{2}{3} \right) \div \left(3\frac{1}{5} \div 1\frac{2}{3} \right) \right] \div 2\frac{1}{3} = \left[\left(\frac{(4 \times 5) + 2}{5} \div \frac{(1 \times 3) + 2}{3} \right) \div \left(\frac{(3 \times 5) + 1}{5} \div \frac{(1 \times 3) + 2}{3} \right) \right] \div \frac{(2 \times 3) + 1}{3}$

$= \left[\left(\frac{20 + 2}{5} \div \frac{3 + 2}{3} \right) \div \left(\frac{15 + 1}{5} \div \frac{3 + 2}{3} \right) \right] \div \frac{6 + 1}{3} = \left[\left(\frac{22}{5} \div \frac{5}{3} \right) \div \left(\frac{16}{5} \div \frac{5}{3} \right) \right] \div \frac{7}{3} = \left[\left(\frac{22}{5} \times \frac{3}{5} \right) \div \left(\frac{16}{5} \times \frac{3}{5} \right) \right] \div \frac{7}{3}$

$= \left[\left(\frac{22 \times 3}{5 \times 5} \right) \div \left(\frac{16 \times 3}{5 \times 5} \right) \right] \div \frac{7}{3} = \left[\left(\frac{66}{25} \right) \div \left(\frac{48}{25} \right) \right] \div \frac{7}{3} = \left[\frac{66}{25} \div \frac{48}{25} \right] \div \frac{7}{3} = \left[\frac{66}{25} \times \frac{25}{48} \right] \div \frac{7}{3} = \left[\frac{\overset{33}{\cancel{66}} \times \overset{1}{\cancel{25}}}{\underset{1}{\cancel{25}} \times \underset{24}{\cancel{48}}} \right] \div \frac{7}{3} = \left[\frac{33 \times 1}{1 \times 24} \right] \div \frac{7}{3}$

$= \left[\frac{33}{24} \right] \div \frac{7}{3} = \frac{33}{24} \div \frac{7}{3} = \frac{33}{24} \times \frac{3}{7} = \frac{33 \times \overset{1}{\cancel{3}}}{\underset{8}{\cancel{24}} \times 7} = \frac{33 \times 1}{8 \times 7} = \mathbf{\frac{33}{56}}$

Section 5.5 Solutions:

1. $\left(4\frac{1}{2} \div 2\frac{3}{5} \right) \times 2\frac{3}{4} = \left(\frac{(4 \times 2) + 1}{2} \div \frac{(2 \times 5) + 3}{5} \right) \times \frac{(2 \times 4) + 3}{4} = \left(\frac{8 + 1}{2} \div \frac{10 + 3}{5} \right) \times \frac{8 + 3}{4} = \left(\frac{9}{2} \div \frac{13}{5} \right) \times \frac{11}{4} = \left(\frac{9}{2} \times \frac{5}{13} \right) \times \frac{11}{4}$

$= \left(\frac{9 \times 5}{2 \times 13} \right) \times \frac{11}{4} = \left(\frac{45}{26} \right) \times \frac{11}{4} = \frac{45}{26} \times \frac{11}{4} = \frac{45 \times 11}{26 \times 4} = \frac{495}{104} = \mathbf{4\frac{79}{104}}$

2. $1\frac{3}{8} + \left(2\frac{1}{5} \div 1\frac{4}{5} \right) = \frac{(1 \times 8) + 3}{8} + \left(\frac{(2 \times 5) + 1}{5} \div \frac{(1 \times 5) + 4}{5} \right) = \frac{8 + 3}{8} + \left(\frac{10 + 1}{5} \div \frac{5 + 4}{5} \right) = \frac{11}{8} + \left(\frac{11}{5} \div \frac{9}{5} \right) = \frac{11}{8} + \left(\frac{11}{5} \times \frac{5}{9} \right)$

$= \frac{11}{8} + \left(\frac{11 \times \overset{1}{\cancel{5}}}{\underset{1}{\cancel{5}} \times 9} \right) = \frac{11}{8} + \left(\frac{11 \times 1}{1 \times 9} \right) = \frac{11}{8} + \left(\frac{11}{9} \right) = \frac{11}{8} + \frac{11}{9} = \frac{(11 \times 9) + (11 \times 8)}{8 \times 9} = \frac{99 + 88}{72} = \frac{187}{72} = \mathbf{2\frac{43}{72}}$

3. $\left(1\frac{3}{4} \times 2\frac{1}{3} \right) \div 1\frac{2}{5} = \left(\frac{(1 \times 4) + 3}{4} \times \frac{(2 \times 3) + 1}{3} \right) \div \frac{(1 \times 5) + 2}{5} = \left(\frac{4 + 3}{4} \times \frac{6 + 1}{3} \right) \div \frac{5 + 2}{5} = \left(\frac{7}{4} \times \frac{7}{3} \right) \div \frac{7}{5} = \left(\frac{7 \times 7}{4 \times 3} \right) \div \frac{7}{5}$

$= \left(\frac{49}{12} \right) \div \frac{7}{5} = \frac{49}{12} \div \frac{7}{5} = \frac{49}{12} \times \frac{5}{7} = \frac{\overset{7}{\cancel{49}} \times 5}{12 \times \underset{1}{\cancel{7}}} = \frac{7 \times 5}{12 \times 1} = \frac{35}{12} = \mathbf{2\frac{11}{12}}$

4. $\left(2\frac{3}{4} - 2\frac{1}{4} \right) + 1\frac{3}{4} = \left(\frac{(2 \times 4) + 3}{4} - \frac{(2 \times 4) + 1}{4} \right) + \frac{(1 \times 4) + 3}{4} = \left(\frac{8 + 3}{4} - \frac{8 + 1}{4} \right) + \frac{4 + 3}{4} = \left(\frac{11}{4} - \frac{9}{4} \right) + \frac{7}{4} = \left(\frac{11 - 9}{4} \right) + \frac{7}{4}$

$= \left(\frac{2}{4} \right) + \frac{7}{4} = \frac{2}{4} + \frac{7}{4} = \frac{2 + 7}{4} = \frac{9}{4} = \mathbf{2\frac{1}{4}}$

5. $3\frac{1}{5} \div \left(4\frac{2}{3} + 1\frac{1}{3}\right) = \frac{(3\times5)+1}{5} \div \left(\frac{(4\times3)+2}{3} + \frac{(1\times3)+1}{3}\right) = \frac{15+1}{5} \div \left(\frac{12+2}{3} + \frac{3+1}{3}\right) = \frac{16}{5} \div \left(\frac{14}{3} + \frac{4}{3}\right) = \frac{16}{5} \div \left(\frac{14+4}{3}\right)$

$= \frac{16}{5} \div \left(\frac{18}{3}\right) = \frac{16}{5} \div \frac{18}{3} = \frac{16}{5} \times \frac{3}{18} = \frac{16 \times \overset{1}{\cancel{3}}}{5 \times \cancel{18}}_{\,6} = \frac{16 \times 1}{5 \times 6} = \frac{\overset{8}{\cancel{16}}}{\underset{15}{\cancel{30}}} = \frac{8}{15}$

6. $\left(2\frac{2}{3} \times 1\frac{1}{2}\right) + \left(2\frac{4}{5} \times 3\frac{1}{2}\right) = \left(\frac{(2\times3)+2}{3} \times \frac{(1\times2)+1}{2}\right) + \left(\frac{(2\times5)+4}{5} \times \frac{(3\times2)+1}{2}\right) = \left(\frac{6+2}{3} \times \frac{2+1}{2}\right) + \left(\frac{10+4}{5} \times \frac{6+1}{2}\right)$

$= \left(\frac{8}{3} \times \frac{3}{2}\right) + \left(\frac{14}{5} \times \frac{7}{2}\right) = \frac{\overset{4}{\cancel{8}} \times \overset{1}{\cancel{3}}}{\underset{1}{\cancel{3}} \times \underset{1}{\cancel{2}}} + \frac{\overset{7}{\cancel{14}} \times 7}{5 \times \underset{1}{\cancel{2}}} = \left(\frac{4\times1}{1\times1}\right) + \left(\frac{7\times7}{5\times1}\right) = \left(\frac{4}{1}\right) + \left(\frac{49}{5}\right) = \frac{4}{1} + \frac{49}{5} = \frac{(4\times5)+(49\times1)}{1\times5}$

$= \frac{20+49}{5} = \frac{69}{5} = 13\frac{4}{5}$

7. $\left(3\frac{3}{4} \div 2\frac{3}{5}\right) \div \left(1\frac{4}{5} \times 1\frac{2}{3}\right) = \left(\frac{(3\times4)+3}{4} \div \frac{(2\times5)+3}{5}\right) \div \left(\frac{(1\times5)+4}{5} \times \frac{(1\times3)+2}{3}\right) = \left(\frac{12+3}{4} \div \frac{10+3}{5}\right) \div \left(\frac{5+4}{5} \times \frac{3+2}{3}\right)$

$= \left(\frac{15}{4} \div \frac{13}{5}\right) \div \left(\frac{9}{5} \times \frac{5}{3}\right) = \left(\frac{15}{4} \times \frac{5}{13}\right) \div \frac{\overset{3}{\cancel{9}} \times \overset{1}{\cancel{5}}}{\underset{1}{\cancel{5}} \times \underset{1}{\cancel{3}}} = \left(\frac{15\times5}{4\times13}\right) \div \left(\frac{3\times1}{1\times1}\right) = \left(\frac{75}{52}\right) \div \left(\frac{3}{1}\right) = \frac{75}{52} \div \frac{3}{1} = \frac{75}{52} \times \frac{1}{3} = \frac{\overset{25}{\cancel{75}} \times 1}{52 \times \underset{1}{\cancel{3}}}$

$= \frac{25\times1}{52\times1} = \frac{25}{52}$

8. $\left(2\frac{1}{8} \times 1\frac{2}{5}\right) \div \left(2\frac{3}{5} + 2\frac{1}{5}\right) = \left(\frac{(2\times8)+1}{8} \times \frac{(1\times5)+2}{5}\right) \div \left(\frac{(2\times5)+3}{5} + \frac{(2\times5)+1}{5}\right) = \left(\frac{16+1}{8} \times \frac{5+2}{5}\right) \div \left(\frac{10+3}{5} + \frac{10+1}{5}\right)$

$= \left(\frac{17}{8} \times \frac{7}{5}\right) \div \left(\frac{13}{5} + \frac{11}{5}\right) = \left(\frac{17\times7}{8\times5}\right) \div \left(\frac{13+11}{5}\right) = \left(\frac{119}{40}\right) \div \left(\frac{24}{5}\right) = \frac{119}{40} \div \frac{24}{5} = \frac{119}{40} \times \frac{5}{24} = \frac{119 \times \overset{1}{\cancel{5}}}{\underset{8}{\cancel{40}} \times 24} = \frac{119 \times 1}{8 \times 24}$

$= \frac{119}{192}$

9. $\left(1\frac{2}{3} + 3\frac{1}{4}\right) \div \left(2\frac{3}{5} - 1\frac{1}{3}\right) = \left(\frac{(1\times3)+2}{3} + \frac{(3\times4)+1}{4}\right) \div \left(\frac{(2\times5)+3}{5} - \frac{(1\times3)+1}{3}\right) = \left(\frac{3+2}{3} + \frac{12+1}{4}\right) \div \left(\frac{10+3}{5} - \frac{3+1}{3}\right)$

$= \left(\frac{5}{3} + \frac{13}{4}\right) \div \left(\frac{13}{5} - \frac{4}{3}\right) = \left(\frac{(5\times4)+(13\times3)}{3\times4}\right) \div \left(\frac{(13\times3)-(4\times5)}{5\times3}\right) = \left(\frac{20+39}{12}\right) \div \left(\frac{39-20}{15}\right) = \left(\frac{59}{12}\right) \div \left(\frac{19}{15}\right) = \frac{59}{12} \div \frac{19}{15}$

$= \frac{59}{12} \times \frac{15}{19} = \frac{59 \times \overset{5}{\cancel{15}}}{\underset{4}{\cancel{12}} \times 19} = \frac{59\times5}{4\times19} = \frac{295}{76} = 3\frac{67}{76}$

10. $\left[\left(3\frac{1}{2} - 1\frac{2}{3}\right) + 1\frac{2}{5}\right] \times 2\frac{1}{3} = \left[\left(\frac{(3\times2)+1}{2} - \frac{(1\times3)+2}{3}\right) + \frac{(1\times5)+2}{5}\right] \times \frac{(2\times3)+1}{3} = \left[\left(\frac{6+1}{2} - \frac{3+2}{3}\right) + \frac{5+2}{5}\right] \times \frac{6+1}{3}$

$= \left[\left(\frac{7}{2} - \frac{5}{3}\right) + \frac{7}{5}\right] \times \frac{7}{3} = \left[\left(\frac{(7\times3)-(5\times2)}{2\times3}\right) + \frac{7}{5}\right] \times \frac{7}{3} = \left[\left(\frac{21-10}{6}\right) + \frac{7}{5}\right] \times \frac{7}{3} = \left[\left(\frac{11}{6}\right) + \frac{7}{5}\right] \times \frac{7}{3} = \left[\frac{11}{6} + \frac{7}{5}\right] \times \frac{7}{3}$

$= \left[\frac{(11\times5)+(7\times6)}{6\times5}\right] \times \frac{7}{3} = \left[\frac{55+42}{30}\right] \times \frac{7}{3} = \left[\frac{97}{30}\right] \times \frac{7}{3} = \frac{97}{30} \times \frac{7}{3} = \frac{97\times7}{30\times3} = \frac{679}{90} = 7\frac{49}{90}$

Chapter 6 Solutions:

Section 6.1 Solutions:

1. $\dfrac{2}{5} + 0.01 = \dfrac{2}{5} + \dfrac{1}{100} = \dfrac{(2 \times 100) + (1 \times 5)}{5 \times 100} = \dfrac{200 + 5}{500} = \dfrac{\overset{41}{\cancel{205}}}{\underset{100}{\cancel{500}}} = \mathbf{\dfrac{41}{100}}$

2. $\dfrac{3}{8} + \dfrac{0.2}{0.06} + 1 = \left(\dfrac{3}{8} + \dfrac{0.2}{0.06}\right) + 1 = \left(\dfrac{3}{8} + \dfrac{\frac{2}{10}}{\frac{6}{100}}\right) + \dfrac{1}{1} = \left(\dfrac{3}{8} + \dfrac{2 \times 100}{10 \times 6}\right) + \dfrac{1}{1} = \left(\dfrac{3}{8} + \dfrac{\overset{10}{\cancel{200}}}{\underset{3}{\cancel{60}}}\right) + \dfrac{1}{1} = \left(\dfrac{3}{8} + \dfrac{10}{3}\right) + \dfrac{1}{1}$

   $= \left(\dfrac{(3 \times 3) + (10 \times 8)}{8 \times 3}\right) + \dfrac{1}{1} = \left(\dfrac{9 + 80}{24}\right) + \dfrac{1}{1} = \left(\dfrac{89}{24}\right) + \dfrac{1}{1} = \dfrac{89}{24} + \dfrac{1}{1} = \dfrac{(89 \times 1) + (1 \times 24)}{24 \times 1} = \dfrac{89 + 24}{24} = \dfrac{113}{24} = \mathbf{4\dfrac{17}{24}}$

3. $\dfrac{3}{5} + \dfrac{1.5}{0.2} + \dfrac{3}{0.4} = \left(\dfrac{3}{5} + \dfrac{1.5}{0.2}\right) + \dfrac{3}{0.4} = \left(\dfrac{3}{5} + \dfrac{\frac{15}{10}}{\frac{2}{10}}\right) + \dfrac{3}{\frac{4}{10}} = \left(\dfrac{3}{5} + \dfrac{15 \times 10}{10 \times 2}\right) + \dfrac{3 \times 10}{1 \times 4} = \left(\dfrac{3}{5} + \dfrac{\overset{15}{\cancel{150}}}{\underset{2}{\cancel{20}}}\right) + \dfrac{\overset{15}{\cancel{30}}}{\underset{2}{\cancel{4}}} = \left(\dfrac{3}{5} + \dfrac{15}{2}\right) + \dfrac{15}{2}$

   $= \left(\dfrac{(3 \times 2) + (15 \times 5)}{5 \times 2}\right) + \dfrac{15}{2} = \left(\dfrac{6 + 75}{10}\right) + \dfrac{15}{2} = \left(\dfrac{81}{10}\right) + \dfrac{15}{2} = \dfrac{81}{10} + \dfrac{15}{2} = \dfrac{(81 \times 2) + (15 \times 10)}{10 \times 2} = \dfrac{162 + 150}{20} = \dfrac{\overset{78}{\cancel{312}}}{\underset{5}{\cancel{20}}} = \dfrac{78}{5}$

   $= \mathbf{15\dfrac{3}{5}}$

4. $\left(\dfrac{1}{2} + \dfrac{3}{4}\right) + \dfrac{0.8}{1.2} = \left(\dfrac{(1 \times 4) + (3 \times 2)}{2 \times 4}\right) + \dfrac{\frac{8}{10}}{\frac{12}{10}} = \left(\dfrac{4 + 6}{8}\right) + \dfrac{8 \times 10}{10 \times 12} = \left(\dfrac{10}{8}\right) + \dfrac{\overset{2}{\cancel{80}}}{\underset{3}{\cancel{120}}} = \dfrac{\overset{5}{\cancel{10}}}{\underset{4}{\cancel{8}}} + \dfrac{2}{3} = \dfrac{5}{4} + \dfrac{2}{3} = \dfrac{(5 \times 3) + (2 \times 4)}{4 \times 3}$

   $= \dfrac{15 + 8}{12} = \dfrac{23}{12} = \mathbf{1\dfrac{11}{12}}$

5. $5.5 + \dfrac{3}{5} + \dfrac{0.2}{0.5} = \left(5.5 + \dfrac{3}{5}\right) + \dfrac{0.2}{0.5} = \left(\dfrac{55}{10} + \dfrac{3}{5}\right) + \dfrac{\frac{2}{10}}{\frac{5}{10}} = \left(\dfrac{\overset{11}{\cancel{55}}}{\underset{2}{\cancel{10}}} + \dfrac{3}{5}\right) + \dfrac{2 \times 10}{10 \times 5} = \left(\dfrac{11}{2} + \dfrac{3}{5}\right) + \dfrac{\overset{2}{\cancel{20}}}{\underset{5}{\cancel{50}}} = \left(\dfrac{11}{2} + \dfrac{3}{5}\right) + \dfrac{2}{5}$

   $= \left(\dfrac{(11 \times 5) + (3 \times 2)}{2 \times 5}\right) + \dfrac{2}{5} = \left(\dfrac{55 + 6}{10}\right) + \dfrac{2}{5} = \left(\dfrac{61}{10}\right) + \dfrac{2}{5} = \dfrac{61}{10} + \dfrac{2}{5} = \dfrac{(61 \times 5) + (2 \times 10)}{10 \times 5} = \dfrac{305 + 20}{50} = \dfrac{\overset{13}{\cancel{325}}}{\underset{2}{\cancel{50}}} = \dfrac{13}{2}$

   $= \mathbf{6\dfrac{1}{2}}$

6. $\left(\dfrac{6}{8} + \dfrac{1}{8} + \dfrac{3}{8}\right) + \dfrac{0.4}{0.08} = \left(\dfrac{6 + 1 + 3}{8}\right) + \dfrac{\frac{4}{10}}{\frac{8}{100}} = \left(\dfrac{10}{8}\right) + \dfrac{4 \times 100}{10 \times 8} = \dfrac{\overset{5}{\cancel{10}}}{\underset{4}{\cancel{8}}} + \dfrac{\overset{5}{\cancel{400}}}{\underset{1}{\cancel{80}}} = \dfrac{5}{4} + \dfrac{5}{1} = \dfrac{(5 \times 1) + (5 \times 4)}{4 \times 1} = \dfrac{5 + 20}{4} = \dfrac{25}{4}$

   $= \mathbf{6\dfrac{1}{4}}$

7. $\left(\dfrac{3}{4} + \dfrac{0.2}{0.1}\right) + \left(\dfrac{1}{0.1} + \dfrac{1}{5}\right) = \left(\dfrac{3}{4} + \dfrac{\frac{2}{10}}{\frac{1}{10}}\right) + \left(\dfrac{1}{\frac{1}{10}} + \dfrac{1}{5}\right) = \left(\dfrac{3}{4} + \dfrac{2 \times 10}{10 \times 1}\right) + \left(\dfrac{1 \times 10}{1 \times 1} + \dfrac{1}{5}\right) = \left(\dfrac{3}{4} + \dfrac{\overset{2}{\cancel{20}}}{\underset{1}{\cancel{10}}}\right) + \left(\dfrac{10}{1} + \dfrac{1}{5}\right)$

   $= \left(\dfrac{3}{4} + \dfrac{2}{1}\right) + \left(\dfrac{(10 \times 5) + (1 \times 1)}{1 \times 5}\right) = \left(\dfrac{(3 \times 1) + (2 \times 4)}{4 \times 1}\right) + \left(\dfrac{50 + 1}{5}\right) = \left(\dfrac{3 + 8}{4}\right) + \left(\dfrac{51}{5}\right) = \left(\dfrac{11}{4}\right) + \dfrac{51}{5} = \dfrac{11}{4} + \dfrac{51}{5}$

$$= \frac{(11 \times 5) + (51 \times 4)}{4 \times 5} = \frac{55 + 204}{20} = \frac{259}{20} = \mathbf{12\frac{19}{20}}$$

8. $\dfrac{0.04}{1.2} + \left(2.2 + \dfrac{4}{5}\right) = \dfrac{\dfrac{4}{100}}{\dfrac{12}{10}} + \left(\dfrac{22}{10} + \dfrac{4}{5}\right) = \dfrac{4 \times 10}{100 \times 12} + \left(\dfrac{(22 \times 5) + (4 \times 10)}{10 \times 5}\right) = \dfrac{\overset{1}{\cancel{40}}}{\underset{30}{\cancel{1200}}} + \left(\dfrac{110 + 40}{50}\right) = \dfrac{1}{30} + \left(\dfrac{150}{50}\right)$

$$= \frac{1}{30} + \frac{\overset{3}{\cancel{150}}}{\underset{1}{\cancel{50}}} = \frac{1}{30} + \frac{3}{1} = \frac{(1 \times 1) + (3 \times 30)}{30 \times 1} = \frac{1 + 90}{30} = \frac{91}{30} = \mathbf{3\frac{1}{30}}$$

9. $\left(\dfrac{1}{4} + \dfrac{5}{3}\right) + \left(\dfrac{1}{0.4} + \dfrac{5}{0.2}\right) = \left(\dfrac{(1 \times 3) + (5 \times 4)}{4 \times 3}\right) + \left(\dfrac{\dfrac{1}{1}}{\dfrac{4}{10}} + \dfrac{\dfrac{5}{1}}{\dfrac{2}{10}}\right) = \left(\dfrac{3 + 20}{12}\right) + \left(\dfrac{1 \times 10}{1 \times 4} + \dfrac{5 \times 10}{1 \times 2}\right) = \left(\dfrac{23}{12}\right) + \left(\dfrac{\overset{5}{\cancel{10}}}{\underset{2}{\cancel{4}}} + \dfrac{\overset{25}{\cancel{50}}}{\underset{1}{\cancel{2}}}\right)$

$$= \frac{23}{12} + \left(\frac{5}{2} + \frac{25}{1}\right) = \frac{23}{12} + \left(\frac{(5 \times 1) + (25 \times 2)}{2 \times 1}\right) = \frac{23}{12} + \left(\frac{5 + 50}{2}\right) = \frac{23}{12} + \left(\frac{55}{2}\right) = \frac{23}{12} + \frac{55}{2} = \frac{(23 \times 2) + (55 \times 12)}{12 \times 2}$$

$$= \frac{46 + 660}{24} = \frac{\overset{353}{\cancel{706}}}{\underset{12}{\cancel{24}}} = \frac{353}{12} = \mathbf{29\frac{5}{12}}$$

10. $\left(\dfrac{1}{4} + \dfrac{3}{2}\right) + \left(\dfrac{0.2}{0.04} + 2\right) = \left(\dfrac{(1 \times 2) + (3 \times 4)}{4 \times 2}\right) + \left(\dfrac{\dfrac{2}{10}}{\dfrac{4}{100}} + \dfrac{2}{1}\right) = \left(\dfrac{2 + 12}{8}\right) + \left(\dfrac{2 \times 100}{10 \times 4} + \dfrac{2}{1}\right) = \left(\dfrac{14}{8}\right) + \left(\dfrac{\overset{5}{\cancel{200}}}{\underset{1}{\cancel{40}}} + \dfrac{2}{1}\right)$

$$= \frac{\overset{7}{\cancel{14}}}{\underset{4}{\cancel{8}}} + \left(\frac{5}{1} + \frac{2}{1}\right) = \frac{7}{4} + \left(\frac{5 + 2}{1}\right) = \frac{7}{4} + \left(\frac{7}{1}\right) = \frac{7}{4} + \frac{7}{1} = \frac{(7 \times 1) + (7 \times 4)}{4 \times 1} = \frac{7 + 28}{4} = \frac{35}{4} = \mathbf{8\frac{3}{4}}$$

Section 6.2 Solutions:

1. $\dfrac{3}{8} - \dfrac{0.12}{0.3} = \dfrac{3}{8} - \dfrac{\dfrac{12}{100}}{\dfrac{3}{10}} = \dfrac{3}{8} - \dfrac{12 \times 10}{100 \times 3} = \dfrac{3}{8} - \dfrac{\overset{2}{\cancel{120}}}{\underset{5}{\cancel{300}}} = \dfrac{3}{8} - \dfrac{2}{5} = \dfrac{(3 \times 5) - (2 \times 8)}{8 \times 5} = \dfrac{15 - 16}{40} = -\dfrac{\mathbf{1}}{\mathbf{40}}$

2. $\dfrac{0.3}{0.5} - \dfrac{4}{6} - 3 = \left(\dfrac{0.3}{0.5} - \dfrac{4}{6}\right) - 3 = \left(\dfrac{\dfrac{3}{10}}{\dfrac{5}{10}} - \dfrac{4}{6}\right) - \dfrac{3}{1} = \left(\dfrac{3 \times 10}{10 \times 5} - \dfrac{4}{6}\right) - \dfrac{3}{1} = \left(\dfrac{\overset{3}{\cancel{30}}}{\underset{5}{\cancel{50}}} - \dfrac{\overset{2}{\cancel{4}}}{\underset{3}{\cancel{6}}}\right) - \dfrac{3}{1} = \left(\dfrac{3}{5} - \dfrac{2}{3}\right) - \dfrac{3}{1}$

$$= \left(\frac{(3 \times 3) - (2 \times 5)}{5 \times 3}\right) - \frac{3}{1} = \left(\frac{9 - 10}{15}\right) - \frac{3}{1} = \left(\frac{-1}{15}\right) - \frac{3}{1} = -\frac{1}{15} - \frac{3}{1} = \frac{(-1 \times 1) - (3 \times 15)}{15 \times 1} = \frac{-1 - 45}{15} = \frac{-46}{15} = -\left(\mathbf{3\frac{1}{15}}\right)$$

3. $\left(\dfrac{5}{6} - \dfrac{1}{6}\right) - 1.25 = \left(\dfrac{5 - 1}{6}\right) - \dfrac{125}{100} = \left(\dfrac{4}{6}\right) - \dfrac{\overset{5}{\cancel{125}}}{\underset{4}{\cancel{100}}} = \dfrac{\overset{2}{\cancel{4}}}{\underset{3}{\cancel{6}}} - \dfrac{5}{4} = \dfrac{2}{3} - \dfrac{5}{4} = \dfrac{(2 \times 4) - (5 \times 3)}{3 \times 4} = \dfrac{8 - 15}{12} = -\dfrac{\mathbf{7}}{\mathbf{12}}$

4. $\left(\dfrac{5}{2} - \dfrac{0.01}{0.4}\right) - \dfrac{3}{5} = \left(\dfrac{5}{2} - \dfrac{\dfrac{1}{100}}{\dfrac{4}{10}}\right) - \dfrac{3}{5} = \left(\dfrac{5}{2} - \dfrac{1 \times 10}{100 \times 4}\right) - \dfrac{3}{5} = \left(\dfrac{5}{2} - \dfrac{\overset{1}{\cancel{10}}}{\underset{40}{\cancel{400}}}\right) - \dfrac{3}{5} = \left(\dfrac{5}{2} - \dfrac{1}{40}\right) - \dfrac{3}{5} = \left(\dfrac{(5 \times 40) - (1 \times 2)}{2 \times 40}\right) - \dfrac{3}{5}$

$$= \left(\frac{200 - 2}{80}\right) - \frac{3}{5} = \left(\frac{198}{80}\right) - \frac{3}{5} = \frac{\overset{99}{\cancel{198}}}{\underset{40}{\cancel{80}}} - \frac{3}{5} = \frac{99}{40} - \frac{3}{5} = \frac{(99 \times 5) - (3 \times 40)}{40 \times 5} = \frac{495 - 120}{200} = \frac{\overset{15}{\cancel{375}}}{\underset{8}{\cancel{200}}} = \frac{15}{8} = \mathbf{1\frac{7}{8}}$$

5. $\dfrac{3}{4} - \dfrac{1}{3} - 0.2 = \left(\dfrac{3}{4} - \dfrac{1}{3}\right) - 0.2 = \left(\dfrac{3}{4} - \dfrac{1}{3}\right) - \dfrac{\overset{1}{\cancel{2}}}{\underset{5}{\cancel{10}}} = \left(\dfrac{(3 \times 3) - (1 \times 4)}{4 \times 3}\right) - \dfrac{1}{5} = \left(\dfrac{9 - 4}{12}\right) - \dfrac{1}{5} = \left(\dfrac{5}{12}\right) - \dfrac{1}{5} = \dfrac{5}{12} - \dfrac{1}{5}$

$$= \frac{(5 \times 5) - (1 \times 12)}{12 \times 5} = \frac{25 - 12}{60} = \mathbf{\frac{13}{60}}$$

6. $\frac{5}{6} - \left(\frac{1}{10} - 0.01\right) = \frac{5}{6} - \left(\frac{1}{10} - \frac{1}{100}\right) = \frac{5}{6} - \left(\frac{(1 \times 100) - (1 \times 10)}{10 \times 100}\right) = \frac{5}{6} - \left(\frac{100 - 10}{1000}\right) = \frac{5}{6} - \left(\frac{90}{1000}\right) = \frac{5}{6} - \frac{\overset{9}{\cancel{90}}}{\underset{100}{\cancel{1000}}}$

$$= \frac{5}{6} - \frac{9}{100} = \frac{(5 \times 100) - (9 \times 6)}{6 \times 100} = \frac{500 - 54}{600} = \frac{\overset{223}{\cancel{446}}}{\underset{300}{\cancel{600}}} = \mathbf{\frac{223}{300}}$$

7. $8.5 - \frac{2}{10} - \frac{0.4}{0.5} = \left(8.5 - \frac{2}{10}\right) - \frac{0.4}{0.5} = \left(\frac{85}{10} - \frac{2}{10}\right) - \frac{\frac{4}{10}}{\frac{5}{10}} = \left(\frac{85 - 2}{10}\right) - \frac{4 \times 10}{10 \times 5} = \left(\frac{83}{10}\right) - \frac{\overset{4}{\cancel{40}}}{\underset{5}{\cancel{50}}} = \frac{83}{10} - \frac{4}{5}$

$$= \frac{(83 \times 5) - (4 \times 10)}{10 \times 5} = \frac{415 - 40}{50} = \frac{\overset{15}{\cancel{375}}}{\underset{2}{\cancel{50}}} = \frac{15}{2} = \mathbf{7\frac{1}{2}}$$

8. $12.5 - \left(\frac{3}{7} - \frac{2}{3}\right) = \frac{125}{10} - \left(\frac{3}{7} - \frac{2}{3}\right) = \frac{\overset{25}{\cancel{125}}}{\underset{2}{\cancel{10}}} - \left(\frac{(3 \times 3) - (2 \times 7)}{7 \times 3}\right) = \frac{25}{2} - \left(\frac{9 - 14}{21}\right) = \frac{25}{2} - \left(\frac{-5}{21}\right) = \frac{25}{2} - \frac{-5}{21} = \frac{25}{2} + \frac{5}{21}$

$$= \frac{(25 \times 21) + (5 \times 2)}{2 \times 21} = \frac{525 + 10}{42} = \frac{535}{42} = \mathbf{12\frac{31}{42}}$$

9. $\frac{0.2}{0.04} - \left(\frac{0.1}{2} - \frac{0.1}{4}\right) = \frac{\frac{2}{10}}{\frac{4}{100}} - \left(\frac{\frac{1}{10}}{\frac{2}{1}} - \frac{\frac{1}{10}}{\frac{4}{1}}\right) = \frac{2 \times 100}{10 \times 4} - \left(\frac{1 \times 1}{10 \times 2} - \frac{1 \times 1}{10 \times 4}\right) = \frac{\overset{5}{\cancel{200}}}{\underset{1}{\cancel{40}}} - \left(\frac{1}{20} - \frac{1}{40}\right) = \frac{5}{1} - \left(\frac{(1 \times 40) - (1 \times 20)}{20 \times 40}\right)$

$$= \frac{5}{1} - \left(\frac{40 - 20}{800}\right) = \frac{5}{1} - \left(\frac{20}{800}\right) = \frac{5}{1} - \frac{\overset{1}{\cancel{20}}}{\underset{40}{\cancel{800}}} = \frac{5}{1} - \frac{1}{40} = \frac{(5 \times 40) - (1 \times 1)}{1 \times 40} = \frac{200 - 1}{40} = \frac{199}{40} = \mathbf{4\frac{39}{40}}$$

10. $\left(\frac{8}{3} - \frac{4}{3}\right) - \left(\frac{0.4}{0.12} - \frac{2}{3}\right) = \left(\frac{8 - 4}{3}\right) - \left(\frac{\frac{4}{10}}{\frac{12}{100}} - \frac{2}{3}\right) = \left(\frac{4}{3}\right) - \left(\frac{4 \times 100}{10 \times 12} - \frac{2}{3}\right) = \frac{4}{3} - \left(\frac{\overset{10}{\cancel{400}}}{\underset{3}{\cancel{120}}} - \frac{2}{3}\right) = \frac{4}{3} - \left(\frac{10}{3} - \frac{2}{3}\right)$

$$= \frac{4}{3} - \left(\frac{10 - 2}{3}\right) = \frac{4}{3} - \left(\frac{8}{3}\right) = \frac{4}{3} - \frac{8}{3} = \frac{4 - 8}{3} = \frac{-4}{3} = -\left(\mathbf{1\frac{1}{3}}\right)$$

Section 6.3 Solutions:

1. $\frac{3}{5} \times \frac{0.05}{0.1} = \frac{3}{5} \times \frac{\frac{5}{100}}{\frac{1}{10}} = \frac{3}{5} \times \frac{5 \times 10}{100 \times 1} = \frac{3}{5} \times \frac{\overset{1}{\cancel{50}}}{\underset{2}{\cancel{100}}} = \frac{3}{5} \times \frac{1}{2} = \frac{3 \times 1}{5 \times 2} = \mathbf{\frac{3}{10}}$

2. $5 \times \frac{0.22}{0.001} \times \frac{1}{100} = \frac{5}{1} \times \frac{\frac{22}{100}}{\frac{1}{1000}} \times \frac{1}{100} = \frac{5}{1} \times \frac{22 \times 1000}{100 \times 1} \times \frac{1}{100} = \frac{5}{1} \times \frac{\overset{220}{\cancel{22000}}}{\underset{1}{\cancel{100}}} \times \frac{1}{100} = \frac{5}{1} \times \frac{220}{1} \times \frac{1}{100} = \frac{5 \times \overset{11}{\cancel{220}} \times 1}{1 \times 1 \times \underset{5}{\cancel{100}}}$

$$= \frac{5 \times 11 \times 1}{1 \times 1 \times 5} = \frac{\overset{11}{\cancel{55}}}{\underset{1}{\cancel{5}}} = \frac{11}{1} = \mathbf{11}$$

3. $\left(\frac{2}{8} \times 0.4\right) \times \frac{10}{2} = \left(\frac{2}{8} \times \frac{4}{10}\right) \times \frac{10}{2} = \left(\frac{\overset{1}{\cancel{2}} \times \overset{1}{\cancel{4}}}{\underset{2}{\cancel{8}} \times \underset{5}{\cancel{10}}}\right) \times \frac{\overset{5}{\cancel{10}}}{\underset{1}{\cancel{2}}} = \left(\frac{1 \times 1}{2 \times 5}\right) \times \frac{5}{1} = \left(\frac{1}{10}\right) \times \frac{5}{1} = \frac{1}{10} \times \frac{5}{1} = \frac{1 \times 5}{10 \times 1} = \frac{\overset{1}{\cancel{5}}}{\underset{2}{\cancel{10}}} = \mathbf{\frac{1}{2}}$

4. $\dfrac{2}{0.04} \times \left(\dfrac{0.5}{0.01} \times \dfrac{1}{4}\right) = \dfrac{\frac{2}{1}}{\frac{4}{100}} \times \left(\dfrac{\frac{5}{10}}{\frac{1}{100}} \times \dfrac{1}{4}\right) = \dfrac{2\times100}{1\times4} \times \left(\dfrac{5\times100}{10\times1} \times \dfrac{1}{4}\right) = \dfrac{\overset{50}{\cancel{200}}}{\underset{1}{\cancel{4}}} \times \left(\dfrac{\overset{50}{\cancel{500}}}{\underset{1}{\cancel{10}}} \times \dfrac{1}{4}\right) = \dfrac{50}{1} \times \left(\dfrac{50}{1} \times \dfrac{1}{4}\right)$

$= \dfrac{50}{1} \times \left(\dfrac{\overset{25}{\cancel{50}}\times1}{1\times\underset{2}{\cancel{4}}}\right) = \dfrac{50}{1} \times \left(\dfrac{25\times1}{1\times2}\right) = \dfrac{50}{1} \times \left(\dfrac{25}{2}\right) = \dfrac{50}{1} \times \dfrac{25}{2} = \dfrac{\overset{25}{\cancel{50}}\times25}{1\times\underset{1}{\cancel{2}}} = \dfrac{25\times25}{1\times1} = \dfrac{625}{1\times1} = \mathbf{625}$

5. $\dfrac{5}{8} \times 0.8 \times \dfrac{3}{0.05} = \dfrac{5}{8} \times \dfrac{8}{10} \times \dfrac{\frac{3}{1}}{\frac{5}{100}} = \dfrac{5}{8} \times \dfrac{8}{10} \times \dfrac{3\times100}{1\times5} = \dfrac{5}{8} \times \dfrac{8}{10} \times \dfrac{300}{5} = \dfrac{\overset{1}{\cancel{5}}\times\overset{1}{\cancel{8}}\times\overset{30}{\cancel{300}}}{\underset{1}{\cancel{8}}\times\underset{1}{\cancel{10}}\times\underset{1}{\cancel{5}}} = \dfrac{1\times1\times30}{1\times1\times1} = \dfrac{30}{1} = \mathbf{30}$

6. $\left(\dfrac{5}{3}\times0\right) \times \left(0.3\times\dfrac{1}{0.03}\right) = \mathbf{0}$

7. $\dfrac{7}{3} \times \left(\dfrac{1}{0.7} \times \dfrac{0.3}{5}\right) = \dfrac{7}{3} \times \left(\dfrac{\frac{1}{1}}{\frac{7}{10}} \times \dfrac{\frac{3}{10}}{\frac{5}{1}}\right) = \dfrac{7}{3} \times \left(\dfrac{1\times10}{1\times7} \times \dfrac{3\times1}{10\times5}\right) = \dfrac{7}{3} \times \left(\dfrac{10}{7} \times \dfrac{3}{50}\right) = \dfrac{7}{3} \times \left(\dfrac{\overset{1}{\cancel{10}}\times3}{7\times\underset{5}{\cancel{50}}}\right) = \dfrac{7}{3} \times \left(\dfrac{1\times3}{7\times5}\right)$

$= \dfrac{7}{3} \times \left(\dfrac{3}{35}\right) = \dfrac{7}{3} \times \dfrac{3}{35} = \dfrac{\overset{1}{\cancel{7}}\times\overset{1}{\cancel{3}}}{\underset{1}{\cancel{3}}\times\underset{5}{\cancel{35}}} = \dfrac{1\times1}{1\times5} = \mathbf{\dfrac{1}{5}}$

8. $\left(\dfrac{5}{1}\times\dfrac{1}{3}\right) \times \left(0.03\times\dfrac{10}{0.2}\right) = \left(\dfrac{5\times1}{1\times3}\right) \times \left(\dfrac{3}{100}\times\dfrac{\frac{10}{1}}{\frac{2}{10}}\right) = \left(\dfrac{5}{3}\right) \times \left(\dfrac{3}{100}\times\dfrac{10\times10}{1\times2}\right) = \dfrac{5}{3} \times \left(\dfrac{3}{100}\times\dfrac{100}{2}\right) = \dfrac{5}{3} \times \left(\dfrac{3\times\overset{1}{\cancel{100}}}{\underset{1}{\cancel{100}}\times2}\right)$

$= \dfrac{5}{3} \times \left(\dfrac{3\times1}{1\times2}\right) = \dfrac{5}{3} \times \left(\dfrac{3}{2}\right) = \dfrac{5}{3} \times \dfrac{3}{2} = \dfrac{5\times\overset{1}{\cancel{3}}}{\underset{1}{\cancel{3}}\times2} = \dfrac{5\times1}{1\times2} = \dfrac{5}{2} = \mathbf{2\dfrac{1}{2}}$

9. $\dfrac{4}{3} \times \dfrac{0.3}{2} \times \dfrac{10}{0.1} \times 0.4 = \dfrac{4}{3} \times \dfrac{\frac{3}{10}}{2} \times \dfrac{\frac{10}{1}}{\frac{1}{10}} \times \dfrac{4}{10} = \dfrac{4}{3} \times \dfrac{3\times1}{10\times2} \times \dfrac{10\times10}{1\times1} \times \dfrac{4}{10} = \dfrac{4}{3} \times \dfrac{3}{20} \times \dfrac{100}{1} \times \dfrac{4}{10} = \dfrac{4\times\overset{1}{\cancel{3}}\times\overset{10}{\cancel{100}}\times4}{\underset{1}{\cancel{3}}\times\underset{5}{\cancel{20}}\times1\times\underset{1}{\cancel{10}}}$

$= \dfrac{4\times1\times10\times1}{1\times5\times1\times1} = \dfrac{\overset{8}{\cancel{40}}}{\underset{1}{\cancel{5}}} = \dfrac{8}{1} = \mathbf{8}$

10. $\left(\dfrac{3}{8}\times0.2\right) \times \left(2\times\dfrac{8}{6}\times\dfrac{1}{0.04}\right) = \left(\dfrac{3}{8}\times\dfrac{2}{10}\right) \times \left(\dfrac{2}{1}\times\dfrac{8}{6}\times\dfrac{\frac{1}{1}}{\frac{4}{100}}\right) = \left(\dfrac{3\times2}{8\times10}\right) \times \left(\dfrac{2}{1}\times\dfrac{8}{6}\times\dfrac{1\times100}{1\times4}\right) = \left(\dfrac{3\times1}{4\times10}\right) \times \left(\dfrac{2}{1}\times\dfrac{8}{6}\times\dfrac{100}{4}\right)$

$= \left(\dfrac{3}{40}\right) \times \left(\dfrac{2\times\overset{1}{\cancel{8}}\times\overset{2}{\cancel{100}}}{1\times\underset{3}{\cancel{6}}\times\underset{1}{\cancel{4}}}\right) = \dfrac{3}{40} \times \left(\dfrac{1\times2\times100}{1\times3\times1}\right) = \dfrac{3}{40} \times \left(\dfrac{200}{3}\right) = \dfrac{3}{40} \times \dfrac{200}{3} = \dfrac{\overset{1}{\cancel{3}}\times\overset{5}{\cancel{200}}}{40\times\underset{1}{\cancel{3}}}\!\!\!\phantom{\underset{1}{1}} = \dfrac{1\times5}{1\times1} = \dfrac{5}{1} = \mathbf{5}$

Section 6.4 Solutions:

1. $\dfrac{5}{4} \div \dfrac{0.4}{1.2} = \dfrac{5}{4} \div \dfrac{\frac{4}{10}}{\frac{12}{10}} = \dfrac{5}{4} \div \dfrac{4\times10}{10\times12} = \dfrac{5}{4} \div \dfrac{\overset{1}{\cancel{40}}}{\underset{3}{\cancel{120}}} = \dfrac{5}{4} \div \dfrac{1}{3} = \dfrac{5}{4} \times \dfrac{3}{1} = \dfrac{5\times3}{4\times1} = \dfrac{15}{4} = \mathbf{3\dfrac{3}{4}}$

2. $0.2 \div \dfrac{5}{8} = \dfrac{2}{10} \div \dfrac{5}{8} = \dfrac{2}{10} \times \dfrac{8}{5} = \dfrac{\overset{1}{\cancel{2}}\times8}{\underset{5}{\cancel{10}}\times5} = \dfrac{1\times8}{5\times5} = \mathbf{\dfrac{8}{25}}$

3. $\left(\dfrac{1}{0.1} \div 1\right) \div 0.6 = \left(\dfrac{\frac{1}{1}}{\frac{1}{10}} \div \dfrac{1}{1}\right) \div \dfrac{6}{10} = \left(\dfrac{1\times10}{1\times1} \div \dfrac{1}{1}\right) \div \dfrac{\overset{3}{\cancel{6}}}{\underset{5}{\cancel{10}}} = \left(\dfrac{10}{1} \div \dfrac{1}{1}\right) \div \dfrac{3}{5} = \left(\dfrac{10}{1} \times \dfrac{1}{1}\right) \div \dfrac{3}{5} = \left(\dfrac{10\times1}{1\times1}\right) \div \dfrac{3}{5} = \left(\dfrac{10}{1}\right) \div \dfrac{3}{5}$

$= \dfrac{10}{1} \div \dfrac{3}{5} = \dfrac{10}{1} \times \dfrac{5}{3} = \dfrac{10\times5}{1\times3} = \dfrac{50}{3} = \mathbf{16\dfrac{2}{3}}$

4. $\left(\dfrac{9}{8} \div \dfrac{3}{8}\right) \div \dfrac{0.2}{0.3} = = \left(\dfrac{9}{8} \times \dfrac{8}{3}\right) \div \dfrac{\frac{2}{10}}{\frac{3}{10}} = = \left(\dfrac{\overset{3}{\cancel{9}}\times\overset{1}{\cancel{8}}}{\underset{1}{\cancel{8}}\times\underset{1}{\cancel{3}}}\right) \div \dfrac{2\times10}{10\times3} = = \left(\dfrac{3\times1}{1\times1}\right) \div \dfrac{20}{30} = = \left(\dfrac{3}{1}\right) \div \dfrac{\overset{2}{\cancel{20}}}{\underset{3}{\cancel{30}}} = = \dfrac{3}{1} \div \dfrac{2}{3} = \dfrac{3}{1} \times \dfrac{3}{2} = \dfrac{3\times3}{1\times2}$

$= \dfrac{9}{2} = \mathbf{4\dfrac{1}{2}}$

5. $\left(\dfrac{1}{0.04} \div \dfrac{1}{2}\right) \div 5 = \left(\dfrac{\frac{1}{1}}{\frac{4}{100}} \div \dfrac{1}{2}\right) \div \dfrac{5}{1} = \left(\dfrac{1\times100}{1\times4} \div \dfrac{1}{2}\right) \div \dfrac{5}{1} = \left(\dfrac{\overset{25}{\cancel{100}}}{\underset{1}{\cancel{4}}} \div \dfrac{1}{2}\right) \div \dfrac{5}{1} = \left(\dfrac{25}{1} \div \dfrac{1}{2}\right) \div \dfrac{5}{1} = \left(\dfrac{25}{1} \times \dfrac{2}{1}\right) \div \dfrac{5}{1}$

$= \left(\dfrac{25\times2}{1\times1}\right) \div \dfrac{5}{1} = \left(\dfrac{50}{1}\right) \div \dfrac{5}{1} = \dfrac{50}{1} \div \dfrac{5}{1} = \dfrac{50}{1} \times \dfrac{1}{5} = \dfrac{\overset{10}{\cancel{50}}\times1}{1\times\underset{1}{\cancel{5}}} = \dfrac{10\times1}{1\times1} = \dfrac{10}{1} = \mathbf{10}$

6. $\left(\dfrac{4}{6} \div 0.3\right) \div \dfrac{2}{9} = \left(\dfrac{4}{6} \div \dfrac{3}{10}\right) \div \dfrac{2}{9} = \left(\dfrac{4}{6} \times \dfrac{10}{3}\right) \div \dfrac{2}{9} = \left(\dfrac{4\times\overset{5}{\cancel{10}}}{\underset{3}{\cancel{6}}\times3}\right) \div \dfrac{2}{9} = \left(\dfrac{4\times5}{3\times3}\right) \div \dfrac{2}{9} = \left(\dfrac{20}{9}\right) \div \dfrac{2}{9} = \dfrac{20}{9} \div \dfrac{2}{9} = \dfrac{20}{9} \times \dfrac{9}{2}$

$= \dfrac{\overset{10}{\cancel{20}}\times\overset{1}{\cancel{9}}}{\underset{1}{\cancel{9}}\times\underset{1}{\cancel{2}}} = \dfrac{10\times1}{1\times1} = \dfrac{10}{1} = \mathbf{10}$

7. $\left(\dfrac{0.8}{2.4} \div 0.02\right) \div \dfrac{5}{10} = \left(\dfrac{\frac{8}{10}}{\frac{24}{10}} \div \dfrac{2}{100}\right) \div \dfrac{5}{10} = \left(\dfrac{8\times10}{10\times24} \div \dfrac{2}{100}\right) \div \dfrac{5}{10} = \left(\dfrac{\overset{1}{\cancel{80}}}{\underset{3}{\cancel{240}}} \div \dfrac{\overset{1}{\cancel{2}}}{\underset{50}{\cancel{100}}}\right) \div \dfrac{\overset{1}{\cancel{5}}}{\underset{2}{\cancel{10}}} = \left(\dfrac{1}{3} \div \dfrac{1}{50}\right) \div \dfrac{1}{2}$

$= \left(\dfrac{1}{3} \times \dfrac{50}{1}\right) \div \dfrac{1}{2} = \left(\dfrac{1\times50}{3\times1}\right) \div \dfrac{1}{2} = \left(\dfrac{50}{3}\right) \div \dfrac{1}{2} = \dfrac{50}{3} \div \dfrac{1}{2} = \dfrac{50}{3} \times \dfrac{2}{1} = \dfrac{50\times2}{3\times1} = \dfrac{100}{3} = \mathbf{33\dfrac{1}{3}}$

8. $\left(0.04 \div \dfrac{2}{10}\right) \div \dfrac{1}{5} = \left(\dfrac{4}{100} \div \dfrac{2}{10}\right) \div \dfrac{1}{5} = \left(\dfrac{4}{100} \times \dfrac{10}{2}\right) \div \dfrac{1}{5} = \left(\dfrac{\overset{1}{\cancel{4}}\times\overset{5}{\cancel{10}}}{\underset{25}{\cancel{100}}\times\underset{1}{\cancel{2}}}\right) \div \dfrac{1}{5} = \left(\dfrac{1\times5}{25\times1}\right) \div \dfrac{1}{5} = \left(\dfrac{5}{25}\right) \div \dfrac{1}{5} = \dfrac{\overset{1}{\cancel{5}}}{\underset{5}{\cancel{25}}} \div \dfrac{1}{5}$

$= \dfrac{1}{5} \div \dfrac{1}{5} = \dfrac{1}{5} \times \dfrac{5}{1} = \dfrac{1\times5}{5\times1} = \dfrac{\overset{1}{\cancel{5}}}{\underset{1}{\cancel{5}}} = \dfrac{1}{1} = \mathbf{1}$

9. $0.2 \div \left(\dfrac{1}{8} \div \dfrac{1}{4}\right) = \dfrac{2}{10} \div \left(\dfrac{1}{8} \times \dfrac{4}{1}\right) = \dfrac{\overset{1}{\cancel{2}}}{\underset{5}{\cancel{10}}} \div \left(\dfrac{1\times\overset{1}{\cancel{4}}}{\underset{2}{\cancel{8}}\times1}\right) = \dfrac{1}{5} \div \left(\dfrac{1\times1}{2\times1}\right) = \dfrac{1}{5} \div \left(\dfrac{1}{2}\right) = \dfrac{1}{5} \div \dfrac{1}{2} = \dfrac{1}{5} \times \dfrac{2}{1} = \mathbf{\dfrac{2}{5}}$

10. $\left(\dfrac{1}{5} \div \dfrac{4}{5}\right) \div \left(0.2 \div \dfrac{0.1}{0.04}\right) = \left(\dfrac{1}{5} \times \dfrac{5}{4}\right) \div \left(\dfrac{2}{10} \div \dfrac{\frac{1}{10}}{\frac{4}{100}}\right) = \left(\dfrac{1\times\overset{1}{\cancel{5}}}{\underset{1}{\cancel{5}}\times4}\right) \div \left(\dfrac{2}{10} \div \dfrac{1\times100}{10\times4}\right) = \left(\dfrac{1\times1}{1\times4}\right) \div \left(\dfrac{2}{10} \div \dfrac{100}{40}\right)$

$= \left(\dfrac{1}{4}\right) \div \left(\dfrac{2}{10} \times \dfrac{40}{100}\right) = \left(\dfrac{1}{4}\right) \div \left(\dfrac{2\times\overset{1}{\cancel{40}}}{\underset{5}{\cancel{10}}\times\underset{25}{\cancel{100}}}\right) = \dfrac{1}{4} \div \left(\dfrac{1\times10}{5\times25}\right) = \dfrac{1}{4} \div \left(\dfrac{10}{125}\right) = \dfrac{1}{4} \div \dfrac{10}{125} = \dfrac{1}{4} \times \dfrac{125}{10} = \dfrac{1\times\overset{25}{\cancel{125}}}{4\times\underset{2}{\cancel{10}}} = \dfrac{1\times25}{4\times2}$

$$= \frac{25}{8} = 3\frac{1}{8}$$

Section 6.5 Solutions:

1. $\left(\frac{1}{4} + \frac{3}{2}\right) \div 0.7 = \left(\frac{(1\times2)+(3\times4)}{4\times2}\right) \div \frac{\frac{7}{10}}{\frac{2}{1}} = \left(\frac{2+12}{8}\right) \div \frac{7\times1}{10\times2} = \left(\frac{14}{8}\right) \div \frac{7}{20} = \frac{14}{8} \div \frac{7}{20} = \frac{14}{8} \times \frac{20}{7} = \frac{\overset{2}{\cancel{14}}\times \overset{5}{\cancel{20}}}{\underset{2}{\cancel{8}}\times \underset{1}{\cancel{7}}} = \frac{2\times5}{2\times1}$

$$= \frac{\overset{5}{\cancel{10}}}{\underset{1}{\cancel{2}}} = \frac{5}{1} = 5$$

2. $\left(\frac{0.2}{1.4} + 2\right) \times \frac{1}{4} = \left(\frac{\frac{2}{10}}{\frac{14}{10}} + \frac{2}{1}\right) \times \frac{1}{4} = \left(\frac{2\times10}{10\times14} + \frac{2}{1}\right) \times \frac{1}{4} = \left(\frac{\overset{1}{\cancel{20}}}{\underset{7}{\cancel{140}}} + \frac{2}{1}\right) \times \frac{1}{4} = \left(\frac{1}{7} + \frac{2}{1}\right) \times \frac{1}{4} = \left(\frac{(1\times1)+(2\times7)}{7\times1}\right) \times \frac{1}{4}$

$$= \left(\frac{1+14}{7}\right) \times \frac{1}{4} = \left(\frac{15}{7}\right) \times \frac{1}{4} = \frac{15}{7} \times \frac{1}{4} = \frac{15\times1}{7\times4} = \frac{15}{28}$$

3. $\left(\frac{1}{5} \times 0.5\right) + \frac{1}{10} = \left(\frac{1}{5} \times \frac{5}{10}\right) + \frac{1}{10} = \left(\frac{1\times \overset{1}{\cancel{5}}}{\underset{1}{\cancel{5}}\times 10}\right) + \frac{1}{10} = \left(\frac{1\times1}{1\times10}\right) + \frac{1}{10} = \left(\frac{1}{10}\right) + \frac{1}{10} = \frac{1}{10} + \frac{1}{10} = \frac{1+1}{10} = \frac{\overset{1}{\cancel{2}}}{\underset{5}{\cancel{10}}} = \frac{1}{5}$

4. $\left(\frac{3}{5} + \frac{2}{3}\right) \times \frac{0.1}{1.5} = \left(\frac{(3\times3)+(2\times5)}{5\times3}\right) \times \frac{\frac{1}{10}}{\frac{15}{10}} = \left(\frac{9+10}{15}\right) \times \frac{1\times10}{10\times15} = \left(\frac{19}{15}\right) \times \frac{10}{150} = \frac{19}{15} \times \frac{10}{150} = \frac{19\times \overset{1}{\cancel{10}}}{15\times \underset{15}{\cancel{150}}} = \frac{19\times1}{15\times15}$

$$= \frac{19}{225}$$

5. $\left(\frac{5}{3} - \frac{1}{3}\right) \div \frac{2.8}{0.12} = \left(\frac{5-1}{3}\right) \div \frac{\frac{28}{10}}{\frac{12}{100}} = \left(\frac{4}{3}\right) \div \frac{28\times100}{10\times12} = \frac{4}{3} \div \frac{\overset{70}{\cancel{2800}}}{\underset{3}{\cancel{120}}} = \frac{4}{3} \div \frac{70}{3} = \frac{4}{3} \times \frac{3}{70} = \frac{\overset{2}{\cancel{4}}\times \overset{1}{\cancel{3}}}{\underset{1}{\cancel{3}}\times \underset{35}{\cancel{70}}} = \frac{2\times1}{1\times35} = \frac{2}{35}$

6. $\left(\frac{3}{8} \times 4\right) \div \frac{0.05}{0.1} = \left(\frac{3}{8} \times \frac{4}{1}\right) \div \frac{\frac{5}{100}}{\frac{1}{10}} = \left(\frac{3\times4}{8\times1}\right) \div \frac{5\times10}{100\times1} = \left(\frac{12}{8}\right) \div \frac{50}{100} = \frac{\overset{3}{\cancel{12}}}{\underset{2}{\cancel{8}}} \div \frac{\overset{1}{\cancel{50}}}{\underset{2}{\cancel{100}}} = \frac{3}{2} \div \frac{1}{2} = \frac{3}{2} \times \frac{2}{1} = \frac{3\times \overset{1}{\cancel{2}}}{\underset{1}{\cancel{2}}\times1} = \frac{3\times1}{1\times1}$

$$= \frac{3}{1} = 3$$

7. $\left(\frac{0.3}{2.4} \times \frac{1}{3} \times 2\right) \div \frac{1}{4} = \left(\frac{\frac{3}{10}}{\frac{24}{10}} \times \frac{1}{3} \times \frac{2}{1}\right) \div \frac{1}{4} = \left(\frac{3\times10}{10\times24} \times \frac{1}{3} \times \frac{2}{1}\right) \div \frac{1}{4} = \left(\frac{30}{240} \times \frac{1}{3} \times \frac{2}{1}\right) \div \frac{1}{4} = \left(\frac{\overset{1}{\cancel{30}}\times1\times2}{\underset{8}{\cancel{240}}\times3\times1}\right) \div \frac{1}{4}$

$$= \left(\frac{1\times1\times \overset{1}{\cancel{2}}}{\underset{4}{\cancel{8}}\times3\times1}\right) \div \frac{1}{4} = \left(\frac{1\times1\times1}{4\times3\times1}\right) \div \frac{1}{4} = \left(\frac{1}{12}\right) \div \frac{1}{4} = \frac{1}{12} \div \frac{1}{4} = \frac{1}{12} \times \frac{4}{1} = \frac{1\times \overset{1}{\cancel{4}}}{\underset{3}{\cancel{12}}\times1} = \frac{1\times1}{3\times1} = \frac{1}{3}$$

8. $\left(\frac{3}{5} \times \frac{0.1}{4.4}\right) + 400 = \left(\frac{3}{5} \times \frac{\frac{1}{10}}{\frac{44}{10}}\right) + \frac{400}{1} = \left(\frac{3}{5} \times \frac{1\times10}{10\times44}\right) + \frac{400}{1} = \left(\frac{3}{5} \times \frac{10}{440}\right) + \frac{400}{1} = \left(\frac{3\times \overset{1}{\cancel{10}}}{5\times \underset{44}{\cancel{440}}}\right) + \frac{400}{1} = \left(\frac{3\times1}{5\times44}\right) + \frac{400}{1}$

$$= \left(\frac{3}{220}\right) + \frac{400}{1} = \frac{3}{220} + \frac{400}{1} = \frac{(3\times1)+(400\times220)}{220\times1} = \frac{3+88000}{220} = \frac{88003}{220} = 400\frac{3}{220}$$

9. $\left(\dfrac{1}{4}+\dfrac{2}{3}\right)\times\left(\dfrac{0.5}{0.02}\times\dfrac{1}{5}\right) = \left(\dfrac{(1\times3)+(2\times4)}{4\times3}\right)\times\left(\dfrac{\frac{5}{10}}{\frac{2}{100}}\times\dfrac{1}{5}\right) = \left(\dfrac{3+8}{12}\right)\times\left(\dfrac{5\times100}{10\times2}\times\dfrac{1}{5}\right) = \left(\dfrac{11}{12}\right)\times\left(\dfrac{500}{20}\times\dfrac{1}{5}\right)$

$= \dfrac{11}{12}\times\left(\dfrac{\overset{25}{\cancel{500}}\times1}{\cancel{20}\times5}\right) = \dfrac{11}{12}\times\left(\dfrac{25\times1}{1\times5}\right) = \dfrac{11}{12}\times\left(\dfrac{25}{5}\right) = \dfrac{11}{12}\times\dfrac{25}{5} = \dfrac{11\times\overset{5}{\cancel{25}}}{12\times\underset{1}{\cancel{5}}} = \dfrac{11\times5}{12\times1} = \dfrac{55}{12} = \mathbf{4\dfrac{7}{12}}$

10. $\left[\left(\dfrac{5}{3}\times\dfrac{0.2}{1.2}\right)\div\dfrac{4}{9}\right]+\dfrac{3}{2} = \left[\left(\dfrac{5}{3}\times\dfrac{\frac{2}{10}}{\frac{12}{10}}\right)\div\dfrac{4}{9}\right]+\dfrac{3}{2} = \left[\left(\dfrac{5}{3}\times\dfrac{2\times10}{10\times12}\right)\div\dfrac{4}{9}\right]+\dfrac{3}{2} = \left[\left(\dfrac{5}{3}\times\dfrac{20}{120}\right)\div\dfrac{4}{9}\right]+\dfrac{3}{2} = \left[\left(\dfrac{5\times\overset{1}{\cancel{20}}}{3\times\underset{6}{\cancel{120}}}\right)\div\dfrac{4}{9}\right]+\dfrac{3}{2}$

$= \left[\left(\dfrac{5\times1}{3\times6}\right)\div\dfrac{4}{9}\right]+\dfrac{3}{2} = \left[\left(\dfrac{5}{18}\right)\div\dfrac{4}{9}\right]+\dfrac{3}{2} = \left[\dfrac{5}{18}\div\dfrac{4}{9}\right]+\dfrac{3}{2} = \left[\dfrac{5}{18}\times\dfrac{9}{4}\right]+\dfrac{3}{2} = \left[\dfrac{5\times\overset{1}{\cancel{9}}}{\underset{2}{\cancel{18}}\times4}\right]+\dfrac{3}{2} = \left[\dfrac{5\times1}{2\times4}\right]+\dfrac{3}{2} = \left[\dfrac{5}{8}\right]+\dfrac{3}{2}$

$= \dfrac{5}{8}+\dfrac{3}{2} = \dfrac{(5\times2)+(3\times8)}{8\times2} = \dfrac{10+24}{16} = \dfrac{\overset{17}{\cancel{34}}}{\underset{8}{\cancel{16}}} = \dfrac{17}{8} = \mathbf{2\dfrac{1}{8}}$

Chapter 7 Solutions:

Section 7.1 Solutions:

1. $\dfrac{2}{3}+2\dfrac{1}{3} = \dfrac{2}{3}+\dfrac{(2\times 3)+1}{3} = \dfrac{2}{3}+\dfrac{6+1}{3} = \dfrac{2}{3}+\dfrac{7}{3} = \dfrac{2+7}{3} = \dfrac{\overset{3}{\cancel{9}}}{\underset{1}{\cancel{3}}} = \dfrac{3}{1} = \mathbf{3}$

2. $1\dfrac{1}{3}+2\dfrac{1}{5}+\dfrac{5}{6} = \left(1\dfrac{1}{3}+2\dfrac{1}{5}\right)+\dfrac{5}{6} = \left(\dfrac{(1\times 3)+1}{3}+\dfrac{(2\times 5)+1}{5}\right)+\dfrac{5}{6} = \left(\dfrac{3+1}{3}+\dfrac{10+1}{5}\right)+\dfrac{5}{6} = \left(\dfrac{4}{3}+\dfrac{11}{5}\right)+\dfrac{5}{6}$

$= \left(\dfrac{(4\times 5)+(11\times 3)}{3\times 5}\right)+\dfrac{5}{6} = \left(\dfrac{20+33}{15}\right)+\dfrac{5}{6} = \left(\dfrac{53}{15}\right)+\dfrac{5}{6} = \dfrac{53}{15}+\dfrac{5}{6} = \dfrac{(53\times 6)+(5\times 15)}{15\times 6} = \dfrac{318+75}{90} = \dfrac{\overset{131}{\cancel{393}}}{\underset{30}{\cancel{90}}} = \dfrac{131}{30}$

$= \mathbf{4\dfrac{11}{30}}$

3. $1\dfrac{1}{5}+2\dfrac{1}{3}+4 = \left(1\dfrac{1}{5}+2\dfrac{1}{3}\right)+4 = \left(\dfrac{(1\times 5)+1}{5}+\dfrac{(2\times 3)+1}{3}\right)+\dfrac{4}{1} = \left(\dfrac{5+1}{5}+\dfrac{6+1}{3}\right)+\dfrac{4}{1} = \left(\dfrac{6}{5}+\dfrac{7}{3}\right)+\dfrac{4}{1}$

$= \left(\dfrac{(6\times 3)+(7\times 5)}{5\times 3}\right)+\dfrac{4}{1} = \left(\dfrac{18+35}{15}\right)+\dfrac{4}{1} = \left(\dfrac{53}{15}\right)+\dfrac{4}{1} = \dfrac{53}{15}+\dfrac{4}{1} = \dfrac{(53\times 1)+(4\times 15)}{15\times 1} = \dfrac{53+60}{15} = \dfrac{113}{15} = \mathbf{7\dfrac{8}{15}}$

4. $\dfrac{3}{4}+\left(1\dfrac{1}{4}+2\dfrac{1}{3}\right) = \dfrac{3}{4}+\left(\dfrac{(1\times 4)+1}{4}+\dfrac{(2\times 3)+1}{3}\right) = \dfrac{3}{4}+\left(\dfrac{4+1}{4}+\dfrac{6+1}{3}\right) = \dfrac{3}{4}+\left(\dfrac{5}{4}+\dfrac{7}{3}\right) = \dfrac{3}{4}+\left(\dfrac{(5\times 3)+(7\times 4)}{4\times 3}\right)$

$= \dfrac{3}{4}+\left(\dfrac{15+28}{12}\right) = \dfrac{3}{4}+\left(\dfrac{43}{12}\right) = \dfrac{3}{4}+\dfrac{43}{12} = \dfrac{(3\times 12)+(43\times 4)}{4\times 12} = \dfrac{36+172}{48} = \dfrac{\overset{13}{\cancel{208}}}{\underset{3}{\cancel{48}}} = \dfrac{13}{3} = \mathbf{4\dfrac{1}{3}}$

5. $\left(2\dfrac{1}{6}+\dfrac{3}{8}\right)+12 = \left(\dfrac{(2\times 6)+1}{6}+\dfrac{3}{8}\right)+\dfrac{12}{1} = \left(\dfrac{12+1}{6}+\dfrac{3}{8}\right)+\dfrac{12}{1} = \left(\dfrac{13}{6}+\dfrac{3}{8}\right)+\dfrac{12}{1} = \left(\dfrac{(13\times 8)+(3\times 6)}{6\times 8}\right)+\dfrac{12}{1}$

$= \left(\dfrac{104+18}{48}\right)+\dfrac{12}{1} = \left(\dfrac{122}{48}\right)+\dfrac{12}{1} = \dfrac{\overset{61}{\cancel{122}}}{\underset{24}{\cancel{48}}}+\dfrac{12}{1} = \dfrac{61}{24}+\dfrac{12}{1} = \dfrac{(61\times 1)+(12\times 24)}{24\times 1} = \dfrac{61+288}{24} = \dfrac{349}{24} = \mathbf{14\dfrac{13}{24}}$

6. $\left(3\dfrac{1}{5}+2\dfrac{1}{2}\right)+\dfrac{4}{5} = \left(\dfrac{(3\times 5)+1}{5}+\dfrac{(2\times 2)+1}{2}\right)+\dfrac{4}{5} = \left(\dfrac{15+1}{5}+\dfrac{4+1}{2}\right)+\dfrac{4}{5} = \left(\dfrac{16}{5}+\dfrac{5}{2}\right)+\dfrac{4}{5} = \left(\dfrac{(16\times 2)+(5\times 5)}{5\times 2}\right)+\dfrac{4}{5}$

$= \left(\dfrac{32+25}{10}\right)+\dfrac{4}{5} = \left(\dfrac{57}{10}\right)+\dfrac{4}{5} = \dfrac{57}{10}+\dfrac{4}{5} = \dfrac{(57\times 5)+(4\times 10)}{10\times 5} = \dfrac{285+40}{50} = \dfrac{\overset{13}{\cancel{325}}}{\underset{2}{\cancel{50}}} = \dfrac{13}{2} = \mathbf{6\dfrac{1}{2}}$

7. $1\dfrac{3}{5}+\left(\dfrac{2}{3}+\dfrac{4}{3}+\dfrac{1}{3}\right) = \dfrac{(1\times 5)+3}{5}+\left(\dfrac{2+4+1}{3}\right) = \dfrac{5+3}{5}+\left(\dfrac{7}{3}\right) = \dfrac{8}{5}+\dfrac{7}{3} = \dfrac{(8\times 3)+(7\times 5)}{5\times 3} = \dfrac{24+35}{15} = \dfrac{59}{15} = \mathbf{3\dfrac{14}{15}}$

8. $3\dfrac{1}{4}+\left(2\dfrac{1}{2}+5\right) = \dfrac{(3\times 4)+1}{4}+\left(\dfrac{(2\times 2)+1}{2}+\dfrac{5}{1}\right) = \dfrac{12+1}{4}+\left(\dfrac{4+1}{2}+\dfrac{5}{1}\right) = \dfrac{13}{4}+\left(\dfrac{5}{2}+\dfrac{5}{1}\right) = \dfrac{13}{4}+\left(\dfrac{(5\times 1)+(5\times 2)}{2\times 1}\right)$

$= \dfrac{13}{4}+\left(\dfrac{5+10}{2}\right) = \dfrac{13}{4}+\left(\dfrac{15}{2}\right) = \dfrac{13}{4}+\dfrac{15}{2} = \dfrac{(13\times 2)+(15\times 4)}{4\times 2} = \dfrac{26+60}{8} = \dfrac{\overset{43}{\cancel{86}}}{\underset{4}{\cancel{8}}} = \dfrac{43}{4} = \mathbf{10\dfrac{3}{4}}$

9. $\left(\dfrac{1}{3}+2\dfrac{1}{3}\right)+\dfrac{4}{6} = \left(\dfrac{1}{3}+\dfrac{(2\times 3)+1}{3}\right)+\dfrac{\overset{2}{4}}{\underset{3}{6}} = \left(\dfrac{1}{3}+\dfrac{6+1}{3}\right)+\dfrac{2}{3} = \left(\dfrac{1}{3}+\dfrac{7}{3}\right)+\dfrac{2}{3} = \left(\dfrac{1+7}{3}\right)+\dfrac{2}{3} = \left(\dfrac{8}{3}\right)+\dfrac{2}{3} = \dfrac{8}{3}+\dfrac{2}{3} = \dfrac{8+2}{3}$

$= \dfrac{10}{3} = 3\dfrac{1}{3}$

10. $\left[\left(\dfrac{4}{5}+2\dfrac{1}{3}\right)+1\dfrac{1}{3}\right]+22 = \left[\left(\dfrac{4}{5}+\dfrac{(2\times 3)+1}{3}\right)+\dfrac{(1\times 3)+1}{3}\right]+\dfrac{22}{1} = \left[\left(\dfrac{4}{5}+\dfrac{6+1}{3}\right)+\dfrac{3+1}{3}\right]+\dfrac{22}{1} = \left[\left(\dfrac{4}{5}+\dfrac{7}{3}\right)+\dfrac{4}{3}\right]+\dfrac{22}{1}$

$= \left[\left(\dfrac{(4\times 3)+(7\times 5)}{5\times 3}\right)+\dfrac{4}{3}\right]+\dfrac{22}{1} = \left[\left(\dfrac{12+35}{15}\right)+\dfrac{4}{3}\right]+\dfrac{22}{1} = \left[\left(\dfrac{47}{15}\right)+\dfrac{4}{3}\right]+\dfrac{22}{1} = \left[\dfrac{47}{15}+\dfrac{4}{3}\right]+\dfrac{22}{1}$

$= \left[\dfrac{(47\times 3)+(4\times 15)}{15\times 3}\right]+\dfrac{22}{1} = \left[\dfrac{141+60}{45}\right]+\dfrac{22}{1} = \left[\dfrac{201}{45}\right]+\dfrac{22}{1} = \dfrac{201}{45}+\dfrac{22}{1} = \dfrac{(201\times 1)+(22\times 45)}{45\times 1} = \dfrac{201+990}{45}$

$= \dfrac{\overset{397}{\cancel{1191}}}{\underset{15}{\cancel{45}}} = \dfrac{397}{15} = 26\dfrac{7}{15}$

Section 7.2 Solutions:

1. $5\dfrac{2}{3}-\dfrac{1}{6} = \dfrac{(5\times 3)+2}{3}-\dfrac{1}{6} = \dfrac{15+2}{3}-\dfrac{1}{6} = \dfrac{17}{3}-\dfrac{1}{6} = \dfrac{(17\times 6)-(1\times 3)}{3\times 6} = \dfrac{102-3}{18} = \dfrac{\overset{11}{\cancel{99}}}{\underset{2}{\cancel{18}}} = \dfrac{11}{2} = 5\dfrac{1}{2}$

2. $7\dfrac{1}{2}-\dfrac{2}{3}-1\dfrac{5}{8} = \left(7\dfrac{1}{2}-\dfrac{2}{3}\right)-1\dfrac{5}{8} = \left(\dfrac{(7\times 2)+1}{2}-\dfrac{2}{3}\right)-\dfrac{(1\times 8)+5}{8} = \left(\dfrac{14+1}{2}-\dfrac{2}{3}\right)-\dfrac{8+5}{8} = \left(\dfrac{15}{2}-\dfrac{2}{3}\right)-\dfrac{13}{8}$

$= \left(\dfrac{(15\times 3)-(2\times 2)}{2\times 3}\right)-\dfrac{13}{8} = \left(\dfrac{45-4}{6}\right)-\dfrac{13}{8} = \left(\dfrac{41}{6}\right)-\dfrac{13}{8} = \dfrac{41}{6}-\dfrac{13}{8} = \dfrac{(41\times 8)-(13\times 6)}{6\times 8} = \dfrac{328-78}{48} = \dfrac{\overset{125}{\cancel{250}}}{\underset{24}{\cancel{48}}} = \dfrac{125}{24}$

$= 5\dfrac{5}{24}$

3. $\dfrac{2}{6}-3\dfrac{5}{6}-1\dfrac{1}{6} = \dfrac{2}{6}-\dfrac{(3\times 6)+5}{6}-\dfrac{(1\times 6)+1}{6} = \dfrac{2}{6}-\dfrac{18+5}{6}-\dfrac{6+1}{6} = \dfrac{2}{6}-\dfrac{23}{6}-\dfrac{7}{6} = \dfrac{2-23-7}{6} = \dfrac{\overset{-14}{\cancel{-28}}}{\underset{3}{\cancel{6}}} = \dfrac{-14}{3} = -\left(4\dfrac{2}{3}\right)$

4. $6\dfrac{2}{3}-1\dfrac{1}{2}-5 = \left(6\dfrac{2}{3}-1\dfrac{1}{2}\right)-5 = \left(\dfrac{(6\times 3)+2}{3}-\dfrac{(1\times 2)+1}{2}\right)-\dfrac{5}{1} = \left(\dfrac{18+2}{3}-\dfrac{2+1}{2}\right)-\dfrac{5}{1} = \left(\dfrac{20}{3}-\dfrac{3}{2}\right)-\dfrac{5}{1}$

$= \left(\dfrac{(20\times 2)-(3\times 3)}{3\times 2}\right)-\dfrac{5}{1} = \left(\dfrac{40-9}{6}\right)-\dfrac{5}{1} = \left(\dfrac{31}{6}\right)-\dfrac{5}{1} = \dfrac{31}{6}-\dfrac{5}{1} = \dfrac{(31\times 1)-(5\times 6)}{6\times 1} = \dfrac{31-30}{6} = \dfrac{1}{6}$

5. $\left(4\dfrac{1}{3}-\dfrac{3}{5}\right)-12 = \left(\dfrac{(4\times 3)+1}{3}-\dfrac{3}{5}\right)-\dfrac{12}{1} = \left(\dfrac{12+1}{3}-\dfrac{3}{5}\right)-\dfrac{12}{1} = \left(\dfrac{13}{3}-\dfrac{3}{5}\right)-\dfrac{12}{1} = \left(\dfrac{(13\times 5)-(3\times 3)}{3\times 5}\right)-\dfrac{12}{1}$

$= \left(\dfrac{65-9}{15}\right)-\dfrac{12}{1} = \left(\dfrac{56}{15}\right)-\dfrac{12}{1} = \dfrac{56}{15}-\dfrac{12}{1} = \dfrac{(56\times 1)-(12\times 15)}{15\times 1} = \dfrac{56-180}{15} = \dfrac{-124}{15} = -\left(8\dfrac{4}{15}\right)$

6. $1\dfrac{2}{3}-\dfrac{3}{5}-\dfrac{1}{4} = \left(1\dfrac{2}{3}-\dfrac{3}{5}\right)-\dfrac{1}{4} = \left(\dfrac{(1\times 3)+2}{3}-\dfrac{3}{5}\right)-\dfrac{1}{4} = \left(\dfrac{3+2}{3}-\dfrac{3}{5}\right)-\dfrac{1}{4} = \left(\dfrac{5}{3}-\dfrac{3}{5}\right)-\dfrac{1}{4} = \left(\dfrac{(5\times 5)-(3\times 3)}{3\times 5}\right)-\dfrac{1}{4}$

$= \left(\dfrac{25-9}{15}\right)-\dfrac{1}{4} = \left(\dfrac{16}{15}\right)-\dfrac{1}{4} = \dfrac{16}{15}-\dfrac{1}{4} = \dfrac{(16\times 4)-(1\times 15)}{15\times 4} = \dfrac{64-15}{60} = \dfrac{49}{60}$

7. $7\frac{1}{3} - \left(\frac{3}{4} - \frac{1}{4}\right) = \frac{(7 \times 3) + 1}{3} - \left(\frac{3-1}{4}\right) = \frac{21+1}{3} - \left(\frac{2}{4}\right) = \frac{22}{3} - \frac{\overset{1}{\underset{2}{\cancel{2}}}}{\underset{2}{\cancel{4}}} = \frac{22}{3} - \frac{1}{2} = \frac{(22 \times 2) - (1 \times 3)}{3 \times 2} = \frac{44-3}{6} = \frac{41}{6} = \mathbf{6\frac{5}{6}}$

8. $\left(\frac{2}{5} - 1\frac{1}{2}\right) - \frac{3}{4} = \left(\frac{2}{5} - \frac{(1 \times 2) + 1}{2}\right) - \frac{3}{4} = \left(\frac{2}{5} - \frac{2+1}{2}\right) - \frac{3}{4} = \left(\frac{2}{5} - \frac{3}{2}\right) - \frac{3}{4} = \left(\frac{(2 \times 2) - (3 \times 5)}{5 \times 2}\right) - \frac{3}{4} = \left(\frac{4-15}{10}\right) - \frac{3}{4}$

$= \left(\frac{-11}{10}\right) - \frac{3}{4} = -\frac{11}{10} - \frac{3}{4} = \frac{(-11 \times 4) - (3 \times 10)}{10 \times 4} = \frac{-44-30}{40} = \frac{\overset{-37}{\cancel{-74}}}{\underset{20}{\cancel{40}}} = \frac{-37}{20} = -\left(\mathbf{1\frac{17}{20}}\right)$

9. $\left(3\frac{5}{6} - 8\right) - 1\frac{1}{6} = \left(\frac{(3 \times 6) + 5}{6} - \frac{8}{1}\right) - \frac{(1 \times 6) + 1}{6} = \left(\frac{18+5}{6} - \frac{8}{1}\right) - \frac{6+1}{6} = \left(\frac{23}{6} - \frac{8}{1}\right) - \frac{7}{6} = \left(\frac{(23 \times 1) - (8 \times 6)}{6 \times 1}\right) - \frac{7}{6}$

$= \left(\frac{23-48}{6}\right) - \frac{7}{6} = \left(\frac{-25}{6}\right) - \frac{7}{6} = -\frac{25}{6} - \frac{7}{6} = \frac{-25-7}{6} = \frac{\overset{-16}{\cancel{-32}}}{\underset{3}{\cancel{6}}} = -\frac{16}{3} = -\left(\mathbf{5\frac{1}{3}}\right)$

10. $\left(4\frac{2}{3} - \frac{1}{6}\right) - \left(\frac{3}{4} - \frac{1}{3}\right) = \left(\frac{(4 \times 3) + 2}{3} - \frac{1}{6}\right) - \left(\frac{(3 \times 3) - (1 \times 4)}{4 \times 3}\right) = \left(\frac{12+2}{3} - \frac{1}{6}\right) - \left(\frac{9-4}{12}\right) = \left(\frac{14}{3} - \frac{1}{6}\right) - \left(\frac{5}{12}\right)$

$= \left(\frac{(14 \times 6) - (1 \times 3)}{3 \times 6}\right) - \frac{5}{12} = \left(\frac{84-3}{18}\right) - \frac{5}{12} = \left(\frac{81}{18}\right) - \frac{5}{12} = \frac{\overset{27}{\cancel{81}}}{\underset{6}{\cancel{18}}} - \frac{5}{12} = \frac{27}{6} - \frac{5}{12} = \frac{(27 \times 12) - (5 \times 6)}{6 \times 12} = \frac{324-30}{72}$

$= \frac{\overset{49}{\cancel{294}}}{\underset{12}{\cancel{72}}} = \frac{49}{12} = \mathbf{4\frac{1}{12}}$

Section 7.3 Solutions:

1. $\frac{2}{8} \times 1\frac{1}{4} = \frac{2}{8} \times \frac{(1 \times 4) + 1}{4} = \frac{2}{8} \times \frac{4+1}{4} = \frac{2}{8} \times \frac{5}{4} = \frac{\overset{1}{2} \times 5}{8 \times \underset{2}{\cancel{4}}} = \frac{1 \times 5}{8 \times 2} = \mathbf{\frac{5}{16}}$

2. $2\frac{1}{5} \times 5\frac{1}{3} \times \frac{3}{11} = \frac{(2 \times 5) + 1}{5} \times \frac{(5 \times 3) + 1}{3} \times \frac{3}{11} = \frac{10+1}{5} \times \frac{15+1}{3} \times \frac{3}{11} = \frac{11}{5} \times \frac{16}{3} \times \frac{3}{11} = \frac{\overset{1}{\cancel{11}} \times 16 \times \overset{1}{\cancel{3}}}{5 \times \underset{1}{\cancel{3}} \times \underset{1}{\cancel{11}}} = \frac{1 \times 16 \times 1}{5 \times 1 \times 1} = \frac{16}{5}$

$= \mathbf{3\frac{1}{5}}$

3. $\left(1\frac{1}{3} \times 2\frac{1}{3}\right) \times \frac{3}{8} = \left(\frac{(1 \times 3) + 1}{3} \times \frac{(2 \times 3) + 1}{3}\right) \times \frac{3}{8} = \left(\frac{(1 \times 3) + 1}{3} \times \frac{(2 \times 3) + 1}{3}\right) \times \frac{3}{8} = \left(\frac{3+1}{3} \times \frac{6+1}{3}\right) \times \frac{3}{8} = \left(\frac{4}{3} \times \frac{7}{3}\right) \times \frac{3}{8}$

$= \left(\frac{4 \times 7}{3 \times 3}\right) \times \frac{3}{8} = \left(\frac{28}{9}\right) \times \frac{3}{8} = \frac{28}{9} \times \frac{3}{8} = \frac{\overset{7}{\cancel{28}} \times \overset{1}{\cancel{3}}}{\underset{3}{\cancel{9}} \times \underset{2}{\cancel{8}}} = \frac{7 \times 1}{3 \times 2} = \frac{7}{6} = \mathbf{1\frac{1}{6}}$

4. $\left(\frac{5}{8} \times 1\frac{1}{3}\right) \times \left(\frac{3}{8} \times \frac{4}{5}\right) = \left(\frac{5}{8} \times \frac{(1 \times 3) + 1}{3}\right) \times \left(\frac{3 \times \overset{1}{\cancel{4}}}{\underset{2}{\cancel{8}} \times 5}\right) = \left(\frac{5}{8} \times \frac{3+1}{3}\right) \times \left(\frac{3 \times 1}{2 \times 5}\right) = \left(\frac{5}{8} \times \frac{4}{3}\right) \times \left(\frac{3}{10}\right) = \left(\frac{5 \times \overset{1}{\cancel{4}}}{\underset{2}{\cancel{8}} \times 3}\right) \times \frac{3}{10}$

$= \left(\frac{5 \times 1}{2 \times 3}\right) \times \frac{3}{10} = \left(\frac{5}{6}\right) \times \frac{3}{10} = \frac{5}{6} \times \frac{3}{10} = \frac{\overset{1}{\cancel{5}} \times \overset{1}{\cancel{3}}}{\underset{2}{\cancel{6}} \times \underset{2}{\cancel{10}}} = \frac{1 \times 1}{2 \times 2} = \mathbf{\frac{1}{4}}$

5. $15 \times \left(5\frac{1}{2} \times \frac{2}{11}\right) = \frac{15}{1} \times \left(\frac{(5 \times 2) + 1}{2} \times \frac{2}{11}\right) = \frac{15}{1} \times \left(\frac{10+1}{2} \times \frac{2}{11}\right) = \frac{15}{1} \times \left(\frac{11}{2} \times \frac{2}{11}\right) = \frac{15}{1} \times \left(\frac{\overset{1}{\cancel{11}} \times \overset{1}{\cancel{2}}}{\underset{1}{\cancel{2}} \times \underset{1}{\cancel{11}}}\right) = \frac{15}{1} \times \left(\frac{1 \times 1}{1 \times 1}\right)$

$$= \frac{15}{1} \times \left(\frac{1}{1}\right) = \frac{15}{1} \times \frac{1}{1} = \frac{15 \times 1}{1 \times 1} = \frac{15}{1} = \mathbf{15}$$

6. $\left(1\frac{1}{4} \times 2\frac{1}{3}\right) \times \left(1\frac{1}{5} \times \frac{2}{7}\right) = \left(\frac{(1 \times 4)+1}{4} \times \frac{(2 \times 3)+1}{3}\right) \times \left(\frac{(1 \times 5)+1}{5} \times \frac{2}{7}\right) = \left(\frac{4+1}{4} \times \frac{6+1}{3}\right) \times \left(\frac{5+1}{5} \times \frac{2}{7}\right)$

$= \left(\frac{5}{4} \times \frac{7}{3}\right) \times \left(\frac{6}{5} \times \frac{2}{7}\right) = \left(\frac{5 \times 7}{4 \times 3}\right) \times \left(\frac{6 \times 2}{5 \times 7}\right) = \left(\frac{35}{12}\right) \times \left(\frac{12}{35}\right) = \frac{35}{12} \times \frac{12}{35} = \frac{\overset{1}{\cancel{35}} \times \overset{1}{\cancel{12}}}{\underset{1}{\cancel{12}} \times \underset{1}{\cancel{35}}} = \frac{1 \times 1}{1 \times 1} = \frac{1}{1} = \mathbf{1}$

7. $\left(5 \times \frac{3}{5} \times \frac{1}{4}\right) \times \left(\frac{2}{3} \times 2\frac{1}{2}\right) = \left(\frac{5}{1} \times \frac{3}{5} \times \frac{1}{4}\right) \times \left(\frac{2}{3} \times \frac{(2 \times 2)+1}{2}\right) = \left(\frac{\overset{1}{\cancel{5}} \times 3 \times 1}{1 \times \underset{1}{\cancel{5}} \times 4}\right) \times \left(\frac{2}{3} \times \frac{5}{2}\right) = \left(\frac{1 \times 3 \times 1}{1 \times 1 \times 4}\right) \times \left(\frac{\overset{1}{\cancel{2}} \times 5}{3 \times \underset{1}{\cancel{2}}}\right)$

$= \left(\frac{3}{4}\right) \times \left(\frac{1 \times 5}{3 \times 1}\right) = \frac{3}{4} \times \left(\frac{5}{3}\right) = \frac{3}{4} \times \frac{5}{3} = \frac{\overset{1}{\cancel{3}} \times 5}{4 \times \underset{1}{\cancel{3}}} = \frac{1 \times 5}{4 \times 1} = \frac{5}{4} = \mathbf{1\frac{1}{4}}$

8. $2\frac{1}{3} \times \left(\frac{3}{8} \times 1\frac{4}{7}\right) = \frac{(2 \times 3)+1}{3} \times \left(\frac{3}{8} \times \frac{(1 \times 7)+4}{7}\right) = \frac{6+1}{3} \times \left(\frac{3}{8} \times \frac{7+4}{7}\right) = \frac{7}{3} \times \left(\frac{3}{8} \times \frac{11}{7}\right) = \frac{7}{3} \times \left(\frac{3 \times 11}{8 \times 7}\right) = \frac{7}{3} \times \left(\frac{33}{56}\right)$

$= \frac{7}{3} \times \frac{33}{56} = \frac{\overset{1}{\cancel{7}} \times \overset{11}{\cancel{33}}}{\underset{1}{\cancel{3}} \times \underset{8}{\cancel{56}}} = \frac{1 \times 11}{1 \times 8} = \frac{11}{8} = \mathbf{1\frac{3}{8}}$

9. $1\frac{1}{5} \times \frac{2}{3} \times \frac{1}{6} \times \frac{5}{4} = \frac{(1 \times 5)+1}{5} \times \frac{2}{3} \times \frac{1}{6} \times \frac{5}{4} = \frac{5+1}{5} \times \frac{2}{3} \times \frac{1}{6} \times \frac{5}{4} = \frac{6}{5} \times \frac{2}{3} \times \frac{1}{6} \times \frac{5}{4} = \frac{\overset{1}{\cancel{6}} \times \overset{1}{\cancel{2}} \times 1 \times \overset{1}{\cancel{5}}}{\underset{1}{\cancel{5}} \times 3 \times \underset{1}{\cancel{6}} \times \underset{2}{\cancel{4}}} = \frac{1 \times 1 \times 1 \times 1}{1 \times 3 \times 1 \times 2} = \mathbf{\frac{1}{6}}$

10. $3\frac{1}{3} \times \left[\frac{2}{3} \times \frac{5}{2} \times \left(1\frac{1}{5} \times 0\right)\right] = \mathbf{0}$

Section 7.4 Solutions:

1. $2\frac{1}{3} \div \frac{5}{6} = \frac{(2 \times 3)+1}{3} \div \frac{5}{6} = \frac{6+1}{3} \div \frac{5}{6} = \frac{7}{3} \div \frac{5}{6} = \frac{7}{3} \times \frac{6}{5} = \frac{7 \times \overset{2}{\cancel{6}}}{\underset{1}{\cancel{3}} \times 5} = \frac{7 \times 2}{1 \times 5} = \frac{14}{5} = \mathbf{2\frac{4}{5}}$

2. $2\frac{3}{5} \div 6 = \frac{(2 \times 5)+3}{5} \div \frac{6}{1} = \frac{10+3}{5} \div \frac{6}{1} = \frac{13}{5} \div \frac{6}{1} = \frac{13}{5} \times \frac{1}{6} = \frac{13 \times 1}{5 \times 6} = \mathbf{\frac{13}{30}}$

3. $\frac{6}{10} \div 2\frac{4}{5} = \frac{\overset{3}{\cancel{6}}}{\underset{5}{\cancel{10}}} \div \frac{(2 \times 5)+4}{5} = \frac{3}{5} \div \frac{10+4}{5} = \frac{3}{5} \div \frac{14}{5} = \frac{3}{5} \times \frac{5}{14} = \frac{3 \times \overset{1}{\cancel{5}}}{\underset{1}{\cancel{5}} \times 14} = \frac{3 \times 1}{1 \times 14} = \mathbf{\frac{3}{14}}$

4. $5 \div \left(\frac{1}{3} \div \frac{3}{5}\right) = \frac{5}{1} \div \left(\frac{1}{3} \times \frac{5}{3}\right) = \frac{5}{1} \div \left(\frac{1 \times 5}{3 \times 3}\right) = \frac{5}{1} \div \left(\frac{5}{9}\right) = \frac{5}{1} \div \frac{5}{9} = \frac{5}{1} \times \frac{9}{5} = \frac{\overset{1}{\cancel{5}} \times 9}{1 \times \underset{1}{\cancel{5}}} = \frac{1 \times 9}{1 \times 1} = \frac{9}{1} = \mathbf{9}$

5. $\frac{1}{8} \div \left(1\frac{1}{4} \div \frac{3}{5}\right) = \frac{1}{8} \div \left(\frac{(1 \times 4)+1}{4} \div \frac{3}{5}\right) = \frac{1}{8} \div \left(\frac{4+1}{4} \div \frac{3}{5}\right) = \frac{1}{8} \div \left(\frac{5}{4} \div \frac{3}{5}\right) = \frac{1}{8} \div \left(\frac{5}{4} \times \frac{5}{3}\right) = \frac{1}{8} \div \left(\frac{5 \times 5}{4 \times 3}\right) = \frac{1}{8} \div \left(\frac{25}{12}\right)$

$= \frac{1}{8} \div \frac{25}{12} = \frac{1}{8} \times \frac{12}{25} = \frac{1 \times \overset{3}{\cancel{12}}}{\underset{2}{\cancel{8}} \times 25} = \frac{1 \times 3}{2 \times 25} = \mathbf{\frac{3}{50}}$

6. $\left(\frac{3}{7} \div \frac{4}{7}\right) \div 2\frac{3}{4} = \left(\frac{3}{7} \times \frac{7}{4}\right) \div \frac{(2 \times 4)+3}{4} = \left(\frac{3 \times \overset{1}{\cancel{7}}}{\underset{1}{\cancel{7}} \times 4}\right) \div \frac{8+3}{4} = \left(\frac{3 \times 1}{1 \times 4}\right) \div \frac{11}{4} = \left(\frac{3}{4}\right) \div \frac{11}{4} = \frac{3}{4} \div \frac{11}{4} = \frac{3}{4} \times \frac{4}{11} = \frac{3 \times \overset{1}{\cancel{4}}}{\underset{1}{\cancel{4}} \times 11}$

$= \frac{3 \times 1}{1 \times 11} = \mathbf{\frac{3}{11}}$

7. $\frac{5}{6} \div \left(1\frac{1}{5} \div \frac{4}{5}\right) = \frac{5}{6} \div \left(\frac{(1\times5)+1}{5} \div \frac{4}{5}\right) = \frac{5}{6} \div \left(\frac{5+1}{5} \div \frac{4}{5}\right) = \frac{5}{6} \div \left(\frac{6}{5} \div \frac{4}{5}\right) = \frac{5}{6} \div \left(\frac{6}{5} \times \frac{5}{4}\right) = \frac{5}{6} \div \left(\frac{\overset{3}{6}\times\overset{1}{5}}{\underset{1}{5}\times\underset{2}{4}}\right) = \frac{5}{6} \div \left(\frac{3\times1}{1\times2}\right)$

$= \frac{5}{6} \div \left(\frac{3}{2}\right) = \frac{5}{6} \div \frac{3}{2} = \frac{5}{6} \times \frac{2}{3} = \frac{5\times\overset{1}{2}}{\underset{3}{6}\times3} = \frac{5\times1}{3\times3} = \frac{5}{9}$

8. $\left(3\frac{1}{8} \div \frac{5}{6}\right) \div 12 = \left(\frac{(3\times8)+1}{8} \div \frac{5}{6}\right) \div \frac{12}{1} = \left(\frac{24+1}{8} \div \frac{5}{6}\right) \div \frac{12}{1} = \left(\frac{25}{8} \div \frac{5}{6}\right) \div \frac{12}{1} = \left(\frac{25}{8} \times \frac{6}{5}\right) \div \frac{12}{1} = \left(\frac{\overset{5}{25}\times\overset{3}{6}}{\underset{4}{8}\times\underset{1}{5}}\right) \div \frac{12}{1}$

$= \left(\frac{5\times3}{4\times1}\right) \div \frac{12}{1} = \left(\frac{15}{4}\right) \div \frac{12}{1} = \frac{15}{4} \div \frac{12}{1} = \frac{15}{4} \times \frac{1}{12} = \frac{\overset{5}{15}\times1}{4\times\underset{4}{12}} = \frac{5\times1}{4\times4} = \frac{5}{16}$

9. $\left(1\frac{1}{4} \div \frac{3}{45}\right) \div \frac{2}{5} = \left(\frac{(1\times4)+1}{4} \div \frac{3}{45}\right) \div \frac{2}{5} = \left(\frac{4+1}{4} \div \frac{3}{45}\right) \div \frac{2}{5} = \left(\frac{5}{4} \div \frac{3}{45}\right) \div \frac{2}{5} = \left(\frac{5}{4} \times \frac{45}{3}\right) \div \frac{2}{5} = \left(\frac{5\times\overset{15}{45}}{4\times\underset{1}{3}}\right) \div \frac{2}{5}$

$= \left(\frac{5\times15}{4\times1}\right) \div \frac{2}{5} = \left(\frac{75}{4}\right) \div \frac{2}{5} = \frac{75}{4} \div \frac{2}{5} = \frac{75}{4} \times \frac{5}{2} = \frac{75\times5}{4\times2} = \frac{375}{8} = 46\frac{7}{8}$

10. $\left(1\frac{5}{8} \div 5\right) \div \left(2\frac{3}{4} \div \frac{1}{2}\right) = \left(\frac{(1\times8)+5}{8} \div \frac{5}{1}\right) \div \left(\frac{(2\times4)+3}{4} \div \frac{1}{2}\right) = \left(\frac{8+5}{8} \div \frac{5}{1}\right) \div \left(\frac{8+3}{4} \div \frac{1}{2}\right) = \left(\frac{13}{8} \div \frac{5}{1}\right) \div \left(\frac{11}{4} \div \frac{1}{2}\right)$

$= \left(\frac{13}{8} \times \frac{1}{5}\right) \div \left(\frac{11}{4} \times \frac{2}{1}\right) = \left(\frac{13\times1}{8\times5}\right) \div \left(\frac{11\times\overset{1}{2}}{\underset{2}{4}\times1}\right) = \left(\frac{13}{40}\right) \div \left(\frac{11\times1}{2\times1}\right) = \frac{13}{40} \div \left(\frac{11}{2}\right) = \frac{13}{40} \div \frac{11}{2} = \frac{13}{40} \times \frac{2}{11} = \frac{13\times\overset{1}{2}}{\underset{20}{40}\times11}$

$= \frac{13\times1}{20\times11} = \frac{13}{220}$

Section 7.5 Solutions:

1. $\left(\frac{2}{3} \times 4\frac{1}{5}\right) + 2\frac{3}{4} = \left(\frac{2}{3} \times \frac{(4\times5)+1}{5}\right) + \frac{(2\times4)+3}{4} = \left(\frac{2}{3} \times \frac{20+1}{5}\right) + \frac{8+3}{4} = \left(\frac{2}{3} \times \frac{21}{5}\right) + \frac{11}{4} = \left(\frac{2\times\overset{7}{21}}{\underset{1}{3}\times5}\right) + \frac{11}{4}$

$= \left(\frac{2\times7}{1\times5}\right) + \frac{11}{4} = \left(\frac{14}{5}\right) + \frac{11}{4} = \frac{14}{5} + \frac{11}{4} = \frac{(14\times4)+(11\times5)}{5\times4} = \frac{56+55}{20} = \frac{111}{20} = 5\frac{11}{20}$

2. $\frac{8}{7} \times \left(2\frac{1}{3} \div 1\frac{4}{5}\right) = \frac{8}{7} \times \left(\frac{(2\times3)+1}{3} \div \frac{(1\times5)+4}{5}\right) = \frac{8}{7} \times \left(\frac{6+1}{3} \div \frac{5+4}{5}\right) = \frac{8}{7} \times \left(\frac{7}{3} \div \frac{9}{5}\right) = \frac{8}{7} \times \left(\frac{7}{3} \times \frac{5}{9}\right) = \frac{8}{7} \times \left(\frac{7\times5}{3\times9}\right)$

$= \frac{8}{7} \times \left(\frac{35}{27}\right) = \frac{8}{7} \times \frac{35}{27} = \frac{8\times\overset{5}{35}}{\underset{1}{7}\times27} = \frac{8\times5}{1\times27} = \frac{40}{27} = 1\frac{13}{27}$

3. $12 + \left(3\frac{1}{2} - 1\frac{1}{4}\right) = \frac{12}{1} + \left(\frac{(3\times2)+1}{2} - \frac{(1\times4)+1}{4}\right) = \frac{12}{1} + \left(\frac{6+1}{2} - \frac{4+1}{4}\right) = \frac{12}{1} + \left(\frac{7}{2} - \frac{5}{4}\right) = \frac{12}{1} + \left(\frac{(7\times4)-(5\times2)}{2\times4}\right)$

$= \frac{12}{1} + \left(\frac{28-10}{8}\right) = \frac{12}{1} + \left(\frac{18}{8}\right) = \frac{12}{1} + \frac{\overset{9}{18}}{\underset{4}{8}} = \frac{12}{1} + \frac{9}{4} = \frac{(12\times4)+(9\times1)}{1\times4} = \frac{48+9}{4} = \frac{57}{4} = 14\frac{1}{4}$

4. $5 \div \left(\frac{4}{9} \times 3\frac{2}{5}\right) = \frac{5}{1} \div \left(\frac{4}{9} \times \frac{(3\times5)+2}{5}\right) = \frac{5}{1} \div \left(\frac{4}{9} \times \frac{15+2}{5}\right) = \frac{5}{1} \div \left(\frac{4}{9} \times \frac{17}{5}\right) = \frac{5}{1} \div \left(\frac{4\times17}{9\times5}\right) = \frac{5}{1} \div \left(\frac{68}{45}\right) = \frac{5}{1} \div \frac{68}{45}$

$$= \frac{5}{1} \times \frac{45}{68} = \frac{5 \times 45}{1 \times 68} = \frac{225}{68} = 3\frac{21}{68}$$

5. $\left(\frac{4}{5} + 5\frac{1}{6}\right) - \left(2\frac{1}{3} - \frac{2}{3}\right) = \left(\frac{4}{5} + \frac{(5 \times 6) + 1}{6}\right) - \left(\frac{(2 \times 3) + 1}{3} - \frac{2}{3}\right) = \left(\frac{4}{5} + \frac{30 + 1}{6}\right) - \left(\frac{6 + 1}{3} - \frac{2}{3}\right) = \left(\frac{4}{5} + \frac{31}{6}\right) - \left(\frac{7}{3} - \frac{2}{3}\right)$

$$= \left(\frac{(4 \times 6) + (31 \times 5)}{5 \times 6}\right) - \left(\frac{7 - 2}{3}\right) = \left(\frac{24 + 155}{30}\right) - \left(\frac{5}{3}\right) = \left(\frac{179}{30}\right) - \left(\frac{5}{3}\right) = \frac{179}{30} - \frac{5}{3} = \frac{(179 \times 3) - (5 \times 30)}{30 \times 3} = \frac{537 - 150}{90}$$

$$= \frac{\overset{43}{\cancel{387}}}{\underset{10}{\cancel{90}}} = \frac{43}{10} = 4\frac{3}{10}$$

6. $\left(\frac{2}{3} \times \frac{5}{4}\right) \div \left(\frac{3}{4} \times 2\frac{1}{3}\right) = \left(\frac{\overset{1}{2} \times 5}{3 \times \underset{2}{\cancel{4}}}\right) \div \left(\frac{3}{4} \times \frac{(2 \times 3) + 1}{3}\right) = \left(\frac{1 \times 5}{3 \times 2}\right) \div \left(\frac{3}{4} \times \frac{6 + 1}{3}\right) = \left(\frac{5}{6}\right) \div \left(\frac{3}{4} \times \frac{7}{3}\right) = \frac{5}{6} \div \left(\frac{\overset{1}{\cancel{3}} \times 7}{4 \times \underset{1}{\cancel{3}}}\right)$

$$= \frac{5}{6} \div \left(\frac{1 \times 7}{4 \times 1}\right) = \frac{5}{6} \div \left(\frac{7}{4}\right) = \frac{5}{6} \div \frac{7}{4} = \frac{5}{6} \times \frac{4}{7} = \frac{5 \times \overset{2}{\cancel{4}}}{\underset{3}{\cancel{6}} \times 7} = \frac{5 \times 2}{3 \times 7} = \frac{10}{21}$$

7. $\left(\frac{4}{5} + 1\frac{1}{2}\right) \times \frac{3}{8} = \left(\frac{4}{5} + \frac{(1 \times 2) + 1}{2}\right) \times \frac{3}{8} = \left(\frac{4}{5} + \frac{2 + 1}{2}\right) \times \frac{3}{8} = \left(\frac{4}{5} + \frac{3}{2}\right) \times \frac{3}{8} = \left(\frac{(4 \times 2) + (3 \times 5)}{5 \times 2}\right) \times \frac{3}{8} = \left(\frac{8 + 15}{10}\right) \times \frac{3}{8}$

$$= \left(\frac{23}{10}\right) \times \frac{3}{8} = \frac{23}{10} \times \frac{3}{8} = \frac{23 \times 3}{10 \times 8} = \frac{69}{80}$$

8. $\left(2\frac{1}{3} \times 1\frac{1}{5} \times \frac{5}{4}\right) \div \frac{3}{8} = \left(\frac{(2 \times 3) + 1}{3} \times \frac{(1 \times 5) + 1}{5} \times \frac{5}{4}\right) \div \frac{3}{8} = \left(\frac{6 + 1}{3} \times \frac{5 + 1}{5} \times \frac{5}{4}\right) \div \frac{3}{8} = \left(\frac{7}{3} \times \frac{6}{5} \times \frac{5}{4}\right) \div \frac{3}{8} = \left(\frac{7 \times \overset{2}{\cancel{6}} \times \overset{1}{\cancel{5}}}{\underset{1}{\cancel{3}} \times \underset{1}{\cancel{5}} \times 4}\right) \div \frac{3}{8}$

$$= \left(\frac{7 \times 2 \times 1}{1 \times 1 \times 4}\right) \div \frac{3}{8} = \left(\frac{14}{4}\right) \div \frac{3}{8} = \frac{\overset{7}{\cancel{14}}}{\underset{2}{\cancel{4}}} \div \frac{3}{8} = \frac{7}{2} \div \frac{3}{8} = \frac{7}{2} \times \frac{8}{3} = \frac{7 \times \overset{4}{\cancel{8}}}{\underset{1}{\cancel{2}} \times 3} = \frac{7 \times 4}{1 \times 3} = \frac{28}{3} = 9\frac{1}{3}$$

9. $\left(\frac{2}{3} + \frac{1}{3}\right) \times \left(2\frac{3}{8} \times 4\right) = \left(\frac{2 + 1}{3}\right) \times \left(\frac{(2 \times 8) + 3}{8} \times \frac{4}{1}\right) = \left(\frac{3}{3}\right) \times \left(\frac{16 + 3}{8} \times \frac{4}{1}\right) = \frac{\overset{1}{\cancel{3}}}{\underset{1}{\cancel{3}}} \times \left(\frac{19}{8} \times \frac{4}{1}\right) = \frac{1}{1} \times \left(\frac{19 \times \overset{1}{\cancel{4}}}{\underset{2}{\cancel{8}} \times 1}\right) = \frac{1}{1} \times \left(\frac{19 \times 1}{2 \times 1}\right)$

$$= \frac{1}{1} \times \left(\frac{19}{2}\right) = \frac{1}{1} \times \frac{19}{2} = \frac{1 \times 19}{1 \times 2} = \frac{19}{2} = 9\frac{1}{2}$$

10. $\left(4\frac{2}{3} - \frac{1}{6}\right) \div \left(\frac{6}{25} \times \frac{5}{3}\right) = \left(\frac{(4 \times 3) + 2}{3} - \frac{1}{6}\right) \div \left(\frac{\overset{2}{\cancel{6}} \times \overset{1}{\cancel{5}}}{\underset{5}{\cancel{25}} \times \underset{1}{\cancel{3}}}\right) = \left(\frac{12 + 2}{3} - \frac{1}{6}\right) \div \left(\frac{2 \times 1}{5 \times 1}\right) = \left(\frac{14}{3} - \frac{1}{6}\right) \div \left(\frac{2}{5}\right)$

$$= \left(\frac{(14 \times 6) - (1 \times 3)}{3 \times 6}\right) \div \frac{2}{5} = \left(\frac{84 - 3}{18}\right) \div \frac{2}{5} = \left(\frac{81}{18}\right) \div \frac{2}{5} = \frac{81}{18} \div \frac{2}{5} = \frac{81}{18} \times \frac{5}{2} = \frac{\overset{9}{\cancel{81}} \times 5}{\underset{2}{\cancel{18}} \times 2} = \frac{9 \times 5}{2 \times 2} = \frac{45}{4} = 11\frac{1}{4}$$

Chapter 8 Solutions:

Section 8.1 Solutions:

1. $3\dfrac{2}{5} + \dfrac{0.01}{0.5} = \dfrac{(3\times5)+2}{5} + \dfrac{\frac{1}{100}}{\frac{5}{10}} = \dfrac{15+2}{5} + \dfrac{1\times10}{100\times5} = \dfrac{17}{5} + \dfrac{\frac{1}{10}}{\frac{500}{50}} = \dfrac{17}{5} + \dfrac{1}{50} = \dfrac{(17\times50)+(1\times5)}{5\times50} = \dfrac{850+5}{250} = \dfrac{\overset{171}{\cancel{855}}}{\underset{50}{\cancel{250}}}$

   $= \dfrac{171}{50} = 3\dfrac{21}{50}$

2. $0.12 + 6\dfrac{2}{10} = \dfrac{12}{100} + \dfrac{(6\times10)+2}{10} = \dfrac{12}{100} + \dfrac{60+2}{10} = \dfrac{\overset{3}{\cancel{12}}}{\underset{25}{\cancel{100}}} + \dfrac{\overset{31}{\cancel{62}}}{\underset{5}{\cancel{10}}} = \dfrac{3}{25} + \dfrac{31}{5} = \dfrac{(3\times5)+(31\times25)}{25\times5} = \dfrac{15+775}{125} = \dfrac{\overset{158}{\cancel{790}}}{\underset{25}{\cancel{125}}}$

   $= \dfrac{158}{25} = 6\dfrac{8}{25}$

3. $\dfrac{0.03}{0.5} + 3\dfrac{4}{5} = \dfrac{\frac{3}{100}}{\frac{5}{10}} + \dfrac{(3\times5)+4}{5} = \dfrac{3\times10}{100\times5} + \dfrac{15+4}{5} = \dfrac{\overset{3}{\cancel{30}}}{\underset{50}{\cancel{500}}} + \dfrac{19}{5} = \dfrac{3}{50} + \dfrac{19}{5} = \dfrac{(3\times5)+(19\times50)}{50\times5} = \dfrac{15+950}{250} = \dfrac{\overset{193}{\cancel{965}}}{\underset{50}{\cancel{250}}}$

   $= \dfrac{193}{50} = 3\dfrac{43}{50}$

4. $\left(3\dfrac{1}{2} + 2\dfrac{3}{4}\right) + \dfrac{0.8}{1.2} = \left(\dfrac{(3\times2)+1}{2} + \dfrac{(2\times4)+3}{4}\right) + \dfrac{\frac{8}{10}}{\frac{12}{10}} = \left(\dfrac{6+1}{2} + \dfrac{8+3}{4}\right) + \dfrac{8\times10}{10\times12} = \left(\dfrac{7}{2} + \dfrac{11}{4}\right) + \dfrac{\overset{2}{\cancel{80}}}{\underset{3}{\cancel{120}}}$

   $= \left(\dfrac{(7\times4)+(11\times2)}{2\times4}\right) + \dfrac{2}{3} = \left(\dfrac{28+22}{8}\right) + \dfrac{2}{3} = \left(\dfrac{50}{8}\right) + \dfrac{2}{3} = \dfrac{\overset{25}{\cancel{50}}}{\underset{4}{\cancel{8}}} + \dfrac{2}{3} = \dfrac{25}{4} + \dfrac{2}{3} = \dfrac{(25\times3)+(2\times4)}{4\times3} = \dfrac{75+8}{12} = \dfrac{83}{12}$

   $= 6\dfrac{11}{12}$

5. $3\dfrac{5}{8} + \dfrac{0.02}{0.14} + \dfrac{0.2}{0.5} = \left(3\dfrac{5}{8} + \dfrac{0.02}{0.14}\right) + \dfrac{0.2}{0.5} = \left(\dfrac{(3\times8)+5}{8} + \dfrac{\frac{2}{100}}{\frac{14}{100}}\right) + \dfrac{\frac{2}{10}}{\frac{5}{10}} = \left(\dfrac{24+5}{8} + \dfrac{2\times100}{100\times14}\right) + \dfrac{2\times10}{10\times5} = \left(\dfrac{29}{8} + \dfrac{\overset{1}{\cancel{200}}}{\underset{7}{\cancel{1400}}}\right) + \dfrac{\overset{2}{\cancel{20}}}{\underset{5}{\cancel{50}}}$

   $= \left(\dfrac{29}{8} + \dfrac{1}{7}\right) + \dfrac{2}{5} = \left(\dfrac{(29\times7)+(1\times8)}{8\times7}\right) + \dfrac{2}{5} = \left(\dfrac{203+8}{56}\right) + \dfrac{2}{5} = \left(\dfrac{211}{56}\right) + \dfrac{2}{5} = \dfrac{211}{56} + \dfrac{2}{5} = \dfrac{(211\times5)+(2\times56)}{56\times5}$

   $= \dfrac{1055+112}{280} = \dfrac{1167}{280} = 4\dfrac{47}{280}$

6. $\left(3\dfrac{6}{8} + 5\dfrac{1}{8}\right) + \dfrac{0.4}{0.08} = \left(\dfrac{(3\times8)+6}{8} + \dfrac{(5\times8)+1}{8}\right) + \dfrac{\frac{4}{10}}{\frac{8}{100}} = \left(\dfrac{24+6}{8} + \dfrac{40+1}{8}\right) + \dfrac{4\times100}{10\times8} = \left(\dfrac{30}{8} + \dfrac{41}{8}\right) + \dfrac{\overset{40}{\cancel{400}}}{\underset{8}{\cancel{80}}} = \left(\dfrac{71}{8}\right) + \dfrac{40}{8}$

   $= \dfrac{71}{8} + \dfrac{40}{8} = \dfrac{71+40}{8} = \dfrac{111}{8} = 13\dfrac{7}{8}$

7. $\left(5\dfrac{3}{4} + \dfrac{0.2}{0.1}\right) + 0.24 = \left(\dfrac{(5\times4)+3}{4} + \dfrac{\frac{2}{10}}{\frac{1}{10}}\right) + \dfrac{24}{100} = \left(\dfrac{20+3}{4} + \dfrac{2\times10}{10\times1}\right) + \dfrac{24}{100} = \left(\dfrac{23}{4} + \dfrac{\overset{2}{\cancel{20}}}{\underset{1}{\cancel{10}}}\right) + \dfrac{\overset{6}{\cancel{24}}}{\underset{25}{\cancel{100}}} = \left(\dfrac{23}{4} + \dfrac{2}{1}\right) + \dfrac{6}{25}$

   $= \left(\dfrac{(23\times1)+(2\times4)}{4\times1}\right) + \dfrac{6}{25} = \left(\dfrac{23+8}{4}\right) + \dfrac{6}{25} = \left(\dfrac{31}{4}\right) + \dfrac{6}{25} = \dfrac{31}{4} + \dfrac{6}{25} = \dfrac{(31\times25)+(6\times4)}{4\times25} = \dfrac{775+24}{100} = \dfrac{799}{100}$

$$= 7\frac{99}{100}$$

8. $\dfrac{0.04}{1.2} + \left(4\dfrac{5}{6} + 2\dfrac{4}{5}\right) = \dfrac{\frac{4}{100}}{\frac{12}{10}} + \left(\dfrac{(4\times6)+5}{6} + \dfrac{(2\times5)+4}{5}\right) = \dfrac{4\times10}{100\times12} + \left(\dfrac{24+5}{6} + \dfrac{10+4}{5}\right) = \dfrac{\overset{1}{\cancel{40}}}{\underset{30}{\cancel{1200}}} + \left(\dfrac{29}{6} + \dfrac{14}{5}\right)$

$\qquad = \dfrac{1}{30} + \left(\dfrac{(29\times5)+(14\times6)}{6\times5}\right) = \dfrac{1}{30} + \left(\dfrac{145+84}{30}\right) = \dfrac{1}{30} + \left(\dfrac{229}{30}\right) = \dfrac{1}{30} + \dfrac{229}{30} = \dfrac{1+229}{30} = \dfrac{\overset{23}{\cancel{230}}}{\underset{3}{\cancel{30}}} = \dfrac{23}{3} = 7\dfrac{2}{3}$

9. $3\dfrac{2}{7} + \left(\dfrac{0.2}{0.04} + 0.4\right) = \dfrac{(3\times7)+2}{7} + \left(\dfrac{\frac{2}{10}}{\frac{4}{100}} + \dfrac{4}{10}\right) = \dfrac{21+2}{7} + \left(\dfrac{2\times100}{10\times4} + \dfrac{4}{10}\right) = \dfrac{23}{7} + \left(\dfrac{\overset{5}{\cancel{200}}}{\underset{1}{\cancel{40}}} + \dfrac{\overset{2}{\cancel{4}}}{\underset{5}{\cancel{10}}}\right) = \dfrac{23}{7} + \left(\dfrac{5}{1} + \dfrac{2}{5}\right)$

$\qquad = \dfrac{23}{7} + \left(\dfrac{(5\times5)+(2\times1)}{1\times5}\right) = \dfrac{23}{7} + \left(\dfrac{25+2}{5}\right) = \dfrac{23}{7} + \left(\dfrac{27}{5}\right) = \dfrac{23}{7} + \dfrac{27}{5} = \dfrac{(23\times5)+(27\times7)}{7\times5} = \dfrac{115+189}{35} = \dfrac{304}{35} = 8\dfrac{24}{35}$

10. $\left(3\dfrac{1}{4} + 2\dfrac{4}{5}\right) + \left(\dfrac{0.12}{0.4} + \dfrac{0.5}{0.2}\right) = \left(\dfrac{(3\times4)+1}{4} + \dfrac{(2\times5)+4}{5}\right) + \left(\dfrac{\frac{12}{100}}{\frac{4}{10}} + \dfrac{\frac{5}{10}}{\frac{2}{10}}\right) = \left(\dfrac{12+1}{4} + \dfrac{10+4}{5}\right) + \left(\dfrac{12\times10}{100\times4} + \dfrac{5\times10}{10\times2}\right)$

$\qquad = \left(\dfrac{13}{4} + \dfrac{14}{5}\right) + \left(\dfrac{\overset{3}{\cancel{120}}}{\underset{10}{\cancel{400}}} + \dfrac{\overset{5}{\cancel{50}}}{\underset{2}{\cancel{20}}}\right) = \left(\dfrac{(13\times5)+(14\times4)}{4\times5}\right) + \left(\dfrac{3}{10} + \dfrac{5}{2}\right) = \left(\dfrac{65+56}{20}\right) + \left(\dfrac{(3\times2)+(5\times10)}{10\times2}\right) = \left(\dfrac{121}{20}\right) + \left(\dfrac{6+50}{20}\right)$

$\qquad = \dfrac{121}{20} + \left(\dfrac{56}{20}\right) = \dfrac{121}{20} + \dfrac{\overset{14}{\cancel{56}}}{\underset{5}{\cancel{20}}} = \dfrac{121}{20} + \dfrac{14}{5} = \dfrac{(121\times5)+(14\times20)}{20\times5} = \dfrac{605+280}{100} = \dfrac{\overset{177}{\cancel{885}}}{\underset{20}{\cancel{100}}} = \dfrac{177}{20} = 8\dfrac{17}{20}$

Section 8.2 Solutions:

1. $2\dfrac{1}{6} - \dfrac{0.02}{0.5} = \dfrac{(2\times6)+1}{6} - \dfrac{\frac{2}{100}}{\frac{5}{10}} = \dfrac{12+1}{6} - \dfrac{2\times10}{100\times5} = \dfrac{13}{6} - \dfrac{\overset{1}{\cancel{20}}}{\underset{25}{\cancel{500}}} = \dfrac{13}{6} - \dfrac{1}{25} = \dfrac{(13\times25)-(1\times6)}{6\times25} = \dfrac{325-6}{150} = \dfrac{319}{150}$

$\qquad = 2\dfrac{19}{150}$

2. $\dfrac{0.03}{1.5} - 4\dfrac{2}{3} = \dfrac{\frac{3}{100}}{\frac{15}{10}} - \dfrac{(4\times3)+2}{3} = \dfrac{3\times10}{100\times15} - \dfrac{12+2}{3} = \dfrac{\overset{1}{\cancel{30}}}{\underset{50}{\cancel{1500}}} - \dfrac{14}{3} = \dfrac{1}{50} - \dfrac{14}{3} = \dfrac{(1\times3)-(14\times50)}{50\times3} = \dfrac{3-700}{150} = \dfrac{-697}{150}$

$\qquad = -\left(4\dfrac{97}{150}\right)$

3. $12.2 - 3\dfrac{4}{5} = \dfrac{122}{10} - \dfrac{(3\times5)+4}{5} = \dfrac{\overset{61}{\cancel{122}}}{\underset{5}{\cancel{10}}} - \dfrac{15+4}{5} = \dfrac{61}{5} - \dfrac{19}{5} = \dfrac{61-19}{5} = \dfrac{42}{5} = 8\dfrac{2}{5}$

4. $\left(3\dfrac{1}{2} - 1\dfrac{3}{4}\right) - \dfrac{1.8}{0.9} = \left(\dfrac{(3\times2)+1}{2} - \dfrac{(1\times4)+3}{4}\right) - \dfrac{\frac{18}{10}}{\frac{9}{10}} = \left(\dfrac{6+1}{2} - \dfrac{4+3}{4}\right) - \dfrac{18\times10}{10\times9} = \left(\dfrac{7}{2} - \dfrac{7}{4}\right) - \dfrac{\overset{2}{\cancel{180}}}{\underset{1}{\cancel{90}}}$

$\qquad = \left(\dfrac{(7\times4)-(7\times2)}{2\times4}\right) - \dfrac{2}{1} = \left(\dfrac{28-14}{8}\right) - \dfrac{2}{1} = \left(\dfrac{14}{8}\right) - \dfrac{2}{1} = \dfrac{\overset{7}{\cancel{14}}}{\underset{4}{\cancel{8}}} - \dfrac{2}{1} = \dfrac{7}{4} - \dfrac{2}{1} = \dfrac{(7\times1)-(2\times4)}{4\times1} = \dfrac{7-8}{4} = -\dfrac{1}{4}$

5. $2\dfrac{3}{8} - \dfrac{1.2}{0.06} - \dfrac{0.2}{0.5} = \left(2\dfrac{3}{8} - \dfrac{1.2}{0.06}\right) - \dfrac{0.2}{0.5} = \left(\dfrac{(2\times 8)+3}{8} - \dfrac{\frac{12}{10}}{\frac{6}{100}}\right) - \dfrac{\frac{2}{10}}{\frac{5}{10}} = \left(\dfrac{16+3}{8} - \dfrac{12\times 100}{10\times 6}\right) - \dfrac{2\times 10}{10\times 5} = \left(\dfrac{19}{8} - \dfrac{\overset{20}{\cancel{1200}}}{\underset{1}{\cancel{60}}}\right) - \dfrac{\overset{2}{\cancel{20}}}{\underset{5}{\cancel{50}}}$

$= \left(\dfrac{19}{8} - \dfrac{20}{1}\right) - \dfrac{2}{5} = \left(\dfrac{(19\times 1)-(20\times 8)}{8\times 1}\right) - \dfrac{2}{5} = \left(\dfrac{19-160}{8}\right) - \dfrac{2}{5} = \left(\dfrac{-141}{8}\right) - \dfrac{2}{5} = \dfrac{-141}{8} - \dfrac{2}{5} = \dfrac{-141}{8} - \dfrac{2}{5}$

$= \dfrac{(-141\times 5)-(2\times 8)}{8\times 5} = \dfrac{-705-16}{40} = \dfrac{-721}{40} = -\left(\mathbf{18\dfrac{1}{40}}\right)$

6. $\left(5\dfrac{2}{8} - 1\dfrac{3}{8}\right) - \dfrac{0.4}{0.08} = \left(\dfrac{(5\times 8)+2}{8} - \dfrac{(1\times 8)+3}{8}\right) - \dfrac{\frac{4}{10}}{\frac{8}{100}} = \left(\dfrac{40+2}{8} - \dfrac{8+3}{8}\right) - \dfrac{4\times 100}{10\times 8} = \left(\dfrac{42}{8} - \dfrac{11}{8}\right) - \dfrac{\overset{5}{\cancel{400}}}{\underset{1}{\cancel{80}}} = \left(\dfrac{42-11}{8}\right) - \dfrac{5}{1}$

$= \left(\dfrac{31}{8}\right) - \dfrac{5}{1} = \dfrac{31}{8} - \dfrac{5}{1} = \dfrac{(31\times 1)-(5\times 8)}{8\times 1} = \dfrac{31-40}{8} = \dfrac{-9}{8} = -\left(\mathbf{1\dfrac{1}{8}}\right)$

7. $\left(15\dfrac{3}{4} - 0.12\right) - \dfrac{0.8}{1.2} = \left(\dfrac{(15\times 4)+3}{4} - \dfrac{12}{100}\right) - \dfrac{\frac{8}{10}}{\frac{12}{10}} = \left(\dfrac{60+3}{4} - \dfrac{\overset{3}{\cancel{12}}}{\underset{25}{\cancel{100}}}\right) - \dfrac{8\times 10}{10\times 12} = \left(\dfrac{63}{4} - \dfrac{3}{25}\right) - \dfrac{\overset{2}{\cancel{80}}}{\underset{3}{\cancel{120}}}$

$= \left(\dfrac{(63\times 25)-(3\times 4)}{4\times 25}\right) - \dfrac{2}{3} = \left(\dfrac{1575-12}{100}\right) - \dfrac{2}{3} = \left(\dfrac{1563}{100}\right) - \dfrac{2}{3} = \dfrac{1563}{100} - \dfrac{2}{3} = \dfrac{(1563\times 3)-(2\times 100)}{100\times 3} = \dfrac{4689-200}{300}$

$= \dfrac{4489}{300} = \mathbf{14\dfrac{289}{300}}$

8. $\dfrac{0.24}{1.2} - \left(2\dfrac{3}{5} - 3\dfrac{4}{9}\right) = \dfrac{\frac{24}{100}}{\frac{12}{10}} - \left(\dfrac{(2\times 5)+3}{5} - \dfrac{(3\times 9)+4}{9}\right) = \dfrac{24\times 10}{100\times 12} - \left(\dfrac{10+3}{5} - \dfrac{27+4}{9}\right) = \dfrac{\overset{1}{\cancel{240}}}{\underset{5}{\cancel{1200}}} - \left(\dfrac{13}{5} - \dfrac{31}{9}\right)$

$= \dfrac{1}{5} - \left(\dfrac{(13\times 9)-(31\times 5)}{5\times 9}\right) = \dfrac{1}{5} - \left(\dfrac{117-155}{45}\right) = \dfrac{1}{5} - \left(\dfrac{-38}{45}\right) = \dfrac{1}{5} - \dfrac{-38}{45} = \dfrac{1}{5} + \dfrac{38}{45} = \dfrac{(1\times 45)+(38\times 5)}{5\times 45} = \dfrac{45+190}{225}$

$= \dfrac{\overset{47}{\cancel{235}}}{\underset{45}{\cancel{225}}} = \dfrac{47}{45} = \mathbf{1\dfrac{2}{45}}$

9. $3\dfrac{1}{8} - \left(\dfrac{0.8}{0.04} - 1.2\right) = \dfrac{(3\times 8)+1}{8} - \left(\dfrac{\frac{8}{10}}{\frac{4}{100}} - \dfrac{12}{10}\right) = \dfrac{24+1}{8} - \left(\dfrac{8\times 100}{10\times 4} - \dfrac{12}{10}\right) = \dfrac{25}{8} - \left(\dfrac{\overset{200}{\cancel{800}}}{\underset{10}{\cancel{40}}} - \dfrac{12}{10}\right) = \dfrac{25}{8} - \left(\dfrac{200}{10} - \dfrac{12}{10}\right)$

$= \dfrac{25}{8} - \left(\dfrac{200-12}{10}\right) = \dfrac{25}{8} - \left(\dfrac{188}{10}\right) = \dfrac{25}{8} - \dfrac{\overset{94}{\cancel{188}}}{\underset{5}{\cancel{10}}} = \dfrac{25}{8} - \dfrac{94}{5} = \dfrac{(25\times 5)-(94\times 8)}{8\times 5} = \dfrac{125-752}{40} = \dfrac{-627}{40} = -\left(\mathbf{15\dfrac{27}{40}}\right)$

10. $\left(15.8 - 2\dfrac{3}{5}\right) - \left(\dfrac{0.12}{0.3} - \dfrac{0.5}{0.15}\right) = \left(\dfrac{158}{10} - \dfrac{(2\times 5)+3}{5}\right) - \left(\dfrac{\frac{12}{100}}{\frac{3}{10}} - \dfrac{\frac{5}{10}}{\frac{15}{100}}\right) = \left(\dfrac{158}{10} - \dfrac{10+3}{5}\right) - \left(\dfrac{12\times 10}{100\times 3} - \dfrac{5\times 100}{10\times 15}\right)$

$= \left(\dfrac{\overset{79}{\cancel{158}}}{\underset{5}{\cancel{10}}} - \dfrac{13}{5}\right) - \left(\dfrac{\overset{2}{\cancel{120}}}{\underset{5}{\cancel{300}}} - \dfrac{\overset{10}{\cancel{500}}}{\underset{3}{\cancel{150}}}\right) = \left(\dfrac{79}{5} - \dfrac{13}{5}\right) - \left(\dfrac{2}{5} - \dfrac{10}{3}\right) = \left(\dfrac{79-13}{5}\right) - \left(\dfrac{(2\times 3)-(10\times 5)}{5\times 3}\right) = \left(\dfrac{66}{5}\right) - \left(\dfrac{6-50}{15}\right)$

$$= \frac{66}{5} - \left(\frac{-44}{15}\right) = \frac{66}{5} - \frac{-44}{15} = \frac{66}{5} + \frac{44}{15} = \frac{(66 \times 15) + (44 \times 5)}{5 \times 15} = \frac{990 + 220}{75} = \frac{\overset{242}{\cancel{1210}}}{\underset{15}{\cancel{75}}} = \frac{242}{15} = \mathbf{16\frac{2}{15}}$$

Section 8.3 Solutions:

1. $2\frac{1}{5} \times \frac{0.04}{0.8} = \frac{(2 \times 5) + 1}{5} \times \frac{\frac{4}{100}}{\frac{8}{10}} = \frac{10 + 1}{5} \times \frac{4 \times 10}{100 \times 8} = \frac{11}{5} \times \frac{40}{800} = \frac{11 \times \overset{1}{\cancel{40}}}{5 \times \underset{20}{\cancel{800}}} = \frac{11 \times 1}{5 \times 20} = \frac{\mathbf{11}}{\mathbf{100}}$

2. $\frac{0.22}{0.001} \times 2\frac{4}{5} = \frac{\frac{22}{100}}{\frac{1}{1000}} \times \frac{(2 \times 5) + 4}{5} = \frac{22 \times 1000}{100 \times 1} \times \frac{10 + 4}{5} = \frac{22000}{100} \times \frac{14}{5} = \frac{\overset{220}{\cancel{22000}} \times 14}{\underset{1}{\cancel{100}} \times 5} = \frac{220 \times 14}{1 \times 5} = \frac{\overset{616}{\cancel{3080}}}{\underset{1}{\cancel{5}}} = \frac{616}{1}$

    $= \mathbf{616}$

3. $3\frac{1}{8} \times 0.4 = \frac{(3 \times 8) + 1}{8} \times \frac{4}{10} = \frac{24 + 1}{8} \times \frac{4}{10} = \frac{25}{8} \times \frac{4}{10} = \frac{\overset{5}{\cancel{25}} \times \overset{1}{\cancel{4}}}{\underset{2}{\cancel{8}} \times \underset{2}{\cancel{10}}} = \frac{5 \times 1}{2 \times 2} = \frac{5}{4} = \mathbf{1\frac{1}{4}}$

4. $2\frac{3}{7} \times \left(\frac{0.6}{0.01} \times 3\frac{1}{5}\right) = \frac{(2 \times 7) + 3}{7} \times \left(\frac{\frac{6}{10}}{\frac{1}{100}} \times \frac{(3 \times 5) + 1}{5}\right) = \frac{14 + 3}{7} \times \left(\frac{6 \times 100}{10 \times 1} \times \frac{15 + 1}{5}\right) = \frac{17}{7} \times \left(\frac{600}{10} \times \frac{16}{5}\right)$

    $= \frac{17}{7} \times \left(\frac{\overset{60}{\cancel{600}} \times 16}{\underset{1}{\cancel{10}} \times 5}\right) = \frac{17}{7} \times \left(\frac{60 \times 16}{1 \times 5}\right) = \frac{17}{7} \times \left(\frac{960}{5}\right) = \frac{17}{7} \times \frac{960}{5} = \frac{17 \times \overset{192}{\cancel{960}}}{7 \times \underset{1}{\cancel{5}}} = \frac{17 \times 192}{7 \times 1} = \frac{3264}{7} = \mathbf{466\frac{2}{7}}$

5. $3\frac{5}{8} \times \frac{1.2}{0.05} \times 14.8 = \frac{(3 \times 8) + 5}{8} \times \frac{\frac{12}{10}}{\frac{5}{100}} \times \frac{148}{10} = \frac{24 + 5}{8} \times \frac{12 \times 100}{10 \times 5} \times \frac{148}{10} = \frac{29}{8} \times \frac{1200}{50} \times \frac{148}{10} = \frac{29 \times \overset{24}{\cancel{1200}} \times \overset{37}{\cancel{148}}}{\underset{2}{\cancel{8}} \times \underset{1}{\cancel{50}} \times 10}$

    $= \frac{29 \times 24 \times 37}{2 \times 1 \times 10} = \frac{\overset{6438}{\cancel{25752}}}{\underset{5}{\cancel{20}}} = \frac{6438}{5} = \mathbf{1287\frac{3}{5}}$

6. $0.002 \times \left(2\frac{3}{5} \times \frac{0.8}{0.04}\right) = \frac{2}{1000} \times \left(\frac{(2 \times 5) + 3}{5} \times \frac{\frac{8}{10}}{\frac{4}{100}}\right) = \frac{2}{1000} \times \left(\frac{10 + 3}{5} \times \frac{8 \times 100}{10 \times 4}\right) = \frac{\overset{1}{\cancel{2}}}{\underset{500}{\cancel{1000}}} \times \left(\frac{13}{5} \times \frac{\overset{20}{\cancel{800}}}{\underset{1}{\cancel{40}}}\right)$

    $= \frac{1}{500} \times \left(\frac{13}{5} \times \frac{20}{1}\right) = \frac{1}{500} \times \left(\frac{13 \times \overset{4}{\cancel{20}}}{\underset{1}{\cancel{5}} \times 1}\right) = \frac{1}{500} \times \left(\frac{13 \times 4}{1 \times 1}\right) = \frac{1}{500} \times \left(\frac{52}{1}\right) = \frac{1}{500} \times \frac{52}{1} = \frac{1 \times \overset{13}{\cancel{52}}}{\underset{125}{\cancel{500}} \times 1} = \frac{1 \times 13}{125 \times 1} = \frac{\mathbf{13}}{\mathbf{125}}$

7. $2\frac{1}{3} \times \left(5\frac{6}{15} \times \frac{0.3}{0.15}\right) = \frac{(2 \times 3) + 1}{3} \times \left(\frac{(5 \times 15) + 6}{15} \times \frac{\frac{3}{10}}{\frac{15}{100}}\right) = \frac{6 + 1}{3} \times \left(\frac{75 + 6}{15} \times \frac{3 \times 100}{10 \times 15}\right) = \frac{7}{3} \times \left(\frac{81}{15} \times \frac{300}{150}\right)$

    $= \frac{7}{3} \times \left(\frac{81 \times \overset{2}{\cancel{300}}}{15 \times \underset{1}{\cancel{150}}}\right) = \frac{7}{3} \times \left(\frac{81 \times 2}{15 \times 1}\right) = \frac{7}{3} \times \left(\frac{162}{15}\right) = \frac{7}{3} \times \frac{162}{15} = \frac{7 \times \overset{54}{\cancel{162}}}{\underset{1}{\cancel{3}} \times 15} = \frac{7 \times 54}{1 \times 15} = \frac{378}{15} = \mathbf{25\frac{3}{15}}$

8. $\left(3\frac{5}{7} \times \frac{1.8}{2.48}\right) \times \left(0.12 \times 3\frac{10}{12}\right) = \left(\frac{(3 \times 7) + 5}{7} \times \frac{\frac{18}{10}}{\frac{248}{100}}\right) \times \left(\frac{12}{100} \times \frac{(3 \times 12) + 10}{12}\right) = \left(\frac{21 + 5}{7} \times \frac{18 \times 100}{10 \times 248}\right) \times \left(\frac{12}{100} \times \frac{36 + 10}{12}\right)$

$$= \left(\frac{26}{7} \times \frac{1800}{2480}\right) \times \left(\frac{12}{100} \times \frac{46}{12}\right) = \left(\frac{26 \times \overset{45}{\cancel{1800}}}{7 \times \underset{62}{\cancel{2480}}}\right) \times \left(\frac{\overset{1}{\cancel{12}} \times \overset{23}{\cancel{46}}}{\underset{50}{\cancel{100}} \times \underset{1}{\cancel{12}}}\right) = \left(\frac{26 \times 45}{7 \times 62}\right) \times \left(\frac{1 \times 23}{50 \times 1}\right) = \left(\frac{1170}{434}\right) \times \left(\frac{23}{50}\right) = \frac{1170}{434} \times \frac{23}{50}$$

$$= \frac{\overset{585}{\cancel{1170}} \times 23}{\underset{217}{\cancel{434}} \times 50} = \frac{\overset{117}{\cancel{585}} \times 23}{217 \times \underset{10}{\cancel{50}}} = \frac{117 \times 23}{217 \times 10} = \frac{2691}{2170} = 1\frac{521}{2170}$$

9. $$5\frac{2}{3} \times \frac{0.3}{12.8} \times 4\frac{9}{13} = \frac{(5 \times 3)+2}{3} \times \frac{\frac{3}{10}}{\frac{128}{10}} \times \frac{(4 \times 13)+9}{13} = \frac{15+2}{3} \times \frac{3 \times 10}{10 \times 128} \times \frac{52+9}{13} = \frac{17}{3} \times \frac{30}{1280} \times \frac{61}{13} = \frac{17 \times \overset{3}{\cancel{30}} \times 61}{3 \times \underset{128}{\cancel{1280}} \times 13}$$

$$= \frac{17 \times \overset{1}{\cancel{3}} \times 61}{\underset{1}{\cancel{3}} \times 128 \times 13} = \frac{17 \times 1 \times 61}{1 \times 128 \times 13} = \frac{1037}{1664}$$

10. $$\left(2\frac{3}{8} \times \frac{0.1}{0.01}\right) \times \left(1\frac{2}{3} \times 1\frac{4}{5}\right) = \left(\frac{(2 \times 8)+3}{8} \times \frac{\frac{1}{10}}{\frac{1}{100}}\right) \times \left(\frac{(1 \times 3)+2}{3} \times \frac{(1 \times 5)+4}{5}\right) = \left(\frac{16+3}{8} \times \frac{1 \times 100}{10 \times 1}\right) \times \left(\frac{3+2}{3} \times \frac{5+4}{5}\right)$$

$$= \left(\frac{19}{8} \times \frac{100}{10}\right) \times \left(\frac{5}{3} \times \frac{9}{5}\right) = \left(\frac{19 \times \overset{10}{\cancel{100}}}{8 \times \underset{1}{\cancel{10}}}\right) \times \left(\frac{\overset{1}{\cancel{5}} \times \overset{3}{\cancel{9}}}{\underset{1}{\cancel{3}} \times \underset{1}{\cancel{5}}}\right) = \left(\frac{19 \times 10}{8 \times 1}\right) \times \left(\frac{1 \times 3}{1 \times 1}\right) = \left(\frac{190}{8}\right) \times \left(\frac{3}{1}\right) = \frac{190}{8} \times \frac{3}{1} = \frac{\overset{95}{\cancel{190}} \times 3}{\underset{4}{\cancel{8}} \times 1} = \frac{95 \times 3}{4 \times 1}$$

$$= \frac{285}{4} = 71\frac{1}{4}$$

Section 8.4 Solutions:

1. $$1\frac{3}{4} \div \frac{0.4}{1.2} = \frac{(1 \times 4)+3}{4} \div \frac{\frac{4}{10}}{\frac{12}{10}} = \frac{4+3}{4} \div \frac{4 \times 10}{10 \times 12} = \frac{7}{4} \div \frac{\overset{1}{\cancel{40}}}{\underset{3}{\cancel{120}}} = \frac{7}{4} \div \frac{1}{3} = \frac{7 \times 3}{4 \times 1} = \frac{21}{4} = 5\frac{1}{4}$$

2. $$0.4 \div 2\frac{3}{8} = \frac{4}{10} \div \frac{(2 \times 8)+3}{8} = \frac{\overset{2}{\cancel{4}}}{\underset{5}{\cancel{10}}} \div \frac{16+3}{8} = \frac{2}{5} \div \frac{19}{8} = \frac{2}{5} \times \frac{8}{19} = \frac{2 \times 8}{5 \times 19} = \frac{16}{95}$$

3. $$\left(\frac{0.05}{0.1} \div 2\frac{5}{8}\right) \div 0.6 = \left(\frac{\frac{5}{100}}{\frac{1}{10}} \div \frac{(2 \times 8)+5}{8}\right) \div \frac{6}{10} = \left(\frac{5 \times 10}{100 \times 1} \div \frac{16+5}{8}\right) \div \frac{6}{10} = \left(\frac{\overset{1}{\cancel{50}}}{\underset{2}{\cancel{100}}} \div \frac{21}{8}\right) \div \frac{\overset{3}{\cancel{6}}}{\underset{5}{\cancel{10}}} = \left(\frac{1}{2} \div \frac{21}{8}\right) \div \frac{3}{5}$$

$$= \left(\frac{1}{2} \times \frac{8}{21}\right) \div \frac{3}{5} = \left(\frac{1 \times \overset{4}{\cancel{8}}}{\underset{1}{\cancel{2}} \times 21}\right) \div \frac{3}{5} = \left(\frac{1 \times 4}{1 \times 21}\right) \div \frac{3}{5} = \left(\frac{4}{21}\right) \div \frac{3}{5} = \frac{4}{21} \div \frac{3}{5} = \frac{4}{21} \times \frac{5}{3} = \frac{4 \times 5}{21 \times 3} = \frac{20}{63}$$

4. $$\left(1\frac{3}{8} \div 2\frac{6}{8}\right) \div \frac{0.2}{0.3} = \left(\frac{(1 \times 8)+3}{8} \div \frac{(2 \times 8)+6}{8}\right) \div \frac{\frac{2}{10}}{\frac{3}{10}} = \left(\frac{8+3}{8} \div \frac{16+6}{8}\right) \div \frac{2 \times 10}{10 \times 3} = \left(\frac{11}{8} \div \frac{22}{8}\right) \div \frac{\overset{2}{\cancel{20}}}{\underset{3}{\cancel{30}}} = \left(\frac{11}{8} \times \frac{8}{22}\right) \div \frac{2}{3}$$

$$= \left(\frac{\overset{1}{\cancel{11}} \times \overset{1}{\cancel{8}}}{\underset{1}{\cancel{8}} \times \underset{2}{\cancel{22}}}\right) \div \frac{2}{3} = \left(\frac{1 \times 1}{1 \times 2}\right) \div \frac{2}{3} = \left(\frac{1}{2}\right) \div \frac{2}{3} = \frac{1}{2} \div \frac{2}{3} = \frac{1}{2} \times \frac{3}{2} = \frac{1 \times 3}{2 \times 2} = \frac{3}{4}$$

5. $$\left(\frac{0.1}{0.04} \div 3\frac{1}{2}\right) \div 5\frac{2}{3} = \left(\frac{\frac{1}{10}}{\frac{4}{100}} \div \frac{(3 \times 2)+1}{2}\right) \div \frac{(5 \times 3)+2}{3} = \left(\frac{1 \times 100}{10 \times 4} \div \frac{6+1}{2}\right) \div \frac{15+2}{3} = \left(\frac{\overset{5}{\cancel{100}}}{\underset{2}{\cancel{40}}} \div \frac{7}{2}\right) \div \frac{17}{3} = \left(\frac{5}{2} \div \frac{7}{2}\right) \div \frac{17}{3}$$

$$= \left(\frac{5}{2} \times \frac{2}{7}\right) \div \frac{17}{3} = \left(\frac{5 \times \overset{1}{2}}{\underset{1}{2} \times 7}\right) \div \frac{17}{3} = \left(\frac{5 \times 1}{1 \times 7}\right) \div \frac{17}{3} = \left(\frac{5}{7}\right) \div \frac{17}{3} = \frac{5}{7} \div \frac{17}{3} = \frac{5}{7} \times \frac{3}{17} = \frac{5 \times 3}{7 \times 17} = \frac{\mathbf{15}}{\mathbf{119}}$$

6. $\left(2\frac{5}{6} \div 0.3\right) \div 1\frac{2}{9} = \left(\frac{(2 \times 6) + 5}{6} \div \frac{3}{10}\right) \div \frac{(1 \times 9) + 2}{9} = \left(\frac{12 + 5}{6} \div \frac{3}{10}\right) \div \frac{9 + 2}{9} = \left(\frac{17}{6} \div \frac{3}{10}\right) \div \frac{11}{9} = \left(\frac{17}{6} \times \frac{10}{3}\right) \div \frac{11}{9}$

$$= \left(\frac{17 \times \overset{5}{10}}{\underset{3}{6} \times 3}\right) \div \frac{11}{9} = \left(\frac{17 \times 5}{3 \times 3}\right) \div \frac{11}{9} = \left(\frac{85}{9}\right) \div \frac{11}{9} = \frac{85}{9} \div \frac{11}{9} = \frac{85}{9} \times \frac{9}{11} = \frac{85 \times \overset{1}{9}}{\underset{1}{9} \times 11} = \frac{85 \times 1}{1 \times 11} = \frac{85}{11} = 7\frac{\mathbf{8}}{\mathbf{11}}$$

7. $\left(\frac{0.8}{2.4} \div 0.04\right) \div 2\frac{4}{5} = \left(\frac{\frac{8}{10}}{\frac{24}{10}} \div \frac{4}{100}\right) \div \frac{(2 \times 5) + 4}{5} = \left(\frac{8 \times 10}{10 \times 24} \div \frac{4}{100}\right) \div \frac{10 + 4}{5} = \left(\frac{\overset{1}{80}}{\underset{3}{240}} \div \frac{\overset{1}{4}}{\underset{25}{100}}\right) \div \frac{14}{5} = \left(\frac{1}{3} \div \frac{1}{25}\right) \div \frac{14}{5}$

$$= \left(\frac{1}{3} \times \frac{25}{1}\right) \div \frac{14}{5} = \left(\frac{1 \times 25}{3 \times 1}\right) \div \frac{14}{5} = \left(\frac{25}{3}\right) \div \frac{14}{5} = \frac{25}{3} \div \frac{14}{5} = \frac{25}{3} \times \frac{5}{14} = \frac{25 \times 5}{3 \times 14} = \frac{125}{42} = 2\frac{\mathbf{41}}{\mathbf{42}}$$

8. $\left(0.04 \div 3\frac{1}{10}\right) \div 3\frac{1}{5} = \left(\frac{4}{100} \div \frac{(3 \times 10) + 1}{10}\right) \div \frac{(3 \times 5) + 1}{5} = \left(\frac{4}{100} \div \frac{30 + 1}{10}\right) \div \frac{15 + 1}{5} = \left(\frac{\overset{1}{4}}{\underset{25}{100}} \div \frac{31}{10}\right) \div \frac{16}{5} = \left(\frac{1}{25} \div \frac{31}{10}\right) \div \frac{16}{5}$

$$= \left(\frac{1}{25} \times \frac{10}{31}\right) \div \frac{16}{5} = \left(\frac{1 \times \overset{2}{10}}{\underset{5}{25} \times 31}\right) \div \frac{16}{5} = \left(\frac{1 \times 2}{5 \times 31}\right) \div \frac{16}{5} = \left(\frac{2}{155}\right) \div \frac{16}{5} = \frac{2}{155} \div \frac{16}{5} = \frac{2}{155} \times \frac{5}{16} = \frac{\overset{1}{2} \times \overset{1}{5}}{\underset{31}{155} \times \underset{8}{16}} = \frac{1 \times 1}{31 \times 8}$$

$$= \frac{\mathbf{1}}{\mathbf{248}}$$

9. $0.2 \div \left(3\frac{1}{8} \div 2\frac{1}{4}\right) = \frac{2}{10} \div \left(\frac{(3 \times 8) + 1}{8} \div \frac{(2 \times 4) + 1}{4}\right) = \frac{2}{10} \div \left(\frac{24 + 1}{8} \div \frac{8 + 1}{4}\right) = \frac{\overset{1}{2}}{\underset{5}{10}} \div \left(\frac{25}{8} \div \frac{9}{4}\right) = \frac{1}{5} \div \left(\frac{25}{8} \times \frac{4}{9}\right)$

$$= \frac{1}{5} \div \left(\frac{25 \times \overset{1}{4}}{8 \times 9} \right) = \frac{1}{5} \div \left(\frac{25 \times 1}{2 \times 9}\right) = \frac{1}{5} \div \left(\frac{25}{18}\right) = \frac{1}{5} \div \frac{25}{18} = \frac{1}{5} \times \frac{18}{25} = \frac{1 \times 18}{5 \times 25} = \frac{\mathbf{18}}{\mathbf{125}}$$

10. $\left(3\frac{1}{5} \div 4\frac{4}{5}\right) \div \left(0.02 \div \frac{0.12}{0.4}\right) = \left(\frac{(3 \times 5) + 1}{5} \div \frac{(4 \times 5) + 4}{5}\right) \div \left(\frac{2}{100} \div \frac{\frac{12}{100}}{\frac{4}{10}}\right) = \left(\frac{15 + 1}{5} \div \frac{20 + 4}{5}\right) \div \left(\frac{2}{100} \div \frac{12 \times 10}{100 \times 4}\right)$

$$= \left(\frac{16}{5} \div \frac{24}{5}\right) \div \left(\frac{\overset{1}{2}}{\underset{50}{100}} \div \frac{\overset{3}{120}}{\underset{10}{400}}\right) = \left(\frac{16}{5} \times \frac{5}{24}\right) \div \left(\frac{1}{50} \div \frac{3}{10}\right) = \left(\frac{\overset{2}{16} \times \overset{1}{5}}{\underset{1}{5} \times \underset{3}{24}}\right) \div \left(\frac{1}{50} \times \frac{10}{3}\right) = \left(\frac{2 \times 1}{1 \times 3}\right) \div \left(\frac{1 \times \overset{1}{10}}{\underset{5}{50} \times 3}\right) = \left(\frac{2}{3}\right) \div \left(\frac{1 \times 1}{5 \times 3}\right)$$

$$= \left(\frac{2}{3}\right) \div \left(\frac{1}{15}\right) = \frac{2}{3} \div \frac{1}{15} = \frac{2}{3} \times \frac{15}{1} = \frac{2 \times \overset{5}{15}}{\underset{1}{3} \times 1} = \frac{2 \times 5}{1 \times 1} = \frac{10}{1} = \mathbf{10}$$

Section 8.5 Solutions:

1. $\left(2\frac{1}{4} + 3\frac{3}{5}\right) \div \frac{0.4}{0.24} = \left(\frac{(2 \times 4) + 1}{4} + \frac{(3 \times 5) + 3}{5}\right) \div \frac{\frac{4}{10}}{\frac{24}{100}} = \left(\frac{8 + 1}{4} + \frac{15 + 3}{5}\right) \div \frac{4 \times 100}{10 \times 24} = \left(\frac{9}{4} + \frac{18}{5}\right) \div \frac{\overset{5}{400}}{\underset{3}{240}}$

$$= \left(\frac{(9 \times 5) + (18 \times 4)}{4 \times 5}\right) \div \frac{5}{3} = \left(\frac{45 + 72}{20}\right) \div \frac{5}{3} = \left(\frac{117}{20}\right) \div \frac{5}{3} = \frac{117}{20} \div \frac{5}{3} = \frac{117}{20} \times \frac{3}{5} = \frac{117 \times 3}{20 \times 5} = \frac{351}{100} = 3\frac{\mathbf{51}}{\mathbf{100}}$$

2. $\left(\dfrac{0.2}{1.4}+2\dfrac{3}{8}\right)\times 3\dfrac{1}{4} = \left(\dfrac{\frac{2}{10}}{\frac{14}{10}}+\dfrac{(2\times 8)+3}{8}\right)\times\dfrac{(3\times 4)+1}{4} = \left(\dfrac{2\times 10}{10\times 14}+\dfrac{16+3}{8}\right)\times\dfrac{12+1}{4} = \left(\dfrac{20}{140}+\dfrac{19}{8}\right)\times\dfrac{13}{4} = \left(\dfrac{1}{7}+\dfrac{19}{8}\right)\times\dfrac{13}{4}$

$= \left(\dfrac{(1\times 8)+(19\times 7)}{7\times 8}\right)\times\dfrac{13}{4} = \left(\dfrac{8+133}{56}\right)\times\dfrac{13}{4} = \left(\dfrac{141}{56}\right)\times\dfrac{13}{4} = \dfrac{141}{56}\times\dfrac{13}{4} = \dfrac{141\times 13}{56\times 4} = \dfrac{1833}{224} = \mathbf{8\dfrac{41}{224}}$

3. $\left(2\dfrac{1}{5}\times 0.5\right)+4\dfrac{3}{10} = \left(\dfrac{(2\times 5)+1}{5}\times\dfrac{5}{10}\right)+\dfrac{(4\times 10)+3}{10} = \left(\dfrac{10+1}{5}\times\dfrac{5}{10}\right)+\dfrac{40+3}{10} = \left(\dfrac{11}{5}\times\dfrac{5}{10}\right)+\dfrac{43}{10} = \left(\dfrac{11\times\overset{1}{\cancel{5}}}{\underset{1}{\cancel{5}}\times 10}\right)+\dfrac{43}{10}$

$= \left(\dfrac{11\times 1}{1\times 10}\right)+\dfrac{43}{10} = \left(\dfrac{11}{10}\right)+\dfrac{43}{10} = \dfrac{11}{10}+\dfrac{43}{10} = \dfrac{11+43}{10} = \dfrac{\overset{27}{\cancel{54}}}{\underset{5}{\cancel{10}}} = \dfrac{27}{5} = \mathbf{5\dfrac{2}{5}}$

4. $\left(1\dfrac{3}{5}-3\dfrac{2}{3}\right)\times\dfrac{0.1}{1.5} = \left(\dfrac{(1\times 5)+3}{5}-\dfrac{(3\times 3)+2}{3}\right)\times\dfrac{\frac{1}{10}}{\frac{15}{10}} = \left(\dfrac{5+3}{5}-\dfrac{9+2}{3}\right)\times\dfrac{1\times 10}{10\times 15} = \left(\dfrac{8}{5}-\dfrac{11}{3}\right)\times\dfrac{\overset{1}{\cancel{10}}}{\underset{15}{\cancel{150}}}$

$= \left(\dfrac{(8\times 3)-(11\times 5)}{5\times 3}\right)\times\dfrac{1}{15} = \left(\dfrac{24-55}{15}\right)\times\dfrac{1}{15} = \left(\dfrac{-31}{15}\right)\times\dfrac{1}{15} = \dfrac{-31}{15}\times\dfrac{1}{15} = \dfrac{-31\times 1}{15\times 15} = -\mathbf{\dfrac{31}{225}}$

5. $\left(4\dfrac{5}{3}-3\dfrac{1}{3}\right)\div\dfrac{4.8}{0.12} = \left(\dfrac{(4\times 3)+5}{3}-\dfrac{(3\times 3)+1}{3}\right)\div\dfrac{\frac{48}{10}}{\frac{12}{100}} = \left(\dfrac{12+5}{3}-\dfrac{9+1}{3}\right)\div\dfrac{48\times 100}{10\times 12} = \left(\dfrac{17}{3}-\dfrac{10}{3}\right)\div\dfrac{4800}{120}$

$= \left(\dfrac{17-10}{3}\right)\div\dfrac{\overset{40}{\cancel{4800}}}{\underset{1}{\cancel{120}}} = \left(\dfrac{7}{3}\right)\div\dfrac{40}{1} = \dfrac{7}{3}\div\dfrac{40}{1} = \dfrac{7}{3}\times\dfrac{1}{40} = \dfrac{7\times 1}{3\times 40} = \mathbf{\dfrac{7}{120}}$

6. $\left(2\dfrac{3}{8}\times 2\dfrac{6}{14}\right)\div\dfrac{0.01}{0.6} = \left(\dfrac{(2\times 8)+3}{8}\times\dfrac{(2\times 14)+6}{14}\right)\div\dfrac{\frac{1}{100}}{\frac{6}{10}} = \left(\dfrac{16+3}{8}\times\dfrac{28+6}{14}\right)\div\dfrac{1\times 10}{100\times 6} = \left(\dfrac{19}{8}\times\dfrac{34}{14}\right)\div\dfrac{10}{600}$

$= \left(\dfrac{19\times\overset{17}{\cancel{34}}}{8\times 14}\atop 7\right)\div\dfrac{\overset{1}{\cancel{10}}}{\underset{60}{\cancel{600}}} = \left(\dfrac{19\times 17}{8\times 7}\right)\div\dfrac{1}{60} = \left(\dfrac{323}{56}\right)\div\dfrac{1}{60} = \dfrac{323}{56}\div\dfrac{1}{60} = \dfrac{323}{56}\times\dfrac{60}{1} = \dfrac{323\times\overset{15}{\cancel{60}}}{\underset{14}{\cancel{56}}\times 1} = \dfrac{323\times 15}{14\times 1} = \dfrac{4845}{14}$

$= \mathbf{346\dfrac{1}{14}}$

7. $\left(\dfrac{0.3}{2.4}\times 4\dfrac{1}{3}\right)\div 3\dfrac{1}{4} = \left(\dfrac{\frac{3}{10}}{\frac{24}{10}}\times\dfrac{(4\times 3)+1}{3}\right)\div\dfrac{(3\times 4)+1}{4} = \left(\dfrac{3\times 10}{10\times 24}\times\dfrac{12+1}{3}\right)\div\dfrac{12+1}{4} = \left(\dfrac{30}{240}\times\dfrac{13}{3}\right)\div\dfrac{13}{4} = \left(\dfrac{\overset{1}{\cancel{30}}\times 13}{\underset{8}{\cancel{240}}\times 3}\right)\div\dfrac{13}{4}$

$= \left(\dfrac{1\times 13}{8\times 3}\right)\div\dfrac{13}{4} = \left(\dfrac{13}{24}\right)\div\dfrac{13}{4} = \dfrac{13}{24}\div\dfrac{13}{4} = \dfrac{13}{24}\times\dfrac{4}{13} = \dfrac{\overset{1}{\cancel{13}}\times\overset{1}{\cancel{4}}}{\underset{6}{\cancel{24}}\times\underset{1}{\cancel{13}}} = \dfrac{1\times 1}{6\times 1} = \mathbf{\dfrac{1}{6}}$

8. $\left(2\dfrac{3}{5}\times\dfrac{0.1}{1.4}\right)+4\dfrac{7}{3} = \left(\dfrac{(2\times 5)+3}{5}\times\dfrac{\frac{1}{10}}{\frac{14}{10}}\right)+\dfrac{(4\times 3)+7}{3} = \left(\dfrac{10+3}{5}\times\dfrac{1\times 10}{10\times 14}\right)+\dfrac{12+7}{3} = \left(\dfrac{13}{5}\times\dfrac{10}{140}\right)+\dfrac{19}{3} = \left(\dfrac{13\times\overset{1}{\cancel{10}}}{5\times\underset{14}{\cancel{140}}}\right)+\dfrac{19}{3}$

$= \left(\dfrac{13\times 1}{5\times 14}\right)+\dfrac{19}{3} = \left(\dfrac{13}{70}\right)+\dfrac{19}{3} = \dfrac{13}{70}+\dfrac{19}{3} = \dfrac{(13\times 3)+(19\times 70)}{70\times 3} = \dfrac{39+1330}{210} = \dfrac{1369}{210} = \mathbf{6\dfrac{109}{210}}$

9. $\left(3\frac{1}{5}+2\frac{2}{5}\right)\times\left(\dfrac{0.5}{0.08}\times 4\frac{1}{3}\right) = \left(\dfrac{(3\times 5)+1}{5}+\dfrac{(2\times 5)+2}{5}\right)\times\left(\dfrac{\frac{5}{10}}{\frac{8}{100}}\times\dfrac{(4\times 3)+1}{3}\right) = \left(\dfrac{15+1}{5}+\dfrac{10+2}{5}\right)\times\left(\dfrac{5\times 100}{10\times 8}\times\dfrac{12+1}{3}\right)$

$= \left(\dfrac{16}{5}+\dfrac{12}{5}\right)\times\left(\dfrac{500}{80}\times\dfrac{13}{3}\right) = \left(\dfrac{16+12}{5}\right)\times\left(\dfrac{\overset{25}{\cancel{500}}\times 13}{\underset{4}{\cancel{80}}\times 3}\right) = \left(\dfrac{28}{5}\right)\times\left(\dfrac{25\times 13}{4\times 3}\right) = \dfrac{28}{5}\times\left(\dfrac{325}{12}\right) = \dfrac{28}{5}\times\dfrac{325}{12} = \dfrac{\overset{7}{\cancel{28}}\times\overset{65}{\cancel{325}}}{\underset{1}{\cancel{5}}\times\underset{3}{\cancel{12}}}$

$= \dfrac{7\times 65}{1\times 3} = \dfrac{455}{3} = \mathbf{151\frac{2}{3}}$

10. $\left[\left(2\frac{1}{3}\times\dfrac{0.2}{1.2}\right)\div 3\frac{4}{5}\right]-1\frac{1}{2} = \left[\left(\dfrac{(2\times 3)+1}{3}\times\dfrac{\frac{2}{10}}{\frac{12}{10}}\right)\div\dfrac{(3\times 5)+4}{5}\right]-\dfrac{(1\times 2)+1}{2} = \left[\left(\dfrac{6+1}{3}\times\dfrac{2\times 10}{10\times 12}\right)\div\dfrac{15+4}{5}\right]-\dfrac{2+1}{2}$

$= \left[\left(\dfrac{7}{3}\times\dfrac{20}{120}\right)\div\dfrac{19}{5}\right]-\dfrac{3}{2} = \left[\left(\dfrac{7\times\overset{1}{\cancel{20}}}{3\times\underset{6}{\cancel{120}}}\right)\div\dfrac{19}{5}\right]-\dfrac{3}{2} = \left[\left(\dfrac{7\times 1}{3\times 6}\right)\div\dfrac{19}{5}\right]-\dfrac{3}{2} = \left[\left(\dfrac{7}{18}\right)\div\dfrac{19}{5}\right]-\dfrac{3}{2} = \left[\dfrac{7}{18}\div\dfrac{19}{5}\right]-\dfrac{3}{2}$

$= \left[\dfrac{7}{18}\times\dfrac{5}{19}\right]-\dfrac{3}{2} = \left[\dfrac{7\times 5}{18\times 19}\right]-\dfrac{3}{2} = \left[\dfrac{35}{342}\right]-\dfrac{3}{2} = \dfrac{35}{342}-\dfrac{3}{2} = \dfrac{(35\times 2)-(3\times 342)}{342\times 2} = \dfrac{70-1026}{684} = \dfrac{\overset{-239}{\cancel{-956}}}{\underset{171}{\cancel{684}}} = \dfrac{-239}{171}$

$= -\left(1\dfrac{68}{171}\right)$

Chapter 9 Solutions:

Section 9.1 Solutions:

1. $1\frac{2}{5} + \frac{3}{5} + 0.5 = \left(1\frac{2}{5} + \frac{3}{5}\right) + 0.5 = \left(\frac{(1\times 5)+2}{5} + \frac{3}{5}\right) + \frac{5}{10} = \left(\frac{5+2}{5} + \frac{3}{5}\right) + \frac{\overset{1}{\cancel{5}}}{\underset{2}{\cancel{10}}} = \left(\frac{7}{5} + \frac{3}{5}\right) + \frac{1}{2} = \left(\frac{7+3}{5}\right) + \frac{1}{2}$

$= \left(\frac{10}{5}\right) + \frac{1}{2} = \frac{\overset{2}{\cancel{10}}}{\underset{1}{\cancel{5}}} + \frac{1}{2} = \frac{2}{1} + \frac{1}{2} = \frac{(2\times 2)+(1\times 1)}{1\times 2} = \frac{4+1}{2} = \frac{5}{2} = 2\frac{1}{2}$

2. $2\frac{1}{3} + \frac{3}{4} + \frac{0.12}{0.1} = \left(2\frac{1}{3} + \frac{3}{4}\right) + \frac{0.12}{0.1} = \left(\frac{(2\times 3)+1}{3} + \frac{3}{4}\right) + \frac{\frac{12}{100}}{\frac{1}{10}} = \left(\frac{6+1}{3} + \frac{3}{4}\right) + \frac{12\times 10}{100\times 1} = \left(\frac{7}{3} + \frac{3}{4}\right) + \frac{120}{100}$

$= \left(\frac{(7\times 4)+(3\times 3)}{3\times 4}\right) + \frac{\overset{6}{\cancel{120}}}{\underset{5}{\cancel{100}}} = \left(\frac{28+9}{12}\right) + \frac{6}{5} = \left(\frac{37}{12}\right) + \frac{6}{5} = \frac{37}{12} + \frac{6}{5} = \frac{(37\times 5)+(6\times 12)}{12\times 5} = \frac{185+72}{60} = \frac{257}{60} = 4\frac{17}{60}$

3. $1\frac{3}{5} + \frac{0.3}{0.8} + 6 = \left(1\frac{3}{5} + \frac{0.3}{0.8}\right) + 6 = \left(\frac{(1\times 5)+3}{5} + \frac{\frac{3}{10}}{\frac{8}{10}}\right) + \frac{6}{1} = \left(\frac{5+3}{5} + \frac{3\times 10}{10\times 8}\right) + \frac{6}{1} = \left(\frac{8}{5} + \frac{30}{80}\right) + \frac{6}{1}$

$= \left(\frac{(8\times 80)+(30\times 5)}{5\times 80}\right) + \frac{6}{1} = \left(\frac{640+150}{400}\right) + \frac{6}{1} = \left(\frac{790}{400}\right) + \frac{6}{1} = \frac{\overset{79}{\cancel{790}}}{\underset{40}{\cancel{400}}} + \frac{6}{1} = \frac{79}{40} + \frac{6}{1} = \frac{(79\times 1)+(6\times 40)}{40\times 1} = \frac{79+240}{40}$

$= \frac{319}{40} = 7\frac{39}{40}$

4. $4\frac{3}{5} + \frac{3}{8} + \frac{0.1}{1.2} + 4 = \left(4\frac{3}{5} + \frac{3}{8}\right) + \left(\frac{0.1}{1.2} + 4\right) = \left(\frac{(4\times 5)+3}{5} + \frac{3}{8}\right) + \left(\frac{\frac{1}{10}}{\frac{12}{10}} + \frac{4}{1}\right) = \left(\frac{20+3}{5} + \frac{3}{8}\right) + \left(\frac{1\times 10}{10\times 12} + \frac{4}{1}\right)$

$= \left(\frac{23}{5} + \frac{3}{8}\right) + \left(\frac{10}{120} + \frac{4}{1}\right) = \left(\frac{(23\times 8)+(3\times 5)}{5\times 8}\right) + \left(\frac{(10\times 1)+(4\times 120)}{120\times 1}\right) = \left(\frac{184+15}{40}\right) + \left(\frac{10+480}{120}\right) = \left(\frac{199}{40}\right) + \left(\frac{490}{120}\right)$

$= \frac{199}{40} + \frac{\overset{49}{\cancel{490}}}{\underset{12}{\cancel{120}}} = \frac{199}{40} + \frac{49}{12} = \frac{(199\times 12)+(49\times 40)}{40\times 12} = \frac{2388+1960}{480} = \frac{\overset{1087}{\cancel{4348}}}{\underset{120}{\cancel{480}}} = \frac{1087}{120} = 9\frac{7}{120}$

5. $\frac{2}{8} + \frac{3}{8} + 1\frac{1}{5} + 2.8 = \left(\frac{2}{8} + \frac{3}{8}\right) + \left(1\frac{1}{5} + 2.8\right) = \left(\frac{2+3}{8}\right) + \left(\frac{(1\times 5)+1}{5} + \frac{28}{10}\right) = \left(\frac{5}{8}\right) + \left(\frac{5+1}{5} + \frac{\overset{14}{\cancel{28}}}{\underset{5}{\cancel{10}}}\right) = \frac{5}{8} + \left(\frac{6}{5} + \frac{14}{5}\right)$

$= \frac{5}{8} + \left(\frac{6+14}{5}\right) = \frac{5}{8} + \left(\frac{20}{5}\right) = \frac{5}{8} + \frac{20}{5} = \frac{(5\times 5)+(20\times 8)}{8\times 5} = \frac{25+160}{40} = \frac{\overset{37}{\cancel{185}}}{\underset{8}{\cancel{40}}} = \frac{37}{8} = 4\frac{5}{8}$

6. $\left(\frac{3}{4} + 2\right) + \left(1\frac{1}{5} + 0.5\right) = \left(\frac{3}{4} + \frac{2}{1}\right) + \left(\frac{(1\times 5)+1}{5} + \frac{5}{10}\right) = \left(\frac{(3\times 1)+(2\times 4)}{4\times 1}\right) + \left(\frac{5+1}{5} + \frac{\overset{1}{\cancel{5}}}{\underset{2}{\cancel{10}}}\right) = \left(\frac{3+8}{4}\right) + \left(\frac{6}{5} + \frac{1}{2}\right)$

$= \left(\frac{11}{4}\right) + \left(\frac{(6\times 2)+(1\times 5)}{5\times 2}\right) = \frac{11}{4} + \left(\frac{12+5}{10}\right) = \frac{11}{4} + \left(\frac{17}{10}\right) = \frac{11}{4} + \frac{17}{10} = \frac{(11\times 10)+(17\times 4)}{4\times 10} = \frac{110+68}{40} = \frac{\overset{89}{\cancel{178}}}{\underset{20}{\cancel{40}}} = \frac{89}{20}$

$= 4\frac{9}{20}$

7. $\dfrac{3}{5}+1\dfrac{1}{2}+2.4+\dfrac{6}{10} = \left(\dfrac{3}{5}+1\dfrac{1}{2}\right)+\left(2.4+\dfrac{6}{10}\right) = \left(\dfrac{3}{5}+\dfrac{(1\times 2)+1}{2}\right)+\left(\dfrac{24}{10}+\dfrac{6}{10}\right) = \left(\dfrac{3}{5}+\dfrac{2+1}{2}\right)+\left(\dfrac{24+6}{10}\right) = \left(\dfrac{3}{5}+\dfrac{3}{2}\right)+\left(\dfrac{30}{10}\right)$

$= \left(\dfrac{(3\times 2)+(3\times 5)}{5\times 2}\right)+\dfrac{\overset{3}{\cancel{30}}}{\underset{1}{\cancel{10}}} = \left(\dfrac{6+15}{10}\right)+\dfrac{3}{1} = \left(\dfrac{21}{10}\right)+\dfrac{3}{1} = \dfrac{21}{10}+\dfrac{3}{1} = \dfrac{(21\times 1)+(3\times 10)}{10\times 1} = \dfrac{21+30}{10} = \dfrac{51}{10} = \mathbf{5\dfrac{1}{10}}$

8. $2\dfrac{3}{4}+\dfrac{1}{5}+\dfrac{3}{8}+0.4+3\dfrac{2}{3} = \left(2\dfrac{3}{4}+\dfrac{1}{5}\right)+\left(\dfrac{3}{8}+0.4\right)+3\dfrac{2}{3} = \left(\dfrac{(2\times 4)+3}{4}+\dfrac{1}{5}\right)+\left(\dfrac{3}{8}+\dfrac{4}{10}\right)+\dfrac{(3\times 3)+2}{3}$

$= \left(\dfrac{8+3}{4}+\dfrac{1}{5}\right)+\left(\dfrac{3}{8}+\dfrac{4}{10}\right)+\dfrac{9+2}{3} = \left(\dfrac{11}{4}+\dfrac{1}{5}\right)+\left(\dfrac{3}{8}+\dfrac{4}{10}\right)+\dfrac{11}{3} = \left(\dfrac{(11\times 5)+(1\times 4)}{4\times 5}\right)+\left(\dfrac{(3\times 10)+(4\times 8)}{8\times 10}\right)+\dfrac{11}{3}$

$= \left(\dfrac{55+4}{20}\right)+\left(\dfrac{30+32}{80}\right)+\dfrac{11}{3} = \left(\dfrac{59}{20}\right)+\left(\dfrac{62}{80}\right)+\dfrac{11}{3} = \dfrac{59}{20}+\dfrac{62}{80}+\dfrac{11}{3} = \left(\dfrac{59}{20}+\dfrac{62}{80}\right)+\dfrac{11}{3} = \left(\dfrac{(59\times 80)+(62\times 20)}{20\times 80}\right)+\dfrac{11}{3}$

$= \left(\dfrac{4720+1240}{1600}\right)+\dfrac{11}{3} = \left(\dfrac{5960}{1600}\right)+\dfrac{11}{3} = \dfrac{\overset{149}{\cancel{5960}}}{\underset{40}{\cancel{1600}}}+\dfrac{11}{3} = \dfrac{149}{40}+\dfrac{11}{3} = \dfrac{(149\times 3)+(11\times 40)}{40\times 3} = \dfrac{447+440}{120} = \dfrac{887}{120}$

$= \mathbf{7\dfrac{47}{120}}$

9. $\left(\dfrac{3}{7}+2\dfrac{1}{7}\right)+\left(3\dfrac{4}{5}+1\dfrac{2}{5}\right)+\dfrac{0.1}{0.01} = \left(\dfrac{3}{7}+\dfrac{(2\times 7)+1}{7}\right)+\left(\dfrac{(3\times 5)+4}{5}+\dfrac{(1\times 5)+2}{5}\right)+\dfrac{\dfrac{1}{10}}{\dfrac{1}{100}}$

$= \left(\dfrac{3}{7}+\dfrac{14+1}{7}\right)+\left(\dfrac{15+4}{5}+\dfrac{5+2}{5}\right)+\dfrac{1\times 100}{10\times 1} = \left(\dfrac{3}{7}+\dfrac{15}{7}\right)+\left(\dfrac{19}{5}+\dfrac{7}{5}\right)+\dfrac{\overset{10}{\cancel{100}}}{\underset{1}{\cancel{10}}} = \left(\dfrac{3+15}{7}\right)+\left(\dfrac{19+7}{5}\right)+\dfrac{10}{1}$

$= \left(\dfrac{18}{7}\right)+\left(\dfrac{26}{5}\right)+\dfrac{10}{1} = \dfrac{18}{7}+\dfrac{26}{5}+\dfrac{10}{1} = \left(\dfrac{18}{7}+\dfrac{26}{5}\right)+\dfrac{10}{1} = \left(\dfrac{(18\times 5)+(26\times 7)}{7\times 5}\right)+\dfrac{10}{1} = \left(\dfrac{90+182}{35}\right)+\dfrac{10}{1}$

$= \left(\dfrac{272}{35}\right)+\dfrac{10}{1} = \dfrac{272}{35}+\dfrac{10}{1} = \dfrac{(272\times 1)+(10\times 35)}{35\times 1} = \dfrac{272+350}{35} = \dfrac{622}{35} = \mathbf{17\dfrac{27}{35}}$

10. $\dfrac{3}{5}+\left(\dfrac{3.2}{1.6}+3\dfrac{2}{3}\right)+\left(\dfrac{0.3}{2.6}+2\right) = \dfrac{3}{5}+\left(\dfrac{\dfrac{32}{10}}{\dfrac{16}{10}}+\dfrac{(3\times 3)+2}{3}\right)+\left(\dfrac{\dfrac{3}{10}}{\dfrac{26}{10}}+\dfrac{2}{1}\right) = \dfrac{3}{5}+\left(\dfrac{32\times 10}{10\times 16}+\dfrac{9+2}{3}\right)+\left(\dfrac{3\times 10}{10\times 26}+\dfrac{2}{1}\right)$

$= \dfrac{3}{5}+\left(\dfrac{\overset{2}{\cancel{320}}}{\underset{1}{\cancel{160}}}+\dfrac{11}{3}\right)+\left(\dfrac{\overset{3}{\cancel{30}}}{\underset{26}{\cancel{260}}}+\dfrac{2}{1}\right) = \dfrac{3}{5}+\left(\dfrac{2}{1}+\dfrac{11}{3}\right)+\left(\dfrac{3}{26}+\dfrac{2}{1}\right) = \dfrac{3}{5}+\left(\dfrac{(2\times 3)+(11\times 1)}{1\times 3}\right)+\left(\dfrac{(3\times 1)+(2\times 26)}{26\times 1}\right)$

$= \dfrac{3}{5}+\left(\dfrac{6+11}{3}\right)+\left(\dfrac{3+52}{26}\right) = \dfrac{3}{5}+\left(\dfrac{17}{3}\right)+\left(\dfrac{55}{26}\right) = \dfrac{3}{5}+\dfrac{17}{3}+\dfrac{55}{26} = \left(\dfrac{3}{5}+\dfrac{17}{3}\right)+\dfrac{55}{26} = \left(\dfrac{(3\times 3)+(17\times 5)}{5\times 3}\right)+\dfrac{55}{26}$

$= \left(\dfrac{9+85}{15}\right)+\dfrac{55}{26} = \left(\dfrac{94}{15}\right)+\dfrac{55}{26} = \dfrac{94}{15}+\dfrac{55}{26} = \dfrac{(94\times 26)+(55\times 15)}{15\times 26} = \dfrac{2444+825}{390} = \dfrac{3269}{390} = \mathbf{8\dfrac{149}{390}}$

Section 9.2 Solutions:

1. $2\dfrac{1}{6}-\dfrac{3}{5}-\dfrac{1.4}{0.4} = \left(2\dfrac{1}{6}-\dfrac{3}{5}\right)-\dfrac{1.4}{0.4} = \left(\dfrac{(2\times 6)+1}{6}-\dfrac{3}{5}\right)-\dfrac{\dfrac{14}{10}}{\dfrac{4}{10}} = \left(\dfrac{12+1}{6}-\dfrac{3}{5}\right)-\dfrac{14\times 10}{10\times 4} = \left(\dfrac{13}{6}-\dfrac{3}{5}\right)-\dfrac{\overset{7}{\cancel{140}}}{\underset{2}{\cancel{40}}}$

$$= \left(\frac{(13 \times 5) - (3 \times 6)}{6 \times 5} \right) - \frac{7}{2} = \left(\frac{65 - 18}{30} \right) - \frac{7}{2} = \left(\frac{47}{30} \right) - \frac{7}{2} = \frac{47}{30} - \frac{7}{2} = \frac{(47 \times 2) - (7 \times 30)}{30 \times 2} = \frac{94 - 210}{60} = \frac{\overset{-29}{-116}}{\underset{15}{60}} = \frac{-29}{15}$$

$$= -\left(1\frac{14}{15} \right)$$

2. $\frac{5}{8} - 2\frac{4}{5} - 0.1 = \left(\frac{5}{8} - 2\frac{4}{5} \right) - 0.1 = \left(\frac{5}{8} - \frac{(2 \times 5) + 4}{5} \right) - \frac{1}{10} = \left(\frac{5}{8} - \frac{10 + 4}{5} \right) - \frac{1}{10} = \left(\frac{5}{8} - \frac{14}{5} \right) - \frac{1}{10}$

$$= \left(\frac{(5 \times 5) - (14 \times 8)}{8 \times 5} \right) - \frac{1}{10} = \left(\frac{25 - 112}{40} \right) - \frac{1}{10} = \left(\frac{-87}{40} \right) - \frac{1}{10} = \frac{-87}{40} - \frac{1}{10} = \frac{(-87 \times 10) - (1 \times 40)}{40 \times 10} = \frac{-870 - 40}{400}$$

$$= \frac{\overset{-91}{-910}}{\underset{40}{400}} = \frac{-91}{40} = -\left(2\frac{11}{40} \right)$$

3. $\left(1\frac{3}{4} - 0.2 \right) - \frac{2}{3} = \left(\frac{(1 \times 4) + 3}{4} - \frac{2}{10} \right) - \frac{2}{3} = \left(\frac{4 + 3}{4} - \frac{2}{10} \right) - \frac{2}{3} = \left(\frac{7}{4} - \frac{\overset{1}{2}}{\underset{5}{10}} \right) - \frac{2}{3} = \left(\frac{7}{4} - \frac{1}{5} \right) - \frac{2}{3} = \left(\frac{(7 \times 5) - (1 \times 4)}{4 \times 5} \right) - \frac{2}{3}$

$$= \left(\frac{35 - 4}{20} \right) - \frac{2}{3} = \left(\frac{31}{20} \right) - \frac{2}{3} = \frac{31}{20} - \frac{2}{3} = \frac{(31 \times 3) - (2 \times 20)}{20 \times 3} = \frac{93 - 40}{60} = \frac{53}{60}$$

4. $\left(4\frac{2}{3} - 8 \right) - \frac{0.01}{0.1} = \left(\frac{(4 \times 3) + 2}{3} - \frac{8}{1} \right) - \frac{\frac{1}{100}}{\frac{1}{10}} = \left(\frac{12 + 2}{3} - \frac{8}{1} \right) - \frac{1 \times 10}{100 \times 1} = \left(\frac{14}{3} - \frac{8}{1} \right) - \frac{10}{100} = \left(\frac{(14 \times 1) - (8 \times 3)}{3 \times 1} \right) - \frac{1}{10}$

$$= \left(\frac{14 - 24}{3} \right) - \frac{1}{10} = \left(\frac{-10}{3} \right) - \frac{1}{10} = \frac{-10}{3} - \frac{1}{10} = \frac{(-10 \times 10) - (1 \times 3)}{3 \times 10} = \frac{-100 - 3}{30} = \frac{-103}{30} = -\left(3\frac{13}{30} \right)$$

5. $1\frac{3}{5} - \left(\frac{1}{8} - \frac{0.14}{0.2} \right) = \frac{(1 \times 5) + 3}{5} - \left(\frac{1}{8} - \frac{\frac{14}{100}}{\frac{2}{10}} \right) = \frac{5 + 3}{5} - \left(\frac{1}{8} - \frac{14 \times 10}{100 \times 2} \right) = \frac{8}{5} - \left(\frac{1}{8} - \frac{\overset{7}{140}}{\underset{10}{200}} \right) = \frac{8}{5} - \left(\frac{1}{8} - \frac{7}{10} \right)$

$$= \frac{8}{5} - \left(\frac{(1 \times 10) - (7 \times 8)}{8 \times 10} \right) = \frac{8}{5} - \left(\frac{10 - 56}{80} \right) = \frac{8}{5} - \left(\frac{-46}{80} \right) = \frac{8}{5} - \frac{-46}{80} = \frac{8}{5} + \frac{\overset{23}{46}}{\underset{40}{80}} = \frac{8}{5} + \frac{23}{40} = \frac{(8 \times 40) + (23 \times 5)}{5 \times 40}$$

$$= \frac{320 + 115}{200} = \frac{\overset{87}{435}}{\underset{40}{200}} = \frac{87}{40} = 2\frac{7}{40}$$

6. $7 - \frac{2}{3} - 1\frac{1}{4} - 0.25 = \left(7 - \frac{2}{3} \right) + \left(-1\frac{1}{4} - 0.25 \right) = \left(\frac{7}{1} - \frac{2}{3} \right) + \left(-\frac{(1 \times 4) + 1}{4} - \frac{25}{100} \right) = \left(\frac{(7 \times 3) - (2 \times 1)}{1 \times 3} \right) + \left(-\frac{4 + 1}{4} - \frac{25}{100} \right)$

$$= \left(\frac{21 - 2}{3} \right) + \left(-\frac{5}{4} - \frac{\overset{1}{25}}{\underset{4}{100}} \right) = \left(\frac{19}{3} \right) + \left(-\frac{5}{4} - \frac{1}{4} \right) = \frac{19}{3} + \left(\frac{-5 - 1}{4} \right) = \frac{19}{3} + \left(\frac{-6}{4} \right) = \frac{19}{3} + \frac{-6}{4} = \frac{19}{3} - \frac{6}{4}$$

$$= \frac{(19 \times 4) - (6 \times 3)}{3 \times 4} = \frac{76 - 18}{12} = \frac{\overset{29}{58}}{\underset{6}{12}} = \frac{29}{6} = 4\frac{5}{6}$$

7. $\left(3\frac{2}{3} - \frac{1}{3} \right) - \left(0.9 - \frac{2}{5} \right) = \left(\frac{(3 \times 3) + 2}{3} - \frac{1}{3} \right) - \left(\frac{9}{10} - \frac{2}{5} \right) = \left(\frac{9 + 2}{3} - \frac{1}{3} \right) - \left(\frac{(9 \times 5) - (2 \times 10)}{10 \times 5} \right) = \left(\frac{11}{3} - \frac{1}{3} \right) - \left(\frac{45 - 20}{50} \right)$

$$= \left(\frac{11 - 1}{3} \right) - \left(\frac{25}{50} \right) = \left(\frac{10}{3} \right) - \frac{\overset{1}{25}}{\underset{2}{50}} = \frac{10}{3} - \frac{1}{2} = \frac{(10 \times 2) - (1 \times 3)}{3 \times 2} = \frac{20 - 3}{6} = \frac{17}{6} = 2\frac{5}{6}$$

8. $\left(\dfrac{1}{3}-1\dfrac{1}{4}\right)-\left(\dfrac{4}{5}-\dfrac{1}{5}\right)-0.6 = \left(\dfrac{1}{3}-\dfrac{(1\times4)+1}{4}\right)-\left(\dfrac{4-1}{5}\right)-\dfrac{6}{10} = \left(\dfrac{1}{3}-\dfrac{4+1}{4}\right)-\left(\dfrac{3}{5}\right)-\dfrac{\overset{3}{\cancel{6}}}{\underset{5}{\cancel{10}}} = \left(\dfrac{1}{3}-\dfrac{5}{4}\right)-\dfrac{3}{5}-\dfrac{3}{5}$

$= \left(\dfrac{(1\times4)-(5\times3)}{3\times4}\right)-\left(\dfrac{3}{5}+\dfrac{3}{5}\right) = \left(\dfrac{4-15}{12}\right)-\left(\dfrac{3+3}{5}\right) = \left(\dfrac{-11}{12}\right)-\left(\dfrac{6}{5}\right) = \dfrac{-11}{12}-\dfrac{6}{5} = \dfrac{(-11\times5)-(6\times12)}{12\times5} = \dfrac{-55-72}{60}$

$= \dfrac{-127}{60} = -\left(\mathbf{2\dfrac{7}{60}}\right)$

9. $\left[4-\left(\dfrac{2}{5}-1\dfrac{2}{3}\right)\right]-0.04 = \left[\dfrac{4}{1}-\left(\dfrac{2}{5}-\dfrac{(1\times3)+2}{3}\right)\right]-\dfrac{4}{100} = \left[\dfrac{4}{1}-\left(\dfrac{2}{5}-\dfrac{3+2}{3}\right)\right]-\dfrac{\overset{1}{\cancel{4}}}{\underset{25}{\cancel{100}}} = \left[\dfrac{4}{1}-\left(\dfrac{2}{5}-\dfrac{5}{3}\right)\right]-\dfrac{1}{25}$

$= \left[\dfrac{4}{1}-\left(\dfrac{(2\times3)-(5\times5)}{5\times3}\right)\right]-\dfrac{1}{25} = \left[\dfrac{4}{1}-\left(\dfrac{6-25}{15}\right)\right]-\dfrac{1}{25} = \left[\dfrac{4}{1}-\left(\dfrac{-19}{15}\right)\right]-\dfrac{1}{25} = \left[\dfrac{4}{1}-\dfrac{-19}{15}\right]-\dfrac{1}{25} = \left[\dfrac{4}{1}+\dfrac{19}{15}\right]-\dfrac{1}{25}$

$= \left[\dfrac{(4\times15)+(19\times1)}{1\times15}\right]-\dfrac{1}{25} = \left[\dfrac{60+19}{15}\right]-\dfrac{1}{25} = \left[\dfrac{79}{15}\right]-\dfrac{1}{25} = \dfrac{79}{15}-\dfrac{1}{25} = \dfrac{(79\times25)-(1\times15)}{15\times25} = \dfrac{1975-15}{375} = \dfrac{\overset{392}{\cancel{1960}}}{\underset{75}{\cancel{375}}}$

$= \dfrac{392}{75} = \mathbf{5\dfrac{17}{75}}$

10. $\left[\left(5\dfrac{2}{3}-1\dfrac{1}{4}\right)-0.2\right]-\dfrac{2}{5} = \left[\left(\dfrac{(5\times3)+2}{3}-\dfrac{(1\times4)+1}{4}\right)-\dfrac{2}{10}\right]-\dfrac{2}{5} = \left[\left(\dfrac{15+2}{3}-\dfrac{4+1}{4}\right)-\dfrac{2}{10}\right]-\dfrac{2}{5} = \left[\left(\dfrac{17}{3}-\dfrac{5}{4}\right)-\dfrac{2}{10}\right]-\dfrac{2}{5}$

$= \left[\left(\dfrac{(17\times4)-(5\times3)}{3\times4}\right)-\dfrac{2}{10}\right]-\dfrac{2}{5} = \left[\left(\dfrac{68-15}{12}\right)-\dfrac{2}{10}\right]-\dfrac{2}{5} = \left[\left(\dfrac{53}{12}\right)-\dfrac{2}{10}\right]-\dfrac{2}{5} = \left[\dfrac{53}{12}-\dfrac{2}{10}\right]-\dfrac{2}{5}$

$= \left[\dfrac{(53\times10)-(2\times12)}{12\times10}\right]-\dfrac{2}{5} = \left[\dfrac{530-24}{120}\right]-\dfrac{2}{5} = \left[\dfrac{506}{120}\right]-\dfrac{2}{5} = \dfrac{\overset{253}{\cancel{506}}}{\underset{60}{\cancel{120}}}-\dfrac{2}{5} = \dfrac{253}{60}-\dfrac{2}{5} = \dfrac{(253\times5)-(2\times60)}{60\times5}$

$= \dfrac{1265-120}{300} = \dfrac{\overset{229}{\cancel{1145}}}{\underset{60}{\cancel{300}}} = \dfrac{229}{60} = \mathbf{3\dfrac{49}{60}}$

Section 9.3 Solutions:

1. $\dfrac{3}{5}\times1\dfrac{2}{3}\times0.2 = \dfrac{3}{5}\times\dfrac{(1\times3)+2}{3}\times\dfrac{2}{10} = \dfrac{3}{5}\times\dfrac{3+2}{3}\times\dfrac{2}{10} = \dfrac{3}{5}\times\dfrac{5}{3}\times\dfrac{2}{10} = \dfrac{\overset{1}{\cancel{3}}\times\overset{1}{\cancel{5}}\times\overset{1}{\cancel{2}}}{\underset{1}{\cancel{5}}\times\underset{1}{\cancel{3}}\times\underset{5}{\cancel{10}}} = \dfrac{1\times1\times1}{1\times1\times5} = \mathbf{\dfrac{1}{5}}$

2. $1\dfrac{3}{8}\times\dfrac{2}{3}\times0.5 = \dfrac{(1\times8)+3}{8}\times\dfrac{2}{3}\times\dfrac{5}{10} = \dfrac{8+3}{8}\times\dfrac{2}{3}\times\dfrac{5}{10} = \dfrac{11}{8}\times\dfrac{2}{3}\times\dfrac{5}{10} = \dfrac{11\times\overset{1}{\cancel{2}}\times\overset{1}{\cancel{5}}}{\underset{4}{\cancel{8}}\times3\times\underset{2}{\cancel{10}}} = \dfrac{11\times1\times1}{4\times3\times2} = \mathbf{\dfrac{11}{24}}$

3. $\dfrac{1}{3}\times\dfrac{3}{4}\times0.04\times1\dfrac{2}{3} = \dfrac{1}{3}\times\dfrac{3}{4}\times\dfrac{4}{100}\times\dfrac{(1\times3)+2}{3} = \dfrac{1}{3}\times\dfrac{3}{4}\times\dfrac{4}{100}\times\dfrac{3+2}{3} = \dfrac{1}{3}\times\dfrac{3}{4}\times\dfrac{4}{100}\times\dfrac{5}{3} = \dfrac{1\times\overset{1}{\cancel{3}}\times\overset{1}{\cancel{4}}\times\overset{1}{\cancel{5}}}{\underset{1}{\cancel{3}}\times\underset{1}{\cancel{4}}\times\underset{20}{\cancel{100}}\times3}$

$= \dfrac{1\times1\times1\times1}{1\times1\times20\times3} = \mathbf{\dfrac{1}{60}}$

4. $\left(2\dfrac{1}{5}\times\dfrac{3}{11}\times1\dfrac{1}{3}\right)\times\dfrac{0.2}{0.01} = \left(\dfrac{(2\times5)+1}{5}\times\dfrac{3}{11}\times\dfrac{(1\times3)+1}{3}\right)\times\dfrac{\dfrac{2}{10}}{\dfrac{1}{100}} = \left(\dfrac{10+1}{5}\times\dfrac{3}{11}\times\dfrac{3+1}{3}\right)\times\dfrac{2\times100}{10\times1}$

$= \left(\dfrac{11}{5}\times\dfrac{3}{11}\times\dfrac{4}{3}\right)\times\dfrac{\overset{20}{\cancel{200}}}{\underset{1}{\cancel{10}}} = \left(\dfrac{\overset{1}{\cancel{11}}\times\overset{1}{\cancel{3}}\times4}{5\times\underset{1}{\cancel{11}}\times\underset{1}{\cancel{3}}}\right)\times\dfrac{20}{1} = \left(\dfrac{1\times1\times4}{5\times1\times1}\right)\times\dfrac{20}{1} = \left(\dfrac{4}{5}\right)\times\dfrac{20}{1} = \dfrac{4}{5}\times\dfrac{20}{1} = \dfrac{4\times\overset{4}{\cancel{20}}}{\underset{1}{\cancel{5}}\times1} = \dfrac{4\times4}{1\times1} = \dfrac{16}{1} = \mathbf{16}$

5. $0.08 \times \left(\frac{1}{4} \times 2\frac{1}{4}\right) = \frac{8}{100} \times \left(\frac{1}{4} \times \frac{(2 \times 4)+1}{4}\right) = \frac{\overset{2}{8}}{\underset{25}{100}} \times \left(\frac{1}{4} \times \frac{8+1}{4}\right) = \frac{2}{25} \times \left(\frac{1}{4} \times \frac{9}{4}\right) = \frac{2}{25} \times \left(\frac{1 \times 9}{4 \times 4}\right) = \frac{2}{25} \times \left(\frac{9}{16}\right)$

$= \frac{2}{25} \times \frac{9}{16} = \frac{2 \times 9}{25 \times \underset{8}{16}} = \frac{1 \times 9}{25 \times 8} = \frac{\mathbf{9}}{\mathbf{200}}$

6. $\left(2\frac{4}{5} \times 1\frac{2}{3}\right) \times \left(\frac{5}{8} \times \frac{0.4}{0.05}\right) = \left(\frac{(2 \times 5)+4}{5} \times \frac{(1 \times 3)+2}{3}\right) \times \left(\frac{5}{8} \times \frac{\frac{4}{10}}{\frac{5}{100}}\right) = \left(\frac{10+4}{5} \times \frac{3+2}{3}\right) \times \left(\frac{5}{8} \times \frac{4 \times 100}{10 \times 5}\right)$

$= \left(\frac{14}{5} \times \frac{5}{3}\right) \times \left(\frac{5}{8} \times \frac{400}{50}\right) = \left(\frac{14 \times \overset{1}{5}}{\underset{1}{5} \times 3}\right) \times \left(\frac{5 \times \overset{8}{400}}{8 \times \underset{1}{50}}\right) = \left(\frac{14 \times 1}{1 \times 3}\right) \times \left(\frac{5 \times 8}{8 \times 1}\right) = \left(\frac{14}{3}\right) \times \left(\frac{40}{8}\right) = \frac{14}{3} \times \frac{40}{8} = \frac{14 \times \overset{5}{40}}{3 \times \underset{1}{8}} = \frac{14 \times 5}{3 \times 1}$

$= \frac{70}{3} = \mathbf{23\frac{1}{3}}$

7. $\frac{20}{27} \times 1\frac{3}{4} \times \frac{3}{6} \times \frac{0.008}{0.04} = \frac{20}{27} \times \frac{(1 \times 4)+3}{4} \times \frac{3}{6} \times \frac{\frac{8}{1000}}{\frac{4}{100}} = \frac{20}{27} \times \frac{4+3}{4} \times \frac{3}{6} \times \frac{8 \times 100}{1000 \times 4} = \frac{20}{27} \times \frac{7}{4} \times \frac{3}{6} \times \frac{800}{4000}$

$= \frac{\overset{5}{20} \times 7 \times \overset{1}{3} \times \overset{1}{800}}{27 \times \underset{1}{4} \times \underset{2}{6} \times \underset{5}{4000}} = \frac{5 \times 7 \times 1 \times 1}{27 \times 1 \times 2 \times 5} = \frac{\overset{7}{35}}{\underset{54}{270}} = \frac{\mathbf{7}}{\mathbf{54}}$

8. $\left(2\frac{3}{5} \times 0.2\right) \times \left(\frac{5}{13} \times \frac{0.2}{0.24}\right) = \left(\frac{(2 \times 5)+3}{5} \times \frac{2}{10}\right) \times \left(\frac{5}{13} \times \frac{\frac{2}{10}}{\frac{24}{100}}\right) = \left(\frac{10+3}{5} \times \frac{2}{10}\right) \times \left(\frac{5}{13} \times \frac{2 \times 100}{10 \times 24}\right)$

$= \left(\frac{13}{5} \times \frac{2}{10}\right) \times \left(\frac{5}{13} \times \frac{200}{240}\right) = \left(\frac{13 \times \overset{1}{2}}{5 \times \underset{5}{10}}\right) \times \left(\frac{5 \times \overset{5}{200}}{13 \times \underset{6}{240}}\right) = \left(\frac{13 \times 1}{5 \times 5}\right) \times \left(\frac{5 \times 5}{13 \times 6}\right) = \left(\frac{13}{25}\right) \times \left(\frac{25}{78}\right) = \frac{13}{25} \times \frac{25}{78} = \frac{\overset{1}{13} \times \overset{1}{25}}{\underset{1}{25} \times \underset{6}{78}}$

$= \frac{1 \times 1}{1 \times 6} = \frac{\mathbf{1}}{\mathbf{6}}$

9. $\left(3\frac{2}{3} \times \frac{1}{11} \times 0.9\right) \times \frac{1}{27} = \left(\frac{(3 \times 3)+2}{3} \times \frac{1}{11} \times \frac{9}{10}\right) \times \frac{1}{27} = \left(\frac{9+2}{3} \times \frac{1}{11} \times \frac{9}{10}\right) \times \frac{1}{27} = \left(\frac{11}{3} \times \frac{1}{11} \times \frac{9}{10}\right) \times \frac{1}{27}$

$= \left(\frac{\overset{1}{11} \times 1 \times \overset{3}{9}}{\underset{1}{3} \times \underset{1}{11} \times 10}\right) \times \frac{1}{27} = \left(\frac{1 \times 1 \times 3}{1 \times 1 \times 10}\right) \times \frac{1}{27} = \left(\frac{3}{10}\right) \times \frac{1}{27} = \frac{3}{10} \times \frac{1}{27} = \frac{\overset{1}{3} \times 1}{10 \times \underset{9}{27}} = \frac{1 \times 1}{10 \times 9} = \frac{\mathbf{1}}{\mathbf{90}}$

10. $\left(\frac{0.5}{1.5} \times 2\frac{1}{10} \times 0.8\right) \times \left(\frac{1}{21} \times \frac{1}{0.4}\right) = \left(\frac{\frac{5}{10}}{\frac{15}{10}} \times \frac{(2 \times 10)+1}{10} \times \frac{8}{10}\right) \times \left(\frac{1}{21} \times \frac{1}{\frac{4}{10}}\right) = \left(\frac{5 \times 10}{10 \times 15} \times \frac{20+1}{10} \times \frac{8}{10}\right) \times \left(\frac{1}{21} \times \frac{1 \times 10}{1 \times 4}\right)$

$= \left(\frac{50}{150} \times \frac{21}{10} \times \frac{8}{10}\right) \times \left(\frac{1}{21} \times \frac{10}{4}\right) = \left(\frac{\overset{1}{50} \times 21 \times \overset{4}{8}}{\underset{3}{150} \times \underset{5}{10} \times 10}\right) \times \left(\frac{1 \times \overset{5}{10}}{21 \times \underset{2}{4}}\right) = \left(\frac{1 \times 21 \times 4}{3 \times 5 \times 10}\right) \times \left(\frac{1 \times 5}{21 \times 2}\right) = \left(\frac{84}{150}\right) \times \left(\frac{5}{42}\right) = \frac{84}{150} \times \frac{5}{42}$

$= \frac{\overset{2}{84} \times \overset{1}{5}}{\underset{30}{150} \times \underset{1}{42}} = \frac{2 \times 1}{30 \times 1} = \frac{\overset{1}{2}}{\underset{15}{30}} = \frac{\mathbf{1}}{\mathbf{15}}$

Section 9.4 Solutions:

1. $\left(1\frac{1}{5} \div 25\right) \div \frac{0.1}{0.25} = \left(\frac{(1\times5)+1}{5} \div \frac{25}{1}\right) \div \frac{\frac{1}{10}}{\frac{25}{100}} = \left(\frac{5+1}{5} \div \frac{25}{1}\right) \div \frac{1\times100}{10\times25} = \left(\frac{6}{5} \div \frac{25}{1}\right) \div \frac{\overset{2}{\cancel{100}}}{\underset{50}{\cancel{250}}} = \left(\frac{6}{5} \times \frac{1}{25}\right) \div \frac{2}{5}$

     $= \left(\frac{6\times1}{5\times25}\right) \div \frac{2}{5} = \left(\frac{6}{125}\right) \div \frac{2}{5} = \frac{6}{125} \div \frac{2}{5} = \frac{6}{125} \times \frac{5}{2} = \frac{\overset{3}{\cancel{6}}\times\overset{1}{\cancel{5}}}{\underset{25}{\cancel{125}}\times\underset{1}{\cancel{2}}} = \frac{3\times1}{25\times1} = \mathbf{\frac{3}{25}}$

2. $\left(2\frac{1}{3} \div 0.5\right) \div \frac{1}{3} = \left(\frac{(2\times3)+1}{3} \div \frac{5}{10}\right) \div \frac{1}{3} = \left(\frac{6+1}{3} \div \frac{5}{10}\right) \div \frac{1}{3} = \left(\frac{7}{3} \div \frac{5}{10}\right) \div \frac{1}{3} = \left(\frac{7}{3} \times \frac{10}{5}\right) \div \frac{1}{3} = \left(\frac{7\times\overset{2}{\cancel{10}}}{3\times\underset{1}{\cancel{5}}}\right) \div \frac{1}{3}$

     $= \left(\frac{7\times2}{3\times1}\right) \div \frac{1}{3} = \left(\frac{14}{3}\right) \div \frac{1}{3} = \frac{14}{3} \div \frac{1}{3} = \frac{14}{3} \times \frac{3}{1} = \frac{14\times\overset{1}{\cancel{3}}}{\underset{1}{\cancel{3}}\times1} = \frac{14\times1}{1\times1} = \frac{14}{1} = \mathbf{14}$

3. $\left(2\frac{3}{4} \div \frac{2}{6}\right) \div 1.1 = \left(\frac{(2\times4)+3}{4} \div \frac{2}{6}\right) \div \frac{11}{10} = \left(\frac{8+3}{4} \div \frac{2}{6}\right) \div \frac{11}{10} = \left(\frac{11}{4} \div \frac{2}{6}\right) \div \frac{11}{10} = \left(\frac{11}{4} \times \frac{6}{2}\right) \div \frac{11}{10} = \left(\frac{11\times\overset{3}{\cancel{6}}}{4\times\underset{1}{\cancel{2}}}\right) \div \frac{11}{10}$

     $= \left(\frac{11\times3}{4\times1}\right) \div \frac{11}{10} = \left(\frac{33}{4}\right) \div \frac{11}{10} = \frac{33}{4} \div \frac{11}{10} = \frac{33}{4} \times \frac{10}{11} = \frac{\overset{3}{\cancel{33}}\times\overset{5}{\cancel{10}}}{\underset{2}{\cancel{4}}\times\underset{1}{\cancel{11}}} = \frac{3\times5}{2\times1} = \frac{15}{2} = \mathbf{7\frac{1}{2}}$

4. $\left(\frac{2}{3} \div 1\frac{1}{3}\right) \div \left(0.3 \div \frac{1}{6}\right) = \left(\frac{2}{3} \div \frac{(1\times3)+1}{3}\right) \div \left(\frac{3}{10} \times \frac{6}{1}\right) = \left(\frac{2}{3} \div \frac{3+1}{3}\right) \div \left(\frac{3\times\overset{3}{\cancel{6}}}{\underset{5}{\cancel{10}}\times1}\right) = \left(\frac{2}{3} \div \frac{4}{3}\right) \div \left(\frac{3\times3}{5\times1}\right) = \left(\frac{2}{3} \times \frac{3}{4}\right) \div \left(\frac{9}{5}\right)$

     $= \left(\frac{2\times\overset{1}{\cancel{3}}}{\underset{1}{\cancel{3}}\times\underset{2}{\cancel{4}}}^{\,1}\right) \div \frac{9}{5} = \left(\frac{1\times1}{1\times2}\right) \div \frac{9}{5} = \left(\frac{1}{2}\right) \div \frac{9}{5} = \frac{1}{2} \div \frac{9}{5} = \frac{1}{2} \times \frac{5}{9} = \frac{1\times5}{2\times9} = \mathbf{\frac{5}{18}}$

5. $0.05 \div \left(2\frac{1}{3} \div 7\right) = \frac{5}{100} \div \left(\frac{(2\times3)+1}{3} \div \frac{7}{1}\right) = \frac{\overset{1}{\cancel{5}}}{\underset{20}{\cancel{100}}} \div \left(\frac{6+1}{3} \div \frac{7}{1}\right) = \frac{1}{20} \div \left(\frac{7}{3} \div \frac{7}{1}\right) = \frac{1}{20} \div \left(\frac{7}{3} \times \frac{1}{7}\right) = \frac{1}{20} \div \left(\frac{\overset{1}{\cancel{7}}\times1}{3\times\underset{1}{\cancel{7}}}\right)$

     $= \frac{1}{20} \div \left(\frac{1\times1}{3\times1}\right) = \frac{1}{20} \div \left(\frac{1}{3}\right) = \frac{1}{20} \div \frac{1}{3} = \frac{1}{20} \times \frac{3}{1} = \frac{1\times3}{20\times1} = \mathbf{\frac{3}{20}}$

6. $\left(\frac{2}{3} \div 0.2\right) \div \left(1\frac{1}{3} \div 4\right) = \left(\frac{2}{3} \div \frac{2}{10}\right) \div \left(\frac{(1\times3)+1}{3} \div \frac{4}{1}\right) = \left(\frac{2}{3} \times \frac{10}{2}\right) \div \left(\frac{3+1}{3} \div \frac{4}{1}\right) = \left(\frac{\overset{1}{\cancel{2}}\times10}{3\times\underset{1}{\cancel{2}}}\right) \div \left(\frac{4}{3} \div \frac{4}{1}\right)$

     $= \left(\frac{1\times10}{3\times1}\right) \div \left(\frac{4}{3} \times \frac{1}{4}\right) = \left(\frac{10}{3}\right) \div \left(\frac{\overset{1}{\cancel{4}}\times1}{3\times\underset{1}{\cancel{4}}}\right) = \frac{10}{3} \div \left(\frac{1\times1}{3\times1}\right) = \frac{10}{3} \div \left(\frac{1}{3}\right) = \frac{10}{3} \div \frac{1}{3} = \frac{10}{3} \times \frac{3}{1} = \frac{10\times\overset{1}{\cancel{3}}}{\underset{1}{\cancel{3}}\times1} = \frac{10\times1}{1\times1} = \mathbf{10}$

7. $\left(2\frac{4}{3} \div 1\frac{2}{3}\right) \div \left(\frac{3}{4} \div 0.1\right) = \left(\frac{(2\times3)+4}{3} \div \frac{(1\times3)+2}{3}\right) \div \left(\frac{3}{4} \div \frac{1}{10}\right) = \left(\frac{6+4}{3} \div \frac{3+2}{3}\right) \div \left(\frac{3}{4} \times \frac{10}{1}\right) = \left(\frac{10}{3} \div \frac{5}{3}\right) \div \left(\frac{3\times\overset{5}{\cancel{10}}}{\underset{2}{\cancel{4}}\times1}\right)$

     $= \left(\frac{10}{3} \times \frac{3}{5}\right) \div \left(\frac{3\times5}{2\times1}\right) = \left(\frac{\overset{2}{\cancel{10}}\times\overset{1}{\cancel{3}}}{\underset{1}{\cancel{3}}\times\underset{1}{\cancel{5}}}\right) \div \left(\frac{15}{2}\right) = \left(\frac{2\times1}{1\times1}\right) \div \frac{15}{2} = \left(\frac{2}{1}\right) \div \frac{15}{2} = \frac{2}{1} \div \frac{15}{2} = \frac{2}{1} \times \frac{2}{15} = \frac{2\times2}{1\times15} = \mathbf{\frac{4}{15}}$

8. $\left(\frac{5}{8} \div 3\frac{1}{8}\right) \div 0.2 = \left(\frac{5}{8} \div \frac{(3\times8)+1}{8}\right) \div \frac{2}{10} = \left(\frac{5}{8} \div \frac{24+1}{8}\right) \div \frac{2}{10} = \left(\frac{5}{8} \div \frac{25}{8}\right) \div \frac{2}{10} = \left(\frac{5}{8} \times \frac{8}{25}\right) \div \frac{\overset{1}{\cancel{2}}}{\underset{5}{\cancel{10}}} = \left(\frac{\overset{1}{\cancel{5}}\times\overset{1}{\cancel{8}}}{\underset{1}{\cancel{8}}\times\underset{5}{\cancel{25}}}\right) \div \frac{1}{5}$

$$= \left(\frac{1 \times 1}{1 \times 5}\right) \div \frac{1}{5} = \left(\frac{1}{5}\right) \div \frac{1}{5} = \frac{1}{5} \div \frac{1}{5} = \frac{1}{5} \times \frac{5}{1} = \frac{1 \times \overset{1}{\cancel{5}}}{\cancel{5} \times 1} = \frac{1 \times 1}{1 \times 1} = \mathbf{1}$$

9. $\left(3\frac{1}{4} \div \frac{2}{16}\right) \div \left(1\frac{2}{3} \div \frac{1}{0.3}\right) = \left(\frac{(3 \times 4)+1}{4} \div \frac{2}{16}\right) \div \left(\frac{(1 \times 3)+2}{3} \div \frac{1}{\frac{3}{10}}\right) = \left(\frac{12+1}{4} \div \frac{2}{16}\right) \div \left(\frac{3+2}{3} \div \frac{1 \times 10}{1 \times 3}\right)$

$$= \left(\frac{13}{4} \div \frac{2}{16}\right) \div \left(\frac{5}{3} \div \frac{10}{3}\right) = \left(\frac{13}{4} \times \frac{16}{2}\right) \div \left(\frac{5}{3} \times \frac{3}{10}\right) = \left(\frac{13 \times \overset{4}{\cancel{16}}}{\cancel{4} \times 2}\right) \div \left(\frac{\overset{1}{\cancel{5}} \times \overset{1}{\cancel{3}}}{\cancel{3} \times \cancel{10}}\right) = \left(\frac{13 \times 4}{1 \times 2}\right) \div \left(\frac{1 \times 1}{1 \times 2}\right) = \left(\frac{52}{2}\right) \div \left(\frac{1}{2}\right)$$

$$= \frac{52}{2} \div \frac{1}{2} = \frac{52}{2} \times \frac{2}{1} = \frac{52 \times \overset{1}{\cancel{2}}}{\cancel{2} \times 1} = \frac{52 \times 1}{1 \times 1} = \frac{52}{1} = \mathbf{52}$$

10. $12 \div \left[1\frac{1}{3} \div \left(\frac{1}{5} \div 0.5\right)\right] = \frac{12}{1} \div \left[\frac{(1 \times 3)+1}{3} \div \left(\frac{1}{5} \div \frac{5}{10}\right)\right] = \frac{12}{1} \div \left[\frac{3+1}{3} \div \left(\frac{1}{5} \times \frac{10}{5}\right)\right] = \frac{12}{1} \div \left[\frac{4}{3} \div \left(\frac{1 \times \overset{2}{\cancel{10}}}{5 \times \cancel{5}}\right)\right]$

$$= \frac{12}{1} \div \left[\frac{4}{3} \div \left(\frac{1 \times 2}{5 \times 1}\right)\right] = \frac{12}{1} \div \left[\frac{4}{3} \div \left(\frac{2}{5}\right)\right] = \frac{12}{1} \div \left[\frac{4}{3} \div \frac{2}{5}\right] = \frac{12}{1} \div \left[\frac{4}{3} \times \frac{5}{2}\right] = \frac{12}{1} \div \left[\frac{\overset{2}{\cancel{4}} \times 5}{3 \times \cancel{2}}\right] = \frac{12}{1} \div \left[\frac{2 \times 5}{3 \times 1}\right] = \frac{12}{1} \div \left[\frac{10}{3}\right]$$

$$= \frac{12}{1} \div \frac{10}{3} = \frac{12}{1} \times \frac{3}{10} = \frac{\overset{6}{\cancel{12}} \times 3}{1 \times \cancel{10}} = \frac{6 \times 3}{1 \times 5} = \frac{18}{5} = \mathbf{3\frac{3}{5}}$$

Section 9.5 Solutions:

1. $\left(2\frac{4}{5} - \frac{1}{5}\right) \div 45 = \left(\frac{(2 \times 5)+4}{5} - \frac{1}{5}\right) \div \frac{45}{1} = \left(\frac{10+4}{5} - \frac{1}{5}\right) \div \frac{45}{1} = \left(\frac{14}{5} - \frac{1}{5}\right) \div \frac{45}{1} = \left(\frac{14-1}{5}\right) \div \frac{45}{1} = \left(\frac{13}{5}\right) \div \frac{45}{1}$

$$= \frac{13}{5} \div \frac{45}{1} = \frac{13}{5} \times \frac{1}{45} = \frac{13 \times 1}{5 \times 45} = \mathbf{\frac{13}{225}}$$

2. $\left(1\frac{1}{4} + \frac{2}{3}\right) \times \frac{0.24}{0.2} = \left(\frac{(1 \times 4)+1}{4} + \frac{2}{3}\right) \times \frac{\frac{24}{100}}{\frac{2}{10}} = \left(\frac{4+1}{4} + \frac{2}{3}\right) \times \frac{24 \times 10}{100 \times 2} = \left(\frac{5}{4} + \frac{2}{3}\right) \times \frac{\overset{6}{\cancel{240}}}{\underset{5}{\cancel{200}}} = \left(\frac{(5 \times 3)+(2 \times 4)}{4 \times 3}\right) \times \frac{6}{5}$

$$= \left(\frac{15+8}{12}\right) \times \frac{6}{5} = \left(\frac{23}{12}\right) \times \frac{6}{5} = \frac{23}{12} \times \frac{6}{5} = \frac{23 \times \overset{1}{\cancel{6}}}{\underset{2}{\cancel{12}} \times 5} = \frac{23 \times 1}{2 \times 5} = \frac{23}{10} = \mathbf{2\frac{3}{10}}$$

3. $\frac{3}{8} \times \left(3\frac{2}{5} - 0.2\right) = \frac{3}{8} \times \left(\frac{(3 \times 5)+2}{5} - \frac{2}{10}\right) = \frac{3}{8} \times \left(\frac{15+2}{5} - \frac{\overset{1}{\cancel{2}}}{\underset{5}{\cancel{10}}}\right) = \frac{3}{8} \times \left(\frac{17}{5} - \frac{1}{5}\right) = \frac{3}{8} \times \left(\frac{17-1}{5}\right) = \frac{3}{8} \times \left(\frac{16}{5}\right) = \frac{3}{8} \times \frac{16}{5}$

$$= \frac{3 \times \overset{2}{\cancel{16}}}{\underset{1}{\cancel{8}} \times 5} = \frac{3 \times 2}{1 \times 5} = \frac{6}{5} = \mathbf{1\frac{1}{5}}$$

4. $3\frac{1}{8} - \left(\frac{0.12}{0.6} + \frac{2}{3}\right) = \frac{(3 \times 8)+1}{8} - \left(\frac{\frac{12}{100}}{\frac{6}{10}} + \frac{2}{3}\right) = \frac{24+1}{8} - \left(\frac{12 \times 10}{100 \times 6} + \frac{2}{3}\right) = \frac{25}{8} - \left(\frac{\overset{1}{\cancel{120}}}{\underset{5}{\cancel{600}}} + \frac{2}{3}\right) = \frac{25}{8} - \left(\frac{1}{5} + \frac{2}{3}\right)$

$$= \frac{25}{8} - \left(\frac{(1 \times 3)+(2 \times 5)}{5 \times 3}\right) = \frac{25}{8} - \left(\frac{3+10}{15}\right) = \frac{25}{8} - \left(\frac{13}{15}\right) = \frac{25}{8} - \frac{13}{15} = \frac{(25 \times 15)-(13 \times 8)}{8 \times 15} = \frac{375-104}{120} = \frac{271}{120}$$

$$= 2\frac{31}{120}$$

5. $\left(1\frac{1}{4}+\frac{2}{3}\right)\times\left(\frac{1}{0.2}\times\frac{1}{5}\right) = \left(\frac{(1\times4)+1}{4}+\frac{2}{3}\right)\times\left(\frac{1}{\frac{2}{10}}\times\frac{1}{5}\right) = \left(\frac{4+1}{4}+\frac{2}{3}\right)\times\left(\frac{1\times10}{1\times2}\times\frac{1}{5}\right) = \left(\frac{5}{4}+\frac{2}{3}\right)\times\left(\frac{10}{2}\times\frac{1}{5}\right)$

$= \left(\frac{(5\times3)+(2\times4)}{4\times3}\right)\times\left(\frac{10\times1}{2\times5}\right) = \left(\frac{15+8}{12}\right)\times\left(\frac{10}{10}\right) = \left(\frac{23}{12}\right)\times\frac{10}{10} = \frac{23}{12}\times\frac{10}{10} = \frac{23\times\overset{1}{10}}{12\times\underset{1}{10}} = \frac{23\times1}{12\times1} = \frac{23}{12} = 1\frac{11}{12}$

6. $\left(\frac{2}{3}+2\frac{2}{3}\right)\div\left(15\times\frac{1}{5}\right) = \left(\frac{2}{3}+\frac{(2\times3)+2}{3}\right)\div\left(\frac{15}{1}\times\frac{1}{5}\right) = \left(\frac{2}{3}+\frac{6+2}{3}\right)\div\left(\frac{15}{1}\times\frac{1}{5}\right) = \left(\frac{2}{3}+\frac{8}{3}\right)\div\left(\frac{\overset{3}{15}\times1}{1\times\underset{1}{5}}\right)$

$= \left(\frac{2+8}{3}\right)\div\left(\frac{3\times1}{1\times1}\right) = \left(\frac{10}{3}\right)\div\left(\frac{3}{1}\right) = \frac{10}{3}\div\frac{3}{1} = \frac{10}{3}\times\frac{1}{3} = \frac{10\times1}{3\times3} = \frac{10}{9} = 1\frac{1}{9}$

7. $\left[\left(4\frac{1}{7}-\frac{1}{4}\right)\times0.02\right]\div\frac{1}{14} = \left[\left(\frac{(4\times7)+1}{7}-\frac{1}{4}\right)\times\frac{2}{100}\right]\div\frac{1}{14} = \left[\left(\frac{28+1}{7}-\frac{1}{4}\right)\times\frac{2}{100}\right]\div\frac{1}{14} = \left[\left(\frac{29}{7}-\frac{1}{4}\right)\times\frac{\overset{1}{2}}{\underset{50}{100}}\right]\div\frac{1}{14}$

$= \left[\left(\frac{(29\times4)-(1\times7)}{7\times4}\right)\times\frac{1}{50}\right]\div\frac{1}{14} = \left[\left(\frac{116-7}{28}\right)\times\frac{1}{50}\right]\div\frac{1}{14} = \left[\left(\frac{109}{28}\right)\times\frac{1}{50}\right]\div\frac{1}{14} = \left[\frac{109}{28}\times\frac{1}{50}\right]\div\frac{1}{14}$

$= \left[\frac{109\times1}{28\times50}\right]\div\frac{1}{14} = \left[\frac{109}{1400}\right]\div\frac{1}{14} = \frac{109}{1400}\div\frac{1}{14} = \frac{109}{1400}\times\frac{14}{1} = \frac{109\times\overset{1}{14}}{\underset{100}{1400}\times1} = \frac{109\times1}{100\times1} = \frac{109}{100} = 1\frac{9}{100}$

8. $\left[\left(2\frac{1}{5}+\frac{1.5}{0.01}\right)\div\frac{1}{5}\right]\times4 = \left[\left(\frac{(2\times5)+1}{5}+\frac{\frac{15}{10}}{\frac{1}{100}}\right)\div\frac{1}{5}\right]\times\frac{4}{1} = \left[\left(\frac{10+1}{5}+\frac{15\times100}{10\times1}\right)\div\frac{1}{5}\right]\times\frac{4}{1} = \left[\left(\frac{11}{5}+\frac{\overset{750}{1500}}{\underset{5}{10}}\right)\div\frac{1}{5}\right]\times\frac{4}{1}$

$= \left[\left(\frac{11}{5}+\frac{750}{5}\right)\div\frac{1}{5}\right]\times\frac{4}{1} = \left[\left(\frac{11+750}{5}\right)\div\frac{1}{5}\right]\times\frac{4}{1} = \left[\left(\frac{761}{5}\right)\div\frac{1}{5}\right]\times\frac{4}{1} = \left[\frac{761}{5}\times\frac{5}{1}\right]\times\frac{4}{1} = \left[\frac{761\times\overset{1}{5}}{\underset{1}{5}\times1}\right]\times\frac{4}{1}$

$= \left[\frac{761\times1}{1\times1}\right]\times\frac{4}{1} = \left[\frac{761}{1}\right]\times\frac{4}{1} = \frac{761}{1}\times\frac{4}{1} = \frac{761\times4}{1} = \frac{3044}{1} = \mathbf{3044}$

9. $\left(2\frac{1}{5}-\frac{1}{5}\right)\div\left(0.2\times\frac{3}{5}\right) = \left(\frac{(2\times5)+1}{5}-\frac{1}{5}\right)\div\left(\frac{2}{10}\times\frac{3}{5}\right) = \left(\frac{10+1}{5}-\frac{1}{5}\right)\div\left(\frac{\overset{1}{2}\times3}{\underset{5}{10}\times5}\right) = \left(\frac{11}{5}-\frac{1}{5}\right)\div\left(\frac{1\times3}{5\times5}\right)$

$= \left(\frac{11-1}{5}\right)\div\left(\frac{3}{25}\right) = \left(\frac{10}{5}\right)\div\frac{3}{25} = \frac{10}{5}\div\frac{3}{25} = \frac{10}{5}\times\frac{25}{3} = \frac{10\times\overset{5}{25}}{\underset{1}{5}\times3} = \frac{10\times5}{1\times3} = \frac{50}{3} = \mathbf{16\frac{2}{3}}$

10. $2.8\div\left[\left(2\frac{1}{6}+\frac{2}{3}\right)+\frac{1}{18}\right] = \frac{28}{10}\div\left[\left(\frac{(2\times6)+1}{6}+\frac{2}{3}\right)+\frac{1}{18}\right] = \frac{28}{10}\div\left[\left(\frac{12+1}{6}+\frac{2}{3}\right)+\frac{1}{18}\right] = \frac{\overset{14}{28}}{\underset{5}{10}}\div\left[\left(\frac{13}{6}+\frac{2}{3}\right)+\frac{1}{18}\right]$

$= \frac{14}{5}\div\left[\left(\frac{(13\times3)+(2\times6)}{6\times3}\right)+\frac{1}{18}\right] = \frac{14}{5}\div\left[\left(\frac{39+12}{18}\right)+\frac{1}{18}\right] = \frac{14}{5}\div\left[\left(\frac{51}{18}\right)+\frac{1}{18}\right] = \frac{14}{5}\div\left[\frac{51}{18}+\frac{1}{18}\right] = \frac{14}{5}\div\left[\frac{51+1}{18}\right]$

$= \frac{14}{5}\div\left[\frac{52}{18}\right] = \frac{14}{5}\div\frac{52}{18} = \frac{14}{5}\times\frac{18}{52} = \frac{14\times\overset{9}{18}}{5\times\underset{26}{52}} = \frac{14\times9}{5\times26} = \frac{\overset{63}{126}}{\underset{65}{130}} = \frac{63}{65}$

Index

A

Absolute value, *51, 54*
    definition, *xii*
Addend, *1*
    definition, *xii*
Addition
    associative property of, *8*
    commutative property of, *8*
    definition, *xii*
Algebraic approach, *1, 80, 132, 204*
    definition, *xii*
Associative property, *8, 28*
    definition, *xii*

B

Brackets, *1, 12-50*
    definition, *xii*
    use of in addition, *12-16*
    use of in addition, subtraction,
        multiplication, and division, *45-50*
    use of in division, *38-42*
    use of in multiplication, *31-35*
    use of in subtraction, *22-27*

C

Case
    definition, *xii*
Change
    decimal fractions to integer fractions, *71-76*
    definition, *xii*
    improper fractions to mixed fractions, *54-60*
    mixed fractions to integer fractions, *77-79*
Common denominator
    definition, *xii*
Common fraction
    definition, *xii*
Commutative property, *8, 28*
    definition, *xii*
Complex fraction, *76*
    definition, *xii*
Conversion
    definition, *xii*
Convert, *51*
    definition, *xii*

D

Decimal factions, *52, 132-203, 266, 370, 424*

adding, *132-150*
    definition, *xii*
    dividing, *181-191*
    multiplying, *170-180*
    solving mixed operations using, *192-203*
    subtracting, *151-169*
Decimal and mixed fractions, *370-423*
    adding, *370-381*
    dividing, *402-411*
    multiplying, *393-401*
    solving mixed operations using, *412-423*
    subtracting, *382-392*
Decimal number, *52*
    definition, *xii*
Decimal point, *52*
    definition, *xiii*
Denominator, *51*
    definition, *xiii*
Difference, *2*
    definition, *xiii*
Distributive property, *28*
    definition, *xiii*
Dividend, *5, 54-59*
    definition, *xiii*
Division
    definition, *xiii*
Divisor, *5, 54-60*
    definition, *xiii*

E

Equal, *53*
    definition, *xiii*
Equivalent fractions, *53*
    definition, *xiii*
Even number, *61-62, 65-70*
    definition, *xiii*
Exact order, *91*
    definition, *xiii*
Exponential notation, *52*
    definition, *xiii*

F

Factor, *4*
    definition, *xiii*
Fraction, *51*
    definition, *xiii*

About the Author

Said Hamilton received his B.S. degree in electrical engineering from Oklahoma State University and Master's degree, also in electrical engineering, from University of Texas at Austin. He has taught a number of math and engineering courses as a visiting lecturer at University of Oklahoma, Department of Mathematics, and as a faculty member at Rose State College, Department of Engineering Technology, at Midwest City, Oklahoma. He is currently working in the field of aerospace technology and has published numerous technical papers.

Order Form
call 1-800-209-8186 to order
Or: Use the order form

Last Name _____ First Name _____ M.I. _____

Address _____

City _____ State _____ Zip Code _____

No. of Books	Book Price ($49.95)	Total Price
		$
	Subtotal	$
	Shipping and Handling (Add $4.50 for the first book $3.00 for each additional book)	$
	Sales Tax Va. residents add 4.5% ($49.95 × 0.045 = $2.25)	$
	Total Payment	$

Enclosed is:

A check ☐   Master Card ☐

VISA ☐   American Express ☐

Account Number _____ Expiration Date _____

Signature _____

Make checks payable to Hamilton Education Guides.

Please send completed form to:

Hamilton Education Guides

P.O. Box 681

Vienna, Va. 22183

Watch for these other Hamilton Education Guides:

- Mastering Algebra: An Introduction
- Mastering Algebra: Intermediate Level
- Mastering Algebra: Advanced Level